SCOTT FORESMAN • ADDISON WESLEY

Mathematics

Authors

Randall I. Charles
Janet H. Caldwell
Mary Cavanagh
Dinah Chancellor
Alma B. Ramirez

Warren Crown
Jeanne F. Ramos
Kay Sammons
Jane F. Schielack

Francis (Skip) Fennell
William Tate
Mary Thompson
John A. Van de Walle

Consulting Mathematicians

Edward J. Barbeau
Professor of Mathematics
University of Toronto
Toronto, Ontario, Canada

David M. Bressoud
DeWitt Wallace Professor of Mathematics
Macalester College
Saint Paul, Minnesota

Gary Lippman
Professor of Mathematics and Computer Science
California State University Hayward
Hayward, California

PEARSON
Scott Foresman

Editorial Offices: Glenview, Illinois • Parsippany, New Jersey • New York, New York

Sales Offices: Boston, Massachusetts • Duluth, Georgia • Glenview, Illinois
Coppell, Texas • Sacramento, California • Mesa, Arizona

Reading Consultants

Peter Afflerbach
Professor and Director of The Reading Center
University of Maryland
College Park, Maryland

Donald J. Leu
John and Maria Neag
Endowed Chair in Literacy and Technology
University of Connecticut
Storrs, Connecticut

Reviewers

Mary Bacon
Mathematics Specialist
East Baton Rouge Parish School System
Baton Rouge, Louisiana

Cheryl Baker
Mathematics Teacher
Norton Middle School
Norton, Ohio

Marcelline A. Barron
Curriculum Leader Math and Science, K–5
Fairfield Public Schools
Fairfield, Connecticut

Mary Connery-Simmons
Mathematics Specialist
Springfield Massachusetts Public Schools
Springfield, Massachusetts

Anthony C. Dentino
Supervisor of Curriculum
Brick Township Schools
Brick, New Jersey

Dawn Evans
Mathematics Teacher
Bret Harte Elementary School
Chicago, Illinois

Sam Hanson
Teacher
Totem Falls Elementary
Snohomish, Washington

Allison Harris
Professional Development School Coach
Seattle Public Schools
Seattle, Washington

Pamela Renee Hill NBCT
Teacher
Durham Public Schools
Durham, North Carolina

Catherine Kuhns
Teacher
Country Hills Elementary
Coral Springs, Florida

Madeleine A. Madsen
District Curriculum Resource
Community
Consolidated School District 59
Arlington Heights, Illinois

Lynda M. Penry
Teacher
Wright Elementary
Ft. Walton Beach, Florida

Deanna P. Rigdon
District Math Curriculum Specialist, Grades 3–4
Granite School District
Salt Lake City, Utah

Thomas Romero
Principal
Adams Elementary
Wapato, Washington

Wendy Siegel
Mathematics Coordinator K–12
Orchard Park Middle School
Orchard Park, New York

Sandra Smith
Teacher
Cheat Lake Elementary
Morgantown, West Virginia

Rochelle A. Solomon
Mathematics Resource Teacher
Cleveland Municipal School District
Cleveland, Ohio

Frank L. Sparks
Curriculum Design and Support Specialist, Secondary Mathematics
New Orleans Public Schools
New Orleans, Louisiana

Beth L. Spivey
Lead Teacher, Elementary Mathematics
Wake County Public School System
Raleigh, North Carolina

Paula Spomer
Teacher
Chisholm Elementary
Edmond, Oklahoma

Robert Trammel
Math Consultant
Fort Wayne Community Schools
Fort Wayne, Indiana

Annemarie Tuffner
Mathematics Lead Teacher, K–12
Neshaminy School District
Langhorne, Pennsylvania

Judy L. Wright
Curriculum and Staff Development Specialist
Columbus Public Schools
Columbus, Ohio

Theresa Zieles
Teacher
Indianapolis Public School 88
Indianapolis, Indiana

ISBN: 0-328-26367-2

1 2 3 4 5 6 7 8 9 10 V063 15 14 13 11 10 09 08 07 06

CHAPTER 1

Place Value and Money

Instant Check System
- Diagnosing Readiness, 2
- Warm Up, daily
- Talk About It, daily
- Check, daily
- Diagnostic Checkpoint, 15, 27, 43

Test Prep
- Mixed Review and Test Prep, daily
- Test Talk, daily, 44
- Cumulative Review and Test Prep, 50

Reading For Math Success — Reading Helps!
- Reading Helps, 12, 24, 38
- Key Vocabulary and Concept Review, 46

Writing in Math
- Writing in Math exercises, daily

DK Problem-Solving Applications, 40

Discovery Channel School — Discover Math in Your World, 19

Additional Resources
- Learning with Technology, 37
- Enrichment, 7
- Chapter 1 Test, 48
- Reteaching, 52
- More Practice, 56

CHAPTER 2

Adding and Subtracting Whole Numbers and Money

Instant Check System
- Diagnosing Readiness, 60
- Warm Up, daily
- Talk About It, daily
- Check, daily
- Diagnostic Checkpoint, 75, 93, 105

Test Prep
- Mixed Review and Test Prep, daily
- Test Talk, daily, 106
- Cumulative Review and Test Prep, 112

Reading For Math Success / Reading Helps!
- Reading for Math Success, 88
- Reading Helps, 90, 94
- Key Vocabulary and Concept Review, 108

Writing in Math
- Writing in Math exercises, daily

Problem-Solving Applications, 102

Discovery Channel School: Discover Math in Your World, 67

Additional Resources
- Learning with Technology, 85
- Practice Game, 79
- Enrichment, 71
- Chapter 2 Test, 110
- Reteaching, 114
- More Practice, 118

CHAPTER 3

Multiplication and Division Concepts and Facts

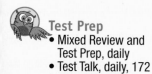

Instant Check System
- Diagnosing Readiness, 122
- Warm Up, daily
- Talk About It, daily
- Check, daily
- Diagnostic Checkpoint, 145, 159, 171

Test Prep
- Mixed Review and Test Prep, daily
- Test Talk, daily, 172
- Cumulative Review and Test Prep, 178

Reading For Math Success
Reading Helps!
- Reading for Math Success, 138
- Reading Helps, 140, 156
- Key Vocabulary and Concept Review, 174

Writing in Math
- Writing in Math exercises, daily

Problem-Solving Applications, 168

Discovery Channel School
Discover Math in Your World, 163

Additional Resources
- Learning with Technology, 127
- Practice Game, 131
- Enrichment, 135
- Chapter 3 Test, 176
- Reteaching, 180
- More Practice, 184

Instant Check System
- Diagnosing Readiness, 188
- Warm Up, daily
- Talk About It, daily
- Check, daily
- Diagnostic Checkpoint, 203, 225, 237

Test Prep
- Mixed Review and Test Prep, daily
- Test Talk, daily, 238
- Cumulative Review and Test Prep, 244

Reading For Math Success
Reading Helps!
- Reading for Math Success, 220
- Reading Helps, 198, 222
- Key Vocabulary and Concept Review, 240

Writing in Math
- Writing in Math exercises, daily
- Writing to Compare, 198

Problem-Solving Applications, 234

Discovery Channel School
Discover Math in Your World, 215

Additional Resources
- Learning with Technology, 219
- Practice Game, 211
- Enrichment, 195, 229
- Chapter 4 Test, 242
- Reteaching, 246
- More Practice, 250

CHAPTER 4

Time, Data, and Graphs

CHAPTER 5

Multiplying by One-Digit Numbers

Instant Check System
- Diagnosing Readiness, 254
- Warm Up, daily
- Talk About It, daily
- Check, daily
- Diagnostic Checkpoint, 269, 285, 295

Test Prep
- Mixed Review and Test Prep, daily
- Test Talk, daily, 296
- Cumulative Review and Test Prep, 302

Reading For Math Success
Reading Helps!
- Reading for Math Success, 276
- Reading Helps, 278, 290
- Key Vocabulary and Concept Review, 298

Writing in Math
- Writing in Math exercises, daily

DK Problem-Solving Applications, 292

Discovery Channel School Discover Math in Your World, 273

Additional Resources
- Learning with Technology, 267
- Practice Game, 261
- Enrichment, 267
- Chapter 5 Test, 300
- Reteaching, 304
- More Practice, 308

Instant Check System
- Diagnosing Readiness, 312
- Warm Up, daily
- Talk About It, daily
- Check, daily
- Diagnostic Checkpoint, 331, 347

Test Prep
- Mixed Review and Test Prep, daily
- Test Talk, daily, 348
- Cumulative Review and Test Prep, 354

Reading For Math Success
Reading Helps!
- Reading for Math Success, 324
- Reading Helps, 326, 342
- Key Vocabulary and Concept Review, 350

Writing in Math
- Writing in Math exercises, daily
- Writing to Explain, 342

Problem-Solving Applications, 344

DISCOVERY CHANNEL SCHOOL
Discover Math in Your World, 335

Additional Resources
- Learning with Technology, 319
- Enrichment, 323
- Chapter 6 Test, 352
- Reteaching, 356
- More Practice, 360

CHAPTER 6

Multiplying by Two-Digit Numbers

CHAPTER

7 Dividing

Instant Check System
- Diagnosing Readiness, 364
- Warm Up, daily
- Talk About It, daily
- Check, daily
- Diagnostic Checkpoint, 379, 401, 415

Test Prep
- Mixed Review and Test Prep, daily
- Test Talk, daily, 416
- Cumulative Review and Test Prep, 422

Reading For Math Success — Reading Helps!
- Reading for Math Success, 394
- Reading Helps, 384, 396
- Key Vocabulary and Concept Review, 418

Writing in Math
- Writing in Math exercises, daily

Problem-Solving Applications, 412

Discovery Channel School: Discover Math in Your World, 383

Additional Resources
- Learning with Technology, 377, 389, 411
- Practice Game, 371
- Chapter 7 Test, 420
- Reteaching, 424
- More Practice, 428

Geometry and Measurement

Instant Check System
- Diagnosing Readiness, 432
- Warm Up, daily
- Talk About It, daily
- Check, daily
- Diagnostic Checkpoint, 451, 463, 481

Test Prep
- Mixed Review and Test Prep, daily
- Test Talk, daily, 482
- Cumulative Review and Test Prep, 488

Reading For Math Success — Reading Helps!
- Reading for Math Success, 472
- Reading Helps, 460, 474
- Key Vocabulary and Concept Review, 484

Writing in Math
- Writing in Math exercises, daily
- Writing to Describe, 460

Problem-Solving Applications, 478

Discovery Channel School — Discover Math in Your World, 447

Additional Resources
- Learning with Technology, 455
- Practice Game, 437
- Enrichment, 443, 467, 471
- Chapter 8 Test, 486
- Reteaching, 490
- More Practice, 494

CHAPTER 9

Fraction Concepts

Instant Check System
- Diagnosing Readiness, 498
- Warm Up, daily
- Talk About It, daily
- Check, daily
- Diagnostic Checkpoint, 515, 529, 543

Test Prep
- Mixed Review and Test Prep, daily
- Test Talk, daily, 544
- Cumulative Review and Test Prep, 550

Reading For Math Success — Reading Helps!
- Reading for Math Success, 510
- Reading Helps, 512, 538
- Key Vocabulary and Concept Review, 546

Writing in Math
- Writing in Math exercises, daily
- Writing to Explain, 538

Problem-Solving Applications, 540

Discovery Channel School — Discover Math in Your World, 507

Additional Resources
- Learning with Technology, 519
- Practice Game, 527
- Enrichment, 533
- Chapter 9 Test, 548
- Reteaching, 552
- More Practice, 556

Instant Check System
- Diagnosing Readiness, 560
- Warm Up, daily
- Talk About It, daily
- Check, daily
- Diagnostic Checkpoint, 573, 587, 605

Test Prep
- Mixed Review and Test Prep, daily
- Test Talk, daily, 606
- Cumulative Review and Test Prep, 612

Reading For Math Success
Reading Helps!
- Reading for Math Success, 582
- Reading Helps, 584, 600
- Key Vocabulary and Concept Review, 608

Writing in Math
- Writing in Math exercises, daily

Problem-Solving Applications, 602

Discovery Channel School
Discover Math in Your World, 571

Additional Resources
- Learning with Technology, 581
- Practice Game, 599
- Enrichment, 567, 577
- Chapter 10 Test, 610
- Reteaching, 614
- More Practice, 618

CHAPTER 10

Fraction Operations and Customary Measurement

CHAPTER 11

Decimals and Metric Measurement

Instant Check System
- Diagnosing Readiness, 622
- Warm Up, daily
- Talk About It, daily
- Check, daily
- Diagnostic Checkpoint, 635, 651, 669

Test Prep
- Mixed Review and Test Prep, daily
- Test Talk, daily, 670
- Cumulative Review and Test Prep, 676

Reading For Math Success — Reading Helps!
- Reading for Math Success, 646
- Reading Helps, 648, 662
- Key Vocabulary and Concept Review, 672

Writing in Math
- Writing in Math exercises, daily
- Writing to Explain, 662

DK Problem-Solving Applications, 666

Discovery Channel School — Discover Math in Your World, 627

Additional Resources
- Learning with Technology, 641
- Enrichment, 645, 661
- Chapter 11 Test, 674
- Reteaching, 678
- More Practice, 682

CHAPTER 12

Graphing and Probability

Instant Check System
- Diagnosing Readiness, 686
- Warm Up, daily
- Talk About It, daily
- Check, daily
- Diagnostic Checkpoint, 699, 719

Test Prep
- Mixed Review and Test Prep, daily
- Test Talk, daily, 720
- Cumulative Review and Test Prep, 726

Reading For Math Success — Reading Helps!
- Reading for Math Success, 712
- Reading Helps, 696, 714
- Key Vocabulary and Concept Review, 722

Writing in Math
- Writing in Math exercises, daily

Problem-Solving Applications, 716

Discovery Channel School — Discover Math in Your World, 703

Additional Resources
- Learning with Technology, 709
- Enrichment, 695
- Chapter 12 Test, 724
- Reteaching, 728
- More Practice, 731

What can help you get higher test scores?
Turn the page to find out.

Test-Taking Strategies

Remember these six test-taking strategies that will help you do well on tests. These strategies are also taught in the Test Talk before each chapter test.

Understand the Question

- **Look for important words.**
- **Turn the question into a statement: "I need to find out..."**

1. Which letter does NOT have a line of symmetry?

A. 

B. 

C. 

D. 

1. What are some important words in the problem that tell you what the problem is about?

2. What important word in the problem is highlighted using capital letters?

3. Turn the question into a statement that begins with "I need to find out . . .".

Get Information for the Answers

- **Get information from text.**
- **Get information from pictures, maps, diagrams, tables, graphs.**

2. Liza has a slice of pizza for lunch every day. Each day she has a different crust and topping combination. The menu shows Liza's choices. How many possible combinations of one topping and one crust does she have? Explain.

Pizza Place

CRUST CHOICES	TOPPING CHOICES
Deep Dish	Pepperoni
Thin	Onion
	Green Pepper
	Mushrooms
	Cheese

____

____

____

____

4. What information from the picture is needed to solve the problem?

5. What information in the text is needed to solve the problem?

Most strategies can be used with any type of test item.

Plan How to Find the Answer

- **Think about problem-solving skills and strategies.**
- **Choose computation methods.**

3. Norene rode her bike 3 blocks to meet Maria at the park. Norene and Maria spent 20 minutes riding their bikes along the park's bike path. Then they played on the swings for 15 minutes. Then after talking for 10 minutes, Norene rode her bike home. How much time did Norene spend at the park with Maria?

A. 25 minutes

B. 30 minutes

C. 45 minutes

D. 48 minutes

6. Tell how you would use the following problem-solving skills and strategies as you solve the problem.

- Identify extra or missing information.
- Choose an operation.
- Draw a picture.

7. Which of the following computation methods is best to use to solve this problem?

- Mental math
- Paper and pencil
- Calculator

Use the strategy below with multiple-choice test items.

Make Smart Choices

- **Eliminate wrong answers.**
- **Try working backward from an answer.**
- **Check answers for reasonableness; estimate.**

4. Jorge picked 96 apples at the Red Apple orchard. He will share the apples with his 3 younger brothers. How many apples will each of the 4 brothers receive if they each receive the same amount?

A. 14 apples

B. 24 apples

C. 32 apples

D. 93 apples

8. Which answer choices can you eliminate because you are sure they are wrong answers? Explain.

9. How could you use multiplication to work backward from an answer to see if it is correct?

10. How could you estimate the answer? Is the correct answer close to the estimate?

Use these two strategies when you have to write an answer.

Use Writing in Math

- **Make your answer brief but complete.**
- **Use words from the problem and use math terms accurately.**
- **Describe steps in order.**
- **Draw pictures if they help you explain your thinking.**

5. How many diagonals does a pentagon have? Explain how you found your answer.

Work space

11. What words from the problem will you use in your response?

12. What steps could you describe in your response?

13. How can drawing a picture help you explain your thinking?

Improve Written Answers

- **Check if your answer is complete.**
- **Check if your answer is clear and easy to follow.**
- **Check if your answer makes sense.**

6. Jared has been saving money he has earned each week. If he continues to save the same amount each week, what will his total savings be by week 4? Explain how you found your answer.

Week	1	2	3	4
Total	\$2.75	\$5.50	\$8.25	

I found a pattern in the table.
Jared's total savings
by Week 4 will be \$11.00.

14. Is the answer that is given worth 4 points, using the rubric that is shown on the next page? Explain.

15. If the answer is not worth 4 points, tell how to improve the answer.

Scoring Rubric

4 points

Full credit: 4 points

The answer is correct. A full explanation is given as to how the answer is found.

3 points

Partial credit: 3 points

The answer is correct, but the explanation does not fully explain how the answer was found.

2 points

Partial credit: 2 points

The answer is correct or the explanation is correct, but not both.

1 point

Partial credit: 1 point

A solution is attempted, but the answer is incorrect. The explanation is unclear.

0 points

No credit: 0 points

The solution is completely incorrect or missing.

For more on Test-Taking Strategies, see the following Test Talk pages.

Test-Taking Strategies

Test Prep

As you use your book, look for these features that help you prepare for tests.

Test Talk before each chapter test teaches Test-Taking Strategies.

TEST TALK

Think It Through
- I will **check if the answer is complete.**
- I will **check if the answer makes sense.**

Test Talk: Think It Through within lessons helps you do the kind of thinking you need to do when you take a test.

Mixed Review and Test Prep

Mixed Review and Test Prep at the end of lessons gives you practice with the kind of items on tests.

Take It to the NET
Test Prep
www.scottforesman.com

Take It to the Net: Test Prep at the end of lessons offers online test prep.

Cumulative Review and Test Prep

Cumulative Review and Test Prep at the end of chapters helps you remember content you'll need to know when you take tests.

CHAPTER 1

Place Value and Money

DIAGNOSING READINESS

A Vocabulary

(Grade 3)

Choose the best term from the box.

1. In 784, the 7 is in the _?_ place, the 8 is in the _?_ place, and the 4 is in the _?_ place.

2. The number 2,346 is _?_ than the number 1,875.

3. A _?_ is worth 5 cents.

Vocabulary

- **ones**
- **tens**
- **hundreds**
- **greater**
- **less**
- **penny**
- **nickel**
- **dime**

B Numbers in the Hundreds and Thousands

(Grade 3)

Write the word form for each number.

4. 648 **5.** 256 **6.** 138

7. 574 **8.** 1,803 **9.** 3,720

Write each number in standard form.

10. Three hundred forty-five

11. Six hundred ninety-one

12. Four thousand, nine hundred two

Do You Know...

What is the world's largest vegetable crop?

You will find out in Lesson 1-14.

C Rounding

(Grade 3)

13. What number is halfway between 20 and 30?

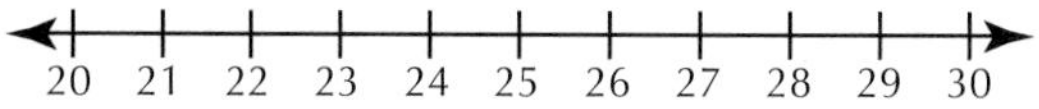

14. What number is halfway between 600 and 700?

15. What number is halfway between 800 and 900?

Round each number to the nearest ten.

16. 46 **17.** 22 **18.** 89

19. 138 **20.** 367 **21.** 874

22. Is 236 closer to 230 or 240?

D Count the Money

(Grade 3)

Count each money amount.

23. 

24. 

25. 

Key Idea
There are many ways to represent a number.

Vocabulary
- expanded form
- standard form
- word form
- digits
- period

Numbers in the Thousands

WARM UP

What number is shown?

1. 
2. 30 + 2
3. 10 + 10 + 3

LEARN

What are some ways to represent numbers in the thousands?

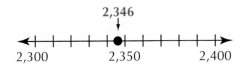

Here are different ways to represent 2,346.

Place-value blocks:

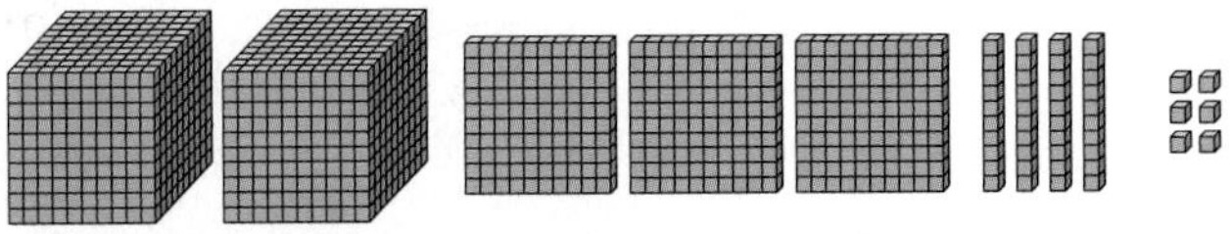

2 thousands 3 hundreds 4 tens 6 ones

Number line:

Expanded form: 2,000 + 300 + 40 + 6
2 thousands + 3 hundreds + 4 tens + 6 ones
$(2 \times 1{,}000) + (3 \times 100) + (4 \times 10) + (6 \times 1)$

Standard form: 2,346

Word form: two thousand, three hundred forty-six

Digits are the symbols used to write numbers: 0, 1, 2, 3, 4, 5, 6, 7, 8, and 9.

In 2,346, the digit 3 has a **value** of 300 because it is in the hundreds place.

Talk About It

1. Which digit is in the thousands place in 2,346?

How do you read and write numbers in the thousands?

A place-value chart can help you read and write numbers. Each group of 3 digits, starting from the right, forms a **period.** Periods are separated by commas.

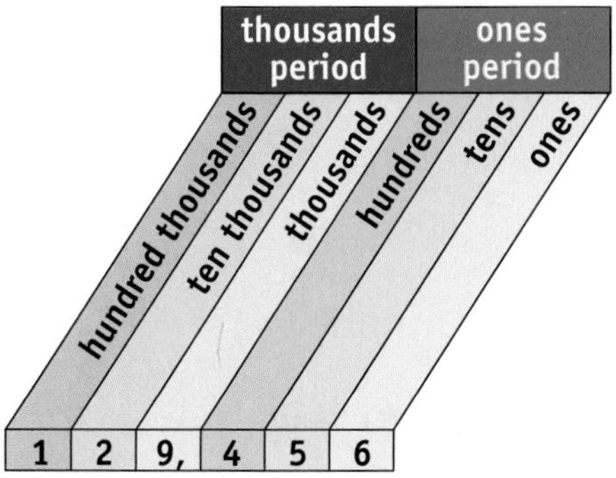

Race-car speedways in Georgia, Indiana, and Texas have more than 120,000 seats.

Example

Write the expanded form for the number in the place-value chart. Then write the standard form and the word form.

Expanded form: 100,000 + 20,000 + 9,000 + 400 + 50 + 6

Standard form: 129,456

Word form: one hundred twenty-nine thousand, four hundred fifty-six

Talk About It

2. In 129,456, which digits are in the thousands period?

3. What is the value of the 9 in 129,456? the 5? the 1?

CHECK

For another example, see Set 1-1 on p. 52.

Write each number in standard form.

1. two hundred fourteen thousand, five hundred three 214,563

2. 300,000 + 20,000 + 7,000 + 400 + 5 327,405

Write the word form and tell the value of the red digit for each number.

3. 456,963 **4.** 803,254 **5.** 940,037 **6.** 37,204

7. Number Sense Draw a picture of place-value blocks to show 1,751.

For more practice, see Set 1-1 on p. 56.

A Skills and Understanding

Write each number in standard form.

8. 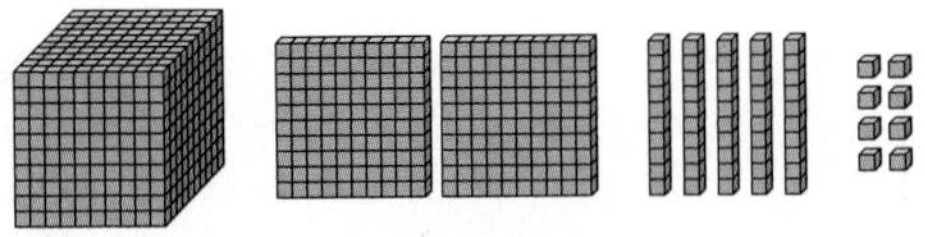

9. 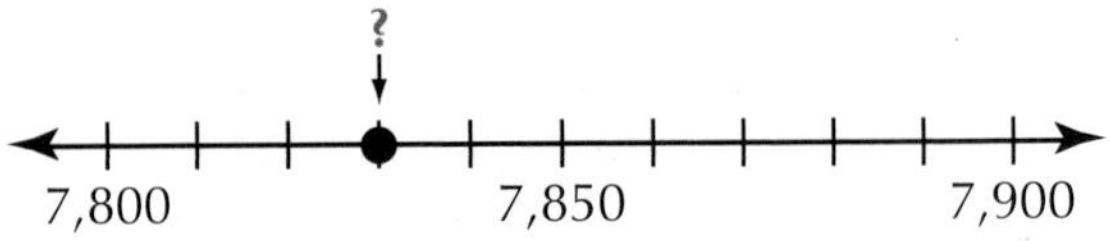

10. 6 ten thousands + 1 thousand + 0 hundreds + 9 tens + 3 ones

Write the word form and tell the value of the red digit for each number.

11. 7,425 **12.** 53,203 **13.** 352,915 **14.** 925,163

15. 60,234 **16.** 196,350 **17.** 473,512 **18.** 230,777

19. Number Sense Write a six-digit number with a 0 in the thousands place and a 3 in the hundreds place.

B Reasoning and Problem Solving

What will the odometer at the right show after the car has traveled an additional

An odometer displays the total distance a car, truck, or other vehicle has traveled. Odometers can be either electronic or mechanical.

20. 1 mile? **21.** 10 miles?

22. 100 miles? **23.** 1,000 miles?

24. What is 1,000 less than 23,906?

25. Reasoning What is the greatest 6-digit number you can write? What is the least?

26. **Writing in Math** Is the explanation below correct? If not, tell why and write a correct response.

Explain why the 6 in 267,423 has a value of 60,000.

Thousands			Ones		
Hundred Thousands	Ten Thousands	Thousands	Hundreds	Tens	Ones
2	6	7	4	2	3

The 6 is in the ten thousands place and 6 ten thousands make 60,000.

Think It Through
I can **use a chart** to explain my thinking.

PRACTICE

C Extensions

27. Use the clues below to find the mystery number.

___ ___, ___ 4 ___

- The number is between 30,000 and 40,000.
- The digit in the tens place is 4.
- The digit in the thousands place is 3 more than the digit in the tens place.
- The value of the digit in the hundreds place is 900.
- The digit in the ones place is the sum of 3 and 2.

Mixed Review and Test Prep

Take It to the NET
Test Prep
www.scottforesman.com

28. 3 + 9 **29.** 8 + 7 **30.** 12 + 5 **31.** 14 + 32

32. Round 368 to the nearest hundred.

A. 300 **B.** 360 **C.** 400 **D.** 460

Practice Game

Guess My Number!

Players: 2
Materials: paper and pencil for each player

1. Player 1 thinks of a 4-digit number and secretly writes it down.

2. Player 2 asks questions about the digits in the number. Questions should have a **Yes** or **No** answer. Here are some sample questions.

- Is the digit in the tens place less than 5?
- Are any of the digits in the number a 7?

3. Player 1 keeps a tally of the number of questions asked. Player 2 is allowed no more than 20 questions.

4. After the number is found, players change roles.

5. If the number is not guessed after 20 questions, Player 1 says the number aloud and then players change roles.

Key Idea
Place value can help you read and understand numbers in the millions.

Understanding Greater Numbers

LEARN

What are some ways to represent numbers in the millions?

In 2000, the population of the United States was about 281,420,000 people.

Example A

Write the expanded form for 281,420,000. Then write the word form. Use a place-value chart.

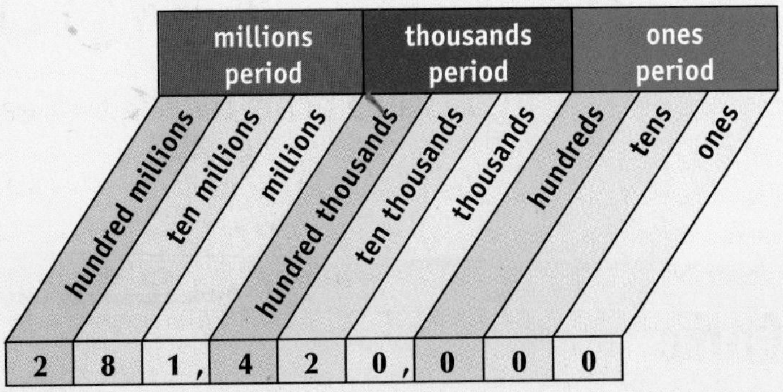

millions period
thousands period
ones period
hundred millions
ten millions
millions
hundred thousands
ten thousands
thousands
hundreds
tens
ones
2 8 1 , 4 2 0 , 0 0 0

Expanded form: 200,000,000 + 80,000,000 + 1,000,000 + 400,000 + 20,000

Word form: Two hundred eighty-one *million*, four hundred twenty *thousand*

Example B

Write the value of the red digits in 354,726,219.

The 5 is in the ten millions place. Its value is 50,000,000.

The 7 is in the hundred thousands place. Its value is 700,000.

WARM UP

For 1–4 write the value of the digit 3.

1. 103,789
2. 392,554
3. 8,032
4. 230,148

Talk About It

1. How does using commas to separate periods help you read large numbers?

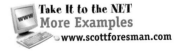

Take It to the NET
More Examples
www.scottforesman.com

In 1790, the U.S. Census counted about 4,000,000 people.

CHECK

For another example, see Set 1-2 on p. 52.

1. Write three million, five hundred thousand, seventeen in standard form.
2. Write the word form and tell the value of the red digit for 147,036,267.
3. **Number Sense** In the number 352,100,978, which digit has the greatest value?

TEST TALK

Think It Through
I can **make a chart** to read and write large numbers.

PRACTICE

For more practice, see Set 1-2 on p. 56.

A Skills and Understanding

Write 70,000,000 + 5,000,000 + 20,000 + 1,000 + 300 + 40 + 6 in

4. standard form. 7,52 1,346
5. word form. Not enough space

Write the word form and tell the value of the red digit for each number.

6. 85,204,062
7. 5,180,246
8. 397,002,035
9. 928,269,926

10. **Number Sense** Write the number that is one million more than 14,035,390.

B Reasoning and Problem Solving

Write the word form for the number of vehicles made in

11. Germany.
12. U.S.
13. Japan.

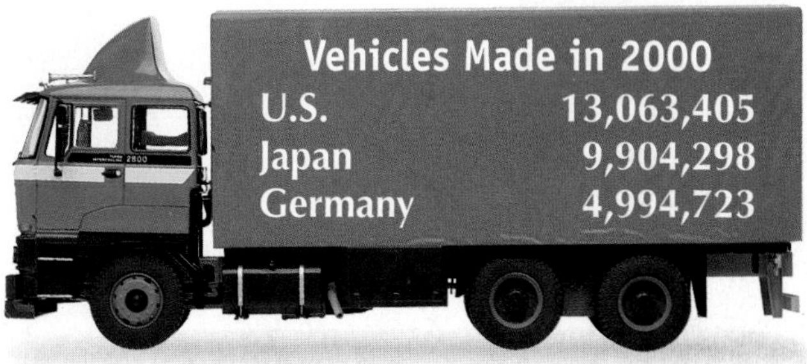

Vehicles Made in 2000	
U.S.	13,063,405
Japan	9,904,298
Germany	4,994,723

14. **Writing in Math** Write an 8-digit number with 3 in the hundred thousands place and 7 in the hundreds place.

Mixed Review and Test Prep

Take It to the NET
Test Prep
www.scottforesman.com

15. Write five hundred three thousand, two hundred sixty-four in standard form.
16. **Algebra** Find the missing number in 8 + ▢ = 12.

A. 3 **B.** 4 **C.** 5 **D.** 20

Key Idea
Place value can help you understand number patterns.

Place-Value Patterns

> **WARM UP**
>
> Write each number in standard form.
>
> 1. 20,000 + 4,000 + 300 + 7
> 2. 3,000,000 + 50,000 + 200 + 40

LEARN

Can you name the same number in different ways?

Our place-value system is based on groups of ten.

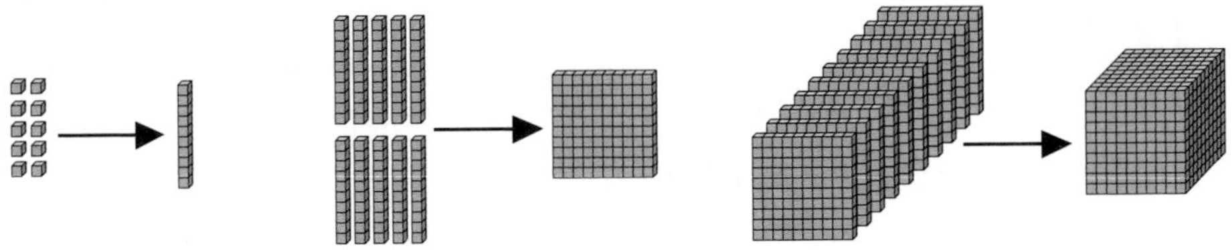

10 ones = 1 ten   10 tens = 1 hundred   10 hundreds = 1 thousand

Example A

Name 2,300 in two different ways.

	What You **Show**	What You **Say**
One Way	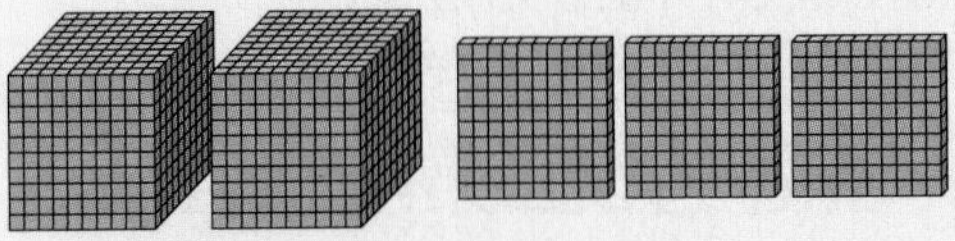	two thousand, three hundred
Another Way	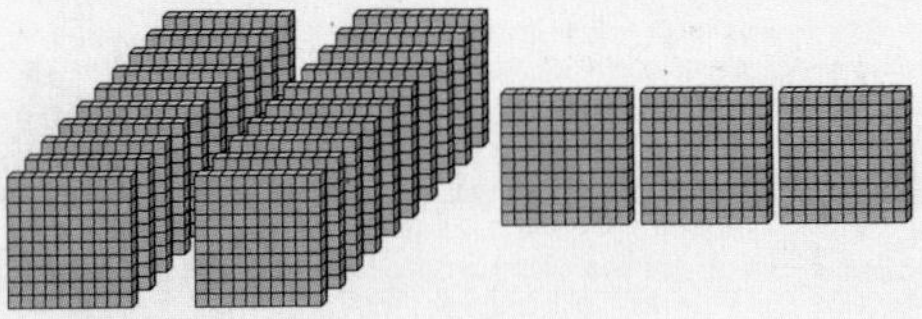	twenty-three hundreds

Example B

Write 520 in two different ways.

520 five hundred twenty or 520 fifty-two tens

Talk About It

1. Explain why 520 equals 52 tens.
2. How many hundreds are in 20,000?

CHECK

For another example, see Set 1-3 on p. 52.

Write each number in two different ways.

1. 800 **2.** 960 **3.** 1,400 **4.** 36,000

5. Number Sense How many tens are in 5,280?

PRACTICE

For more practice, see Set 1-3 on p. 56.

A Skills and Understanding

Write each number in two different ways.

6. 200 **7.** 470 **8.** 1,300 **9.** 56,000

10. 6,000 **11.** 7,200 **12.** 3,900 **13.** 84,000

14. 900 **15.** 350 **16.** 6,800 **17.** 21,000

18. Number Sense What is the least number of place-value blocks that you need to show 3,010? What is the greatest number?

B Reasoning and Problem Solving

A local newspaper prints 1,800 copies each day. How many stacks of newspapers would there be if the papers were stacked in

19. hundreds? **20.** tens?

For 21–23, look for a pattern. Then find the next three numbers.

21. 2,938 3,038 3,138

22. 12,720 12,820 12,920

23. 1,999 1,989 1,979

24. Betsy made a chain of 3,000 links. She takes off 100 links. How many links are left in the chain?

25. Writing in Math Tell what you need to add to change 348,725 to 348,825. Explain.

Mixed Review and Test Prep

Take It to the NET
Test Prep
www.scottforesman.com

26. Write the word form for 1,023,607.

27. Write 70,000,000 + 80,000 + 4,000 + 20 + 5 in standard form.

A. 78,425 **B.** 784,025 **C.** 70,084,025 **D.** 70,804,025

Problem-Solving Skill

Reading Helps!

Identifying steps in a process
can help you with...
the *Read and Understand* phase of the problem-solving process.

Key Idea
Read and Understand is the first phase of the problem-solving process.

Read and Understand

LEARN

What steps can help you understand a problem?

State Names Use the chart below.
How many state names begin with a vowel?

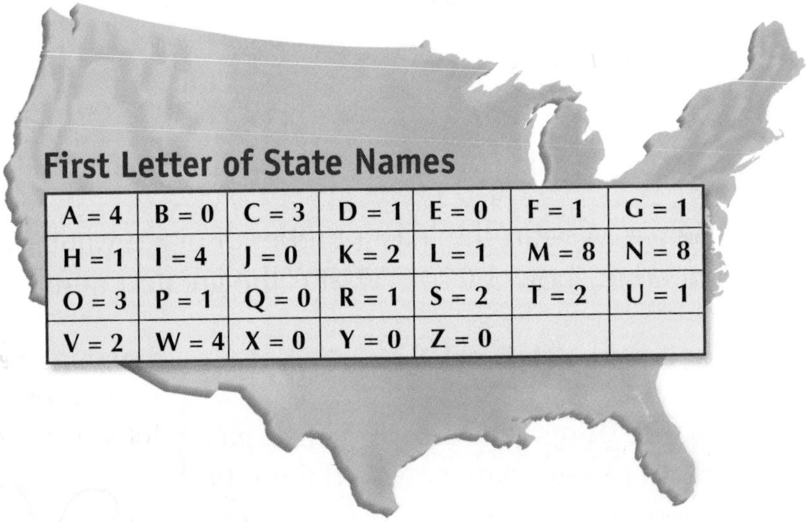

First Letter of State Names

A = 4	B = 0	C = 3	D = 1	E = 0	F = 1	G = 1
H = 1	I = 4	J = 0	K = 2	L = 1	M = 8	N = 8
O = 3	P = 1	Q = 0	R = 1	S = 2	T = 2	U = 1
V = 2	W = 4	X = 0	Y = 0	Z = 0		

Read and Understand

Step 1: What do you know?

- Tell the problem in your own words.

  The number of states with names beginning with each letter is given.

- Identify key facts and details.

  A, E, I, O, and U are vowels. From the chart, A = 4, E = 0, I = 4, O = 3, and U = 1.

Step 2: What are you trying to find?

- Tell what the question is asking.

  How many states have names that begin with an A, E, I, O, or U?

- Show the main idea.

A	E	I	O	U
4	0	4	3	1

← Add these numbers.

Talk About It

1. Give the answer in a complete sentence.

CHECK

For another example, see Set 1-4 on p. 53.

For 1–3, use the Country Names problem.

1. **Step 1:** What do you know?
   - **a.** Tell what you know in your own words.
   - **b.** Identify key facts and details.
2. **Step 2:** What are you trying to find?
   - **a.** Tell what the question is asking.
   - **b.** Show the main idea.
3. Solve the problem.

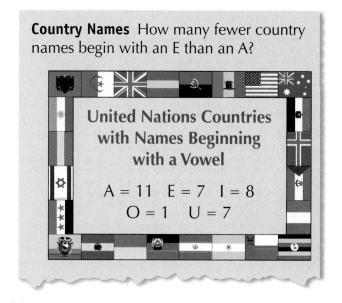

Country Names How many fewer country names begin with an E than an A?

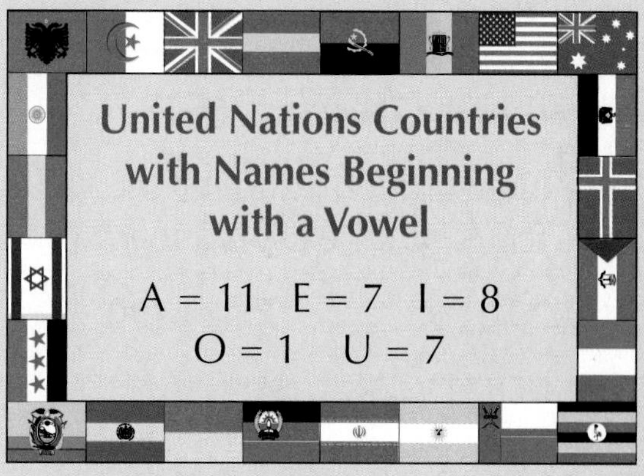

United Nations Countries with Names Beginning with a Vowel
A = 11 E = 7 I = 8
O = 1 U = 7

PRACTICE

For more practice, see Set 1-4 on p. 57.

For 4–6, use the Month Names problem.

4. **Step 1:** What do you know?
   - **a.** Tell what you know in your own words.
   - **b.** Identify key facts and details.
5. **Step 2:** What are you trying to find?
   - **a.** Tell what the question is asking.
   - **b.** Show the main idea.
6. Solve the problem.

Month Names How many more months begin with the letter J than begin with the letter M?

First Letter of Month Names

A = 2	D = 1	F = 1
J = 3	M = 2	N = 1
O = 1	S = 1	

For 7–9, use the bar graph at the right.

7. Emily has how many more tops than Thomas?
8. How many tops do Emily, Thomas, and Jaz have together?
9. **Writing in Math** Thomas and Jaz together have how many more tops than Emily? Explain.

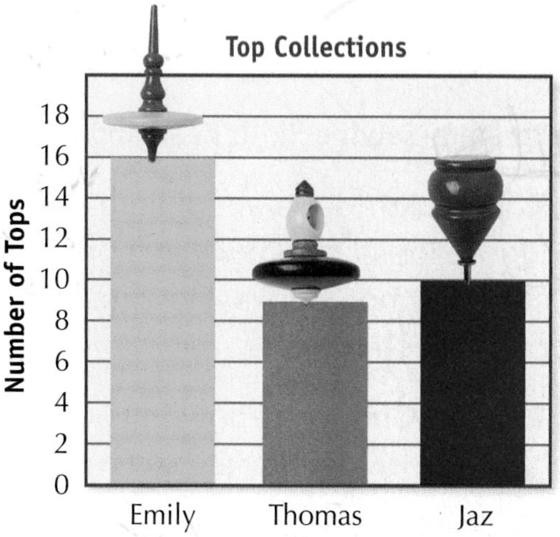

Review

Do You Know How?

Do You Understand?

Numbers in the Thousands (1-1)

Write the word form and tell the value of the red digit for each number.

1. 5,264 **2.** 46,790

3. 236,821 **4.** 356,225

A Tell how you found the value of the red digit in Exercise 2.

B Describe the periods in 75,874,110.

Understanding Greater Numbers (1-2)

Write each number in standard form.

5. Eight million, four hundred five thousand, one hundred twelve

6. 30,000,000 + 2,000,000 + 4,000 + 200 + 90 + 6

C Write the number that is 100,000 more than the number in Exercise 5.

D Write a number that has a 6 in the millions place and a 3 in the ten thousands place.

Place-Value Patterns (1-3)

Write each number in two different ways.

7. 500 **8.** 850

9. 4,800 **10.** 3,100

11. 62,000 **12.** 18,000

E Tell how you found two names for 4,800.

F Find the next three numbers.

6,792 6,802 6,812

Problem-Solving Skill: Read and Understand (1-4)

Notebooks Maria and Juan have 9 notebooks together. Each one has at least 2 notebooks. How many could each have?

13. Tell what you know in your own words. Identify key facts and details.

14. Tell what the question is asking.

G Show the main idea in the Notebooks problem.

H Solve the Notebooks problem. Explain what you did.

Diagnostic Checkpoint

MULTIPLE CHOICE

Test Talk — Think It Through
I can **identify the main idea** in a question by finding key words like *not*.

1. How many hundreds are in 19,000? (1-3)

A. 19,000 **B.** 1,900 **C.** 190 **D.** 19

2. Which of the following does NOT represent 1,472? (1-1)

A. one thousand, four hundred seventy-two

B. 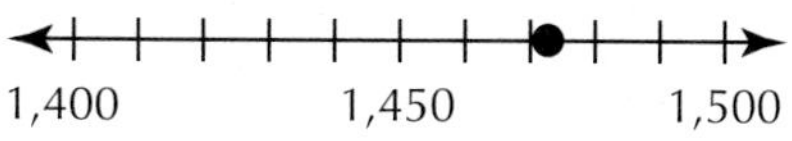

C. 1,000 + 400 + 20 + 7

D. 

FREE RESPONSE

Write each number in standard form.

3. five hundred six thousand, two hundred fifteen

4. 200,000 + 80,000 + 1,000 + 300

Write the word form and tell the value of the red digit for each number. (1-1 and 1-2)

5. 6,482 **6.** 25,815 **7.** 932,744 **8.** 36,109,562

Look for a pattern. Find the next three numbers. (1-3)

9. 1,500 2,500 3,500 **10.** 4,815 4,915 5,015

Use the Squares problem for 11–12. (1-4)

Squares Show how to divide a square into 4 equal parts so that each part is NOT a square.

11. Step 1: What do you know?

a. Tell what you know in your own words.

b. Identify key facts and details.

12. Step 2: What are you trying to find?

a. Tell what the question is asking.

b. Show the main idea.

Writing in Math

13. Explain why the 7 in 47,205,162 has a value of 7,000,000. (1-2)

14. Explain how to write 3,200 in two different ways. (1-3)

Key Idea
Place value can help you compare and order numbers.

Comparing and Ordering Numbers

WARM UP

Which number is greater?

1. 317 or 371
2. 893 or 389
3. 655 or 565

LEARN

How do you compare two numbers?

You can use a number line to compare two numbers. On a number line, numbers to the right are greater.

Example A

Which ocean has a greater depth, the Atlantic Ocean at 28,232 feet or the Pacific Ocean at 35,840 feet?

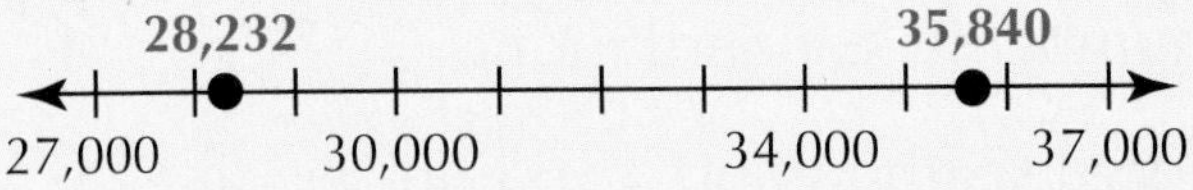

Since 35,840 is to the right of 28,232, 35,840 > 28,232. The Pacific Ocean has a greater depth than the Atlantic Ocean.

TEST TALK

Think It Through

I **remember** that the symbol > means "is greater than" and the symbol < means "is less than."

You can use place value to compare numbers.

Example B

Which ocean has a greater depth, the Atlantic Ocean at 28,232 feet or the Indian Ocean at 23,376 feet?

STEP 1	STEP 2
Write the numbers, lining up places. Begin at the left and compare.	Find the first place where the digits are different and compare.
28,232 23,376	28,232 23,376 8 thousands > 3 thousands so 28,232 > 23,376.

The Atlantic Ocean has a greater depth than the Indian Ocean.

Talk About It

1. Which place would you use to compare 35,840 and 28,232?

How can you order numbers?

You can use place value to order numbers.

Example C

Order the numbers below from greatest to least.

23,376 35,840 17,881

STEP 1	STEP 2	STEP 3
Line up the places. Begin at the left. Find the greatest number.	Compare the other numbers.	Write the numbers from greatest to least.
23,376 35,840 17,881	23,376 17,881	35,840 23,376 17,881
35,840 is the greatest.	$23{,}376 > 17{,}881$	

In order from greatest to least, the numbers are 35,840, 23,376, and 17,881.

Talk About It

2. If the numbers in Example C were shown on a number line, which one would be farthest to the right? Why?

3. How would you order the numbers below from least to greatest? Explain.

32,450 324,500 3,245

Take It to the NET
More Examples
www.scottforesman.com

CHECK

For another example, see Set 1-5 on p. 53.

Compare. Write $>$ or $<$ for each ●.

1. 4,869 ● 4,709 **2.** 25,033 ● 25,013 **3.** 847,260 ● 748,350

Order the numbers from greatest to least.

4. 37,256 36,955 37,276

5. 210,415 21,390 120,475

6. Number Sense Write three numbers that are greater than 25,000 but less than 26,000.

PRACTICE

For more practice, see Set 1-5 on p. 57.

A Skills and Understanding

Compare. Write > or < for each ●.

7. 6,249 ● 6,384 **8.** 36,256 ● 8,889 **9.** 1,743,265 ● 1,734,652

10. 5,280 ● 2,580 **11.** 48,524 ● 48,425 **12.** 18,263,014 ● 19,632,114

Order the numbers from least to greatest.

13. 276,106 274,108 275,210 **14.** 12,073 12,007 12,401

15. Number Sense Write three numbers that are greater than 470,000 but less than 471,000.

B Reasoning and Problem Solving

Math and Social Studies

Which ocean has the greater area:

16. Atlantic or Indian? **17.** Arctic or Indian?

18. Put the oceans in order from the one with the greatest area to the one with the least.

Data File

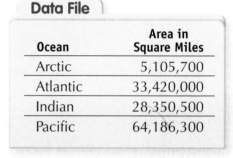

Ocean	Area in Square Miles
Arctic	5,105,700
Atlantic	33,420,000
Indian	28,350,500
Pacific	64,186,300

19. Which point on the number line represents 3,285?

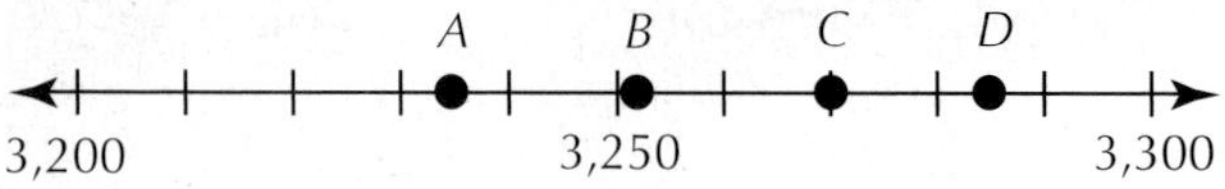

20. Order the numbers from least to greatest.

3,270 3,285 3,250 3,235

21. **Writing in Math** Is the explanation below correct? If not, tell why and write a correct response.

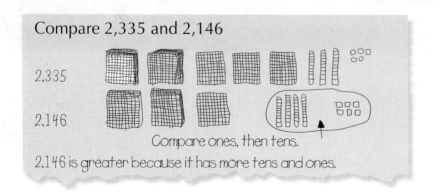

Compare 2,335 and 2,146

2,146 is greater because it has more tens and ones.

Think It Through
I can **use objects** or **draw pictures** to explain my thinking.

PRACTICE

C Extensions

22. Use the digits 2, 3, and 7 to make as many 3-digit numbers as you can. Put the numbers in order from least to greatest.

23. Use the digits 8, 8, 2, and 2 to make as many 4-digit numbers as you can. Put the numbers in order from greatest to least.

Mixed Review and Test Prep

Take It to the NET
Test Prep
www.scottforesman.com

Write each number in two different ways.

24. 600 **25.** 190 **26.** 5,400 **27.** 28,000

28. Which number has a 2 in the millions place?

A. 25,432,601 **B.** 32,580,000 **C.** 64,270,100 **D.** 75,128,000

Discovery CHANNEL SCHOOL™

Discover Math in Your World

A Colossal Achievement

The Colosseum in Rome, Italy, was built more than 1,900 years ago. It consisted of 4 levels and 80 entrances. The Romans invented the ticket system to seat thousands of spectators quickly. Each ticket had an entrance number, a level number, and a seat number.

1. Were there more or less than 100 entrances to the Colosseum?

2. Was the Colosseum built more or less than 1,000 years ago?

3. The ticket system helped to seat over 3,666 spectators per minute. Is this number greater than or less than 3,600?

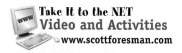

Take It to the NET
Video and Activities
www.scottforesman.com

Key Idea
Place value can help you round numbers.

Vocabulary
• rounding

Rounding Numbers

WARM UP

Round to the nearest 10.

1. 132
2. 258
3. 761
4. 250

LEARN

How do you round numbers?

Rounding replaces one number with another number that tells about how many or how much.

You can use a number line to round numbers.

Example A

Round 26,415 to the nearest thousand.

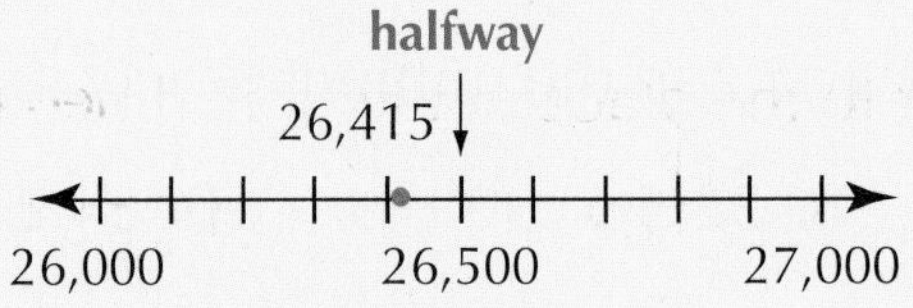

Since 26,415 is closer to 26,000 than 27,000, 26,415 rounds to 26,000.

You can use place value to round numbers.

Step 1 Look at the digit to the right of the rounding place. If it is 5 or more, add 1 to the rounding digit. If it is less than 5, leave the rounding digit alone.

Step 2 Change the digits to the right of the rounding place to zeros.

Example B

Round 26,808 to the nearest thousand.

thousands place ↓

$26,\underline{8}08$ The digit to the right is $\underline{8}$. Since $8 > 5$, add 1 to the digit in the thousands place.

27,000

Example C

Round 534,043 to the nearest hundred thousand.

hundred thousands place ↓

$5\underline{3}4,043$ The digit to the right is $\underline{3}$. Since $3 < 5$, leave the digit in the hundred thousands place alone.

500,000

Talk About It

1. Name a 3-digit and a 4-digit number that each round to 1,000.

Take It to the NET
More Examples
www.scottforesman.com

CHECK

For another example, see Set 1-6 on p. 53.

Round each number to the place of the underlined digit.

1. $4,\underline{5}35$ 2. $\underline{9},243$ 3. $4\underline{6},925$
4. $\underline{4}3,705$ 5. $\underline{8}15,578$ 6. $2,6\underline{7}0,322$
7. **Number Sense** Write 4 numbers that round to 300 when rounded to the nearest hundred.

TEST TALK

Think It Through
I can **draw a picture** of a number line to find the closest number.

PRACTICE

For more practice, see Set 1-6 on p. 57.

A Skills and Understanding

Round each number to the place of the underlined digit.

8. $5,\underline{6}90$ 9. $\underline{2},585$ 10. $\underline{7}2,932$ 11. $4\underline{7},172$
12. $\underline{1}6,555$ 13. $5\underline{4},995$ 14. $\underline{6}91,843$ 15. $4,30\underline{5},344$
16. **Number Sense** Write four numbers that would round to 2,000 when rounded to the nearest thousand.

B Reasoning and Problem Solving

17. Round 11,900,000 to the nearest million.
18. **Reasoning** To what place do you think the number 11,900,000 is rounded? Explain.
19. **Writing in Math** You want to round 3,546 to the nearest hundred. How does it help to know what number is halfway between 3,500 and 3,600?

During the 2000–2001 theater season, about 11,900,000 people attended a Broadway play.

Mixed Review and Test Prep

Take It to the NET
Test Prep
www.scottforesman.com

Compare. Write > or <.

20. 8,765 ● 7,865 21. 46,200 ● 46,220 22. 27,914,106 ● 28,094,610
23. Which number has an 8 in the thousands place?

A. 37,386 **B.** 36,846 **C.** 8,236 **D.** 87,246

Lesson 1-7

Key Idea
Place-value relationships can help you estimate how much.

Materials
- grid paper or e tools
- scissors
- tape

TEST TALK

Think It Through
I can **use objects** to understand numbers.

The Size of Numbers

LEARN

WARM UP

Write < or > for each ◯.

1. 3,456 ◯ 3,477
2. 16,463 ◯ 16,436
3. 136,002 ◯ 136,012

Activity

How much is a million?

a. Work in 10 groups. Each group cuts 10-by-10 grids from graph paper to make 100-grids.

b. Each group tapes its 100-grids together to make 1,000-strips. How many 100-grids are needed for each 1,000-strip?

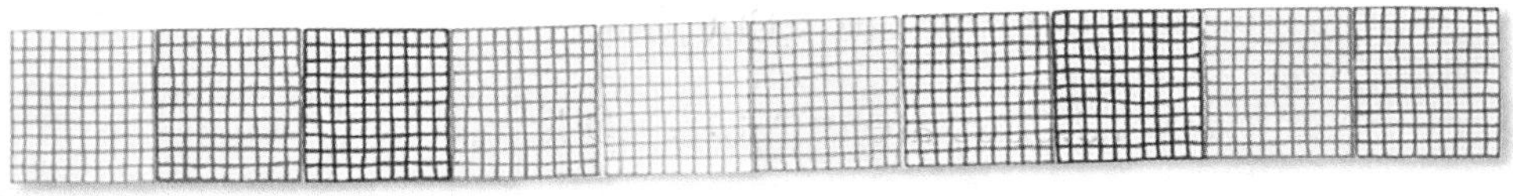

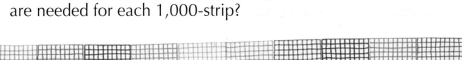

c. Each group makes enough 1,000 strips to form one 10,000-mat. How many 1,000-strips does each group need?

d. Put your 10,000-mat together with mats from the other 9 groups. How many squares are there?

e. Suppose your class put their 100,000-mats together with mats from 9 other classes. How many squares will there be? Copy and fill in the chart to find out.

Number of Classes	Number of 10,000-Mats	Number of 1,000-Strips	Number of Squares
1	10	100	100,000
2	20	200	200,000
3			
10			

Talk About It

1. Describe the number patterns you see in the chart.

CHECK

For another example, see Set 1-7 on p. 53.

Use reasoning or counting to answer each question.

1. How many 1,000s are in 100,000?
2. How many 10,000s are in 100,000?
3. **Number Sense** How many 50,000s are in 400,000? Explain.

PRACTICE

For more practice, see Set 1-7 on p. 57.

A Skills and Understanding

About how many grains of rice are in

4. 6 cups? 5. 8 cups? 6. 10 cups?

There are about 10,000 grains of rice in one cup.

7. How many 1,000s are in 1,000,000?
8. How many 10,000s are in 1,000,000?
9. How many 100,000s are in 1,000,000?
10. **Number Sense** How many 10,000s are in 500,000? Explain.

B Reasoning and Problem Solving

Would you use hundreds, thousands, or millions to count these objects? Tell why.

11. The number of math books in your school
12. The number of people in the United States
13. The number of pets in your town
14. **Writing in Math** A factory can produce 30,000 pairs of sneakers each day. About how many days will it take to produce 300,000 pairs? Explain.

Mixed Review and Test Prep

Take It to the NET
Test Prep
www.scottforesman.com

15. Round 87,267 to the nearest thousand and ten thousand.
16. Which digit is in the ten millions place in 148,265,000?

A. 1 **B.** 4 **C.** 6 **D.** 8

Problem-Solving Skill

Key Idea
Plan and Solve is the second phase of the problem-solving process.

Reading Helps!
Identifying steps in a process
can help you with...
the *Plan and Solve* phase of the problem-solving process.

Plan and Solve

LEARN

How can you make a plan to solve a problem?

Beautiful View It costs 50¢ to use a viewing machine. The machine can take any combination of quarters, dimes, and nickels. How many ways can you put 50¢ in this machine?

Plan and Solve

Step 1: Choose a strategy.
Think about which strategy or strategies might work.

Q	D	N	Q	D	N
2	0	0	0	4	2
1	2	1	0	3	4
1	1	3	0	2	6
1	0	5	0	1	8
0	5	0	0	0	10

STRATEGIES

- **Show What You Know**
  - Draw a Picture
  - Make an Organized List
  - Make a Table
  - Make a Graph
  - Act It Out or Use Objects
- **Look for a Pattern**
- **Try, Check, and Revise**
- **Write a Number Sentence**
- **Use Logical Reasoning**
- **Solve a Simpler Problem**
- **Work Backward**

Choose a tool

Step 2: Stuck? Don't give up.
Try the tips at the right if you get stuck.

Step 3: Answer the question.
There are 10 ways to make change for 50 cents using quarters, dimes, and nickels.

TEST TALK

Think It Through

- Reread the problem.
- Tell the problem in your own words.
- Tell what you know.
- Identify key facts and details.
- Show the main idea.
- Try a different strategy.
- Retrace your steps.

✓ Talk About It

1. Would another strategy work? Explain.

CHECK

For another example, see Set 1-8 on p. 54.

Numbers Find two numbers that have a sum of 20 and a difference of 8.

1. Name the strategy Micky used.
2. Give the answer in a complete sentence.

Micky

Try $12 + 8 = 20$ $\quad 12 - 8 = 4$ $\quad$ no
Try $13 + 7 = 20$ $\quad 13 - 7 = 6$ $\quad$ no
Try $14 + 6 = 20$ $\quad 14 - 6 = 8$ $\quad$ yes

PRACTICE

For more practice, see Set 1-8 on p. 58.

Feeder Fish A tank had 18 fish for feeding turtles. Sam put 27 more fish in the tank. How many fish are in the tank now?

Ann

18 + 27 = number of fish
45 fish

3. Name the strategy Ann used to solve the Feeder Fish problem.
4. Give the answer to the Feeder Fish problem in a complete sentence.

Tacos Tacos are made with corn or flour tortillas and either beef, chicken, or bean fillings. How many different tacos are possible?

Ronaldo

corn-beef flour-beef
corn-chicken flour-chicken
corn-beans flour-beans
6 tacos

Carrie

2 beef
2 chicken
+ 2 bean
6 tacos

5. Name the strategy Ronaldo used to solve the Tacos problem.
6. Name the strategy Carrie used to solve the Tacos problem.
7. Give the answer to the Tacos problem in a complete sentence.

Writing in Math Answer the questions at the right for the

8. Numbers problem.
9. Feeder Fish problem.

Reading and Understanding Problems

STEP 1 What do you know?

STEP 2 What are you trying to find?

Section B: Lessons 1-5 through 1-8

Review

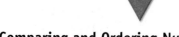

Do You Know How?

Do You Understand?

Comparing and Ordering Numbers (1-5)

Compare. Write > or < for each ●.

1. 2,346 < 2,436

2. 15,983 < 16,352

3. 935,261 < 953,261

A Explain how you compared the numbers in Exercise 2.

B Explain how you could use a number line in Exercise 1.

Rounding Numbers (1-6)

Round each number to the nearest thousand and ten thousand.

4. 28,263 **5.** 48,765

6. 511,358 **7.** 926,510

C Explain why 6,243 is closer to 6,000 than 7,000.

D Tell how you rounded a number to the nearest thousand.

The Size of Numbers (1-7)

How many thousands equal each?

8. 30,000 **9.** 70,000

10. 800,000 **11.** 500,000

12. 1,000,000 **13.** 2,000,000

E How many 10,000s equal 80,000?

F Would you use hundreds, thousands, or millions to give the total number of cars in your state? Explain.

Problem-Solving Skill: Plan and Solve (1-8)

14. Balloons Tina had 2 balloons. After she bought a new package, she had 12 balloons. After she bought another package, she had 22 balloons. How many balloons will she have after she buys one more package?

2, 12, 22,
+10 + 10 32 balloons

G Name the strategy that was used to solve the Balloons problem.

H What is another way you could solve the problem?

Diagnostic Checkpoint

MULTIPLE CHOICE

1. Which number is greater than 58,246? (1-5)

   A. 58,236 **B.** 57,246 **C.** 58,426 **D.** 58,146

2. How many hundreds equal 46,000? (1-7)

   A. 46 **B.** 460 **C.** 4,600 **D.** 46,000

Think It Through

I can **turn the question into a statement** like, "I need to find a number greater than 58,246."

FREE RESPONSE

For 3-5, use the data file at the right. Which state had the greater population in 2000? (1-5)

3. Texas or New York
4. New York or Florida
5. Round the population of Virginia to the nearest hundred thousand. (1-5)

Data File

State	2000 Population
Florida	15,982,378
New York	18,976,467
Texas	20,851,820
Virginia	7,078,515

Each flower bed has 100 tulips. How many tulips are in

6. 7 flower beds?
7. 40 flower beds? (1-7)

Schools In 1999, Illinois had 3,169 elementary schools while New York had 3,081. Which state had a greater number of elementary schools?

8. Solve the Schools problem. Write the answer in a complete sentence. (1-8)
9. Explain how you compared the numbers in the Schools problem.

Writing in Math

10. Explain how to order 56,087, 56,901, 57,543, and 56,672 from greatest to least. (1-5)
11. Explain how you could use place value to round 3,169 to the nearest thousand. (1-6)

Key Idea
A dime is one-tenth of a dollar, and a penny is one-hundredth of a dollar.

Vocabulary
- tenth
- hundredth
- decimal point

Using Money to Understand Decimals

WARM UP

Write the value of the red digit for each number.

1. 2,348
2. 159,762
3. 648,295

LEARN

How are decimals related to money?

Ten dimes equal one dollar. A dime is one **tenth** of a dollar.

0.1
one tenth

One hundred pennies equal one dollar. A penny is one **hundredth** of a dollar.

0.01
one hundredth

You can use a place-value chart to relate decimals and money.

dollars (ones)		dimes (tenths)	pennies (hundredths)
$4	.	9	5

decimal point

Read: four dollars *and* ninety-five cents.

Example

Here are two ways to show $4.95.

$4.95 = 4 dollars + 9 dimes + 5 pennies
= 4 ones + 9 tenths + 5 hundredths

$4.95 = 4 dollars + 95 pennies
= 4 ones + 95 hundredths

Talk About It

1. Why is a dime one tenth of a dollar?
2. Why is a penny one hundredth of a dollar?

Take It to the NET
More Examples
www.scottforesman.com

CHECK ✓

For another example, see Set 1-9 on p. 54.

Copy and complete.

1. $2.85 = ■ dollars + ■ dimes + ■ pennies
2.85 = ■ ones + ■ tenths + ■ hundredths

2. $5.37 = ■ dollars + ■ pennies
5.37 = ■ ones + ■ hundredths

3. Number Sense Write seven and forty-three hundredths with a decimal point.

PRACTICE

For more practice, see Set 1-9 on p. 58.

A Skills and Understanding

Copy and complete.

4. $4.25 = ■ dollars + ■ dimes + ■ pennies
4.25 = ■ ones + ■ tenths + ■ hundredths

5. $1.09 = ■ dollars + ■ dimes + ■ pennies
1.09 = ■ ones + ■ tenths + ■ hundredths

6. $8.16 = ■ dollars + ■ pennies
8.16 = ■ ones + ■ hundredths

7. Write 2 dollars, 8 dimes, 4 pennies with a dollar sign and decimal point.

8. Number Sense Which is more, 3 dimes and 2 pennies or 2 dimes and 3 pennies?

B Reasoning and Problem Solving

How could you use only dollars, dimes and pennies to buy

9. the collar? **10.** the hat?

11. Writing in Math Explain why the 7 in $8.47 represents hundredths of a dollar.

Mixed Review and Test Prep

Take It to the NET
Test Prep
www.scottforesman.com

12. Rosa knows that each album has about 100 pages. There are 30 albums. Estimate the total number of pages.

13. Round 784,692 to the nearest thousand.

A. 780,000 **B.** 784,000 **C.** 785,000 **D.** 790,000

Key Idea
When counting money, it is often easiest to start with the bills or coins that have the largest value.

Counting Money

LEARN

How do you count money?

WARM UP

Find the value of

1. 3 dimes.
2. 2 quarters.
3. 7 dimes and 2 pennies.

Example A

Suppose you have these coins and bills in your pocket: one penny, two nickels, one dime, five quarters, two $1 bills, one $5 bill, and one $10 bill. How much money do you have?

First, count the bills. Start with the bill of greatest value.

$10.00 ⟶ $15.00 ⟶ $16.00 ⟶ **$17.00**

Four quarters make another dollar.

$17.25 ⟶ $17.50 ⟶ $17.75 ⟶ **$18.00**

Then count the remaining coins. Start with the coin of the greatest value.

$18.25 → $18.35 → $18.40 → $18.45 → **$18.46**

Write: $18.46

Say: eighteen dollars and forty-six cents

Example B

How can you make $21.30 with the fewest bills and coins?

Start with the largest possible bill. Then keep using the largest possible bills or coins.

Use one $20 bill, one $1 bill, one quarter, and one nickel.

Talk About It

1. Explain why the four quarters in Example A were counted together.

Quarters and dimes minted prior to 1965 contained 90% silver.

CHECK ✓

For another example, see Set 1-10 on p. 54.

Count the money. Write each amount with a dollar sign and a decimal point.

1. two \$1 bills, 4 dimes, 8 pennies **2.** one \$5 bill, 3 quarters, 1 dime

Tell how to make each money amount with the fewest bills and coins.

3. \$4.65 **4.** \$17.48 **5.** \$1.99 **6.** \$28.32

7. Reasoning Ed has one \$10 bill, one \$5 bill, 4 dollars, 3 quarters, and 2 dimes. Stacy has three \$5 bills, three \$1 bills, and 8 quarters. Who has more money?

PRACTICE

For more practice, see Set 1-10 on p. 58.

A Skills and Understanding

Count the money. Write each amount with a dollar sign and a decimal point.

8. four \$1 bills, 1 quarter, 2 nickels **9.** one \$5 bill, two \$1 bills, 3 dimes

Tell how to make each money amount with the fewest bills and coins.

10. \$3.25 **11.** \$26.72 **12.** \$8.19 **13.** \$14.56

14. Reasoning How could you make \$41.15 with exactly three bills and three coins?

B Reasoning and Problem Solving

15. Algebra Ms. Mendez has \$0.93 in her change purse. She has 9 coins. She has two more dimes than quarters. What coins does she have?

16. Writing in Math How many different ways can you make \$0.35 using only nickels and dimes? Explain.

Mixed Review and Test Prep

Take It to the NET
Test Prep
www.scottforesman.com

17. \$6.47 = ▢ dollars + ▢ dimes + ▢ pennies
6.47 = ▢ ones + ▢ tenths + ▢ hundredths

18. Each wrestler weighs about 200 pounds. Estimate the weight of 10 wrestlers.

A. 200 pounds **B.** 1,000 pounds **C.** 2,000 pounds **D.** 20,000 pounds

Key Idea
You can count up from the cost to make change.

TEST TALK

Think It Through
When making change, think about **what coins and bills are needed to count up to the amount paid.**

Making Change

✔ WARM UP

Write each amount with a dollar sign and decimal point.

1. **4 dollars, 2 quarters, 1 dime**
2. **2 dollars, 3 dimes**

LEARN

How can you make change?

When you make change, you count money.

Example A

Eric buys flowers for $2.68 and pays three $1 bills. How much change does he get?

Count on from $2.68.

Cost **Amount paid**

$2.68 → $2.69 → $2.70 → $2.75 → **$3.00**

Eric's change is a quarter, a nickel, and 2 pennies, or $0.32.

Example B

Ms. Feld buys seed packets for $7.45 and pays with a $10 bill. How much change does she get?

Count on from $7.45.

Cost **Amount paid**

$7.45 → $7.50 → $7.75 → $8.00 → $9.00 → **$10.00**

Ms. Feld's change is 2 dollars, 2 quarters, and a nickel, or $2.55.

✔ Talk About It

1. In Example B, what change would Ms. Feld get if she paid with a $20 bill?

CHECK

List the coins and bills you would use to make change for each purchase paid for with the amount shown. Then write the amount with a dollar sign and decimal point.

1. Cost: $8.25

2. Cost $13.52

3. Cost $18.79

4. Reasoning Suppose you buy an item that costs $3.23. Why might you pay with a $5 bill, two dimes, and 3 pennies?

PRACTICE

For more practice, see Set 1-11 on p. 59.

A Skills and Understanding

List the coins and bills you would use to make change for each purchase paid for with the amount shown. Then write the amount with a dollar sign and decimal point.

5. Cost $16.94

6. Cost $24.05

7. Cost $37.98

8. Number Sense Suppose you buy an item that costs $1.96. Why might you pay with two $1 bills and 1 penny?

B Reasoning and Problem Solving

How much change should you get from $20 when you buy

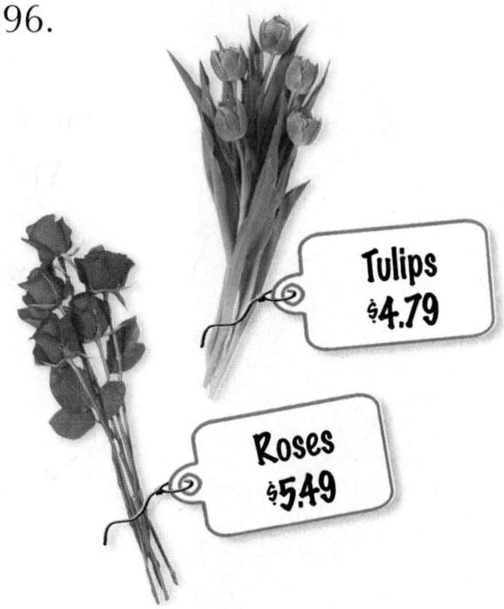

9. the tulips?

10. the roses?

11. Writing in Math Ken pays with a $20 bill for an item that costs $12.73. What is the least number of coins and bills he could get as change? Explain.

Mixed Review and Test Prep

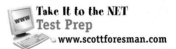

Take It to the NET
Test Prep
www.scottforesman.com

12. How many 100s equal 100,000?

13. Which of the following is seven and twenty-one hundredths?

A. 7.021 **B.** 7.21 **C.** 72.1 **D.** 721

Key Idea
A grid can be used to show tenths and hundredths.

Materials
Decimal models

TEST TALK

Think It Through
Look at the place value of the last digit at the right to read a decimal.

More About Decimals

WARM UP

Tell the value of the red digit in each number.

1. 34,636
2. 2,579
3. 264,203

LEARN

How can you show, read, and write tenths and hundredths?

You can use grids to show how to read and write decimals.

Example A

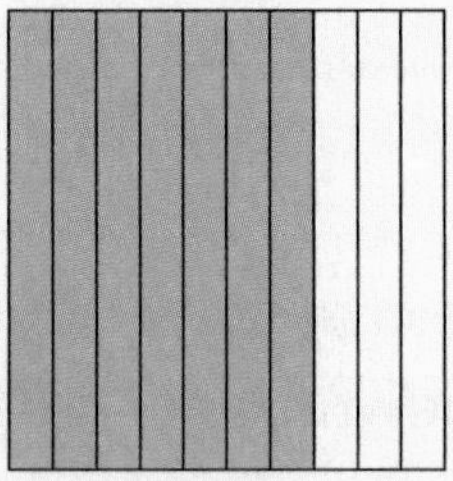

Ones		Tenths
0	.	7

7 out of 10 parts are shaded.

Read: seven tenths

Write: 0.7

Example B

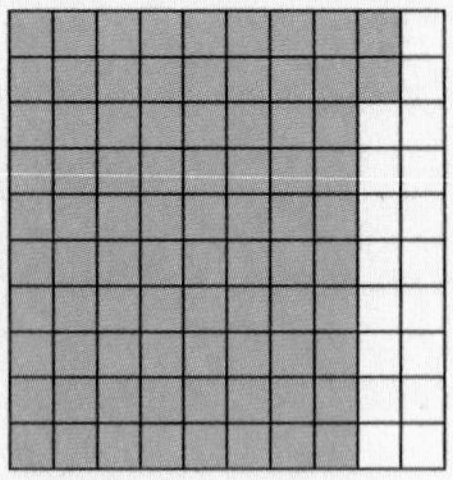

Ones		Tenths	Hundredths
0	.	8	2

82 out of 100 parts are shaded.

Read: eighty-two hundredths

Write: 0.82

Talk About It

1. Why is each part of the grid in Example A equal to one tenth?
2. How is one part of the grid in Example B like a penny?

How are tenths and hundredths related?

What part is shaded? Here's what Scott and Marie thought.

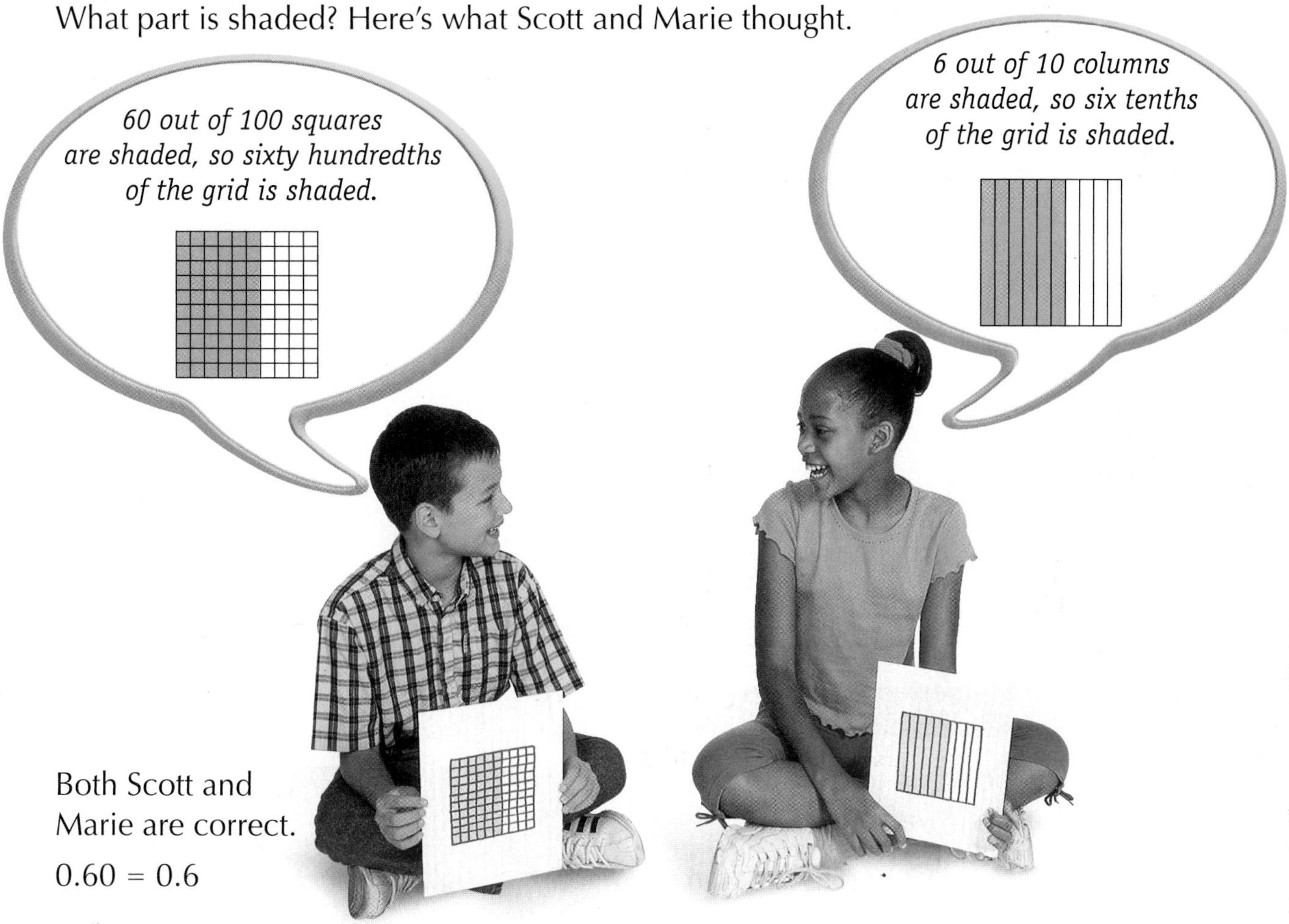
60 out of 100 squares are shaded, so sixty hundredths of the grid is shaded.
6 out of 10 columns are shaded, so six tenths of the grid is shaded.

Both Scott and Marie are correct.

0.60 = 0.6

Talk About It

3. How does Scott's grid show both 0.60 and 0.6?

4. How many hundredths equal 10 tenths?

CHECK

For another example, see Set 1-12 on p. 55.

Write the word form and decimal for each shaded part.

1. 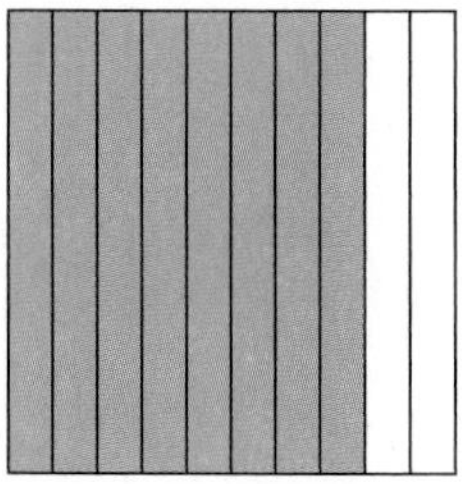

2. 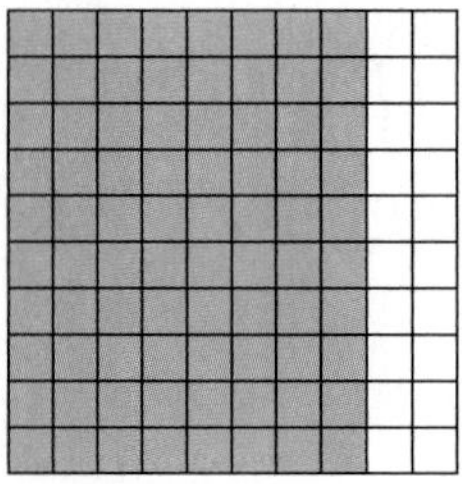

3. 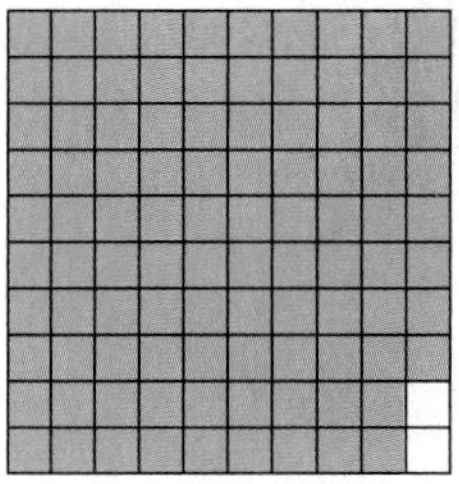

Draw and shade a grid to show each decimal.

4. 0.55 **5.** 0.5 **6.** 0.05 **7.** 0.50 **8.** 0.33

9. Number Sense Which is greater, 0.3 or 0.03? Explain.

PRACTICE

For more practice, see Set 1-12 on p. 59.

A Skills and Understanding

Write the word form and decimal for each shaded part.

10. 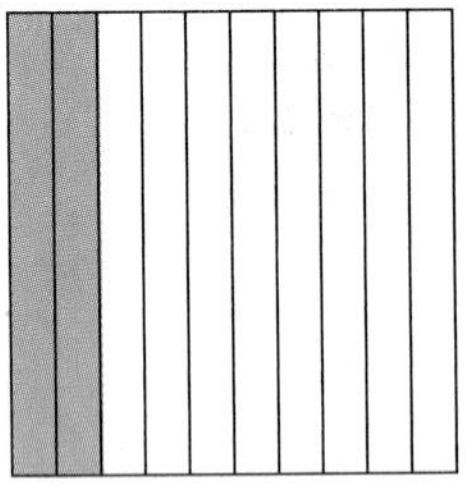

11. 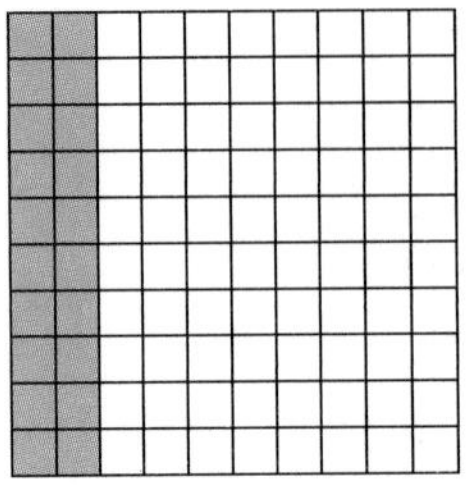

12. 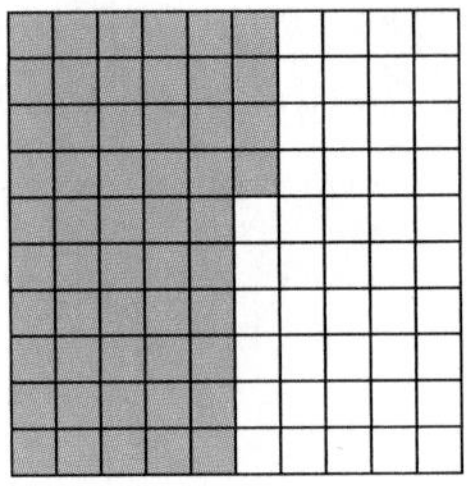

Draw and shade a grid to show each decimal.

13. 0.3 **14.** 0.68 **15.** 0.90 **16.** 0.14 **17.** 0.71

18. Number Sense Explain why 0.7 = 0.70.

B Reasoning and Problem Solving

Math and Science

For 19–21, shade a grid to show the part of the land covered with forests.

19. In 1972, about 0.32 of the land on Earth was covered with forests.

20. In 2001, about 0.29 of the land on Earth was covered with forests.

21. Use the information at the right to show the part of land in the United States that is covered with forests.

22. Tina collected 4 gallons of maple sap one day and 3 gallons the next day. If each gallon makes 4 ounces of maple syrup, how many ounces of syrup can Tina make in all?

23. **Writing in Math** Explain why 2 tenths is larger than 2 hundredths. Use hundredths grids or money to help.

In the United States, forests cover about 0.25 of the land.

PRACTICE

24. Writing in Math Is the explanation below correct? If not, tell why and write a correct response.

> Are 0.30 and 0.3 equal? Explain.
>
> No, 0.30 is greater than 0.3 because 30 is greater than 3.

TEST TALK
Think It Through
I should always **check my answer.**

C Extensions

Patterns Write the next two numbers in each pattern.

25. 0.1, 0.3, 0.5,

26. 0.24, 0.23, 0.22,

Mixed Review and Test Prep

Take It to the NET
Test Prep
www.scottforesman.com

27. A customer pays for a \$6.89 purchase with a \$20 bill. What coins and bills could you give in change?

28. How much money is a \$5 bill, a quarter, a dime, a nickel and 3 pennies?

A. \$5.18 **B.** \$5.33 **C.** \$5.43 **D.** \$6.18

Learning with Technology

The Money eTool

With the two-part workspace selected, build \$5.01 in the top half of the screen and \$1.96 in the bottom half. Add money to the bottom half of the screen until it equals the amount in the top half. Keep track of what you add.

1. How much money did you add to \$1.96 to get \$5.01?

2. If an item costs \$1.96, why would you give the cashier \$5.01 instead of \$5.00?

3. A box of pens costs \$6.98. Why would you give the cashier \$10.03 instead of \$10.00?

Problem-Solving Skill

Key Idea
Look Back and Check is the final phase of the problem-solving process.

Reading Helps!
Identifying steps in a process
can help you with...
the *Look Back and Check* phase of the problem-solving process.

Look Back and Check

LEARN

What are the last steps in solving a problem?

The Private Plane
A plane rises into the air at 400 feet each second. How many seconds will it take the plane to reach 2,000 feet?

Seconds	Feet	Height
1 sec	400	400
1 sec	400	800
1 sec	400	1,200
1 sec	400	1,600
1 sec	400	2,000

It will take 5 seconds.

Look Back and Check

Step 1: Have you checked your answer?

- Did you answer the right question?

Yes, I want to know the total number of seconds.

- Use estimation and reasoning to decide if the answer makes sense.

I counted by 400s to get 2,000. The answer is reasonable.

Step 2: Have you checked your work?

- Look back at your work and compare it against the information in the problem.

I gave the total number of seconds, 5 seconds.

- Check that you used the correct operation or procedure.

Counting by 400 to get to 2,000 showed how many seconds were needed.

Talk About It

1. Tammy's work is shown at the right. Did she answer the right question? Explain.

Tammy
2,000 + 400 = 2,400
The total is 2,400 feet.

CHECK

For another example, see Set 1-13 on p. 55.

For 1–4, use the Four Towns problem.

1. Did Pat answer the right question?

2. Does Pat's work match the information in the problem?

3. Did Pat use a correct procedure?

4. Is Pat's answer reasonable? Explain.

Four Towns Four towns are on the same road that runs east and west. York is west of Martinsville but east of Central. Dallastown is east of Martinsville. What is the order of these towns from west to east?

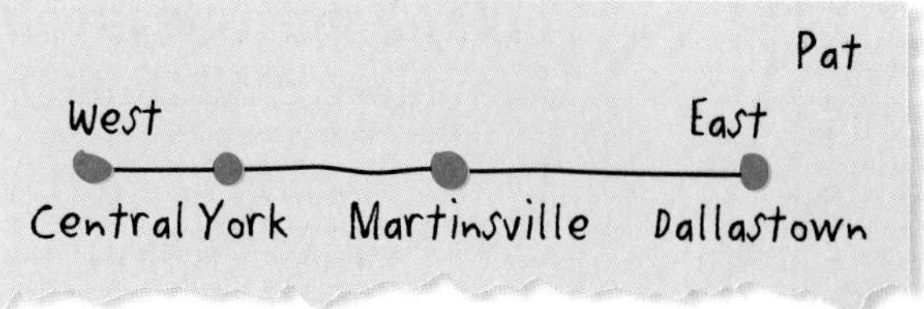

PRACTICE

For another example, see Set 1-13 on p. 59.

Use the Stickers problem for 5–8.

5. Did Sarah answer the right question?

6. Does Sarah's work match the information in the problem?

7. Did Sarah use a correct procedure?

8. Is Sarah's answer reasonable?

Sarah

3 + 4 + 1 = 8

Mr. Richardson has 80 stickers.

Stickers How many stickers does Mr. Richardson have in all?

Mr. Richardson's Stickers

On sheets	♥ ♥ ♥
On rolls	♥ ♥ ♥ ♥
In boxes	♥

Each ♥ = 10 stickers.

Use the Sweatshirt problem for 9–11.

9. Solve the Sweatshirt problem. Give the answer to the problem in a complete sentence.

10. Check your answer. Did you answer the right question? Is your answer reasonable?

11. **Writing in Math** Explain how you can check your work.

Sweatshirt Dawn buys a sweatshirt. The total cost is $12.65. She pays with a $10 bill and a $5 bill. How much change should she receive?

Lesson 1-14

Problem-Solving Applications

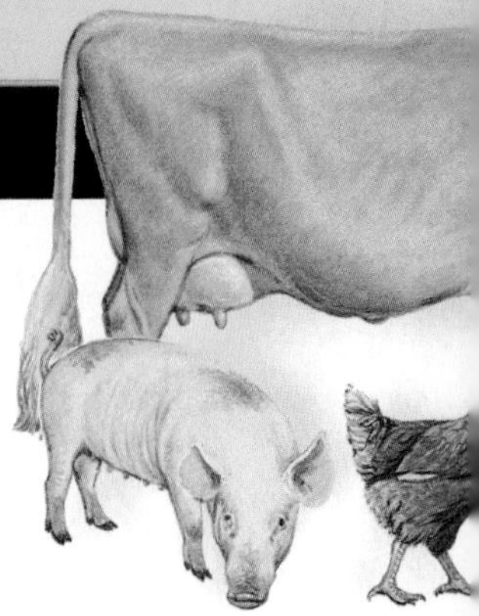

Food for One Day As the world's population increases, the amount of food needed each day will increase. Each day, farms supply tons of food. A vast network of trains, trucks, and ships moves the food around the globe. Just imagine if all this food were put in one place!

Trivia Each day, American farmers feed over 98,000,000 cattle, 61,000,000 pigs, 7,800,000 sheep, and 313,000,000 hens.

1 Use the data above. Write the word form for the number of cattle, pigs, sheep, and hens that are fed in the U.S. each day.

2 All the tomatoes harvested in the world in one day weigh about 234,000 tons. Write the numbers that are 1,000 more and 1,000 less than 234,000.

Key Facts
Food Harvested Daily

Food	Tons
• Peas	13,200
• Pineapples	35,000
• Potatoes	801,000
• Corn	1,800,000
• Tomatoes	234,000
• Onions	98,000

Using Key Facts

3 Order the amounts of food harvested daily from greatest to least. What is the world's largest vegetable crop?

Good News/Bad News
More than $478,000 worth of breath freshener is sold daily, but each day the world produces 24,000 tons of garlic.

Dorling Kindersley

4 Every day, 159,000 tons of bananas are picked. What number is in the ten-thousands place?

5 **Writing in Math** Use data from this lesson to write a word problem involving place value. Give the answer in a complete sentence.

6 The world's grape harvest weighs about 342 million pounds each day. Write that number in standard form.

7 **Decision Making** Suppose you want to eat less than 600 calories for lunch. Which foods would you choose to eat? How many calories would your lunch have?

Food	Calories
Milk	137
Orange juice	111
Hamburger	330
Taco	220
Hot dog	214
Potato chips	148
Pretzels	111
Orange	65
Yogurt	228
Apple	81

Review

Do You Know How?

Do You Understand?

Using Money to Understand Decimals (1-9)
Counting Money (1-10)

Write each amount with a dollar sign and decimal point.

1. one $1 bill, 5 dimes, 4 pennies

2. one $10 bill, 5 quarters, 2 nickels

A Tell how to make $6.36 with the fewest bills and coins.

B Write one and fifty-four hundredths with a decimal point.

Making Change (1-11)

List the coins and bills you would use to make change. Then write the amount with a dollar sign and decimal point.

3. Cost $2.95 **4.** Cost $3.26

C Tell another way you could give change in Exercise 4.

D When making change, do you start with coins or bills? Why?

More About Decimals (1-12)

Draw and shade a grid to show each decimal.

5. 0.7 **6.** 0.68 **7.** 0.30

E Write the word name for 0.68.

F Explain why 0.4 = 0.40.

Problem-Solving Skill: Look Back and Check (1-13)

Train A train is traveling 17 miles. It stops after 8 miles. How much farther does it need to go?

Nate

8 + ____ = 17

8 + 9 = 17 9 more miles

8. Did Nate answer the right question?

G Tell how you decided if Nate answered the right question.

H Explain how to check Nate's work.

Diagnostic Checkpoint

TEST TALK

Think It Through

I should **understand the vocabulary** in a question.

MULTIPLE CHOICE

1. How many tenths are in 34.75? (1-9)

A. 3 **B.** 4 **C.** 5 **D.** 7

2. How much change would you get for a purchase of \$8.74 if you paid with a \$20 bill? (1-11)

A. \$10.26 **B.** \$10.36 **C.** \$11.26 **D.** \$11.36

FREE RESPONSE

Copy and complete. (1-9)

3. \$5.67 = ___ dollars + ___ dimes + ___ pennies
5.67 = ___ ones + ___ tenths + ___ hundredths

Tell how to make each money amount with the fewest bills and coins. (1-10)

4. \$1.47 **5.** \$4.85 **6.** \$14.26 **7.** \$27.12

8. How much change would you get for a purchase of \$1.39 if you paid with a \$10.00 bill? (1-11)

9. Write the word name and decimal for the shaded part. (1-12)

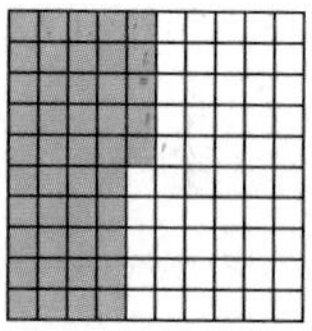

Writing in Math

10. Explain how to make \$17.68 with the fewest bills and coins. (1-10)

Use the Coins problem for 11–12.

Coins How many ways can you make 12 cents?

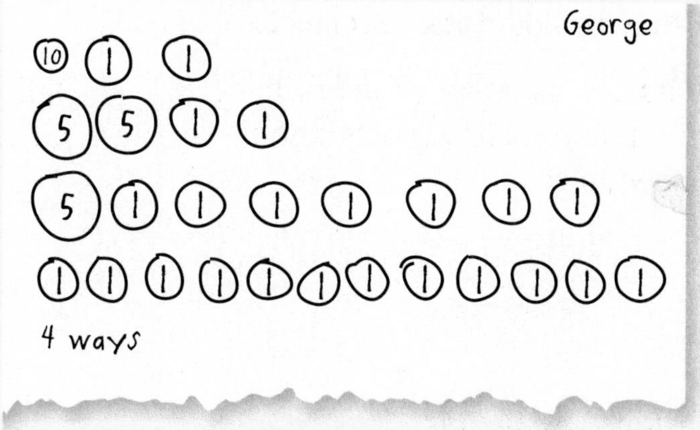

11. Did George answer the right question? (1-13)

12. Does George's work match the information in the problem? (1-13)

Test-Taking Strategies

- **Understand the question.**
- Get information for the answer.
- Plan how to find the answer.
- Make smart choices.
- Use writing in math.
- Improve written answers.

Understand the Question

Before you can answer a test question you have to understand it. The steps used with the problem below will help you understand what the question is asking.

1. Dorothy made this chart to compare the distances between some cities in the United States.

Distance Between Cities

Cities	Distance (in miles)
Orlando, FL to Cleveland, OH	1,050
Los Angeles, CA to Des Moines, IA	1,710
Atlanta, GA, to Boston, MA	1,110
New York, NY to Denver, CO	1,790

Which list below orders the distances from **least** to **greatest?**

A. 1,790 1,710 1,050 1,110

B. 1,050 1,110 1,710 1,790

C. 1,110 1,050 1,710 1,790

D. 1,050 1,790 1,710 1,110

Understand the question.

- Look for important words (words that tell what the problem is about and highlighted words).

__Least__ and __greatest__ are in bold type. __Least__ is written first. So, the smallest number in the list should come first, and the __greatest__ number should come last.

- Turn the question into a statement that begins: "I need to find...."

I need to find the list that orders the numbers from least to greatest.

2. Bradley counted 9 windows on the first floor of a building. The building has 8 floors and each floor has about the same number of windows. Which is the best estimate for the number of windows in the building?

A. about 20

B. about 50

C. about 70

D. about 200

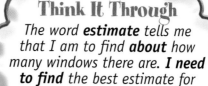

Think It Through

*The word **estimate** tells me that I am to find **about** how many windows there are. **I need to find** the best estimate for the number of windows in the building.*

Now it's your turn.

For each problem, identify important words. Finish the statement, "I need to find...."

3. Florida has the fourth largest population of the 50 states. One source reported it to be 15,982,378.

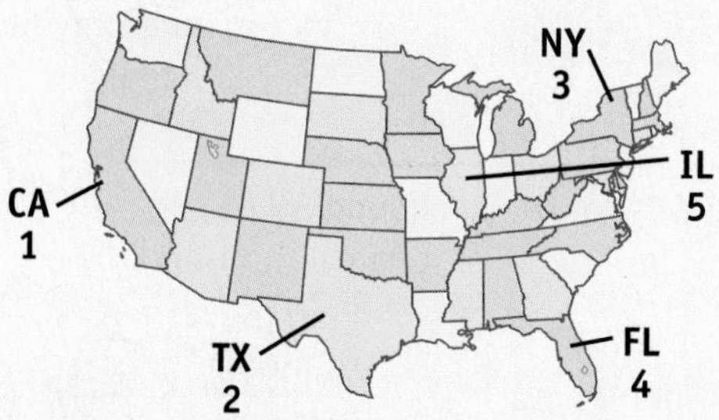

Which digit is in the hundred thousands place?

A. 9

B. 7

C. 8

D. 5

4. Shelly is riding the bike trail shown below. She had gone 5 miles when she arrived at Crystal River.

Which is the best estimate for the length of the bike trail?

A. 10 miles

B. 14 miles

C. 6 miles

D. 20 miles

Key Vocabulary and Concept Review

In our school,
each period is 50 minutes.
In a number, each **period** has 3 digits, starting from the right. (p. 8)

Self Check

Read and understand numbers. (Lessons 1-1, 1-2, 1-3)

A **place-value** chart can help you tell the amount each **digit** represents.

millions			thousands			ones		
hundred millions	ten millions	millions	hundred thousands	ten thousands	thousands	hundreds	tens	ones
6	0	1	3	2	7	8	5	4

Expanded form: 600,000,000 + 1,000,000 + 300,000 + 20,000 + 7,000 + 800 + 50 + 4
Standard form: 601,327,854
Word form: six hundred one million, three hundred twenty-seven thousand, eight hundred fifty-four

The **value** of the digit 8 is 800. 800 can also be written as 80 tens.

1. Write the word form and expanded form for 42,306,987.

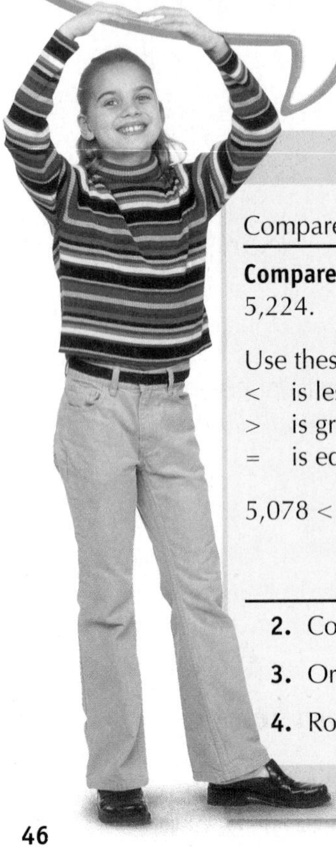
Rounded numbers
usually contain round zeros.
Rounding is showing a number to the nearest ten, hundred, and so on. (p. 20)

Self Check

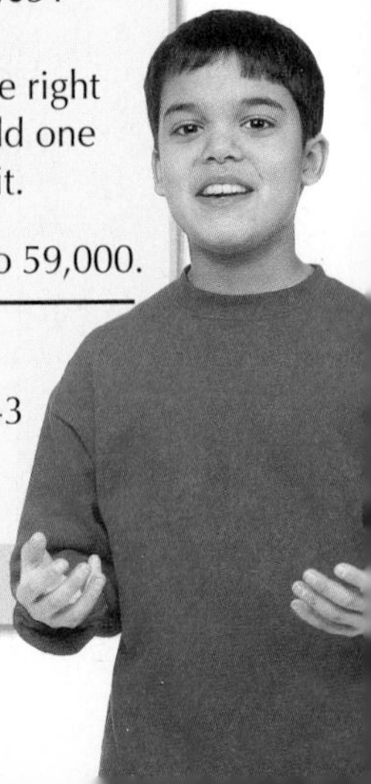
Our new car
has standard equipment.
Standard form is the usual way we write numbers. (p. 4)

Compare, order, and round numbers. (Lessons 1-5, 1-6)

Compare 5,078 and 5,224.

Use these symbols:
< is less than
> is greater than
= is equal to.

5,078 < 5,224

Order 52,672, 58,681, and 36,185, from least to greatest.

Compare pairs of numbers. 58,681 is the greatest, and 36,185 is the least.

36,185 52,672 58,681

Round 58,651 to the nearest thousand.

Find the rounding place. 58,**6**51

Since the digit to the right is greater than 5, add one to the rounding digit.

So, 58,651 rounds to 59,000.

2. Compare 7,714 and 7,641.

3. Order these numbers from least to greatest. 462,500 491,266 460,743

4. Round 634,219 to the nearest ten thousand.

Self Check

Use money to understand decimals. (Lessons 1-9, 1-10, 1-11, 1-12)

dollars (ones)		dimes (tenths)	pennies (hundredths)
$2	.	6	4

decimal point

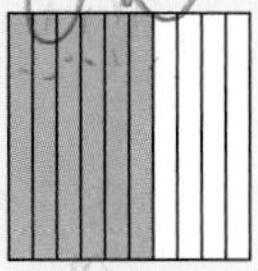

0.6
six tenths

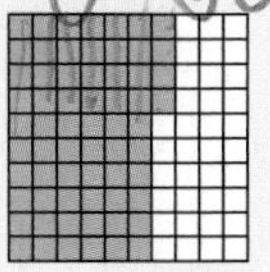

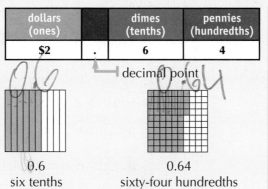

0.64
sixty-four hundredths

Ali bought a binder for $3.88. She paid with a $5 bill. How much change did she get?

Count up from $3.88.

$3.88 $3.89 $3.90 $4.00 $5.00

Ali got back $1.12.

Tenth contains the word "ten," and hundredth contains the word "hundred."

If you split something into 10 equal parts you get ***tenths.*** *If there are 100 equal parts, you get* ***hundredths.*** *(p. 34)*

5. A grid has 37 shaded squares out of 100. Write a decimal for the shaded part.

6. A purchase of $2.43 is made with a $5 bill. List the coins and bills you could use to make change.

Self Check

Use steps in a process to solve problems. (Lessons 1-4, 1-7, 1-8, 1-13)

Viv estimated that there are 50 pens in a box. About how many are in 4 boxes?

Read and understand.

I want to know about how many pens are in 4 boxes.

Plan and solve.

Make a table.

1 box	50
2 boxes	100
3 boxes	150
4 boxes	200

There are about 200 pens.

Look back and check.

I answered the question. The answer is reasonable because I counted by 50s to get 200.

7. A jet travels 600 miles per hour. How long will it take to travel 3,000 miles?

Answers: **1.** forty-two million, three hundred six thousand, nine hundred eighty-seven; 40,000,000 + 2,000,000 + 300,000 + 6,000 + 900 + 80 + 7 **2.** 7,714 > 7,641 **3.** 460,743 462,500 491,266 **4.** 630,000 **5.** 0.37 **6.** Sample answer: 2 pennies, 1 nickel, 2 quarters, 2 one-dollar bills **7.** 5 hours

Chapter Test

MULTIPLE CHOICE

Choose the correct letter for each answer.

1. How much change would you get for a purchase of $6.79, if you paid with a $10 bill?

A. $2.29 **C.** $4.20

B. $3.21 **D.** $4.21

2. Round 571,092 to the nearest ten thousand.

A. 570,000 **C.** 580,000

B. 571,000 **D.** 600,000

3. What is another way of naming 65,000?

A. 65 tens **C.** 65 thousands

B. 65 hundreds **D.** 65 ten thousands

4. What is the value of the red digit?

97,065

A. 90 **C.** 90,000

B. 9,000 **D.** 900,000

5. Find the next three numbers in the pattern:

3,410, 3,430, 3,450, ■, ■, ■

A. 3,460, 3,470, 3,480

B. 3,450, 3,480, 3,510

C. 3,470, 3,490, 3,510

D. 3,480, 3,510, 3,540

6. Write 3 dollars, no dimes, and 2 pennies with a dollar sign and decimal point.

A. $3.02 **C.** $3.22

B. $3.20 **D.** $3.23

7. Which number sentence is TRUE?

A. $4{,}768 < 2{,}109$

B. $22{,}489 > 22{,}498$

C. $96{,}587 > 96{,}855$

D. $65{,}984 < 66{,}489$

TEST TALK

Think It Through

- I need to **read each problem carefully.**
- I should **watch for words like true, false or not.**

8. Count the money.

A. $10.63 **C.** $13.63

B. $13.33 **D.** $103.63

9. Order the numbers from least to greatest.

157,661 156,671 156,761

A. 157,661, 156,671, 156,761

B. 156,671, 156,761, 157,661

C. 156,761, 156,671, 157,661

D. 157,661, 156,761, 156,671

10. Which number does NOT come between 2,538 and 2,637?

A. 2,583 **C.** 2,638

B. 2,573 **D.** 2,539

FREE RESPONSE

How much change would you get from a $10 bill for each purchase?

11. $3.01 **12.** $6.17

Round each number to the place of the underlined digit.

13. <u>8</u>13,928 **14.** 2,3<u>9</u>9,001

Compare. Use <, >, or =.

15. 104,872 ◯ 104,827

16. 41,982,324 ◯ 41,892,324

A theater had 2,400 programs printed for a play. How many boxes of programs would there be if the programs were packed in

17. hundreds? **18.** tens?

Write each in expanded and word form.

19. 330,584 **20.** 45,678,971

Copy and complete.

21. $8.56 = ▭ dollars + ▭ dimes + ▭ pennies

8.56 = ▭ ones + ▭ tenths + ▭ hundredths

22. Write the word form and decimal for the shaded part.

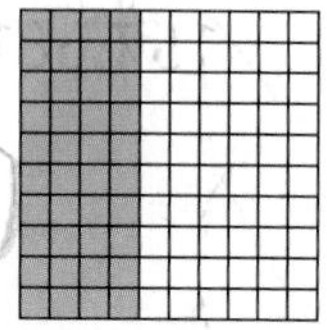

23. Order these numbers from least to greatest.

4,238 4,282 4,283 4,239

24. Write five million, four hundred sixty-seven thousand, seventeen in standard form.

Writing in Math

For 25–29, use the Pocket Change problem.

> **Pocket Change** Victoria has 1 quarter, 1 dime, 3 nickels, and 4 pennies in her pocket. Can she combine the coins in different ways to make all amounts up to 50 cents?

25. Write what you know.

26. Write what you are trying to find.

27. Could Victoria combine coins to make 56 cents? Why or why not?

28. Solve the problem and write your answer in a complete sentence. What strategy did you use to complete the problem?

> **TEST TALK**
>
> **Think It Through**
> - I should look for key words.
> - I will need to try different combinations.

29. Check your answer. Did you answer the right question? Explain how you checked your answer.

Cumulative Review and Test Prep

Number and Operation

MULTIPLE CHOICE

1. Bobby buys a baseball ticket for $13.65. He pays with a $20 bill. How much change does he get back?

   A. $6.35 **C.** $7.15

   B. $7.00 **D.** $7.35

2. Find 8 + 9 + 4.

   A. 18 **B.** 19 **C.** 21 **D.** 28

3. Notebooks cost $3. If Jan buys 4 notebooks, how much will it cost?

   A. $3

   B. $4

   C. $7

   D. $12

TEST TALK

Think It Through
I can **draw a picture** to help explain my thinking.

FREE RESPONSE

4. Write these numbers in order from greatest to least.

   67,098 66,236 67,381 67,715

5. How many thousands equal 400,000?

6. Tell how to make $14.33 with the fewest bills and coins.

Writing in Math

7. Explain how to round 219,076 to the nearest thousand and ten thousand.

Geometry and Measurement

MULTIPLE CHOICE

8. Find the perimeter of the rectangle.

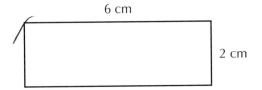

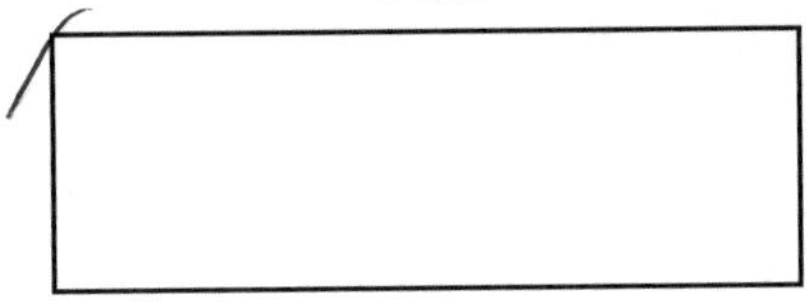

   A. 8 cm **C.** 14 cm

   B. 12 cm **D.** 16 cm

9. Name the figure.

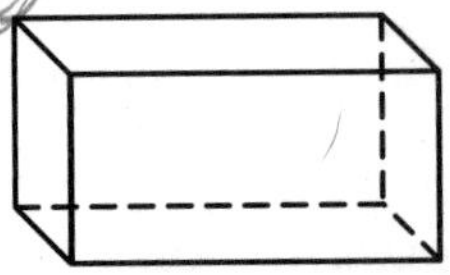

   A. rectangular prism

   B. cube

   C. sphere **D.** cylinder

10. Which figure does not have a line of symmetry?

   A.  **C.** 

   B. 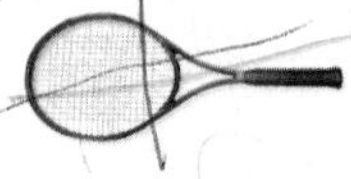 **D.** 

FREE RESPONSE

11. A football field is 100 yards long. How many feet long is the football field?

12. Erin went to the movie that started at 2:30 P.M. The movie ended at 3:50 P.M. How long was the movie?

Writing in Math

13. Give an example of an item that you would measure in meters, and an example of an item you would measure in centimeters. Explain your choices.

Data Analysis and Probability

MULTIPLE CHOICE

14. Predict the color you are most likely to pull out.

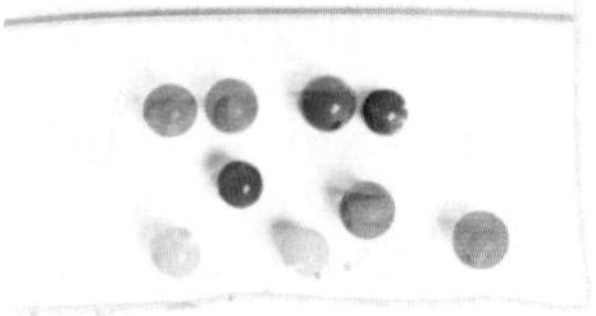

A. blue **C.** yellow

B. red **D.** orange

15. What are the chances you will pick a blue marble from the bag of marbles shown in Question 14?

A. impossible **C.** likely

B. unlikely **D.** certain

FREE RESPONSE

Use the line plot for 16–17.

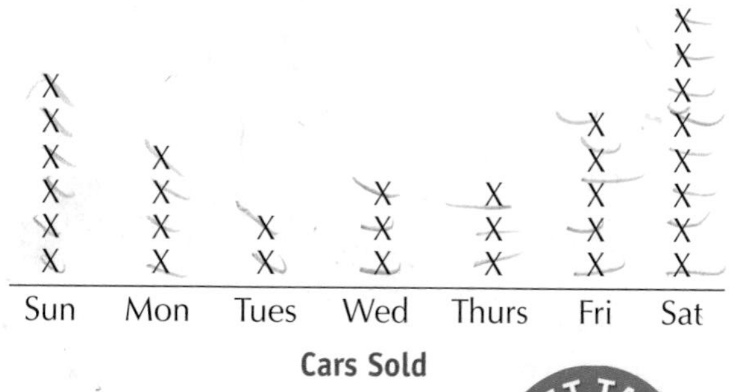

16. On what day were the most cars sold?

17. How many cars were sold in all?

TEST TALK
Think It Through
I should look for key words like IN ALL.

Writing in Math

18. Explain what kind of graph you would choose to display data about the temperatures for a week.

Algebra

MULTIPLE CHOICE

19. Dave scored 2 points in his first basketball game, 5 points in his second game, and 8 points in his third game. If the pattern continues, how many points should he score in his fifth game?

A. 11 **B.** 14 **C.** 15 **D.** 18

20. Solve 12 − ▢ = 7.

A. 5 **B.** 7 **C.** 12 **D.** 19

21. Solve 14 + ▢ = 25.

A. 9 **B.** 11 **C.** 15 **D.** 39

FREE RESPONSE

22. Fill in the table with the missing numbers. Then write the rule.

In	6	8	10	12	14
Out	2		6		10

23. Eliza strings a necklace with 3 blue beads, 2 green beads, 4 purple beads, and then repeats the pattern. If she uses 15 blue beads in her necklace, how many beads did she use altogether?

Writing in Math

24. Write the fact family for 9, 5, and 14. Explain how you know.

Reteaching

Set 1-1 (pages 4–7)

Tell the value of the red digit for the number 678,802.

678 is in the thousands period and 802 is in the ones period.

The 7 is in the ten thousands place. Its value is 70,000.

Remember periods can help you read large numbers.

Tell the value of the red digit for each number.

1. 56,098

2. 932,744

3. 121,212

4. 67,945

5. 986,003

6. 25,815

7. 72,709

8. 540,327

Set 1-2 (pages 8–9)

Write 70,000,000 + 2,000,000 + 500,000 + 6,000 + 300 + 10 + 4 in standard form.

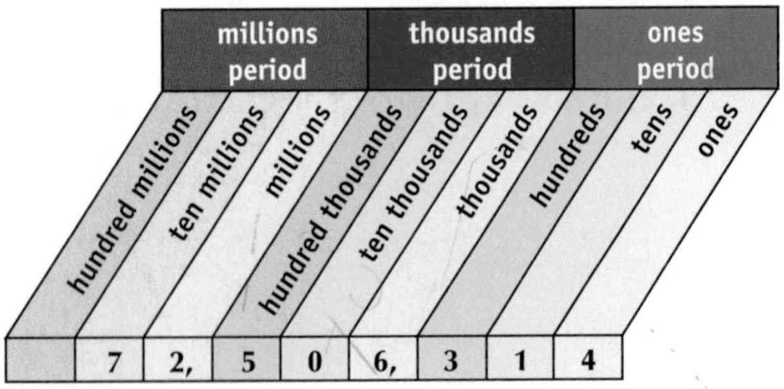

millions period
thousands period
ones period
hundred millions
ten millions
millions
hundred thousands
ten thousands
thousands
hundreds
tens
ones
7
2,
5
0
6,
3
1
4

The standard form is 72,506,314.

Remember to put a zero as a place holder if there is a place without a value.

Write each number in standard form.

1. 800,000,000 + 50,000,000 + 6,000,000 + 500,000 + 30,000 + 2,000 + 700 + 90 + 1

2. Forty million, seven hundred forty-four thousand, one hundred three.

3. 3,000,000 + 200,000 + 40,000 + 600 + 70 + 7

Set 1-3 (pages 10–11)

Name 37,000 in two different ways.

37,000 thirty-seven thousands

or

37,000 three hundred seventy hundreds

Remember that our number system is based on groups of ten.

Name each number in two different ways.

1. 740

2. 1,800

3. 2,700

4. 500

5. 6,300

6. 91,000

Set 1-4 (pages 12–13)

Tell the problem in your own words and tell what the question is asking.

Runner Karl ran 3 miles on Monday, 2 miles on Thursday, and 4 miles on Saturday. How far did he run in all?

How far Karl ran on three different days is given. I need to find how far he ran all three days.

Remember that you need to read and understand a problem before you try to solve it.

Use the Runner problem for 1–3.

1. Identify key facts and details.
2. Show the main idea.
3. Solve the problem.

Set 1-5 (pages 16–19)

Write > or < for each ●.

45,671,256 ● 45,672,132

45,671,256

45,672,132

1 thousand < 2 thousands

So, 45,671,256 < 45,672,132.

Remember that a number line can be used to compare numbers.

Write > or < for each ●.

1. 62,967 ● 65,834
2. 8,921 ● 8,931
3. 98,360,371 ● 98,450,284

Set 1-6 (pages 20–21)

Round 676,532 to the nearest ten thousand.

676,532

Find the rounding place. Look at the digit to the right. Add 1 to the rounding digit since 6 > 5.

676,532 is about 680,000.

Remember that you can use the halfway number to find the closer number.

Round to the nearest ten thousand.

1. 82,953
2. 526,562
3. 333,333
4. 99,601
5. 23,199
6. 705,821

Set 1-7 (pages 22–23)

How many hundreds equal 700,000?

7 hundreds = 700
70 hundreds = 7,000
700 hundreds = 70,000
7,000 hundreds = 700,000

So, 7,000 hundreds = 700,000.

Remember you can use place value to estimate large numbers.

How many hundreds equal each?

1. 8,000
2. 50,000
3. 300,000
4. Four million

Set 1-8 (pages 24–25)

Tom and Amy have 16 video games together. Amy has 2 more than Tom. How many does each have?

Leo

Try 6 + 10 = 16   10 − 6 = 4 no
Try 7 + 9 = 16   9 − 7 = 2 yes
Amy 9, Tom 7

Remember that there are many strategies you can use to solve a problem.

1. Tell what strategy Leo used to solve the problem.
2. Write the answer to the problem in a complete sentence.
3. What other strategy could you use to solve the problem?

Set 1-9 (pages 28–29)

Write 5 dollars, 4 dimes, and 2 pennies with a dollar sign and a decimal point.

dollars (ones)	.	dimes (tenths)	pennies (hundredths)
\$5	**.**	**4**	**2**

\$5.42

Remember a dime is one tenth of a dollar and a penny is one hundredth of a dollar.

Write each amount with a dollar sign and decimal point.

1. 6 dollars, 2 dimes, 6 pennies
2. no dollars, 7 dimes, 5 pennies
3. 7 dollars, no dimes, 3 pennies

Set 1-10 (pages 30–31)

Count the money. Write the amount with a dollar sign and decimal point.

Count the bills: \$5, \$6, \$7, \$8.
Count the coins. Start with the dimes, then continue with the nickels: 10, 20, 25, 30, 35 cents.

That is 8 dollars and 35 cents or \$8.35.

Remember it is often easiest to count money when you count the bills or coins with the largest value first.

Count the money. Write the amount with a dollar sign and decimal point.

1. two \$5 bills, one dollar, 1 quarter, 3 dimes
2. three dollars, 4 quarters, 6 nickels
3. three \$5 bills, four dollars, 4 dimes, 4 nickels
4. four dollars, 2 quarters, 4 dimes, 1 nickel, 5 pennies

Set 1-11 (pages 32–33)

Macy bought $7.32 in groceries. She paid with a $10.00 bill. List the coins and bills you give as change. Write the amount with a dollar sign and decimal point.

Start with the amount.	$7.32
Give her 3 pennies.	$7.35
Give her 1 nickel.	$7.40
Give her 1 dime.	$7.50
Give her 2 quarters.	$8.00
Give her two $1 bills.	$10.00

The total change is $2.68.

Remember to start with the purchase price and count up to the amount given when you make change.

List the bills and coins you would give as change from a $10 bill for each purchase. Write the amount with a dollar sign and decimal point.

1. $9.23 **2.** $5.82

3. $1.46 **4.** $4.91

5. $0.65 **6.** $2.74

Set 1-12 (pages 34–37)

Write the word form and decimal for the shaded part.

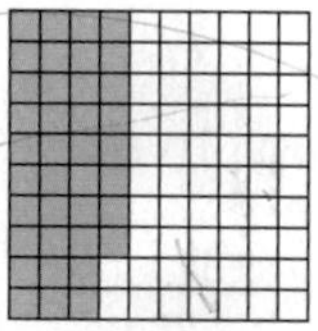

38 out of 100 parts are shaded.

Word form: Thirty-eight hundredths

Decimal: 0.38

Remember that the first two places after the decimal point are tenths and hundredths.

Write the word form and decimal for the shaded part.

1.

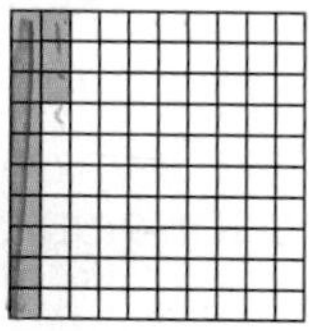

2.

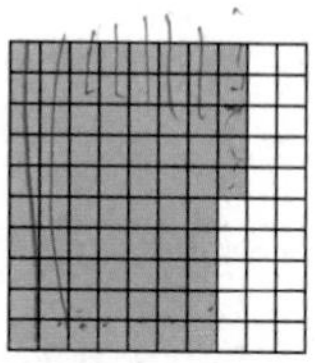

3.

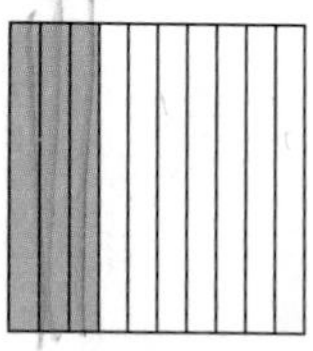

4.

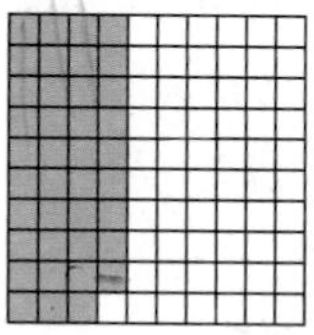

Set 1-13 (pages 38–39)

Solve.

How much is 2 quarters, 3 dimes, and 5 pennies?

Kevin

quarters: 25, 50
dimes: 60, 70, 80
pennies: 85

Remember to check your answer and your work.

1. Did Kevin answer the right question?
2. Does Kevin's work match the information in the problem?
3. Is Kevin's answer reasonable?

More Practice

Set 1-1 (pages 4–7)

Write each number in standard form.

1. 800,000 + 6,000 + 500 + 30 + 2
2. four hundred ten thousand, nineteen
3. 90,000 + 3,000 + 600 + 80 + 4
4. fifty-five thousand, eight hundred five

Tell the value of the red digit for each number.

5. 589,030 6. 7,267 7. 812,274 8. 34,672 9. 605,980

10. Jonathan's school collected 21,707 cans of food. Write this number in words.

Set 1-2 (pages 8–9)

Write each number in standard form.

1. Four hundred thirty-five million, nine hundred five thousand, eight hundred seventeen
2. One hundred two million, five hundred forty-seven thousand, nine hundred five
3. 80,000,000 + 5,000,000 + 30,000 + 6,000 + 700 + 3
4. 100,000,000 + 4,000,000 + 700,000 + 60,000 + 800 + 30 + 9

Tell the value of the red digit for each number.

5. 429,703,214 6. 36,109,562 7. 735,812,903 8. 216,843,725

9. The population of Pennsylvania in the year 2000 was 12,281,054. Write this number in words.

Set 1-3 (pages 10–11)

Name each number in two different ways.

1. 49,000 2. 8,000 3. 920 4. 2,200 5. 70,000

Look for a pattern. Find the next three numbers.

6. 4,963 4,973 4,983 7. 5,206 5,106 5,006 8. 22,396 21,396 20,396

9. The library has 65,000 books. How many bookshelves would the library need if each bookshelf held 100 books?

Set 1-4 (pages 12–13)

Use the Bookstore problem for 1–3.

1. **Step 1:** What do you know?
   - **a.** Tell what you know in your own words.
   - **b.** Identify key facts and details.
2. **Step 2:** What are you trying to find?
   - **a.** Tell what the question is asking.
   - **b.** Show the main idea.
3. Solve the problem.

> **Bookstore** Lance bought two books for $6 each and two bookmarks for $1 each. How much did he spend in all?

Set 1-5 (pages 16–19)

Compare. Write > or < for each ●.

1. 98,854 ● 98,584 **2.** 703,759 ● 730,759

3. 31,863,032 ● 31,853,032

4. Put the states in order from the one with the greatest population to the one with the least population.

Data File

State	2000 Population
Alabama	4,447,100
Colorado	4,301,261
Louisiana	4,468,976

Set 1-6 (pages 20–21)

Round each number to the place of the underlined digit.

1. 97,$\underline{3}$89 **2.** $\underline{6}$84,023 **3.** 10$\underline{9}$,355 **4.** $\underline{3}$0,525

5. 4$\underline{5}$,103 **6.** 8$\underline{9}$9,934 **7.** 7$\underline{3}$,782 **8.** $\underline{5}$29,605

9. The library has 45,582 books. Round this number to the nearest thousand and ten thousand.

Set 1-7 (pages 22–23)

Write how many buttons are in each.

1. 8 bags **2.** 50 bags **3.** 100 bags

4. If Danika bought 100 bags for her store, how many buttons would she have?

More Practice

Set 1-8 (pages 24–25)

Use the Bracelets problem for 1–2.

1. Name the strategy Thomas used to solve the Bracelets problem.
2. Give the answer to the Bracelets problem in a complete sentence.

Bracelets Karolyn can make 3 bracelets in one hour. How many hours will it take her to make enough bracelets for all 15 girls in her club?

Thomas

hours	1	2	3	4	5
bracelets	3	6	9	12	15

5 hours.

Set 1-9 (pages 28–29)

Copy and complete.

1. $9.75 = ___ dollars + ___ dimes + ___ pennies
   9.75 = ___ ones + ___ tenths + ___ hundredths
2. $1.30 = ___ dollars + ___ dimes + ___ pennies
   1.30 = ___ ones + ___ tenths + ___ hundredths

Write each with a dollar sign and a decimal point.

3. 9 dollars, 3 dimes, 2 pennies
4. 5 dollars, 7 dimes, 3 pennies
5. 4 dollars, no dimes, 4 pennies
6. 6 dollars, 2 dimes, 8 pennies
7. Write four and seventy-five hundredths with a decimal point.

Set 1-10 (pages 30–31)

Count the money. Write each amount with a dollar sign and decimal point.

1. Five $5 bills, 3 quarters, 1 penny
2. Three $1 bills, 7 dimes, 3 nickels

Tell how to make each money amount with the fewest bills and coins.

3. $27.89
4. $4.24
5. $11.11
6. $19.67
7. Jill has six $1 bills, 2 quarters, 3 dimes, and 4 pennies. Mark has one $5 bill, one $1 bill, 2 quarters, 5 nickels, and 3 pennies. Who has more money?

Take It to the NET
More Practice
www.scottforesman.com

Set 1-11 (pages 32–33)

Tell how you would give change from a $20.00 bill for each purchase. List the bills and coins you would use and give the amount with a dollar sign and decimal point.

1. $18.76 **2.** $13.58 **3.** $1.23 **4.** $0.93 **5.** $6.37

6. Sue buys a book for $16.84 and pays for it with a $20 bill. How much change does she get back?

Set 1-12 (pages 34–37)

Write the word form and decimal for each shaded part.

1.
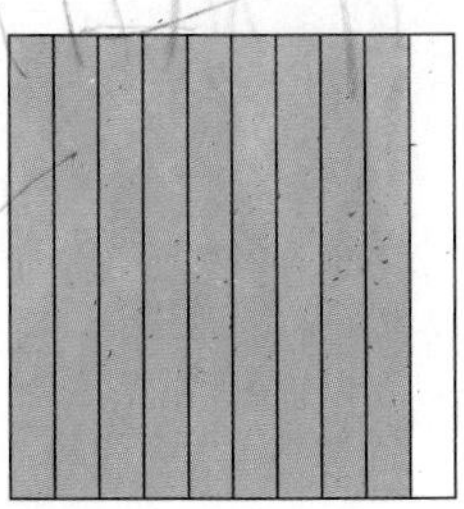

2.
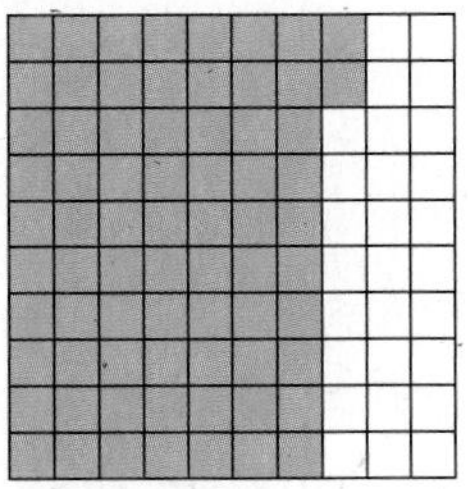

3.
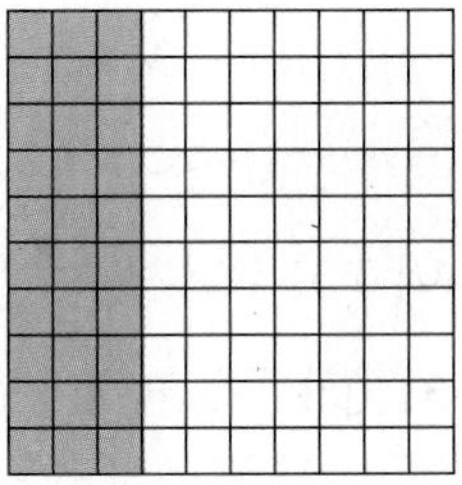

Draw and shade a grid to show each decimal.

4. 0.80 **5.** 0.19 **6.** 0.45 **7.** 0.87 **8.** 0.73

9. How many hundredths equal 8 tenths?

Set 1-13 (pages 38–39)

Use the Next Number problem for 1–3.

1. Solve the problem. Give the answer to the problem in a complete sentence.

2. Check your answer. Did you answer the right question? Is your answer reasonable?

3. Check your work. Does your work match the information in the problem? Did you use correct operations and procedures?

> **Next Number** If Maury continues the pattern, what will the next 3 numbers be?
>
> 32, 33, 35, 38, 42, 47 __, __, __

CHAPTER 2

Adding and Subtracting Whole Numbers and Money

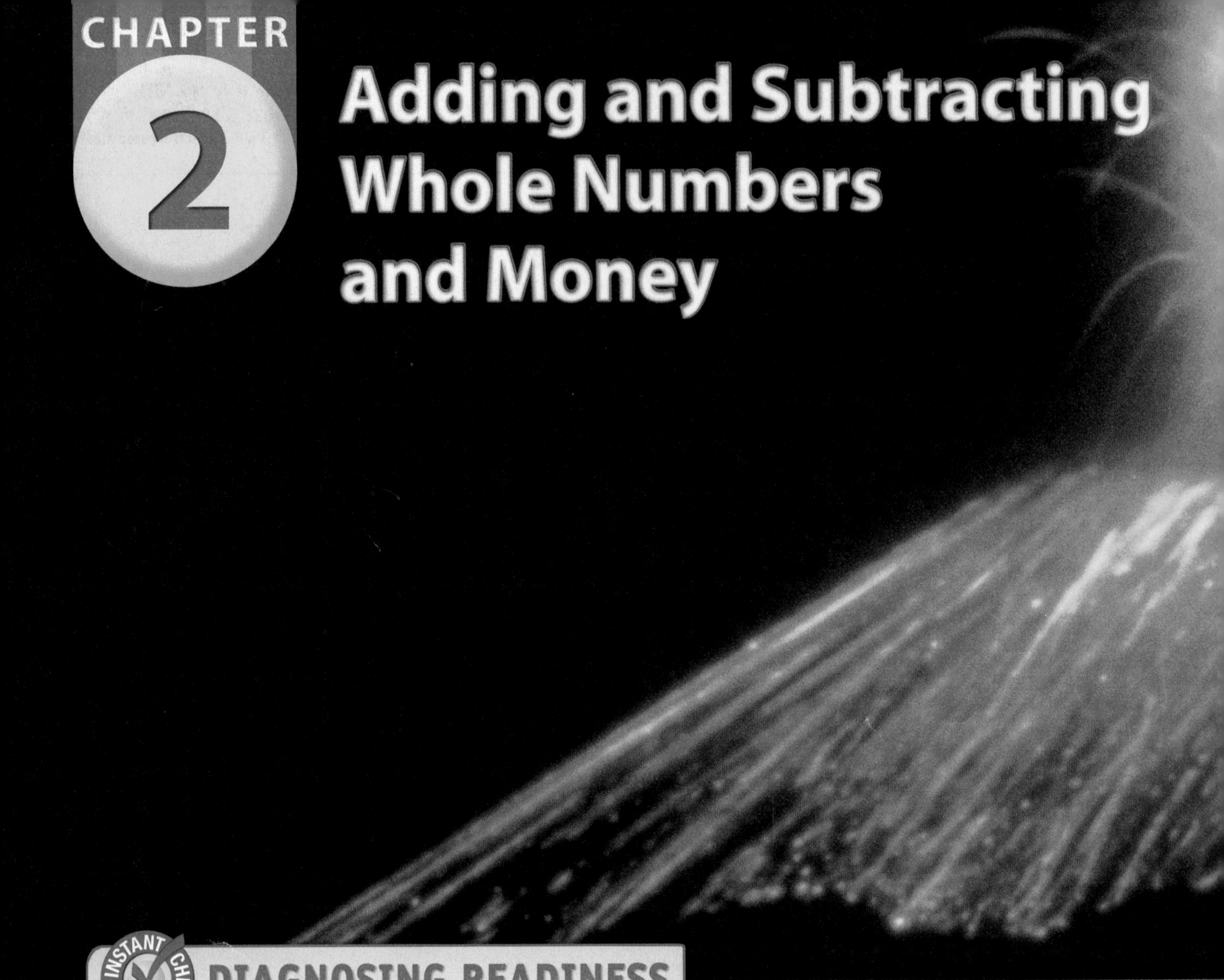

DIAGNOSING READINESS

A Vocabulary

(Grade 3, pages 4–5, 30–31)

Choose the best term from the box.

1. In 5,837, the 8 is in the __?__ place and the 5 is in the __?__ place.

2. The __?__ of 30 and 20 is 50, and the __?__ of 30 and 20 is 10.

3. In $3.98, the __?__ is between the 3 and the 9.

Vocabulary

- **decimal point** *(p. 30)*
- **sum** *(Gr. 3)*
- **difference** *(Gr. 3)*
- **thousands** *(p. 4)*
- **hundreds** *(p. 4)*
- **tens** *(p. 4)*

B Rounding

(Grade 3)

Round each number to the nearest ten.

4. 24 **5.** 95 **6.** 62

7. 451 **8.** 208 **9.** 5,479

Round each number to the nearest hundred.

10. 483 **11.** 150 **12.** 742

13. 8,236 **14.** 6,399 **15.** 9,281

16. What number is halfway between 700 and 800?

Do You Know...

How tall did the Paricutin volcano grow during its 9 years of eruptions?

You will find out in Lesson 2-14.

C Addition and Subtraction Facts

(Grade 3)

17. 4 + 4 **18.** 7 + 2 **19.** 8 + 6

20. 9 + 7 **21.** 6 + 7 **22.** 9 + 8

23. 7 − 3 **24.** 10 − 2 **25.** 15 − 6

26. 11 − 4 **27.** 16 − 9 **28.** 17 − 8

29. Find the sum of 5 and 2.

30. Katie had 14 picture books. She gave 9 to her little brother. How many did she have left?

D Counting Money

(pages 30–31)

Count the money. Write each amount with a dollar sign and decimal point.

31. Three $1 bills, 5 dimes, 4 pennies

32. Seven $1 bills, 2 quarters, 3 nickels, 1 penny

33. Two $10 bills, three $1 bills, 4 dimes

34. Three $10 bills, 7 dimes, 8 pennies

35. Two $5 bills, 3 nickels

Key Idea
Numbers can be broken apart and combined in many ways.

Vocabulary
- Commutative Property of Addition
- Associative Property of Addition
- Identity Property of Addition
- breaking apart
- compensation
- addends
- sum

TEST TALK

Think It Through
- I can **get information from the picture** to solve the problem.
- I need **an exact answer.**

Mental Math: Adding

WARM UP

1. 5 + 7
2. 20 + 40
3. 50 + 35
4. 90 + 50

LEARN

How can you add with mental math?

Max has $182. Does he have enough money to buy a wetsuit and a snorkel?

There are many ways to add using mental math. Properties explain why you can break numbers apart and add in any order.

Commutative Property of Addition	Associative Property of Addition	Identity Property of Addition
You can add two numbers in any order.	You can change the grouping of numbers you add.	The sum of any number and zero is that same number.
5 + 7 = 7 + 5	(3 + 2) + 8 = 3 + (2 + 8)	4 + 0 = 4

Example

Add $145 + $39 using mental math.

One Way

Toni used **breaking apart** to make a ten.

$145 + $39
Adding 5s is easy. 39 = 5 + 34
145 + 5 = 150
150 + 34 = 184
So, 145 + 39 = 184

Another Way

Damian made tens and then used **compensation.**

$145 + $39
145 + 40 = 185
I added 1 too many, so I will subtract 1.
185 − 1 = 184

Max does not have enough money to buy both items.

$184 is the **sum** and $145 and $39 are **addends.**

Talk About It

1. Is it easier to add 145 + 40 or 145 + 39?

CHECK

For another example, see Set 2-1 on p. 114.

Add. Use mental math.

1. 78 + 44 **2.** 224 + 0 **3.** 175 + 26 **4.** 2,000 + 4,000

5. Reasoning How can you write 46 + (8 + 4) to make it easier to add?

PRACTICE

For more practice, see Set 2-1 on p. 118

A Skills and Understanding

Add. Use mental math.

6. 54 + 29 **7.** 36 + 48 **8.** 234 + 39 **9.** 475 + 197

10. 578 + 153 **11.** 619 + 281 **12.** 500 + 700 **13.** 0 + 387

14. 293 + 467 **15.** 585 + 348 **16.** 6,000 + 3,000 **17.** 918 + 122

18. Reasoning How can you write 68 + (2 + 36) to make it easier to add?

B Reasoning and Problem Solving

Use mental math to find the cost of

19. the bed and the chair.

20. the lamp and the table.

21. Which item is the most expensive?

22. Writing in Math Explain how you could add 436 + 298 using mental math. (Hint: Change 298 to an easier number.)

Mixed Review and Test Prep

Take It to the NET
Test Prep
www.scottforesman.com

Use the Reading problem for 23–24.

23. Solve the problem. Give the answer in a complete sentence.

24. Check your answer. Did you answer the right question? Is your answer reasonable?

Reading Each day at school, Julia read 3 chapters. If she did this for two 5-day weeks, how many chapters did she read at school?

25. Amy has three $5 bills, two $1 bills, 5 quarters, and 2 nickels. How much money does she have in all?

A. $17.35 **B.** $17.85 **C.** $18.10 **D.** $18.35

Key Idea
Changing to a simpler problem or counting on can help you subtract with mental math.

Vocabulary
- difference
- compensation (p. 62)

TEST TALK

Think It Through
I can think about subtracting 10s **to solve simpler problems.**

Mental Math: Subtracting

WARM UP

Add. Use mental math.

1. 83 + 19
2. 250 + 600
3. 27 + 41

LEARN

How can you subtract using a simpler problem?

School Play Fairfield Elementary has 98 fourth-grade students. Fifteen of these students were in the school play. The rest watched. How many fourth-grade students watched the play?

You can subtract mentally by breaking apart numbers.

Example A

Subtract 98 − 15.

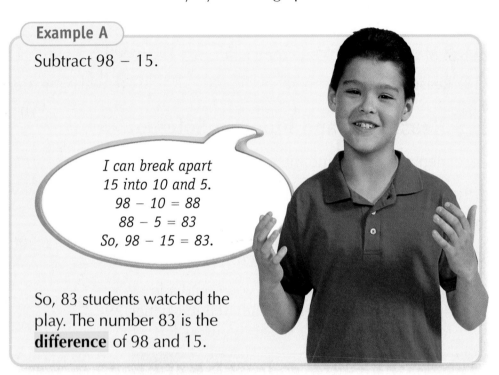

I can break apart 15 into 10 and 5.
98 − 10 = 88
88 − 5 = 83
So, 98 − 15 = 83.

So, 83 students watched the play. The number 83 is the **difference** of 98 and 15.

You can also use **compensation** to subtract.

Example B

Subtract 172 − 58.

	What You **Think**	What You **Say**
STEP 1	It's easy to subtract 60.	172 − 60 = 112
STEP 2	I subtracted 2 too many, so I will add 2.	112 + 2 = 114 So, 172 − 58 = 114.

Talk About It

1. What simpler problems were used to subtract 172 − 58?
2. How could you use breaking apart to find 98 − 15?
3. How could you use compensation to find 134 − 19?

How can you subtract using counting on?

Example C

Subtract 500 − 285. Use mental math.

What You **Think**	What You **Say**
What can I add to 285 to get the next ten?	285 + 5 = 290
What can I add to 290 to get to the next hundred?	290 + 10 = 300
What can I add to 300 to get to 500?	300 + 200 = 500
How much did I add in all?	5 + 10 + 200 = 215 So, 500 − 285 = 215.

Talk About It

4. What is the next ten after 285?
5. Why does 5 + 10 + 200 equal 500 − 285?

CHECK

For another example, see Set 2-2 on p. 114.

Subtract. Use mental math.

1. 76 − 12 **2.** 96 − 78 **3.** 400 − 36 **4.** 244 − 56

5. 67 − 15 **6.** 306 − 99 **7.** 143 − 58 **8.** 600 − 125

9. Number Sense How can you find 174 − 49 using mental math?

PRACTICE

For more practice, see Set 2-2 on p. 118.

A Skills and Understanding

Subtract. Use mental math.

10. 65 − 23	**11.** 91 − 59	**12.** 64 − 21	**13.** 80 − 14
14. 56 − 18	**15.** 100 − 44	**16.** 672 − 341	**17.** 430 − 293
18. 910 − 128	**19.** 438 − 86	**20.** 978 − 662	**21.** 579 − 33
22. 500 − 87	**23.** 435 − 213	**24.** 388 − 216	**25.** 130 − 42

26. Number Sense If you counted on to find 840 − 399, what number would you add to 399 first?

B Reasoning and Problem Solving

Math and Social Studies

Use mental math for 27–30.

How many more silver medals were won by

27. the United States than Norway?

28. Germany than Russia?

29. How many more gold medals were won by the U.S. and Canada combined than by Germany?

30. How many medals did each country win in all?

Data File

Top Medal Winners 2002 Winter Olympics

Country	Gold	Silver	Bronze
Germany	12	16	7
United States	10	13	11
Norway	11	7	6
Canada	6	3	8
Russia	6	6	4

31. **Writing in Math** Is the explanation below correct? If not, tell why and write a correct response.

Explain how you could use mental math to subtract 146 − 38.

146 − 36 = 110
110 − 2 = 108
So, 146 − 38 = 108

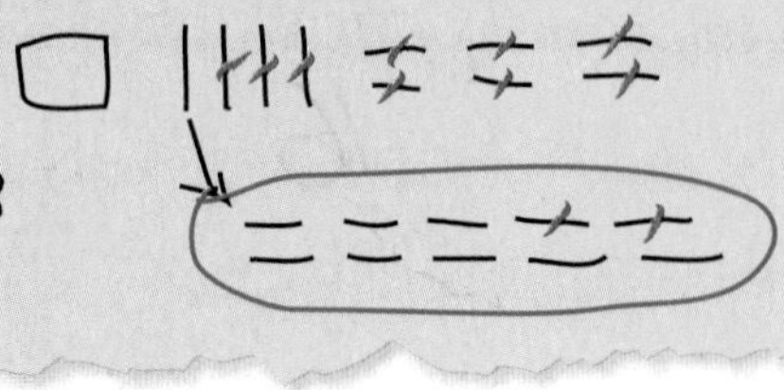

TEST TALK

Think It Through
I can **draw a picture** to explain my thinking.

PRACTICE

C Extensions

Subtract. Use mental math.

32. 1,748 – 295 **33.** 5,480 – 2,360 **34.** 3,540 – 1,993 **35.** 29,365 – 8,214

Mixed Review and Test Prep

Take It to the NET
Test Prep
www.scottforesman.com

Add. Use mental math.

36. 14 + 27 **37.** 58 + 37 **38.** 337 + 449 **39.** 593 + 298

40. Round 365,735 to the nearest ten thousand.

A. 300,000 **B.** 360,000 **C.** 370,000 **D.** 400,000

Discovery Channel School

Discover Math in Your World

Volcano on a Plate

Earth's crust is not a solid mass. It is composed of plates that slide by, collide with, and override each other. As a result of plate movements, world geography has changed slowly, but constantly.

1. Earth's major plates range in thickness from 80 to 402 kilometers. Use mental math to calculate this difference in thickness.

2. Most volcanoes occur along plate boundaries. Of the world's 850 active volcanoes, about 638 of them occur around the Pacific plate. About how many occur elsewhere?

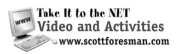

Take It to the NET
Video and Activities
www.scottforesman.com

Key Idea
To estimate, you change numbers to ones that are easy to add and subtract.

Vocabulary
- rounding (p. 20)
- front-end estimation

TEST TALK

Think It Through
I only need **to know about how much so I can** estimate.

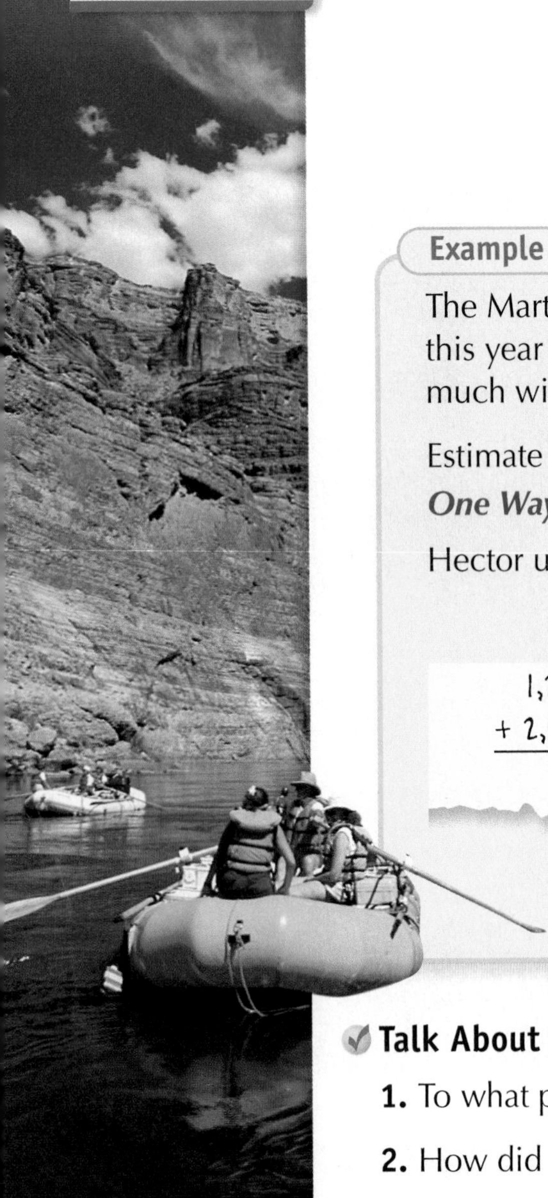

Estimating Sums and Differences

WARM UP

Round each number to the place of the underlined digit.

1. <u>4</u>72 2. <u>9</u>36
3. <u>8</u>,256 4. <u>5</u>,803

LEARN

How can you estimate sums?

The Martins are planning their vacations. They want to have an estimate of the cost.

1 day	**Rafting Trip**	$279
5 days	**Camping and Rafting Trip** Includes rafting, camping supplies, and food.	$1,248
7 days	**Canoeing, Inn to Inn Trip** Includes canoe rental, meals, nightly stays at inns.	$2,579

Example A

The Martin family decided to purchase the 5-days package this year and the 7-days package next year. About how much will they spend in all?

Estimate $1,248 + $2,579.

One Way

Hector used **rounding.**

$$\begin{array}{r} 1{,}248 \\ +\ 2{,}579 \\ \hline \end{array} \qquad \begin{array}{r} 1{,}200 \\ +\ 2{,}600 \\ \hline 3{,}800 \end{array}$$

They will spend about $3,800.

Another Way

Sonya used **front-end estimation.**

$$\begin{array}{r} 1{,}248 \\ +\ 2{,}579 \\ \hline \end{array} \qquad \begin{array}{r} 1{,}000 \\ +\ 2{,}000 \\ \hline 3{,}000 \end{array}$$

They will spend about $3,000.

Talk About It

1. To what places did Hector round 1,248 and 2,579?
2. How did Sonya get 1,000 and 2,000 for her estimate?

How can you estimate differences?

About how much more is the 7-days package than the 5-days package?

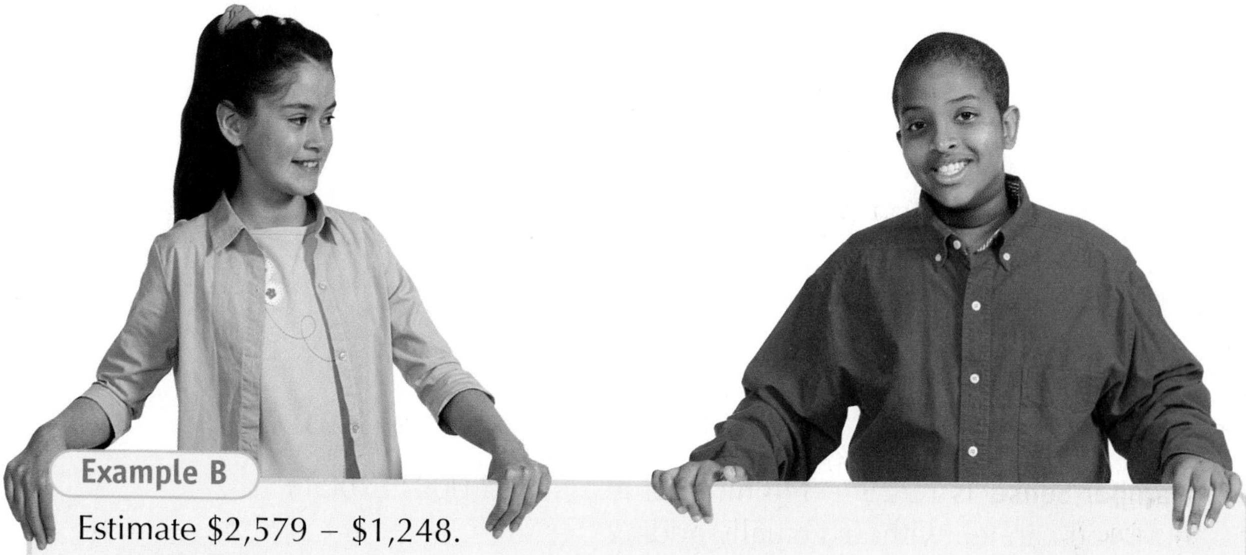

Example B

Estimate \$2,579 − \$1,248.

One Way

Amy used **rounding.**

$$\begin{array}{r} 2{,}579 \\ -\ 1{,}248 \\ \hline \end{array} \qquad \begin{array}{r} 2{,}600 \\ -\ 1{,}200 \\ \hline 1{,}400 \end{array}$$

The cost of the 7-days package is about \$1,400 more.

Another Way

Ross used **front-end estimation.**

$$\begin{array}{r} 2{,}579 \\ -\ 1{,}248 \\ \hline \end{array} \qquad \begin{array}{r} 2{,}000 \\ -\ 1{,}000 \\ \hline 1{,}000 \end{array}$$

The cost of the 7-days package is about \$1,000 more.

Talk About It

3. To what places did Amy round 2,579 and 1,248?

4. How did Ross get 2,000 and 1,000 for his estimate?

Take It to the NET
More Examples
www.scottforesman.com

CHECK

For another example, see Set 2-3 on p.114.

Estimate each sum or difference.

1. 365 + 526 **2.** 1,429 + 8,294 **3.** 762 − 375 **4.** 8,925 − 4,079

5. Number Sense Is 826 − 575 more or less than 300? Explain how you can tell without actually subtracting.

For more practice, see Set 2-3 on p. 118.

A Skills and Understanding

Estimate each sum or difference.

6. 438 + 85	**7.** 919 − 191	**8.** 787 − 222	**9.** 813 + 290
10. 6,742 + 884	**11.** 4,374 − 1,614	**12.** 28,807 − 3,499	**13.** 3,352 + 2,116

14. 649 − 98 **15.** 555 + 42 **16.** 709 + 486 **17.** 836 − 252

18. 5,961 − 3,179 **19.** 27,832 + 18,445 **20.** 75,629 + 3,331 **21.** 73,295 − 9,750

22. Number Sense Is 1,725 + 346 more or less than 2,000? Explain how you can tell without actually adding.

B Reasoning and Problem Solving

Math and Science

A light-year is the distance light can travel in a year. Light travels over 186,000 miles in one second, so it travels very far in one year. About how many light-years is a roundtrip (there and back) from Earth to

Data File

Distances from Earth

Star	Light Years
Andromedae	199
Polaris	431
Rigel	773

23. Polaris? **24.** Rigel?

About how much farther is it from Earth to

25. Rigel than to Andromedae? **26.** Polaris than to Andromedae?

27. Writing in Math Is the explanation below correct? If not, tell why and write a correct response.

> Estimate 837 + 252.
>
> I used front-end estimation.
>
> 800
> + 200
> 10,000
>
> 837 + 252 is about 10,000.

TEST TALK

Think It Through

I should always check that my **answer is reasonable.**

PRACTICE

C Extensions

Estimate each sum or difference.

28. 2,637,249 + 5,824,593

29. 3,456,875 − 1,842,126

30. 735,428 − 265,306

31. 675,450 + 525,304

Mixed Review and Test Prep

Take It to the NET
Test Prep
www.scottforesman.com

32. 55 − 13 **33.** 915 + 337 **34.** 825 − 756 **35.** 300 − 223

36. Write 7,000,000 + 40,000 + 500 + 3 in standard form.

A. 7,453 **B.** 7,040,503 **C.** 7,453,000 **D.** 7,040,503

Enrichment

Venn Diagrams

A **Venn Diagram** uses circles to show the relationship between sets of data or objects. Circles overlap **(intersect)** when some data belong to more than one group.

1. Which students belong to all three clubs?
2. To what clubs does Brian belong?

School Clubs

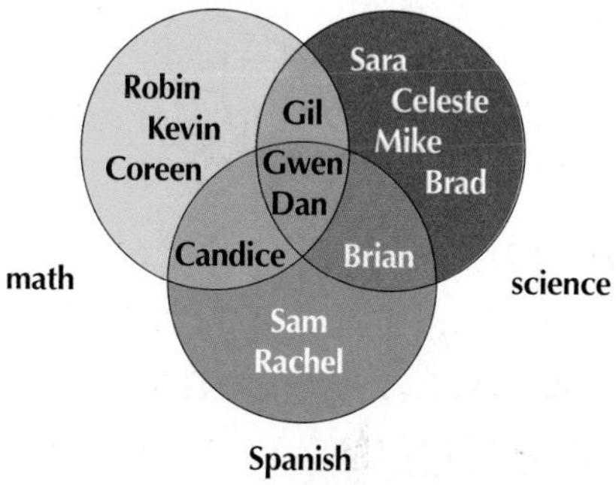

Enrichment

Inequalities

Number sentences that use the symbols >, <, ≥, and ≤ are called *inequalities*.

The symbol ≤ is read "is less than or equal to."
The whole numbers 0, 1, 2, 3, 4, and **5** make the number sentence, □ ≤ 5, true.

The symbol ≥ is read "is greater than or equal to."
The whole numbers **3,** 4, 5, 6, 7, 8, . . . make the number sentence, □ ≥ 3, true.

For 1–4, list 5 whole numbers that will make each number sentence true.

1. □ ≤ 7 **2.** □ ≥ 4 **3.** □ ≥ 1 **4.** □ ≤ 12

Key Idea
You can tell if your estimate is over or under the actual result by thinking about how you changed the numbers.

Vocabulary
- overestimate
- underestimate

TEST TALK

Think It Through
I can estimate if I only need **to know about how much.**

Overestimates and Underestimates

WARM UP

Estimate each sum or difference.

1. 44 + 27
2. 3,283 + 493
3. 8,091 − 1,765

LEARN

How can you tell if your estimate is too much or too little?

An estimate that is greater than the exact answer is an **overestimate.** An estimate that is less than the exact answer is an **underestimate.**

Tell whether each estimate is an overestimate or an underestimate. Explain.

Example A

$$\begin{array}{r} 825 \\ +\ 346 \\ \hline \end{array} \qquad \begin{array}{r} 800 \\ +\ 300 \\ \hline 1{,}100 \end{array}$$

Since both numbers were replaced with lesser numbers, 1,100 is an underestimate. The exact sum is greater than 1,100.

Example B

$$\begin{array}{r} 4{,}825 \\ +\ 2{,}517 \\ \hline \end{array} \qquad \begin{array}{r} 5{,}000 \\ +\ 3{,}000 \\ \hline 8{,}000 \end{array}$$

Since both numbers were replaced with greater numbers, 8,000 is an overestimate. The exact sum is less than 8,000.

Example C

$$\begin{array}{r} 372 \\ +\ 238 \\ \hline \end{array} \qquad \begin{array}{r} 400 \\ +\ 200 \\ \hline 600 \end{array}$$

Since 372 was replaced with a greater number and 238 was replaced with a lesser number, it is difficult to tell whether 600 is an overestimate or an underestimate.

Example D

$$\begin{array}{r} 575 \\ -\ 138 \\ \hline \end{array} \qquad \begin{array}{r} 600 \\ -\ 100 \\ \hline 500 \end{array}$$

Since the first number was replaced with a greater number and the second number was replaced with a lesser number, 500 is an overestimate. The exact difference is less than 500.

Example E

$$\begin{array}{r} 9{,}286 \\ -\ 6{,}529 \\ \hline \end{array} \qquad \begin{array}{r} 9{,}000 \\ -\ 7{,}000 \\ \hline 2{,}000 \end{array}$$

Since the first number was replaced with a lesser number and the second number was replaced with a greater number, 2,000 is an underestimate. The exact difference is greater than 2,000.

Example F

$$\begin{array}{r} 784 \\ -\ 498 \\ \hline \end{array} \qquad \begin{array}{r} 800 \\ -\ 500 \\ \hline 300 \end{array}$$

Since both numbers were replaced with greater numbers, it is difficult to tell whether 300 is an overestimate or an underestimate.

Talk About It

1. In Example D, explain why 500 is an overestimate.

CHECK

For another example, see Set 2-4 on p. 114.

Estimate each sum or difference. Then, if possible, tell whether your estimate is an overestimate or an underestimate.

1. 903 − 417 **2.** 98 + 271 **3.** 767 + 214 **4.** 8,724 − 3,973

5. Number Sense Martha estimated 743 + 235 by adding 700 + 200. Is this an overestimate or an underestimate?

PRACTICE

For more practice, see Set 2-4 on p. 119.

A Skills and Understanding

Estimate each sum or difference. Then, if possible, tell whether your estimate is an overestimate or an underestimate.

6. 76 − 21 **7.** 351 + 382 **8.** 135 + 609 **9.** 6,827 − 3,753

10. 525 − 96 **11.** 13 + 84 **12.** 5,095 + 2,495 **13.** 5,340 − 1,819

14. 739 − 413 **15.** 1,782 + 5,505 **16.** 2,723 + 2,613 **17.** 6,832 − 4,314

18. Number Sense Mike estimated 732 + 293 by adding 700 + 300. Can Mike tell if his estimate is an overestimate or an underestimate? Explain.

B Reasoning and Problem Solving

19. Sarah needs $275 for a new bicycle. She has saved $122. Then she earned $82 babysitting. About how much more money does Sarah need? Then tell whether your estimate is an overestimate or an underestimate.

20. Writing in Math Rachel estimated 485 + 762 by adding 500 + 800. Explain why Rachel's estimate is an overestimate.

Mixed Review and Test Prep

Take It to the NET
Test Prep
www.scottforesman.com

Estimate each sum or difference.

21. 77 + 341 **22.** 750 + 619 **23.** 809 − 166 **24.** 479 − 251

25. Cami bought a book for $4.62. How much change would she get if she paid with a $10.00 bill?

A. $4.62 **B.** $5.38 **C.** $5.48 **D.** $6.48

Review

Do You Know How?

Do You Understand?

Mental Math: Adding (2-1)

Add. Use mental math.

1. 14 + 68 **2.** 85 + 27

3. 43 + 25 **4.** 56 + 29

5. 685 + 448 **6.** 489 + 263

7. 253 + 147 **8.** 637 + 314

A Tell what method you used to find the sum in Exercise 4.

B Explain how you could use mental math to add 48 + 29.

Mental Math: Subtracting (2-2)

Subtract. Use mental math.

9. 82 − 48 **10.** 94 − 51

11. 78 − 33 **12.** 826 − 219

13. 300 − 165 **14.** 948 − 596

15. 425 − 257 **16.** 140 − 118

C Tell what method you used to find the difference in Exercise 10.

D Explain two different ways you could find 75 − 28 using mental math.

Estimating Sums and Differences (2-3)

Estimate each sum or difference.

17. 374 − 109 **18.** 511 − 168

19. 5,426 − 980 **20.** 6,819 − 2,343

21. 852 + 465 **22.** 790 + 173

E Tell how you estimated the difference in Exercise 20.

F Explain how to use rounding to estimate the sum in Exercise 21.

Overestimates and Underestimates (2-4)

Estimate each sum or difference.

23. 465 + 384 **24.** 87 − 18

25. 696 + 118 **26.** 112 + 706

27. 628 − 136 **28.** 3,924 − 2,263

G Is the estimate you got in Exercise 23 an overestimate or an underestimate? Explain.

H Explain why you can't always tell if an estimate is an overestimate or an underestimate.

Diagnostic Checkpoint

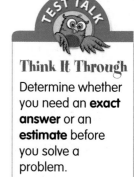

MULTIPLE CHOICE

1. Rick read a book with 135 pages. Brad read a book with 295 pages. About how many pages did they read together? (2-3)

   A. 200 pages **B.** 400 pages **C.** 600 pages **D.** 800 pages

2. Crystal collected 58 cans for the food drive. Audra collected 37 cans. How many more cans did Crystal collect than Audra? (2-2)

   A. 11 cans **B.** 21 cans **C.** 27 cans **D.** 95 cans

TEST TALK

Think It Through
Determine whether you need an **exact answer** or an **estimate** before you solve a problem.

FREE RESPONSE

Add or subtract. Use mental math. (2-1 and 2-2)

3. 75 + 49 **4.** 203 + 55 **5.** 98 − 35 **6.** 381 − 176

7. 198 + 586 **8.** 900 − 445 **9.** 678 − 263 **10.** 466 + 321

Estimate each sum or difference. Then, tell whether your estimate is an overestimate or an underestimate. (2-4)

11. 723 − 156 **12.** 651 + 236 **13.** 5,978 + 2,574 **14.** 7,729 − 3,199

Use the information at the right for 15–17.

Pages Read in 1 Week

Grade	Boys	Girls
Third	825	749
Fourth	975	967
Fifth	1,008	1,024

15. How many pages did the third-grade students read? (2-1)

16. About how many pages did the fourth- and fifth-grade girls read? (2-3)

Writing in Math

17. Estimate how many pages the fifth grade read. Is your estimate an overestimate or an underestimate? Explain how you know. (2-4)

18. Explain how you can use estimation to decide which has the greater difference: 939 − 397 or 763 − 417. (2-3)

19. Tricia estimated 3,635 + 4,187 with front-end estimation. She got 7,000. Is this an overestimate or an underestimate? Explain. (2-4)

Key Idea
You can add numbers by adding ones, then tens, then hundreds, and then thousands.

TEST TALK

Think It Through
- I can **draw a picture** to show the main idea.
- I should add when joining groups of different sizes.

Adding Whole Numbers and Money

WARM UP

Estimate each sum.

1. 27 + 62
2. 205 + 630
3. 31 + 95
4. 89 + 14
5. Josie has one \$10 bill, two \$5 bills, 3 quarters, 3 nickels, and 2 pennies. How much money does she have?

LEARN

How do you add whole numbers using paper and pencil?

Sports Cards Marcie and Josh collect sports cards. Marcie has 275 cards and Josh has 137. How many cards do they have together?

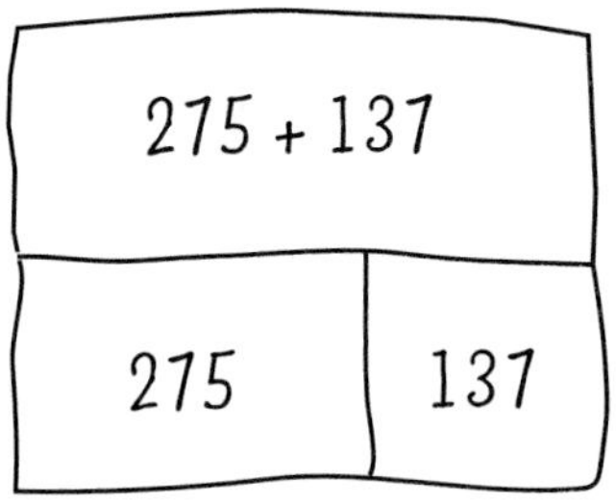

Example A

Add 275 + 137.

Estimate: 300 + 100 = 400

STEP 1	STEP 2	STEP 3
Add the ones. Regroup if necessary.	Add the tens. Regroup if necessary.	Add the hundreds.
$\begin{array}{r} {}^{1} \\ 275 \\ +\ 137 \\ \hline 2 \end{array}$	$\begin{array}{r} {}^{1\,1} \\ 275 \\ +\ 137 \\ \hline 12 \end{array}$	$\begin{array}{r} {}^{1\,1} \\ 275 \\ +\ 137 \\ \hline 412 \end{array}$

The sum 412 is reasonable because it is close to the estimate 400. Marcie and Josh have 412 cards together.

Talk About It

1. Explain how the tens were regrouped in Step 2.
2. Why is there no regrouping in Step 3?

How do you add larger numbers and money?

Example B

Add 7,376 + 2,719.

Estimate:
7,000 + 3,000 = 10,000

Add each place from right to left, regrouping as needed.

$$\begin{array}{r} {\scriptstyle 1\ \ 1\ \ \ \ } \\ 7{,}376 \\ +\ 2{,}719 \\ \hline 10{,}095 \end{array}$$

The sum 10,095 is reasonable because it is close to the estimate of 10,000.

Example C

Add 54,842 + 37,585.

Estimate:
50,000 + 40,000 = 90,000

Add each place from right to left, regrouping as needed.

$$\begin{array}{r} {\scriptstyle 1\,1\ 1\ \ \ \ \ \ } \\ 54{,}842 \\ +\ 37{,}585 \\ \hline 92{,}427 \end{array}$$

The sum 92,427 is reasonable because it is close to the estimate of 90,000.

Example D

Add \$36.25 + \$12.94.

Estimate: \$40 + \$10 = \$50

Add as you would whole numbers.

$$\begin{array}{r} {\scriptstyle 1\ \ \ \ \ \ \ \ \ \ } \\ \$36.25 \\ +\ \ \ 12.94 \\ \hline \$49.19 \end{array}$$

Place the dollar sign and decimal point in the answer.

The sum \$49.19 is reasonable because it is close to the estimate of \$50.

Example E

Add \$125.98 + \$690.50.

Estimate: \$100 + \$700 = \$800

Add as you would whole numbers.

$$\begin{array}{r} {\scriptstyle 1\ \ 1\ \ \ \ \ \ \ \ \ \ } \\ \$125.98 \\ +\ \ \ 690.50 \\ \hline \$816.48 \end{array}$$

Place the dollar sign and decimal point in the answer.

The sum is reasonable because it is close to the estimate of \$800.

Talk About It

3. How is adding money different than adding whole numbers?

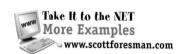

Take It to the NET
More Examples
www.scottforesman.com

CHECK

For another example, see Set 2-5 on p. 115.

1. $\begin{array}{r} 567 \\ +\ 395 \\ \hline \end{array}$

2. $\begin{array}{r} 861 \\ +\ 3{,}192 \\ \hline \end{array}$

3. $\begin{array}{r} 13{,}926 \\ +\ \ \ 4{,}832 \\ \hline \end{array}$

4. $\begin{array}{r} 1{,}994 \\ +\ \ \ 226 \\ \hline \end{array}$

5. $\begin{array}{r} \$25.29 \\ +\ \ \ 36.84 \\ \hline \end{array}$

6. **Number Sense** Meg added 8,250 + 250 and got a sum of 10,500. Is this reasonable? Explain.

PRACTICE

For more practice, see Set 2-5 on p. 119.

A Skills and Understanding

7. 214 + 87

8. 856 + 163

9. 7,123 + 2,891

10. 4,068 + 941

11. 32,325 + 1,995

12. 19,433 + 70,318

13. $81.82 + 1.98

14. $58.35 + 29.66

15. 806 + 495

16. 5,555 + 5,555

17. 62,009 + 9,093

18. $3.19 + $49.23

19. 612 + 307

20. 3,196 + 4,508

21. $9.23 + $15.12

22. $2.51 + $3.38

23. Number Sense Mary adds 3,692 and 5,245. Should her answer be greater or less than 10,000?

B Reasoning and Problem Solving

Math and Music

Altogether, how many stations play

24. Oldies or Spanish music?

25. Country or Top-40 music?

26. Country or Oldies music?

27. Do more stations play Country music than the other three types of music combined? Tell how you know.

28. **Writing in Math** Is the explanation below correct? If not, tell why and write a correct response.

> Explain how to add 92 + 39.
>
> 1
> 92   2 ones + 9 ones = 11 ones or 1 ten 1 one
> \+ 39   1 ten + 9 tens + 3 tens = 13 tens
> 10,031   or 1 hundred 3 tens

Data File

U.S. Commercial Radio in 2001

Type of Music	Number of Stations
Country	2,190
Oldies	785
Spanish	574
Top-40	468

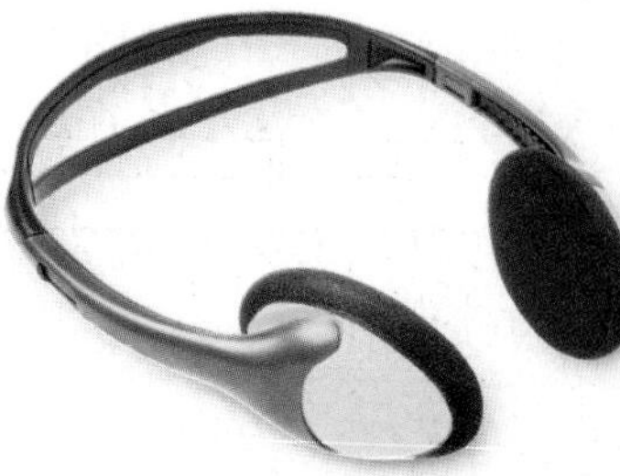

TEST TALK

Think It Through
I should always check **that my answer is reasonable.**

PRACTICE

C Extensions

29. 354,926 + 275,450

30. 478,395 + 855,268

31. 7,243,526 + 1,968,978

32. \$189.65 + 575.89

Mixed Review and Test Prep

Take It to the NET
Test Prep
www.scottforesman.com

Estimate each sum or difference. Then tell whether your estimate is an overestimate or an underestimate.

33. 856 − 150 **34.** 432 + 527 **35.** 1,549 + 3,683 **36.** 7,219 − 2,026

37. What is the value of the 6 in the number 869,024?

A. 6 **B.** 60 **C.** 6,000 **D.** 60,000

Practice Game

Close call

Players: 2–3

Materials: Number cards 0–9 (10 cards per player) Recording sheet

1. Ten cards numbered 0–9 are placed face down in front of each player.
2. Each player takes 6 cards and makes two 3-digit addends.
3. Players record the addends and sum on their record sheet.
4. Players return the cards to their decks, shuffle them, and draw six new cards.
5. Players add the sums from Rounds 1 and 2 and then add the sum of Round 3 to find the final total. The player with the highest final total after 3 rounds is the winner.

Key Idea
You can add more than two numbers by adding one place at a time.

TEST TALK

Think It Through
- I need to **get information from the table** to solve the problem.
- I need **an exact answer.**

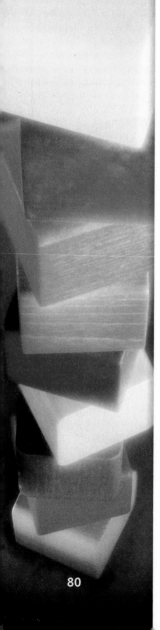

Column Addition

WARM UP

1. 375 + 285
2. 273 + 774
3. 178 + 992
4. 526 + 487

LEARN

How do you add more than two numbers?

What is the total number of elementary schools in Florida, Idaho, Texas, and Virginia?

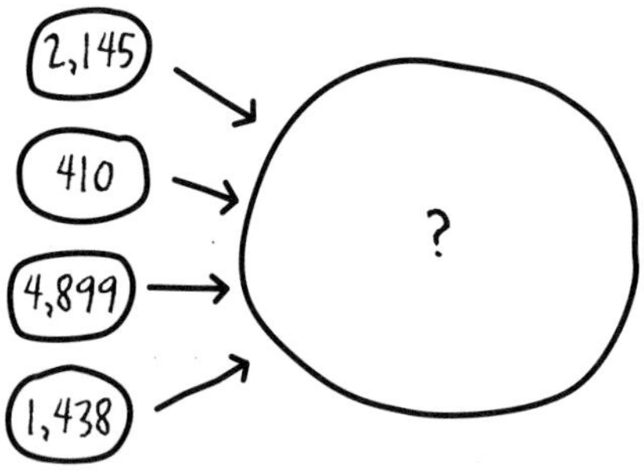

Data File

State	Number of Elementary Schools
Florida	2,145
Idaho	410
Texas	4,899
Virginia	1,438

Example

Add 2,145 + 410 + 4,899 + 1,438.

Estimate: 2,000 + 400 + 5,000 + 1,000 = 8,400

STEP 1

Add the ones. Regroup if necessary.

$$\begin{array}{r} {}^{2} \\ 2{,}145 \\ 410 \\ 4{,}899 \\ +\ 1{,}438 \\ \hline 2 \end{array}$$

STEP 2

Add the tens. Regroup if necessary.

$$\begin{array}{r} {}^{1\,2} \\ 2{,}145 \\ 410 \\ 4{,}899 \\ +\ 1{,}438 \\ \hline 92 \end{array}$$

STEP 3

Add the hundreds and thousands. Regroup if necessary.

$$\begin{array}{r} {}^{1\ \,1\,2} \\ 2{,}145 \\ 410 \\ 4{,}899 \\ +\ 1{,}438 \\ \hline 8{,}892 \end{array}$$

The sum 8,892 is reasonable because it is close to the estimate of 8,400. The four states have a total of 8,892 elementary schools.

Talk About It

1. Why is it easier to add the 1 and the 9 in the tens column first in Step 2?

CHECK ✓

For another example, see Set 2-6 on p. 115.

1.	2.	3.	4.	5.
413	$26.07	24	4,196	$119.00
126	4.91	206	6,804	63.00
+ 184	+ 19.38	+ 817	+19,912	+ 476.00

6. **Number Sense** If you know that the sum of 29, 92, and 83 is 204, what do you know about the sum of 92, 29, and 83?

PRACTICE

For more practice, see Set 2-6 on p. 119.

A Skills and Understanding

7.	8.	9.	10.	11.
286	$84.81	956	76,117	$284.90
219	15.24	1,341	8,982	76.15
+ 83	+ 3.62	+ 6,470	+ 11,046	+ 42.19

12.	13.	14.	15.	16.
69	$20.32	2,844	613	$275.25
358	19.75	3,916	824	36.19
97	6.42	104	176	1.05
+ 523	+ 3.18	+ 2,753	+ 202	+ 1.10

17. **Number Sense** Thomas added 295 + 307 + 488 and got 780. Is this sum reasonable?

B Reasoning and Problem Solving

Use the information at the right for 18–19.

Class Fundraisers
Flower Sale $25.03
Bake Sale $85.25
Car Wash $129.50
Walk-a-Thon $64.79

18. How much money did the class raise in all?

19. Was more money raised at the car wash or at the flower sale and bake sale combined?

20. **Writing in Math** Toby added 2,712 + 4,379 + 5,241. Should her answer be more or less than 10,000?

Mixed Review and Test Prep

Take It to the NET
Test Prep
www.scottforesman.com

Add.

21. 4,679 + 3,443 **22.** 63,774 + 8,261 **23.** $99.17 + $10.38 **24.** $44.95 + $3.95

25. How many hundreds equal 10,000?

A. 10 **B.** 100 **C.** 1,000 **D.** 10,000

Key Idea
You can subtract numbers by subtracting ones, then tens, then hundreds, and then thousands.

Vocabulary
- inverse operations

TEST TALK

Think It Through
- I need to **get information from the text of the problem** to solve.
- I should subtract when I am **comparing amounts.**

Subtracting Whole Numbers and Money

WARM UP

Estimate each difference.

1. 83 − 27
2. 295 − 217
3. $3.87 − $1.18

LEARN

How do you subtract whole numbers using paper and pencil?

Roller Coasters The tallest roller coaster in the world is in California. It is 415 feet tall. The next tallest roller coaster is in Australia. It is 377 feet tall. How much taller is the tallest roller coaster than the second tallest roller coaster?

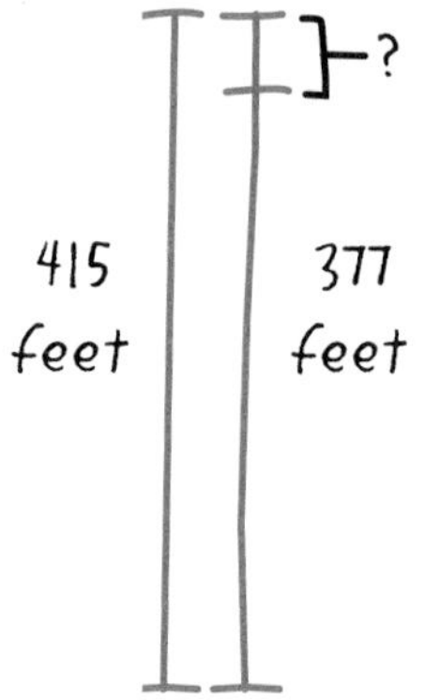

Example A

Find 415 − 377.

Estimate: 420 − 380 = 40

STEP 1	STEP 2	
Regroup if necessary. Subtract the ones.	Regroup if necessary. Subtract the tens. Subtract the hundreds.	Check your answer.
0 15 4 ~~1~~ ~~5~~ − 3 7 7 8	3 10 15 ~~4~~ ~~1~~ ~~5~~ − 3 7 7 3 8	1 1 377 + 38 415 The answer checks.

The tallest roller coaster is 38 feet taller than the second tallest roller coaster.

You can add to check the difference because addition and subtraction are **inverse operations.** They undo each other.

Talk About It

1. If 415 − ☐ = 38, then ☐ + 377 = 415.

How do you subtract across zeros?

Example B

Find 504 − 278.

Estimate: 500 − 300 = 200

One Way

Ken regrouped hundreds to tens and then tens to ones.

```
   9
 4 10 14
 5  0  4
-2  7  8
--------
 2  2  6
```

5 hundreds + 0 tens = 4 hundreds + 10 tens

10 tens + 4 ones = 9 tens + 14 ones

Another Way

Vanessa thought of 504 as 50 tens + 4 ones.

```
 4 9 14
 5 0 4
-2 7 8
------
 2 2 6
```

50 tens + 4 ones = 49 tens + 14 ones

Talk About It

2. Explain the two ways to regroup in Example B.

How do you subtract larger numbers and money?

Example C

Find 5,000 − 2,781.

Estimate: 5,000 − 3,000 = 2,000

```
     9  9
 4  10 10 10
 5,  0  0  0
-2,  7  8  1
------------
 2,  2  1  9
```

Regroup from thousands to subtract the ones.

Example D

Find $72.50 − $24.99.

Estimate: $70 − $20 = $50

```
   6 11  14 10
  $7  2.  5  0
-     2 4. 9  9
--------------
  $4  7.  5  1
```

Subtract as you would whole numbers. Place the dollar sign and decimal point in the answer.

Talk About It

3. Tell how to use addition to check the answer in Example D.

Take It to the NET
More Examples
www.scottforesman.com

CHECK

For another example, see Set 2-7 on p. 115.

Subtract.

1. 960 − 392

2. 8,668 − 669

3. 4,000 − 196

4. 7,804 − 6,926

5. $70.14 − 46.31

6. Number Sense Explain how you would regroup to subtract 302 − 85.

PRACTICE

A Skills and Understanding

Subtract.

7. 803 − 79

8. 5,891 − 3,993

9. 6,000 − 3,704

10. 6,740 − 651

11. $73.86 − 4.95

12. $9.00 − 4.61

13. 7,795 − 948

14. 7,001 − 3,220

15. 3,975 − 3,899

16. $30.00 − 16.48

17. 714 − 395 **18.** 9,070 − 4,675 **19.** 2,006 − 1,156 **20.** $56.01 − $39.22

21. 405 − 186 **22.** 8,123 − 1,483 **23.** 7,613 − 6,948 **24.** $88.25 − $9.36

25. Reasoning Rudy subtracts 7,205 from 10,285. Should his answer be greater or less than 3,000? Explain.

B Reasoning and Problem Solving

26. In the book, *Kate Shelley: Bound for Legend,* Kate is 15 years old when the bridge collapses in 1881. In what year was she born?

When a 700-foot railroad bridge collapsed during a terrible storm, Kate warned the railroad company of the collapse.

27. Ben scored 9,345 points playing his favorite computer game. Drew scored 8,715 points playing the same game. How many more points did Ben score than Drew?

Math and Social Studies

How many more fire departments are

28. all career than mostly career?

29. all volunteer than all career?

30. mostly volunteer than mostly career?

31. How many fire departments are not all volunteer?

32. How many fire departments are there in all?

Data File

U.S. Fire Departments

Type	Number
All Career	1,871
Mostly Career	1,397
Mostly Volunteer	3,848
All Volunteer	19,238

33. Writing in Math Is Jeff's explanation below correct? If not, tell why and write a correct response.

Explain how to subtract 248 from 500.

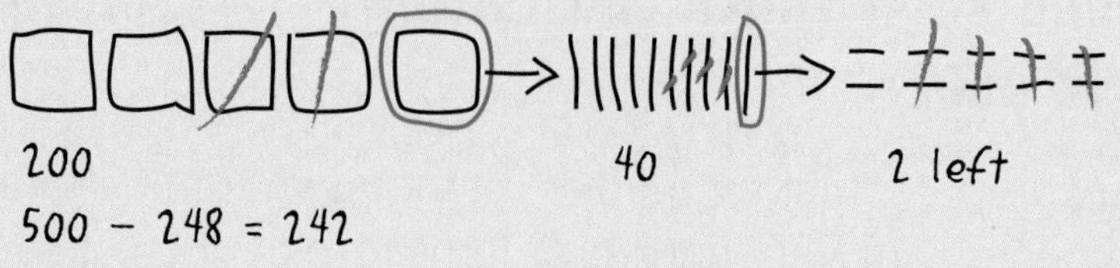

TEST TALK

Think It Through
I can **use a picture** to explain my thinking.

Mixed Review and Test Prep

Take It to the NET
Test Prep
www.scottforesman.com

Add.

34. 846 + 51 + 59

35. \$14.37 + 7.45 + 4.71

36. 4,884 + 634 + 4,026

37. 123 + 994 + 425

38. \$132.08 + 263.00 + 411.10

39. Show 1 dollar and 4 pennies with a dollar sign and decimal point.

A. \$0.14 **B.** \$1.04 **C.** \$1.40 **D.** \$10.40

Learning with Technology

The Place-Value Blocks eTool

Before you begin, estimate and record each difference. With the odometer off, stamp each number in the problem. Break down thousands, hundreds, and tens as needed. Check the actual difference against your estimate. Try different strategies to get your estimates and the actual differences as close to each other as you can.

1. 183 − 25 **2.** 789 − 15

3. 582 − 396 **4.** 6,026 − 1,135

5. 3,447 − 1,724 **6.** 6,615 − 2,345

Key Idea
You can use mental math, paper and pencil, or a calculator to solve addition and subtraction problems.

Materials
- calculator

Choose a Computation Method

WARM UP

Add or subtract.

1. 725 + 725
2. 310 − 85
3. 600 − 250
4. 1,400 + 350

LEARN

How do you know which calculation method to use?

When you compute, first try mental math. Next, think about using paper and pencil. For very hard problems, use a calculator.

TEST TALK

Think It Through

- I can **solve problems in more than one way.**
- Sometimes using mental math or paper and pencil are faster than using a calculator.

Example A

An order was placed for 10 backboards, hoops, and nets. The cost was \$1,480 plus \$110 in tax. What was the total cost?

This is easy to do in my head. I'll use **mental math.**

1,480 + 100 = 1,580

1,580 + 10 = 1,590

Total cost: \$1,590

Example B

The sports store paid \$11,125 for basketball equipment. It sold all of the equipment for \$16,375. Find the difference of these prices.

There are no regroupings. I'll use **paper and pencil.**

$$\begin{array}{r} \$16,375 \\ -\ \ 11,125 \\ \hline \$5,250 \end{array}$$

Difference: \$5,250

Example C

The sports store had total weekly sales of \$10,367, \$22,143, and \$29,251 for 3 weeks. What are the total sales for these 3 weeks?

There are a lot of regroupings. I'll use a **calculator.**

Press:
10367 [+]
22143 [+]
29251 [ENTER =]

Display: 61761

Total sales: \$61,761

Talk About It

1. Why would you use mental math in Example A?
2. When would you use a calculator?

CHECK

For another example, see Set 2-8 on p. 116.

Add or subtract. Tell what computation method you used.

1. 47,800 + 26,500

2. 60,000 − 30,000

3. 25,842 − 17,318

4. $3,539 + 1,883

5. Number Sense Kit used a calculator to find 3,648 − 257. She got 1,078. Is this answer reasonable? Explain.

PRACTICE

For more practice, see Set 2-8 on p. 120.

A Skills and Understanding

Add or subtract. Tell what computation method you used.

6. $8,657 + 6,988

7. 78,136 − 59,645

8. 90,000 − 20,000

9. 37,997 + 9,875

10. 16,835 + 84,997

11. $5,871 − 2,757

12. 73,240 + 16,760

13. 23,001 + 6,000

14. 37,481 − 35,081 **15.** $8,450 − $7,000 **16.** 72,560 + 21,040 **17.** 43,832 + 15,598

18. Number Sense Explain why you would use mental math to add 50,000 and 8,300.

B Reasoning and Problem Solving

19. Use the data at the right. How much more is the basketball backboard than the two basketballs combined?

20. Writing in Math Explain why you would not use a calculator to find 8,000 − 2,000.

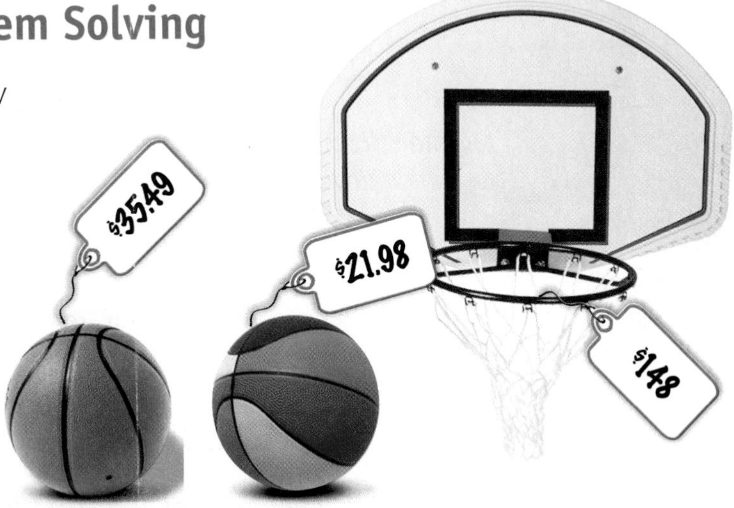

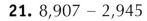

Mixed Review and Test Prep

Take It to the NET
Test Prep
www.scottforesman.com

21. 8,907 − 2,945

22. 8,000 − 6,237

23. $68.42 − $4.68

24. Which number is NOT greater than 67,845?

A. 67,846 **B.** 67,945 **C.** 67,880 **D.** 67,842

Reading For Math Success

Predict and Generalize

Predicting and generalizing when you read in math can help you use the **problem-solving strategy, *Look for a Pattern,*** in the next lesson.

In reading, predicting and generalizing can help you figure out what comes next in a story. In math, predicting and generalizing can help you figure out what comes next in a pattern.

First figure out how to get the second figure from the first figure.

Predict the next figure.

Next figure out how to get the third figure from the second figure.

First Second Third Fourth Fifth

Set the first clock ahead 15 minutes to get the second clock.

Set the second clock ahead 15 minutes to get the third clock.

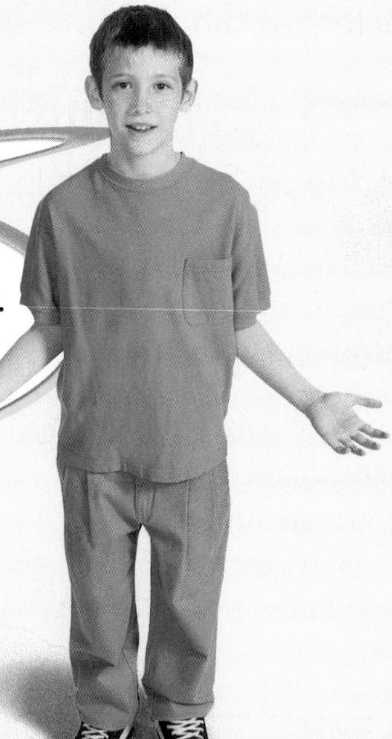

Generalize *to describe the* ***pattern:*** *the hands advance 15 minutes each time. Then* ***predict.*** *The sixth clock will show 3:15.*

1. What time will the seventh clock show?
2. If the pattern were the same but the first clock showed 6:30, what time would the third clock show?

For 3–6, use the picture at the right.

3. How can you get the second row from the first row?

4. How can you get the third row from the second row?

5. Writing in Math Generalize by describing the pattern.

6. Predict the number of suns that will be in the fourth row.

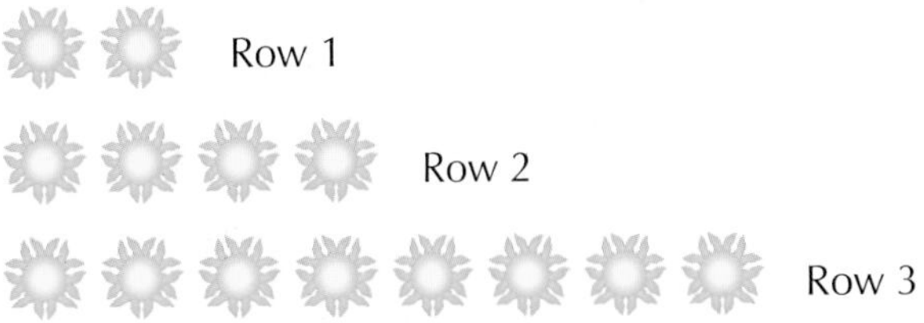

For 7–10, use the picture below.

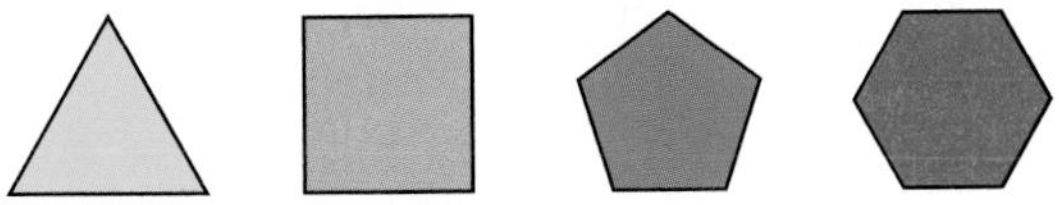

7. Starting at the left, how is the second polygon different from the first?

8. How is the third polygon different from the second?

9. Writing in Math Generalize by describing the pattern.

10. Predict what the fifth and sixth polygons will be.

For 11–15, use the pictures at the right.

11. In the row of houses, how can you get the third address from the first two?

12. In the fireman's hats, how can you get the third number from the first two?

13. Predict the missing number on the football jersey.

14. Generalize to describe the pattern.

15. Writing in Math Use the pattern to make your own picture. Explain how your picture follows the pattern.

Problem-Solving Strategy

Key Idea
Learning how and when to look for a pattern can help you solve problems.

TEST TALK

Think It Through
I can use the pattern of shaded triangles to **predict** the next three shapes.

Reading Helps!

Predicting and generalizing

can help you with...

the problem-solving strategy, *Look for a Pattern*

Look for a Pattern

LEARN

How can you use patterns?

Patterns are found in buildings, nature, and mathematics among other things.

Example A

Look for a pattern. Draw the next three shapes.

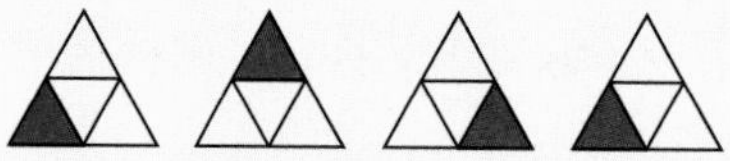

The shaded part seems to rotate.

The next three would be:

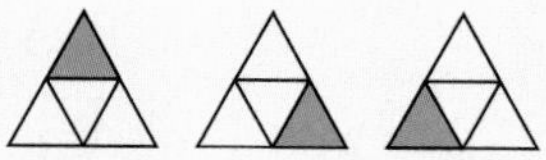

Example B

Look for a pattern. Copy and complete each number sentence.

10 + 1 = 11
100 + 10 + 1 = 111
1,000 + 100 + 10 + 1 = ■
10,000 + 1,000 + 100 + 10 + 1 = ■

All the digits in the sum are the same.

1,000 + 100 + 10 + 1 = **1,111**
10,000 + 1,000 + 100 + 10 + 1 = **11,111**

Talk About It

1. What is the pattern in Example A?

CHECK

For another example, see Set 2-9 on p. 116.

1. Look for a pattern. Draw the next two shapes.

2. Look for a pattern. Tell the missing numbers.
2, 4, 6, 8, ■, ■, ■

For more practice, see Set 2-9 on p. 120.

Look for a pattern. Draw the next two shapes.

3. 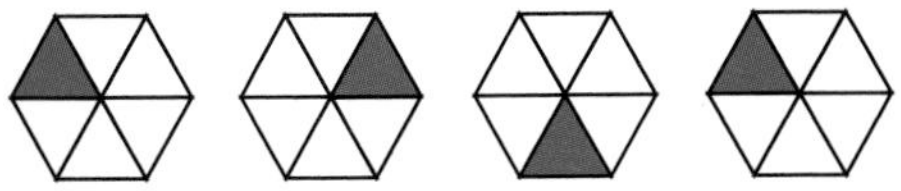

4. 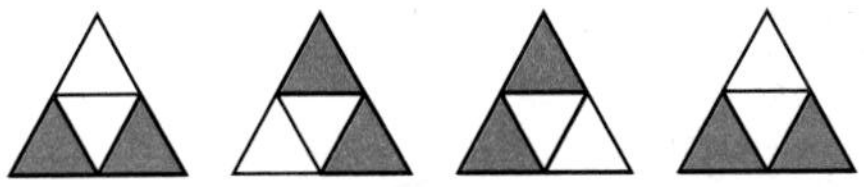

5. 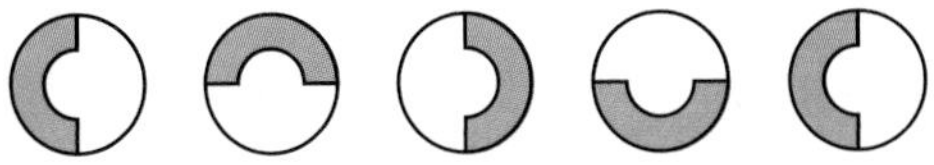

6. 

Look for a pattern. Tell the missing numbers.

7. 1, 3, 5, 7, ___, ___, ___

8. 1, 2, 4, 7, 11, ___, ___, ___

9. 1, 4, 5, 8, 9, ___, ___, ___

10. 2, 7, 9, 14, 16, ___, ___, ___

11. 3, 6, 9, 12, ___, ___, ___

12. 4, 10, 16, 22, ___, ___, ___

Look for a pattern. Copy and complete each number sentence.

13. 40 + 4 = 44
400 + 4 = 404
4,000 + 4 = ___
40,000 + 4 = ___

14. 70 + 7 = 77
707 + 70 = 777
7,007 + 770 = ___
70,707 + 7,070 = ___

15. 500 + 5 = 505
55,000 + 55 = ___
5,550,000 + 555 = ___

The year 2002 was a palindrome. Palindromes are words, sentences, or numbers that are the same written backward and forward.

16. What is the next year that will be a palindrome?

17. What was the last year before 2002 that was a palindrome?

18. Each campsite in a campground has an even number. If the campsites are numbered in order and the first campsite is number 2, what number is the ninth campsite?

Reasoning Look for patterns in the rows of the tables. Find the missing numbers.

19.

A	B	C
3	8	11
5	11	16
7		17
	14	23
10		25
15	20	

20.

A	B	C
9	4	5
10	2	
12		2
16	5	11
20	8	12
25		15

21. **Writing in Math** Suppose there are 16 spoons arranged in this pattern: big spoon, little spoon, big spoon, little spoon, and so on. Is the last spoon a big spoon or a little spoon? Explain.

Review

Do You Know How?

Adding Whole Numbers and Money (2-5)
Column Addition (2-6)

1. $\begin{array}{r} \$69.24 \\ +\ 23.81 \\ \hline \end{array}$

2. $\begin{array}{r} 3,816 \\ +\ 4,494 \\ \hline \end{array}$

3. $\begin{array}{r} 231 \\ 452 \\ +\ 175 \\ \hline \end{array}$

4. $\begin{array}{r} 19,881 \\ 6,521 \\ +\ 31,107 \\ \hline \end{array}$

Subtracting Whole Numbers and Money (2-7)

5. $\begin{array}{r} \$2.32 \\ -\ 1.86 \\ \hline \end{array}$

6. $\begin{array}{r} 306 \\ -\ 187 \\ \hline \end{array}$

7. $\begin{array}{r} 9,184 \\ -\ 8,285 \\ \hline \end{array}$

8. $\begin{array}{r} 8,014 \\ -\ 6,289 \\ \hline \end{array}$

Choose a Computation Method (2-8)

9. $\begin{array}{r} 31,553 \\ +\ 60,000 \\ \hline \end{array}$

10. $\begin{array}{r} 72,008 \\ -\ 16,971 \\ \hline \end{array}$

11. $\begin{array}{r} 21,000 \\ -\ 19,984 \\ \hline \end{array}$

12. $\begin{array}{r} 49,250 \\ +\ 23,250 \\ \hline \end{array}$

Problem-Solving Strategy: Look for a Pattern (2-9)

Look for a pattern. Tell the missing numbers.

13. 1, 5, 9, 13, ▢, ▢, ▢

14. 2, 5, 8, 11, ▢, ▢, ▢

15. 1, 3, 4, 6, 7, ▢, ▢, ▢

16. 3, 8, 13, 18, 23, ▢, ▢, ▢

Do You Understand?

A Tell how you regrouped in Exercise 1.

B Describe an easy way to add the tens in Exercise 3.

C Tell how subtracting money amounts is the same as subtracting whole numbers.

D Explain why your answer is reasonable in Exercise 8.

E Tell which computation method you used for each exercise.

F Write two numbers that you would add using mental math.

G Describe the pattern in Exercises 13 and 14.

H Explain how you would complete the number sentence.

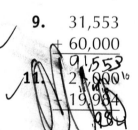

800 + ▢ + 8 = 888

Diagnostic Checkpoint

Think It Through
I can **estimate** to make sure my **answer is reasonable.**

MULTIPLE CHOICE

1. William bought a helmet for $116.34, a pair of gloves for $39.32, and goggles for $49.47. How much did he spend in all? (2-6)

A. $105.13 **B.** $155.66 **C.** $195.13 **D.** $205.13

2. The 4th grade collected 5,053 cans of food. The 3rd grade collected 4,964 cans. How many more cans did the 4th grade collect than the 3rd grade? (2-7)

A. 89 cans **B.** 99 cans **C.** 109 cans **D.** 1,089 cans

FREE RESPONSE

Add or subtract. (2-5, 2-6, and 2-7)

3. 5,098 + 3,995

4. 593 + 672

5. $8.12 − 4.25

6. 6,000 − 2,451

7. 806 − 458

8. 782 + 297 + 11

9. 2,546 + 9,862 + 6,974

10. $56.93 + 78.23 + 50.00

11. 12,000 + 7,000

12. 8,965 − 2,435

13. How many pages are in all four books combined? (2-6)

14. How many more pages are in the book about France than the book about Germany? (2-7) 130

Api's Travel Books

Books	Pages
France	826
Germany	696
Italy	516
Switzerland	392

Look for a pattern. Draw the next two shapes. (2-9)

15. 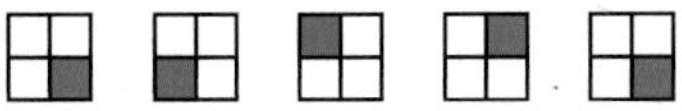

16. 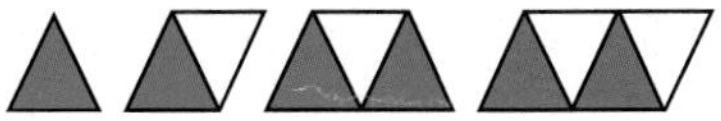

Writing in Math

17. Joe bought two stamp collections. One had 7,519 stamps. The other had 10,381 stamps. How many stamps did Joe buy? Explain which computation method you used and why. (2-8)

18. Mary's sister said these numbers: 4, 8, 12, 16. Tell the next two numbers and explain the pattern she used. (2-9)

Algebra

Key Idea
Translating words to numerical expressions can help you solve problems.

Vocabulary
- number expression

Translating Words to Expressions

Reading Helps!

Drawing conclusions can help you with... translating words to expressions.

LEARN

How do you translate words to number expressions?

Sharks There are 350 species of sharks. Of these, only 42 species are known to have attacked humans. Write a number expression that shows how many types of sharks have not attacked humans.

Read and Understand

A **number expression** contains numbers and at least one operation. Some examples of number expressions are below.

46 + 58   16 ÷ 4   4 × 5 + 8   8 × 6   24 + 15 + 12

To write a number expression for the Sharks problem, think about parts and wholes.

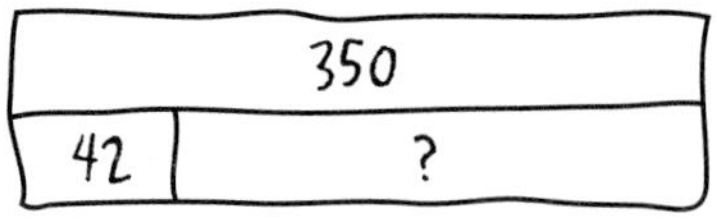

Plan and Solve

What You **Think:** 350 less 42   What You **Write:** 350 − 42

Look Back and Check

The number expression 350 − 42 shows that 42 less than 350 is the number of species of sharks that have not attacked humans.

Other Examples

Phrase	Number Expression
12 red pens combined with 8 blue pens	12 + 8
38 girls, but 14 fewer boys	38 − 14
68 more than 37	37 + 68

Talk About It

1. What other word phrase could you use for the Sharks problem?

CHECK

For another example, see Set 2-10 on p. 116.

Write a number expression for each phrase.

1. 272 pages minus 28 pages
2. 25 apples combined with 32 peaches
3. 16 more than 29 students
4. 57 red marbles, but 19 fewer blue marbles
5. **Reasoning** If you have 5 more pens than pencils, do you have 5 fewer pencils than pens? Explain.

PRACTICE

For more practice, see Set 2-10 on p. 121.

Write a number expression for each phrase.

6. \$27 increased by \$9
7. the total of 25 cars, 4 buses, and 9 trucks
8. 7 bicycles, but 12 more tricycles
9. 168 is how much more than 95?
10. 135 less than 264 days
11. 352 inches decreased by 24 inches

Use the graph for 12–16. Write a number expression and then solve.

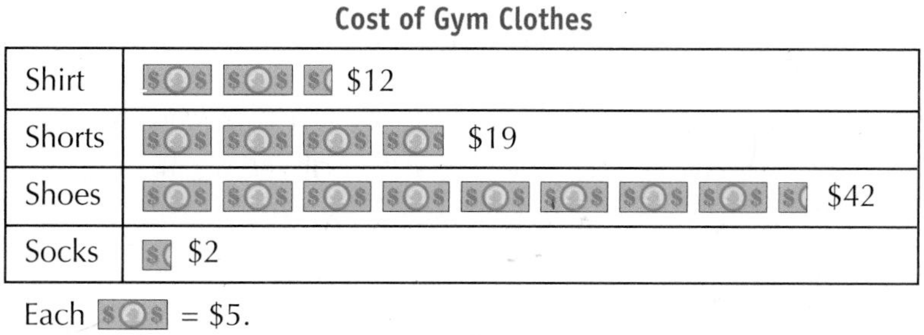

12. How much do the shirt and shoes cost together?
13. How much more are the shoes than the shorts?
14. How much would the shirt cost if the price was increased by \$3?
15. How much would the shoes cost if the price was decreased by \$9?
16. How much do the clothes cost altogether?

Choose the number expression that matches the situation.

17. Westwood Elementary had 276 students. Then, 8 more students came. How many students were there then?

    276 − 8   276 + 8

18. Ms. Johnson had 78 sheets of poster board at the beginning of the year. The class used 49 sheets. How many sheets were left?

    78 − 49   78 + 49

Writing in Math Write two phrases for each number expression.

19. 41 − 36
20. 74 − 65
21. 472 + 135
22. 16 + 28 + 56

Algebra

Key Idea
Number expressions with more than one operation use parentheses to tell which operation to do first.

TEST TALK

Think It Through
I can **write a number expression** to solve the problem.

Matching Words and Number Expressions

WARM UP

1. 8 + 2	2. 15 + 9
3. 16 − 4	4. 32 − 25

LEARN

How can you use number expressions?

Parentheses ( ) tell which operation to do first in a number expression.

Example A

Pia had $20. She spent $7 and then earned $9. How much did she have left?

STEP 1	Write a number expression.	**(20 − 7) + 9** ↑ Pia spent $7 first.
STEP 2	Find the value of the expression.	Do the operation in parentheses first. **(20 − 7) + 9** ↓ **13 + 9 = 22**

Pia had $22 left.

Talk About It

1. What do parentheses in number expressions tell you to do?

CHECK

For another example, see Set 2-11 on p. 117.

Choose the number expression that matches the words. Then find its value.

1. Jennifer had 30 stickers. She gave out 7 on Monday and 5 on Tuesday.

(30 − 7) − 5 or 30 − (7 − 5)

2. Jim made 8 potholders, sold 5, and then made 4 more.

8 − (5 + 4) or (8 − 5) + 4

3. **Number Sense** Do 12 − (2 + 6) and (12 − 2) + 6 have the same value? Explain.

For more practice, see Set 2-11 on p. 121.

A Skills and Understanding

Choose the number expression that matches the words. Then find its value.

4. Kurt earned \$12 and \$7 and then spent \$4.

12 − (7 + 4) or (12 + 7) − 4

5. Trina made 9 baskets. She gave 3 baskets to Sue and 2 to Jonna.

9 − (3 − 2) or (9 − 3) − 2

6. Mario had 12 stamps. He bought 9 stamps and then gave Ted 5 of the stamps.

12 − (9 − 5) or (12 + 9) − 5

7. Jane had 36 paper cups. She used 17 cups at the party and then bought 8 more cups.

36 − (17 + 8) or (36 − 17) + 8

8. Number Sense Does (9 − 5) + 2 or 9 − (5 + 2) have a value of 2? Explain.

B Reasoning and Problem Solving

Choose the number expression that matches the words. Then, find its value.

9. How many more representatives does Illinois have than Maine and Oklahoma combined?

(18 − 2) + 5 or 18 − (2 + 5)

10. The representatives of Michigan and Maine agreed to support a bill. Then the representatives of Oklahoma joined them. How many representatives supported the bill then?

(15 + 2) − 5 or (15 + 2) + 5

Data File

U.S. House of Representatives

State	Number of Representatives
Illinois	18
Michigan	15
Maine	2
Oklahoma	5

The U.S. Census figures determine the number of each state's congressional representatives.

11. Writing in Math Explain why the values of (10 − 4) − 2 and 10 − (4 − 2) are not the same.

Mixed Review and Test Prep

Take It to the NET
Test Prep
www.scottforesman.com

12. Look for a pattern. Draw the next two shapes.

13. Round 678,312 to the nearest thousand.

A. 678,000 **B.** 678,300 **C.** 679,000 **D.** 680,000

Algebra

Key Idea
Some expressions have variables as well as numbers.

Vocabulary
- variable
- algebraic expression

Evaluating Expressions

WARM UP

1. 7 + 5
2. 32 + 5
3. 14 − 6
4. 48 − 12

LEARN

How can you evaluate expressions with addition and subtraction?

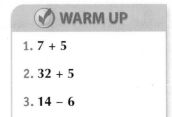

A **variable** is a symbol that stands for a number. Expressions with variables are called **algebraic expressions.** These are algebraic expressions.

★ + 8   ◆ − 12 $32 + n$ $x + 1$

To evaluate an expression, substitute a value for the variable and then compute.

Example A

Evaluate ★ + 8 when ★ = 6.

Substitute 6 for ★. Then add.

★ + 8
↓
6 + 8 = 14

Example B

Evaluate ◆ − 12 when ◆ = 42.

Substitute 42 for ◆. Then subtract.

◆ − 12
↓
42 − 12 = 30

Example C

There are 32 people signed up for painting classes. The table shows how many will be taking classes if n more people sign up, for different values of n. Find the missing number in the table.

Substitute 12 for n in the expression $32 + n$.

$32 + n$
↓
$32 + 12 = 44$

The missing number is 44.

n	$32 + n$	
4	36	← 32 + 4
7	39	← 32 + 7
12	?	

Talk About It

1. What is the value of ★ + 8 when ★ = 6?

2. In Example C, explain why 36 is next to 4 in the table.

CHECK

For another example, see Set 2-12 on p.117.

Evaluate each expression for $k = 5$.

1. $k + 19$ **2.** $k - 2$ **3.** $13 + k$ **4.** $k + 100$ **5.** $8 - k$

6. Number Sense Does the expression ✣ + 7 have a greater value when ✣ = 4 or when ✣ = 14?

PRACTICE

For more practice, see Set 2-12 on p. 121.

A Skills and Understanding

Evaluate each expression for $x = 20$.

7. $x + 32$ **8.** $x + 7$ **9.** $400 + x$ **10.** $x - 5$ **11.** $64 - x$

Find the missing numbers in each table.

12.

✱	6 + ✱
4	10
7	
24	
100	

13.

z	$z - 7$
47	
36	29
30	
24	

14.

m	$m + 16$
4	
7	
34	50
100	

B Reasoning and Problem Solving

15. Tina has $40 saved. The table shows how much she will have if she saves d dollars more, for different values of d. Copy and complete the table.

DOLLARS SAVED	TOTAL DOLLARS
d	$40 + d$
8	
12	
	65
32	

16. Traci earns $6 baby-sitting and $2 washing dishes. She spends $4. How much money does she have left?

17. Writing in Math Explain how to evaluate $x + 16$ for $x = 8$.

Mixed Review and Test Prep

Take It to the NET
Test Prep
www.scottforesman.com

18. Choose the number expression that matches the words. Then find its value. Mason bought 14 pencils. He gave 8 away and then bought 4 more.

$14 - (8 + 4)$ or $(14 - 8) + 4$

19. What is the next number in the pattern? 3,478 3,488 3,498

A. 3,408 **B.** 3,488 **C.** 3,508 **D.** 3,598

Algebra

Key Idea
To solve an equation, find the value of the variable that makes the equation true.

Vocabulary
- equation
- solution
- solve

TEST TALK

Think It Through
- I can **use mental math** to solve an equation.
- I can **try, check, and revise** to solve an equation.

Solving Addition and Subtraction Equations

WARM UP

Evaluate each expression for $x = 10$.

1. $x + 8$ **2.** $x + 42$

3. $x - 4$ **4.** $70 - x$

LEARN

How can you find the value of the variable that makes an equation true?

An **equation** is a number sentence that uses the equal sign (=) to show that two expressions have the same value. The following are equations.

$8 + 9 = 17$ $100 - 40 = 60$ $x + 3 = 7$ $\square - 5 = 12$

The **solution** to an equation is the value of the variable that makes the equation true. When you find the solution to an equation that has a variable, you **solve** the equation.

	Example A		Example B
	Solve. $9 + n = 24$		Solve. $k - 30 = 50$
STEP 1 Use mental math.	9 plus what number equals 24?		What number minus 30 equals 50?
STEP 2 Try.	Try $n = 13$ $9 + n$ ↓ $9 + 13 = 22$	Try $n = 15$ $9 + n$ ↓ $9 + 15 = 24$	Try $k = 80$ $k - 30$ ↓ $80 - 30 = 50$
STEP 3 Check and revise, if necessary.	Does 9 + 13 equal 24? *No*	Does 9 + 15 equal 24? *Yes*	Does 80 − 30 equal 50? *Yes*
	The solution is $n = 15$.		The solution is $k = 80$.

Talk About It

1. What is the solution to $9 + n = 24$?

2. Explain how to solve $k - 30 = 50$.

CHECK

For another example, see Set 2-13 on p. 117.

Solve each equation.

1. $* - 8 = 7$ **2.** $m + 300 = 700$ **3.** $y - 4 = 9$ **4.** $9 + \square = 12$

5. Number Sense Is the solution of $n + 5 = 35$ greater or less than 35? Explain how you know.

PRACTICE

For more practice, see Set 2-13 on p. 121.

A Skills and Understanding

Solve each equation.

6. $a - 6 = 19$ **7.** $c + 6 = 11$ **8.** $h - 25 = 50$ **9.** $9 + d = 23$

10. $60 + p = 70$ **11.** $m - 200 = 100$ **12.** $t - 3 = 12$ **13.** $28 - r = 15$

14. $b + 3 = 9$ **15.** $z - 5 = 4$ **16.** $w + 400 = 600$ **17.** $e - 8 = 8$

18. Number Sense Is $t = 11$ a reasonable solution of $t - 9 = 10$?

B Reasoning and Problem Solving

19. After Rebecca bought a dog collar for $4, she had $6 left. How much money did she have to start? Let d = the amount of money she had to start. Use the equation $d - 4 = 6$ to solve the problem.

20. Reasonableness Marissa solved the equation $k - 15 = 45$ and got $k = 30$. Is this solution reasonable? Explain.

21. Writing in Math Explain how the pan balance on the right shows the equation $a + 2 = 6$. Solve the equation and tell what the solution means.

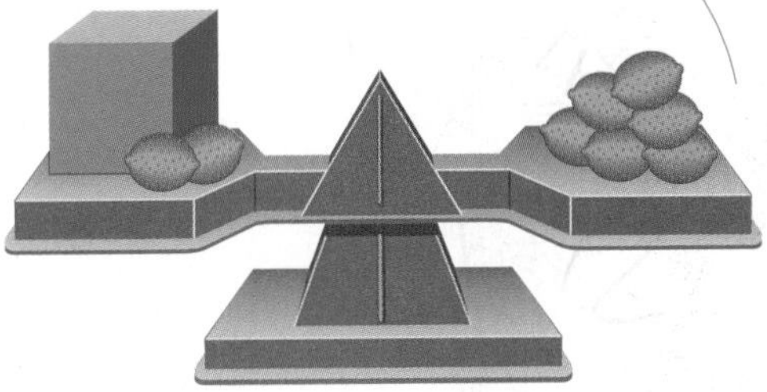

Mixed Review and Test Prep

Take It to the NET
Test Prep
www.scottforesman.com

Evaluate each expression for $w = 30$.

22. $w - 12$ **23.** $w + 6$ **24.** $w - 21$ **25.** $14 + w$ **26.** $52 - w$

27. Add $67.09 + $5.95.

A. $61.14 **B.** $62.94 **C.** $72.94 **D.** $73.04

Problem-Solving Applications

Mountains Some mountains are formed when large sections of the earth move. Others are made by volcanic eruptions. Mountains are beautiful places to hike, ski, and enjoy nature.

Trivia In 1943, a farmer in Mexico noticed a crack in his field. Lava began to pour out of the crack and in 6 days the cone of the volcano had grown to 500 feet! This volcano is called Paricutin.

1 By the time Paricutin reached 500 feet it had gained world-wide attention. It grew to 1,100 feet in the first year. In 1952, Paricutin became dormant. By this time its cone had grown another 290 feet. How tall did Paricutin grow during 9 years of eruptions?

2 Each year, more than 500,000 people go mountain climbing. What number is 100,000 more than 500,000? 1,000 more? 10 more?

Using Key Facts

3 Which mountains have a greater difference in height: Mount Aconcagua and Mount Cook, or Mount Everest and Mount Kilimanjaro?

Key Facts

Mountain	Height
•Mt. Cook	12,316 ft
•Matterhorn	14,690 ft
•Mt. Kilimanjaro	19,340 ft
•Mt. McKinley	20,320 ft
•Mt. Aconcagua	22,834 ft
•Mt. Everest	29,035 ft

Good News/Bad News *As warm moist air is blown up one side of a mountain, rain often falls, helping lush forests to grow. Unfortunately, this leaves little moisture left in the air for it to rain on the other side of the mountain, and so desert conditions may exist there.*

4 **Writing in Math** Use the data in the Key Facts to write your own word problem. Solve it and write the answer in a complete sentence.

5 **Decision Making** Suppose you have $40 to buy supplies for a one-day hike in the mountains. What will you buy? How much money will you have left?

Item	Cost
Pocket knife	$25
First-aid kit	$12
Sunglasses	$10
100 feet of rope	$15
Flashlight	$9
Energy bar	$2
Compass	$10
Map	$5

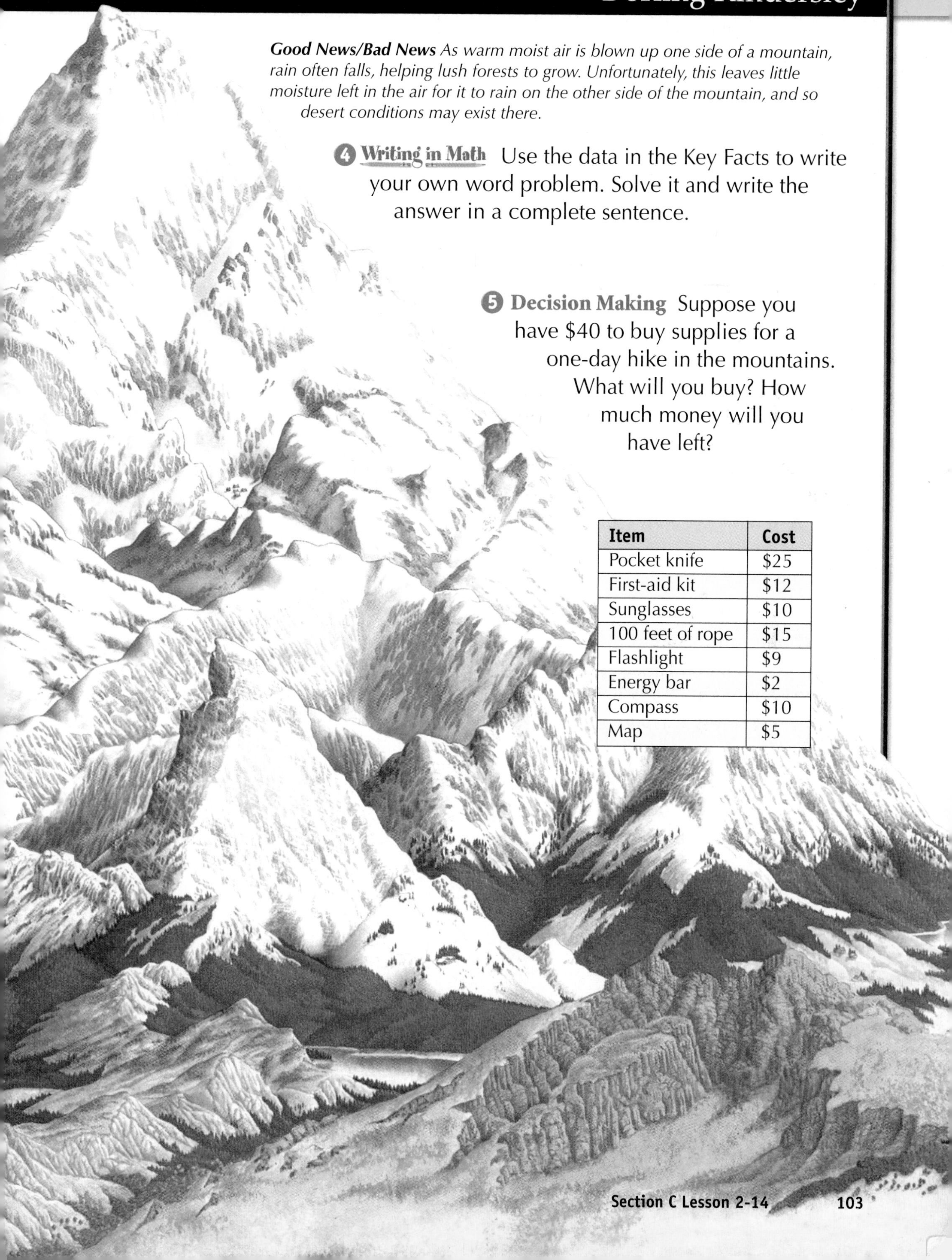

Review

Do You Know How?

Do You Understand?

Translating Words to Expressions (2-10)

Write a number expression for each phrase.

1. 181 trees minus 4 trees
2. $375 increased by $28
3. 47 cars combined with 27 cars

A Tell how you wrote the number expression in Exercise 1.

B Explain how you knew which operation to use in Exercise 2.

Matching Words and Number Expressions (2-11)

Choose the number expression that matches the words. Then, find its value.

4. Jake had $18. He spent $4. Then he earned $12 more mowing. How much money does he have now?

   $18 - (4 + 12)$ or $(18 - 4) + 12$

C Explain how to find the values of $(8 - 5) + 2$ and $8 - (5 + 2)$.

D Is the value of $(2 + 8) + 5$ the same as $2 + (8 + 5)$? Explain.

Evaluating Expressions (2-12)

Evaluate each expression for $h = 9$.

5. $h + 16$
6. $h + 43$
7. $100 + h$
8. $h - 7$
9. $h - 9$
10. $25 - h$

E Tell how you evaluated the expressions in Exercises 5 and 8.

F Explain why the expression $n + 7$ has a different value when $n = 8$ than when $n = 10$.

Solving Addition and Subtraction Equations (2-13)

Solve each equation.

11. $6 + r = 14$
12. $m + 14 = 21$
13. $b - 8 = 9$
14. $w - 20 = 60$
15. $y + 5 = 12$
16. $n - 50 = 50$

G Explain why $n = 6$ is the solution to $n + 8 = 14$.

H Explain why 40 is NOT a solution to $w - 20 = 60$.

Diagnostic Checkpoint

TEST TALK

Think It Through
I can turn the question into a statement, "I need to…."

MULTIPLE CHOICE

1. Choose the expression that matches the words. Haley had 8 bracelets. She gave 6 away and then made 2 more. (2-11)

A. $8 + (6 - 2)$ **C.** $(8 + 6) - 2$

B. $8 - (6 + 2)$ **D.** $(8 - 6) + 2$

2. Danny spent \$6 on a book. He had \$8 left. How much money did he have to start? Use $d - 6 = 8$ to solve. (2-13)

A. \$2 **B.** \$8 **C.** \$12 **D.** \$14

FREE RESPONSE

Choose the number expression that matches the words. Then find its value. (2-11)

3. Leo had 24 invitations. He gave out 19 and then bought 12 more.

$(24 - 19) + 12$ or $24 + (19 - 12)$

4. Mandy made 13 bookmarks. She gave 3 to her sister and then 2 to her brother.

$13 - (3 - 2)$ or $(13 - 3) - 2$

5. Find the missing numbers in the table on the right. (2-12)

s	9	14	27	32
s + 13				45

Solve each equation. (2-13)

6. $18 + a = 24$ **7.** $c + 5 = 14$ **8.** $k - 9 = 8$ **9.** $13 - m = 6$

For 10–11, use the information at the right. Write a number expression. Then solve. (2-10)

10. How many more books does the fourth grade need to collect to reach the goal of 40 books?

11. How many books have the fourth- and fifth-grade classes collected together?

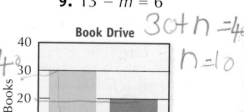

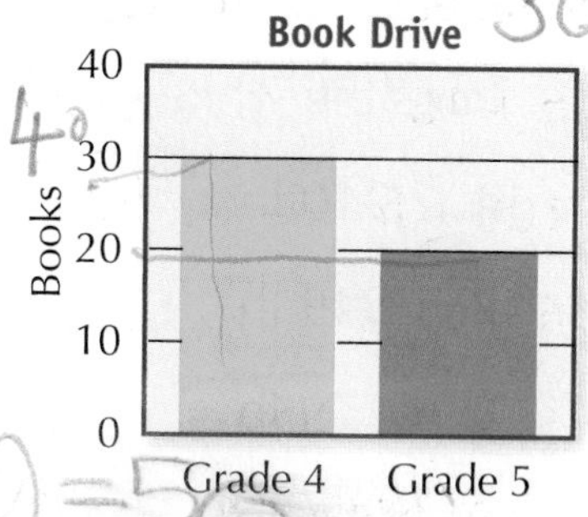

Writing in Math

12. Explain how to find the values of $(14 - 7) - 3$ and $14 - (7 - 3)$. (2-11)

13. Explain how to evaluate $t - 5$ for $t = 14$. (2-12)

CHAPTER 2
Test Talk

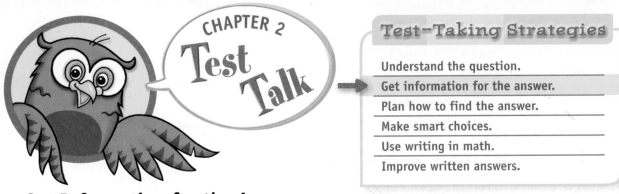

Test-Taking Strategies

- Understand the question.
- Get information for the answer.
- Plan how to find the answer.
- Make smart choices.
- Use writing in math.
- Improve written answers.

Get Information for the Answer

After you understand a test question, you need to get information for the answer. Some test questions do not contain all the information you need in the text. You may need to look for more information in a picture, map, diagram, table, or graph.

1. The table shows some of the biggest sharks ever caught.

Kind of Shark	Weight	Year Caught
Bignose shark	370 lb	1993
Blue shark	454 lb	1996
Shortfin mako	1,115 lb	1988
Thresher shark	506 lb	2003
Tiger shark	1,780 lb	1964
White shark	2,664 lb	1959

Compare the weights of the white shark and the shortfin mako shark. How much more does the white shark weigh?

A. 2,210 lb

B. 1,549 lb

C. 3,779 lb

D. 1,559 lb

Understand the question.

I need to find how much more the white shark weighed than the shortfin mako shark.

Get information for the answer.

- Look for important information in the text.

  In this problem, the text does not contain any numbers I need to find my answer.

- Look for important information in pictures, maps, diagrams, tables, or graphs.

I can find the weights of the white shark and the shortfin mako shark in the table.

2. Which expression should be used to calculate Thomas Jefferson's age when he died?

Thomas Jefferson
Born: 1743 Died: 1826

Think It Through

I need to find which expression could be used to find Thomas Jefferson's age. I can get the year he was born and the year he died from the caption under the photo.

A. 1743 − 1826

B. 1746 + 1826

C. 1826 + 1743

D. 1826 − 1743

Now it's your turn.

For each problem, tell what information is needed to solve the problem.

3. Wendy bought a sweater and a pair of jeans at Fashion City.

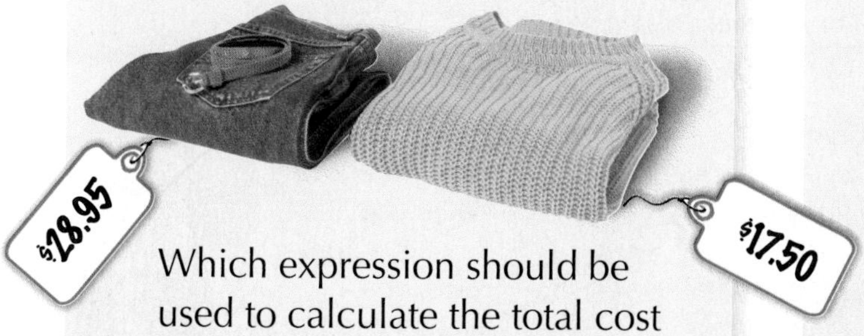

Which expression should be used to calculate the total cost of the sweater and the jeans?

A. \$28.95 − \$17.50

B. \$28.95 + \$17.50

C. \$17.50 + \$7.98

D. \$28.95 − \$7.98

4. Tim's family drove from Orlando to Miami. Pat's family drove from Tampa to Orlando. Tim's family drove how many more miles than Pat's family?

A. 150

B. 155

C. 300

D. 320

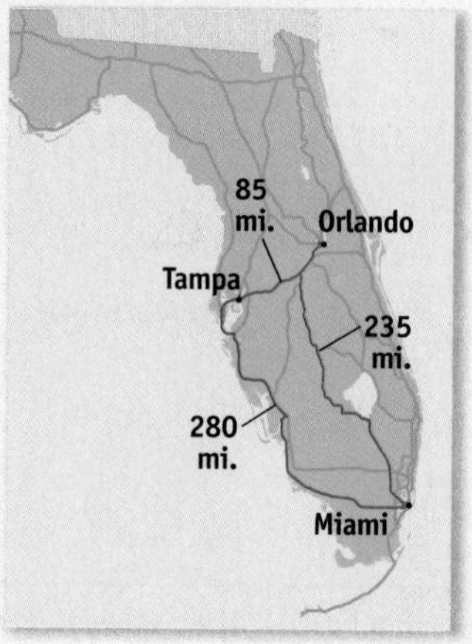

Key Vocabulary and Concept Review

My dad rides the commuter train both ways to work.

The ***Commutative Property of Addition*** *says you can add in any order. (p. 62)*

Self Check

Mental math helps you find sums and differences. (Lessons 2-1, 2-2)

Use properties.

Commutative Property of Addition

3 + 6 = 6 + 3

Associative Property of Addition

2 + (5 + 4) = (2 + 5) + 4

Use **breaking apart.**

327 + 24 — Break apart 24 to make a ten.

327 + 3 + 21

330 + 21

351

So, 327 + 24 = 351. (327 and 24 are the addends; 351 is the sum.)

Use **compensation.**

144 − 28 = ▢

144 − 30 = 114 — Subtract 30.

114 + 2 = 116 — Then add 2.

So, 144 − 28 = 116. (116 is the difference.)

1. Use mental math to find 436 + 46 and 179 − 48.

My mom is compensated for the extra hours she works.

Compensation *is an adjustment yo make to the numbers you're computing with. (p. 62)*

Self Check

Estimate sums and differences and then add or subtract. (Lessons 2-3, 2-4, 2-5, 2-6, 2-7)

Add 1,634 + 428.

Use **front-end estimation.**
2,000 + 400 = 2,400

```
    1
  2,234
+   428
  2,662
```

Add each column starting with the ones. Regroup if necessary.

2,000 is an **underestimate.**

Subtract $35.12 − 13.45.

Estimate by rounding.
$40 − $10 = $30

```
     10
    4 0 12
  $3 5.1 2
−   1 3.4 5
  $2 1.6 7
```

Subtract each column starting with the ones. Regroup if necessary.

$30 is an **overestimate.**

Subtract 4,000 − 2,376.

Estimate by rounding.
4,000 − 2,000 = 2,000

```
     9  9
  3 10 10 10
  4, 0  0  0
− 2, 3  7  6
  1, 6  2  4
```

When you subtract across zeros, you may have to regroup the hundreds or thousands first.

Use **inverse operations** to check.
1,624 + 2,376 = 4,000

2. Find 1,486 + 3,908, $60.07 − 13.58, and 413 + 677 + 21.

Self Check

You can choose a computation method or look for a pattern to solve problems. (Lessons 2-8, 2-9)

The county fair had a total attendance of 95,877 people. There were 42,126 adults that attended the fair. How many children attended the fair?

$$\begin{array}{r} 95{,}877 \\ -\ 42{,}126 \\ \hline 53{,}751 \end{array}$$

There are no regroupings, use paper and pencil.

There were 53,751 children at the county fair.

Look for a pattern. Find the missing numbers.

2, 6, 10, ▪, ▪, ▪

+4 +4 +4 +4 +4

2 6 10 **14** **18** **22**

3. At the fair, the Morton family spent \$24 on entrance tickets, \$36 on ride tickets, and \$55 on food. How much did they spend in all?

Evaluate sounds like it contains "value."
*To **evaluate an expression** means to find out what it's worth. (p. 98)*

My lunch varies from day to day.
*The value of a **variable** changes in different situations. (p. 98)*

Self Check

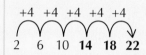

Many problems involve expressions and equations. (Lessons 2-10, 2-11, 2-12, 2-13)

Number Expression

Martha borrowed 2 books and 5 books and then returned 3 books.

$(2 + 5) - 3$

To find the value of the expression, do the operation in the **parentheses** first.

$(2 + 5) - 3 = 4$

Algebraic Expression

Evaluate $n - 14$ for $n = 30$.

Substitute 30 for the **variable.**

$n - 14$

↓

$30 - 14 = 16$

Equation

Solve $y + 13 = 18$.

Try 3. Does $3 + 13 = 18$? *No.*
Try 5. Does $5 + 13 = 18$? *Yes.*

The **solution** is $y = 5$.

4. Find the value of $(6 - 3) + 8$.
5. Evaluate $m + 12$ for $m = 7$ and solve $p - 6 = 11$.

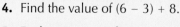

Answers: 1. 482; 131 2. 5,394; \$46.49; 1,111 3. \$115 4. 11 5. 19; $p = 17$

Chapter Test

MULTIPLE CHOICE

Choose the correct letter for each answer.

1. Find 5,000 − 3,245.

A. 1,755 **C.** 2,245
B. 2,755 **D.** 8,245

2. Marisa practiced basketball drills for 87 minutes and foul shots for 42 minutes. How many more minutes did she spend practicing drills than foul shots?

A. 14 **B.** 25 **C.** 45 **D.** 129

3. Find \$89.56 + \$55.31.

A. \$34.25 **C.** \$144.87
B. \$134.87 **D.** \$159.56

4. Erin wrapped 97 gifts at the mall during the holiday fundraiser. Mike wrapped 113 gifts. About how many gifts did they wrap altogether?

A. 100 **C.** 200
B. 150 **D.** 300

5. Find 37,899 + 41,231.

A. 79,103 **C.** 79,190
B. 79,130 **D.** 82,541

6. When the circus came to town, it was seen by 3,127 children and 2,818 adults. How many more children than adults saw the circus?

A. 309 **C.** 1,319
B. 939 **D.** 1,717

7. Find 1,435 + 698 + 314 + 2,076.

A. 4,209 **C.** 4,528
B. 4,523 **D.** 6,903

8. Martin bought a pair of jeans for \$42.99, a coat for \$127.45, and a sweater for \$32.09. How much money did he spend altogether?

TEST TALK
Think It Through
I'll **watch for key words like HOW MANY MORE and IN ALL.**

A. \$75.08 **C.** \$213.43
B. \$202.53 **D.** \$254.90

9. Dave spent \$13 on a compact disc. He had \$5 left. How much money did he have to start? Use $n - 13 = 5$ to solve.

A. \$8 **C.** \$15
B. \$14 **D.** \$18

10. Rachel had 10 muffins, and made 12 more. Then she gave 5 away. Choose the expression that indicates how many muffins Rachel has left.

A. (10 + 12) − 5 **C.** (12 − 10) + 5
B. 10 + (12 + 5) **D.** 10 − (12 + 5)

11. Which number goes in the ☐ to complete the pattern?

3, 6, 12, 24, ☐, 96

A. 27 **B.** 36 **C.** 48 **D.** 63

FREE RESPONSE

Use mental math to add or subtract.

12. 567 + 381

13. 751 − 207

Estimate each sum or difference. Then tell if your estimate is an overestimate or an underestimate.

14. 687 + 301

15. 7,321 − 5,012

Add or subtract.

16. \$45.99 − \$32.22

17. 1,894 + 234 + 5,412

Look for a pattern. Write the next 3 numbers.

18. 4, 8, 12, ▢, ▢, ▢

19. 5, 10, 20, 40, ▢, ▢, ▢

Write a number expression for each phrase.

20. \$151 decreased by \$21

21. 405 books and 232 more

Evaluate each expression for $x = 4$.

22. $x + 15$

23. $57 - x$

Solve each equation.

24. $3 + n = 27$

25. $t - 40 = 80$

26. Tia was planting flowers in a row by following the order below. If she continues the same pattern, what are the next two flowers she will plant?

daisy, daisy, lily, lily, daisy, daisy, lily, ?, ?

Writing in Math

27. Jason made a table to keep track of how many cans he collected. On what day will Jason have more than 100 cans? Explain how you know.

TEST TALK

Think It Through

- I will look for a pattern.
- I will **check my work** to verify my answer.

Jason's Can Collection

Day	Total Number of Cans Collected
1	15
2	30
3	45

Solve the problem below, then tell which computation method you used and why.

28. The fourth-grade students from three different schools are going on a field trip. Eastern Elementary has 121 fourth-graders, Western Elementary has 118 fourth-graders, and Northern Elementary has 129 fourth-graders. How many fourth-grade students are there in all?

29. Clare said that (12 − 4) − 2 is the same as 12 − (4 − 2). Is she correct? Explain.

Cumulative Review and Test Prep

Number and Operation

MULTIPLE CHOICE

1. Find 975 − 451.

A. 424 **C.** 1,324

B. 524 **D.** 1,426

2. Jack had 136 nails in his toolbox and he bought 240 more. How many nails does Jack have in all?

A. 236 **C.** 376

B. 367 **D.** 474

3. Between what two numbers would 180,243 appear?

A. 170,940 and 180,240

B. 180,135 and 180,235

C. 180,234 and 180,254

D. 180,342 and 180,432

TEST TALK

Think It Through

I can **eliminate wrong answers.**

FREE RESPONSE

4. Find \$712 + \$139. Tell what computation method you used.

5. Meredith bought a bike on sale for \$227. The original price was \$350. How much did Meredith save by buying the bike on sale?

Writing in Math

6. Explain how you could subtract 176 − 49 using mental math.

Geometry and Measurement

MULTIPLE CHOICE

7. A local market sold 356 pounds of pumpkin on Saturday and 415 pounds on Sunday. How many more pounds of pumpkin did the market sell on Sunday than on Saturday?

A. 59 **C.** 169

B. 60 **D.** 771

8. Which unit of measure is best for measuring the length of a crayon?

A. inch **C.** yard

B. foot **D.** mile

FREE RESPONSE

9. What is the temperature?

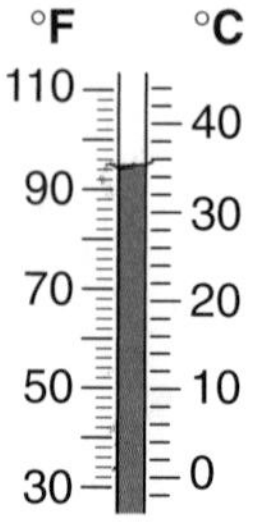

10. Write slide, flip, or turn.

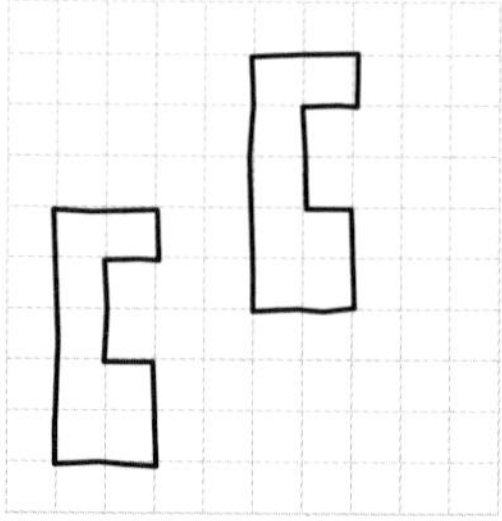

Writing in Math

11. Explain how to find the perimeter of the following figure.

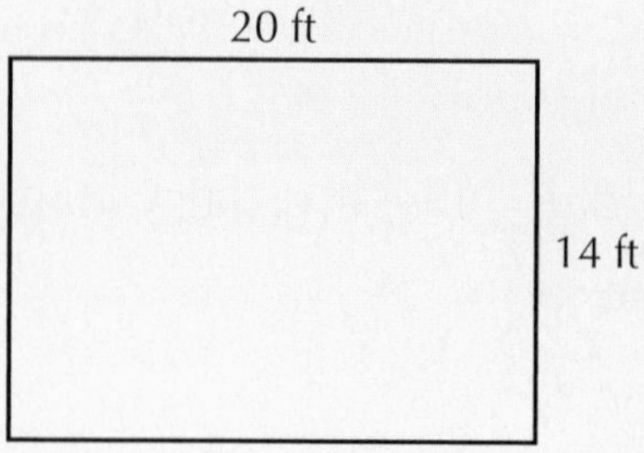

Data Analysis and Probability

MULTIPLE CHOICE

12. Which color is the spinner most likely to land on?

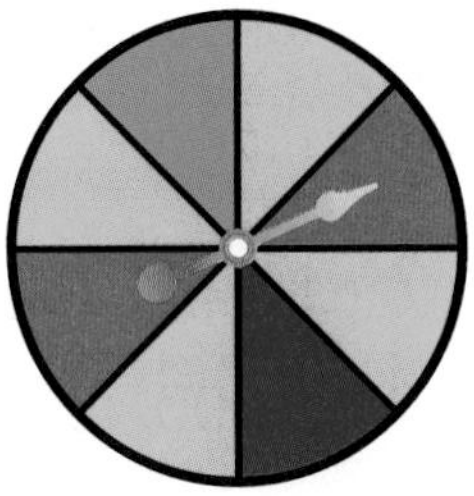

A. red

B. blue

C. orange

D. green

13. How many possible outcomes are on the spinner in Question 12?

A. 1 **B.** 3 **C.** 4 **D.** 8

FREE RESPONSE

Use the bar graph for Items 14–16.

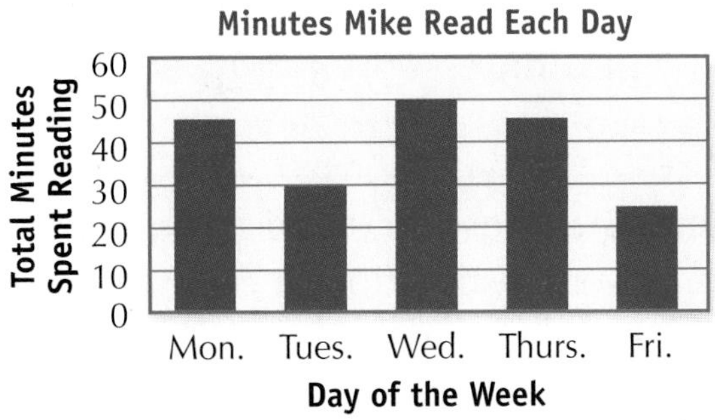

14. On what day did Mike spend the most time reading?

15. How many more minutes did Mike spend reading on Wednesday than on Tuesday?

TEST TALK

Think It Through

I should **check my answers to be sure they are reasonable.**

Writing in Math

16. On what days do you suppose Mike was busy with other activities? Explain.

Algebra

MULTIPLE CHOICE

17. Solve $14 + y = 49$.

A. $y = 35$ **C.** $y = 63$

B. $y = 46$ **D.** $y = 71$

18. Amy decided to start collecting coins. She collected 3 coins the first week, 5 coins the second week, and 7 coins the third week. If she continues this pattern, how many coins will she have in all by the end of the sixth week?

A. 15 **B.** 27 **C.** 35 **D.** 48

FREE RESPONSE

19. Write a number expression to match the words.

Carol had 9 tomato plants, and bought 5 more.

20. Draw the next two shapes in the pattern.

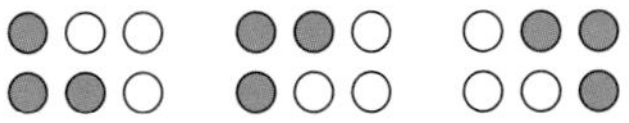

21. Look for the pattern and write the missing numbers.

5, 10, 16, 23, 31, ▢, ▢, ▢

Writing in Math

22. Tom solved $n - 16 = 9$ by saying $n = 7$. Was he correct? If not, give the correct solution and explain how you found it.

Chapter 2
Reteaching

Set 2-1 (pages 62–63)

Add 191 + 212. Use mental math.

Use breaking apart.

191 + 212

191 + (9 + 203)

(191 + 9) + 203

200 + 203 = 403

Remember that when you use compensation, you must adjust the sum.

1. 48 + 64 **2.** 599 + 235

3. 200 + 700 **4.** 854 + 351

5. 476 + 229 **6.** 7,000 + 4,000

7. 800 + 300 **8.** \$165 + \$29

Set 2-2 (pages 64–67)

Subtract 614 − 297. Use mental math.

Use compensation.

614 − 300 = 314

314 + 3 = 317

So, 614 − 297 = 317

Subtract 300. I subtracted 3 too many, so I will add 3.

Remember that you can use compensation, breaking apart, or counting on to subtract with mental math.

1. 83 − 46 **2.** 295 − 78

3. 495 − 257 **4.** 800 − 144

5. 738 − 99 **6.** 326 − 128

Set 2-3 (pages 68–71)

Estimate 8,847 − 1,384.

Use rounding.

$$\begin{array}{rcr} 8{,}847 & \rightarrow & 9{,}000 \\ -\ 1{,}384 & \rightarrow & -\ 1{,}000 \\ \hline & & 8{,}000 \end{array}$$

The difference is about 8,000.

Remember that you can use rounding or front-end estimation to estimate sums and differences.

1. 568 + 288 **2.** 1,844 + 3,096

3. 44,834 + 2,954 **4.** 887 − 198

5. 9,472 − 3,562 **6.** 2,846 + 5,012

7. 61,752 − 3,122 **8.** 7,639 + 216

Set 2-4 (pages 72–73)

Estimate. Tell whether the estimate is an overestimate or an underestimate.

$$\begin{array}{rcr} 3{,}626 & \rightarrow & 4{,}000 \\ +\ 4{,}904 & \rightarrow & +\ 5{,}000 \\ \hline & & 9{,}000 \end{array}$$

Since both numbers were replaced with greater numbers, 9,000 is an overestimate. The exact sum is less than 9,000.

Remember that an underestimate is less than the exact answer.

1. 272 + 398 **2.** 429 + 196

3. 6,212 + 2,441 **4.** 758 − 284

5. 5,623 − 1,276 **6.** 8,360 − 3,449

Set 2-5 (pages 76–79)

Add 74,862 + 15,829.

Estimate: 70,000 + 20,000 = 90,000

$$\begin{array}{r} {}^{1\,1\;\;1}\\ 74{,}862 \\ +\ 15{,}829 \\ \hline 90{,}691 \end{array}$$

The sum 90,691 is reasonable because it is close to the estimate 90,000.

Remember to place the decimal point and dollar sign in the answer when you add money.

1. 7,683 + 239
2. 9,256 + 4,772
3. 65,023 + 19,889
4. \$56.72 + 97.19
5. 3,985 + 9,348
6. \$4.57 + \$7.95

Set 2-6 (pages 80–81)

Find 1,931 + 5,917 + 7,996.

Estimate: 2,000 + 6,000 + 8,000 = 16,000

$$\begin{array}{r} {}^{2\;1\,1}\\ 1{,}931 \\ 5{,}917 \\ +\ 7{,}996 \\ \hline 15{,}844 \end{array}$$

Add numbers one place at a time, from right to left. Regroup if necessary.

The sum 15,844 is reasonable because it is close to the estimate of 16,000.

Remember that you can add in any order.

1. 276 + 749 + 337
2. 6,892 + 6,103 + 4,288
3. 1,764 + 3,994 + 5,036
4. \$546 + 678 + 70

Set 2-7 (pages 82–85)

Find 5,884 − 3,995.

Estimate: 6,000 − 4,000 = 2,000

$$\begin{array}{r} {}^{4\;\;7\;17\,14}\\ \not{5},\not{8}\,\not{8}\,\not{4} \\ -\,3,\,9\,9\,5 \\ \hline 1,\,8\,8\,9 \end{array} \quad \text{check:} \quad \begin{array}{r} {}^{1\;1\,1}\\ 3{,}995 \\ +\ 1{,}889 \\ \hline 5{,}884 \end{array}$$

The difference 1,889 is reasonable because it is close to the estimate 2,000.

Remember that you may need to regroup before you subtract.

1. 605 − 248
2. 7,275 − 397
3. 56,002 − 23,783
4. \$68.23 − 15.79
5. 7,000 − 4,562
6. \$57.00 − \$9.95
7. 9,989 − 2,656
8. 8,347 − 3,064
9. 6,000 − 3,891
10. \$69.50 − \$23.12

Chapter 2
Reteaching

Set 2-8 (pages 86–87)

Add or subtract. Tell what method you used.

Art had 2,313 pennies. His aunt gave him 1,003 more pennies. How many pennies does he have now?

You could use mental math.

2,313 + 1,000 = 3,313

3,313 + 3 = 3,316

Art has 3,316 pennies.

Remember that you can use mental math, paper and pencil, or a calculator to solve addition and subtraction problems.

1. Jake had 776 stamps. He gave 399 stamps away. How many stamps did he have left?
2. Ms. Kay has $171.25 in the bank. She has $91.69 in her purse. How much money does she have in all?

Set 2-9 (pages 90–91)

Look for a pattern. Tell the missing numbers.

1, 8, 15, 22, ■, ■, ■

Step 1: Find a pattern.	**Step 2:** Finish the pattern.
1 + 7 = 8	22 + 7 = 29
8 + 7 = 15	29 + 7 = 36
15 + 7 = 22	36 + 7 = 43

The missing numbers are 29, 36, and 43.

Remember that in some patterns you do not add the *same* number every time.

1. 1, 7, 13, 19, ■, ■, ■
2. 3, 7, 11, 15, ■, ■, ■
3. 2, 3, 5, 8, 12, 17, ■, ■, ■
4. 4, 5, 7, 8, 10, 11, 13, ■, ■, ■
5. 2, 5, 8, 11, ■, ■, ■
6. 1, 9, 17, 25, ■, ■, ■
7. 1, 4, 8, 11, 15, 18, ■, ■, ■

Set 2-10 (pages 94–95)

Write a number expression for each phrase.

365 days and 28 more days

365 + 28

$249 needed, $175 saved

249 − 175

Remember that writing a number expression can help you solve problems.

1. 36 is how much more than 12?
2. $425 increased by $58
3. 114 ounces decreased by 6 ounces
4. 185 adults, but 36 students fewer
5. 19 pencils combined with 23 pens

Set 2-11 (pages 96–97)

Choose the expression that matches the words. Then find its value.

Lisa had \$8. She earned \$12 babysitting. Then she spent \$5 at the movies. How much did she have left?

$8 + (12 - 5)$ or $(8 + 12) - 5$

Lisa earned \$12 first, so $(8 + 12) - 5$ is the correct expression.

$(8 + 12) - 5$
$20 \quad - 5 = 15$

Lisa had \$15.

Remember to do the operation in the parentheses first.
Choose the number expression that matches the words. Then find its value.

1. Bo had 16 invitations. He sent 9 in the mail. He handed out 5 in school.

   $16 - (9 - 5)$ or $(16 - 9) - 5$

2. Tom made 24 bookmarks. He gave 13 to friends. Then, he made 11 more.

   $(24 - 13) + 11$ or $24 - (13 + 11)$

Set 2-12 (pages 98–99)

Evaluate $d + 15$ when $d = 12$.

Substitute 12 for d. Then add.

$d + 15$
↓
$12 + 15 = 27$

Remember that you replace the variable with a number to find the value of the expression.

Evaluate each expression for $m = 8$.

1. $m + 12$ **2.** $m + 34$

3. $25 - m$ **4.** $m - 4$

Set 2-13 (pages 100–101)

Solve $k + 16 = 35$.

Use mental math: What number plus 16 equals 35?

Try: $k = 15$ $k + 16$
↓
$15 + 16 = 31$

Check: Does $15 + 16$ equal 35? *No*

Revise: $k = 19$ $k + 16$
↓
$19 + 16 = 35$

Check: Does $19 + 16 = 35$? *Yes*

The solution is $k = 19$.

Remember that after one try, you might need to revise and try again to solve an equation.

1. $12 + x = 27$ **2.** $h + 9 = 39$

3. $800 + p = 813$ **4.** $a - 5 = 16$

5. $w - 10 = 30$ **6.** $x - 5 = 5$

7. $n + 40 = 120$ **8.** $k - 30 = 20$

9. $z - 24 = 32$ **10.** $t + 5 = 19$

11. $m - 18 = 35$ **12.** $y + 42 = 81$

More Practice

Set 2-1 (pages 62–63)

Add. Use mental math.

1. 76 + 58 **2.** 40 + 60 **3.** 24 + 39 **4.** 95 + 47

5. 38 + 235 **6.** 125 + 46 **7.** 300 + 400 **8.** 216 + 232

9. 399 + 465 **10.** 925 + 118 **11.** 616 + 334 **12.** 8,000 + 5,000

13. The local post office sold 243 stamps on Monday and 278 stamps on Tuesday. How many stamps did the post office sell in all?

Set 2-2 (pages 64–67)

Subtract. Use mental math.

1. 87 − 68 **2.** 78 − 35 **3.** 61 − 19 **4.** 649 − 25

5. 282 − 98 **6.** 357 − 160 **7.** 815 − 604 **8.** 400 − 327

9. 531 − 214 **10.** 870 − 436 **11.** 935 − 326 **12.** 768 − 345

13. A sports store had 538 baseballs. They sold 125 baseballs to the junior league. How many baseballs did the store have then?

Set 2-3 (pages 68–71)

Estimate each sum or difference.

1. $\begin{array}{r} 318 \\ +\ 239 \\ \hline \end{array}$ **2.** $\begin{array}{r} 927 \\ +\ \ 13 \\ \hline \end{array}$ **3.** $\begin{array}{r} 941 \\ -\ 753 \\ \hline \end{array}$ **4.** $\begin{array}{r} 446 \\ -\ 133 \\ \hline \end{array}$

5. $\begin{array}{r} 8{,}264 \\ -\ 5{,}729 \\ \hline \end{array}$ **6.** $\begin{array}{r} 68{,}294 \\ -\ 25{,}169 \\ \hline \end{array}$ **7.** $\begin{array}{r} 4{,}625 \\ +\ 3{,}872 \\ \hline \end{array}$ **8.** $\begin{array}{r} 29{,}426 \\ +\ 50{,}248 \\ \hline \end{array}$

9. 515 + 321 **10.** 4,687 + 809 **11.** 729 − 275

12. 8,874 − 1,982 **13.** 5,724 + 2,395 **14.** 18,844 + 30,956

15. 8,593 − 4,682 **16.** 94,742 − 35,623 **17.** 8,073 + 4,875

18. Cole had \$676. He spent \$157 on school clothes. About how much money does Cole have left?

19. Tina likes a dress that costs \$46, a skirt that costs \$38, and a blouse that costs \$29. About how much more are the skirt and blouse together than the dress?

Take It to the NET
More Practice
www.scottforesman.com

Set 2-4 (pages 72–73)

Estimate each sum or difference. Then, if possible, tell whether your estimate is an overestimate or an underestimate.

1. 21 + 72 **2.** 458 + 381 **3.** 371 − 109 **4.** 853 − 682

5. 286 + 377 **6.** 5,481 + 3,270 **7.** 937 − 496 **8.** 6,098 − 5,314

9. 3,723 + 3,296 **10.** 3,326 + 2,497 **11.** 7,608 − 1,254 **12.** 5,983 − 2,401

13. Chance had 5,125 cards in his collection. He bought his friend's collection of 3,408 cards. About how many cards does Chance have now?

Set 2-5 (pages 76–79)

Add.

1. 861 + 129

2. 7,777 + 625

3. 9,321 + 5,939

4. $10.85 + 9.95

5. $36.73 + 65.50

6. 43,901 + 7,899

7. 27,832 + 46,079

8. 55,875 + 18,068

9. $61.94 + 98.44

10. $58.96 + 47.69

11. Eddie had $82.93 in his savings account. He put in another $19.75. How much money did Eddie have in his savings account then?

Set 2-6 (pages 80–81)

Add.

1. 994 + 39 + 207

2. 7,902 + 693 + 1,196

3. 5,592 + 9,210 + 8,432

4. $65.92 + 4.58 + 25.25

5. $43.98 + 12.81 + 67.21

6. 6,821 + 9,324 + 11,964

7. 76,211 + 10,973 + 8,994

8. 31,867 + 22,095 + 16,908

9. $567.03 + 33.96 + 119.95

10. $21.74 + 32.98 + 40.03

11. There were 19,034 books checked out from the library in June, 25,784 books checked out in July, and 23,218 books checked out in August. How many total books were checked out in these three months?

Chapter 2
More Practice

Set 2-7 (pages 82–85)

Subtract.

1. 861 − 456
2. 901 − 732
3. 4,872 − 983
4. \$60.26 − 4.51
5. \$45.18 − 32.99
6. 8,003 − 2,976
7. 35,720 − 4,891
8. 98,337 − 29,759
9. \$83.11 − 26.75
10. \$52.02 − 35.85
11. Jim found a stereo on sale for \$123. The original price was \$150. How much will he save if he buys it on sale?

Set 2-8 (pages 86–87)

Add or subtract. Tell what method you used.

1. 65,000 + 17,000
2. 32,875 + 44,986
3. 80,999 − 20,198
4. 67,034 − 49,275
5. One month, the pet store ordered 5,500 crickets. The next month 4,500 crickets were ordered. How many crickets were ordered in all?

Set 2-9 (pages 90–91)

Look for a pattern. Draw the next two shapes.

1. 

2. 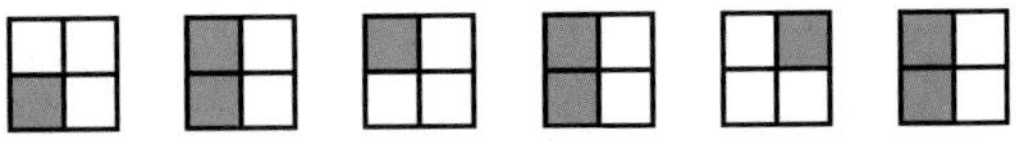

Copy and complete each number sentence.

3. 80 + 8 = 88
   800 + 8 = 808
   8,000 + 8 = □
   80,000 + 8 = □

4. 20 + 2 = 22
   200 + 20 + 2 = 222
   2,000 + 200 + 20 + 2 = □
   20,000 + 2,000 + 200 + 20 + 2 = □

5. Suppose you save \$1 in January, \$2 in February, and \$3 in March. If you continue this pattern, how much money will you have saved in a year?

6. Anton's number pattern is shown below. What are the next 3 numbers in his pattern?

   1, 3, 6, 10, 15, □, □, □

Take It to the NET
More Practice
www.scottforesman.com

Set 2-10 (pages 94–95)

Write a number expression for each phrase.

1. 482 pounds of potatoes, but 249 fewer pounds of onions
2. 125 sheets of paper increased by 500 sheets of paper
3. The total of \$246, \$379, and \$543
4. \$574 decreased by \$298

Set 2-11 (pages 96–97)

Choose the number expression that matches the words. Then find its value.

1. Liza earned \$32. She spent \$13, then earned \$15.

   $(32 - 13) + 15$ or $32 - (13 + 15)$

2. Jackson made 15 sand castles. The waves ruined 6, then his brother ruined 4.

   $15 - (6 - 4)$ or $(15 - 6) - 4$

3. Mandy had 9 stickers. She bought 3 more. Then she gave her sister 5 stickers.

   $(9 + 3) - 5$ or $9 - (3 + 5)$

4. Travis had 24 toy cars. He bought 8 more. Then he gave his brother 5 cars.

   $(24 + 8) - 5$ or $24 - (8 + 5)$

Set 2-12 (pages 98–99)

Evaluate each expression for $n = 7$.

1. $n + 23$
2. $n - 7$
3. $9 + n$
4. $n + 500$
5. $13 - n$

Evaluate each expression for $x = 25$.

6. $8 + x$
7. $55 - x$
8. $x + 100$
9. $19 + x$
10. $x - 18$
11. **Number Sense** Does the expression $a + 17$ have a greater value when $a = 9$ or $a = 12$? Explain.

Set 2-13 (pages 100–101)

Solve each equation.

1. $h + 8 = 13$
2. $w - 2 = 6$
3. $t - 5 = 7$
4. $14 + p = 17$
5. $200 + s = 600$
6. $a - 25 = 10$
7. $d - 40 = 40$
8. $m + 4 = 21$
9. **Number Sense** Is the solution of $7 + h = 28$ greater or less than 22? Explain how you know.

CHAPTER 3

Multiplication and Division Concepts and Facts

DIAGNOSING READINESS

INSTANT CHECK SYSTEM™

A Vocabulary
(Grade 3)

Choose the best term from the box.

1. You multiply numbers to find a __?__.
2. The answer in division is called the __?__.
3. A number you multiply is a __?__.
4. The number you divide by is the __?__.

Vocabulary

- **product** *(Gr. 3)*
- **quotient** *(Gr. 3)*
- **divisor** *(Gr. 3)*
- **factor** *(Gr. 3)*

B Skip Counting
(Grade 3)

Write the missing numbers in each pattern.

5. 2, 4, 6, □, 10, □
6. 10, 20, □, 40, □, 60
7. 3, 5, 7, □, 11, □
8. 9, □, □, 36, 45, 54
9. 5, 10, □, □, 25, 30
10. 7, □, 21, □, 35, 42
11. Write the first 6 numbers in a pattern if you start with 5 and skip count by 3s.

Do You Know...

How many hours does a bear sleep each day?

You will find out in Lesson 3-15.

C Arrays

(Grade 3)

Copy each array of counters and circle equal groups of 4.

12. 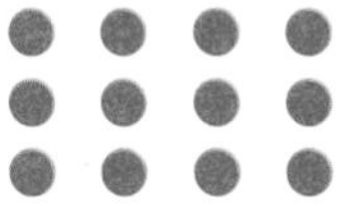

13. 

14. 

15. 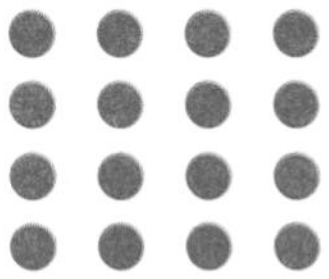

16. Look at Exercise 14. How many groups are circled? How many counters are there in all?

D Evaluating Expressions

(pages 98–99)

Evaluate each expression for $n = 2$.

17. $4 + n$

18. $8 - n$

19. $32 + n$

20. $45 - n$

21. $n - 1$

22. $17 - n$

23. What is the value of $x + 70$ when $x = 30$?

24. Rich thinks the expression shown below equals 20. Bob thinks it is equal to 8. Who is correct and why?

$12 + 4 - (2 + 6)$

Key Idea
When groups or rows are equal, you can multiply to find the total.

Vocabulary
- array
- factor
- product

TEST TALK

Think It Through
I need to ask **"What do I know?"** and **"What do I need to find out?"**

Meanings for Multiplication

WARM UP

Find each sum.

1. 3 + 3
2. 4 + 4 + 4
3. 5 + 5 + 5 + 5
4. 2 + 2 + 2 + 2 + 2

LEARN

How can multiplication be used when equal groups are combined?

Multiplication can be used to find the total when you know the number of equal groups and the number in each group.

Example A

Joy is baking muffins. She has 4 rows with 6 muffins in each row. How many muffins does she have in all?

Objects arranged in equal rows form an **array.** You can multiply to find the total number because the rows are equal.

4 rows of 6

6 + 6 + 6 + 6 = 24

4 × 6 = 24

factors **product**

Joy has 24 muffins.

Example B

Joy put the muffins on 3 plates with 8 muffins on each plate. How many muffins does she have in all?

You can multiply to find the total because the number of muffins on each plate is the same. They are equal groups.

3 groups of 8

8 + 8 + 8 = 24

3 × 8 = 24

factors **product**

Joy has 24 muffins.

Talk About It

1. Name the factors in Examples A and B.
2. **Number Sense** If Joy had 4 plates of muffins with 5 on each plate, how many muffins would she have?

How can multiplication be used when you only know the number in one group?

Multiplication can be used to compare the size of one group to another.

Example C

Joy ate 3 muffins. Her brother Karl ate twice as many. How many muffins did Karl eat?

Twice as many means two times as many.

$2 \times 3 = 6$

Karl ate 6 muffins.

Talk About It

3. What does each factor in Example C stand for?
4. How could you use addition to find the number of muffins Karl ate?

CHECK

For another example, see Set 3-1 on p. 180.

Write an addition sentence and a multiplication sentence for each picture.

1. 

2. 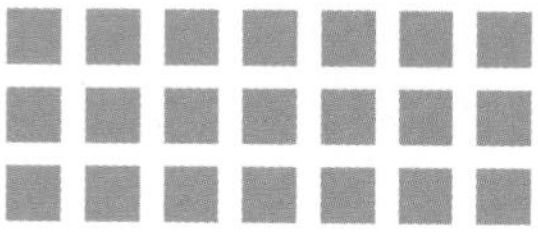

3. 

4. 

5. 

6. XXXX
XXXX
XXXX
XXXX

7. Draw two pictures for 6×3. Use an array for one picture and equal groups for the other. Give the product.
8. **Number Sense** How could you use multiplication to find $9 + 9 + 9$?

Think It Through
I'll think of the **number of equal groups** as the first factor and the **number in each group** as the second factor.

PRACTICE

For more practice, see Set 3-1 on p. 184.

A Skills and Understanding

Write an addition sentence and a multiplication sentence for each picture.

9. 

10. 

11. 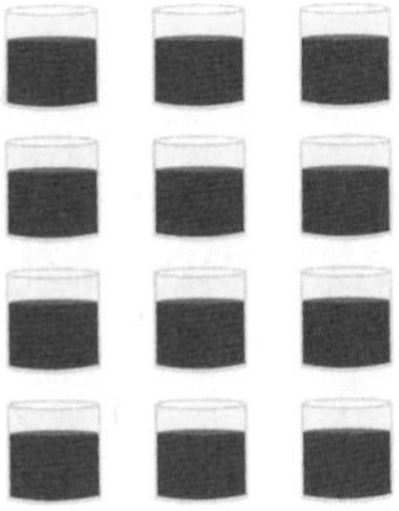

Write a multiplication sentence for each addition sentence.

12. $6 + 6 + 6 + 6 = 24$ 13. $9 + 9 = 18$ 14. $5 + 5 + 5 + 5 + 5 + 5 + 5 = 35$

15. Draw two pictures to show 6×5. Use an array for one picture and equal groups for the other.

16. **Number Sense** How could you use addition to find 3×4?

B Reasoning and Problem Solving

Math and Music

The Star-Spangled Banner, written by Francis Scott Key, became our national anthem in 1931. It was written in 1814 at Fort McHenry, Maryland.

Fort McHenry, Maryland

17. There are 4 verses in *The Star-Spangled Banner*. Each verse has 8 lines. How many lines are in the anthem?

18. The entrance fee to Fort McHenry for adults over 17 years old is $5. How much would it cost for 5 adults to enter?

19. **Writing in Math** Dana wrote 5×3 to find $3 + 3 + 3 + 3 + 3$. Is she correct? Explain.

Think It Through
I need to **compare** multiplication and addition.

C Extensions

20. **Understanding Operations** You can use a number line to multiply. The number line below shows $2 \times 4 = 8$. Use the number line to find 3×3.

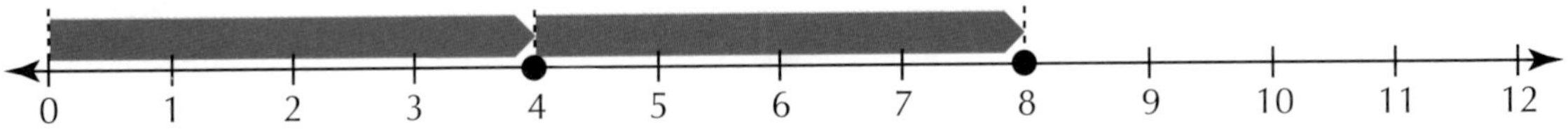

Mixed Review and Test Prep

Take It to the NET
Test Prep
www.scottforesman.com

Write the rule. Then complete the table.

21. Rule: ________

In	Out
26	21
32	27
48	43
56	
61	

22. Rule: ________

In	Out
12	23
15	26
24	35
32	
49	

23. Rule: ________

In	Out
17	8
25	16
32	23
46	
58	

24. Rounded to the nearest thousand, which number does NOT round to 18,000?

A. 18,327 **B.** 18,511 **C.** 17,777 **D.** 17,519

Learning with Technology

Using a Spreadsheet/Data/Grapher eTool

Each block in a spreadsheet is called a *cell*. Cells are named by the column letter and row number. In the spreadsheet below, cell C3 is highlighted.

Create a spreadsheet with the values shown at right.

	A	B	C	D
1	factor	×1	×2	×5
2	4	4	8	20
3	6	6	**12**	30
4	8	8	16	40

1. What appears in cell B4?

2. What appears in cell A3?

3. Name the cell that contains the product 4 × 1.

4. Name the cell than contains the product 6 × 5.

5. What number would appear in cell C5?

6. What number would appear in cell D6?

7. Name three cells that have the same number.

Key Idea
Patterns can help you remember multiplication facts.

Vocabulary
- multiple
- Zero Property of Multiplication
- Identity Property of Multiplication
- Commutative Property of Multiplication

Materials
- hundred chart

TEST TALK

Think It Through
I can **use patterns** to help me find the facts for 2, 5, 9.

Patterns in Multiplying by 0, 1, 2, 5, and 9

WARM UP

Find the pattern. Fill in the blanks.

1. 2, 4, 6, ___, ___, ___
2. 5, 10, 15, ___, ___, ___
3. 9, 18, 27, ___, ___, ___
4. 10, 20, 30, ___, ___, ___

LEARN

What are the patterns for multiples of 2, 5, and 9?

A **multiple** is the product of any two whole numbers.

Activity

1	2	3	4	5	6	7	8	9	10
11	12	13	14	15	16	17	18	19	20
21	22	23	24	25	26	27	28	29	30
31	32	33	34	35	36	37	38	39	40
41	42	43	44	45	46	47	48	49	50
51	52	53	54	55	56	57	58	59	60
61	62	63	64	65	66	67	68	69	70
71	72	73	74	75	76	77	78	79	80
81	82	83	84	85	86	87	88	89	90
91	92	93	94	95	96	97	98	99	100

a. Copy and complete the hundred chart shown above.

b. Many things come in pairs, such as socks and mittens. Skip count by 2s. Put a triangle around each multiple of 2. What pattern do you see in the multiples of 2?

c. Skip count by 5s. Put a square around each multiple of 5. What pattern do you see in the multiples of 5?

d. Skip count by 9s. Put a circle around each multiple of 9. What pattern do you see in the multiples of 9?

e. What patterns do you see for the numbers that have both triangles and squares?

f. Explain how you know that 73 is not a multiple of 5.

g. Explain how you know that 89 is not a multiple of 9.

What are the patterns for multiples of 0 and 1?

	Example A	Example B	Example C
What You **See**	 3 groups of 0	 1 group of 2	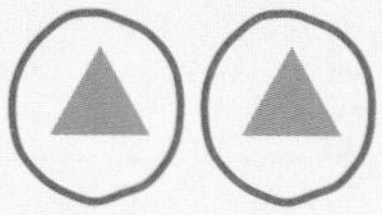 2 groups of 1
What You **Write**	$3 \times 0 = 0$	$1 \times 2 = 2$	$2 \times 1 = 2$

I know that if
5 × 3 = 15, then
3 × 5 = 15.

Multiplication properties can help you remember basic facts.

Zero Property of Multiplication
The product of any number and zero is zero.

Identity Property of Multiplication
The product of any number and one is that number.

Commutative Property of Multiplication
Two numbers can be multiplied in any order and the product is the same.

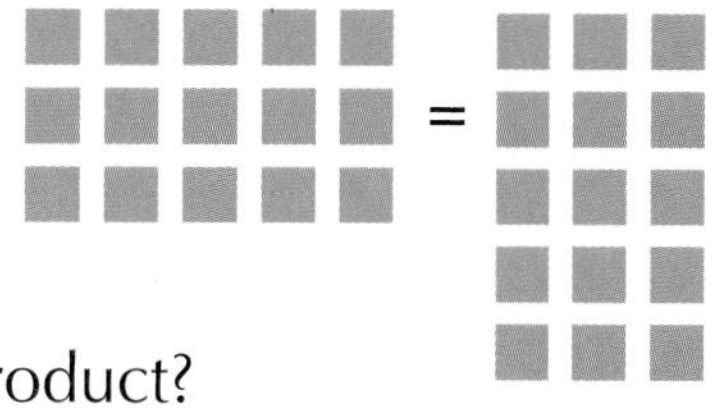
=

Talk About It

1. When you multiply any number by 1, what is the product?
2. Which property can help you find the missing number in ▢ $\times 157 = 0$?
3. Which two examples above show the Commutative Property of Multiplication?

Take It to the NET
More Examples
www.scottforesman.com

CHECK

For another example, see Set 3-2 on p. 180.

1. 5×3
2. 9×7
3. 2×0
4. 2×7
5. 1×1
6. 0×9
7. 5×6
8. 8×1
9. 9×5
10. 5×2
11. **Number Sense** How do you know that $23 \times 89 = 89 \times 23$ without finding the products?

PRACTICE

For more practice, see Set 3-2 on p. 184.

A Skills and Understanding

12. 5×6 **13.** 9×2 **14.** 6×0 **15.** 2×8 **16.** 8×5

17. 5×7 **18.** 3×1 **19.** 8×9 **20.** 5×5 **21.** 4×9

22. 1×9 **23.** 3×0 **24.** 9×6 **25.** 2×5 **26.** 0×4

Algebra Find the missing number. Tell which property can help you.

27. $3 \times 2 = 2 \times \square$ **28.** $\square \times 2 = 0$ **29.** $\square \times 1 = 7$

30. **Number Sense** Tina has 5 boxes with 4 pencils in each box. Trey has 4 boxes with 5 pencils in each. Who has more pencils? Explain.

B Reasoning and Problem Solving

Use the data in the table for 31–33.

Type of Sticker	Number in a Package
Star	8
Heart	9
Rainbow	5
Daisy	2

31. How many heart stickers are there in 3 packages?

32. How many rainbow stickers do you get if you buy 8 packages?

33. Julie buys a package of stars and a package of hearts. How many stickers does she get?

Math and Science

Spiders are sometimes mistaken for insects. The Data File at the right lists two differences between spiders and insects.

Data File

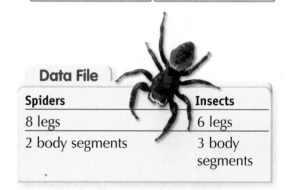

Spiders	Insects
8 legs	6 legs
2 body segments	3 body segments

34. How many legs do 5 spiders have in all?

35. How many body segments do 8 insects have in all?

36. How many legs do 2 spiders and 5 insects have in all?

37. **Number Sense** The product of two numbers is 0. Can you name one of the factors? Explain.

38. **Writing in Math** The product of two numbers is 63. One of the numbers is 63. Tina says the other number is 0. Is she correct? Explain.

C Extensions

39. Describe two more patterns on the hundred chart that you made for the activity on page 128.

Mixed Review and Test Prep

Take It to the NET
Test Prep
www.scottforesman.com

Write an addition sentence and a multiplication sentence for each picture.

40. 

41. 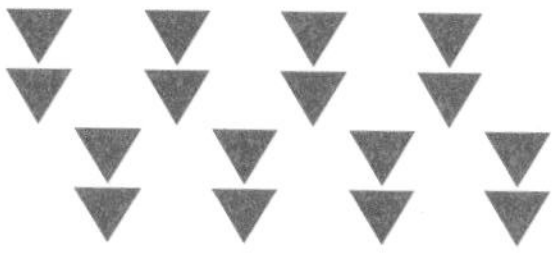

42. 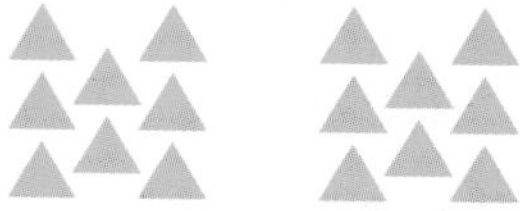

43. **Algebra** Which of the following is the solution to $m - 4 = 20$?

A. $m = 5$ **B.** $m = 16$ **C.** $m = 24$ **D.** $m = 80$

Practice Game

Brain or Battery

Players: 3

Materials: Number cards 1–23 (1 set), calculator

1. The dealer draws 2 cards from the deck and simultaneously places them face up saying, "Go."
2. One player uses the calculator to find the product; the other player computes the product mentally.
3. The dealer decides which of the two players is first to say the correct product and will award that player both cards.
4. The winner is the player with the most cards when all cards have been played.

Key Idea
You can use multiplication facts you know to help you find the products for other facts.

Vocabulary
- Distributive Property

Using Known Facts to Find Unknown Facts

WARM UP

1. 2×9
2. 5×7
3. 8×5
4. 6×1
5. 7×2
6. 3×5

LEARN

How can I break apart facts?

The **Distributive Property** shows that you can break apart facts to find the product.

Phil is making a tile-top table. He needs 3 rows of 6 tiles. How many tiles does he need in all?

Example A

Find 3×6.

What You **Show**	What You **Think**	What You **Write**
 $3 \times 6 = (2 \times 6) + (1 \times 6)$	3 rows of 6 is the same as 2 rows of 6 and 1 row of 6. $2 \times 6 = 12$ $1 \times 6 = 6$ $12 + 6 = 18$	$3 \times 6 = 18$ **Phil needs 18 tiles in all.**

Example B

Find 7×8.

What You **Show**	What You **Think**	What You **Write**
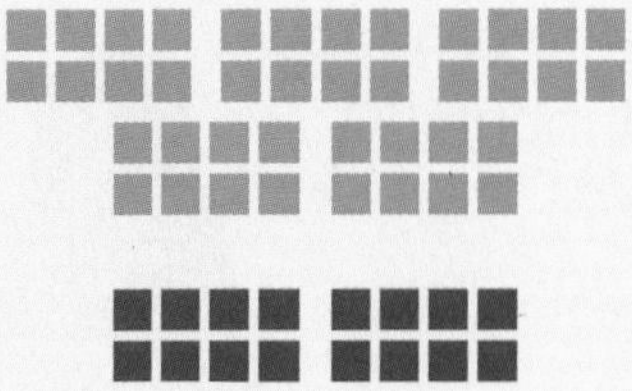 $7 \times 8 = (5 \times 8) + (2 \times 8)$	7 groups of 8 is the same as 5 groups of 8 and 2 groups of 8. $5 \times 8 = 40$ $2 \times 8 = 16$ $40 + 16 = 56$	$7 \times 8 = 56$

Talk About It

1. What two facts were used to find 3×6?

2. Explain how you can use $2 \times 6 = 12$ to find 4×6.

Are there different ways to break apart a fact?

You can use facts you know to break apart a fact.

Show two ways to find 6×7.

Julia's Way

I think of the first factor as telling how many rows there are.

To find 6×7, I think of 6 rows as **5** rows and **1** row.

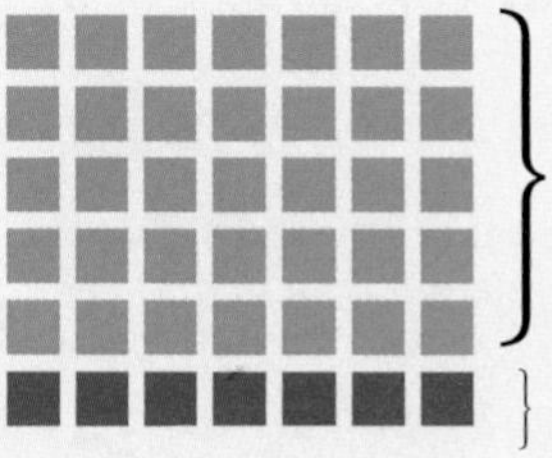

$\mathbf{5} \times 7 = 35$

$\mathbf{1} \times 7 = 7$

$35 + 7 = 42$, so $6 \times 7 = 42$.

Ricky's Way

Sometimes I want to break apart the second factor, so I think about columns instead of rows.

To find 6×7, I think of 7 columns as **5** columns and **2** columns.

$6 \times \mathbf{5} = 30$ $\quad 6 \times \mathbf{2} = 12$

$30 + 12 = 42$, so $6 \times 7 = 42$.

Talk About It

3. Is Julia's method or Ricky's method easier for you? Explain.

4. Explain how you would find 3×7 by breaking apart 3.

5. Explain how you would find 3×7 by breaking apart 7.

Take It to the NET
More Examples
www.scottforesman.com

CHECK

For another example, see Set 3-3 on p. 180.

Use breaking apart to find each product.

1. 4×3 **2.** 8×3 **3.** 5×9 **4.** 8×8 **5.** 6×4

6. 7×7 **7.** 4×7 **8.** 3×3 **9.** 3×9 **10.** 7×1

11. Number Sense How can you use $3 \times 5 = 15$ to help you find 6×5?

PRACTICE

For more practice, see Set 3-3 on p. 184.

A Skills and Understanding

Use breaking apart to find each product.

12. 7×8 **13.** 9×4 **14.** 6×2 **15.** 8×4 **16.** 4×5

17. 8×5 **18.** 9×7 **19.** 7×3 **20.** 6×9 **21.** 0×6

22. 4×4 **23.** 8×6 **24.** 3×9 **25.** 5×6 **26.** 9×9

27. Number Sense Jay says that after he multiplied 6×9, he knew 7×9 as well. What does he mean?

B Reasoning and Problem Solving

Reasoning Compare. Use <, >, or = to fill in each ○.

28. 9×8 ○ 8×9 **29.** 8×6 ○ 5×8 **30.** 8×3 ○ 4×6

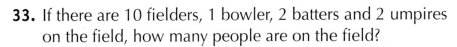

Math and Social Studies

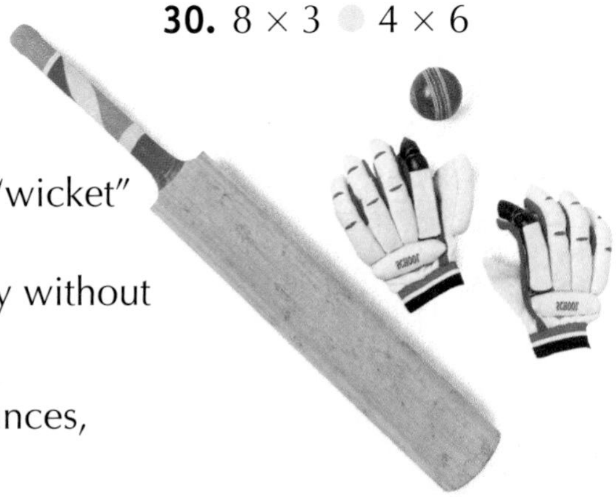

In cricket, a batter must run to a marker called a "wicket" to score a run. If a ball is hit to the boundary, the batter scores 4 runs. If a ball is hit to the boundary without a bounce, the batter scores 6 runs.

31. If 5 balls are batted to the boundary with bounces, how many runs are scored?

32. If 4 balls are batted to the boundary without bouncing, how many runs are scored?

33. If there are 10 fielders, 1 bowler, 2 batters and 2 umpires on the field, how many people are on the field?

34. **Writing in Math** Isabel says that 6×8 and 8×6 are alike in some ways and different in other ways. What does she mean?

Think It Through
I can **use a property** to explain my thinking.

C Extensions

A **prime number** has exactly two factors, 1 and itself. A **composite number** has more than two factors. List all the factors for each number. Tell whether each number is prime or composite.

35. 20 **36.** 14 **37.** 17 **38.** 12 **39.** 19 **40.** 3

41. 24 **42.** 18 **43.** 11 **44.** 15 **45.** 10 **46.** 4

Mixed Review and Test Prep

Take It to the NET
Test Prep
www.scottforesman.com

Find each product.

47. 2×8 **48.** 5×9 **49.** 9×0 **50.** 3×6

51. Which number is less than 4,565?

A. 4,565 **B.** 4,655 **C.** 4,556 **D.** 4,665

Enrichment

Properties of Equality

An equation is like a pan balance. Whatever is done to one side must also be done to the other side in order for the pans to stay balanced.

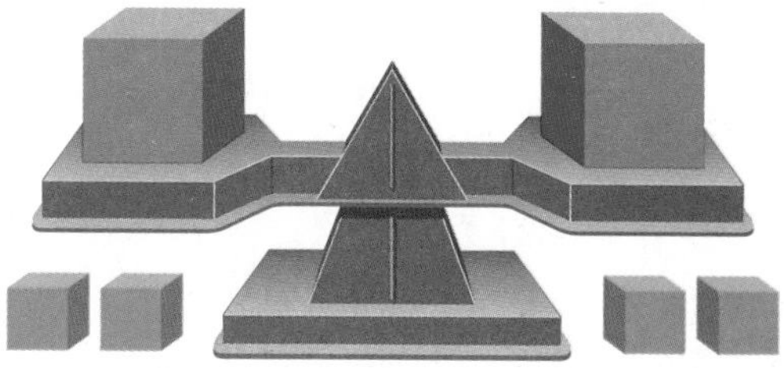

The properties of equality describe how equations remain balanced.

Properties of Equality

Property	Meaning	Example
Addition Property of Equality; Subtraction Property of Equality	You can add or subtract the same number on both sides of an equation and the two sides will remain equal.	You know: $3 + 4 = 7$. So, $3 + 4 + \mathbf{2} = 7 + \mathbf{2}$. You know: $8 + 5 = 13$. So, $(8 + 5) - \mathbf{6} = 13 - \mathbf{6}$.
Multiplication Property of Equality; Division Property of Equality	You can multiply or divide by the same number on both sides of an equation and the two sides will remain equal.	You know: $2 \times 5 = 10$. So, $2 \times 5 \times \mathbf{4} = 10 \times \mathbf{4}$. You know: $12 + 9 = 21$ So, $(12 + 9) \div \mathbf{3} = 21 \div \mathbf{3}$.

For 1–3, answer yes or no. Use the Properties of Equality to help.

You know:	Does:
1. $52 + 46 = 98$	$52 + 46 + 61 = 98 - 61$?
2. $60 \div 4 = 15$	$(60 \div 4) \times 5 = 15 \times 5$?
3. $10 \times 14 = 140$	$(10 \times 14) \times 2 = 140 \times 2$?

Key Idea
Patterns can help you remember multiplication facts.

Materials
- calculator

Multiplying by 10, 11, and 12

✓ WARM UP

1. 3 × 0
2. 2 × 7
3. 8 × 1
4. 0 × 5
5. 9 × 2
6. 6 × 1

LEARN

Activity

What are patterns for multiples of 10, 11, and 12?

a. Use a calculator to find each missing product.

1 × 10 = 10	1 × 11 = 11	1 × 12 = 12
2 × 10 = 20	2 × 11 = 22	2 × 12 = 24
3 × 10 = ▭	3 × 11 = ▭	3 × 12 = ▭
4 × 10 = ▭	4 × 11 = ▭	4 × 12 = ▭
5 × 10 = ▭	5 × 11 = ▭	5 × 12 = ▭
6 × 10 = ▭	6 × 11 = ▭	6 × 12 = ▭
7 × 10 = ▭	7 × 11 = ▭	7 × 12 = ▭
8 × 10 = ▭	8 × 11 = ▭	8 × 12 = ▭
9 × 10 = ▭	9 × 11 = ▭	9 × 12 = ▭
10 × 10 = ▭	10 × 11 = ▭	10 × 12 = ▭
11 × 10 = ▭	11 × 11 = ▭	11 × 12 = ▭
12 × 10 = ▭	12 × 11 = ▭	12 × 12 = ▭

b. Describe a rule that tells how to find each multiple of 10.

c. Explain how you can use breaking apart to find 7 × 12.

d. Describe a rule that tells how to find each multiple of 11.

e. Describe how to use breaking apart to find 6 × 11.

f. Describe a rule that tells how to find each multiple of 12.

TEST TALK

Think It Through
I can **look for a pattern** to find a rule.

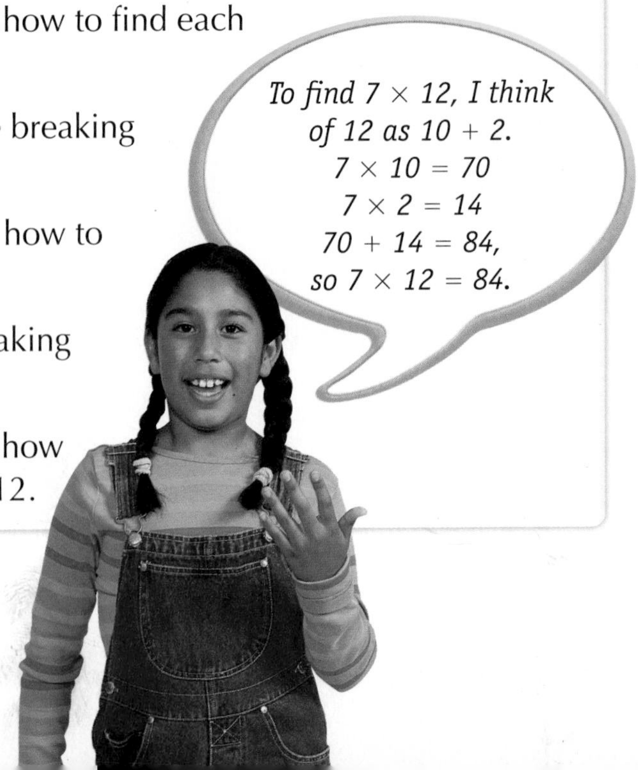

To find 7 × 12, I think of 12 as 10 + 2.
7 × 10 = 70
7 × 2 = 14
70 + 14 = 84,
so 7 × 12 = 84.

CHECK ✓

For another example, see Set 3-4 on p. 180.

1. 4×11 **2.** 12×3 **3.** 10×8 **4.** 6×12 **5.** 11×12

6. Number Sense How can you use 8×10 to help you find 8×12?

PRACTICE

For more practice, see Set 3-4 on p. 184.

A Skills and Understanding

7. 5×11 **8.** 4×10 **9.** 12×8 **10.** 11×9 **11.** 10×11

12. 10×12 **13.** 12×5 **14.** 11×6 **15.** 2×12 **16.** 7×11

17. 9×11 **18.** 4×12 **19.** 11×11 **20.** 1×11 **21.** 10×7

22. Number Sense Carlton said that 11×12 is 1,212. Is this reasonable?

B Reasoning and Problem Solving

TEST TALK

Think It Through
I know **one dozen equals 12.**

How many eggs are in

23. 3 dozen? **24.** 5 dozen?

25. 8 dozen? **26.** one gross (12 dozen)?

27. Number Sense Decide without counting whether the photo on page 136 shows less than, more than, or exactly one dozen eggs.

Reasoning Use the following information for 28–30.

George has 9 coins.

28. If all of George's coins are dimes, how much money does he have?

29. If all of George's coins are nickels, how much money does he have?

30. If George has 4 nickels and 5 dimes, how much money does he have?

31. Writing in Math Which factor would you break apart to find 7×12? Explain.

Mixed Review and Test Prep

Take It to the NET
Test Prep
www.scottforesman.com

32. 2×8 **33.** 5×9 **34.** 9×0

35. 6×7 **36.** 4×3 **37.** 7×8

38. Write a multiplication sentence for $8 + 8 + 8 + 8$.

A. 2×8 **B.** 4×8 **C.** 5×8 **D.** 8×8

Reading For Math Success

Understand Graphic Sources: Tables and Charts

Understanding graphic sources such as tables and charts when you read in math can help you use the **problem-solving strategy, *Make a Table,*** in the next lesson.

In reading, understanding tables can help you understand what you read. In math, understanding tables can help you solve problems.

*Read the **title** to find out in general what the table is about.*

This title tells you the table is about Sports Max Stores.

Sports Max Stores

State	Ohio	Florida	Texas	Illinois
Number of stores	14	22	17	11
Number of employees	242	315	260	171

*The other information in the **table** are the entries. They reveal specific information.*

These headings tell what the data is about.

The entry 260 is in the column for Texas and the row for employees. So there are 260 employees in the Texas stores.

*The headings describe the different types of data in the **table.** In some tables, the headings go across. In others, the headings go down.*

1. How many Sports Max stores are in Illinois?
2. Tell all the information given in the table about Sports Max stores in Florida.

For 3–6, use the Mountain Heights table at the right.

3. What is the table about?

4. What type of data is in the table?

5. Writing in Math Write a sentence that gives some specific information displayed in the table.

6. What is the height of Mount McKinley?

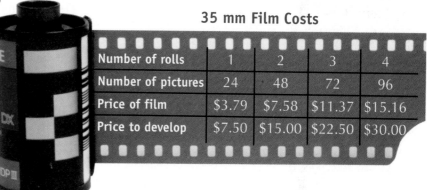

Mountain Heights

Mountain	Height (ft)
Everest	29,035
McKinley	20,320
Kilimanjaro	19,340
Matterhorn	14,690
Rainier	14,410
Pikes Peak	14,110

For 7–9, use the table at the right.

7. How much does it cost to develop 2 rolls of film?

8. How many pictures are on 3 rolls?

9. How many rolls of film can be developed for $30.00?

35 mm Film Costs

Number of rolls	1	2	3	4
Number of pictures	24	48	72	96
Price of film	$3.79	$7.58	$11.37	$15.16
Price to develop	$7.50	$15.00	$22.50	$30.00

For 10–15, use the chart below.

10. What type of information is given in a schedule?

11. What do you think ***duration*** means? Explain your thinking.

12. Which tours start at 1:00 P.M.?

13. What does ***hr*** mean?

14. What information does ****Meals included*** tell you?

15. Writing in Math Tell all the information given about tours to the museums.

Welcome to Chicago Tours

Tour Schedule

Tour	Times	Duration
Downtown Chicago	10:00 A.M., 2:00 P.M.	3 hr
Chicago River cruise	9:00 A.M., 11:00 A.M., 1:00 P.M.	1.5 hr
Lake Michigan cruise*	10:00 A.M., 1:00 P.M., 7:00 P.M.	3 hr
Museums*	9:00 A.M., 11:30 A.M.	4.5 hr
Zoos*	8:00 A.M.	5 hr

*Meals included

Problem-Solving Strategy

Key Idea
Learning how and when to make a table can help you solve problems.

Reading Helps!

Understanding graphic sources such as tables and charts

can help you with...

the problem-solving strategy, *Make a Table.*

Make a Table

LEARN

How do you make a table to solve a problem?

Library Fines The Riverside Library charges 5¢ if a book is one day overdue, 10¢ if a book is two days overdue, 15¢ if a book is three days overdue, and so on. What fine does the librarian charge for a book that is 7 days overdue?

Read and Understand

What do you know? The fine for 1 day is 5¢, for 2 days is 10¢, for 3 days is 15¢, and so on.

What are you trying to find? Find the fine for 7 days.

Plan and Solve

What strategy will you use? **Strategy: Make a table.**

How to Make a Table

Step 1 Set up the table with the correct labels.

Days							
Fine							

Step 2 Enter known data in the table.

Days	1	2	3				
Fine	5¢	10¢	15¢				

Step 3 Look for a pattern. Extend the table.

Days	1	2	3	4	5	6	7
Fine	5¢	10¢	15¢	20¢	25¢	30¢	35¢

Step 4 Find the answer in the table.

Days	1	2	3	4	5	6	7
Fine	5¢	10¢	15¢	20¢	25¢	30¢	35¢

Answer: The fine for 7 days is 35¢.

Look Back and Check

Is your answer reasonable? Yes, the answer makes sense because $7 \times 5 = 35$.

Talk About It

1. In the Library Fines problem, what are the labels for the table?
2. What patterns were used to complete the table?

When might you make a table?

Rides at the Fair Phil and Marcy spent all day Saturday at the fair. Phil rode 3 rides each half hour and Marcy rode 2 rides each half hour. How many rides had Marcy ridden when Phil rode 24 rides?

Rides for Phil	3	6	9	12	15	18	21	24
Rides for Marcy	2	4	6	8	10	12	14	16

When to Make a Table

Think about making a table when:

You have two or more quantities.

- Days and Fines
- Rides for Phil and Rides for Marcy

The amounts for each quantity change using a pattern.

- The fine for each day was 5¢ more than the previous day.
- Phil rode 3 rides each half hour, Marcy rode 2 rides each half hour.

Talk About It

3. What are the two quantities in the Rides at the Fair problem?
4. What patterns do you see in the table?
5. Give the answer to the problem in a complete sentence.

CHECK

For another example, see Set 3-5 on p. 181.

1. Copy and complete the table for the Bottle Factory problem.

Bottle Factory At a bottle factory, 4 bottles are capped every 30 seconds. How many bottles are capped in 3 minutes?

Time	30 sec	1 min	1 min 30 sec	2 min	
Bottles	4	8	12		

2. Make and use a table to solve the Stuffing Envelopes problem.

Stuffing Envelopes Jack and Jay stuffed envelopes for their mother's company. Jack stuffed 4 envelopes per minute. Jay stuffed 3 per minute. How many envelopes did Jay stuff when Jack stuffed 32 envelopes?

For more practice, see Set 3-5 on p. 185.

A Using the Strategy

Completing a Table to Solve a Problem Copy and complete the table to solve the problem. Write the answer in a complete sentence.

3. A store sells school-supply packs that contain 5 pencils and 2 pens. A customer bought enough packs to get 30 pencils. How many pens did the customer get?

Pencils	5	10	15	20		
Pens	2	4				

4. When Gino visited his aunt, she gave him 10¢ the first day, 20¢ the second day, 30¢ the third day, and so on. How much did she give him on the sixth day of his visit?

Day	1	2	3	4		
Money	10¢	20¢	30¢			

Making a Table to Solve a Problem For 5–7 make a table. Use it to find the answer. Write the answer in a complete sentence.

5. At a car wash, Jim washed 8 cars per hour, and David washed 6 cars per hour. How many cars did Jim wash while David washed 24 cars?

6. Video Villa charges $8 to rent 3 videotapes. A customer asked how many tapes she could rent for $32. What should the clerk answer?

7. Leo's Pizza restaurant offers a $3 discount for every 10 pizzas ordered. Kyle's family ordered 60 pizzas from Leo's Pizza last year. What was the total value of the discounts they should receive?

8. Decision Making A purchasing agent is ordering 56 T-shirts with a special design. Should she order from Shirt City or from T-Time? Explain.

Shirt City
10 T-shirts $80
20 T-shirts $160
50 T-shirts $400
For each additional T-shirt add $9.
T-Time
8 T-shirts $72
24 T-shirts $216
48 T-shirts $432
For each additional T-shirt add $10.

B Mixed Strategy Practice

Solve each problem.

9. Each house on Drew's street has an address that is 4 more than the house before it. If the first house has an address of 135, what is the address of the fifth house?

10. Suppose you have 28 paper clips. How many rows can you make if you continue the pattern shown below?

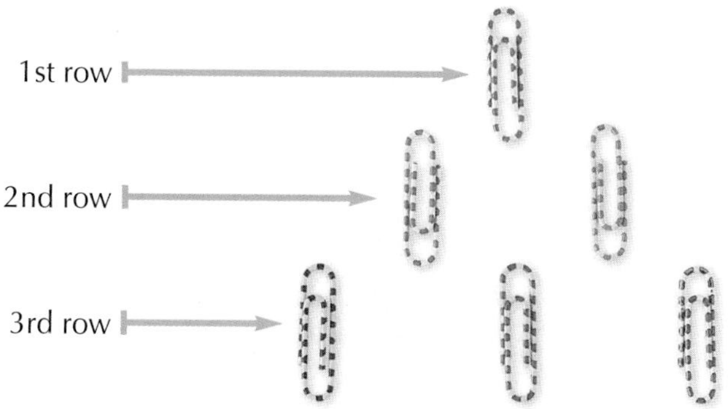

11. Writing in Math Solve the Dog and Cat problem. Write a paragraph to convince a classmate that your answer is correct.

Dog and Cat A pet shop has 3 cats and 2 dogs. The clerk wants to put 1 dog and 1 cat in the window. In how many ways can she choose 1 cat and 1 dog?

STRATEGIES

- **Show What You Know**
  - Draw a Picture
  - Make an Organized List
  - Make a Table
  - Make a Graph
  - Act It Out or Use Objects
- **Look for a Pattern**
- **Try, Check, and Revise**
- **Write a Number Sentence**
- **Use Logical Reasoning**
- **Solve a Simpler Problem**
- **Work Backward**

Choose a tool

TEST TALK

Think It Through

Stuck? Don't give up.

Try these!

- Reread the problem.
- Tell what you know.
- Identify key facts and details.
- Tell the problem in your own words.
- Show the main idea.
- Try a different strategy.
- Retrace your steps.

Mixed Review and Test Prep

Take It to the NET
Test Prep
www.scottforesman.com

12. 6 × 4 **13.** 7 × 5 **14.** 0 × 6 **15.** 3 × 7 **16.** 8 × 6

17. What is the value of the underlined digit in the number 26,051?

A. 6 **B.** 60 **C.** 6,000 **D.** 60,000

18. What is the value of the underlined digit in the number 13,946,255?

A. 3,000 **B.** 30,000 **C.** 300,000 **D.** 3,000,000

19. What is a reasonable estimate for 8,892 + 2,388?

A. 11,000 **B.** 16,000 **C.** 100,000 **D.** 110,000

Review

Do You Know How?

Do You Understand?

Meanings for Multiplication (3-1)

Draw two pictures to show each product. Use arrays in one and groups in the other.

1. 3 × 4

2. 2 × 8

3. 5 × 3

4. 6 × 4

A Explain how you decided to draw each picture. Explain how you decided how many rows and groups to draw.

B Explain how to find a number that is three times as great as 7.

Patterns in Multiplying by 0, 1, 2, 5, and 9 (3-2)

5. 5 × 7

6. 9 × 4

7. 8 × 9

8. 1 × 9

9. 0 × 4

10. 6 × 2

C Tell another multiplication fact that has the same product as 0 × 4.

D Explain how to use the fives pattern to find 7 × 5.

Using Known Facts to Find Unknown Facts (3-3)
Multiplying by 10, 11, and 12 (3-4)

11. 6 × 7

12. 3 × 6

13. 4 × 8

14. 7 × 8

15. 12 × 7

16. 11 × 4

E Explain how you can use 10 × 9 to find 12 × 9.

F Explain how you can use 2 × 3 to find 4 × 3.

Problem-Solving Strategy: Make a Table (3-5)

17. Make and use a table to solve the Chairs problem.

Chairs Jack washed 6 chairs in one hour. Telly washed 8 chairs in one hour. How many chairs will Jack have washed when Telly has washed 40 chairs?

G Tell what you know. Identify the known facts.

H Explain how a table can help you solve the problem.

Diagnostic Checkpoint

MULTIPLE CHOICE

1. Tia found 7 seashells. Tamara found 3 times as many. How many seashells did Tamara find? (3-1)

A. 10 seashells **B.** 14 seashells **C.** 21 seashells **D.** 28 seashells

2. Which does NOT have the same product as 4×2? (3-2)

A. 0×8 **B.** 2×4 **C.** 8×1 **D.** 1×8

FREE RESPONSE

Write an addition sentence and a multiplication sentence for each set of pictures. (3-1)

3. 

4. 

5. 

6. Write a multiplication sentence for $8 + 8 + 8 + 8 + 8 = 40$. (3-1)

Multiply. (3-2, 3-3, 3-4)

7. 6×0 **8.** 8×5 **9.** 4×6 **10.** 7×6 **11.** 9×1

12. 10×5 **13.** 9×2 **14.** 3×7 **15.** 12×6 **16.** 8×6

Algebra Find the missing number. Tell which property can help you. (3-2 and 3-3)

17. $8 \times 4 = \square \times 8$ **18.** $8 \times \square = 8$ **19.** $\square \times 7 = 0$

20. Sam earned \$7.00 an hour and Lisa earned \$8.00 an hour. Lisa and Sam worked the same number of hours. Sam earned \$49, how much did Lisa earn? (3-5)

Writing in Math

21. Use breaking apart to find 4×9. Explain what you did. (3-3)

22. How can you use the fact $3 \times 6 = 18$ to find 6×6? (3-3)

Key Idea
Divide to find the number of equal groups and the number in each group.

Vocabulary
- divide
- divisor
- dividend
- quotient

TEST TALK

Think It Through
- **I know** the total number of beads.
- What do **I need to find?**

Meanings for Division

WARM UP

1. 9×6
2. 8×3
3. 5×7
4. 4×6
5. 10×3
6. 2×8

LEARN

What does it mean to divide?

You can **divide** to find the number in each group or the number of equal groups.

Example A

Nicole has 24 beads. She is making 4 bracelets, all with the same number of beads. How many beads should each bracelet have?

What You **Think**	What You **Show**	What You **Write**
Think about sharing. Put 24 beads into 4 equal groups. How many beads are in each group?	4 equal groups 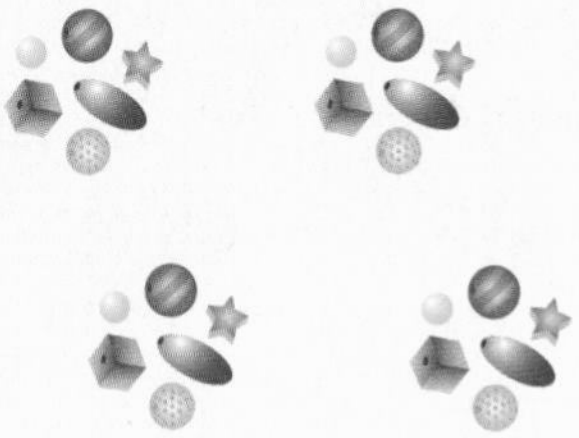	divisor ↓ $24 \div 4 = 6$ ↑ dividend ↑ quotient Each bracelet should have 6 beads.

Example B

Nicole has 24 beads. She decides to use 6 beads for each bracelet. How many bracelets can she make?

What You **Think**	What You **Show**	What You **Write**
Think about repeated subtraction. Put 24 beads in groups of 6. How many groups can you make?	6 in each group 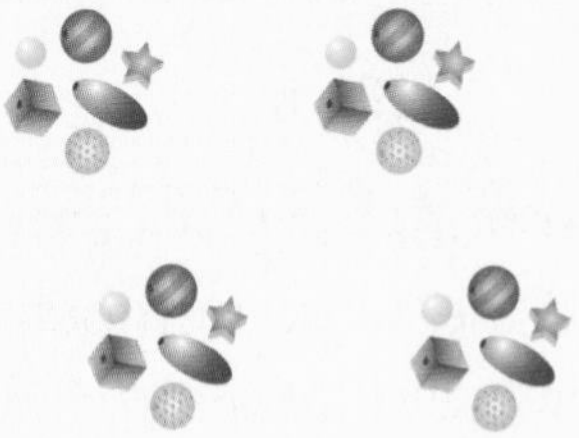	divisor → $6\overline{)24}$ ← dividend; 4 ← quotient Nicole can make 4 bracelets.

Talk About It

1. In Example A, what does the dividend represent? the divisor? the quotient?
2. Explain how you can use repeated subtraction to find $20 \div 4$.

CHECK ✓

For another example, see Set 3-6 on p. 181.

Draw pictures to solve each problem.

1. You put 28 cards into 4 piles. How many cards are in each pile?
2. You need to arrange 32 people into rows of 8. How many rows can you make?
3. **Number Sense** You divide 12 cups into 4 groups and get 3 cups in each group. If you divide the 12 cups into 2 groups instead, would each group have more or fewer than 3 cups? Explain.

PRACTICE

For another example, see Set 3-6 on p. 185.

A Skills and Understanding

Draw pictures to solve each problem.

4. You want to plant 20 trees in 4 rows. How many trees should you put in each row?
5. A box holds 8 candles. How many boxes can you fill with 32 candles? How many boxes can you fill with 48 candles?
6. **Number Sense** You have 18 toys to pass out equally to a group of children. Does each child get more toys if there are 6 children or if there are 9 children? Explain.

B Reasoning and Problem Solving

7. Twelve players came to soccer practice. They formed two teams with the same number of players on each team. How many players were on each team?
8. **Writing in Math** Write a problem about equal groups that can be solved using 64 ÷ 8.
9. **Writing in Math** How can repeated subtraction help you find 54 ÷ 9?

Mixed Review and Test Prep

Take It to the NET
Test Prep
www.scottforesman.com

Write the value of each underlined digit.

10. 7$\underline{8}$9 **11.** 6,$\underline{2}$54 **12.** $\underline{1}$50,400 **13.** $\underline{3}$4,209,528

14. Find 4 × 8.

A. 16 **B.** 24 **C.** 32 **D.** 40

Key Idea
Multiplication and division are related in the same way that addition and subtraction are related.

Vocabulary
- fact family
- inverse operations

Materials
- grid paper or e tools

TEST TALK

Think It Through
I can **draw an array** to show multiplication and division. An array has the same number of objects in each row and column.

Relating Multiplication and Division

WARM UP

1. 8 × 5
2. 3 × 7
3. 2 × 6
4. 4 × 10
5. 4 × 7
6. 7 × 9

LEARN

Activity

How are multiplication and division related?

For each question, use grid paper to draw an array and write a number sentence.

a. Sam buys stamps at the post office. He has 4 rows with 3 stamps in each row. How many stamps does he have in all?

b. Sam has 12 stamps altogether. The stamps are in 4 rows. How many stamps are in each row?

Multiplication and division are **inverse operations.** They undo each other.

What is a fact family?

Fact families connect multiplication and division. A **fact family** shows all the related multiplication and division facts for a set of numbers. You can use fact families to help you remember division facts.

This is the fact family for 7, 8, and 56.

$7 \times 8 = 56$ $56 \div 7 = 8$

$8 \times 7 = 56$ $56 \div 8 = 7$

Talk About It

1. How are the sentences in a fact family related?

2. Write the fact family for 2, 7, and 14.

CHECK

For another example, see Set 3-7 on p. 181.

Copy and complete each fact family.

1. $7 \times ■ = 42$ $42 \div 6 = ■$ $42 \div ■ = ■$ $■ \times ■ = 42$

2. $4 \times ■ = 28$ $28 \div ■ = ■$ $28 \div ■ = ■$ $■ \times ■ = 28$

Write a fact family for each set of numbers.

3. 6, 8, 48 **4.** 5, 7, 35 **5.** 3, 6, 18

6. Number Sense Is $2 \times 6 = 12$ part of the fact family for 3, 4, and 12?

PRACTICE

For more practice, see Set 3-7 on p. 185.

A Skills and Understanding

Copy and complete each fact family.

7. $5 \times ■ = 30$ $30 \div 6 = ■$ $■ \times ■ = 30$ $30 \div ■ = ■$

8. $8 \times ■ = 72$ $72 \div 9 = ■$ $■ \times ■ = 72$ $72 \div ■ = ■$

Write a fact family for each set of numbers.

9. 2, 7, 14 **10.** 4, 8, 32 **11.** 7, 7, 49 **12.** 5, 8, 40

13. Number Sense If you know that $6 \times 9 = 54$, what division facts do you know?

B Reasoning and Problem Solving

14. The United States flag has one star for each state. Write the fact family for the array of stars shown in the 1822 U.S. flag shown at the right.

15. Writing in Math Explain why the fact family for 64 and 8 has only two number sentences.

Mixed Review and Test Prep

Take It to the NET
Test Prep
www.scottforesman.com

Fill in the ●. Use > or <.

16. 86 ● 96 **17.** 532 ● 530 **18.** 5,055 ● 5,505

19. Sean has 12 toy cars. He divided them evenly between two boxes. How many cars are in each box?

A. $12 \div 3 = 4$ **B.** $12 \div 6 = 2$ **C.** $12 \div 2 = 6$ **D.** $12 \div 4 = 3$

Key Idea
Thinking about multiplication can help you divide.

TEST TALK

Think It Through
I can write a related multiplication fact to help me divide.

Division Facts

WARM UP

1. 9 × 4	2. 3 × 8
3. 2 × 9	4. 5 × 10
5. 5 × 7	6. 7 × 8

LEARN

How can you use multiplication to divide?

Apples Emma and her father are packing apples grown on their farm. They pack 48 apples in each box. Each tray in the box holds 8 apples. How many trays are in each box?

Example

Find 48 ÷ 8.

What You **Think**	What You **Say**	What You **Write**
What number times 8 equals 48? ▢ × 8 = 48 6 times 8 equals 48. 6 × 8 = 48	48 divided by 8 is what number? *or* How many times does 8 go into 48?	48 ÷ 8 = 6 or $8\overline{)48}$ with quotient 6

There are 6 trays in each box.

Talk About It

1. Why is division used to solve the Apples problem?
2. Why is the multiplication fact 6 × 8 = 48 helpful?
3. What multiplication fact could you use to help you find 21 ÷ 3?

Take It to the NET
More Examples
www.scottforesman.com

CHECK

For more practice, see Set 3-8 on p. 182.

1. $14 \div 2$ **2.** $12 \div 3$ **3.** $5\overline{)25}$ **4.** $7\overline{)35}$ **5.** $9\overline{)36}$

6. Number Sense A number divided by 7 is 7. What is the number? How do you know?

PRACTICE

For more practice, see Set 3-8 on p. 186.

A Skills and Understanding

7. $8 \div 4$ **8.** $15 \div 5$ **9.** $42 \div 6$ **10.** $54 \div 9$ **11.** $63 \div 7$

12. $4\overline{)40}$ **13.** $2\overline{)12}$ **14.** $6\overline{)18}$ **15.** $8\overline{)72}$ **16.** $4\overline{)16}$

17. Reasoning If $45 \div 9 = 5$, what is $45 \div 5$? Explain.

B Reasoning and Problem Solving

18. A large box of cereal costs \$3. How many boxes can you buy for \$12?

19. Tim exercised for 2 hours each day from Monday through Friday. For how many hours did Tim exercise?

20. Each finger has 3 bones and each thumb has 2 bones. How many bones are in 8 fingers and 2 thumbs?

21. Number Sense Is the quotient of $24 \div 3$ greater than or less than the quotient of $15 \div 3$? Explain how you know without actually finding the quotients.

22. Writing in Math Is the quotient of $36 \div 4$ greater than or less than the quotient of $36 \div 9$? Explain how you know without actually finding the quotients.

Mixed Review and Test Prep

Take It to the NET
Test Prep
www.scottforesman.com

23. \$4.53 + \$0.45 **24.** \$16.09 + \$4.72 **25.** \$45 + \$2.50

26. $\begin{array}{r} 451 \\ -\ 266 \\ \hline \end{array}$ **27.** $\begin{array}{r} 3{,}042 \\ -\ \ \ 128 \\ \hline \end{array}$ **28.** $\begin{array}{r} 9{,}006 \\ -\ 4{,}787 \\ \hline \end{array}$

29. What number sentence is NOT part of the fact family for 2, 10, and 20?

A. $20 \div 2 = 10$ **B.** $10 \times 2 = 20$ **C.** $20 \div 10 = 2$ **D.** $2 \times 5 = 10$

Key Idea
Thinking about multiplication can help you divide with zero and one.

Special Quotients

WARM UP

1. 8 × 10
2. 7 × 1
3. 1 × 5
4. 0 × 3
5. 10 × 1
6. 12 × 0

LEARN

How can you divide with 1 and 0?

Example A

	What You **Think**	What You **Write**
A pizza is cut into 6 slices. How many people can each eat one slice of pizza? Find 6 ÷ 1.	What number times 1 equals 6? **Rule:** Any number divided by 1 is that number.	6 × 1 = 6 6 ÷ 1 = 6 The pizza can feed 6 people.

Example B

A pizza is cut into 8 slices. How many pieces each will 8 people get? Find 8 ÷ 8.	8 times what number equals 8? **Rule:** Any number divided by itself (except 0) is 1.	8 × 1 = 8 8 ÷ 8 = 1 Each person gets 1 slice.

Example C

Find 0 ÷ 2.	Two times what number equals 0? **Rule:** Zero divided by any number (except 0) is 0.	2 × 0 = 0 0 ÷ 2 = 0

Example D

Find 5 ÷ 0.	Zero times what number equals 5? **Rule:** You cannot divide by 0.	**0 × ? = 5** **5 ÷ 0 cannot be done.**

TEST TALK

Think It Through
I can **draw a picture** to help me solve a problem.

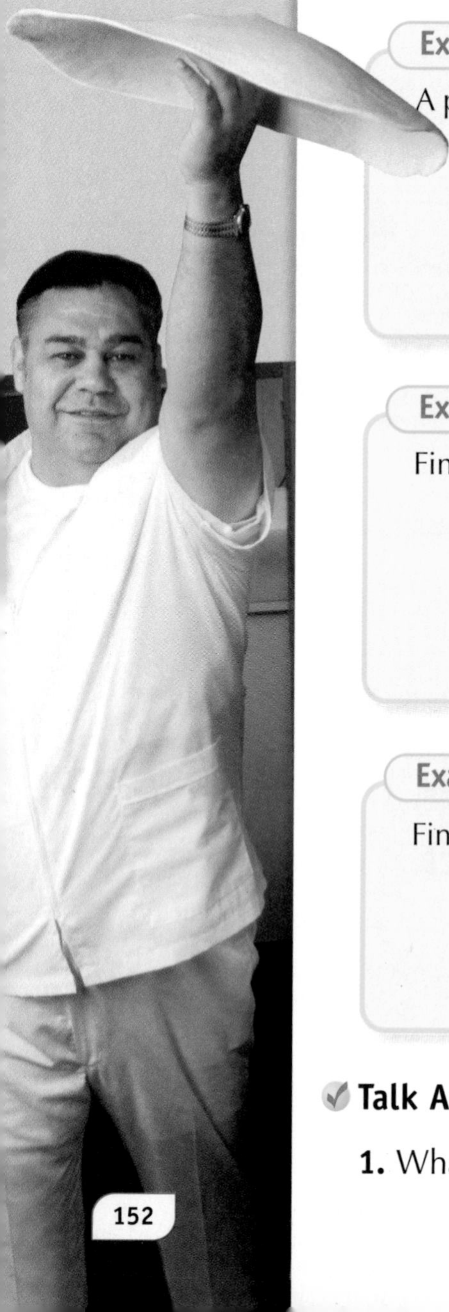

Talk About It

1. What multiplication sentence can help you find 6 ÷ 1? 0 ÷ 2?

CHECK

For another example, see Set 3-9 on p. 182.

1. 0 ÷ 8 **2.** 5 ÷ 5 **3.** 1)3 **4.** 6)0 **5.** 1)1

6. Number Sense Can you put 4 counters into zero rows? Explain.

PRACTICE

For more practice, see Set 3-9 on p. 186.

A Skills and Understanding

7. 8 ÷ 1 **8.** 0 ÷ 4 **9.** 0 ÷ 6 **10.** 2 ÷ 2 **11.** 0 ÷ 2

12. 1)7 **13.** 1)5 **14.** 10)0 **15.** 5)0 **16.** 1)3

Compare. Use >, <, or = for each ●.

17. 3 ÷ 3 ● 0 ÷ 5 **18.** 6 ÷ 1 ● 6 ÷ 6 **19.** 2 ÷ 2 ● 0 ÷ 2

20. 0 ÷ 8 ● 0 ÷ 9 **21.** 1 ÷ 1 ● 7 ÷ 1 **22.** 5 ÷ 5 ● 4 ÷ 4

23. Number Sense Write a fact family for 1, 1, 1.

B Reasoning and Problem Solving

24. Twelve people want to share the pizza shown. How many slices does each person get?

25. Pamela has already read 32 of the 41 chapters in her book. How many more chapters does she have to read? If she reads one chapter each day, how many days will it take her to finish the book?

26. Number Sense If ■ ÷ ▲ = 0, what do you know about ■?

27. Writing in Math Write a word problem in which 7 is divided by 7 and another problem in which 7 is divided by 1.

TEST TALK

Think It Through

I'm **dividing,** so my problem will be about **sharing between equal groups.**

Mixed Review and Test Prep

Take It to the NET
Test Prep
www.scottforesman.com

28. 4)12 **29.** 6)54 **30.** 4)28 **31.** 5)25

32. 3)27 **33.** 7)35 **34.** 5)40 **35.** 9)36

36. Hal has 58 cents in one pocket and 37 cents in another pocket. How much money does he have in all?

A. 85 cents **B.** 95 cents **C.** $1.15 **D.** $95

Key Idea
Multiplication and division describe real situations.

Multiplication and Division Stories

WARM UP

1. 15 ÷ 3
2. 20 ÷ 5
3. 28 ÷ 4
4. 16 ÷ 2
5. 42 ÷ 7
6. 72 ÷ 9

LEARN

How can you write a story?

Suzette is making a quilt. The pattern she is using is shown below.

Example A

Use Suzette's quilt to write a multiplication story for 3 × 5 = 15.

Suzette's quilt has 3 rows with 5 large squares in each row. How many large squares does it have in all?

Example B

Use Suzette's quilt to write a division story for 35 ÷ 5 = 7.

Suzette has 35 tiny solid blue squares. She needs 5 tiny blue squares for each patterned square. How many patterned squares can she make with the tiny solid blue squares?

TEST TALK

Think It Through
- I can **multiply when I combine equal groups.**
- I can **divide when I need to find the number in each group.**

Talk About It

1. Is there only one correct story for a given multiplication or division fact? Explain.
2. Write a story about Suzette's quilt for 15 ÷ 3 = 5 and for 15 ÷ 5 = 3.
3. Write a multiplication story about the squares in the quilt. What number sentence would you use to solve your story?

CHECK

For another example, see Set 3-10 on p. 182.

Use the data in the table to write a multiplication or division story for each number fact. Solve.

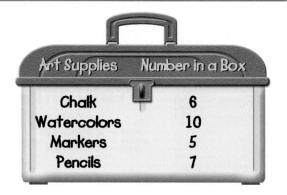

Art Supplies	Number in a Box
Chalk	6
Watercolors	10
Markers	5
Pencils	7

1. $6 \times 7 = 42$ **2.** $10 \div 5 = 2$

3. Number Sense Would you need more boxes of markers or boxes of chalk to have 30 of each?

PRACTICE

For more practice, see Set 3-10 on p. 186.

A Skills and Understanding

Reasoning Write a multiplication or division story for each number fact. Solve.

4. $2 \times 6 = 12$ **5.** $24 \div 8 = 3$ **6.** $5 \times 8 = 40$ **7.** $32 \div 4 = 8$

B Reasoning and Problem Solving

Use the data in the table to write a multiplication or division story for each number fact. Solve.

Groceries	Number in a Bag
Apples	9
Bananas	4
Carrots	7
Potatoes	10
Oranges	8
Grapefruit	3

8. $7 \times 9 = 63$ **9.** $4 \times 8 = 32$ **10.** $8 \times 9 = 72$

11. $24 \div 3 = 8$ **12.** $36 \div 4 = 9$ **13.** $10 \div 1 = 10$

14. The product of two numbers is 36. Their sum is 13. What are the numbers?

15. Tim needs 5 boards that are each 3 feet long. He has two 10-foot boards to cut them from. Will that be enough?

16. Writing in Math Write two different division stories for $28 \div 4 = 7$.

Mixed Review and Test Prep

Take It to the NET
Test Prep
www.scottforesman.com

17. Algebra Find $3 \times n$ when $n = 0$.

18. Find $56 \div 7$.

A. 5 **B.** 6 **C.** 7 **D.** 8

19. Find $18 \div 6$.

A. 2 **B.** 3 **C.** 4 **D.** 5

Problem-Solving Skill

Key Idea
Identifying hidden questions helps you solve multiple-step problems.

Reading Helps!
Identifying sequence of events
can help you with...
identifying hidden questions in multiple-step problems.

Multiple-Step Problems

LEARN

How can finding hidden questions help solve a problem?

Baseball Cards Trisha and her brother, Kyle, collect and sell baseball cards. Kyle has 6 cards to sell. Trisha has 3 cards to sell. If they sell the cards for 8¢ each, how much money will they get all together?

Here are two ways to solve the Baseball Cards problem.

Read and Understand

Solution 1

Hidden Question: How many cards did they have to sell all together?

Trisha has 3 cards. Kyle has 6 cards.

3 + 6 = 9

They had 9 cards to sell.

Question in the Problem: If they sell the cards for 8¢ each, how much money would they get together?

9 cards × 8¢ each = 72¢

Kyle and Trisha will get 72¢ together.

Solution 2

Hidden Question 1: How much money would Trisha get for selling her cards?

3 cards × 8¢ each = 24¢

Hidden Question 2: How much money would Kyle get for selling his cards?

6 cards × 8¢ each = 48¢

Question in the Problem: If they sell the cards for 8¢ each, how much money would they get together?

24¢ + 48¢ = 72¢

Kyle and Trisha get 72¢ together.

Talk About It

1. Do you like Solution 1 or Solution 2 better? Why?

CHECK ✓

For another example, see Set 3-11 on p. 182.

Write and answer the hidden question or questions. Then solve the problem. Write your answer in a complete sentence.

1. Rita and Toby ride bikes on a 3-mile course. Last week Rita rode the course 6 times and Toby rode it 4 times. How much farther did Rita ride than Toby?

2. Rachel has 12 tomato plants and 18 pepper plants for her garden. She plans to put 6 plants in a row. How many rows does she need in all for the tomatoes and peppers?

PRACTICE

For another example, see Set 3-11 on p. 186.

Write and answer the hidden question or questions. Then solve the problem. Write your answer in a complete sentence.

3. Kara spent $12 to rent 3 video games. Her brother, Karl, spent $12 to rent 6 movies. How much more did it cost to rent one game than to rent one movie?

4. A train boxcar has 8 wheels. How many more wheels are on 6 boxcars than on 6 bicycles?

Use the data at the right for 5–6.

5. Gina and her family bought 4 chicken sandwiches and 4 salads at Diner Delight. They paid $1 sales tax. How much did they spend?

6. Jill's family spent $20 at the diner, not including tax. They bought 2 hamburgers, 2 chicken sandwiches, and some salads. How many salads did they buy?

Diner Delight	
Hamburger	$3
Chicken Sandwich	$4
French Fries	$2
Salad	$2

7. **Writing in Math** Use the data at the right to write a problem about going to the movies that has a hidden question. Then solve the problem.

Metro Movies Ticket Prices

	Matinee (before 3 P.M.)	Evening
Children Under 12	$3	$5
Adults	$5	$8
Seniors	$3	$6

Review

Do You Know How?

Do You Understand?

Meanings for Division (3-6)

Draw pictures to solve each problem.

1. Three people share 12 tacos. How many tacos does each person get?
2. How many pairs can be made from 18 socks?

A Explain how you solved each problem. Explain whether you thought of division as sharing or as repeated subtraction.

B Explain how to find 28 ÷ 4 with repeated subtraction.

Relating Multiplication and Division (3-7)
Multiplication and Division Stories (3-10)

Write a fact family for each set of numbers.

3. 2, 5, 10
4. 6, 6, 36
5. Write four related stories to represent the facts in Exercise 3.

C Explain how the fact family for Exercise 3 is different than the fact family for Exercise 4.

D Explain how the stories for each fact family are related to each other.

Division Facts (3-8)
Special Quotients(3-9)

6. 36 ÷ 4
7. 49 ÷ 7
8. 0 ÷ 8
9. 3 ÷ 3
10. 20 ÷ 5
11. 9 ÷ 1

E What multiplication facts could you have used to find 36 ÷ 4 and 49 ÷ 7?

F How is 8 ÷ 0 different from 0 ÷ 8?

Problem-Solving Skill: Multiple-Step Problems (3-11)

12. Pedro buys 6 packages of batteries. There are 4 batteries in each package. He uses 8 batteries in his flashlight. How many batteries does he have left?

G Identify the hidden question.

H Explain how you could solve the problem another way.

Diagnostic Checkpoint

MULTIPLE CHOICE

1. Which multiplication fact can help you find $24 \div 8$? (3-8)

A. 2×8 **B.** 3×8 **C.** 4×6 **D.** 4×8

2. Find $0 \div 9$. (3-9)

A. 0 **B.** 1 **C.** 9 **D.** cannot be done

3. Ella is putting 15 red chairs and 30 blue chairs in rows. She plans to put 5 chairs in each row. How many rows of chairs will she make? (3-11)

A. 6 rows **B.** 7 rows **C.** 8 rows **D.** 9 rows

FREE RESPONSE

Divide. (3-8 and 3-9)

4. 3)0 **5.** 7)7 **6.** 4)24 **7.** 8)40 **8.** 9)54

9. $15 \div 3$ **10.** $18 \div 2$ **11.** $40 \div 4$ **12.** $6 \div 1$ **13.** $0 \div 4$

14. Write the fact family for 7, 8, and 56. (3-7)

Use the graph at the right for 15–17. Write your answer in a complete sentence. (3-11)

15. How many more fourth graders like to ride scooters than skateboards?

16. How many more fourth graders like to ride bicycles than skateboards?

17. How many fourth graders' favorite rides are skateboards or scooters?

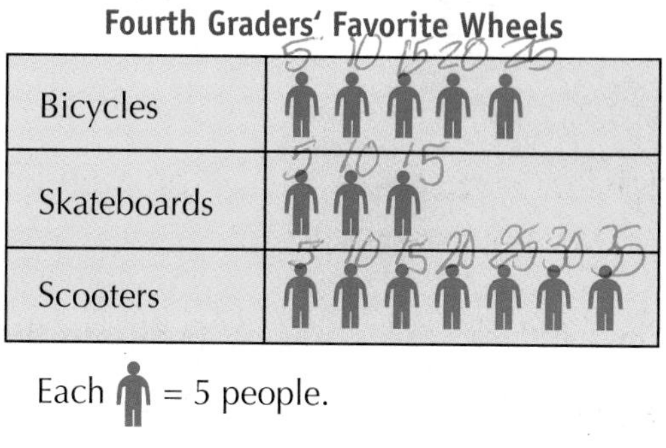

Writing in Math

18. Draw a picture to show how you can use an array to find $27 \div 9$. Explain how you can find the quotient with repeated subtraction and your array. (3-6)

19. Write two different division stories for $8 \div 4$. (3-10)

20. Describe a situation in which 5 is divided by 5. (3-9)

Algebra

Key Idea
Expressions can help you solve problems.

Vocabulary
- variable (p. 98)

TEST TALK

Think It Through
I can **draw a picture** to model a problem.

Writing and Evaluating Expressions

WARM UP

Evaluate each expression for $n = 11$.

1. $n + 7$
2. $n + 19$
3. $11 - n$
4. $24 - n$

LEARN

How can you use expressions to solve problems?

When a variable is used in a multiplication expression, the times sign (×) is usually not used. For example, *4 times n* is usually written as $4n$. Division expressions can be written in different ways. For example, *m divided by 4* can be written as $m \div 4$ or $\frac{m}{4}$.

Example A

The train at the zoo has 6 cars. How many people does the train hold if each car holds n people?

Write an expression.

STEP 1 Let n = the number of people each car holds.

Number of cars ↓ 6 × People in each car ↓ n

The train holds $6n$ people.

Evaluate the expression.

STEP 2 If each car holds 4 people, how many people does the train hold?

Evaluate $6n$ for $n = 4$.

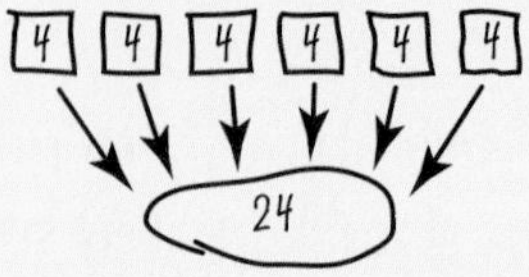

$6n$ Substitute 4 for n.
↓
$6 \times 4 = 24$ Multiply.

If each car holds 4 people, the train holds 24 people.

Example B

Each car on the train holds 8 people. How many cars are needed to hold x people?

Write an expression.

STEP 1 Let x = the number of people in all.

Number of people ↓ x ÷ People in each car ↓ 8

The train needs $x \div 8$ cars to hold x people.

Evaluate the expression.

STEP 2 How many cars are needed to hold 24 people?

Evaluate $x \div 8$ for $x = 24$.

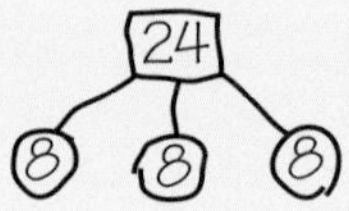

$x \div 8$ Substitute 24 for x.
↓
$24 \div 8 = 3$ Divide.

The train needs 3 cars to hold 24 people.

Talk About It

1. Explain what the variable, n, represents in Example A.
2. To evaluate $6n$ for $n = 3$, would you multiply or divide?
3. Evaluate $6n$ for $n = 5$ and $n \div 8$ for $n = 56$.

How can you evaluate expressions with more than one operation?

Some expressions may contain grouping symbols, such as parentheses ( ). When an expression involves more than one operation, do the computation inside the parentheses first.

Example C

Evaluate $(3t) + 1$ for $t = 2$.

Substitute 2 for t.

Do the computations inside the parentheses first.

$(3 \times t) + 1$

↓

$(3 \times 2) + 1$

↓

$6 \quad + 1 = 7$

Example D

Evaluate $(k + 2) \div 4$ for $k = 18$.

Substitute 18 for k.

Do the computations inside the parentheses first.

$(k + 2) \quad \div 4$

↓

$(18 + 2) \div 4$

↓

$20 \quad \div 4 = 5$

Talk About It

4. To evaluate $(3 \times 2) + 1$, which operation do you do first?
5. To evaluate $(18 + 2) \div 4$, which operation do you do first?
6. Evaluate $(3 \times t) + 1$ for $t = 5$ and $(k + 2) \div 4$ for $k = 10$.

CHECK

For another example, see Set 3-12 on p. 183.

Evaluate each expression for $n = 8$.

1. $5n$ **2.** $\frac{n}{2}$ **3.** $16 \div n$ **4.** $(n \div 4) + 7$

5. Reasoning Write an expression to represent the amount of money in d dimes. Draw a picture that shows the main idea. Then evaluate the expression for $d = 8$.

PRACTICE

For more practice, see Set 3-12 on p. 187.

A Skills and Understanding

Evaluate each expression for $m = 9$.

6. $7m$ **7.** $m \div 3$ **8.** $2m$ **9.** $10m$

Evaluate each expression for $x = 2$.

10. $\frac{x}{1}$ **11.** $5x$ **12.** $6x$ **13.** $\frac{12}{x}$

Evaluate each expression.

14. $(m \div 8) - 2$ for $m = 48$ **15.** $9 \times (n + 2)$ for $n = 1$ **16.** $(k - 10) \div 5$ for $k = 40$

17. Reasoning Write an expression for the number of nickels in c cents. Draw a picture that shows the main idea. Then evaluate your expression for $c = 45$.

B Reasoning and Problem Solving

18. Thomas bought 4 puzzle books plus some comic books. Each book was \$2. The total cost, including c comic books is $2 \times (4 + c)$. Find the total cost if Thomas bought 3 comic books.

Math and Music

Hush Little Baby is a popular nursery rhyme in the United States. Each verse has 2 lines. The second line of each verse has 10 syllables.

19. If there are 6 verses in *Hush Little Baby,* how many lines are there?

20. Write an expression to represent the total number of lines in the nursery rhyme. Let n = the number of verses.

21. What is the total number of syllables in the second lines of 6 verses?

22. Write an expression to represent the total number of syllables in the second lines of r verses.

Hush Little Baby

Hush, little baby, don't say a word.
Papa's gonna buy you a mockingbird.

And if that mockingbird won't sing,
Papa's gonna buy you a diamond ring.

And if that diamond ring
turns brass,
Papa's gonna buy you
a looking glass.

And if that looking glass gets broke,
Papa's gonna buy you a billy goat.

And if that billy goat won't pull,
Papa's gonna buy you a cart and bull.

And if that cart and bull fall down,
You'll still be the sweetest
baby in town.

23. Writing in Math Sam wrote the expression $12 \div x$ to represent the number of inches in x feet. Is Sam's expression correct? Explain.

C Extensions

24. Evaluate $(4 + 6) \times (n - 3)$ for $n = 8$.

Rewrite each expression with parentheses to make the statement true.

25. $9 + 12 \div 3 = 7$

26. $2 \times 5 - 3 = 4$

Mixed Review and Test Prep

Take It to the NET
Test Prep
www.scottforesman.com

27. Kendra has 12 tulip bulbs and 28 daffodil bulbs. She plans to plant them in rows with 4 of the same kind of bulb in each row. How many more rows of daffodils will she have than rows of tulips?

28. Jay's stamp collection includes 35 stamps from Mexico, 45 stamps from Canada, and more than 100 stamps from the United States. Which of these is a reasonable estimate for the total number of stamps in Jay's collection?

A. Fewer than 60 stamps

B. Between 60 and 100 stamps

C. Between 100 and 160 stamps

D. More than 160 stamps

Discovery Channel School™

Discover Math in Your World

Age, Height, and Weight

When a Douglas fir is about 120 years old, 150 feet tall, and between 3,000 and 4,000 pounds in weight, it is cut down for lumber.

1. A decade is 10 years. How many decades old is a Douglas fir when it is cut down for lumber?

2. Use the multiplication facts you know to calculate the number of 6-foot sections in 30 feet. Then find the number of 6-foot sections in 150 feet.

Take It to the NET
Video and Activities
www.scottforesman.com

Algebra

Key Idea
You can describe a rule for patterns with words or symbols.

Materials
- tiles

Find a Rule

WARM UP

1. Evaluate $x + 10$ for $x = 4, 5, 9, 12,$ and 30.
2. Evaluate $n - 3$ for $n = 8, 13, 15, 22,$ and 25.

LEARN

How can you find a rule?

A rule tells how one quantity is related to another.

Activity

a. Use tiles to build each shape at the right. Record your results in the table.

Figure	1	2	3	4
Number of tiles	1	4	9	

Figure 1

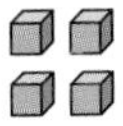

Figure 2

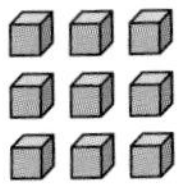

Figure 3

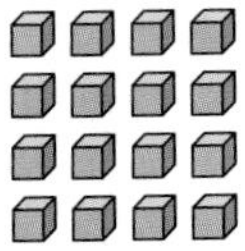

Figure 4

b. Use tiles to make the fourth figure. Draw it and complete the table.

c. Extend the table to figure 8. Complete the extended table.

d. If you know the figure number, how can you find the number of tiles?

Example

Complete the table. Start with the number in the IN column. What rule tells you how to find the number in the OUT column? Write the rule.

IN	OUT
6	3
8	4
12	6
16	
n	

What You Think

6 ÷ 2 = 3

8 ÷ 2 = 4

12 ÷ 2 = 6

16 ÷ 2 = 8

A rule is *divide by 2*.

What You Write

IN	OUT
6	3
8	4
12	6
16	8
n	$n \div 2$

The rule *divide by 2* is written as $n \div 2$.

Talk About It

1. Explain why the rule in the example is divide by 2 and not multiply by 2.

CHECK

For another example, see Set 3-13 on p. 183.

1. **Reasoning** Copy and complete the table to represent the pattern in the figures at the right. Describe the pattern in words and write the rule.

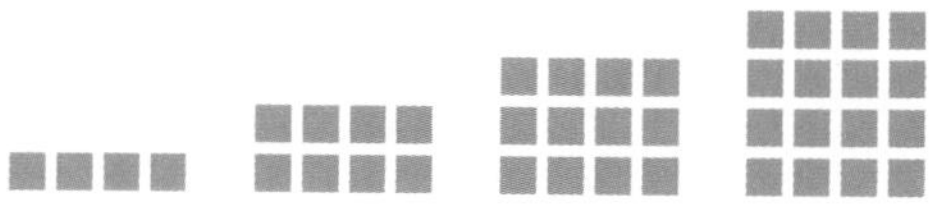

Figure 1 Figure 2 Figure 3 Figure 4

Figure	1			
Tiles	4			

PRACTICE

For more practice, see Set 3-13 on p. 187.

A Skills and Understanding

Copy and complete each table. Write the rule.

2.

In	9	7	5	2	*n*
Out	18	14	10		

3.

In	4	12	20	36	*n*
Out	1	3	5		

4. **Reasoning** Copy and complete the table to represent the pattern in the figures. Describe the pattern in words and write a rule.

Figure 1 Figure 2 Figure 3

Figure				
Tiles				

B Reasoning and Problem Solving

One month Mark saved $3 and his mother added $9 to it. The next month, he saved $5 and his mother added $15. The third month he saved $2 and she added $6.

Mark	3	5	2	7	*d*
Mom	9	15	6		

5. Copy and complete the table to show how much Mark's mom added to Mark's savings next month when Mark saved $7.

6. **Writing in Math** Write a rule to show how much Mark's mom added to Mark's savings when he saved *d* dollars. Explain how you found the rule.

Mixed Review and Test Prep

Take It to the NET
Test Prep
www.scottforesman.com

7. **Writing in Math** Write a division story about riding a bus to school that uses $18 \div 2 = 9$.

8. Find the value of $n \div 6$ when $n = 18$.

A. 3 **B.** 13 **C.** 24 **D.** 36

Algebra

Key Idea
To solve an equation, find the value of the variable that makes the equation true.

Vocabulary
- equation (p. 100)
- solution (p. 100)

Solving Multiplication and Division Equations

WARM UP

Evaluate each expression for $x = 3$.

1. $x + 7$
2. $x + 19$
3. $11 - x$
4. $24 - x$

LEARN

How can you solve an equation?

Example A

Solve the equation $5c = 30$ by testing these values for c: 3, 4, 5, and 6.

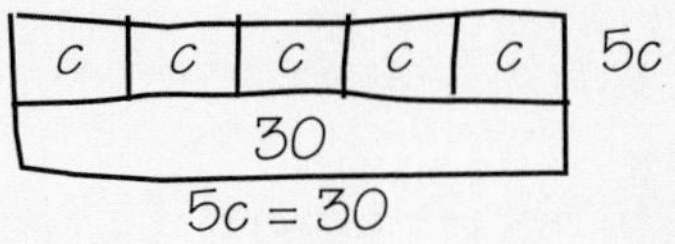

Try Find $5c$ Does $5c = 30$?	$c = 4$ $5 \times 4 = 20$ No	$c = 5$ $5 \times 5 = 25$ No	$c = 6$ $5 \times 6 = 30$ Yes

The solution to the equation is $c = 6$, because $5 \times 6 = 30$.

TEST TALK

Think It Through
If you use **mental math,** you may not have to test every value.
Think: 5 times what number is 30?

Example B

Solve the equation $m \div 7 = 4$ by testing these values for m: 21, 28, and 35.

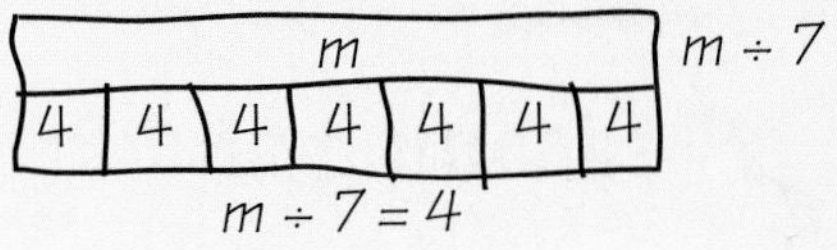

Try: Find $m \div 7$: Does $m \div 7 = 4$?	$m = 21$ $21 \div 7 = 3$ No	$m = 28$ $28 \div 7 = 4$ Yes	$m = 35$ $35 \div 7 = 5$ No

The solution to the equation is $m = 28$, because $28 \div 7 = 4$.

Talk About It

1. Explain how $c = 6$ makes the equation $5 \times c = 30$ true.
2. Solve the equation $35 \div m = 7$ by testing these values for m: 1, 5, and 7.

Take It to the NET
More Examples
www.scottforesman.com

CHECK

For another example, see Set 3-14 on p. 183.

Solve each equation by testing these values for k: 4, 5, 6.

1. $k \div 2 = 2$ **2.** $8k = 48$ **3.** $6 \div k = 1$ **4.** $9k = 45$

5. Number Sense Without testing values, explain why the solution to $m \div 2 = 5$ must be greater than 5.

PRACTICE

For more practice, see Set 3-14 on p. 187.

A Skills and Understanding

Solve each equation by testing these values for t: 1, 2, 5, and 10.

6. $9t = 18$ **7.** $\frac{20}{t} = 4$ **8.** $10t = 10$ **9.** $\frac{t}{2} = 5$

Solve each equation by testing these values for n: 4, 6, 28, 36.

10. $2n = 12$ **11.** $n \div 4 = 9$ **12.** $24 \div n = 6$ **13.** $n \div 7 = 4$

Solve each equation by testing these values for x: 5, 9, 20, 27.

14. $x \div 9 = 3$ **15.** $7x = 63$ **16.** $11x = 99$ **17.** $50 \div x = 10$

B Reasoning and Problem Solving

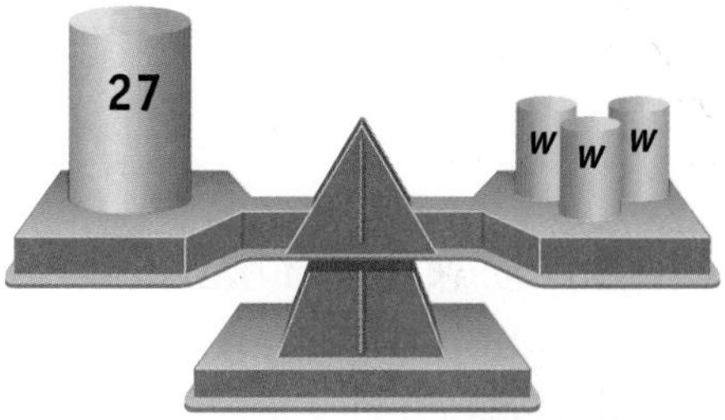

18. Write an equation for the pan balance shown at the right. Solve the equation by testing these values for w: 9, 10, 11.

19. Carlos put the same number of party treats in each of 8 bags. He used 32 party treats. Solve the equation $8t = 32$ by testing these values for t: 3, 4, 5, and 6 to find how many treats Carlos put in each bag.

20. Writing in Math Without testing values, explain why the solution to $4k = 8$ must be less than 8.

Mixed Review and Test Prep

Take It to the NET
Test Prep
www.scottforesman.com

Evaluate each expression.

21. $m \div 5$ for $m = 45$ **22.** $n - 5$ for $n = 7$ **23.** $(2k) + 16$ for $k = 4$

24. Which is the rule for the table?

In	8	5	3	2	n
Out	56	35	21	14	

A. $n \div 7$ **C.** $n \div 8$

B. $7n$ **D.** $8n$

Problem-Solving Applications

Sleeping Animals Scientists are not sure why we need to sleep, but it is clear that we do. In fact, our bodies are affected more quickly by a lack of sleep than a lack of food. Sleep appears to be a time when the body repairs itself and parts of the brain rest.

Trivia Some birds, dolphins, seals, and manatees have the ability to have half of their brain fall asleep while the other half stays awake.

1 A ground squirrel sleeps 14 hours per day. A bear sleeps 6 hours less per day. How many hours does a bear sleep each day?

2 A gorilla sleeps 4 times longer than a horse. If a horse sleeps 3 hours per day, how long does a gorilla sleep?

3 **Writing in Math** Write a division or multiplication problem about the sleeping habits of different animals. Give the answer in a complete sentence.

4 An Asian elephant sleeps 4 hours each day. An African elephant sleeps 3 hours a day. How many more hours will an Asian elephant sleep in a week than an African elephant?

5 A big brown bat sleeps 5 times as long as a cow. A cow sleeps 4 hours less each day than a rabbit sleeps. If a rabbit sleeps an average of 8 hours each day, how long does a big brown bat sleep per day?

Using Key Facts

6 Order the animals by how much they typically sleep each day from least to greatest. Then order the animals by size from least to greatest. Are the lists the same? Is there a relationship in this data between size and sleep? If so, describe the relationship.

Key Facts
Animal Size and Sleep

Animal	Possible Weight	Sleep Per Day
• Baboon	90 lb	10 hr
• Guinea pig	1 lb	8 hr
• Hamster	1/4 lb	14 hr
• Sheep	350 lb	4 hr
• Gray seal	800 lb	6 hr
• Giant armadillo	130 lb	18 hr

7 Decision Making If school starts at 8:00 A.M., and you need 10 hours of sleep each night, what would be an acceptable bedtime? Explain your reasoning and do not forget to allow time to eat breakfast. (Hint: Use a clock to help you count the hours.)

Good News/Bad News
Caffeine in coffee and soda can help you to stay up late, but a lack of sleep can lead to irritability and poor school performance.

Review

Do You Know How?

Writing and Evaluating Expressions (3-12)

Evaluate each expression.

1. $4m$ for $m = 9$

2. $k \div 3$ for $k = 12$

3. $(y - 9) \times 3$ for $y = 15$

4. $24 \div (n - 2)$ for $n = 8$

Do You Understand?

A How did you know which operation to do first in Exercise 3?

B Write an expression you could use to find the number of chairs in *n* rows if there are 10 chairs in each row. Use your expression to find the number of chairs in 4 rows.

Find a Rule (3-13)

Copy and complete each table. Write the rule.

5.

In	2	4	5	8	*n*
Out	14	28	35		

6.

In	9	6	4	2	*n*
Out	72	48	32		

C Tell how you found each rule.

D Explain how you know to use multiplication and not division in a rule when the IN number is less than the OUT number.

Solving Multiplication and Division Equations (3-14)

Solve each equation by testing these values for *m*: 2, 3, 5, 6

7. $2m = 6$

8. $9m = 45$

9. $30 \div m = 10$

10. $4m = 20$

Solve each equation by testing these values for *n*: 4, 6, 12, 24, 30

11. $n \div 3 = 8$

12. $42 \div n = 7$

13. $n \div 3 = 10$

14. $2n = 24$

E Explain how you knew the solution for Exercise 10 was not 2.

F Explain why the solution to Exercise 13 must be greater than 10.

Chapter 3 Section C

Diagnostic Checkpoint

MULTIPLE CHOICE

1. Evaluate $(12 \div m)$ for $m = 2$. (3-12)

A. 3 **B.** 4 **C.** 5 **D.** 6

2. Which is the solution to $7k = 42$? (3-14)

A. 3 **B.** 4 **C.** 6 **D.** 7

FREE RESPONSE

Copy and complete each table. Write the rule. (3-13)

3.

In	4	6	7	8	n
Out	12	18	21		

4.

In	64	56	40	8	n
Out	8	7	5		

Evaluate each expression for $n = 8$. (3-12)

5. $2n$ **6.** $9n$ **7.** $n \div 8$ **8.** $n - 2$ **9.** $16 - n$

10. To evaluate $5 \times (4 + 6)$, which operation do you do first? (3-12)

11. To evaluate $(10 \times 3) - 4$, which operation do you do first? (3-12)

Evaluate each expression.

12. $(t + 6) \div 4$ for $t = 22$ **13.** $(y + 9) \times 3$ for $y = 3$ **14.** $5 \times (n - 2)$ for $n = 10$

Solve each equation by testing these values for k: 1, 2, 3, and 6. (3-14)

15. $7k = 21$ **16.** $12 \div k = 4$ **17.** $18 \div k = 9$ **18.** $6k = 6$

Writing in Math

19. Copy and complete the table that represents the pattern in the figures below. Describe the pattern in words and write a rule. (3-13)

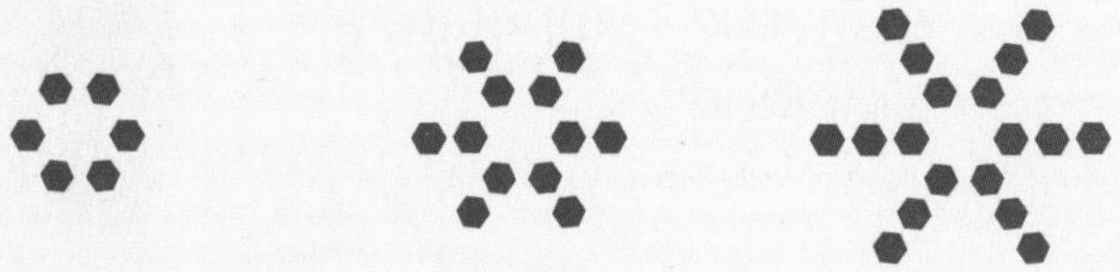

Figure 1 Figure 2 Figure 3

Figure	1		
Tiles	6		

20. Marion runs 4 miles every day. She uses the expression $4n$ to describe how much she runs. Explain what the variable n represents. Write a problem that can be solved using the equation $4n = 28$. (3-12)

Test-Taking Strategies

- Understand the question.
- Get information for the answer.
- → Plan how to find the answer.
- Make smart choices.
- Use writing in math.
- Improve written answers.

Plan How to Find the Answer

After you understand a test question and get needed information, you need to plan how to find the answer. Think about problem-solving skills and strategies and computation methods you know.

1. The table below shows the number of grams of protein in skim milk. It also shows how many cups of milk provide the protein.

Protein in Skim Milk

Number of Cups of Skim Milk	Number of Grams of Protein
1	9
2	18
3	27

Nino drank 6 cups of milk. How many grams of protein did he get from the milk?

A. 9

B. 12

C. 34

D. 54

Understand the question.

I need to find *the number of grams of protein in 6 cups of skim milk.*

Gather information for the answer.

The numbers I need are in the ***table.***

Plan how to find the answer.

- Think about problem-solving skills and strategies.

  I should ***look for a pattern*** *in the numbers in the second column. What is the difference between the first and second numbers? between the second and third numbers?*

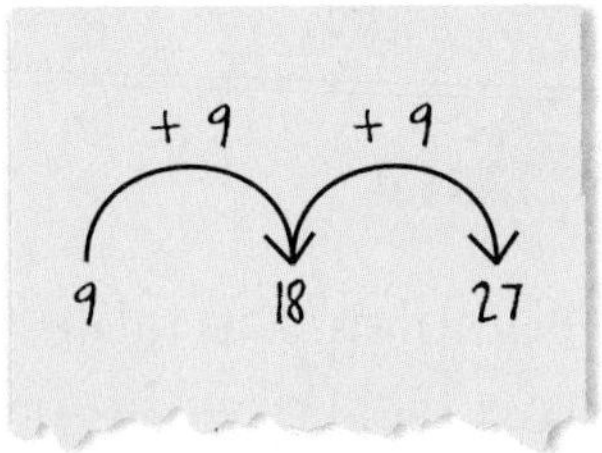

- Choose computation methods.

I can ***use mental math*** *to find the next 3 numbers.*

2. Laurie needs to rent a power sander. The table below shows the charges for renting various tools.

Tool Rental Charges

Tool	Cost per Hour
Power saw	$9
Power sander	$8
Electric drill	$6

Let *h* represent the number of hours Laurie rents the sander. Which expression could be used to represent the amount of money she will need to pay?

A. $8 + *h* **C.** $8 ÷ *h*

B. $8 × *h* **D.** $8 − *h*

Think It Through

I need to find an expression that can be used to find how much Laurie will pay to rent a sander. The text tells me that h represents the number of hours Laurie rents the sander. The table tells me the cost per hour. I can draw a picture to show the main idea.

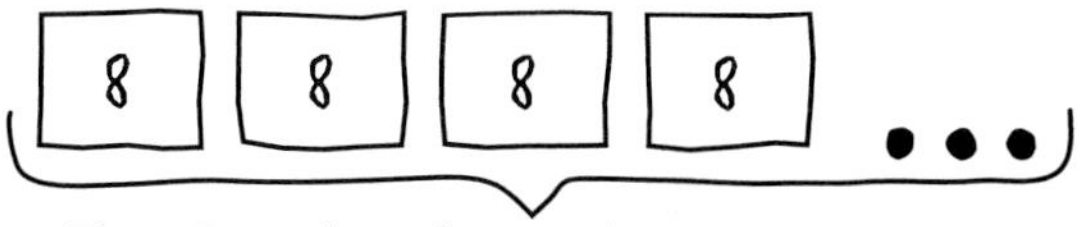

Then I need to choose the expression that matches my picture. For this problem I don't have to compute anything.

Now it's your turn.

For each problem, describe a plan for finding the answer.

3. Kevin is making cheese omelettes. He is following this recipe.

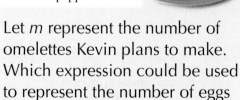

Cheese Omelettes

3 eggs
1/2 cup milk
1 tablespoon butter
1/4 cup cheddar cheese
salt and pepper

Let *m* represent the number of omelettes Kevin plans to make. Which expression could be used to represent the number of eggs Kevin will need?

A. 3 − *m* **C.** 3 ÷ *m*

B. 3 + *m* **D.** 3 × *m*

4. The table below shows the number of plastic bugs that come in *Kritters* games. It also shows how many games are needed to have that many bugs.

Bugs in *Kritters* Games

Kritters games	1	2	3	4
Number of plastic bugs	6	12	18	24

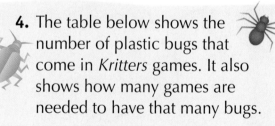

How many bugs are in 7 games?

A. 42 **C.** 30

B. 36 **D.** 6

Chapter 3

Key Vocabulary and Concept Review

Array sounds like "arrangement."

*An **array** is an arrangement of objects in equal rows. (p. 124)*

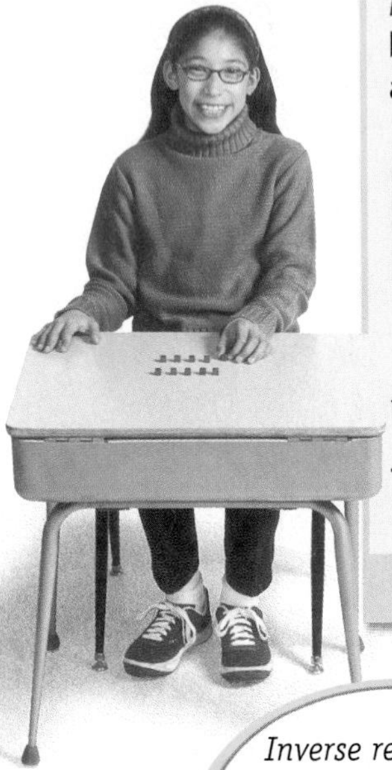

Self Check

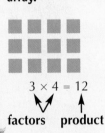

Use models, patterns, and properties to find products. (Lessons 3-1, 3-2, 3-3, 3-4)

Multiplication can be modeled by an **array.**

3 × 4 = 12

factors **product**

Multiples have patterns.

1 × 11 = 11
2 × 11 = 22
3 × 11 = 33
4 × 11 = 44
5 × 11 = 55

Here are some important properties.

Zero Property of Multiplication	4 × 0 = 0
Identity Property of Multiplication	9 × 1 = 9
Commutative Property of Multiplication	7 × 3 = 3 × 7
Distributive Property	6 × 5 = (5 × 5) + (1 × 5)

1. Find 8 × 6, 3 × 12, and 7 × 10.

We're identical twins.

*The **Identity Property of Multiplication** says that a number stays the same when you multiply it by 1. (p. 129)*

Inverse reminds me of the word "reverse."

***Inverse operations** undo each other. (p. 286)*

Self Check

Think about fact families and stories when you divide. (Lessons 3-6, 3-7, 3-8, 3-9, 3-10)

Write a division story for 14 ÷ 2. Then solve the problem.

Mr. Iverson has 14 toys for 2 children. How should he **divide** them up?

Think: What number times 2 equals 14?

▢ × 2 = 14
7 × 2 = 14

Each child should get 7 toys.

Multiplication and division are **inverse operations.** This is shown in a fact family.

7 × 2 = 14   14 ÷ 2 = 7
2 × 7 = 14   14 ÷ 7 = 2

14 ÷ 2 = 7

dividend **divisor** **quotient**

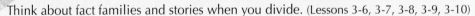

2. Write a division story for 32 ÷ 8. Then solve the problem.

My puzzle book gives the solutions at the back.
The **solution** to an equation is the number that makes it true. (p. 166)

Self Check

Expressions, equations, and tables are used to solve problems. (Lessons 3-12, 3-13, 3-14)

Evaluate $(n + 2) \div 3$ for $n = 25$.

Substitute 25 for n. Work inside the parentheses first.

$(n + 2) \div 3$
↓
$(25 + 2) \div 3$
↓
$27 \div 3 = 9$

Complete the table and write the rule.

In	3	2	8	6	m
Out	15	10	40		

Rule: Multiply by 5.

In	3	2	8	6	m
Out	15	10	40	**30**	**5m**

Solve $4y = 24$.

Try 3. Does $4 \times 3 = 24$? *No.*
Try 7. Does $4 \times 7 = 24$? *No.*
Try 6. Does $4 \times 6 = 24$? *Yes.*

The **solution** is $y = 6$.

3. Evaluate $(k - 3) \times 8$ for $k = 7$ and solve $a \div 8 = 6$.

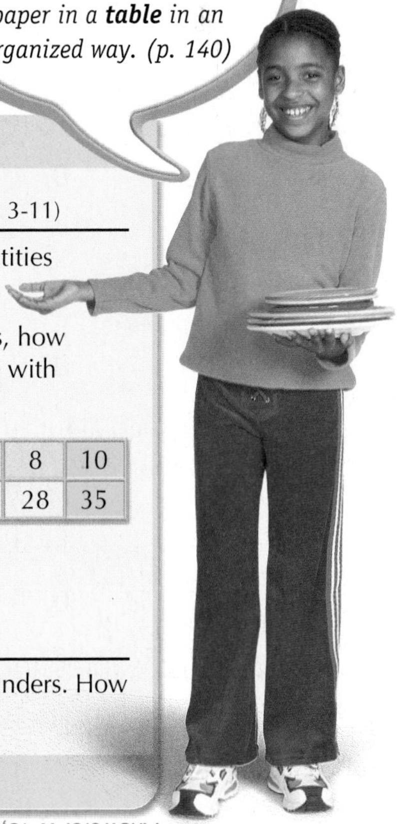

At home, I put dishes on a table in an organized way.
In math, I put information on paper in a **table** in an organized way. (p. 140)

Self Check

Look for hidden questions or make a table to solve problems. (Lessons 3-5, 3-11)

Sometimes you need to answer the hidden question before you solve the problem.

Two slices of bread are needed for each sandwich. How much bread do you need for 5 turkey sandwiches and 3 ham sandwiches?

Answer the hidden question: What is the total number of sandwiches? $3 + 5 = 8$

Then solve the problem. $8 \times 2 = 16$

You need 16 slices of bread.

Make a **table** when quantities change using a pattern.

If 2 pies contain 7 apples, how many pies can you make with 35 apples?

Pies	2	4	6	8	10
Apples	7	14	21	28	35

You can make 10 pies.

4. Each binder costs \$3. Curtis bought 4 yellow binders and 2 green binders. How much did he spend for the binders?

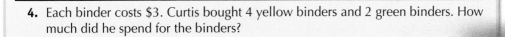

Answers: 1. 48; 36; 70 2. Accept all reasonable stories; 4 3. 32; 48 4. \$18

Chapter Test

MULTIPLE CHOICE

Choose the correct letter for each answer.

1. Which number sentence is equal to $5 + 5 + 5 + 5 = 20$?

A. $5 \times 5 = 20$ **C.** $20 - 5 = 5$

B. $4 \times 5 = 20$ **D.** $20 + 5 = 25$

2. What is the product of 8 and 6?

A. 2 **C.** 48

B. 14 **D.** 56

3. Use breaking apart to find 4×12.

A. 8 **C.** 40

B. 16 **D.** 48

4. You put the same number of roses into 4 vases. If you use a total of 36 roses, how many are in each vase?

A. 8 **C.** 32

B. 9 **D.** 40

5. Find $42 \div 6$.

A. 5 **C.** 7

B. 6 **D.** 8

6. What is the quotient of 24 divided by 8?

A. 2 **C.** 4

B. 3 **D.** 5

7. Evaluate the expression $5m$, for $m = 6$.

A. 11 **C.** 40

B. 30 **D.** 56

8. Which of the following is NOT part of the same fact family?

A. $2 \times 3 = 6$

B. $6 - 3 = 3$

C. $6 \div 2 = 3$

D. $3 \times 2 = 6$

TEST TALK

Think It Through

- I should **look for words like not or except.**
- I need to **read each answer choice carefully.**

9. Find $4 \div 0$.

A. 0 **C.** 4

B. 1 **D.** cannot be done

10. Which multiplication property says that two numbers can be multiplied in any order and the product is the same?

A. Distributive Property

B. Identity Property

C. Commutative Property

D. Zero Property

11. Mr. Levin bought 8 CDs. Each CD cost \$12. How much did he spend in all?

A. \$20 **C.** \$84

B. \$60 **D.** \$96

12. In $20 \div 4 = 5$, what is 4 called?

A. quotient **C.** divisor

B. dividend **D.** factor

FREE RESPONSE

Evaluate each expression for $x = 8$.

13. $3x$

14. $x \div 2$

15. $72 \div x$

16. $11x$

Solve each equation by testing these values for n: 2, 3, 4, 5, and 6.

17. $7 \times n = 35$

18. $54 \div n = 9$

Find each product.

19. 4×3

20. 9×9

21. 0×12

22. 7×11

23. 8×8

24. 10×6

Find each quotient.

25. $18 \div 6$

26. $49 \div 7$

27. $32 \div 4$

28. $72 \div 6$

29. $80 \div 8$

30. $56 \div 7$

31. Mrs. Allen planted 6 apple trees in each row of her orchard. Draw a picture and write an expression you could use to find the number of apple trees in n rows. Then use your expression to find the number of apple trees in 5 rows.

32. Complete the table. Write the rule.

Week	1	2	3	4	n
Deposit	$10	$20	$30		

Writing in Math

33. Write a multiplication story for 7×3.

34. Write and answer the hidden question or questions. Then solve the problem.

Tommy bought 4 comic books, and Brenda bought 5 comic books. Each comic book costs $3. How much money did they spend altogether?

TEST TALK

Think It Through

- **Look for key facts and details** to tell what the problem is asking.
- **Identify the sequence of events** to find the hidden question.

35. Make a table to solve this problem.

A party favor store sells packs that contain 6 invitations and 8 envelopes. A customer bought enough packs to get 40 envelopes. How many invitations did the customer get?

Cumulative Review and Test Prep

Number and Operation

MULTIPLE CHOICE

1. What is the value of the underlined digit in $9\underline{8},752$?

A. 8 ten-thousands

B. 8 thousands

C. 8 hundreds

D. 8 tens

2. What is the quotient of $72 \div 9$?

A. 6 **C.** 8

B. 7 **D.** 9

3. Which of the following is NOT part of the same fact family?

A. $3 \times 4 = 12$ **C.** $12 \div 3 = 4$

B. $12 - 4 = 3$ **D.** $4 \times 3 = 12$

FREE RESPONSE

4. Write these numbers in order from greatest to least.

4,838 4,383 4,883 4,833

5. William earned $28.50 for doing chores. He spent $12 on a pizza and $2.50 on a magazine. How much money did he have left?

Writing in Math

6. Explain how to use an array to show the product of 7×5.

TEST TALK

Think It Through
I can **draw pictures** to model problems.

Geometry and Measurement

MULTIPLE CHOICE

7. Which of these figures appear to be congruent?

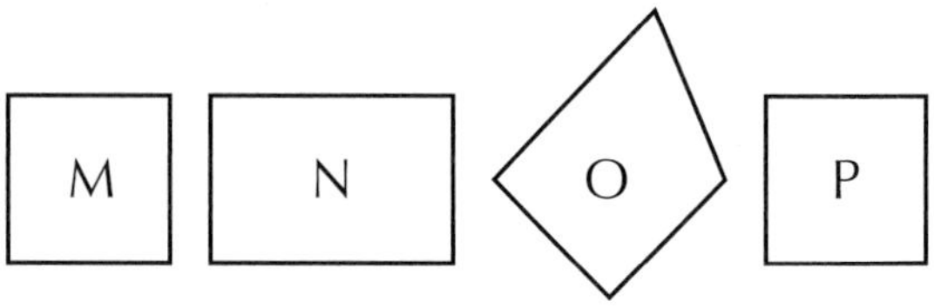

A. O and P

B. M and N

C. P and M

D. N and O

8. Which of the following is NOT a metric unit used to measure length?

A. meter **C.** centimeter

B. liter **D.** kilometer

9. How many angles are in a triangle?

A. 1 **C.** 3

B. 2 **D.** 4

FREE RESPONSE

10. What solid figure has 6 square faces, 12 edges, and 8 corners?

11. Juanita was 30 minutes late to the soccer game. The game started at 4:00 P.M. At what time did she get to the game?

Writing in Math

12. Explain the difference between a triangle and a square.

Data Analysis and Probability

MULTIPLE CHOICE

13. On which color is the spinner most likely to stop?

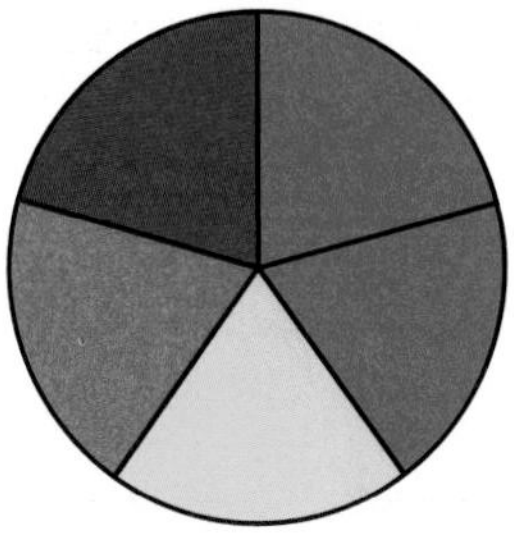

A. green

B. yellow

C. red

D. purple

14. If you spin the spinner above, what is the probability that it will stop on red?

A. $\frac{1}{4}$ **C.** $\frac{1}{3}$

B. $\frac{1}{5}$ **D.** $\frac{4}{5}$

FREE RESPONSE

Use the grid for 15–17.

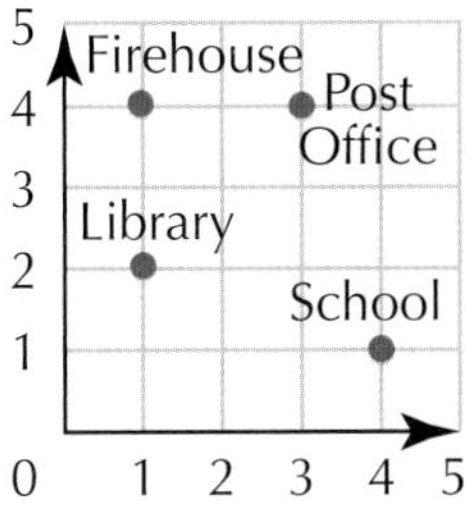

15. Which building is located at point (1, 2)?

16. Starting at the post office, Tom walked 2 units left and 2 units down. Which building did he reach?

Writing in Math

17. Describe how to get from the firehouse to the post office. Be sure to tell which directions to move and how many units.

Algebra

MULTIPLE CHOICE

18. Evaluate the expression $9m$ for $m = 7$.

A. 2 **C.** 63

B. 16 **D.** 97

19. Solve $56 \div n = 8$ by testing these values for n: 3, 4, 7, and 8.

A. $n = 3$ **C.** $n = 7$

B. $n = 4$ **D.** $n = 8$

20. Bryant had 25 baseball cards. He gave several to his brother. Which expression models this situation?

A. $25 - n$ **C.** $25 + n$

B. $n - 25$ **D.** $25 \div n$

FREE RESPONSE

21. What is the rule?

In	18	16	14	12
Out	9	8	7	6

22. Miranda planted a 3-foot tall tree. The next year it was 5 feet tall. The year after that it was 7 feet tall. If this pattern continues, how tall will Miranda's tree be 10 years after she planted it?

> **TEST TALK**
>
> **Think It Through**
>
> I need to **read the problem carefully** and **look for patterns.**

Writing in Math

23. Explain how to evaluate the expression $(30 + 6) \div 4$.

Reteaching

Set 3-1 (pages 124–127)

Write an addition sentence and a multiplication sentence.

7 + 7 + 7 = 21

3 × 7 = 21

Remember you can multiply when adding the same number over and over.

1. 

2. 

Set 3-2 (pages 128–131)

Find 6 × 0.

When you multiply any number by 0, the product is 0.

6 × 0 = 0

Remember you can change the order of the factors when you multiply.

1. 8 × 9 **2.** 3 × 7

3. 6 × 1 **4.** 2 × 0

5. 5 × 5 **6.** 0 × 1

Set 3-3 (pages 132–135)

Find 7 × 8 using breaking apart.

7 groups of 8 equals 5 groups of 8 and 2 groups of 8.

7 × 8 = (5 × 8) + (2 × 8)

= 40 + 16

= 56

Remember you can use breaking apart to remember multiplication facts.

1. 6 × 4 **2.** 4 × 9

3. 7 × 3 **4.** 8 × 7

5. 4 × 4 **6.** 6 × 6

7. 6 × 8 **8.** 4 × 7

Set 3-4 (pages 136–137)

Find 6 × 12 using breaking apart.

6 groups of 12 equals 6 groups of 10 and 6 groups of 2.

6 × 12 = (6 × 10) + (6 × 2)

= 60 + 12

= 72

Remember you can use patterns or breaking apart to multiply.

1. 5 × 10 **2.** 11 × 3

3. 4 × 11 **4.** 12 × 2

5. 10 × 9 **6.** 12 × 6

7. 10 × 10 **8.** 11 × 11

Set 3-5 (pages 140–141)

How do you make a table to solve a problem?

On the average, Griffin jogs 3 blocks every 8 minutes. How many minutes will it take Griffin to jog 15 blocks?

- Set up the table and enter known data in the table.
- Look for a pattern. Extend the table.
- Find the answer in the table.

Blocks	3	6	9	12	15
Minutes	8	16	24	32	40

It will take 40 minutes for Griffin to jog 15 blocks.

Remember you can make a table to solve a problem.

1. Marlene reads 6 pages in her book each night. Her mother reads 9 pages in her book. How many pages will Marlene's mother have read when Marlene has finished reading 48 pages?
2. Tucker uses 8 ounces of pet food to feed his pet hamsters each day. How many days will it take Tucker to use a 64-ounce bag of food?

Set 3-6 (pages 146–147)

Phillipe is setting up 6 chairs in each row. He has set up 18 chairs so far. How many rows has he made?

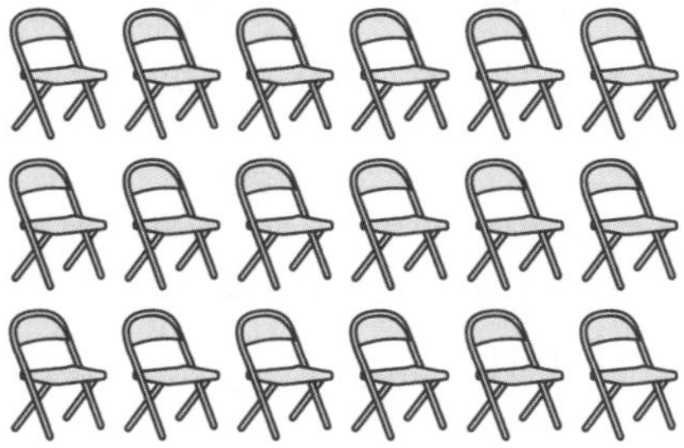

18 ÷ 6 = 3

Remember you can think about sharing or repeated subtraction to divide.

1. The soccer club has 24 balls for 8 teams to share equally. How many balls should each team get?
2. Maureen has 27 feet of rope for the picnic. How many 9-foot jump ropes can she make?

Set 3-7 (pages 148–149)

Write a fact family for 4, 5, and 20.

$4 \times 5 = 20$

$5 \times 4 = 20$

$20 \div 4 = 5$

$20 \div 5 = 4$

Remember a fact family shows all the related facts for a set of numbers.

Write a fact family for each set of numbers.

1. 2, 6, 12
2. 3, 8, 24
3. 5, 5, 25
4. 9, 4, 36

Set 3-8 (pages 150–151)

Find 63 ÷ 7.

What number times 7 equals 63?

9 × 7 = 63

So, 63 ÷ 7 = 9

Remember you can use multiplication facts to help remember division facts.

1. 45 ÷ 9 **2.** 42 ÷ 6

3. 32 ÷ 4 **4.** 63 ÷ 9

5. 35 ÷ 7 **6.** 56 ÷ 7

Set 3-9 (pages 152–153)

Find 9 ÷ 9 and 5 ÷ 1.

Any number divided by itself, except 0, is 1. So, 9 ÷ 9 = 1.

Any number divided by 1 is that number. So, 5 ÷ 1 = 5.

Remember zero divided by any number is zero, but you cannot divide by zero.

1. 3 ÷ 1 **2.** 4 ÷ 4

3. 0 ÷ 6 **4.** 7 ÷ 7

5. 5 ÷ 1 **6.** 3 ÷ 3

Set 3-10 (pages 154–155)

Write a story for 16 ÷ 2.

Think of division as sharing.

Sarah is putting 16 lemons equally in two bags. How many lemons is she putting in each bag?

Remember multiplication and division stories describe real situations.

Write a multiplication or division story for each number fact. Solve.

1. 6 × 4 **2.** 7 × 5 **3.** 10 ÷ 2

Set 3-11 (pages 156–157)

How can you use hidden questions to solve the problem?

Answer the hidden questions first. Then solve the problem.

Kara and Karl spent $3 each to go to the Zoo and $7 each to go to the water park. How much more did it cost for both of them to go to the water park than the zoo?

$7 − $3 = $4

2 × $4 = $8

Remember some problems involve more than one step.

Write and answer the hidden question or questions. Then solve the problem.

1. Last month, Amy spent $12 on movie tickets. Her brother Ali, spent $9. Each ticket costs $3. How many tickets did they buy in all?

2. Jane and Maria made several 5-mile bike rides. Last week, Jane biked 15 miles and Maria biked 20 miles. How many more rides did Maria make than Jane.

Set 3-12 (pages 160–163)

Evaluate $7k$ for $k = 9$.

Substitute 9 for k. Then do the computation.

$7k$

7×9

$7 \times 9 = 63$

When $k = 9$, $7k = 63$.

Remember to do the computation inside the parentheses first.

Evaluate each expression.

1. $8m$ for $m = 3$

2. $\frac{k}{2}$ for $k = 10$

3. $5n$ for $n = 8$

4. $\frac{28}{y}$ for $y = 4$

5. $\frac{t}{6}$ for $t = 0$

6. $\frac{x}{5}$ for $x = 55$

Evaluate $7 \times (k - 4)$ for each value of k.

7. $k = 7$ **8.** $k = 5$ **9.** $k = 4$

Set 3-13 (pages 164–165)

Complete the table. Write the rule.

In	3	4	6	9	n
Out	12	16	24		

Think: $4 \times 3 = 12$, $4 \times 4 = 16$
$4 \times 5 = 20$, and $4 \times 6 = 24$.

A rule is multiply by 4.

$4 \times 9 = 36$

In	3	4	6	9	n
Out	12	16	24	36	$4n$

Remember a rule must fit all the numbers in the table.

Complete the table. Write the rule.

1.

In	7	21	35	42	n
Out	1	3	5		

2.

In	72	54	45	27	n
Out	8	6	5		

3.

In	1	4	7	10	n
Out	5	20	35		

Set 3-14 (pages 166–167)

Solve $36 \div n = 4$ by testing these values for n: 6, 9.

Try $n = 6$: Does $36 \div \mathbf{6} = 4$? *No*

Try $n = 9$: Does $36 \div \mathbf{9} = 4$? *Yes*

The solution to the equation is $n = 9$.

Remember the solution makes the equation true.

Solve each equation by testing these values for m: 3, 4, 6, and 8.

1. $5m = 20$

2. $24 \div m = 4$

Solve each equation by testing these values for n: 2, 3, 4, and 6.

3. $6n = 36$

4. $12 \div n = 3$

5. $15 \div n = 5$

6. $7n = 21$

More Practice

Set 3-1 (pages 124–127)

Write an addition sentence and a multiplication sentence for each picture.

1. 

2. 

3. 

4. Three players each scored 4 goals. How many goals were scored altogether?

Set 3-2 (pages 128–131)

1. 5×7 2. 8×2 3. 7×0 4. 2×6

5. 4×8 6. 1×3 7. 2×9 8. 5×8

9. **Algebra** Find the missing number. Tell which property can help you. $5 \times 6 = \square \times 5$

Set 3-3 (pages 132–135)

1. 3×8 2. 8×4 3. 6×3 4. 6×8

5. The new computer lab has 4 rows of computers with 6 computers in each row. How many computers are in the new lab?

4×6=24

Set 3-4 (pages 136–137)

1. 10×6 2. 12×3 3. 5×11 4. 7×10

5. 12×8 6. 10×6 7. 11×12 8. 10×9

9. Mr. Bird is exactly 6 feet tall. What is his height in inches?

Set 3-5 (pages 140–143)

Copy and complete the table to solve the problem. Write the answer in a complete sentence.

1. Tyrone can type 9 words on his computer each minute. How many minutes will it take him to type 54 words?

Minutes	1	2	3	4
Words typed	9	18		

2. Amanda can wrap 6 packages in one hour. How many packages can she wrap in 4 hours?

Hours	1	2	3	4
Packages	6	12		

3. It takes Terrence 3 minutes to walk each block on his way home from school. If he lives 5 blocks from school, how long does it take him to walk home?

Block	1	2	3	4
Minutes	3	6		

Set 3-6 (pages 146–147)

Write a division sentence to solve each problem.

1. One can holds 3 tennis balls. How many cans are needed to hold 15 balls?
2. Taylor has 40 stamps to put on 5 pages in his stamp collection. How many stamps should he put on each page if he wants the same number of stamps on each page?

Set 3-7 (pages 148–149)

Copy and complete each fact family.

1. $9 \times \square = 18$ $\quad 18 \div 2 = \square$
   $\square \times \square = 18$ $\quad 18 \div \square = \square$
2. $7 \times \square = 56$ $\quad 56 \div 7 = \square$
   $\square \times \square = 56$ $\quad 56 \div \square = \square$
3. $6 \times \square = 48$ $\quad 48 \div 8 = \square$
   $\square \times \square = 48$ $\quad 48 \div \square = \square$
4. $8 \times \square = 32$ $\quad 32 \div 8 = \square$
   $\square \times \square = 32$ $\quad 32 \div \square = \square$

Write a fact family for each set of numbers.

5. 5, 9, 45
6. 1, 10, 10
7. 9, 9, 81
8. 6, 7, 42
9. 3, 9, 27
10. 8, 9, 72

Chapter 3

More Practice

Set 3-8 (pages 150–151)

1. $8 \div 2$ **2.** $24 \div 4$ **3.** $14 \div 7$ **4.** $36 \div 9$

5. $5\overline{)50}$ **6.** $3\overline{)12}$ **7.** $6\overline{)36}$ **8.** $8\overline{)56}$

9. $4\overline{)16}$ **10.** $35 \div 5$ **11.** $16 \div 2$ **12.** $7\overline{)56}$

13. $9\overline{)54}$ **14.** $3\overline{)24}$ **15.** $48 \div 8$ **16.** $42 \div 6$

17. A table in the school library has space for 4 students. How many tables are needed for a class of 20 students?

Set 3-9 (pages 152–153)

1. $9 \div 1$ **2.** $0 \div 5$ **3.** $2 \div 2$ **4.** $8 \div 0$

5. $1\overline{)4}$ **6.** $1\overline{)0}$ **7.** $5\overline{)10}$ **8.** $7\overline{)28}$

9. Five friends want to share 5 tacos equally. How many tacos should each friend get?

Set 3-10 (pages 154–155)

Use the data in the table to write multiplication or division stories for each number sentence.

Craft Beads

Color	Blue	Yellow	Green	Black
Number in Each Bag	8	5	6	3

1. $3 \times 5 = 15$ **2.** $2 \times 8 = 16$ **3.** $24 \div 3 = 8$ **4.** $30 \div 6 = 5$

Set 3-11 (pages 156–157)

Write and answer the hidden question or questions. Then solve the problem. Write your answer in a complete sentence.

1. Olga made 4 clown decorations and Leo made 5 lion decorations. Each decoration used 3 balls of cotton. How many balls of cotton did they use in all?

2. Steve and Marie made several 2-mile walking trips to the store. Last week, Steve walked 8 miles and Marie walked 12 miles. How many more trips did Marie make than Steve?

3. Tyrone bought 3 packages of pens and 2 packages of pencils. There are 4 pens in each package and 5 pencils in each package. How many more pens than pencils did Tyrone buy?

Set 3-12 (pages 160–163)

Evaluate each expression for $n = 8$.

1. $n \div 4$ **2.** $6n$ **3.** $\frac{40}{n}$ **4.** $0 \div n$

Evaluate each expression for $n = 7$.

5. $8n$ **6.** $\frac{49}{n}$ **7.** $\frac{n}{7}$ **8.** $4n$

Evaluate each expression for $n = 10$.

9. $n \div 5$ **10.** $\frac{0}{n}$ **11.** $(n - 5) \times 3$ **12.** $(n \div 2) - 3$

Evaluate each expression.

13. $4 \times (m - 5)$ for $m = 12$ **14.** $11 - (2k)$ for $k = 3$ **15.** $(n \div 3) + 5$ for $n = 27$

16. Write an expression for the number of oranges in each bag when 12 oranges are put in b bags.

Set 3-13 (pages 164–165)

Copy and complete each table. Write the rule.

1.

In	6	15	24	30	n
Out	2	5	8		

2.

In	0	1	5	7	n
Out	0	9	45		

3. Copy and complete the table at the right to represent the pattern in the figures below. Describe the pattern in words and write a rule.

Figure					n
Hexagons					

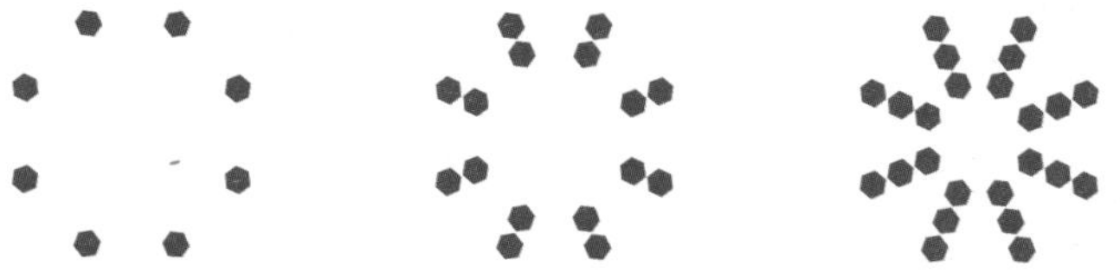

Figure 1 Figure 2 Figure 3

Set 3-14 (pages 166–167)

Solve each equation by testing these values for n: 2, 3, 8, 9.

1. $3n = 27$ **2.** $8 \div n = 4$ **3.** $16 \div n = 8$

4. $4n = 32$ **5.** $9n = 72$ **6.** $9 \div n = 3$

7. Ken put 24 markers into holders with the same number of markers in each. Each holder contained 6 markers. Solve the equation $24 \div h = 6$ to find how many holders Ken used.

CHAPTER 4

Time, Data, and Graphs

DIAGNOSING READINESS

A Vocabulary
(grade 3)

Choose the best term from the box.

1. A __?__ is used to tell time.
2. An analog clock always has a __?__ hand and an __?__ hand.
3. A __?__ uses pictures or symbols to show information.
4. A __?__ uses bars to show information.

Vocabulary

- **clock** *(gr. 3)*
- **hour** *(gr. 3)*
- **minute** *(gr. 3)*
- **bar graph** *(gr. 3)*
- **pictograph** *(gr. 3)*

B Finding Patterns
(pages 10, 90)

Look for a pattern. Find the next three numbers.

5. 6, 12, 18
6. 4, 8, 12
7. 150, 250, 350
8. 500, 600, 700
9. 48, 50, 52
10. 45, 50, 55
11. 25, 50, 75
12. 30, 32, 34

What number is halfway between

13. 40 and 50?
14. 600 and 800?
15. 12 and 16?
16. 200 and 400?
17. How many hundreds are in 538?
18. 480 = ▢ tens

Do You Know...

How fast do tsunamis move in deep water?

You will find out in Lesson 4-15.

C Ordering Numbers
(pages 16–19)

Order the numbers from least to greatest.

19. 3, 8, 4, 7, 9

20. 12, 18, 10, 14

21. 21, 12, 25, 27

22. 42, 47, 45, 52

23. 132, 123, 321

24. 576, 765, 657

25. 248, 252, 276, 284, 225, 267

26. 678, 876, 682, 732, 741, 887

27. 1,246, 1,319, 1,209, 1,240

28. A number is greater than 38 and less than 45. The tens digit and the ones digit are the same. What is the number?

D Subtracting Whole Numbers *(pages 82–85)*

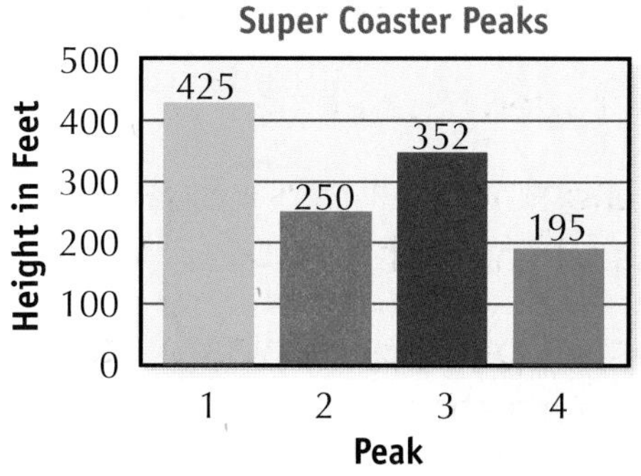

Use the bar graph. How much higher is

29. Peak 1 than Peak 3?

30. Peak 3 than Peak 4?

31. Peak 2 than Peak 4?

32. Peak 3 than Peak 2?

Key Idea
Time can be shown and read in different ways.

Vocabulary
- analog clock
- digital clock
- A.M.
- P.M.

TEST TALK

Think It Through
I know that I can use the words **quarter** for 15 minutes and **half** for 30 minutes

Telling Time

WARM UP

Write the number that is ten more than each number.

1. 24
2. 56
3. 32
4. 98

LEARN

How do you say the time?

A clock that displays time using hands is called an **analog clock.** A clock that displays time using numbers is called a **digital clock.**

Analog Clock

Digital Clock

You can say the same time in different ways. You can write the time as 4:45 or 15 minutes to 5.

Remember, **A.M.** includes times from midnight until noon, and **P.M.** includes times from noon until midnight. Five minutes past midnight is 12:05 A.M. and five minutes past noon is 12:05 P.M.

Example A

Estimate the time.

It's about ten after 9 or 9:10.

Example B

Julie eats breakfast at 7:30. Is it A.M. or P.M.?

Julie eats breakfast in the morning, between midnight and noon. So she eats breakfast at 7:30 A.M.

Talk About It

1. What is something you might do at 12:05 P.M.? 12:05 A.M.?

CHECK

For another example, see Set 4-1 on p. 246.

Write the time shown on each clock in two ways.

1. 

2. 

3. 

4. 

5. **Number Sense** Write a reasonable time for going to school. Include A.M. or P.M.

PRACTICE

For more practice, see Set 4-1 on p. 250.

A Skills and Understanding

Write the time shown on each clock in two ways.

6. 

7. 

8. 

9. 

10. **Number Sense** Write a reasonable time for playing outside. Include A.M. or P.M.

B Reasoning and Problem Solving

11. Tia has soccer practice on Tuesdays and Thursdays at 4:00. Is her practice at 4:00 A.M. or 4:00 P.M.?

12. **Reasoning** The digits displayed in the clock at the right are increasing in consecutive order. List 4 other times when this is true.

13. **Estimation** Write the time shown on each clock in Exercises 7 and 9, to the nearest 5 minutes and to the nearest half hour.

14. **Writing in Math** Could the time 5:63 be displayed on a digital clock? Explain.

Mixed Review and Test Prep

Take It to the NET
Test Prep
www.scottforesman.com

15. **Algebra** Evaluate 24 ÷ n when $n = 4$.

16. **Algebra** Solve the equation $5a = 35$ by testing these values for a: 6, 7, 8, 9.

A. $a = 6$ **B.** $a = 7$ **C.** $a = 8$ **D.** $a = 9$

Key Idea
Time can be measured in different units.

Vocabulary
- second
- minute
- hour
- century
- millennium
- day
- week
- month
- year
- leap year
- decade

Materials
- clock or watch with a second hand

Units of Time

WARM UP

Write $>$ or $<$ for each ●.

1. 35 ● 12 + 12 + 12
2. 7 × 3 ● 24

LEARN

Activity

How much time is it?

a. Watch a clock or wristwatch for one minute. The second hand goes all the way around the face of the clock each minute.

b. Work with a Partner Without looking at a clock or wristwatch, try to guess when one minute has passed. Ask your partner to watch the clock and tell you how much time actually passed.

c. How close was your estimate of a minute to an actual minute?

d. With your partner, make a list of things you can do in

one second. one minute. one hour.

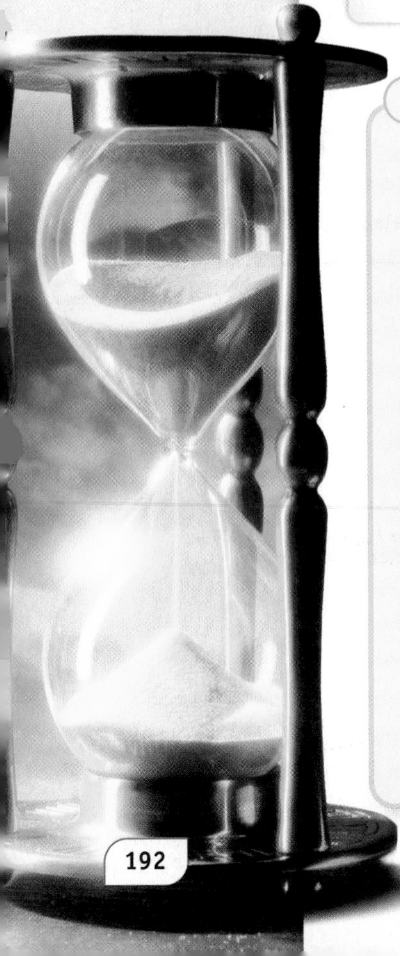

Example A

It takes about one **second** to

clap your hands once.

It takes about one **minute** to

feed your fish.

It takes about one **hour** to

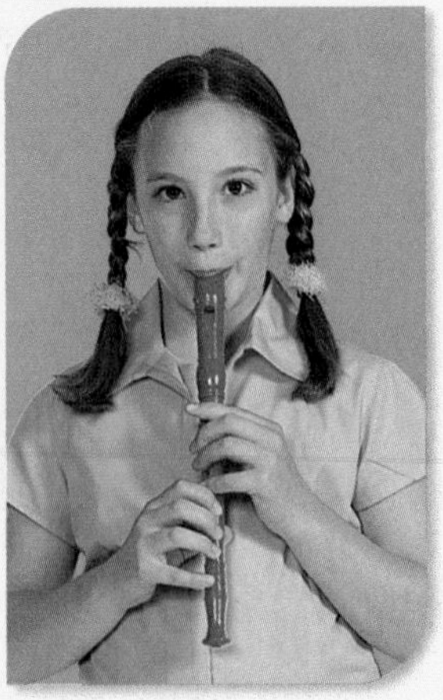

take a music lesson.

Example B

About one **century** ago...

About one **millennium** ago...

How do you compare time?

A second is a very short unit of time and a millennium is a very long unit of time.

You can use the information in the table at the right to compare different amounts of time.

Units of Time

1 minute = 60 seconds
1 hour = 60 minutes
1 **day** = 24 hours
1 **week** = 7 days
1 **month** = about 4 weeks
1 **year** = 52 weeks
1 year = 12 months
1 year = 365 days
1 **leap year** = 366 days
1 **decade** = 10 years
1 century = 100 years
1 millennium = 1,000 years

Example C

Which is longer, 2 years or 100 weeks?

According to the table, 1 year = 52 weeks.

1 year = 52 weeks
2 years = 104 weeks

$$\begin{array}{r} 52 \\ +\ 52 \\ \hline 104 \end{array}$$

104 weeks > 100 weeks
2 years > 100 weeks

So, 2 years is longer than 100 weeks.

Talk About It

1. Have you lived a decade? Tell how you decided.

CHECK

For another example, see Set 4-2 on p. 246.

Write >, <, or = for each ⬤.

1. 23 months ⬤ 2 years **2.** 10 decades ⬤ 1 century **3.** 125 seconds ⬤ 2 minutes

4. Number Sense You are telling a friend the time of a movie. Should you tell her the time to the nearest day, hour, minute, or second?

PRACTICE

For more practice, see Set 4-2 on p. 250.

A Skills and Understanding

Write >, <, or = for each ●.

5. 36 years ● 3 decades **6.** 15 weeks ● 3 months **7.** 1 minute ● 65 seconds

8. 52 weeks ● 360 days **9.** 3 weeks ● 21 days **10.** 1 millennium ● 9 centuries

11. Number Sense About how long does it take to brush your teeth?

B Reasoning and Problem Solving

Math and Social Studies

12. A **score** is 20 years. How many years is four score and seven years?

Write >, <, or = for each ●.

13. 4 score and 7 years ● 5 decades

14. 4 score and 7 years ● 87 years

15. **Writing in Math** Is the explanation below correct? If not, tell why and write a correct response.

> Which is longer 725 days or 2 years? Explain how you decided.
>
> 365 days = 1 year
> 725 > 720
> 725 days > 2 years
> 725 days is longer.
>
> $$\begin{array}{r} \overset{1}{365} \\ +\ 365 \\ \hline 720 \end{array}$$

President Lincoln was 52 years old at the time of his inauguration.

TEST TALK

Think It Through
I should **check if my answer is complete.**

C Extensions

There are 4 **time zones** in the continental United States. They are the Eastern, Central, Mountain, and Pacific time zones. If it is 8:00 P.M. in the Eastern time zone, it is 7:00 P.M. Central time, 6:00 P.M. Mountain time, and 5:00 P.M. Pacific time.

16. What time zone do you live in?

It is 9:00 A.M. Central time. What time is it in the

17. Pacific time zone? **18.** Eastern time zone? **19.** Mountain time zone?

Mixed Review and Test Prep

Take It to the NET
Test Prep
www.scottforesman.com

20. Write a reasonable time for soccer practice to start. Include A.M. or P.M.

21. Algebra Solve $n \div 4 = 8$ by testing these values for n: 4, 12, 28, 32.

A. $n = 4$ **B.** $n = 12$ **C.** $n = 28$ **D.** $n = 32$

Enrichment

Roman Numerals

In ancient Rome, letters were used to represent numbers. The letters Romans used are shown in the chart at the right. Today, some watches and clocks use Roman numerals.

I	=	1
V	=	5
X	=	10
L	=	50
C	=	100
D	=	500
M	=	1,000

Most Roman numeral clocks show the number 4 as IIII, not IV.

Here is how to read Roman numerals. When the letters are the same, add their values.

III = 1 + 1 + 1 = 3

When a letter is to the right of a letter of greater value, add the values of the letters.

VIII = 5 + 3 = 8

When a letter is to the left of a letter of greater value, subtract the values of the letters.

IX = 10 − 1 = 9

Write the time shown on each clock.

1. 

2. 

3. 

4. 

Find the value of each set of Roman numerals.

5. LX **6.** XL **7.** CXXXVI **8.** MMIV

Key Idea
You can use time to tell how long something takes.

Vocabulary
• elapsed time

Elapsed Time

LEARN

How do you find and use elapsed time?

Annette started a triathlon at 10:45 A.M. and finished at 1:05 P.M. How long did it take her to run the race?

Elapsed time is the amount of time that passes between the beginning of an event and the end of the event.

WARM UP

Find 15 more than each number.

1. 25 2. 30 3. 60

Find 15 less than each number.

4. 35 5. 40 6. 60

Triathlon

Swim	1.5 km
Bike	40 km
Run	10 km

TEST TALK

Think It Through
I can solve elapsed time problems in **more than one way.**

Example A

Find the elapsed time from 10:45 A.M. to 1:05 P.M.

Jen's Way

10:45 A.M. to 11:00 A.M. is 15 minutes.
11:00 A.M. to 1:00 P.M. is 2 hours.
1:00 to 1:05 is 5 minutes.
That's 2 hours and 20 minutes in all.

Ken's Way

10:45 A.M. to 12:45 P.M. is 2 hours.
12:45 to 1:05 is 20 minutes.
That's 2 hours and 20 minutes in all.

Example B

Jerry completed a triathlon in 2 hours and 22 minutes. He started at 11:50 A.M. What time did he finish?

Jerry started at 11:50 A.M. Count 2 hours to 1:50 P.M. Count 10 minutes to 2:00 P.M. Count another 12 minutes to 2:12 P.M.

Jerry finished the race at 2:12 P.M.

Talk About It

1. In Example A, how long did it take Annette to complete the triathlon?

2. Could you solve the problem in Example B another way? Explain.

Take It to the NET
More Examples
www.scottforesman.com

CHECK

For another example, see Set 4-3 on p. 246.

Find each elapsed time.

1. Start: 10:00 A.M.
   Finish: 1:35 P.M.
2. Start: 2:35 P.M.
   Finish: 5:55 P.M.
3. Start: 8:22 P.M.
   Finish: 11:10 P.M.
4. Write the time the clock will show in 30 minutes.
5. **Number Sense** Is the elapsed time from 4:35 P.M. to 8:25 P.M. more or less than four hours? Explain.

PRACTICE

For more practice, see Set 4-3 on p. 250.

A Skills and Understanding

Find each elapsed time.

6. Start: 4:00 P.M.
   Finish: 7:42 P.M.
7. Start: 11:15 A.M.
   Finish: 1:45 P.M.
8. Start: 5:52 P.M.
   Finish: 7:17 P.M.

Write the time each clock will show in 45 minutes.

9. 
10. 
11. 
12. 

13. **Number Sense** Is the elapsed time from 3:40 P.M. to 5:50 P.M. more or less than two hours? Explain.

B Reasoning and Problem Solving

14. In practice, Annette started at 1:45 P.M. and finished at 4:12 P.M. How long did it take her to finish the practice triathlon?
15. **Writing in Math** Jake finished his bike ride at 1:20 P.M. He had ridden for 2 hours and 40 minutes. What time did he start the bike ride? Explain how you found the answer.

Mixed Review and Test Prep

Take It to the NET
Test Prep
www.scottforesman.com

16. Write the time shown on each clock in Exercises 9–12, in two ways.
17. Which of the following is a reasonable amount of time for watching a movie?

    A. 2 days **B.** 2 hours **C.** 2 minutes **D.** 2 seconds

Lesson 4-4

Problem-Solving Skill

Reading Helps!

Comparing and contrasting
can help you with...
writing to compare.

Key Idea
There are specific things you can do to write a good comparison in math.

Writing to Compare

LEARN

How do you write a good comparison?

Bus Stops Two buses travel from the mall to midtown. They travel the same route but do not stop at all of the same places. Write two statements that compare the data in the bus schedules.

STOP	MALL	A	B	C	D	E	F	G	H	MIDTOWN
Bus 101	7:05	–	7:15	7:24	–	7:45	8:00	8:10	8:18	8:30
Bus 102	7:30	7:35	–	7:50	–	–	7:55	8:00	–	8:25

TEST TALK

Think It Through
I must make sure that I have read the information in the table correctly.

Writing a Math Comparison

- Look closely at the data to find how it is alike and how it is different.
- Sometimes you can do calculations and compare results.
- Use contrast words such as *fewer, later, however,* or *but*.

Bus 102 makes fewer stops than Bus 101.

Bus 101 takes 1 hour and 25 minutes to go from the mall to midtown, but Bus 102 takes ony 55 minutes.

✓ Talk About It

1. What other comparison statements could be made using the schedules?
2. Do you think the statement "Bus 102 and Bus 101 begin at the mall and end at midtown" could be used to answer the Bus Stops problem? Explain why or why not.

CHECK

For another example, see Set 4-4 on p. 246.

1. Write two statements comparing the times in the flight schedule.

Flight Number	1176	1177	1178	1179	1180
DEPART San Francisco	11:05 A.M.	12:14 P.M.	1:35 P.M.	2:45 P.M.	4:05 P.M.
ARRIVE Los Angeles	12:32 P.M.	1:43 P.M.	3:02 P.M.	4:16 P.M.	5:35 P.M.

PRACTICE

For more practice, see Set 4-4 on p. 250.

Beach Middle School
Daily Schedule

Class 1	8:15 A.M. to 9:20 A.M.
Class 2	9:25 A.M. to 10:15 A.M.
Class 3	10:20 A.M. to 11:10 A.M.
A Lunch	11:10 A.M. to 11:40 A.M.
B Lunch	11:40 A.M. to 12:10 P.M.
Class 4	12:15 P.M. to 1:05 P.M.
Class 5	1:10 P.M. to 2:00 P.M.
Class 6	2:05 P.M. to 2:55 P.M.

Cinema House
Evening Movie Schedule

		Movie A	Movie B	Movie C
Showing 1	Start	6:05	4:45	5:00
	End	7:35	6:50	6:45
Showing 2	Start	7:55	7:10	7:05
	End	9:25	9:15	8:50
Showing 3	Start	9:45	9:30	9:10
	End	11:15	11:35	10:55

Use the Beach School Daily Schedule for 2–3.

2. Write a statement comparing the time spent for A lunch and the time spent for B Lunch.

3. Write two statements comparing data in the daily schedule.

Use the Cinema House Evening Movie Schedule for 4–5.

4. Write a statement comparing the longest movie and the shortest movie.

5. Write two other statements comparing the data in the Cinema House Schedule.

6. The bar graph at the right shows the amount Katie saved each month from July through December. Write two statements comparing the data in the graph.

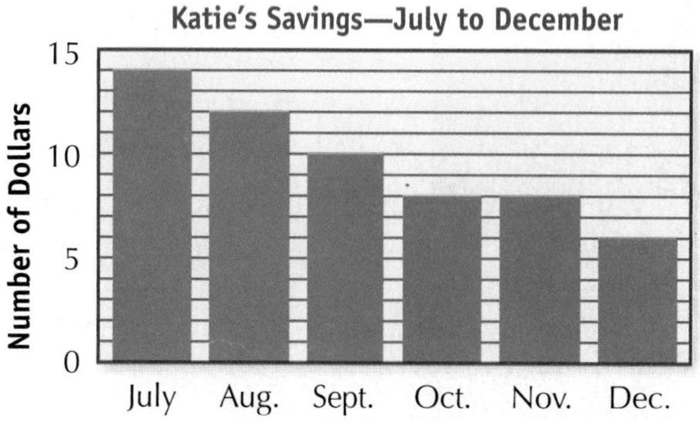

7. Writing in Math Write a problem that can be solved using any of the schedules in this lesson. Solve your problem.

Key Idea
A calendar helps you keep track of days, weeks, and months.

Vocabulary
- ordinal numbers

Calendars

WARM UP

Add 7 to each number.

1. 8 2. 19 3. 4
4. 21 5. 17 6. 24

LEARN

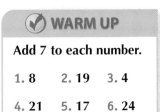

How can a calendar help you solve problems?

Vacation The Arnolds are leaving for vacation on the first Saturday in August. They will be gone two weeks. What date will they return home?

August						
S	M	T	W	T	F	S
			1	2	3	4
5	6	7	8	9	10	11
12	13	14	15	16	17	18
19	20	21	22	23	24	25
26	27	28	29	30	31	

Move down one row on a calendar and you have counted one week or seven days. Move down two rows for two weeks. The Arnolds will return home on August 18.

Numbers like first, sixth, and eighteenth are **ordinal numbers.** Ordinal numbers are used to tell order. August 10 is the second Friday in August.

Example A

What date is one week before August 24?

Find August 24 on the calendar. Count up one row. One week before August 24 is August 17.

Example B

What day of the week is July 30?

July has 31 days. August 1 is on Wednesday. So, July 31 is Tuesday, and July 30 is Monday.

Talk About It

1. How can you use the calendar to find two weeks before August 22?

CHECK ✓

For another example, see Set 4-5 on p. 247.

Use the August calendar on page 200. Find the date

1. two weeks after August 13.

2. of the fifth Friday of August.

3. **Number Sense** How could you find the date one week before August 9, without using a calendar?

PRACTICE

For more practice, see Set 4-5 on p. 251.

A Skills and Understanding

Use the April and May calendars at the right. Find the date

4. two weeks after May 11.

5. one week before April 23.

6. three weeks after April 18.

7. of the third Monday in May.

8. **Number Sense** Find the date two weeks after June 5, without a calendar.

April

S	M	T	W	T	F	S
			1	2	3	4
5	6	7	8	9	10	11
12	13	14	15	16	17	18
19	20	21	22	23	24	25
26	27	28	29	30		

May

S	M	T	W	T	F	S
					1	2
3	4	5	6	7	8	9
10	11	12	13	14	15	16
17	18	19	20	21	22	23
24/31	25	26	27	28	29	30

B Reasoning and Problem Solving

You can use the rhyme at the right to remember the number of days in each month.

Thirty days hath September,
April, June, and November.
All the rest have thirty-one.
Excepting February alone,
Which hath but twenty-eight, in fine,
Till leap year gives it twenty-nine.

9. How many days are there in June?

10. How many months have 31 days?

Use the April and May calendars above for 11–12.

11. Suppose you take an art class that meets every other Friday. The first class is on April 10. What are the next three meeting dates?

12. **Writing in Math** About how many weeks is it from April 18 to May 14? Explain how you decided.

Mixed Review and Test Prep

Take It to the NET
Test Prep
www.scottforesman.com

13. Find the elapsed time from 9:35 A.M. to 7:15 P.M.

14. Which amount of time is longer than 2 years?

A. 21 months **B.** 600 days **C.** 103 weeks **D.** 25 months

Review

Do You Know How?

Do You Understand?

Telling Time (4-1)

Write the time shown on each clock in two ways.

1. 

2. 

A Tell how you could use *before* or *after* to say each time.

B Describe some things you might do at 8:30 A.M. and at 8:30 P.M.

Units of Time (4-2)

Write >, <, or = for each ○.

3. 1 year ○ 11 months

4. 2 days ○ 50 hours

5. 12 months ○ 370 days

C Tell how you decided which amount of time was greater in Exercise 4.

D About how long does a movie last? Explain why you used the units you did.

Elapsed Time (4-3)
Problem-Solving Skill: Writing to Compare (4-4)

6. Find the length of time scheduled for each game.

Saturday's Soccer Schedule

Game	Start	End
A: Under 12	9:00 A.M.	10:15 A.M.
B: Under 14	10:30 A.M.	12:10 P.M.
C: Under 10	12:30 P.M.	1:35 P.M.

E Tell how you found the time scheduled for the Under 14 game.

F Write two statements comparing the times in the soccer schedule.

Calendars (4-5)

Find the date

7. one week after November 12.

8. two weeks after February 9.

9. one week before December 21.

G Tell how you found the date in Exercise 9, without a calendar.

H Why do you need to know how many days are in January to find the date 2 weeks after January 19?

Diagnostic Checkpoint

TEST TALK

Think It Through
For multiple choice items, first **eliminate any unreasonable answers.**

MULTIPLE CHOICE

1. **Estimation** Which of the following could you do in one minute? (4-2)

   A. run a mile **C.** jump rope 20 times

   B. take a bath **D.** mow the lawn

2. Which of the following is NOT a way to say the time on the clock at the right? (4-1)

   A. nine forty-five **C.** quarter of nine

   B. quarter of ten **D.** fifteen minutes before ten

FREE RESPONSE

Write >, <, or = for each ●. (4-2)

3. 7 weeks ● 2 months **4.** 175 seconds ● 3 minutes **5.** 2 days ● 40 hours

For 6–8, use the schedule at the right. (4-3)

How long does it take the train to get from

6. Millville to Watertown? **7.** Trent to Happy?

8. How long does the train stay at Trent?

Millville Express		
Station	**Arrival**	**Departure**
Millville	9:10 A.M.	9:25 A.M.
Watertown	12:18 P.M.	12:35 P.M.
Trent	3:06 P.M.	3:25 P.M.
Happy	5:52 P.M.	6:30 P.M.

Use the June calendar for 9–11. (4-5)

Find the date

9. of the second Monday in June.

10. one week before June 11.

11. two weeks after June 18.

June

S	M	T	W	T	F	S
	1	2	3	4	5	6
7	8	9	10	11	12	13
14	15	16	17	18	19	20
21	22	23	24	25	26	27
28	29	30				

Writing in Math

12. About how long has the United States of America been a country? Give three reasonable estimates using years, decades, and centuries. (4-2)

13. Write two statements comparing the data in the Millville Express schedule. (4-4)

Key Idea
Pictographs use pictures to display data.

Vocabulary
- data
- pictograph
- key

Materials
- grid paper

TEST TALK

Think It Through
I can **read the graph** to compare data.

Pictographs

WARM UP

How many tens in each?

1. 47   2. 85

How many thousands in each?

3. 1,825   4. 7,021

LEARN

How do pictographs display data?

Pieces of information collected are called **data.** A **pictograph** uses pictures or symbols to show data. The **key** tells what quantity each symbol represents.

Daily Calcium Needed

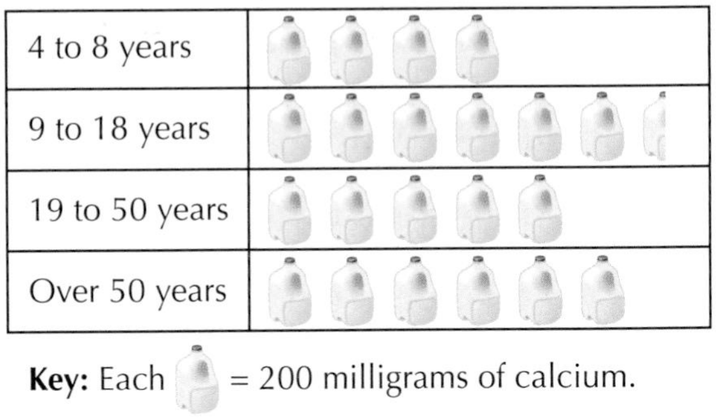

	Example A	Example B
	How much calcium a day do 9- to 18-year olds need?	How much more calcium do 9- to 18-year olds need than 4- to 8-years olds each day?
What You **Think**	Look in the row next to 9 to 18 years. There are 6 complete cartons and half of another one. Count: 200, 400, 600, 800, 1,000, 1,200 The half carton is 100 more. 1,200 + 100 = 1,300	There are two and a half more full cartons of milk next to 9- to 18-years than next to 4- to 8- years. 200 + 200 + 100 = 500
What You **Write**	People who are 9 to 18 years old need 1,300 milligrams of calcium a day.	People who are 9 to 18 years old need 500 more milligrams of calcium a day than people who are 4 to 8 years old.

Talk About It

1. How does the key help you read the pictograph?

CHECK ✓

For another example, see Set 4-6 on p. 247.

How many milligrams of calcium are in

1. 1 cup of milk? **2.** 1 cup of refried beans?

3. About how many more milligrams of calcium are in 8 ounces of fruit-flavored yogurt than one ounce of cheddar cheese?

4. Number Sense If each symbol on a pictograph equals 100 milligrams, how many symbols would you need to show 250 milligrams?

Calcium in Foods

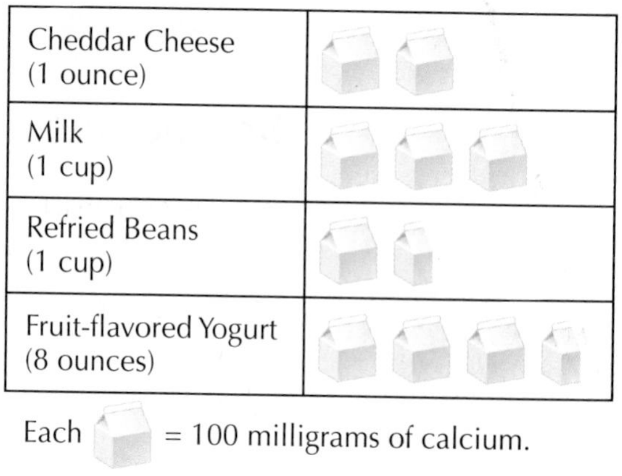

Cheddar Cheese (1 ounce)
Milk (1 cup)
Refried Beans (1 cup)
Fruit-flavored Yogurt (8 ounces)
Each = 100 milligrams of calcium.

PRACTICE

For more practice, see Set 4-6 on p. 251.

A Skills and Understanding

How many people prefer a vacation

5. at a lake? **6.** in the mountains?

7. How many more people prefer to vacation at a theme park than a historic site?

8. Number Sense Do more or less than twice as many people prefer a historic sites vacation than a lake vacation? Explain.

Favorite Vacation Getaways

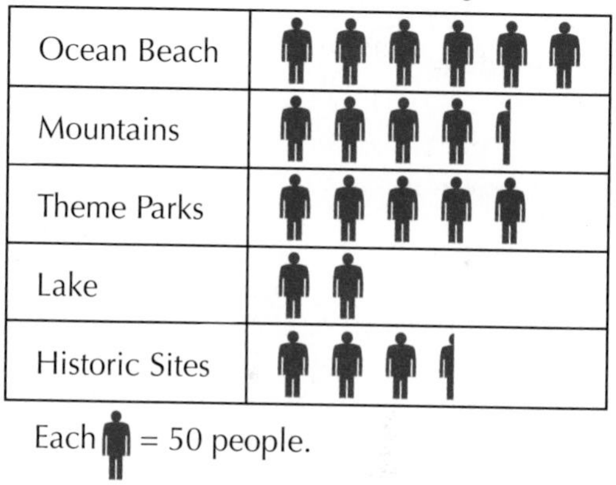

B Reasoning and Problem Solving

9. Use the pictograph on page 204. How much more calcium do people over 50 need than people 19 to 50 years old?

10. Make a pictograph of the data on Summer 2004 Visitors. Let each symbol equal 500 visitors.

11. Writing in Math To make a pictograph of the summer visitors data, explain why you would want each symbol to equal 500 or 1,000 visitors rather than 10 or 100.

Summer 2004 Visitors

Place	Number of Visitors
Sandy Beach	4,000
Rocky Lake	2,500
Colonial City	5,000
Great Water Fall	1,500
Sooner Mountain	3,000

Mixed Review and Test Prep

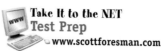

Take It to the NET
Test Prep
www.scottforesman.com

12. If January 16 is on a Friday, what is the date of the next Friday?

13. 48 ÷ 6

A. 6 **B.** 7 **C.** 8 **D.** 9

All text pages available online and on CD-ROM.

Key Idea
A line plot displays data along a number line.

Vocabulary
- line plot
- outlier

TEST TALK

Think It Through
I can **get information from the graph** to answer questions.

Line Plots

WARM UP

What number should be written at each point?

1. *A* 2. *B*

LEARN

How do line plots display data?

A **line plot** displays data along a number line. Each X represents one number in the data. In the line plot below, each X represents one zoo.

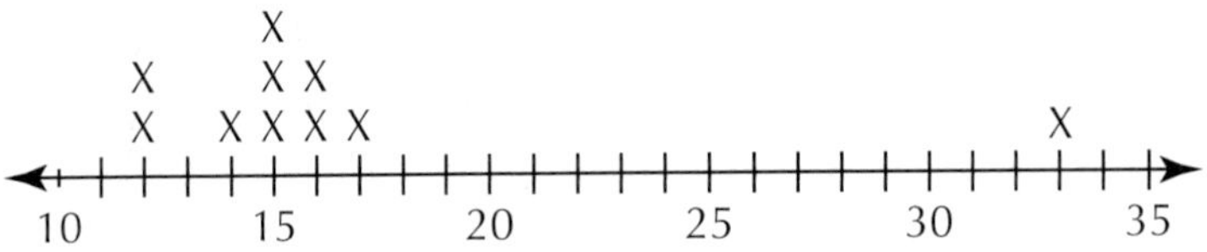

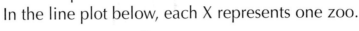

Zoo Budgets in Millions of Dollars

Example A

Read the line plot.

Since there are 2 Xs above the 16, 2 of the zoos have budgets of $16 million.

The most Xs are above the 15, so the most common budget is $15 million.

The greatest budget shown is $33 million and the least budget shown is $12 million.

An **outlier** is a number in a data set that is very different from the rest of the numbers.

Example B

Identify the outlier in the data set shown in the line plot.

In the line plot, the number 33 is far away from the rest of the numbers.

The budget of $33 million is an outlier.

Talk About It

1. **Reasoning** Is there an outlier in the following data set? If so, what is it? Explain.

   17, 25, 29, 18, 32, 4, 25, 29, 25

CHECK ✓

For another example, see Set 4-7 on p. 247.

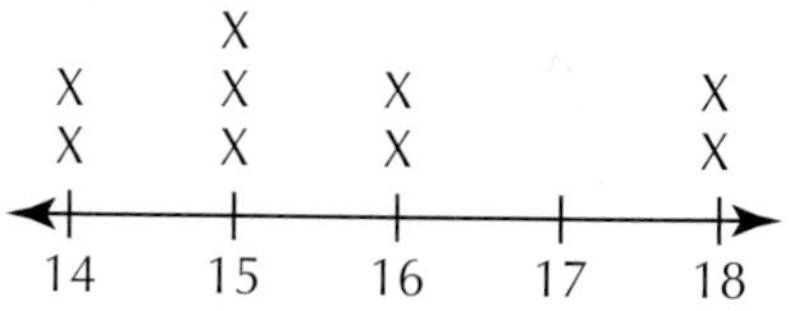

Giraffe Heights in Feet

1. How many of the giraffes are 16 feet tall?
2. What is the most common height of the giraffes?
3. What is the tallest giraffe shown on the line plot?
4. **Number Sense** Is there an outlier in the data set? Explain.

PRACTICE

For more practice, see Set 4-7 on p. 251.

A Skills and Understanding

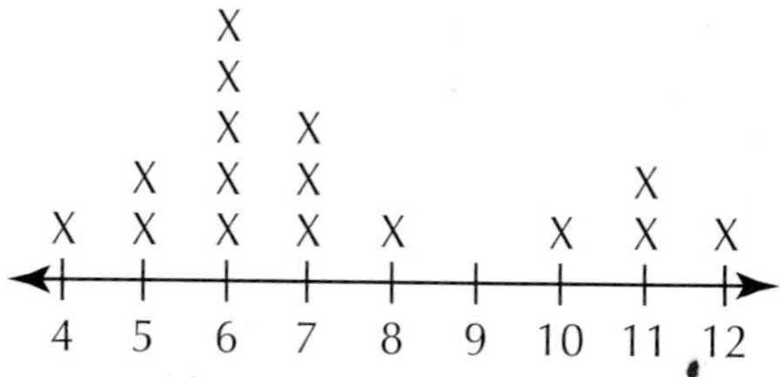

Chin-Ups by Fourth Graders

5. How many fourth graders did 5 chin-ups?
6. How many chin-ups did most fourth graders do?
7. What is the most chin-ups done by a fourth grader?
8. **Number Sense** Suppose another student did chin-ups and that number was added to the line plot. Predict if the number would be more or less than 12. Explain.

B Reasoning and Problem Solving

9. Use the line plot on page 206. How many more zoos have a budget of $15 million than $14 million?

Eighteen states had budgets less than $10 billion in 1998. For 10–11, use the budget data for these states at the right.

10. Make a line plot of the data.
11. **Writing in Math** Is there an outlier in the data set? Explain.

Data File

State Budgets

State	Billions	State	Billions
Alaska	$7	New Hampshire	$4
Delaware	$5	New Mexico	$9
Hawaii	$7	North Dakota	$3
Idaho	$5	Rhode Island	$5
Kansas	$9	South Dakota	$3
Maine	$6	Utah	$9
Montana	$4	Vermont	$3
Nebraska	$6	West Virginia	$8
Nevada	$8	Wyoming	$3

Mixed Review and Test Prep

Take It to the NET
Test Prep
www.scottforesman.com

12. Use the table above. Make a pictograph showing the budgets in Alaska, Idaho, New Mexico, and Vermont. Let each dollar sign symbol equal $1 billion.
13. Round 2,836 to the nearest hundred.

A. 3,000 **B.** 2,900 **C.** 2,800 **D.** 2,700

Key Idea
Data can be organized in bar graphs.

Vocabulary
- bar graph
- scale
- interval

Materials
- grid paper or e tools

Bar Graphs

WARM UP

Round each number to the nearest hundred.

1. 456
2. 623
3. 796
4. 154

LEARN

How do you read a bar graph?

A **bar graph** uses bars to show data.

Numbers that show the units used on a graph are the **scale.**

The **interval** of the scale is 50.

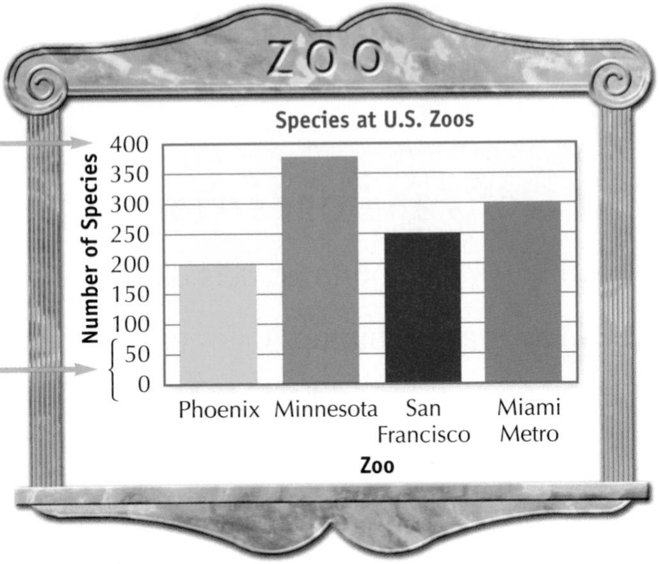

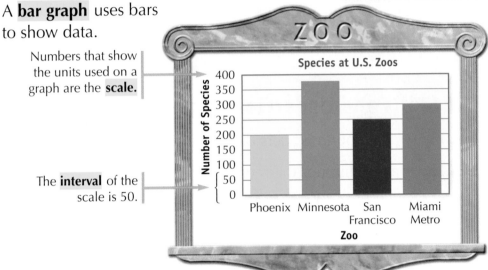

	Example A	Example B
	About how many species of animals are in the Minnesota Zoo?	How many more species are in the Miami Metro Zoo than the Phoenix Zoo?
What You **Think**	The bar above Minnesota Zoo is about halfway between the numbers 350 and 400 on the scale.	Skip count by 50s from the top of the bar above Phoenix Zoo until you are even with the top of the bar above Miami Metro Zoo. Count: 50, 100.
What You **Write**	The Minnesota Zoo has about 375 species of animals.	Miami Metro Zoo has 100 more species of animals than the Phoenix Zoo.

Talk About It

1. What is the interval on the scale in the bar graph above?
2. **Reasoning** How can you decide which zoo has 250 species of animals?

Activity

How do you make a bar graph to display data?

a. Make a bar graph to display the data on animal heights.

Data File

Animal Heights	
Asian Elephant	9 feet
African Elephant	11 feet
Lion	3 feet
Rhinoceros	6 feet

Copy and complete the graph at the right. The first two steps have been done for you.

Step 1: Choose a scale.

Step 2: Draw and label the side and bottom of the graph.

Step 3: Draw a bar on the graph for each animal height in the data file.

Step 4: Give the graph a title. The title should describe the subject of the graph.

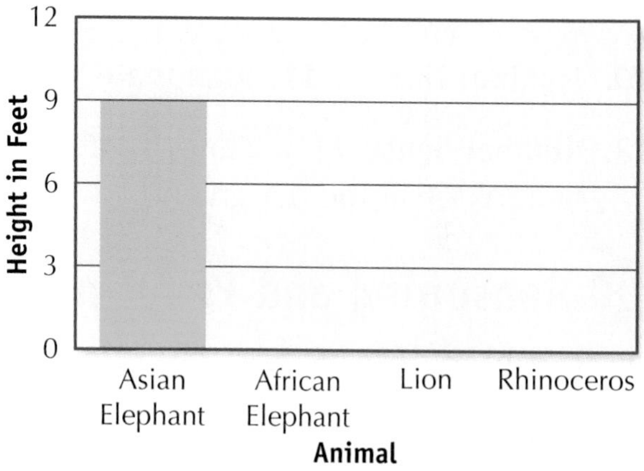

b. Explain how you drew the bar for the

African elephant. lion. rhinoceros.

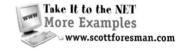

Take It to the NET
More Examples
www.scottforesman.com

CHECK

For another example, see Set 4-8 on p. 248.

Use the bar graph on the right for 1–4.

What is the average lifespan of

1. a dog? **2.** a pig?

3. About how much longer does a lion live than a giraffe?

4. Which animals have the same average life span?

5. Number Sense The average lifespan of a gorilla is 20 years. If you included a gorilla on the graph, would the bar be taller or shorter than the bar for the lion?

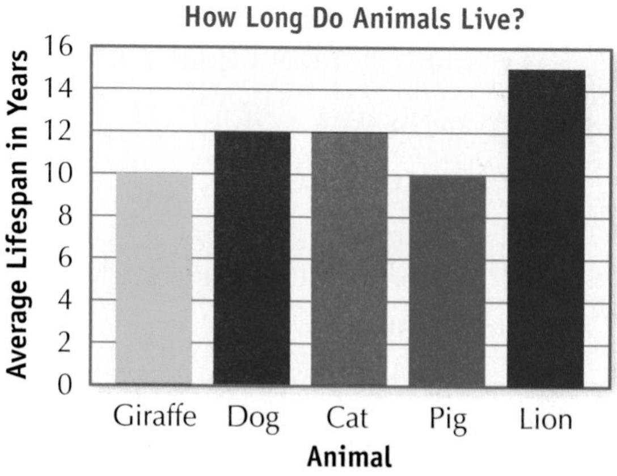

PRACTICE

For more practice, see Set 4-8 on p. 251.

A Skills and Understanding

Use the bar graph on the right for 6–12.

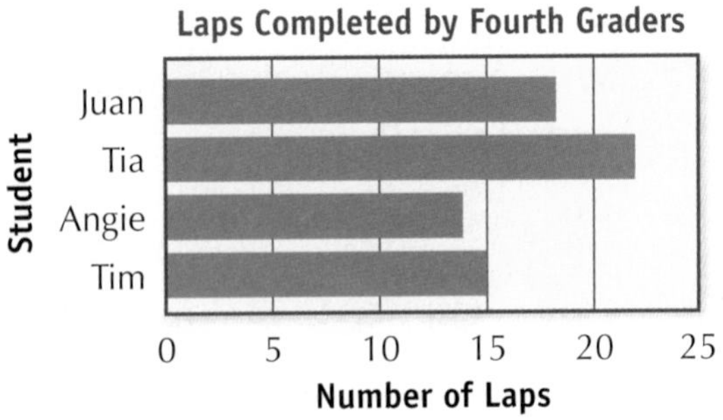

How many laps were completed by

6. Tim? **7.** Juan?

Who completed

8. 14 laps? **9.** 22 laps?

How many more laps were completed by

10. Tia than Tim? **11.** Juan than Angie? **12.** Juan than Tim?

13. Number Sense How can you tell who completed the most laps by looking at the bar graph?

B Reasoning and Problem Solving

14. Use the bar graph on page 208. About how many more species of animals are in the Minnesota Zoo than the San Francisco Zoo?

Math and Music

15. Use the data file at the right. Draw a bar graph. Label the side Number of States and the bottom Number of U.S. Symphony Orchestras.

16. Make a pictograph showing the number of symphonies in Arizona, Illinois, Florida, Ohio, and New York. Let each symbol equal 2 orchestras.

Data File

U.S. Symphony Orchestras

Number	States
7	NY
6	CA, FL
5	OH, TX
3	CO, IL, TN
2	AZ, CT, GA, IN, MI, MN, MO, NC, OK, PA, VA, WA
1	AL, DC, KY, LA, MA, MD, ME, NE, NJ, NM, OR, RI, UT, WI, WV

17. Writing in Math Is the explanation below correct? If not, tell why and write a correct response.

How much more does Lady weigh than Sonny?

Lady weighs one more pound than Sonny because I count up one line from the top of Sonny's bar to the top of Lady's bar.

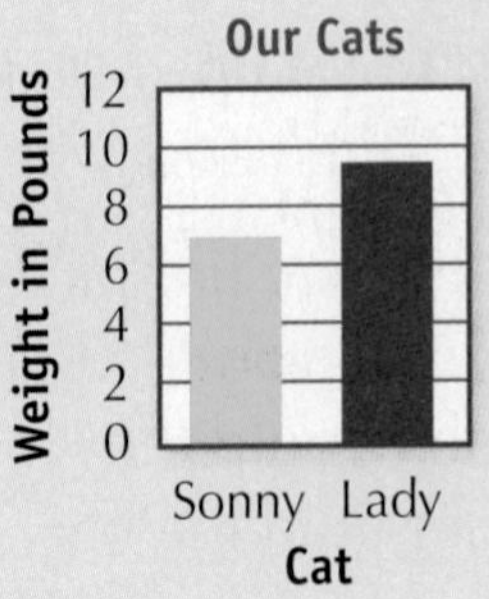

TEST TALK

Think It Through
I should always **check the scale of the graph.**

C Extensions

A **histogram** is a bar graph that shows how many values appear within intervals of the data. Use the histogram on the right for 18–20.

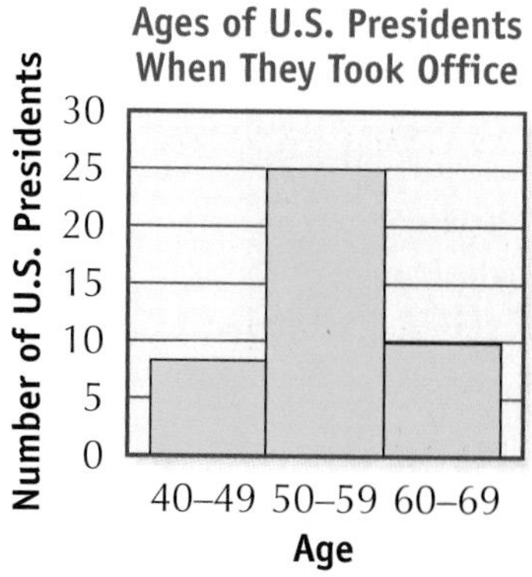

When they took office, how many U.S. Presidents were

18. 50 to 59 years old?

19. 60 to 69 years old?

20. Estimation About how many U.S. Presidents were 40 to 49 years old when they took office?

Mixed Review and Test Prep

Take It to the NET
Test Prep
www.scottforesman.com

21. Use the data file on page 210. Draw a line plot of the data for the number of states with 3 to 7 symphony orchestras.

22. Find the product of 9 and 5.

A. 40 **B.** 45 **C.** 48 **D.** 50

Practice Game

Bar Graph Game

Players: 2–5

Materials: Two number cubes, numbered 1–6
Markers or colored pencils

Players take turns tossing two number cubes. If the sum of the cubes is a multiple of 3, the player draws a bar the length of the sum and tosses the cubes again. Only sums that are multiples of 3 can be used to start a bar. If a multiple of 3 is not tossed, the number cubes are passed to the next player. The first player whose bar crosses line 36 wins the game.

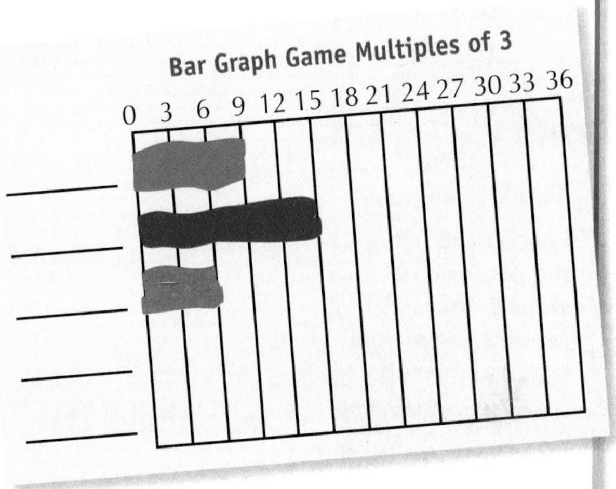

Variation: Players change the target multiple from 3 to 2 or 4.

Algebra

Key Idea

A coordinate grid helps you locate points.

Vocabulary

- coordinate grid
- ordered pair
- plot

Materials

- first-quadrant grid paper or e tools

Graphing Ordered Pairs

WARM UP

What number should be written at each point?

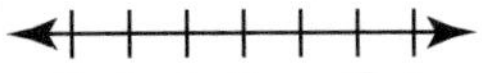

1. *A* **2.** *B* **3.** *C*

LEARN

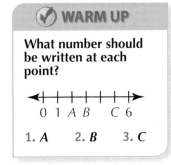

How do you name a point?

Archaeologists search for objects to find out about life in earlier civilizations. A **coordinate grid** allows them to use points to identify the location of objects they find.

An **ordered pair** is a pair of numbers that names a point on a coordinate grid.

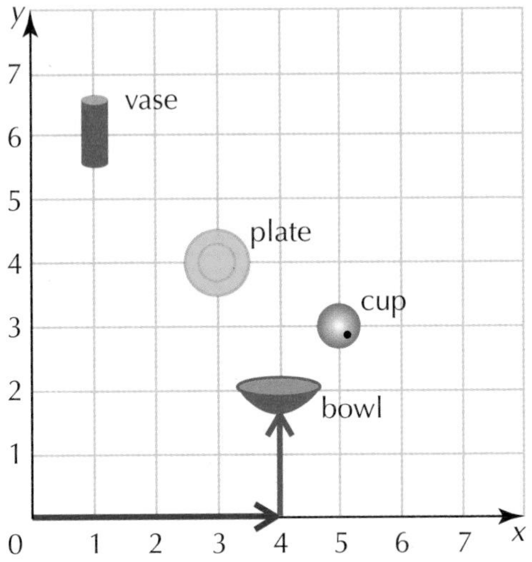

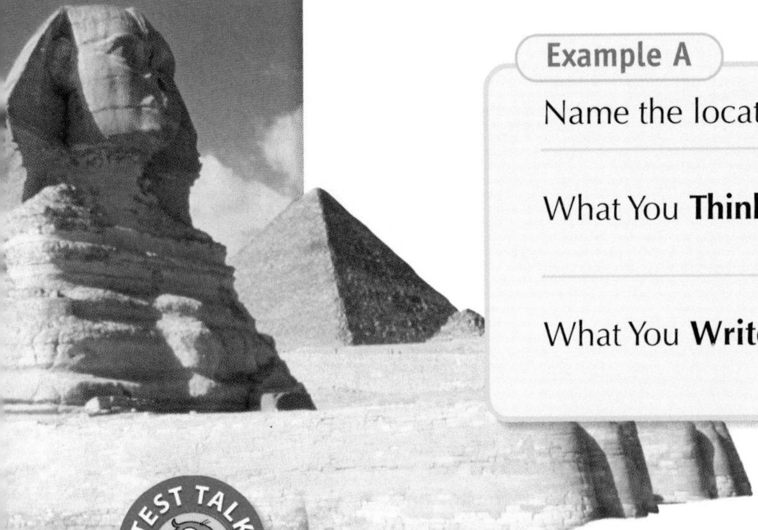

Example A

Name the location of the bowl.

What You **Think**	Start at 0. Move right **4** spaces. Then move up **2** spaces.
What You **Write**	The bowl is at (**4**, **2**).

The first number in an ordered pair tells how far to the right of zero the point is.

Ordered Pair: (4, 2)

The second number in an ordered pair tells how far up from zero the point is.

TEST TALK

Think It Through

I need to **identify the sequence of steps in the process.** Move right first, and then up.

Talk About It

1. After moving right 4 spaces, how far do you need to move up to get to the bowl?

2. Which way do you always move first, right or up?

How do you locate a point using an ordered pair?

Example B

What object is located at the point (3, 4)?

What You **Think**	• Start at 0. Since the first number in the ordered pair is **3**, move right 3 units. • Since the second number in the ordered pair is **4**, move up 4 units
What You **Write**	The plate is located at (3, 4).

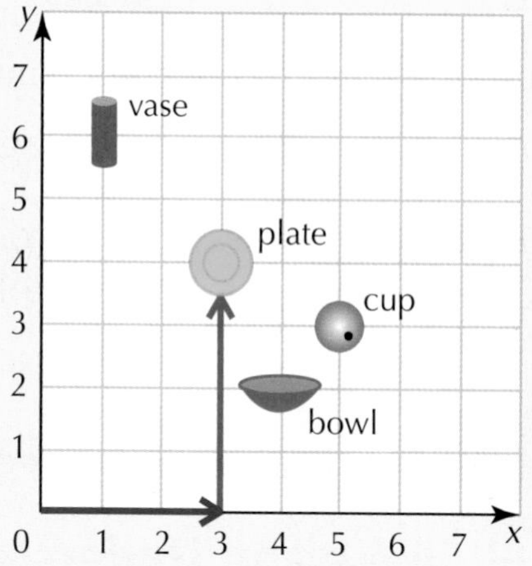

To **plot** a point, locate and mark the point named by an ordered pair on a grid.

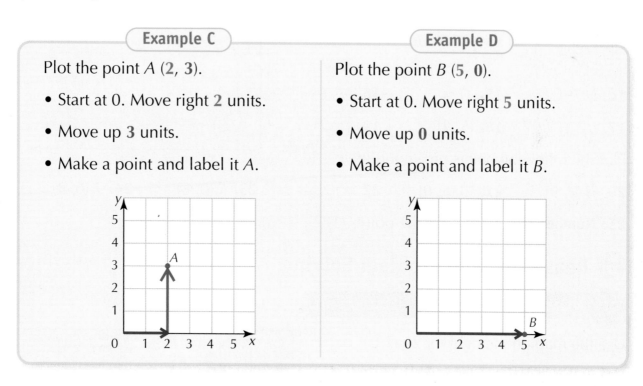

Example C

Plot the point *A* (**2**, **3**).

- Start at 0. Move right **2** units.
- Move up **3** units.
- Make a point and label it *A*.

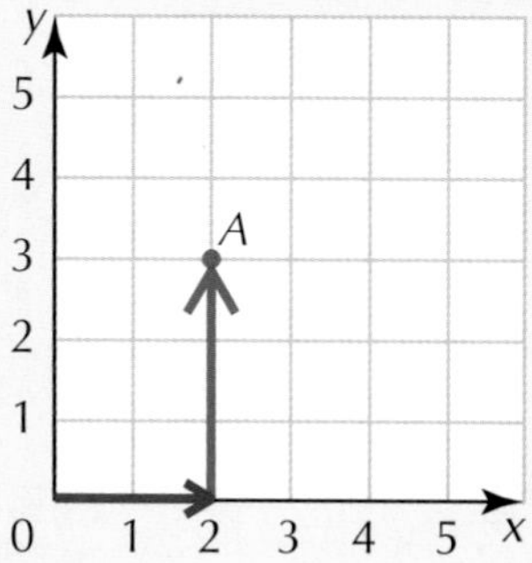

Example D

Plot the point *B* (**5**, **0**).

- Start at 0. Move right **5** units.
- Move up **0** units.
- Make a point and label it *B*.

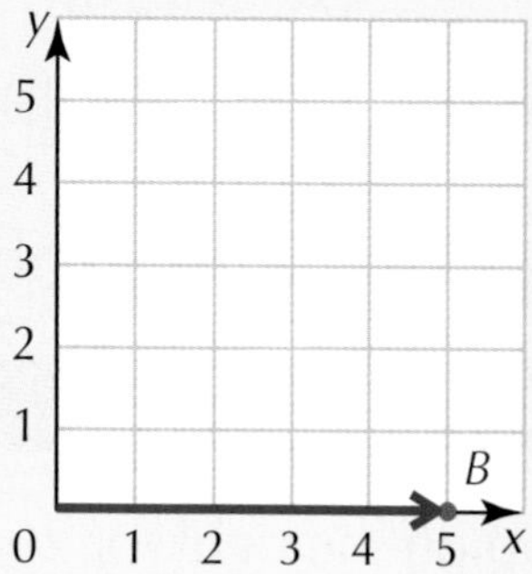

Talk About It

3. What does the 3 in the ordered pair (3, 4) tell you to do? What does the 4 tell you?

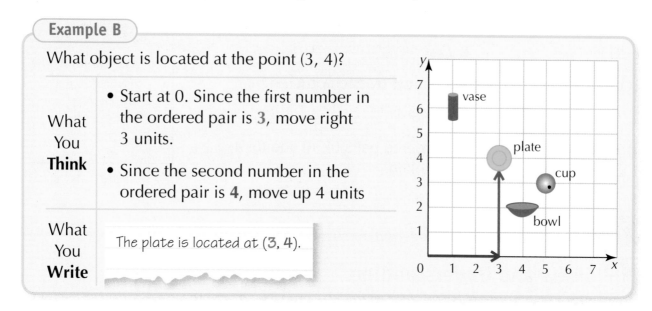

4. In Example B, what object is located at (5, 3)?

Take It to the NET
More Examples
www.scottforesman.com

CHECK

For another example, see Set 4-9 on p. 248.

Name the ordered pair for each point.

1. *B* **2.** *D* **3.** *F*

Give the letter of the point named by each ordered pair.

4. (3, 6) **5.** (2, 4) **6.** (3, 0)

7. Number Sense Do the ordered pairs (4, 6) and (6, 4) name the same point? Explain.

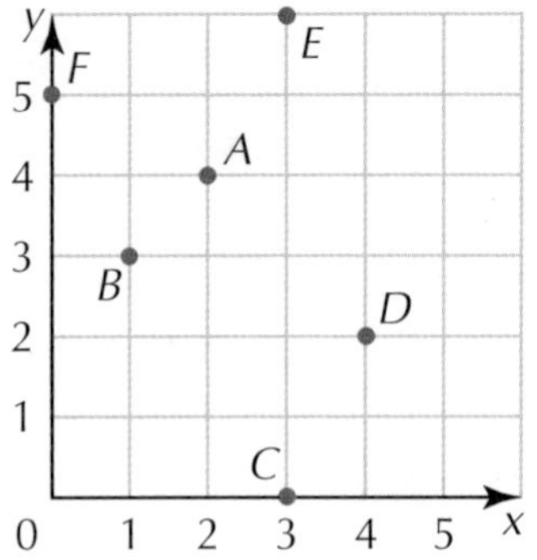

PRACTICE

For more practice, see Set 4-9 on p. 252.

A Skills and Understanding

Name the ordered pair for each point.

8. *B* **9.** *D* **10.** *G*

11. *K* **12.** *M* **13.** *E*

Give the letter of the point named by each ordered pair.

14. (1, 9) **15.** (0, 4) **16.** (7, 6)

17. (8, 3) **18.** (5, 9) **19.** (1, 2)

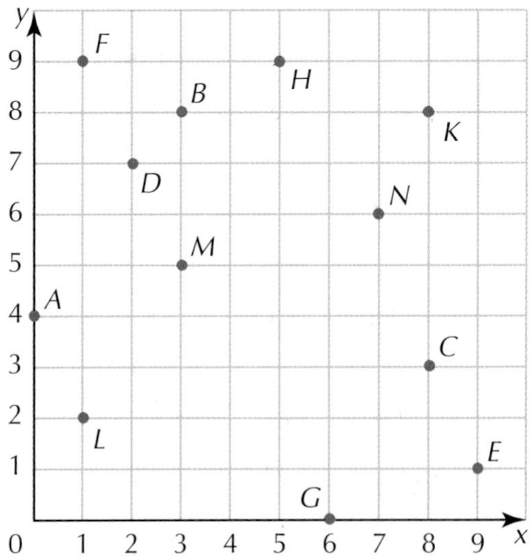

Plot the following points on a coordinate grid.

20. *P* (2, 9) **21.** *Q* (5, 0) **22.** *R* (7, 4) **23.** *S* (0, 8) **24.** *T* (6, 3)

25. Number Sense How are the points (1, 2), (1, 5), and (1, 7) alike?

B Reasoning and Problem Solving

Math and Social Studies

Use the map on the right for 26–29.

Name the ordered pair for the location of

26. the White House. **27.** the Lincoln Memorial.

What is located at

28. (7, 6)? **29.** (8, 3)?

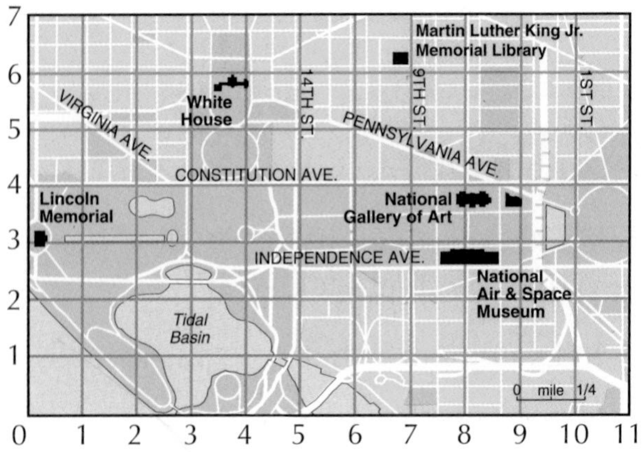

PRACTICE

30. **Writing in Math** Explain how to plot P (2, 1).

C Extensions

Draw a coordinate grid to plot each set of points. Look for a pattern. What do you notice about the points?

31. (1, 3), (2, 6), (3, 9)

32. (2, 4), (3, 5), (4, 6), (0, 2)

33. (1, 6), (2, 7), (4, 9)

TEST TALK

Think It Through

- I need to **get information from the graph.**
- I am **writing to explain** my answer.

Mixed Review and Test Prep

Take It to the NET
Test Prep
www.scottforesman.com

34. Make a pictograph using the data at the right.

35. Write seven and forty-three hundredths in standard form.

A. 7,430 **C.** 7.43

B. 740.30 **D.** 7.043

Data File

Object	Number Found
Vases	5
Plates	3
Bones	4
Spoons	3
Bowls	3

Discovery CHANNEL SCHOOL

Discover Math in Your World

Tug of Water

The moon affects the tides.

Find the elapsed time between first and second high tides.

High Tides Times

	Day	First High Tide	Second High Tide
1.	Friday	2:46 A.M.	3:19 P.M.
2.	Saturday	3:41 A.M.	4:19 P.M.
3.	Sunday	4:39 A.M.	5:23 P.M.
4.	Monday	5:42 A.M.	6:31 P.M.

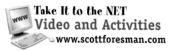

Take It to the NET
Video and Activities
www.scottforesman.com

Algebra

Key Idea
Line graphs help you see changes in data over time.

Vocabulary
- line graph
- trend

Materials
- grid paper or e tools

Line Graphs

LEARN

WARM UP

Draw a coordinate grid and plot each point.

1. *A* (1, 2) 2. *B* (0, 3)
3. *C* (3, 2) 4. *D* (4, 5)

How do you read and interpret a line graph?

A **line graph** connects points to show how data changes over time. The line graph on the right shows the population of the United States from 1790 to 1830, the first five decades of the census.

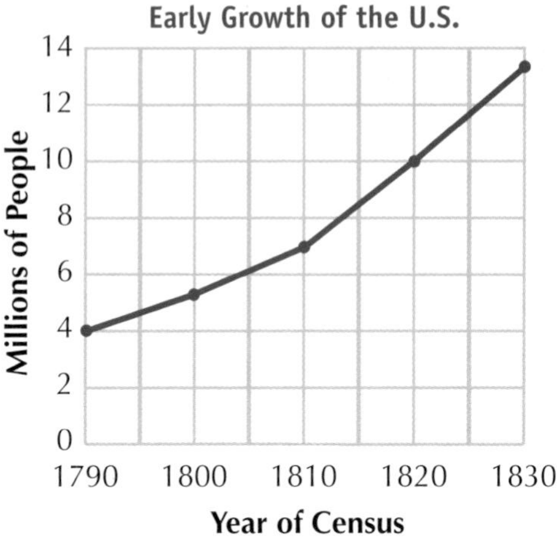

TEST TALK

Think It Through
- I need to **get information from the graph** to answer the questions.
- I **can look for a pattern** to find the trend.

Example A

When was the population of the United States about 6 million?

The grid line for 6 million crosses the graph between 1800 and 1810, at 1805.

The population was about 6 million in 1805.

In a line graph, when the line goes up from left to right, there is an **increase** in the data. When the line goes down, there is a **decrease.** The increase or decrease indicates the **trend** in the data.

Example B

Did the U.S. population increase more between 1790 and 1800 or between 1810 and 1820?

The line between 1810 and 1820 goes up more sharply than the line between 1790 and 1800.

The U.S. population increased more between 1810 and 1820 than between 1790 and 1800.

Example C

What was the trend in the population?

The line generally goes up from left to right.

The trend in the population was to increase.

Talk About It

1. What is the interval on each scale in the graph on page 216?

2. Would you expect the population in 1840 to be more or less than 13 million? Explain.

How do you make a line graph?

Draw a line graph about Marissa's Bike Race.

Data File

Marissa's Bike Race

Minutes from Start	Miles from Finish
0	4
5	3
9	2
14	1
20	0

Example D

STEP 1

Choose an interval for each scale. Draw and label the side and bottom of the graph. Put time on the bottom.

STEP 2

Plot a point for each row in the data file. Plot (0, 4), (5, 3), and so on.

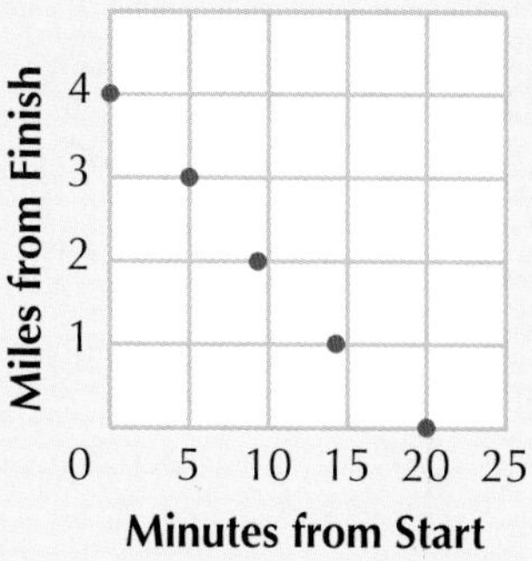

STEP 3

Draw a line from each point to the next one, in order.

STEP 4

Give the graph a title. The title should describe the subject of the graph.

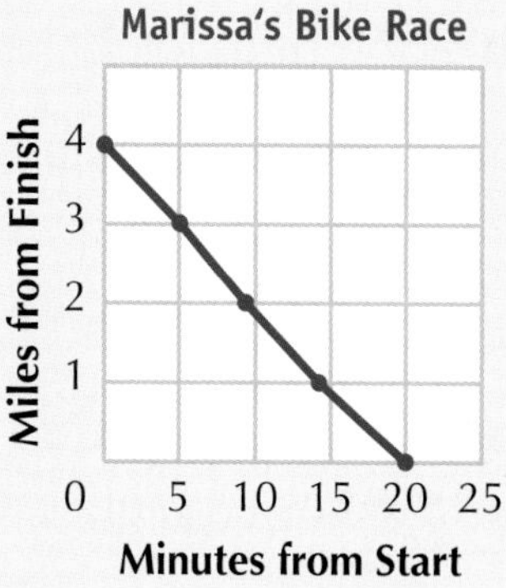

Talk About It

3. What is the interval on each scale in the graph?

4. Explain how to plot the point for Marissa's distance 9 minutes after the race started.

Take It to the NET
More Examples
www.scottforesman.com

CHECK

For another example, see Set 4-10 on p. 248.

Use the line graph on the right for 1–4.

About how far did the canoe travel in the first

1. four minutes? **2.** 12 minutes?

3. About how long did it take the canoe to travel 10,000 feet?

4. Reasoning What is the trend in the data?

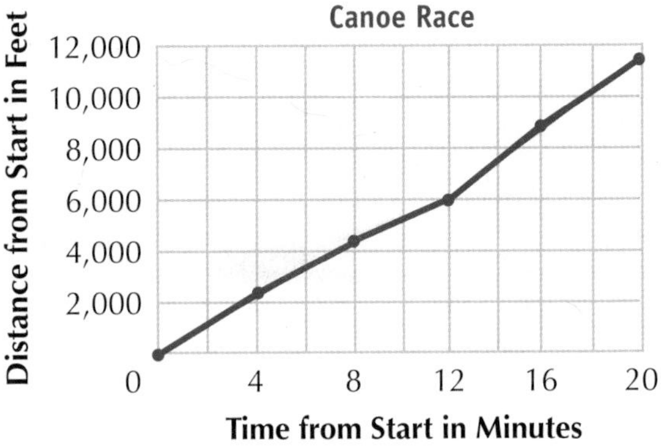

PRACTICE

For more practice, see Set 4-10 on p. 252.

A Skills and Understanding

5. Earl is a Beagle puppy. Draw a line graph about Earl's first year. Put age along the bottom of the graph.

6. Reasoning Use the line graph on page 217. What is the trend in the data? Did Marissa's distance from the finish increase or decrease over time?

Earl's First Year

Age in Months	Mass in Kilograms
0	Less than 1
2	3
4	7
6	9
8	10
10	11
12	12

B Reasoning and Problem Solving

Math and Science

Use the graph at the right for 7–12.

About how many species of mammals were listed as endangered

7. in 1996? **8.** in 2000? **9.** in 1982?

10. Estimation About when were 60 species of mammals listed as endangered?

11. Did the number of species of mammals listed as endangered increase more between 1988 and 1992 or between 1992 and 1996?

12. Reasoning What is the trend in the data?

13. Writing in Math Explain how a line graph shows changes over time.

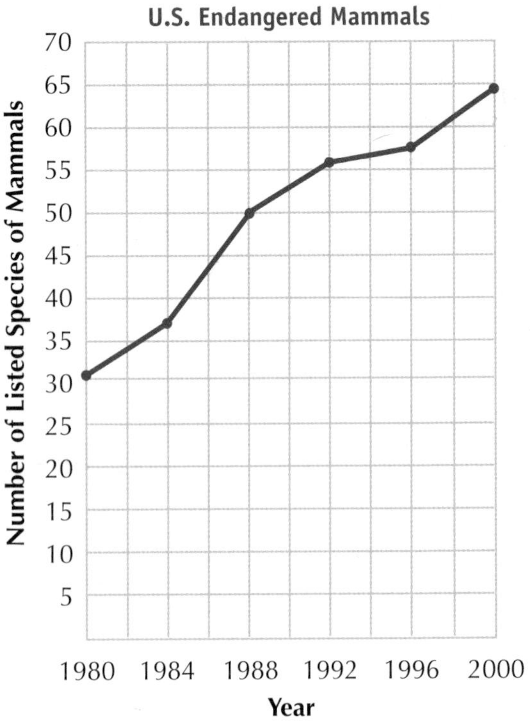

Mixed Review and Test Prep

Take It to the NET
Test Prep
www.scottforesman.com

Draw a coordinate grid and plot the following points.

14. A (2, 7) **15.** B (6, 3) **16.** C (0, 9) **17.** D (8, 0) **18.** E (3,4)

19. Henry rode in a bike-a-thon. He started the ride at 10:30 A.M. and finished at 12:25 P.M. How long did he ride in the bike-a-thon?

A. 55 minutes

B. 1 hour 5 minutes

C. 1 hour 55 minutes

D. 2 hours 5 minutes

Learning with Technology

Spreadsheet/Data/Grapher eTool Features

Marco surveyed 25 friends about their favorite type of bug and recorded the results in the chart to the right.

Favorite Bug

Grasshopper	6
Cricket	3
Ladybug	11
Ant	2
Praying Mantis	3

Create a spreadsheet from Marco's chart, entering the data in the order it appears. Generate a bar graph and print it if possible. Then, sort the data in ascending order and generate a bar graph of the sorted data.

1. How do the sorted data graph and the original graph differ?

2. How are the sorted data graph and the original graph the same?

Reading For Math Success

Understand Graphic Sources: Graphs

Understanding graphic sources such as graphs when you read in math can help you use the **problem-solving strategy, *Make a Graph,*** in the next lesson.

In reading, understanding graphs can help you understand what you read. In math, understanding graphs can help you solve problems.

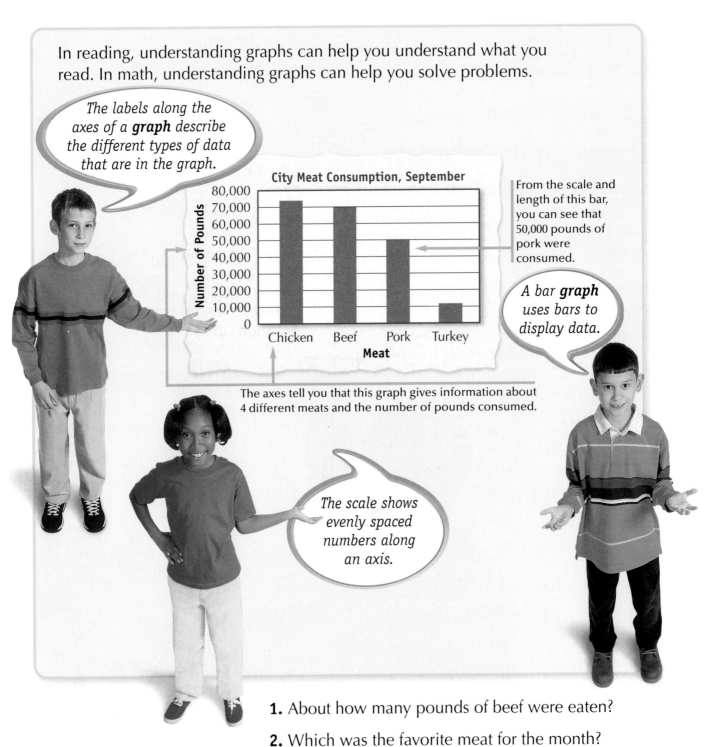

The labels along the axes of a **graph** describe the different types of data that are in the graph.
City Meat Consumption, September
Number of Pounds
80,000
70,000
60,000
50,000
40,000
30,000
20,000
10,000
0
Chicken
Beef
Pork
Turkey
Meat
From the scale and length of this bar, you can see that 50,000 pounds of pork were consumed.
A bar **graph** uses bars to display data.
The axes tell you that this graph gives information about 4 different meats and the number of pounds consumed.
The scale shows evenly spaced numbers along an axis.

1. About how many pounds of beef were eaten?

2. Which was the favorite meat for the month?

For 3–5, use the pictograph at the right.

3. How many newspapers are represented by each newspaper? by each half a newspaper?
4. Which scout troop recycled the most newspapers?
5. **Writing in Math** About how many newspapers were recycled altogether? Explain how you found your answer.

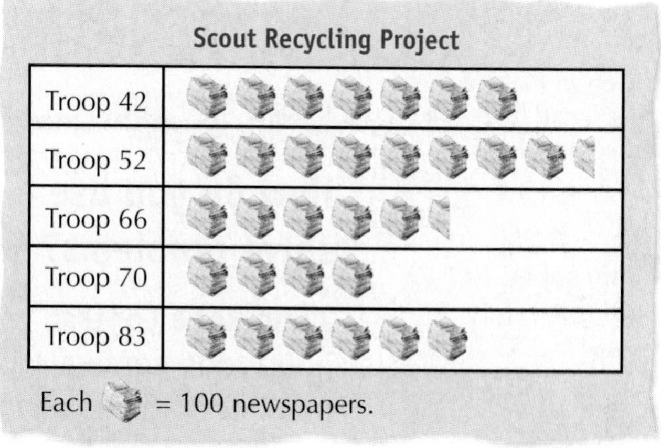

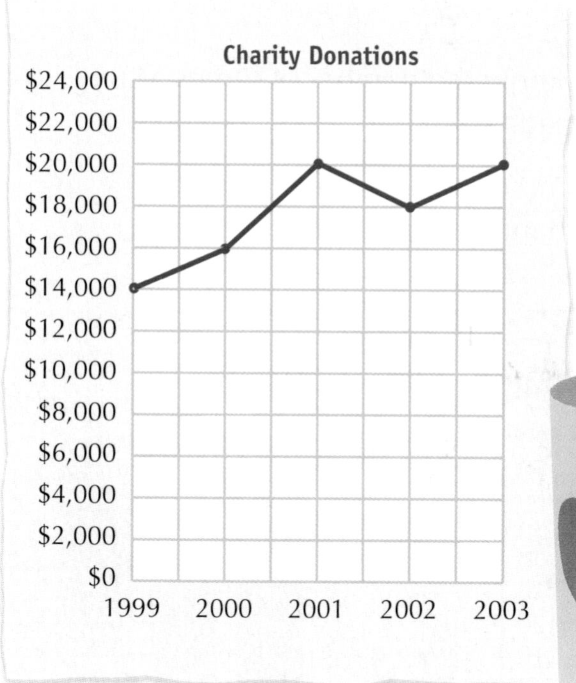

For 6–9, use the line graph at the left.

6. How much money was donated in 2001?
7. During which year did donations decrease from the previous year?
8. During which two years were donations the same?

For 9–11, use the bar graph at the right.

9. How many wins did the Lions have?
10. Describe the graph's scale.
11. **Writing in Math** Which two teams had the same number of wins? How can you tell from the bar graph?

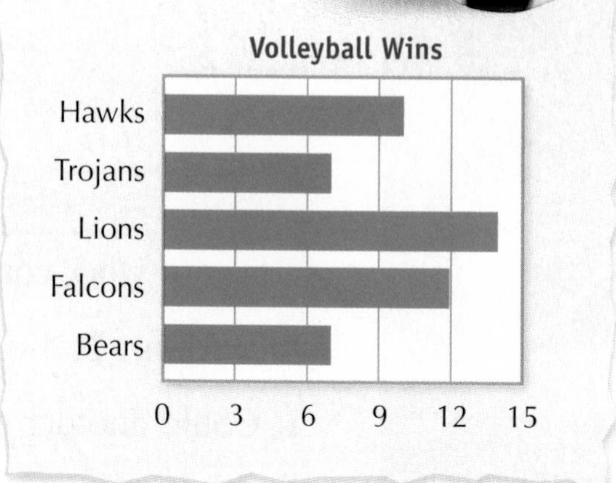

Problem-Solving Strategy

Reading Helps!

Understanding graphic sources such as tables and graphs

can help you with...

the problem-solving strategy, *Make a Graph.*

Key Idea
Learning how and when to make a graph can help you solve problems.

Materials
- grid paper
or e tools

Make a Graph

LEARN

How do you use a graph to solve problems?

Jump Rope Contest Mary was in a jump rope contest. How did her number of jumps change over the five days of the contest?

Day	Jumps
Monday	25
Tuesday	34
Wednesday	55
Thursday	32
Friday	68

Read and Understand

What do you know? I know the number of jumps Mary made each day.

What are you trying to find? Find how the number of jumps changed over the five days.

Plan and Solve

What strategy will you use? **Strategy: Make a graph.**

Step 1 Set up the bar graph.
Step 2 Enter known data.
Step 3 Read the graph. Look for a pattern.

Mary's Jump Rope Contest Results

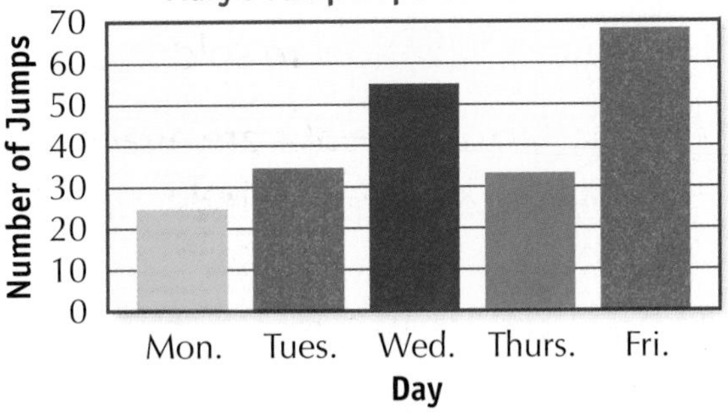

Answer: The number of jumps increased each day from Monday through Wednesday. But then it dropped on Thursday. On Friday it went up to the highest yet.

Look Back and Check

Is your work correct? Yes, the bar graph shows the correct data.

✓ Talk About It

1. Could another type of graph have been used ? Explain.

CHECK

For another example, see Set 4-11 on p. 249.

Copy and complete the graph to solve each problem.

1. Juanita is practicing the ring toss. Between which two days did she improve the most?

Juanita's Ring Toss Practice
Hits out of 20

Monday	Tuesday	Wednesday	Thursday
10	12	15	16

Each ◯ = 2 hits.

2. During which month did Judson visit the park the most?

Judson's Park Passes

Date	May 1	June 1	July 1	August 1
Passes Left	20	18	10	4

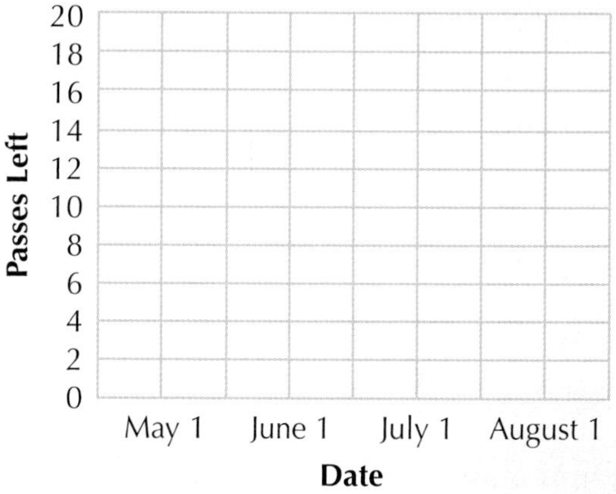

PRACTICE

For more practice, see Set 4-11 on p. 252.

Solve. Write your answer in a complete sentence.

3. Sean made a table to show how many tickets for the school play were sold each day. Between which 2 days did ticket sales increase the most?

School Play Tickets

Day	Number Sold
Monday	17
Tuesday	20
Wednesday	22
Thursday	22
Friday	26

4. How many tickets were sold in all?

5. At a car factory, 4 bolts are attached every 15 seconds. How many bolts are attached in 2 minutes?

6. Tell the missing numbers.
8, 12, 16, 20, ▢, ▢, ▢

7. Use the tally chart at the right. How many more of the people who signed the Declaration of Independence were farmers than were physicians?

8. How many people signed the Declaration of Independence?

Occupation of People Who Signed The Declaration of Independence

Lawyer or Judge	卌 卌 卌 卌 卌 |||
Farmer	卌 ||||
Merchant	卌 卌
Physician	||||
Other	卌 ||

Section B: Lessons 4-6 through 4-11

Review

Do You Know How?

Do You Understand?

Pictographs (4-6)
Line Plots (4-7) and Bar Graphs (4-8)

Use the information in the table.

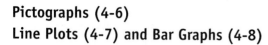

Tiger Basketball

Year	Wins
2000	6
2001	5
2002	8
2003	6
2004	8

1. Make a pictograph.

2. Make a line plot.

3. Make a bar graph.

A Explain how you chose the value of each symbol for the pictograph.

B Tell how you chose the scale for the bar graph.

Graphing Ordered Pairs (4-9)

Name the ordered pair for each point.

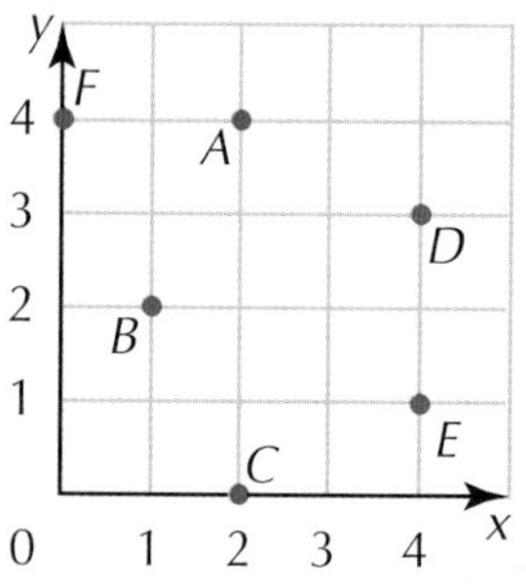

4. *A* **5.** *C*

6. *E* **7.** *F*

8. Give the letter of the point named by (1, 2).

C Tell how you found the ordered pair for Exercise 4.

D Explain how to find the point named by the ordered pair (4, 3).

Line Graphs (4-10); Problem-Solving Strategy: Make a Graph (4-11)

9. Make a line graph of the data.

Banana Slug Harvey's Race

Seconds from Start	0	20	40	60
Centimeters from Start	0	5	12	16

10. How long did it take Harvey to crawl about 14 centimeters?

11. During which 20 seconds did Harvey crawl the farthest?

12. During which 20 seconds did Harvey crawl the least?

E Tell how you made your line graph. Explain why you chose the scales you did.

F Describe the trend in the data.

Diagnostic Checkpoint

MULTIPLE CHOICE

1. If each symbol on a pictograph represents 10 people, how many symbols would you need to represent 60 people? (4-6)

A. 1 symbol **B.** 6 symbols **C.** 7 symbols **D.** 10 symbols

FREE RESPONSE

Use the bar graph at the right for 2–4. (4-8)

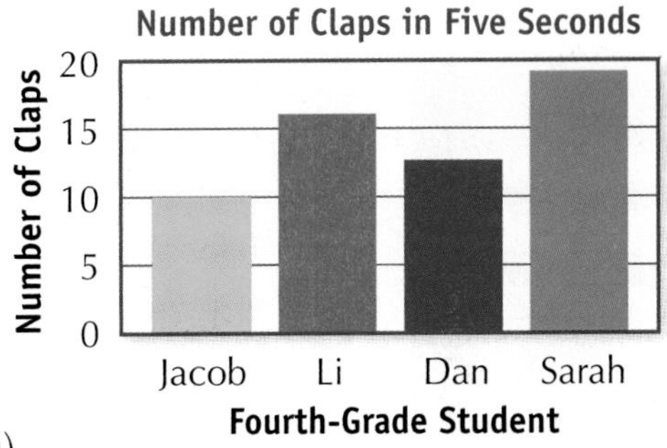

2. Who clapped the most?

3. How many more times did Sarah clap than Jacob?

4. Who clapped 16 times in 5 seconds? (4-8)

Plot the following points on a coordinate grid. (4-9)

5. *A* (1, 7) **6.** *B* (8, 5) **7.** *C* (0, 6)

For 8–9, use the following times, in seconds, for students in the 100-meter dash: 15, 16, 17, 16, 18, 15, 16, 17

8. Make a line plot of the data. (4-7)

9. What was the most common time? (4-11)

10. According to the line graph below, how many new Broadway productions were there in the 1998 season? (4-10)

Think It Through
Get information from the graph to answer the question.

Writing in Math

11. Use the line graph at the right. How did the number of new Broadway productions change from the 1988 to the 1998 seasons? Explain how you can tell. (4-10)

12. Describe the trend in the data shown in the line graph. Has the number of new productions generally been increasing or decreasing since 1968? (4-10)

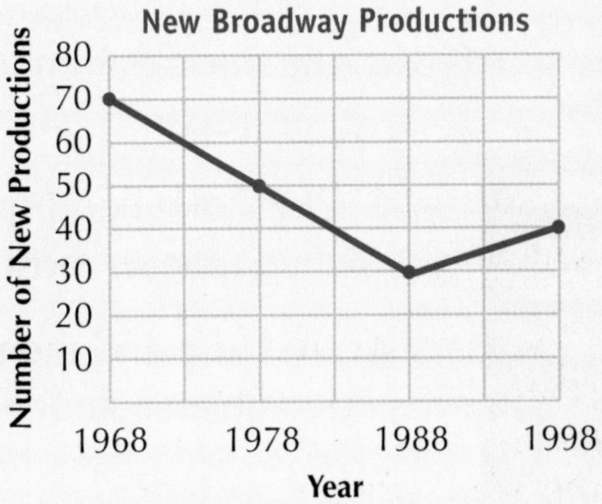

Key Idea

You can summarize data by using median, mode, or range.

Vocabulary

- median
- mode
- range

Materials

- centimeter ruler

TEST TALK

Think It Through

I can **use logical reasoning** to find the median. I can count from each end to find the middle number.

Median, Mode, and Range

WARM UP

Write each set of numbers in order from least to greatest.

1. 26, 35, 42, 29, 36, 48, 38
2. 61, 16, 68, 58, 85, 72, 27
3. 243, 234, 342, 235, 253

LEARN

Activity

What are median, mode, and range?

a. With a partner, measure your hand span to the nearest centimeter. Measure the distance from the tip of your little finger to the tip of your thumb.

b. Record your data on a class line plot.

c. What is the shortest hand span in your class? What is the longest hand span?

d. What is the difference between the longest hand span and the shortest hand span? This difference is the **range** of the hand spans.

e. List the hand spans in order from shortest to longest and find the middle number. The middle number is the **median** of the hand spans.

f. Does one hand span occur more often than the rest? The one that appears most often is the **mode** of the hand spans.

g. Measure and then find the median, mode, and range of foot lengths for students in your class.

The **median** is the middle number when the data are listed in order. The **mode** is the number or numbers that occur most often in the data. The **range** is the difference between the greatest and least number in the data.

How do you find and use median, mode, and range?

Example A

Find the median, mode, and range for the heights in inches of each group of fourth graders.

Group 1: 53, 57, 50, 57, 48, 55, 56, 59, 50

Group 2: 59, 52, 54, 52, 53

	STEP 1	STEP 2	STEP 3
	To find the median, list the data in order from least to greatest, and find the middle number.	To find the mode, find the number or numbers that occur most often.	To find the range, subtract the greatest value minus the least value.
Group 1	48, 50, 50, 53, **55**, 56, 57, 57, 59 The median of Group 1 is 55.	The modes of Group 1 are 50 and 57.	59 − 48 = 11 The range of Group 1 is 11.
Group 2	52, 52, **53**, 54, 59 The median of Group 2 is 53.	The mode of Group 2 is 52.	59 − 52 = 7 The range of Group 2 is 7.

Talk About It

1. In Example A, how many numbers are less than the 55 shown in blue? How many numbers are greater than the 55 shown in blue?
2. Within which group are the heights more the same? Explain how you can use the range to help you decide.
3. Why does Group 1 have 2 modes and Group 2 have 1 mode?

CHECK

For another example, see Set 4-12 on p. 249.

Find the median, mode, and range of each set of data.

1. 8, 5, 7, 4, 3, 7, 2
2. 12, 15, 18, 15, 14
3. 23, 26, 28, 27, 25, 29, 30
4. **Reasoning** Is there always a mode in a set of data? Explain your thinking.

For more practice, see Set 4-12 on p. 253.

lls and Understanding

F nedian, mode, and range of each set of data.

9, 9, 3, 5, 6

6. 68, 64, 72, 68, 70

7. 65, 67, 66, 68, 65

, 4, 5, 2, 1, 1, 5
, 1, 2, 4, 3, 1

9. 34, 37, 42, 41, 38, 37
36, 36, 39, 32, 36

10. 16, 17, 16, 19, 23, 8
15, 25, 9, 12, 16

nber Sense Could 18 be the median of 9, 4, 18, 3, and 6?
plain why or why not.

easoning and Problem Solving

ne line plot on the right for 12–13.

Find the median, mode, and range of the hand spans for students in Ms. Angler's class.

13. Reasoning Ms. Angler's hand span is 21 centimeters. If you include this measure would the mode change? Would the range change? Explain your thinking.

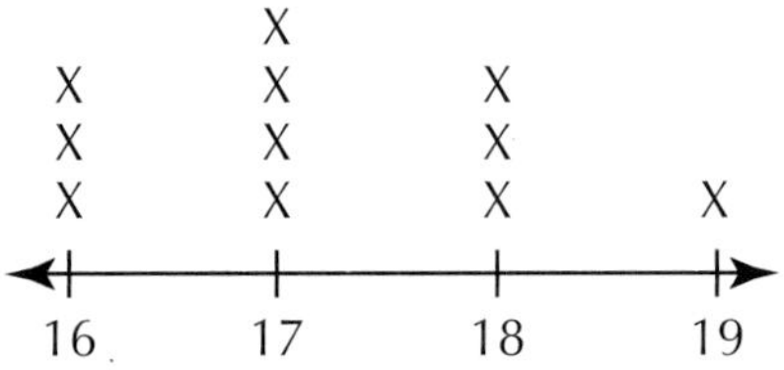

Hand Spans of Students in Ms. Angler's Fourth Grade Class In Centimeters

Math and Science

Nine Largest National Champion Trees

Girth in inches	998	950	761	707	505	644	546	442	451
Height in feet	275	321	159	191	281	83	108	232	219
Crown spread in feet	107	80	45	96	71	85	118	29	39

National Champion Trees are the largest known tree of each U.S. species. For the nine largest National Champion Trees, find the median and the range of the

14. girths, the distance around the trunk of the tree at $4\frac{1}{2}$ feet above the ground.

15. heights, the distance from the base to the top of the tree.

16. crown spreads, the spread of the branches.

17. **Writing in Math** Ryan said the median of the data set 42, 48, 46, 45, 42 is 46 because 46 is the middle number. Is he correct? Explain.

PRACTICE

C Extensions

Use the line graph at the right for 18–19.

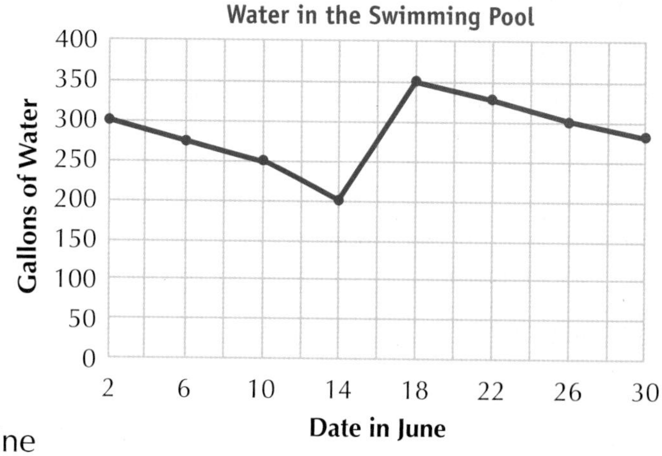

18. What was the greatest number of gallons of water in the swimming pool? What was the least number of gallons of water in the pool? What was the range of the water in the pool?

19. Reasoning Explain how to use the line graph to find the range of the data.

Mixed Review and Test Prep

Take It to the NET
Test Prep
www.scottforesman.com

20. Use the line graph above. How much water was in the swimming pool on June 10th?

21. 7×8

A. 56 **B.** 49 **C.** 48 **D.** 42

Enrichment

Stem-and-Leaf Plots

The heights in inches of nine basketball players are 74, 67, 71, 75, 69, 75, 75, 68, 71. You can use a stem-and-leaf plot to organize and compare data.

Height in Inches

Stem	Leaves
6	7 8 9
7	1 1 4 5 5 5

Each **stem** stands for the first digit of a number.

Write the tens digits in order from least to greatest.

Each **leaf** stands for the second digit of a number.

Shows 67, 68, and 69.

Write the ones digits in order from least to greatest.

1. Are more players taller or shorter than 70 inches?

2. What is the mode of the heights?

3. What is the median for the heights?

4. What is the range of the heights?

5. Make a stem-and-leaf plot for the following heights.
49, 55, 61, 58, 54, 48, 60, 54

Key Idea
Taking a survey helps you find out information to solve a problem or answer a question.

Vocabulary
- survey

TEST TALK

Think It Through
I can **make a tally chart** to record the results of my survey. Remember, 𝍸 equals 5.

Data from Surveys

WARM UP

1. Count the tallies to find how many students like each color.

Red	𝍸 |||
Blue	||||
Orange	𝍸 ||

LEARN

What is a survey?

Jim and Julie want to know what kinds of movies their classmates like to see. They decide to take a **survey.** When you ask different people the same question and record their answers you are taking a **survey.**

Jim asked his classmates,

"What is your favorite kind of movie?"

Here are his results in a tally chart.

Favorite Type of Movie

Action	||	2
Animated	𝍸		6
Comedy	𝍸		6
Sports	𝍸	5
Drama			1

Julie asked her classmates,

"Would you rather see a drama, comedy, or action movie?"

Here are her results in a tally chart.

Favorite Type of Movie

Drama	𝍸	5
Comedy	𝍸 ||	7
Action	|||	3

Talk About It

1. Do you know if Julie's classmates like animated movies? Why?
2. **Reasoning** What type of movies would most of Jim's classmates like to see?

Activity

How do you take a survey?

Take a class survey to find out how many siblings your classmates have.

a. Write a survey question.

b. Make a tally chart to record the data. Ask your classmates the survey question and record their answers on the chart.

c. Count the tallies.

d. Explain the results of your survey.

CHECK ✓

For another example, see Set 4-13 on p. 249.

Use the data in the tally chart at the right.

1. How many people in the survey liked the MindTwisters website best?
2. How many people were surveyed?
3. Which website is the favorite of more people than any other?
4. **Number Sense** If twice as many people were surveyed, how many do you think would say they liked AwesomeMath best? Explain.

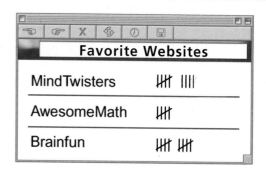

Favorite Websites

MindTwisters	𝍸 𝍷𝍷𝍷𝍷
AwesomeMath	𝍸
Brainfun	𝍸 𝍸

PRACTICE

For more practice, see Set 4-13 on p. 253.

A Skills and Understanding

Use the data in the tally chart at the right.

5. How many people in the survey liked cats best?
6. How many people were surveyed?
7. According to the data, which type of pet is the favorite of more people than any other?
8. **Number Sense** If ten times as many people were surveyed, how many do you think would say they liked fish best? Explain.

Favorite Type of Pet

Dog	𝍸 𝍸 𝍷𝍷
Cat	𝍸 𝍷𝍷𝍷𝍷
Fish	𝍷𝍷𝍷𝍷
Gerbil	𝍷𝍷𝍷
Turtle	𝍷𝍷

B Reasoning and Problem Solving

9. Make a bar graph of the data on favorite websites.
10. Take a survey to find the favorite sport of 20 people. Write the question you ask. Give your results in a tally chart.
11. **Writing in Math** Design your own survey. Explain what you are trying to find out. Write a survey question. Ask the question and record your answers in a tally chart. Explain what you found out.

Mixed Review and Test Prep

Take It to the NET
Test Prep
www.scottforesman.com

12. Find the median, mode, and range of 24, 36, 28, 25, 42, 18, 25.
13. Write seven million, fifty thousand, two hundred three in standard form.

A. 75,203 **B.** 750,203 **C.** 7,050,203 **D.** 7,500,203

Key Idea
The idea you get when you first look at a graph may not be correct.

Vocabulary
- scale (p. 208)

Misleading Graphs

WARM UP

Find the next number in each pattern.

1. 32, 42, 52, ...
2. 15, 20, 25, ...
3. 16, 18, 20...

LEARN

How can you tell if a graph is misleading?

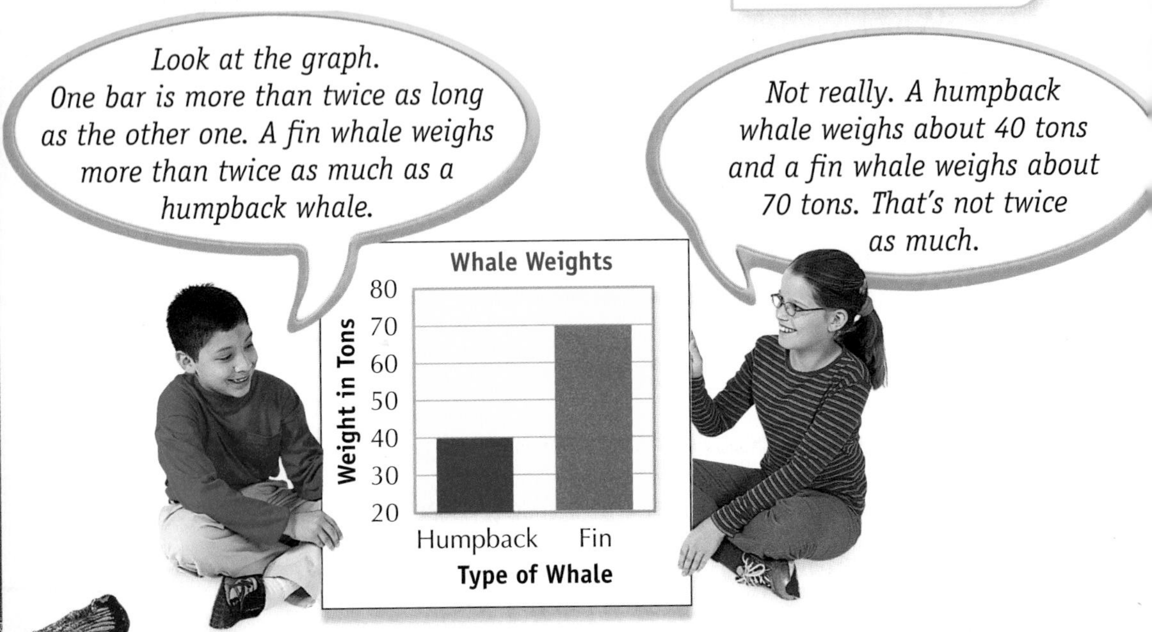

The graph is misleading because the scale does not start at zero.

Example

Which graph makes you think that the number of T-shirts sold each year by Ms. Bolt's classes increased quickly? Why does it seem this way?

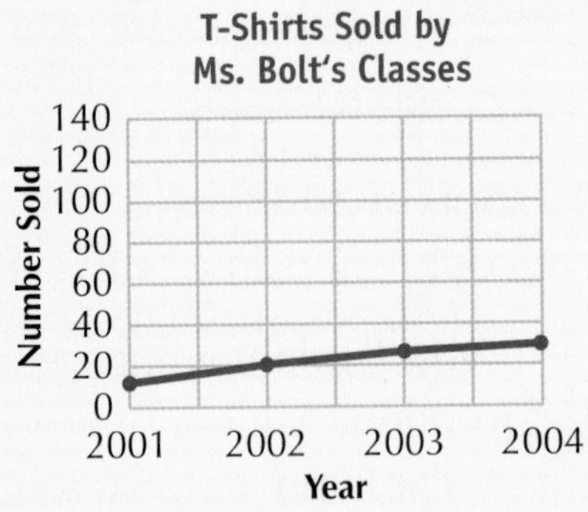

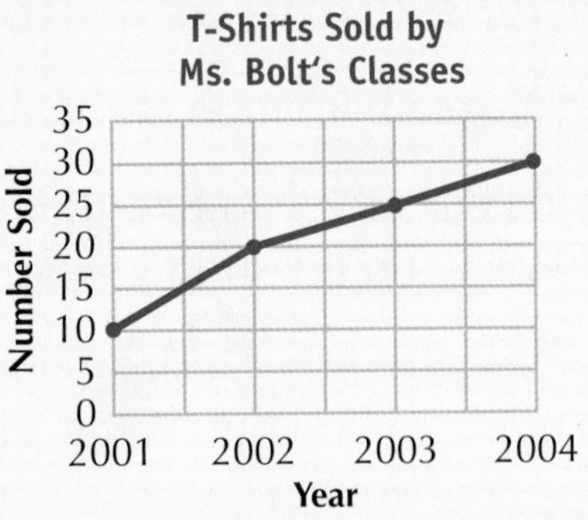

The second graph makes you think the number sold increased quickly. The scale is by 5s and the other scale is by 20s.

TEST TALK

Think It Through
I can decide whether or not a graph is misleading by **looking carefully at the scale.**

Talk About It

1. Why is the Whale Weights graph misleading?

CHECK ✓

For another example, see Set 4-14 on p. 249.

Use the bar graph at the right for 1–4.

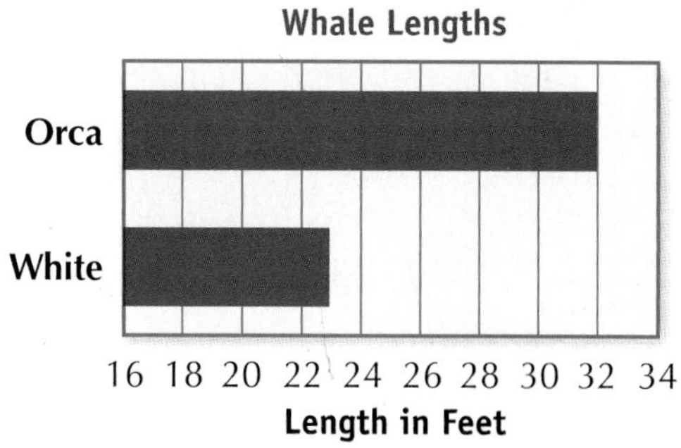

1. Looking at the graph, about how many times as long is the orca whale as the white whale?

2. About how long is each whale?

3. Is the orca whale more than twice as long as the white whale?

4. **Reasoning** Why is the graph misleading?

PRACTICE

For more practice, see Set 4-14 on p. 253.

A Skills and Understanding

Use the bar graph at the right for 5–7.

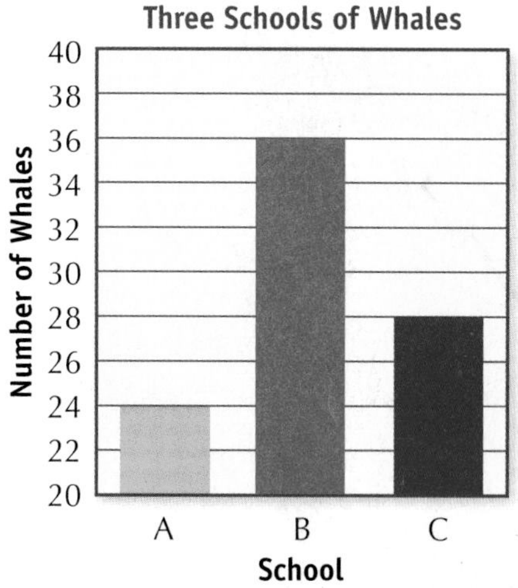

5. Looking at the graph, about how many times as many whales does there seem to be in School B as in School A? How many whales are in School B? School A?

6. Looking at the graph, about how many times as many whales do there seem to be in School B as in School C? How many whales are in School B? School C?

7. Why is the graph misleading?

B Reasoning and Problem Solving

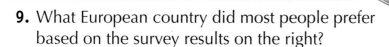

8. **Writing in Math** For the data in the Plant Growth table, would a line graph with a scale of 0 to 20 by 2s or 0 to 10 by 1s make you think that the plant grew more quickly? Explain.

Plant Growth

Day	4	6	8	10
Height in Inches	2	5	7	9

Mixed Review and Test Prep

Take It to the NET
Test Prep
www.scottforesman.com

9. What European country did most people prefer based on the survey results on the right?

Favorite European Country

England	𝍸 𝍸 ||
France	𝍸 |
Sweden	||

10. 36 ÷ 4

A. 6 **B.** 8 **C.** 9 **D.** 10

Problem-Solving Applications

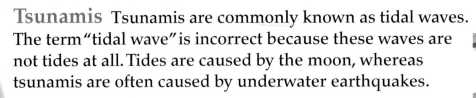

Tsunamis Tsunamis are commonly known as tidal waves. The term "tidal wave" is incorrect because these waves are not tides at all. Tides are caused by the moon, whereas tsunamis are often caused by underwater earthquakes.

Trivia On June 15, 1896, an 80-foot tsunami struck the Japanese island of Honshu. The same tsunami crossed the ocean in less than 10 hours and hit the California coast with a height of more than 9 feet.

1. The 1896 tsunami struck Honshu at about 8:00 P.M. What was the time twelve hours before the tsunami struck?

2. Japan has 4,628 miles of coastline. The 1896 tsunami destroyed 175 miles of coastline. How much of the coastline was left unharmed?

3. The 1896 tsunami approached the island of Honshu at 7:55 P.M. People began to search the wreckage at 8:25 P.M. How much time had elapsed?

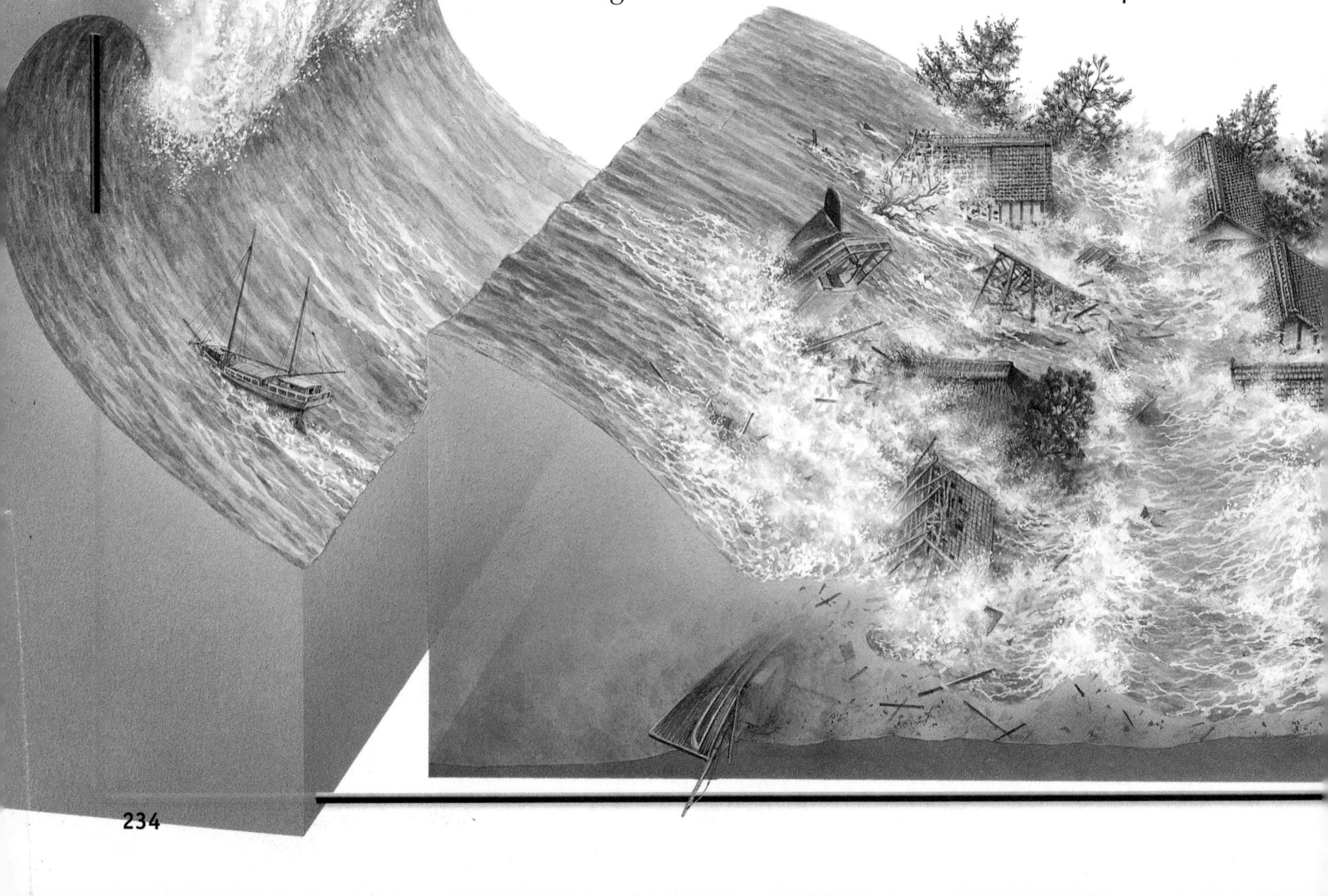

Using Key Facts

4 Find the median height of the tsunamis in the table.

Key Facts
Tsunamis

Year	Location	Time of Day	Height of Wave
•1923	Japan	2:58 A.M.	12.1 m
•1933	Japan	5:31 P.M.	29.3 m
•1960	Chile	7:11 P.M.	25.0 m
•1976	Philippines	4:11 P.M.	5.0 m
•1992	Indonesia	5:29 A.M.	26.2 m

5 As tsunamis travel from the deep ocean to more shallow water, they slow down. At a depth of 1,000 meters they travel at 356 kilometers per hour. This is 400 kilometers per hour slower than their speed in deeper ocean water. How fast do tsunamis travel in deep ocean water?

6 **Writing in Math** Use the data from this lesson to write your own word problem. Answer the question in a complete sentence.

7 **Decision Making** What kind of graph would be best for showing the heights of the tsunamis in the table? Make the graph of your choice.

Good News/Bad News
Ocean buoys and seismographs can be used to detect the formation of tsunamis. This gives people time to escape to higher land, but nothing can be done to prevent the destruction of property along the coast.

Review

Do You Know How?

Median, Mode, and Range (4-12)

The data below give the number of runs scored in each game by the Thomasville Tigers baseball team, for 2 years.

2003: 2, 5, 0, 1, 4, 2, 1, 1, 3, 1, 4
2004: 1, 2, 8, 4, 2, 0, 3, 2, 0, 3, 1

Find the median, mode, and range of the runs scored by the Tigers

1. in 2003. **2.** in 2004.

Do You Understand?

A Tell how you found the median for 2003.

B Compare the ranges of the data for 2003 and 2004. What does the range tell you about the data sets?

Data from Surveys (4-13)

The tally chart shows the results of a survey.

Hours of Sleep Each Night

8	𝍸 |
9	𝍸 ||
10	||

3. How many people were surveyed?

4. How many hours do most people sleep?

C Tell how you found how many people were surveyed.

D Write a survey question you might ask your classmates.

Misleading Graphs (4-14)

Use the bar graph below for 5–6.

5. How many times as many school lunches does it seem were sold on Tuesday than Monday?

6. How many lunches were sold each day?

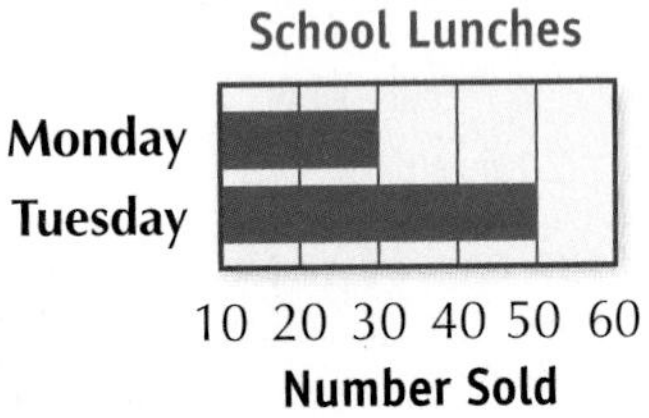

E Were twice as many lunches sold on Tuesday as Monday? Explain.

F Explain why the School Lunches graph is misleading.

Diagnostic Checkpoint

> **TEST TALK**
>
> **Think It Through**
> For multiple choice questions, **eliminate unreasonable answers** first.

MULTIPLE CHOICE

1. The following are the arm spans in inches of seven fourth-graders. Find the median. 51, 48, 45, 52, 50, 51, 39 (4-12)

A. 13 in. **B.** 48 in. **C.** 50 in. **D.** 51 in.

2. Use the tally chart on the right. How many students were surveyed? (4-13)

A. 48 **C.** 45

B. 40 **D.** 38

Students' Favorite Sport to Play

Baseball	𝍸 𝍸 𝍸
Basketball	𝍸 |||
Soccer	𝍸 𝍸 𝍸 ||

FREE RESPONSE

For 3–4, use the tally chart above. (4-13)

3. How many students' favorite sport was basketball?

4. What is the favorite sport of more students than any other?

Find the median, mode, and range of each set of data. (4-12)

5. 8, 9, 12, 15, 9, 10, 14, 9, 16

6. 56, 39, 28, 26, 48, 42, 48

Use the bar graph on the right for 7–8. (4-14)

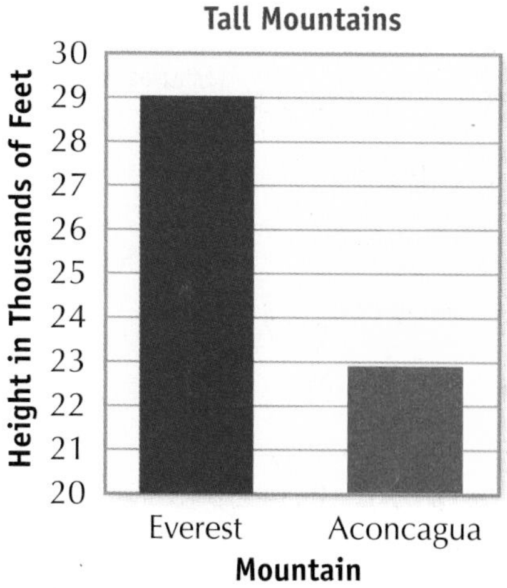

7. Looking at the graph, about how many times as tall as Aconcagua does Everest seem?

8. About how tall is each mountain?

Writing in Math

9. Use the table. For which continent are the heights of the nine tallest mountains more the same? Explain. (4-12)

Nine Tallest Mountains

	Africa	North America
Median	14,979 ft	17,930 ft
Range	5,459 ft	3,349 ft

10. Describe how you would take a survey to find out the favorite school lunch of all the fourth-grade students in your school. (4-13)

Test-Taking Strategies

- Understand the question.
- Get information for the answer.
- Plan how to find the answer.
- Make smart choices.
- Use writing in math.
- Improve written answers.

Make Smart Choices

To answer a multiple-choice test question, you need to choose an answer from answer choices. The steps below will help you make a smart choice.

1. The line graph below shows the number of students who attended Hill School for the 1997–2002 school years.

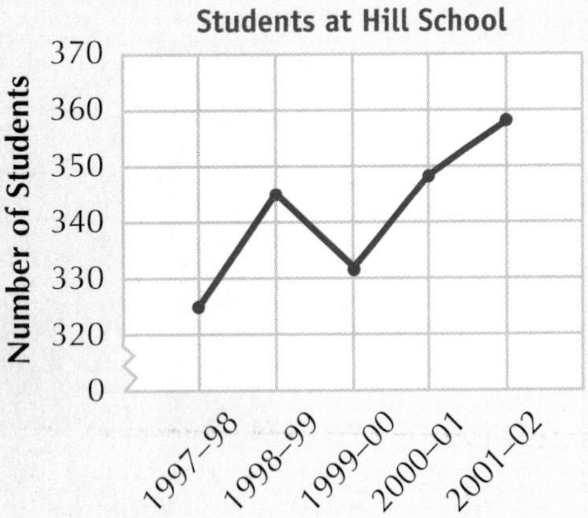

According to the information in the graph, during which school year did Hill School have the second fewest number of students?

A. 1997–1998

B. 1998–1999

C. 1999–2000

D. 2000–2001

Understand the question.

*I need to find out which school year had the **second fewest** students.*

Gather information for the answer.

*The **graph** shows the number of students in each school year.*

Plan how to find the answer.

*The answer is in the graph, so I need to **read the graph** carefully.*

Make Smart Choices.

- Eliminate wrong answers.
- Try working backward from an answer.
- Check answers for reasonableness.

The year 2001–2002 had the greatest number of students, so answer choice D is wrong.

The year 1997–1998 had the fewest number of students, so answer choice A is wrong.

That leaves either B or C as the correct answer. I'll compare the points on the graph to make the right choice. The point for 1999–2000 is the second lowest, so that's the year that had the second fewest number of students.

The correct answer is C, 1999–2000.

2. Point P on the grid below can be identified by which coordinates?

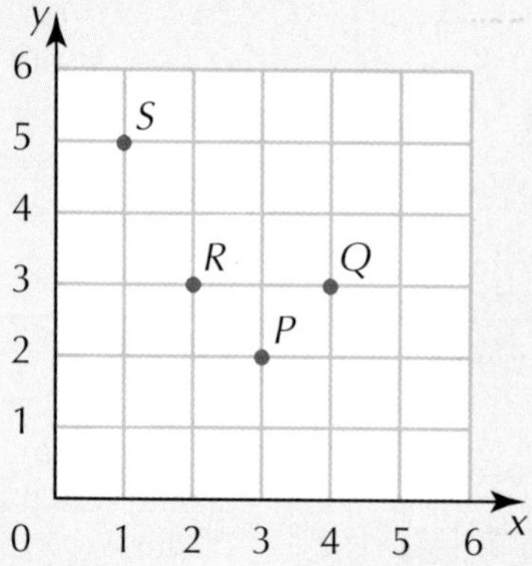

A. (1, 5)

B. (2, 3)

C. (3, 2)

D. (4, 3)

Think It Through

I need to find the coordinates of point P. I can work backward from each answer choice by moving my finger to the point named by the order pair.

First I'll try (1, 5). I wound up at point S, so answer choice A is wrong.

Next, try (2, 3). That's point R, so answer choice B is wrong.

Try (3, 2). That's it. I wound up at point P. The correct answer is C, (3, 2).

Now it's your turn.

For each problem, give the answer and explain how you made your choice.

3. The pictograph below shows the number of lifeguards stationed at four beaches in Stonecrest County.

Stonecrest Lifeguards

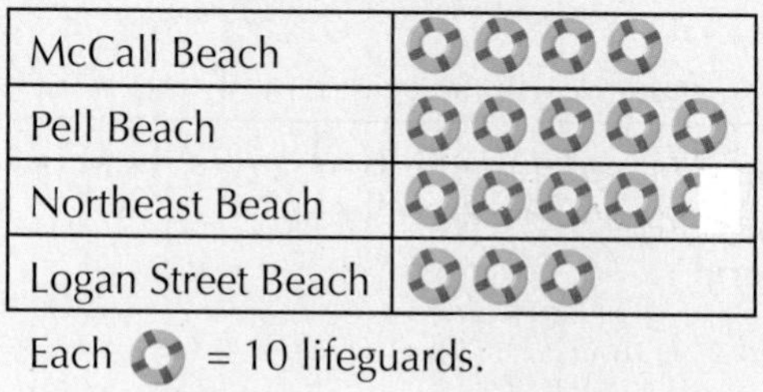

Which beach has 45 lifeguards?

A. McCall

B. Pell

C. Northeast

D. Logan Street

4. Point W on the grid below can be identified by which coordinates?

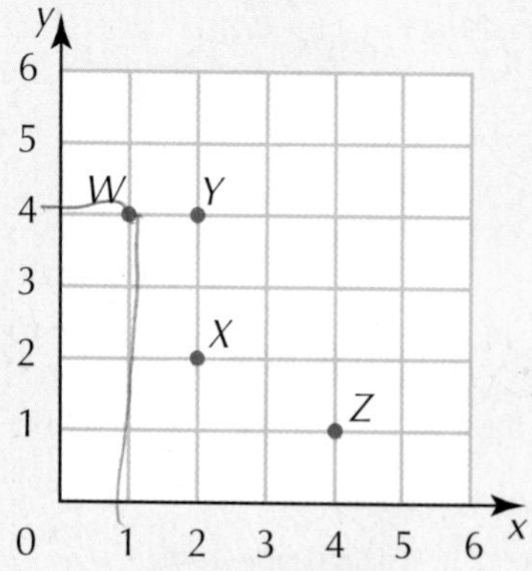

A. (2, 4)

B. (1, 4)

C. (4, 1)

D. (2, 2)

Key Vocabulary and Concept Review

Digital contains the word "digit."

*A **digital clock** shows the digits of the present time. An **analog** clock has a face.* *(p. 190)*

Self Check

Measure and compare time. (Lessons 4-1, 4-2, 4-3, 4-4, 4-5)

Find the **elapsed time.**

Start: 11:00 A.M.   Finish: 2:18 P.M.

analog clock   **digital clock**

11:00 A.M. to 2:00 P.M.:
3 hours
2:00 P.M. to 2:18 P.M.:
18 minutes

The elapsed time is
3 hours and 18 minutes

What is the date a week after October 13?

October

S	M	T	W	T	F	S
	1	2	3	4	5	6
7	8	9	10	11	12	13
14	15	16	17	18	19	20
21	22	23	24	25	26	27
28	29	30	31			

October 20 is a week after October 13. It is the third Saturday in October.

Third is an **ordinal number.**

1 minute = 60 seconds
1 hour = 60 minutes
1 day = 24 hours
1 week = 7 days
1 month = about 4 weeks
1 year = 52 weeks
1 year = 12 months
1 year = 365 days
1 leap year = 366 days
1 decade = 10 years
1 century = 100 years
1 millennium = 1,000 years

Ordinal sounds like "order."

***Ordinal numbers** are used to tell order.* *(p. 202)*

1. Find the elapsed time from 10:00 P.M. to 12:15 A.M.
2. What is the date 2 weeks before October 23?
3. Write two statements comparing the units of time given in the table above.

Our track coach plots the course we run in practice.

*To **plot** a point you mark its location.* *(p. 215)*

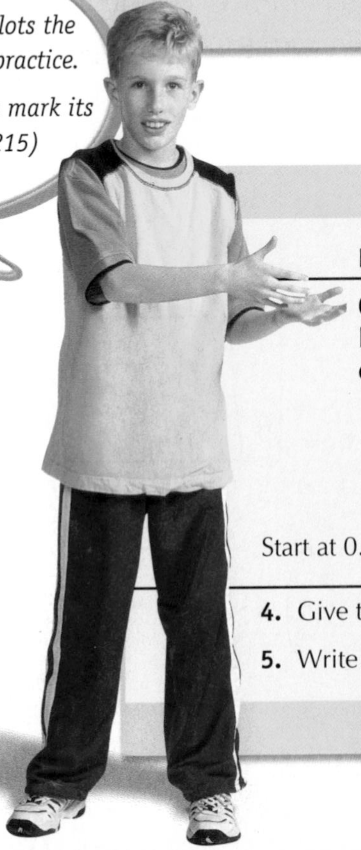

Self Check

Locate points on a coordinate grid. (Lesson 4-9)

Ordered pairs are used to name locations and **plot** points on a **coordinate grid.**

Point *C* is at (1, 7).

Start at 0.   Move 1 space to the right.   Move 7 spaces up.

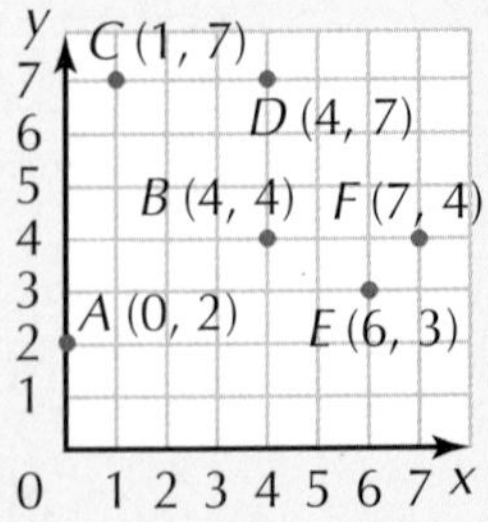

4. Give the letter of the point named by (4, 4).
5. Write the ordered pair that describes the location of point *A*.

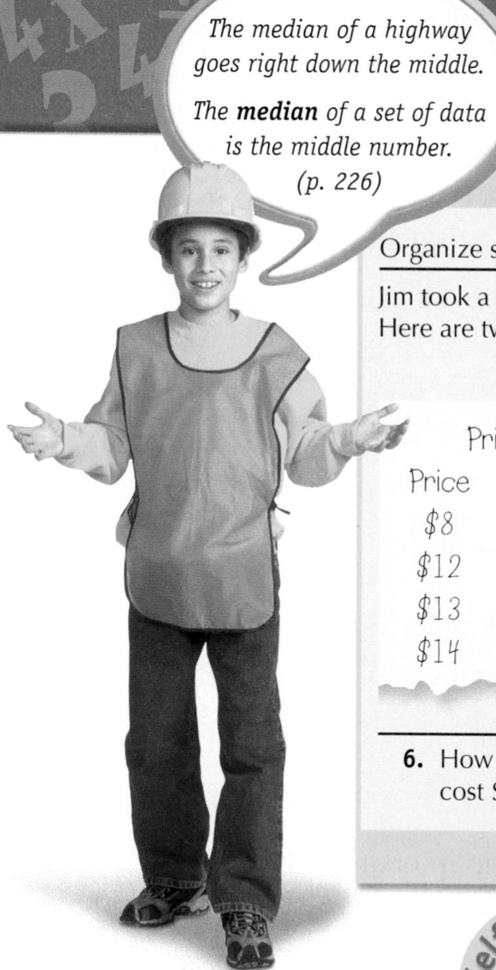

Self Check

Organize survey results. (Lessons 4-7, 4-12, 4-13)

Jim took a **survey** and asked, "How Much Did Your Cap Cost?" Here are two ways to display the results.

Tally Chart

Prices of Caps

Price	Tally	Number
$8	I	1
$12	II	2
$13	~~IIII~~ I	6
$14	II	2

Line Plot

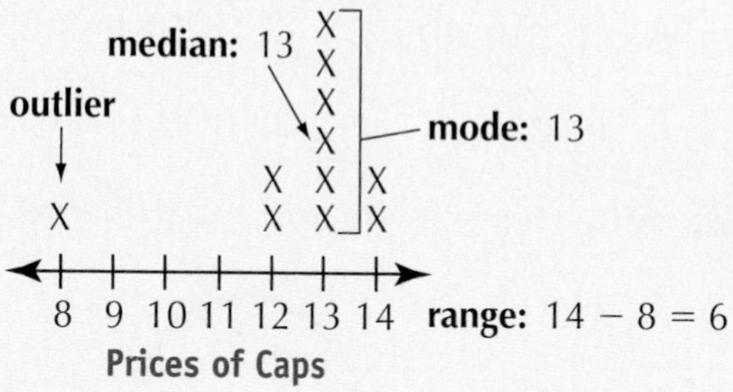

6. How many caps cost less than $13? How many cost $10?

Self Check

Make and analyze graphs to help solve problems. (Lessons 4-6, 4-8, 4-10, 4-11, 4-14)

Pictograph

Bar Graph

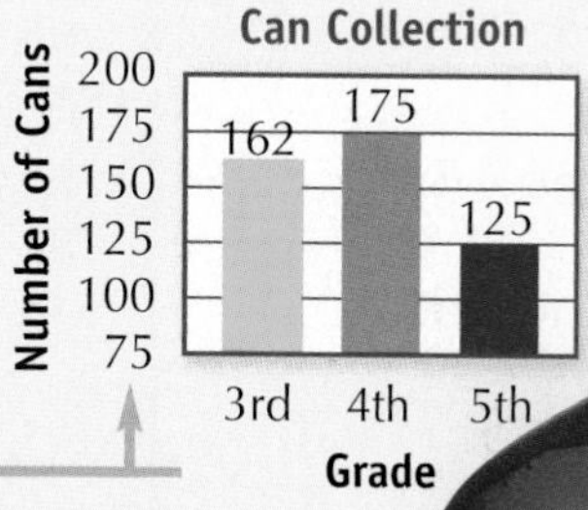

The **interval** is 25. This graph is misleading because the **scale** does not start at zero.

Line Graph

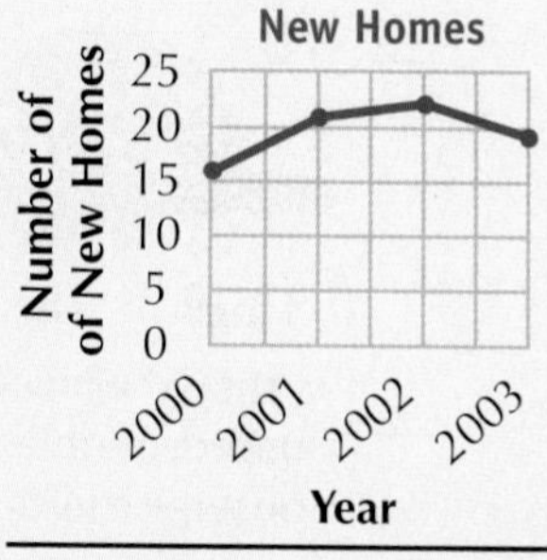

You can see the **trend** of the **data.** There is an **increase** from 2000 to 2002 and a **decrease** from 2002 to 2003.

7. How many computers did Moy sell?

Answers: 1. 2 hours 15 minutes 2. October 9th 3. Answers will vary. 4. B 5. (0,2) 6. 3; 0 7. 15

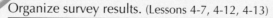

Chapter Test

MULTIPLE CHOICE

Choose the correct letter for each answer.

1. Which is greater than 50 weeks?

   A. 10 months **C.** 300 days

   B. 1 year **D.** 600 hours

2. What time is shown on this clock?

   A. 3:30

   B. 6:45

   C. 9:30

   D. 9:45

3. An event starts at 11:00 A.M. and ends at 1:15 P.M. Find the elapsed time.

   A. 1 hr 15 min **C.** 10 hr 15 min

   B. 2 hr 15 min **D.** 10 hr 45 min

4. Find the date one week after June 5.

   A. June 10 **C.** June 15

   B. June 12 **D.** June 19

Use the pictograph below for 5.

School Milk Sales

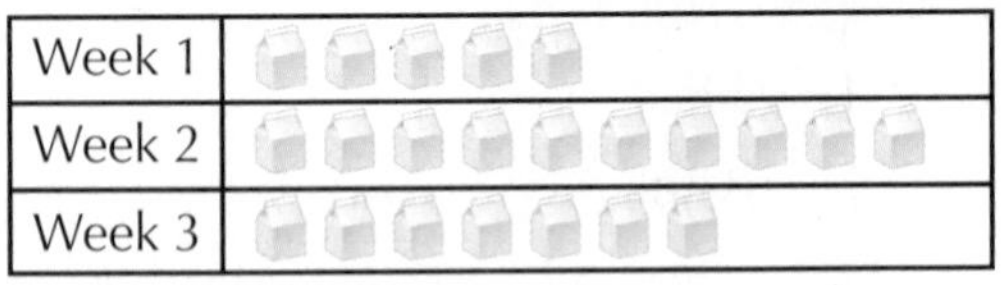

Each [carton] = 100 milk cartons.

5. How many more milk cartons were sold during Week 2 than Week 3?

   A. 150 **C.** 250

   B. 200 **D.** 300

For 6–7, use the line graph below.

James's Bike Race

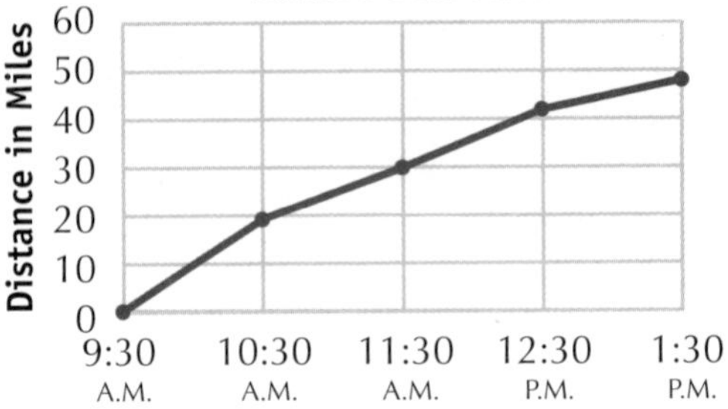

6. During which one-hour period did James bike the farthest?

   A. 1st hour **C.** 3rd hour

   B. 2nd hour **D.** 4th hour

7. What is the interval of the line graph's scale?

   A. 20 **B.** 15 **C.** 10 **D.** 5

8. Starting at 0 on a coordinate grid, which of the following directions would plot the ordered pair (2, 3)?

   A. Move up 2 units and right 3 units.

   B. Move right 5 units.

   C. Move up 3 units.

   D. Move right 2 units and up 3 units.

9. What is the outlier in this data set?

   16, 18, 46, 19, 20, 17, 22, 18

   A. 18 **C.** 22

   B. 19 **D.** 46

10. What is the mode in this data set?

    42, 44, 56, 42, 50

    A. 14 **B.** 42 **C.** 44 **D.** 56

TEST TALK

Think It Through

I should **eliminate unreasonable answer choices.**

FREE RESPONSE

Write the time shown on each clock in two ways.

11. 

12. 

13. What time will it be 55 minutes after the time shown on the clock in item 12?

Write <, >, or = for ●.

14. 1 minute ● 68 seconds

15. 2 decades ● 4 years

Find the median, mode, and range of each data set.

16. 5, 3, 8, 8, 4, 6, 7

17. 34, 38, 42, 38, 40

Find each elapsed time.

18. Start: 4:16 P.M.
Finish: 5:00 P.M.

19. Start: 7:52 A.M.
Finish: 8:27 A.M.

For 20–21, use the information in the table.

Sharks Football

Year	Wins
2000	8
2001	5
2002	10
2003	7
2004	10

20. Make a pictograph.

21. Make a line plot.

Name the ordered pair for each point.

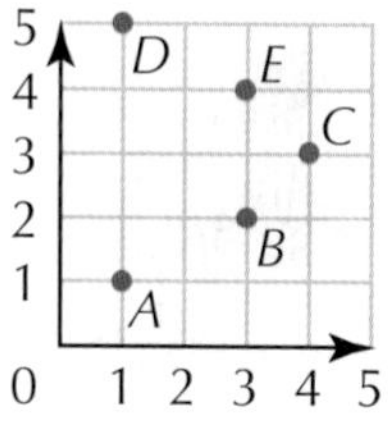

22. *E*

23. *C*

24. Give the letter of the point named by (1, 5).

25. Make a bar graph to solve the Work problem.

Work How did the number of hours Linda worked change over 5 weeks?

TEST TALK

Think It Through
I can **look for a pattern** to solve the problem.

Linda's Work Hours

Week	1	2	3	4	5
Hours	23	25	27	29	31

Writing in Math

26. Explain the steps you would follow to survey your classmates on their favorite ice cream flavor.

27. How is the bar graph below misleading?

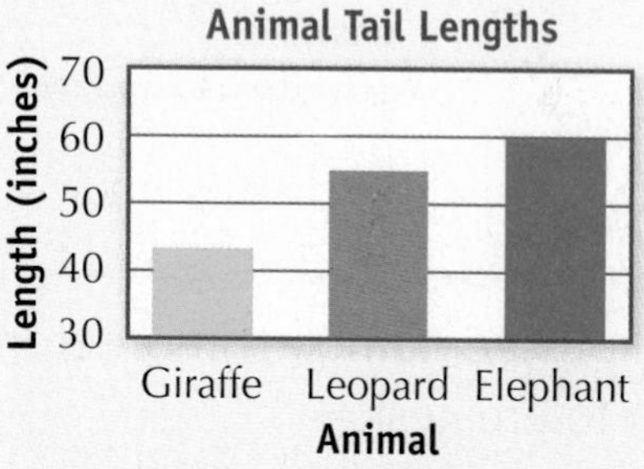

28. Write two sentences comparing the times in the museum tour schedule.

Museum Tour Schedule	
Tour 1	9:00 A.M. to 10:15 A.M.
Tour 2	10:30 A.M. to 11:30 A.M.
Tour 3	12:00 P.M. to 1:15 P.M.
Tour 4	1:30 P.M. to 2:30 P.M.
Tour 5	3:00 P.M. to 4:15 P.M.

Cumulative Review and Test Prep

Number and Operation

MULTIPLE CHOICE

1. What is three million, ninety-eight thousand, four hundred five written in standard form?

A. 39,845 **C.** 3,098,450

B. 3,098,405 **D.** 3,980,405

2. Estimate 6,742 − 2,938.

A. 2,000 **C.** 4,000

B. 3,000 **D.** 5,000

3. What is the quotient of 54 ÷ 9?

A. 5

B. 6

C. 9

D. 45

TEST TALK

Think It Through
I can **use logic to eliminate wrong answers.**

FREE RESPONSE

4. Write these numbers in order from least to greatest.

75,175 75,715 75,571 75,751

5. Round 27,649 to the nearest thousand.

6. Carlos bought a camera for $28.75 and two rolls of film for $4.50 each. How much did Carlos spend in all?

Writing in Math

7. Explain how you can break numbers apart to find the product 8 × 12.

Geometry and Measurement

MULTIPLE CHOICE

8. Which of these figures has a line of symmetry drawn through it?

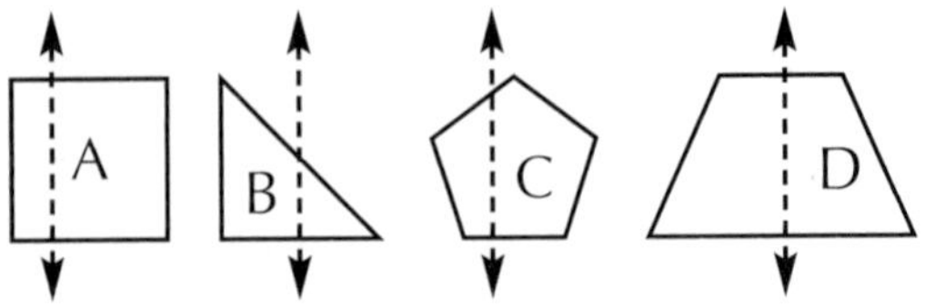

A. Figure A **C.** Figure C

B. Figure B **D.** Figure D

9. Which of the following is NOT greater than 5 weeks?

A. 1 month **C.** 40 days

B. 4 weeks 10 days **D.** 2 months

10. What time is shown on the clock?

A. 2:35

B. 6:10

C. 7:10

D. 7:35

FREE RESPONSE

11. Find the date three weeks after May 3rd.

12. A rectangle is 8 inches long and 5 inches wide. What is the perimeter of the rectangle?

Writing in Math

13. Explain two ways to find the elapsed time from 10:45 A.M. to 1:20 P.M.

Data Analysis and Probability

MULTIPLE CHOICE

14. What point on this coordinate grid is named by the ordered pair (3, 4)?

A. *C*

B. *E*

C. *B*

D. *D*

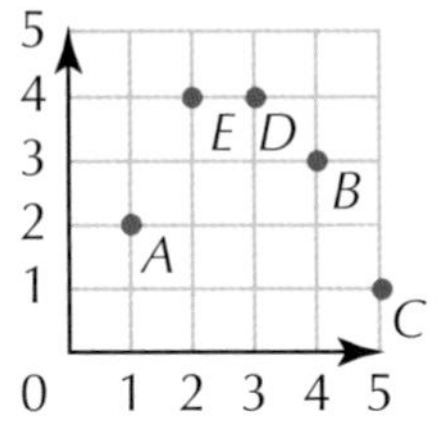

15. A bag has 3 red marbles, 2 blue marbles, 4 black marbles, and 3 green marbles. Which color marble are you most likely to pick?

A. red
B. blue
C. black
D. green

FREE RESPONSE

Use the line graph for Items 16–18.

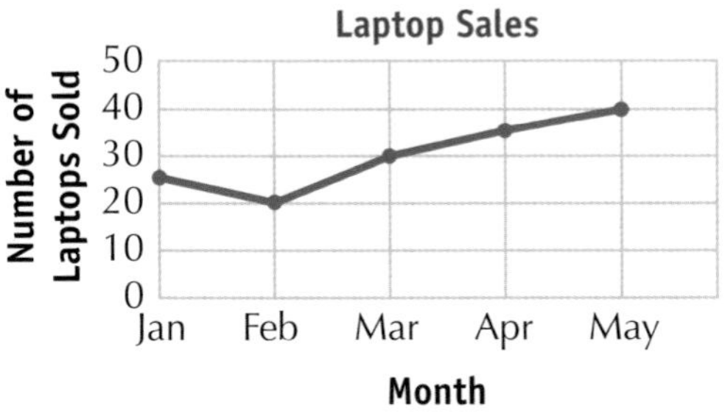

16. In which month were the most laptops sold? the least?

17. What was the total number of laptops sold from January through May?

Writing in Math

18. Between which two months did laptop sales increase the most? Explain how you used the graph to find your answer.

Algebra

MULTIPLE CHOICE

Think It Through

I can **work backwards** from the answer to find the missing number.

19. Solve $47 - n = 38$.

A. $n = 7$

B. $n = 8$

C. $n = 9$

D. $n = 10$

20. Evaluate the expression $3 \times m$ for $m = 9$.

A. 12
B. 24
C. 27
D. 36

21. Which multiplication property explains why $3 \times 9 = 9 \times 3$?

A. Commutative Property

B. Distributive Property

C. Identity Property

D. Zero Property

FREE RESPONSE

22. The 24 desks in the classroom are arranged in *n* equal rows. Write an expression to show the number of desks in each row. Then use the expression to find how many desks are in each row if there are 6 rows.

Writing in Math

23. Complete the table. Then explain the pattern you used to find the distance traveled in 4 hours.

Time	1 h	2 h	3 h	4 h
Distance	9 mi	18 mi	27 mi	

Chapter 4
Reteaching

Set 4-1 (pages 190–191)

Write the time shown on the clock.

eight fifteen,
quarter after eight, or fifteen after eight

Remember you say "after" for times up to half past the hour.

Write the time shown in two ways.

1. 

2. 

Set 4-2 (pages 192–195)

Write >, <, or = for ●.

14 months ● 50 weeks

12 months = 1 year
So, 14 months is more than a year.
52 weeks = 1 year
So, 50 weeks is less than a year.

14 months > 50 weeks

Remember time can be measured in many different units.

Write >, <, or = for each ●.

1. 3 hours ● 185 minutes
2. 106 weeks ● 2 years
3. 2 months ● 70 days

Set 4-3 (pages 196–197)

Find the elapsed time from 11:48 A.M. to 1:15 P.M.

Count 1 hour from 11:48 A.M. to 12:48 P.M.
Count ahead 12 minutes from 12:48 P.M. to 1:00 P.M. Count 15 minutes to 1:15 P.M.
Add the minutes: 12 + 15 = 27

The elapsed time is 1 hour 27 minutes.

Remember elapsed time tells the amount of time that has passed.

Find each elapsed time.

1. Start: 2:00 P.M. Finish: 3:45 P.M.
2. Start: 10:16 A.M. Finish: 11:28 A.M.
3. Start: 9:48 P.M. Finish: 1:28 A.M.

Set 4-4 (pages 198–199)

Write a comparison statement for the data in the schedule.

Monty's Visit to Aunt Kim's
11:00 A.M. - 11:43 A.M. Drive
noon - 12:25 P.M. Lunch
12:45 P.M. -1:05 P.M. Play volleyball
1:10 P.M. - 2:10 P.M. Hike

Monty will spend more time driving to Aunt Kim's than eating lunch.

Remember to use contrast words like "fewer," "later," "however," or "but."

1. How long does Monty plan to play volleyball?
2. Write two other statements comparing the data in the schedule at the left.

Set 4-5 (pages 200–201)

What is the date two weeks after March 10?

March						
S	M	T	W	T	F	S
1	2	3	4	5	6	7
8	9	10	11	12	13	14
15	16	17	18	19	20	21
22	23	24	25	26	27	28
29	30	31				

Find March 10. Move down 2 rows for 2 weeks. Two weeks later is March 24.

Remember that you can move down one row on a calendar to find the date one week later and up one row to find the date one week earlier.

Find the date

1. two weeks after March 20.

2. two weeks before March 16.

3. Reasoning What day of the week is April first?

Set 4-6 (pages 204–205)

How many more pounds of paper were recycled in January than March?

Recycling Paper

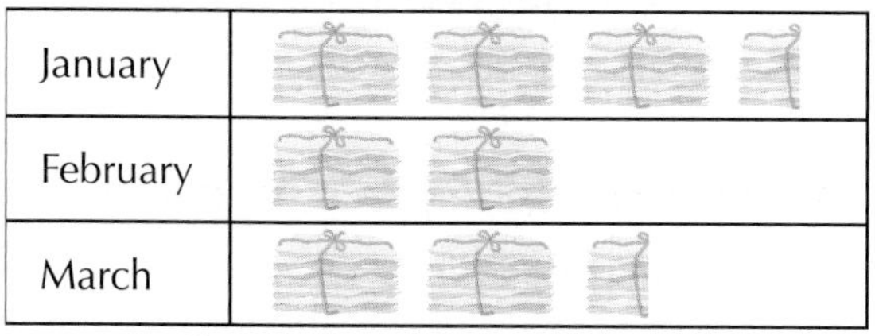

Each  = 100 pounds of paper.

There is one more bundle next to January than March. So, 100 more pounds of paper were recycled in January than March.

Remember that the key on a pictograph tells you what each symbol represents.

How many pounds of paper were recycled in

1. February? **2.** March?

3. How many more pounds of paper were recycled in January than in February?

4. During which month was the least amount of paper recycled?

Set 4-7 (pages 206–207)

Use the line plot. How many Super Readers read 9 books?

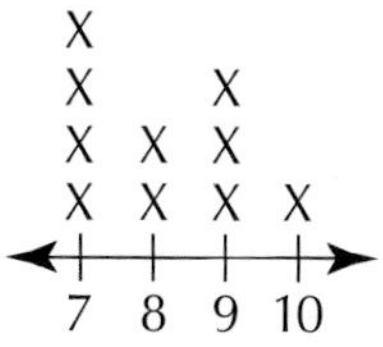

Super Readers Club Books Read This Year

There are 3 Xs above the 9, so 3 Super Readers read 9 books.

Remember that each X in a line plot stands for one number in the data.

How many Super Readers read

1. 8 books? **2.** 7 books?

3. What is the greatest number of books read by a Super Reader?

4. Number Sense Is there an outlier in the data? Explain.

Reteaching

Set 4-8 (pages 208–211)

Which animal has 32 teeth?

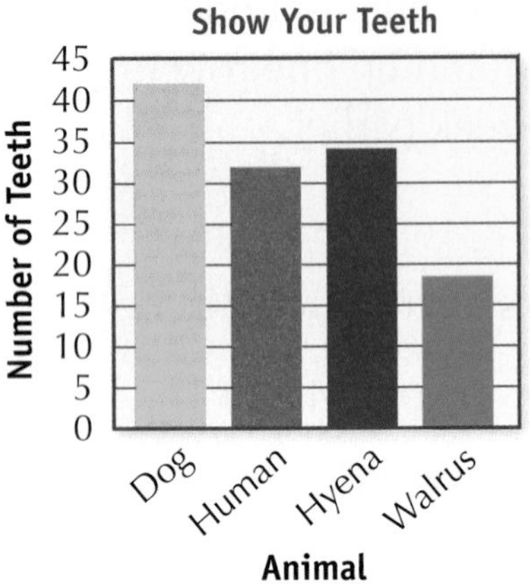

The bar that is just above the line for 30 is the one for humans. Humans have 32 teeth.

Remember to use a scale that starts at 0 and goes beyond the highest number in the data when you draw a bar graph.

1. What is the graph about?
2. What is the scale of the graph?
3. Which animal has 34 teeth?
4. About how many more teeth does a dog have than a human?

Set 4-9 (pages 212–215)

Name the ordered pair for point *A*.

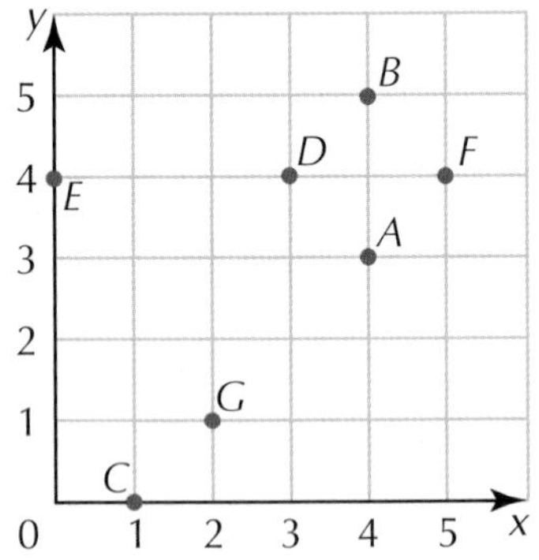

To get from 0 to *A*, you go right 4 units and up 3 units. The ordered pair for *A* is (4, 3).

Remember that the first number in an ordered pair tells how far to move right

Name the ordered pair for each point.

1. *G*
2. *D*
3. *C*

Give the letter of the point named by each ordered pair.

4. (4, 5)
5. (5, 4)
6. (0, 4)

Set 4-10 (pages 216–219)

In what year were there about 50 million subscribers?

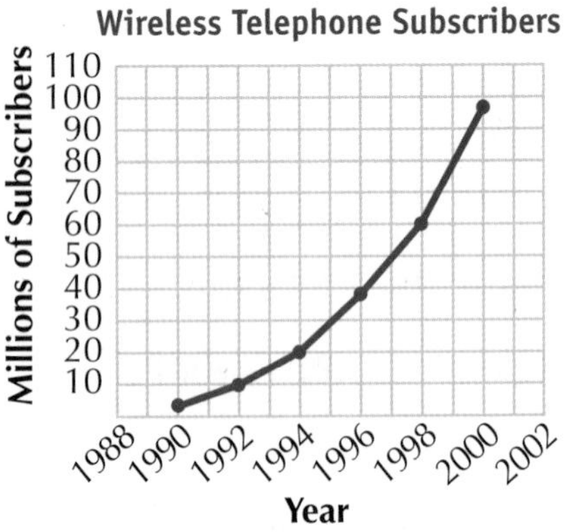

The graph crosses the grid line for 50 million about halfway between 1996 and 1998.

There were about 50 million wireless telephone subscribers in 1997.

Remember that line graphs show changes in data over time.

1. In what year were there about 60 million wireless telephone subscribers?
2. Between which two years did the number of subscribers increase the most?
3. What is the trend in the data?

Set 4-11 (pages 222–223)

Is Stacey's trip away from home or toward home?

Stacey's Trip

Minutes	0	2	4	6	8
Miles from Home	5	4	2	1	0

Draw a graph.

The trip is toward home.

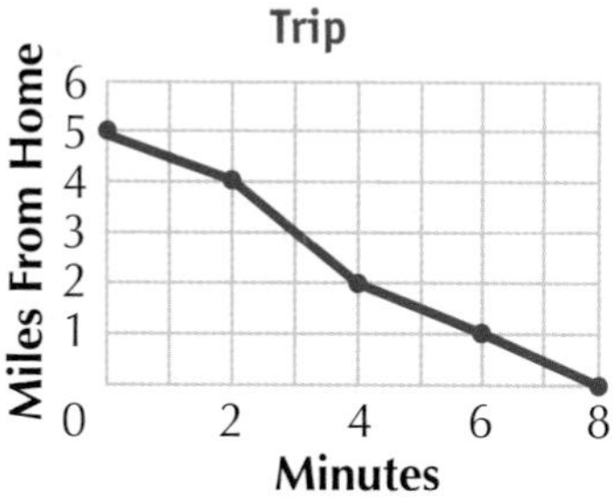

Remember that you can solve problems by making a graph.

1. How did Stacey's distance from home change from minute to minute?
2. During which 2 minutes did Stacey travel the most?

Set 4-12 (pages 226–229)

Find the median, mode, and range of the data: 15, 12, 9, 11, 10.

Put the data in order: 9, 10, 11, 12, 15

The median is the middle number, 11. There is no mode. The range is $15 - 9 = 6$.

Remember that the median is the middle number when the data are in order.

Find the median, mode, and range.

1. 6, 7, 5, 7, 9
2. 347, 350, 339
3. 17, 18, 18, 12, 3
4. 724, 564, 649

Set 4-13 (pages 230–231)

How many people in the survey liked to watch basketball best?

Nine people liked to watch basketball best.

Favorite Sport to Watch

Football	𝍸 𝍸 II
Baseball	IIII
Basketball	𝍸 IIII

Remember that you can answer a question by taking a survey.

1. How many people in the survey liked to watch baseball best?
2. Which sport was named by more people than any other sport?

Set 4-14 (pages 232–233)

Looking at the graph, how many times faster does a cheetah run than a cat?

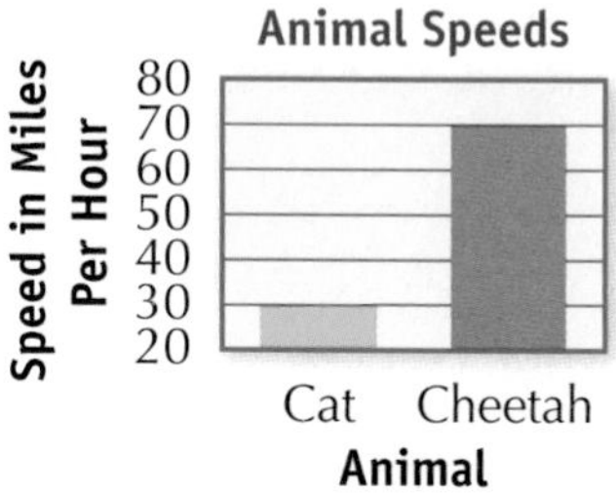

The cheetah seems to run 5 times faster than a cat.

Remember a graph can be misleading.

1. Is the cheetah 5 times faster than a cat?
2. Why is the graph misleading?

More Practice

Set 4-1 (pages 190–191)

Write the time shown on each clock in two ways.

1. 

2. 

3. 

4. 

5. **Number Sense** Write a reasonable time for eating lunch. Include A.M. or P.M.

Set 4-2 (pages 192–195)

Write >, <, or = for each ●.

1. 52 years ● 5 decades

2. 35 days ● 5 weeks

3. 30 months ● 2 years

4. 18 decades ● 2 centuries

5. 1 year ● 1 leap year

6. 3 days ● 70 hours

7. **Number Sense** About how long does it take you to get to school?

Set 4-3 (pages 196–197)

Find each elapsed time.

1. Start: 7:25 P.M.
Finish: 9:15 P.M.

2. Start: 8:15 A.M.
Finish: 3:05 P.M.

3. Start: 8:18 A.M.
Finish: 11:05 A.M.

4. Start: 9:30 A.M.
Finish: 10:45 A.M.

5. Start: noon
Finish: 2:00 A.M.

6. Start: 3:38 P.M.
Finish: 4:26 P.M.

7. A power failure stopped the clock at 8:05. The power returned after 45 minutes. To what time should you set the clock?

Set 4-4 (pages 198–199)

Use the schedule.

How much time is planned for

1. traveling?

2. touring the museum?

3. lunch?

4. visiting the park?

5. **Writing in Math** Write two statements comparing the data in the Field Trip Schedule.

Field Trip Schedule

Activity	Start	Finish
Travel	8:10 A.M.	9:25 A.M.
Tour museum	9:30 A.M.	11:15 A.M.
Lunch	11:30 A.M.	12:20 P.M.
Visit park	12:30 P.M.	1:10 P.M.

Take It to the NET
More Practice
www.scottforesman.com

Set 4-5 (pages 200–201)

1. Find the date two weeks before October 20th.

2. **Reasoning** What day of the week is the last day of September?

October

S	M	T	W	T	F	S
		1	2	3	4	5
6	7	8	9	10	11	12
13	14	15	16	17	18	19
20	21	22	23	24	25	26
27	28	29	30	31		

Set 4-6 (pages 204–205)

How many umbrellas were rented on

1. Saturday?
2. Monday?

How many more umbrellas were rented

3. on Saturday than Friday?
4. on Sunday than Wednesday?

5. On what day were the most umbrellas rented?

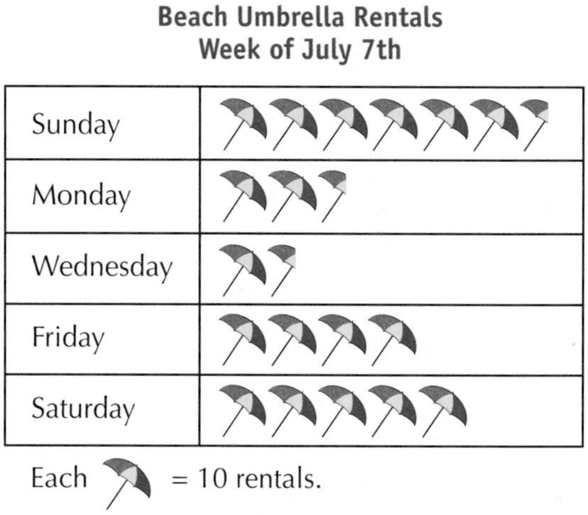

Set 4-7 (pages 206–207)

Use the line plot at the right.

1. What is the most common number of books read?

In October how many students read

2. 4 books?
3. 2 books?

4. **Reasoning** What is the greatest number of books read?

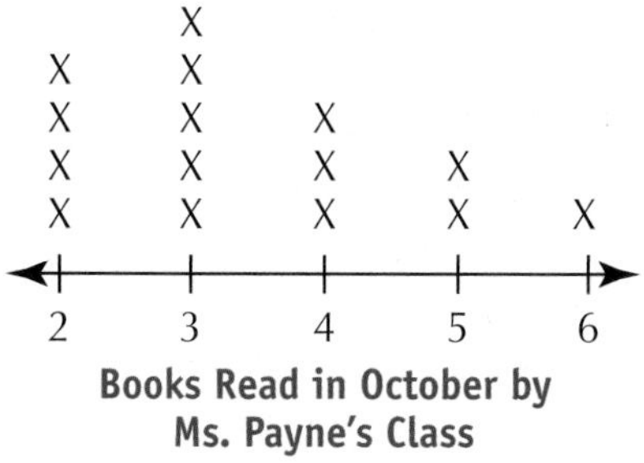

Set 4-8 (pages 208–211)

Use the bar graph at the right.

How many students were absent on

1. Wednesday?
2. Tuesday?

How many more students were absent on Thursday

3. than Friday?
4. than Tuesday?

5. On what day were the most students absent?

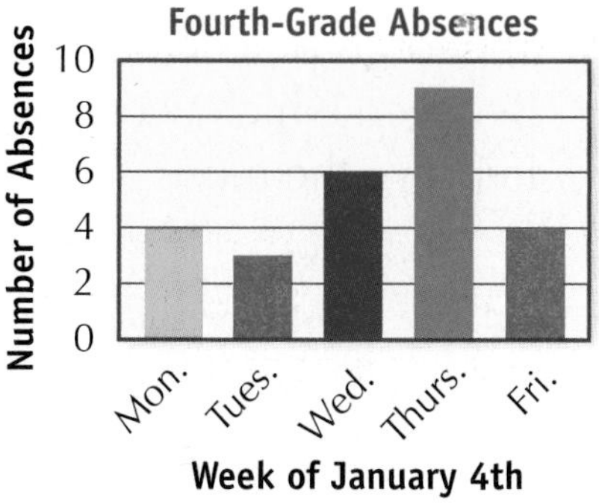

More Practice

Set 4-9 (pages 212–215)

Name the ordered pair for each point.

1. *B* **2.** *E* **3.** *F*

Give the letter of the point named by each ordered pair.

4. (1, 1) **5.** (5, 4) **6.** (4, 0)

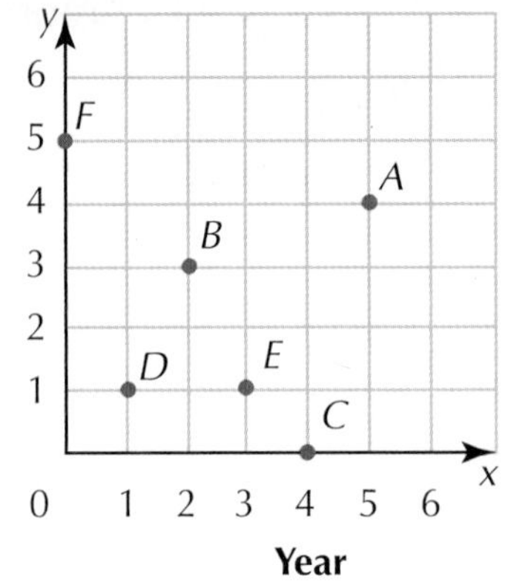

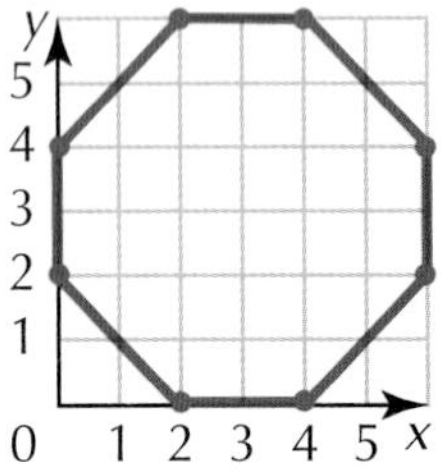

7. List the ordered pairs you could use to make the shape at the left.

Set 4-10 (pages 216–219)

The line graph shows the number of music CDs shipped and sold over several years.

About how many music CDs were shipped in

1. 1992? **2.** 2000?

3. In what year were about 710 million music CDs shipped?

4. Did the number of CDs shipped increase more between 1992 and 1994 or between 1998 and 2000?

5. Reasoning What is the trend in the data?

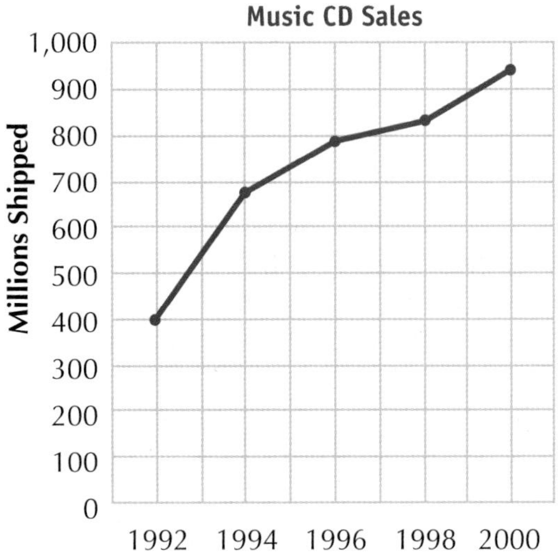

Set 4-11 (pages 222–223)

Copy and complete the graph to solve the problem.

1. Shelton is practicing the long jump. Between which two days did he improve the most?

Shelton's Long Jump
Best Daily Jump in Inches

Monday	Tuesday	Wednesday	Thursday
34	40	43	52

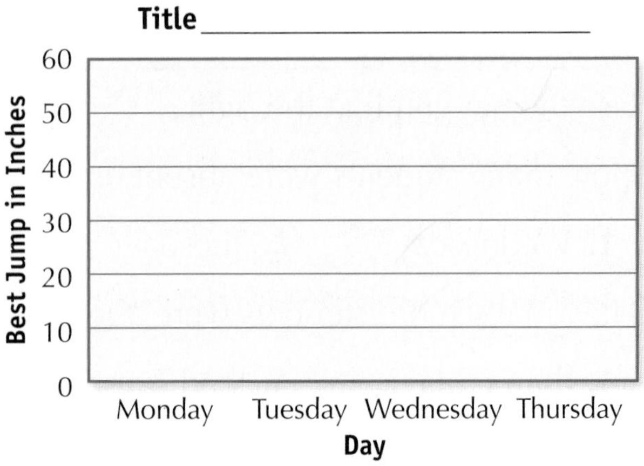

Set 4-12 (pages 226–227)

Find the median, mode, and range of each set of data.

1. 43, 45, 44, 45, 42
2. 8, 7, 6, 7, 7, 5, 5
3. 83, 82, 79, 90, 82
4. 2, 1, 1, 3, 1, 1, 7, 2, 4
5. 53, 52, 58, 52, 60, 52, 58
6. 293, 300, 304, 298, 293
7. 592, 600, 704, 691, 625, 648, 691, 595, 656
8. 28, 30, 28, 25, 32, 24, 36, 32, 29, 25, 32, 38, 26
9. 3, 9, 10, 8, 4, 4, 2, 7, 1, 5, 3, 4, 6, 3, 2, 4, 8
10. **Number Sense** If 10 is added to the data in Exercise 2, would the range change? What if 6 is added instead? Explain.

Set 4-13 (pages 230–231)

Use the data in the tally chart at the right for 1–4.

Favorite Color

Red	~~IIII~~ ~~IIII~~
Blue	~~IIII~~ III
Green	~~IIII~~ I
Orange	IIII
Purple	II

1. How many people in the survey liked blue best?
2. How many people were surveyed?
3. Which color is the favorite of more people than any other?
4. **Reasoning** If twice as many people were surveyed, how many do you think would say they liked orange best? Explain.
5. **Writing in Math** Take a survey to find out the favorite color of students in your class. Write down the question you ask. Give your results on a tally chart.

Set 4-14 (pages 232–233)

Use the bar graph at the right.

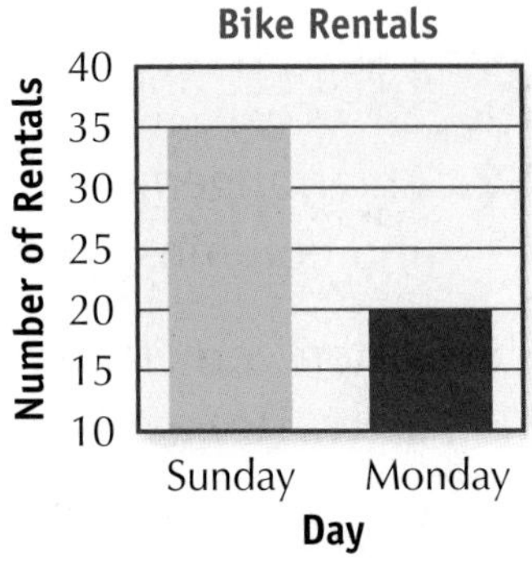

1. Looking at the graph, about how many times as many bikes does it seem were rented on Sunday than on Monday?
2. How bikes were rented each day?
3. Were twice as many bikes rented on Sunday as on Monday?
4. **Reasoning** Why is the Bike Rentals graph misleading?

CHAPTER

5 Multiplying by One-Digit Numbers

DIAGNOSING READINESS

A Vocabulary

(pages 20, 124)

Choose the best term from the box.

1. In the number sentence 4 × 7 = 28, 4 is a _?_ and 28 is a _?_.

2. An arrangement of objects in rows and columns is called a(n) _?_.

3. When you estimate to the nearest 10 or 100, you may use _?_.

Vocabulary

- **array** *(p. 124)*
- **factor** *(p. 124)*
- **rounding** *(p. 20)*
- **product** *(p. 124)*

B Multiplication Facts

(pages 128–135)

4. 4 × 5 **5.** 6 × 7 **6.** 8 × 4

7. 7 × 8 **8.** 9 × 6 **9.** 6 × 8

10. 9 × 7 **11.** 7 × 7 **12.** 8 × 9

13. Draw an array to show 4 × 8.

14. There are 5 glue sticks in each box. How many glue sticks are there in 7 boxes?

Do You Know...

How long would it take to fill the fuel tank of a jumbo jet at your local gas station?

You'll find out in Lesson 5-12.

C Rounding

(pages 20–21)

15. What number is halfway between 40 and 50?

16. What number is halfway between 300 and 400?

Round each number to the nearest hundred.

17. 436 **18.** 765 **19.** 652

20. 149 **21.** 351 **22.** 599

23. Explain how to round 549 to the hundreds place.

D Multiplying by 10, 100, or 1,000 *(Grade 3)*

24. 5×10 **25.** 8×10

26. 6×10 **27.** 2×100

28. 3×100 **29.** 7×100

30. $4 \times 1{,}000$ **31.** $9 \times 1{,}000$

32. Carrie's goal is to bicycle 100 miles each day for 5 days. How far will she have bicycled if she meets her goal?

Key Idea
A pattern can help you multiply by numbers like 40, 300, or 8,000.

Vocabulary
- product (p. 124)

Materials
- calculator

TEST TALK

Think It Through
I can **look for a pattern** to find a rule.

$3 \times 6 = 18$
$3 \times 60 = 180$
$3 \times 600 = 1{,}800$
$3 \times 6{,}000 = \square$

Multiplying by Multiples of 10, 100, or 1,000

WARM UP

1. 8×4
2. 6×6
3. 5×7
4. 8×6
5. 3×9
6. 7×4

LEARN

Activity

What's the rule?

a. Use a calculator to find each missing product.

$3 \times 4 = 12$	$2 \times 3 = 6$	$4 \times 7 = 28$
$3 \times 40 = \square$	$2 \times 30 = \square$	$4 \times 70 = \square$
$3 \times 400 = \square$	$2 \times 300 = \square$	$4 \times 700 = \square$
$3 \times 4{,}000 = \square$	$2 \times 3{,}000 = \square$	$4 \times 7{,}000 = \square$

b. Find each product without a calculator. Then check your answers with a calculator.

4×8	7×5	6×9
4×80	7×50	6×90
4×800	7×500	6×900
$4 \times 8{,}000$	$7 \times 5{,}000$	$6 \times 9{,}000$

c. Describe a rule that tells how to find each product.

Does your rule always work?

I get it! There are 2 zeros in 400. So by my rule, the product will always have exactly 2 zeros.
Not always. It depends.

When you multiply by 400, how many zeros are in the product? Read what Tom and Sue thought.

Talk About It

1. **Reasoning** Who's correct? Use 6×400 and 5×400 to decide. Explain.
2. How many zeros do the products of 5×200, 5×600, and 5×800 have?

CHECK ✓

For another example, see Set 5-1 on p. 304.

Find each product. Use mental math.

1. $4 \times 70 = \square$ **2.** $5 \times 600 = \square$ **3.** $7 \times 4{,}000 = \square$

4. Number Sense Tell what number goes in the blank. To find $4 \times 7{,}000$, multiply 4 and 7. Then write $\square$ zeros at the end.

PRACTICE

For more practice, see Set 5-1 on p. 308.

A Skills and Understanding

Find each product. Use mental math.

5. 2×30 **6.** 10×7 **7.** 4×80 **8.** 7×50 **9.** 8×50

10. 5×200 **11.** 200×8 **12.** 6×600 **13.** 9×500 **14.** 4×800

15. $3 \times 2{,}000$ **16.** $7 \times 4{,}000$ **17.** $9 \times 5{,}000$ **18.** $8{,}000 \times 8$ **19.** $4 \times 5{,}000$

20. Number Sense Tell what number goes in the blank. To find 3×600, multiply 3 and 6. Then write $\square$ zeros at the end.

B Reasoning and Problem Solving

Compared to a hand, an arm has 20 times as many miles of blood vessels and a whole human body has 6,000 times as many. How many miles are in the

21. arm? **22.** whole human body?

23. Writing in Math Explain why the product for 6×500 has three zeros when there are only two zeros in 500.

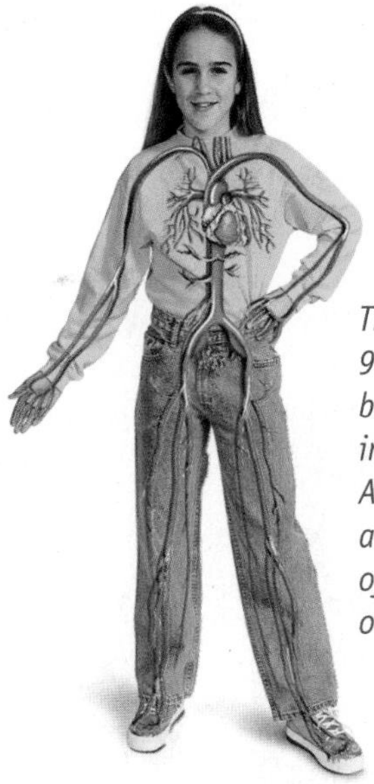

There are 9 miles of blood vessels in the hand. An adult has about 6 quarts of blood in his or her body.

Mixed Review and Test Prep

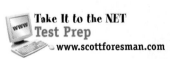

Take It to the NET
Test Prep
www.scottforesman.com

24. Writing in Math Explain why the graph at the right is misleading.

Popcorn Comparison

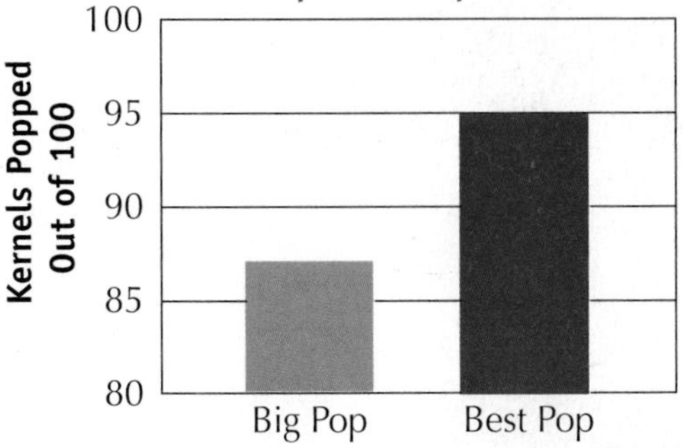

25. Which of these numbers is equal to 20 hundreds?

A. 20 **C.** 2,000

B. 200 **D.** 20,000

Key Idea
To estimate, use factors you can multiply mentally.

Vocabulary
- rounding (p. 20)
- compatible numbers
- underestimate (p. 72)
- overestimate (p. 72)

Estimating Products

WARM UP

Round to the place with the underlined digit.

1. 68
2. 52
3. 81
4. 35
5. 465
6. 350
7. Estimate the total cost of a $498 TV and a $217 VCR.

LEARN

Exact answer or estimate?

The panda eats 150 pounds of bamboo in a weekend. A zookeeper has four 26-pound sacks of bamboo. Is this enough to feed the panda for the weekend?

Have

(26) (26) (26) (26)

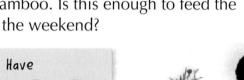

Need 150
Estimate 4 x 26. Then compare that estimate to 150.

TEST TALK

Think It Through
- I only need an **estimate** because I just need to know if there's enough.
- I can **draw a picture** to show the main idea.

What are some ways to estimate?

Example A

Estimate 4 × 26.

Compatible numbers are numbers that are easy to compute with mentally.

One Way

Lucy used **rounding.**

I rounded 26 to 30.
4 x 26
4 x 30 = 120
So, 4 x 26 is about 120.

Since 26 was rounded to 30, Lucy found an overestimate. The exact product is less than 120.

Another Way

Al used **compatible numbers.**

I replaced 26 with 25.
4 x 26
4 x 25 = 100
So, 4 x 26 is about 100.

Since 26 was adjusted to 25, Al found an underestimate. The exact product is greater than 100.

Both estimates are less than 150. The zookeeper needs 150 pounds, so he does not have enough food for the weekend.

These examples involve larger numbers.

Rabbits

- Each eats 8 ounces of food daily.
- Each weighs 2 pounds.

Giraffe

- Eats 243 times as much as one rabbit daily.
- Weighs 2,179 times as much as one rabbit.

Example B

About how many ounces of food does the giraffe eat daily?

Estimate 8×243 using compatible numbers.

$$\mathbf{8 \times 243}$$

$$\downarrow$$

$$\mathbf{8 \times 250 = 2{,}000}$$

Four 250s is 1,000. Eight 250s is 2,000. So, 8×243 is about 2,000.

The giraffe eats about 2,000 ounces of food daily.

Example C

About how many pounds does the giraffe weigh?

Estimate $2 \times 2{,}179$ using rounding.

$$\mathbf{2 \times 2{,}179}$$

$$\downarrow$$

$$\mathbf{2 \times 2{,}000 = 4{,}000}$$

2,179 rounds to 2,000. So, $2 \times 2{,}179$ is about 4,000.

The giraffe weighs about 4,000 pounds.

Talk About It

1. In Example A, which compatible numbers did Al use?
2. In Example B, is 2,000 an underestimate or an overestimate?
3. **Reasoning** In Example C, how do you know if the exact answer for $2 \times 2{,}179$ is closer to $2 \times 2{,}000 = 4{,}000$ or to $2 \times 3{,}000 = 6{,}000$?

CHECK

For another example, see Set 5-2 on p. 304.

Estimate each product.

1. 5×82 **2.** 53×3 **3.** 6×33 **4.** 4×678 **5.** 463×7

6. Number Sense Estimate to decide if 4×68 is less than or greater than 280. Tell how you decided.

For more practice, see Set 5-2 on p. 308.

A Skills and Understanding

7. 6 × 34 is close to 6 × ▢.

8. 7 × 284 is close to 7 × ▢.

Estimate each product.

9. 4 × 56	**10.** 9 × 62	**11.** 8 × 105	**12.** 3 × 97	**13.** 4 × 77
14. 6 × 82	**15.** 26 × 5	**16.** 7 × 395	**17.** 5 × 625	**18.** 9 × 58
19. 6 × 145	**20.** 59 × 6	**21.** 4 × 677	**22.** 8 × 804	**23.** 3 × 75
24. 8 × 458	**25.** 2 × 399	**26.** 7 × 998	**27.** 9 × 5,064	**28.** 8 × 949

29. Number Sense Estimate to decide if 6 × 412 is less than or greater than 2,400. Tell how you decided.

B Reasoning and Problem Solving

Math and Science

Use the bar graph at the right for 30–35. Elephants are the largest land animals. Estimate how much of each food a zoo elephant eats in 6 months.

30. Carrots

31. Apples

32. Pellets

33. Hay

34. Estimate how many pounds of food a zoo elephant eats in 1 month.

35. A zoo elephant eats about how many more pounds of hay than apples in a month?

36. **Writing in Math** Is the explanation below correct? If not, tell why and write a correct explanation.

> Is the exact answer to 7 × 234 closer to 7 × 200 = 1,400 or to 7 × 300 = 2,100? Explain.
>
> I think the exact answer to 7 x 234 is closer to 2,100 because 234 is greater than 200.

Amount of Food Eaten by a Zoo Elephant in One Month

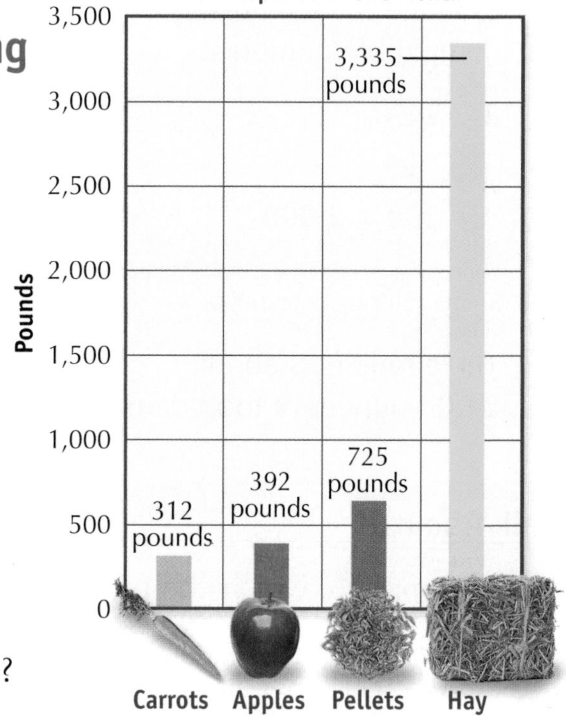

A newborn elephant can weigh about 200 pounds.

TEST TALK

Think It Through

- I will **check if the answer is complete.**
- I will **check if the answer makes sense.**

C Extensions

Number Sense In 37–39, use estimation to help you find two numbers whose product is between

37. 1,200 and 1,500.

38. 600 and 800.

39. 5,000 and 10,000.

Mixed Review and Test Prep

Take It to the NET
Test Prep
www.scottforesman.com

Find each answer.

40. 453 + 5,788

41. 3,000 × 8

42. \$25.13 − \$18.45

43. A rectangle has how many sides?

44. How many quarts are in a gallon?

45. Which of these sums is closest to 28 + 69?

A. 20 + 60
B. 20 + 70
C. 30 + 60
D. 30 + 70

46. **Algebra** If $n = 37$, what is the value of $87 + n - 9$?

A. 41
B. 78
C. 115
D. 133

47. **Writing in Math** Ann has an older sister named Ruth. Let *a* represent Ann's age. Write a problem that the equation $a + 3 = 15$ might be used to solve.

48. Ed is 28 and drives 18 miles roundtrip to work. About how many miles does he live from work?

A. 9 miles
B. 10 miles
C. 14 miles
D. 46 miles

Practice Game

The Multiplication Estimation Game

Players: 4 **Material:** Spinner numbered 1–8

Players take turns. On each turn, a player spins the spinner 4 times to get 4 digits that can be placed in any blank.

▯ × ▯▯▯

The player estimates the product using rounding. That estimate is the number of points the player gets on that turn. The first player to get 50,000 points wins.

Key Idea
The ways you find products mentally depends on the kinds of numbers in the calculation.

Vocabulary
- breaking apart (p. 62)
- compatible numbers (p. 258)

Mental Math

WARM UP

1. 40 × 2
2. 60 + 8
3. 70 − 7
4. 200 × 3
5. 500 × 4
6. 160 + 28

LEARN

What are some ways to multiply mentally?

Example A

Find 2 × 64 by **breaking apart** numbers.

STEP 1 Use place value to break apart 64 into 60 and 4.

64 = 60 + 4

STEP 2 Think of 2 × 64 as 2 × 60 and 2 × 4.

(2 × 60) + (2 × 4)
120 + 8

STEP 3 Add the partial products to get the total.
120 + 8 = 128

2 × 64 = 128

Example B

Find 18 × 3 by using **compatible numbers.**

STEP 1 Substitute a compatible number for 18 that is easy to multiply by 3.

18 × 3
↓ Add 2 to make 20.
20 × 3

STEP 2 Find the new product.

20 × 3 = 60

STEP 3 Now adjust. Subtract 2 groups of 3.
60 − 6 = 54.

18 × 3 = 54

I get it. 18 × 3 means 18 groups of 3.

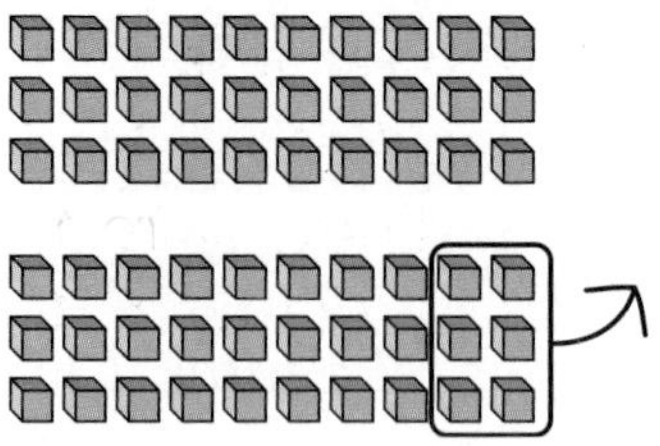

Since I found 20 groups of 3, I need to subtract 2 groups of 3 for the final answer.

Talk About It

1. Can you find 3 × 18 by breaking apart? Explain.
2. Why are 20 and 3 compatible numbers?
3. How can you find 4 × 19 using compatible numbers?

CHECK ✓

For another example, see Set 5-3 on p. 304.

Use the break apart method to find each product mentally.

1. 4×36 **2.** 8×52 **3.** 63×2 **4.** 81×4 **5.** 41×92

Use compatible numbers to find each product mentally.

6. 3×32 **7.** 28×5 **8.** 4×79 **9.** 58×3 **10.** 8×59

11. Number Sense Which method would you use to find 48×6? Explain.

PRACTICE

For more practice, see Set 5-3 on p. 308.

A Skills and Understanding

Use mental math to find each product.

12. 32×6 **13.** 7×19 **14.** 8×61 **15.** 59×5 **16.** 4×15

17. 51×9 **18.** 99×8 **19.** 32×5 **20.** 3×72 **21.** 29×6

22. 7×39 **23.** 59×3 **24.** 38×6 **25.** 5×71 **26.** 83×4

27. 9×81 **28.** 5×29 **29.** 9×21 **30.** 6×51 **31.** 5×78

32. Number Sense How would you find 26×8 mentally?

B Reasoning and Problem Solving

33. Algebra In $a \times c = 128$, a is a one-digit number and c is a two-digit number. What numbers could a and c represent?

34. Writing in Math The tall tale of Paul Bunyan says he was 3 times as tall as a 28-foot tree. The horns on his ox, Babe, were 4 times as wide as a 25-foot river. How tall was Paul? How wide were Babe's horns? Explain how you found your answers.

Mixed Review and Test Prep

Take It to the NET
Test Prep
www.scottforesman.com

Find each answer.

35. $2,500 - 375$ **36.** $906 + 48$ **37.** $314 + 108 + 36$

38. Which is a reasonable estimate for $8,892 + 2,388$?

A. 11,000 **B.** 16,000 **C.** 100,000 **D.** 110,000

Key Idea
To find a product like 5 × 3, you can build an array and break it into two simpler parts.

Vocabulary
- array (p. 124)
- partial products

Materials
- place-value blocks

or e tools

TEST TALK

Think It Through
- I can **choose multiplication** when I'm joining equal groups.
- I can **use objects** to **solve a simpler problem.**

Using Arrays to Multiply

WARM UP

1. 8 + 30
2. 7 + 140
3. 14 + 70
4. 56 + 120
5. 6 + 130
6. 72 + 130
7. Jenny planted 5 rows of tulips with 8 in each row and 5 rows of petunias with 6 in each row. How many flowers did she plant in all?

LEARN

Activity

How do you multiply using an array?

An array is an arrangement of objects in equal rows. The picture shows an array of windows. Here's how to find the product of 5 × 15 using an array of place-value blocks.

Step 1: Use place-value blocks to build the array.

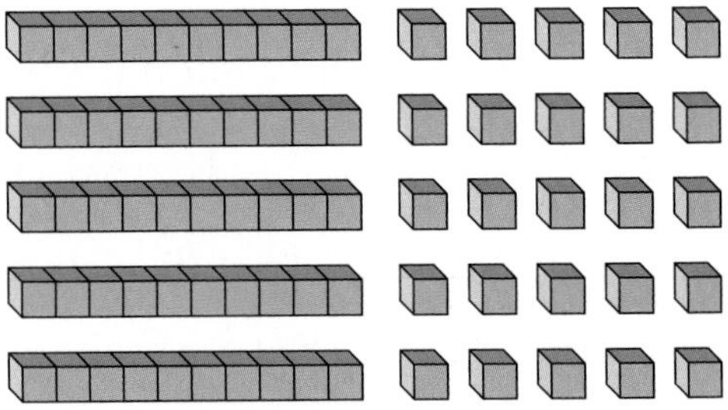

5 rows with 1 ten and 5 ones in each.

Step 2: Break apart the array into ones and tens.

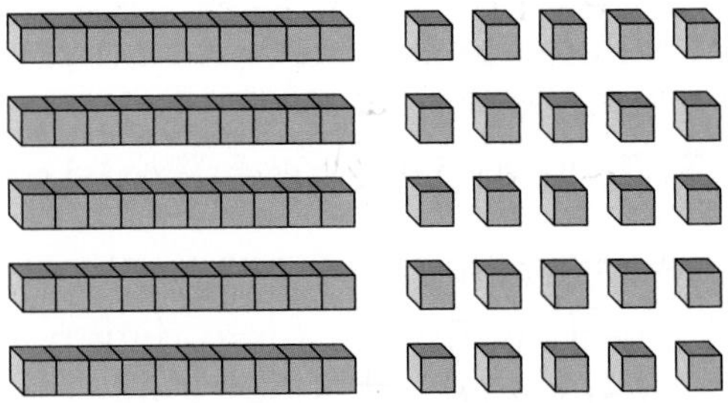

5 rows, 1 ten in each
5 × 10 = 50

5 rows, 5 ones in each
5 × 5 = 25

Step 3: Add the tens and ones. Give the product.

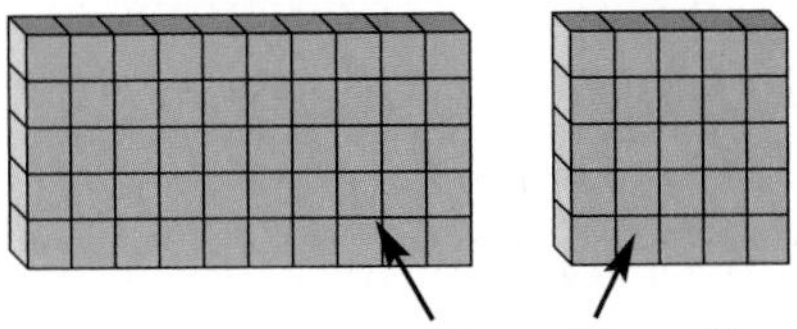

50 + 25 = 75
So 5 × 15 = 75.

a. Use place-value blocks to build each array. Follow the steps above to find each product.

2 × 14   3 × 16   2 × 24   3 × 12   2 × 32

b. Explain how breaking apart the array for 2 × 24 into tens and ones is like solving two simpler problems. What are the simpler problems?

Activity

How do you record what you showed with the array?

Here is one way to record what you do using an array of place-value blocks to find the product for 2×26.

What You **Show**	What You **Write**
2×26 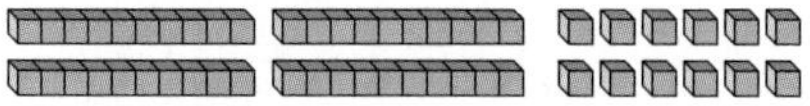 $2 \times 20 = 40$ $2 \times 6 = 12$ $40 + 12 = 52$	26 × 2 12 2 × 6 ones 40 2 × 2 tens 52

The numbers 12 and 40 are called **partial products;** 52 is the product.

a. Use place-value blocks to build each array. Follow the method above to find each product.

2×16 3×26 2×21 3×13 2×22

b. In the array shown above, where do you see 12? 40?

c. What are the partial products for each product above? What is the product?

Take It to the NET
More Examples
www.scottforesman.com

CHECK

For another example, see Set 5-4 on p. 305.

Use blocks or draw a picture to build an array.
Then copy and complete the calculation.

1. 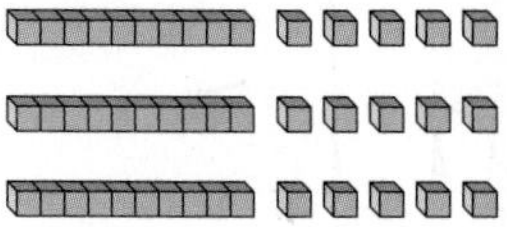

15
× 3

2. 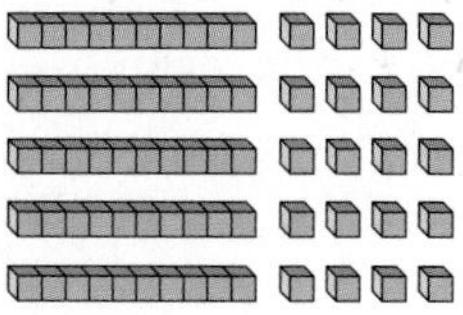

14
× 5

3. 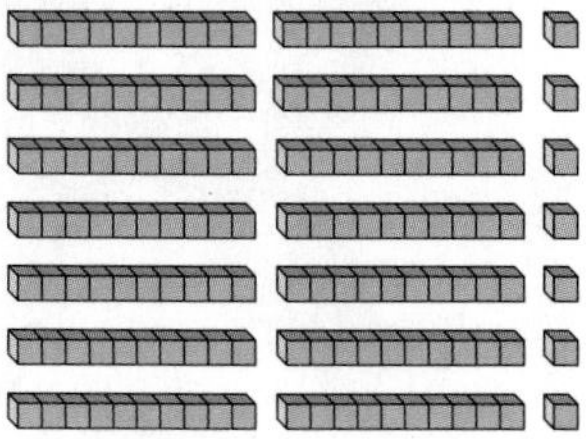

21
× 7

4. 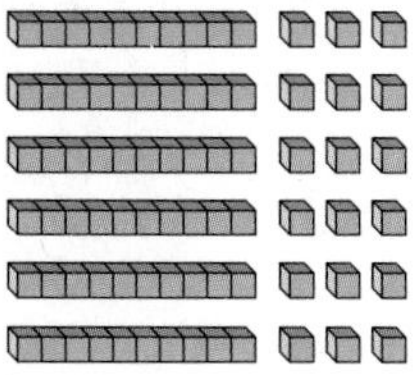

13
× 6

Think It Through
I'll **draw pictures** to show blocks. I'll draw segments for tens and dots for ones.

or

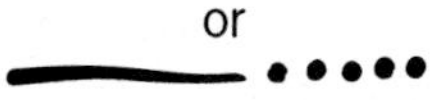

5. Number Sense What two simpler problems can you use to find 3×24? (Hint: Think about tens and ones.)

PRACTICE

For more practice, see Set 5-4 on p. 309.

A Skills and Understanding

Use the array to find the partial products and the product. Copy and complete the calculation.

6. 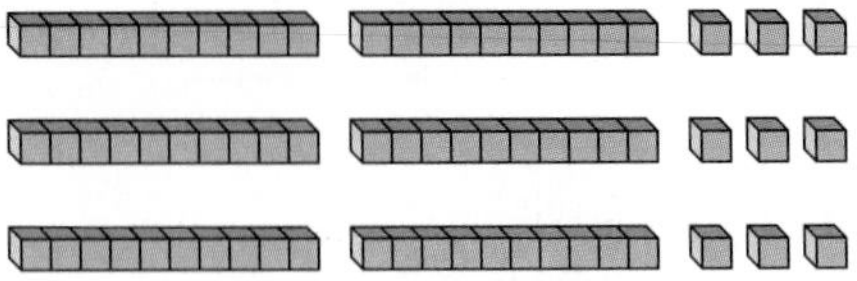

$$\begin{array}{r} 23 \\ \times\ 3 \\ \hline \blacksquare \\ \blacksquare\blacksquare \\ \hline \blacksquare\blacksquare \end{array}$$

7. 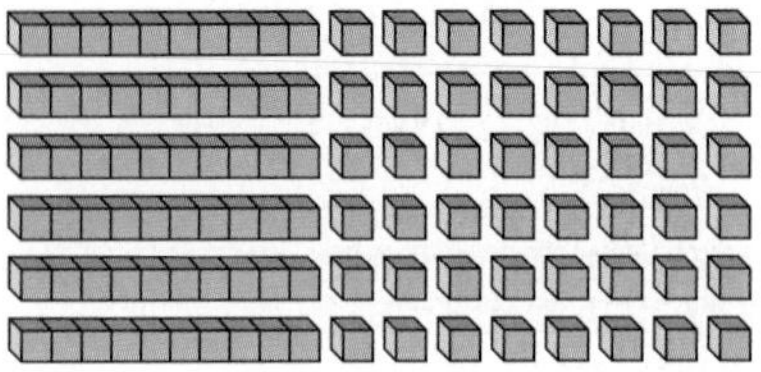

$$\begin{array}{r} 18 \\ \times\ 6 \\ \hline \blacksquare\blacksquare \\ \blacksquare\blacksquare \\ \hline \blacksquare\blacksquare\blacksquare \end{array}$$

8. $\begin{array}{r} 16 \\ \times\ 3 \\ \hline \blacksquare\blacksquare \\ \blacksquare\blacksquare \\ \hline \blacksquare\blacksquare \end{array}$

9. $\begin{array}{r} 12 \\ \times\ 4 \\ \hline \blacksquare \\ \blacksquare\blacksquare \\ \hline \blacksquare\blacksquare \end{array}$

10. $\begin{array}{r} 25 \\ \times\ 2 \\ \hline \blacksquare\blacksquare \\ \blacksquare\blacksquare \\ \hline \blacksquare\blacksquare \end{array}$

11. $\begin{array}{r} 18 \\ \times\ 3 \\ \hline \blacksquare\blacksquare \\ \blacksquare\blacksquare \\ \hline \blacksquare\blacksquare \end{array}$

12. 2×17

13. 5×14

14. 3×26

15. 3×27

16. Number Sense Into what two simpler problems can you break apart 5×38? (Hint: Think about tens and ones.)

B Reasoning and Problem Solving

Math and Art

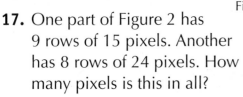

In the late 19th century, Leo Gausson painted *House on the Bank of the River* using dots of paint. In 2001, a computer artist drew Figure 2. The computer stored the picture using arrays of squares called pixels.

House on the Bank of the River

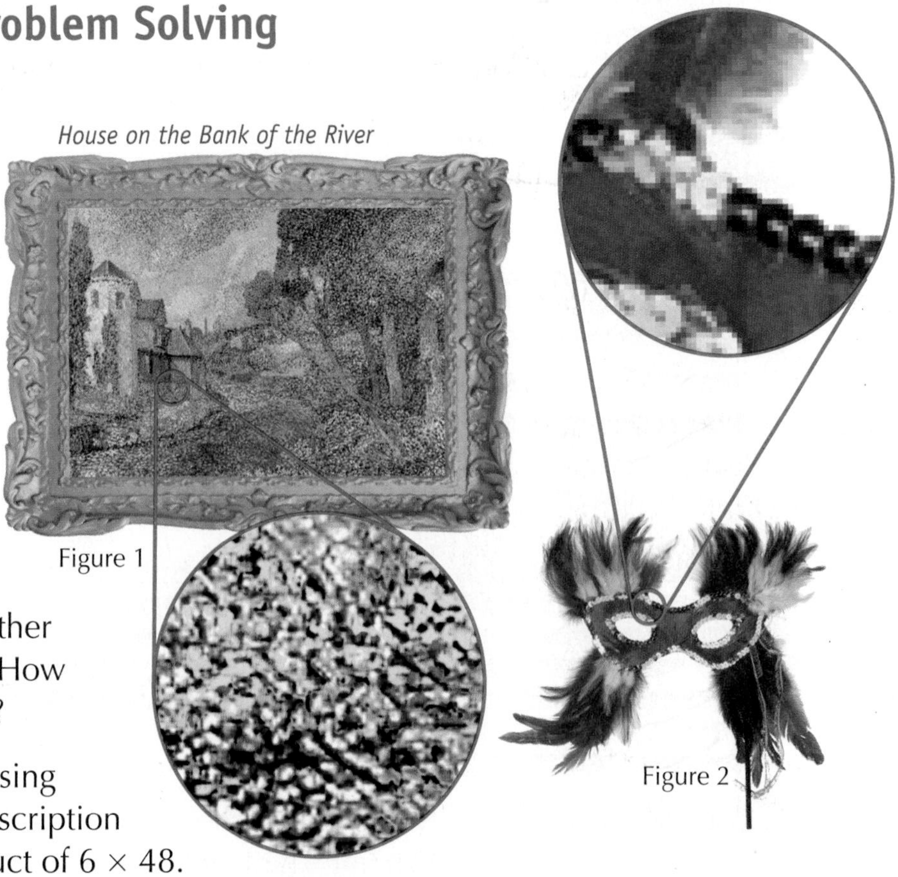

Figure 1

Figure 2

17. One part of Figure 2 has 9 rows of 15 pixels. Another has 8 rows of 24 pixels. How many pixels is this in all?

18. Writing in Math Without using actual blocks, write a description of the array for the product of 6×48.

Mixed Review and Test Prep

Take It to the NET
Test Prep
www.scottforesman.com

Use mental math to find each product.

19. 19×4 **20.** 99×6 **21.** 7×41 **22.** 2×38

23. Which of these answers is correct?

A. $2 \times 8 = 48$ **B.** $9 \times 8 = 74$ **C.** $39 - 10 = 19$ **D.** $40 + 8 = 48$

Enrichment

The Distributive Property

Algebra As shown below, the Distributive Property lets you break problems such as 3×21 into two simpler problems.

What You See	Why It Works	
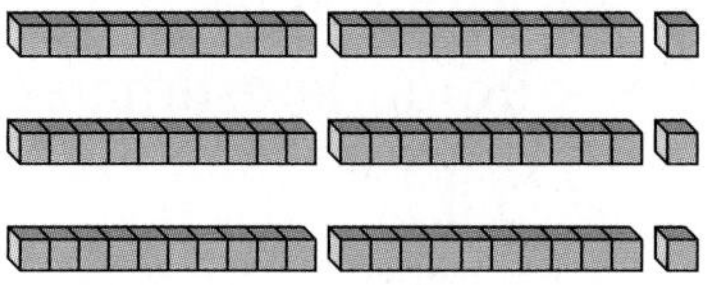	$3 \times 21 = 3 \times (20 + 1)$	Break 21 apart using place value.
	$= (3 \times 20) + (3 \times 1)$	Distributive Property
	$= 60 + 3$	Find each product.
	$= 63$	Add the products.

Show how the Distributive Property can be used to find each product.

1. 4×35 **2.** 7×36 **3.** 6×52 **4.** 8×43

Learning with Technology

Using Arrays to Multiply

Find the product 4×23 using the array workspace of the Place-Value Blocks eTool. To find 4×23, draw a box 23 units wide and 4 units tall. Begin filling the box with rows of 2 ten blocks and 3 unit blocks.

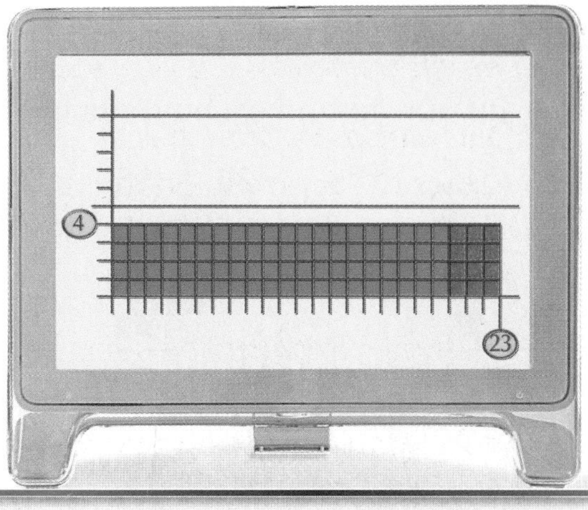

1. How do the number of ones, tens, and odometer total change as you build the array?

For 2–4, estimate each product first. Then check the odometer total against your estimate.

2. 5×13 **3.** 6×52 **4.** 7×73

Section A: Lessons 5-1 through 5-4

Review

Do You Know How?

Do You Understand?

Multiplying by Multiples of 10, 100, or 1,000 (5-1)

Find each product.

1. 3 × 40 **2.** 5 × 200

3. 6 × 7,000 **4.** 4 × 500

5. 7 × 400 **6.** 2 × 6,000

A Explain how you found the answer to Exercise 3.

B If you are multiplying by 400, when will the product have more than 2 zeros? Tell why.

Estimating Products (5-2)

Estimate each product.

7. 2 × 47 **8.** 5 × 355

9. 6 × 705 **10.** 3 × 73

11. 5 × 584 **12.** 8 × 99

C Describe two ways to estimate 4 × 23.

D Is your estimate for Exercise 9 an overestimate or an underestimate? Explain.

Mental Math (5-3)

Use mental math to find each product.

13. 48 × 3 **14.** 7 × 24

15. 73 × 2 **16.** 9 × 65

17. 22 × 8 **18.** 39 × 5

E Tell for which exercises you used breaking apart.

F Tell how you could use compatible numbers to find the product in Exercise 14.

Using Arrays to Multiply (5-4)

Use an array to find each product.

19.
```
  35
×  2
----
  ■■
  ■■
----
  ■■
```

20.
```
  16
×  8
----
  ■■
  ■■
----
 ■■■
```

G What are the partial products in Exercises 19 and 20?

H What two simpler problems can you use to find 4 × 53?

Diagnostic Checkpoint

TEST TALK

Think It Through
For multiple-choice items, first **eliminate any unreasonable answers.**

MULTIPLE CHOICE

1. An airline ticket to Paris costs $400. What is the cost of 5 tickets? (5-1)

A. $200 **B.** $1,000 **C.** $2,000 **D.** $2,500

2. Which is the best estimate of 48×9? (5-2)

A. 500 **B.** 600 **C.** 700 **D.** 800

FREE RESPONSE

Use mental math to find each product. (5-1, 5-3)

3. 6×10 **4.** 8×50 **5.** $2 \times 5{,}000$ **6.** 7×700 **7.** 3×900

8. 2×48 **9.** 6×19 **10.** 5×99 **11.** 8×31 **12.** 4×103

Estimate each product. (5-2)

13. 8×46 **14.** 5×14 **15.** 5×815 **16.** 2×889 **17.** 4×606

Use blocks or draw a picture to build an array. Then give each product. (5-4)

18. 27×3 **19.** 12×5 **20.** 48×4 **21.** 74×7

Use the pictograph at the right for 22–25. (5-1)

How far are two round-trips from New York to

22. Berlin? **23.** Honolulu?

24. Juneau? **25.** Cape Town?

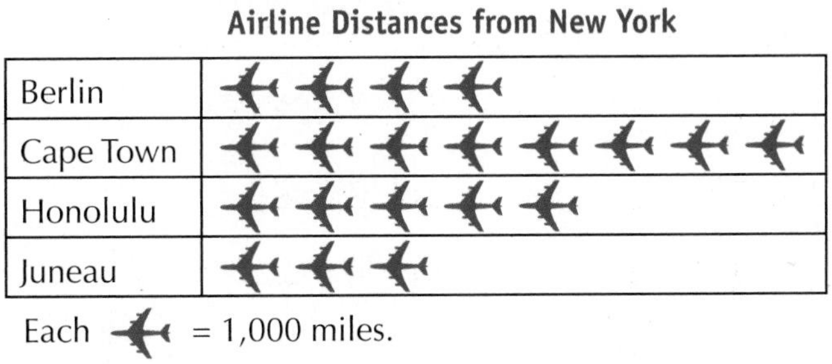

Writing in Math

26. Explain how you can tell how many zeros are in the product of 3×700. (5-1)

27. Is $6 \times 7{,}204$ greater than or less than 42,000? Tell how you decided without finding an exact answer. (5-2)

28. Explain how to find 5×18 by breaking it into two simpler problems. (5-4)

Key Idea
To find a product like 3 × 26, break it into simpler problems.

Multiplying Two-Digit and One-Digit Numbers

WARM UP

1. 8 × 4
2. 6 × 6
3. 5 × 7
4. 8 × 6
5. 3 × 9
6. 7 × 4

LEARN

What data do you need?

When air travel began, it was much slower than it is today. How far would the 1903 plane travel in 3 seconds?

Data File

History of Flight

Year	Event	Speed (feet per second)
1783	First balloon flight	3
1804	First model glider	5
1903	First powered flight	26
1966	First jumbo jet	851

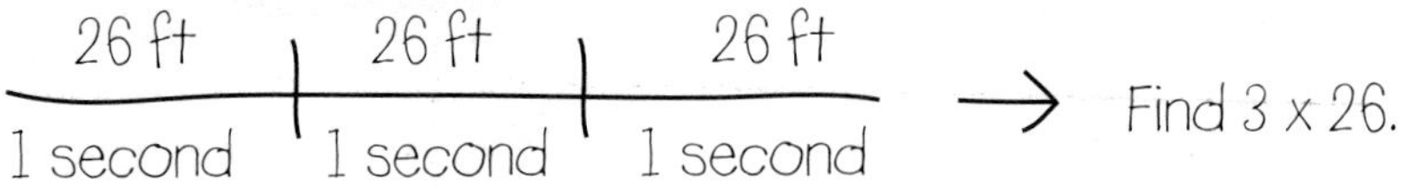

TEST TALK

Think It Through

- I need data **from the story** *and* **data from the table.**
- I can **draw a picture to show the problem.**

How do you multiply with paper and pencil?

Example A

Find 3 × 26.

	What You **Think**	What You **Write**
STEP 1 Multiply the ones. Regroup if necessary.	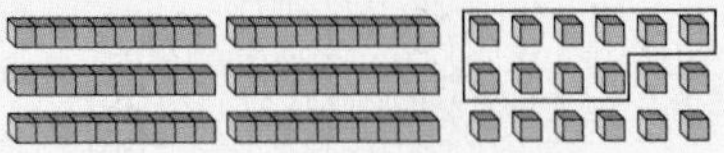 **3** × **6** = **18** ones. Regroup 18 ones as 1 ten 8 ones.	see below
STEP 2 Multiply the tens. Add any extra tens.	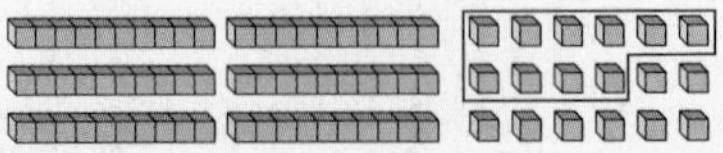 **3** × **2** tens = **6** tens **6** tens + **1** ten = **7** tens	see below

Step 1, What You Write:

```
  1
 26
x 3
 --
  8
```

Step 2, What You Write:

```
  1
 26
x 3
 --
 78
```

The 1903 plane would travel 78 feet in 3 seconds.

Example B	Example C	Example D
No regrouping	3-digit product	3-digit product with regrouping
$\begin{array}{r} 43 \\ \times\ 2 \\ \hline 86 \end{array}$	$\begin{array}{r} 61 \\ \times\ 4 \\ \hline 244 \end{array}$	$\begin{array}{r} ^{4} \\ 36 \\ \times\ 7 \\ \hline 252 \end{array}$

TEST TALK

Think It Through

I can **do it another way** by showing all partial products.

$$\begin{array}{r} 36 \\ \times\ 7 \\ \hline 42 \\ 210 \\ \hline 252 \end{array}$$

Talk About It

1. In Example A, Step 2, what two numbers were multiplied first? What number was added?

2. In Example D, is it really 7×3 or 7×30?

Is the answer reasonable?

Example E

Is 78 a reasonable answer for 3×26?

Exact: $3 \times 26 = 78$

↓

Estimate: $3 \times 30 = 90$

Round 26 to 30.
Since 78 is close to 90, the answer is reasonable.

Talk About It

3. To estimate 3×26, suppose you used 3×25 instead of 3×30. What would your estimate be?

4. Number Sense Is 282 a reasonable answer for 6×47? Estimate to decide.

Take It to the NET
More Examples
www.scottforesman.com

CHECK

For another example, see Set 5-5 on p. 305.

Find each product. Decide if your answer is reasonable.

1. $\begin{array}{r} 12 \\ \times\ 6 \\ \hline \end{array}$ **2.** $\begin{array}{r} 18 \\ \times\ 7 \\ \hline \end{array}$ **3.** $\begin{array}{r} 72 \\ \times\ 5 \\ \hline \end{array}$ **4.** $\begin{array}{r} 49 \\ \times\ 8 \\ \hline \end{array}$ **5.** $\begin{array}{r} 63 \\ \times\ 3 \\ \hline \end{array}$

6. $\begin{array}{r} 66 \\ \times\ 8 \\ \hline \end{array}$ **7.** $\begin{array}{r} 94 \\ \times\ 5 \\ \hline \end{array}$ **8.** $\begin{array}{r} 37 \\ \times\ 4 \\ \hline \end{array}$ **9.** $\begin{array}{r} 78 \\ \times\ 7 \\ \hline \end{array}$ **10.** $\begin{array}{r} 53 \\ \times\ 9 \\ \hline \end{array}$

11. Number Sense Gary said that $3 \times 54 = 222$. Estimate to check. If Gary's answer is wrong, find the correct answer.

For more practice, see Set 5-5 on p. 309.

A Skills and Understanding

Find each product. Decide if your answer is reasonable.

12. 15×5	**13.** 14×6	**14.** 28×3	**15.** 34×7	**16.** 43×4
17. 94×3	**18.** 32×5	**19.** 18×7	**20.** 77×7	**21.** 45×6
22. 23×7	**23.** 88×9	**24.** 56×4	**25.** 82×8	**26.** 63×4
27. 4×42	**28.** 6×76	**29.** 4×47	**30.** 3×92	**31.** 7×29
32. 9×24	**33.** 5×43	**34.** 55×7	**35.** 4×61	**36.** 68×7
37. 34×8	**38.** 6×72	**39.** 37×8	**40.** 55×6	**41.** 9×89

42. Number Sense Jo said $7 \times 68 = 476$. Estimate to check. If her answer is wrong, find the correct answer.

43. Estimation Use estimation to decide which has the greater product: 906×3 or 806×4.

B Reasoning and Problem Solving

Math and Social Studies

Modern airplanes are much larger than the Wright Brothers' plane in 1903 and can travel much farther.

Data File

Jumbo Jet		Wright Brothers' Plane
196 feet	**Wingspan**	40 feet
63 feet	**Height**	12 feet
6,000 miles	**Flying Range**	60 miles

44. A jumbo jet's wingspan is how much greater than the wingspan of the Wright Brothers' plane?

45. Would 100 trips in the Wright Brothers' plane take you as far as one trip in a jumbo jet? Explain.

46. Would 5 of the Wright Brothers' planes on top of each other be as tall as a jumbo jet? Explain.

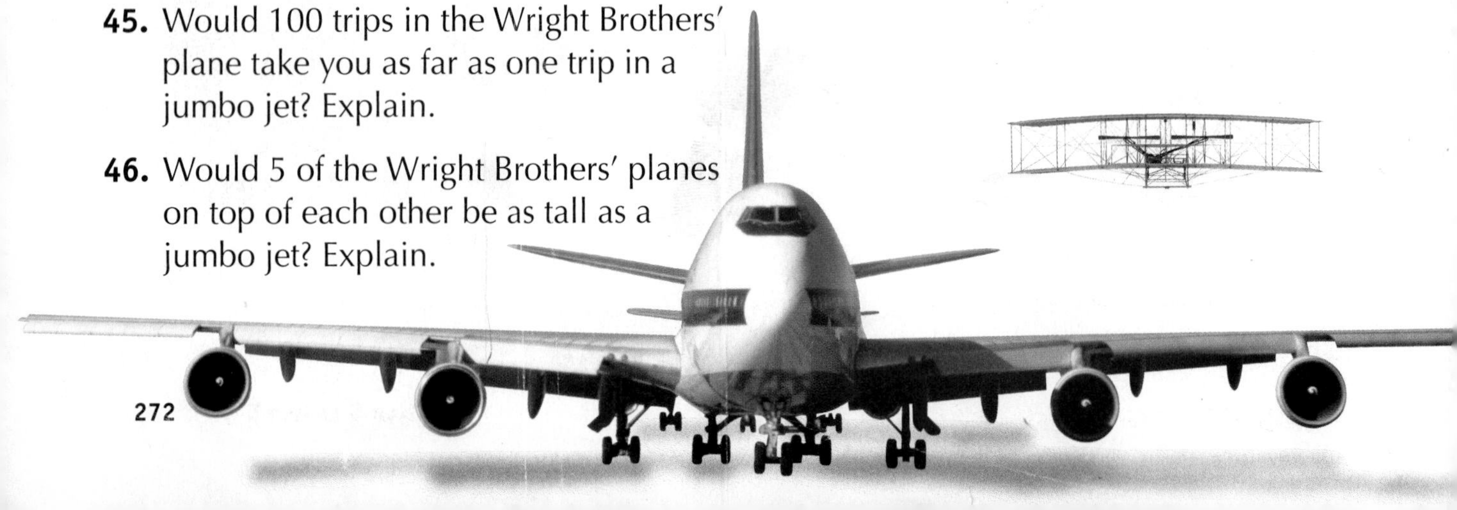

PRACTICE

47. **Writing in Math** Is the explanation below correct? If not, tell why and write a correct response.

> Explain why the steps for finding 4 × 34 make sense.
>
> $$\begin{array}{r} ^{1} \\ 34 \\ \times \ \ 4 \\ \hline 136 \end{array}$$
>
> 4 x 4 ones = 16 ones, or 1 ten 6 ones.
> Write the 1 in the tens column.
> 4 x 3 tens = 12 tens.
> 12 tens + 1 ten = 13 tens.
> The answer is 13 tens 6 ones, or 136.

TEST TALK

Think It Through
I can **draw pictures to explain my thinking.**

C Extensions

48. Write a question that can be answered using the Data File on page 272 and one or more operations. Find the answer.

Mixed Review and Test Prep

Take It to the NET
Test Prep
www.scottforesman.com

49. Draw a picture of an array for 4 × 36. Then find the product.

50. Find 7,006 − 428.

A. 6,578 **B.** 6,582 **C.** 7,422 **D.** 7,434

Discovery CHANNEL SCHOOL™

Discover Math in Your World

It's All Up in the Air

Today's hot air balloons can last about 500 hours. They use about 15 gallons of fuel an hour.

1. If a pilot flies 65 hours per year, will she fly more or less than 500 hours in 7 years?

2. If a pilot flies 90 hours per year, will he fly more or less than 500 hours in 5 years?

3. How many gallons of fuel would be needed for 8 hours of flying?

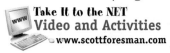

Take It to the NET
Video and Activities
www.scottforesman.com

Fire-resistant materials similar to what firefighters and racecar drivers wear are used for the lower portion of hot air balloons.

Key Idea
To find a product like 6 × 125, break apart 125 using place value.

Multiplying Three-Digit and One-Digit Numbers

WARM UP

1. 24 × 2
2. 21 × 4
3. 27 × 3
4. 10 × 5
5. 37 × 7
6. 59 × 6

LEARN

How do you multiply larger numbers?

The steps for multiplying a 2-digit number by a 1-digit number can be extended to multiplying a 3-digit number by a 1-digit number.

	Example A	Example B
STEP 1 Multiply the ones. Regroup if necessary.	3 125 × 6 0	6 208 × 8 4
STEP 2 Multiply the tens. Add any extra tens. Regroup if necessary.	1 3 125 × 6 50	6 208 × 8 64
STEP 3 Multiply the hundreds. Add any extra hundreds.	1 3 125 × 6 750	6 208 × 8 1,664

TEST TALK

Think It Through
I can **multiply another way.**

125
× 6
30
120
600
750

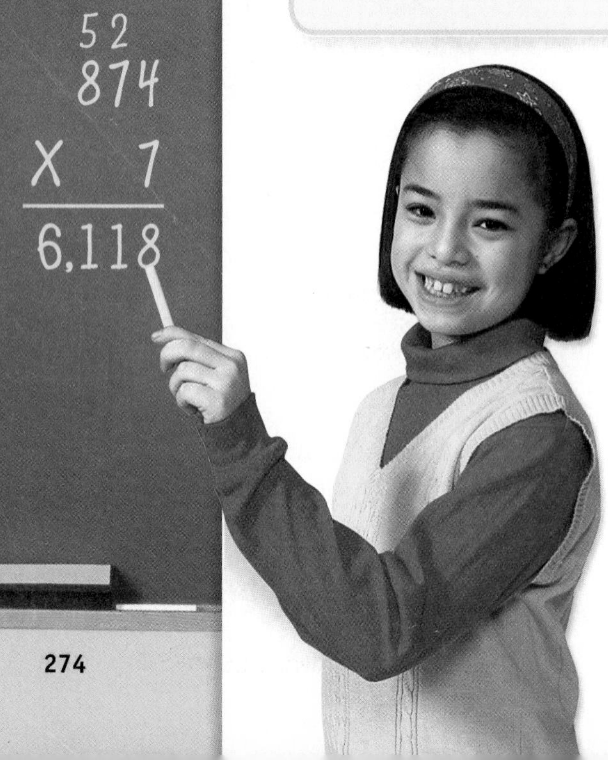

Talk About It

1. In Example A, Step 3, is it really 6 × 1 or 6 × 100? Explain.
2. In Example B, Step 2, what two numbers were multiplied first? What number was added to this product?
3. **Estimation** How can you estimate each product in the examples above?

CHECK

For another example, see Set 5-6 on p. 305.

Find each product. Estimate to check reasonableness.

1. 423×2 **2.** 506×4 **3.** 821×3 **4.** 159×5 **5.** 624×7

6. Number Sense How could you use the product of 103 and 5 to find the product of 206 and 5?

PRACTICE

For more practice, see Set 5-6 on p. 309.

A Skills and Understanding

Find each product. Estimate to check reasonableness.

7. 406×5 **8.** 511×9 **9.** 293×9 **10.** 804×8

11. 146×3 **12.** 302×9 **13.** 525×2 **14.** 203×7

15. 9×608 **16.** 7×778 **17.** 6×451 **18.** 3×409

19. 5×935 **20.** 2×673 **21.** 8×667 **22.** 4×873

23. Number Sense Is 261×5 greater than or less than 1,000? Explain.

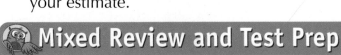

B Reasoning and Problem Solving

Smaller animals have faster heart rates than larger animals.

A squirrel's heart can beat 245 times per minute. How many times will the squirrel's heart beat in

24. 3 minutes? **25.** 5 minutes? **26.** 8 minutes?

27. Writing in Math Find a reasonable value for n if the estimated product of n and 998 is 5,000. Tell how you found your estimate.

Mixed Review and Test Prep

Take It to the NET
Test Prep
www.scottforesman.com

Find each product.

28. 6×200 **29.** $8 \times 4,000$ **30.** 42×7 **31.** 5×84

32. Algebra Give the next three numbers in this pattern: 2, 6, 10, 14, ▢, ▢, ▢

A. 15, 16, 17 **B.** 16, 18, 20 **C.** 18, 22, 26 **D.** 18, 24, 28

Reading For Math Success

Predict and Verify

Predicting and verifying when you read in math can help you use the **problem-solving strategy, *Try, Check, and Revise,*** in the next lesson.

In reading, predicting and verifying help you think about what comes next in a story. In math, predicting and verifying help you try different answers and check if they are correct.

To **verify** it, use information in the problem and **check** if it works.

Kim is twice as old as Tyler. The sum of their ages is 24 years. How old is Tyler?

Predict	*Verify*		
Predict Tyler's age.	**Multiply to find Kim's age.**	**Find the sum of their ages.**	**Compare the sum to 24.**
10	$10 \times 2 = 20$	$10 + 20 = 30$	too high
4	$4 \times 2 = 8$	$4 + 8 = 12$	too low
7	$7 \times 2 = 14$	$7 + 14 = 21$	too low
8	$8 \times 2 = 16$	$8 + 16 = 24$	correct

***Predict** a reasonable answer to **try** out.*

*Use the results of your first prediction to **revise** your prediction. Continue predicting and verifying until you find an answer that works.*

1. Which statement in the problem tells you that the first prediction is too high?
2. Why was the prediction of 4 for Tyler's age too low?

For 3–6, use the problem below and the picture at the right.

There are 3 times as many apple pies as cherry pies for sale at the fair. There are 20 pies in all. How many cherry pies are there?

3. Make a prediction for the number of cherry pies.
4. **Writing in Math** Explain how you can verify your prediction.
5. If your prediction was not the correct solution, make a second prediction and check if it works.
6. How many cherry pies are there?

For 7–9, use the problem below.

At basketball practice, Maya and Veronica made 30 foul shots in all. Maya made 4 more than Veronica. How many foul shots did Veronica make?

7. Predict the number of foul shots that Veronica made and verify your prediction.
8. **Writing in Math** Do you need to revise your prediction? Explain why or why not.
9. How many foul shots did Veronica make?

For 10–12, use the problem below and the sign at the right.

Mr. Rafael bought two different small pizzas and a large pizza for a party. He spent $40. Which pizzas did he buy?

10. Predict Mr. Rafael's choices for the two small pizzas and the large pizza. Verify your prediction.
11. Do you need to revise your prediction? If so, make a second prediction and check if it works.
12. **Writing in Math** Which pizzas did Mr. Rafael buy? Explain how you knew when you had solved the problem.

Key Idea
The strategy Try, Check, and Revise can help you solve problems.

Try, Check, and Revise

Reading Helps!
Predicting and verifying
can help you with...
the problem-solving strategy, *Try, Check, and Revise.*

LEARN

How do you try, check, and revise?

Sale Suzanne spent $27, not including tax, on dog supplies. She bought two of one item and one other item. What did she buy?

Dog Supplies Sale!

Leash	$8
Collar	$6
Bowls	$7
Medium Beds	$15
Toys	$12

Read and Understand

What do you know?
She bought three items.
Two of the items were the same.
The prices are in the sign.
She paid $27 for all three.

What are you trying to find?
What three items did she buy?

Plan and Solve

What strategy will you use?
Strategy: Try, Check, and Revise

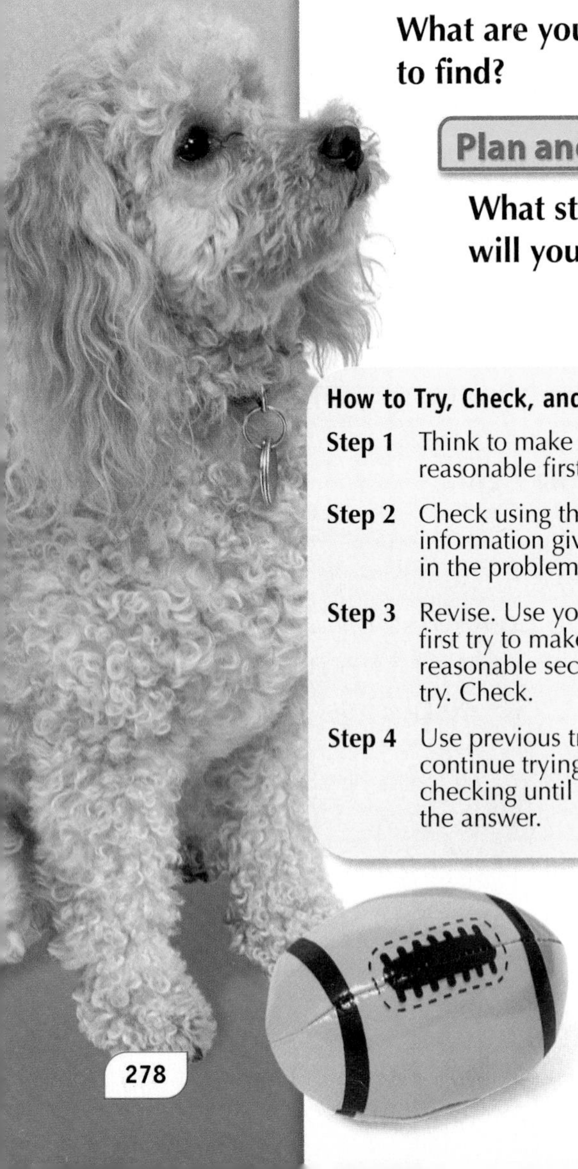

How to Try, Check, and Revise

Step 1 Think to make a reasonable first try.

Step 2 Check using the information given in the problem.

Step 3 Revise. Use your first try to make a reasonable second try. Check.

Step 4 Use previous tries to continue trying and checking until you get the answer.

Two beds are too much. I'll try one. Then I'll try 2 of the smaller items. I'll try leashes first.

$8 + $8 + $15 = $31
That's too high, but very close.

If I keep the bed, I need to come down $4 total or $2 for each item. I'll try the collars.

$6 + $6 + $15 = $27   That's it!

Answer: She bought two collars and one medium bed.

Look Back and Check

Is your work correct?
Yes, the sum is $27 and there are two of one item and one of another item.

Talk About It

1. How do you know two beds are too much?
2. In the second try, what number was the same from the first try? What was changed?

When might you try, check, and revise?

Puppy Count There were 16 dogs in the veterinarian's office. There were three times as many adult dogs as puppies. How many adult dogs and how many puppies were in the office?

Solution

Try 5 puppies. Then $3 \times 5 = 15$ adult dogs.
$5 + 15 = 20$ That's too high.

Try 4 puppies. Then $3 \times 4 = 12$ adult dogs.
$4 + 12 = 16$ That's right!

When to Try, Check, and Revise

Think about using try, check, and revise when:

Some quantities are being combined to find a total.

- Sale items from the pet store
- Number of adult dogs and puppies

You do not know which or how many of the items are used to get the total.

Talk About It

3. Why would 6 puppies not have been a good number for the second try?

CHECK

Use the first try to help you make a second try. Finish solving the problem.

1. Ella's mom brought 24 cartons of orange and grape juice to the park. There were twice as many cartons of orange juice as there were of grape juice. How many of each kind did she bring?

   Try 6 grape juice.
   Then, $2 \times 6 = 12$ orange juice.
   $6 + 12 = 18$ That's too low.

2. In football, a team can score 2, 3, 6, 7, or 8 points. The bulldogs scored 3 times and had 13 points. How did they score their points?

   Try $3 + 3 + 8 = 14$.
   That's too high.

PRACTICE

For another example, see Set 5-7 on p. 310.

A Using the Strategy

Use the data at the right for 3–5.

Finishing the Solution Use the first try to help you make a second try. Finish solving the problem.

3. Anthony spent $15 at Fun Town, before tax. He bought 3 different items. What did he buy?

> Try $9 + $2 + $5 = $16.
> That's too high.

Fun Town

Jump Rope	$2
Skateboard	$25
Basketball	$8
Football	$6
Baseball	$5
Bat	$9

Use Try, Check, and Revise to Solve Problems Try, check, and revise to solve each problem. Write the answer in a complete sentence.

4. Amy spent $35, before tax, on 4 items at Fun Town. Two of her four items were the same. What did she buy?

5. Nick spent $30 before tax, at Fun Town. He bought two of one item and two of another item. What did he buy?

6. Jason put 27 pictures on 6 pages of his photo album. Each page holds 3 large, 4 medium-sized, or 6 small pictures. He had some pictures of each size. How many of each size picture did Jason have?

Math and Social Studies

Every state has two senators, but the number of members of the House of Representatives from each state depends on the state's population. Suppose all the representatives from each of 3 states vote to pass a new law. Which of the states in the data file might they be if there are a total of

7. 56 votes?

8. 73 votes?

9. 37 votes?

10. 44 votes?

Data File

U.S. House of Representatives 108th Congress

State	Members
California	53
Florida	25
Indiana	9
Michigan	15
North Carolina	13
Ohio	18
Virginia	11

For more practice, see Set 5-7 on p. 310.

B Mixed Strategy Practice

Solve each problem. Write the answer in a complete sentence.

11. Ms. Angle's class spends the same amount of time each morning on math, reading, and science. The morning schedule is shown below. How long does Ms. Angle's class spend on each subject?

Ms. Angle's Class Schedule

Opening		10 minutes
Reading		?
Math		?
Recess		20 minutes
Science		?
Total		165 minutes

12. Sam earned $7 an hour and Lisa earned $8 an hour. Lisa and Sam worked the same number of hours. Sam earned $49. How much did Lisa earn?

13. Nancy lines up 18 paperweights in her collection. The paperweights follow this pattern: small, large, large, small, large, large, small, and so on. Is the last paperweight large or small?

14. Writing in Math Use the Fun Town data on page 280. Write a problem that could be solved by using try, check, and revise.

STRATEGIES

- **Show What You Know**
  - Draw a Picture
  - Make an Organized List
  - Make a Table
  - Make a Graph
  - Act It Out or Use Objects
- **Look for a Pattern**
- **Try, Check, and Revise**
- **Write a Number Sentence**
- **Use Logical Reasoning**
- **Solve a Simpler Problem**
- **Work Backward**

Choose a tool

Think It Through

Stuck? I won't give up! I can:

- Reread the problem.
- Tell what I know.
- Identify key facts and details.
- Tell the problem in my own words.
- Show the main idea.
- Try a different strategy.
- Retrace my steps.

Mixed Review and Test Prep

Take It to the NET
Test Prep
www.scottforesman.com

15. 235×8

16. 704×6

17. 915×7

18. 43×9

19. $3{,}000 \times 8$

Algebra Find the value of each expression for $x = 48$.

20. $x - 29$ **21.** $x + 34$ **22.** $2x$ **23.** $x \div 6$

24. Which of the following does NOT equal 8×12?

A. 80 + 24 **B.** 80 + 16 **C.** 64 + 32 **D.** 96

Key Idea
Use mental math, paper and pencil, or a calculator, depending on the numbers involved.

Materials
• calculator

Choose a Computation Method

WARM UP

1. 30 × 2
2. 73 × 5
3. 16 × 6
4. 38 × 7
5. 36 × 5
6. 95 × 4
7. Do four $48 shirts cost more than a $200 jacket? Explain.

LEARN

When do you use different methods?

When you compute, try mental math. Next, think about paper and pencil. For very hard problems, use a calculator.

Data File

Solar Panels	Cost
Small	$1,150
Medium	$2,006
Large	$2,374

TEST TALK

Think It Through
Before I do a calculation, I should **decide which method makes sense.**

Example A

What do 4 medium solar panels cost?

4 × $2,006 = ▢

This is easy to do in my head. I'll use **mental math.**

4 × 6 is 24.
4 × 2,000 is 8,000.
So, 4 × $2,006 is $8,024.

Cost: $8,024

Example B

What do 3 small solar panels cost?

3 × $1,150 = ▢

There are not a lot of regroupings. I'll use **paper and pencil.**

$$\begin{array}{r} \overset{1}{1{,}150} \\ \times \quad 3 \\ \hline 3{,}450 \end{array}$$

Cost: $3,450

Example C

What do 8 large solar panels cost?

8 × $2,374 = ▢

There are lots of regroupings. I'll use a **calculator.**

Press: 8 [×] **2374** [=]

Display: 18992

Cost: $18,992

Talk About It

1. Why is 8 × 2,374 a more difficult computation than 4 × 2,006?
2. Why would you not use a calculator to find 2 × 4,301?

CHECK ✓

For another example, see Set 5-8 on p. 306.

Find each product. Tell what computation method you used.

1. $4,010 \times 3$ **2.** $3,759 \times 8$ **3.** $\$1,907 \times 6$ **4.** $2,987 \times 4$ **5.** $\$5,221 \times 7$

6. Number Sense Roman used paper and pencil to find $8,004 \times 8$. Could he have found the answer a faster way? Explain.

PRACTICE

For more practice, see Set 5-8 on p. 310.

A Skills and Understanding

Find each product. Tell what computation method you used.

7. $3,597 \times 9$ **8.** $6,923 \times 5$ **9.** $8,041 \times 3$ **10.** $7,002 \times 9$ **11.** $3,812 \times 9$

12. $6,020 \times 3$ **13.** $5,003 \times 6$ **14.** $4,874 \times 7$ **15.** $3,220 \times 4$ **16.** $8,108 \times 9$

17. Number Sense Why is using a calculator not a good way to find $3 \times 4,200$?

B Reasoning and Problem Solving

In a 3-year period, how many units come from

18. oil? **19.** coal? **20.** natural gas?

21. Writing in Math Would it make more sense to use mental math to find $4,008 \times 3$ or to find $2,971 \times 5$? Explain your reasoning.

Data File

Energy Consumption Estimate for 2005

Source	Units*
Oil	4,141
Coal	2,415
Natural Gas	2,588
Other	1,559

*10 trillion British Thermal Units

Mixed Review and Test Prep

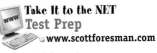

Take It to the NET
Test Prep
www.scottforesman.com

In 22–24, give the missing numbers for each pattern.

22. 26, 52, 104, □, □, □ **23.** 10, 40, 160, □, □, □ **24.** 4, 20, 100, □, □, □

25. Nate and Jay spent a total of $85 for shoes. Nate spent $17 more than Jay. How much did each spend?

26. How many windows are in a 9-story building if there are 28 windows per story?

A. 19 windows **B.** 37 windows **C.** 182 windows **D.** 252 windows

Review

Do You Know How?

Do You Understand?

Multiplying Two-Digit and One-Digit Numbers (5-5)

1. 79×5

2. 46×7

3. 63×3

4. 58×4

5. 36×6

6. 72×2

A Is $40 \times 6 = 240$ a good estimate to check Exercise 5? Tell why.

B Use estimation to decide which has a greater product, 308×4 or 202×7.

Multiplying Three-Digit and One-Digit Numbers (5-6)

7. 519×4

8. 337×2

9. 181×9

10. 268×6

11. 503×5

12. 421×8

C Explain the step you followed to regroup the ones into tens in Exercise 8.

D Is 100×9 a good estimate to check Exercise 9? Tell why.

Problem-Solving Strategy: Try, Check, and Revise (5-7)

13. Try, check, and revise to solve the problem. Write the answer in a complete sentence.

School Supplies Troy and Anna spent a total of \$32 for school supplies. Troy spent \$4 more than Anna. How much did each spend?

E If your first try was not correct, tell how you revised it to solve the problem.

F Explain why checking your answer is an important step in solving problems.

Choose a Computation Method (5-8)

Find each product. Tell which method you used.

14. $3{,}629 \times 9$

15. $7{,}200 \times 4$

16. $5{,}000 \times 7$

17. $6{,}132 \times 3$

G For Exercises 14 and 15, explain how you chose the computation method.

H Explain why you would not use a calculator to find the product in Exercise 16.

Diagnostic Checkpoint

MULTIPLE CHOICE

1. Find the product of 67 and 4. (5-5)

A. 188 **B.** 248 **C.** 268 **D.** 328

2. There are 7 days in one week. How many days are there in 26 weeks? (5-5)

A. 142 days **B.** 144 days **C.** 164 days **D.** 182 days

FREE RESPONSE

Find each product. Decide if your answer is reasonable. (5-5, 5-6)

3. $\begin{array}{r} 22 \\ \times\ 6 \\ \hline \end{array}$ **4.** $\begin{array}{r} 27 \\ \times\ 5 \\ \hline \end{array}$ **5.** $\begin{array}{r} 109 \\ \times\ 3 \\ \hline \end{array}$ **6.** $\begin{array}{r} 522 \\ \times\ 8 \\ \hline \end{array}$

7. $\begin{array}{r} 229 \\ \times\ 7 \\ \hline \end{array}$ **8.** $\begin{array}{r} 640 \\ \times\ 4 \\ \hline \end{array}$ **9.** $\begin{array}{r} 58 \\ \times\ 7 \\ \hline \end{array}$ **10.** $\begin{array}{r} 221 \\ \times\ 5 \\ \hline \end{array}$

Find each product. Tell what computation method you used. (5-8)

11. $\begin{array}{r} 1{,}000 \\ \times\ 6 \\ \hline \end{array}$ **12.** $\begin{array}{r} 8{,}748 \\ \times\ 7 \\ \hline \end{array}$ **13.** $\begin{array}{r} 5{,}231 \\ \times\ 3 \\ \hline \end{array}$

14. Mr. Jackson had 40 cookie jars in his collection. He had 4 times as many large jars as small jars. How many small jars and large jars were in his collection? (5-7)

15. Wendy gave a total of 10 treats to her dogs. She gave her large dog 2 more treats than she gave her small dog. How many treats did she give to each dog?

Think It Through
I should **reread the problem to make sure I answered the question.**

Writing in Math

16. Explain how you can use estimation to decide which has the greater product: 296 × 5 or 396 × 4. (5-6)

17. Write a question that could be answered using multiplication. (5-5, 5-6, 5-7)

18. Suppose you used a calculator to find 8,562 × 7 and got 5,992. Explain how you could tell that this is not the right answer. (5-8)

Key Idea
The steps for multiplying money are almost identical to the steps for multiplying whole numbers.

Multiplying Money

WARM UP

1. 214 × 2
2. 103 × 5
3. 447 × 3
4. 6 × 220
5. 801 × 9
6. 4 × 732

LEARN

When do you multiply?

What is the cost of 3 chicken and noodles meals?

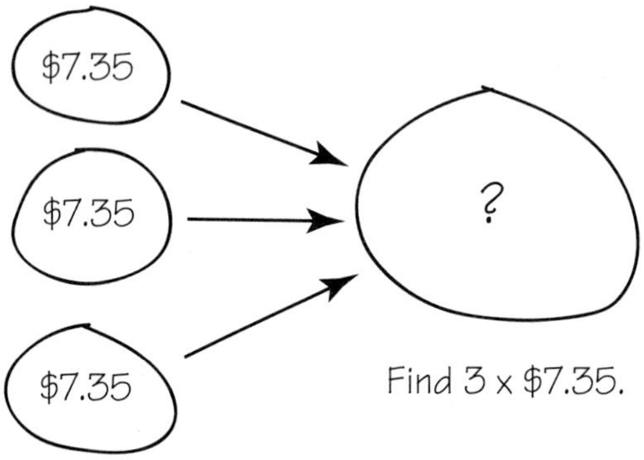

Specials
Chicken and Noodles $7.35
Chicken and Rice $7.15
Chicken and Potatoes $6.25

TEST TALK

Think It Through

- I can **multiply when I combine equal groups.**
- I can **draw a picture** to show the main idea.

Example

STEP 1 Multiply the same way as with whole numbers.

$$\begin{array}{r} \scriptsize{1\,1} \\ \$7.35 \\ \times \quad 3 \\ \hline 2205 \end{array}$$

STEP 2 Write the answer in dollars and cents.

$$\begin{array}{r} \scriptsize{1\,1} \\ \$7.35 \\ \times \quad 3 \\ \hline \$22.05 \end{array}$$

It costs $22.05 to buy 3 chicken and noodles meals.

Talk About It

1. How many digits are to the right of the point used to separate dollars and cents?
2. **Reasonableness** Is $22.05 reasonable? How can you estimate 3 × $7.35 to decide?

CHECK ✓

For another example, see Set 5-9 on p. 307.

1. $2.36 × 4

2. $5.08 × 3

3. $76.59 × 7

4. $18.03 × 9

5. Number Sense Use the data on page 286. Is $35.00 enough to buy 5 chicken and noodles meals? Explain.

PRACTICE

For more practice, see Set 5-9 on p. 311.

A Skills and Understanding

6. $1.37 × 7

7. $2.70 × 4

8. $34.75 × 5

9. $20.04 × 6

10. $14.99 × 8

11. 5 × $32.75 **12.** 9 × $2.21 **13.** 3 × $4.75 **14.** 4 × $51.27 **15.** $9.39 × 4

16. Number Sense Use the data on page 286. Is $14.00 enough to buy 2 chicken and rice meals? Explain.

B Reasoning and Problem Solving

Find each cost.

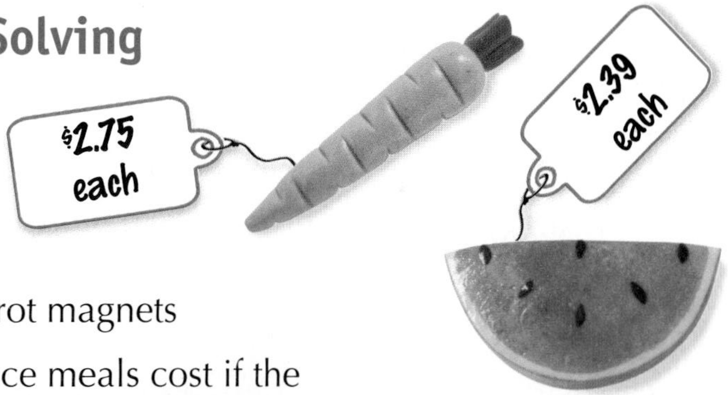

17. 2 watermelon magnets

18. 4 watermelon magnets

19. 9 carrot magnets **20.** 7 carrot magnets

21. How much would 5 chicken and rice meals cost if the tax on one meal is $0.18? Use the data on page 286.

For 22–23, use the menu at the right. Prices include tax.

PIZZA TIME! Menu

	Pizza	Juice
small	$3.25	$0.75
medium	$5.50	$1.25
large	$7.95	$1.75

22. How much more would 4 large pizzas cost than 4 small pizzas?

23. Writing in Math Would $10 buy a medium pizza and two medium juices? Explain.

Mixed Review and Test Prep

Take It to the NET
Test Prep
www.scottforesman.com

24. 18 ÷ 9 **25.** 54 × 6 **26.** 60 ÷ 12 **27.** 64 ÷ 8 **28.** 325 × 4

29. Find 3,004 × 6.

A. 1,824 **B.** 12,024 **C.** 18,024 **D.** 18,240

Algebra

Key Idea
When you multiply 3 factors, you can use properties to save you time.

Vocabulary
- Commutative Property of Multiplication (p. 129)
- Associative Property of Multiplication

Multiplying Three Factors

WARM UP

1. 10 × 3
2. 8 × 7
3. 30 × 3
4. 5 × 40
5. 9 × 70
6. 10 × 6

LEARN

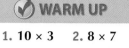

How can you make multiplication easier?

When you multiply three numbers, you can start with any two numbers to make the computation easier. The two properties below explain why this works.

Commutative Property of Multiplication

You can multiply two numbers in any order.

$5 \times 6 = 6 \times 5$

Associative Property of Multiplication

You can change the grouping of factors.

$(5 \times 2) \times 3 = 5 \times (2 \times 3)$

Show three ways to find 25 × 2 × 4.

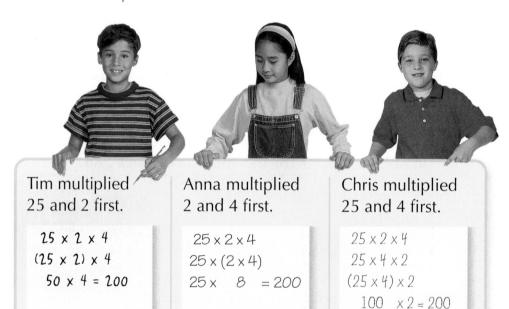

Tim multiplied 25 and 2 first.

25 × 2 × 4
(25 × 2) × 4
50 × 4 = 200

Anna multiplied 2 and 4 first.

25 × 2 × 4
25 × (2 × 4)
25 × 8 = 200

Chris multiplied 25 and 4 first.

25 × 2 × 4
25 × 4 × 2
(25 × 4) × 2
100 × 2 = 200

TEST TALK

Think It Through
I should always check if there's a way to **make a computation easier.**

Talk About It

1. What property did Chris use to go from 25 × 2 × 4 to 25 × 4 × 2?
2. Tim and Chris said it's easier to find the answer if you first use the 25. Why do you think they said this?

CHECK

For another example, see Set 5-10 on p. 307.

1. 5 × 2 × 3 **2.** 50 × 3 × 2 **3.** 4 × 20 × 2 **4.** 3 × 3 × 30

5. Number Sense For 25 × 3 × 2, is it easier to first find 25 × 3 or 25 × 2 in your head? Why?

PRACTICE

For more practice, see Set 5-10 on p. 311.

A Skills and Understanding

6. 7 × 5 × 2 **7.** 4 × 6 × 5 **8.** 4 × 3 × 10 **9.** 8 × 100 × 2

10. 4 × 25 × 4 **11.** 80 × 6 × 1 **12.** 40 × 3 × 3 **13.** 9 × 4 × 5

14. 3 × 50 × 6 **15.** 3 × 60 × 3 **16.** 250 × 7 × 2 **17.** 4 × 500 × 6

18. Number Sense For 4 × 8 × 5, does finding 4 × 5 = 20 first make the problem easier than finding 4 × 8 = 32 first? Explain.

B Reasoning and Problem Solving

19. Show three ways to find 3 × 30 × 2.

20. How many stamps are in 1 section of the collection?

Stamp Collection
1 section = 5 pages
1 page = 9 rows
1 row = 8 stamps

21. Writing in Math What is the cost of a page of 9 rows of 5¢ stamps if there are 8 stamps per row? Explain two different ways to solve the problem.

TEST TALK

Think It Through
- My answer should be **brief but complete.**
- I should **explain the steps in order.**

C Extensions

22. Reasoning When there are two different operations in a calculation, can you start with either operation and always get the same answer? Try (5 × 30) − 2 and 5 × (30 − 2) to decide.

23. What is the cost of 8 cartons of pens if there are 5 boxes per carton, 5 pens per box, and each pen costs $2?

Mixed Review and Test Prep

Take It to the NET
Test Prep
www.scottforesman.com

Use mental math to find each answer.

24. 450 + 19 **25.** 985 − 400 **26.** 9 × $7.33 **27.** 5 × $1.98

28. Which of these lengths is NOT greater than 2 feet?

A. 30 inches **B.** 20 inches **C.** 3 yards **D.** 1 yard

Problem-Solving Skill

Reading Helps!

Identifying the main idea can help you with...

choosing an operation.

Key Idea
Understanding when to choose a particular operation can help you solve problems.

Choose an Operation

LEARN

What helps you choose an operation?

Yo-Yo Facts A yo-yo was taken into space by NASA first in 1985 and again in 1992.

A very large yo-yo was made by a high-school class in Indiana in 1990. It weighed 6 times as much as Pete. Pete weighs 136 pounds. To help you **choose an operation,** first identify the main idea in the problem.

	Example A	Example B
Read and Understand	How much did the large yo-yo weigh?	It was how many years between the first and second time a yo-yo was taken into space?
Show the main idea.	[136] Pete's weight: 136 pounds [136][136][136] [136][136][136] Yo-yo's weight: 6 times as much	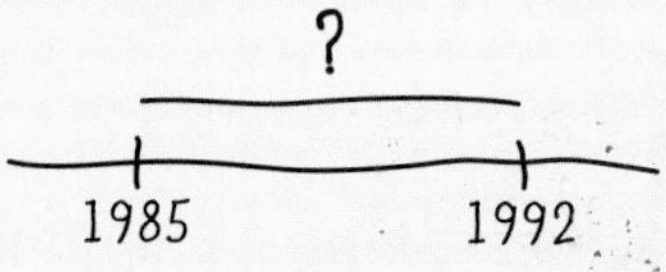
Plan and Solve		
Choose an operation.	Multiply to find "times as much." **136 × 6 = ▢** Pete's weight · Times as much · Yo-yo's weight	Subtract to compare the numbers. **1992 − 1985 = ▢** 2nd time in space · 1st time in space · Years in between

Talk About It

1. Give the answer to each problem above in a complete sentence.

2. **Number Sense** Jack said he can use addition to solve the problem in Example B. Would he be correct? Explain.

CHECK ✓

For another example, see Set 5-11 on p. 307.

The picture shows the main idea. Use the picture to choose an operation and solve the problem.

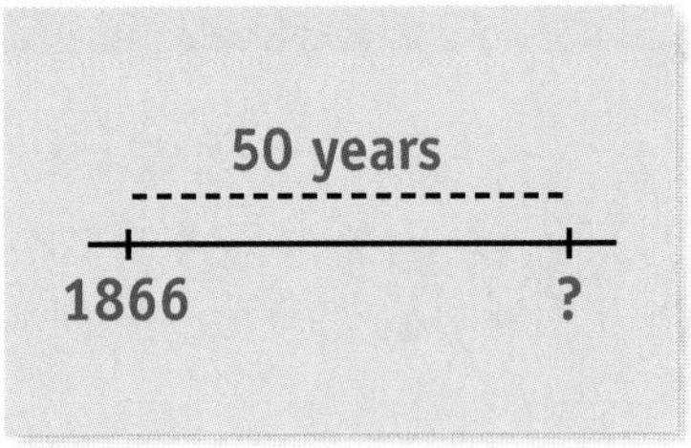

1. Yo-yos first appeared in the United States in 1866, but the name "yo-yo" was first used 50 years later. It's from a Filipino word for "come-come" or "to return." In what year did the yo-yo get its name?

PRACTICE

For more practice, see Set 5-11 on p. 311.

Draw a picture to show the main idea. Then choose an operation and solve the problem.

2. Use the data at the right. How much more is a ton of dimes worth than a ton of pennies?
3. Police officers walk about 1,632 miles per year. Mail carriers walk about 1,056 miles per year. How many more miles does a police officer walk in a year than a mail carrier?
4. If there are 24 hours in a day, how many hours are in 1 week?
5. Maria saved 56 dimes and 3 times as many pennies. How many pennies did she save?

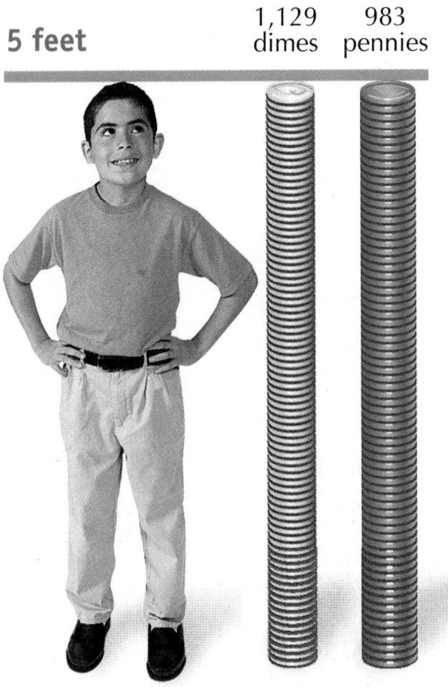

6. Use the data at the right. There are how many more dimes than pennies in a 5-foot stack?
7. **Writing in Math** Use the data below. There are how many more penny stacks in a ton than dime stacks? Explain how you found your answer.

> **A ton of pennies:**
> 360 stacks that are 5 feet tall
> **A ton of dimes:**
> 350 stacks that are 5 feet tall

Problem-Solving Applications

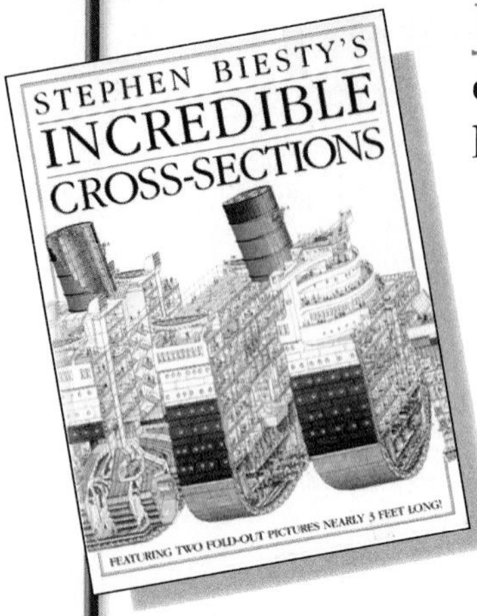
STEPHEN BIESTY'S
INCREDIBLE
CROSS-SECTIONS
FEATURING TWO FOLD-OUT PICTURES NEARLY 5 FEET LONG!

Jumbo Jet The 747 is one of the world's largest jets. It can carry more than 400 people at one time. Starting in 1969, 747s have flown more than 3 billion passengers 35 billion miles!

Trivia The economy section of a 747 is longer than the entire first flight made by Orville and Wilbur Wright at Kitty Hawk, North Carolina, in 1903.

1. A 747 holds 4,774 times as much fuel as Jo's car. Jo fills her car's tank in 3 minutes. At this rate, how long would it take Jo to fill a 747's tanks?

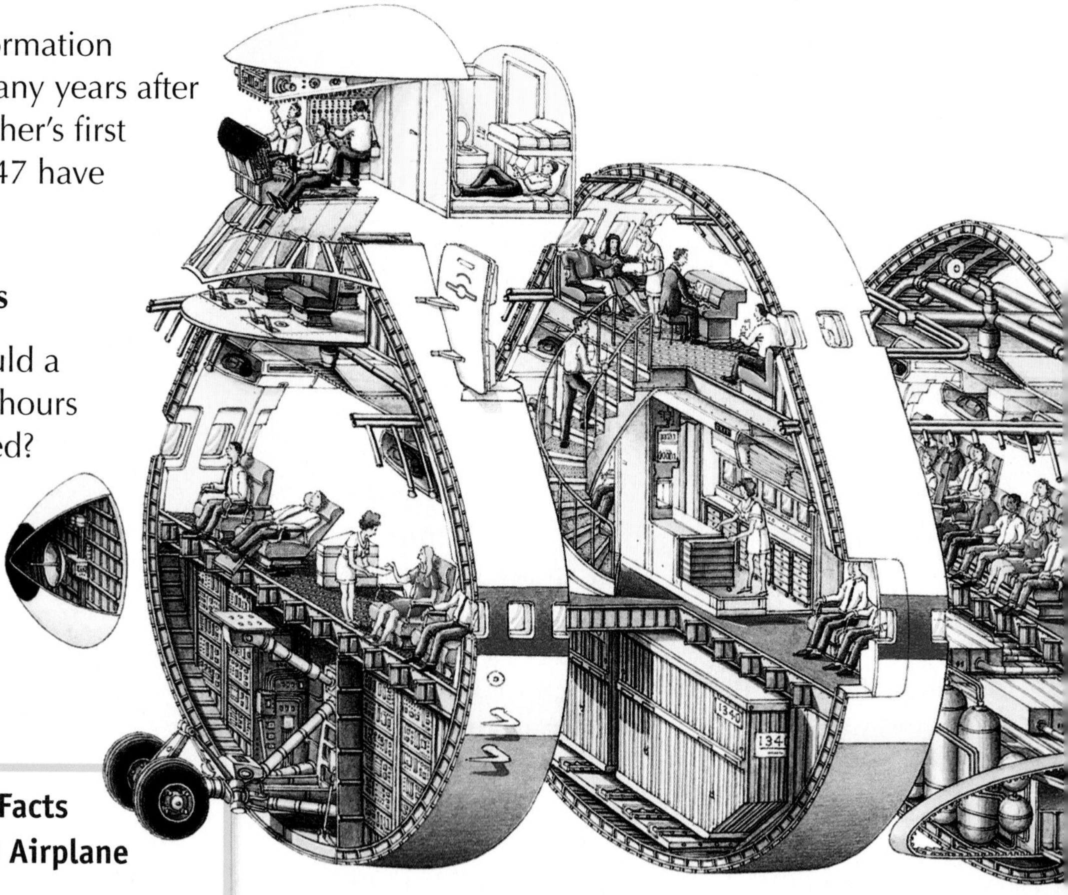

2. Use the information above. How many years after the Wright brother's first flight did the 747 have its first flight?

Using Key Facts

3. How far could a 747 travel in 4 hours at cruising speed?

Key Facts
747-400 Airplane

- 18 wheels
- 6 million parts
- 171 miles of wires
- 211 feet 5 inches wide
- 231 feet 10 inches long
- Typically cruises at 567 mph
- Maximum weight is 875,000 lb

4. One food cart has 12 slots. Each slot holds 2 food trays. How many food trays are in 8 food carts?

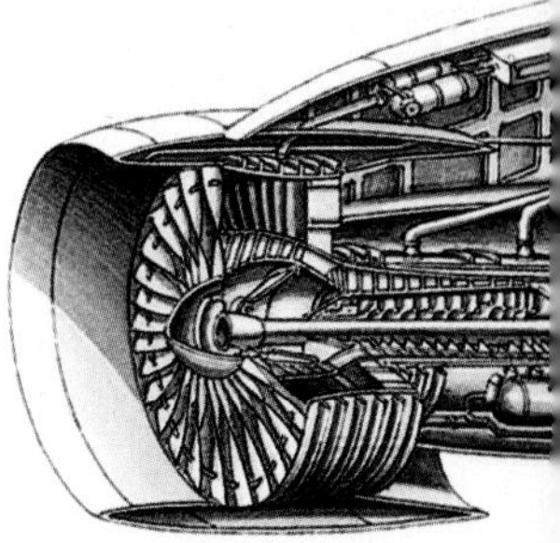

5 For a long flight, more than 5 tons of food and beverages are prepared. How many pounds of food and beverages is this? (Remember, 1 ton = 2,000 pounds.)

6 **Decision Making** Suppose you won $2,000 for you and a friend to take some airline trips. What trips would you take? How much money would you have left over?

Destination	Round-Trip Cost
Chicago	$296
New York	$239
Los Angeles	$349
Orlando	$189
Hawaii	$625

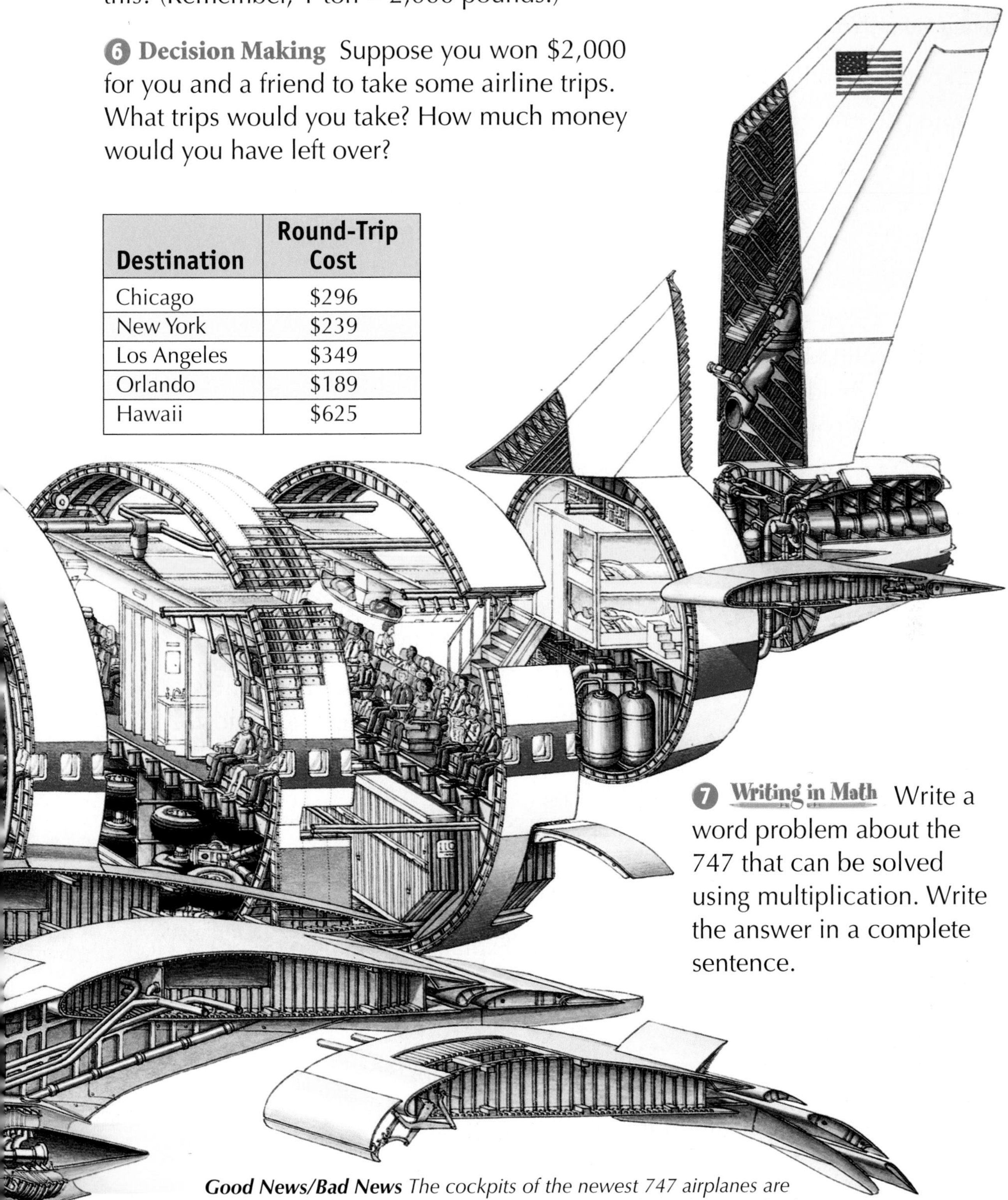

7 **Writing in Math** Write a word problem about the 747 that can be solved using multiplication. Write the answer in a complete sentence.

Good News/Bad News *The cockpits of the newest 747 airplanes are less complicated than the cockpits in earlier models. Unfortunately, the pilots still need to know how to use 365 lights, gauges, and switches.*

Review

Do You Know How?

Multiplying Money (5-9)

Find each product. Estimate to check.

1. $\begin{array}{r} \$2.39 \\ \times \quad 8 \\ \hline \end{array}$

2. $\begin{array}{r} \$57.40 \\ \times \quad 5 \\ \hline \end{array}$

3. $\begin{array}{r} \$6.95 \\ \times \quad 3 \\ \hline \end{array}$

4. $\begin{array}{r} \$20.50 \\ \times \quad 4 \\ \hline \end{array}$

5. Adults pay $7.75 to go to the movies and children pay $4.50. How much would it cost for 2 adults and 4 children to see a movie?

Do You Understand?

A What two symbols must you always include in the answer for money problems?

B Explain how you found the answer to Exercise 5.

Multiplying Three Factors (5-10)

Find each product.

6. $8 \times 5 \times 4$
7. $6 \times 70 \times 5$
8. $10 \times 2 \times 7$
9. $7 \times 2 \times 5$
10. $2 \times 150 \times 8$
11. $40 \times 5 \times 9$
12. $3 \times 4 \times 25$
13. $500 \times 2 \times 6$

C Tell which numbers you multiplied first to find each product.

D Explain how the Associative Property can help you find the product in Exercise 12.

Problem-Solving Skill: Choose an Operation (5-11)

14. For the following problem, draw a picture to show the main idea. Then choose an operation, and solve the problem.

    Map On Lance's map, each inch represents 13 miles. The airport is 4 inches from the state park. How many miles is this?

E Explain the picture you drew. How does it show the main idea?

F How does your picture help you choose an operation?

Diagnostic Checkpoint

TEST TALK

Think It Through
Keep a steady pace. **Skip hard problems and come back to them later.**

MULTIPLE CHOICE

1. Find the product of $2 \times 8 \times 50$. (5-10)

A. 800 **B.** 600 **C.** 500 **D.** 400

2. A car wash costs $3.50. Elliot washed 5 cars and Sam washed 4 cars. How much money did the boys earn altogether? (5-9, 5-12)

A. $9.00 **B.** $17.50 **C.** $27.50 **D.** $31.50

FREE RESPONSE

Find each product. (5-9)

3. $\begin{array}{r} \$1.81 \\ \times \quad 6 \\ \hline \end{array}$ **4.** $\begin{array}{r} \$3.09 \\ \times \quad 4 \\ \hline \end{array}$ **5.** $\begin{array}{r} \$21.50 \\ \times \quad 5 \\ \hline \end{array}$ **6.** $\begin{array}{r} \$59.99 \\ \times \quad 3 \\ \hline \end{array}$

Find each product. (5-10)

7. $4 \times 6 \times 6$ **8.** $7 \times 3 \times 10$ **9.** $2 \times 250 \times 2$ **10.** $25 \times 7 \times 4$

For 11–13, use the Capitol Visitors problem. (5-11)

Capitol Visitors In the spring, as many as 875 visitors can tour the Capitol building each hour. How many visitors can tour the Capitol in 8 hours?

11. Draw a picture to show the main idea.

12. What operation will you use?

13. Solve the problem.

Use the table at the right for 14–15.

14. How many light bulbs are in 1 case? 3 cases? (5-10, 5-11)

15. How much would a box of light bulbs cost if one package costs $3.29? (5-11)

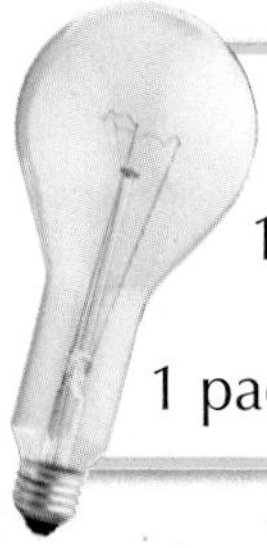

Light Bulbs

1 case = 10 boxes
1 box = 8 packages
1 package = 4 light bulbs

16. Amanda bought 3 posters. Each poster cost $5.95, including tax. How much did she spend in all? (5-9, 5-11)

Writing in Math

17. Explain what steps you would use to find $\$48 \times 6$ mentally. (5-9)

18. Give 3 ways to find $4 \times 20 \times 3$. Which way do you find the easiest? Explain your answer. (5-10)

Test-Taking Strategies

- Understand the question.
- Get information for the answer.
- Plan how to find the answer.
- Make smart choices.
- ➡ Use writing in math.
- Improve written answers.

Use Writing in Math

Sometimes a test question asks for a written answer, such as an explanation, a description, or a comparison. See how one student followed the steps below to answer this test item by writing in math.

1. To solve this problem, you must ESTIMATE. Do NOT find the exact answer.

ESTIMATE the number of books in the bookcase.

Estimate: ____________________

On the lines below, explain how you made your estimate.

____

____

Understand the question.
***I need to find** an estimate for the number of books in the bookcase and explain how I made my estimate.*

Gather information for the answer.
*I'll need to get information from the **text** and the **picture.***

Plan how to find the answer.
*Each section of the bookcase has about the same number of books. So, I can **use multiplication.***

Use writing in math.

- Make your answer brief but complete.
- Use words from the problem and use math terms accurately.
- Describe steps in order.
- Draw pictures if they help to explain your thinking.

Estimate: 90 books

On the lines below, explain how you made your estimate.

First, I counted 15 books in the first section. Next, I counted 6 sections that held the books.

15 15 15 15 15 15

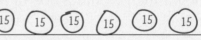

Then I multiplied 15 x 6. I got the estimate of 90 books.

2. The table below shows the number of miles a dolphin can swim. It also shows the number of hours it takes the dolphin to swim that far. Complete the pattern in the table to find how many miles a dolphin can swim in 4 hours.

Dolphin Swimming Patterns

Number of hours	1	2	3	4
Number of miles	20	40	60	

Answer: 80 miles

On the lines below, explain how the number of miles a dolphin swims changes as the number of hours changes.

The number of miles the dolphin swims increases by 20 miles each hour.

Think It Through

I have found the pattern: the missing number is 80. Now I need to explain or describe the pattern in the table.

The problem asks me to tell how the number of miles changes as the number of hours changes. I will begin by using words from the problem.

The number of miles the dolphin swims increases by 20 miles each hour.

Now it's your turn.

For each problem, give a complete response.

3. To solve this problem, you must ESTIMATE. Do NOT find the exact answer.

ESTIMATE the number of nickels. Then explain how you found your estimate.

4. The table below shows the cost to rent a bike.

Town Center Bike Rental

Number of hours	1	2	3	4	5
Price	$8	$16	$24	$32	

Find the price to rent a bike for 5 hours. Then explain how the price changes as the number of hours changes.

Chapter 5

Key Vocabulary and Concept Review

There are around 500 students at my school.

*Remember, **rounding** is showing a number to the nearest ten, hundred, and so on.* *(p. 258)*

Self Check

Use mental math to estimate and find products. (Lessons 5-1, 5-2, 5-3)

Estimate 8 × 24. Then find the actual product.

Use **rounding** to estimate.	Or use **compatible numbers** to estimate.	Use breaking apart to find the actual product.
24 rounds to 20.	24 is close to 25.	8 × 24
8 × 24 is about	8 × 24 is about	8 × 20 + 8 × 4
8 × 20 = 160 To find 8 × 20, find 8 × 2, then write one zero.	8 × 25 = 200.	160 + 32
		192

1. Use mental math to estimate 7 × 32. Then find the actual product.

People who work together easily are compatible.

***Compatible numbers** are numbers that are easy to compute with mentally.* *(p. 164)*

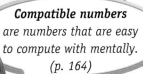

Partial contains the word "part".

*A **partial product** is part of the product.* *(p. 169)*

Self Check

Follow steps when you multiply. (Lessons 5-4, 5-5, 5-6, 5-9)

Show the **partial products** 21 and 350.

```
   53
×   7
   21
  350
  371
```

Or record your work this way by multiply ones, then tens, and so on.

```
  2          12
  53         239
×  7       ×   3
 371         717
```

Multiply money like whole numbers.

```
  1  1
 $26.18
×     2
 $52.36
```

Put $ and . in the product.

2. Find 6 × 487 and 3 × $24.62.

My mom commutes to work the same distance in both directions.

The ***Commutative Property of Multiplication*** *says the order of factors does not affect the product. Example:* $5 \times 6 = 6 \times 5$ *(p. 190)*

Self Check

Choose a computation method or use properties to multiply. (Lessons 5-8, 5-10)

Use paper and pencil when there are not a lot of regroupings.

$$\begin{array}{r} \overset{1}{2{,}120} \\ \times \quad 5 \\ \hline 10{,}600 \end{array}$$

Use the **Commutative Property.**

$40 \times 7 \times 5$

$40 \times 5 \times 7$ Switch the 5 and 7.

200×7

1,400

Use the **Associative Property.**

$17 \times 5 \times 2$

$17 \times (5 \times 2)$ Start with the 5 and 2.

17×10

1,700

3. Find $1{,}302 \times 4$ and $500 \times 9 \times 2$ and $30 \times 3 \times 5$.

My dad is grouped with his associates at work.

The ***Associative Property of Multiplication*** *says the way factors are grouped does not affect the product. Example:* $5 \times (2 \times 3) = (5 \times 2) \times 3$ *(p. 190)*

Self Check

Try, check, and revise or choose operations to solve problems. (Lessons 5-7, 5-11)

Use the given facts to try and check one answer. Then revise and try again if needed.

Maria is twice as old as Ben. The sum of their ages is 18 years. How old is Ben?

Try	Check	
Ben is 8.	$8 \times 2 = 16$; $8 + 16 = 24$	too high
Ben is 5.	$5 \times 2 = 10$; $5 + 10 = 15$	too low
Ben is 6.	$6 \times 2 = 12$; $6 + 12 = 18$	correct

Ben is 6 years old.

To choose an operation, identify the main idea using a picture.

Jane drives 13 miles to work. Gina drives 3 times as far. How far does Gina drive?

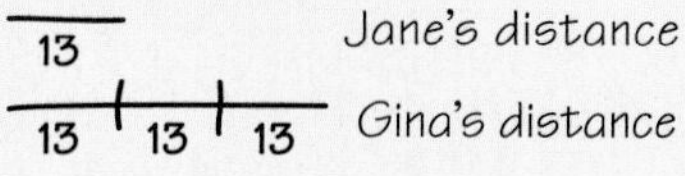

Gina drives 39 miles.

4. Andy paid a total of $28 for a T-shirt and a pair of shorts. The shorts cost 3 times as much as the T-shirt. How much did the T-shirt cost?

Answers: 1. Possible estimate: 210; 224 2. 2,992; $73.86 3. 5,208; 9,000; 450 4. $7

CHAPTER 5

Chapter Test

MULTIPLE CHOICE

Choose the correct letter for each answer.

1. Find 4 × 5,000.

   A. 200 **C.** 20,000

   B. 2,000 **D.** 200,000

2. Which is the most reasonable estimate for 8 × 612?

   A. 480 **C.** 4,800

   B. 540 **D.** 5,400

3. What product does this array show?

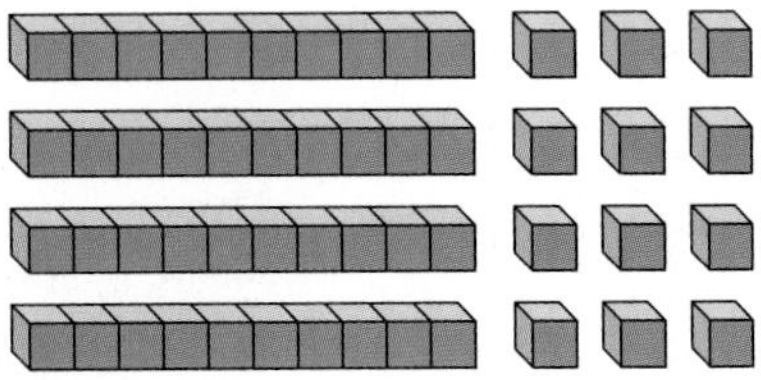

   A. 4 × 3

   B. 4 × 13

   C. 10 × 13

   D. 3 × 43

4. Use mental math to find 19 × 7.

   A. 26 **C.** 143

   B. 133 **D.** 763

5. Multiply 86 × 5.

   A. 91 **C.** 400

   B. 340 **D.** 430

6. Find the product of 7 and 134.

   A. 938 **C.** 948

   B. 942 **D.** 72,128

7. Which product is NOT the same as 5 × 9 × 2?

   A. 45 × 2

   B. 5 × 18

   C. 10 × 9

   D. 5 × 20

> **TEST TALK**
>
> **Think It Through**
> - I should **look for words like *not* and *except* in questions.**
> - I need to **read each answer choice carefully.**

8. Max has 2 times as many baseball cards as Cal. Together they have 60 baseball cards. How many baseball cards does Cal have?

   A. 15 **B.** 20 **C.** 60 **D.** 180

9. Which computation method would be most appropriate to find 2 × 8,000?

   A. Use mental math.

   B. Use paper and pencil.

   C. Use a calculator.

   D. Use a number line.

10. If one compact disc sells for $9.85 including tax, what is the total cost of 3 discs?

    A. $27.45 **C.** $28.55

    B. $27.55 **D.** $29.55

11. Each row of seats in a theater has 24 chairs. If the first 8 rows are completely filled with people, how many people are in the first 8 rows?

    A. 32 people **C.** 192 people

    B. 162 people **D.** 212 people

FREE RESPONSE

Estimate each product.

12. 6×82

13. 109×8

Find each product using mental math.

14. 500×8

15. 3×99

16. $3{,}000 \times 5$

17. 9×101

Find each product.

18. $\begin{array}{r} 46 \\ \times \quad 5 \\ \hline \end{array}$

19. $\begin{array}{r} 606 \\ \times \quad 7 \\ \hline \end{array}$

20. $\begin{array}{r} \$70.60 \\ \times \qquad 9 \\ \hline \end{array}$

21. $\begin{array}{r} 2{,}321 \\ \times \qquad 3 \\ \hline \end{array}$

22. $6 \times \$1.95$

23. 53×8

24. $2 \times 62 \times 5$

25. $78 \times 8 \times 0$

26. $3 \times 100 \times 5$

27. $1 \times 8 \times 20$

28. $4 \times 5 \times 50$

29. $25 \times 9 \times 4$

30. At a cruising speed of 490 miles per hour, how far can a plane travel in 3 hours?

31. A small airplane model costs \$8.99. Find the cost of 4 small airplane models.

32. There are 6 boxes of paper in the storeroom. Each box contains 8 packages, and each package contains 500 sheets. How many sheets of paper are there in all in the storeroom?

Writing in Math

33. Draw an array to find 3×14. Give the product and explain how you found it.

34. Try, check, and revise to solve the Pizza problem.

Pizza Yesterday, Sam's Café sold 4 times as many cheese pizzas as pepperoni pizzas. They sold a total of 30 cheese and pepperoni pizzas. How many of each kind of pizza did Sam's Café sell yesterday? Explain how you chose the numbers for your first try.

TEST TALK

Think It Through

- I need to **write my steps in order.**
- My answer and explanation should be **brief but complete.**

35. Draw a picture to show the main idea. Then choose an operation and solve the Coins problem.

Coins Katy has saved 32 quarters and four times as many dimes. How many dimes has Katy saved?

Cumulative Review and Test Prep

Number and Operation

MULTIPLE CHOICE

1. Perry spent \$18 on color markers. He bought 2 yellow markers, 3 pink markers, and 4 blue markers. If each marker cost the same amount, how much did each marker cost?

A. \$2 **B.** \$3 **C.** \$6 **D.** \$9

2. What is the product of 47×5?

A. 235 **C.** 252

B. 240 **D.** 255

3. Round 236,184 to the nearest ten thousand.

A. 200,000 **C.** 240,000

B. 230,000 **D.** 300,000

FREE RESPONSE

4. Write these numbers in order from least to greatest.

3,022 2,331 3,113 2,311

5. Tell how to make \$16.38 with the fewest bills and coins.

6. Tia bought a poster on sale for \$5.39. The poster originally cost \$7.89. How much money did Tia save?

Writing in Math

7. Draw an array to show 4×14. Give the product and explain how you found it.

Geometry and Measurement

MULTIPLE CHOICE

8. Chip started a 3-mile race at 3:30 P.M. He crossed the finish line at 4:05 P.M. How long did it take Chip to run the race?

> **TEST TALK**
> **Think It Through**
> I need to **identify the sequence of events** in the problem.

A. 25 minutes

B. 35 minutes

C. 1 hour and 25 minutes

D. 1 hour and 35 minutes

9. How many cups are in 1 quart?

A. 2 cups **C.** 8 cups

B. 4 cups **D.** 16 cups

FREE RESPONSE

10. A car weighs 1,780 pounds. The driver weighs 165 pounds. There are two 20-pound packages in the back seat. What is the total weight of the car with the driver and packages inside?

Writing in Math

11. Use geometric terms to describe one common characteristic of the shapes in each group.

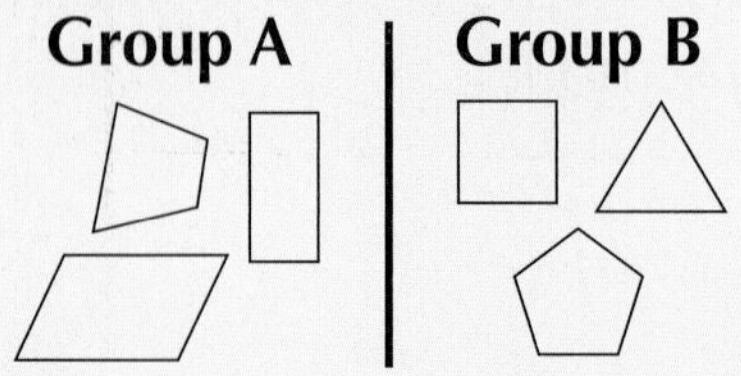

Data Analysis and Probability

MULTIPLE CHOICE

12. If you spin the spinner below 20 times, which color would you probably land on most often?

A. green

B. blue

C. red

D. yellow

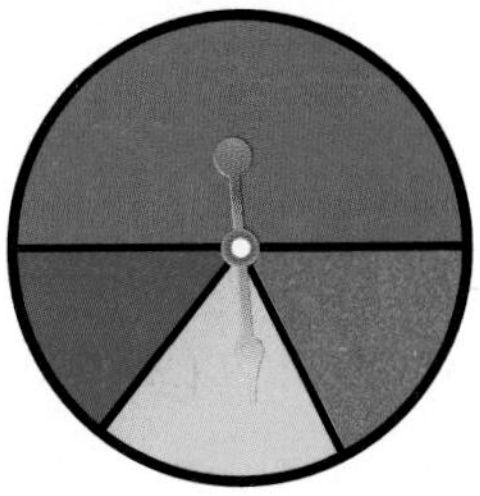

13. What is the range of this data set?
4, 3, 7, 10, 3, 5, 6

A. 3 **B.** 5 **C.** 7 **D.** 10

FREE RESPONSE

Use the pictograph for 14–17.

Bushels of Apples Sold

Each  = 20 bushels.

14. On which day were the most bushels of apples sold?

15. How many more bushels were sold on Saturday than on Sunday?

16. How many bushels were sold in all?

Writing in Math

17. On Monday, 100 bushels of apples were sold. Explain how you would show this data on the pictograph.

Algebra

MULTIPLE CHOICE

18. Which number sentence is NOT in the same fact family as $63 \div 7 = 9$?

A. $63 \div 9 = 7$

B. $9 \times 7 = 63$

C. $9 \times 3 = 27$

D. $7 \times 9 = 63$

TEST TALK

Think It Through
I should **watch for words like NOT or EXCEPT.**

19. Solve $n + 31 = 52$ by testing these values for n: 12, 21, 83, 1,612.

A. $n = 12$ **C.** $n = 83$

B. $n = 21$ **D.** $n = 1{,}612$

20. Terry ran 1 lap on Monday, 4 laps on Tuesday, and 7 laps on Wednesday. If he continues this pattern, how many laps will Terry run on Friday?

A. 9 laps **C.** 13 laps

B. 10 laps **D.** 16 laps

FREE RESPONSE

21. What is the rule for this table?

In	3	4	5	6
Out	12	16	20	24

Writing in Math

22. Give the missing number in the number pattern 63, 54, 45, ▢, 27. Explain how you found your answer.

Reteaching

Set 5-1 (pages 256–257)

Find 6×500.

Use mental math. Look for patterns in the factors and products.

$6 \times 5 = 30$

$6 \times \mathbf{50} = 3\mathbf{00}$

$6 \times \mathbf{500} = 3\mathbf{000}$

Remember that when the product of a basic fact contains a zero, that zero is not part of the pattern.

Find each product. Use mental math.

1. 3×40 = 120 **2.** 8×90 = 720

3. 5×300 = 1500 **4.** $4 \times 8{,}000$ = 32000

5. 7×60 = 420 **6.** $9 \times 4{,}000$ = 36000

7. $6 \times 8{,}000$ = 48000 **8.** 4×500 = 2000

Set 5-2 (pages 258–261)

Estimate 4×458.

One Way: Rounding

4×458
↓
$4 \times 500 = 2{,}000$

Another Way: Compatible Numbers

4×458
↓
$4 \times 450 = 1{,}800$

Think: Two 450s is 900. So, four 450s is 1,800.

Remember that compatible numbers are numbers that are easy to compute with in your head.

Estimate each product.

1. 3×22 **2.** 7×157

3. 6×732 **4.** 9×588

5. $5 \times 1{,}260$ **6.** $8 \times 4{,}657$

7. 4×290 **8.** $2 \times 3{,}501$

9. 7×699 **10.** 6×112

11. $2 \times 4{,}011$ **12.** 5×253

Set 5-3 (pages 262–263)

Find 4×52 by using breaking apart.

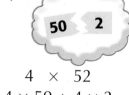

50 **2**

4×52
$4 \times 50 + 4 \times 2$
$200 + 8$
208

Find 78×6 by using compatible numbers.

78×6
↓
$80 \times 6 = 480$
$480 - 12 = 468$

Subtract the 2 extra groups of 6.

Remember when using compatible numbers, you need to add or subtract the extra groups from the new product to get the actual product.

1. 6×38 **2.** 5×42

3. 7×53 **4.** 9×87

5. 2×55 **6.** 4×76

7. 3×65 **8.** 8×29

Set 5-4 (pages 264–267)

Find 4 × 12.

Use blocks or draw a picture to build an array.

$$\begin{array}{r} 12 \\ \times\ 4 \\ \hline 8 \\ 40 \\ \hline 48 \end{array}$$

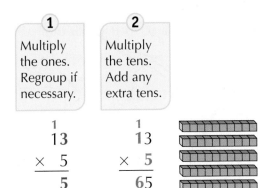

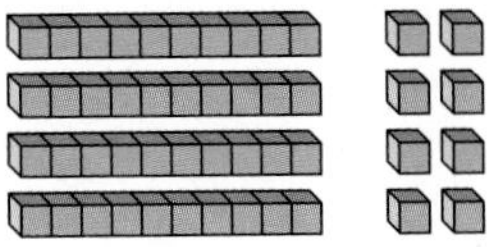

4 × 10 = 40 **4 × 2 = 8**

40 + 8 = 48

Remember to check that your picture accurately shows the numbers that are being multiplied.

1. 22 × 6
2. 28 × 3
3. 75 × 5
4. 53 × 4
5. 88 × 2
6. 21 × 6

Set 5-5 (pages 270–273)

Find 5 × 13.

1 Multiply the ones. Regroup if necessary.

2 Multiply the tens. Add any extra tens.

$$\begin{array}{r} {}^{1} \\ 13 \\ \times\ 5 \\ \hline 5 \end{array} \qquad \begin{array}{r} {}^{1} \\ 13 \\ \times\ 5 \\ \hline 65 \end{array}$$

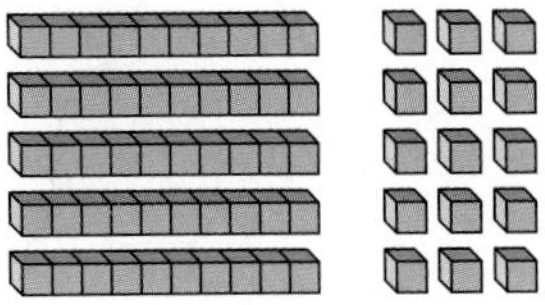

5 × 13 = 65

Remember that you can use an array to help you multiply. Check your answer with an estimate.

1. 18 × 2
2. 48 × 5
3. 33 × 6
4. 97 × 7
5. 62 × 4
6. 25 × 8

Set 5-6 (pages 274–275)

Find 768 × 6.

1 Multiply the ones. Regroup if necessary.

2 Multiply the tens. Add any extra tens. Regroup if necessary.

3 Multiply the hundreds. Add any extra hundreds.

$$\begin{array}{r} {}^{4} \\ 768 \\ \times\ 6 \\ \hline 8 \end{array} \qquad \begin{array}{r} {}^{4\,4} \\ 768 \\ \times\ 6 \\ \hline 08 \end{array} \qquad \begin{array}{r} {}^{4\,4} \\ 768 \\ \times\ 6 \\ \hline 4{,}608 \end{array}$$

Remember to check your answer with an estimate.

1. 239 × 4
2. 980 × 8
3. 485 × 3
4. 186 × 7
5. 228 × 2
6. 391 × 5

Set 5-7 (pages 278–281)

Five horses needed 9 new shoes. Each needed at least one, none needed all 4, at least one horse needed 3 shoes, and at least one horse needed 2 new shoes. How many horses needed 2 new shoes?

Try, check and revise.

Try 3 + 3 + 2 + 1 + 1 = 10
That's too high. Use one less shoe.

Try 3 + 2 + 2 + 1 + 1 = 9
That's right!

Two horses needed 2 new shoes.

Remember that checking lets you see if your first guess is too high or too low.

Ken has a collection of 24 small toy cars to put in a display case with 5 shelves. He wants to use all 5 shelves.

1. If he wants to put either 4 or 6 cars on a shelf, how many shelves should have 6 cars?
2. If he wants to put either 4 or 8 cars on a shelf, how many shelves should have 8 cars?

Set 5-8 (pages 282–283)

Find each product.

7 × 4,050
Use mental math.

7 × 50 is 350.
7 × 4,000 is 28,000.
So, 7 × 4,050 is 28,350.

3 × 2,240

Use paper and pencil. There are not a lot of regroupings.

```
  2,240
×     3
  6,720
```

9 × 6,856

Use a calculator. There are lots of regroupings.

9 [×] **6,856** [=]

61704

Remember to think first about which calculation method would work best for each problem.

1. 4,582 × 6

2. 9,000 × 3

3. $7,500 × 5

4. 2,331 × 4

5. 2,021 × 3

6. 5,924 × 8

7. 4,000 × 9

8. 3,807 × 2

9. 1,241 × 2

10. 6,037 × 8

11. 2,001 × 6

12. 4 × $5,050

13. 8 × 1,111

14. 5 × $2,798

15. 3 × 4,999

16. 4 × $2,020

17. 9 × 5,861

18. 8 × $6,000

Set 5-9 (pages 286–287)

Find 8 × $3.57.

1 Multiply the same way as with whole numbers.

$$\begin{array}{r} {}^{4\,5} \\ \$3.57 \\ \times \quad 8 \\ \hline 2856 \end{array}$$

2 Write the answer in dollars and cents.

$$\begin{array}{r} {}^{4\,5} \\ \$3.57 \\ \times \quad 8 \\ \hline \$28.56 \end{array}$$

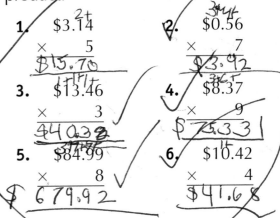

Remember that multiplication problems with dollars and cents need a dollar sign and a decimal point in the product.

1. $3.14 × 5
2. $0.56 × 7
3. $13.46 × 3
4. $8.37 × 9
5. $84.99 × 8
6. $10.42 × 4

Set 5-10 (pages 288–289)

Find 15 × 4 × 5.

Start with any two numbers. Then multiply by the third number.

15 × 4 × 5

(15 × 4) × 5

60 × 5

300

Remember that you can multiply factors in any order. You can also change the grouping of factors.

1. 6 × 15 × 5
2. 10 × 3 × 8
3. 6 × 60 × 9
4. 2 × 150 × 5
5. 40 × 3 × 4
6. 2 × 8 × 500
7. 25 × 7 × 4
8. 4 × 42 × 5

Set 5-11 (pages 290–291)

An orchard has 3 times as many apple trees as cherry trees. If there are 52 cherry trees, how many apple trees are there?

Draw a picture to show the main idea of the problem.

Use your picture to help choose an operation.

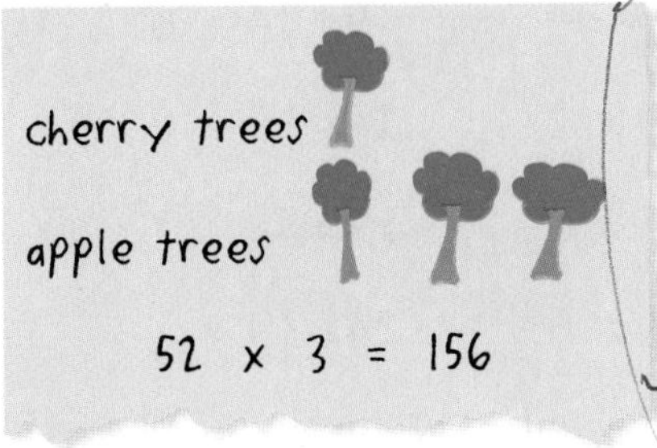

There are 156 apple trees.

Remember to draw a picture of the main idea before you choose an operation.

1. An office ordered 6 copy machines. Each machine weighed 108 pounds. Find the total weight of the order.
2. Celia has four weeks to save $58 for her vacation. The first week she saved $10, the second $21, and the third week $17. How much more money does she need to save?

Chapter 5

More Practice

Set 5-1 (pages 256–257)

Find each product. Use mental math.

1. 4 × 200 **2.** 9 × 50 **3.** 3 × 6,000 **4.** 6 × 800 **5.** 8 × 40

6. 2 × 5,000 **7.** 6 × 90 **8.** 4 × 800 **9.** 2 × 4,000 **10.** 3 × 500

11. 5 × 6,000 **12.** 9 × 900 **13.** 7 × 5,000 **14.** 9 × 300 **15.** 6 × 30

16. 9 × 400 **17.** 8 × 7,000 **18.** 7 × 800 **19.** 5 × 70 **20.** 4 × 600

21. 6 × 4,000 **22.** 5 × 300 **23.** 2 × 900 **24.** 8 × 5,000 **25.** 3 × 700

26. Maggie can type 50 words per minute. How many words can she type in 8 minutes?

400

Set 5-2 (pages 258–261)

Estimate each product.

1. 6 × 38 **2.** 7 × 465 **3.** 4 × 721 **4.** 5 × 885 **5.** 62 × 4

6. 5,500 × 8 **7.** 2 × 77 **8.** 223 × 4 **9.** 3 × 399 **10.** 7 × 125

11. 9 × 45 **12.** 3 × 820 **13.** 975 × 5 **14.** 722 × 3 **15.** 6 × 34

16. 7 × 6,210 **17.** 8,051 × 2 **18.** 5 × 46 **19.** 28 × 7 **20.** 508 × 9

21. 5 × 499 **22.** 512 × 8 **23.** 6 × 21 **24.** 2 × 799 **25.** 189 × 5

26. Andy and his family spent 5 nights at a hotel. Each night cost $85. About how much did the family pay for their stay at the hotel?

$425

Set 5-3 (pages 262–263)

Find each product. Use mental math.

1. 21 × 8 **2.** 32 × 6 **3.** 49 × 5 **4.** 51 × 7 **5.** 81 × 9

6. 8 × 38 **7.** 4 × 26 **8.** 3 × 88 **9.** 34 × 6 **10.** 72 × 7

11. 5 × 90 **12.** 7 × 85 **13.** 67 × 2 **14.** 15 × 8 **15.** 23 × 5

16. 99 × 9 **17.** 39 × 7 **18.** 22 × 6 **19.** 5 × 17 **20.** 4 × 60

21. 9 × 16 **22.** 82 × 5 **23.** 84 × 6 **24.** 39 × 7 **25.** 6 × 45

26. Dina buys 2 hamburger buns for each of the 27 people she has invited to a barbecue. How many hamburger buns does she buy?

Take It to the NET
More Practice
www.scottforesman.com

Set 5-4 (pages 264–267)

Use blocks or draw a picture to build an array. Then find each product.

1. 17×3
2. 28×2
3. 14×5
4. 22×6
5. 23×3
6. 34×2
7. 21×7
8. 18×4
9. 24×4
10. 19×2
11. 12×6
12. 20×5
13. 31×3
14. 15×4
15. 32×7
16. Dina is planting seeds in 4 pots. If she puts 16 seeds into each pot, how many seeds has she planted?

Set 5-5 (pages 270–273)

Find each product. Decide if your answer is reasonable.

1. 54×4
2. 28×7
3. 66×2
4. 75×4
5. 36×5
6. 82×6
7. 91×9
8. 55×8
9. 72×2
10. 61×3
11. 59×6
12. 24×8
13. 3×44
14. 39×7
15. 4×98
16. On the Internet you have found 18 articles on pandas. If it takes 3 minutes to access and print each article, how many minutes will it take to access and print all the articles?

Set 5-6 (pages 274–275)

Find each product. Estimate to check reasonableness.

1. 164×2
2. 608×8
3. 710×9
4. 314×5
5. 815×6
6. 117×9
7. 291×3
8. 844×6
9. 472×5
10. 157×7
11. 955×3
12. 9×197
13. 6×344
14. 347×2
15. 987×3
16. A container of yogurt has 225 calories. How many calories are there in 6 containers of yogurt?

Set 5-7 (pages 278–281)

Try, check, and revise to solve each problem. Write the answer in a complete sentence.

Gerbil Supplies	
Food	$5 a bag
Wood chips	$4 a bag
Toys	$2 each

1. Tandy spent $13, before tax, on 4 items for her gerbil. What did she buy?

2. Thomas spent $15, before tax, on 4 items for his gerbil. What did he buy?

3. Roger took all the wheels off his old bicycles and tricycles. He got 14 wheels off of 6 cycles. How many of each type of cycle did he have?

4. Peter's birthday is 50 days before his father's. If his father's birthday is August 11, when is Peter's birthday?

JUNE

S	M	T	W	T	F	S
						1
2	3	4	5	6	7	8
9	10	11	12	13	14	15
16	17	18	19	20	21	22
23	24	25	26	27	28	29
30						

JULY

S	M	T	W	T	F	S
	1	2	3	4	5	6
7	8	9	10	11	12	13
14	15	16	17	18	19	20
21	22	23	24	25	26	27
28	29	30	31			

AUGUST

S	M	T	W	T	F	S
				1	2	3
4	5	6	7	8	9	10
11	12	13	14	15	16	17
18	19	20	21	22	23	24
25	26	27	28	29	30	31

SEPTEMBER

S	M	T	W	T	F	S
1	2	3	4	5	6	7
8	9	10	11	12	13	14
15	16	17	18	19	20	21
22	23	24	25	26	27	28
29	30					

5. Hannah bought a hat for $7.50 and jeans for $15.95. She had to borrow a dollar from one of her friends in order to pay for her $3.50 lunch. How much money did Hannah start with?

Set 5-8 (pages 282–283)

Find each product. Choose a computation method, then tell which method you used.

1. 2,005 × 3
2. 2,874 × 6
3. $9,042 × 3
4. 5,000 × 8
5. 8,312 × 2
6. $7,040 × 4
7. 1,023 × 7
8. 4,874 × 8
9. $3,660 × 5
10. $1,999 × 4
11. 7,000 × 2
12. 6,736 × 3
13. 8,004 × 6
14. 4,004 × 8
15. Jeanne used a calculator to find 1,021 × 4. Would you use a calculator? Explain. Find the product.

Set 5-9 (pages 286–287)

Find each product.

1. $\$0.89 \times 7$
2. $\$4.67 \times 8$
3. $\$0.55 \times 3$
4. $\$8.90 \times 6$
5. $\$3.28 \times 2$
6. $\$17.34 \times 4$
7. $\$77.91 \times 6$
8. $\$12.63 \times 5$
9. $\$82.99 \times 9$
10. $\$41.32 \times 3$
11. $\$35.47 \times 5$
12. $\$22.15 \times 7$
13. $\$78.09 \times 6$
14. $\$31.50 \times 8$
15. $\$11.25 \times 6$
16. $\$10.45 \times 2$
17. $\$2.56 \times 9$
18. $8 \times \$46.78$
19. $6 \times \$37.30$
20. $\$8.95 \times 6$
21. $3 \times \$3.89$
22. $7 \times \$1.98$
23. $4 \times \$25.50$
24. Shirts cost \$11.57 each at Shirt Express. How much will 4 shirts cost?

Set 5-10 (pages 288–289)

Find each product.

1. $50 \times 5 \times 4$
2. $4 \times 81 \times 2$
3. $7 \times 8 \times 4$
4. $6 \times 40 \times 3$
5. $8 \times 47 \times 5$
6. $100 \times 7 \times 6$
7. $60 \times 2 \times 7$
8. $75 \times 8 \times 2$
9. $3 \times 4 \times 33$
10. $53 \times 2 \times 5$
11. $4 \times 25 \times 2$
12. $28 \times 4 \times 5$
13. $2 \times 6 \times 5$
14. $10 \times 2 \times 25$
15. $35 \times 2 \times 2$
16. $2 \times 45 \times 5$
17. Laurie can bake 2 dozen cookies each day. If she bakes cookies for 5 days, how many cookies will she bake?

Set 5-11 (pages 290–291)

1. A deli made 46 sandwiches in the morning, 21 sandwiches in the afternoon, and 29 sandwiches in the evening. How many sandwiches did the deli make in all?
2. Martha bought 3 packages of plastic forks and 4 packages of paper plates. There are 75 plates in a package. How many paper plates did Martha buy?
3. Roberto's grandmother was born in 1946. Roberto was born in 1994. How much older is Roberto's grandmother than Roberto?

CHAPTER 6

Multiplying by Two-Digit Numbers

DIAGNOSING READINESS

A Vocabulary

(pages 124–125, 258–259, 266–267)

Choose the best term from the box.

1. An arrangement of objects in equal rows is called an __?__.
2. Numbers that are easy to compute with mentally are called __?__.
3. The __?__ Property of Multiplication allows you to multiply two numbers in any order.

Vocabulary

- **rounding** *(p. 258)*
- **compatible numbers** *(p. 266)*
- **Commutative** *(p. 266)*
- **array** *(p. 124)*
- **Associative** *(p. 266)*

B Patterns With Multiples of 10

(pages 256–257)

Write each missing number.

4. 10 20 ▢ 40 ▢ 60
5. 30 60 90 ▢ ▢ 180
6. 70 140 210 ▢ 350 ▢
7. 80 ▢ 240 ▢ 400 480
8. 500 1,000 ▢ ▢ 2,500
9. Look at Exercise 4. If the pattern continued, what number would be the tenth term?

Do You Know...

About how many meals do crocodiles eat in their lifetime?

You'll find out in Lesson 6-10.

C Estimating Products

(pages 258–259)

Estimate each product.

10. 27 × 3 **11.** 38 × 9

12. 92 × 7 **13.** 18 × 6

14. 83 × 8 **15.** 33 × 4

16. 986 × 9 **17.** 723 × 6

18. 765 × 5 **19.** 832 × 7

20. 855 × 3 **21.** 632 × 8

22. 295 × 2 **23.** 304 × 5

D Multiplying by One-Digit Numbers

(pages 274-275)

24. 315 × 4 **25.** 687 × 9

26. 909 × 8 **27.** 796 × 5

28. 234 × 7 **29.** 874 × 6

30. 6,258 × 2 **31.** 7,452 × 5

32. 3,084 × 3 **33.** 1,025 × 5

34. If one pack of blank CDs costs $9.95, what will 3 packs cost, excluding tax?

Key Idea
Basic facts and place value can help you multiply numbers like 50 and 300.

TEST TALK

Think It Through
- I can **use what I know.** There are 50 states.
- The number 3,000 is **an estimate,** so 150,000 is an estimate, too.

Multiplying Multiples of Ten

WARM UP

1. 3 × 20
2. 4 × 80
3. 8 × 100
4. 5 × 400
5. 2 × 500
6. 9 × 7,000

LEARN

How do you multiply with mental math?

Find the total number of schools in the United States if each state had the same number of schools as Florida. Then find the total if each state had the same number of schools as Michigan.

Data File

Elementary and Secondary Schools 1999–2000 (to the nearest thousand)

California	9,000
Florida	3,000
Michigan	4,000

You can use a pattern to multiply with mental math.

Example A

Florida: Find 50 × 3,000.

$5 \times 3 = 15$
$5 \times 30 = 150$
$50 \times 30 = 1{,}500$
$50 \times 300 = 15{,}000$
$50 \times 3{,}000 = 150{,}000$

The number of zeros in both factors equals the number of zeros in the product.

There would be 150,000 schools.

Example B

Michigan: Find 50 × 4,000

$5 \times 4 = 20$
$5 \times 40 = 200$
$50 \times 40 = 2{,}000$
$50 \times 400 = 20{,}000$
$50 \times 4{,}000 = 200{,}000$

When the product of a basic fact includes zero, the zero is not part of the pattern.

There would be 200,000 schools.

Talk About It

1. Explain the pattern for finding 50 × 3,000.
2. When you multiply 50 × 4,000, how many zeros are in the product? Why?

CHECK ✓

For another example, see Set 6-1 on p. 356.

Multiply. Use mental math.

1. 20 × 60 **2.** 40 × 500 **3.** 80 × 2,000 **4.** 20 × 4,000

5. Number Sense Tell what numbers go in the blanks. To find 70 × 600, multiply __?__ and __?__. Then write __?__ zeros at the end.

PRACTICE

For more practice, see Set 6-1 on p. 360.

A Skills and Understanding

Multiply. Use mental math.

6. 80 × 60 **7.** 20 × 90 **8.** 30 × 400 **9.** 80 × 400

10. 60 × 300 **11.** 40 × 600 **12.** 70 × 500 **13.** 20 × 300

14. 50 × 9,000 **15.** 90 × 3,000 **16.** 40 × 4,000 **17.** 30 × 7,000

18. Number Sense How many zeros are in the product of 50 × 8,000? Explain how you know.

B Reasoning and Problem Solving

For 19–21, use the graph on the right. Find the number of schools in the United States if each state had the same number of schools as

19. Texas. **20.** Oklahoma.

21. Would there be more or less than 90,000 schools if each state had the same number of schools as Ohio?

22. Algebra Evaluate $30n$ when $n = 9,000$.

23. Writing in Math Explain why the product of 60 and 5,000 has five zeros when 60 has one zero and 5,000 has three zeros.

Elementary and Secondary Schools 1999–2000 (to the nearest thousand)

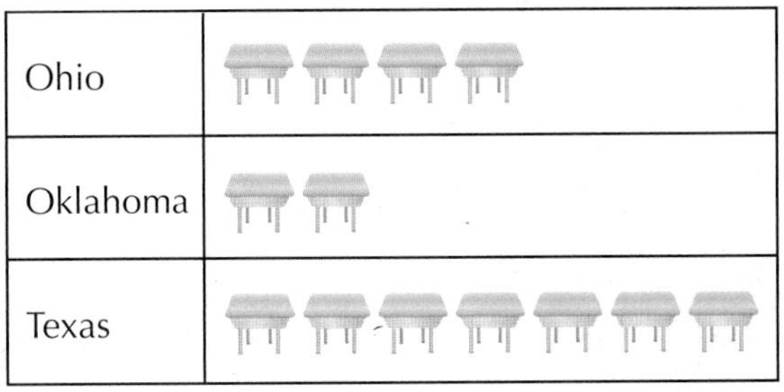

Each [desk] = 1,000 schools.

Mixed Review and Test Prep

Take It to the NET
Test Prep
www.scottforesman.com

24. How many minutes are in 8 hours?

25. Estimation Estimate 6 × 835.

A. 48 **B.** 480 **C.** 4,800 **D.** 48,000

Key Idea
To estimate, use factors you can multiply easily with mental math.

Vocabulary
- rounding (p. 20)
- compatible numbers (p. 258)
- underestimate (p. 72)
- overestimate (p. 72)
- range (p. 226)

TEST TALK

Think It Through
- I **need an estimate** because I only need to know about how many times the station orbits Earth in a year.
- I need to **use what I know.** There are 52 weeks in a year.

Estimating Products

WARM UP
1. 20 × 200 2. 30 × 800
3. 40 × 30 4. 60 × 400

LEARN

What are some ways to estimate?

The International Space Station orbits Earth every 92 minutes when it is 206 nautical miles (about 382 kilometers) above Earth. So, it orbits Earth about 109 times each week.

Example A

About how long does it take the International Space Station to orbit Earth 12 times?

Estimate 12 × 92.

Thomas used **rounding.**

12 x 92
↓ ↓
10 x 90 = 900

Since both numbers were replaced with lesser numbers, 900 is an **underestimate.** The exact answer is greater than 900.

It takes a little more than 900 minutes for the International Space Station to orbit Earth 12 times.

Example B

About how many times does the International Space Station orbit Earth in one year (52 weeks)?

Estimate 52 × 109.

Kelly used **compatible numbers.**

5 × 11 is easy to multiply.

52 x 109
↓ ↓
50 x 110 = 5,500

Since 52 was replaced with a lesser number and 109 was replaced with a greater number, it is difficult to tell whether 5,500 is an **overestimate** or an underestimate.

The International Space Station orbits Earth about 5,500 times a year.

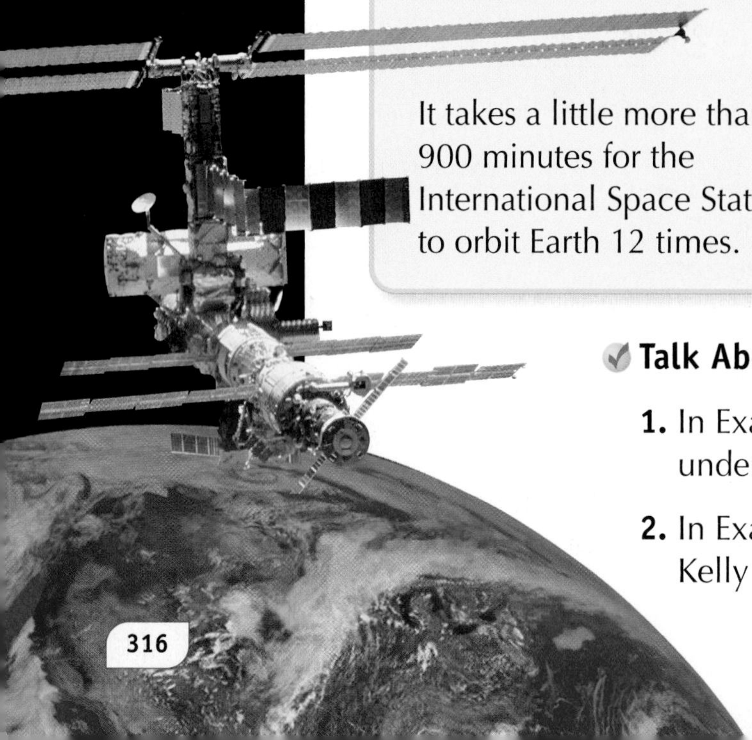

Talk About It

1. In Example A, how do you know 900 is an underestimate?

2. In Example B, what compatible numbers did Kelly use?

C Extensions

Estimate each product.

28. 18 × 4,216 **29.** 22 × 5,291 **30.** 1,882 × 37 **31.** 52 × 3,925

Mixed Review and Test Prep

Take It to the NET
Test Prep
www.scottforesman.com

Multiply. Use mental math.

32. 90 × 40 **33.** 50 × 800 **34.** 70 × 4,000 **35.** 4 × 30

36. Writing in Math Anna is 3 years old and Joan is 32 months old. Who is older? Explain.

37. Elizabeth bought 4 books. Each book cost $2.35. How much did she spend?

A. $8.20 **B.** $8.40 **C.** $9.20 **D.** $9.40

Learning with Technology

Using a Spreadsheet/Data/Grapher eTool to Multiply by Multiples of 10, 100, and 1,000

Enter the information given at the right into your Spreadsheet. Then copy the contents of A2, B3, and C2 down to the fifth row. Write down the products.

Repeat the steps above using the factors below.

1. 24 × 5

2. 24 × 6

3. 24 × 7

4. What do you notice about each product, as the number of zeros in one factor increased?

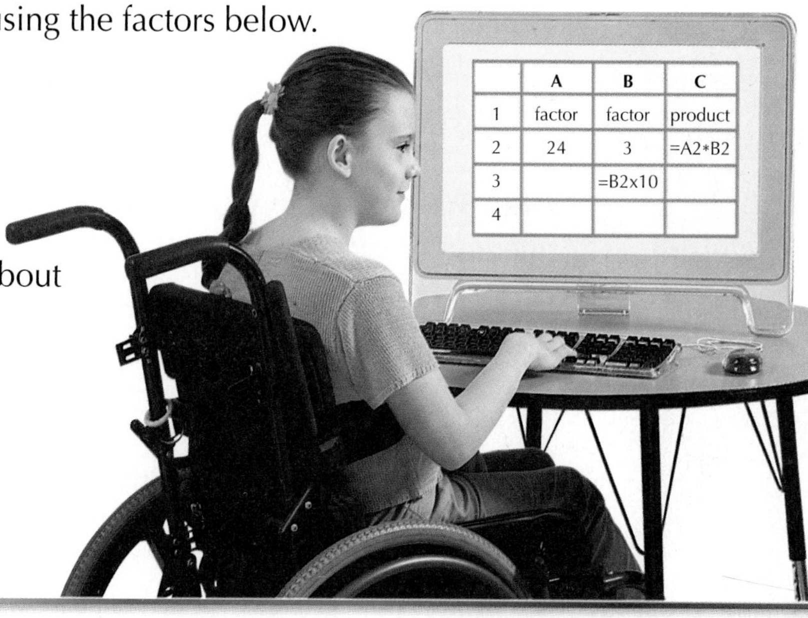

	A	B	C
1	factor	factor	product
2	24	3	=A2*B2
3		=B2x10	
4			

Key Idea
To find a product like 14 × 23, you can use an array and break the problem into four simpler problems.

Vocabulary
- partial products (p. 264)

Materials
- grid paper
- ruler or straightedge or e tools

TEST TALK

Think It Through
I can **use a model** and **solve simpler problems** to multiply.

Using Arrays to Multiply

WARM UP

1. 8 × 20
2. 3 × 30
3. 20 × 90
4. 70 × 40

LEARN

Crops, windows, and marching bands are a few of the things that come in arrays.

Activity

How do you multiply using an array?

A large marching band marched in 23 rows, with 14 members in each row. How many members were in the marching band?

Remember that you can multiply by solving simpler problems and adding together **partial products.** Here's how to find the product 14 × 23 using an array.

Step 1: Use grid paper. Draw a rectangle 23 units long and 14 units wide.

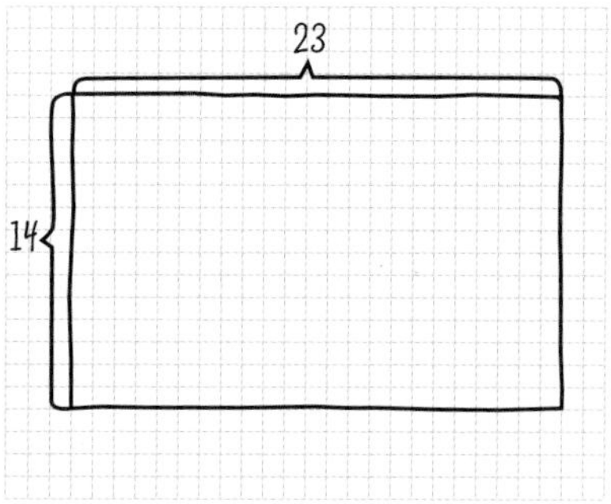

Step 2: Separate the rectangle by tens and ones for each factor. Find the number of squares in each smaller rectangle.

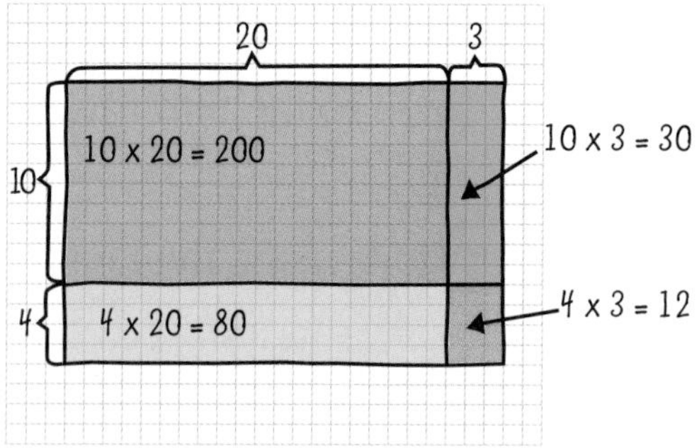

Step 3: Add the numbers of squares in the four rectangles.

$$\begin{array}{r} 12 \\ 80 \\ 30 \\ +\ 200 \\ \hline 322 \end{array}$$

a. Use grid paper to draw each rectangle. Follow the steps above to find each product.

15 × 12   16 × 24   18 × 35   26 × 29

b. Explain how breaking apart the rectangle for 14 × 23 into smaller rectangles is like solving four simpler problems. What are the simpler problems?

Activity

How do you record what you showed with the array?

Here is one way to record what you do with grid paper and an array to find the product for 24 × 27.

What You **Show**	What You **Write**
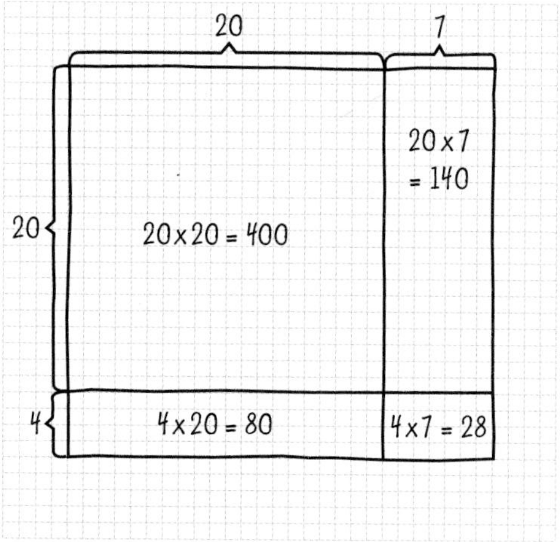	27 x 24 28 80 140 + 400 648

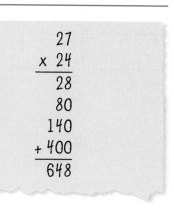

a. Use grid paper to draw each rectangle. Follow the method above to find each product.

17 × 25   19 × 32   21 × 29   12 × 38

b. Explain how breaking apart the rectangle for 24 × 27 into smaller rectangles is like solving four simpler problems. What are the simpler problems?

CHECK ✓

For another example, see Set 6-3 on p. 357.

Use grid paper to draw a rectangle. Then copy and complete the calculation.

1. 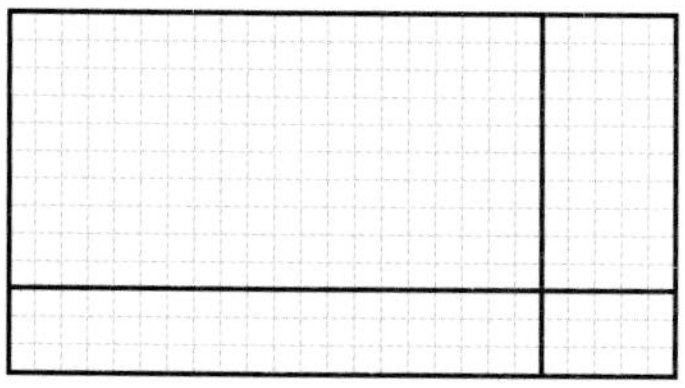

$$\begin{array}{r} 25 \\ \times\ 13 \\ \hline \end{array}$$

2. 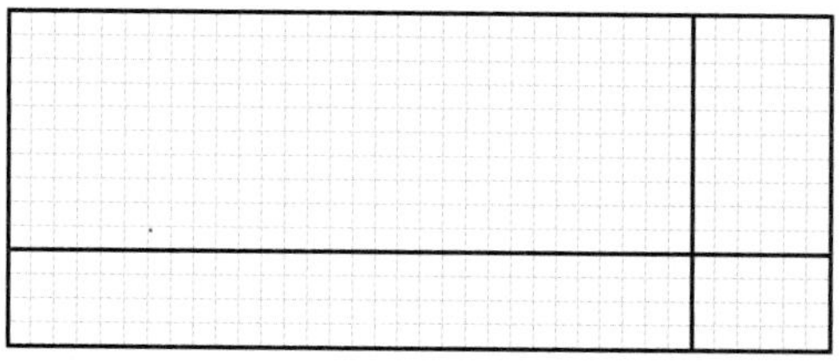

$$\begin{array}{r} 36 \\ \times\ 14 \\ \hline \end{array}$$

3. Number Sense What four simpler problems can you use to find 32 × 48?

4. Number Sense What four simpler problems can you use to find 35 × 34?

 For more practice, see Set 6-3 on p. 361.

A Skills and Understanding

Use grid paper to draw a rectangle. Then copy and complete the calculation.

5. 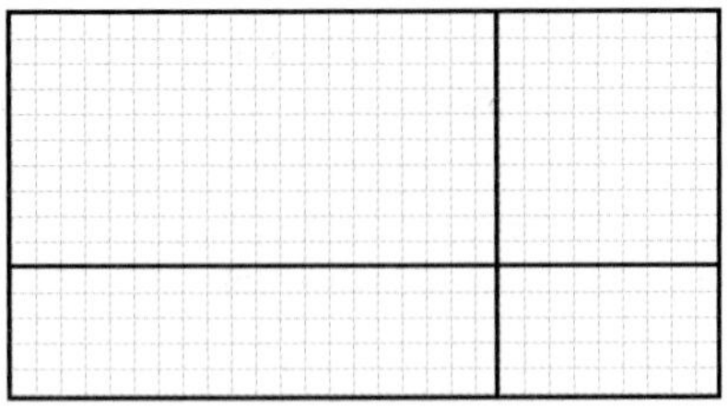

$$\begin{array}{r} 29 \\ \times\ 15 \\ \hline \square\square \\ \square\square\square \\ \square\square \\ \square\square\square \\ \hline \square\square\square \end{array}$$

6. 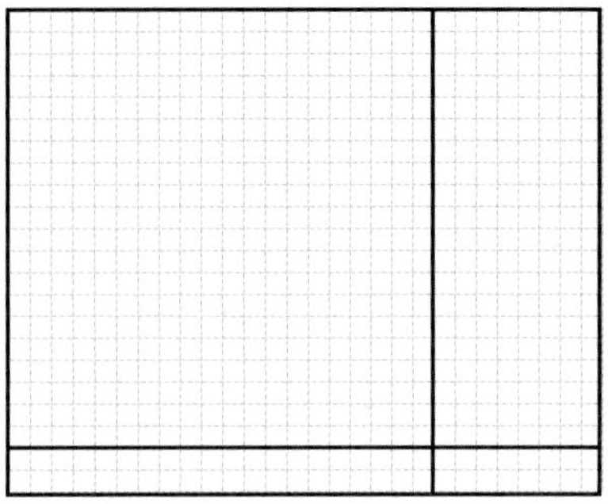

$$\begin{array}{r} 28 \\ \times\ 22 \\ \hline \square\square \\ \square\square \\ \square\square\square \\ \square\square\square \\ \hline \square\square\square \end{array}$$

7.
$$\begin{array}{r} 35 \\ \times\ 16 \\ \hline \square\square \\ \square\square\square \\ \square\square \\ \square\square\square \\ \hline \square\square\square \end{array}$$

8.
$$\begin{array}{r} 19 \\ \times\ 27 \\ \hline \square\square \\ \square\square \\ \square\square\square \\ \square\square\square \\ \hline \square\square\square \end{array}$$

9.
$$\begin{array}{r} 34 \\ \times\ 25 \\ \hline \square\square \\ \square\square\square \\ \square\square \\ \square\square\square \\ \hline \square\square\square \end{array}$$

10.
$$\begin{array}{r} 23 \\ \times\ 18 \\ \hline \square\square \\ \square\square\square \\ \square\square \\ \square\square\square \\ \hline \square\square\square \end{array}$$

11. 14×43 **12.** 24×34 **13.** 33×37 **14.** 13×46

15. Number Sense What four simpler problems can you use to find 42×56?

B Reasoning and Problem Solving

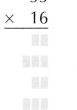

Math and Science

December has 31 days. In December, a Nile hippopotamus eats how many pounds

16. of hay? **17.** of kale?

18. of herbivore pellets? **19.** of food in all?

20. How many more pounds of hay than herbivore pellets does a Nile Hippopotamus eat in December?

21. **Writing in Math** Use an array to explain how the product of 12×24 is like the products of 2×24 plus 10×24.

Data File

What a Nile Hippopotamus Eats

Food	Pounds per Day
Hay	40
Herbivore pellets	14
Kale	2

PRACTICE

C Extensions

Use grids to find each product. Then answer the question.

22. Does $26 \times 24 = 24 \times 26$?

23. Does $12 \times 43 = 43 \times 12$?

Mixed Review and Test Prep

Take It to the NET
Test Prep
www.scottforesman.com

Estimation Estimate each product.

24. 49×39

25. 71×52

26. 246×43

27. 85×368

28. Tate read from 5:17 P.M. to 6:32 P.M. How long did he read?

A. 15 min **B.** 45 min **C.** 1 hr 15 min **D.** 1 hr 45 min

Enrichment

Perfect Squares

Materials: Counters

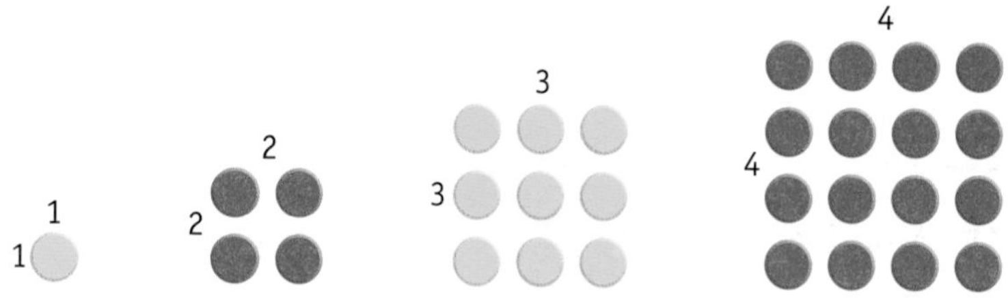

The first four perfect square numbers are 1, 4, 9, and 16. They are called **perfect squares** because they name square-shaped arrays.

1. Use counters or x's to build all the perfect squares from 1 to 100.

2. How many perfect squares did you build?

3. Is 50 a perfect square? Explain why or why not.

4. Find 3 perfect squares greater than 100.

Reading For Math Success

Understand Graphic Sources: Lists

Understanding graphic sources such as lists when you read in math can help you use the **problem-solving strategy, *Make an Organized List,*** in the next lesson.

In reading, understanding lists can help you understand what you read. In math, understanding lists can help you solve problems.

Carl made an organized list to show all the possible combinations of a vase and flowers that he could make.

Vase	Flowers
glass	roses
glass	lilies
glass	tulips
ceramic	roses
ceramic	lilies
ceramic	tulips

There are 6 different possible combinations.

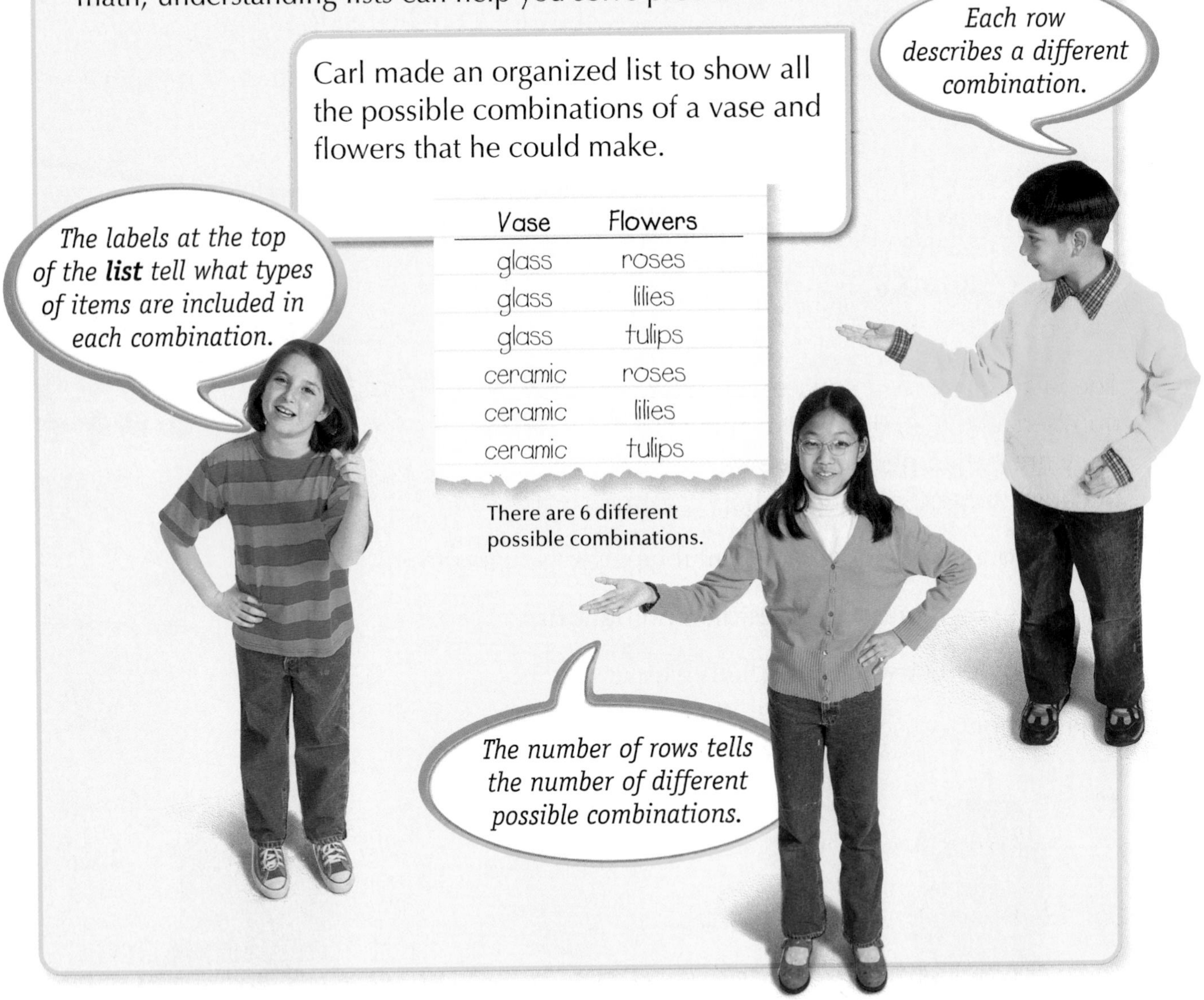
Each row describes a different combination.
*The labels at the top of the **list** tell what types of items are included in each combination.*
The number of rows tells the number of different possible combinations.

1. How many different vases did Carl have to choose from?
2. Why do you think Carl wrote glass vase in the first three rows of his list before writing ceramic vase?
3. How could Carl have organized his list in a different way.

For 4–7, use the problem below and the list at the right.

Eileen and her 4 friends want to ride a Ferris wheel. Each seat holds 2 people. Eileen made a list to show all the possible combinations of 2 friends that can ride together on the same seat.

Friend 1	Friend 2
Eileen	Jon
Eileen	Frank
Eileen	Helen
Eileen	Tracy
Jon	Frank
Jon	Helen
Jon	Tracy
Frank	Helen
Frank	Tracy
Helen	Tracy

4. What is the maximum number of friends that can ride together on the same seat?
5. How many different possible combinations of 2 friends can ride together on the same seat?
6. How many of these combinations include Eileen? Jon? Frank? Helen? Tracy?
7. **Writing in Math** When Eileen made her list, why didn't she add another row listing Tracy's name first?

For 8–11, use the problem below and the list at the right.

Billy has only enough money to buy 3 books. The books he can choose from include a poetry book, a mystery book, a biography, and a history book.

Book 1	Book 2	Book 3
poetry	mystery	biography
poetry	mystery	history
poetry	biography	history
mystery	biography	history

8. From how many different books is Billy choosing?
9. How many different combinations of 3 books are possible?
10. How many different combinations include the mystery book and the biography?
11. **Writing in Math** How could Billy have organized his list in a different way?

For 12–14, use the list at the right.

Nesita bought 3 different plants. She is trying to decide what order to plant them in her flowerbed.

1st Plant	2nd Plant	3rd Plant
daisy	tulip	lily
daisy	lily	tulip
tulip	lily	daisy
tulip	daisy	lily
lily	daisy	tulip
lily	tulip	daisy

12. What plants did Nesita buy?
13. How many different orders are possible?
14. **Writing in Math** Describe how Nesita organized her list.

Problem-Solving Strategy

Key Idea
Learning how and when to make an organized list can help you solve problems.

Make an Organized List

Reading Helps!
Understanding graphic sources such as lists
can help you with...
the problem-solving strategy, *Make an Organized List.*

LEARN

How do you make an organized list?

Map Coloring To color any map so that no adjoining sections are the same color, you need at most four colors. If you use red for one color, how many four-color combinations are possible? Other colors are purple, yellow, green, and orange.

Read and Understand

What do you know? There are 4 color choices besides red. The order of the colors does not matter.

What are you trying to find? Find how many ways there are to choose 3 colors from 4 choices.

Plan and Solve

What strategy will you use? **Strategy: Make an Organized List**

How to Make an Organized List
Step 1 Identify the items to be combined.
Step 2 Choose one of the items. Find combinations keeping that item fixed.
Step 3 Repeat Step 2 as often as needed.

Use Red, Purple, Yellow, Green, and Orange. Red has to be in each combination.

List the choices with Red and Purple.
Red, Purple, Yellow, Green
Red, Purple, Yellow, Orange
Red, Purple, Green, Orange

Red, Yellow, Green, Orange is the only other choice.

Answer: There are 4 possible combinations.

Look Back and Check

Is your work correct? Yes, each combination uses red. The way the list is organized shows that all ways were found.

Talk About It

1. Why is Red, Purple, Green, Yellow not another choice?
2. Why is making an organized list helpful?

When might you make an organized list?

Class Representatives Ralph, Kyle, Dora, and Kay are running for class representatives. The two students with the highest number of votes will be elected. How many outcomes for the election are possible? (Hint: It does not matter who has the most votes between the two highest.)

Solution

Ralph-Kyle
Ralph-Dora   Kyle-Dora
Ralph-Kay   Kyle-Kay   Dora-Kay

Six outcomes are possible.

When to Make an Organized List

Think about making an organized list when:

You are asked to find combinations of two or more items.

- Colors: Red, purple, yellow, green, and orange
- People: Ralph, Kyle, Dora, Kay

There are enough items that organizing the list is helpful.

Talk About It

3. Why is it not necessary to list Kyle-Ralph?

4. How is the list above organized?

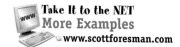

Take It to the NET
More Examples
www.scottforesman.com

CHECK

For another example, see Set 6-4 on p. 357.

For 1–2, use the start of the organized list. Finish solving the problem.

1. Pets Katie has a dog, a cat, and a goldfish. She feeds them in a different order each day. How many different orders are possible?

dog, cat, goldfish
dog, goldfish, cat,

2. Quintuplets Ben, Kari, Kristi, Jami, and Juli are quintuplets. Two of them must help their mother at her business each Saturday. How many combinations are possible?

Ben-Kari   Ben-Kristi
Kari-Kristi

For more practice, see Set 6-4 on p. 361.

A Using the Strategy

Finishing an Organized List Use the start of the organized list. Finish solving the problem.

3. Katie, Tom, Ahmet, and Josie are running for class president. The one with the second most votes will be vice president. How many outcomes are possible for the election?

President is first and VP is second.
Katie-Tom Katie-Ahmet Katie-Josie

Making an Organized List to Solve Problems Make an organized list to solve the problem. Write the answer in a complete sentence.

4. Andrea and Calvin are decorating for a party. They want to use two colors of crepe paper. Their choices are red, blue, green, orange, and yellow. How many ways can they choose two colors?

5. Use the data on the right. How many ways can you buy 200 marbles?

10 marbles 50 marbles 100 marbles

Math and Social Studies

The President of the United States appoints people to head departments within the executive branch of the government. These people are members of the President's cabinet. George Washington's first cabinet had the 4 members listed at the right.

The First Cabinet

Secretary of State	Thomas Jefferson
Secretary of War	Henry Knox
Secretary of the Treasury	Alexander Hamilton
Attorney General	Edmund Randolph

6. How many ways could the first cabinet be listed in a newspaper if Thomas Jefferson were listed first?

7. President Washington appointed the first cabinet in 1789. How many years ago was that?

Suppose some of the first cabinet members held a meeting. How many combinations are possible if

8. two members met?

9. three members met?

PRACTICE

B Mixed Strategy Practice

Solve each problem. Write the answer in a complete sentence.

10. How many ways can you make change for a dollar using only quarters, dimes, and nickels, if you use at most 3 nickels?

11. Tracey and Teri are playing a game. When Tracey says 3, Teri says 6. When Tracey says 8, Teri says 16. When Tracey says 5, what will Teri say?

12. Kara and Karl worked in the orchards picking peaches. Kara picked 9 bushels a day and Karl picked 11 bushels a day. How many bushels had Karl picked when Kara picked 81 bushels?

13. Alex can have his drum lessons on Tuesdays, Wednesdays, or Thursdays. The available times are 4:00, 5:00, and 6:00. Make a list of the days and times Alex can take his drum lesson.

14. **Writing in Math** The school newspaper has a total of 20 articles and ads. There are 8 more articles than ads. How many articles are there? How many ads are there? Explain how you solved the problem.

STRATEGIES

- **Show What You Know**
  - Draw a Picture
  - Make an Organized List
  - Make a Table
  - Make a Graph
  - Act It Out or Use Objects
- **Look for a Pattern**
- **Try, Check, and Revise**
- **Write a Number Sentence**
- **Use Logical Reasoning**
- **Solve a Simpler Problem**
- **Work Backward**

Choose a tool

TEST TALK

Think It Through

Stuck? I won't give up! I can:

- Reread the problem.
- Tell what I know.
- Identify key facts and details.
- Tell the problem in my own words.
- Show the main idea.
- Try a different strategy.
- Retrace my steps.

Mixed Review and Test Prep

Take It to the NET
Test Prep
www.scottforesman.com

15. Use the grid to find the partial products and the product. Copy and complete the calculation.

```
   27
 × 14
   ▢▢
   ▢▢
   ▢▢
  ▢▢▢
 ----
  ▢▢▢
```

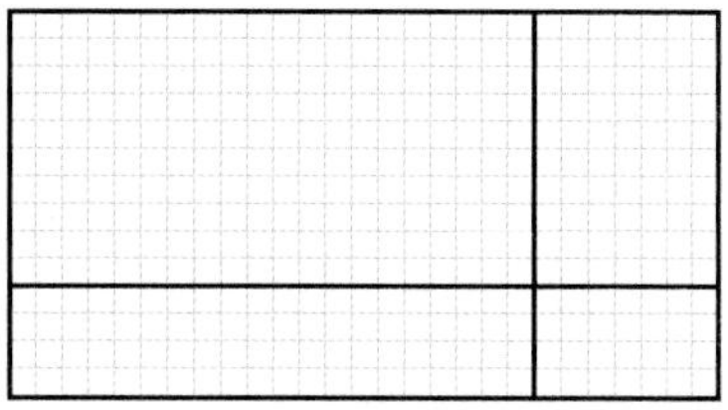

16. Jason had \$20. He spent \$11.19 at the store and \$1.25 on food. How much money did he have left?

A. \$7.56 **B.** \$8.56 **C.** \$8.66 **D.** \$11.19

Section A: Lessons 6-1 through 6-4

Review

Do You Know How?

Multiplying Multiples of Ten (6-1)
Estimating Products (6-2)

Multiply. Use mental math.

1. 30 × 30 **2.** 20 × 700

3. 50 × 5,000 **4.** 80 × 9,000

Estimate each product.

5. 22 × 32 **6.** 39 × 68

7. 53 × 108 **8.** 445 × 71

9. 36 × 243 **10.** 26 × 389

Do You Understand?

A Tell how you found the product in Exercise 2.

B Describe how to estimate 47 × 28 by finding a range for the product.

Using Arrays to Multiply (6-3)

Use grid paper to draw a rectangle. Then copy and complete the calculation.

11.

```
     35
   × 23
   ----
     ▒▒   3 × 5
     ▒▒   3 × 30
    ▒▒▒   20 × 5
  + ▒▒▒   20 × 30
   ----
    ▒▒▒
```

12.

```
     21
   × 28
   ----
      ▒   8 × 1
    ▒▒▒   8 × 20
     ▒▒   20 × 1
  + ▒▒▒   20 × 20
   ----
    ▒▒▒
```

13. 17 × 23 **14.** 28 × 15

C Tell how you found the product in Exercise 13.

D What four simpler problems can you use to find 74 × 56?

Problem-Solving Strategy: Make an Organized List (6-4)

15. Make and use an organized list to solve the Pizza problem.

Pizza Myra has onions, mushrooms, broccoli, and green peppers. How many combinations of 3 different vegetables can she put on a pizza?

E Tell how you used an organized list to solve the problem.

F Why is an organized list useful for this type of problem?

Diagnostic Checkpoint

Think It Through
I can estimate to make sure my **answer is reasonable.**

MULTIPLE CHOICE

1. There are 20 students in Mr. Cheng's class. If each student collects 40 rocks, how many rocks will the class have? (6-1)

A. 40 rocks **B.** 60 rocks **C.** 600 rocks **D.** 800 rocks

2. Josie has 12 packages of beads. Each package has 36 beads. How many beads does Josie have? (6-3)

A. 48 beads **B.** 108 beads **C.** 432 beads **D.** 3,672 beads

FREE RESPONSE

Multiply. Use mental math. (6-1)

3. 90×70 **4.** 60×70 **5.** $3{,}000 \times 20$ **6.** 80×800

7. 30×500 **8.** 40×60 **9.** 90×300 **10.** $5{,}000 \times 20$

Estimate each product. (6-2)

11. 21×11 **12.** 38×19 **13.** 26×242 **14.** 33×446

Copy and complete. (6-3)

15.	**16.**	**17.**	**18.**
13	19	24	38
× 22	× 31	× 25	× 18
▢	▢	▢▢	▢▢
▢▢	▢▢	▢▢▢	▢▢▢
▢▢	▢▢▢	▢▢	▢▢
▢▢▢	▢▢▢	▢▢▢	▢▢▢
▢▢▢	▢▢▢	▢▢▢	▢▢▢

19. Todd, Martin, Dallas, Seth, Josh, and Carlo are friends. How many combinations are possible for the boys to get in groups of three for a project? Make an organized list.

Writing in Math

20. Explain why the product of 60×500 has more zeros than the product of 60×700. (6-1)

21. Explain how to estimate 47×62 by finding a range. (6-2)

Key Idea
To find a product like 17 × 25, break it into simpler problems.

Multiplying Two-Digit Numbers

WARM UP

1. 395×3
2. 482×9
3. 432×6
4. 125×10

LEARN

How do you multiply with paper and pencil?

Example A

If 17 farms each had 25 goats, how many goats would all the farms have together?

(25) (25) (25) (25) (25) (25) (25) (25) . . . .
17 groups

Since each farm has 25 goats, you can multiply.

	What You **Think**	What You **Write**
STEP 1 Multiply the ones. Regroup if necessary.	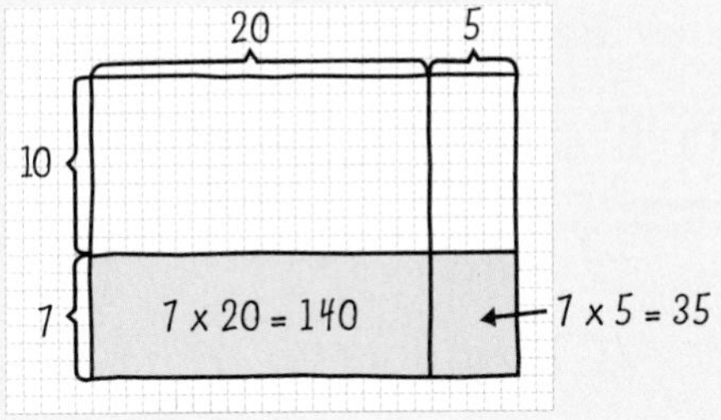 7 × 5 ones = 35 ones. Regroup 35 ones as 3 tens 5 ones. 7 × 2 tens = 14 tens. 14 tens + 3 tens 5 ones = 17 tens 5 ones.	3 25 × 17 175
STEP 2 Multiply the tens. Regroup if necessary.	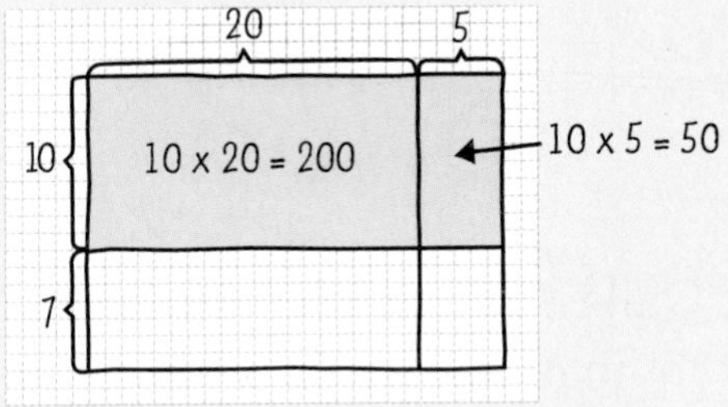 1 ten × 5 ones = 5 tens. 1 ten × 2 tens = 20 tens. 5 tens + 20 tens = 25 tens or 250.	3 25 × 17 175 250
STEP 3 Add the partial products.	5 ones + 0 ones = 5 ones 7 tens + 5 tens = 12 tens Regroup 12 tens as 1 hundred 2 tens. 1 hundred + 1 hundred + 2 hundreds = 4 hundreds	3 25 × 17 ¹175 250 425

TEST TALK

Think It Through

I need an **exact answer.**

I can multiply **another way** by showing all partial products.

$$\begin{array}{r} 25 \\ \times\ 17 \\ \hline 35 \\ 140 \\ 50 \\ 200 \\ \hline 425 \end{array}$$

Talk About It

1. Why do you place a zero in the ones place in Step 2?

2. Explain how to estimate 17×25.

Take It to the NET
More Examples
www.scottforesman.com

Is the answer reasonable?

You can use an estimate to make sure your answer is reasonable.

Example B

If 26 farms each had 39 sheep, how many sheep would there be in all?

Multiply 26×39.

Estimate: $30 \times 40 = 1{,}200$

The product is less than 1,200.

Multiply by the ones. Place a zero in the ones place. Then multiply by the tens.

$$\begin{array}{r} {}^{1}_{5} \\ 39 \\ \times\ 26 \\ \hline 234 \\ 780 \\ \hline 1{,}014 \end{array}$$

$6 \times 39 = 234$

$20 \times 39 = 780$

The product 1,014 is reasonable because it is a little less than the estimate 1,200.

There would be 1,014 sheep.

Example C

If 70 farms each had 82 cows, how many cows would there be in all?

Multiply 70×82.

Estimate: $70 \times 80 = 5{,}600$

The product is greater than 5,600.

Since $0 \times 82 = 0$, you can just put a zero in the ones place.

$$\begin{array}{r} {}^{1} \\ 82 \\ \times\ 70 \\ \hline 5{,}740 \end{array}$$

The product 5,740 is reasonable because it is a little greater than the estimate 5,600.

There would be 5,740 cows.

Talk About It

3. In Example C, how do you know 5,740 is a reasonable answer?

4. Is 385 a reasonable answer for 31×56? Explain.

CHECK

For another example, see Set 6-5 on p. 358.

1. $\begin{array}{r} 39 \\ \times 25 \\ \hline \end{array}$ **2.** $\begin{array}{r} 69 \\ \times 28 \\ \hline \end{array}$ **3.** $\begin{array}{r} 47 \\ \times 80 \\ \hline \end{array}$ **4.** $\begin{array}{r} 86 \\ \times 31 \\ \hline \end{array}$ **5.** $\begin{array}{r} 53 \\ \times 79 \\ \hline \end{array}$

6. Number Sense Sam multiplied 42×70 and got a product of 294. Explain why Sam's answer is not reasonable.

PRACTICE

For more practice, see Set 6-5 on p. 362.

A Skills and Understanding

7. $\begin{array}{r} 63 \\ \times 38 \\ \hline \end{array}$
8. $\begin{array}{r} 22 \\ \times 79 \\ \hline \end{array}$
9. $\begin{array}{r} 86 \\ \times 40 \\ \hline \end{array}$
10. $\begin{array}{r} 55 \\ \times 73 \\ \hline \end{array}$
11. $\begin{array}{r} 39 \\ \times 68 \\ \hline \end{array}$
12. $\begin{array}{r} 21 \\ \times 24 \\ \hline \end{array}$
13. $\begin{array}{r} 63 \\ \times 58 \\ \hline \end{array}$
14. $\begin{array}{r} 74 \\ \times 35 \\ \hline \end{array}$
15. $\begin{array}{r} 19 \\ \times 50 \\ \hline \end{array}$
16. $\begin{array}{r} 47 \\ \times 88 \\ \hline \end{array}$
17. $\begin{array}{r} 98 \\ \times 34 \\ \hline \end{array}$
18. $\begin{array}{r} 66 \\ \times 28 \\ \hline \end{array}$
19. $\begin{array}{r} 54 \\ \times 42 \\ \hline \end{array}$
20. $\begin{array}{r} 83 \\ \times 52 \\ \hline \end{array}$
21. $\begin{array}{r} 37 \\ \times 70 \\ \hline \end{array}$

22. **Number Sense** Lateisha is multiplying 27 × 25. How does she know the product must be less than 1,000?

B Reasoning and Problem Solving

23. Each egg carton holds two dozen eggs. A dozen is 12. How many eggs are in 14 cartons?

Math and Social Studies

A year is 52 weeks. How much money does an American family spend in a year to feed a child who is

24. 6 to 8 years old?
25. 15 to 17 years old?
26. 9 to 14 years old?
27. 3 to 5 years old?
28. In four weeks, how much more money does a family spend to feed a child who is 16 years old than a child who is 7 years old?

Data File

Money Spent by an American Family to Feed a Child

Age of Child	Weekly Amount
3–5 years	$23
6–8 years	$30
9–14 years	$35
15–17 years	$39

29. **Writing in Math** Is the explanation below correct? If not, tell why and write a correct response. If it is correct, draw a picture to show the product.

> Explain how to find the product of 72 and 26.
>
> I multiply the ones. Then, I multiply the tens.
>
> $\begin{array}{r} 72 \\ \times\ 26 \\ \hline 432 \\ 144 \\ \hline 576 \end{array}$

TEST TALK

Think It Through

- I should **describe all the steps,** in order.
- I should always check that my **answer is reasonable.**

C Extensions

Algebra Evaluate each expression when $n = 75$.

30. $12n$ **31.** $36n$ **32.** $28n$ **33.** $56n$ **34.** $87n$

Mixed Review and Test Prep

Take It to the NET
Test Prep
www.scottforesman.com

35. Liz has a blue, a green, a yellow, and a purple sticker. List the different ways can she put them in her sticker book if she puts the green sticker first.

36. Writing in Math Gabby estimated 81×89 and got 7,200. Is this reasonable? Explain.

37. Matt wrote the numbers 3, 7, 11, and 15. What are the next three numbers in his pattern?

A. 16, 17, 18 **B.** 18, 21, 24 **C.** 19, 23, 27 **D.** 20, 24, 28

Discovery CHANNEL SCHOOL

Discover Math in Your World

One Fierce Lizard

Komodo dragons are considered the world's largest lizards and fiercest predators. They are carnivores, or meat-eaters, and have been known to eat deer, goats, and even other lizards.

1. An elephant can smell water from over 5,000 feet away. A Komodo dragon can smell prey from 5 times this distance. From how far away can a Komodo dragon smell prey?

2. A Komodo dragon may have a mass of 98 grams when it hatches. A one-year-old dragon may have a mass that is 87 times as much. What is the possible mass of a one-year-old Komodo dragon?

Take It to the NET
Video and Activities
www.scottforesman.com

Key Idea
To find a product like 18 × 245, break apart 18 and 245 using place value.

Multiplying Greater Numbers

WARM UP

1. $\begin{array}{r} 205 \\ \times\ 10 \\ \hline \end{array}$
2. $\begin{array}{r} 319 \\ \times\ 9 \\ \hline \end{array}$
3. $\begin{array}{r} 24 \\ \times\ 30 \\ \hline \end{array}$
4. $\begin{array}{r} 83 \\ \times\ 18 \\ \hline \end{array}$

LEARN

How do you multiply greater numbers by two-digit numbers?

Microscopes cost $245 each.

How much money does Lincoln Elementary School need to buy 28 microscopes?

Example

Multiply 28 × 245.

Estimate: 30 × 250 = 7,500.

The product is less than 7,500.

STEP 1

Multiply the ones. Regroup if necessary.

$$\begin{array}{r} {}^{3\,4} \\ 245 \\ \times\ 28 \\ \hline 1960 \end{array}$$

STEP 2

Place a zero in the ones place. Multiply the tens. Regroup if necessary.

$$\begin{array}{r} {}^{1} \\ {}^{3\,4} \\ 245 \\ \times\ 28 \\ \hline 1960 \\ 4900 \end{array}$$

STEP 3

Add the partial products.

$$\begin{array}{r} {}^{1} \\ {}^{3\,4} \\ 245 \\ \times\ 28 \\ \hline 1960 \\ 4900 \\ \hline 6{,}860 \end{array}$$

The product 6,860 is reasonable because it is a little less than the estimate of 7,500.

Talk About It

1. How much money does Lincoln Elementary School need to buy the microscopes?
2. Why is there a zero in the ones place in Step 2?

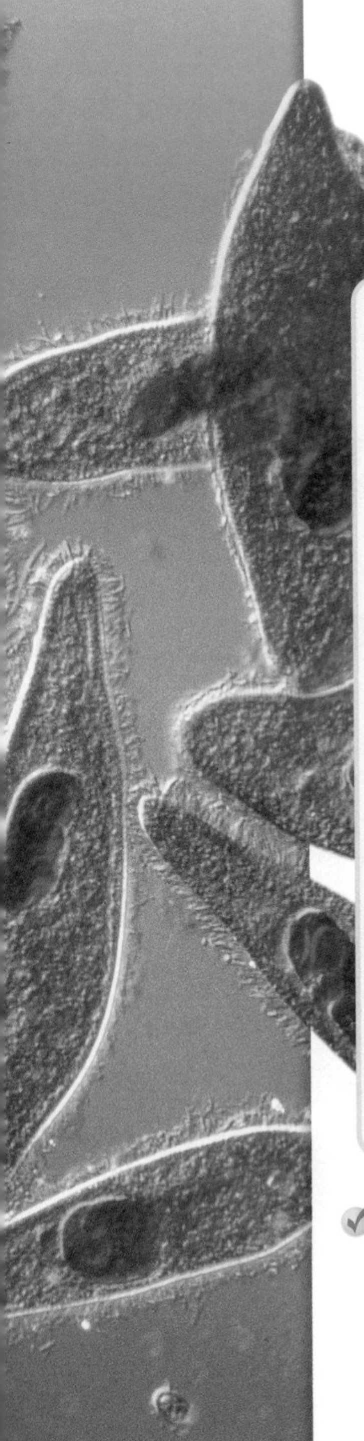

CHECK

For another example, see Set 6-6 on p. 358.

1. 123×36 **2.** 621×23 **3.** 525×44 **4.** 293×58 **5.** 372×70

6. Number Sense Is 60,232 a reasonable answer for 19 × 328? Explain.

PRACTICE

For more practice, see Set 6-6 on p. 362.

A Skills and Understanding

7. 607×68 **8.** 474×19 **9.** 191×98 **10.** 765×82 **11.** 176×73

12. 393×54 **13.** 637×82 **14.** 505×26 **15.** 224×34 **16.** 919×23

17. 213×29 **18.** 721×58 **19.** 382×64 **20.** 857×32 **21.** 409×45

22. Number Sense Is 7,788 a reasonable answer for 48 × 649? Explain.

B Reasoning and Problem Solving

Use the bar graph for 23–26.

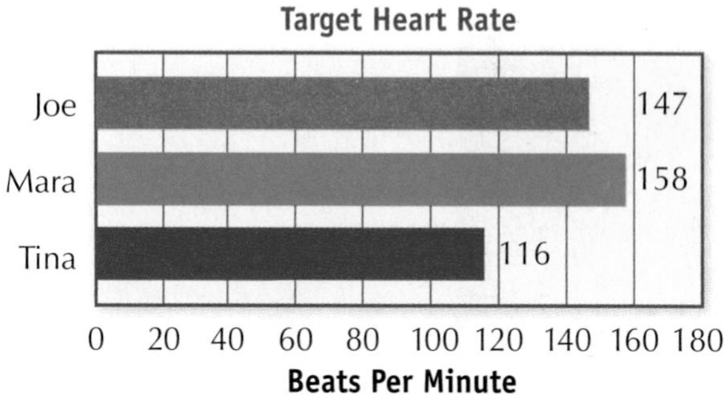

Find how many times each person's heart beats in 15 minutes at the target heart rate.

23. Joe **24.** Mara

In 20 minutes, how many more times does

25. Mara's heart beat than Tina's?

26. Joe's heart beat than Tina's?

27. Writing in Math How could you use the product 6 × 207 = 1,242 to find the product 12 × 207?

Mixed Review and Test Prep

Take It to the NET
Test Prep
www.scottforesman.com

28. 37×83 **29.** 52×76 **30.** 29×48 **31.** 70×80 **32.** 518×3

33. Algebra Evaluate $b + 19$, when $b = 13$.

A. 6 **B.** 12 **C.** 22 **D.** 32

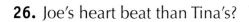

Key Idea
You can use mental math, paper and pencil, or a calculator to multiply depending on the numbers involved and the situation.

Materials
- calculator

Choose a Computation Method

WARM UP

1. 40×80
2. 3×250
3. 205×9
4. 73×28

LEARN

How do you use different methods?

When you multiply, try using mental math first. Next, think about using paper and pencil. For very hard problems, use a calculator.

Weekly Store Sales

Video Super Store	$2,000
Town Video	$905
Eastgate Video	$1,837

TEST TALK

Think It Through
Before I do a calculation, I should **decide which method makes sense.**

Example A

What are Video Super Store's total sales for 10 weeks?

$10 \times \$2{,}000 = \square$

This is easy to do in my head. I'll use **mental math.**

10 × 2,000 is 2,000 with one more zero, or 20,000.

Total Sales: $20,000

Example B

What are Eastgate Video's total sales for a year? Remember, 1 year = 52 weeks.

$52 \times \$1{,}837 = \square$

There are lots of regroupings. I'll use a **calculator.**

Press:

52 [×] 1837 [ENTER =]

Display:

95524

Total Sales: $95,524

Example C

What are Town Video's total sales for a quarter of a year (13 weeks)?

$13 \times 905 = \square$

There are not a lot of regroupings. I'll use **paper and pencil.**

$$\begin{array}{r} \scriptstyle 1 \\ 905 \\ \times \ 13 \\ \hline 2715 \\ 9050 \\ \hline 11{,}765 \end{array}$$

Total Sales: $11,765

Talk About It

1. Why is $10 \times 2{,}000$ an easier computation than 13×905?
2. Why would you not use a calculator to find 20×320?

CHECK

For another example, see Set 6-7 on p. 358.

Multiply. Tell what method you used.

1. 500×30
2. 426×79
3. $1{,}980 \times 17$
4. 316×21
5. 250×40

6. **Number Sense** Cal used a calculator to find 300×90. Could he have used a faster method? Explain.

PRACTICE

For more practice, see Set 6-7 on p. 363.

A Skills and Understanding

Multiply. Tell what method you used.

7. 61×15
8. $2{,}364 \times 21$
9. 900×90
10. 61×30
11. 878×33
12. $1{,}182 \times 45$
13. 50×400
14. 684×20
15. 369×64
16. 202×12

17. **Number Sense** Explain how you could use mental math to find $40 \times 60 \times 25$.

B Reasoning and Problem Solving

Use the pictograph at the right for 18–19. How much rain and snow would you expect to fall in

18. Berlin in 175 years?
19. Manila in 8 years?

20. **Writing in Math** Explain when you would choose to use paper and pencil to multiply.

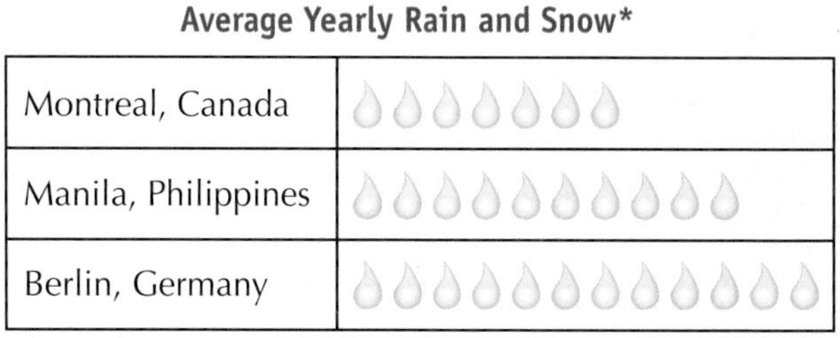

Each [drop] = 5 inches.
*Rounded to the nearest inch.

Mixed Review and Test Prep

Take It to the NET
Test Prep
www.scottforesman.com

21. Multiply 19×79. Decide if your answer is reasonable.

22. Use the pictograph above. How much more rain and snow fall in a year in Berlin than Manila?

A. 10 inches **B.** 22 inches **C.** 9 feet **D.** 22 feet

Key Idea
The steps for multiplying money are almost identical to the steps for multiplying whole numbers.

Multiplying Money

WARM UP

1. 5 × 300
2. 10 × 483
3. 285 × 7
4. 29 × 22

LEARN

When do you multiply?

Use the data at the right. Kristen skated 18 hours last month. She owns her own skates. How much did she spend in all?

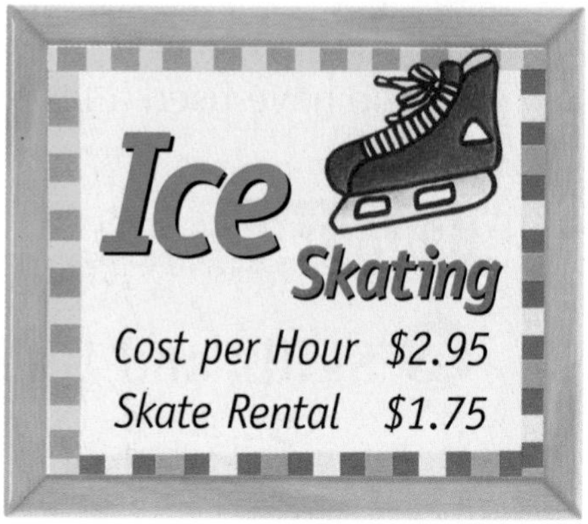

($2.95) ($2.95) ($2.95) . . . . . .
18 groups of $2.95

TEST TALK

Think It Through
I can **multiply when I combine equal groups.**

Example

Find 18 × $2.95.

Estimate: 20 × $3 = $60

The product should be less than $60.

STEP 1 Multiply as you would with whole numbers.

$$\begin{array}{r} {}^{7\ 4}\\ \$2.95 \\ \times\quad 18 \\ \hline 2360 \\ 2950 \\ \hline 5310 \end{array}$$

Multiply the ones and then multiply the tens.

STEP 2 Write the answer in dollars and cents.

$$\begin{array}{r} {}^{7\ 4}\\ \$2.95 \\ \times\quad 18 \\ \hline 2360 \\ 2950 \\ \hline \$53.10 \end{array}$$

The product $53.10 is reasonable because it is a little less than $60.

Kristen spent $53.10 in all on skating.

Talk About It

1. Why isn't $11.73 a reasonable answer for 34 × $3.45?

CHECK

For another example, see Set 6-8 on p. 359.

1. \$3.65 × 15 **2.** \$5.25 × 28 **3.** \$6.82 × 31 **4.** \$1.95 × 42 **5.** \$2.37 × 26

6. Number Sense Is \$9.86 a reasonable product for 17 × \$5.80? Explain how you can use an estimate to decide.

PRACTICE

For more practice, see Set 6-8 on p. 363.

A Skills and Understanding

7. \$4.43 × 15 **8.** \$1.19 × 56 **9.** \$2.26 × 23 **10.** \$3.91 × 31 **11.** \$6.35 × 18

12. \$5.50 × 25 **13.** \$3.48 × 42 **14.** \$2.10 × 76 **15.** \$7.14 × 59 **16.** \$3.33 × 44

17. \$2.86 × 62 **18.** \$3.75 × 29 **19.** \$5.23 × 37 **20.** \$6.09 × 51 **21.** \$4.95 × 16

22. Number Sense Mike multiplies 25 × \$5.75. Which of the following is most likely the product, \$14.37, \$143.75, or \$1437.50? Explain.

B Reasoning and Problem Solving

How much did a person earn for working 35 hours at minimum wage in

23. 1990? **24.** 1970? **25.** 2000? **26.** 1980?

27. How much more did a worker earn for 8 hours of work in 2000 than 1990?

Data File

Federal Minimum Wage for Each Hour Worked

1970	\$1.45
1980	\$3.10
1990	\$3.80
2000	\$5.15

28. *Writing in Math* Mark multiplied 32 × \$4.35 and got an answer of \$13.92. Is this reasonable? What might Mark have done wrong?

Mixed Review and Test Prep

Take It to the NET
Test Prep
www.scottforesman.com

29. Solve. Tell which computation method you used.

Tina bought 20 packages of stickers. Each package had 250 stickers. How many stickers did she buy?

30. The arena has 23,452 seats. For a hockey game, 17,986 tickets were sold. How many tickets were not sold?

A. 5,466 tickets **B.** 5,566 tickets **C.** 6,466 tickets **D.** 14,534 tickets

Problem-Solving Skill

Reading Helps!

Identifying steps in a process
can help you with...
writing to explain.

Key Idea
There are specific things you can do to write a good explanation in math.

TEST TALK

Think It Through
- Sometimes a table will help me see how the numbers change.
- I can figure out the pattern by studying the table.

Writing to Explain

LEARN

How do you write a good explanation?

When you write to explain a pattern, you need to tell how a change in one quantity results in the change of another quantity.

Popping Corn Americans eat over 18.5 billion quarts of popcorn each year. Every man, woman, and child in the United States would have to eat 73 quarts a year to consume 18.5 billion quarts of popcorn. Suppose Lucy eats 73 quarts of popcorn each year. Complete the pattern in the table to show how many quarts of popcorn Lucy would have eaten after 4, 5, and 6 years.

Number of years	1	2	3	4	5	6
Number of quarts of popcorn	73	146	219			

Explain how the number of quarts of popcorn eaten changes as the number of years changes.

Writing a Math Explanation

- Tell how one quantity changes as the other quantity changes. This is the explanation of the pattern.
- Include specific examples to support your answer.

As the number of years increases by 1, the number of quarts of popcorn increases by 73.

So, after 4 years, Lucy would have eaten 219 + 73 = 292 quarts. After 5 years she would have eaten 292 + 73 = 365 quarts. After 6 years, she would have eaten 365 + 73 = 438 quarts of popcorns.

Talk About It

1. When explaining a pattern, why is it important to tell how one quantity changes as the other quantity changes?
2. Explain how you could use multiplication to find the number of quarts of popcorn Lucy would have eaten after 10 years.

CHECK ✓

For another example, see Set 6-9 on p. 359.

1. Some single cells divide as shown in the picture at the right. Copy the table and use the pattern to complete it.

Number of divisions	0	1	2	3	4	5	6
Number of cells	1	2	4	8			

Explain how the number of cells changes as the number of divisions changes.

Start:

1 cell

1st division
2 cells

2nd division
4 cells

3rd division
8 cells

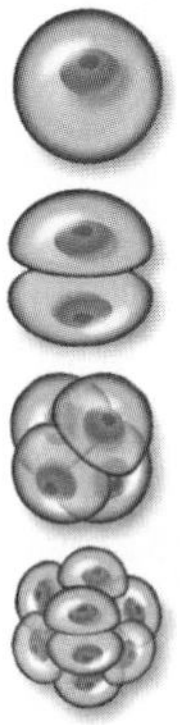

PRACTICE

For more practice, see Set 6-9 on p. 363.

Write to explain.

2. Copy the table and use the pattern to complete it. Explain how the number of days changes as the number of weeks changes.

Weeks	1	2	3	4	5	6
Days	7	14	21			

3. Bert is building a brick patio using the pattern shown at the right. Explain how the number of red bricks increases as the number of gray bricks increases. If Bert uses 8 gray center bricks, how many red bricks will he need?

4. Algebra Use the number sentences at the right. What numbers replace ●, ▲, and ■? Explain how you found these numbers.

A. ● + ● = 16

B. ▲ + ■ = 16

C. ▲ + ● = 10

5. Use the pictograph to find how many baseball cards Trent has. Show your computation neatly. Explain how you found your answer.

Baseball Card Collections

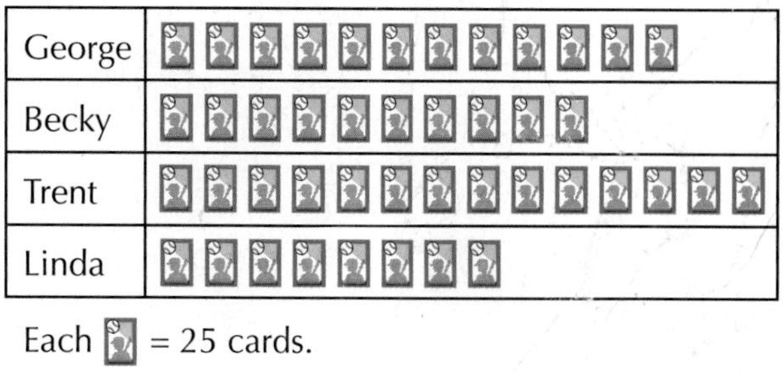

Lesson 6-10

Problem-Solving Applications

DORLING KINDERSLEY EYEWITNESS BOOKS
REPTILE
Discover the intriguing world of reptiles – their natural history, habits, and lifestyles
COLIN McCARTHY

Reptiles Reptiles come in many forms, including turtles, snakes, lizards, and alligators. Some are feared. Some are adored. Perhaps no other group of animals causes such different and strong reactions from people.

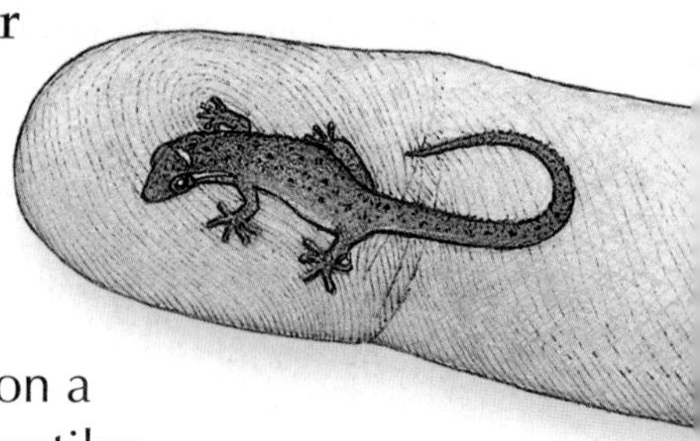

Trivia The smallest reptile is a type of gecko that grows to be just $\frac{3}{4}$ of an inch long. It can curl up comfortably on a dime. It would take about 8 of these reptiles to weigh as much as a paper clip.

1. There are about 7 times as many known species of tortoises as there are of sea turtles. If there are 7 species of sea turtles, about how many species of tortoises are known?

2. Some crocodiles live for 100 years. They eat about 50 meals per year. About how many meals will some crocodiles eat in their lifetime?

3. The Komodo dragon is the largest lizard. It is about 10 times as long as the tokay lizard. If a tokay lizard is 31 centimeters long, how long is a Komodo dragon?

Dorling Kindersley

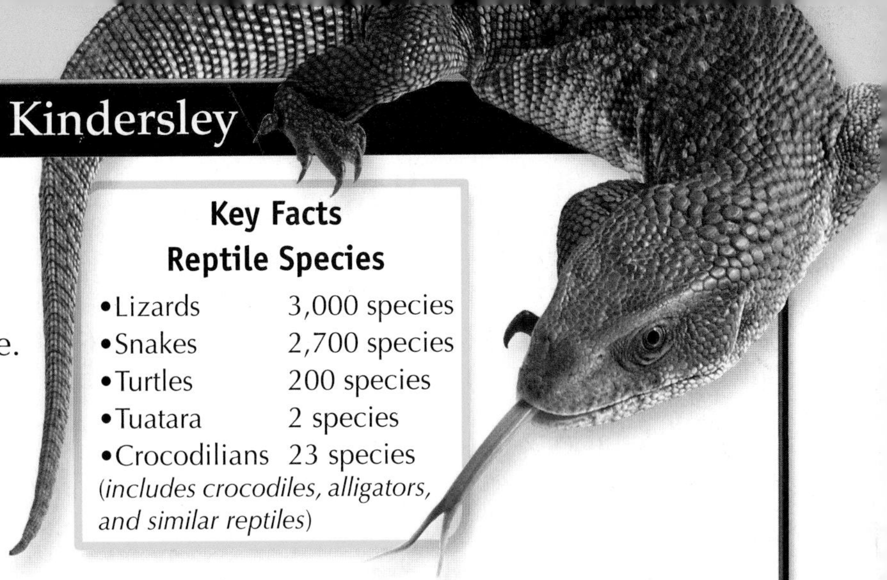

Key Facts
Reptile Species

- Lizards 3,000 species
- Snakes 2,700 species
- Turtles 200 species
- Tuatara 2 species
- Crocodilians 23 species

(includes crocodiles, alligators, and similar reptiles)

4 Humans are usually born with 33 vertebrae in their spine. Some snakes have more than 12 times as many vertebrae. How many vertebrae do these snakes have?

5 Sea turtles can swim 15 miles in one hour. At this rate, how far can a sea turtle swim in 6 hours?

Using Key Facts

6 How many more species of lizards are there than snakes? Use mental math.

7 **Writing in Math** Skip says there are about 9 times as many species of turtles as there are crocodilians. Steve says there are only about 6 times as many turtles as crocodilians. Who is correct? Explain your answer.

8 **Decision Making** Consider the reptiles in the table. Which would you choose as a pet? How much would it cost to buy the reptile, habitat kit, and food for 3 months?

Reptile	Cost	Habitat Kit	Food (per month)
Tortoise	$100	$50	$20
Chameleon	$75	$100	$20
Python	$60	$80	$12
Monitor	$75	$150	$25

Good News/Bad News *Since cold-blooded reptiles do not use the energy from food to keep warm, they do not have to eat as much as mammals. Unfortunately, they can live only where the environment can keep them warm.*

Review

Do You Know How?

Do You Understand?

Multiplying by Two-Digit Numbers (6-5); Multiplying Greater Numbers (6-6); Multiplying Money (6-8)

1. 23 × 45
2. 78 × 32
3. 142 × 19
4. 202 × 37
5. 153 × 42
6. 815 × 45
7. $2.15 × 23
8. $1.99 × 28

A Tell how you found each product in Exercises 3 and 7.

B Explain how you know your answer is reasonable in Exercise 2.

Choose a Computation Method (6-7)

Multiply. Tell what method you used.

9. 67 × 30
10. 1,492 × 57
11. 300 × 40
12. 25 × 11
13. 37 × 111
14. 64 × 935

C Why did you choose the computation method you did to find the product in Exercise 12?

D Explain why you would not use a calculator to find the product in Exercise 11.

Problem-Solving Skill: Writing to Explain (6-9)

15. The table shows the cost of ride tickets at Funland Park. Copy the table and complete the pattern. Explain how the cost changes as the number of tickets changes.

Number of Tickets	Cost
1	$1.25
2	$2.50
3	$3.75
4	
5	
6	

E How does making a table help you explain a pattern?

F How much would 10 ride tickets cost at Funland?

Chapter 6 Section B

Diagnostic Checkpoint

TEST TALK

Think It Through
I should always **check that my answer is reasonable.**

MULTIPLE CHOICE

1. Mr. Orr bought 36 bundles of firewood. Each bundle had 15 pieces of wood. How many pieces of firewood did Mr. Orr buy? (6-5)

A. 186 **B.** 216 **C.** 510 **D.** 540

2. 218 strands of wicker are needed to make one placemat. How many strands are needed to make 25 place mats? (6-6)

A. 1,526 **B.** 5,410 **C.** 5,450 **D.** 5,460

FREE RESPONSE

Multiply. Decide if your answer is reasonable. (6-5 and 6-6)

3. 63×38

4. 89×47

5. 142×18

6. 197×23

Multiply. Tell what method you used. (6-7)

7. $3{,}921 \times 15$

8. 900×90

9. 28×21

10. 570×30

Use the information at the right for 11–14. (6-8)

What is the cost of

11. 34 packages of beads?

12. 23 sewing kits?

13. 46 yards of material?

14. 12 rolls of ribbon?

Items at a Craft Store

Item	Price
Package of Beads	$2.25
Roll of Ribbon	$1.97
Yard of Material	$3.25
Sewing Kit	$5.74

Writing in Math

15. Make a table showing the cost of fruit pops. Explain how the cost changes as the number of fruit pops purchased changes. (6-9)

16. Write a question that could be answered by multiplying 15 × $1.85. (6-8)

Test-Taking Strategies

- Understand the question.
- Get information for the answer.
- Plan how to find the answer.
- Make smart choices.
- Use writing in math.
- **Improve written answers.**

Improve Written Answers

You can follow the tips below to learn how to improve written answers on a test. It is important to write a clear answer and include only information needed to answer the question.

The rubric below is a scoring guide for Test Question 1.

Scoring Rubric

4 points — **Full credit: 4 points**
The list and explanation are both correct.

3 points — **Partial credit: 3 points**
The list has 4 or 5 outcomes, and the explanation is correct.

2 points — **Partial credit: 2 points**
The list has at least 4 outcomes or the explanation is correct, but not both.

1 point — **Partial credit: 1 point**
The list has 2 or 3 outcomes, and the explanation is incorrect.

0 points — **No credit: 0 points**
The list has 0 or 1 outcome, and the explanation is incorrect.

1. Carl, Allen, and Marty want a drink at the water fountain.

In the space below, list all the different ways these three students could line up. You may use the first letter of each student's name in your list (for example, C, A, M).

On the lines below, explain how you made your list.

____

____

____

Improve Written Answers

- Check if your answer is complete.

  In order to ***get as many points as possible,*** *I must make a list* and *explain how I did it.*

- Check if your answer makes sense.

  I need to ***check that my list is complete.*** *Does it show every possible arrangement?*

- Check if your explanation is clear and easy to follow.

*I should reread my explanation to check that I have **accurately and clearly** described how I made the list. Did I **describe the steps in order?** Have I included unnecessary information.*

Anne used the scoring rubric on page 348 to score a student's answer to Test Question 1. The student paper is shown below.

1st	2nd	3rd
C	A	M
C	M	A
A	C	M
A	M	C

On the lines below, explain how you made your list.

First, I chose Carl and found all the arrangements with Carl first. Then I repeated this with each of the other two boys.

Think It Through

The answer is incomplete. The student did not list the arrangements with Marty first: M, A, C and M, C, A. The explanation is correct and clear. Since the list has 4 outcomes, and the explanation is correct, the answer gets 3 points.

Now it's your turn.

Score the student's paper. If it does not get 4 points, rewrite it so that it does.

2. Paul is ordering a submarine sandwich. He can choose any two of these four fillings: ham, turkey, cheese, beef.

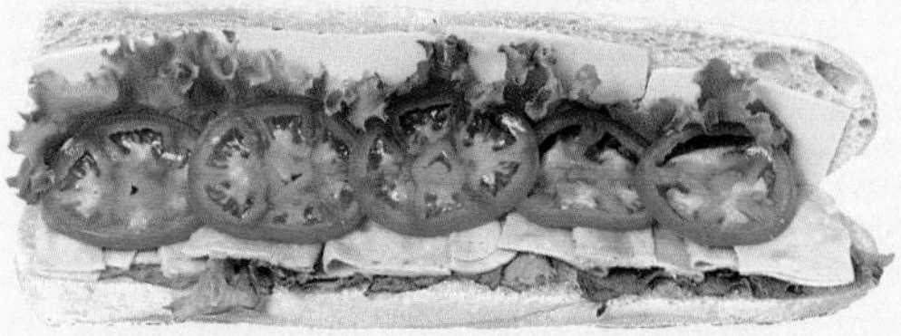

Make a list to show all the choices Paul has for the two fillings. You may use the first letter of each filling in your list (for example, H, T, C, B).

HT
HC
HB

On the lines below, explain how you made your list.

I matched up the first filling, ham, with each of the others.

Chapter 6

Key Vocabulary and Concept Review

The price of lunch at school ranges from \$1.59 to \$3.00.

*A **range** tells you roughly where the answer lies.* *(p. 317)*

Self Check

Estimate products. (Lesson 6-2)

Estimate 42 × 26.

Use **rounding.**	Use **compatible numbers.**	Find a **range.**
42 × 26 ↓ ↓ 40 × 30 = 1,200	42 × 26 ↓ ↓ 40 × 25 = 1,000	42 × 26 (Use lesser numbers.) ↓ ↓ 40 × 20 = 800 42 × 26 (Use greater numbers.) ↓ ↓ 50 × 30 = 1,500 The product is between 800 and 1,500.

1. Estimate 42 × 68 by finding a range.

My car model kit came with lots of parts.

*Remember, a **partial product** is part of the product.* *(p. 320)*

Self Check

Follow steps in order when you multiply. (Lessons 6-5, 6-6, 6-8)

Multiply the ones. Regroup if necessary.	Multiply the tens. Regroup if necessary.	Add the partial products.	Multiply money like whole numbers.
$\begin{array}{r} \overset{2\,\overset{1}{4}}{} \\ 537 \\ \times\ \ 26 \\ \hline 3222 \end{array}$	$\begin{array}{r} \overset{2\,\overset{1}{4}}{} \\ 537 \\ \times\ \ 26 \\ \hline 3222 \\ 10740 \end{array}$	$\begin{array}{r} \overset{2\,\overset{1}{4}}{} \\ 537 \\ \times\ \ 26 \\ \hline 3222 \\ +\ 10740 \\ \hline 13{,}962 \end{array}$	$\begin{array}{r} \overset{1}{} \\ \$4.13 \\ \times\ \ 25 \\ \hline 2065 \\ +\ 8260 \\ \hline \$103.25 \end{array}$ Place \$ and . in the product.

2. Find 72 × 38, 491 × 16, and 54 × \$2.79.

Self Check

Use different computation methods to find products. (Lessons 6-1, 6-7)

Find 30 × 6,000.

Use mental math. Think about patterns.

$3 \times 6 = 18$
$3 \times 6\mathbf{0} = 18\mathbf{0}$
$3\mathbf{0} \times 6\mathbf{0} = 1{,}8\mathbf{00}$
$3\mathbf{0} \times 6\mathbf{00} = 18{,}\mathbf{000}$
$3\mathbf{0} \times 6{,}\mathbf{000} = 18\mathbf{0{,}000}$

Find 204 × 32.

There are not a lot of regroupings. Use paper and pencil.

$$\begin{array}{r} \scriptstyle 1 \\ 204 \\ \times\ 32 \\ \hline 408 \\ +\ 6120 \\ \hline 6{,}528 \end{array}$$

Find 39 × 2,478.

There are a lot of regroupings. Use a calculator.

Press:

39 [×] 2478 [ENTER =]

Display: 96642

So, 39 × 2,478 = 96,642.

Our teacher likes us to keep our desks organized so we can find things.

3. Find 80 × 700, 12 × 470, and 89 × 963.

*An **organized list** helps me find different combinations or arrangements. (p. 326)*

Self Check

Write to explain or make organized lists to solve problems. (Lessons 6-4, 6-9)

Make an **organized list** to show the ways things can be combined or arranged.

How many ways can Kay, Carl, and Paco sit together at the play?

Kay, Carl, Paco
Kay, Paco, Carl
Carl, Kay, Paco
Carl, Paco, Kay
Paco, Kay, Carl
Paco, Carl, Kay

There are 6 ways.

When you are asked to explain, a flow chart can help organize your thoughts.

Make a flow chart to show how you found your answer to the problem at the left.

I listed the orders that start with Kay.
↓
I listed the orders that start with Carl.
↓
I listed the orders that start with Paco.

4. How many ways can you choose 2 colors from red, blue, green, and pink?

Answers: 1. 2,400 to 3,500 2. 2,736; 7,856; $150.66 3. 56,000; 5,640; 85,707 4. 6 ways

Chapter Test

MULTIPLE CHOICE

Choose the correct letter for each answer.

1. Use mental math to multiply $30 \times 4{,}000$.

A. 120 **C.** 12,000

B. 1,200 **D.** 120,000

2. Which is the most reasonable estimate for 17×231?

A. 2,000 **C.** 20,000

B. 4,000 **D.** 40,000

3. What product does this array show?

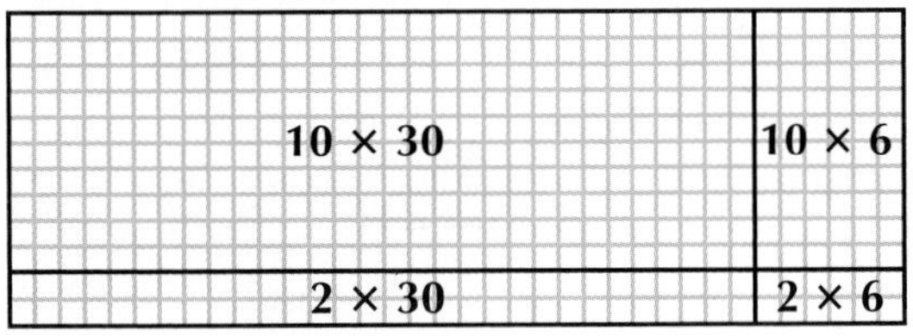

A. 12×36 **C.** 2×36

B. $12 + 36$ **D.** 12×63

4. Find 42×18.

A. 60 **C.** 746

B. 378 **D.** 756

5. Find the product of 34 and 116.

A. 150 **C.** 3,824

B. 812 **D.** 3,944

6. Find 20×400.

A. 800 **C.** 80,000

B. 8,000 **D.** 800,000

7. Which computation method would be best for finding $63 \times 5{,}279$?

A. Use mental math.

B. Use paper and pencil.

C. Use a calculator.

D. Use a number line.

Think It Through

- I need to **read each problem carefully.**
- I should **watch for words like true, false or not.**

8. Which number sentence is TRUE?

A. $6 \times 40 = 2{,}400$

B. $60 \times 40 = 2{,}400$

C. $60 \times 400 = 2{,}400$

D. $60 \times 4{,}000 = 2{,}400$

9. Tim estimated that 32×81 is about 2,400. Which of the following is TRUE about Tim's estimate?

A. 2,400 is an underestimate.

B. The range for the estimated product is 2,400.

C. 2,400 is an overestimate.

D. It is difficult to tell whether 2,400 is an overestimate or an underestimate.

10. A bookstore just got a shipment of 35 paperback books. Each book cost \$4.29. What was the total cost of the shipment?

A. \$35.00 **C.** \$150.15

B. \$39.29 **D.** \$1,501.50

FREE RESPONSE

Estimate each product. Tell whether your estimate is an overestimate or an underestimate.

11. 56×78

12. 23×451

Multiply. Use mental math.

13. 40×80

14. $60 \times 3{,}000$

15. $2{,}000 \times 90$

16. 700×50

Find each product.

17. $\begin{array}{r} \$2.38 \\ \times \quad 51 \\ \hline \end{array}$

18. $\begin{array}{r} 105 \\ \times \ 47 \\ \hline \end{array}$

19. $\begin{array}{r} 99 \\ \times 12 \\ \hline \end{array}$

20. $\begin{array}{r} 13 \\ \times 19 \\ \hline \end{array}$

21. What computation method would you use to find $38 \times 5{,}349$?

22. A factory produces 275 cars a week. How many cars does the factory produce each year? Remember that there are 52 weeks in a year.

23. There are 32 sections in a sports arena. Each section has about 185 seats. Estimate the total number of seats in the sports arena.

24. Draw an array that could be used to find 16×21.

Writing in Math

25. Explain how you would break numbers apart to find 76×54.

26. Make an organized list to solve this problem.

Carter has room for only three birdhouses in his garden. He has a brown birdhouse, a red birdhouse, a white birdhouse, and a black birdhouse. How many different combinations of birdhouses does Carter have to choose from?

> **TEST TALK**
>
> **Think It Through**
> - I can **use a flow chart** to help show my thinking.
> - I will **write my steps in order.**

27. Solve this problem. Show your computation. Then explain how you found your answer.

A taxi service charges a \$2.00 fee and \$0.75 per mile. Melissa rode in the taxi for 13 miles. How much did the taxi service charge Melissa in all?

Number and Operation

MULTIPLE CHOICE

1. Carol bought 4 packs of paper plates and 3 packs of paper cups. Each pack of plates cost $2.75, and each pack of cups cost $1.99. How much did Carol spend in all?

   A. $16.97 **C.** $5.03
   B. $16.21 **D.** $4.74

2. Which number is NOT between 4,783 and 4,873?

   A. 4,787 **C.** 4,788
   B. 4,878 **D.** 4,837

FREE RESPONSE

3. Write one hundred seventy-nine thousand, two hundred four in standard form.

4. Estimate 67×235 by finding a range.

5. There are 359 students in the third grade, 395 students in the fourth grade, and 393 students in the fifth grade. Write the grades in order from the greatest number of students to the least number of students.

> **TEST TALK**
> **Think It Through**
> I should check that my answer makes sense.

Writing in Math

6. Explain how to find $80 \times 4,000$ using mental math.

Geometry and Measurement

MULTIPLE CHOICE

7. Which of these figures is a rectangular prism?

   A. 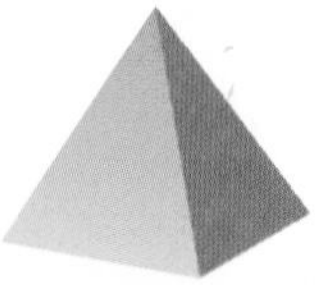
   C. 
   B. 
   D. 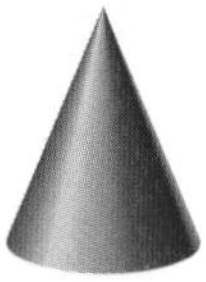

8. Which of the following time periods is greater than 30 months?

   A. 2 years **C.** 156 weeks
   B. 712 days **D.** 1 leap year

FREE RESPONSE

Use the clock at the right for 9–10.

9. Write the time shown in two different ways.

10. What time is 50 minutes past the time shown on the clock?

11. Emily made a yard sale sign that has 5 equal sides and 5 corners. What was the shape of Emily's sign?

Writing in Math

12. Kelly's train left Station 1 at 9:45 A.M. It arrived at Station 2 at 12:10 P.M. How long did it take the train to travel from Station 1 to Station 2? Explain how you found your answer.

Data Analysis and Probability

MULTIPLE CHOICE

13. What is the range of the data shown on this line plot?

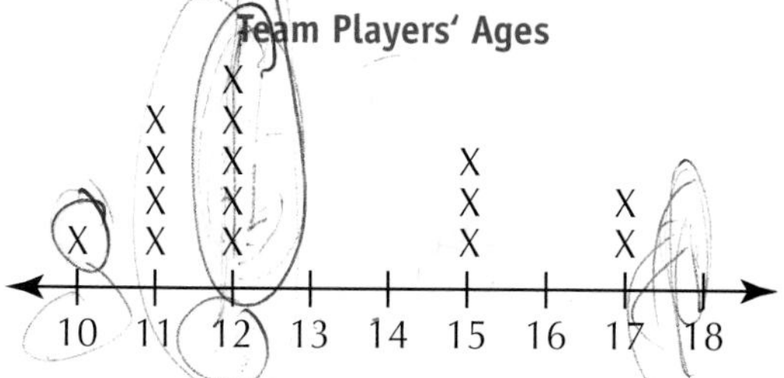

A. 7 **B.** 10 **C.** 12 **D.** 17

14. A number cube is labeled 1 through 6. If you toss the number cube once, which of the following is a certain outcome?

A. The number is odd.

B. The number is less than 7.

C. The number is even.

D. The number is greater than 1.

FREE RESPONSE

Use the coordinate grid for Items 15–17.

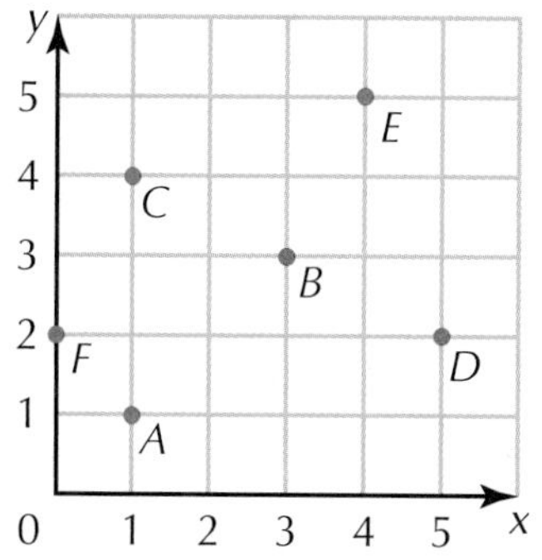

Name the ordered pair for each point.

15. *C* **16.** *A* **17.** *B*

Writing in Math

18. How are the ordered pairs for points *D* and *F* alike?

Algebra

MULTIPLE CHOICE

19. Find the missing number in the pattern.

7, 14, 28, ▢, 112

A. 48

B. 56

C. 94

D. 214

TEST TALK

Think It Through
For multiple-choice items, first **eliminate any unreasonable answers.**

20. Which number expression models the phrase "$237 decreased by $19"?

A. 237 + 19 **C.** 237 − 19

B. 19 + 237 **D.** 19 − 237

21. Solve 14 + n = 21.

A. $n = 3$ **C.** $n = 14$

B. $n = 7$ **D.** $n = 35$

FREE RESPONSE

22. What is the rule for this table?

In	22	23	24	25
Out	13	14	15	16

Writing in Math

23. Allen is making a beaded necklace by following the pattern below. If he continues the same pattern, what are the next two beads he will use? Explain your answer.

red, red, black, blue, blue, red, red, __?__, __?__

Chapter 6

Reteaching

Set 6-1 (pages 314–315)

Find 80 × 500.

Use mental math. Look for patterns in the factors and products.

8 × 5 = 40

8 × **50** = 40**0**

80 × **50** = 4,**000**

Remember that the number of zeros in both factors equals the number of zeros in the product, except when there is a zero in the basic fact.

1. 50 × 70 = 350 **2.** 30 × 600

3. 80 × 80 = 640 **4.** 90 × 8,000

5. 60 × 9,000 = 54000 **6.** 20 × 500

7. 40 × 50 **8.** 70 × 2,000

9. 70 × 7,000 **10.** 90 × 600

11. 20 × 80 **12.** 40 × 3,000

13. 30 × 5,000 **14.** 60 × 300

15. 80 × 2,000 **16.** 50 × 600

Set 6-2 (pages 316–319)

Estimate 37 × 44.

One way: Rounding

37 × 44
↓ ↓
40 × 40 = 1,600

Another way: Finding a range

Underestimate.	Overestimate.
37 × 44 ↓ ↓ 30 × 40 = 1,200	37 × 44 ↓ ↓ 40 × 50 = 2,000

The product 37 × 44 is between 1,200 and 2,000.

Remember that you also can use compatible numbers to estimate.

Estimate each product.

1. 17 × 76 **2.** 52 × 81

3. 49 × 23 **4.** 37 × 173

5. 845 × 62 **6.** 75 × 204

7. 28 × 315 **8.** 61 × 488

Estimate each product by finding a range.

9. 26 × 67 **10.** 33 × 74

11. 81 × 46 **12.** 51 × 711

13. 863 × 21 **14.** 483 × 65

15. 43 × 126 **16.** 68 × 63

17. 527 × 18 **18.** 293 × 13

Set 6-3 (pages 320–323)

Use grid paper to draw a rectangle. Then copy and complete the calculation.

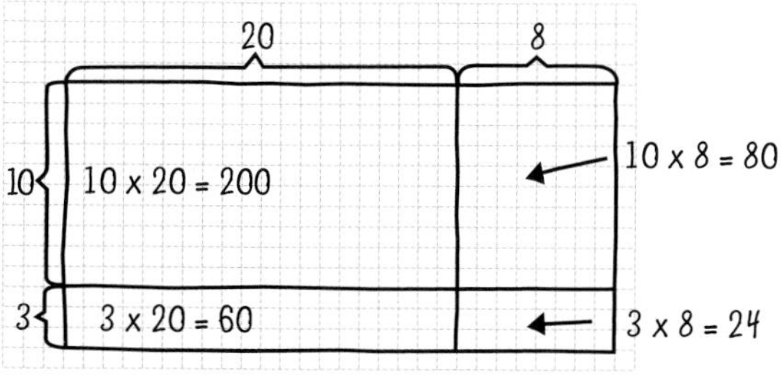

$$\begin{array}{rl} 28 & \\ \times\ 13 & \\ \hline 24 & \leftarrow 3 \times 8 \\ 60 & \leftarrow 3 \times 20 \\ 80 & \leftarrow 10 \times 8 \\ 200 & \leftarrow 10 \times 20 \\ \hline 364 & \end{array}$$

Remember that you can multiply by solving simpler problems and adding partial products.

1. $\begin{array}{r} 14 \\ \times\ 17 \\ \hline ■■ \\ ■■ \\ ■■ \\ ■■■ \\ \hline ■■■ \end{array}$

2. $\begin{array}{r} 23 \\ \times\ 19 \\ \hline ■■ \\ ■■■ \\ ■■ \\ ■■■ \\ \hline ■■■ \end{array}$

3. 16 × 24
4. 21 × 13
5. 22 × 31
6. 25 × 18
7. 18 × 14
8. 13 × 13
9. 17 × 25
10. 15 × 12

Set 6-4 (pages 326–329)

Make an organized list to solve the problem.

Libby, Cate, Mitch, and Ryan are choosing partners for a game. How many ways can they make groups of two?

1 Identify the people to be grouped.

Libby, Cate, Mitch, and Ryan

2 Choose a person. Find combinations.

Libby, Cate
Libby, Mitch
Libby, Ryan

3 Repeat Step 2 as often as needed.

Libby, Cate		
Libby, Mitch	**Cate, Mitch**	
Libby, Ryan	**Cate, Ryan**	**Mitch, Ryan**

They can make 6 groups of two.

Remember the way you organize a list can help you find all the possibilities in a problem.

1. Robin has red, blue, green, and black markers. How many different ways can she use two markers to make a poster?
2. Veronica, Tonya, and Suzie each make each of the others a bracelet. How many bracelets will be made?
3. Kyle has ham, chicken, and turkey. How many ways can he choose two types of meat for a sandwich?
4. Robert has one mystery, one science fiction, one historical fiction, and one poetry book. How many different ways are possible for him to read the books?

Chapter 6

Reteaching

Set 6-5 (pages 332–335)

Find 87 × 25.

$$\begin{array}{rl} \scriptstyle 1 & \\ \scriptstyle 3 & \\ 87 & \\ \times\ 25 & \\ \hline 435 & 5 \times 87 = 435 \\ 1740 & 20 \times 87 = 1740 \\ \hline 2{,}175 & \end{array}$$

Remember that when you multiply by the tens, there will be a zero in the ones place.

1. $\begin{array}{r} 49 \\ \times\ 63 \\ \hline \end{array}$
2. $\begin{array}{r} 25 \\ \times\ 25 \\ \hline \end{array}$
3. $\begin{array}{r} 46 \\ \times\ 72 \\ \hline \end{array}$
4. $\begin{array}{r} 34 \\ \times\ 56 \\ \hline \end{array}$
5. $\begin{array}{r} 19 \\ \times\ 86 \\ \hline \end{array}$
6. $\begin{array}{r} 27 \\ \times\ 32 \\ \hline \end{array}$

Set 6-6 (pages 336–337)

Find 35 × 398.

1 Multiply the ones. Regroup if necessary.

$$\begin{array}{r} \scriptstyle 44 \\ 398 \\ \times\ \ 35 \\ \hline 1990 \end{array}$$

2 Place a zero in the ones place. Multiply the tens. Regroup.

$$\begin{array}{r} \scriptstyle 22 \\ \scriptstyle 44 \\ 398 \\ \times\ \ 35 \\ \hline 1990 \\ 11940 \end{array}$$

3 Add the partial products.

$$\begin{array}{r} \scriptstyle 22 \\ \scriptstyle 44 \\ 398 \\ \times\ \ 35 \\ \hline 1990 \\ 11940 \\ \hline 13{,}930 \end{array}$$

Remember that you add partial products to find a product.

1. $\begin{array}{r} 216 \\ \times\ \ 48 \\ \hline \end{array}$
2. $\begin{array}{r} 634 \\ \times\ \ 29 \\ \hline \end{array}$
3. $\begin{array}{r} 575 \\ \times\ \ 67 \\ \hline \end{array}$
4. $\begin{array}{r} 482 \\ \times\ \ 56 \\ \hline \end{array}$
5. $\begin{array}{r} 703 \\ \times\ \ 23 \\ \hline \end{array}$
6. $\begin{array}{r} 745 \\ \times\ \ 37 \\ \hline \end{array}$
7. $\begin{array}{r} 341 \\ \times\ \ 42 \\ \hline \end{array}$
8. $\begin{array}{r} 607 \\ \times\ \ 15 \\ \hline \end{array}$

Set 6-7 (pages 338–339)

Multiply. Tell what method you used.

31 × 212

There are no regroupings. Use pencil and paper.

$$\begin{array}{r} 212 \\ \times\ \ \ 31 \\ \hline 212 \\ 6360 \\ \hline 6{,}572 \end{array}$$

Remember that you can use mental math, a calculator, or pencil and paper to multiply.

1. $\begin{array}{r} 210 \\ \times\ \ 80 \\ \hline \end{array}$
2. $\begin{array}{r} 123 \\ \times\ \ 21 \\ \hline \end{array}$
3. $\begin{array}{r} 300 \\ \times\ \ 40 \\ \hline \end{array}$
4. $\begin{array}{r} 988 \\ \times\ \ 79 \\ \hline \end{array}$
5. $\begin{array}{r} 404 \\ \times\ \ 20 \\ \hline \end{array}$
6. $\begin{array}{r} 3{,}745 \\ \times\ \ \ \ 67 \\ \hline \end{array}$

Set 6-8 (pages 340–341)

Find 34 × $2.45.

```
   1 1
   1 2
 $2.45   Multiply as you would with
×   34   whole numbers.
   980
  7350   Place the dollar sign and
$83.30   decimal point in the answer.
```

Remember that multiplication problems with dollars and cents need a dollar sign and a decimal point in the product.

1. $3.37 × 24
2. $4.15 × 24
2. $1.96 × 42
3. $2.84 × 25
5. $3.27 × 19
6. $6.20 × 26

Set 6-9 (pages 342–343)

When you write to explain a pattern, follow these steps.

Step 1: Find two pieces of information that will help you find a pattern. (Length of each side and the perimeter.)

Step 2: Tell how one quantity changes and the other changes. Give examples.

Joan earns $16 an hour. She started the table below to find out how much she earns for 1, 2, and 3 hours of work.

How much does she earn for 4, 5, and 6 hours? Write to explain your answers.

Hours	1	2	3	4	5	6
Earnings	$16	$32	$48			

As the number of hours increases by 1, Joan's salary increases by $16.
So, after 4 hours, Joan earned $48 + $16 = $64. After 5 hours, she earned $64 + $16 = $80. After 6 hours, she earned $80 + $16 = $96.

Remember that studying a table might help you figure out a pattern.

1. Copy the table and use the pattern to complete it. Explain how the perimeter of a square changes as the length of each side changes.

Length of Each Side of a Square	Perimeter of the Square
1 in.	4 in.
2 in.	8 in.
3 in.	12 in.
4 in.	
5 in.	
6 in.	

2. How much more money would you earn in a year if you received $2 a day than if you received $12 a week? Assume it is not a leap year. Remember there are 365 days or 52 weeks in a year.

Chapter 6

More Practice

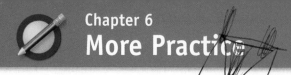

Set 6-1 (pages 314–315)

Multiply. Use mental math.

1. 20 × 80	**2.** 60 × 300	**3.** 80 × 70	**4.** 30 × 7,000
5. 90 × 500	**6.** 40 × 6,000	**7.** 50 × 20	**8.** 70 × 900
9. 50 × 50	**10.** 70 × 5,000	**11.** 40 × 800	**12.** 20 × 7,000
13. 60 × 200	**14.** 90 × 700	**15.** 60 × 90	**16.** 80 × 5,000
17. 90 × 80	**18.** 50 × 300	**19.** 30 × 4,000	**20.** 60 × 500

There are 30 beads in each bag. How many beads would Ella have if she bought

21. 20 bags?	**22.** 40 bags?	**23.** 60 bags?	**24.** 80 bags?

There are 200 stickers on a roll. How many stickers are on

25. 10 rolls?	**26.** 30 rolls?	**27.** 50 rolls?	**28.** 70 rolls?

29. Henry bought 40 boxes of envelopes. Each box had 40 envelopes. How many envelopes did he buy?

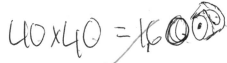

Set 6-2 (pages 316–319)

Estimate each product.

1. 53 × 42	**2.** 39 × 16	**3.** 34 × 54	**4.** 18 × 31
5. 23 × 802	**6.** 46 × 46	**7.** 521 × 51	**8.** 636 × 47
9. 81 × 881	**10.** 298 × 65	**11.** 317 × 71	**12.** 48 × 762

Estimate each product by finding a range.

13. 21 × 43	**14.** 68 × 35	**15.** 91 × 56	**16.** 82 × 14
17. 33 × 51	**18.** 77 × 23	**19.** 69 × 426	**20.** 34 × 613
21. 283 × 49	**22.** 270 × 33	**23.** 505 × 88	**24.** 464 × 55
25. 248 × 87	**26.** 28 × 387	**27.** 758 × 42	**28.** 16 × 129

29. Mrs. Libby bought 19 boxes of facial tissue for her classroom. Each box has 144 tissues. Estimate the number of tissues that Mrs. Libby has by finding a range.

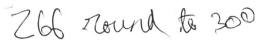

Take It to the NET
More Practice
www.scottforesman.com

Set 6-3 (pages 320–323)

Use grid paper to draw a rectangle. Then copy and complete the calculation.

1. $\begin{array}{r} 12 \\ \times\ 24 \\ \hline \end{array}$

2. $\begin{array}{r} 15 \\ \times\ 17 \\ \hline \end{array}$

3. $\begin{array}{r} 21 \\ \times\ 21 \\ \hline \end{array}$

4. $\begin{array}{r} 16 \\ \times\ 13 \\ \hline \end{array}$

5. $\begin{array}{r} 22 \\ \times\ 14 \\ \hline \end{array}$

6. $\begin{array}{r} 18 \\ \times\ 13 \\ \hline \end{array}$

7. $\begin{array}{r} 11 \\ \times\ 31 \\ \hline \end{array}$

8. $\begin{array}{r} 23 \\ \times\ 24 \\ \hline \end{array}$

9. 21 × 19
10. 12 × 14
11. 34 × 12
12. 25 × 19
13. 15 × 23
14. 27 × 35
15. 18 × 26
16. 33 × 15

17. There are 22 slices in one loaf of bread. How many slices are in 12 loaves of bread?

Set 6-4 (pages 326–329)

Make an organized list to solve the problem. Write the answer in a complete sentence.

1. Jackie has a red picture frame, a blue picture frame, and a purple picture frame. How many different ways can she arrange them in a row on a shelf?

2. Courtney has blue plates, yellow plates, red plates, and green plates. She wants to use two different-colored plates for her party. From how many different combinations does she have to choose?

3. Marcus, Dustin, Aaron, and Gavin are trying out for a team. Only 3 boys will make the team. How many different ways can they be picked for the team?

4. Only 3 types of fruit can be put in the salad. Jewell has strawberries, grapes, pineapple, and bananas. How many different salads could she make?

More Practice

Set 6-5 (pages 332–335)

1. 58×19	**2.** 67×85	**3.** 92×74	**4.** 28×49	**5.** 39×56
6. 97×61	**7.** 25×52	**8.** 36×36	**9.** 69×42	**10.** 78×52
11. 45×25	**12.** 29×83	**13.** 72×66	**14.** 57×30	**15.** 94×23
16. 12×36	**17.** 33×43	**18.** 26×13	**19.** 71×39	**20.** 53×64

21. There are 24 flour tortillas in a package. The soccer club bought 18 packages of tortillas to make burritos to sell in the concession stand during the game. How many burritos can they make?

22. Mrs. Wiley bought 34 boxes of raisins for the elementary school picnic. Each box weighed 15 ounces. How much did the raisins weigh in all?

Set 6-6 (pages 336–337)

1. 246×18	**2.** 837×42	**3.** 174×25	**4.** 529×63	**5.** 413×46
6. 303×76	**7.** 473×84	**8.** 612×39	**9.** 777×44	**10.** 547×52
11. 398×71	**12.** 642×82	**13.** 955×23	**14.** 243×19	**15.** 708×57
16. 271×17	**17.** 325×24	**18.** 118×39	**19.** 538×42	**20.** 494×63

21. Roger has 17 photo albums. Each album holds 128 photos. How many photos does Roger need to fill all the albums?

22. Reasoning Today is Lisa's 12th birthday. How many weeks has she lived?

Set 6-7 (pages 338–339)

Multiply. Tell what method you used.

1. 21×13
2. 978×96
3. 46×31
4. 300×20
5. $7{,}683 \times 65$
6. 700×30
7. $1{,}001 \times 19$
8. 202×21
9. $3{,}598 \times 78$
10. $2{,}300 \times 10$
11. 45×32
12. $2{,}967 \times 29$
13. 270×20
14. 800×70
15. 386×88
16. There are 1,296 inches of tape in 1 roll. How many inches of tape are in a dozen rolls? (Hint: A dozen is 12.)

1,152

Set 6-8 (pages 340–341)

1. $\$1.65 \times 32$
2. $\$3.19 \times 14$
3. $\$5.24 \times 55$
4. $\$2.08 \times 49$
5. $\$4.37 \times 28$
6. $\$8.06 \times 72$
7. $\$2.23 \times 17$
8. $\$6.62 \times 87$
9. $\$5.15 \times 23$
10. $\$3.41 \times 48$
11. $\$2.93 \times 28$
12. $\$7.14 \times 63$
13. $\$9.09 \times 26$
14. $\$4.50 \times 35$
15. $\$2.76 \times 33$
16. Mr. Brown bought 24 packages of markers. Each package cost \$2.79. How much did Mr. Brown spend on markers?

Set 6-9 (pages 342–343)

Write to explain.

1. Rex works in a grocery. He is making the display at the right using cans of soup. Copy the table and use the pattern to complete it.

Row 3
Row 2
Row 1

Row number	1	2	3	4	5	6
Number of cans	8	7	6			

Explain how the number of cans in a row changes as the number of the row changes.

2. Extend the table. Which row will have 1 can?

CHAPTER 7

Dividing

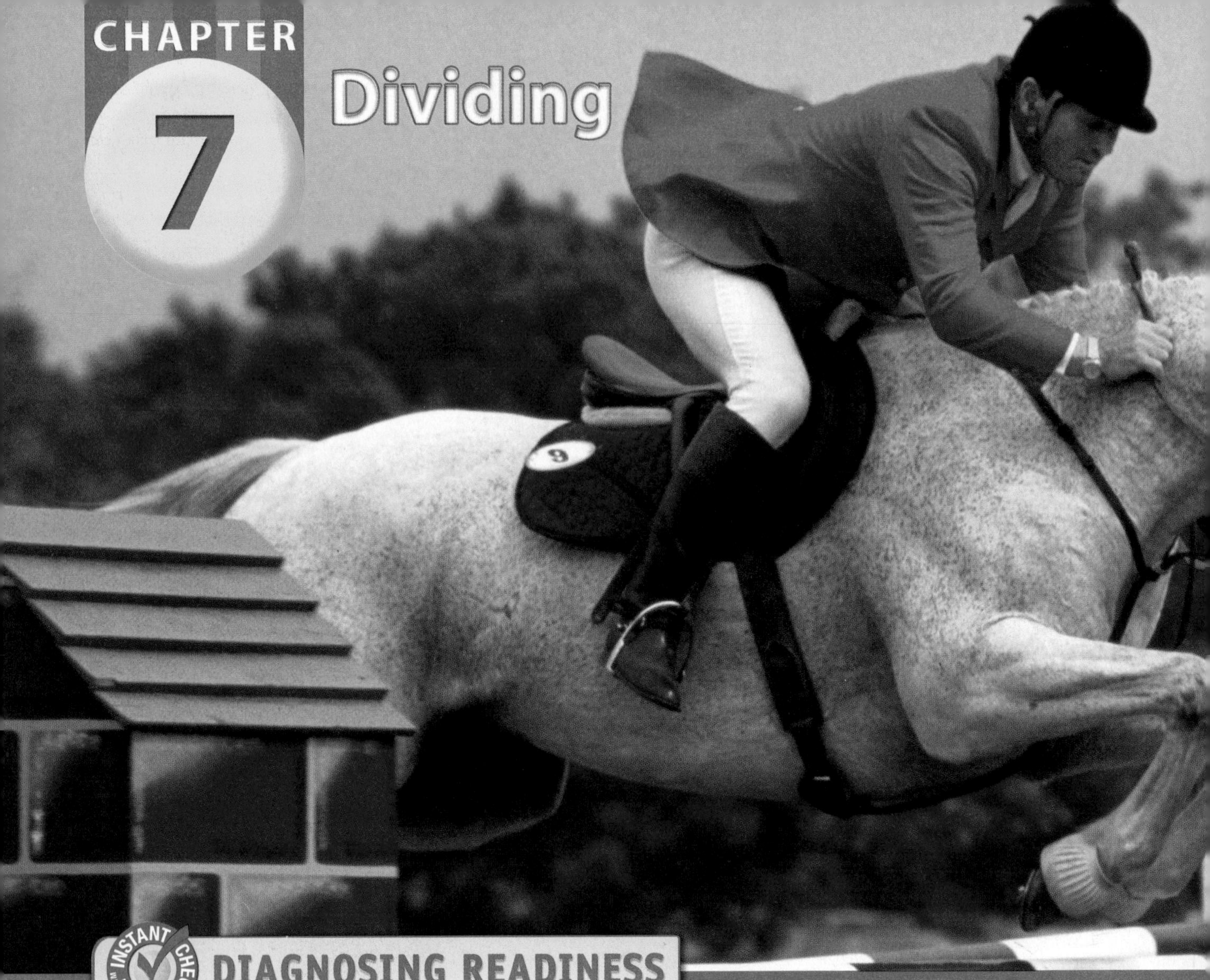

DIAGNOSING READINESS

A Vocabulary

(pages 124, 146, 148)

Choose the best term from the box.

1. In the number sentence 18 ÷ 6 = 3, 18 is the __?__, 6 is the __?__, and 3 is the __?__.

2. In the number sentence 5 × 8 = 40, 5 is a __?__.

3. Multiplication and division are __?__.

Vocabulary

- **factor (p. 124)**
- **dividend (p. 146)**
- **divisor (p. 146)**
- **quotient (p. 146)**
- **inverse operations (p. 148)**

B Multiplying by Multiples of 10, 100, or 1,000 *(pages 256–257)*

4. 7 × 40

5. 2 × 900

6. 3 × 800

7. 5 × 200

8. 4 × 6,000

9. 9 × 7,000

10. How does knowing that 7 × 3 = 21 help you multiply 7 by 30? by 300? by 3,000?

Do You Know...

How tall was the tallest horse on record?

You will find out in Lesson 7-15.

C Division Facts

(pages 150–151)

11. $12 \div 2$ **12.** $20 \div 4$ **13.** $9 \div 3$

14. $42 \div 7$ **15.** $27 \div 9$ **16.** $36 \div 6$

17. $5\overline{)45}$ **18.** $8\overline{)48}$ **19.** $7\overline{)63}$

Write a division sentence to solve each problem.

20. Tina wants to put 4 coins into each change purse. How many purses does she need to hold 24 coins?

21. Travis is arranging his 15 small cars in 3 rows. How many cars should he put in each row?

D Multiplying

(pages 270–271)

Estimate each product. Then, multiply.

22. 5×31 **23.** 3×25

24. 2×167 **25.** 8×249

26. 6×419 **27.** 42×376

28. Is 252 a reasonable answer for 7×36? Estimate to decide.

29. The music teacher got 3 boxes of hats for the chorus. Each box had 35 hats. How many hats were there in all?

Key Idea
Basic facts and place-value patterns can help you find quotients like 1,800 ÷ 6 easily.

Vocabulary
- quotient (p. 146)

Materials
- calculator

Using Patterns to Divide Mentally

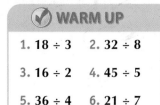

WARM UP

1. 18 ÷ 3
2. 32 ÷ 8
3. 16 ÷ 2
4. 45 ÷ 5
5. 36 ÷ 4
6. 21 ÷ 7

LEARN

Activity

What's the rule?

a. Use a calculator to find each **quotient.** Look for a pattern.

15 ÷ 3 = 5	**35 ÷ 5 = 7**	**40 ÷ 8 = 5**
150 ÷ 3 =	**350 ÷ 5 =**	**400 ÷ 8 =**
1,500 ÷ 3 =	**3,500 ÷ 5 =**	**4,000 ÷ 8 =**
15,000 ÷ 3 =	**35,000 ÷ 5 =**	**40,000 ÷ 8 =**

b. Find each quotient without a calculator. Then check your answers with a calculator.

81 ÷ 9	**18 ÷ 6**	**30 ÷ 5**
810 ÷ 9	**180 ÷ 6**	**300 ÷ 5**
8,100 ÷ 9	**1,800 ÷ 6**	**3,000 ÷ 5**
81,000 ÷ 9	**18,000 ÷ 6**	**30,000 ÷ 5**

c. Describe a rule that tells how to find the quotient.

TEST TALK

Think It Through
I can **look for a pattern** to find a rule.

How can you divide mentally?

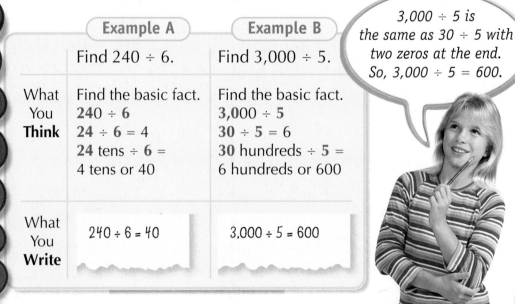

	Example A	Example B
	Find 240 ÷ 6.	Find 3,000 ÷ 5.
What You **Think**	Find the basic fact. **240 ÷ 6** **24** ÷ **6** = 4 **24** tens ÷ **6** = 4 tens or 40	Find the basic fact. **3,000 ÷ 5** **30** ÷ **5** = 6 **30** hundreds ÷ **5** = 6 hundreds or 600
What You **Write**	240 ÷ 6 = 40	3,000 ÷ 5 = 600

3,000 ÷ 5 is the same as 30 ÷ 5 with two zeros at the end. So, 3,000 ÷ 5 = 600.

Talk About It

1. Find 2,400 ÷ 6 and 24,000 ÷ 6.

CHECK

For another example, see Set 7-1 on p. 424.

Use patterns to find each quotient.

1. 36 ÷ 6 =
   360 ÷ 6 =
   3,600 ÷ 6 =
   36,000 ÷ 6 =

2. 54 ÷ 9 =
   540 ÷ 9 =
   5,400 ÷ 9 =
   54,000 ÷ 9 =

3. 10 ÷ 5 =
   100 ÷ 5 =
   1,000 ÷ 5 =
   10,000 ÷ 5 =

4. 30 ÷ 6 =
   300 ÷ 6 =
   3,000 ÷ 6 =
   30,000 ÷ 6 =

5. **Number Sense** How is dividing 280 by 4 like dividing 28 by 4?

PRACTICE

For more practice, see Set 7-1 on p. 428.

A Skills and Understanding

Divide. Use mental math.

6. 240 ÷ 4
7. 4,000 ÷ 5
8. 63,000 ÷ 7
9. 7,200 ÷ 8
10. 140 ÷ 2
11. 1,800 ÷ 3
12. 49,000 ÷ 7
13. 2,000 ÷ 4
14. 420 ÷ 6
15. 6,400 ÷ 8
16. 45,000 ÷ 5
17. 1,000 ÷ 2
18. **Number Sense** How is dividing 2,100 by 7 like dividing 21 by 7? How is dividing 2,100 by 7 like dividing 210 by 7?

B Reasoning and Problem Solving

Use the map at the right for 19–20. Assume you drive the same number of miles each hour.

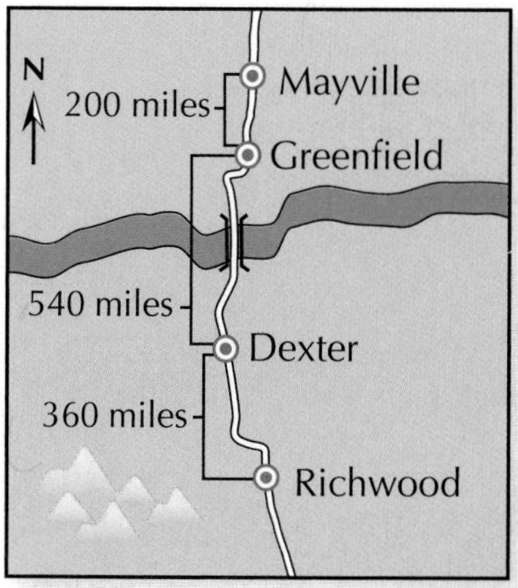

19. How many miles do you drive each hour, if you drive from Mayville to Greenfield in 4 hours? if you drive from Greenfield to Dexter in 9 hours?
20. **Writing in Math** Is it reasonable to be able to drive from Dexter to Richwood in 4 hours? Explain why or why not.

Mixed Review and Test Prep

Take It to the NET
Test Prep
www.scottforesman.com

21. 35 × 17
22. $2.43 × 38
23. $4.72 × 65
24. 1,284 × 56
25. Evaluate 6*n* when *n* = 10.

   A. 4 **B.** 16 **C.** 60 **D.** 610

Key Idea
There are different ways to estimate quotients.

Vocabulary
- compatible numbers (p. 62)
- overestimate (p. 72)
- underestimate (p. 72)

Estimating Quotients

WARM UP

Round to the place with the underlined digit.

1. 5$\underline{2}$7
2. 5,$\underline{8}$75
3. $\underline{6}$74
4. $\underline{2}$,347
5. $\underline{1}$48
6. 8,$\underline{9}$25

LEARN

Exact answer or estimate?

Antique Dolls Aunt Glenna has decided to give her collection of 310 antique dolls to her 8 nieces. She wants to give each niece the same number of dolls. She wants to know about how many dolls she will give to each niece.

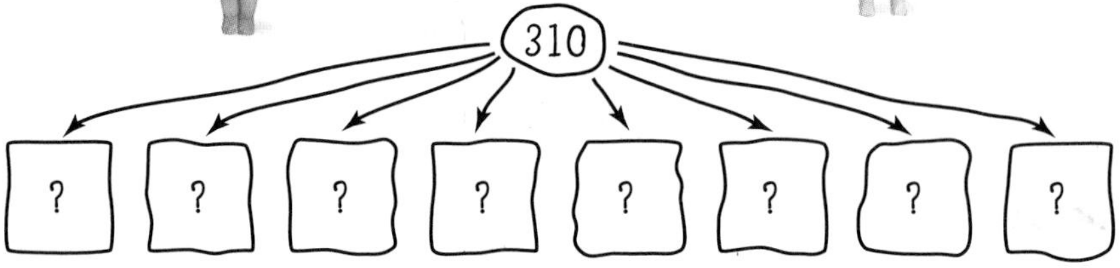

TEST TALK

Think It Through
- I can **draw a picture** to show the main idea.
- I need only an **estimate** because I just need to know about how many dolls each niece will get.

What are some ways to estimate quotients?

Example A

Estimate 310 ÷ 8.

One Way	*Another Way*
Mark used **compatible numbers.**	Nina thought about multiplication.
I adjusted 310 to 320 because 32 ÷ 8 = 4.	I thought, 8 times what number is about 310?
320 ÷ 8 = 40	8 × 4 = 32, so 8 × 40 = 320.
So, 310 ÷ 8 is about 40.	So, 310 ÷ 8 is about 40.

A good estimate is about 40 dolls for each niece.

Talk About It

1. Why did Mark adjust 310 to 320?

2. Why is division the operation needed to solve the Antique Dolls problem on page 368?

Take It to the NET
More Examples
www.scottforesman.com

Is your estimate an overestimate or an underestimate?

Anna, Ahmet, Emily, and Dan earned \$115 working in their neighborhood. They need to estimate 115 ÷ 4 to find about how much each of them will get.

Example B

Anna found an **underestimate.**

Exact: 115 ÷ 4   115 is changed to a lesser number.

↓

Estimate: 100 ÷ 4 = 25

So the estimate of \$25 is less than the exact answer.

Example C

Ahmet found an **overestimate.**

Exact: 115 ÷ 4   115 is changed to a greater number.

↓

Estimate: 120 ÷ 4 = 30

So the estimate of \$30 is greater than the exact answer.

Talk About It

3. Would you rather use an underestimate or an overestimate to know how much money to expect? Explain.

4. To estimate 760 ÷ 8, Juan adjusts 760 to 720. Find his estimate. Is this an overestimate or an underestimate?

CHECK

For another example, see Set 7-2 on p. 424.

Estimate each quotient. Tell whether you found an overestimate or an underestimate.

1. \$79 ÷ 4   **2.** 439 ÷ 7   **3.** 603 ÷ 3   **4.** 182 ÷ 8

5. Number Sense Give two different sets of compatible numbers you can use to estimate the quotient of 262 ÷ 4.

For more practice, see Set 7-2 on p. 428.

A Skills and Understanding

Estimate each quotient. Tell whether you found an overestimate or an underestimate.

6. 58 ÷ 3	**7.** 159 ÷ 2	**8.** 186 ÷ 6	**9.** 535 ÷ 9
10. 582 ÷ 2	**11.** 572 ÷ 7	**12.** 342 ÷ 5	**13.** 452 ÷ 4
14. 289 ÷ 5	**15.** 805 ÷ 9	**16.** 365 ÷ 4	**17.** 391 ÷ 8
18. 361 ÷ 7	**19.** 636 ÷ 8	**20.** 178 ÷ 3	**21.** 431 ÷ 7
22. 928 ÷ 9	**23.** 468 ÷ 9	**24.** 638 ÷ 7	**25.** 117 ÷ 3

26. Number Sense Tina used 250 ÷ 5 = 50 to estimate 225 ÷ 5. Did she get an underestimate or an overestimate? Explain.

B Reasoning and Problem Solving

Math and Everyday Life

Use the graph for 27–30.

Pages in Students' Favorite Books

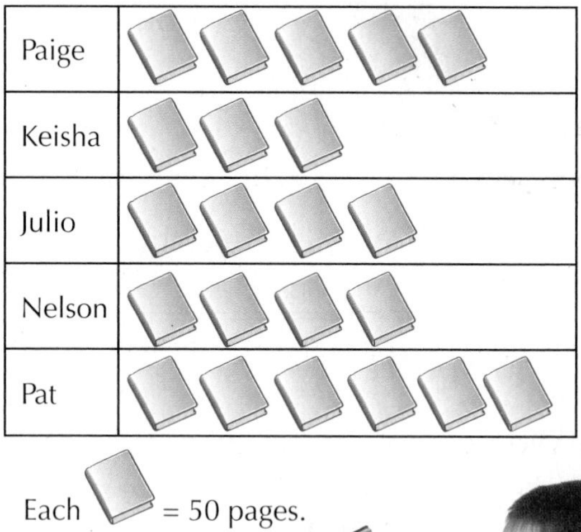

27. If Paige read her book in 7 days, about how many pages did she read each day?

28. If Julio read his book in 6 days, about how many pages did he read each day?

29. If Pat and Keisha both read their books in 7 days, about how many more pages did Pat read each day than Keisha?

30. How many pages are in the five favorite books altogether?

31. **Writing in Math** Rob needs to estimate the quotient of 430 ÷ 6. Tell two different ways that Rob could make a reasonable estimate and find the estimate each way.

C Extensions

Fill in each ◯ with > or <. Explain how you know which quotient is greater, without dividing.

32. 930 ÷ 4 ◯ 762 ÷ 4 **33.** 742 ÷ 8 ◯ 742 ÷ 7

Mixed Review and Test Prep

Take It to the NET
Test Prep
www.scottforesman.com

Find each quotient. Use mental math.

34. 810 ÷ 9 **35.** 1,200 ÷ 3 **36.** 2,500 ÷ 5 **37.** 4,800 ÷ 8

38. A school has 120 fourth graders. How many students will be in each group if they are divided into 3 groups? 4 groups? 6 groups?

39. Which of the following is a reasonable estimate of 7 × 35?

A. 40 **B.** 110 **C.** 140 **D.** 280

Practice Game

Tic-Tac Numbers

Number of players: 2 or more

Materials: Tic-Tac Computation Game Board for each player
spinner marked 2–9
18 markers for each player

The first player spins the spinner and finds a number on the game board that is a multiple of the number on the spinner. The player places a marker on that number. If there are several possible board numbers, the player chooses just one to mark.

Then the second player takes his or her turn.

Play continues until one player has 6 markers in a row on the game board horizontally, vertically, or diagonally. That player wins the game.

Key Idea
Sometimes when you divide, there are some left over.

Vocabulary
- remainder
- divisor (p. 146)

Materials
- counters
  or e tools

TEST TALK

Think It Through
- I can **choose division** when I'm finding equal groups.
- I can **draw a picture to show the problem.**

Dividing with Remainders

WARM UP

Divide.

1. 15 ÷ 3 2. 12 ÷ 4
3. 48 ÷ 8 4. 54 ÷ 9

LEARN

What happens when some are left?

Cameron is arranging 14 chairs into 3 rows so that each row has the same number of chairs. How many chairs are in each row? How many chairs are left over?

The part that is left over is called the **remainder.** The remainder should always be less than the **divisor**.

Example

Find 14 ÷ 3.

What You **Show**	What You **Think**	What You **Write**
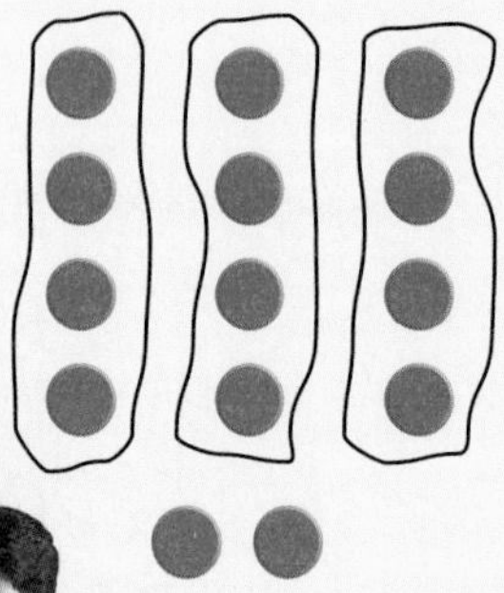	If I put 14 counters in 3 groups, I get 4 in each group.	$3\overline{)14}$ Divide.
	I used 12 counters in the 3 groups.	$\begin{array}{r} 4 \\ 3\overline{)14} \\ \underline{12} \\ 2 \end{array}$ Multiply.
	There are 2 counters left over. This is not enough to put one more in each group. Write the remainder by the quotient.	$\begin{array}{r} 4\text{ R2} \\ 3\overline{)14} \\ \underline{12} \\ 2 \end{array}$ Subtract. Compare. $2 < 3$
	Check: Multiply 4 × 3. Then add 2.	Check: $4 \times 3 = 12$; $12 + 2 = 14$

Talk About It

1. What does the remainder tell?

2. For ▢ ÷ 3, can the remainder be 3? Explain?

Take It to the NET
More Examples
www.scottforesman.com

CHECK ✓

For another example, see Set 7-3 on p. 424.

Use counters or draw pictures. Tell how many items are in each row and how many are left over if the items are divided equally among the rows.

1. 17 chairs
3 rows

2. 23 balls
8 rows

3. 28 books
3 rows

4. 21 disks
6 rows

5. Number Sense When you divide by 4, what remainders are possible? Explain your answer.

PRACTICE

For more practice, see Set 7-3 on p. 428.

A Skills and Understanding

Divide. You may use counters or pictures to help.

6. $4\overline{)25}$ **7.** $7\overline{)30}$ **8.** $5\overline{)28}$ **9.** $9\overline{)29}$ **10.** $8\overline{)73}$

11. $9\overline{)49}$ **12.** $4\overline{)30}$ **13.** $7\overline{)55}$ **14.** $6\overline{)45}$ **15.** $2\overline{)19}$

16. $3\overline{)29}$ **17.** $5\overline{)48}$ **18.** $6\overline{)29}$ **19.** $8\overline{)57}$ **20.** $5\overline{)33}$

21. Number Sense When you divide by 6, can the remainder be 5? Why or why not?

B Reasoning and Problem Solving

22. Room A has 8 rows of chairs with 16 chairs in each row. Room B has 20 rows of chairs with 7 chairs in each row. Which room has more chairs?

23. Algebra If 48 ÷ 7 = 6 Rn, what is the value of n?

24. Writing in Math When 38 desks were arranged into 6 equal rows, there were 8 desks left over. Explain if this is reasonable.

Mixed Review and Test Prep

Take It to the NET
Test Prep
www.scottforesman.com

Find each quotient. Use mental math.

25. 300 ÷ 5 **26.** 1,800 ÷ 2 **27.** 2,400 ÷ 3 **28.** 2,700 ÷ 9

29. Estimate 572 ÷ 8.

A. 70 **B.** 100 **C.** 120 **D.** 200

Key Idea
You can find 2-digit quotients by breaking apart the problem and dividing tens, then ones.

Materials
- place-value blocks or e tools

WARM UP

Divide.

1. 18 ÷ 5
2. 32 ÷ 7
3. 26 ÷ 3
4. 62 ÷ 8
5. 43 ÷ 6
6. 56 ÷ 9

Two-Digit Quotients

LEARN

Activity

How do you find quotients with two digits?

Pencils Pedro has 54 pencils and 3 empty pencil boxes. He wants to put the same number of pencils in each box. How many pencils should he put in each box?

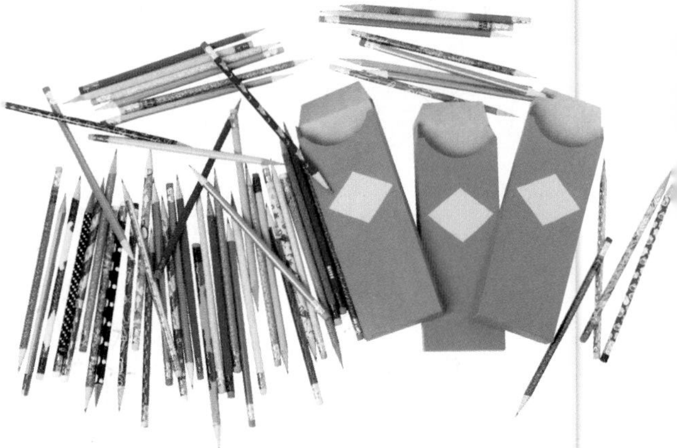

TEST TALK

Think It Through
I can **use objects** or **draw pictures** to divide.

Since Pedro wants to put the pencils into 3 equal groups, he can divide.

Find 54 ÷ 3.

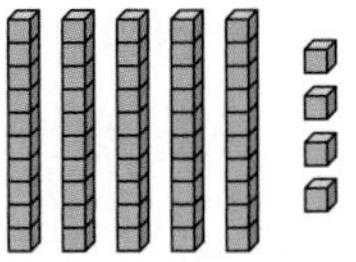

Step 1: Use place-value blocks to show 54.

Step 2: Divide the tens into 3 equal groups. How many tens can you put in each group? How many tens are left over?

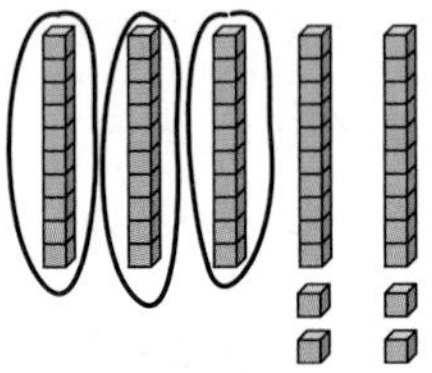

Step 3: Trade the extra tens for ones.

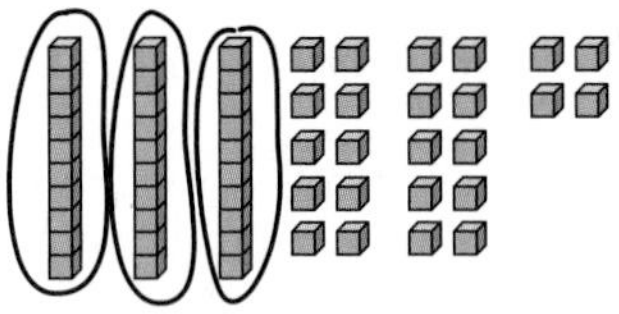

Step 4: Put the ones into the 3 groups so that the same number of ones are in each group. How many ones are in each group?

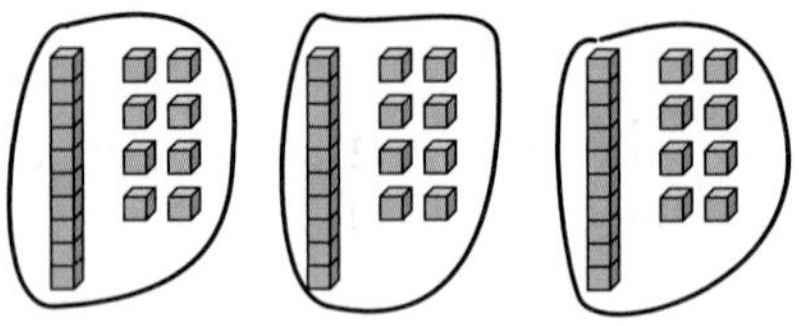

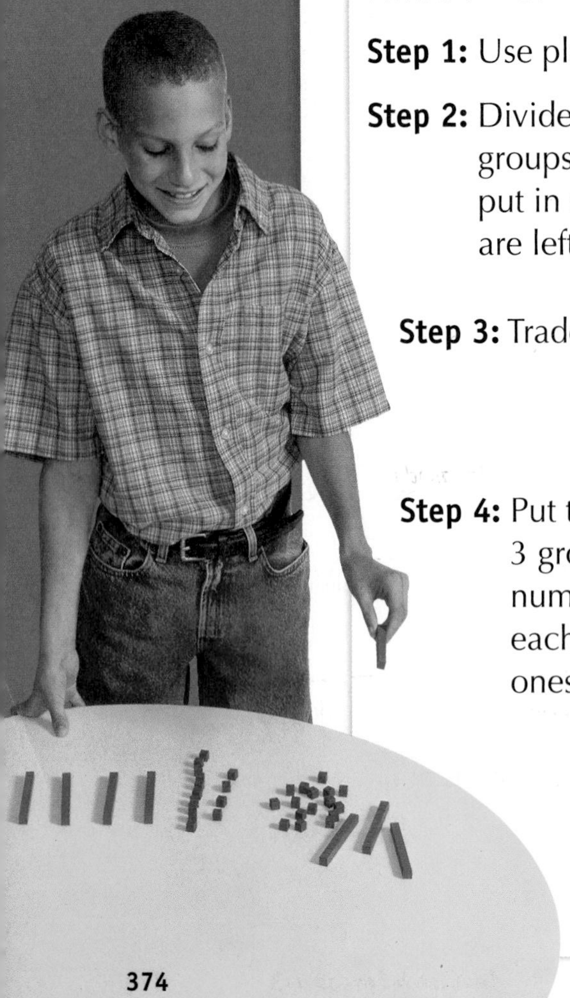

a. What is 54 ÷ 3? How many pencils should Pedro put in each box?

b. Divide. Use place-value blocks.

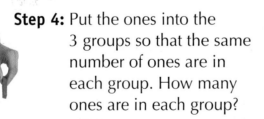

52 ÷ 4   34 ÷ 2   60 ÷ 5

How do you record division?

Example

Find 46 ÷ 3.

	What You **Show**	What You **Think**	What You **Write**
STEP 1 Divide the tens.	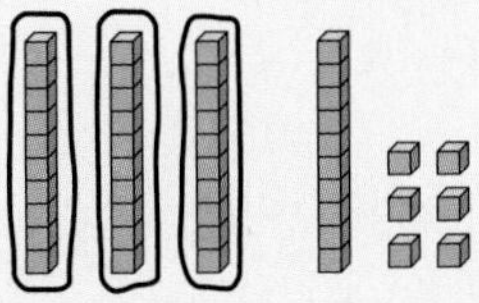	There is 1 ten in each group and 1 ten left over.	1 3)46 -3 1
STEP 2 Regroup by bringing down the ones.	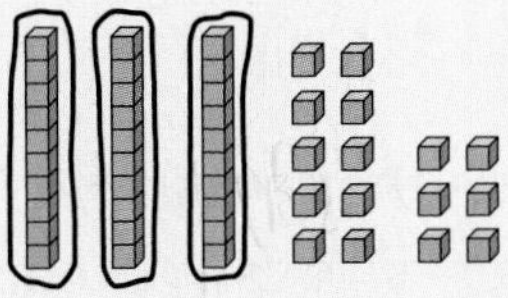	Trade the extra ten for ten ones. The one ten and 6 ones make 16 ones.	1 3)46 -3 16
STEP 3 Divide the ones.	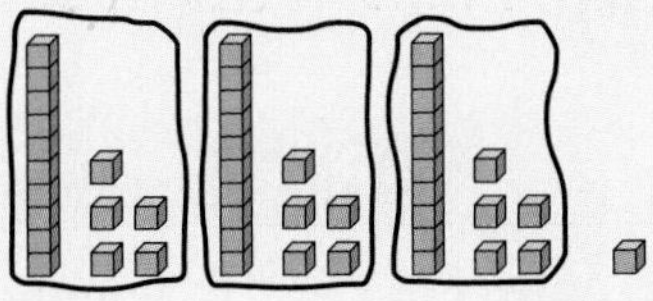	There are 5 ones in each group and 1 one left over.	15 R1 3)46 -3 16 -15 1

46 ÷ 3 = 15 R1

Talk About It

1. After you trade the extra ten for ones, how many ones are there in all?

2. How do you check that 15 R1 is the correct answer?

CHECK

For another example, see Set 7-4 on p. 424.

Use place-value blocks or draw pictures. Tell how many items are in each box and how many are left over.

1. 57 pencils
3 boxes

2. 98 photos
7 boxes

3. 71 CDs
2 boxes

4. 95 calendars
4 boxes

5. Number Sense You have 56 magazines. You divide them equally among some boxes. How many boxes must you use to get fewer than 10 magazines in each box?

PRACTICE

For more practice, see Set 7-4 on p. 428.

A Skills and Understanding

Use place-value blocks or draw pictures. Tell how many oranges are in each bag and how many are left over.

6. 70 oranges
5 bags

7. 63 oranges
3 bags

8. 31 oranges
2 bags

9. 58 oranges
4 bags

Divide. You may use place-value blocks or pictures to help.

10. $5\overline{)90}$ **11.** $2\overline{)78}$ **12.** $6\overline{)85}$ **13.** $3\overline{)77}$ **14.** $4\overline{)84}$

15. $6\overline{)73}$ **16.** $4\overline{)93}$ **17.** $2\overline{)70}$ **18.** $3\overline{)98}$ **19.** $5\overline{)71}$

20. $5\overline{)70}$ **21.** $3\overline{)63}$ **22.** $2\overline{)38}$ **23.** $4\overline{)56}$ **24.** $7\overline{)79}$

25. Number Sense You have 38 oranges. You divide them equally among some bags. What is the greatest number of bags you can use and still get at least 10 oranges in each bag?

B Reasoning and Problem Solving

Math and Art

Use the table at the right for 26–28. Each room within a gallery contains the same number of paintings. How many paintings are in each room of the

Gallery	Number of Rooms	Number of Paintings
Eton	7	91
Sunrise	5	65
Pallet	4	52
Rogers	8	96
Eastern	6	72

26. Eton Gallery? **27.** Rogers Gallery?

28. How many more paintings are in a room of the Sunrise Gallery than a room of the Eastern Gallery?

29. Writing in Math Is the explanation below correct? If not, tell why and write a correct response.

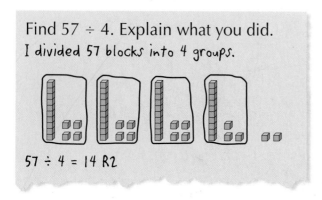

Find 57 ÷ 4. Explain what you did.
I divided 57 blocks into 4 groups.

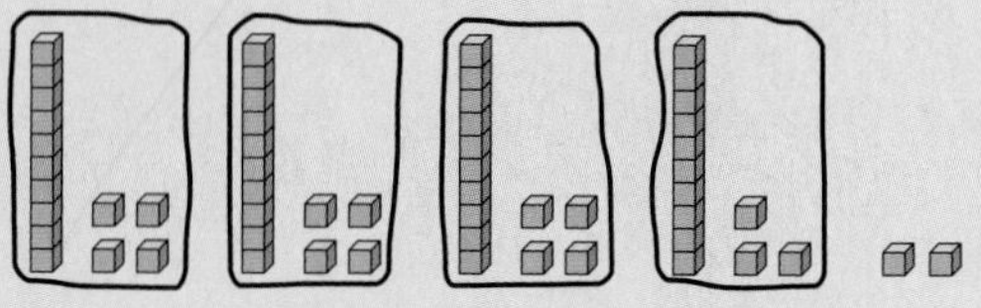

57 ÷ 4 = 14 R2

TEST TALK

Think It Through
I can **use objects** or **draw a picture** to explain my thinking.

PRACTICE

C Extensions

Find the next three numbers in each pattern.

30. 85, 80, 75, ... **31.** 78, 75, 72, ... **32.** 72, 68, 64, ...

Mixed Review and Test Prep

Take It to the NET
Test Prep
www.scottforesman.com

Divide. You may use counters to help.

33. $2\overline{)9}$ **34.** $8\overline{)59}$ **35.** $9\overline{)65}$ **36.** $4\overline{)38}$ **37.** $5\overline{)39}$

38. Find 23 × 548.

A. 2,740 **B.** 11,384 **C.** 12,604 **D.** 12,884

Learning with Technology

Using the Place-Value Blocks eTool to Divide

To divide 137 ÷ 3 using the Place-Value Blocks eTool, stamp the dividend, 137.

Then drag blocks, breaking them as needed, to create three equal groups. The number of groups you create is the divisor.

Count the number of blocks in the equal groups and count how many blocks remain.

1. What does the number of blocks in each group represent?

2. What does the number of blocks left over represent?

3. Will grouping groups of blocks in a pile help in counting?

Use the Place-Value Blocks eTool to divide.

4. 183 ÷ 3 **5.** 222 ÷ 4

6. 87 ÷ 5 **7.** 281 ÷ 5

8. 306 ÷ 8 **9.** 420 ÷ 4

10. 215 ÷ 7 **11.** 563 ÷ 6

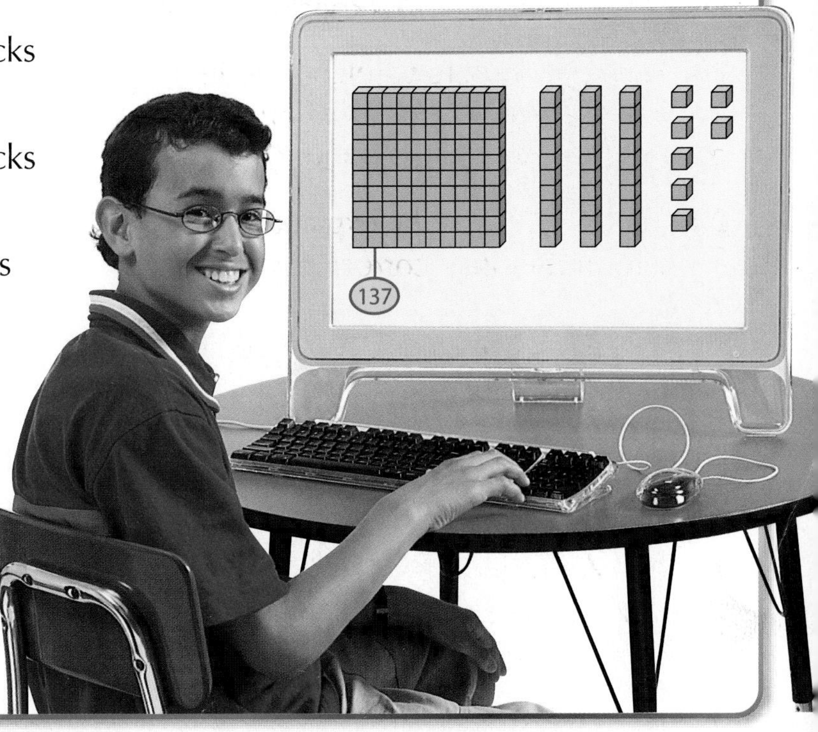

Review

Do You Know How?

Do You Understand?

Using Patterns to Divide Mentally (7-1)

Divide. Use mental math.

1. 210 ÷ 3
2. 800 ÷ 2
3. 4,800 ÷ 6
4. 4,000 ÷ 8
5. 30,000 ÷ 5
6. 36,000 ÷ 4

A Tell how you used mental math to find the quotient for Exercise 5.

B If you divide a number by 5 and the quotient has 1 zero, could the number be 200? 300? 500?

Estimating Quotients (7-2)

Estimate each quotient.

7. 64 ÷ 2
8. 88 ÷ 3
9. 165 ÷ 8
10. 400 ÷ 6
11. 562 ÷ 7
12. 318 ÷ 5

C Tell what method you used to find the estimate for Exercise 8.

D Is your estimate for Exercise 12 an overestimate or an underestimate?

Dividing with Remainders (7-3)

Divide. You may use counters or pictures to help.

13. $2\overline{)13}$
14. $7\overline{)23}$
15. $6\overline{)39}$
16. $4\overline{)19}$
17. $5\overline{)42}$
18. $9\overline{)71}$

E How can you tell that 2R9 is an incorrect answer for Exercise 14?

F Explain why the remainder must be less than the divisor.

Two-Digit Quotients (7-4)

Divide. You may use place-value blocks or pictures to help.

19. $5\overline{)86}$
20. $3\overline{)77}$
21. $4\overline{)76}$
22. $2\overline{)58}$
23. $6\overline{)84}$
24. $4\overline{)50}$

G How can you check that your answer to Exercise 19 is correct?

H In Exercise 20, after you traded the extra tens for ones, how many ones did you have in all?

Diagnostic Checkpoint

Test Talk

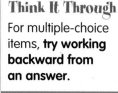

Think It Through
For multiple-choice items, **try working backward from an answer.**

MULTIPLE CHOICE

1. Miguel has 48 markers. He sorts them into 3 piles. How many markers are in each pile? (7-4)

A. 7 **B.** 10 **C.** 15 **D.** 16

2. Which multiplication sentence could help you estimate $354 \div 9$? (7-2)

A. 9×3 **B.** 9×4 **C.** 9×30 **D.** 9×40

FREE RESPONSE

Divide. Use mental math. (7-1)

3. $600 \div 2$ **4.** $200 \div 5$ **5.** $6{,}300 \div 9$ **6.** $9{,}000 \div 3$ **7.** $5{,}600 \div 8$

Divide. You may use counters or pictures to help. (7-3)

8. 3)8 **9.** 8)36 **10.** 4)23 **11.** 6)56 **12.** 7)43

Estimate each quotient. (7-2)

13. 5)206 **14.** 2)38 **15.** 6)352 **16.** 4)192 **17.** 7)291

Divide. You may use place-value blocks or pictures to help. (7-4)

18. 3)42 **19.** 8)92 **20.** 6)74 **21.** 3)52 **22.** 2)95

The shipment of prizes shown at the right needs to be divided equally among 5 stores. (7-1)

23. How many bears should each store get?

24. How many toy cars should each store get?

Writing in Math

25. How can you use the fact that $32 \div 4 = 8$ to divide 32,000 by 4? (7-1)

26. Explain how you know if 30 is an overestimate or an underestimate for $245 \div 7$. (7-2)

27. Write a problem that can be solved by dividing 51 by 4. (7-4)

Key Idea
You can find 2-digit quotients by breaking apart the problem and dividing tens, then ones.

Vocabulary
- dividend (p. 146)
- divisor (p. 146)
- quotient (p. 146)

Dividing Two-Digit Numbers

WARM UP

Estimate each quotient.

1. 62 ÷ 3
2. 38 ÷ 2
3. 248 ÷ 5
4. 179 ÷ 3
5. 502 ÷ 7
6. 732 ÷ 9

LEARN

How do you divide with paper and pencil?

An electronics company gave 76 calculators to Hill Elementary School. If 4 fourth-grade classes shared the calculators equally, how many calculators did each class receive?

Example A

Find 76 ÷ 4.

Estimate: 76 is close to 80 and 80 ÷ 4 is 20, so the quotient is a little less than 20. The quotient has two digits, so start by dividing the tens.

		What You **Think**	What You **Write**
STEP 1	Divide the tens.	7 tens ÷ 4 = 1 ten in each group. 4 tens used, 3 tens left.	1 4)76 Multiply. 1 x 4 −4 Subtract. 7 − 4 3 Compare. 3 < 4
STEP 2	Bring down the ones and divide.	36 ones ÷ 4 = 9 ones in each group	19 4)76 −4↓ 36 Multiply. 9 x 4 −36 Subtract. 0 Compare. 0 < 4
CHECK	Multiply the quotient by the divisor.	The product, 76, is the same as the dividend, 76. The answer checks.	3 19 x 4 76

So, 76 ÷ 4 = 19. Each class received 19 calculators.

TEST TALK

Think It Through

I need to **understand vocabulary.**

19 ← quotient
4)76 ← dividend
↑
divisor

Talk About It

1. Why do you multiply to check division?

Take It to the NET
More Examples
www.scottforesman.com

What if some are left?

Example B

Find $83 \div 3$.

Estimate: 83 is close to 90 and $90 \div 3$ is 30, so the quotient is a little less than 30. The quotient has two digits, so start by dividing the tens.

STEP 1

Divide the tens.

$$\begin{array}{r l} 2 & \\ 3\overline{)83} & \text{Multiply. } 2 \times 3 \\ -6 & \text{Subtract. } 8 - 6 \\ \hline 2 & \text{Compare. } 2 < 3 \end{array}$$

STEP 2

Bring down the ones and divide.

$$\begin{array}{r l} 27 & \\ 3\overline{)83} & \\ -6\downarrow & \\ \hline 23 & \text{Multiply. } 7 \times 3 \\ -21 & \text{Subtract. } 23 - 21 \\ \hline 2 & \text{Compare. } 2 < 3 \end{array}$$

CHECK

Multiply the quotient by the divisor and add the remainder.

$$\begin{array}{r} {}^{2} \\ 27 \\ \times\ 3 \\ \hline 81 \end{array} \qquad \begin{array}{r} 81 \\ +\ 2 \\ \hline 83 \end{array}$$

The answer checks.

So, $83 \div 3 = 27$ R2.

Example C

Find $64 \div 4$.

Estimate: $80 \div 4 = 20$.

$$\begin{array}{r} 16 \\ 4\overline{)64} \\ -4 \\ \hline 24 \\ -24 \\ \hline 0 \end{array}$$

Check: $4 \times 16 = 64$

The answer checks.

Example D

Find $53 \div 2$.

Estimate: $60 \div 2 = 30$.

$$\begin{array}{r} 26\text{ R1} \\ 2\overline{)53} \\ -4 \\ \hline 13 \\ -12 \\ \hline 1 \end{array}$$

Check: $2 \times 26 = 52$
$52 + 1 = 53$.
The answer checks.

Example E

Find $97 \div 8$.

Estimate: $80 \div 8 = 10$.

$$\begin{array}{r} 12\text{ R1} \\ 8\overline{)97} \\ -8 \\ \hline 17 \\ -16 \\ \hline 1 \end{array}$$

Check: $8 \times 12 = 96$
$96 + 1 = 97$.
The answer checks.

Talk About It

2. In Step 1 of Example B, why do you compare the difference, 2, to the divisor, 3?

3. Reasoning Does the quotient $58 \div 6$ have one digit or two digits? Explain how you know without finding the exact answer.

CHECK

For another example, see Set 7-5 on p. 425.

1. $\begin{array}{r} 3\square \\ 2\overline{)64} \\ -6\downarrow \\ \hline 0\square \\ -\square \\ \hline 0 \end{array}$

2. $\begin{array}{r} \square 9 \\ 5\overline{)95} \\ -\square\downarrow \\ \hline \square\square \\ -\square\square \\ \hline 0 \end{array}$

3. $\begin{array}{r} \square\square \text{ R}\square \\ 7\overline{)82} \\ -\square\downarrow \\ \hline \square\square \\ -\square \\ \hline \square \end{array}$

4. $\begin{array}{r} \square\square \text{ R}\square \\ 4\overline{)75} \end{array}$

5. **Number Sense** Explain why 43 ÷ 3 has two digits in the quotient, but 43 ÷ 7 has only one digit in the quotient.

PRACTICE

For more practice, see Set 7-5 on p. 429.

A Skills and Understanding

6. $\begin{array}{r} 2\square \\ 3\overline{)78} \\ -\square\downarrow \\ \hline \square\square \\ -\square\square \\ \hline 0 \end{array}$

7. $\begin{array}{r} \square 6 \\ 5\overline{)80} \\ -\square\downarrow \\ \hline \square 0 \\ -\square 0 \\ \hline 0 \end{array}$

8. $\begin{array}{r} \square\square \text{ R4} \\ 8\overline{)92} \\ -\square\downarrow \\ \hline \square\square \\ -\square \\ \hline \square \end{array}$

9. $\begin{array}{r} \square\square \text{ R}\square \\ 4\overline{)94} \end{array}$

10. $2\overline{)56}$	11. $7\overline{)84}$	12. $5\overline{)74}$	13. $6\overline{)68}$	14. $9\overline{)99}$
15. $4\overline{)58}$	16. $5\overline{)78}$	17. $2\overline{)45}$	18. $3\overline{)64}$	19. $8\overline{)91}$
20. $6\overline{)62}$	21. $2\overline{)74}$	22. $4\overline{)63}$	23. $6\overline{)88}$	24. $7\overline{)83}$
25. $4\overline{)91}$	26. $3\overline{)57}$	27. $6\overline{)76}$	28. $3\overline{)94}$	29. $5\overline{)70}$

30. **Number Sense** Suppose you divided 48 by 5 and got 8 R8. How would you know you made a mistake?

B Reasoning and Problem Solving

Math and Everyday Life

Use the table at the right for Exercises 31–32.

31. If the cartons of juice are divided equally among 3 stores, how many cartons does each store get?

32. If each carton of pudding contains 36 boxes, how many boxes of pudding are there altogether?

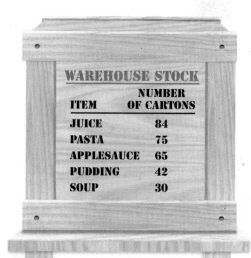

WAREHOUSE STOCK

ITEM	NUMBER OF CARTONS
JUICE	84
PASTA	75
APPLESAUCE	65
PUDDING	42
SOUP	30

PRACTICE

33. Algebra If 79 ÷ 6 = 13 Rn, what is the value of n?

34. Writing in Math Write a problem that could be solved by dividing 74 by 6.

C Extensions

Could 90 cartons of books be divided equally among each of the following numbers of bookstores with no cartons left over or divided up? Explain your answer.

35. 3 stores **36.** 5 stores **37.** 7 stores **38.** 8 stores

Mixed Review and Test Prep

Take It to the NET
Test Prep
www.scottforesman.com

Divide. You may use place-value blocks or pictures to help.

39. $2\overline{)74}$ **40.** $5\overline{)60}$ **41.** $4\overline{)71}$ **42.** $7\overline{)93}$ **43.** $3\overline{)86}$

44. Round 243,872 to the nearest thousand.

A. 240,000 **B.** 243,000 **C.** 243,900 **D.** 244,000

Discovery Channel School — Discover Math in Your World

Not So Lone Wolves

Wolves occupy territories. A wolf pack will defend its territory against other trespassing wolves. Normally, the territory belonging to a pack of wolves is inherited by the offspring of the pack.

1. The average territory held by a Wisconsin wolf pack is about 70 square miles. There are almost 2,100 square miles of official wildlife recreation land in Wisconsin. Estimate the number of packs that could occupy this land.

2. Gray wolves will pursue animals much larger than themselves. The average gray wolf weighs 80 pounds. The average moose weighs 13 times as much. How much does the average moose weigh?

Take It to the NET
Video and Activities
www.scottforesman.com

Problem-Solving Skill

Reading Helps!
Creating graphic organizers
can help you with...
interpreting remainders.

Key Idea
The real-world situation tells how to interpret the remainder.

Interpreting Remainders

LEARN

How do you interpret a remainder in a division problem?

Van Pool There are 86 fourth-grade students in van pools. Each van holds 6 students.

When you solve a problem using division, the real-world situation tells how to **interpret the remainder.**

Example A	Example B	Example C
Read and Understand How many vans will be completely filled?	**Read and Understand** How many students will be in the van that is not filled?	**Read and Understand** How many vans are needed to hold all of the students?
Plan and Solve 86 ÷ 6 = 14 R2 14 vans will be completely filled.	**Plan and Solve** 86 ÷ 6 = 14 R2 Two students will be in the van that is not filled.	**Plan and Solve** 86 ÷ 6 = 14 R2 14 vans are needed.
Look Back and Check 14 vans will have 6 students in each. One van will have fewer than 6 students.	**Look Back and Check** The remainder of 2 tells us there are 2 extra students for another van.	**Look Back and Check** One more van is needed for the 2 extra students. So, 14 + 1 = 15 vans are needed.

✓ Talk About It

1. How many students are in vans that are full?

CHECK

For another example, see Set 7-6 on p. 425.

1. You are setting up tables for a school party. Each table seats 4 people and 58 people are expected.

   A. How many tables will be filled?

   B. How many tables do you need?

2. Kay saved $40 to buy dinosaur models for her collection. Each model costs $3.

   A. How many models can Kay buy?

   B. How much more money will Kay need to buy one more model?

PRACTICE

For more practice, see Set 7-6 on p. 429.

The fourth graders are helping Ms. Marshall's first-grade class make baby chick decorations for spring. Use the decoration at the right for 3–5.

3. How many chicks can the students make with 32 buttons?

4. How many chicks can they make with 85 sticks? How many sticks will be left over?

5. How many balls of cotton do they need in order to make 16 chicks?

For 6–9 use the bar graph below. Three elementary schools collected all the paper that each school throws away in one day. The paper was packed in 6-pound bundles, plus one smaller bundle for any extra paper.

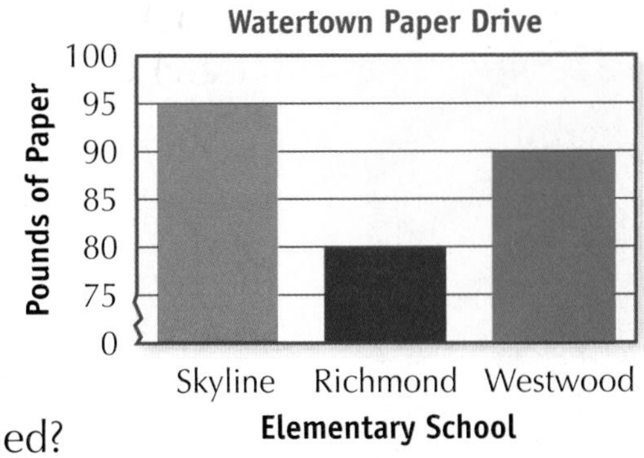

6. How many pounds of paper did each school collect?

7. How many bundles did each school make?

8. How many full bundles were collected in all?

9. **Reasoning** How many full bundles could be made if all of the partial bundles were combined?

10. **Writing in Math** Write a problem that can be solved using $76 \div 3 = 25$ R1.

Key Idea
You can divide larger numbers the same way you divide smaller numbers.

Dividing Three-Digit Numbers

WARM UP

Estimate each quotient.

1. 75 ÷ 4
2. 62 ÷ 3
3. 485 ÷ 5
4. 823 ÷ 4

LEARN

How do you divide larger numbers?

A school bus company has 273 buses and five parking lots. If the company wants to park the same number of buses in each lot, how many buses should be parked in each lot?

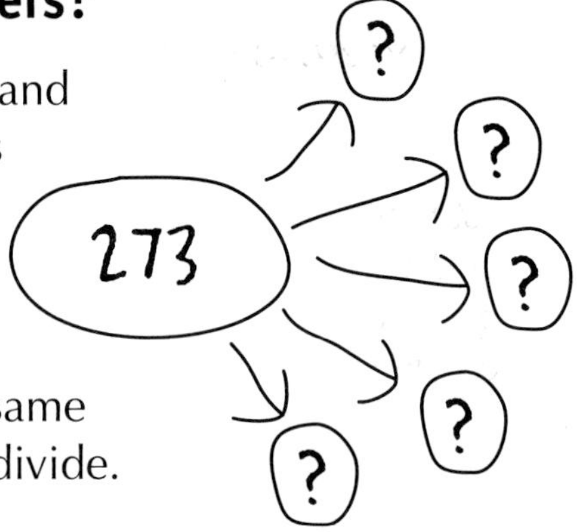

Since the company wants to park the same number of buses in each lot, you can divide.

Example A

Find 273 ÷ 5.

Estimate: 273 is close to 250 and 250 ÷ 5 is 50, so the quotient is a little more than 50.

STEP 1

Divide the tens.

```
   5
5)273   Multiply.
 - 25   Subtract.
    2   Compare. 2 < 5
```

STEP 2

Bring down the ones and divide.

```
   54 R3
5)273
 - 25↓
    23   Multiply.
  - 20   Subtract.
     3   Compare.
         3 < 5
```

CHECK

Multiply the quotient by the divisor and add the remainder.

```
  2
  54      270
×  5    +   3
 270      273
```

The answer checks. The dividend is 273.

So, 273 ÷ 5 = 54 R3.

The company can park 54 buses in each lot. They will have 3 buses left over.

TEST TALK

Think It Through

- I can divide when I need to **find how many in each group.**
- I can **draw a picture** to show the main idea.

Talk About It

1. In Example A, why do you start dividing with the tens?

Take It to the NET
More Examples
www.scottforesman.com

How can you tell where to start dividing?

An estimate can help you decide where to start dividing. If the estimated quotient has 2 digits, start with the tens. If it has 3 digits, start with the hundreds.

When I'm dividing by 5, I see if the number I'm dividing is more or less than 500.

Example B

Tell where to start dividing.

921 ÷ 8

Estimate: 921 is more than 800 and 800 ÷ 8 is 100, so the quotient has three digits. Start by dividing the hundreds.

Example C

Tell where to start dividing.

278 ÷ 3

Estimate: 278 is less than 300 and 300 ÷ 3 is 100, so the quotient has two digits. Start by dividing the tens.

Example D

Find 869 ÷ 7.

Estimate: 869 is close to 700 and 700 ÷ 7 is 100.

STEP 1

Divide the hundreds.

```
   1
7)869    Multiply.
 - 7     Subtract.
   1     Compare.
         1 < 7
```

STEP 2

Bring down the tens and divide.

```
   12
7)869
 - 7↓
   16    Multiply.
 - 14    Subtract.
    2    Compare.
         2 < 7
```

STEP 3

Bring down the ones and divide.

```
   124 R1
7)869
 - 7
   16
 - 14↓
    29   Multiply.
  - 28   Subtract.
     1   Compare.
         1 < 7
```

CHECK

Multiply the quotient by the divisor and add the remainder.

```
  12
  124       868
×   7     +   1
  868       869
```

The answer checks.

869 ÷ 7 = 124 R1

Talk About It

2. Explain how an estimated quotient can help you decide where to start dividing.

CHECK

For another example, see Set 7-7 on p. 425.

1. $6\overline{)156}$, quotient 2▢

2. $9\overline{)327}$, quotient ▢6 R▢

3. $3\overline{)741}$, quotient 24▢

4. $4\overline{)750}$, quotient 18▢ R▢

5. **Number Sense** Without dividing, tell whether 384 ÷ 3 has a two-digit quotient or a three-digit quotient. Explain how you know.

PRACTICE

For more practice, see Set 7-7 on p. 429.

A Skills and Understanding

6. $5\overline{)145}$, quotient 2▢

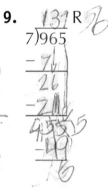

7. $3\overline{)268}$, quotient ▢9 R▢

8. $8\overline{)984}$, quotient ▢2▢

9. $7\overline{)965}$, quotient ▢3▢ R▢

10. $4\overline{)336}$ 11. $7\overline{)861}$ 12. $2\overline{)523}$ 13. $6\overline{)435}$ 14. $8\overline{)426}$

15. $5\overline{)470}$ 16. $2\overline{)931}$ 17. $7\overline{)248}$ 18. $6\overline{)762}$ 19. $8\overline{)995}$

20. $2\overline{)483}$ 21. $9\overline{)819}$ 22. $3\overline{)537}$ 23. $5\overline{)641}$ 24. $4\overline{)396}$

25. **Number Sense** Without dividing, tell whether 420 ÷ 5 has a two-digit or a three-digit quotient. Explain how you know.

B Reasoning and Problem Solving

Math and Everyday Life

26. If 484 buses are parked equally in 4 parking lots, how many buses are in each lot?

27. If a fleet of 531 taxi cabs are divided so 9 cabs are at each stand, how many stands are there?

PRACTICE

28. Algebra If 149 ÷ 6 = 24 R*n*, what is the value of *n*?

29. Writing in Math Write a word problem involving division that has a solution with a remainder of 3.

C Extensions

Fill in each ● with > or <. Look for a pattern.

30. 48 ÷ 3 ● 48 ÷ 4 **31.** 80 ÷ 5 ● 80 ÷ 4 **32.** 75 ÷ 5 ● 75 ÷ 3

Mixed Review and Test Prep

Take It to the NET
Test Prep
www.scottforesman.com

Estimate each quotient. Then, divide and check your answer.

33. $3\overline{)42}$ **34.** $4\overline{)63}$ **35.** $6\overline{)258}$ **36.** $7\overline{)520}$ **37.** $5\overline{)738}$

38. You have 80 CDs to pack into boxes that hold 6 CDs each. How many boxes can you fill?

A. 2 boxes **B.** 12 boxes **C.** 13 boxes **D.** 14 boxes

Learning with Technology

Using a Calculator to Find Remainders

Here is one way to find the quotient and remainder for 298 ÷ 48 using a calculator.

Press: 298 [÷] 48 [ENTER =] Display: 6.2083333

The result, 6.2083333, means the quotient is 6 with a remainder. Use the following key sequence to find the remainder.

Press: 298 [−] [(] 6 [×] 48 [)] [ENTER =] Display: 10

So 298 ÷ 48 = 6 R10

Another way to divide is to use the [Int÷] button. The result shows the remainder as a whole number.

Press: 298 [Int÷] 48 [ENTER =] Display: 6 10

Use a calculator to divide. Write the remainder as a whole number.

1. 847 ÷ 6 **2.** 578 ÷ 63 **3.** 726 ÷ 34 **4.** 923 ÷ 7

Key Idea
The steps for dividing do not change when there are zeros in the quotient.

TEST TALK
Think It Through
I know that 18 and 108 are not the same number.

Zeros in the Quotient

WARM UP
Divide.
1. $52 \div 2$ 2. $640 \div 5$
3. $92 \div 8$ 4. $835 \div 6$
5. $65 \div 9$ 6. $645 \div 7$

LEARN

Do zeros matter?

Example

Find $435 \div 4$.

Estimate: 435 is close to 400 and $400 \div 4$ is 100. The quotient has three digits, so start by dividing the hundreds.

STEP 1
Divide the hundreds.

```
    1
 4)435   Multiply.
  - 4    Subtract.
    0    Compare.
         0 < 4
```

STEP 2
Bring down the tens and divide.

```
    10
 4)435
  - 4↓
    03   Multiply.
   - 0   Subtract.
     3   Compare.
         3 < 4
```

STEP 3
Bring down the ones and divide.

```
    108 R3
 4)435
  - 4
    03
   - 0↓
     35  Multiply.
   - 32  Subtract.
      3  Compare.
         3 < 4
```

CHECK
Multiply the quotient by the divisor and add the remainder.

```
   1 3
   108       432
 ×   4     +   3
   432       435
```

The answer checks.

So, $435 \div 4 = 108$ R3.

I can use a shortcut on problems like $435 \div 4$, as long as I remember the zero in the quotient.

```
    108 R3
 4)435
  - 4
    035  ←— I brought down the 3 and
  - 32      divided. Since 3 ÷ 4 = 0 R3,
      3     I placed a zero in the
            quotient and brought
            down the 5.
```

Talk About It

1. Explain why the quotient 18 R3 is not reasonable for $435 \div 4$.

CHECK ✓

For another example, see Set 7-8 on p. 426.

Divide. Check your answer.

1. 4)812 **2.** 6)627 **3.** 9)931 **4.** 8)877 **5.** 7)814

6. Number Sense How can you tell, without dividing, that 816 ÷ 4 could not be 24?

PRACTICE

For more practice, see Set 7-8 on p. 430.

A Skills and Understanding

Divide. Check your answer.

7. 2)416 **8.** 9)936 **9.** 3)620 **10.** 7)912 **11.** 5)518

12. 5)535 **13.** 3)612 **14.** 7)758 **15.** 2)721 **16.** 4)837

17. 5)548 **18.** 6)243 **19.** 3)926 **20.** 7)735 **21.** 8)857

22. 2)815 **23.** 9)905 **24.** 6)614 **25.** 8)863 **26.** 3)628

27. Number Sense How can you tell, without dividing, that 385 ÷ 5 will have a two-digit quotient?

B Reasoning and Problem Solving

The school cafeteria has 4 coolers. The staff divides the cartons of juice and milk as evenly as possible among the coolers.

28. How many cartons of juice are in each cooler?

29. How many cartons of milk and juice are there altogether?

30. Writing in Math If the staff divides the milk evenly among the coolers and puts all the extra cartons in one cooler, how many cartons of milk are in this cooler? Explain.

Mixed Review and Test Prep

Take It to the NET
Test Prep
www.scottforesman.com

Estimate each quotient. Then divide and check your answer.

31. 3)42 **32.** 4)63 **33.** 6)258 **34.** 7)520 **35.** 5)738

36. Algebra Evaluate $n + 26$ for $n = 45$.

A. 19 **B.** 61 **C.** 71 **D.** 1,170

Key Idea
Dividing money amounts is like dividing whole numbers.

Dividing Money Amounts

WARM UP

1. 732 ÷ 4
2. 873 ÷ 9
3. 280 ÷ 5
4. 882 ÷ 7
5. 614 ÷ 2
6. 960 ÷ 8

LEARN

How do you divide money amounts?

An 8-pack of mountain spring water is on sale for $2.48. What is the cost of each bottle of water?

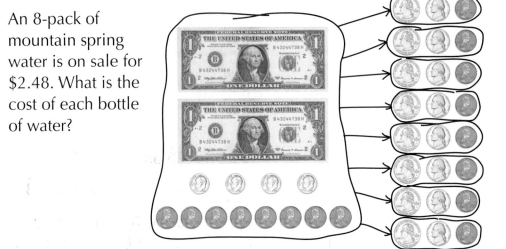

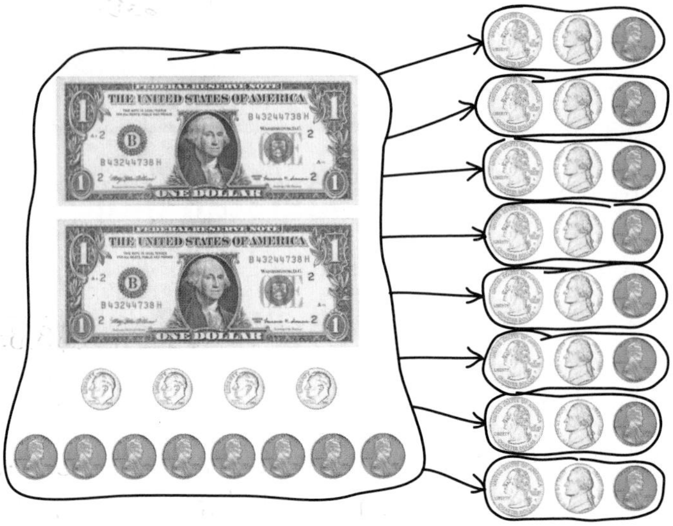

Example

Find $2.48 ÷ 8.

Estimate: Since the 8-pack costs less than $8, each bottle must cost less than $1.

STEP 1	STEP 2	CHECK
Divide the way you would with whole numbers	Show the dollar sign and decimal point in the quotient.	Multiply the quotient by the divisor.
31 8)$2.48 − 2 4 08 − 8 0	$0.31 8)$2.48 − 2 4 08 − 8 0 Move the decimal point straight up.	$0.31 × 8 $2.48 The answer checks.

So, $2.48 ÷ 8 = $0.31. Each bottle of water costs $0.31. Another way to write $0.31 is 31¢.

Talk About It

1. How do you know the quotient is $0.31 and not $3.10 or $31?

CHECK ✓

For another example, see Set 7-9 on p. 426.

Divide. Check your answer.

1. $3\overline{)\$4.62}$ **2.** $7\overline{)\$6.37}$ **3.** $4\overline{)\$7.28}$ **4.** $2\overline{)\$1.36}$ **5.** $8\overline{)\$8.40}$

6. Number Sense Using estimation, how do you know that \$19.50 ÷ 5 is \$3.90 and not \$39?

PRACTICE

For more practice, see Set 7-9 on p. 430.

A Skills and Understanding

Divide. Check your answer.

7. $5\overline{)\$4.65}$ **8.** $9\overline{)\$9.54}$ **9.** $6\overline{)\$8.88}$ **10.** $8\overline{)\$4.40}$ **11.** $3\overline{)\$1.74}$

12. $2\overline{)\$9.32}$ **13.** $7\overline{)\$8.68}$ **14.** $4\overline{)\$1.24}$ **15.** $9\overline{)\$6.03}$ **16.** $5\overline{)\$5.15}$

17. Number Sense When you divide \$7.85 by 6, is the answer a little more than \$1 or a little less than \$1? Explain how you know without finding the exact answer.

B Reasoning and Problem Solving

Packages of Chicken Wings

Number of Pieces	Cost
2	\$1.58
4	\$2.72
6	\$3.96
8	\$4.72

Use the table at the right for 18–21. Find the cost of each chicken wing in the

18. 4-piece package. **19.** 8-piece package.

20. How much more does one chicken wing from the 2-piece package cost than one wing from the 6-piece package?

21. Mr. Juarez bought a 4-piece package of wings and a 6-piece package of wings. How much did he pay for both packages?

22. Writing in Math Explain, as you would to a friend, how to divide \$7.45 by 5.

Mixed Review and Test Prep

Take It to the NET
Test Prep
www.scottforesman.com

Estimate each quotient. Then, divide and check your answer.

23. $8\overline{)492}$ **24.** $3\overline{)754}$ **25.** $4\overline{)439}$ **26.** $6\overline{)382}$ **27.** $5\overline{)628}$

28. Find 0 ÷ 4.

A. 0 **B.** 1 **C.** 4 **D.** cannot be done

Identifying the Main Idea

Identifying the main idea when you read in math can help you use the **problem-solving strategy, *Write a Number Sentence,*** in the next lesson.

In reading, identifying the main idea helps you know what the story is about. In math, the main idea for some story problems is part-part-whole or equal groups with something unknown.

*The **main idea** here is equal groups, with the amount per group unknown.*

A pet shop has 433 fish. This includes 237 freshwater fish. The rest are saltwater fish. The shop has how many saltwater fish?

Whole		Part		Part
433	–	237	=	*n*

The shop put 52 goldfish into 4 tanks with the same number in each tank. How many goldfish were in each tank?

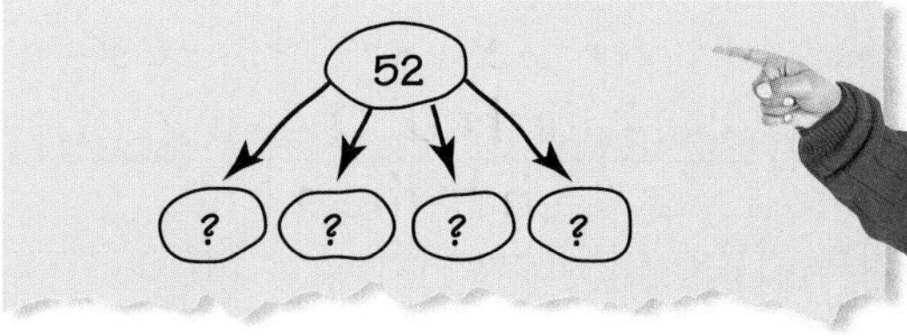

Total amount		Number of groups		Amount per group
52	÷	4	=	*n*

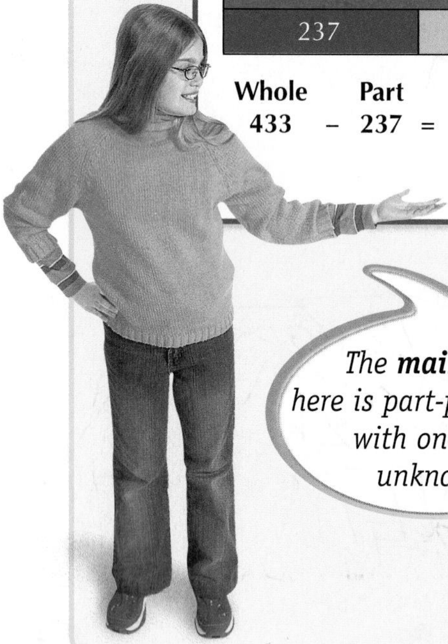

*The **main idea** here is part-part-whole, with one part unknown.*

*Each picture shows the main idea. The main idea helps you know what **number sentence** to write.*

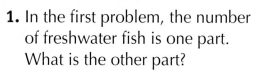

1. In the first problem, the number of freshwater fish is one part. What is the other part?
2. In the second problem, what is the number of groups?

For 3–6, use the problem below and the picture at the right.

Seth bought a package of balloons for a school dance. There are 144 red balloons and the rest of the balloons are white. How many white balloons are there?

3. What is the main idea in this problem?

4. Draw a picture to show the main idea.

5. *Writing in Math* What operation would you use to solve this problem? Explain how you know.

6. Write a number sentence for this problem.

For 7–9, use the problem below.

Claudia baked 120 cookies. She has 5 cookie tins. How many cookies should she put in each tin if she wants each of them to have the same amount?

7. What is the main idea in this problem?

8. Draw a picture to show the main idea.

9. Write a number sentence for this problem.

For 10–13, use the problem below and the table at the right.

Griffin bought 3 boxes of floating candles. How much money did Griffin spend altogether?

Candle Shop

Candle	Candles per Box	Cost
Votive	6	$5.94
Taper	6	$9.48
Floating	3	$5.39

10. What is the main idea in this problem?

11. Draw a picture to show the main idea.

12. Write a number sentence for this problem.

13. *Writing in Math* Use the information in the table to write a part-part-whole problem.

Problem-Solving Strategy

Key Idea
Learning how and when to write a number sentence can help you solve problems.

TEST TALK

Think It Through
The **most important idea** is equal groups, so I should write a division sentence.

Reading Helps!

Identifying the main idea
can help you with...
the problem-solving strategy, *Write a Number Sentence*

Write a Number Sentence

LEARN

How do you write a number sentence to solve a problem?

Compact Disc Player Maria's new CD player can hold 6 discs at a time. If she has 204 CDs, how many times can the player be filled without repeating a CD?

How to Write a Number Sentence

Step 1 Show the main idea in the problem.

Step 2 Decide which operation goes with the main idea.

Step 3 Use a letter to show what you are trying to find. Write a number sentence.

Step 4 Solve the number sentence.

Read and Understand

What do you know? 6 CDs at one time. A total of 204 CDs.

What are you trying to find? Find the number of times the player can be filled.

Plan and Solve

What strategy will you use? **Strategy: Write a number sentence.**

Step 1: Show the main idea.

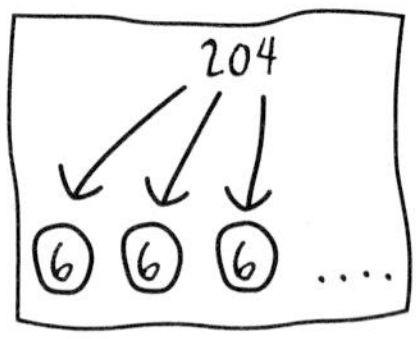

Step 2: Use division since you need to find how many groups of 6 are in 204.

Step 3: Let n equal the number of groups of 6 in 204. Write a number sentence.
$204 \div 6 = n$

Step 4:
Solve $204 \div 6 = n$

```
   34
6)204
 - 18
   24
 - 24
    0
```

Answer: $n = 34$; **The CD player can be filled 34 times without repeating CDs.**

Look Back and Check

Is your answer reasonable? Yes, the answer makes sense because $6 \times 34 = 204$.

Talk About It

1. In the Compact Disc Player problem, what is the total? How many equal groups are there?

2. What does n stand for in Step 3?

When might you write a number sentence?

School Supplies A marker costs \$1.35. A pen costs \$0.75. What is the cost for 2 markers and 1 pen?

When to Write a Number Sentence

Think about writing a number sentence when:

The story describes a situation that can be completed using an operation or operations.

- The total cost is given for 6 equal amounts.
- Costs for markers and pen are combined.

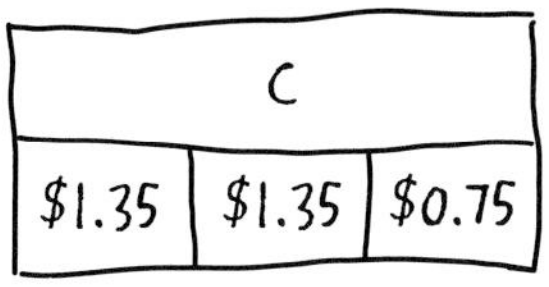

Multiply to find the cost of 2 markers. Then add the cost of the pen.

c = total cost for all 3 items.

$(2 \times \$1.35) + \$0.75 = c$

$\$2.70 + \$0.75 = c$

$\$3.45 = c$

The total cost for 2 markers and 1 pen is \$3.45.

Talk About It

3. Why can multiplication be used to find the cost for two markers?

4. What does c stand for in the School Supplies problem?

CHECK

For another example, see Set 7-10 on p. 426.

Solve the number sentence. Write the answer in a complete sentence.

1. Todd filled bags of grapefruit from a crate. The crate had 52 grapefruits and Todd put 4 grapefruits in each bag. How many bags did he fill?
   b = number of bags filled
   $52 \div 4 = b$

2. Tricia ran 5 times as far as Ali. Ali ran 375 meters. How far did Tricia run?
   t = distance Tricia ran;
   $375 \times 5 = t$

 For another example, see Set 7-10 on p. 430.

A Using the Strategy

Using a Number Sentence to Solve Problems Solve the number sentence. Write the answer in a complete sentence.

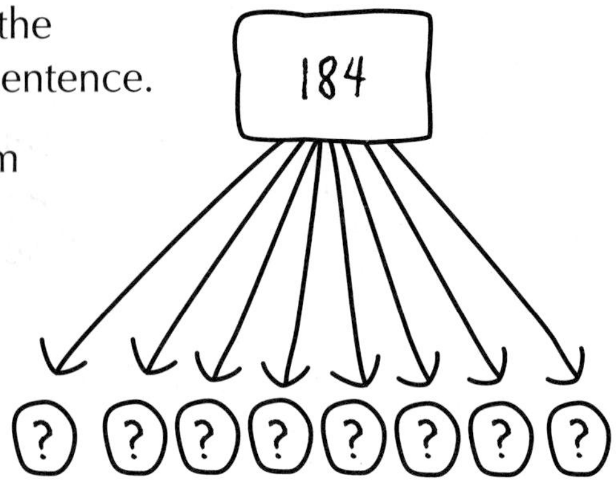

3. There are 8 soccer teams in a league. Each team has the same number of players. There are 184 players altogether. How many are on each team?

   n = the number on each team

   $184 \div 8 = n$

Writing a Number Sentence to Solve Problems For 4–9, use the information at the bottom of this page. Draw a picture to show the main idea for each problem. Use a letter to show what you are trying to find. Then write a number sentence and solve it. Write the answer in a complete sentence.

4. Tom bought an 8-pound bag of potatoes. How much did the potatoes cost per pound?
5. Samantha bought 7 pounds of onions. How much did she pay?
6. Corey bought an 8-pound bag of potatoes and 3 pounds of onions. How much did he spend altogether?
7. How much more is 8 pounds of onions than 8 pounds of potatoes?
8. Chet bought two 8-pound bags of potatoes and 10 pounds of onions. How much did he pay?

B Mixed Strategy Practice

Solve each problem.

9. Janna gave the clerk \$10 for an 8-pound bag of potatoes. How much change should she get?

STRATEGIES

- **Show What You Know**
  Draw a Picture
  Make an Organized List
  Make a Table
  Make a Graph
  Act It Out or Use Objects
- **Look for a Pattern**
- **Try, Check, and Revise**
- **Write a Number Sentence**
- **Use Logical Reasoning**
- **Solve a Simpler Problem**
- **Work Backward**

Choose a tool

PRACTICE

10. A small box of cereal costs $3. A larger box costs twice as much. You spent $15. How many of each did you buy? Explain how you got the answer.

11. At the jazz festival, Neil spent $12 for food, $8.50 for a CD, and $2 for a program. If he had $4 left, how much did he start with?

12. **Writing in Math** Solve the Soccer Colors problem. Write a paragraph to convince a classmate that your answer is correct.

Soccer Colors The soccer team wants to choose team colors from black, light blue, navy, red, green, and yellow. How many sets of two colors can they choose?

TEST TALK

Think It Through

Stuck? I won't give up I can:

- Reread the problem.
- Tell the problem in your own words.
- Tell what you know.
- Identify key facts and details.
- Show the main idea.
- Try a different strategy.
- Retrace your steps.

Mixed Review and Test Prep

Take It to the NET
Test Prep
www.scottforesman.com

Divide. Check your answer.

13. $8\overline{)56}$ **14.** $3\overline{)20}$ **15.** $4\overline{)69}$ **16.** $6\overline{)506}$ **17.** $7\overline{)\$7.63}$

18. How many days are there altogether in April, May, and June?

Use the pictograph at the right for 19–23.

Number of Calendars Sold in December

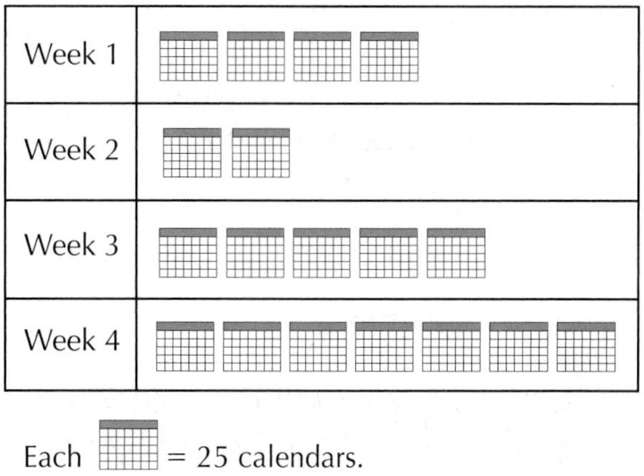

19. How many calendars does each symbol represent?

20. How many more calendars were sold in Week 1 than in Week 2?

21. In which week were the most calendars sold?

22. How many calendars were sold in Weeks 3 and 4 combined?

23. How many calendars were sold in December?

24. Ames School has 32 classrooms. Each classroom has 12 computers. How many computers are in all of the classrooms?

A. 44 computers

B. 96 computers

C. 374 computers

D. 384 computers

Review

Do You Know How?

Do You Understand?

Dividing Two-Digit Numbers (7-5)
Problem Solving: Interpreting Remainders (7-6)

Divide. Check your answer.

1. $3\overline{)81}$ **2.** $2\overline{)72}$ **3.** $4\overline{)60}$

4. $8\overline{)99}$ **5.** $6\overline{)95}$ **6.** $7\overline{)95}$

7. You are buying props for the school play. You need 50 sailor's hats for the chorus. The hats are sold in packages of 4. How many packages should you buy?

A Tell how to check your answers for Exercises 4–6.

B Explain how the remainder affected your answer in Exercise 7.

Dividing Three-Digit Numbers (7-7)
Zeros in the Quotient (7-8)

Divide. Check your answer.

8. $5\overline{)625}$ **9.** $7\overline{)505}$ **10.** $9\overline{)467}$

11. $2\overline{)821}$ **12.** $6\overline{)610}$ **13.** $3\overline{)625}$

14. $8\overline{)824}$ **15.** $4\overline{)540}$ **16.** $7\overline{)447}$

C Tell how you decided where to start dividing in Exercise 8.

D Explain why the quotient 41 R1 is not reasonable for Exercise 11.

Dividing Money Amounts (7-9)
Problem Solving: Write a Number Sentence (7-10)

Divide. Check your answer.

17. $5\overline{)\$7.25}$ **18.** $3\overline{)\$7.44}$ **19.** $7\overline{)\$6.65}$

20. $2\overline{)\$3.56}$ **21.** $4\overline{)\$5.36}$ **22.** $8\overline{)\$8.32}$

23. A package of 8 pencils cost $2.32. What is the cost of each pencil?

24. There are 6 groups of students at the museum. Each group has the same number of students. There are 108 students altogether. How many students are in each group?

E Tell how you place the dollar sign and decimal point when dividing money amounts.

F In Exercise 23, what number sentence could you write to solve the problem?

Diagnostic Checkpoint

TEST TALK

Think It Through
For multiple-choice items, check answers for **reasonableness.**

MULTIPLE CHOICE

1. 628 ÷ 4 (7-7)

A. 15 R2 **B.** 132 **C.** 154 R2 **D.** 157

2. \$7.42 ÷ 7 (7-8 and 7-9)

A. \$0.16 **B.** \$0.18 **C.** \$1.06 **D.** \$1.08

SHORT RESPONSE

Divide. Check your answer. (7-5, 7-7, 7-8, and 7-9)

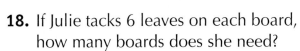

3. $4\overline{)48}$	**4.** $2\overline{)76}$	**5.** $9\overline{)828}$	**6.** $3\overline{)543}$	**7.** $8\overline{)919}$
8. $5\overline{)520}$	**9.** $7\overline{)843}$	**10.** $6\overline{)632}$	**11.** $3\overline{)\$5.76}$	**12.** $9\overline{)\$5.58}$
13. $4\overline{)112}$	**14.** $5\overline{)\$7.95}$	**15.** $6\overline{)495}$	**16.** $3\overline{)873}$	**17.** $4\overline{)812}$

Use the graph at the right for 18–21. For 18 and 19, draw a picture to show the main idea. Then write a number sentence. Write the answer in a complete sentence. (7-6 and 7-10)

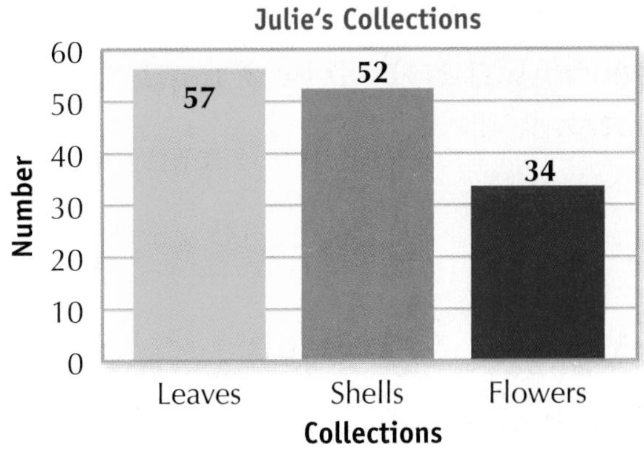

18. If Julie tacks 6 leaves on each board, how many boards does she need?

19. If Julie puts 4 shells on each board, how many boards does she need?

20. If Julie puts 5 flowers on each board, how many flowers will be on the board that is not filled?

21. Julie wants to put her leaves and flowers together in a scrapbook. She puts 3 leaves or 2 flowers on a page. How many pages does she need in all?

Writing in Math

22. Write a problem that could be solved by dividing a three-digit number by a one-digit number. (7-7)

23. You divide 857 ÷ 8 and get 17 R1. How can you tell that you have made a mistake? (7-8)

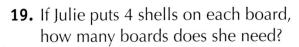

Key Idea
You can use rules to tell if a number is divisible by 2, 3, 5, 9, or 10.

Vocabulary
- divisible
- divisibility rules

Divisibility Rules

WARM UP

Tell if each number is even or odd.

1. 10
2. 16
3. 20
4. 15
5. 23
6. 30
7. 25
8. 40
9. 49

LEARN

How can you tell if one number is divisible by another?

A number is **divisible** by another number if when it is divided there is no remainder.

You can use the **divisibility rules** below to decide if one number is divisible by another.

TEST TALK

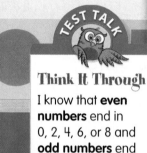

Think It Through
I know that **even numbers** end in 0, 2, 4, 6, or 8 and **odd numbers** end in 1, 3, 5, 7, or 9.

Divisibility Rules

A whole number is divisible by	Some numbers divisible by
2 if the ones digit is even.	**2** are 2, 10, 236.
3 if the sum of its digits is divisible by 3.	**3** are 3, 15, 231.
5 if the ones digit is 0 or 5.	**5** are 5, 20, 145.
9 if the sum of its digits is divisible by 9.	**9** are 9, 36, 189.
10 if the ones digit is 0.	**10** are 10, 80, 340.

Test 285 to see if it is divisible by 2, 3, 5, 9, or 10.

2: The ones digit, 5, is not even, so 285 is not divisible by 2.

3: The sum of the digits is $2 + 8 + 5 = 15$. Since 15 is divisible by 3, 285 is divisible by 3.

5: The ones digit is 5, so 285 is divisible by 5.

9: The sum of the digits, 15, is not divisible by 9, so 285 is not divisible by 9.

10: The ones digit is not 0, so 285 is not divisible by 10.

285 is divisible by 3 and 5.

285		
Divisible by	Yes	No
2		X
3	X	
5	X	
9		X
10		X

Talk About It

1. Explain why 285 is divisible by 3, but not by 9.

CHECK

For another example, see Set 7-11 on p. 427.

Test each number to see if it is divisible by 2, 3, 5, 9, or 10.

1. 54 **2.** 75 **3.** 186 **4.** 480 **5.** 675 **6.** 872

7. Number Sense Explain why all numbers that end in a zero are divisible by 10.

PRACTICE

For more practice, see Set 7-11 on p. 430.

A Skills and Understanding

Test each number to see if it is divisible by 2, 3, 5, 9, or 10.

8. 57 **9.** 68 **10.** 85 **11.** 165 **12.** 384 **13.** 966

14. 572 **15.** 450 **16.** 780 **17.** 822 **18.** 931 **19.** 896

20. Number Sense Are all numbers that are divisible by 10 also divisible by 2? How do you know? Are all numbers that are divisible by 2, also divisible by 10? How do you know?

B Reasoning and Problem Solving

21. Jen has 50 pencils. She wants to put them in bags so that each bag has the same number of pencils. What are three different ways Jen can do this?

22. Sam is packing 138 CDs. Can he place them into 3 boxes so that each box has the same number of CDs? How do you know, without dividing?

23. Writing in Math Explain how you can tell if 260 is divisible by 2, 3, 5, 9 or 10.

Mixed Review and Test Prep

Take It to the NET
Test Prep
www.scottforesman.com

Divide. Check your answer.

24. 3)$1.26 **25.** 8)$1.76 **26.** 2)$1.46 **27.** 5)$8.35 **28.** 9)$1.98

29. Nathan bought 4 packages with 10 baseball cards in each to add to the 180 cards he already had. How many cards does he have now?

A. 190 cards **B.** 200 cards **C.** 210 cards **D.** 220 cards

Key Idea
An average tells what is typical of the numbers in a set of data.

Vocabulary
- mean
- average

Finding Averages

LEARN

WARM UP

Find the median and mode of each set of data. Then find the sum.

1. 5, 7, 7, 6, 4, 3, 8
2. 25, 28, 32, 46, 28
3. 85, 86, 85, 89, 90, 92, 84

How can you find the mean?

Like the median and the mode, the **mean** tells what is typical of the numbers in a set of data. The mean is sometimes called the **average.**

To find an average, all the items are combined and divided equally. The diagram at the right shows that 5 is the average of 7, 4, and 4.

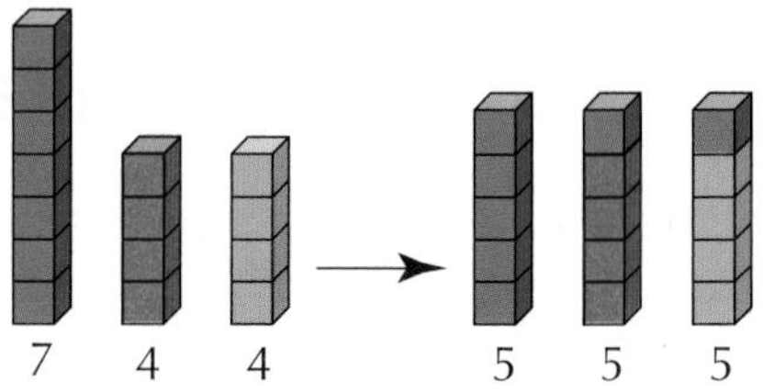

	Example A	Example B
	Marie's 3 test scores in math are 81, 87 and 93. Find her average score.	Marie's test scores in social studies are 84, 78, 92, 86, and 80. Find her average score.
STEP 1 Add the numbers in the set.	$81 + 87 + 93 = 261$	$84 + 78 + 92 + 86 + 80 = 420$
STEP 2 Divide the sum by the number of addends.	$261 \div 3 = 87$ ($3)\overline{261}$: -24, 21, -21, 0) Marie's average score in math is 87.	$420 \div 5 = 84$ ($5)\overline{420}$: -40, 20, -20, 0) Marie's average score in social studies is 84.

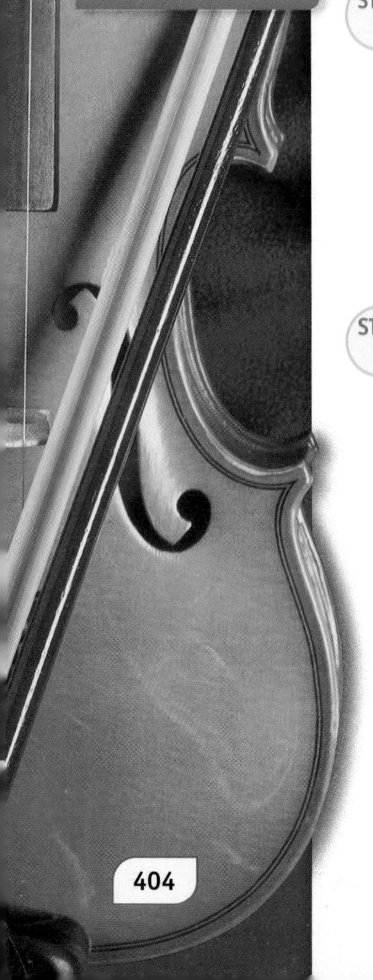

TEST TALK

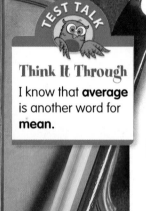

Think It Through
I know that **average** is another word for **mean.**

Talk About It

1. Why do you divide by 3 in Example A and 5 in Example B?

Take It to the NET
More Examples
www.scottforesman.com

CHECK ✓

For another example, see Set 7-12 on p. 427.

Find the average, or mean, of each set of data.

1. 3, 8, 8, 17

2. 15, 38, 25, 22, 40

3. 115, 192, 152

4. **Number Sense** Without computing, what is the average of 17, 17, 17 and 17?

PRACTICE

For more practice, see Set 7-12 on p. 431.

A Skills and Understanding

Find the average, or mean, of each set of data.

5. 25, 93, 35, 92, 40

6. 56, 84, 72, 68

7. 3, 5, 7, 4, 6, 5

8. 165, 248, 136

9. 46, 32, 40, 42

10. 2, 2, 8, 8, 1, 3

11. **Number Sense** Find a set of 3 different numbers that have an average of 45. Could there be another set with the same average?

B Reasoning and Problem Solving

Use the table at the right for 12–14. What was the average number of minutes that Jacob spent each day

Jacob's Schedule in Minutes

Day	*Homework*	*Violin*
Monday	*45*	*25*
Tuesday	*85*	*50*
Wednesday	*30*	*35*
Thursday	*65*	*15*
Friday	*20*	*75*

12. doing homework?

13. practicing the violin?

14. Does Jacob spend more time a day doing homework or practicing violin?

15. **Reasoning** The mean of 3 numbers is 8. Two of the numbers are 12 and 3. What is the third number?

16. **Writing in Math** Do you think the average of 96, 97, 98, and 20 is in the 90s? Explain.

Mixed Review and Test Prep

Take It to the NET
Test Prep
www.scottforesman.com

17. Test to see if 270 is divisible by 2, 3, 5, 9, or 10.

18. $7.44 ÷ 6

A. $1.06 **B.** $1.23 **C.** $1.24 **D.** $1.26

Key Idea
Basic facts and place-value patterns can help you find quotients like 2,100 ÷ 70.

Materials
- calculator

Think It Through
I can **look for a pattern** to find a rule.

63 ÷ 9 = 7 and
630 ÷ 90 = 7

630 ÷ 9 = 70 and
6,300 ÷ 90 = 70

Dividing by Multiples of 10

WARM UP

Divide.

1. 180 ÷ 3
2. 3,200 ÷ 8
3. 160 ÷ 2

LEARN

Activity

What's the rule?

a. Use a calculator to find each quotient. Look for a pattern in the number of zeros.

6 ÷ 3 = 2	12 ÷ 4 = 3	30 ÷ 5 = 6
60 ÷ 3 =	120 ÷ 4 =	300 ÷ 5 =
60 ÷ 30 =	120 ÷ 40 =	300 ÷ 50 =
600 ÷ 30 =	1,200 ÷ 40 =	3,000 ÷ 50 =

b. Find each quotient without a calculator. Then check your answers with a calculator.

48 ÷ 8	21 ÷ 7	20 ÷ 4
480 ÷ 8	210 ÷ 7	200 ÷ 4
480 ÷ 80	210 ÷ 70	200 ÷ 40
4,800 ÷ 80	2,100 ÷ 70	2,000 ÷ 40

c. Describe a rule that tells how to find the quotient.

How can you mentally divide by numbers like 20, 50, and 70?

Here's how Allison and Anthony found 1,800 ÷ 20.

1,800 ÷ 20 is the same as 180 ÷ 2, so 1,800 ÷ 20 is 90.
What times 20 equals 1,800? I know 90 × 20 = 1,800. So, 1,800 ÷ 20 is 90.

Talk About It

1. Which method do you prefer? Why?
2. Explain how you can find 5,400 ÷ 90 mentally.

CHECK

For another example, see Set 7-13 on p. 427.

Divide. Use mental math.

1. 800 ÷ 40 **2.** 1,800 ÷ 30 **3.** 6,300 ÷ 90 **4.** 2,000 ÷ 50

5. Number Sense Name another division problem with the same answer as 1,800 ÷ 30.

PRACTICE

For more practice, see Set 7-13 on p. 431.

A Skills and Understanding

Divide. Use mental math.

6. 90 ÷ 30 **7.** 560 ÷ 80 **8.** 4,200 ÷ 70 **9.** 300 ÷ 60

10. 120 ÷ 20 **11.** 360 ÷ 60 **12.** 270 ÷ 30 **13.** 400 ÷ 80

14. 2,800 ÷ 70 **15.** 7,200 ÷ 90 **16.** 3,200 ÷ 40 **17.** 1,000 ÷ 50

18. Number Sense Name another division problem with the same answer as 160 ÷ 2.

B Reasoning and Problem Solving

Use the data file at the right for 19–21. The Statue of Liberty National Monument is approximately 60 acres in size. About how many times as large is the national monument at:

19. Scott's Bluff? **20.** Navajo?

21. Jewel Cave National Monument in South Dakota is about 20 times as large as the Statue of Liberty National Monument. About how many acres is it?

Data File

National Monument	Approximate Number of Acres
Statue of Liberty (NY/NJ)	60
Navajo (AZ)	360
Scott's Bluff (NE)	3,000

22. Harry is reading a book with 3 chapters. The first chapter is 15 pages long. The second chapter is 17 pages long. There are 60 pages in the book. How many pages are in the third chapter?

23. Writing in Math Write a word problem using the data in the Data File.

Mixed Review and Test Prep

Take It to the NET
Test Prep
www.scottforesman.com

24. Find the mean of 2, 9, 5, 3, 4, 5, 7.

25. The number 357 is divisible by which of the following numbers?

A. 2 **B.** 3 **C.** 5 **D.** 9

Key Idea
You can divide with two-digit divisors like you did with one-digit divisors, but your estimate is even more important.

Vocabulary
- compatible numbers (p. 258)
- rounding (p. 20)

TEST TALK

Think It Through
I can use an estimate to **decide if the answer is reasonable.**

Dividing with Two-Digit Divisors

WARM UP

Divide. Use mental math.

1. $140 \div 20$
2. $350 \div 70$
3. $5,400 \div 60$
4. $4,000 \div 50$
5. $5,600 \div 80$
6. $1,200 \div 30$

LEARN

What is a reasonable estimate?

The 28 students in Mrs. York's fourth-grade class are sharing 202 marbles. How many marbles will each student get?

Example A

Estimate $202 \div 28$.

One Way

Tim used **compatible numbers** and division.

I adjusted 28 to 30 and 202 to 210.

$202 \div 28$
↓ ↓
$210 \div 30 = 7$

So, $202 \div 28$ is about 7.

Another Way

Sue used **rounding** and multiplication.

I rounded 28 to 30. Then, I thought: What number times 30 is about 202?

$6 \times 30 = 180$ and $7 \times 30 = 210$

So, $202 \div 28$ is about 6 or 7.

Example B

Find $202 \div 28$.

Use the estimate of 7.

$$\begin{array}{r} 7\text{ R}6 \\ 28\overline{)202} \\ -\,196 \\ \hline 6 \end{array}$$

Multiply. $7 \times 28 = 196$
Compare. $196 < 202$
Subtract. $202 - 196 = 6$
Compare. $6 < 28$

Check Multiply the divisor by the quotient and add the remainder.

$$\begin{array}{r} {\scriptstyle 5} \\ 28 \\ \times\quad 7 \\ \hline 196 \end{array} \qquad \begin{array}{r} {\scriptstyle 1\,1} \\ 196 \\ +\quad 6 \\ \hline 202 \end{array}$$

The answer checks. 202 is the dividend.

Each student will get 7 marbles and there will be 6 marbles left over.

Talk About It

1. In Example A, which compatible numbers did Tim use?

Take It to the NET
More Examples
www.scottforesman.com

How can you tell if you need to adjust your estimate?

I used 240 ÷ 40 = 6 to estimate and here's what I got.
My remainder is too big. I could make another group of 37, so the quotient should be bigger. I'll try 7.
Nathan
6
37)262
- 222
40 40 > 37
7
37)262
- 259
3 3 < 37

168 > 159, so 4 must be too large. I'll try 3.
I used 160 ÷ 40 = 4 to estimate and here's what I got.
Emily
4
42)159
- 168 168 > 159
3
42)159
- 126 33 < 42
33

Talk About It

2. How could Nathan tell that his estimate was too small?

3. How could Emily tell that her estimate was too large?

CHECK For another example, see Set 7-14 on p. 427.

Estimate each quotient. Then divide.

1. 376 ÷ 53 **2.** 135 ÷ 18 **3.** 190 ÷ 62 **4.** 241 ÷ 33

5. Number Sense How could you tell that 285 ÷ 18 is greater than 10 without dividing? Hint: Think multiplication.

PRACTICE For more practice, see Set 7-14 on p. 431.

A Skills and Understanding

Estimate each quotient. Then divide.

6. 135 ÷ 32 **7.** 244 ÷ 34 **8.** 512 ÷ 56 **9.** 281 ÷ 91

10. $25\overline{)175}$ **11.** $74\overline{)153}$ **12.** $87\overline{)714}$ **13.** $43\overline{)241}$

14. $12\overline{)101}$ **15.** $65\overline{)520}$ **16.** $99\overline{)308}$ **17.** $22\overline{)197}$

18. Number Sense If you divide 344 by 43 and get an answer of 80, how can you tell you made a mistake?

B Reasoning and Problem Solving

Math and Social Studies

In Turkey, many people travel in minibuses, called *dolmus* (dol moosh). The name comes from the Turkish word for stuffed, because the dolmus leave only when they are full. The table shows the number of minibuses and the number of people on several popular city routes.

Minibus Routes

Route	Number of Minibuses	Number of Riders
A	23	207
B	35	245
C	18	144
D	15	165

Use the table above right for 19–22. Find the average number of people who rode each minibus on

19. Route A. **20.** Route B.

21. Route C. **22.** Route D.

PRACTICE

Writing in Math Decide whether or not each estimate needs to be adjusted. Explain how you know.

23. $\begin{array}{r} 5 \\ 56\overline{)275} \end{array}$ **24.** $\begin{array}{r} 7 \\ 45\overline{)362} \end{array}$ **25.** $\begin{array}{r} 9 \\ 38\overline{)345} \end{array}$ **26.** $\begin{array}{r} 3 \\ 68\overline{)198} \end{array}$

C Extensions

Find each two-digit quotient.

27. $15\overline{)165}$ **28.** $36\overline{)576}$ **29.** $19\overline{)456}$ **30.** $23\overline{)805}$

Mixed Review and Test Prep

Take It to the NET
Test Prep
www.scottforesman.com

Test each number to see if it is divisible by 2, 3, 5, 9, or 10.

31. 80 **32.** 72 **33.** 147 **34.** 328 **35.** 486 **36.** 726

37. 3,600 ÷ 40

A. 6 **B.** 9 **C.** 60 **D.** 90

Technology

Using a Calculator to Find Averages

You can use a calculator to find the average of a data set. Use the following key sequence to find the average of 84, 73, 92, 67, and 74:

Press: (84 + 73 + 92 + 67 + 74) ÷ 5 ENTER =

Display: 78

Use your calculator to find the average of each data set listed below.

1. 77, 56, 92, 66, 47, 64

2. 124, 321, 456, 771

3. 87, 67, 45, 67, 98, 55, 46, 63

4. 167, 94, 208, 37, 116, 254

5. 796, 812, 806, 764, 708, 752

6. 1,030, 2,475, 2,125, 1,925, 2,005

Problem-Solving Applications

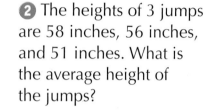

Equestrian Competitions In the Olympics there are 6 major equestrian events. They are team and individual jumping, dressage, and three-day event. The three-day event was recognized as an Olympic event in 1912. This competition tests a horse and rider's endurance, speed and cooperation.

Trivia Equestrian competitions are one of the few Olympic sports in which men and women compete against each other.

1. In the 2000 Olympics, there were 74 riders who qualified for the jumping event but 29 of them were either eliminated or withdrew. How many riders completed the event?

2. The heights of 3 jumps are 58 inches, 56 inches, and 51 inches. What is the average height of the jumps?

3. Bales of hay are typically divided into 10 pieces called flakes. How many bales are equal to 2,500 flakes?

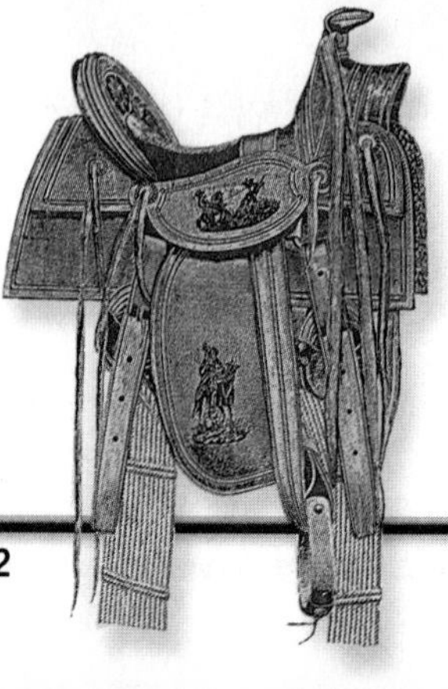

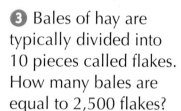

4. **Writing in Math** There are 10 horses in one barn. They are fed twice a day. At each meal, 5 horses eat 6 pounds of grain, 3 horses eat 4 pounds of grain, and 2 horses eat 3 pounds of grain. How much grain is needed to feed the horses each day? Use complete sentences to explain how you found your answer.

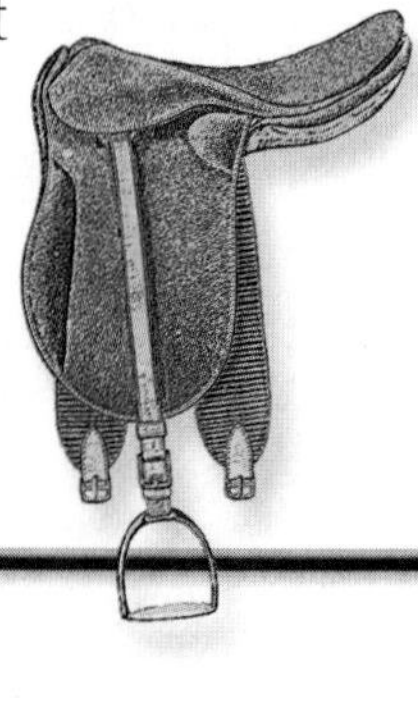

Dorling Kindersley

Key Facts
Jumping Scores

- Rider with the lowest score wins.
- Knocking off a rail scores 4 points.
- The first time the horse refuses to make a jump, 3 points are scored.
- A second refusal scores another 6 points.
- Three refusals results in elimination.

Using Key Facts

5 A rider received 12 points by knocking rails down. How many rails did she knock down?

6 In ancient races, chariots may have traveled more than 9,200 meters. Write the word name for this number.

7 Horses are measured to the top of their shoulders in a unit of length called a hand. A hand is 4 inches. The tallest horse on record was over 84 inches tall. How many hands tall was the tallest horse?

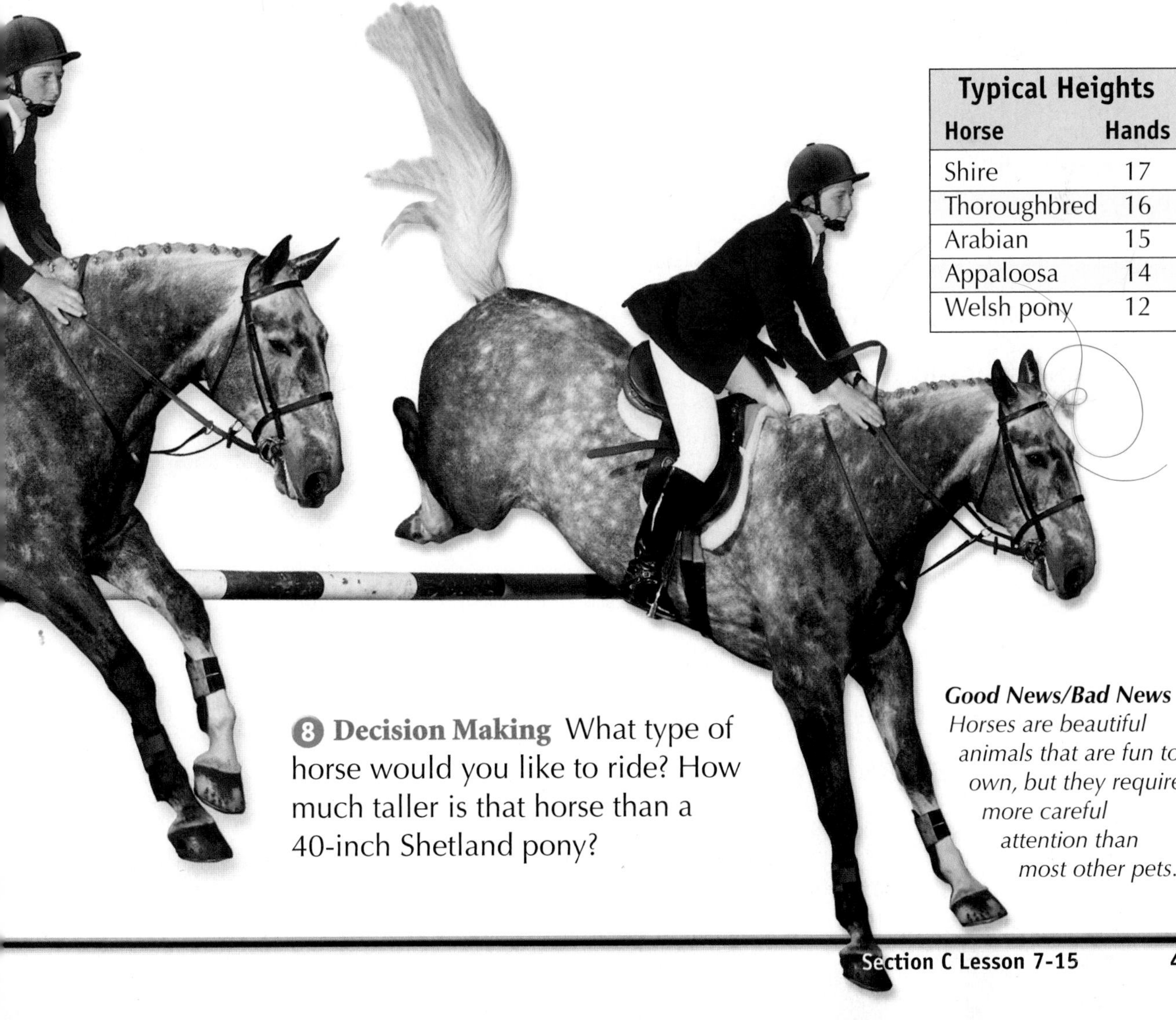

Typical Heights	
Horse	**Hands**
Shire	17
Thoroughbred	16
Arabian	15
Appaloosa	14
Welsh pony	12

8 **Decision Making** What type of horse would you like to ride? How much taller is that horse than a 40-inch Shetland pony?

Good News/Bad News
Horses are beautiful animals that are fun to own, but they require more careful attention than most other pets.

Review

Do You Know How?

Do You Understand?

Divisibility Rules (7-11)

Test each number to see if it is divisible by 2, 3, 5, 9, or 10.

1. 39 **2.** 95 **3.** 420

4. 162 **5.** 746 **6.** 855

A Tell how you know 420 is divisible by 3 but not by 9.

B Is 7 divisible by 7? Explain how you know.

Finding Averages (7-12)

Find the average, or mean, of each set of data.

7. 2, 1, 1, 0

8. 14, 17, 35, 28, 41

9. Group A heights in inches: 46, 45, 42, 51

10. Group B heights in inches: 49, 52, 40

C Tell how you decided which number to divide by to find the average in Exercise 8.

D Name a set of data with four different numbers that has an average of 10.

Dividing by Multiples of 10 (7-13)

Divide. Use mental math.

11. 800 ÷ 20 **12.** 720 ÷ 80

13. 4,900 ÷ 70 **14.** 4,000 ÷ 50

15. 4,800 ÷ 60 **16.** 8,100 ÷ 90

E Tell how you used mental math to find the quotient in Exercise 14.

F Name another division problem with the same quotient as 4,900 ÷ 70.

Dividing with Two-Digit Divisors (7-14)

Estimate each quotient. Then divide.

17. 116 ÷ 19 **18.** 275 ÷ 31

19. 310 ÷ 63 **20.** 144 ÷ 47

21. 165 ÷ 22 **22.** 208 ÷ 54

G Tell what method you used to estimate Exercise 22.

H Explain how you could tell an estimated quotient of 4 is too small for Exercise 17.

Diagnostic Checkpoint

TEST TALK

Think It Through
For multiple-choice items, first **eliminate any unreasonable answers.**

MULTIPLE CHOICE

1. Which of the following numbers is divisible by 3? (7-11)

A. 326 **B.** 143 **C.** 472 **D.** 582

2. What is a reasonable estimate for 389 ÷ 52? (7-14)

A. 4 **B.** 7 **C.** 40 **D.** 70

3. Which has the same quotient as 2,700 ÷ 90? (7-13)

A. 27 ÷ 9 **B.** 270 ÷ 9 **C.** 270 ÷ 90 **D.** 2,700 ÷ 9

FREE RESPONSE

Divide. Use mental math. (7-13)

4. 300 ÷ 30 **5.** 240 ÷ 80 **6.** 2,800 ÷ 40 **7.** 3,000 ÷ 60

Estimate each quotient. Then divide. (7-14)

8. 154 ÷ 22 **9.** 238 ÷ 78 **10.** 248 ÷ 51 **11.** 502 ÷ 86

Use the graph at the right for 12–17.

Basketballs were shipped from 3 different factories. Tell which factory or factories could ship all their basketballs in boxes containing (7-11)

Number of Basketballs Shipped

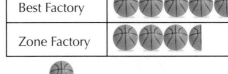

Dunk Factory		276
Best Factory		315
Zone Factory		180

Each (basketball) = 50 basketballs.

12. 2 balls. **13.** 3 balls.

14. 5 balls. **15.** 9 balls.

16. Find the average number of basketballs made at the factories. (7-12)

Writing in Math

17. Dunk Factory shipped all their basketballs in 4 days and Best Factory shipped all their basketballs in 5 days. Which factory averaged shipping more basketballs a day? Explain. (7-12, 7-15)

18. Explain how to estimate 492 ÷ 83. (7-14)

CHAPTER 7
Test Talk

Test-Taking Strategies

- Understand the question.
- Get information for the answer.
- Plan how to find the answer.
- Make smart choices.
- Use writing in math.
- Improve written answers.

Plan How to Find the Answer

After you understand a test question and get needed information, you need to plan how to find the answer. Think about problem-solving skills and strategies and computation methods.

1. The notebook shows Jack's earnings during the summer.

Date
Pay
June 15 $ 9.75
June 29 $ 8.50
July 6 $12.50
July 15 $ 7.75
July 29 $ 8.80
Aug. 10 $10.50
$ 7.20
Total: $65.00

If Jack worked a total of 20 hours, which of the following expressions **best** represents the amount he earned each hour?

A. $n < \$3$

B. $n = \$65$

C. $n > \$3$

D. $n = \$3$

Understand the question.

- Look for important words. Finish the statement "I need to find ..."

I need to find which expression best represents the amount Jack earned each hour.

Get information for the answer.

The picture shows that Jack earned $65. The text says he worked for 20 hours.

Plan how to find the answer.

- Think about problem-solving skills and strategies.

Since I need to separate $65 into 20 equal groups I should divide. I do not need an exact answer, so I can estimate the quotient. I will use compatible numbers to estimate. Then I will choose the expression that best represents my estimate.

- Choose computation methods.

I only need an estimate, so I will use mental math.

2. Which operations can be used in the boxes below to get the least possible result?

1 ▢ 7 ▢ 1

A. + and +

B. × and ×

C. × and +

D. × and −

Think It Through

*I need to find which operations can be used in the boxes in the expression to get the **least** number. I can **work backward** from the given pairs of operations. I will substitute each pair of operations in the expression and see which gives the least result. I can use mental math to evaluate each expression. But since there are several results to keep track of, I'll use paper and pencil instead.*

Now it's your turn.

For each problem, describe a plan for finding the answer.

3. The state of Florida has a total of 67 counties. Of those, 7 counties are named after United States Presidents.

Write an equation that could be used to calculate the number of Florida counties that are NOT named after United States Presidents.

4. Packs of 6 cans of dog food are on sale this week at Pet City.

What operation would you use to find the cost of one can of dog food?

A. addition

B. division

C. multiplication

D. subtraction

Chapter 7

Key Vocabulary and Concept Review

"Over" and "under" are opposites.

Remember, an ***overestimate*** *is greater than the answer, while an* ***underestimate*** *is less. (p. 369)*

Self Check

Use mental math to divide and to estimate quotients. (Lessons 7-1, 7-2, 7-13)

Find 5,600 ÷ 70.

Think of the basic fact: 56 ÷ 7 = 8.
Think of the pattern with zeros: 5,600 ÷ 70 is the same as 560 ÷ 7.

5,600 ÷ 70 = 80

Estimate 412 ÷ 6.

Use compatible numbers: Adjust 412 to 420 because 42 ÷ 6 = 7.

420 ÷ 6 = 70

So, 412 ÷ 6 is about 70.

Since 412 was changed to a greater number, 70 is an **overestimate.**

Estimate 548 ÷ 90.

Use compatible numbers: Adjust 548 to 540 because 54 ÷ 9 = 6.

540 ÷ 90 = 6

So, 548 ÷ 90 is about 6.

Since 548 was changed to a lesser number, 6 is an **underestimate.**

1. Find 160 ÷ 8 and 4,500 ÷ 50.

2. Estimate 224 ÷ 3 and 261 ÷ 50.

When I'm done eating, I save the remainder of the food for leftovers.

When I'm done dividing, the part that is left over is called the ***remainder****. (p. 372)*

Self Check

Follow steps in order when you divide. (Lessons 7-3, 7-4, 7-5, 7-7, 7-8, 7-9, 7-14)

Estimate the quotient to decide what place value to divide first.
Divide, multiply, subtract, compare, and bring down.
If there is a remainder, write it in the quotient.

23 R3	Divide the tens.	106 R2	7 R4	$1.64	Divide money
4)95	Multiply. 2 × 4	7)744	32)228	5)$8.20	like whole
− 8	Subtract. 9 − 8	− 7	− 224	− 5	numbers.
15	Compare. 1 < 4	04	4	32	Then write $
− 12	Bring down the	− 0		− 30	and . in the
3	ones and divide.	44		20	quotient.
	Multiply. 3 × 4	− 42		− 20	
	Subtract. 15 − 12	2		0	
	Compare. 3 < 4				

3. Find 55 ÷ 3, 814 ÷ 4, 119 ÷ 23, and $2.58 ÷ 6.

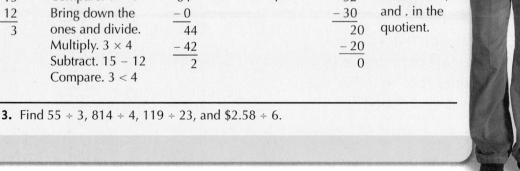

Divisible comes from the word "divide."

A number is ***divisible*** *by another number if there is no remainder after dividing. (p. 402)*

Self Check

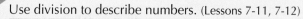

Use division to describe numbers. (Lessons 7-11, 7-12)

Test 78, using the **divisibility rules,** to see if it is **divisible** by 2, 3, 5, 9, or 10.

Divisible by 2?	Yes, 8 is an even number.
Divisible by 3?	Yes, 7 + 8 = 15, and 15 is divisible by 3.
Divisible by 5?	No, the ones digit is not 0 or 5.
Divisible by 9?	No, 7 + 8 = 15, and 15 is not divisible by 9.
Divisible by 10?	No, the ones digit is not 0.

78 is divisible by 2 and 3.

Find the **average,** or **mean,** of this set of data.
8, 6, 5, 4, 7

Add the numbers in the set:
8 + 6 + 5 + 4 + 7 = 30

Divide the sum by the number of addends:
30 ÷ 5 = 6

The average is 6.

4. Test 60 to see if it is divisible by 2, 3, 5, 9, or 10.

5. Find the average of the data set: 12, 16, 15, 18, 12, 17.

I'm an average, or typical, 4th-grader.

The ***average,*** *or* ***mean,*** *of a set of data gives you an idea of what's typical. (p. 404)*

Self Check

Interpret remainders or write number sentences to solve problems. (Lessons 7-6, 7-10)

The real-world situation tells you how to interpret the remainder.

Paul has 50 beads. He will use 8 beads for each necklace. How many necklaces can he make? How many beads will be left over?

50 ÷ 8 = 6 R2

Paul can make 6 necklaces. He will have 2 beads left over.

To write a number sentence, decide which operation goes with the main idea. Use a letter to show what you are trying to find.

Alice bought 3 sticker books for $5.25. How much did she pay for each book?

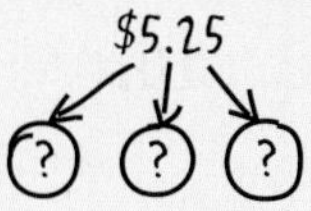

n is the cost for each book.

$5.25 ÷ 3 = *n*
$5.25 ÷ 3 = $1.75

Alice paid $1.75 for each book.

6. If each T-shirt costs $9, how many T-shirts can you buy with $40? How much money will you have left over?

Answers: **1.** 20; 90 **2.** 70; 5 **3.** 18 R1; 203 R2; 5 R4; $0.43
4. Divisible by 2, 3, 5, and 10 **5.** 15 **6.** 4 T-shirts, $4 left over

Chapter Test

MULTIPLE CHOICE

Choose the correct letter for each answer.

1. Use mental math to divide 4,800 ÷ 60.

A. 8 **C.** 800

B. 80 **D.** 8,000

2. Which is the most reasonable estimate for 281 ÷ 9?

A. 3 **C.** 30

B. 4 **D.** 40

3. What division problem do these counters model?

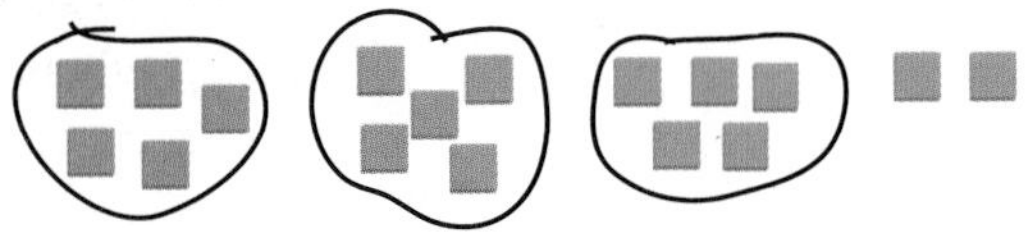

A. 17 ÷ 3 = 5 R2

B. 17 ÷ 5 = 3 R1

C. 15 ÷ 5 = 3

D. 15 ÷ 3 = 3

4. Which of the following is the correct answer and explanation for $4\overline{)58}$?

A. 14 R2, because 14 × 4 = 56 and 56 + 2 = 58

B. 13 R6, because 13 × 4 = 52 and 52 + 6 = 58

C. 12, because 12 × 4 = 58

D. 12, because 5 ÷ 4 = 1 and 8 ÷ 4 = 2

5. Find $8.70 ÷ 5.

A. $0.174 **C.** $1.74

B. $1.70 **D.** $17.40

6. Tammy baked 47 cookies. Each bag will hold 9 cookies. Which of the following is NOT true?

A. Nine cookies will be in every bag.

B. Two cookies will be in the bag not filled.

C. Five bags will be filled.

D. Six bags are needed to hold all the cookies.

7. Find 810 ÷ 6.

A. 13 R3 **C.** 130 R5

B. 13 R30 **D.** 135

8. Which number is divisible by 3?

A. 92 **C.** 123

B. 107 **D.** 241

9. Find the average, or mean, of this data set: 10, 12, 16, 14, 18

A. 8 **B.** 14 **C.** 15 **D.** 70

10. Which number sentence is FALSE?

A. 20 ÷ 4 = 5

B. 200 ÷ 40 = 5

C. 2,000 ÷ 4 = 50

D. 2,000 ÷ 40 = 50

TEST TALK

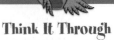

Think It Through

- I need to **read each problem carefully.**
- I should **watch for words like TRUE, FALSE, or NOT.**

11. There were 192 band members marching in the parade. There were 8 band members in each row. Which number sentence would you use to find how many rows of band members were marching in the parade?

A. $192 + 8 = n$ **C.** $192 \times 8 = n$

B. $192 - 8 = n$ **D.** $192 \div 8 = n$

12. Which number sentence checks the quotient of $60 \div 4 = 15$?

A. $60 - 15 = 4$

B. $15 \times 4 = 60$

C. $15 \div 4 = 60$

D. $60 + 15 + 4 = 79$

FREE RESPONSE

Estimate each quotient.

13. $652 \div 9$ **14.** $57 \div 6$

Find each quotient using mental math.

15. $600 \div 3$ **16.** $4{,}900 \div 70$

17. $560 \div 80$ **18.** $3{,}500 \div 5$

Find each quotient.

19. $4\overline{)73}$ **20.** $6\overline{)648}$

21. $7\overline{)\$6.02}$ **22.** $117 \div 23$

23. There are 15 students going on a field trip. Ms. Hubert wants to divide the students into equal groups of 2, 3, or 5. Which size groups can she make without any remaining students?

24. On the last three math quizzes, Sharon scored 77, 83, and 95. What was Sharon's average score?

25. Mr. Cohen bought 7 rosemary plants at the market for \$8.05. How much did each rosemary plant cost? Draw a picture to show the main idea. Then write a number sentence and solve.

A seamstress bought 85 yards of cloth. She needs 4 yards of cloth to make one dress.

26. How many dresses can she make?

27. How much material will she have left over?

TEST TALK

Think It Through

- I need to **choose an operation** to go with the main idea of the problem.
- I need to **check that I answered the question.**

Writing in Math

28. Explain how you know that an estimated quotient of 8 is too large for $317 \div 42$.

29. Each case holds 8 compact discs. If you have 43 compact discs, how many cases will you need to hold all your compact discs? Explain how you found your answer.

30. Explain how you can tell if 156 is divisible by 3 or 5.

Cumulative Review and Test Prep

Number and Operation

MULTIPLE CHOICE

1. Cat food is on sale for $3.54 for 6 cans. What is the cost of one can?

   A. $0.54 **C.** $5.40

   B. $0.59 **D.** $5.90

2. Which is the most reasonable estimate for 258 × 42?

   A. 100 **C.** 10,000

   B. 1,000 **D.** 100,000

3. On Saturday, 3,050 people attended the theater. On Sunday, 2,641 people attended the theater. How many more people attended the theater on Saturday than on Sunday?

   A. 409 **B.** 1,419

   C. 1,409 **D.** 1,611

FREE RESPONSE

4. Write the following numbers in order from least to greatest.

   2,975 2,795 2,579 2,597

5. Test 72 to see if it is divisible by 2, 3, 5, 9, or 10.

Writing in Math

6. Explain how to divide $4.83 by 3.

TEST TALK

Think It Through
- I should **describe the steps in order.**
- My writing should **be complete.**

Geometry and Measurement

MULTIPLE CHOICE

7. What is the elapsed time if both of the clocks below show an A.M. time?

Start End

   A. 2 hours and 35 minutes

   B. 2 hours and 15 minutes

   C. 1 hour and 45 minutes

   D. 1 hour and 15 minutes

8. Which is a solid figure?

   A. pentagon **C.** cube

   B. circle **D.** rectangle

FREE RESPONSE

9. Mr. Lewis drove 325 miles to Capital City. He drove at an average speed of 65 miles per hour. How long did it take Mr. Lewis to drive to Capital City?

10. How is a square different from a triangle?

Writing in Math

11. Phil ran around the perimeter of the park two times. How far did Phil run in all? Explain your answer.

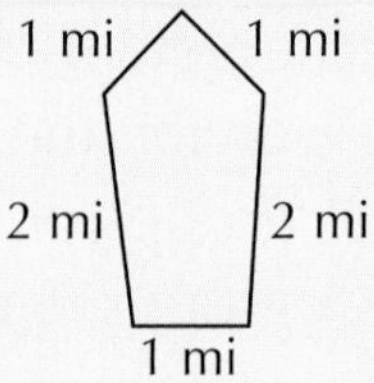

Data Analysis and Probability

MULTIPLE CHOICE

12. What is the mean of the data shown on this line plot?

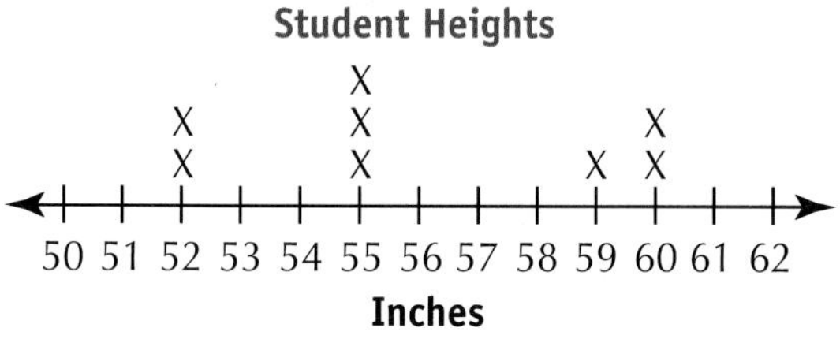

A. 8 in. **C.** 55 in.

B. 52 in. **D.** 56 in.

FREE RESPONSE

13. If you spin the spinner once, is it more likely to land on a number divisible by 2 or a number divisible by 3?

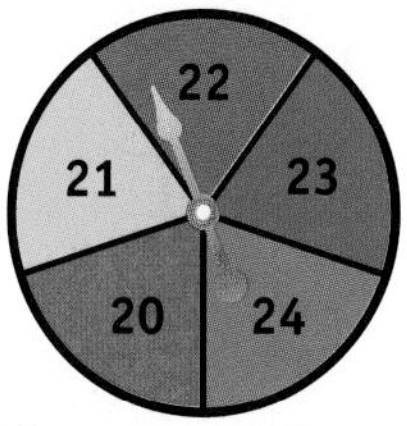

Use the line graph for Items 14–16.

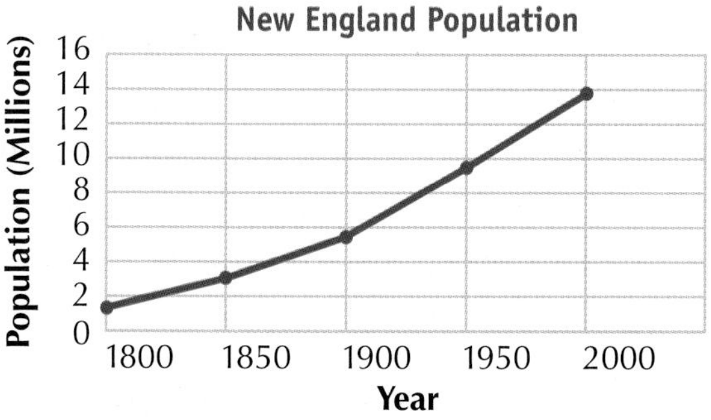

14. What is the interval on the vertical scale in the graph?

15. About how many people lived in New England in 1850?

Writing in Math

16. Describe the trend in the data shown in the line graph.

Algebra

MULTIPLE CHOICE

17. Which is the next number in the pattern?

3, 9, 27, 81, ■

A. 162 **B.** 213 **C.** 243 **D.** 283

18. Which equation does NOT have a solution of $n = 7$?

A. $63 \div n = 9$ **C.** $n + 24 = 31$

B. $8 \times n = 15$ **D.** $14 - n = 7$

19. Evaluate $84 \div m$ for $m = 4$.

A. 12 **B.** 20 **C.** 21 **D.** 22

FREE RESPONSE

20. Complete the table and describe the rule you used.

In	25	35	45	55
Out	5	7	9	

21. Calvin bought 7 postcards for \$2.45. How much did he pay for each postcard? Write a number sentence. Then solve.

Writing in Math

22. Explain how to use patterns to find $4{,}000 \div 8$ and $4{,}000 \div 80$.

Think It Through
I can use basic facts to **look for a pattern** and find a rule.

Reteaching

Set 7-1 (pages 366–367)

Divide 5,600 ÷ 7.

Use mental math.

56 ÷ 7 = 8

56 hundreds ÷ 7 = 8 hundreds, or 800

5,600 ÷ 7 = 800

Remember zeros in the basic fact are NOT part of the pattern.

Divide. Use mental math.

1. 150 ÷ 5
2. 300 ÷ 6
3. 2,700 ÷ 3
4. 7,200 ÷ 9

Set 7-2 (pages 368–371)

Estimate 768 ÷ 9.

One Way: Compatible Numbers

720 ÷ 9 = 80

Another Way: Use Multiplication

9 times what number is about 768?

9 × 90 = 810

Remember basic facts can help you estimate.

Estimate each quotient.

1. 38 ÷ 2
2. 362 ÷ 5
3. $6\overline{)381}$
4. $4\overline{)335}$
5. $3\overline{)192}$
6. $8\overline{)301}$

Set 7-3 (pages 372–373)

Divide 11 ÷ 2.

You may use counters to help.

$$\begin{array}{r} 5\text{ R}1 \\ 2\overline{)11} \\ -10 \\ \hline 1 \end{array}$$

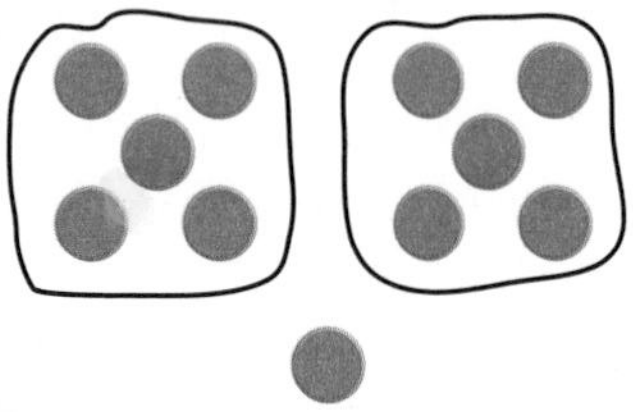

Remember the remainder must be less than the divisor.

Divide. You may use counters or pictures to help.

1. $4\overline{)11}$
2. $7\overline{)17}$
3. $5\overline{)49}$
4. $8\overline{)42}$
5. $9\overline{)37}$
6. $3\overline{)22}$

Set 7-4 (pages 374–377)

Tell how many books are in each stack if 52 books are divided equally among 4 stacks.

Use place-value blocks.

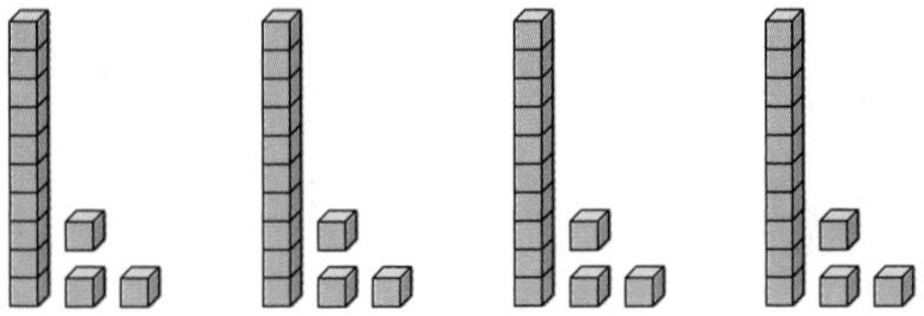

Each stack has 13 books.

Remember to divide the tens and then divide the ones.

Divide. You may use place-value blocks or pictures to help.

1. 44 books
4 stacks

2. 30 books
2 stacks

3. 45 books
3 stacks

4. 65 books
5 stacks

Set 7-5 (pages 380–383)

Divide 86 ÷ 6.

Check your answer.

$$\begin{array}{r} 1 \\ 6\overline{)86} \\ -6 \\ \hline 2 \end{array}$$

Divide.
Multiply.
Subtract.

$$\begin{array}{r} 14 \text{ R2} \\ 6\overline{)86} \\ -6\downarrow \\ \hline 26 \\ -24 \\ \hline 2 \end{array}$$

Bring down the 6.
Divide.
Multiply.
Subtract.

Check:

$$\begin{array}{r} 14 \\ \times\ 6 \\ \hline 84 \end{array} \qquad \begin{array}{r} 84 \\ +\ 2 \\ \hline 86 \end{array}$$

The answer checks.

Remember that an estimate can tell you where to start dividing and if your answer is reasonable.

Divide. Check your answer.

1. $2\overline{)54}$
2. $9\overline{)96}$
3. $7\overline{)80}$
4. $5\overline{)79}$
5. $3\overline{)82}$
6. $4\overline{)7}$
7. $8\overline{)90}$
8. $4\overline{)67}$
9. $5\overline{)83}$
10. $7\overline{)98}$
11. $6\overline{)78}$
12. $5\overline{)66}$

Set 7-6 (pages 384–385)

You need 76 balloons to decorate for the school party. The balloons come in packages of 6. How many packages should you buy?

Find 76 ÷ 6.

76 ÷ 6 = 12 R4

You need to buy 13 packages to have enough balloons.

Remember that the real-world situation tells you how to interpret the remainder.

You have 95 flowers. You plan to use 3 flowers to decorate each table.

1. How many tables can you decorate?
2. If you wear the extra flowers, how many flowers will you wear?

Set 7-7 (pages 386–389)

Find 832 ÷ 6.

Estimate: 832 is more than 600, so the quotient has three digits. Start by dividing the hundreds.

$$\begin{array}{r} 138 \text{ R4} \\ 6\overline{)832} \\ -6 \\ \hline 23 \\ -18 \\ \hline 52 \\ -48 \\ \hline 4 \end{array}$$

Remember that an estimate can tell you where to start dividing.

Divide. Check your answer.

1. $9\overline{)576}$
2. $5\overline{)615}$
3. $4\overline{)341}$
4. $8\overline{)943}$
5. $6\overline{)925}$
6. $2\overline{)357}$
7. $3\overline{)586}$
8. $5\overline{)193}$
9. $7\overline{)825}$
10. $4\overline{)528}$

Chapter 7
Reteaching

Set 7-8 (pages 390–391)

Find 514 ÷ 5.

Estimate: 514 is more than 500 and 500 ÷ 5 = 100, so the quotient has three digits. Start by dividing the hundreds.

$$\begin{array}{r} 102\text{ R}4 \\ 5\overline{)514} \\ -\,5 \\ \hline 01 \\ -\,0 \\ \hline 14 \\ -\,10 \\ \hline 4 \end{array}$$

Check:

$$\begin{array}{r} \overset{1}{1}02 \\ \times\quad 5 \\ \hline 510 \end{array} \qquad \begin{array}{r} 510 \\ +\quad 4 \\ \hline 514 \end{array}$$

The answer checks.

Remember to write zeros in the quotient when needed.

Divide. Check your answer.

1. $8\overline{)825}$ **2.** $2\overline{)612}$

3. $3\overline{)619}$ **4.** $6\overline{)723}$

5. $7\overline{)738}$ **6.** $9\overline{)966}$

7. $4\overline{)827}$ **8.** $3\overline{)540}$

9. $8\overline{)851}$ **10.** $2\overline{)417}$

11. $6\overline{)633}$ **12.** $4\overline{)424}$

Set 7-9 (pages 392–393)

Find \$4.71 ÷ 3.

Estimate: Since \$4.71 is more than \$3, the quotient must be more than \$1.

$$\begin{array}{r} \$1.57 \\ 3\overline{)\$4.71} \\ -\,3 \\ \hline 17 \\ -\,15 \\ \hline 21 \\ -\,21 \\ \hline 0 \end{array}$$

Check:

$$\begin{array}{r} \$1.\overset{2}{5}7 \\ \times\quad 3 \\ \hline \$4.71 \end{array}$$

The answer checks.

Remember, when dividing money amounts, to bring the decimal point straight up into the quotient.

Divide. Check your answer.

1. $4\overline{)\$8.56}$ **2.** $6\overline{)\$5.88}$

3. $7\overline{)\$5.25}$ **4.** $2\overline{)\$7.32}$

5. $5\overline{)\$8.85}$ **6.** $9\overline{)\$4.32}$

7. $8\overline{)\$3.68}$ **8.** $3\overline{)\$6.09}$

9. $6\overline{)\$7.26}$ **10.** $4\overline{)\$5.96}$

Set 7-10 (pages 396–399)

Write a number sentence to solve the problem.

There are 224 players in a softball league. Each team has the same number of players. There are 16 teams. How many are on each team?

n = the number on each team

$224 \div 16 = n$

$n = 14$

Remember to use a letter to show what you are trying to find.

Write a number sentence to solve each problem. Tell what the variable represents.

1. Seven postcards cost \$9.45. How much does each postcard cost?

2. Tina paid \$0.35 for each picture to have 8 pictures developed. How much did she spend in all?

Set 7-11 (pages 402–403)

Test 378 to see if it is divisible by 2, 3, 5, 9, or 10.

The ones digit, 8, is even, so 378 is divisible by 2. The sum of the digits is 3 + 7 + 8 = 18. Since 18 is divisible by 3, 378 is divisible by 3. 18 is divisible by 9, so 378 is divisible by 9. The ones digit is not 0 or 5, so 378 is not divisible by 5 or 10.

378 is divisible by 2, 3, and 9.

Remember that even numbers end in 0, 2, 4, 6, or 8.

Test each number to see if it is divisible by 2, 3, 5, 9, or 10.

1. 48	**2.** 79	**3.** 153
4. 214	**5.** 435	**6.** 682
7. 828	**8.** 102	**9.** 515
10. 720	**11.** 364	**12.** 180

Set 7-12 (pages 404–405)

Find the average, or mean, of 33, 42, 28, and 37.

Add: 33 + 42 + 28 + 37 = 140

Divide: 140 ÷ 4 = 35

The average is 35.

Remember to add the numbers in the data set and then divide by the number of addends.

Find the mean of each data set.

1. 2, 3, 5, 7, 3, 4	**2.** 2, 6, 5, 4, 3, 4
3. 135, 210, 183	**4.** 28, 47, 53, 16

Set 7-13 (pages 406–407)

Divide 2,100 ÷ 30. Use mental math.

2,100 ÷ 30 = 210 ÷ 3

21 tens ÷ 3 = 7 tens, or 70

So, 2,100 ÷ 30 = 70.

Remember you can use patterns with zero to divide by multiples of 10.

Divide. Use mental math.

1. 250 ÷ 50	**2.** 160 ÷ 20
3. 2,400 ÷ 60	**4.** 3,600 ÷ 90

Set 7-14 (pages 408–411)

Divide 334 ÷ 65.

$$\begin{array}{r} 5\text{ R9} \\ 65\overline{)334} \\ -\underline{325} \\ 9 \end{array}$$

Check:

$$\begin{array}{r} 65 \\ \times\ \ 5 \\ \hline 325 \end{array} \qquad \begin{array}{r} \overset{1}{3}25 \\ +\ \ \ 9 \\ \hline 334 \end{array}$$

The answer checks.

Remember you need to check that the remainder is less than the divisor.

1. 87 ÷ 12	**2.** 345 ÷ 49
3. $57\overline{)384}$	**4.** $39\overline{)186}$
5. $68\overline{)562}$	**6.** $82\overline{)225}$
7. $28\overline{)212}$	**8.** $14\overline{)126}$

Chapter 7

More Practice

Set 7-1 (pages 366–367)

Divide. Use mental math.

1. 400 ÷ 2 **2.** 400 ÷ 5 **3.** 180 ÷ 9 **4.** 1,200 ÷ 4 **5.** 1,400 ÷ 7

6. 6,000 ÷ 3 **7.** 1,600 ÷ 8 **8.** 5,400 ÷ 6 **9.** 4,200 ÷ 7 **10.** 1,200 ÷ 2

11. Reasoning If 560 divided by a number is equal to 80, what is that number?

Set 7-2 (pages 368–371)

Estimate each quotient.

1. 115 ÷ 6 **2.** 162 ÷ 3 **3.** 198 ÷ 4 **4.** 223 ÷ 7 **5.** 302 ÷ 9

6. $5\overline{)413}$ **7.** $2\overline{)142}$ **8.** $8\overline{)654}$ **9.** $6\overline{)554}$ **10.** $5\overline{)243}$

11. If you swim about 100 laps of the pool in 5 days, about how many laps do you swim each day?

Set 7-3 (pages 372–373)

Divide. You may use counters to help.

1. $4\overline{)14}$ **2.** $8\overline{)19}$ **3.** $5\overline{)22}$ **4.** $6\overline{)33}$ **5.** $7\overline{)38}$

6. $2\overline{)17}$ **7.** $9\overline{)75}$ **8.** $3\overline{)11}$ **9.** $8\overline{)76}$ **10.** $6\overline{)50}$

11. If 8 people share 26 slices of pizza equally, how many slices does each person get? How many slices are left over?

Set 7-4 (pages 374–377)

Use place-value blocks. Tell how many club members are on each committee if all the members are divided equally among the committees.

1. 75 members, 5 committees **2.** 36 members, 3 committees **3.** 88 members, 8 committees **4.** 84 members, 7 committees

Divide. You may use place-value blocks to help.

5. $3\overline{)78}$ **6.** $2\overline{)38}$ **7.** $6\overline{)90}$ **8.** $4\overline{)80}$ **9.** $9\overline{)99}$

10. Howie has 96 decorations to pack in boxes that hold 6 decorations each. How many boxes does he need?

Take It to the NET
More Practice
www.scottforesman.com

Set 7-5 (pages 380–383)

Copy and complete.

1. $\begin{array}{r} 2\square \\ 3\overline{)81} \\ -6 \\ \hline \square\square \\ -\square\square \\ \hline 0 \end{array}$

2. $\begin{array}{r} \square 7 \\ 5\overline{)85} \\ -\square \\ \hline \square\square \\ -\square\square \\ \hline 0 \end{array}$

3. $\begin{array}{r} \square\square \text{ R}\square \\ 2\overline{)73} \\ -\square \\ \hline \square\square \\ -\square\square \\ \hline \square \end{array}$

4. $\begin{array}{r} \square\square \text{ R}\square \\ 8\overline{)92} \\ -\square \\ \hline \square\square \\ -\square\square \\ \hline \square \end{array}$

Divide. Check your answer.

5. $4\overline{)98}$ 6. $7\overline{)90}$ 7. $5\overline{)83}$ 8. $6\overline{)88}$ 9. $3\overline{)94}$

10. Millville Elementary has 96 fourth-grade students and 4 fourth-grade teachers. If split equally, how many students should be in each class?

Set 7-6 (pages 384–385)

Monica has 55 yards of edging to put around trees. Each tree needs 8 yards of edging.

1. How many trees can be edged?
2. How many yards of edging will Monica have left over?

Steven has 82 ounces of lemonade to put in 6-ounce cups.

3. How many cups does Steven need to hold all the lemonade?
4. How many cups can Steven fill?
5. How many ounces of lemonade will be in the cup that is not filled?

Set 7-7 (pages 386–389)

Divide. Check your answer.

1. $2\overline{)754}$ 2. $7\overline{)441}$ 3. $4\overline{)678}$ 4. $9\overline{)208}$ 5. $8\overline{)574}$

6. $3\overline{)824}$ 7. $5\overline{)937}$ 8. $6\overline{)492}$ 9. $3\overline{)197}$ 10. $4\overline{)253}$

11. A basketball star signed 171 autographs in 3 hours. If she signed the same number each hour, how many autographs did she sign in one hour?

More Practice

Set 7-8 (pages 390–391)

Divide. Check your answer.

1. $3\overline{)321}$ 2. $5\overline{)520}$ 3. $4\overline{)428}$ 4. $7\overline{)724}$ 5. $2\overline{)815}$

6. $6\overline{)657}$ 7. $9\overline{)984}$ 8. $8\overline{)849}$ 9. $5\overline{)652}$ 10. $4\overline{)415}$

11. The 6 musicians in a rock band want to share $648 evenly. How much money should each musician get?

Set 7-9 (pages 392–393)

Divide. Check your answer.

1. $2\overline{)\$8.72}$ 2. $4\overline{)\$6.36}$ 3. $7\overline{)\$6.02}$ 4. $9\overline{)\$2.16}$ 5. $6\overline{)\$1.56}$

6. $8\overline{)\$5.20}$ 7. $9\overline{)\$9.27}$ 8. $5\overline{)\$8.75}$ 9. $3\overline{)\$6.57}$ 10. $5\overline{)\$6.45}$

11. T-shirts are on sale for 3 for $5.25. How much does each T-shirt cost?

Set 7-10 (pages 396–399)

Troy put 3 puppies in a dog carrier. The carrier weighed 20 ounces. Each puppy weighed 8 ounces. How much did the puppies and the carrier weigh in all?

1. Draw a picture to show the main idea in the problem.
2. Which operations will you use to solve the problem?
3. Use a letter for the total weight and write a number sentence.
4. Solve the number sentence.
5. Answer the question in the problem with a complete sentence.

Set 7-11 (pages 402–403)

Test each number to see if it is divisible by 2, 3, 5, 9, or 10.

1. 90 2. 36 3. 83 4. 174 5. 265 6. 424

7. 310 8. 561 9. 738 10. 645 11. 913 12. 834

13. Explain why all numbers that are divisible by 9 are also divisible by 3.

14. Find a number that is divisible by 5 and 9.

15. Find a number that is divisible by 2, 3, and 5.

Take It to the NET
More Practice
www.scottforesman.com

Set 7-12 (pages 404–405)

Find the average, or mean, of each set of data.

1. 3, 7, 4, 2, 4 **2.** 17, 18, 19, 18 **3.** 8, 7, 8, 7, 9, 9

4. 46, 83, 48, 75 **5.** 172, 210, 185 **6.** 36, 48, 72, 25, 64

7. 258, 369, 171 **8.** 37, 259, 92, 132 **9.** 10, 12, 9, 6, 4, 9, 6

The table shows the number of minutes two operators let the Ferris wheel run on four different rides. What is the average number of minutes per ride on the rides operated by

Minutes on the Ferris Wheel

Ride	Operator	
	Sue	Nan
1	3	3
2	5	2
3	4	4
4	4	3

10. Sue? **11.** Nan?

12. Which operator averages longer rides? Explain how you know.

Set 7-13 (pages 406–407)

Divide. Use mental math.

1. 60 ÷ 20 **2.** 160 ÷ 40 **3.** 350 ÷ 50 **4.** 140 ÷ 70

5. 4,200 ÷ 60 **6.** 1,500 ÷ 30 **7.** 6,300 ÷ 70 **8.** 100 ÷ 20

9. 3,200 ÷ 80 **10.** 1,400 ÷ 20 **11.** 5,400 ÷ 60 **12.** 4,500 ÷ 90

13. Name another division problem with the same answer as 2,500 ÷ 50.

14. If you drive 60 miles each hour, how many hours would it take you to drive 480 miles?

Set 7-14 (pages 408–411)

Estimate each quotient. Then divide.

1. 135 ÷ 26 **2.** 300 ÷ 64 **3.** 610 ÷ 94 **4.** 89 ÷ 41

5. 321 ÷ 85 **6.** 378 ÷ 52 **7.** 402 ÷ 76 **8.** 152 ÷ 16

9. $72\overline{)351}$ **10.** $48\overline{)398}$ **11.** $35\overline{)336}$ **12.** $93\overline{)264}$

13. $58\overline{)474}$ **14.** $29\overline{)111}$ **15.** $81\overline{)576}$ **16.** $67\overline{)443}$

17. Explain how you could tell that an estimated quotient of 7 is too large for 139 ÷ 21.

CHAPTER 8

Geometry and Measurement

DIAGNOSING READINESS

A Vocabulary
(Grade 3)

Choose the best term from the box.

1. The __?__ of an object tells how wide it is.
2. The __?__ of an object tells how long it is.
3. Measure the __?__ of an object to find how tall it is.

Vocabulary

- **height** *(Gr. 3)*
- **length** *(Gr. 3)*
- **perimeter** *(Gr. 3)*
- **width** *(Gr. 3)*

B Solid Figures
(Grade 3)

Name the solid figure each object looks like.

4. 

5. 

6. 

7. 

Do You Know...

Is the Sears Tower more than twice the height of the Eiffel Tower?

You will find out in Lesson 8-14.

C Column Addition

(pages 80–81)

8. 18 + 12 + 27

9. 61 + 49 + 38

10. 23 + 58 + 30 + 49

11. 76 + 182 + 51 + 179

12. Shannon added 56 + 97 + 78. Should her answer be greater than or less than 200?

D Multiplying Three Factors

(pages 288–289)

13. $3 \times 5 \times 5$

14. $6 \times 2 \times 4$

15. $1 \times 15 \times 2$

16. $8 \times 8 \times 6$

17. $4 \times 10 \times 9$

18. $20 \times 7 \times 3$

19. Show two ways to find $2 \times 5 \times 4$.

20. Find the product of $3 \times 3 \times 3$.

21. Leo can make 3 dozen bagels an hour. If he makes bagels for 8 hours, how many bagels will he make?

Key Idea
There is a unique connection between solid figures and flat shapes.

Vocabulary
- plane figure
- solid figure
- cube
- edge
- face
- vertex
- rectangular prism
- triangular prism
- pyramid
- rectangular pyramid
- square pyramid
- sphere
- cylinder
- cone
- net

Materials
- set of solids
- scissors
- tape
- dot paper

Relating Solids and Plane Figures

WARM UP

Name the figure. How many corners and sides does each one have?

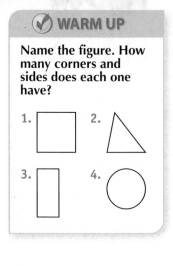

1. 2. 3. 4.

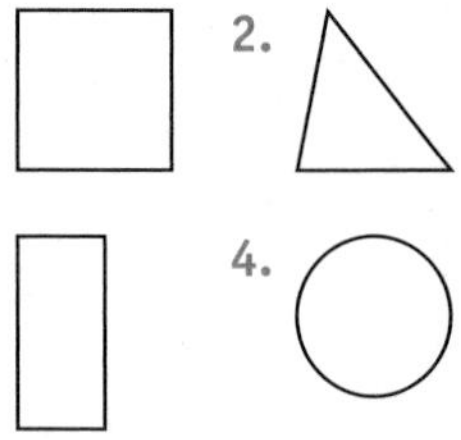

LEARN

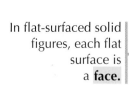

How are solids and flat shapes related?

A square is a flat shape, or **plane figure.** It has just two dimensions, length and width. Six squares can be combined to make a cube, which is a **solid figure.** It has three dimensions, length, width, and height.

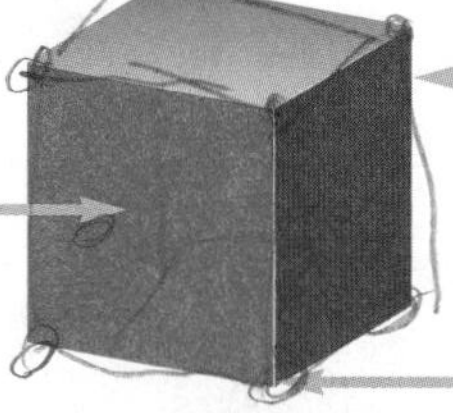

In flat-surfaced solid figures, each flat surface is a **face.**
An **edge** is a line segment where 2 faces meet.
A **vertex** is where 3 or more edges meet. (plural: vertices)

Cube

Solid figures are also called solids or space figures. Here are some other solids that have all flat surfaces.

Rectangular prism

Triangular prism

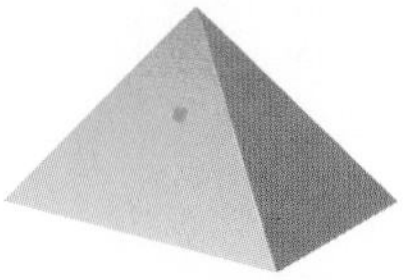
Rectangular pyramid

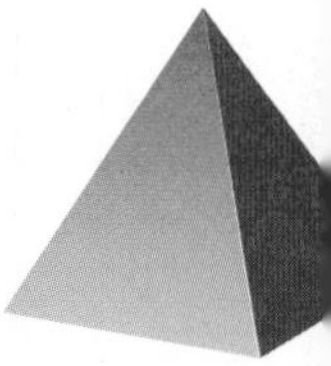
Square pyramid

Here are some solids that have curved surfaces.

Sphere

Cylinder

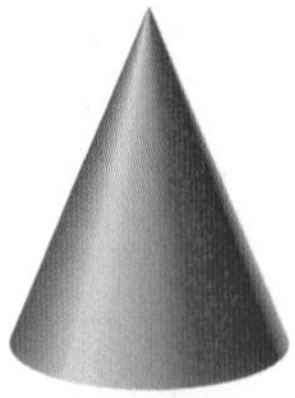
Cone

Talk About It

1. Which solid has no flat surfaces? Which solids have both flat and curved surfaces

Activity

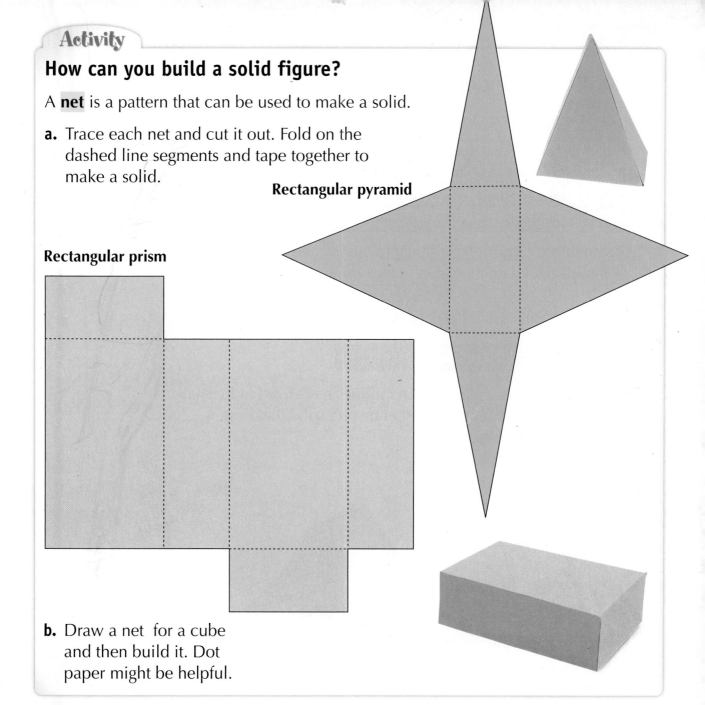

How can you build a solid figure?

A **net** is a pattern that can be used to make a solid.

a. Trace each net and cut it out. Fold on the dashed line segments and tape together to make a solid.

Rectangular pyramid

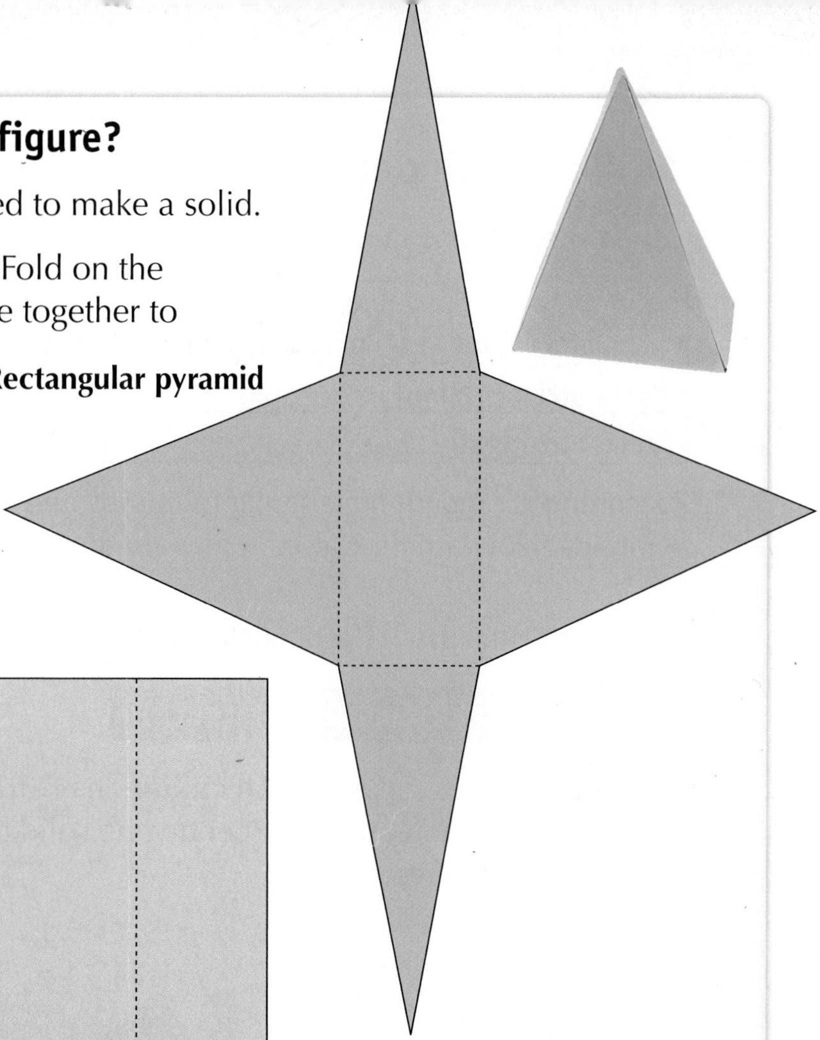

Rectangular prism

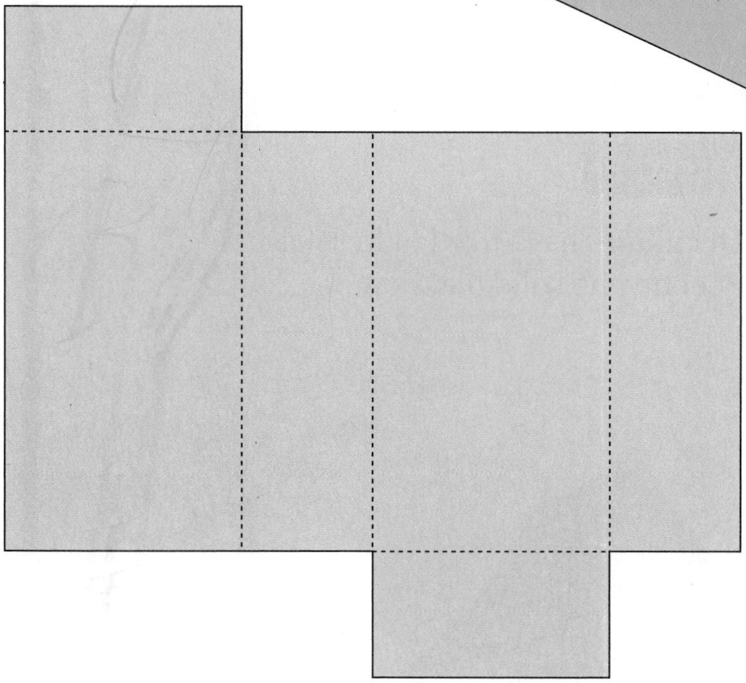

b. Draw a net for a cube and then build it. Dot paper might be helpful.

CHECK

For another example, see Set 8-1 on p. 490.

Copy and complete the table.

	Solid Figure	Number of Faces	Number of Edges	Number of Vertices	Shape(s) of Faces
1.	Cube	6			
2.	Rectangular prism				
3.	Triangular prism				2 triangles and 3 rectangles

4. Reasoning Compare rectangular prisms and triangular prisms. How are they alike? How are they different?

PRACTICE

For more practice, see Set 8-1 on p. 494.

A Skills and Understanding

Copy and complete the table.

	Solid Figure	Number of Faces	Number of Edges	Number of Vertices	Shape(s) of Faces
5.	Rectangular pyramid				
6.	Square pyramid				4 triangles and 1 square

7. Reasoning Compare rectangular pyramids and square pyramids. How are they alike? How are they different?

B Reasoning and Problem Solving

Math and Social Studies

For thousands of years, people of all cultures have lived in tents or have enjoyed them for recreation. Identify the solid that best describes the shape of each tent.

8.

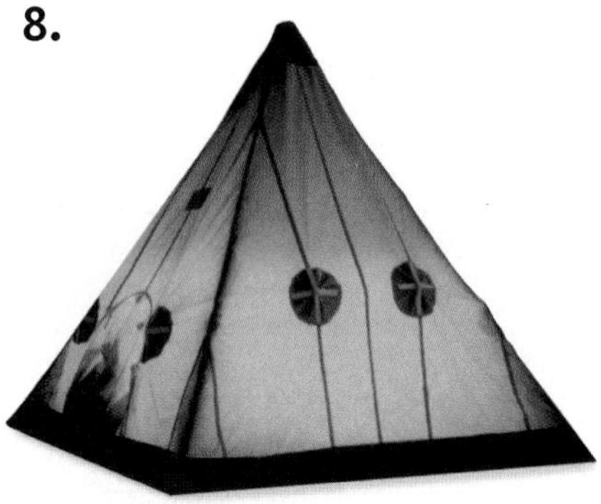

9.

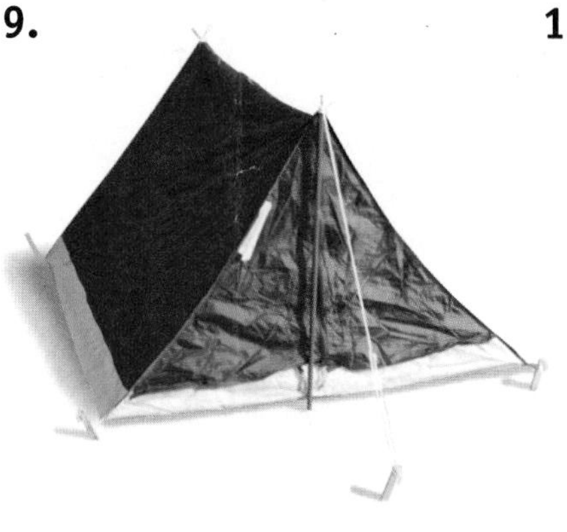

10.

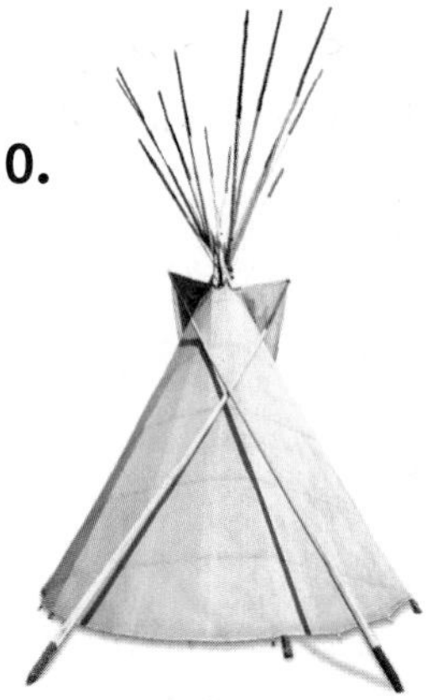

The Lavvu is used by the Sami people of northern Scandinavia.

11. Writing in Math A paint can looks like a cylinder. Which solid does each of these real-life objects look like?

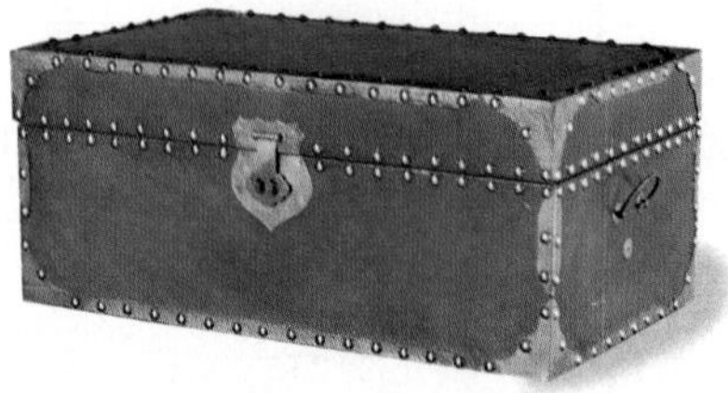

C Extensions

12. Which solids can be combined to make this figure?

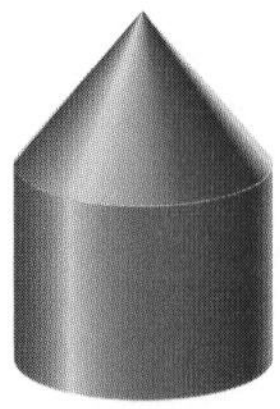

13. Which solids would you get if you cut a triangular prism as shown?

Place a rectangular prism, triangular prism, square pyramid, cone, and cylinder on your desk. Draw how each solid would look if you viewed it from

14. above. **15.** the side. **16.** the bottom.

Mixed Review and Test Prep

Take It to the NET
Test Prep
www.scottforesman.com

Find each answer.

17. \$1.56 ÷ 6 **18.** \$12.07 × 8 **19.** \$17.11 − 12.93 **20.** \$3.52 × 51

21. The fourth-graders are printing poetry booklets. Each booklet is 24 pages. How many booklets can they make from a package of 500 sheets of paper?

A. 2 **B.** 20 **C.** 21 **D.** 24

Practice Game

Abundant Attributes

Number of Players: 2

Materials: Polygon Cards, 1 set
Attribute Cards, 1 set

Players place the polygon cards face up on the playing surface. The attribute cards are placed face down. Player A draws the top attribute card and collects all of the polygons having that attribute. Player B then draws the next attribute card and collects all of the polygons having that attribute. If there is not a polygon with the attribute on the card, the player loses that turn. Play continues until there are no polygon cards left. The winner is the player with more polygon cards.

Key Idea
The name of a polygon tells how many sides it has.

Vocabulary
- polygon
- side
- vertex
- triangle
- quadrilateral
- pentagon
- hexagon
- octagon

Materials
- set of polygons or e tools

Polygons

WARM UP

Describe the faces of each solid figure.

1. 
2. 

LEARN

How do you identify polygons?

A **polygon** is a closed plane figure made up of line segments. Each line segment is a **side.** The point where the sides meet is called a **vertex.** (Vertices means more than one vertex.)

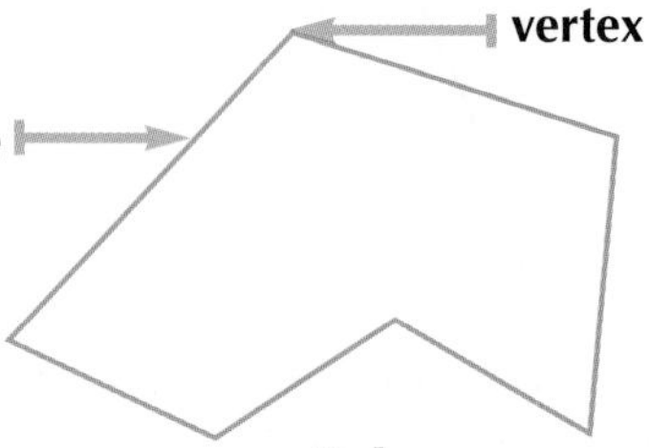

Polygon

Here are some examples of polygons.

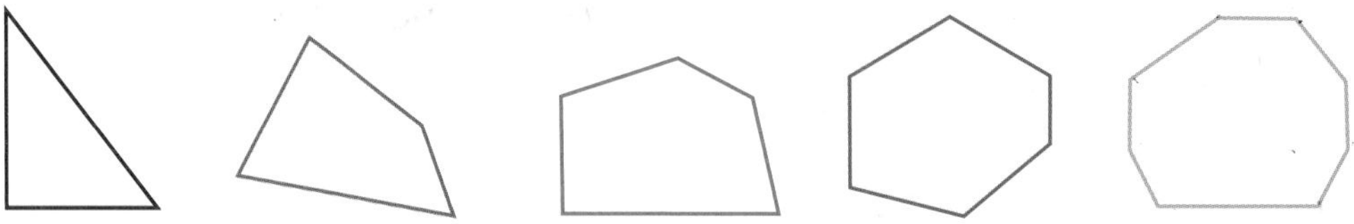

Triangle	**Quadrilateral**	**Pentagon**	**Hexagon**	**Octagon**
3 sides	4 sides	5 sides	6 sides	8 sides

Talk About It

1. Is each figure at the right a polygon? Explain your thinking.

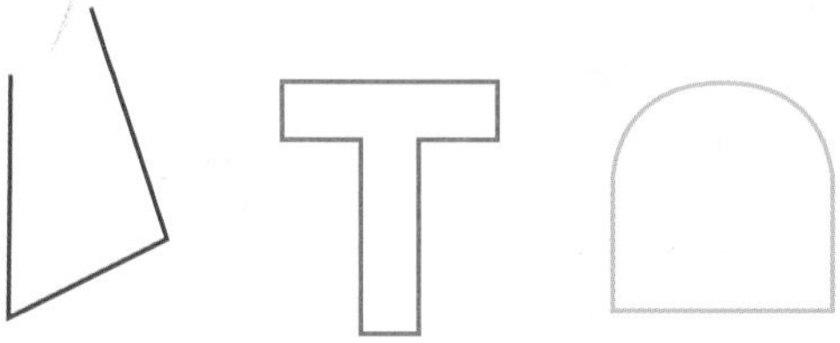

Activity

How can you sort polygons?

a. Sort your set of polygons by the number of sides each polygon has. Put them in piles on a sheet of paper and write the name of the polygon by each pile.

b. **Work with a Partner** Find another way to sort the set of polygons. See if your partner can guess how they were sorted.

TEST TALK

Think It Through
I can **look for a pattern** to help find a rule.

CHECK

For another example, see Set 8-2 on p. 490.

Draw an example of each polygon. How many sides and vertices does each one have?

1. Quadrilateral
2. Hexagon
3. Triangle
4. **Reasoning** If a polygon has 22 sides, how many vertices does it have?

PRACTICE

For more practice, see Set 8-2 on p. 494.

A Skills and Understanding

Draw an example of each polygon. How many sides and vertices does each one have?

5. Octagon
6. Pentagon
7. 10-sided polygon
8. **Reasoning** If a polygon has 35 vertices, how many sides does it have?

B Reasoning and Problem Solving

9. **Reasoning** Tell which polygon comes next in the pattern. Explain why.

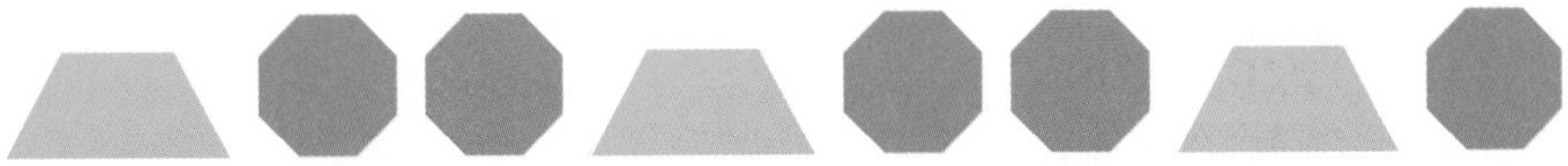

10. Refer to the design at the right. Identify the polygons that are lettered.

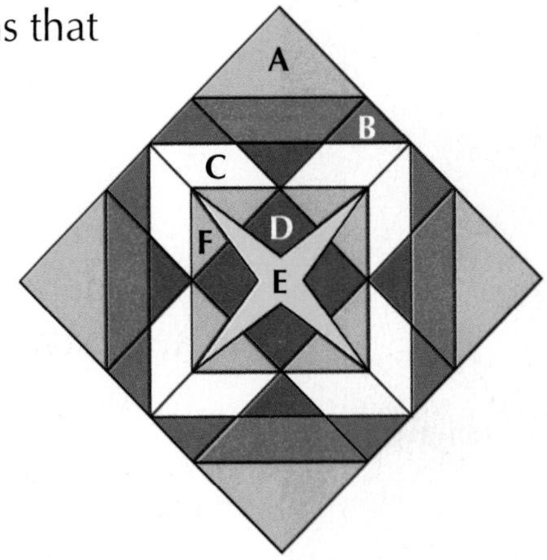

11. **Writing in Math** What rule do you think was used to sort these polygons?

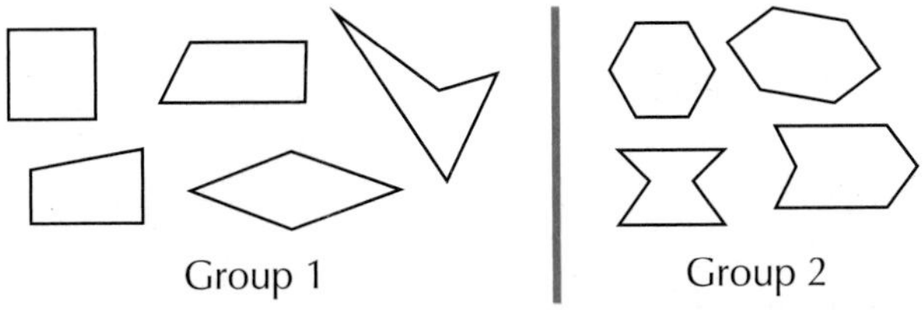

Mixed Review and Test Prep

Take It to the NET
Test Prep
www.scottforesman.com

12. Find the average of 6, 10, 4, and 8.
13. How many faces does a triangular prism have?

A. 2 **B.** 3 **C.** 5 **D.** 6

Key Idea
Geometric terms can be used to describe the location and position of things in our world.

Vocabulary
- point
- line
- line segment
- ray
- angle
- vertex
- right angle
- acute angle
- obtuse angle
- straight angle
- parallel lines
- intersecting lines
- perpendicular lines

Materials
- rulers
- straws or paper strips or e tools
- tape

Lines, Line Segments, Rays, and Angles

WARM UP

How many edges and vertices does each figure have?

1. 
2. 
3. 
4. 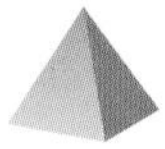

LEARN

What are some important geometric terms?

The table below gives some terms that help describe geometric figures and real-world objects.

Example

	What You **Draw**	What You **Write**	What You **Say**
A **point** is an exact location in space.		A or Point A	point *A*
A **line** is a straight path of points that goes on and on in two directions.	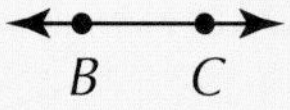	$\overleftrightarrow{BC}$ (or $\overleftrightarrow{CB}$)	line *BC* or line *CB*
A **line segment** is part of a line. It has two endpoints.		$\overline{DE}$ (or $\overline{ED}$)	line segment *DE* or line segment *ED*
A **ray** is part of a line. It has one endpoint and continues on and on in only one direction.	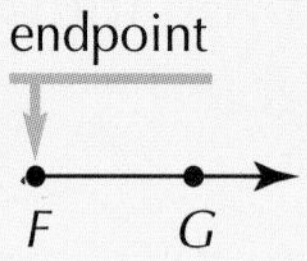	$\overrightarrow{FG}$	ray *FG*
An **angle** is formed by two rays that have the same endpoint. The common endpoint is called the **vertex.**	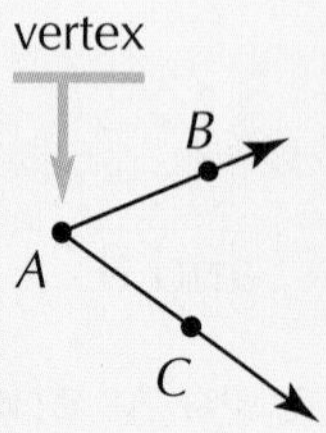	∠BAC (or ∠CAB or ∠A)	angle *BAC* or angle *CAB* or angle *A*

When three letters are used, the middle letter always names the vertex.

✔ Talk About It

1. Why is there one arrow in the drawing of a ray and two arrows in the drawing of a line?

2. What are the names of the rays that form the angle in the table?

Take It to the NET
More Examples
www.scottforesman.com

Activity

What are some special angles and lines?

Angles are given special names depending on their size.

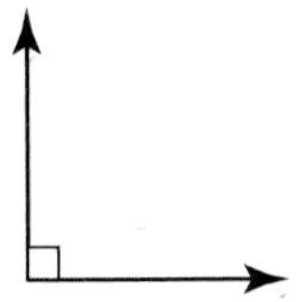

A **right angle** is a square corner.

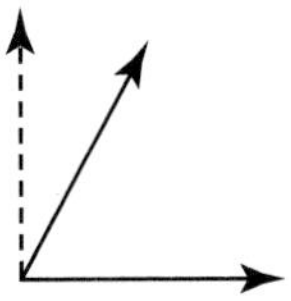

An **acute angle** is less than a right angle.

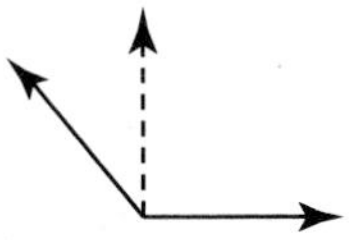

An **obtuse angle** is greater than a right angle.

A **straight angle** forms a straight line.

a. Use straws or paper strips to make each type of angle described above. Tape them on your paper and label them.

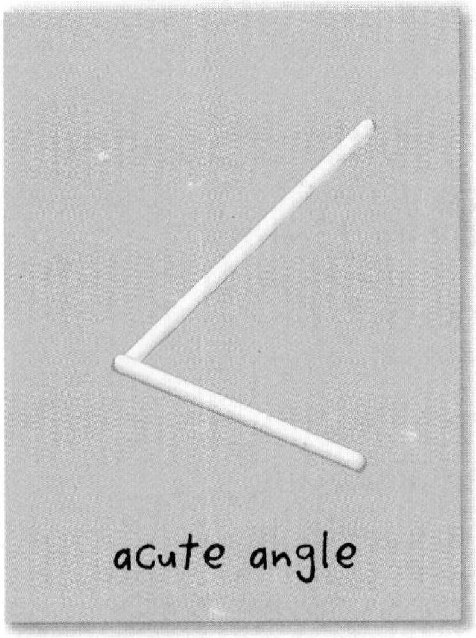

TEST TALK

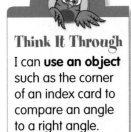

Think It Through

I can **use an object** such as the corner of an index card to compare an angle to a right angle.

Pairs of lines are given special names depending on their relationship.

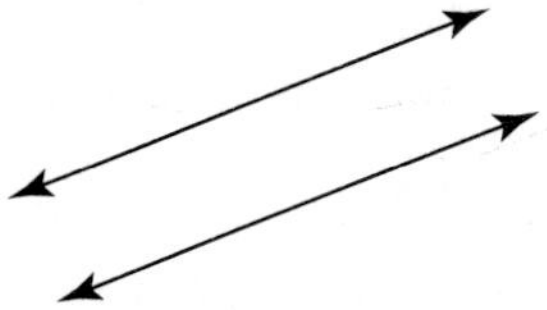

Parallel lines never intersect.

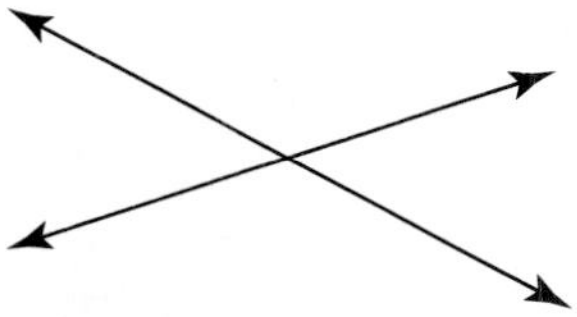

Intersecting lines pass through the same point.

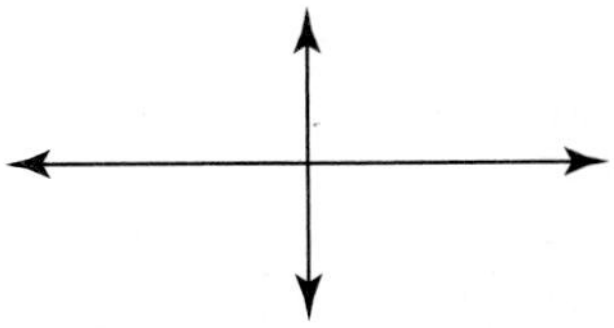

Perpendicular lines are lines that form right angles.

b. Use straws or paper strips to show an example of each pair of lines described above. Tape them on your paper and label them.

CHECK

For another example, see Set 8-3 on p. 490.

Use geometric terms to describe what is shown. Be as specific as possible.

1. 2. 3. 4. 5.

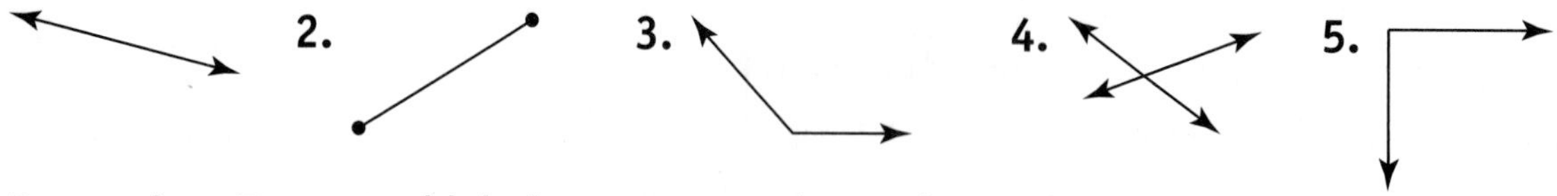

6. **Reasoning** Draw and label ∠*PQR*, a right angle, and ∠*AEF*, an acute angle.

PRACTICE

For more practice, see Set 8-3 on p. 494.

A Skills and Understanding

Use geometric terms to describe what is shown. Be as specific as possible.

7. 8. 9. 10. 11.

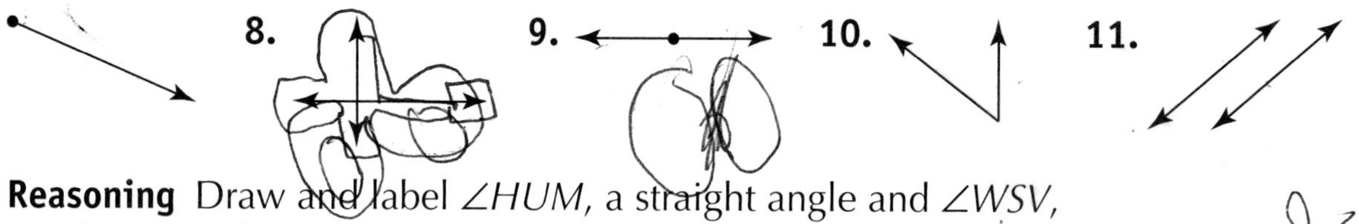

12. **Reasoning** Draw and label ∠*HUM*, a straight angle and ∠*WSV*, an obtuse angle.

B Reasoning and Problem Solving

Use the drawing at the right for 13–15.

13. Name three line segments.

14. Name two rays.

15. Name a right angle, an acute angle, an obtuse angle, and a straight angle.

Math and Social Studies

Use the map of the airport runways at the right. Identify the color of each of the following figures.

16. Obtuse angle
17. Parallel lines
18. Perpendicular lines
19. Acute angle
20. **Writing in Math** Describe something in your classroom that illustrates parallel lines. Describe something that illustrates perpendicular lines.

PRACTICE

C Extensions

The point halfway between the endpoints of a line segment is called the **midpoint.** Identify each midpoint.

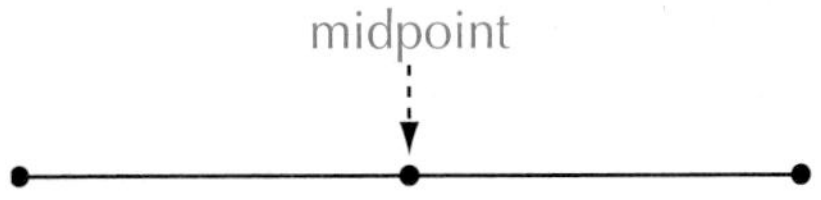

21. 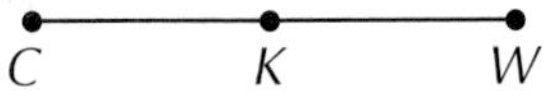

22. 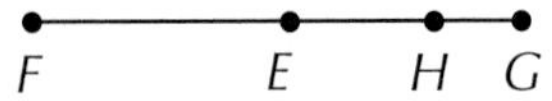

23. 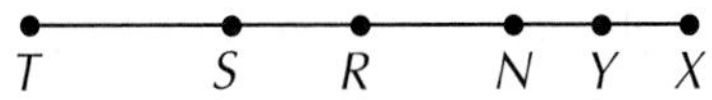

Mixed Review and Test Prep

Take It to the NET
Test Prep
www.scottforesman.com

24. Find the elapsed time from 10:35 A.M. to 1:10 P.M.

25. What is the name of a 6-sided polygon?

A. Octagon **B.** Quadrilateral **C.** Pentagon **D.** Hexagon

Enrichment

Measuring Angles

Materials: Protractor

You can use a protractor to find the size or measure of an angle. An angle is measured in degrees (°). Follow these steps to measure ∠*LMN*.

- Place the center mark of the protractor on vertex *M*.
- Place the zero mark on ray *MN*.
- Notice there are two scales on the protractor.
- Use the scale that starts with zero at $\overrightarrow{MN}$ and follow it to $\overrightarrow{ML}$. $\overrightarrow{ML}$ crosses the protractor at 45°.

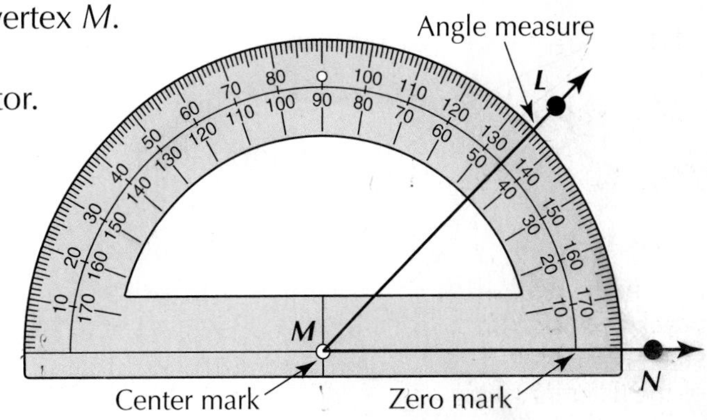

The measure of ∠*LMN* is 45°.

Trace and extend the hands on each clock face. Measure the angles formed.

1. 

2. 

3. 

4. Which angle above is a right angle? What is the measure of a right angle?

5. Which angle above is a straight angle? What is the measure of a straight angle?

Key Idea
There are different ways to classify triangles and quadrilaterals.

Vocabulary
- equilateral triangle
- isosceles triangle
- scalene triangle
- right triangle
- acute triangle
- obtuse triangle
- rectangle
- square
- trapezoid
- parallelogram
- rhombus

Materials
- straws or paper strips or e tools
- scissors
- ruler
- grid paper

TEST TALK

Think It Through
I can **make an organized list** to be sure I have used all the different combinations of lengths.

Triangles and Quadrilaterals

WARM UP

Name each polygon.

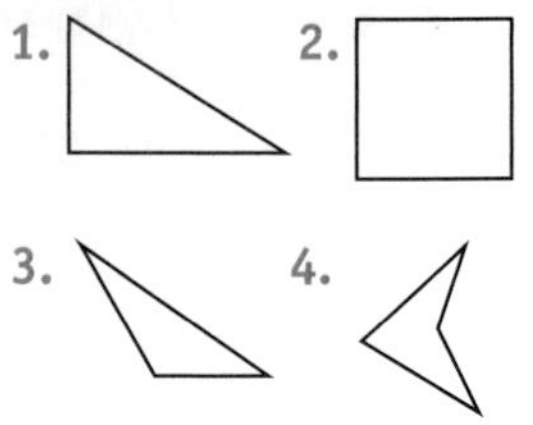

LEARN

Activity

How do you classify triangles?

a. Cut straws or paper strips into the following lengths.

- **1 piece 3 inches long**
- **4 pieces each 4 inches long**
- **1 piece 5 inches long**
- **2 pieces each 6 inches long**

b. Use the 3-inch, 4-inch, and 5-inch pieces to make as many different-shaped triangles as you can. Draw around each one on a sheet of paper. (Hint: Just mark the vertices and then use a ruler to connect them.)

Triangles can be classified by the lengths of their sides.

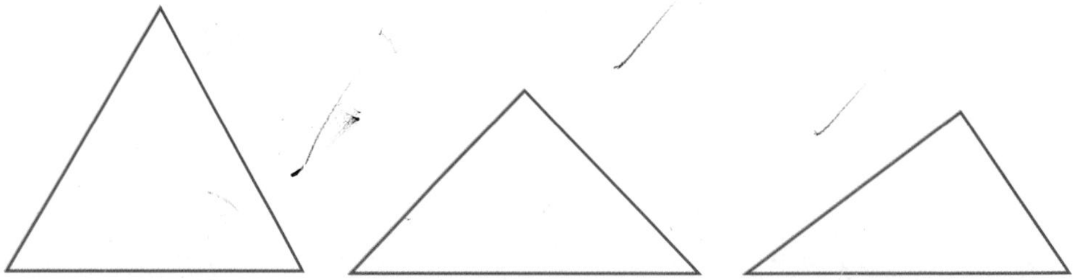

Equilateral triangle	Isosceles triangle	Scalene triangle
All sides are the same length.	At least two sides are the same length.	No sides are the same length.

c. Label each of your triangles as an equilateral, isosceles, or scalene triangle.

Another way to classify triangles is by their angles.

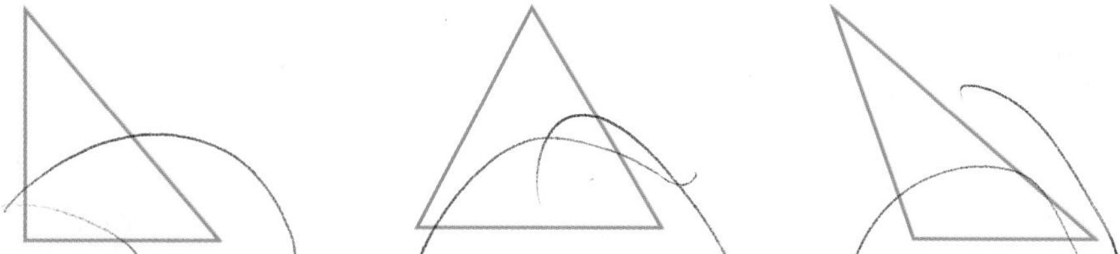

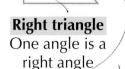

Right triangle
One angle is a right angle

Acute triangle
All three angles are acute angles.

Obtuse triangle
One angle is an obtuse angle.

d. On a sheet of grid paper, use any straws or paper pieces you choose to make one example of each of the triangles above. Draw each triangle and label it right, acute, or obtuse triangle.

e. Describe each of the triangles at the right by its sides and angles.

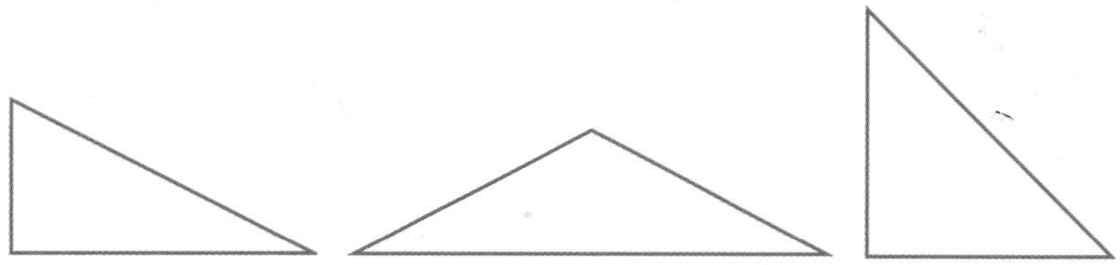

Activity

How do you classify quadrilaterals?

Quadrilaterals can be classified by their angles or pairs of sides.

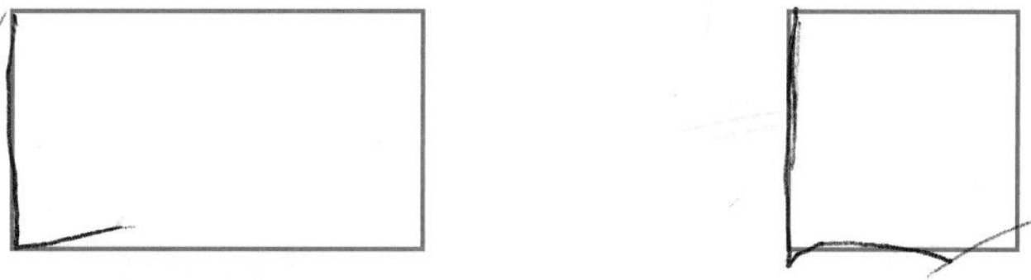

Rectangle
There are four right angles.

Square
There are four right angles and all sides are the same length.

Trapezoid
There is only one pair of parallel sides.

Parallelogram
Opposite sides are parallel.

Rhombus
Opposite sides are parallel and all sides are the same length.

a. On a sheet of grid paper, use some of the straws or paper pieces to make one example of each quadrilateral. Draw and label each quadrilateral.

b. What do you notice about the lengths of the sides in a rectangle? in a parallelogram?

Take It to the NET
More Examples
www.scottforesman.com

CHECK

For another example, see Set 8-4 on p. 491.

Classify each triangle by its sides and then by its angles.

1.  **2.**  **3.** 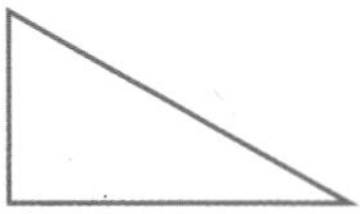 **4.** 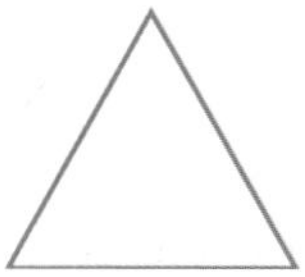 **5.** 

Write the name of each quadrilateral.

6. 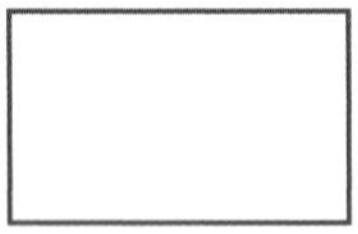 **7.**  **8.** 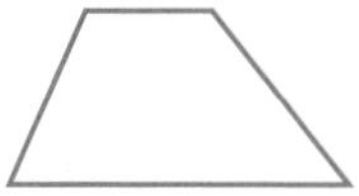 **9.** 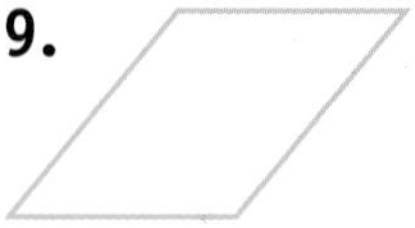 **10.** 

11. Reasoning Can a quadrilateral be both a square and a rectangle? Explain.

PRACTICE

For more practice, see Set 8-4 on p. 494.

A Skills and Understanding

Classify each triangle by its sides and then by its angles.

12. 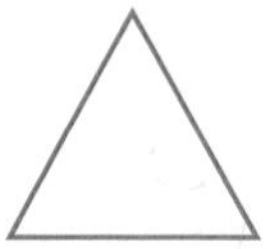 **13.** 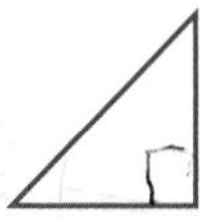 **14.** 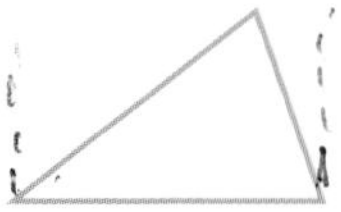 **15.** 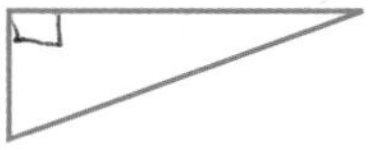 **16.** 

Write the name of each quadrilateral.

17. 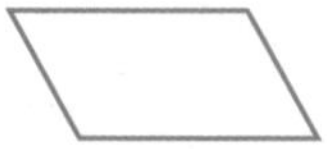 **18.**  **19.** 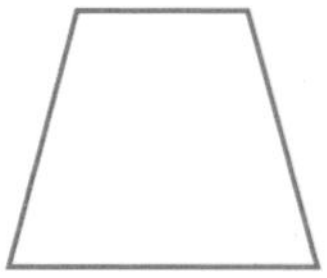 **20.** 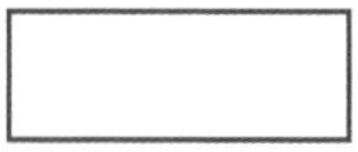 **21.** 

22. Reasoning Can a quadrilateral be both a parallelogram and a rhombus? Explain.

B Reasoning and Problem Solving

Math and Social Studies

Many flags are designed with a variety of geometric figures.

23. Writing in Math Use mathematical terms from this lesson to describe the shapes that are used in each flag.

*The **Czech Republic** is located in central Europe.*

***Chile** is a country in southwest South America.*

C Extensions

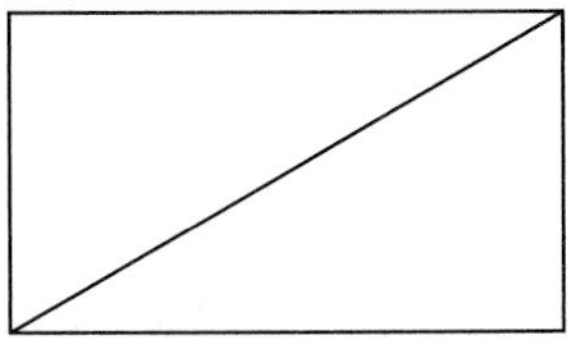

24. Draw a rectangle. Then join one pair of opposite vertices with a line segment.
    a. Classify the resulting triangles by both their sides and angles.
    b. Join the other opposite vertices. Classify the four triangles by both their sides and angles.
    c. Repeat Steps a and b starting with a square.

Mixed Review and Test Prep

Take It to the NET
Test Prep
www.scottforesman.com

25. Kyle bought five binders at $1.49 a piece. Sales tax was 38¢. What was the total price Kyle paid?

26. Draw and label an acute angle, an obtuse angle, a right angle, and a straight angle.

27. What name is given to two lines that do not intersect?

    A. Parallel   B. Intersecting   C. Right   D. Perpendicular

Discovery Channel School — Discover Math in Your World

No Small Plans

Boston's tallest building is a glass tower called the John Hancock Tower. The building's architect, I.M. Pei, designed the floor plan in the shape of a parallelogram.

1. How are a rectangle and a parallelogram the same? How are they different?

2. The corners of a rectangular floor plan are right angles. Describe the corners of the floor plan of the John Hancock Tower.

3. Describe the corners of a floor plan in the shape of a trapezoid and a rhombus.

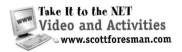

Take It to the NET
Video and Activities
www.scottforesman.com

Key Idea
Circles are plane closed curves that are seen often in the world around us.

Vocabulary
- circle
- center
- radius
- diameter
- chord

Materials
- compass
- ruler or
e tools

Circles

WARM UP

Name each solid.

1. 2. 3. 4.

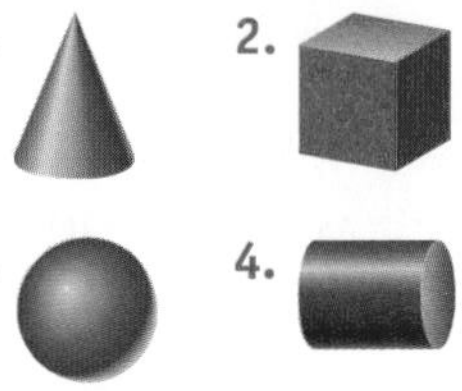

LEARN

Activity

How do you draw and describe circles?

A **circle** is a closed plane figure made up of all the points the same distance from a point called the **center.**

Some line segments have a special relationship with a circle.

A **chord** is any line segment that connects two points on the circle.

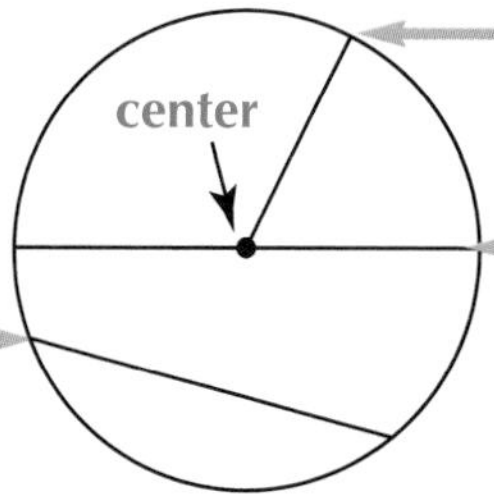

A **radius** is any line segment that connects the center to a point on the circle.

A **diameter** is any line segment that connects two points on the circle and passes through the center.

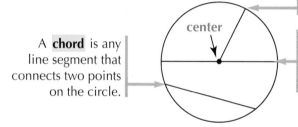

a. Use your compass to draw a large circle.

b. Use a ruler or straightedge to draw and label a radius, a diameter, and a chord.

c. How do you think the length of the diameter compares to the length of the radius? Check your prediction. How did you check it?

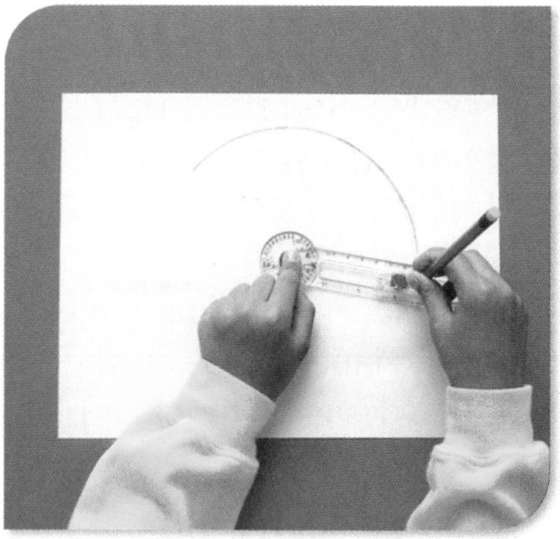

TEST TALK

Think It Through
- I can **draw a picture** to help me describe the parts of a circle.
- I need to **try, check, and revise** my prediction about the diameter and radius.

CHECK

For another example, see Set 8-5 on p. 491.

Use geometric terms to describe what is shown in red.

1. **2.** **3.** **4.** **5.**

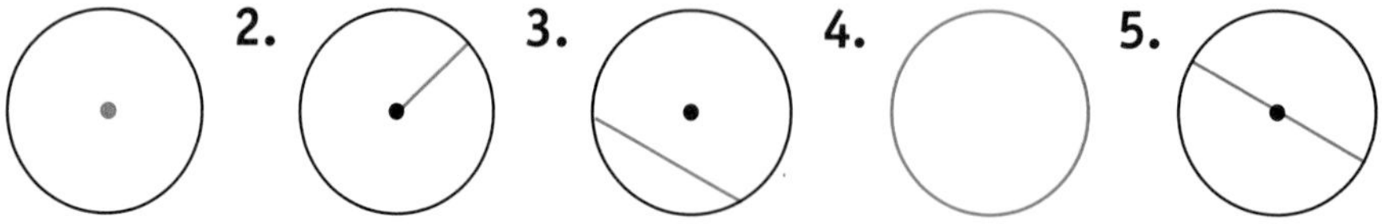

6. Reasoning If the radius of a circle is 7 inches, how long is its diameter?

For more practice, see Set 8-5 on p. 495.

A Skills and Understanding

Use geometric terms to describe what is shown in red.

7. 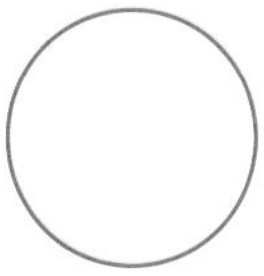

8. 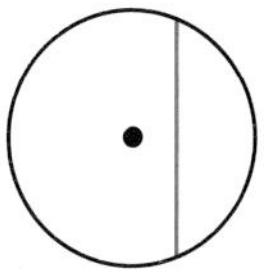

9. 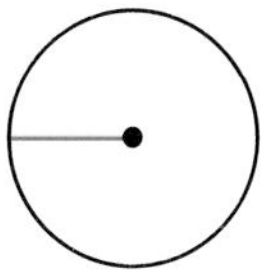

10. 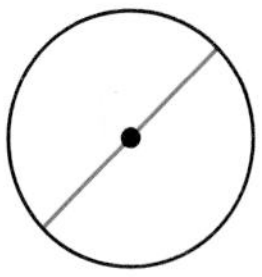

11. 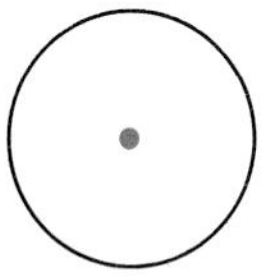

12. **Reasoning** If the diameter of a circle is 20 centimeters, how long is its radius?

B Reasoning and Problem Solving

Find the length of the diameter of each circular object.

13. 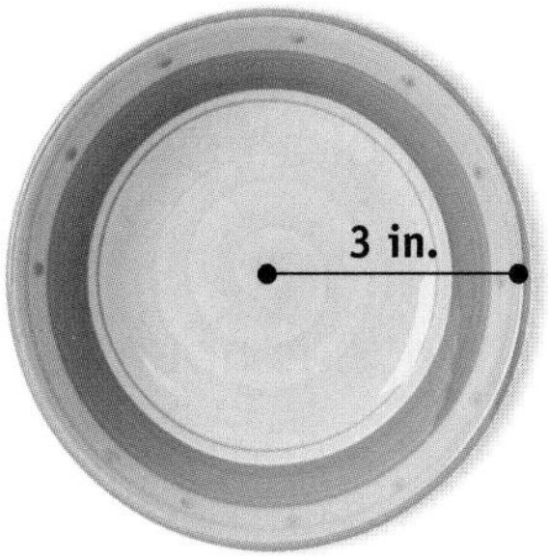

14. 

15. 

16. **Writing in Math** Is the explanation at the right correct? If not, tell why and write a correct response.

Is $\overline{AB}$ a chord?

$\overline{AB}$ is not a chord because it does not pass through the center.

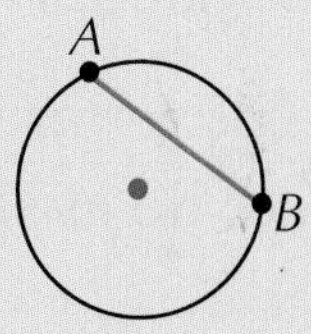

Mixed Review and Test Prep

Take It to the NET
Test Prep
www.scottforesman.com

17. Find the missing numbers in the pattern.

9, 18, 27, 36, ▢, ▢, ▢

18. Evaluate $15m$ for $m = 7$.

A. 22 **B.** 75 **C.** 105 **D.** 157

19. **Writing in Math** Lidia sorted some triangles into two groups. Use geometric terms to describe one characteristic of each group.

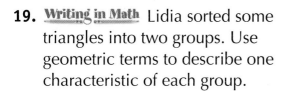

Group 1 Group 2

Section A: Lessons 8-1 through 8-5

Review

Do You Know How?

Do You Understand?

Relating Solids and Plane Figures (8-1)

Name each solid shown.

1. 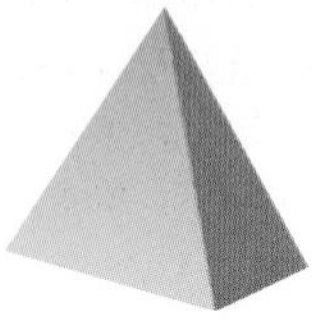

2. 

A How many faces does the solid in Exercise I have?

B How many edges does the solid in Exercise 2 have?

Polygons (8-2)

Draw an example of each polygon. How many sides and vertices does each have?

3. hexagon

4. quadrilateral

5. pentagon

6. octagon

C Draw an example of a figure that is not a polygon.

D Explain why a circle is not a polygon.

Lines, Line Segments, Rays, and Angles (8-3); Circles (8-5)

Use geometric terms to describe what is shown in red. Be as specific as possible.

7. 

8. 

9. 

10. 

E Explain why a line is drawn with two arrows.

F Explain why the line segment in Exercise 9 is both a diameter and a chord.

Triangles and Quadrilaterals (8-4)

Classify each triangle by its sides and then by its angles.

11. 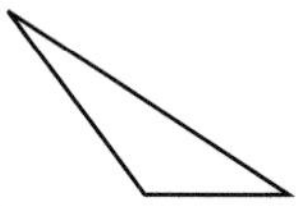

12. 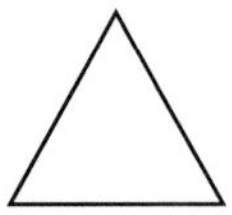

13. Write the name of the quadrilateral.

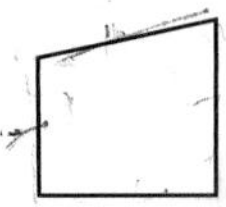

G Tell what you know about the sides and angles of a square.

H Explain why an equilateral triangle is also an isosceles triangle.

Diagnostic Checkpoint

TEST TALK

Think It Through

- I can **use objects** to help identify and describe solids, angles, triangles, and quadrilaterals.
- I should **look for highlighted words, like NOT.**

MULTIPLE CHOICE

1. Which solid does not have a face that is a triangle? (8-1)

A. rectangular prism **C.** rectangular pyramid

B. square pyramid **D.** triangular prism

2. Which of the shapes CANNOT have parallel sides? (8-4)

A. rectangle **B.** rhombus **C.** trapezoid **D.** triangle

FREE RESPONSE

Tell the number of faces, edges, and vertices each solid has. (8-1)

3. square pyramid **4.** triangular prism **5.** rectangular prism **6.** cube

Write the name of the plane figure that describes the shape of each road sign. Be as specific as possible. (8-2, 8-4, and 8-5)

7. 

8. 

9. 

10. 

Use geometric terms to describe what is shown in red. Be as specific as possible. If the figure is a triangle, classify it by its sides and its angles. (8-2, 8-4, and 8-5)

11. 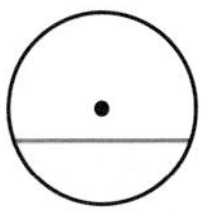

12. 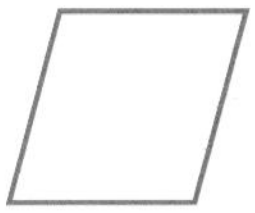

13. 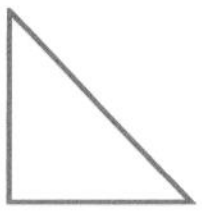

14. 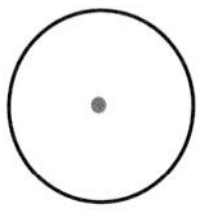

Use the figure at the right for 15–18. (8-3)

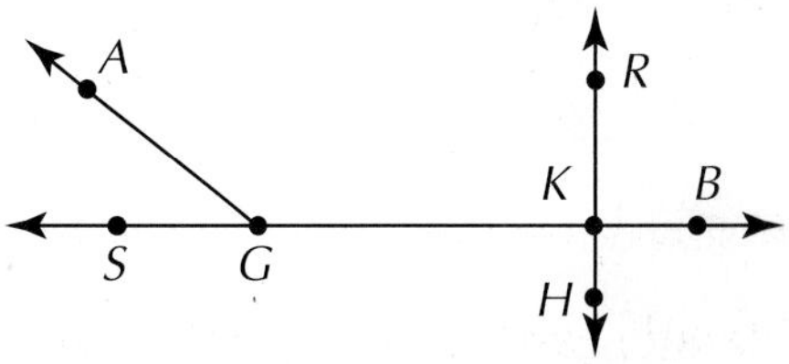

15. Name an acute angle. **16.** Name a ray.

17. Name an obtuse angle. **18.** Name a pair of perpendicular lines.

Writing in Math

19. James said he drew a solid with 6 faces and 8 vertices. Is this possible? If so, draw the solid. If not, explain why it is impossible. (8-1)

20. Draw a net for a square pyramid. Identify each polygon in your net. Be as specific as possible. (8-1 and 8-2)

Key Idea
There are various ways to move a figure to a new position.

Vocabulary
- slide (translation)
- flip (reflection)
- turn (rotation)
- congruent figures

Materials
- set of polygons
- grid paper
- tracing paper or e tools

TEST TALK

Think It Through
- I can **use objects** to explore slides, flips, and turns.
- I can **draw conclusions** from my drawings.

Congruent Figures and Motions

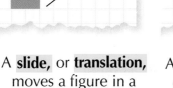

WARM UP

Identify each figure. Be as specific as possible.

1. 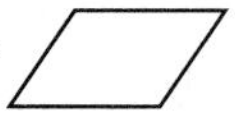
2. 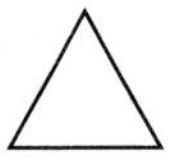
3. 
4. 

LEARN

What are some ways to move a figure?

Here are three different ways to move a plane figure.

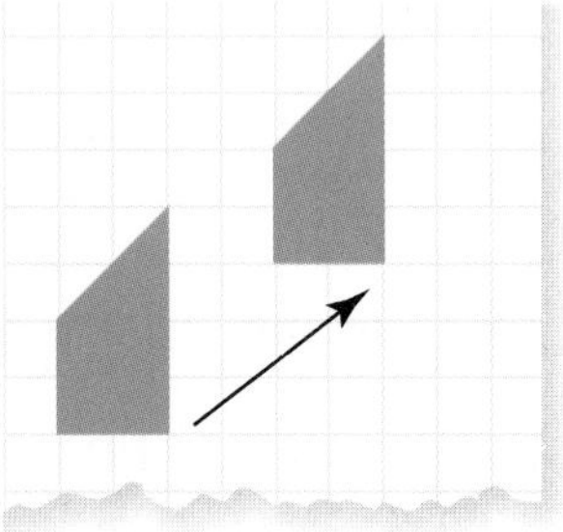

A **slide,** or **translation,** moves a figure in a straight direction.

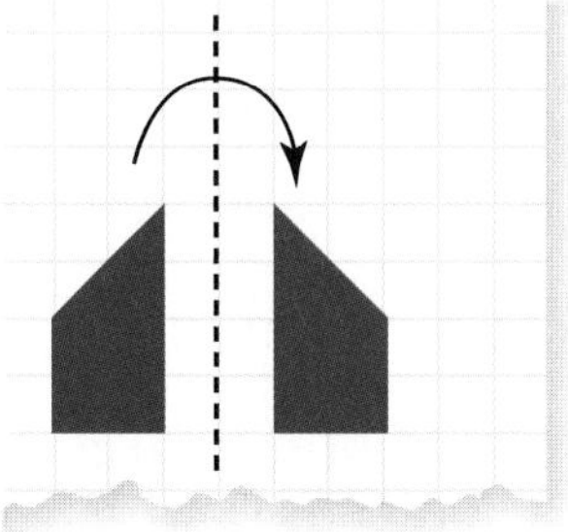

A **flip,** or **reflection,** of a figure gives its mirror image.

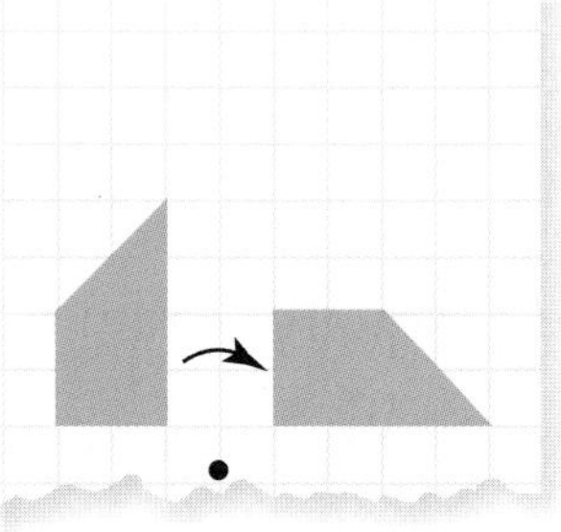

A **turn,** or **rotation,** moves a figure about a point.

Activity

Does moving a figure change its size or shape?

a. Place a polygon on a sheet of grid paper. Trace around it. Slide it to a new position. Then trace around it again.

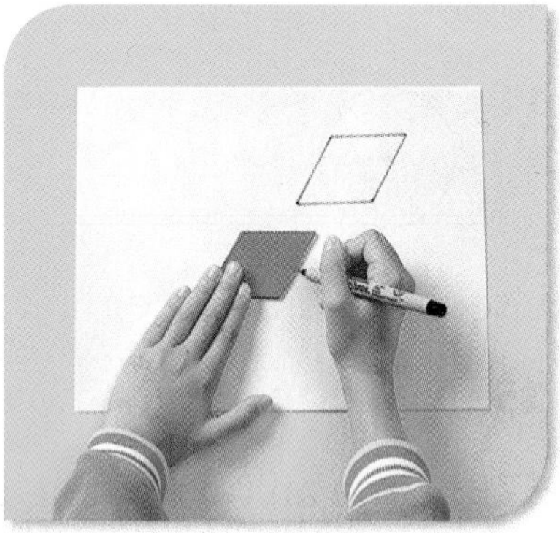

b. Are the two figures the same size? Are they the same shape? Explain how you could use tracing paper or the original polygon to check.

c. Begin again and draw a flip. Did the size or shape of the figure change?

d. Now draw a turn. Did the size or shape of the figure change?

What do you call figures with the same size and shape?

Figures related by a translation (slide), a reflection (flip), or a rotation (turn) have the same size and shape. These figures are **congruent.** You can use tracing paper and slides, flips, or turns to test if two figures are congruent.

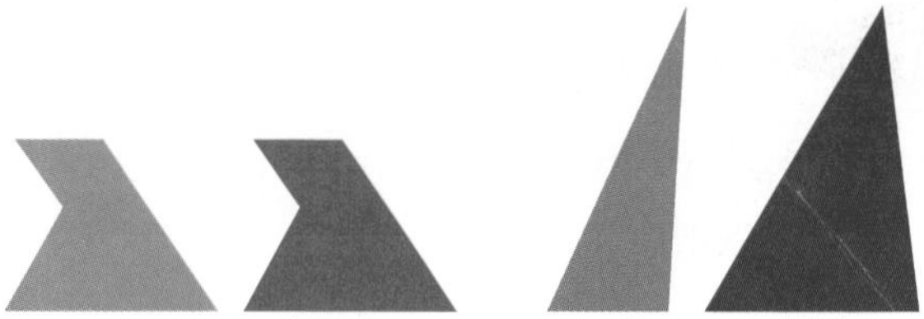

Congruent   Not congruent

Talk About It

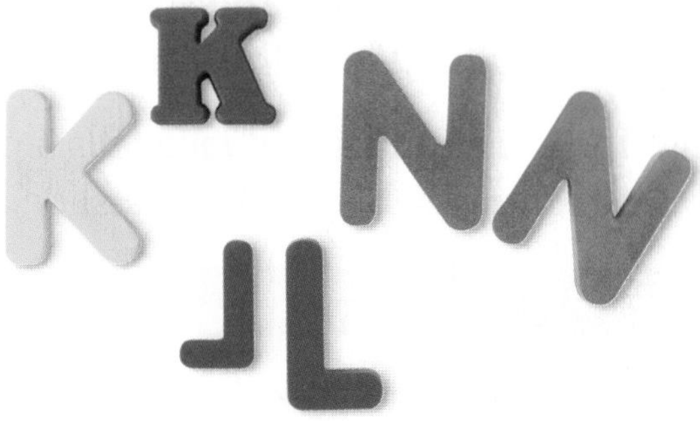

1. Which letters at the right appear to be congruent?

2. Could you use a slide, a flip, or a turn to show that the letters are congruent?

3. How can you tell if two polygons are congruent?

CHECK

For another example, see Set 8-6 on p. 491.

Do the figures in each pair appear to be congruent? If so, tell if they are related by a flip, slide, or turn.

1. 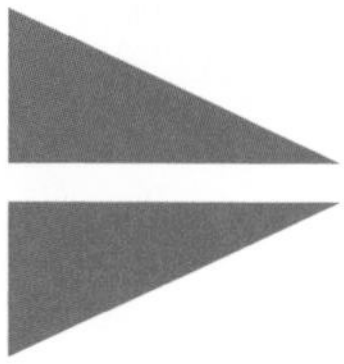

2. 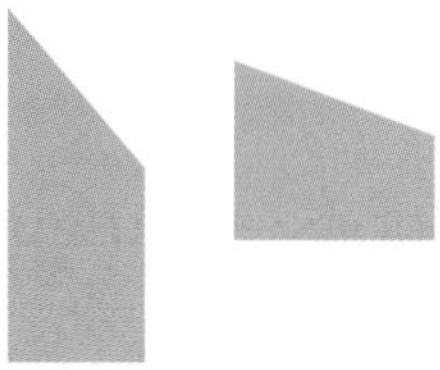

3. 

4. 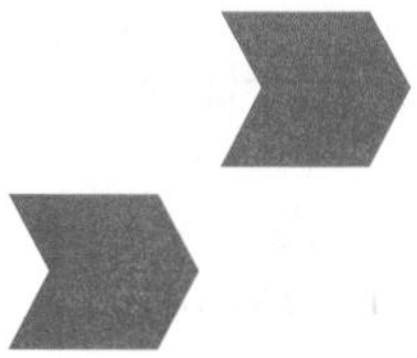

5. Reasoning Could a trapezoid and a square ever be congruent? Explain.

PRACTICE

For more practice, see Set 8-6 on p. 495.

A Skills and Understanding

Do the figures in each pair appear to be congruent? If so, tell if they are related by a flip, slide, or turn.

6. 

7. 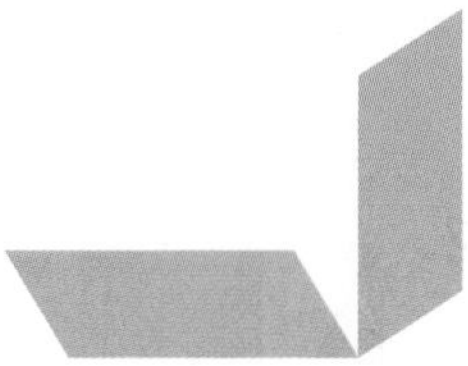

8. 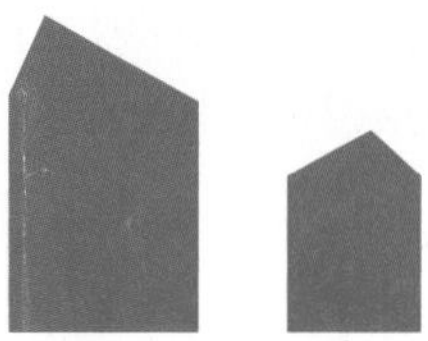

9. 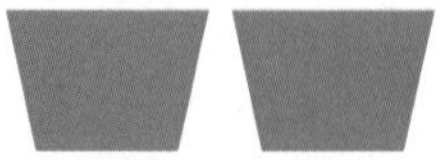

10. Reasoning Could a rectangle and a square ever be congruent? Explain.

PRACTICE

B Reasoning and Problem Solving

11. Describe two objects in your classroom that are congruent.

12. This is how the message at the right looks in a mirror. What does the original message say?

13. Morgan says that if she slides, flips, or turns a circle, the results all look the same. Is she right? Explain.

14. The command *about face* tells a person to face the opposite direction. Is this most like a slide, a flip, or a turn?

Math and Art

Tile patterns, called **tessellations,** can be drawn by sliding, flipping, and turning certain polygons. In each tessellation below, tell whether the red polygons are related by a slide, a flip, or a turn.

15.

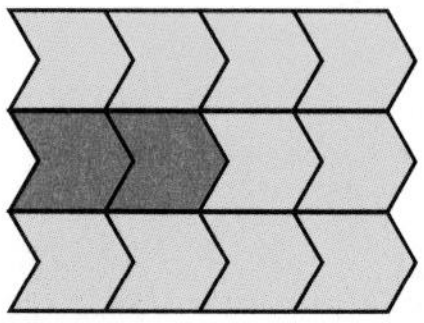

16.

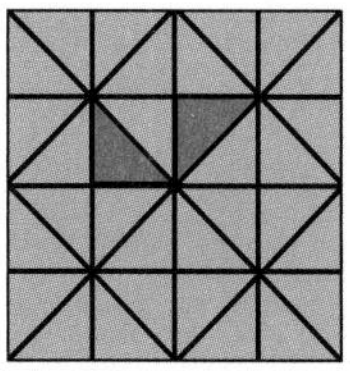

17.

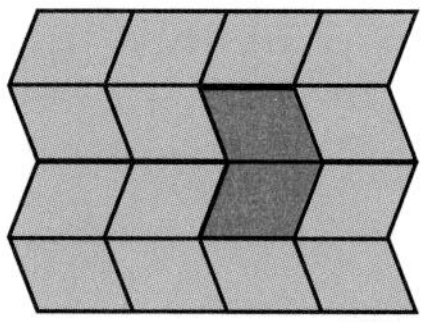

18. Draw your own tessellation. Tell what motions you used to create the pattern.

Writing in Math For each pair of figures, describe everything that is the same and everything that is different. Then tell if the figures are congruent.

19.

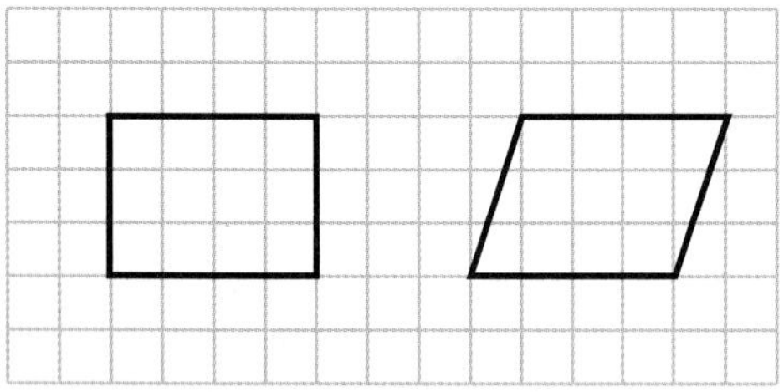

20.

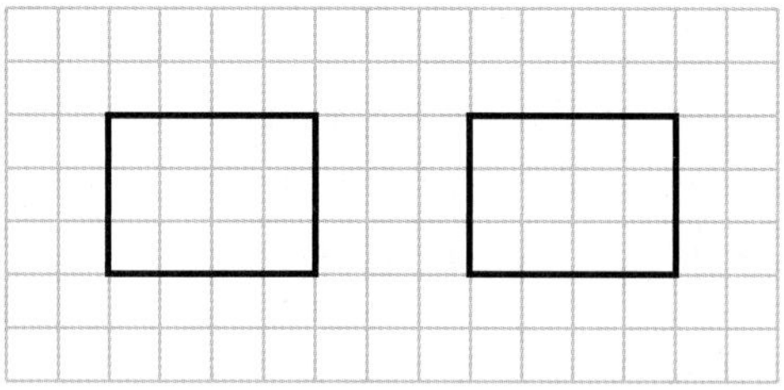

C Extensions

Draw the next figure in each pattern.

21.

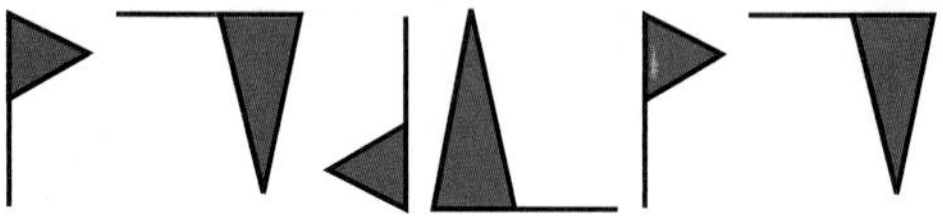

22.

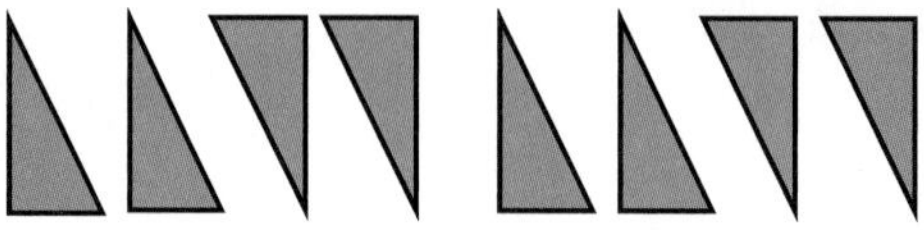

Mixed Review and Test Prep

Take It to the NET
Test Prep
www.scottforesman.com

23. Which solids have some triangular faces?

24. $\overline{GH}$ is a __?__.

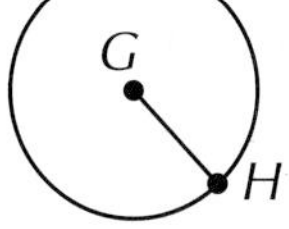

A. chord **C.** center

B. radius **D.** diameter

Learning with Technology

Using the Geometry eTool to Do Transformations

Use the Geometry Drawing eTool to draw a scalene triangle that looks like the one in the picture on the screen at right and label its vertices as shown. Now perform each transformation listed below.

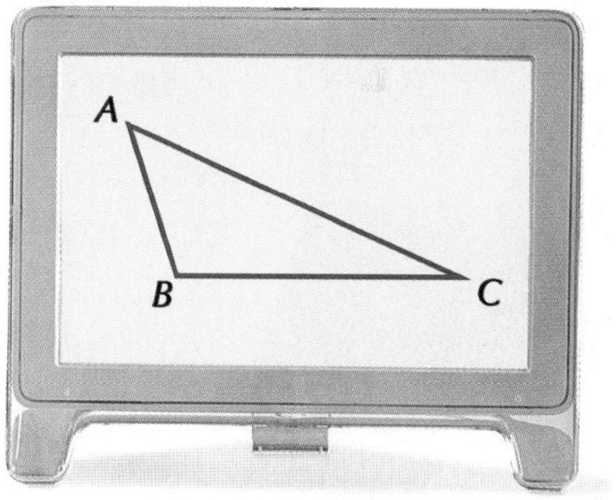

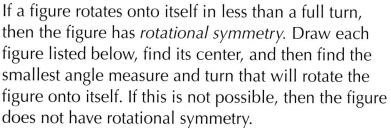

1. Flip $\triangle ABC$ over a line that is parallel to the line containing side BC.

2. Give $\triangle ABC$ a $\frac{1}{4}$ turn (90°), a $\frac{1}{2}$ turn (180°), and a $\frac{3}{4}$ turn (270°).

3. Slide $\triangle ABC$ to the right, to the left, up, and down.

If a figure rotates onto itself in less than a full turn, then the figure has *rotational symmetry.* Draw each figure listed below, find its center, and then find the smallest angle measure and turn that will rotate the figure onto itself. If this is not possible, then the figure does not have rotational symmetry.

4. Rectangle **5.** Square

6. Isosceles triangle **7.** Equilateral triangle

8. Which figures in 4–7 have rotational symmetry?

Key Idea
Some figures have two halves that are congruent.

Vocabulary
- symmetric
- line of symmetry

Materials
- grid paper
- scissors
- set of polygons or e tools

Symmetry

WARM UP

Trace each figure. Then draw a flip.

1. 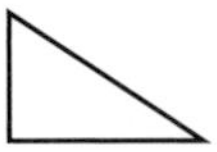

2. 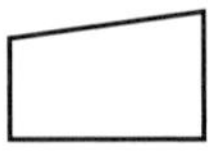

LEARN

Activity

What are symmetric figures?

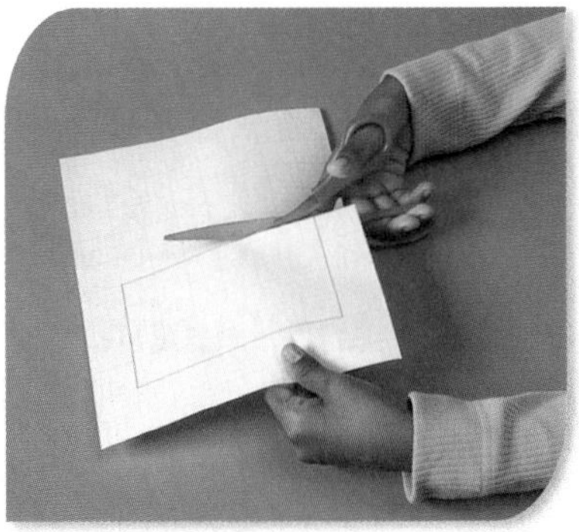

a. On a sheet of grid paper, draw a large rectangle that is not a square and cut it out.

b. Fold the rectangle in half so that the two halves fit on top of each other. Describe the two halves.

c. Open the rectangle. Then fold it a different way so that the two halves fit on top of each other.

A rectangle is a **symmetric** figure because it can be folded into two congruent halves that fit on top of each other. Each of your folds lies along a **line of symmetry.** The rectangle has two lines of symmetry. The W at the right has only one line of symmetry.

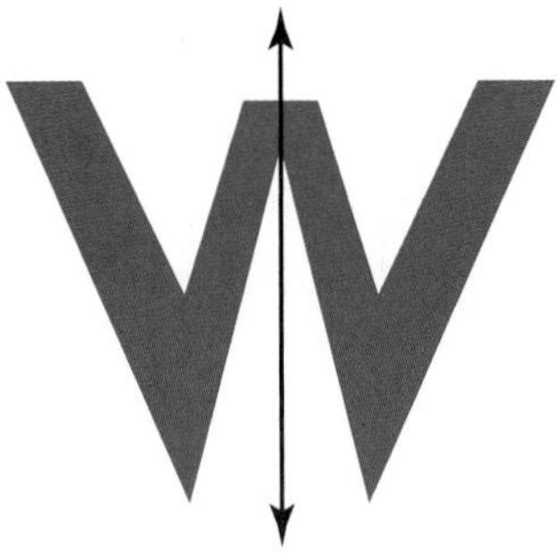

d. Draw and cut out a square. Fold it to find a line of symmetry. Does it have other lines of symmetry? How many?

Activity

How can you draw a symmetric design?

You can use a set of polygons or grid paper to create symmetric designs.

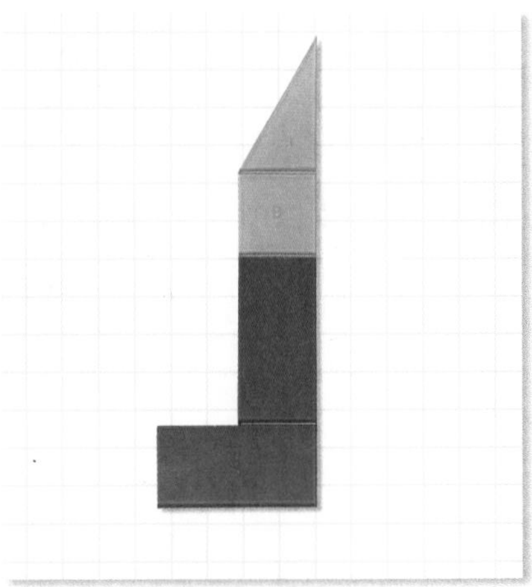

a. Arrange the polygons as shown at the right. Add more pieces to complete the design so that the result has symmetry.

b. Make your own symmetric design with polygons.

CHECK

For another example, see Set 8-7 on p. 492.

How many lines of symmetry does each figure have?

1. 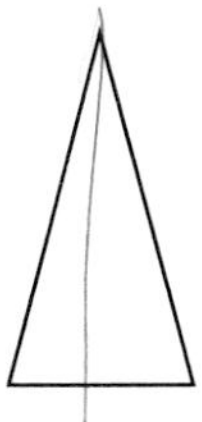

2. 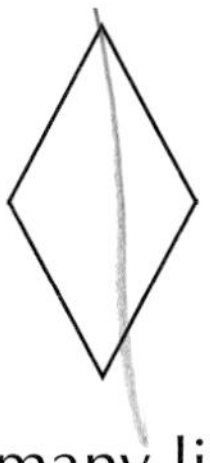

3. 

4. 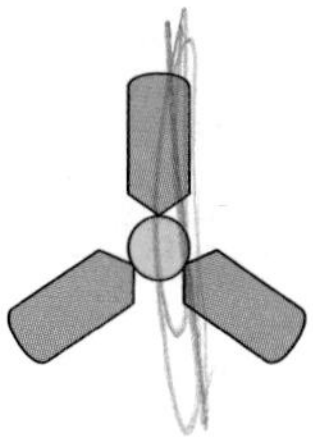

5. 

6. Reasoning How many lines of symmetry does a circle have?

PRACTICE

For more practice, see Set 8-7 on p. 495.

A Skills and Understanding

How many lines of symmetry does each figure have?

7. 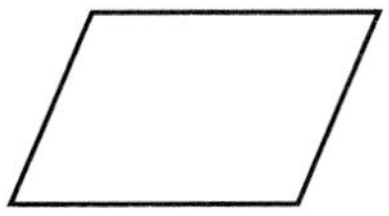

8. 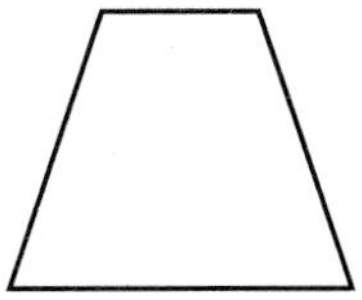

9. 

10. 

11. 

12. Reasoning How many lines of symmetry does a scalene triangle have?

B Reasoning and Problem Solving

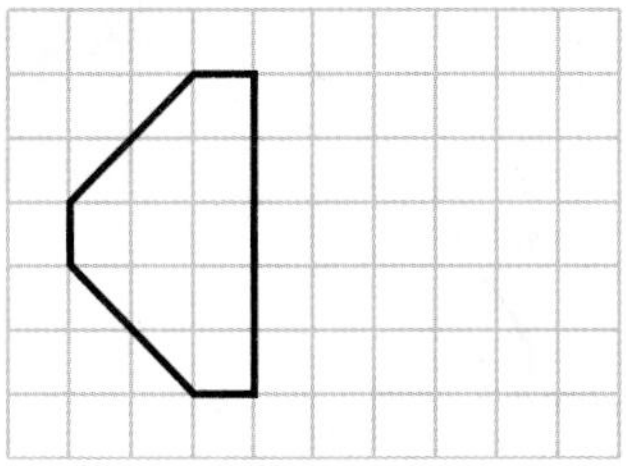

13. Copy the design at the right on grid paper. Then add to it so the result is symmetric.

14. In the musical notation shown, which line is a line of symmetry for the six notes?

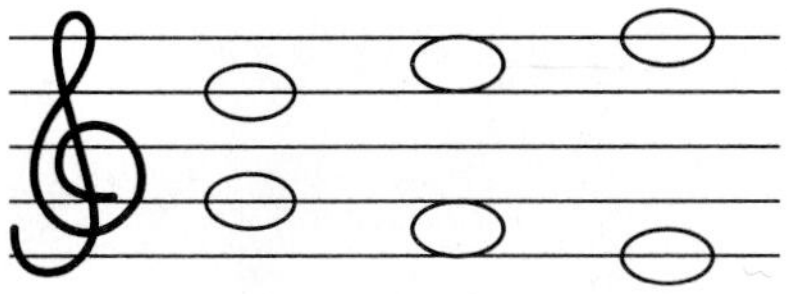

15. Writing in Math Draw a figure that is not symmetric. Explain your reasoning.

Mixed Review and Test Prep

Take It to the NET
Test Prep
www.scottforesman.com

16. What is the value of 2 quarters, 3 dimes, 4 nickels, and 3 pennies?

17. Which two figures appear to be congruent?

A. 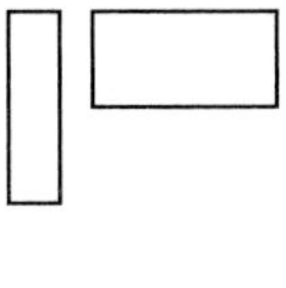

B. 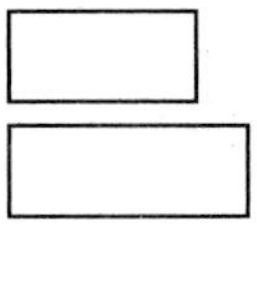

C. 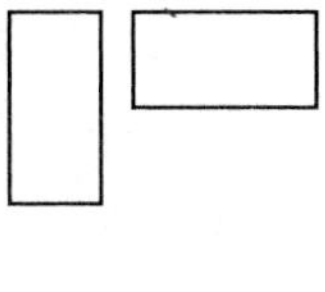

D. 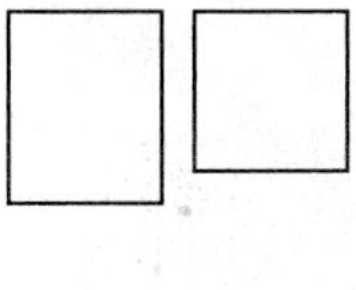

Key Idea
Some figures have the same shape but not necessarily the same size.

Vocabulary
- similar figures

TEST TALK

Think It Through
I need to **classify and categorize** geometric shapes.

Similar Figures

LEARN

What are similar figures?

On her trip to Russia, Jill bought a set of nesting dolls. All of the dolls have the same shape.

Figures that have the same shape are **similar figures.** They may or may not have the same size.

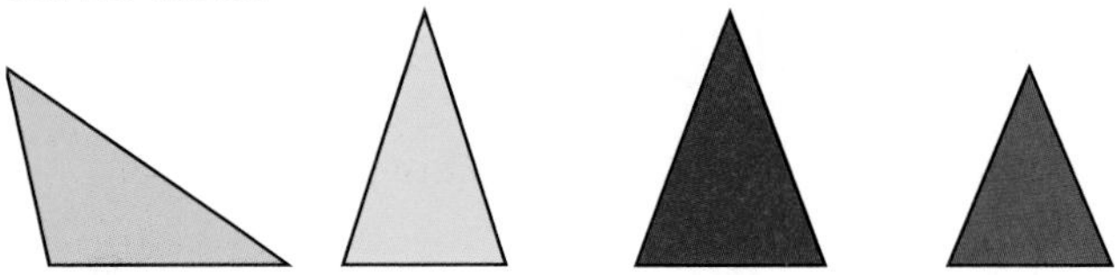

Not similar Similar

These similar figures are also congruent.

Example

Do the figures in each pair appear to be similar?

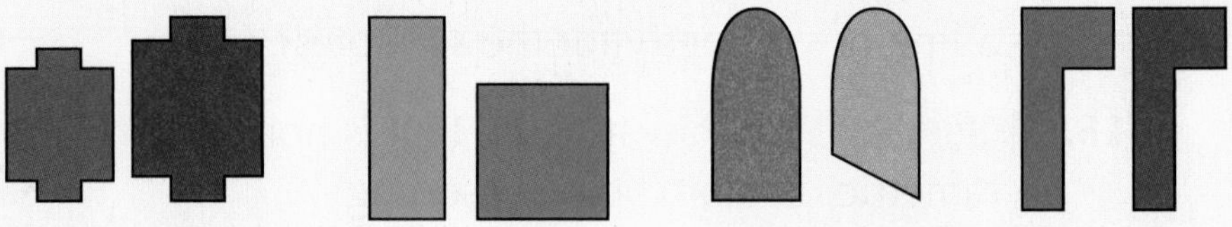

Similar	Not similar	Not similar	Similar
Same shape	Different shape	Different shape	Same size and shape

Talk About It

1. Are the nesting dolls shown above also congruent? Explain.
2. **Reasoning** Do the two triangles at the right appear to be similar? Explain.

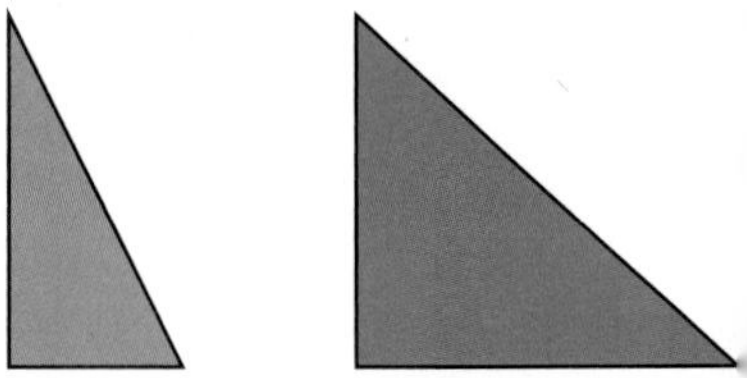

WARM UP

Tell if the figures in each pair are congruent.

1. 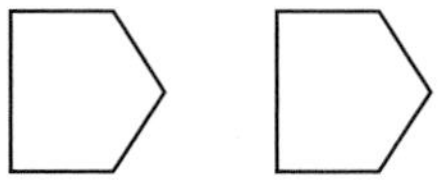

2. 

CHECK

For another example, see Set 8-8 on p. 492.

Do the figures in each pair appear to be similar? If so, are they also congruent?

1. 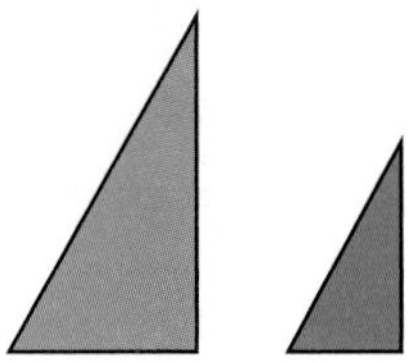

2. 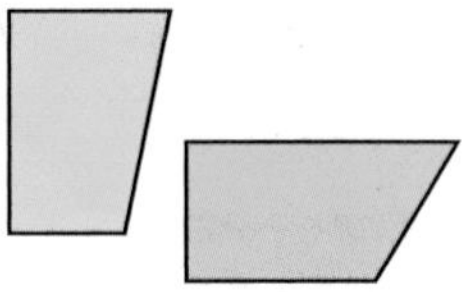

3. 

4. 

5. Reasoning Are all squares similar? Are all rectangles similar? Explain.

PRACTICE

For more practice, see Set 8-8 on p. 496.

A Skills and Understanding

Do the figures in each pair appear to be similar? If so, are they also congruent?

6. 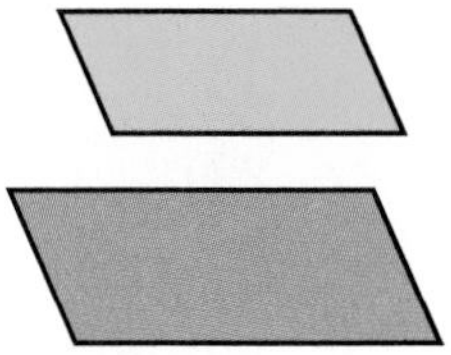

7. 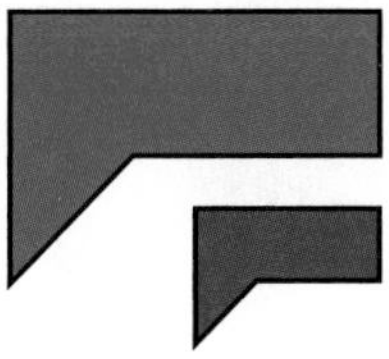

8. 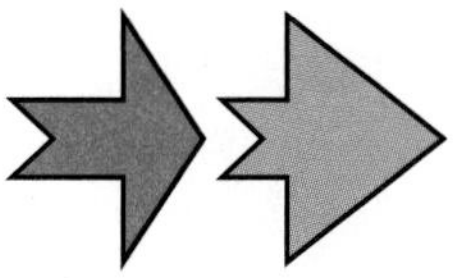

9. 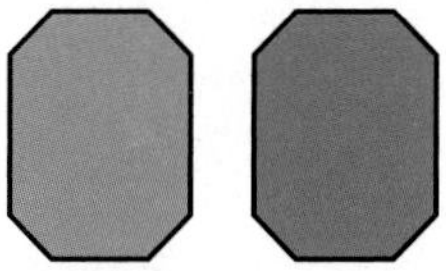

10. Reasoning Are all circles similar? Are all triangles similar? Explain.

B Reasoning and Problem Solving

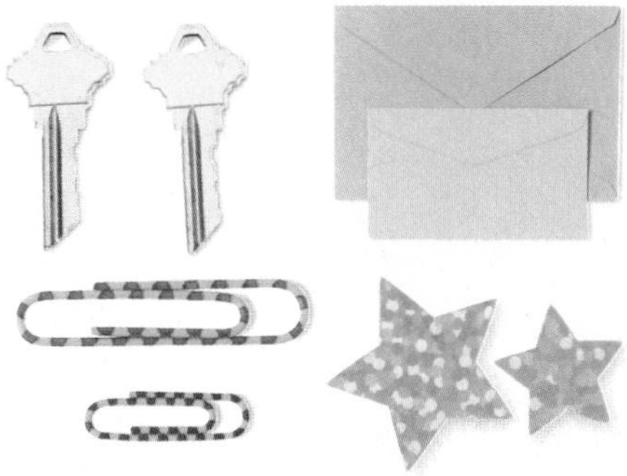

11. Which objects at the right are similar? Which are also congruent?

12. Draw your own example of similar figures.

13. Writing in Math Describe the difference between congruence and similarity.

Mixed Review and Test Prep

Take It to the NET
Test Prep
www.scottforesman.com

14. Draw a figure that has a line of symmetry.

15. Which expression means "six times the sum of four and seven"?

A. $6 \times 4 + 7$ **B.** $6 \times 4 \times 7$ **C.** $6 \times (4 + 7)$ **D.** $(6 \times 4) + 7$

16. Look at the triangle at the right. What part of the figure do the letters *R*, *S*, and *T* represent?

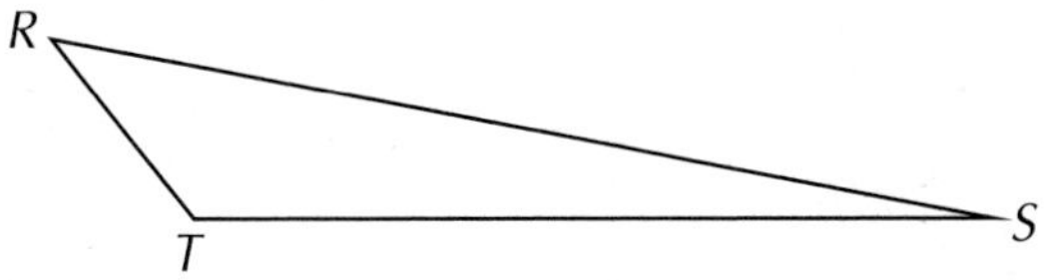

A. sides **C.** faces

B. vertices **D.** segments

Lesson 8-9

Problem-Solving Skill

Reading Helps!

Identifying steps in a process can help you with...

writing to describe.

Key Idea
There are specific things you can do to write a good description in math.

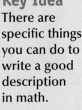

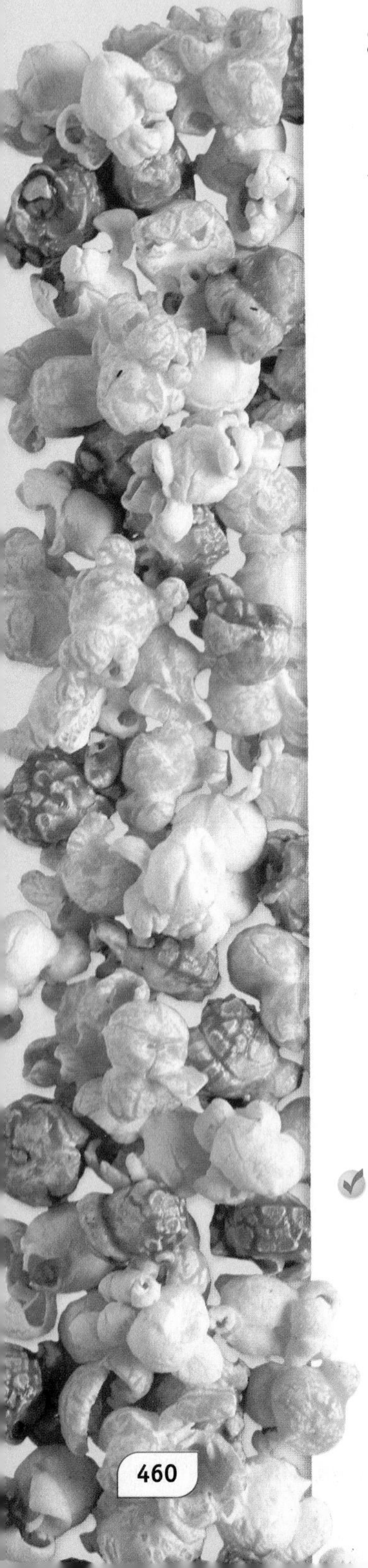

Writing to Describe

LEARN

How do you write a good description?

When you write to describe geometric figures, you need to use geometric terms.

Popcorn Boxes Trent is designing the fronts of the three popcorn boxes shown below. Use geometric terms to describe how a trapezoid, a square, and a rectangle are alike.

Box A

Box B

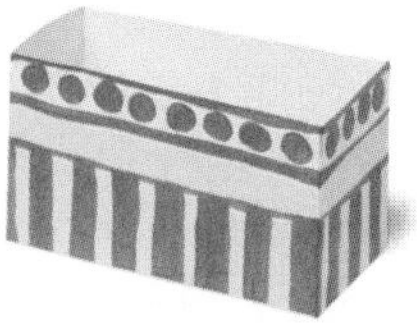

Box C

Writing a Math Description

- Make a list of all the geometric terms that tell about or describe how the shapes are alike.
- Choose the terms to use in your answer.
- Use geometric terms correctly when you write your description.

Geometric terms that describe how the front shapes are alike:

polygons
quadrilaterals
4 angles
2 parallel sides

All the shapes are polygons. Since they all have 4 sides and 4 angles, they are all quadrilaterals. The polygons are a trapezoid, a rectangle, and a square, so they all have at least two sides that are parallel.

Talk About It

1. What words in the description are geometric terms?
2. Look at Boxes A and C. Use geometric terms to describe one way a trapezoid and a rectangle are different.
3. Look at Boxes B and C. Describe one way a rectangle and a square are different.

CHECK

For another example, see Set 8-9 on p. 492.

1. Two team logos are shown below. Write two statements to describe how the logos are alike. Use geometric terms.

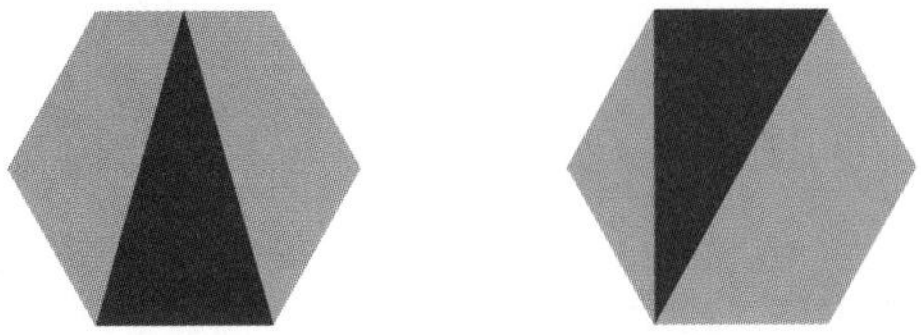

PRACTICE

For more practice, see Set 8-9 on p. 496.

Write to describe. Use geometric terms.

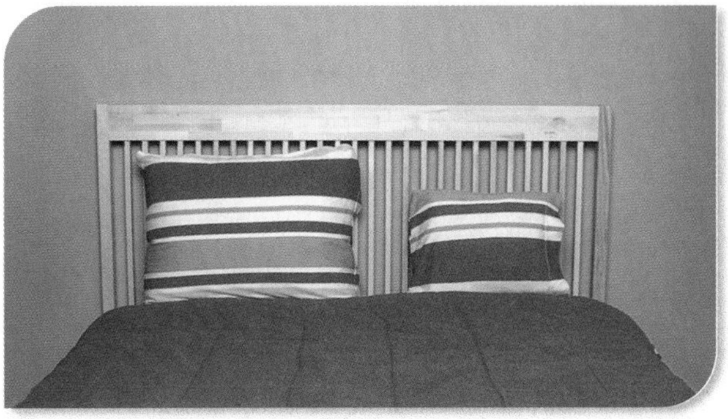

2. Write two statements to describe how the two pillow shapes are alike.

3. Write two statements describing how squares and rectangles are alike. Is a square a special rectangle?

4. Katie sorted four Power Solids into two groups as shown at the right. Describe how the solids in each group are alike. Describe a different way you could sort the four solids.

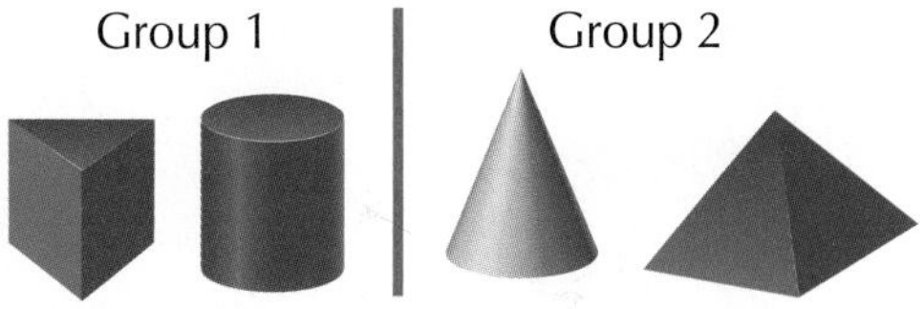

5. Two fourth-grade classes sold rolls of wrapping paper to raise money for a new computer. Every student sold at least 7 rolls. The results are shown below. How do the sales for the two classes compare?

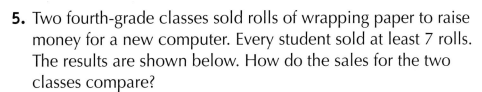

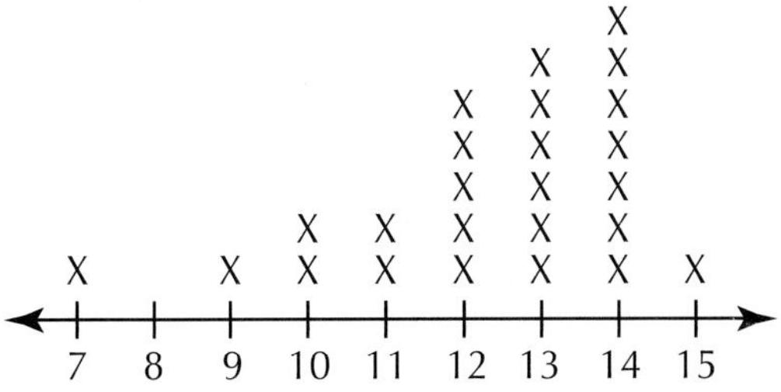

Number of Rolls of Wrapping Paper Sold by Students in Ms. Clark's Class

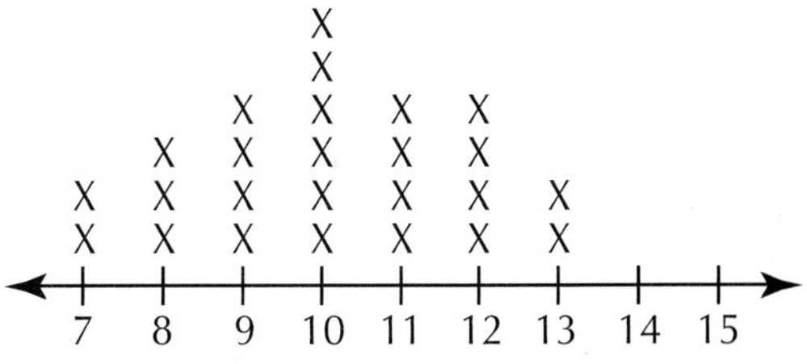

Number of Rolls of Wrapping Paper Sold by Students in Ms. Arnoff's Class

6. Write two statements comparing the shapes of the blocks of cheese at the right.

Review

Do You Know How?

Congruent Figures and Motions (8-6)

Do the figures in each pair appear to be congruent? If so, tell if they are related by a flip, slide, or turn.

1. 

2. 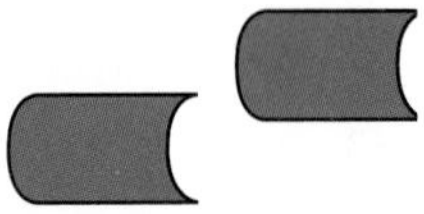

3. 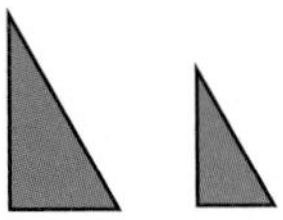

4. 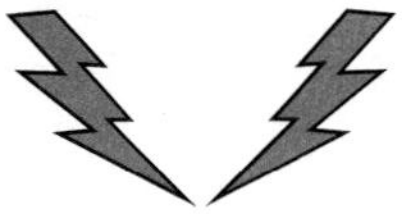

Do You Understand?

A For each pair of congruent figures in Exercises 1–4, explain how you decided each was a flip, slide, or turn.

B Draw a pair of congruent triangles so that one is right and the other is isosceles. What must be true about both triangles?

Symmetry (8-7)

How many lines of symmetry does each figure have?

5. 

6. 

7. 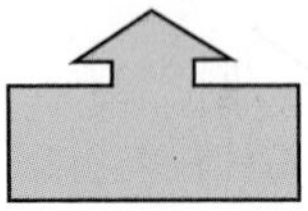

8. 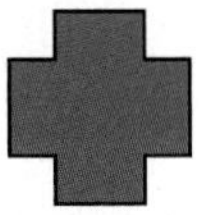

C Are all the figures in Exercises 5–8 symmetric? Explain.

D Draw a figure that is not symmetric.

Similar Figures (8-8)
Problem-Solving Skill: Writing to Describe (8-9)

Do the figures in each pair appear to be similar? If so, are they also congruent?

9. 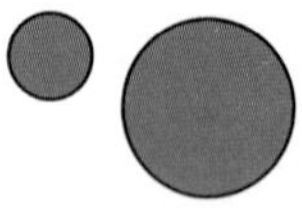

10. 

11. 

12. 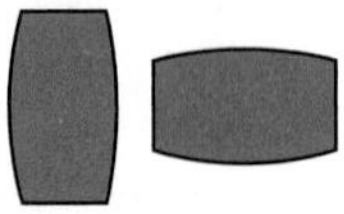

E Tell how you decided if the figures in Exercises 10 and 11 were similar.

F Write two statements describing the figures in Exercise 10.

Diagnostic Checkpoint

Think It Through
I need to look at each answer choice carefully.

MULTIPLE CHOICE

1. Which shape has more than two lines of symmetry? (8-7)

A. 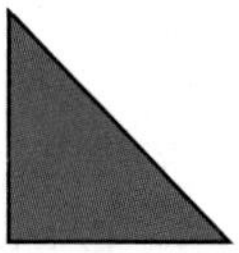 **B.**  **C.**  **D.** 

2. Which figure is a flip of the figure at the right? (8-6)

A. 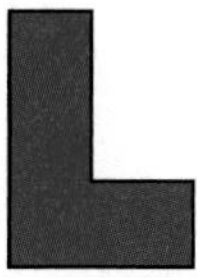 **B.**  **C.** 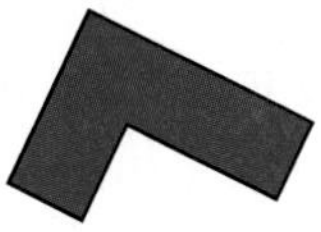 **D.** 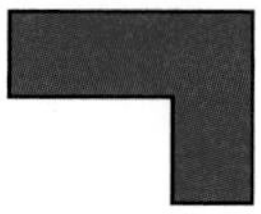

FREE RESPONSE

Do the figures in each pair appear to be similar? If so, are they also congruent? For each pair of congruent figures, tell if they are related by a flip, slide, or turn. (8-6 and 8-8)

3. 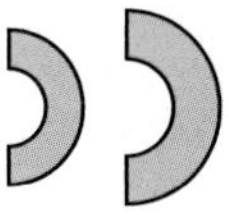 **4.** 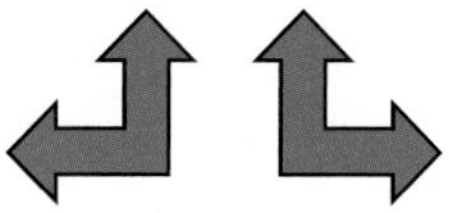 **5.**  **6.** 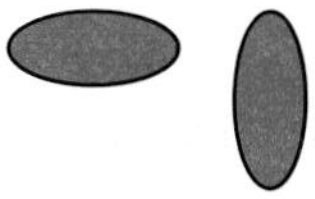

How many lines of symmetry does each figure have? (8-7)

7. 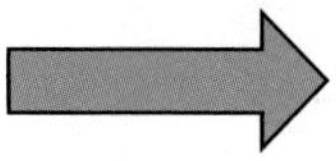 **8.**  **9.**  **10.** 

11. Find the line of symmetry in the figure at the right. Are the two congruent halves of the figure at the right related by a flip, a slide, or a turn? (8-6 and 8-7)

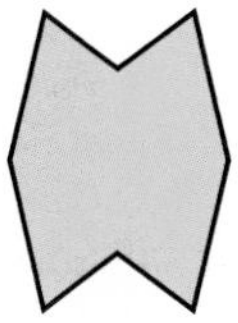

Writing in Math

12. Does a standard playground slide move you in the motion of a slide? Explain why or why not. (8-6)

13. Explain why all equilateral triangles are similar, but not all are congruent. (8-8)

14. Write two statements describing the polygons at the right. (8-9)

Lesson 8-10

Algebra

Key Idea
There are different ways to find the distance around a figure.

Vocabulary
• perimeter

Materials
• straws or paper strips or e tools

TEST TALK

Think It Through
I can **use objects** to help me investigate perimeter.

Perimeter

WARM UP

Name the quadrilateral.

1. I have four right angles, and my sides do not all have the same length.
2. I have four right angles, and my sides all have the same length.

LEARN

Activity

How can you find the perimeter of a figure?

The distance around a figure is its **perimeter.**

a. Work with a partner. Use at least 10 straws or paper strips to make a rectangle. Count the straws to find the perimeter.

b. Have your partner make a rectangle with a different shape that has the same perimeter.

c. Estimate the perimeter of a sheet of paper. Then use straws or paper strips to find the perimeter of the paper. Count the number of straws or paper strips to find the perimeter.

d. Use at least 10 straws or paper strips to make a triangle. Have your partner count the number of straws or paper strips to find the perimeter. Then have your partner make a triangle for you. What is its perimeter?

e. Use 36 straws or paper strips to make a figure. Describe the figure you made. Tell the length of each side.

How can you calculate perimeter?

You can use addition to find the perimeter of a figure. Sometimes you can use a formula.

Example A

Find the perimeter of this hexagon.

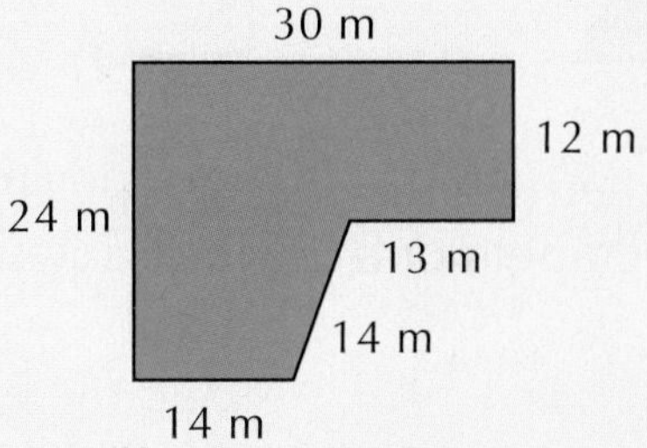

Add the lengths of the sides.

30 + 12 + 13 + 14 + 14 + 24 = 107

The perimeter is 107 meters.

Example B

Find the perimeter of this rectangle.

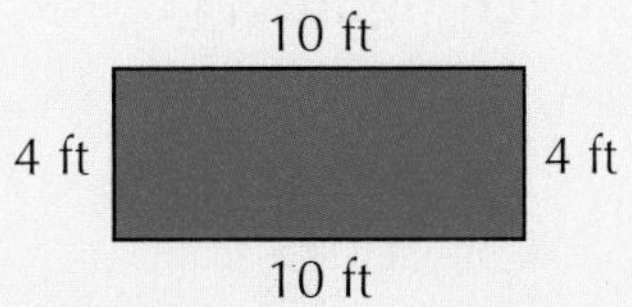

One Way

Emma added.

10 + 4 + 10 + 4 = 28

The perimeter is 28 feet.

Another Way

Miguel used a formula.

$P = 2\ell + 2w$

$P = (2 \times 10) + (2 \times 4)$

$= 20 + 8$

$= 28$

The perimeter is 28 feet.

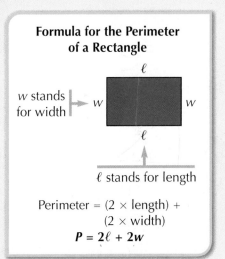

Formula for the Perimeter of a Rectangle

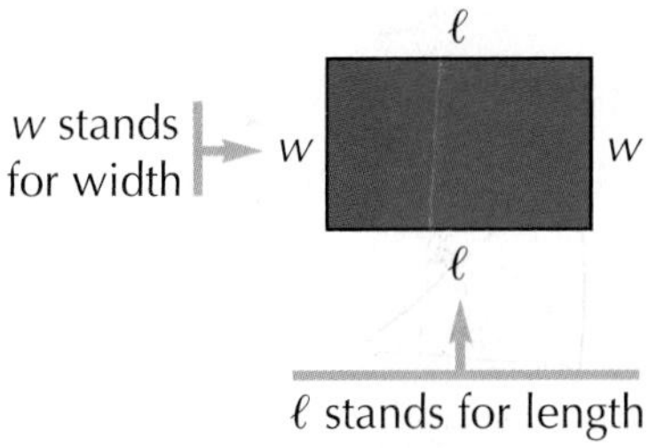

Perimeter = (2 × length) + (2 × width)

$P = 2\ell + 2w$

Talk About It

1. Find the perimeter of the square at the right. How can you use addition to find the answer? How can you use multiplication?

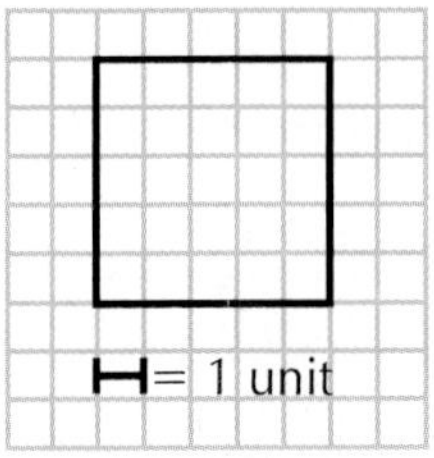

2. Algebra If s stands for the length of the side of a square, why is the formula for the perimeter of a square $P = 4s$?

3. Number Sense Is the perimeter of a square with 22-inch sides more than or less than 100 inches? Estimate to decide.

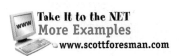

Take It to the NET
More Examples
www.scottforesman.com

CHECK

For another example, see Set 8-10 on p. 493.

Find the perimeter of each figure.

1. 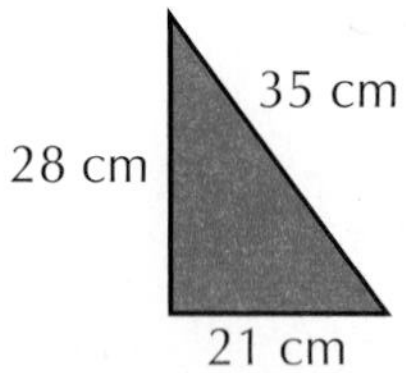

2. 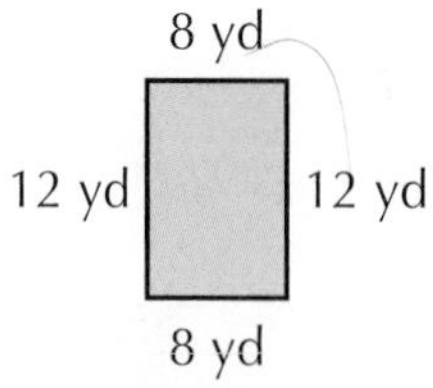

3. 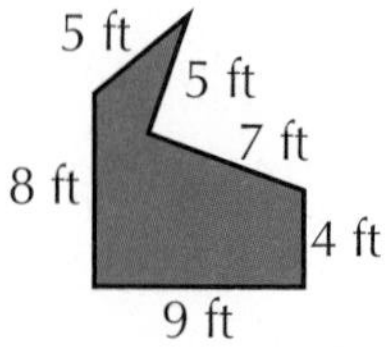

4. 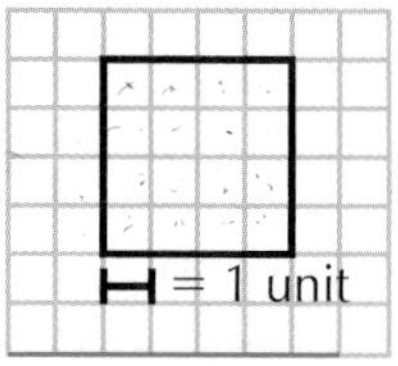

5. **Reasoning** Which has a larger perimeter, a 20-inch by 32-inch rectangle or a 28-inch square?

PRACTICE

For more practice, see Set 8-10 on p. 496.

A Skills and Understanding

Find the perimeter of each figure.

6. 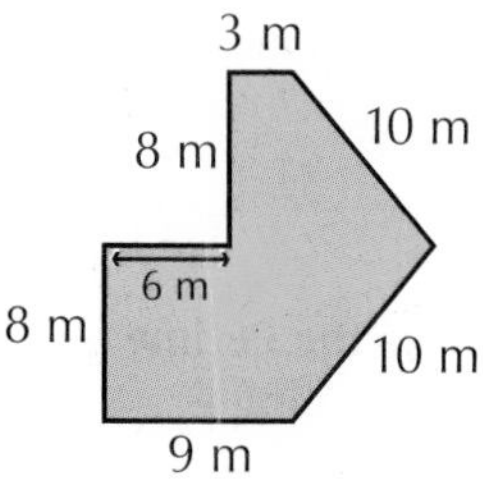

7. 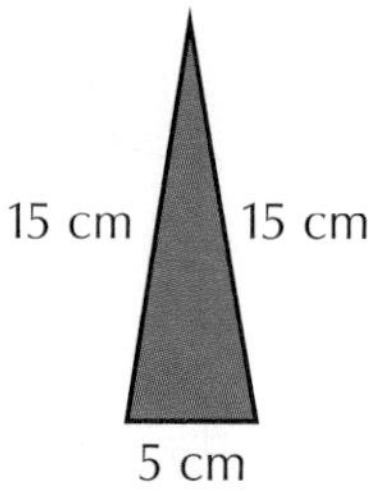

8. 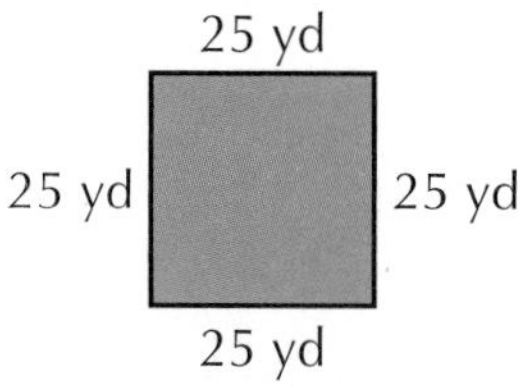

9. 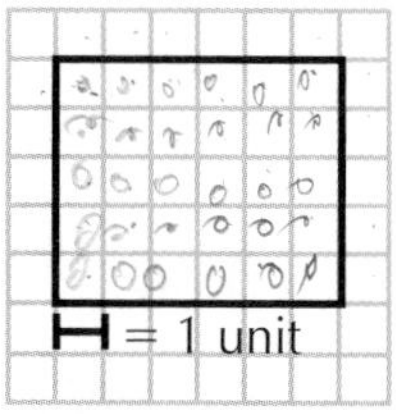

10. **Reasoning** Which has a larger perimeter, a 16-foot by 26-foot rectangle or a 20-foot square?

B Reasoning and Problem Solving

11. The length of one side of a square is 26 inches. What is its perimeter?

12. The perimeter of a rectangle is 32 inches. Its length is 10 inches. What is its width?

Math and Everyday Life

On many farms, children help take care of barnyard animals such as goats. Some people enjoy goat's milk and the cheeses that are made from it.

13. How much fencing is needed for a rectangular goat pen that is 12 feet by 16 feet?

14. **Writing in Math** Describe a situation at home in which you would need to know the perimeter of something.

C Extensions

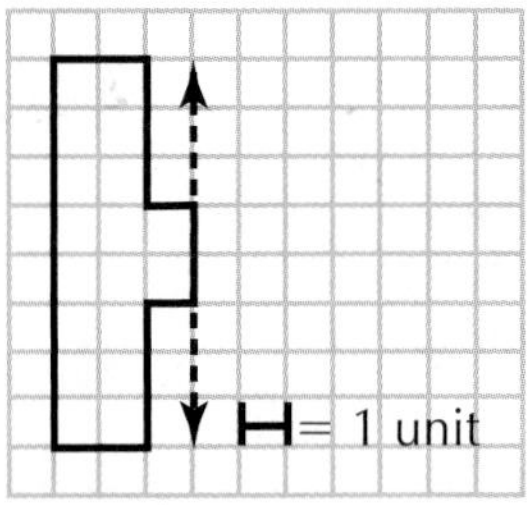

15. Doug drew half the block letter "H" on a grid as shown. The dashed line represents a line of symmetry. Copy Doug's work onto a sheet of grid paper. Complete the other half of the H. Estimate the perimeter. Then find the perimeter of the H.

16. Calculator The perimeter of a square is 1,464 meters. Use a calculator to find the length of a side.

Mixed Review and Test Prep

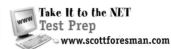

Take It to the NET
Test Prep
www.scottforesman.com

17. Write two statements describing a right triangle.

18. Which number is NOT divisible by 3?

A. 381 **B.** 420 **C.** 451 **D.** 501

Enrichment

Circumference

The perimeter of a circle is called its **circumference.**

1. Copy the table below. Select 4 different-sized circular objects. Measure the diameter and the circumference of each object to the nearest centimeter. Write the measurements in the table.

Object	Diameter (d)	Circumference (C)	$C \div d$

2. For each object, divide the circumference by the diameter. Round the quotient to the nearest whole number. Write the quotient in the last column of the table.

3. Do you notice a pattern when you divide the circumference by the diameter?

4. Estimate the circumference of a circle that has a diameter of 12 inches.

Algebra

Key Idea
There are different ways to count the square units needed to cover a surface.

Vocabulary
- area

Materials
- tiles
- grid paper
  or e tools

Area

LEARN

WARM UP

1. 7 x 9
2. 8 x 8
3. 5 x 7
4. 3 x 9
5. 10 x 14
6. 22 x 17
7. Find the perimeter of a 9-inch by 12-inch rectangle.

Activity

How can you find the area of a figure?

The number of square units needed to cover the region inside a figure is its **area.**

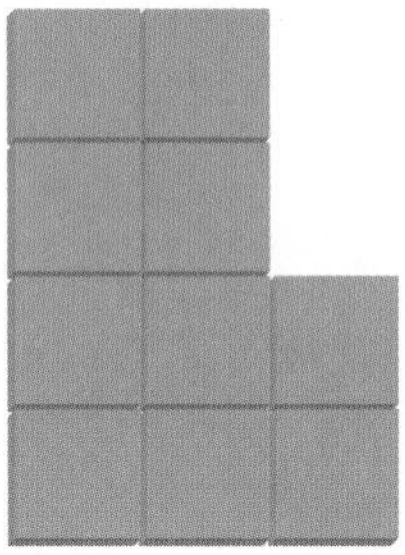

Area = 10 square units

a. Work with a partner. Make two different rectangles using tiles. Count each tile as one square unit. What is the area of each rectangle? What is the perimeter?

b. Slide your rectangles together to make a larger figure. Find the area and perimeter of the new figure.

c. Can you add the areas of the smaller rectangles to get the area of the new figure? Explain.

d. Find the area of the first 2 shapes. Estimate the area of the last 2 shapes. Which figure has the greatest area?

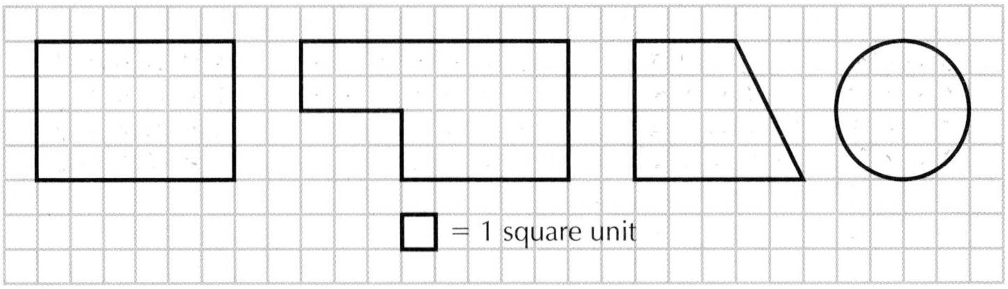

e. Do you have to count each individual square unit to find the area of the rectangle? Explain.

TEST TALK

Think It Through
I can **use logical reasoning** to estimate area. I'll count every two partial grid squares as one whole square.

How can you calculate the area of a figure?

Sometimes you can use multiplication to find the area of a figure.

Example A

Find the area of this rectangle.

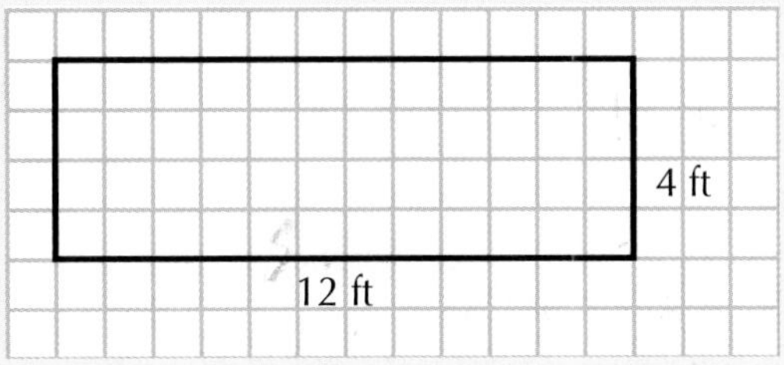

Formula for the Area of a Rectangle

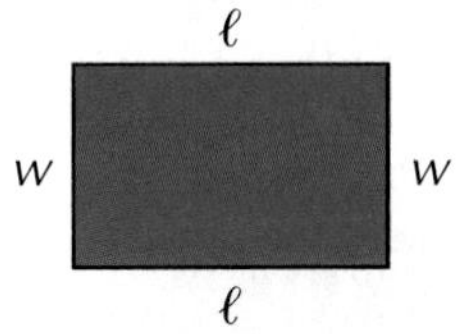

Area = length × width
$A = \ell w$

One Way

John counted the square units.

The area is 48 square feet.

Another Way

Kelly used a formula.

$A = \ell w$

$A = 12 \times 4$

$= 48$

The area is 48 square feet.

Example B

Find the area of this figure.

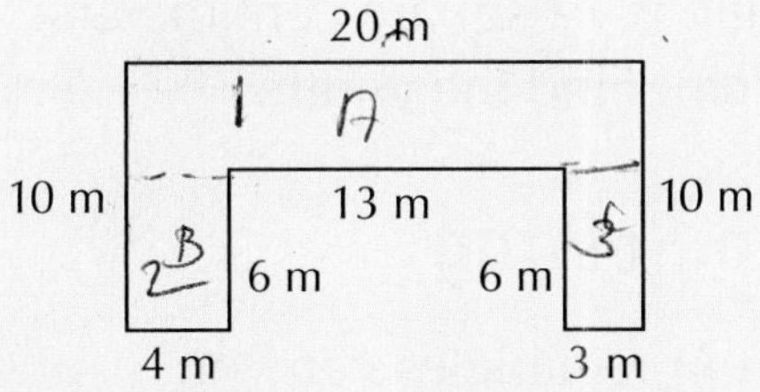

Draw segments to divide the figure into rectangles. Find the area of each rectangle and add.

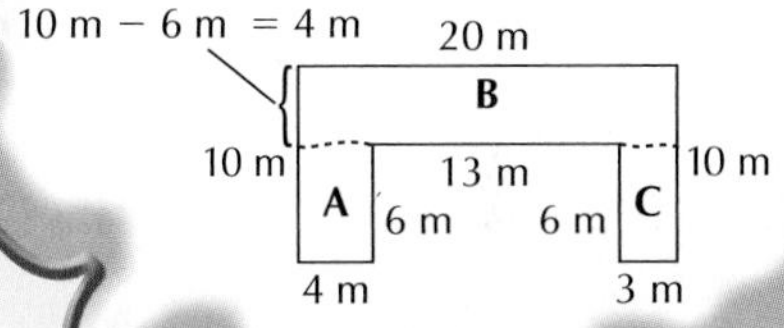

Rectangle A	Rectangle B	Rectangle C
$A = \ell w$	$A = \ell w$	$A = \ell w$
$A = 6 \times 4$	$A = 20 \times 4$	$A = 6 \times 3$
$= 24$	$= 80$	$= 18$

24 + 80 + 18 = 122, so the area of the original figure is 122 square meters.

Talk About It

1. In Example B, what are the dimensions of Rectangle B? Explain.

2. Algebra If s stands for the length of the side of a square, why is the formula for the area of a square $A = s \times s$?

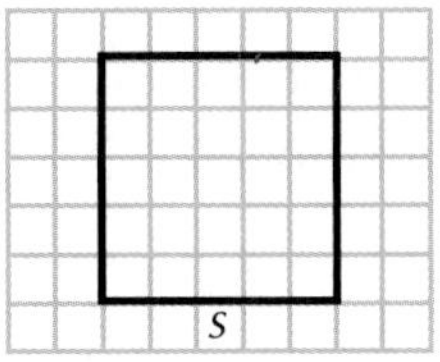

Take It to the NET
More Examples
www.scottforesman.com

CHECK

For another example, see Set 8-11 on p. 493.

Find the area of each figure.

1.

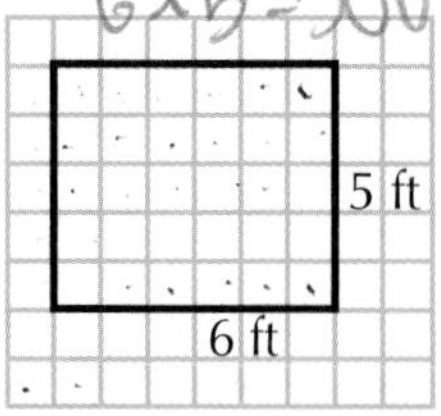

2.

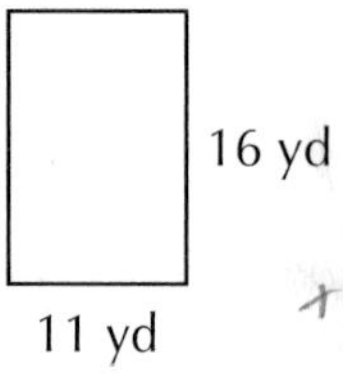

3.

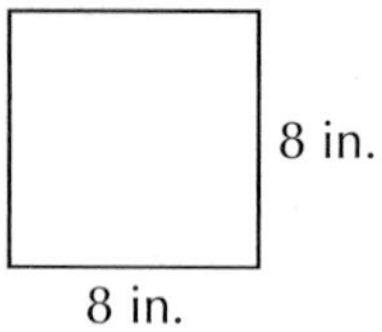

4.

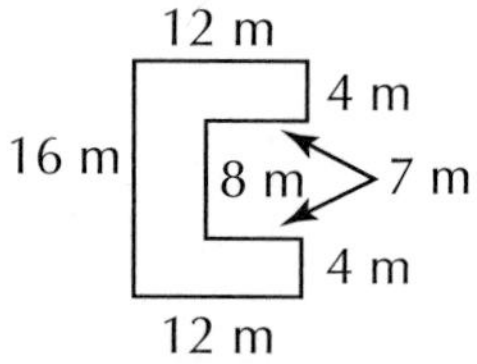

5. **Reasoning** The area of a square is 25 square yards. Find the length of a side.

PRACTICE

For more practice, see Set 8-11 on p. 497.

A Skills and Understanding

Find the area of each figure.

6.

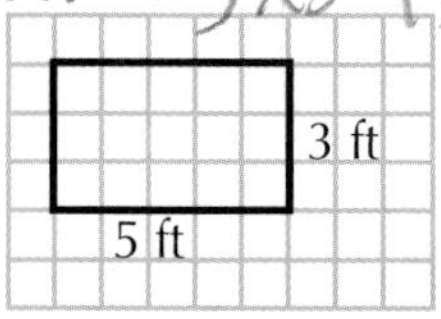

7.

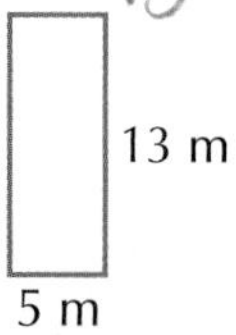

8.

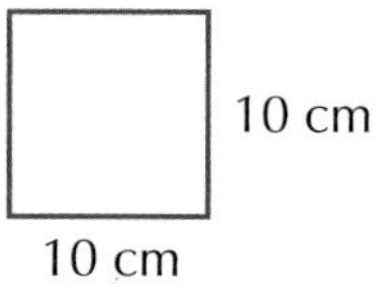

9.

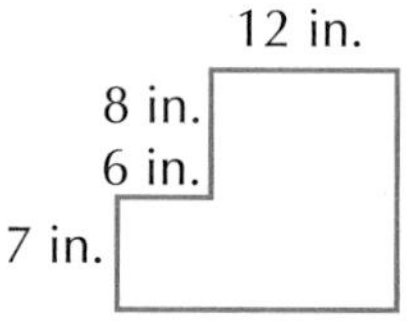

10. **Reasoning** The area of a rectangle is 72 square centimeters. The length of the rectangle is 9 cm. Find the width.

B Reasoning and Problem Solving

11. On grid paper, how many different rectangles can you draw with an area of 12 square units? Do they all have the same perimeter?

12. The perimeter of a square is 20 yd. What is its area?

Math and Everyday Life

The scale drawing at the right shows two minature golf holes.

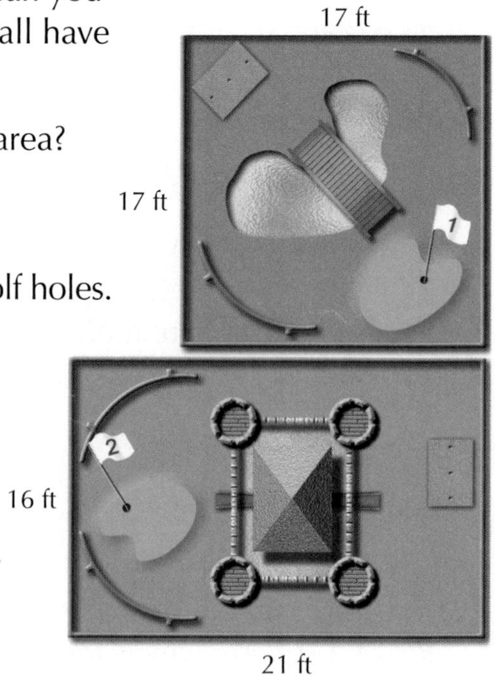

13. Find the area of each golf hole. Which has a greater area, hole 1 or hole 2?

14. Find the perimeter of each golf hole. Which has a greater perimeter, hole 1 or hole 2?

15. Would you want to know the area or perimeter before putting edging around each hole?

16. **Writing in Math** Explain the difference between the perimeter of a figure and the area of a figure.

C Extensions

The **surface area** of a prism is the sum of the areas of all of its faces. Picturing the net for a prism can help you calculate the surface area.

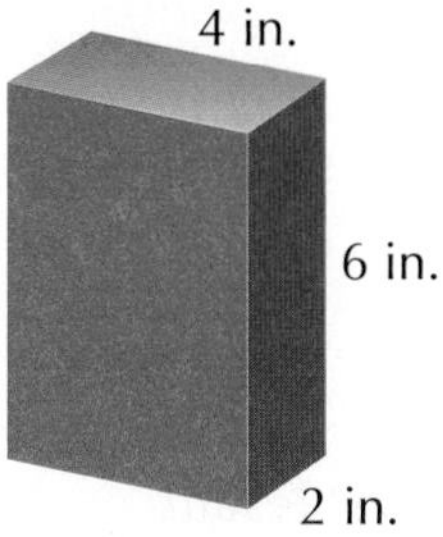

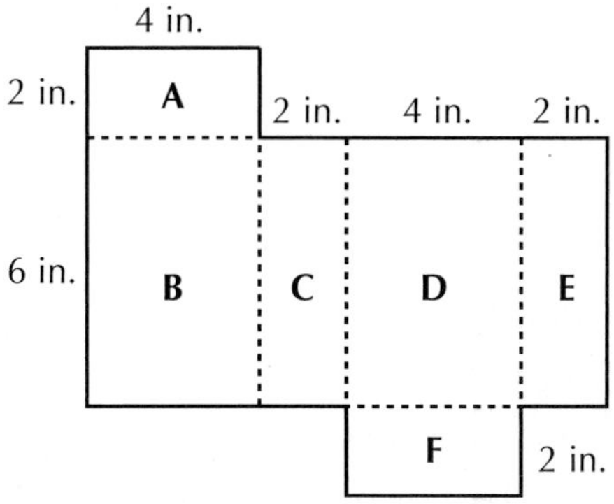

Face	Area
A	8 square inches
B	
C	
D	
E	
F	
Surface area (total)	

17. Copy and complete the table above to find the surface area of the rectangular prism.

Mixed Review and Test Prep

Take It to the NET
Test Prep
www.scottforesman.com

18. Find the median of this data set: 12, 8, 19, 22, 11, 14, 19.

19. What is the perimeter of a square that is 8 inches on one side?

A. 2 inches **B.** 12 inches **C.** 32 inches **D.** 64 inches

Enrichment

Area and Perimeter Using a Geoboard

1. Copy the table. Then use rubber bands to make Polygon A on your geoboard. Find the perimeter and area of Polygon A. Write these numbers in the table.

2. Create two different polygons that have the same perimeter as Polygon A. Call them Polygon B and Polygon C. Find the area of each of these polygons. Write the areas in the table.

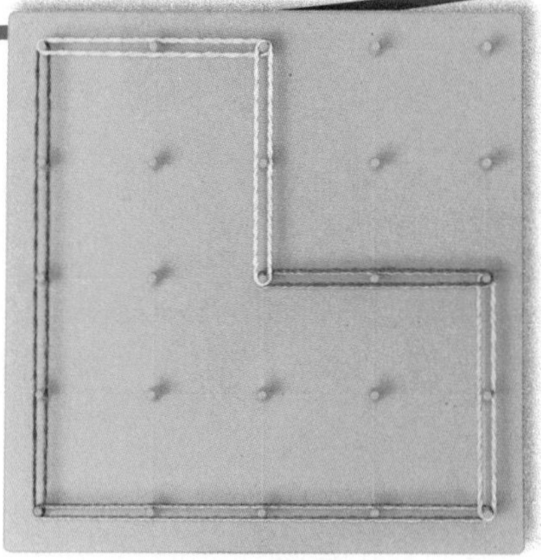

	Perimeter	Area
Polygon A		
Polygon B		
Polygon C		

Reading For Math Success

Visualize

Visualizing when you read in math can help you use the **problem-solving strategy, *Act it Out,*** in the next lesson.

In reading, visualizing can help you "see" what is happening in a story. In math, visualizing can help you "see" what is happening in a problem and act it out to solve the problem.

*When I **visualize** the problem, I see a rectangle with a length of 10 feet and a width of 8 feet.*

Beth is stenciling a border on the walls around the perimeter of her porch. The stencil pattern is 2 feet long. The rectangular room is 10 feet by 8 feet. How many times will Beth repeat the stencil pattern to cover the entire perimeter of her porch?

*I'll **act it out.** I'll let 1 centimeter represent 1 foot and I'll "build" the room with 1-cm paper or plastic squares.*

Then I'll use pieces of straws, 2 cm long each, to represent the pattern.

1. How many squares are needed to represent the length of the room?
2. Why do the pieces of straws need to be 2 cm long?

For 3–5, use the problem below.

A square meeting room is being covered with 1-foot square tiles. The meeting room has a perimeter of 44 feet. How many square tiles will be needed to cover the meeting room floor?

3. Visualize the problem. Describe what you see.

4. Use 1-centimeter paper or plastic squares to represent the problem.

5. **Writing in Math** What are the length and width of the meeting room? How do you know?

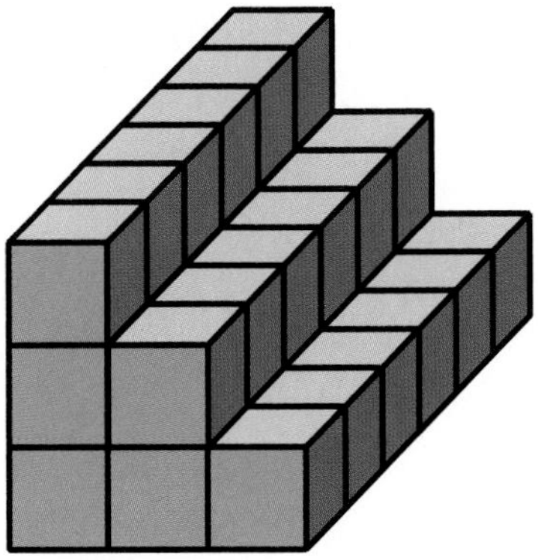

For 6–8, use the problem below.

Following the style of the steps shown at the left, how many cubes are needed to build 5 steps?

6. Visualize the problem. Describe what you see.

7. Use small cubes to represent the problem.

8. **Writing in Math** Would you be able to solve the problem as easily using a drawing? Explain.

For 9–11, use the problem below.

Travis plans to use 12 four-foot sections of fence to enclose a rectangular vegetable garden. What are all the different possible dimensions of the garden?

9. Visualize the problem. Describe what you see.

10. Use straws or strips of paper to represent the problem.

11. **Writing in Math** Describe one arrangement of the fence sections.

Problem-Solving Strategy

Reading Helps!

Visualizing

can help you with...

the problem-solving strategy, *Act It Out*.

Key Idea
Learning how and when to act it out can help you solve problems.

Materials
- straws or paper pieces
- square tiles or e tools

Act It Out

LEARN

How do you act out a problem to solve it?

Kennels Carrie bought 8 ten-foot sections of fence to make a rectangular kennel for her dog. She wants as much space as possible for her dogs. How should she arrange the 80 feet of fence?

Read and Understand

What do you know? Carrie has 8 ten-foot sections, or 80 feet, of fence. She wants the rectangular kennel to be as large as possible.

What are you trying to find? Find how Carrie should arrange the fencing.

Plan and Solve

What strategy will you use? **Strategy: Act It Out**

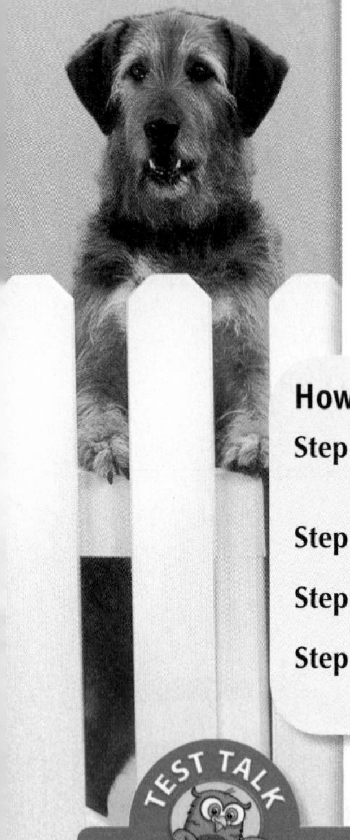

How to Act It Out

Step 1 Choose objects, if needed, to act it out.

Step 2 Show what you know.

Step 3 Act out the problem.

Step 4 Find the answer in your work.

I'll use straws to act it out.

A 10- by-30 foot kennel has an area of 300 square feet. A 20-by-20 kennel has an area of 400 square feet. The 20-by-20 kennel is larger.

TEST TALK

Think It Through
Visualizing the kennel in the problem helps me to **act it out** using straws.

Look Back and Check

Is your work correct? Yes, each kennel has a perimeter of 80 feet.

✓ Talk About It

1. **Reasoning** Can two rectangles have the same perimeter and different areas?

CHECK ✓

For another example, see Set 8-12 on p. 493.

Use tiles to solve the problem. Write the answer in a complete sentence.

1. **Reading Area** Ms. Watson got 42 carpet tiles to make a reading area for her room. Each tile is one foot on each side. Her class wants to put a border around the reading area. How can they arrange the tiles to make the shortest border?

PRACTICE

For more practice, see Set 8-12 on p. 497.

Solve each problem. Write the answer in a complete sentence.

2. Carol and Ron have 10 meters of edging to make a rectangular garden. What length and width should they make the garden to get the greatest area?

3. The economy section of an airplane has 9 seats in each row. The section holds 216 passengers. How many rows of seats are there?

4. **Photo Albums** Laura and Kelly collect pictures of famous people and put the pictures in a photo album. Laura puts 5 pictures in her album each day. Kelly starts collecting the same day as Laura and puts 3 pictures in her album each day. How many pictures does Kelly have in her album when Laura has 25 pictures in hers?

5. How many cubes are needed to build the 7th figure if the pattern continues?

Figure 1

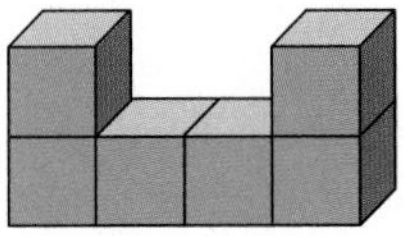

Figure 2

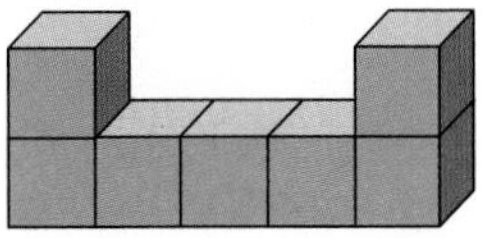

Figure 3

6. How many different rectangles can you make with 24 squares?

7. Mallory has the same number of quarters and nickels. She has $2.10. How many quarters and nickels does she have?

8. Suppose you arrange 48 counters into groups. The first group has 3 counters. Each group after that has 2 more counters than the group before. How many groups do you have?

Algebra

Key Idea
There are different ways to count the cubic units needed to fill a solid figure.

Vocabulary
• volume

Materials
• small cubes
• small boxes

TEST TALK

Think It Through
I can **use objects** to estimate the volume of a solid figure.

Volume

WARM UP

1. 3 × 6 × 4
2. 2 × 2 × 2
3. 10 × 7 × 6
4. 5 × 5 × 12
5. 5 × 5 × 5

LEARN

Activity

How can you measure volume?

The number of cubic units needed to fill a solid figure is its **volume.**

a. Fill a box with as many small cubes as possible. Count each cube as one cubic unit. What is the volume of the box? Is your answer exact or an estimate? Explain.

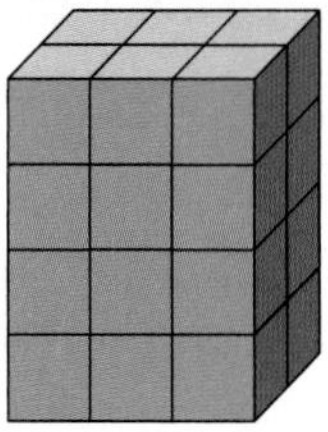

Volume = 24 cubic units

b. How can you use multiplication to find the volume of your box? the box at the right?

How can you find the volume of a rectangular prism?

You can count cubes or use multiplication to find the volume of a rectangular prism.

Example

Find the volume of this rectangular prism.

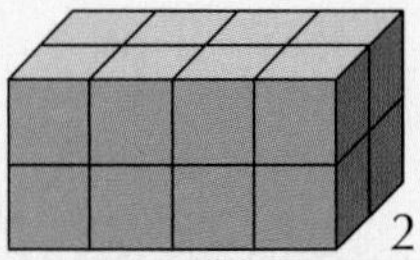

One Way

Lisa counted the cubic units.

The volume is 16 cubic yards.

Another Way

Marta used a formula.

$V = \ell wh$

$V = 4 \times 2 \times 2$

$= 16$

The volume is 16 cubic yards.

Formula for the Volume of a Rectangular Prism

Volume = length × width × height
$V = \ell wh$

CHECK

For another example, see Set 8-13 on p. 493.

Find the volume of each figure.

1.

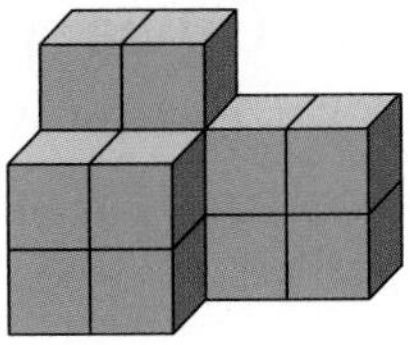

2.

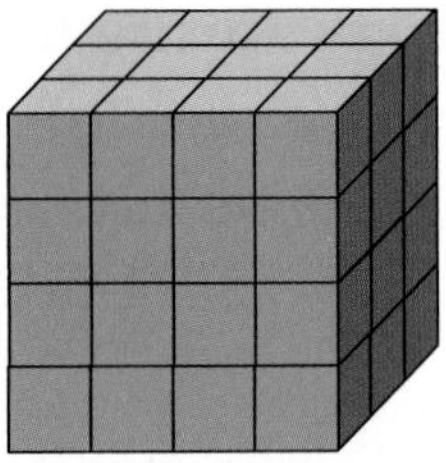

3.

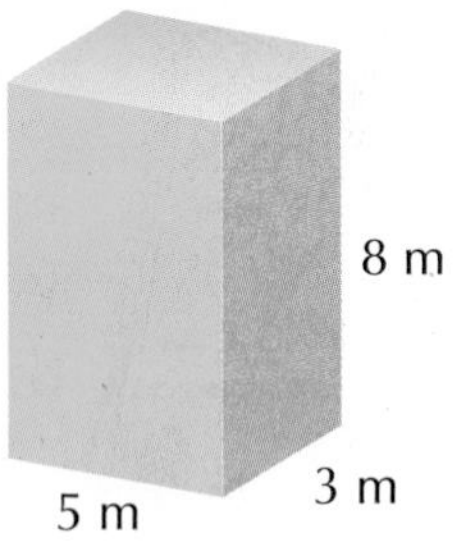

4. Reasoning The length of the edge of a cube is 3 feet. Find the volume. Explain how you found your answer.

PRACTICE

For more practice, see Set 8-13 on p. 497.

A Skills and Understanding

Find the volume of each figure.

5.

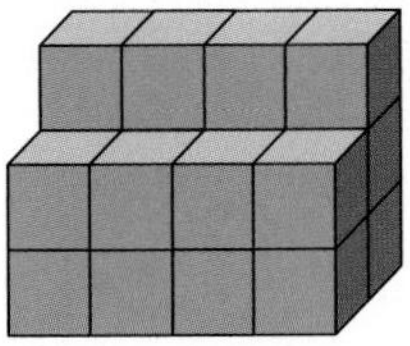

6.

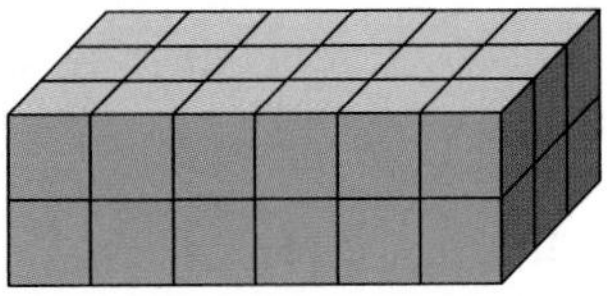

7.

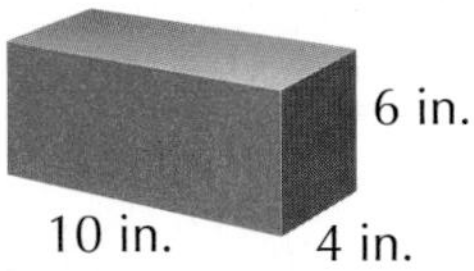

8. Reasoning Find the volumes of figures A and B at the right. How are the volumes related?

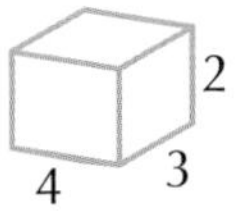

Figure A

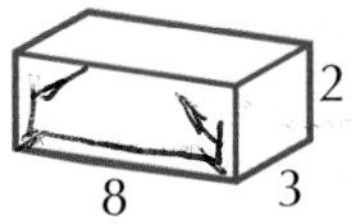

Figure B

B Reasoning and Problem Solving

9. Suppose the box at the right is placed inside the crate. Find how much space is left over inside the crate.

10. Writing in Math A box has a length of 3 yards and a width of 2 yards. Its volume is 30 cubic yards. What is its height? Explain.

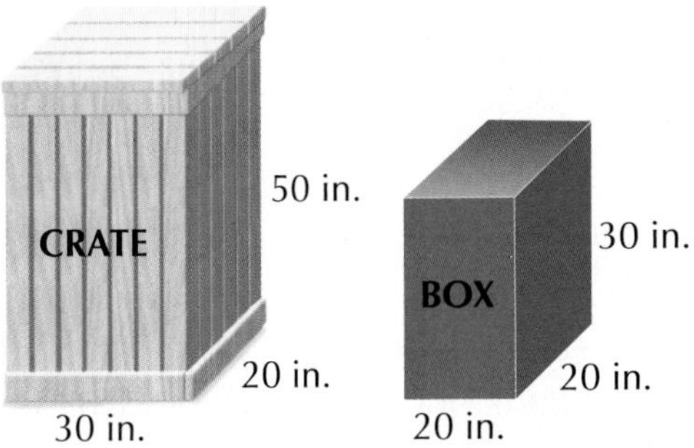

Mixed Review and Test Prep

Take It to the NET
Test Prep
www.scottforesman.com

11. How many lines of symmetry does the figure at the right have?

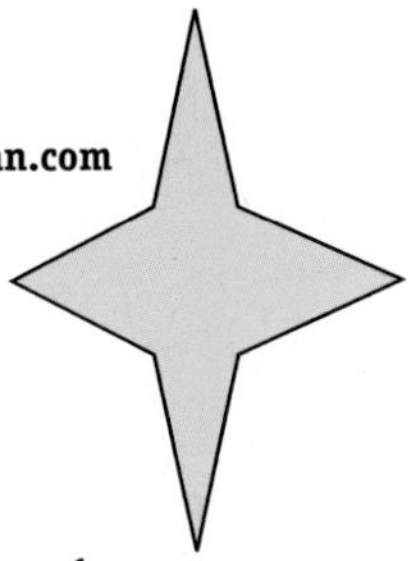

12. What is the perimeter of a square that has an area of 36 feet?

A. 6 feet **B.** 24 feet **C.** 30 feet **D.** 36 feet

Problem-Solving Applications

Tall Buildings Why are tall structures made? Office space is a prime reason, but holding communication antennas is also important. Many are built to inspire awe or to attract tourists. Whatever the reason, tall buildings often become symbols of their cities.

Trivia The Petronas Towers in Malaysia have spires that are higher than the roof of the Sears Tower in Chicago, but the Sears Tower has the highest floor.

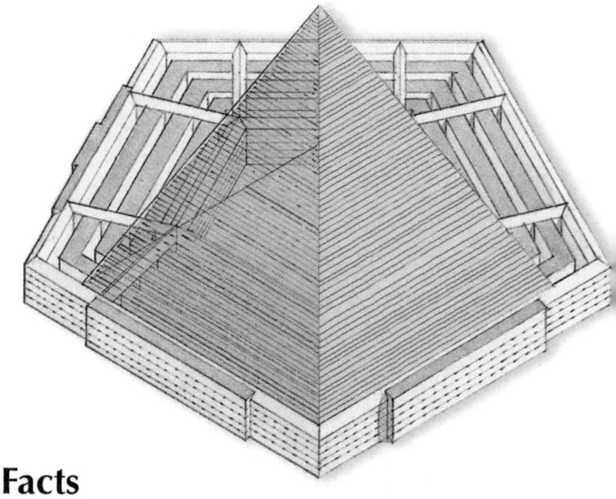

1. The base of the Great Pyramid is a square. Each side is about 755 feet long. Each side of the Pentagon is about 921 feet long. What is the difference between the buildings' perimeters?

2. The base of the Leaning Tower of Pisa is a circle. What is the general shape of the entire tower?

Key Facts
Tall Structures

Structure	Height
• Leaning Tower of Pisa	180 ft
• Statue of Liberty	305 ft
• Great Pyramid	481 ft
• 1 Canada Square	797 ft
• Eiffel Tower	1,052 ft
• Bank of China	1,033 ft
• Chrysler Building	1,046 ft
• Empire State Building	1,250 ft
• Sears Tower	1,453 ft
• CN Tower	1,815 ft
• KTHI-TV Tower	2,063 ft

Using Key Facts

3. About how many times taller is the CN Tower than the Statue of Liberty?

4. How many feet taller is the Sears Tower than the Eiffel Tower? Is the Sears Tower more than twice the height of the Eiffel Tower?

Good News/Bad News *Tall buildings create beautiful skylines, but they can cause city streets to feel closed-in and dark.*

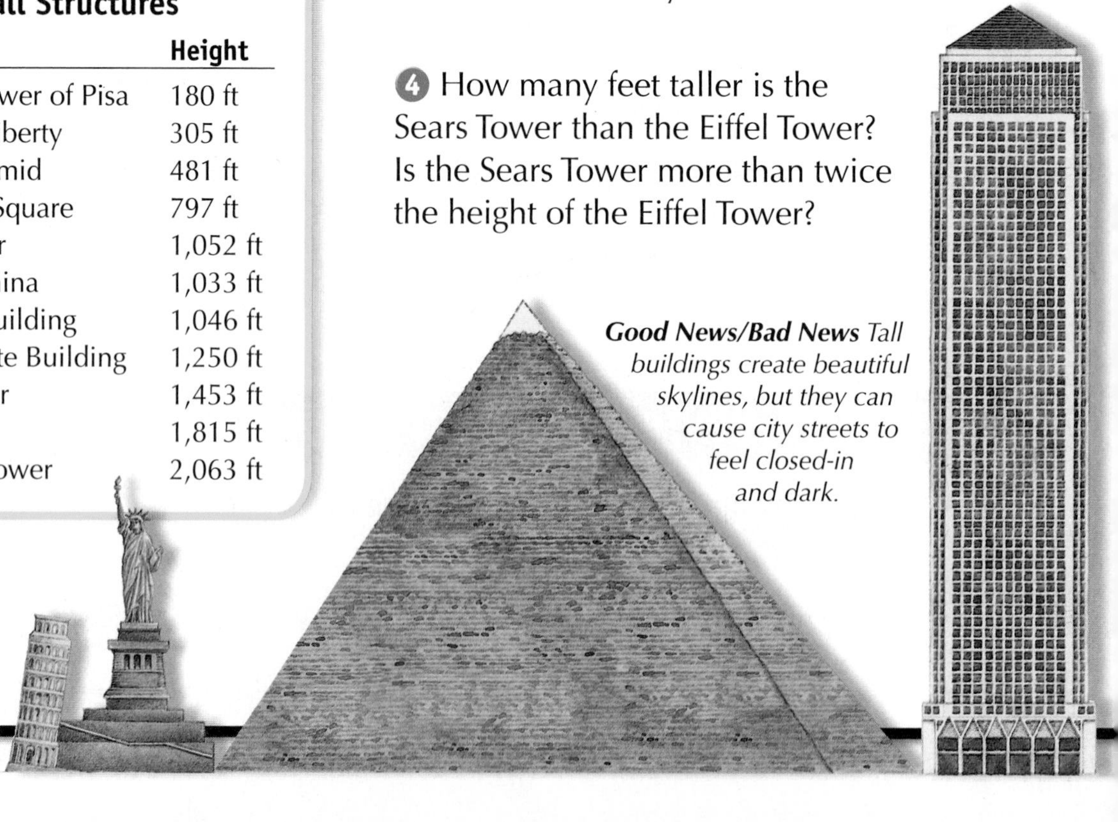

5 **Writing in Math** Describe five different shapes you see in the buildings below.

6 Which three structures shown below do not have symmetry? State their positions from the left starting on page 478.

7 **Decision Making** Draw a skyscraper by using only parallelograms. Draw another skyscraper using only shapes that are not parallelograms. Which skyscraper would be best to build? Explain your answer.

Review

Do You Know How?

Perimeter (8-10)
Area (8-11)

Find the perimeter and area of each figure.

1.

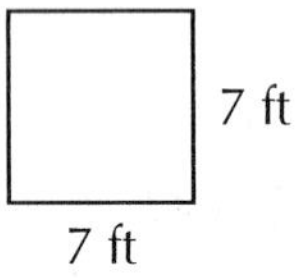

2.

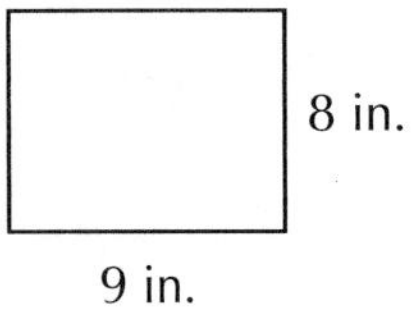

3.

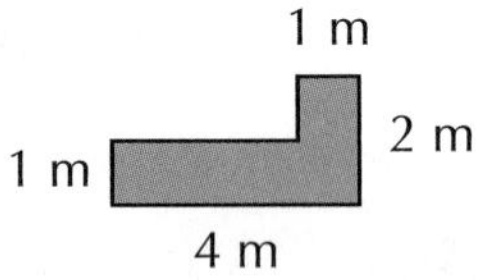

Do You Understand?

A Explain how you found the perimeter in Exercise 2 and the area in Exercise 1.

B What do ℓ and w represent in the formula $P = 2\ell + 2w$?

Problem-Solving Strategy: Act It Out (8-12)

4. Kristen is designing a horse corral that needs to have an area of 105 square meters. What length and width should she make the corral to use the least amount of fence? Assume the length and width must be whole meters.

C Describe how you solved the problem by acting it out.

D Give the lengths and widths of two rectangles that have the same area and different perimeters.

Volume (8-13)

Find the volume of each figure.

5.

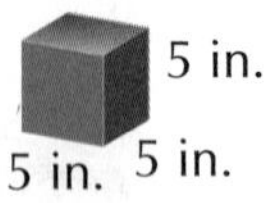

6.

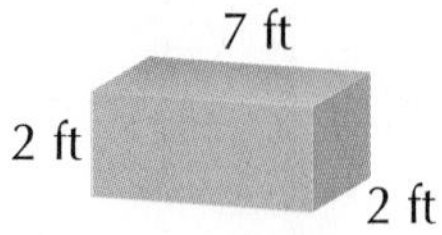

7. A rectangular prism has a length of 6 meters, a width of 2 meters, and a height of 4 meters. What is its volume?

E Explain how you found the volume in Exercise 5.

F Does it matter what order you multiply the lengths of the sides to find volume? Explain your answer.

Chapter 8 Section C

Diagnostic Checkpoint

TEST TALK

Think It Through
I can **use objects** or formulas to find perimeter, area, and volume.

MULTIPLE CHOICE

1. Camille planted a tulip garden in her front yard. The garden was the shape of a rectangle, 4 feet long and 2 feet wide. How many feet of edging will she need to buy if she wants to edge all the way around her garden? (8-10)

A. 6 feet **B.** 8 feet **C.** 10 feet **D.** 12 feet

2. The area of a rectangle is 42 square meters. The width of the rectangle is 6 meters. What is the length? (8-11)

A. 7 meters **B.** 32 meters **C.** 48 meters **D.** 252 meters

FREE RESPONSE

Find the perimeter of each figure. (8-10)

3.
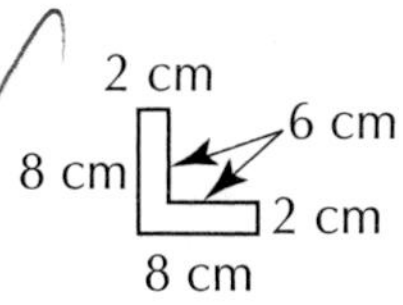

4.
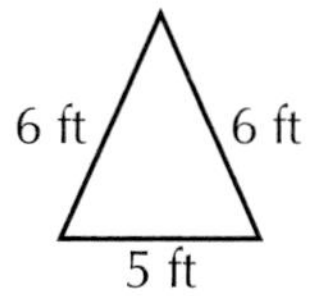

5.
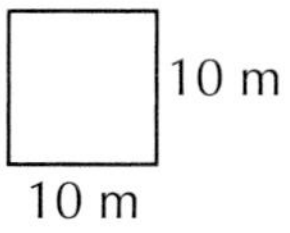

6.
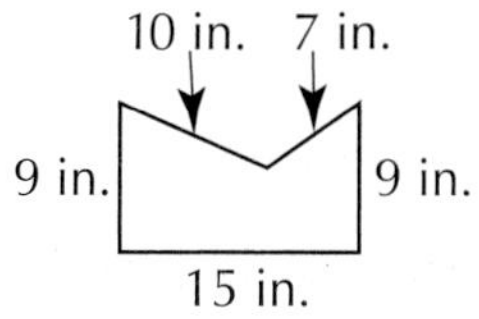

Find the area of each figure. (8-11)

7.
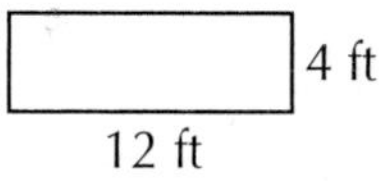

8.
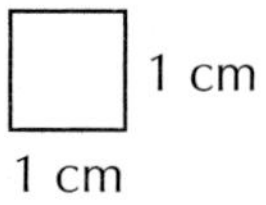

9.
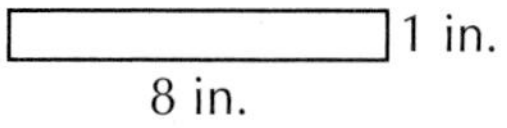

10.
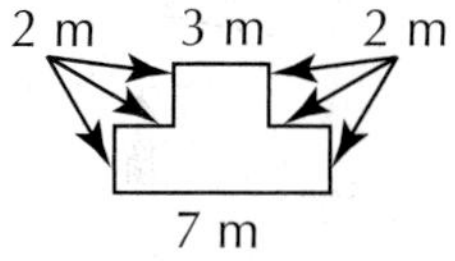

Find the volume of each figure. (8-13)

11.
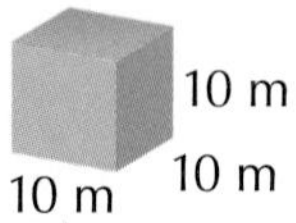

12.
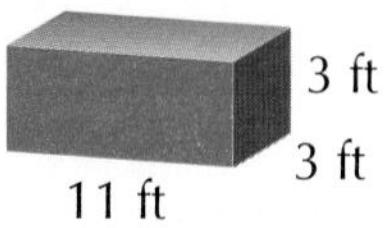

13.
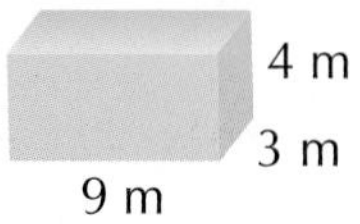

14.
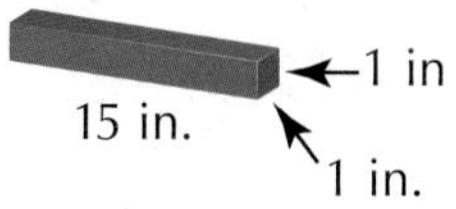

Writing in Math

15. Explain what is wrong with the answer at the right. (8-11)

Find the area.

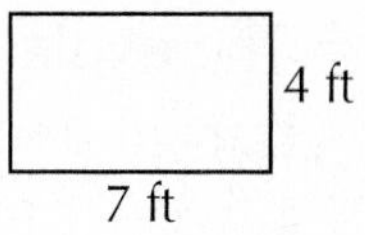

7 + 7 + 4 + 4 = 22
The area is 22 feet.

16. Explain how you can solve the problem below by acting it out. (8-12)

Steven made 3 plaques each day in craft class, and Maria made 2 key chains each day. How many plaques had Steven made when Maria had made 10 key chains?

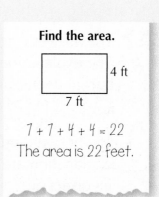

Test-Taking Strategies

- Understand the question.
- Get information for the answer.
- Plan how to find the answer.
- Make smart choices.
- Use writing in math.
- → Improve written answers.

Improve Written Answers

You can follow the tips below to learn how to improve written answers on a test. It is important to write a clear answer and include only information needed to answer the question.

The rubric below is a scoring guide for Test Questions 1 and 2.

Scoring Rubric

4 points

Full credit: 4 points
The answer and explanation are correct.

3 points

Partial credit: 3 points
The answer is correct, but a detail is missing from the explanation.

2 points

Partial credit: 2 points
The answer is correct or the explanation is correct, but not both.

1 point

Partial credit: 1 point
The answer is incorrect. The explanation shows partial understanding.

0 points

No credit: 0 points
The answer and explanation are both incorrect or missing.

1. Hallie drew the block letter "**H**" on the grid below.

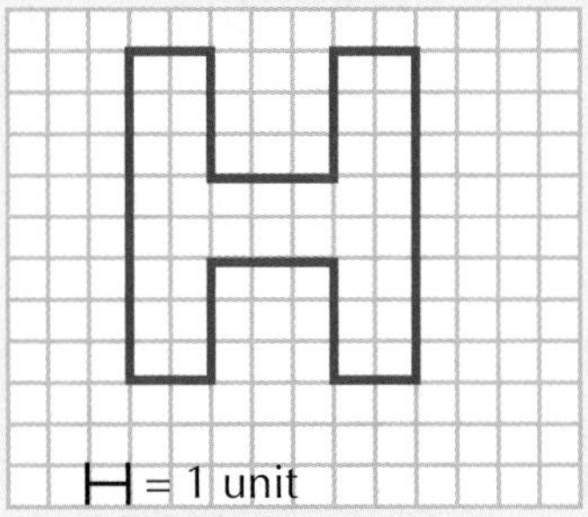

Find the area of the letter "**H**." Explain how you found your answer.

_____________ square units

Improve Written Answers

- Check if your answer is complete.

  *To **get as many points as possible,** I must find the area of the H and explain how I did it.*

- Check if your answer makes sense.

  *Have I used **mathematical terms** correctly to explain how I found the area?*

- Check if your explanation is clear and easy to follow.

  *I should reread my explanation to check that I have **accurately and clearly** explained my work. Have I included only the information called for?*

Jessica used the scoring rubric on page 482 to score a student's answer to Test Question 1. The student's paper is shown below.

Find the area of the letter "**H**." Explain how you found your answer.

___38___ square units

The little squares on the grid are square units. So I counted the little squares to find the area.

Think It Through

The area is correct. The explanation is pretty good, but the student didn't say which little squares were counted. The student should have said that he or she counted the little squares inside the H. Since the answer is correct but a detail is missing from the explanation, the student scores 3 points.

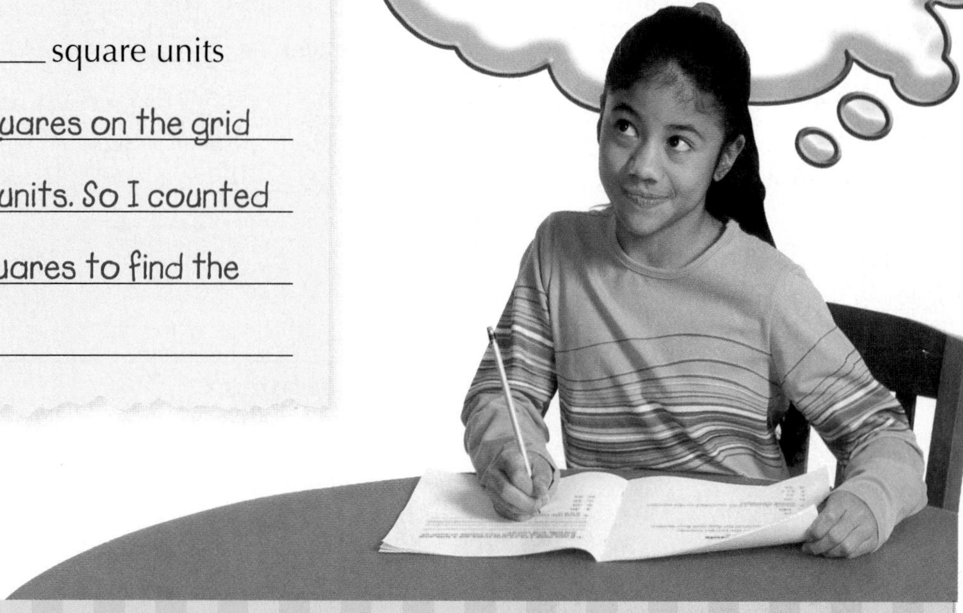

Now it's your turn.

Score the student's paper. If it does not get 4 points, rewrite it so that it does.

2. Lawrence drew the block letter "**L**" on the grid below.

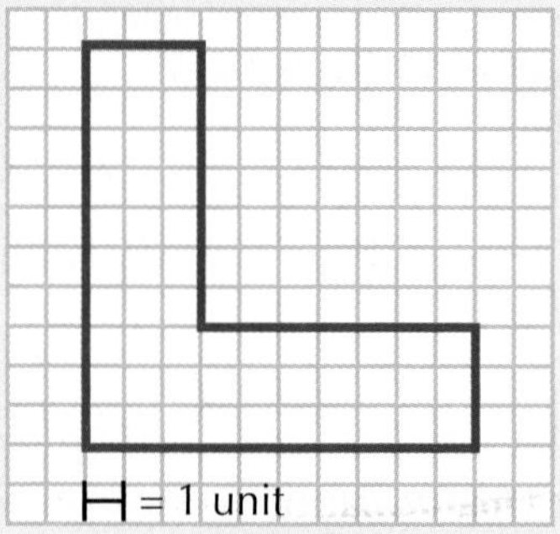

Find the perimeter of the letter "**L**." Then explain how you found your answer.

The perimeter is 51 units. I broke up the L into 2 rectangles. I multiplied 3 x 10 to get the perimeter of one rectangle and 3 x 7 to get the perimeter of the other. Then I added 30 + 21 to get the total perimeter, 51 units.

Key Vocabulary and Concept Review

Self Check

Use geometric terms to describe figures. (Lesson 8-3)

Lines and Parts of Lines

Point: *A* •*A*

Line: $\overleftrightarrow{QS}$

Line segment: $\overline{TU}$

Ray: $\overrightarrow{DE}$

Pairs of Lines

Parallel

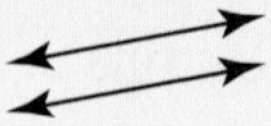

Intersecting

Perpendicular

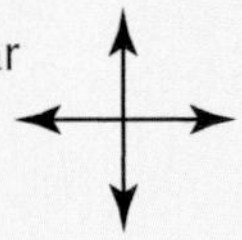

Angles

$\angle XYZ$ vertex

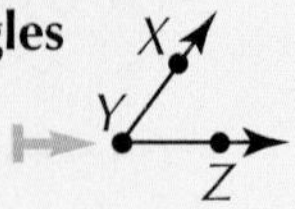

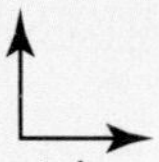

right

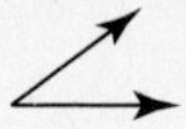

acute

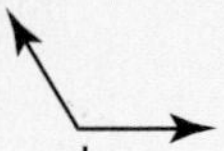

obtuse

straight

1. Name a line segment, a ray, an acute angle, and a pair of perpendicular lines in this diagram.

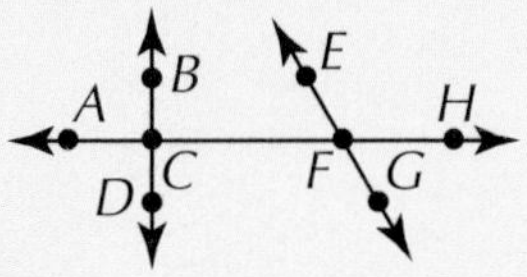

My grandpa uses a plane to smooth flat surfaces. Sometimes he starts with a solid block of wood.

A ***plane figure*** *is flat. A* ***solid figure*** *has 3 dimensions.* *(p. 434)*

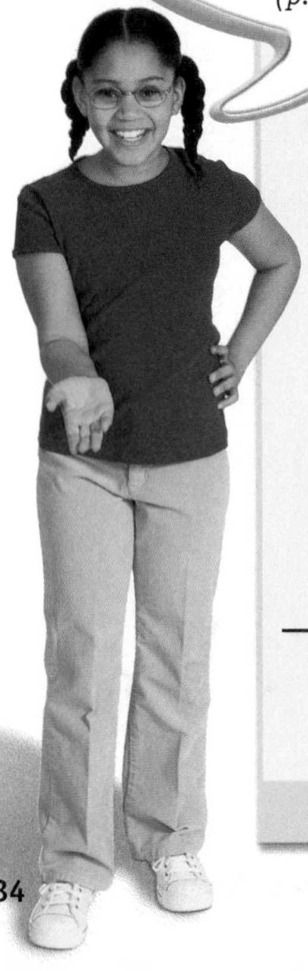

Self Check

Classify geometric figures. (Lessons 8-1, 8-2, 8-4, 8-5)

Identify each figure.

Remember the classifications of **plane** and **solid** figures listed at the right.

Right isosceles triangle

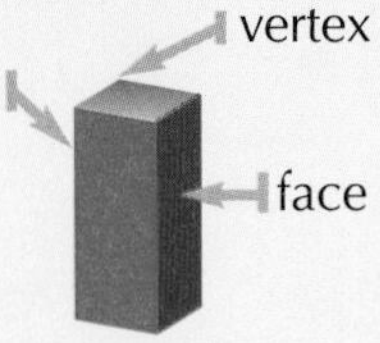

Rectangular prism

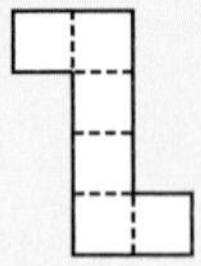

Net for cube

Plane Figures

polygons: triangle, quadrilateral, pentagon, hexagon, octagon

triangles: equilateral, isosceles, scalene, right, acute, obtuse

quadrilaterals: rectangle, square, trapezoid, parallelogram, rhombus

circle

Solid Figures

all flat surfaces: cube, rectangular prism, triangular prism, rectangular pyramid, square pyramid

curved surfaces: sphere, cylinder, cone

2. Identify each figure.

At the park there's a fence around the perimeter of the children's play area.

***Perimeter** is the distance around a flat figure, and **area** is the measurement inside.*

(pps. 464, 468)

Self Check

Measure, compare, and move figures.
(Lessons 8-6, 8-7, 8-8, 8-10, 8-11, 8-13)

6 in.

11 in.

Perimeter: 34 inches
$P = 2\ell + 2w$
Area: 66 square inches
$A = \ell w$

3 in.

8 in. 2 in.

Volume: 48 cubic inches
$V = \ell wh$

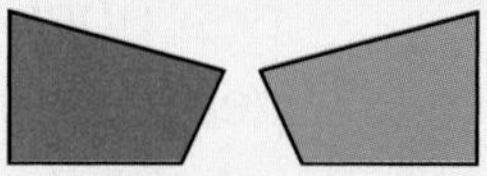

Congruent figures
Same size and shape

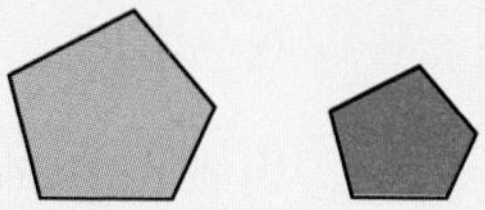

Similar figures Same shape

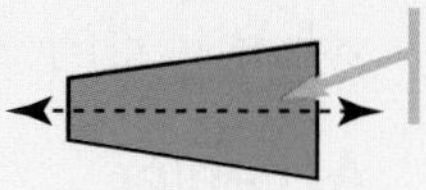

Line of symmetry

Symmetric figure

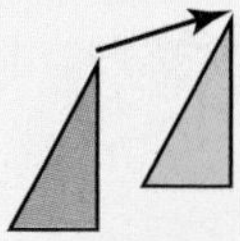

Slide
Translation

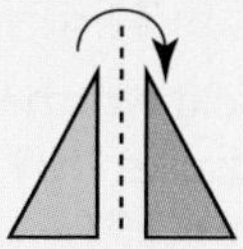

Flip
Reflection

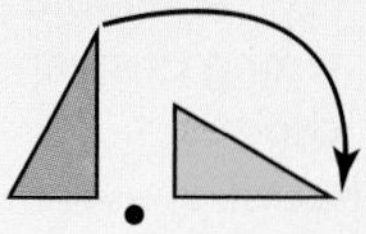

Turn
Rotation

3. Are the green quadrilaterals above related by a slide, a flip, or a turn?

4. Find the perimeter and area of a 4-foot by 9-foot rectangle.

Self Check

Solve problems by writing to describe or acting it out. (Lessons 8-9, 8-12)

Describe two figures by telling how they are the same and how they are different.

Describe these two figures.

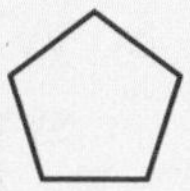

Both polygons are pentagons. The top pentagon has sides that are all the same length, and the bottom one has sides that are different lengths.

Use objects to help you solve a problem.

What are the dimensions of a rectangle that has an area of 18 square units and a perimeter of 22 units?

Use 18 square tiles. Make a rectangle that has a perimeter of 22 units.

The dimensions of the rectangle are 2 units by 9 units.

5. What is the perimeter of a square that has an area of 36 square units?

Answers: **1.** Sample answers: $\overline{CF}$; $\overleftrightarrow{FH}$; $\angle EFC$; $\overleftrightarrow{BD}$ and $\overleftrightarrow{AH}$ **2.** rhombus; obtuse scalene triangle; hexagon; cone **3.** Flip **4.** 26 feet; 36 square feet **5.** 24 units

CHAPTER 8

Chapter Test

MULTIPLE CHOICE

Choose the correct letter for each answer.

Think It Through

- I should **watch for words like NOT and EXCEPT.**
- I can **eliminate wrong answer choices.**

1. Which of the following is NOT true of the solid figure shown below?

A. It has 6 vertices.

B. It is a triangular prism.

C. It has 9 edges.

D. All of its faces are triangles.

2. Which polygon has 5 vertices?

A. triangle **C.** quadrilateral

B. hexagon **D.** pentagon

3. Which of the angles in the figure below is an obtuse angle?

A. ∠*MKL*

B. ∠*JKL*

C. ∠*JKM*

D. ∠*JML*

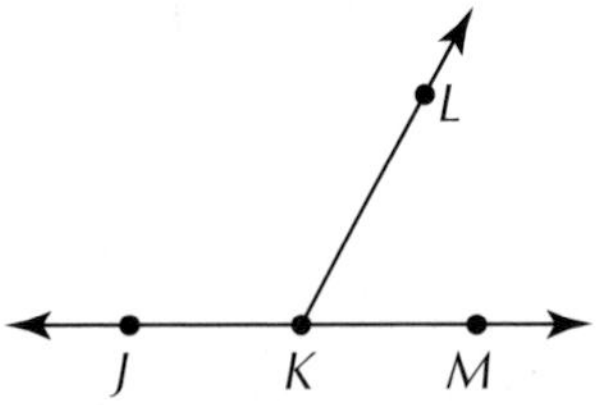

4. Which quadrilateral has only one pair of parallel sides?

A. trapezoid **C.** rhombus

B. rectangle **D.** parallelogram

5. Which of the following best describes, in geometric terms, what happened to the "U"?

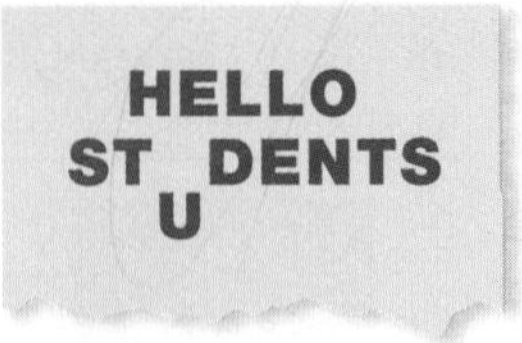

A. slide **C.** turn

B. rotation **D.** flip

6. What geometric term describes what is shown in red?

A. center

B. radius

C. chord

D. diameter

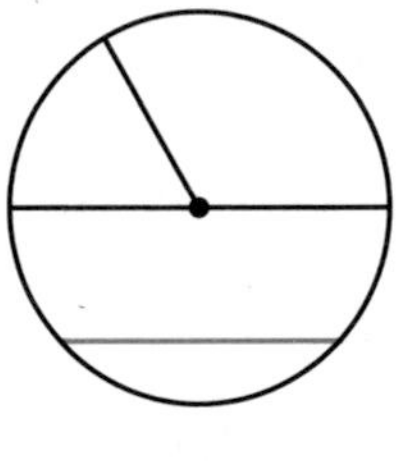

7. Which two figures below appear to be congruent?

A. 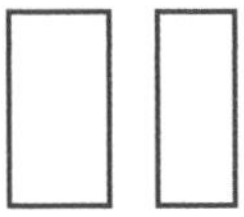

C. 

B. 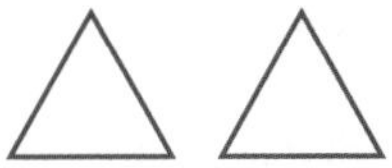

D. 

8. Which dotted line is a line of symmetry?

A. 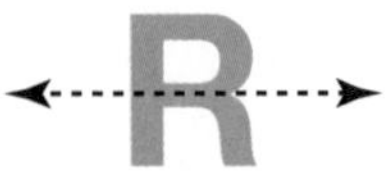

C. 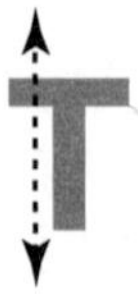

B. 

D. 

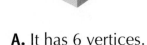

9. What is the perimeter of this figure?

A. 16 feet

B. 32 feet

C. 63 feet

D. 81 feet

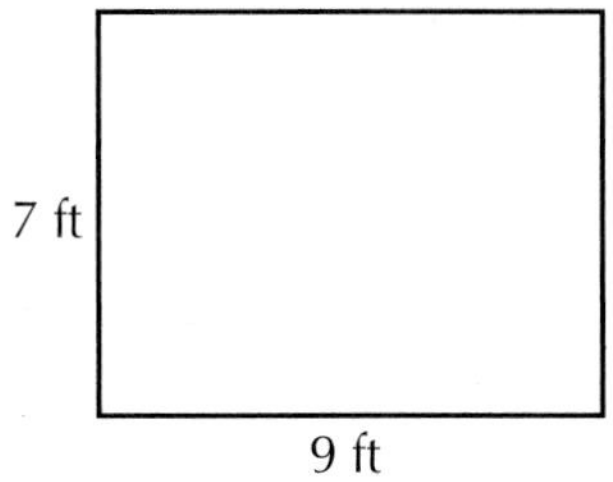

10. What is the area of the shaded figure below?

A. 11 square yards

B. 24 square yards

C. 28 square yards

D. 32 square yards

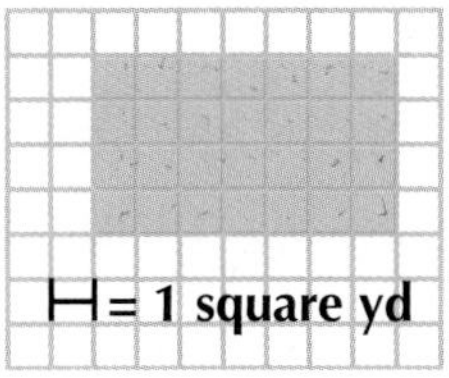

11. What is the volume of this figure?

A. 18 cubic meters

B. 30 cubic meters

C. 210 cubic meters

D. 210 square meters

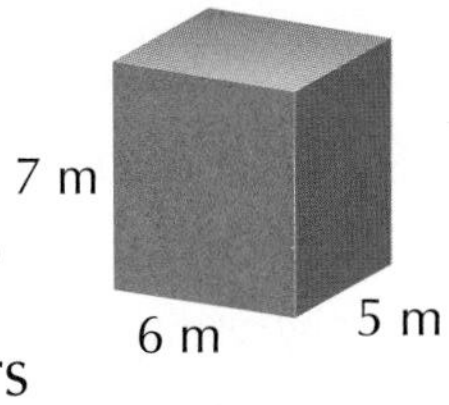

FREE RESPONSE

Draw an example of each polygon. How many sides and vertices does each have?

12. triangle

13. rhombus

14. pentagon

15. hexagon

Find the perimeter and area of each rectangle with the given length and width.

16. $\ell = 9$ ft, $w = 10$ ft

17. $\ell = 12$ m, $w = 8$ m

18. Do the figures at the right appear to be similar? If so, are they also congruent?

For 19–20, use the figure below.

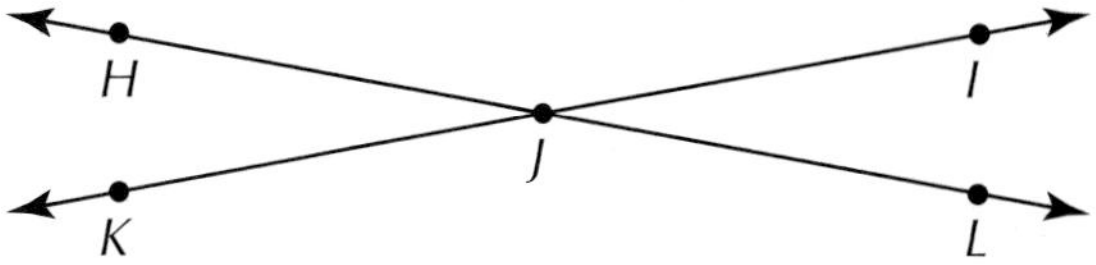

19. Name three different rays.

20. Name an acute angle, an obtuse angle, and a straight angle.

Writing in Math

21. Explain how you could use Act It Out to solve the following problem. Toby has 18 feet of edging to go around a rectangular sandbox. What length and width should Toby make the sandbox to get the most area?

TEST TALK

Think It Through

- I need to **look for words that tell me what the problem is about.**
- I should **draw pictures** to find the answer.

22. Write two statements describing the figures below.

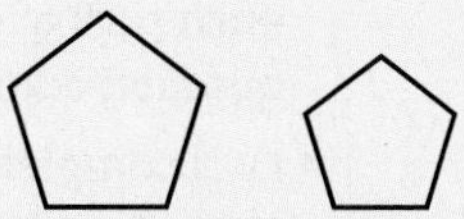

23. How many tiles would be needed to cover a square design with a length of 5 tiles? Explain how you know.

Cumulative Review and Test Prep

Number and Operation

MULTIPLE CHOICE

1. A 6-pack of juice boxes costs \$2.10. What is the cost of one juice box?

A. \$0.30 **C.** \$0.35

B. \$0.33 **D.** \$0.60

2. Which is the most reasonable estimate for 6,125 − 3,921?

A. 2,000 **C.** 4,000

B. 3,000 **D.** 5,000

3. Which number is divisible by 3?

A. 46 **B.** 51 **C.** 79 **D.** 85

FREE RESPONSE

4. There are 60 students going on a field trip to the science museum. Each van can hold 8 students. How many vans are needed to hold all the students going on the trip?

5. Ryan bought 2 T-shirts for \$7 each, 3 pairs of shorts for \$12 each, and 11 pairs of socks for \$2 each. How much did Ryan spend in all?

TEST TALK

Think It Through
- I need to **read each part of the question carefully.**
- I will **complete steps in order.**

Writing in Math

6. Use an array to find 4 × 16. Explain why this method is like solving two simpler problems.

Geometry and Measurement

MULTIPLE CHOICE

7. Which two figures are congruent?

A. 

C. 

B. 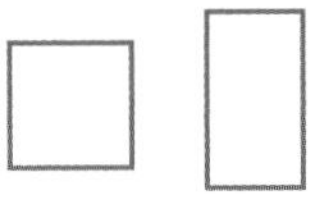

D. 

8. What time will it be 2 hours and 30 minutes after 1:45 P.M.?

A. 2:45 P.M. **C.** 3:45 P.M.

B. 3:15 P.M. **D.** 4:15 P.M.

FREE RESPONSE

9. Use geometric terms to write two statements describing what is shown.

10. What is the name of a five-sided polygon?

11. Tony runs once around a square park every Saturday. Each side of the park is 2 miles long. How far does Tony run each Saturday?

Writing in Math

12. Explain how to find the area of this rectangle in two different ways. Give the area.

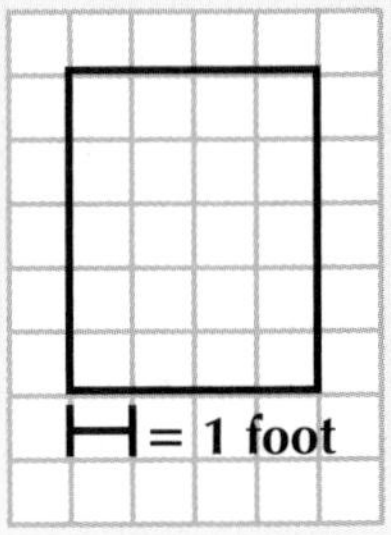

Data Analysis and Probability

MULTIPLE CHOICE

13. What is the range of the data set of team members' ages?

Team Members' Ages

Age	Number
20	||
21	卌
22	卌 |
23	||||
24	||||
25	|

A. 5 **B.** 6 **C.** 20 **D.** 22

14. Find the mode for the team members' ages.

A. 20 **B.** 21 **C.** 22 **D.** 25

FREE RESPONSE

Use the bar graph for 15–16.

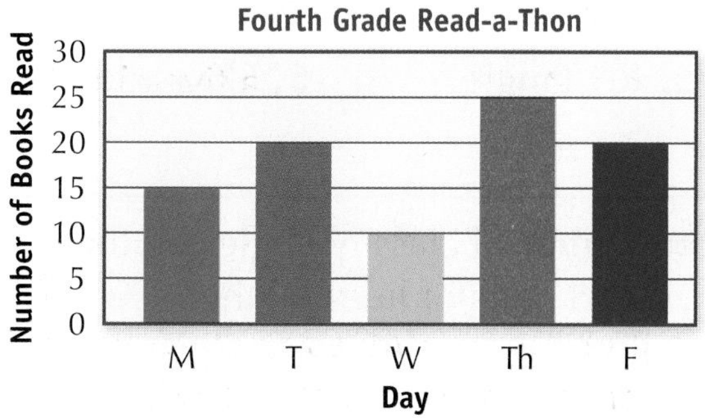

15. On which day did students read the most books?

16. On which days did students read the same number of books?

Writing in Math

17. What other kind of graph could be used to display the data in the bar graph? Explain your answer.

Algebra

MULTIPLE CHOICE

18. Complete the pattern.

1, 4, 16, 64, ■

A. 250 **B.** 256 **C.** 360 **D.** 364

19. Which number sentence is NOT true?

A. $54 \div 9 = 5$ **C.** $27 + 29 = 56$

B. $7 \times 8 = 56$ **D.** $54 - 19 = 35$

20. Which expression models the phrase "36 decreased by a number n"?

A. $n - 36$ **C.** $36 \div n$

B. $36 - n$ **D.** $n \div 36$

FREE RESPONSE

21. Complete the table and describe the rule you used.

In	7	9	11	13
Out	42	54	66	

22. Solve the equation below by testing these values for m: 3, 4, 6, and 8.

$96 \div m = 16$

Writing in Math

23. The Clarks have a rectangular swimming pool in their backyard. It covers 108 square feet of their yard. The pool is 9 feet wide. Find the length of the pool. Explain how you found your answer.

Reteaching

Set 8-1 (pages 434–437)

Name the solid figure shown.

Identify what plane figures form the faces of a solid figure.

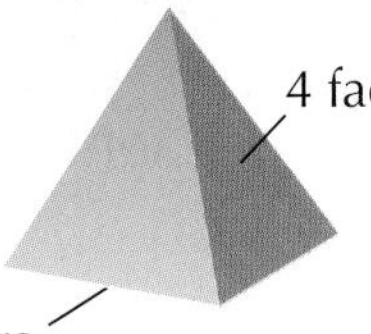

The solid figure is a square pyramid.

It has 4 triangular faces and 1 square face.

Remember that a sphere, cylinder, and cone have curved surfaces.

1. How many faces does a square pyramid have?
2. How many edges does a square pyramid have?
3. How many vertices does a square pyramid have?
4. What plane figure is a face of both a cylinder and a cone?

Set 8-2 (pages 438–439)

Name the polygon shown.

Count the number of sides to identify a polygon.

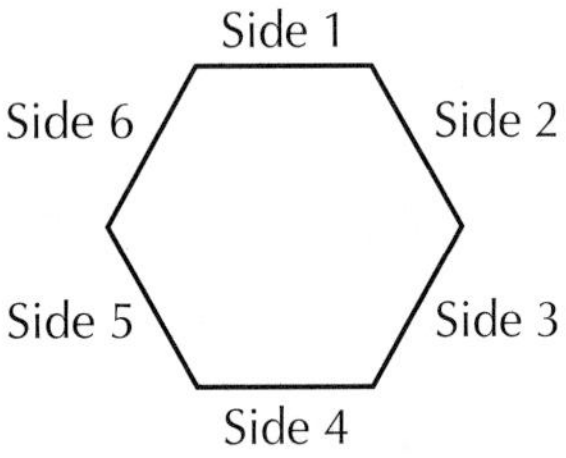

The polygon has 6 sides.

The polygon is a hexagon.

Remember that a polygon has the same number of sides and vertices.

How many sides and vertices does each polygon have?

1. Triangle
2. Square
3. Octagon
4. Pentagon
5. Rectangle
6. Quadrilateral

Set 8-3 (pages 440–443)

Use geometric terms to describe what is shown.

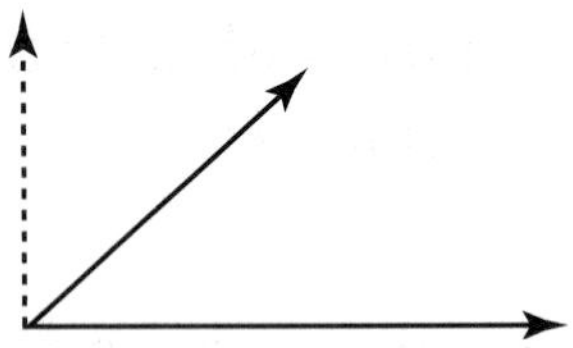

The angle is less than a right angle. It is an acute angle.

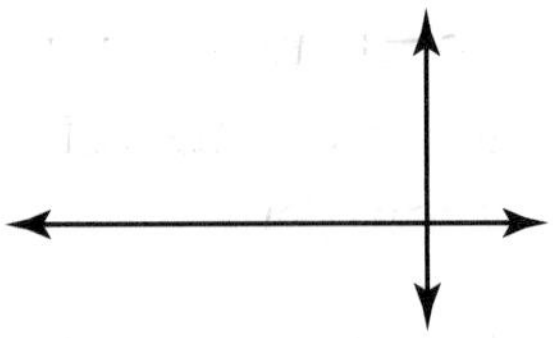

The lines form right angles where they intersect. They are perpendicular lines.

Remember to classify angles by their size and pairs of lines by their relationship.

Use geometric terms to describe what is shown.

1. 
2. 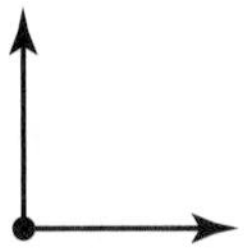
3. 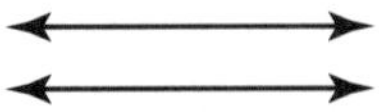
4. 
5. 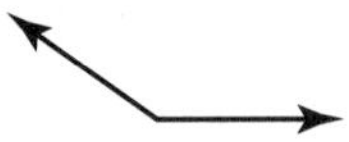
6. 

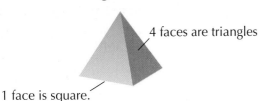

Set 8-4 (pages 444–447)

Classify the triangle by its sides and angles.

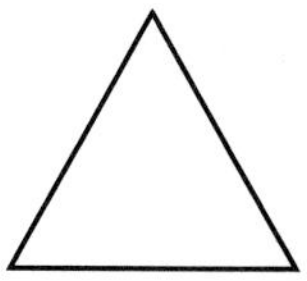

All the sides are the same length. It is an equilateral triangle. All the angles are acute. It is an acute triangle.

Name the quadrilateral.

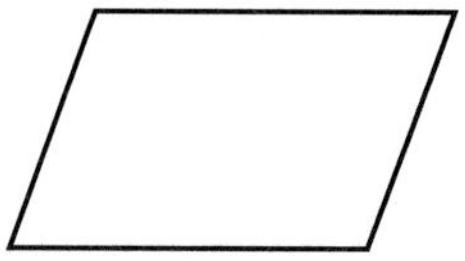

Opposite sides are parallel and the same length. There are no right angles. It is a parallelogram.

Remember that a quadrilateral can be a rectangle, square, trapezoid, parallelogram, or rhombus.

Classify each triangle by its sides and angles, and name each quadrilateral.

1. 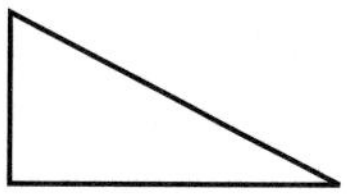

2. 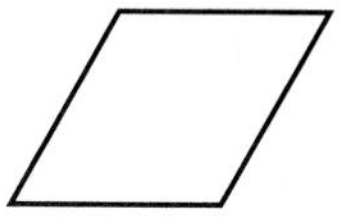

3. 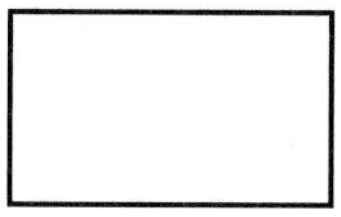

4. 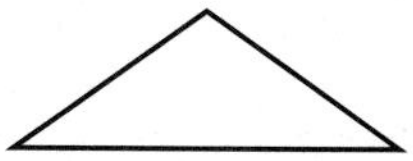

Set 8-5 (pages 448–449)

Use a geometric term to describe what is shown in red.

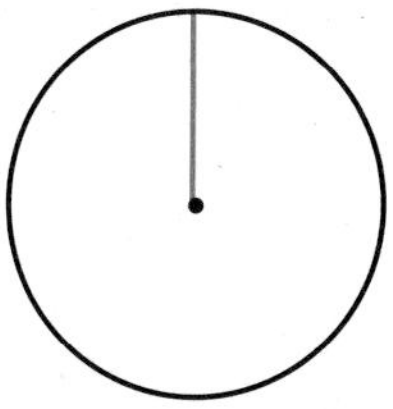

The segment connects the center to a point on the circle.

A radius of the circle is shown in red.

Remember that the length of the diameter of a circle is twice the length of its radius.

Use geometric terms to describe what is shown in red.

1. 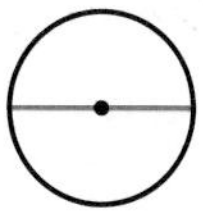

2. 

3. 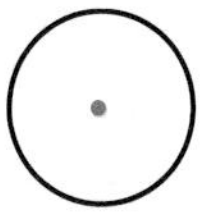

4. 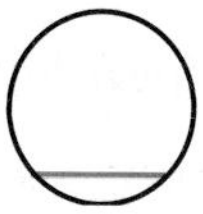

Set 8-6 (pages 452–455)

Are the figures congruent? If so, tell if they are related by a flip, slide, or turn.

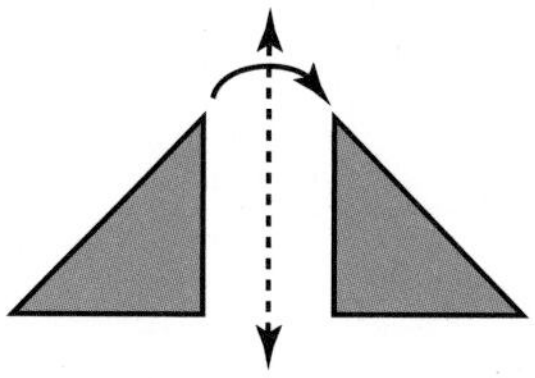

The figures are the same size and shape. The figures are congruent. The first figure is a mirror image of the second figure. The figures are related by a flip.

Remember that you can use slides, flips, and turns to test if two figures are congruent.

Are the figures in each pair congruent? If so, tell if they are related by a flip, slide, or turn.

1. 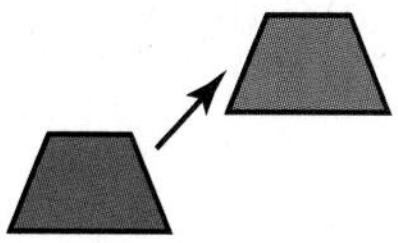

2. 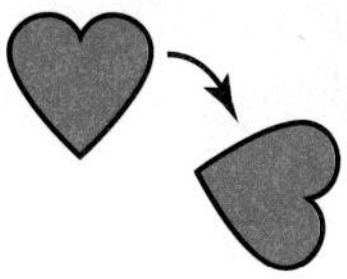

Set 8-7 (pages 456–457)

How many lines of symmetry does the figure have?

Think about folding a figure in half to decide if it has symmetry.

If the figure is folded in half on the vertical line, the two halves are congruent.

The figure has one line of symmetry.

Remember that figures can have more than one line of symmetry.

How many lines of symmetry does each figure have?

1. 

2. 

3. 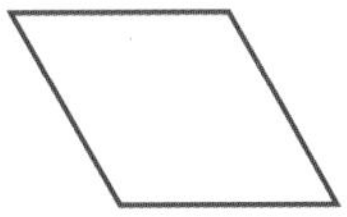

4. 

Set 8-8 (pages 458–459)

Are the figures similar? If so, are they also congruent?

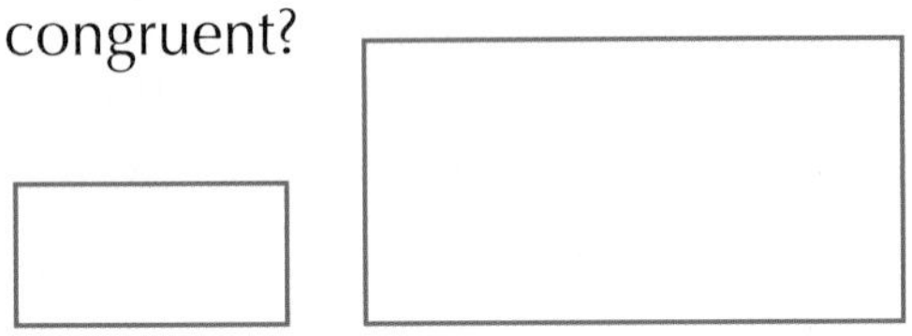

Both figures are rectangles with the same shape. The figures are similar.

The figures are not the same size. The figures are not congruent.

Remember that if two figures are similar and have the same size, they are also congruent.

Are the figures in each pair similar? If so, are they also congruent?

1. 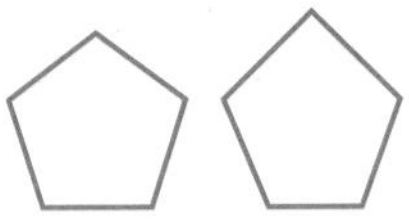

2. 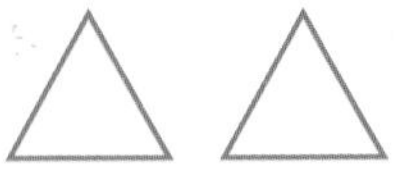

Set 8-9 (pages 460–461)

Describe the figures below.

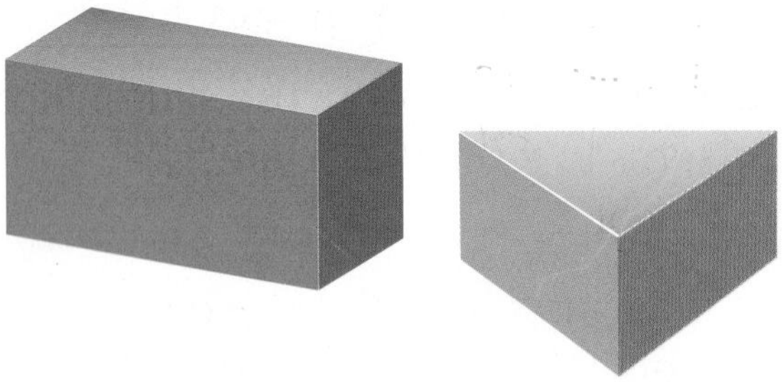

Both figures are prisms. The first figure is a rectangular prism and the second figure is a triangular prism.

Remember to use words like "both," "same," "different," to write descriptions.

Describe the figures below.

1. 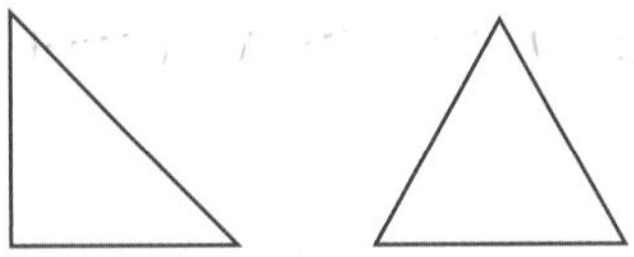

2. 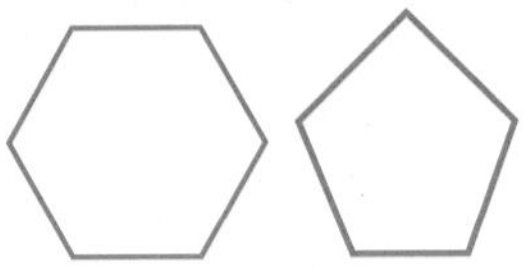

Set 8-10 (pages 464–467)

Find the perimeter of this rectangle.

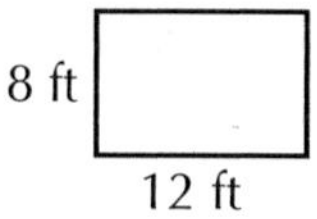

Add the length of the sides or use a formula.

$12 + 8 + 12 + 8 = 40$ ft

$P = 2\ell + 2w$
$P = (2 \times 12) + (2 \times 8)$
$P = 24 + 16$
$P = 40$ ft

P = *perimeter*
ℓ = *length*
w = *width*

Remember that $P = 4s$ is the formula for the perimeter of a square.

Find the perimeter of each figure.

1. 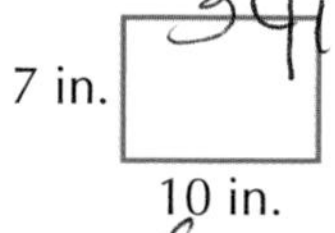

34in

2. 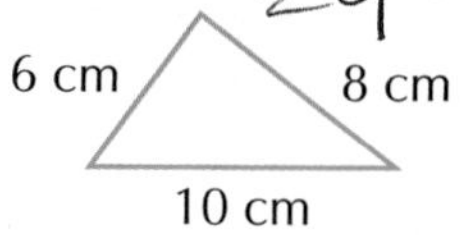

24cm

3. 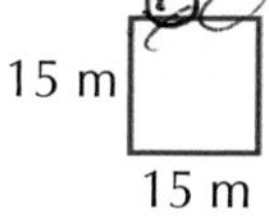

60m

4. 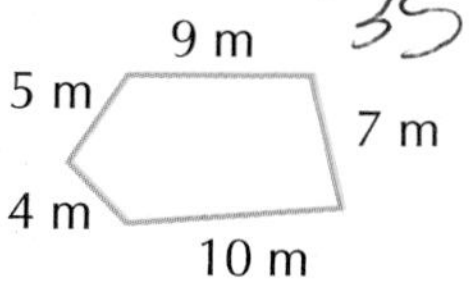

35m

Set 8-11 (pages 468–471)

Find the area of this rectangle.

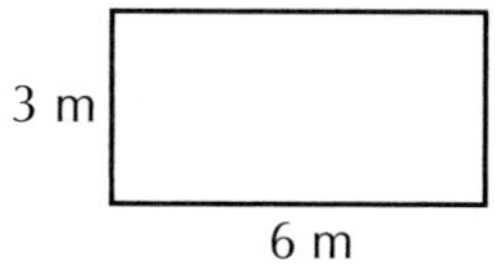

Use a formula:

$A = \ell \times w$
$A = 6 \times 3$
$A = 18$ square meters

A = *area*
ℓ = *length*
w = *width*

Remember that area is always measured in square units.

Find the area of each figure.

1. 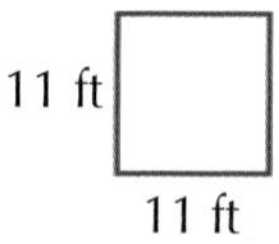

11x11=121ft

2. 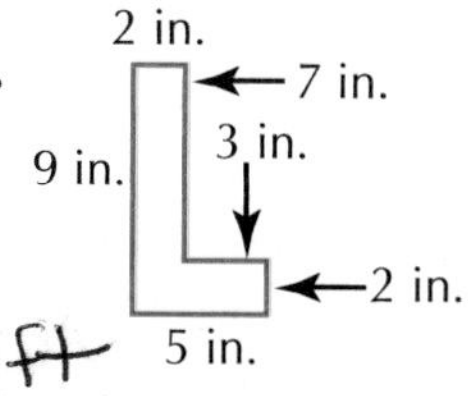

Set 8-12 (pages 474–475)

When you solve a problem by acting it out, follow these steps.

Step 1: Choose objects to act it out.

Step 2: Show what you know.

Step 3: Act out the problem

Step 4: Find the answer in your work.

Remember to know what your objects represent in the problem.

1. Dave has 36 tiles. He wants to put a border around the tiles. How should he arrange the tiles to make the shortest border?

Set 8-13 (pages 476–477)

Find the volume of this rectangular prism.
Volume = length × width × height

$V = \ell \times w \times h$
$V = 5 \times 2 \times 4$
$V = 40$ cubic feet

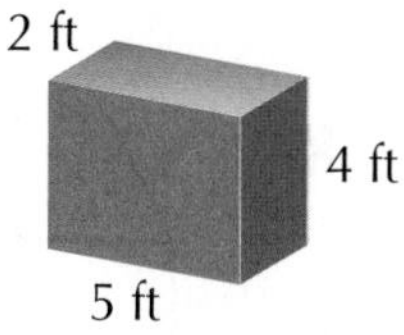

Remember that volume is always measured in cubic units.

1. 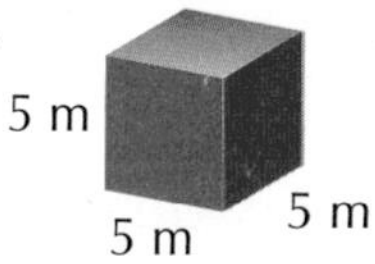

2. 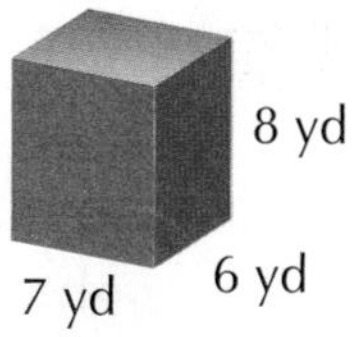

Set 8-1 (pages 434–437)

Name each solid figure. Tell the shape(s) of the faces of each figure.

1. 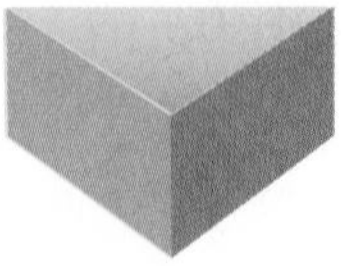

2. 

3. 

4. 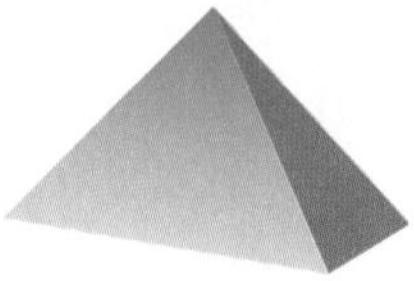

5. From a bag of wooden blocks, Susan chose a cone, a cylinder, and a sphere. What do all of these blocks have in common?

Set 8-2 (pages 438–439)

Draw an example of each polygon. Tell how many sides and vertices each polygon has.

1. triangle
2. hexagon
3. pentagon
4. octagon
5. quadrilateral
6. parallelogram
7. If a polygon has 12 vertices, how many sides does it have?

Set 8-3 (pages 440–443)

Use geometric terms to describe what is shown. Be as specific as possible.

1. 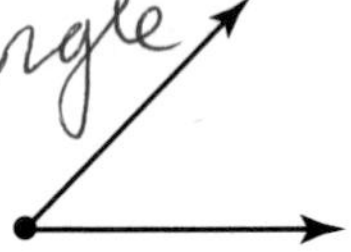
acute angle

2. 
parallel

3. 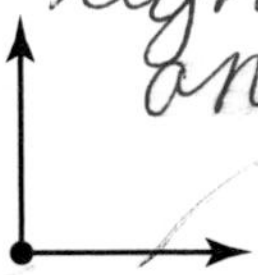
right angle

4. 
ray ~~line~~ ~~segment~~

5. Name three different line segments in the figure at the right.

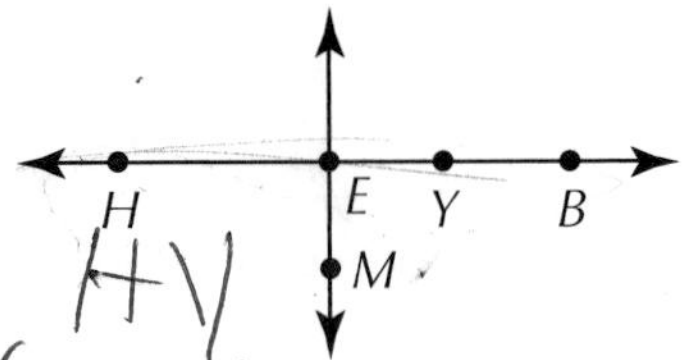

HE, EY, EM, EB, HY, EH, BM, BE, YE, ME

Set 8-4 (pages 444–447)

Classify each triangle by its sides and then by its angles.

1. 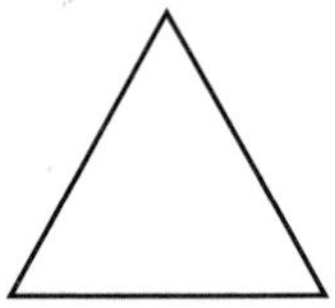

2. 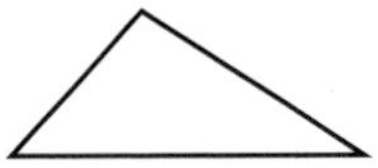

3. 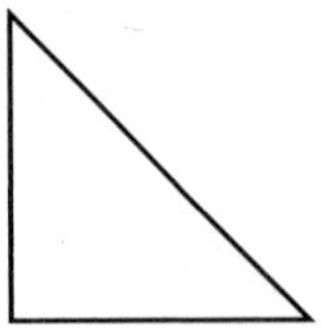

4. 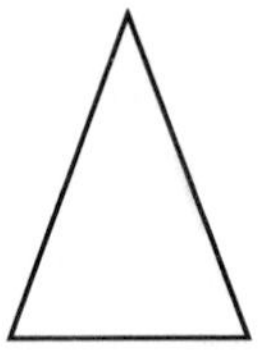

5. Write the name of every quadrilateral in the figure at the right.

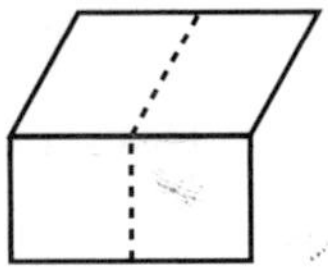

Take It to the NET
More Practice
www.scottforesman.com

Set 8-5 (pages 448–449)

Use geometric terms to describe what is shown in red.

1.
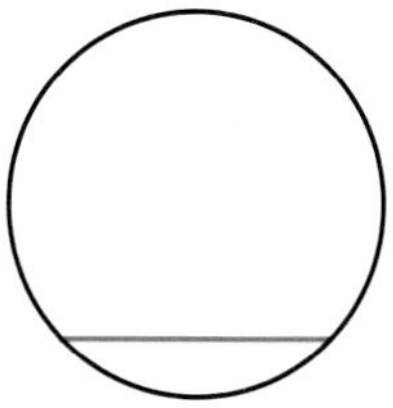

2.
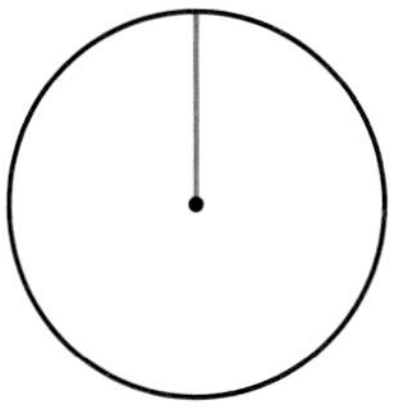

3.
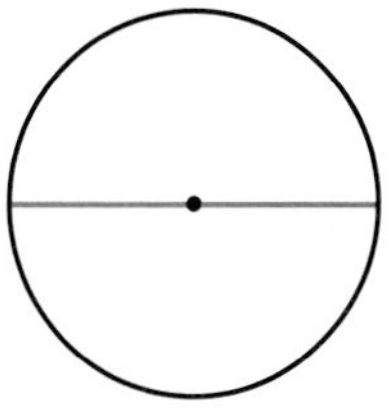

4.
 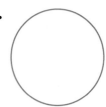

5. The diameter of each wheel on Tony's bicycle is 20 inches. What is the length of the radius on the bike's wheels?

Set 8-6 (pages 452–455)

Are the figures in each pair congruent? If so, tell if they are related by a flip, slide, or turn.

1.
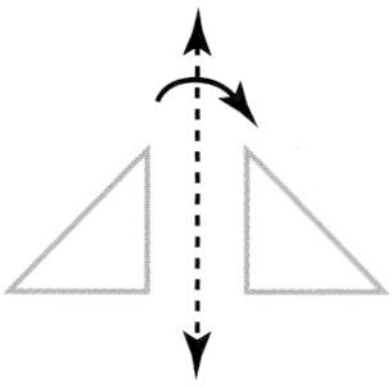

2.
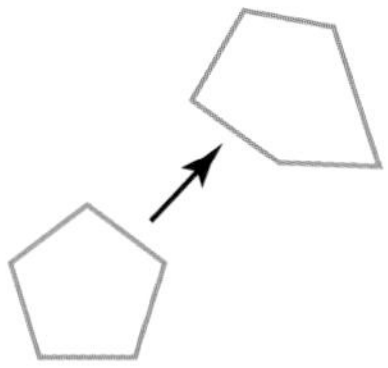

3.
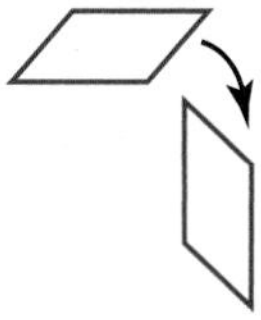

4.

5.

6.
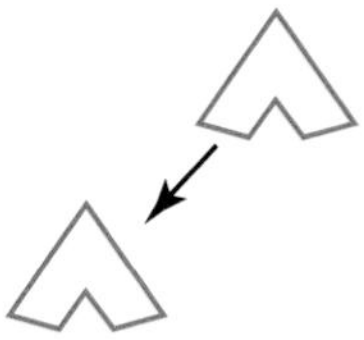

7.
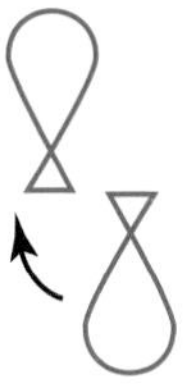

8.
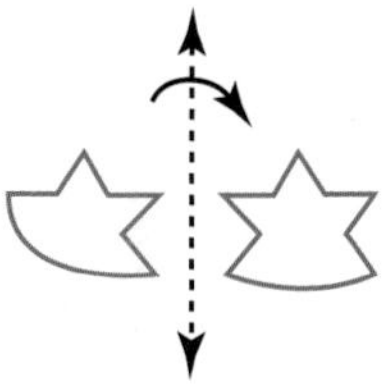

9. Two triangles are congruent. The first triangle is scalene. What do you know about the second triangle?

Set 8-7 (pages 456–457)

How many lines of symmetry does each figure have?

1.
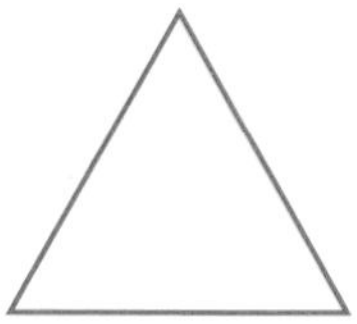

2.
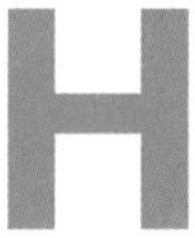

3.

4.
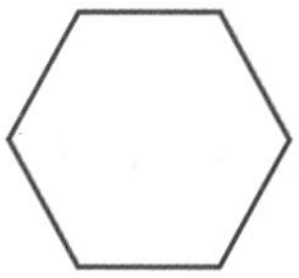

5. The sail on Brandon's model sailboat is an isosceles triangle. How many lines of symmetry does the sail have?

Set 8-8 (pages 458–459)

Are the figures in each pair similar? If so, are they also congruent?

1. 

2. 

3. 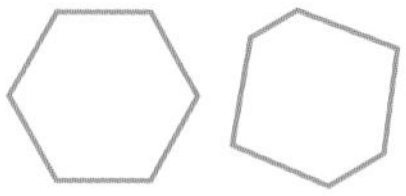

4. 

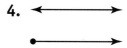

5. In the figure at the right, identify a pair of figures that are congruent and a pair of figures that are similar but not congruent.

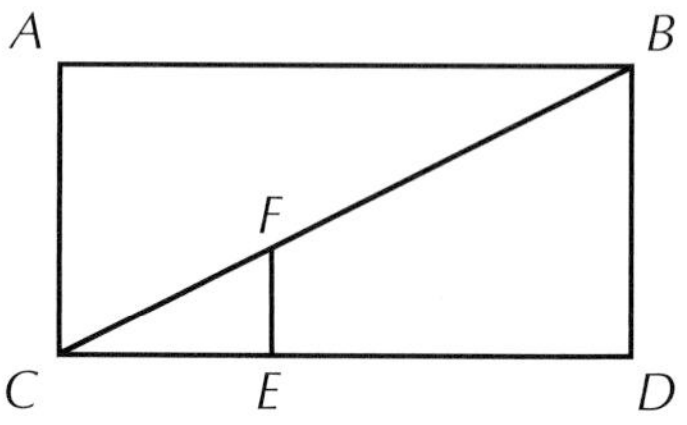

Set 8-9 (pages 460–461)

Write two statements describing each pair of figures.

1. 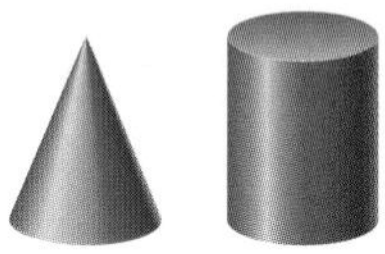

2. 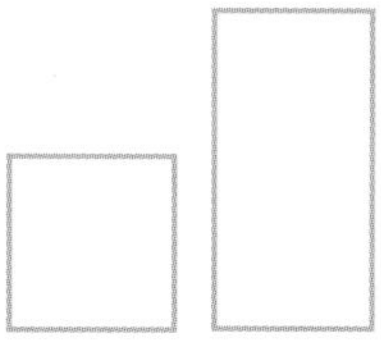

3. 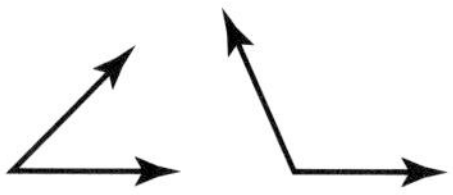

4. 

5. Describe the information displayed in the tables at the right.

In	2	3	4	5
Out	8	9	10	11

In	2	3	4	5
Out	12	18	24	30

Set 8-10 (pages 464–467)

Find the perimeter of each figure.

1. 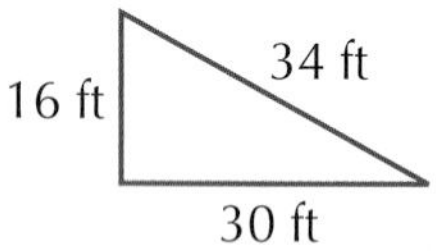

2. 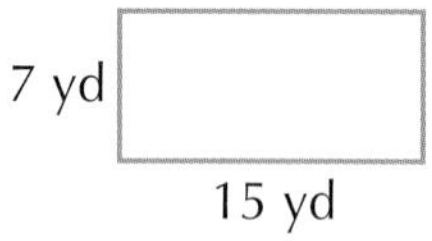

3. 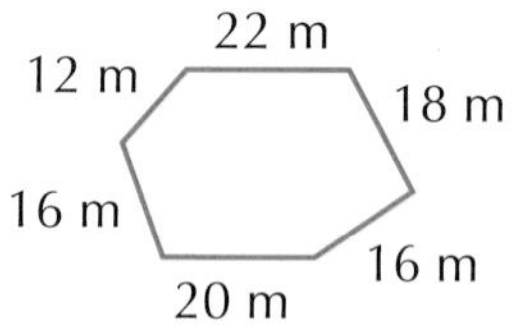

4. 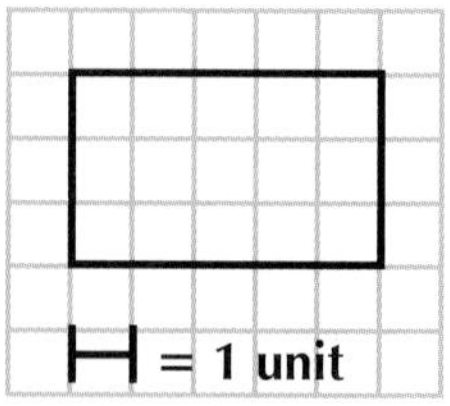

5. The perimeter of a rectangle is 48 inches. Its width is 11 inches. What is the length of the rectangle?

6. The perimeter of a rectangle is 38 yards. Its length is 14 yards. What is the width of the retangle?

Take It to the NET
More Practice
www.scottforesman.com

Set 8-11 (pages 468–471)

Find the area of each rectangle.

1.

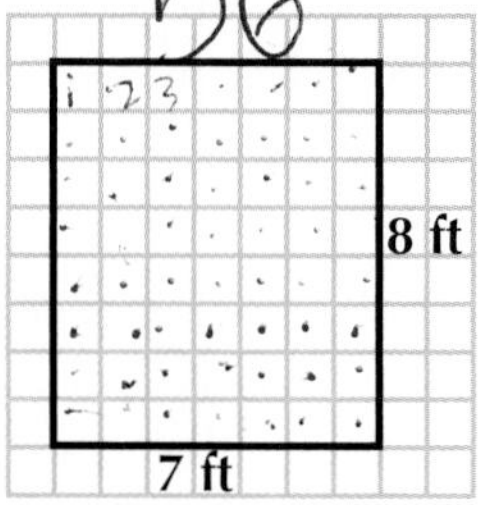

2.

3.

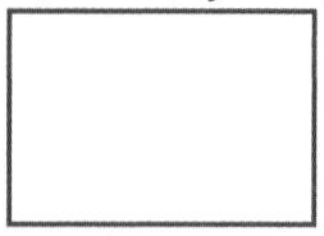

4.

5. The perimeter of a square is 28 feet. What is the area of the square?

6. A rectangle has an area of 54 square cm. The length of the rectangle is 6 cm. What is the width of the rectangle?

Set 8-12 (pages 472–473)

Solve each problem by acting it out. Write the answer in a complete sentence.

1. A restaurant has 8 small square tables. Each side of each table can seat 1 person. Tabitha wants to arrange the small tables to form 1 large rectangular table for a party. She wants to arrange the tables so that the greatest number of people can sit at the large table. How should she arrange the 8 small tables?

2. Mr. Sanchez has 20 feet of fencing to mark the space in his backyard for a rectangular garden. He wants the garden to have the greatest area possible. What should be the length and width of the garden?

Set 8-13 (pages 476–477)

Find the volume of each figure.

1.

2.

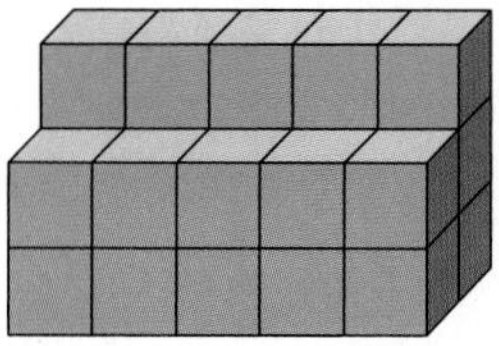

3.

4. The volume of a toy box is 24 cubic feet. Its length is 8 feet, and its width is 3 feet. What is the height of the toy box?

CHAPTER 9

Fraction Concepts

DIAGNOSING READINESS

A Vocabulary

(Grade 3)

Choose the best term from the box.

1. A _?_ describes a part of a whole or set.
2. The _?_ of a fraction tells the number of equal parts in the whole or set.
3. When a shape has three equal parts they are called _?_.

Vocabulary

- **fraction** *(Gr. 3)*
- **denominator** *(Gr. 3)*
- **halves** *(Gr. 3)*
- **mixed number** *(Gr. 3)*
- **numerator** *(Gr. 3)*
- **thirds** *(Gr. 3)*

B Division Facts

(Pages 148–149)

4. $18 \div 3$
5. $24 \div 8$
6. $16 \div 4$
7. $36 \div 9$
8. $25 \div 5$
9. $14 \div 2$
10. $48 \div 6$
11. $56 \div 8$
12. Claudia planted 49 flowers in pots. She planted 7 flowers in each pot. How many pots did Claudia fill in all?
13. Jay rode 32 miles on his bicycle. If it took him 4 hours, how many miles did Jay ride each hour?

CHECK ✓

For another example, see Set 9-1 on p. 552.

1. Write a fraction for the part of the region at the right that is blue.

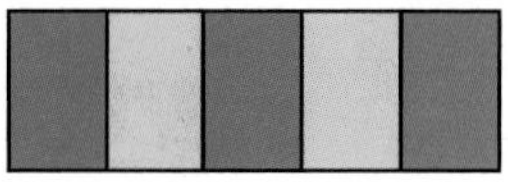

In 2–5, draw a model to show each fraction.

2. $\frac{2}{3}$ **3.** $\frac{3}{8}$ **4.** $\frac{7}{10}$ **5.** $\frac{4}{5}$

6. Number Sense Is $\frac{1}{4}$ of the circle at the right blue? Explain why or why not.

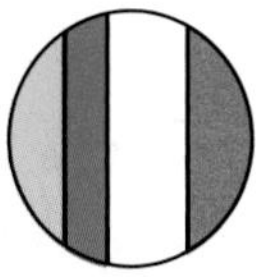

PRACTICE

For more practice, see Set 9-1 on p. 556.

A Skills and Understanding

7. Write a fraction for the part of the region at the right that is green.

In 8–12, draw a model to show each fraction.

8. $\frac{4}{12}$ **9.** $\frac{5}{6}$ **10.** $\frac{4}{7}$ **11.** $\frac{1}{4}$ **12.** $\frac{64}{100}$

13. Number Sense Would you eat more if you ate $\frac{1}{3}$ of a small pizza or $\frac{1}{3}$ of a medium pizza? Explain.

B Reasoning and Problem Solving

For 14–17, write a fraction for the part of each flag that is red.

14.

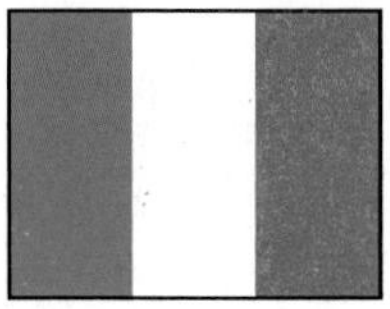

Italy

15.

Indonesia

16.

Taiwan

17.

Austria

18. Writing in Math Suzie says $\frac{2}{3}$ of the rectangle at the right is yellow. Explain why this is not correct.

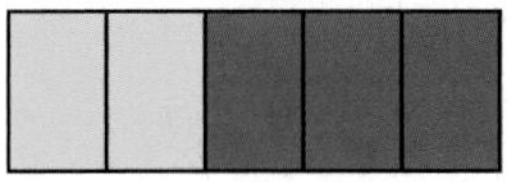

Mixed Review and Test Prep

Take It to the NET
Test Prep
www.scottforesman.com

19. Find the volume of the solid at the right.

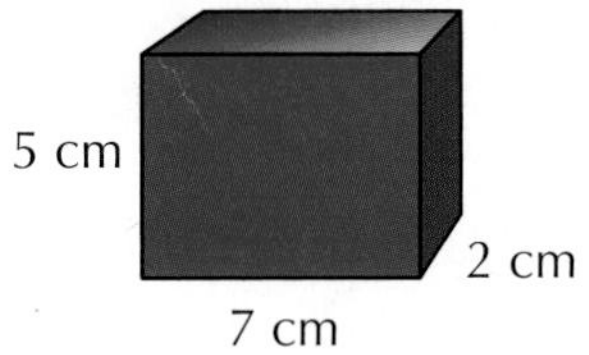

20. 354 ÷ 2

A. 122 **C.** 172

B. 127 **D.** 177

Key Idea
Fractions name parts of a set of objects.

Vocabulary
- fraction (p. 500)
- numerator (p. 500)
- denominator (p. 500)

TEST TALK

Think It Through
I can **draw a picture** to show fractions.

Parts of a Set

WARM UP

Draw a model to show each fraction.

1. $\frac{3}{10}$ 2. $\frac{4}{8}$ 3. $\frac{1}{6}$

LEARN

How do you name and show part of a set?

Example A

What part of the fruit are red pears?

Numerator → 2 ← Number of red pears
Denominator → 5 ← Pieces of fruit in all

Red pears are $\frac{2}{5}$ of the fruit.

You can use a fraction to name a part of a set.

Example B

Show a set with $\frac{7}{10}$ apples.

7 of the 10 pieces of fruit are apples.

Example C

Show a set with $\frac{6}{6}$ apples.

All of the fruit are apples.

Example D

Show a set with $\frac{0}{4}$ apples.

There are no apples in the set.

Talk About It

1. In Example D, why are none of the pieces of fruit apples?

CHECK

For another example, see Set 9-2 on p. 552.

What fraction of each set is blue?

1. 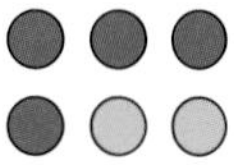 **2.**  **3.** 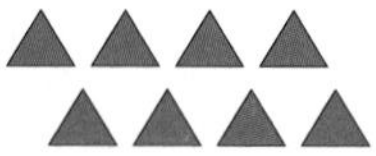 **4.** 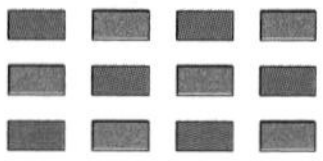

5. Number Sense If $\frac{1}{3}$ of a set is apples, what part is not apples?

For more practice, see Set 9-2 on p. 556.

A Skills and Understanding

What fraction of each set is red?

6. 

7. 

8. 

9. 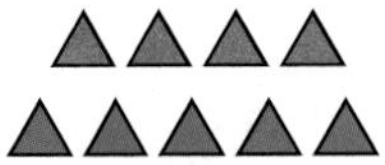

10. 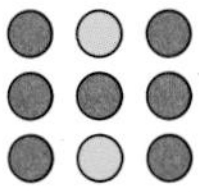

11. 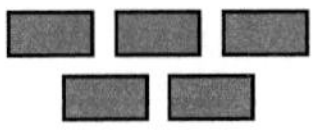

12. 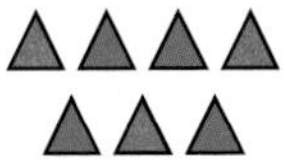

13. 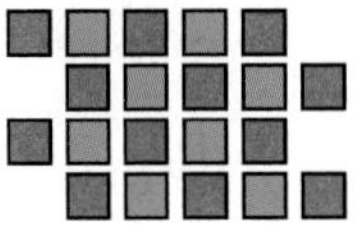

In 14–21, draw a picture to show each fraction as part of a set.

14. $\frac{3}{8}$ **15.** $\frac{1}{6}$ **16.** $\frac{3}{3}$ **17.** $\frac{3}{20}$

18. $\frac{3}{5}$ **19.** $\frac{1}{4}$ **20.** $\frac{6}{10}$ **21.** $\frac{11}{25}$

22. Number Sense *Stellaluna* is a story of a bat that is raised by birds. About $\frac{1}{4}$ of the mammals on Earth are bats. What fraction of mammals are not bats?

B Reasoning and Problem Solving

What fraction of the pieces of fruit at the right are the

23. grapefruit? **24.** strawberries?

25. limes?

26. grapefruits and limes together?

27. strawberries, grapefruit, and limes together?

28. Writing in Math Kevin showed a set of counters with all the counters red. What fraction of Kevin's set was red if he had 5 counters? What if he had 3 counters? Explain.

Mixed Review and Test Prep

Take It to the NET
Test Prep
www.scottforesman.com

29. Write the fraction for the blue part of the region at the right.

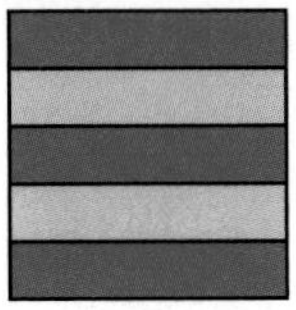

30. 36×48

A. 432 **C.** 1,704

B. 1,628 **D.** 1,728

Key Idea
Fractions name parts of a length.

Materials
- fraction strips or e tools
- straightedge

TEST TALK

Think It Through
I can **use a model** to understand fractions as part of a length.

Fractions, Length, and the Number Line

WARM UP

Draw a model to show each fraction

1. $\frac{2}{3}$
2. $\frac{1}{5}$
3. $\frac{5}{6}$
4. $\frac{7}{8}$

LEARN

Activity

How do you name and show part of a length?

a. Use the red fraction strip for 1 and green fraction strips for $\frac{1}{6}$. Each green strip is what part of the length of the red strip?

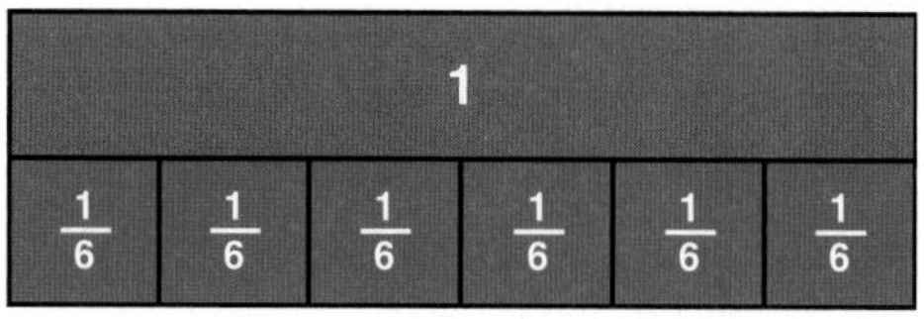

b. Draw a number line that is a little longer than the red strip. Mark the ends of the strip on the number line and label them 0 and 1.

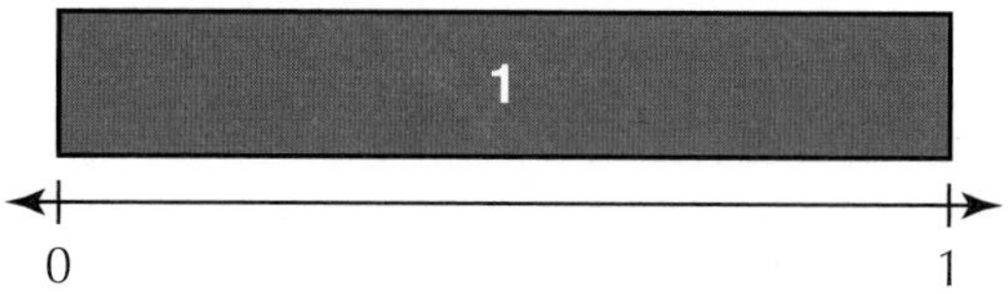

c. Use the green strips to divide the length between 0 and 1 on the number line into 6 equal parts. Label the marks $\frac{1}{6}$, $\frac{2}{6}$, $\frac{3}{6}$, $\frac{4}{6}$, and $\frac{5}{6}$. The number line shows sixths.

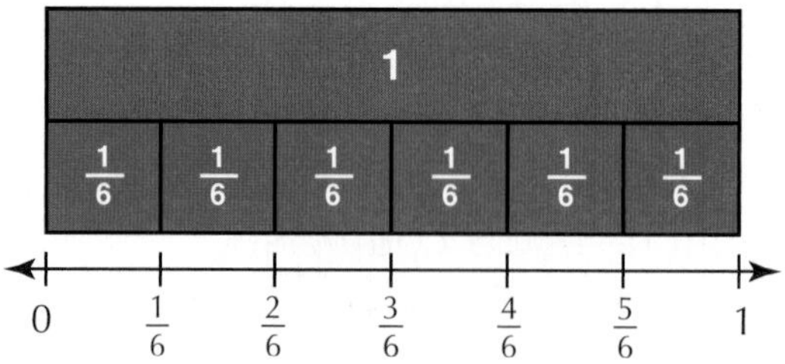

d. Use fraction strips to draw a number line showing each.

Fourths Thirds Tenths Eighths

e. Write a fraction for the part of each length that is green.

 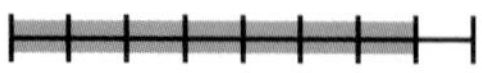 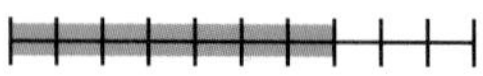

How can you locate and name fractions on a number line?

Example A

Show $\frac{4}{5}$ on a number line.

Draw a number line and label 0 and 1. Then divide the distance between 0 and 1 into 5 equal lengths. Label $\frac{1}{5}$, $\frac{2}{5}$, $\frac{3}{5}$, and $\frac{4}{5}$. Draw a point at $\frac{4}{5}$.

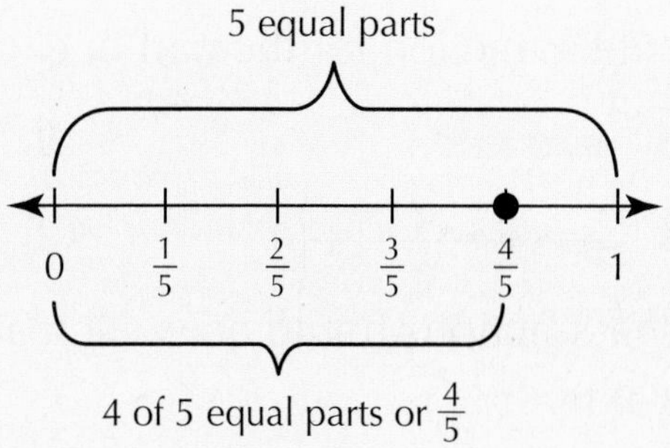

The name of a point on a number line tells the length from 0 to the point.

Example B

What fraction should be written at point A?

There are 4 equal parts between 0 and 1. There are 3 of these equal parts between 0 and point A. So $\frac{3}{4}$ should be written at point A.

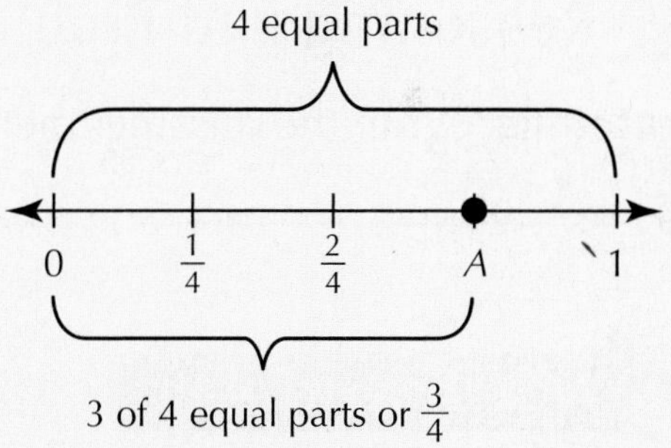

Talk About It

1. In Example B, why should $\frac{3}{4}$ be written at point A?

2. Draw how you show $\frac{2}{3}$ on a number line.

Take It to the NET
More Examples
www.scottforesman.com

CHECK

For another example, see Set 9-3 on p. 552.

Write a fraction for the part of each length that is blue.

1. 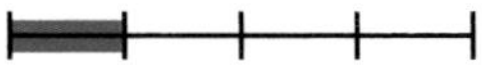 **2.** 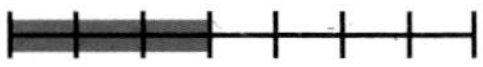 **3.** 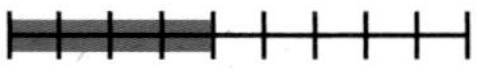

What fraction should be written at each point?

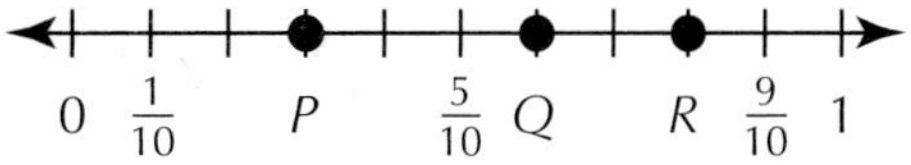

4. P **5.** Q **6.** R

7. Number Sense Explain why $\frac{1}{2}$ should be written at both A and B.

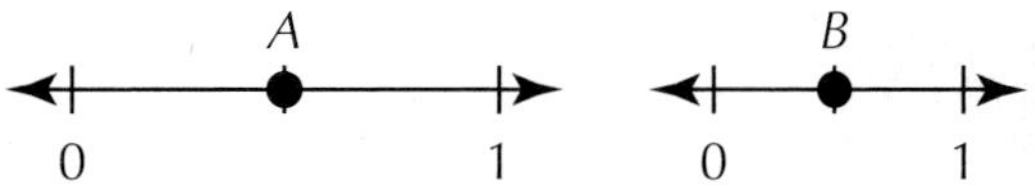

PRACTICE

For more practice, see Set 9-3 on p. 556.

A Skills and Understanding

Write a fraction for the part of each length that is red.

8. 

9. 

10. 

11. 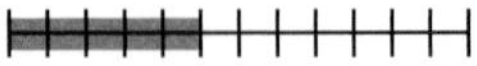

12. 

13. 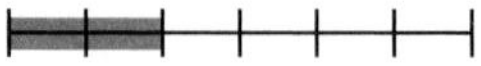

What fraction should be written at each point?

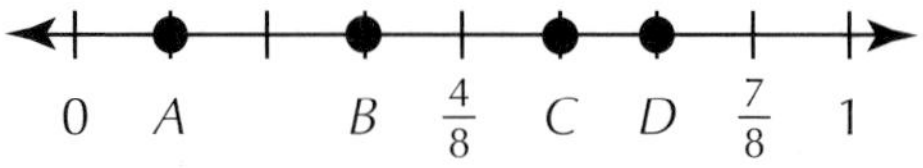

14. *A* **15.** *B* **16.** *C* **17.** *D*

18. Number Sense Draw a picture to show $\frac{1}{3}$ in two different ways. Use fraction strips and a number line.

B Reasoning and Problem Solving

Reasoning Write the missing fractions.

19. 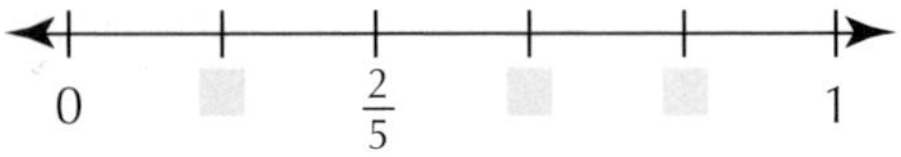

20. 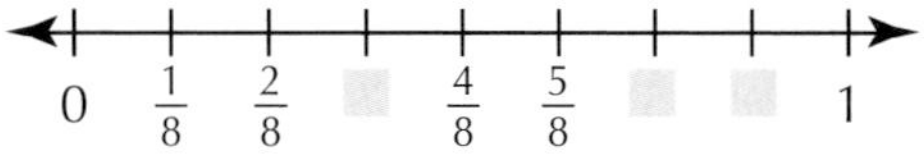

Math and Art

Wallpaper borders usually repeat the same design. For 21–24, write a fraction for the part of the strip that is the pattern. Use the number lines to help.

21. 

22. 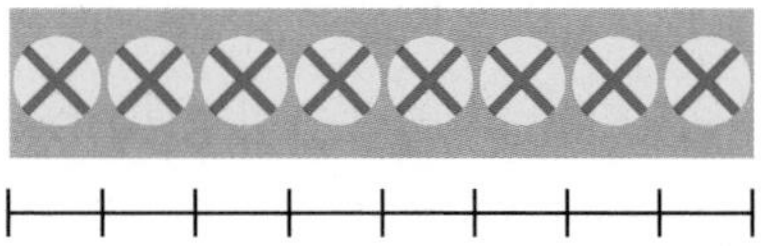

23. 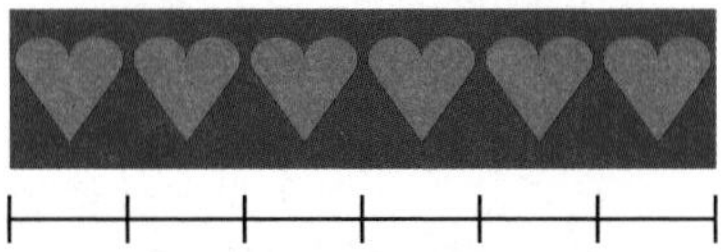

24. 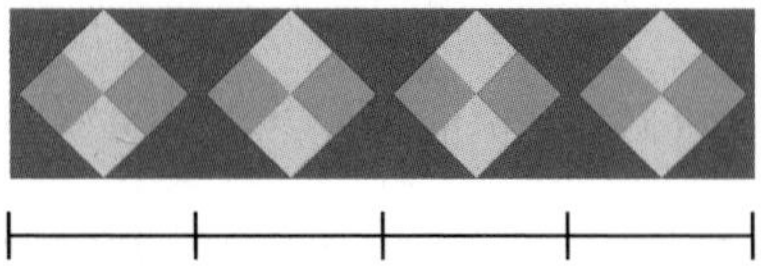

25. Writing in Math Is the explanation below correct? If not, tell why and write a correct response.

Draw a number line to show $\frac{2}{3}$. Explain why it shows $\frac{2}{3}$.

I showed 0 and 1 on a number line. Then I added 3 marks between them and wrote $\frac{2}{3}$ by the second one.

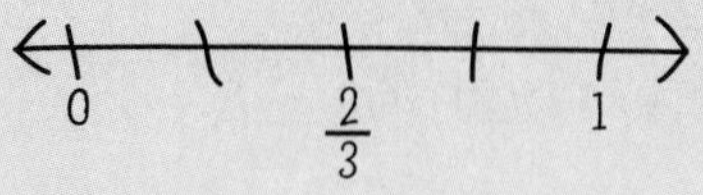

Think It Through

I should **visualize.** I can think, "Is the point I marked $\frac{2}{3}$ of the way from 0 to 1?"

PRACTICE

C Extensions

Tell whether each fraction is closest to 0, 1, or $\frac{1}{2}$.

26. 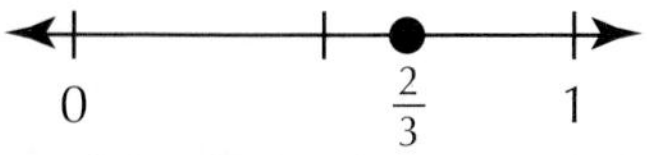

27. 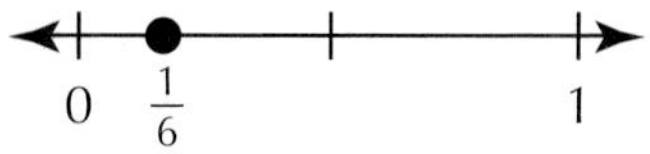

28. 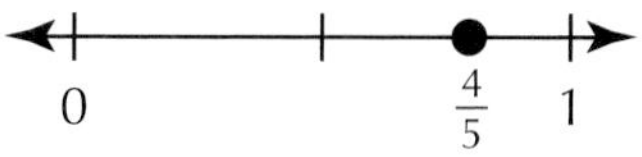

Mixed Review and Test Prep

Take It to the NET
Test Prep
www.scottforesman.com

In 29–32, draw a picture to show each fraction as part of a set.

29. $\frac{2}{8}$ **30.** $\frac{4}{5}$ **31.** $\frac{11}{12}$ **32.** $\frac{7}{20}$

33. Cody had 23 pencils. He shared them equally among 4 friends and kept the extra. How many pencils did each friend get?

A. 4 pencils **B.** 5 pencils **C.** 6 pencils **D.** 92 pencils

Discovery Channel School™

Discover Math in Your World

Big Green

The green turtle is the largest hard-shell turtle in the world. They are named for the color of their body fat. Green turtles often weigh as much as 300 pounds and grow to be almost 4 feet in length. In the United States, they are protected by the Endangered Species Act.

Green turtles cannot pull their head inside of their shell.

1. Of the six species of sea turtles that are present in Australian waters, 3 species are rarely encountered. What fraction of the species are rarely encountered?

2. Green turtles can live to be more than 100 years old. How many months are in 100 years?

Take It to the NET
Video and Activities
www.scottforesman.com

Key Idea
Thinking about benchmark fractions can help you estimate fractional amounts.

Vocabulary
- benchmark fractions

TEST TALK

Think It Through
I only need an **estimate.**

Estimating Fractional Parts

WARM UP

Draw a model to show each fraction.

1. $\frac{1}{6}$ 2. $\frac{3}{4}$
3. $\frac{5}{8}$ 4. $\frac{2}{3}$

LEARN

How do you estimate parts?

Mr. Clarence is harvesting pumpkins from his garden. About what part of the garden still needs to be harvested?

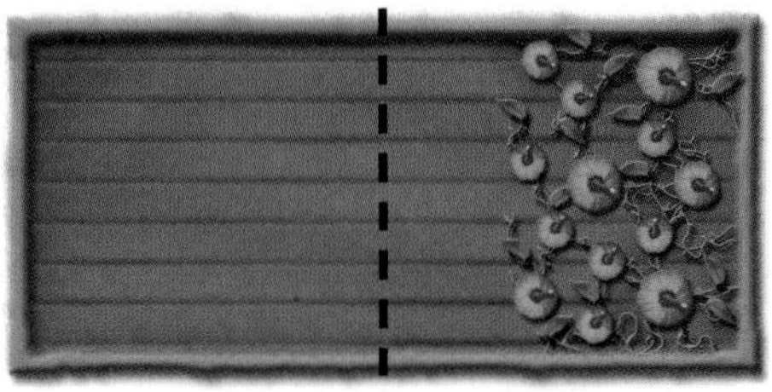

$\frac{1}{2}$

Think about benchmark fractions. **Benchmark fractions** are commonly used fractions such as $\frac{1}{4}$, $\frac{1}{3}$, $\frac{1}{2}$, $\frac{2}{3}$, and $\frac{3}{4}$. Benchmark fractions can be used to estimate fractional parts.

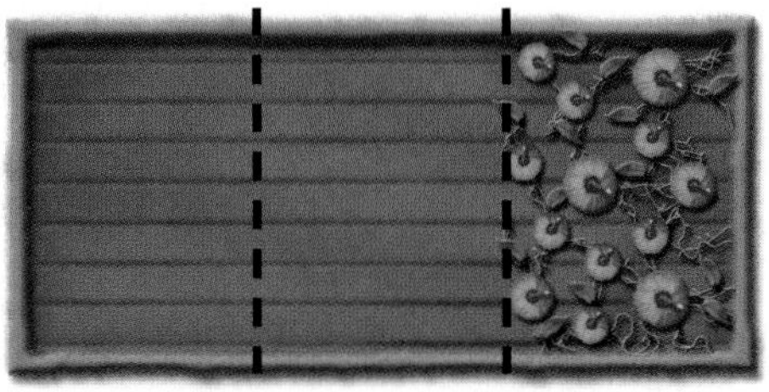

$\frac{1}{3}$

The part of the garden that is left is closest to $\frac{1}{3}$. About $\frac{1}{3}$ of the garden still needs to be harvested.

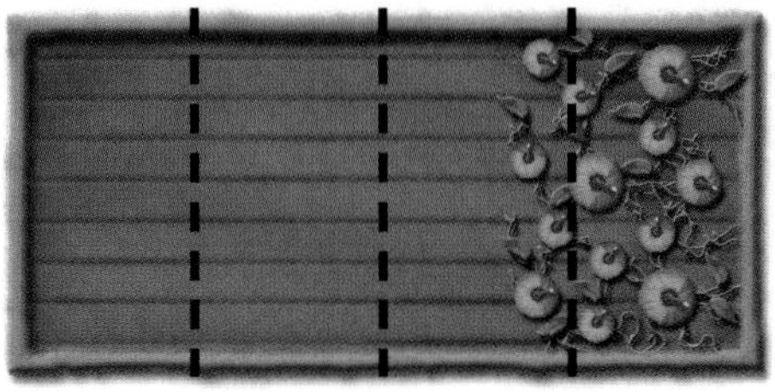

$\frac{1}{4}$

Example

Estimate the fraction that should be written at *A*.

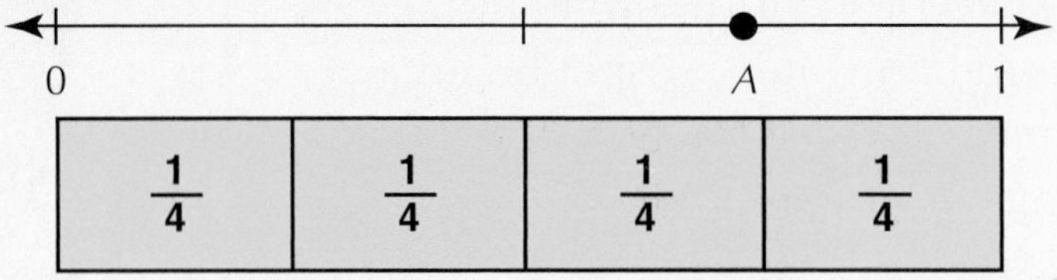

$\frac{3}{4}$ should be written at point *A*.

Think about fraction strips.

Talk About It

1. What is the benchmark fraction in the Example?
2. Estimate the fractional part that is green.

CHECK ✓

For another example, see Set 9-4 on p. 553.

1. Estimate the fractional part of the rectangle that is yellow.

2. Estimate the fraction that should be written at *P*.

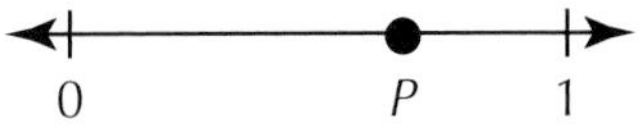

3. Number Sense If more than half of a rectangle is red, is $\frac{1}{3}$ a reasonable estimate for the red part? Explain.

PRACTICE

For more practice, see Set 9-4 on p. 557.

A Skills and Understanding

Estimate the fractional part of each that is green.

4. 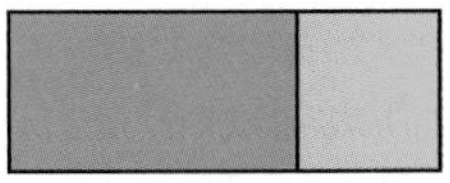

5. 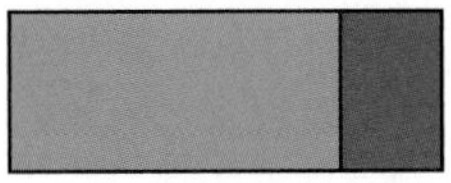

6. 

Estimate the fraction that should be written at each point.

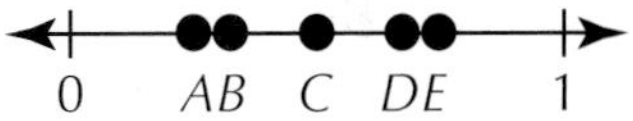

7. *A* **8.** *B* **9.** *C* **10.** *D* **11.** *E*

12. Number Sense Is $\frac{3}{4}$ a reasonable estimate for the green part at the right? Explain.

B Reasoning and Problem Solving

Estimate the part of each garden that has flowers.

13. 

14. 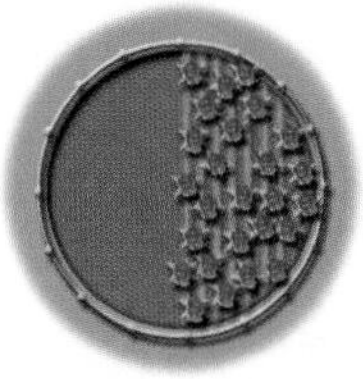

15. 

16. Writing in Math About what part is green in the figure at the right? Explain how you estimated.

Mixed Review and Test Prep

Take It to the NET
Test Prep
www.scottforesman.com

Write a fraction for the part of each length that is green.

17. 

18. 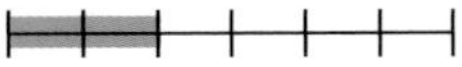

19. 

20. Jason had \$25.15. He spent \$9.73 at the store. How much money did he have left?

A. \$15.42 **B.** \$16.42 **C.** \$24.62 **D.** \$34.88

Understand Graphic Sources: Pictures

Understanding graphic sources such as pictures when you read in math can help you use the **problem-solving strategy, *Draw a Picture,*** in the lesson.

In reading, understanding pictures can help you understand a story. In math, understanding pictures can help you solve problems.

Look for information in the picture.
Fruit Pie
$5.25 for whole pie
or
95¢ per slice
I can get information from the labels and prices in the picture.
I can count to get information. For example, I can count the number of equal slices into which each pie is divided.
Apple $5.25
Berry $5.25
Peach $5.25
Cherry $5.25

1. What is the price of a whole apple pie?
2. Into how many equal slices is each pie divided?
3. What fraction of the peach pie has been purchased?

For 4–7, use the picture at the right.

4. What does the picture show?

5. What labels are in the picture?

6. What is the distance from Dan's home to school?

7. **Writing in Math** If Dan walks from home to the post office, what fraction of the distance from home to school has he walked? Explain how you found your answer.

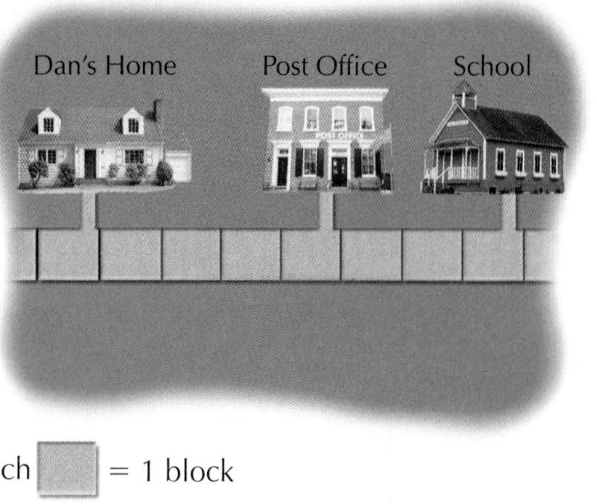

For 8–10, use the picture at the left.

8. Into how many equal slices is each whole roll divided?

9. What is the cost of a whole roll?

10. **Writing in Math** Explain how you would use the picture to find the total cost of a whole fruit roll and 3 slices of another roll.

For 11–13, use the picture at the right.

11. Which box contains the longest nails?

12. How many more nails are in the blue than in the red box?

13. **Writing in Math** Pick two boxes of nails. How are they alike? How are they different?

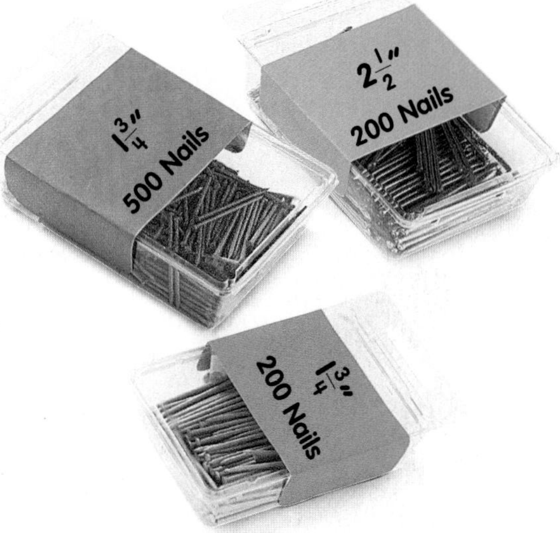

Problem-Solving Strategy

Key Idea
Learning how and when to draw a picture can help you solve problems.

Reading Helps!

Understanding graphic sources such as pictures

can help you with...

the problem-solving strategy, *Draw a Picture.*

Draw a Picture

LEARN

How do you draw a picture to solve a problem?

Race Markers A 5-kilometer run had markers at the starting line and the finish line. Markers were also placed at each kilometer. How many markers were used for the race?

Read and Understand

What do you know? The race was 5 kilometers. Markers were at the starting line and the finish line. Markers showed each kilometer of the race.

What are you trying to find? Find the number of markers used.

Plan and Solve

What strategy will you use? **Strategy: Draw a Picture**

How to Draw a Picture

Step 1 Draw a picture to represent the situation. Do not try to draw the real-world objects.

Step 2 Complete the picture to show the action in the story.

Step 3 Interpret the picture to answer the question in the problem.

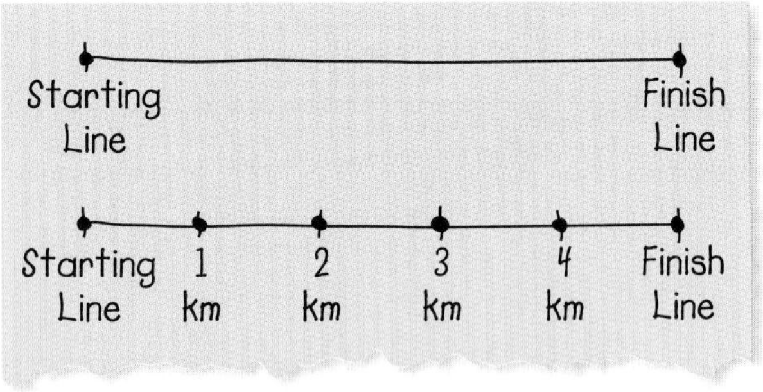

Answer: There were 6 markers used for the race.

Look Back and Check

Is your work correct? Yes, all markers are shown.

Talk About It

1. Zack said the answer was 4 markers. What did he forget to do?

CHECK

For another example, see Set 9-5 on p. 553.

Solve the problem. Write the answer in a complete sentence.

1. **Sharing Sandwiches** Shawn, Heidi, and Missy want to share 2 one-foot-long sandwiches, equally. How much should each of the three friends get?

PRACTICE

For more practice see Set 9-5 on p. 557.

Solve each problem. Write the answer in a complete sentence.

2. **Relay Race** A relay race team has 4 members. Each member runs the same part of a two-mile race. How far does each member run?
3. Wally, Sam, Jack, and Telly arranged their exercise mats in a row. Jack's mat is next to only one other mat. Telly is on the third mat. Sam is not next to Telly. Who is on which mat?
4. **Frame** You buy 16 interlocking strips of wood to make a rectangular bulletin board frame. Each strip is one foot long. What is the greatest area you can frame?
5. The Kennel Club is building a fence around a pen that is 36 feet long and 24 feet wide. They need to put a post at each corner and every 6 feet on a side. How many posts do they need?
6. Manuella's dad promised to add $4 to her savings account for every $10 Manuella saved. If her dad put $24 in her account, how much did Manuella save?
7. **Writing in Math** How many different sandwiches can you make using either chicken or beef and three of the toppings listed below? List the different sandwiches and explain how you made your list.

Build Your Own Sandwich

Choose chicken or beef and 3 toppings.

Pickles • Tomatoes • Lettuce • Sauce

STRATEGIES

- **Show What You Know**
  - Draw a Picture
  - Make an Organized List
  - Make a Table
  - Make a Graph
  - Act It Out or Use Objects
- **Look for a Pattern**
- **Try, Check, and Revise**
- **Write a Number Sentence**
- **Use Logical Reasoning**
- **Solve a Simpler Problem**
- **Work Backward**

Choose a tool

TEST TALK

Think It Through

Stuck? I won't give up. I can:

- Reread the problem.
- Tell what I know.
- Identify key facts and details.
- Tell the problem in my own words.
- Show the main idea.
- Try a different strategy.
- Retrace my steps.

Review

Do You Know How?

Parts of a Region (9-1)
Parts of a Set (9-2)

What fraction of each region or set is blue?

1. 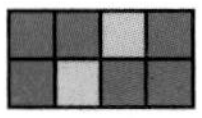

2. 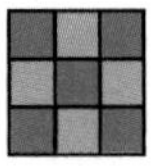

3. 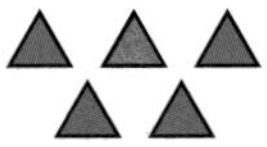

4. 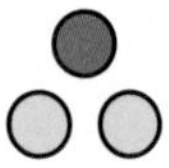

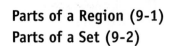

Draw a model to show each fraction as a part of a region and as a part of a set.

5. $\frac{3}{10}$

6. $\frac{7}{12}$

Do You Understand?

A Tell how you found the fractions in Exercises 1 and 3.

B Explain why the model you drew in Exercise 5 may look different than someone else's model.

Fractions, Length, and the Number Line (9-3)
Estimating Fractional Parts (9-4)

Write a fraction for the part of each length that is green.

7. 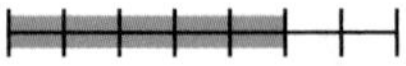

8. 

Estimate the fraction that should be written at each point. 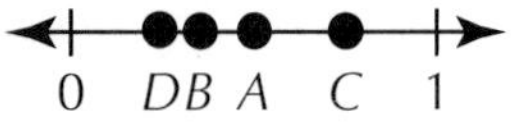

9. *A* **10.** *B* **11.** *C* **12.** *D*

C Tell how you found the fraction in Exercise 7.

D Explain how you would show $\frac{3}{4}$ on a number line.

Problem-Solving Strategy: Draw a Picture (9-5)

13. Make and use a picture to solve the Work problem.

Work How can 8 friends equally share 2 hours of work? How long should each friend work?

E Explain how you used a picture to solve the problem.

F How could 6 friends equally share 2 hours of work?

Diagnostic Checkpoint

TEST TALK

Think It Through
I can **draw a picture** to solve problems.

MULTIPLE CHOICE

1. Megan has 7 red marbles and 8 green marbles. What fraction of Megan's marbles are green? (9-2)

A. $\frac{7}{8}$ **B.** $\frac{7}{15}$ **C.** $\frac{8}{7}$ **D.** $\frac{8}{15}$

2. Mason cut an apple into 8 equal pieces. Ashley ate 2 pieces, Lee ate 3 pieces, and Mason ate 3 pieces. What fraction of the apple did Mason eat? (9-1)

A. $\frac{2}{3}$ **B.** $\frac{2}{8}$ **C.** $\frac{2}{6}$ **D.** $\frac{3}{8}$

FREE RESPONSE

Write a fraction for the part of each region, set, or length that is red. (9-1, 9-2, and 9-3)

3. 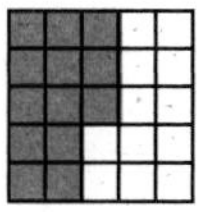

4. 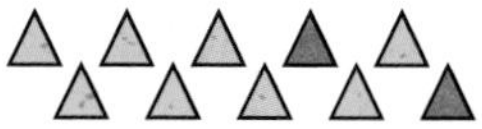

5. 

6. 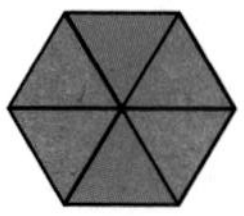

7. 

8. 

9. 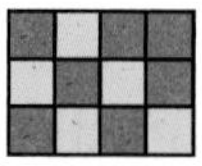

10. 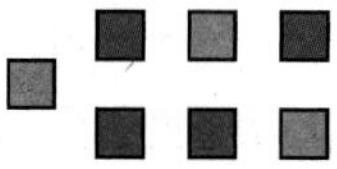

Draw a model to show each fraction as a part of a region and as a part of a set. (9-1 and 9-2)

11. $\frac{1}{3}$ **12.** $\frac{3}{4}$ **13.** $\frac{7}{8}$ **14.** $\frac{2}{5}$

What fraction should be written at each point? (9-3)

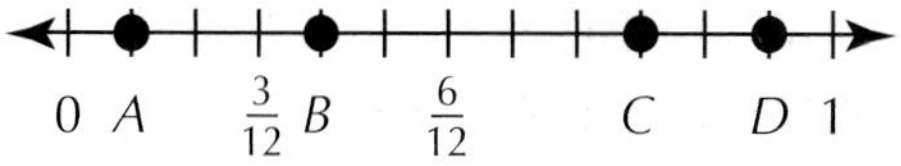

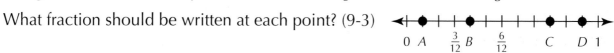

15. *A* **16.** *B* **17.** *C* **18.** *D*

Writing in Math

19. Is $\frac{4}{5}$ of the rectangle on the right yellow? Explain why or why not. (9-1)

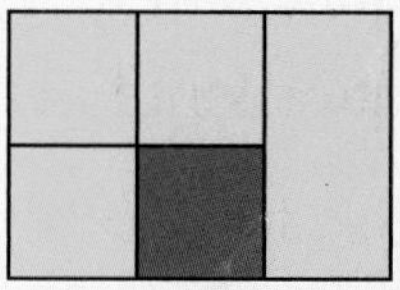

20. Estimate what fractional part of the pizza is left. Explain how you estimated. (9-4)

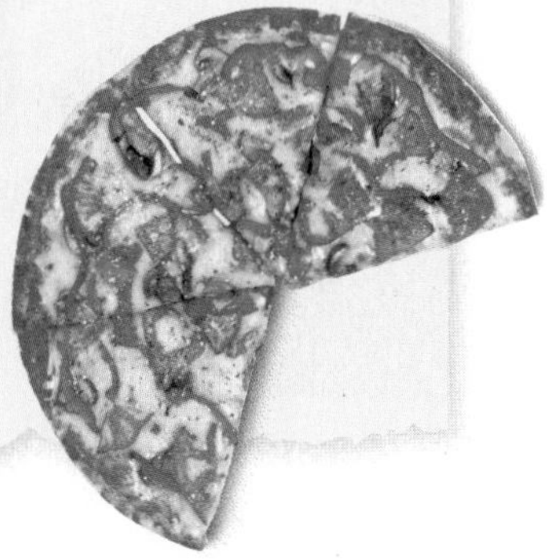

21. Draw a picture to show how 6 people can share 2 pizzas equally. (9-5)

Key Idea
A fraction has many different names.

Vocabulary
- equivalent fractions
- numerator (p. 500)
- denominator (p. 500)

Materials
- fraction strips or e tools

TEST TALK

Think It Through
I can **use a model** to find equivalent fractions.

Equivalent Fractions

WARM UP

Draw a model to show each.

1. $\frac{4}{6}$ as part of a set
2. $\frac{6}{8}$ as part of a length

LEARN

Activity

What are equivalent fractions?

a. Use fraction strips to show $\frac{1}{4}$ and $\frac{2}{8}$ of the red one strip. Are $\frac{1}{4}$ and $\frac{2}{8}$ the same part of the length of the red strip?

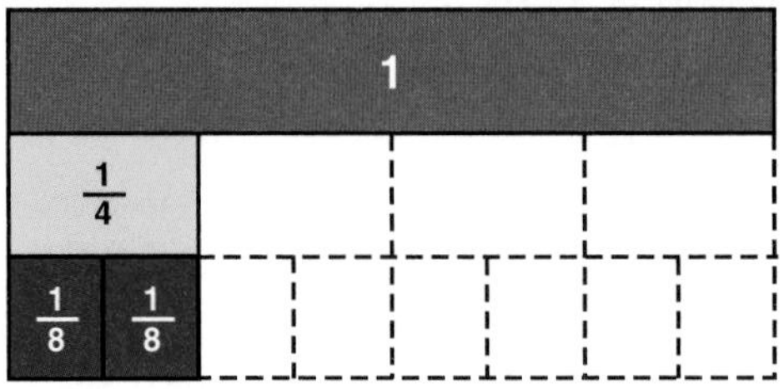

Both $\frac{1}{4}$ and $\frac{2}{8}$ name the same part of the red strip. Fractions that name the same amount are called **equivalent fractions.**

Write $\frac{1}{4} = \frac{2}{8}$.

b. Use fraction strips to find another fraction equivalent to $\frac{1}{4}$ and $\frac{2}{8}$.

c. Use fraction strips to find as many fractions as you can that are equivalent to each fraction below.

$\frac{3}{4}$ $\frac{2}{5}$ $\frac{4}{6}$ $\frac{3}{6}$

d. If $\frac{2}{8}$ and $\frac{3}{12}$ are both equivalent to $\frac{1}{4}$, are they equivalent to each other?

e. Use fraction strips to tell if each pair of fractions is equivalent.

$\frac{4}{5}$ and $\frac{8}{10}$ $\frac{2}{3}$ and $\frac{9}{12}$ $\frac{1}{2}$ and $\frac{5}{10}$

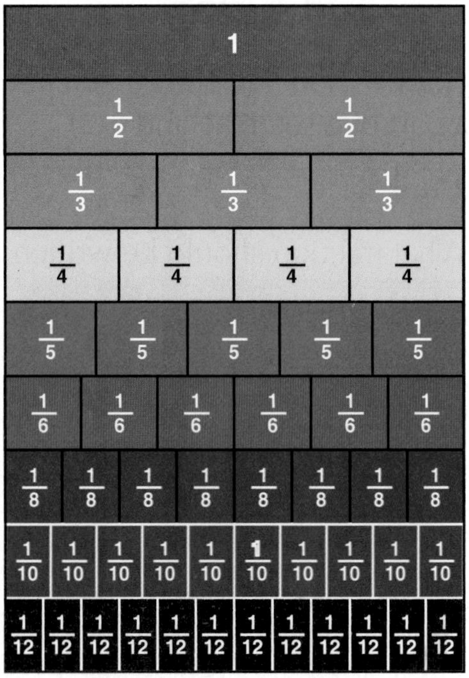

How can you find equivalent fractions?

To find equivalent fractions, multiply the numerator and denominator of a fraction by the same number. But, don't use zero!

Example A

Multiply to find a fraction equivalent to $\frac{2}{5}$.

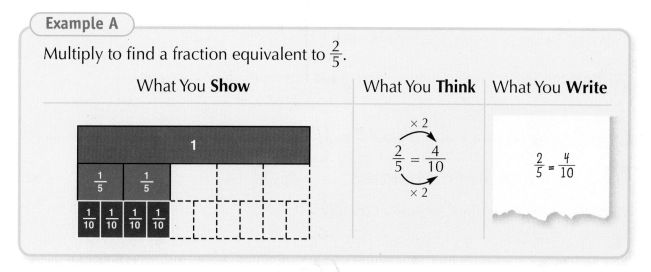

What You **Show**

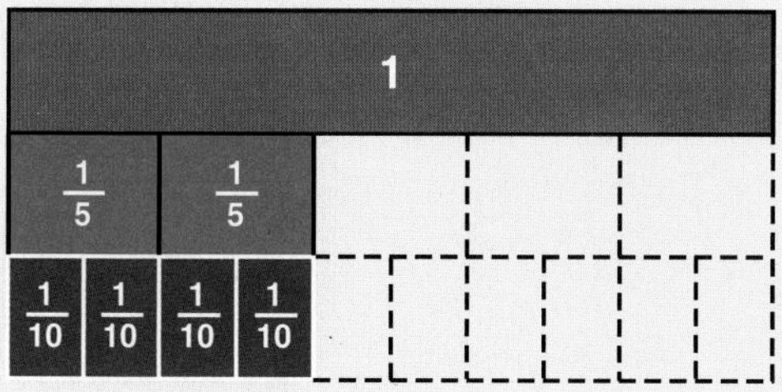

What You **Think**

$\times 2$

$\frac{2}{5} = \frac{4}{10}$

$\times 2$

What You **Write**

$\frac{2}{5} = \frac{4}{10}$

You can also divide the numerator and denominator of a fraction by the same number as long as you don't use zero.

Example B

Divide to find a fraction equivalent to $\frac{4}{6}$.

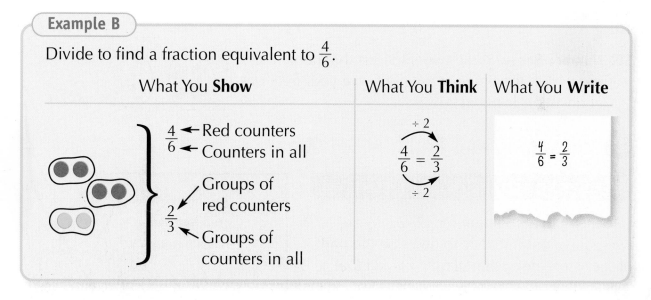

What You **Show**

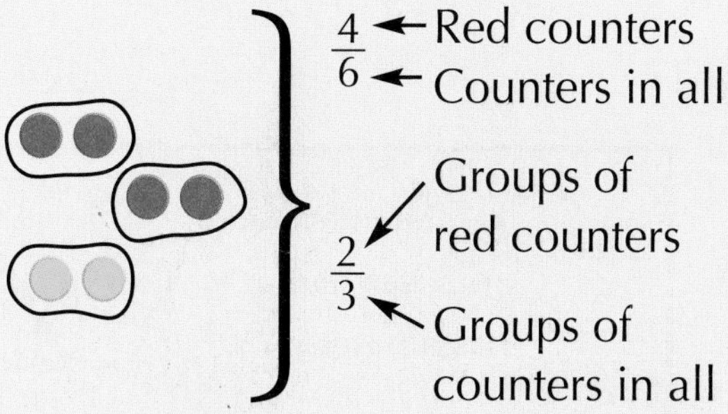

What You **Think**

$\div 2$

$\frac{4}{6} = \frac{2}{3}$

$\div 2$

What You **Write**

$\frac{4}{6} = \frac{2}{3}$

Talk About It

1. In Example B, the numerator and denominator of $\frac{4}{6}$ are divided by 2 to get $\frac{2}{3}$. Is 2 a **factor** of 4 and of 6?
2. If you multiply the numerator and the denominator by 3 instead of 2 to get a fraction equivalent to $\frac{2}{5}$, what fraction would you get?

Take It to the NET
More Examples
www.scottforesman.com

CHECK

For another example, see Set 9-6 on p. 553.

Multiply or divide to find equivalent fractions.

1. $\frac{1}{2} \overset{\times 6}{=} \frac{\square}{\square}$ (× 6)

2. $\frac{3}{4} \overset{\times 3}{=} \frac{\square}{\square}$ (× 3)

3. $\frac{8}{10} \overset{\div 2}{=} \frac{\square}{\square}$ (÷ 2)

4. $\frac{6}{9} \overset{\div 3}{=} \frac{\square}{\square}$ (÷ 3)

5. Number Sense Explain why $\frac{2}{3}$ and $\frac{3}{6}$ are not equivalent fractions.

PRACTICE

For more practice, see Set 9-6 on p. 557.

A Skills and Understanding

Multiply or divide to find equivalent fractions.

6. $\frac{2}{3} \overset{\times 3}{=} \frac{\square}{\square}$ (× 3)

7. $\frac{1}{2} \overset{\times 4}{=} \frac{\square}{\square}$ (× 4)

8. $\frac{9}{15} \overset{\div 3}{=} \frac{\square}{\square}$ (÷ 3)

9. $\frac{4}{10} \overset{\div 2}{=} \frac{\square}{\square}$ (÷ 2)

10. $\frac{5}{6}$ **11.** $\frac{1}{4}$ **12.** $\frac{8}{12}$ **13.** $\frac{2}{8}$ **14.** $\frac{4}{16}$ **15.** $\frac{1}{6}$

16. Number Sense Write two fractions that name the red part in the figure at the right. Are your fractions equivalent? Explain.

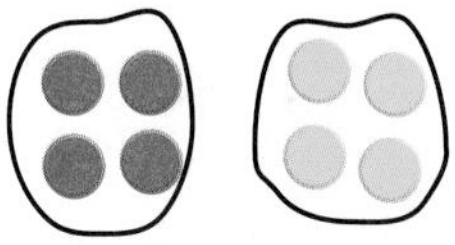

B Reasoning and Problem Solving

Math and Social Studies

Use the map at the right for 17–22. Write two equivalent fractions to describe the part of the states along the Atlantic Ocean that

17. have a name starting with M.

18. have a name starting with N or R.

19. are north of Virginia.

20. have a direction in their name.

21. have a name ending in a vowel.

22. have a two-word name.

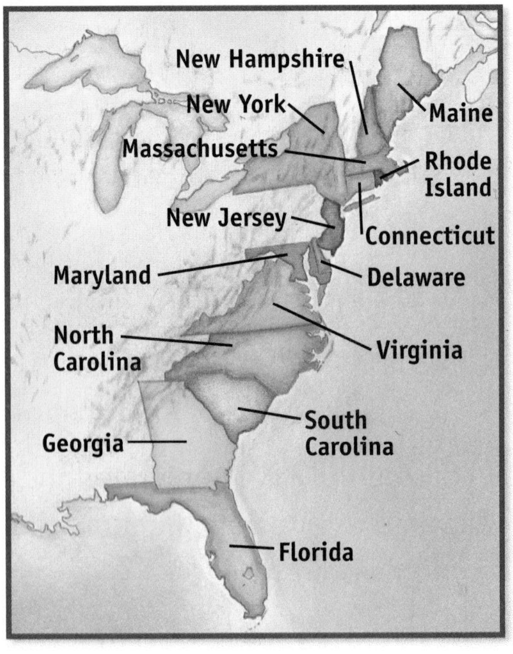

PRACTICE

23. **Writing in Math** Is the explanation below correct? If not tell why and write a correct response.

Draw a picture to show a fraction equivalent to $\frac{8}{10}$. Explain.

I have 10 counters. 8 counters are red. I put them into groups and get $\frac{3}{4}$.

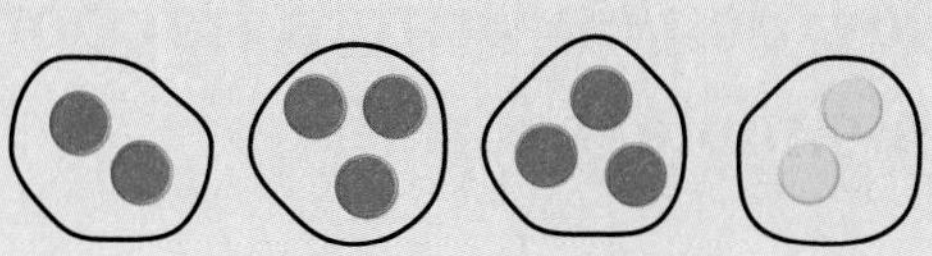

TEST TALK

Think It Through
I should check that my **answer makes sense** by multiplying or dividing.

C Extensions

To find $\frac{2}{3}$ of 9, put 9 counters into 3 groups. Count how many counters are in 2 of the 3 groups. So, $\frac{2}{3}$ of 9 is 6. For 24–27 find each part. You may use counters to help.

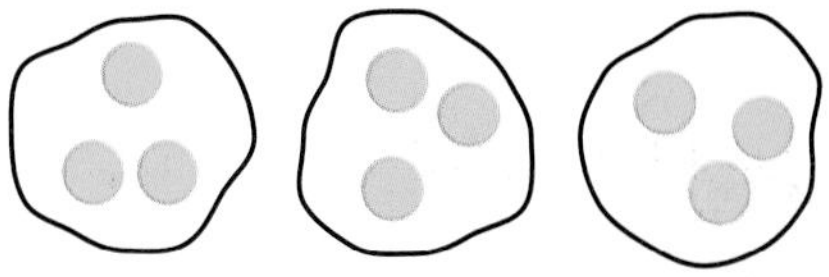

24. $\frac{1}{2}$ of 8 **25.** $\frac{1}{3}$ of 12 **26.** $\frac{2}{5}$ of 10 **27.** $\frac{3}{4}$ of 12

Mixed Review and Test Prep

Take It to the NET
Test Prep
www.scottforesman.com

28. Tracy wants to plant flowers along 9 feet of sidewalk. She plans to place one flower at each end and a flower every foot in between. How many flowers will she plant?

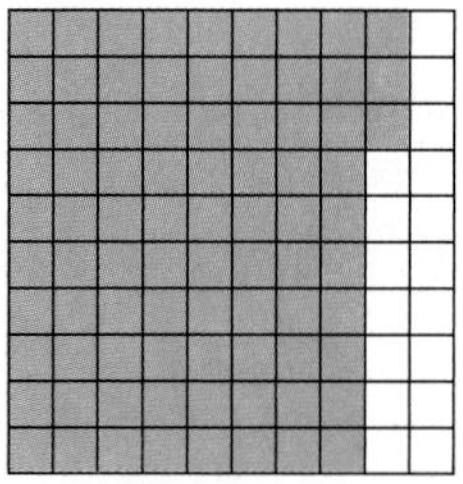

29. Write the decimal for the shaded part at the right.

A. 0.38 **B.** 0.8 **C.** 0.83 **D.** 0.9

Learning with Technology

Using a Calculator to Find Equivalent Fractions

The F↔D key allows you to change between fractions and decimals.

To find an equivalent fraction for $\frac{1}{2}$, press 1 n 2 d ENTER = F↔D.

You will see the decimal equivalent of $\frac{1}{2}$ is 0.5.
Press F↔D again to get a fraction equivalent to 0.5.

For 1–4, use your calculator to find an equivalent fraction.

1. $\frac{3}{4}$ **2.** $\frac{5}{8}$ **3.** $\frac{11}{20}$ **4.** $\frac{9}{50}$

Key Idea
Fractions can be written so that the numerator and denominator have no common factors other than 1.

Vocabulary
- common factor
- simplest form

TEST TALK

Think It Through
- I can find the simplest form in **more than one way.**
- I should **check my answer** to be sure there are no more common factors.

Fractions in Simplest Form

WARM UP

Find equivalent fractions.

1. $\frac{6}{8}$
2. $\frac{4}{10}$
3. $\frac{8}{12}$
4. $\frac{2}{4}$

LEARN

How do you write a fraction in simplest form?

Carrie drew a design on the sidewalk with chalk. What fraction of Carrie's design is blue chalk squares? Write the fraction in the simplest form.

$\frac{8}{12}$ ← Number of blue chalk squares / Total number of chalk squares

Since 4 is a factor of 8 and a factor of 12, it is a **common factor** of 8 and 12. A fraction is in **simplest form** if the numerator and denominator have no common factors other than 1.

Example

Write $\frac{8}{12}$ in simplest form.

One Way

Clint divided twice.

$\frac{8}{12} = \frac{4}{6}$ (÷ 2)

8 and 12 are both even. 2 is a common factor.

$\frac{4}{6} = \frac{2}{3}$ (÷ 2)

I can divide 4 and 6 by 2. I can't divide any more.

Another Way

Roy divided once.

8 and 12 have a common factor of 4.

$\frac{8}{12} = \frac{2}{3}$ (÷ 4)

The only common factor of 2 and 3 is 1.

Carrie's design is $\frac{2}{3}$ blue.

Talk About It

1. How did Clint write $\frac{8}{12}$ in simplest form?
2. Are $\frac{8}{12}$ and $\frac{2}{3}$ equivalent fractions? Explain.

CHECK

For another example, see Set 9-7 on p. 554.

Write each fraction in simplest form. If it is in simplest form, write simplest form.

1. $\frac{3}{6}$ **2.** $\frac{6}{9}$ **3.** $\frac{7}{8}$ **4.** $\frac{4}{7}$ **5.** $\frac{5}{15}$

6. Number Sense Explain how you can tell $\frac{3}{4}$ is in simplest form.

PRACTICE

For more practice, see Set 9-7 on p. 557.

A Skills and Understanding

Write each fraction in simplest form. If it is in simplest form, write simplest form.

7. $\frac{3}{12}$ **8.** $\frac{2}{10}$ **9.** $\frac{4}{8}$ **10.** $\frac{12}{16}$ **11.** $\frac{4}{6}$ **12.** $\frac{2}{5}$

13. $\frac{6}{8}$ **14.** $\frac{3}{16}$ **15.** $\frac{8}{10}$ **16.** $\frac{4}{12}$ **17.** $\frac{3}{7}$ **18.** $\frac{8}{12}$

19. $\frac{9}{10}$ **20.** $\frac{9}{15}$ **21.** $\frac{12}{20}$ **22.** $\frac{5}{6}$ **23.** $\frac{3}{9}$ **24.** $\frac{15}{18}$

25. Number Sense Explain how you can tell $\frac{14}{20}$ is not in simplest form.

B Reasoning and Problem Solving

Write each fraction in simplest form. What fraction of the set of balls are

26. red? **27.** striped? **28.** patterned?

29. Writing in Math What fraction of the balls is blue? Explain how you know this fraction is in simplest form.

Mixed Review and Test Prep

Take It to the NET
Test Prep
www.scottforesman.com

Multiply or divide to find equivalent fractions.

30. $\frac{1}{2} \xrightarrow{\times 7} \frac{\square}{\square}$ (× 7 on numerator and denominator)

31. $\frac{3}{4} \xrightarrow{\times 4} \frac{\square}{\square}$ (× 4 on numerator and denominator)

32. $\frac{12}{15} \xrightarrow{\div 3} \frac{\square}{\square}$ (÷ 3 on numerator and denominator)

33. $\frac{2}{6} \xrightarrow{\div 2} \frac{\square}{\square}$ (÷ 2 on numerator and denominator)

34. What is the perimeter of a rectangle that is 8 inches long and 4 inches wide?

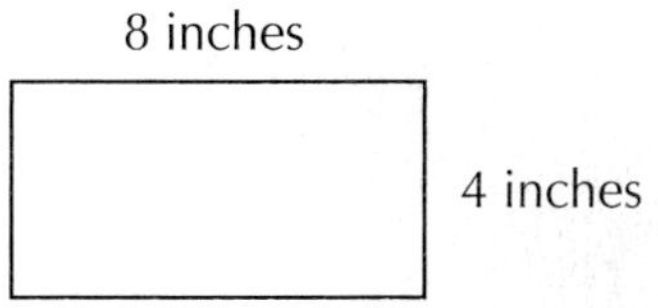

A. 12 inches **C.** 24 inches

B. 20 inches **D.** 32 inches

Key Idea
There are different ways to compare fractions.

Materials
- fraction strips or e tools

TEST TALK

Think It Through
- I can **use a model** to compare fractions.
- I can **look for a pattern** to find a rule.

Using Number Sense to Compare Fractions

WARM UP

Draw a model to show each fraction.

1. $\frac{7}{10}$ as part of a region
2. $\frac{5}{7}$ as part of a set

LEARN

Activity

How do you use fraction strips to compare fractions?

a. Use fraction strips to show $\frac{4}{6}$ and $\frac{5}{6}$. Which is greater?

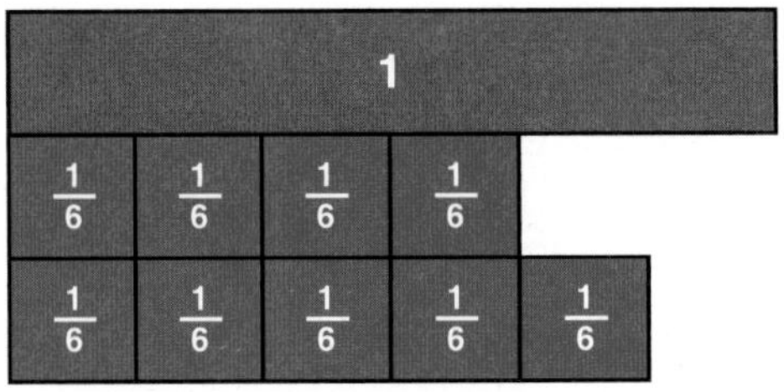

b. Use fraction strips to compare. Then write > or < for each.

$\frac{3}{10}$ ○ $\frac{7}{10}$ $\quad$ $\frac{5}{8}$ ○ $\frac{3}{8}$ $\quad$ $\frac{2}{3}$ ○ $\frac{1}{3}$

c. Write a rule that tells how to compare two fractions with the same denominator.

d. Use fraction strips to show halves and eighths. Decide which fraction with a denominator of 8 equals $\frac{1}{2}$, which fractions are greater than $\frac{1}{2}$, and which fractions are less than $\frac{1}{2}$.

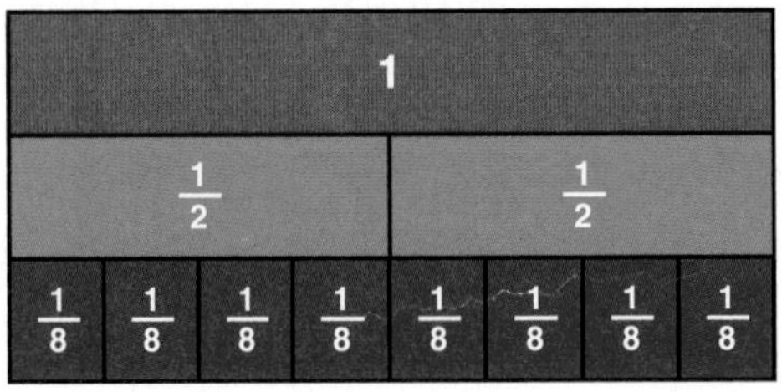

e. Use fraction strips to decide which fraction with a denominator of 10 equals $\frac{1}{2}$, which fractions are less than $\frac{1}{2}$, and which fractions are greater than $\frac{1}{2}$.

f. Use fraction strips. Write > or < for each. Use the first two comparisons to help you find the third.

$\frac{1}{3}$ ○ $\frac{1}{2}$ and $\frac{1}{2}$ ○ $\frac{3}{4}$, so $\frac{1}{3}$ ○ $\frac{3}{4}$

$\frac{5}{8}$ ○ $\frac{1}{2}$ and $\frac{1}{2}$ ○ $\frac{2}{6}$, so $\frac{5}{8}$ ○ $\frac{2}{6}$

CHECK ✓

For another example, see Set 9-8 on p. 554.

Write > or < for each ○. You may use fraction strips to help.

1. $\frac{1}{2}$ ○ $\frac{5}{6}$ **2.** $\frac{3}{10}$ ○ $\frac{1}{2}$ **3.** $\frac{3}{4}$ ○ $\frac{1}{3}$ **4.** $\frac{3}{8}$ ○ $\frac{2}{3}$

5. Number Sense Explain how you can tell that $\frac{9}{12}$ is greater than $\frac{1}{2}$.

PRACTICE

For more practice, see Set 9-8 on p. 558.

A Skills and Understanding

Write > or < for each ○. You may use fraction strips to help.

6. $\frac{1}{4}$ ○ $\frac{1}{8}$ **7.** $\frac{7}{10}$ ○ $\frac{9}{10}$ **8.** $\frac{3}{10}$ ○ $\frac{7}{8}$ **9.** $\frac{5}{12}$ ○ $\frac{1}{2}$

10. $\frac{4}{6}$ ○ $\frac{5}{6}$ **11.** $\frac{1}{3}$ ○ $\frac{1}{4}$ **12.** $\frac{4}{10}$ ○ $\frac{2}{3}$ **13.** $\frac{3}{8}$ ○ $\frac{2}{8}$

14. $\frac{1}{2}$ ○ $\frac{5}{8}$ **15.** $\frac{3}{4}$ ○ $\frac{5}{12}$ **16.** $\frac{7}{12}$ ○ $\frac{11}{12}$ **17.** $\frac{3}{8}$ ○ $\frac{9}{10}$

18. Number Sense Explain how you can tell that $\frac{23}{50}$ is less than $\frac{1}{2}$.

B Reasoning and Problem Solving

The students in Ms. Wilcox's class need to collect leaves from 12 different types of trees. Who has a greater part of their collection completed,

19. Troy or Sandy? **20.** Tina or Aaron?

21. Sandy or Aaron? **22.** Tina or Troy?

23. Reasoning Write > or < for ○. Since $\frac{2}{12} < \frac{1}{3}$ and $\frac{1}{3} < \frac{4}{10}$, $\frac{2}{12}$ ○ $\frac{4}{10}$.

24. Writing in Math Explain how you could decide whether $\frac{5}{8}$ or $\frac{4}{12}$ is greater.

Leaf Collections

Name	Part Completed
Troy	$\frac{1}{4}$
Tina	$\frac{2}{3}$
Sandy	$\frac{3}{4}$
Aaron	$\frac{2}{6}$

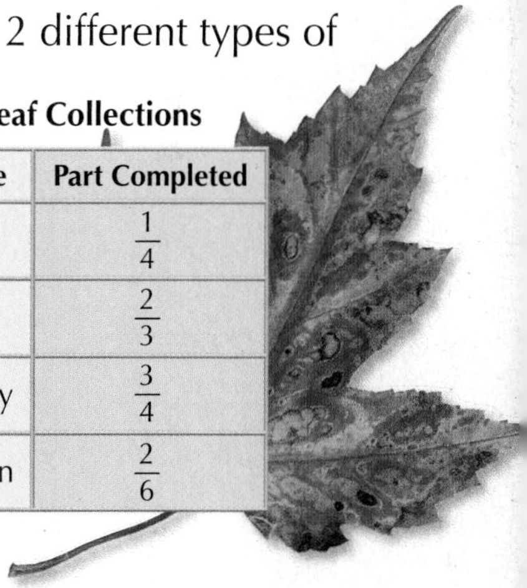

Mixed Review and Test Prep

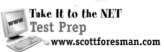

Take It to the NET
Test Prep
www.scottforesman.com

Write each fraction in simplest form.

25. $\frac{9}{12}$ **26.** $\frac{2}{8}$ **27.** $\frac{10}{12}$ **28.** $\frac{6}{12}$ **29.** $\frac{6}{14}$

30. In which set are the numbers in order from least to greatest?

A. 111, 119, 117, 118 **C.** 198, 199, 208, 206

B. 118, 131, 139, 136 **D.** 172, 179, 181, 186

Key Idea
There are different ways to compare and order fractions.

Materials
- fraction strips

or e tools

TEST TALK

Think It Through
I can compare fractions in **more than one way.**

Comparing and Ordering Fractions

WARM UP

Order the numbers from least to greatest

1. 2,345 2,354 2,534
2. 72 78 81 95
3. 617 716 672

LEARN

How do you compare fractions?

Kristina and James weave rugs. Kristina's rug is $\frac{3}{8}$ completed and James's rug is $\frac{3}{4}$ completed.

Example A

Who has a greater part finished, Kristina or James?

Compare $\frac{3}{8}$ and $\frac{3}{4}$.

You can use fraction strips to compare.

$\frac{3}{8} < \frac{3}{4}$

James has a greater part of his rug finished than Kristina.

You also can use number sense or equivalent fractions to compare.

Example B

Compare $\frac{5}{9}$ and $\frac{2}{5}$.

Use number sense.

Compare each fraction to $\frac{1}{2}$.

$\frac{5}{9} > \frac{1}{2}$

$\frac{2}{5} < \frac{1}{2}$

So, $\frac{5}{9} > \frac{2}{5}$.

Example C

Compare $\frac{2}{3}$ and $\frac{5}{6}$.

$\frac{2 \times 2}{3 \times 2} = \frac{4}{6}$

$\frac{2}{3} = \frac{4}{6}$

$\frac{4}{6} < \frac{5}{6}$

So, $\frac{2}{3} < \frac{5}{6}$.

When the denominators are the same, you can compare the numerators.

Talk About It

1. How do the fraction strips in Example A show that $\frac{3}{8} < \frac{3}{4}$
2. In Example B, how can you tell that $\frac{5}{9} > \frac{1}{2}$ and $\frac{2}{5} < \frac{1}{2}$?

How do you order fractions?

Which rug is the longest? Which rug is the shortest?

$\frac{2}{3}$ yard

$\frac{3}{4}$ yard

$\frac{7}{12}$ yard

Example D

Order $\frac{2}{3}$, $\frac{3}{4}$, and $\frac{7}{12}$.

One Way

Use a number line.

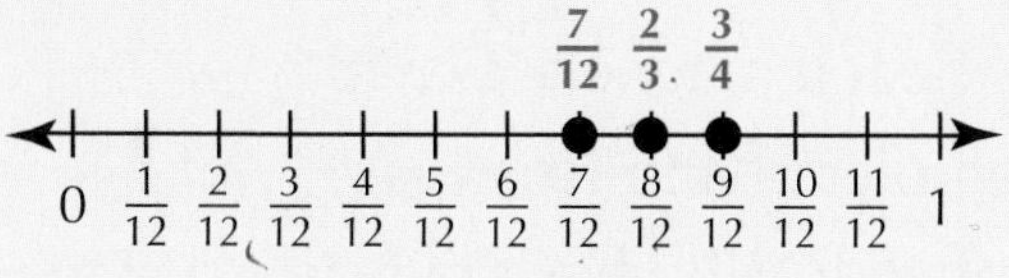

Remember, on a number line, numbers are in order from the least on the left to the greatest on the right.

The fractions in order are $\frac{7}{12}$, $\frac{2}{3}$, $\frac{3}{4}$.

Another Way

Use equivalent fractions.

$$\frac{2 \times 4}{3 \times 4} = \frac{8}{12} \qquad \frac{3 \times 3}{4 \times 3} = \frac{9}{12}$$

From least to greatest: $\frac{7}{12}$, $\frac{8}{12}$, $\frac{9}{12}$.

↓ ↓ ↓

The fractions in order are $\frac{7}{12}$, $\frac{2}{3}$, $\frac{3}{4}$.

The rug that is $\frac{3}{4}$ yard is the longest. The rug that is $\frac{7}{12}$ yard is the shortest.

Talk About It

3. In Example D, how can you tell that $\frac{7}{12}$ is the least using the number line?

CHECK

For another example, see Set 9-9 on p. 554.

Compare. Write >, <, or = for each ●. You can use fraction strips to help.

1. $\frac{1}{2}$ ● $\frac{3}{8}$ **2.** $\frac{2}{3}$ ● $\frac{5}{6}$ **3.** $\frac{3}{4}$ ● $\frac{5}{6}$ **4.** $\frac{7}{10}$ ● $\frac{14}{20}$

Order the numbers from least to greatest.

5. $\frac{2}{3}$, $\frac{1}{2}$, $\frac{5}{12}$ **6.** $\frac{5}{6}$, $\frac{1}{3}$, $\frac{1}{6}$ **7.** $\frac{7}{8}$, $\frac{3}{8}$, $\frac{3}{4}$ **8.** $\frac{1}{3}$, $\frac{1}{6}$, $\frac{3}{4}$

9. Number Sense Bobby drew the picture at the right to show that $\frac{1}{3} > \frac{1}{2}$. What was Bobby's mistake?

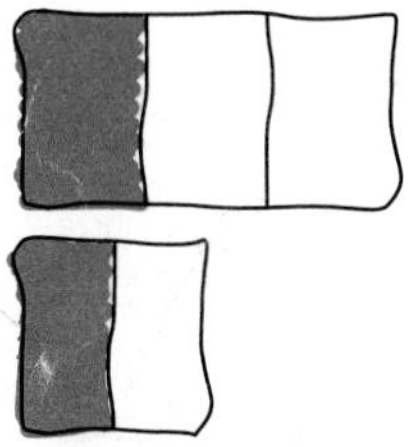

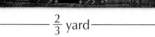

PRACTICE

For more practice, see Set 9-9 on p. 558.

A Skills and Understanding

Compare. Write >, <, or = for each ●.

10. $\frac{5}{12}$ ● $\frac{1}{2}$ **11.** $\frac{3}{4}$ ● $\frac{7}{8}$ **12.** $\frac{1}{6}$ ● $\frac{2}{3}$ **13.** $\frac{5}{6}$ ● $\frac{10}{12}$

14. $\frac{7}{12}$ ● $\frac{3}{4}$ **15.** $\frac{2}{3}$ ● $\frac{5}{12}$ **16.** $\frac{3}{8}$ ● $\frac{2}{3}$ **17.** $\frac{3}{10}$ ● $\frac{7}{8}$

Order the numbers from least to greatest.

18. $\frac{9}{10}, \frac{3}{12}, \frac{2}{6}$ **19.** $\frac{11}{12}, \frac{3}{8}, \frac{1}{2}$ **20.** $\frac{5}{8}, \frac{3}{4}, \frac{1}{3}$ **21.** $\frac{5}{6}, \frac{3}{8}, \frac{7}{12}$

22. $\frac{5}{6}, \frac{3}{10}, \frac{2}{3}$ **23.** $\frac{1}{3}, \frac{1}{4}, \frac{7}{10}$ **24.** $\frac{3}{4}, \frac{1}{3}, \frac{7}{12}$ **25.** $\frac{3}{4}, \frac{7}{8}, \frac{2}{3}$

26. Number Sense Explain why $\frac{2}{3} < \frac{5}{6}$.

B Reasoning and Problem Solving

27. Trent, Carrie, and David are each making a dozen magnets. David has $\frac{1}{2}$ of his completed, Carrie has $\frac{1}{3}$ of hers completed and Trent has $\frac{7}{12}$ of his completed. Who has the greatest part completed? Who has the least?

Math and Social Studies

Use the data file at the right for 28–33. Which state has a greater part of its area in land,

28. Rhode Island or Wisconsin? **29.** Hawaii or Florida?

30. Florida or North Carolina? **31.** Hawaii or North Carolina?

32. Is more or less than half of Hawaii land?

33. Which state has the least part of its area in land, Florida, Hawaii, or North Carolina? Which has the greatest?

34. Writing in Math Is the explanation below correct? If not, tell why and write a correct response.

> Explain how to compare $\frac{6}{10}$ and $\frac{2}{5}$.
>
> $\div 2$: $\frac{6}{10} = \frac{3}{5}$ $\div 2$
>
> $\frac{3}{5} > \frac{2}{5}$
>
> $\frac{6}{10} > \frac{2}{5}$

Data File

State	Part of Area that Is Land
Florida	$\frac{41}{50}$
Hawaii	$\frac{59}{100}$
North Carolina	$\frac{9}{10}$
Rhode Island	$\frac{2}{3}$
Wisconsin	$\frac{5}{6}$

TEST TALK

Think It Through
I can find equivalent fractions in **more than one way.**

PRACTICE

C Extensions

Use Jason's method to compare fractions.

Write > or < for each ●.

35. $\frac{1}{5}$ ● $\frac{1}{6}$ **36.** $\frac{1}{4}$ ● $\frac{1}{2}$

37. $\frac{1}{8}$ ● $\frac{1}{9}$ **38.** $\frac{1}{3}$ ● $\frac{1}{7}$

Jason

$\frac{1}{3} > \frac{1}{4}$ because $3 < 4$

The pieces are bigger when I divide a box into 3 equal pieces than when I divide the same box into 4 pieces.

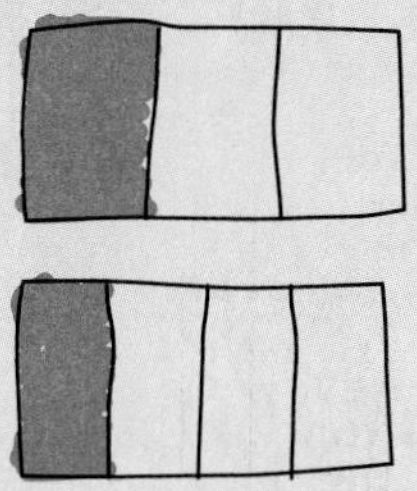

Mixed Review and Test Prep

Take It to the NET
Test Prep
www.scottforesman.com

Write > or < for each ●. You may use fraction strips to help.

39. $\frac{5}{12}$ ● $\frac{1}{12}$ **40.** $\frac{1}{6}$ ● $\frac{1}{3}$ **41.** $\frac{2}{3}$ ● $\frac{1}{2}$ **42.** $\frac{3}{10}$ ● $\frac{7}{12}$

43. 404×8

A. 412 **B.** 3,202 **C.** 3,224 **D.** 3,232

Practice Game

Fraction Action

Number of Players: 2–4

Materials: Fraction Cards

One player deals all the fraction cards, face down, to all players. Each player turns one card over. The player with the greatest fraction wins the round and takes the cards. If there is a tie for the greatest fraction, each player plays another card. The player with the greatest fraction then takes all the cards. Play continues until all of the cards have been used. The winner is the player who has the most cards.

Section B: Lessons 9-6 through 9-9

Review

Do You Know How?

Equivalent Fractions (9-6)

Multiply or divide to find equivalent fractions.

1. $\frac{3}{5} = \frac{\square}{\square}$ (× 2, × 2)

2. $\frac{6}{15} = \frac{\square}{\square}$ (÷ 3, ÷ 3)

3. $\frac{15}{18}$

4. $\frac{3}{4}$

Do You Understand?

A Tell how you found each equivalent fraction in Exercises 3 and 4.

B Explain why $\frac{6}{8}$ and $\frac{9}{12}$ are equivalent fractions.

Fractions in Simplest Form (9-7)

Write each fraction in simplest form. If it is in simplest form, write simplest form.

5. $\frac{2}{6}$

6. $\frac{8}{14}$

7. $\frac{2}{5}$

8. $\frac{6}{10}$

9. $\frac{12}{15}$

10. $\frac{10}{24}$

C Tell how you simplified each fraction.

D Explain how you can tell whether or not $\frac{14}{16}$ is in simplest form.

Using Number Sense to Compare Fractions (9-8)
Comparing and Ordering Fractions (9-9)

Write > or < for each $\bigcirc$.

11. $\frac{5}{12} \bigcirc \frac{7}{12}$

12. $\frac{2}{3} \bigcirc \frac{3}{10}$

13. $\frac{7}{8} \bigcirc \frac{1}{6}$

14. $\frac{3}{4} \bigcirc \frac{7}{8}$

Order the numbers from least to greatest.

15. $\frac{2}{3}, \frac{5}{12}, \frac{5}{6}$

16. $\frac{7}{10}, \frac{1}{4}, \frac{1}{8}$

E Tell how you compared the fractions in Exercise 11.

F Explain how you ordered the fractions in Exercise 15.

Diagnostic Checkpoint

MULTIPLE CHOICE

1. Jo read $\frac{2}{3}$ of a book. Denny said he read more of the same book than Jo. Which could be the fraction of the book that Denny read? (9-9)

   A. $\frac{4}{6}$ **B.** $\frac{7}{9}$ **C.** $\frac{1}{4}$ **D.** $\frac{3}{8}$

2. Mia has 20 marbles. Sixteen of them are red. In simplest form, what fraction of Mia's marbles are red? (9-7)

   A. $\frac{4}{20}$ **B.** $\frac{1}{5}$ **C.** $\frac{8}{10}$ **D.** $\frac{4}{5}$

TEST TALK

Think It Through
I can find equivalent fractions, find simplest form, and compare fractions in **more than one way.**

FREE RESPONSE

Multiply or divide to find equivalent fractions. (9-6)

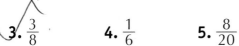

3. $\frac{3}{8}$ **4.** $\frac{1}{6}$ **5.** $\frac{8}{20}$

Write each fraction in simplest form. If it is in simplest form, write simplest form. (9-7)

6. $\frac{5}{10}$ **7.** $\frac{7}{9}$ **8.** $\frac{10}{15}$

Write > or < for each $\bigcirc$. (9-8 and 9-9)

9. $\frac{5}{12} \bigcirc \frac{11}{12}$ **10.** $\frac{7}{8} \bigcirc \frac{3}{10}$ **11.** $\frac{1}{4} \bigcirc \frac{3}{8}$ **12.** $\frac{5}{6} \bigcirc \frac{1}{2}$

Use the information at the right for 13–15. (9-8 and 9-9)

13. Does Ted have more sedimentary or metamorphic rocks?

14. Does Ted have more igneous or sedimentary rocks?

15. Which type of rock does Ted have the most ?

Ted's Rock Collection

Type	Part of Collection
Sedimentary	$\frac{2}{3}$
Igneous	$\frac{2}{15}$
Metamorphic	$\frac{1}{5}$

Writing in Math

16. Joyce and Kelly had sandwiches of the same size. Joyce cut her sandwich into 2 equal pieces and ate both of them. Kelly cut her sandwich into 4 equal pieces and ate 3 pieces. Did they eat the same amount of sandwich? Explain your answer. (9-6)

17. Explain how you could decide whether $\frac{5}{12}$ or $\frac{7}{10}$ is greater. (9-7 and 9-8)

Key Idea
Not all fractions are less than one.

Vocabulary
- mixed numbers
- improper fractions

Materials
- fraction strips or e-tools

Mixed Numbers and Improper Fractions

WARM UP

1. If 3 people share a pizza equally, how much does each person get?

LEARN

Activity

What are mixed numbers and improper fractions?

a. Show 2 wholes and $\frac{1}{4}$ of another whole with fraction strips.

The fraction strips show $2\frac{1}{4}$. A **mixed number** has a whole number and a fraction. $2\frac{1}{4}$ is a mixed number.

b. How many $\frac{1}{4}$ pieces does it take to cover the fraction strips used to show $2\frac{1}{4}$?

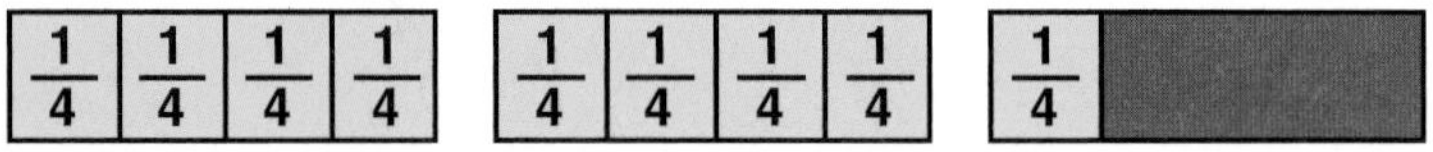

It takes nine $\frac{1}{4}$ pieces to cover $2\frac{1}{4}$. The fraction strips show $2\frac{1}{4} = \frac{9}{4}$.

An **improper fraction** has a numerator greater than or equal to its denominator. $\frac{9}{4}$ is an improper fraction.

c. Use fraction strips. Find an improper fraction that equals each mixed number.

$2\frac{1}{3}$ $\quad 1\frac{7}{10}$ $\quad 3\frac{1}{4}$ $\quad 1\frac{5}{6}$

d. Use fraction strips. Find a mixed number that equals each improper fraction.

$\frac{7}{4}$ $\quad \frac{11}{3}$ $\quad \frac{14}{6}$ $\quad \frac{15}{8}$

e. Can $\frac{6}{3}$ be written as a whole number? Why or why not?

TEST TALK

Think It Through

I can **use a model** to show mixed numbers and improper fractions.

How can you change between improper fractions and mixed numbers?

Example A

Write $2\frac{1}{6}$ as an improper fraction.

One Way

Use fraction strips

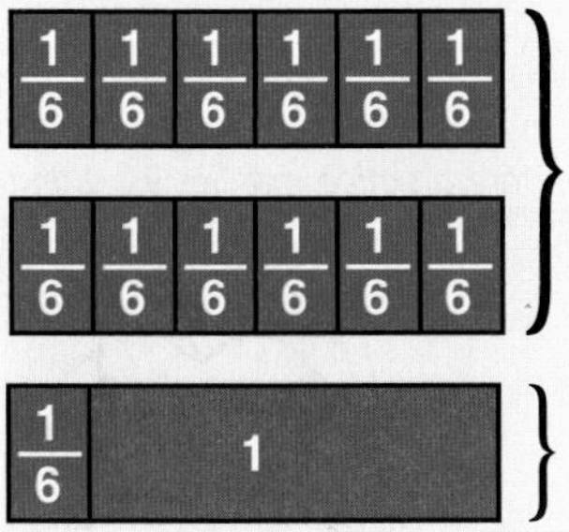

2	×	6	=	12
wholes		sixths in each whole		sixths

Add the other sixth.

12	+	1	=	13
sixths		sixth		sixths

So, $2\frac{1}{6} = \frac{13}{6}$.

Another Way

Use mental math.

Multiply the whole number by the denominator. Then add the numerator.

$2 \times 6 = 12$

$12 + 1 = 13$

Write the sum as the numerator. → $\frac{13}{6}$

The denominator stays the same.

So, $2\frac{1}{6} = \frac{13}{6}$.

Example B

Write $\frac{5}{3}$ as mixed number.

One Way

Use fraction strips. How many wholes can you make with 5 thirds?

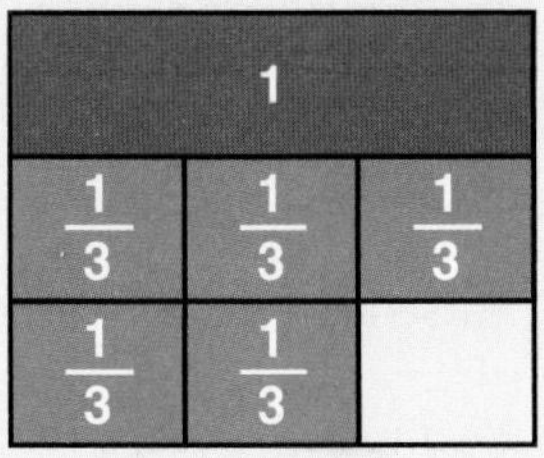

5	÷	3	=	1 R2
thirds		thirds in each whole		one whole and 2 thirds left over

So, $\frac{5}{3} = 1\frac{2}{3}$.

Another Way

Divide the numerator by the denominator.

$$\begin{array}{r} 1\ \text{R}2 \\ 3\overline{)5} \\ -\,3 \\ \hline 2 \end{array}$$

Write the quotient as the whole number. → $1\frac{2}{3}$ ← Write the remainder as the numerator.

The denominator stays the same.

So, $\frac{5}{3} = 1\frac{2}{3}$.

Talk About It

1. How do you change an improper fraction to a mixed number?

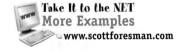

Take It to the NET
More Examples
www.scottforesman.com

CHECK

For another example, see Set 9-10 on p. 555.

Write each mixed number as an improper fraction.

1. $1\frac{3}{8}$ **2.** $2\frac{2}{3}$ **3.** $3\frac{2}{10}$ **4.** $2\frac{5}{12}$

Write each improper fraction as a mixed number or a whole number.

5. $\frac{5}{2}$ **6.** $\frac{12}{4}$ **7.** $\frac{7}{3}$ **8.** $\frac{13}{5}$

9. Number Sense How can you tell if an improper fraction equals a mixed number or a whole number?

PRACTICE

For more practice, see Set 9-10 on p. 558.

A Skills and Understanding

Write each mixed number as an improper fraction.

10. $2\frac{3}{8}$ **11.** $1\frac{1}{2}$ **12.** $4\frac{2}{3}$ **13.** $3\frac{7}{8}$ **14.** $5\frac{1}{4}$

Write each improper fraction as a mixed number or a whole number.

15. $\frac{10}{3}$ **16.** $\frac{13}{8}$ **17.** $\frac{23}{8}$ **18.** $\frac{24}{6}$ **19.** $\frac{23}{4}$

20. $\frac{56}{8}$ **21.** $\frac{12}{5}$ **22.** $\frac{17}{12}$ **23.** $\frac{11}{2}$ **24.** $\frac{93}{10}$

25. Number Sense Write three different improper fractions that equal the whole number 2.

B Reasoning and Problem Solving

Math and Social Studies

People in many countries make and enjoy eating bread. The table shows the amount of flour needed for breads from four different countries.

Bread	Ethnic Origin	Cups of Flour
Brioche	French	$3\frac{1}{2}$
Kulich	Russian	$4\frac{3}{4}$
Limpa Rye	Swedish	$2\frac{3}{4}$
Sally Lunn	English	$5\frac{1}{2}$

If you only had a $\frac{1}{2}$-cup measuring cup, how many times would you need to fill it with flour to make

26. Brioche? **27.** Sally Lunn?

If you only had a $\frac{1}{4}$-cup measuring cup, how many times would you need to fill it with flour to make

28. Kulich? **29.** Limpa Rye?

PRACTICE

30. **Writing in Math** Is the explanation below correct? If not tell why and write a correct response.

> Write $\frac{14}{5}$ as a mixed number.
>
> $5\overline{)14}$ → 2, -10, remainder 4
>
> $\frac{14}{5} = 4\frac{2}{5}$

TEST TALK

Think It Through
I can **check my work** by changing $4\frac{2}{5}$ to an improper fraction.

C Extensions

Multiply or divide to find equivalent mixed numbers.

31. $1\frac{3}{5} = 1\frac{\square}{\square}$ (× 2 numerator, × 2 denominator)

32. $3\frac{1}{4} = 3\frac{\square}{\square}$ (× 5 numerator, × 5 denominator)

33. $2\frac{8}{12} = 2\frac{\square}{\square}$ (÷ 4 numerator, ÷ 4 denominator)

34. $4\frac{9}{12} = 4\frac{\square}{\square}$ (÷ 3 numerator, ÷ 3 denominator)

Mixed Review and Test Prep

Take It to the NET
Test Prep
www.scottforesman.com

Compare. Write > or < for each ●.

35. $\frac{5}{6}$ ● $\frac{1}{2}$ **36.** $\frac{3}{4}$ ● $\frac{5}{12}$ **37.** $\frac{5}{6}$ ● $\frac{3}{8}$ **38.** $\frac{7}{10}$ ● $\frac{4}{5}$

39. $824 \div 4$

A. 26 **B.** 206 **C.** 207 **D.** 3,296

Enrichment

Fractions and Percent

A fraction with a denominator of 100 can be written as a *percent*. Percent means *per 100*. The symbol for percent is %.

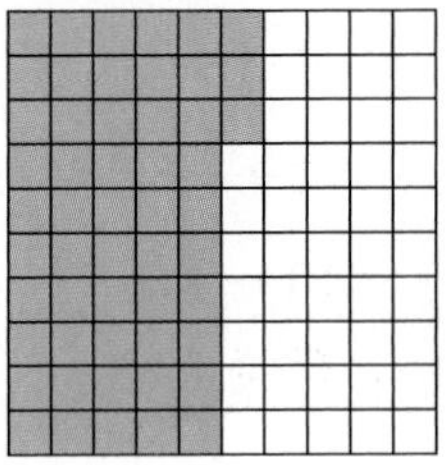

$\frac{53}{100} = 53\%$

Write each fraction with a denominator of 100. Then write the percent.

1. $\frac{1}{2} = \frac{\square}{100} = \square\%$ **2.** $\frac{6}{10} = \frac{\square}{100} = \square\%$ **3.** $\frac{2}{5} = \frac{\square}{100} = \square\%$

4. $\frac{3}{4} = \frac{\square}{100} = \square\%$ **5.** $\frac{41}{50} = \frac{\square}{100} = \square\%$ **6.** $\frac{3}{25} = \frac{\square}{100} = \square\%$

7. Nine out of 25 students in Kelly's room have dogs. What percent of the students have dogs?

Key Idea
There is more than one way to compare mixed numbers.

TEST TALK

Think It Through

- I need to **get information from the picture.**
- I can **use what I know.** Numbers on a number line increase from left to right.

$2 > 1$

Comparing Mixed Numbers

WARM UP

Write each mixed number as an improper fraction.

1. $1\frac{1}{4}$
2. $3\frac{5}{6}$
3. $2\frac{2}{5}$
4. $4\frac{7}{8}$

LEARN

How do you compare mixed numbers?

Amy needs $1\frac{5}{6}$ yards of material to make a skirt. Does she have enough material to make one blue skirt and one red skirt?

$1\frac{2}{3}$ yard blue

$2\frac{1}{3}$ yard red

Example A

Compare $1\frac{5}{6}$ and $2\frac{1}{3}$.

Look at the whole number parts first. $1 < 2$ so $1\frac{5}{6} < 2\frac{1}{3}$.

Amy has enough material to make a red skirt.

Example B

Compare $1\frac{5}{6}$ and $1\frac{2}{3}$.

One Way

Use a number line.

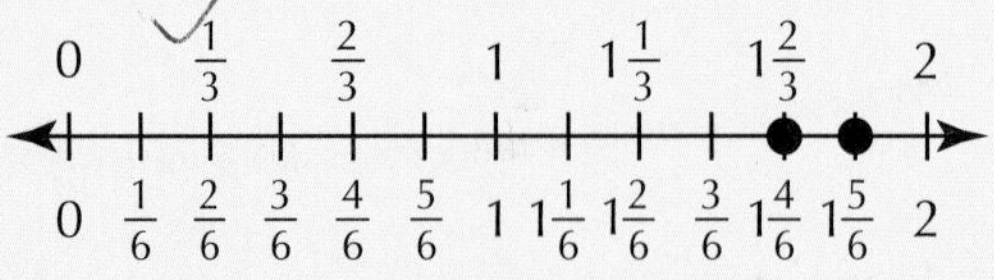

$1\frac{5}{6}$ is to the right of $1\frac{2}{3}$, so $1\frac{5}{6} > 1\frac{2}{3}$.

Another Way

Find fractions with the same denominator.

$$1\frac{2}{3} = 1\frac{4}{6} \quad (\times 2)$$

$1\frac{5}{6} > 1\frac{4}{6}$

because $\frac{5}{6} > \frac{4}{6}$.

So, $1\frac{5}{6} > 1\frac{2}{3}$.

Amy does not have enough material to make a blue skirt.

Talk About It

1. How do you use a number line to compare $1\frac{5}{6}$ and $1\frac{2}{3}$?

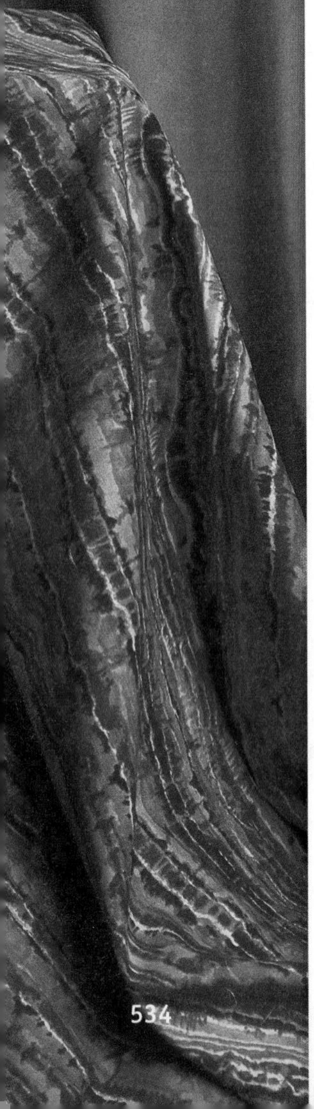

CHECK

For another example, see Set 9-11 on p. 555.

Compare. Write >, <, or = for each ○.

1. $3\frac{1}{4}$ ○ $2\frac{1}{6}$ **2.** $2\frac{3}{4}$ ○ $2\frac{6}{8}$ **3.** $1\frac{1}{5}$ ○ $1\frac{3}{10}$ **4.** $4\frac{1}{3}$ ○ $5\frac{1}{3}$

5. Number Sense $1\frac{7}{12}$ is to the left of $1\frac{3}{4}$ on the number line. Is $1\frac{7}{12}$ less than or greater than $1\frac{3}{4}$? Explain.

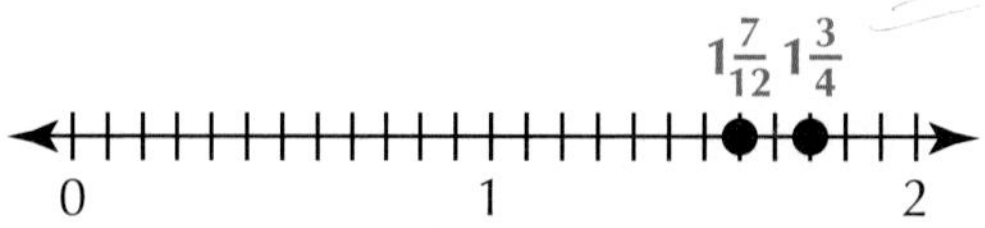

PRACTICE

For more practice, see Set 9-11 on p. 559.

A Skills and Understanding

Compare. Write >, <, or = for each ○.

6. $2\frac{1}{8}$ ○ $1\frac{3}{4}$ **7.** $2\frac{2}{3}$ ○ $2\frac{4}{6}$ **8.** $4\frac{3}{8}$ ○ $4\frac{2}{3}$ **9.** $3\frac{3}{5}$ ○ $2\frac{9}{10}$

10. $1\frac{9}{12}$ ○ $1\frac{5}{6}$ **11.** $5\frac{6}{7}$ ○ $5\frac{2}{5}$ **12.** $2\frac{1}{4}$ ○ $3\frac{1}{4}$ **13.** $3\frac{7}{8}$ ○ $3\frac{3}{4}$

14. Number Sense If $4\frac{4}{5} > 4\frac{3}{10}$, is $4\frac{3}{10} < 4\frac{4}{5}$? Use a number line to explain.

B Reasoning and Problem Solving

Data File

Fishing Contest	Length of fish
John	$20\frac{1}{3}$ in.
Branden	$15\frac{1}{2}$ in.
Garrett	$15\frac{2}{3}$ in.
Walker	$20\frac{1}{2}$ in.

Who caught the larger fish,

15. John or Garrett? **16.** John or Walker?

17. Garrett or Branden? **18.** Branden or Walker?

Reasoning Write the missing numbers.

19.

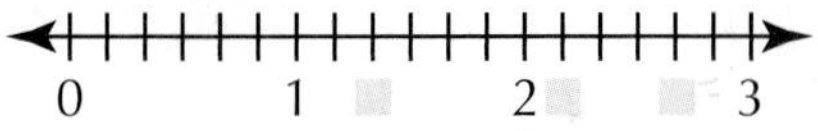

20. Writing in Math Use a number line to explain why $1\frac{3}{8} < 1\frac{1}{2}$.

Mixed Review and Test Prep

Take It to the NET
Test Prep
www.scottforesman.com

Write each mixed number as an improper fraction

21. $4\frac{1}{3}$ **22.** $2\frac{5}{8}$

Write each improper fraction as a mixed or whole number

23. $\frac{9}{2}$ **24.** $\frac{17}{3}$

25. Round 6,982 to the nearest hundred.

A. 6,000 **B.** 6,900 **C.** 6,990 **D.** 7,000

Key Idea
Circle graphs use fractions.

Vocabulary
• circle graph

TEST TALK
Think It Through
• I can **draw conclusions** from the graph.
• I can **use what I know** about fractions to make and read circle graphs.

Circle Graphs

WARM UP
Draw a model to show each fraction.
1. $\frac{1}{2}$ 2. $\frac{1}{4}$ 3. $\frac{1}{3}$

LEARN

How do you make and read a circle graph?

The table shows the favorite type of show named by 16 people. You can use a circle graph to show the data. **Circle graphs** show parts of a whole.

Favorite Type of Show

Type of Show	Number of People
Comedy	7
Drama	3
Game Shows	2
Sports	4

Example A

Make a circle graph to show the data in the table.

STEP 1 Divide a circle into 16 equal parts to represent 16 people.

STEP 2 Shade 7 parts for Comedy, 3 parts for Drama, and so on.

STEP 3 Label each section and write a title for the graph.

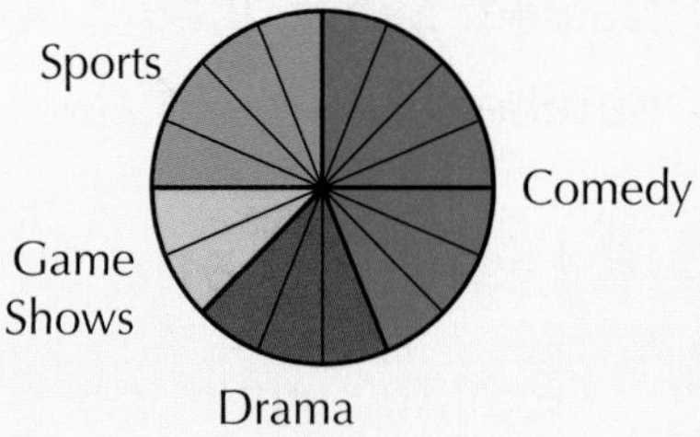

Example B

One fourth of the people liked which type of show?

One fourth of the circle graph is shaded for sports.

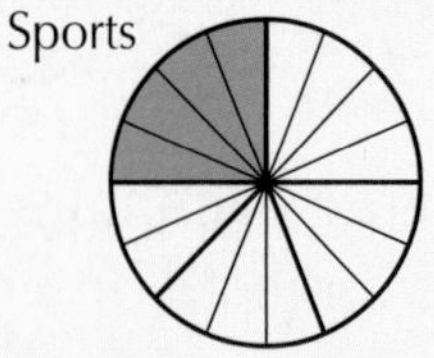

One fourth of the people liked sports shows.

Example C

About what fraction of the people liked sports and game shows combined?

Look at the graph. Think about benchmark fractions.

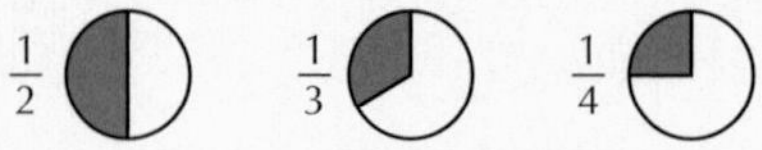

About $\frac{1}{3}$ of the people liked sports and game shows combined.

Talk About It

1. Almost half of the people liked which type of show?

CHECK

For another example, see Set 9-12 on p. 555.

Use the circle graph at the right.

When States Were Admitted to the United States

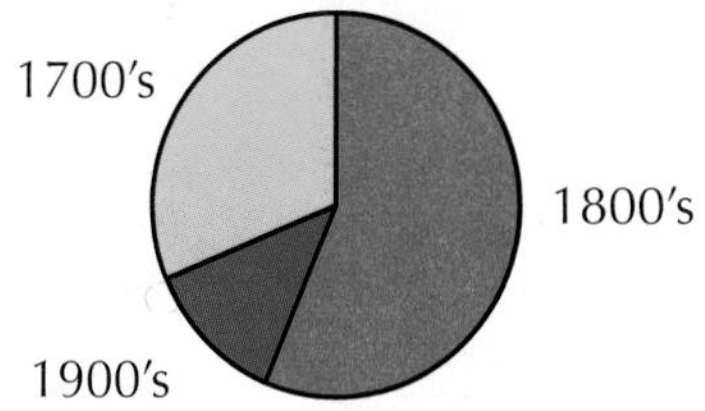

1. About what fraction of the states were admitted to the U.S. in the 1700's?
2. **Number Sense** Were more or less than half of the states admitted during the 1800's?

PRACTICE

For more practice, see Set 9-12 on p. 559.

A Skills and Understanding

For 3–8, use the circle graph at the right.

Beginning Letters of the Names of the Months

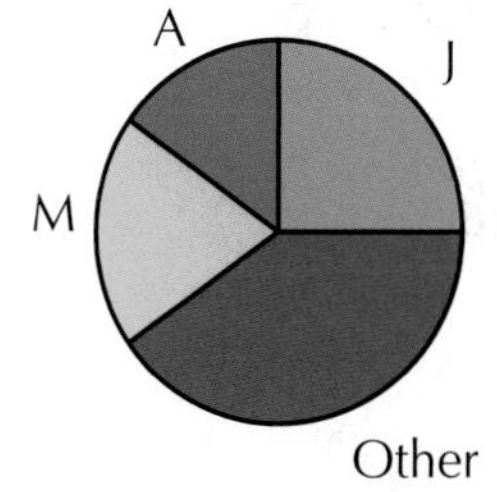

What fraction of the months have names beginning with

3. J?
4. A or M?

Number Sense Do more or less than $\frac{1}{2}$ of the months begin with

5. M, A, or J?
6. a letter other than M, A, or J?

Number Sense Do more or less than $\frac{1}{4}$ of the months begin with

7. A?
8. a letter other than M, A, or J?

B Reasoning and Problem Solving

9. Make a circle graph using the data at the right. Start by dividing a circle into 8 equal parts.
10. Use the circle graph on page 536. Did more or less than $\frac{1}{4}$ of the people like game shows and dramas combined?
11. **Writing in Math** What information can you tell from a circle graph more easily than from a table? Explain.

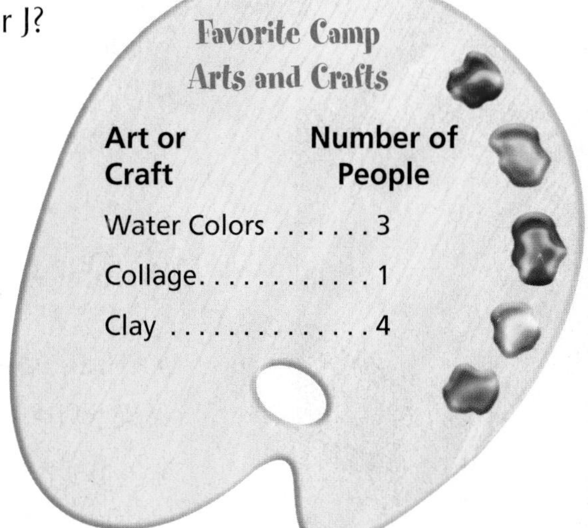

Art or Craft	Number of People
Water Colors	3
Collage	1
Clay	4

Mixed Review and Test Prep

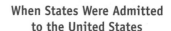

Take It to the NET
Test Prep
www.scottforesman.com

Compare. Write >, or <, or = for each ●.

12. $1\frac{7}{8}$ ● $2\frac{7}{8}$
13. $3\frac{5}{6}$ ● $3\frac{10}{12}$
14. $2\frac{3}{4}$ ● $2\frac{3}{8}$
15. $4\frac{3}{8}$ ● $4\frac{7}{10}$
16. 186 ÷ 4

A. 46 **B.** 46 R2 **C.** 48 **D.** 48 R2

Problem-Solving Skill

Reading Helps!

Identifying steps in a process
can help you with...
the problem-solving strategy, Writing to Explain.

Key Idea
There are specific things you can do to write a good explanation in math.

TEST TALK

Think It Through
- When I write to estimate, I will not get an exact answer.
- I should always check to **make sure my estimate is reasonable.**

Writing to Explain

LEARN

How do you write a good explanation?

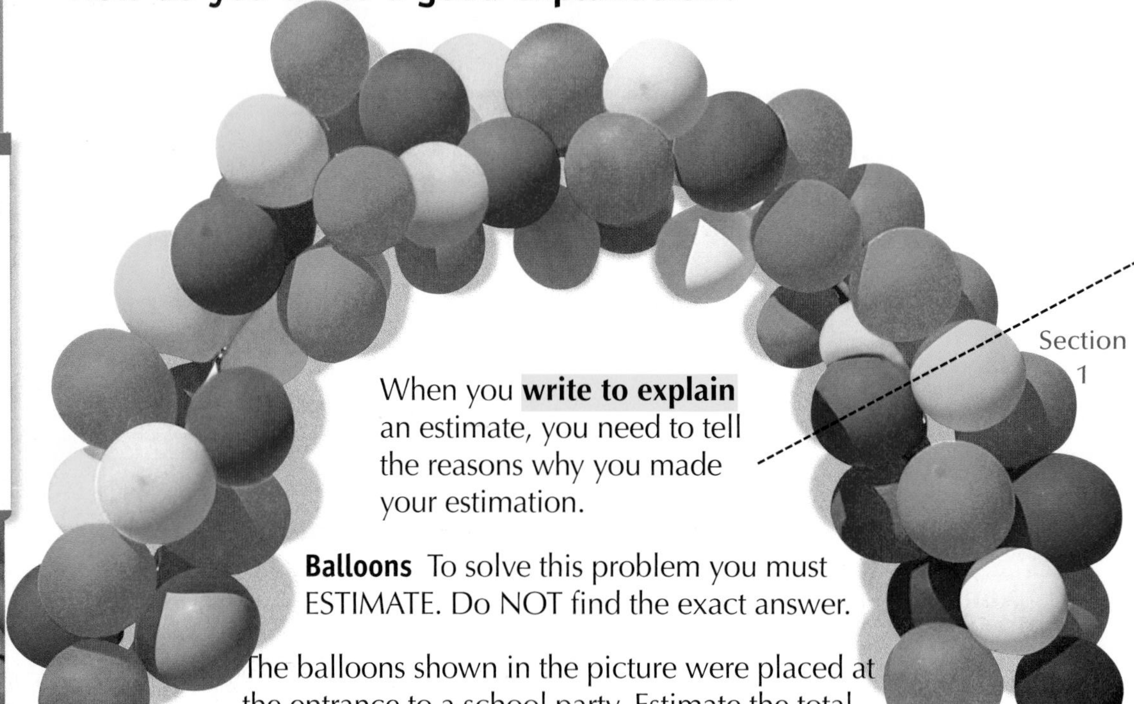

When you **write to explain** an estimate, you need to tell the reasons why you made your estimation.

Balloons To solve this problem you must ESTIMATE. Do NOT find the exact answer.

The balloons shown in the picture were placed at the entrance to a school party. Estimate the total number of red balloons in the complete balloon arch. Explain how you made your estimate.

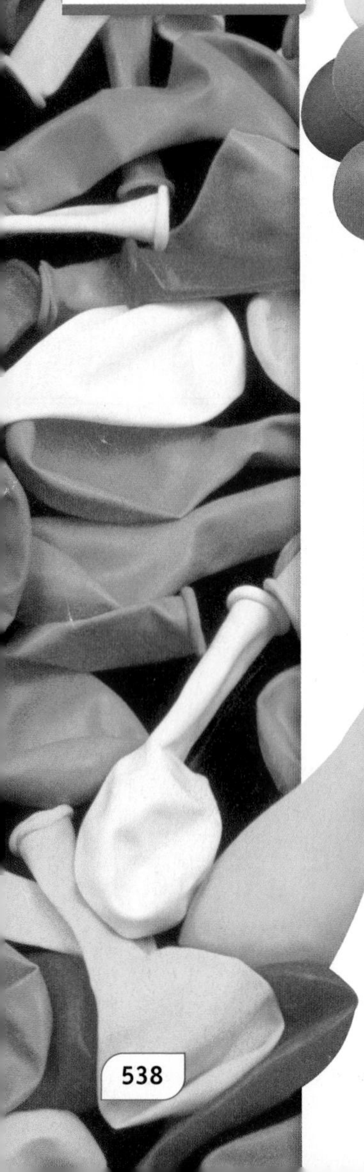

Writing a Math Explanation

- Write your explanation in steps to make it clear.
- Tell what the numbers mean in your explanation.
- Tell why you took certain steps.

Step 1 Section 1 is about $\frac{1}{4}$ of the arch. I counted 5 red balloons in this section.

Step 2 There are 4 fourths in a whole, so if each section has about 5 red balloons, then there are about 4 x 5 or 20 red balloons in the arch.

✔ Talk About It

1. Why is it helpful to break explanations into steps?

CHECK

For another example, see Set 9-13 on p. 555.

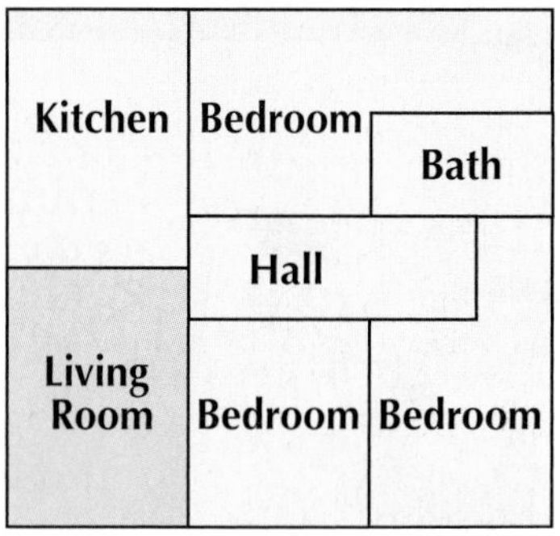

1. The area of the living room in the drawing is 120 square feet. Estimate the total area of the house. Explain how you made your estimate.

2. The area of the kitchen is 120 square feet. Estimate the area of the house that is not the kitchen or living room. Explain how you made your estimate.

PRACTICE

For more practice, see Set 9-13 on p. 559.

To solve these problems, you must ESTIMATE. Write to explain your estimate.

3. Lucy is hiking from camp to Bear Lake on the trail at the right. She has gone about 2 miles. Estimate the total length of the trail. Explain how you made your estimate.

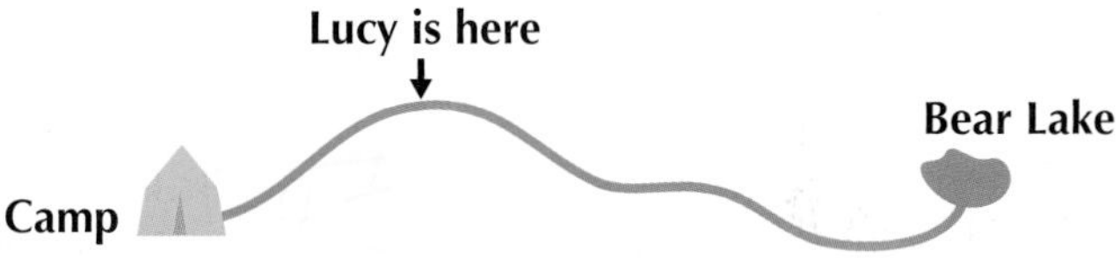

4. Estimate what fraction of the flag is red. Explain how you made your estimate.

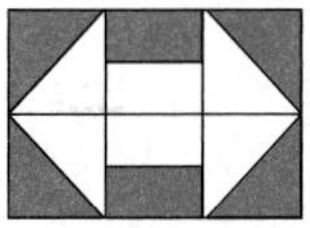

5. Explain why both of the pictures at the right show $\frac{3}{4}$.

6. Place these fractions in order from least to greatest. Explain how you decided.

   $\frac{5}{8}$ $\frac{5}{10}$ $\frac{5}{6}$ $\frac{5}{12}$ $\frac{5}{5}$

7. One hundred people are surveyed about their favorite flower. Of these, 25 say their favorite flower is the daisy. You are drawing a circle graph to show the results of the survey. What fraction of the graph should you make the section for daisies? Explain how you decided.

8. Copy the number line. Estimate the location of each of these fractions and show them on the number line.

   $\frac{1}{3}$ $\frac{1}{4}$ $\frac{5}{6}$ $\frac{3}{4}$

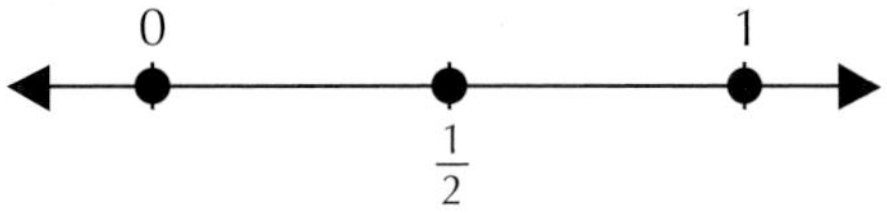

9. About what fraction of the goal have the fund-raisers reached according to the chart at the right? Explain how you estimated.

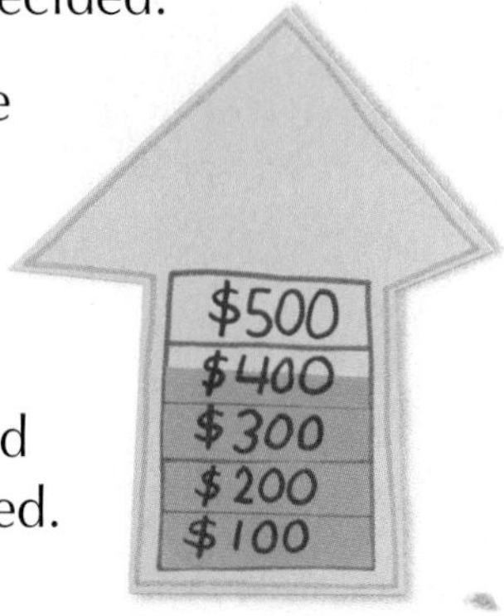

Problem-Solving Applications

LOOK CLOSER
CORAL REEF
A close-up look at the natural world of a coral reef

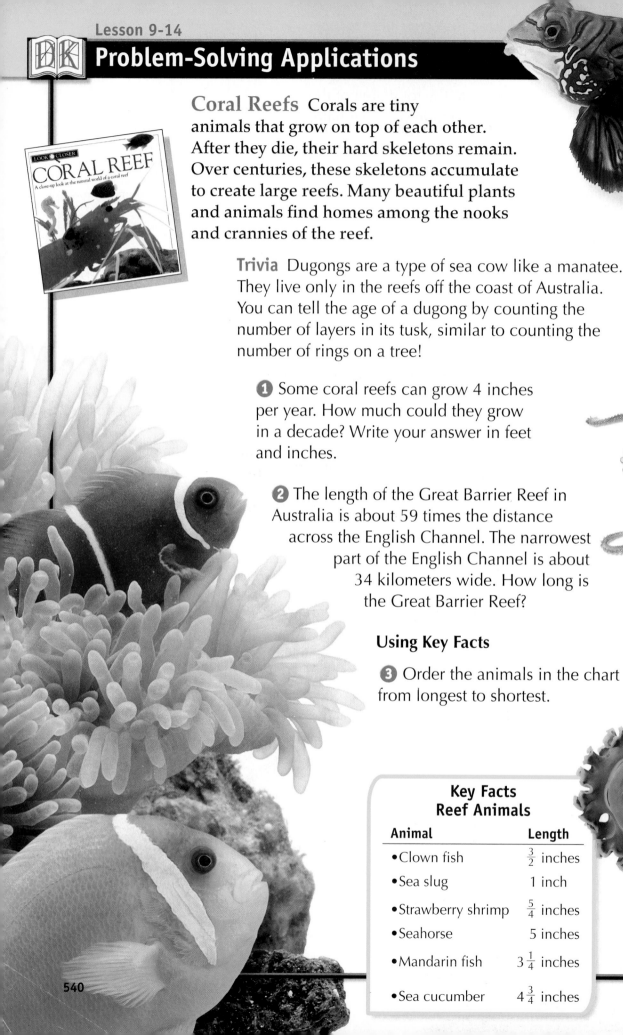

Coral Reefs Corals are tiny animals that grow on top of each other. After they die, their hard skeletons remain. Over centuries, these skeletons accumulate to create large reefs. Many beautiful plants and animals find homes among the nooks and crannies of the reef.

Trivia Dugongs are a type of sea cow like a manatee. They live only in the reefs off the coast of Australia. You can tell the age of a dugong by counting the number of layers in its tusk, similar to counting the number of rings on a tree!

1. Some coral reefs can grow 4 inches per year. How much could they grow in a decade? Write your answer in feet and inches.

2. The length of the Great Barrier Reef in Australia is about 59 times the distance across the English Channel. The narrowest part of the English Channel is about 34 kilometers wide. How long is the Great Barrier Reef?

Using Key Facts

3. Order the animals in the chart from longest to shortest.

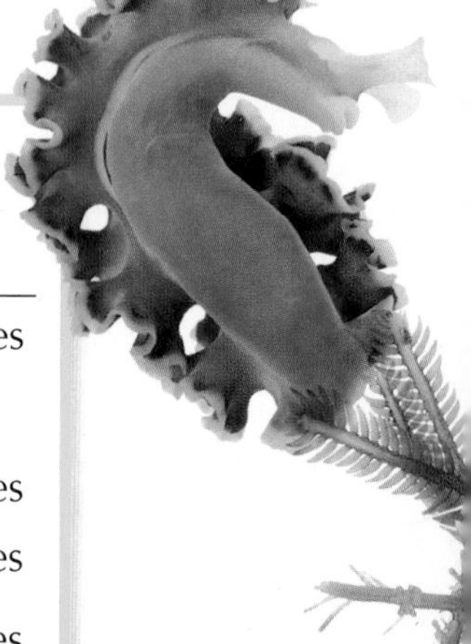

Key Facts
Reef Animals

Animal	Length
• Clown fish	$\frac{3}{2}$ inches
• Sea slug	1 inch
• Strawberry shrimp	$\frac{5}{4}$ inches
• Seahorse	5 inches
• Mandarin fish	$3\frac{1}{4}$ inches
• Sea cucumber	$4\frac{3}{4}$ inches

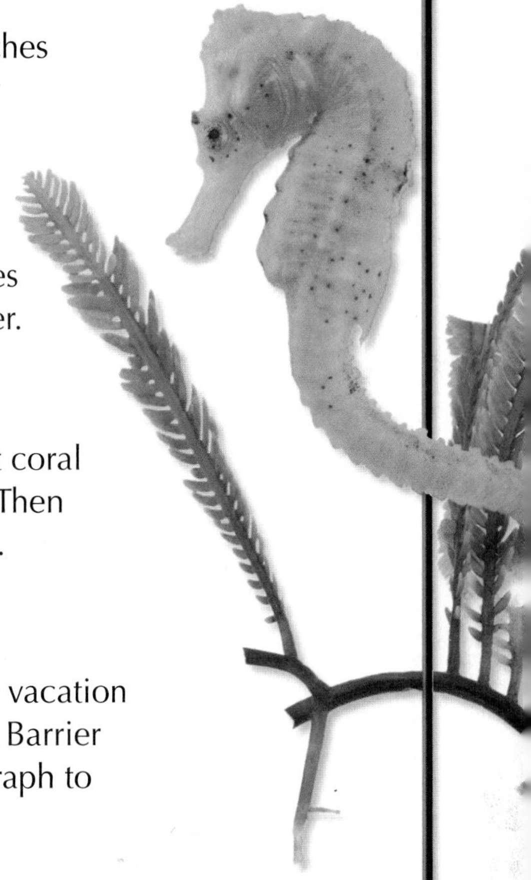

4 A common octopus is about $9\frac{1}{2}$ inches wide. Write this length as an improper fraction.

5 An emperor angelfish is about $\frac{19}{4}$ inches long. Write this number as a mixed number.

6 **Writing in Math** Write a word problem about coral reefs using the information in the Key Facts. Then answer the problem in a complete sentence.

7 **Decision Making** You are going on vacation with a friend's family to see the Great Barrier Reef. Your friend has made a circle graph to show her budget. It looks like this:

Vacation Budget

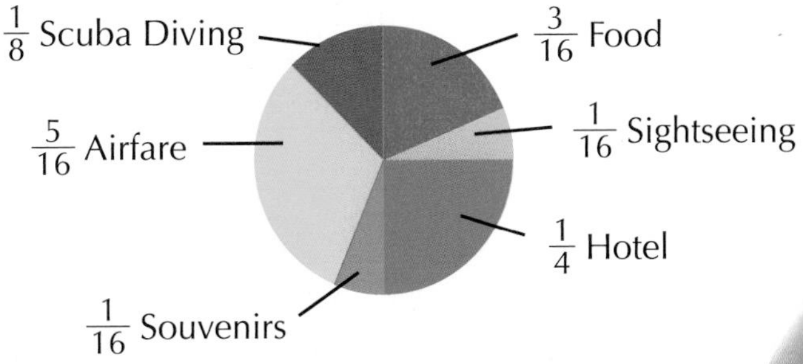

Make a circle graph to show your budget. You can include the same or different categories in your circle graph. Start by dividing the circle into 16 equal parts.

Good News/Bad News *Coral reefs are found in tropical climates where it is very easy to get sunburned. Fortunately, corals produce their own natural sunscreen so they don't get burned!*

Review

Do You Know How?

Mixed Numbers and Improper Fractions (9-10)
Comparing Mixed Numbers (9-11)

Write each improper fraction as a mixed number or a whole number.

1. $\frac{4}{3}$

2. $\frac{17}{6}$

3. $\frac{24}{8}$

4. $\frac{17}{3}$

Compare. Write >, <, or = for each ●.

5. $3\frac{7}{8}$ ● $2\frac{3}{4}$

6. $1\frac{3}{4}$ ● $1\frac{7}{8}$

Do You Understand?

A Tell how you found each answer in Exercises 1 and 3. Explain how an improper fraction can be equal to a whole number.

B Explain how comparing fractions and comparing mixed numbers is alike.

Circle Graphs (9-12)

About what fraction of the people said their favorite fruit was

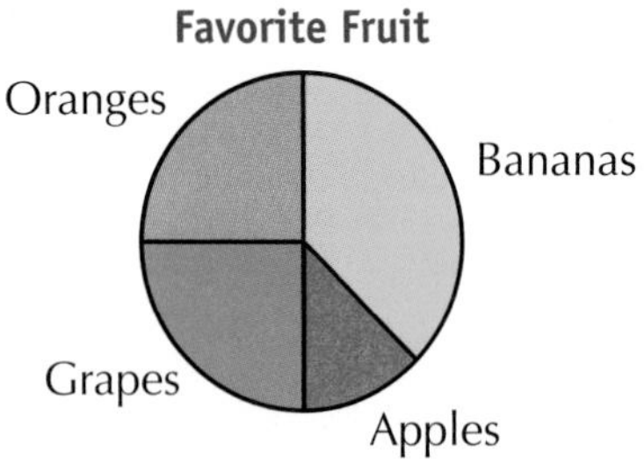

7. bananas?

8. oranges?

9. Did more or less than $\frac{1}{2}$ of the people say their favorite fruit was either apples or grapes?

C Tell the benchmark fractions you used to answer Exercises 7 and 8.

D Explain how you decided whether apples and grapes together are more or less than half.

Problem-Solving Skill: Writing to Explain (9-13)

10. Estimate what fraction of the pie has been eaten. Explain how you made your estimate.

E Explain how using steps can help you make your explanation clear.

F Explain how you know that your answer to Exercise 10 is reasonable.

Diagnostic Checkpoint

Test Talk

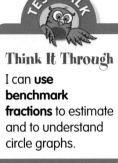

Think It Through

I can **use benchmark fractions** to estimate and to understand circle graphs.

MULTIPLE CHOICE

1. Which number is greater than $3\frac{3}{4}$? (9-11)

A. $2\frac{7}{8}$ **B.** $3\frac{6}{8}$ **C.** $3\frac{1}{2}$ **D.** $3\frac{7}{8}$

2. Write $\frac{31}{6}$ as a mixed number. (9-10)

A. $\frac{1}{6}$ **B.** $4\frac{7}{6}$ **C.** $5\frac{1}{6}$ **D.** $5\frac{1}{3}$

FREE RESPONSE

Write each mixed number as an improper fraction. (9-10)

3. $3\frac{2}{3}$ **4.** $4\frac{5}{6}$ **5.** $1\frac{2}{20}$ **6.** $4\frac{3}{10}$

Write each improper fraction as a mixed number or a whole number. (9-10)

7. $\frac{9}{8}$ **8.** $\frac{11}{3}$ **9.** $\frac{26}{25}$ **10.** $\frac{57}{10}$

Compare. Write $>$, $<$, or $=$ for each ○. (9-11)

11. $3\frac{1}{2}$ ○ $2\frac{1}{2}$ **12.** $1\frac{1}{3}$ ○ $1\frac{2}{6}$ **13.** $4\frac{5}{6}$ ○ $4\frac{11}{12}$ **14.** $2\frac{3}{4}$ ○ $3\frac{1}{4}$

For 15–17, use the information on the right. (9-12)

Soccer Season

The under-10 girls' soccer team scored 3, 2, 0, 2, 2, 1, 2, 3 goals in 8 games.

15. Make a circle graph of the data. Start by dividing a circle into 8 equal parts to represent 8 games.

16. What fraction of the games did the girls score 2 goals?

17. How many goals did the team score one-fourth of the time?

Writing in Math

18. Explain why $2\frac{7}{8}$ is not a reasonable answer for changing $\frac{25}{8}$ to a mixed number. (9-10)

19. Explain what information you can tell from a circle graph more easily than from a list of data. (9-12)

20. About what part is red in the figure at the right? Explain how you estimated. (9-13)

Test-Taking Strategies

- Understand the question.
- Get information for the answer.
- Plan how to find the answer.
- Make smart choices.
- Use writing in math.
- Improve written answers.

Plan How to Find the Answer

After you understand a test question and get needed information, you need to plan how to find the answer. Think about problem-solving skills and strategies and computation methods.

1. Carol uses a set of four different sized measuring cups when she cooks. The cups fit inside one another, with the smallest measure on top, and the largest measure on the bottom.

Which list below orders the cups by size from **greatest** to **least?**

A. $\frac{3}{4}$ cup, $\frac{1}{4}$ cup, $\frac{1}{8}$ cup, $\frac{1}{2}$ cup

B. $\frac{1}{2}$ cup, $\frac{3}{4}$ cup, $\frac{1}{4}$ cup, $\frac{1}{8}$ cup

C. $\frac{1}{8}$ cup, $\frac{3}{4}$ cup, $\frac{1}{4}$ cup, $\frac{1}{2}$ cup

D. $\frac{3}{4}$ cup, $\frac{1}{2}$ cup, $\frac{1}{4}$ cup, $\frac{1}{8}$ cup

Understand the question.

I need to find the list that orders the size of the cups from greatest to least.

Get information for the answer.

From the text and the picture, I know that none of the cups are the same size and that all of the sizes are fractions of a cup.

Plan how to find the answer.

- Think about problem-solving skills and strategies.

*I can **draw a picture** of a number line to help me order the fractions. Or, I can use equivalent fractions to make each fraction have the same denominator and then order the numerators.*

- Choose computation methods.

I'll have to use paper and pencil for either of my plans to order the fractions.

2. Farmers in Florida produce more oranges than in any other state. In fact, about $\frac{8}{10}$ of all the oranges grown in the United States come from Florida.

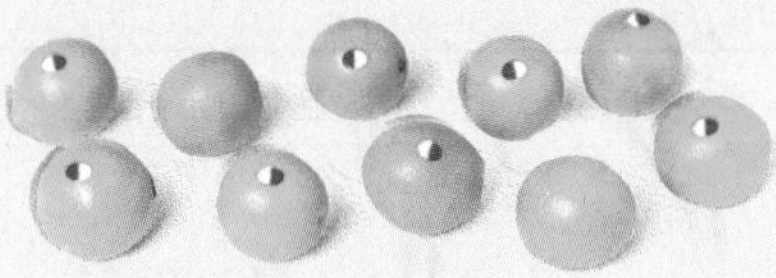

Which fraction has a value equal to $\frac{8}{10}$?

A. $\frac{2}{5}$ **C.** $\frac{4}{5}$

B. $\frac{1}{2}$ **D.** $\frac{10}{5}$

Think It Through

I need to find which fraction has a value equal to $\frac{8}{10}$. The denominator of $\frac{8}{10}$ is 10. I will write an equivalent fraction for each answer with a denominator of 10. The fraction that has a numerator of 8 will be the correct answer. I will use paper and pencil.

Now it's your turn.

For each problem, describe a plan for finding the answer.

3. The state flag of Iowa has blue, white, and red stripes, with a picture of an eagle in the center.

Which fraction below best describes the size of the blue stripe?

A. $\frac{1}{4}$ **C.** $\frac{1}{2}$

B. $\frac{1}{3}$ **D.** $\frac{3}{4}$

4. Allen used this recipe to make trail mix for his camping trip.

Trail Mix Recipe

$1\frac{3}{4}$ lb dried bananas

$1\frac{1}{2}$ lb dried pineapple

$1\frac{3}{8}$ lb raisins

$1\frac{5}{8}$ lb mixed nuts

Which improper fraction shows the amount of raisins he used?

A. $\frac{8}{3}$ **C.** $\frac{18}{3}$

B. $\frac{11}{8}$ **D.** $\frac{13}{8}$

Key Vocabulary and Concept Review

*A **fraction** is used to name part of a region, a set, or a length.*

***Benchmark fractions** are basic fractions such as $\frac{1}{4}$, $\frac{1}{3}$, $\frac{1}{2}$, $\frac{2}{3}$, and $\frac{3}{4}$.* *(p. 508)*

Self Check

Fractions name equal parts of a whole, set, or length. (Lessons 9-1, 9-2, 9-3, 9-4, 9-12)

Write a **fraction** to represent what is shown in red.

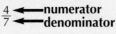

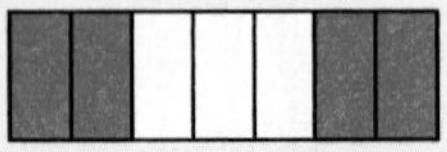

$\frac{4}{7}$ ← **numerator** (4), ← **denominator** (7)

$\frac{3}{8}$

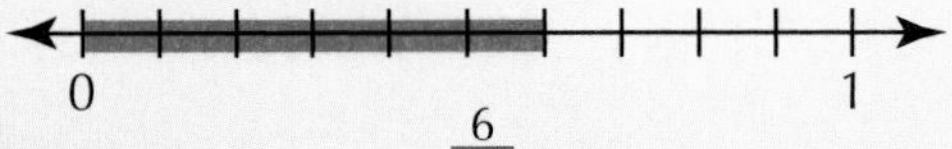

$\frac{6}{10}$

About what fraction of Luisa's car expenses are for repairs?

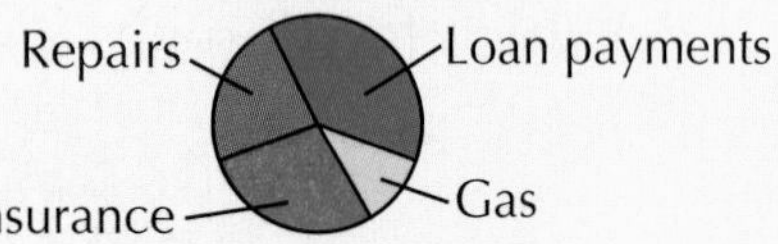

Picture **benchmark fractions.**

About $\frac{1}{4}$ of Luisa's car expenses are for repairs.

1. Write the missing fractions on the number line.

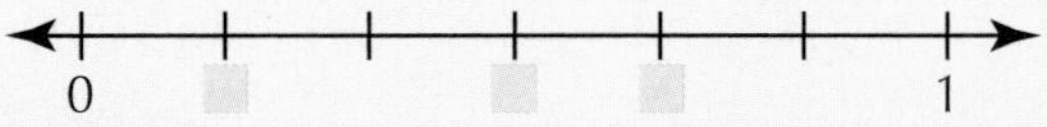

My friends and I have a lot in common.

*A **common factor** is a number that is a factor of two or more numbers.* *(p. 520)*

Self Check

Write equivalent fractions. (Lessons 9-6, 9-7, 9-8, 9-9)

Write an **equivalent fraction** for $\frac{2}{5}$.

Multiply or divide both the numerator and denominator by the same nonzero number.

$\frac{2}{5} = \frac{6}{15}$ (× 3, × 3)

Write $\frac{12}{18}$ in **simplest form.**

Divide the numerator and denominator by a **common factor.**

$\frac{12}{18} = \frac{2}{3}$ (÷ 6, ÷ 6)

Divide again, if necessary, so the only factor of both the numerator and denominator is 1.

Compare $\frac{3}{10}$ and $\frac{1}{3}$.

Use equivalent fractions.

$\frac{3}{10} = \frac{9}{30}$ (× 3, × 3) $\frac{1}{3} = \frac{10}{30}$ (× 10, × 10)

$\frac{9}{30} < \frac{10}{30}$, so $\frac{3}{10} < \frac{1}{3}$.

2. Write $\frac{16}{28}$ in simplest form and compare $\frac{3}{8}$ and $\frac{1}{6}$.

I mix, or combine, ingredients when I bake cookies.

A ***mixed number*** *is a combination of a whole number and a fraction. (p. 530)*

Self Check

Write mixed numbers and improper fractions. (Lessons 9-10, 9-11)

Write a **mixed number** for the fraction strips shown. Then change to an **improper fraction.**

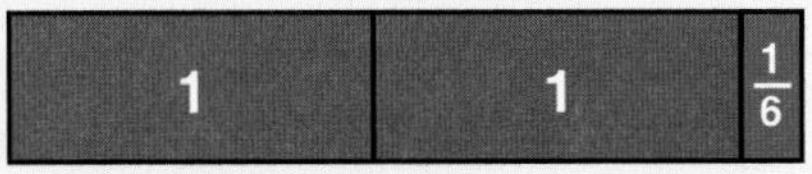

$2\frac{1}{6}$

Multiply the whole number by the denominator. Add the numerator.

$2 \times 6 + 1 = 13$

$2\frac{1}{6} = \frac{13}{6}$

Write $\frac{7}{4}$ as a mixed number.

Divide.

$7 \div 4 = 1 \text{ R}3$

$\frac{7}{4} = 1\frac{3}{4}$

Compare $4\frac{1}{4}$ and $4\frac{1}{3}$.

Use equivalent fractions.

$4\frac{1}{4} = 4\frac{3}{12}$ (× 3) $4\frac{1}{3} = 4\frac{4}{12}$ (× 4)

$4\frac{3}{12} < 4\frac{4}{12}$, so $4\frac{1}{4} < 4\frac{1}{3}$.

3. Write $\frac{8}{3}$ as a mixed number and $3\frac{1}{2}$ as an improper fraction.

If my boots are improper for gym, I'll change.

Sometimes we need to change an ***improper fraction*** *into a whole or mixed number. (p. 530)*

Self Check

Draw a picture and write to explain to solve problems. (Lessons 9-5, 9-13)

Solve a problem by drawing a picture.

Emma is cutting a pie into sixths. If she makes as few cuts as possible, how many will she make?

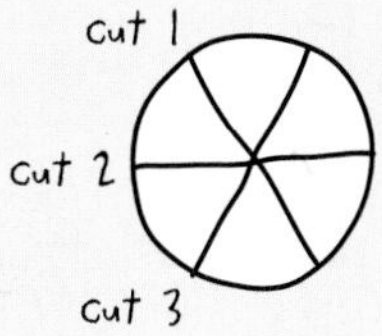

Emma will make 3 cuts.

Describe what you did so your explanation is clear.

Explain how you solved the problem at the left.

I drew a circle to represent the pie. Then I drew lines to divide it into sixths. Each line represents a cut. There are 3 lines, so there would be 3 cuts.

4. Lena is cutting a ribbon into eighths. How many cuts are needed? Explain.

Answers: **1.** $\frac{1}{6}$; $\frac{3}{6}$; $\frac{4}{6}$ **2.** $\frac{4}{7}$; $\frac{3}{8} > \frac{1}{6}$ **3.** $2\frac{2}{3}$; $\frac{7}{2}$ **4.** 7 cuts; explanations will vary.

Chapter Test

MULTIPLE CHOICE

Choose the correct letter for each answer.

1. What fraction of this region is blue?

A. $\frac{1}{2}$ **C.** $\frac{4}{6}$

B. $\frac{4}{5}$ **D.** $\frac{5}{6}$

2. What fraction of this set is red?

A. $\frac{1}{3}$ **C.** $\frac{4}{7}$

B. $\frac{3}{7}$ **D.** $\frac{7}{3}$

3. Which shows $\frac{4}{9}$ of its length shaded green?

A. 

B. 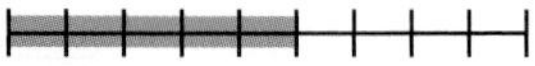

C. 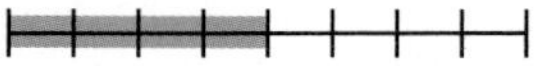

D. 

Think It Through

- I should **read each answer choice carefully.**
- I can **eliminate unreasonable answers.**

4. Which of these fractions is NOT equivalent to $\frac{4}{6}$?

A. $\frac{2}{3}$ **C.** $\frac{8}{12}$

B. $\frac{1}{2}$ **D.** $\frac{12}{18}$

5. What is $\frac{14}{20}$ in simplest form?

A. $\frac{7}{20}$ **C.** $\frac{28}{40}$

B. $\frac{7}{10}$ **D.** $\frac{4}{2}$

6. Estimate the fractional part of this rectangle that is yellow.

A. $\frac{1}{4}$ **C.** $\frac{2}{3}$

B. $\frac{1}{2}$ **D.** $\frac{3}{4}$

7. Which improper fraction is equal to $4\frac{1}{3}$?

A. $\frac{4}{3}$ **C.** $\frac{13}{4}$

B. $\frac{13}{3}$ **D.** $\frac{3}{4}$

8. Which fraction is less than $\frac{2}{5}$?

A. $\frac{1}{3}$ **C.** $\frac{3}{7}$

B. $\frac{4}{9}$ **D.** $\frac{1}{2}$

9. Which of the following is TRUE?

A. $1\frac{1}{4} > 1\frac{1}{3}$ **C.** $2\frac{7}{10} > 2\frac{2}{5}$

B. $\frac{16}{3} = 6\frac{1}{3}$ **D.** $4\frac{4}{7} < 3\frac{6}{7}$

10. Which mixed number is equal to $\frac{18}{4}$?

A. $4\frac{1}{8}$ **C.** $4\frac{1}{2}$

B. $4\frac{1}{4}$ **D.** $8\frac{1}{4}$

11. If you make a circle graph to show the results of the favorite color survey at the right, how many equal parts should you divide your circle into?

Favorite Color Survey

Color	Votes
Red	5
Blue	5
Green	6
Yellow	4

A. 11 **C.** 24

B. 20 **D.** 30

12. Which set of fractions is written in order from least to greatest?

A. $\frac{2}{5}, \frac{3}{4}, \frac{2}{3}$ **C.** $\frac{2}{5}, \frac{2}{3}, \frac{3}{4}$

B. $\frac{3}{4}, \frac{2}{3}, \frac{2}{5}$ **D.** $\frac{2}{3}, \frac{3}{4}, \frac{2}{5}$

FREE RESPONSE

For 13–14, use the circle graph below.

Earth's Land Surface

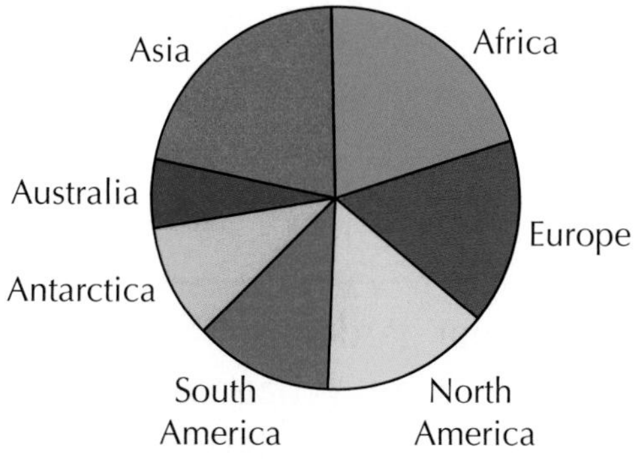

13. Which two continents each cover about one-fourth of Earth's land?

14. About what fraction of Earth's land do Africa and Europe cover combined?

Compare. Write >, <, or = for each ○.

15. $\frac{3}{5}$ ○ $\frac{7}{10}$

16. $2\frac{1}{2}$ ○ $2\frac{5}{9}$

17. $1\frac{1}{6}$ ○ $1\frac{1}{5}$

18. $\frac{19}{3}$ ○ $6\frac{1}{3}$

19. $\frac{3}{8}$ ○ $\frac{4}{10}$

20. $4\frac{1}{2}$ ○ $3\frac{3}{6}$

21. Draw a picture to solve this problem.

Kyle dug a 5-foot-long row in his garden. He planted a seed at the beginning and at the end of the row. He also planted a seed every $\frac{1}{4}$ of a foot along the row. How many seeds did Kyle plant in the row?

Writing in Math

22. The math club used the chart at the right to show how much money they have earned in fundraisers this year. About what fraction of their fund-raising goal has the math club reached? Explain how you estimated.

TEST TALK

Think It Through

- I need to **describe my steps in order.**
- My writing should be **brief but complete.**

23. Tom wrote a fraction equivalent to $\frac{4}{6}$. The numerator was 12. What fraction did Tom write? Explain your answer.

24. Abby, Kevin, and Joe shared a large pizza. Abby ate $\frac{1}{6}$ of it, Kevin ate $\frac{1}{4}$ of it, and Joe ate $\frac{1}{8}$ of it. Who ate the most pizza? Explain.

Cumulative Review and Test Prep

Number and Operation

MULTIPLE CHOICE

1. Diego baked 18 muffins for a bake sale. Twelve of the muffins were bran. What fraction of the muffins were bran?

A. $\frac{18}{12}$ **B.** $\frac{12}{18}$ **C.** $\frac{12}{30}$ **D.** $\frac{18}{30}$

2. What is the product of 16 and 15?

A. 31 **C.** 210

B. 96 **D.** 240

3. What is sixty million, thirty-seven thousand, forty-eight written in standard form?

A. 637,048 **C.** 60,037,480

B. 60,037,048 **D.** 60,370,480

FREE RESPONSE

4. What fraction should be written at point *P* on the number line?

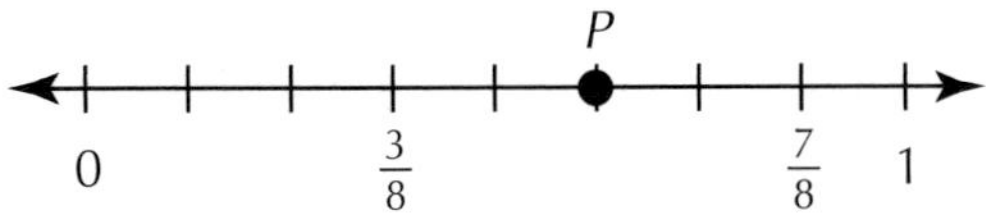

5. Cameron has seven \$1 bills, 3 quarters, and 3 pennies. Charlotte has one \$5 bill, two \$1 bills, 2 quarters, 2 dimes, 1 nickel, and 2 pennies. Who has more money?

Writing in Math

6. Write $4\frac{2}{3}$ as an improper fraction. Explain how you found your answer.

Geometry and Measurement

MULTIPLE CHOICE

7. Which rectangle shows about $\frac{1}{3}$ shaded green?

A.

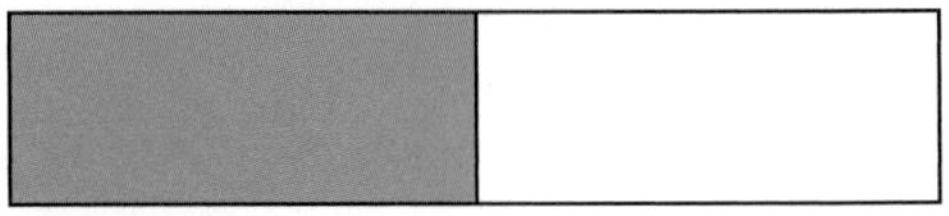

B.

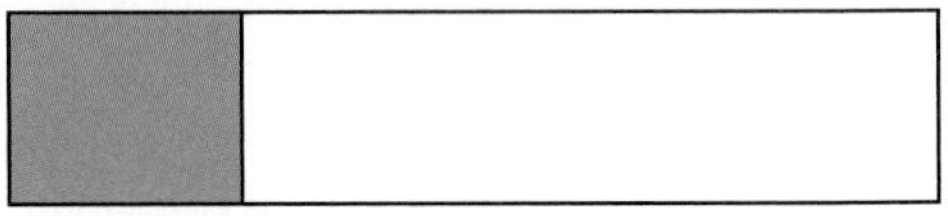

C.

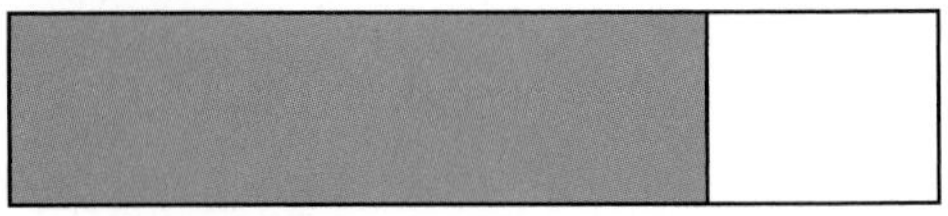

D.

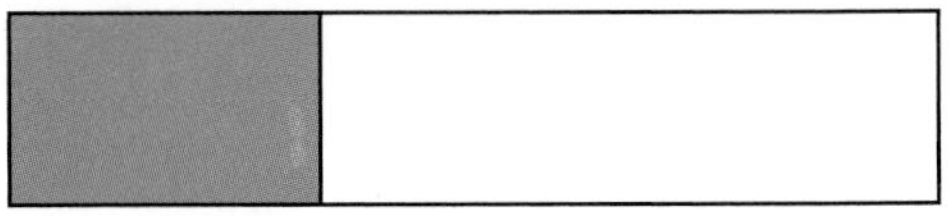

8. Which of the following solid figures has no curved surfaces?

A. sphere **C.** cube

B. cone **D.** cylinder

FREE RESPONSE

9. A rectangular garden is 12 feet long and 10 feet wide. What are the area and perimeter of the garden?

10. How many sides and vertices does a hexagon have?

Writing in Math

11. Explain why all cubes are similar, but not all are congruent.

Data Analysis and Probability

MULTIPLE CHOICE

12. If you spin the spinner below 10 times, which number would you probably land on the most often?

A. 1

B. 2

C. 4

D. 5

13. How many possible outcomes are on the spinner above?

A. 1   **C.** 5

B. 4   **D.** 8

FREE RESPONSE

Use the circle graph for 14–16.

Favorite Color

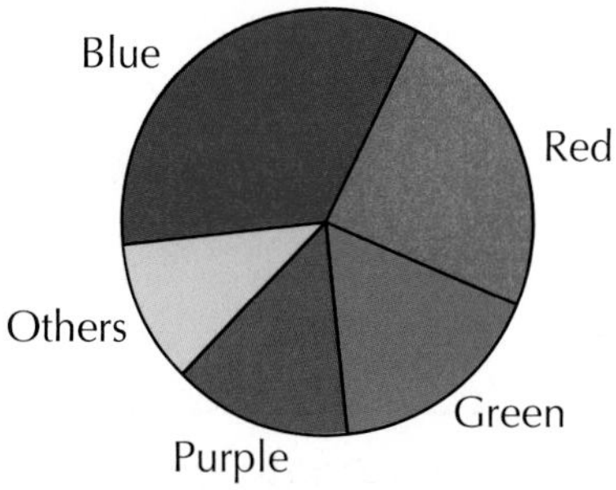

14. What color was chosen by about $\frac{1}{4}$ of the people surveyed?

15. About what fraction of the people surveyed chose green as their favorite color?

Writing in Math

16. Did more or less than $\frac{1}{2}$ of the people say their favorite color was either blue or red? Explain.

Algebra

MULTIPLE CHOICE

TEST TALK

Think It Through

I need to **find a relationship** between the numbers in the pattern.

17. Which number is next in the pattern?

$\frac{1}{2}, \frac{1}{4}, \frac{1}{6}, \frac{1}{8}, \blacksquare$

A. $\frac{1}{2}$ **C.** $\frac{1}{10}$

B. $\frac{1}{9}$ **D.** $\frac{1}{12}$

18. Which equation does NOT have the solution $n = 3$?

A. $51 \div n = 17$ **C.** $59 + n = 62$

B. $n \times 24 = 62$ **D.** $32 - n = 29$

19. Which expression models the phrase "two more than n"?

A. $\frac{1}{2} - n$ **C.** $\frac{1}{2} + n$

B. $n - 2$ **D.** $n + 2$

FREE RESPONSE

20. Complete the table and describe the rule you used.

In	3	4	5	6
Out	9	16	25	

21. Phil has to take 4 steps for every 2 steps that his father takes. When Phil has taken 20 steps, how many steps has his father taken?

Writing in Math

22. Solve this equation for n. Explain how you found the solution.

$6 + n = 25$

Set 9-1 (pages 500–501)

Write a fraction for the part of the region at the right that is green.

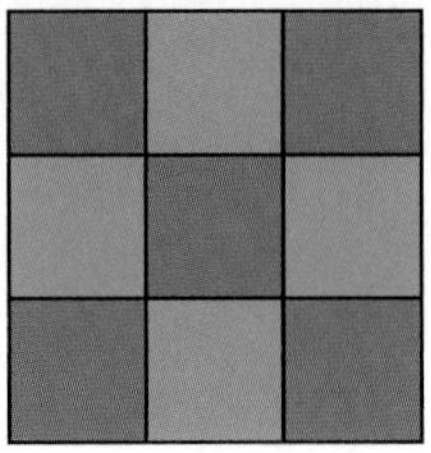

$$\frac{\text{numerator}}{\text{denominator}} = \frac{\text{green parts}}{\text{parts in all}} = \frac{4}{9}$$

$\frac{4}{9}$ of the region is green.

Remember that the numerator tells how many equal parts are described, and the denominator tells how many equal parts in all.

Write a fraction for the part of each region that is blue.

1. 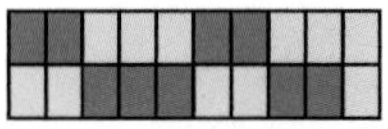

2. 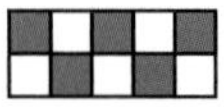

3. 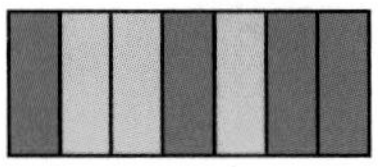

4. 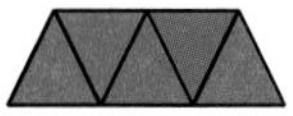

Set 9-2 (pages 502–503)

What fraction of the set at the right is red?

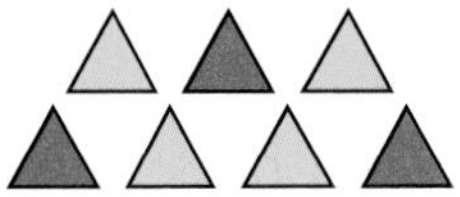

$$\frac{\text{numerator}}{\text{denominator}} = \frac{\text{red triangles}}{\text{triangles in set}} = \frac{3}{7}$$

$\frac{3}{7}$ of the set of triangles is red.

Remember that the numerator is the number above the fraction bar, and the denominator is the number below the fraction bar.

What fraction of each set is yellow?

1. 

2. 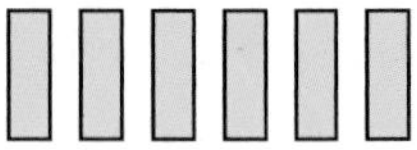

3. 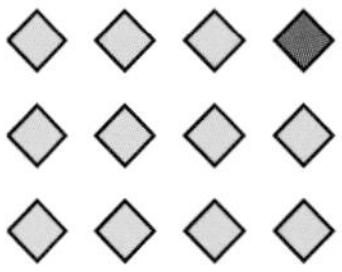

4. 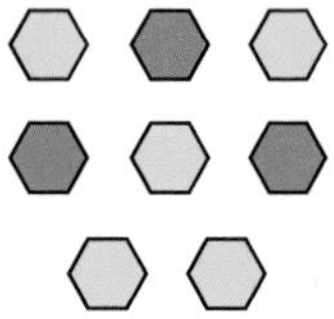

Set 9-3 (pages 504–507)

What fraction should be written at point *D*?

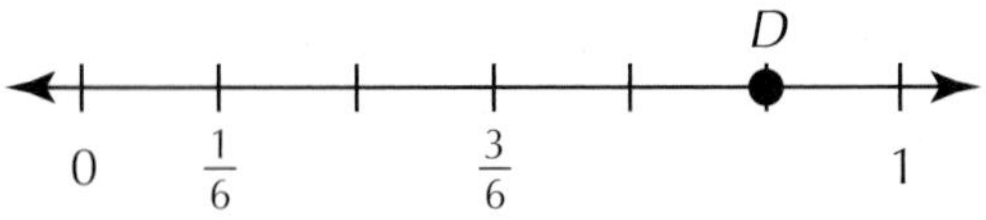

There are 6 equal parts between 0 and 1. There are 5 of these equal parts between 0 and point *D*.

So, $\frac{5}{6}$ should be written at point *D*.

Remember that equally spaced marks between 0 and 1 on a number line form equal parts of a whole.

What fraction should be written at each point?

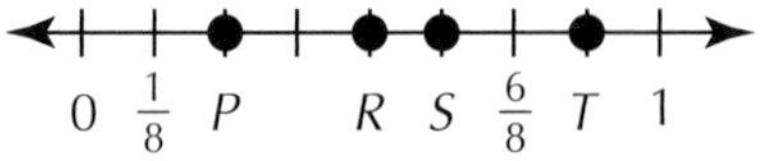

1. *P* **2.** *R* **3.** *S* **4.** *T*

Write a fraction for the part of each length that is blue.

5.  **6.** 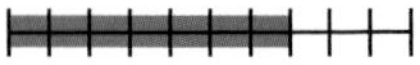

Set 9-4 (pages 508–509)

Estimate the fractional part of the rectangle that is blue.

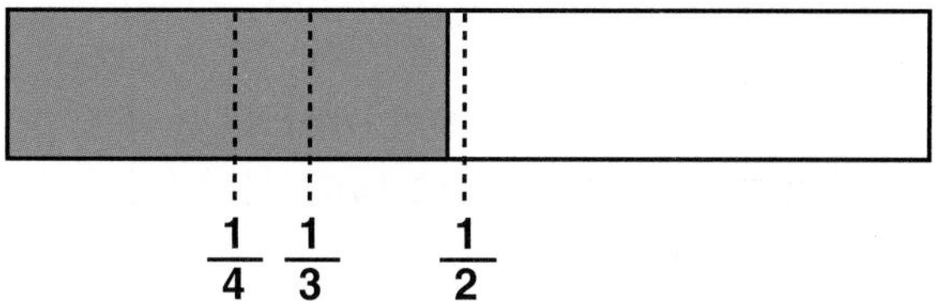

Compare the part that is blue to benchmark fractions. The blue part is less than $\frac{1}{2}$, but more than $\frac{1}{3}$ of the whole rectangle.

About $\frac{1}{2}$ of the rectangle is blue.

Remember that benchmark fractions are basic fractions, such as $\frac{1}{4}$, $\frac{1}{3}$, $\frac{1}{2}$, $\frac{2}{3}$, and $\frac{3}{4}$.

Estimate the fractional part of each rectangle that is green.

1. 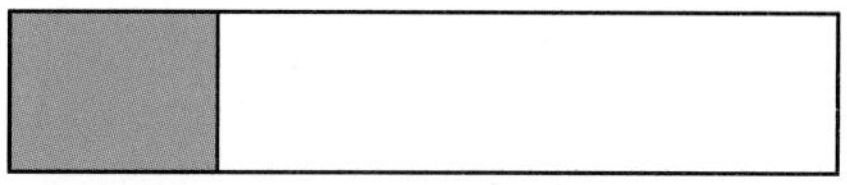

2. 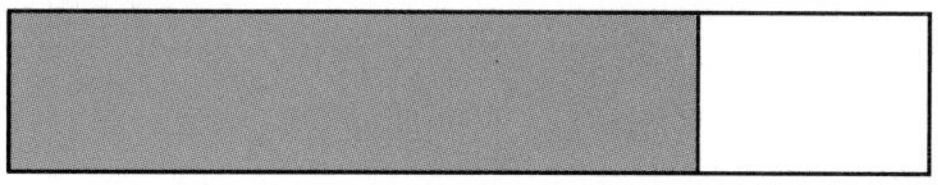

Set 9-5 (pages 512–513)

When you draw a picture to solve a problem, follow these steps.

Step 1: Draw a picture to represent the situation. Do not try to draw the real-world object.

Step 2: Finish the picture to show the action in the story.

Step 3: Interpret the picture to answer the question in the problem.

Remember to label the parts of your picture to show what they represent.

Draw a picture to solve the problem.

1. A 3-mile tunnel has a light at its entrance and exit. It also has a light every $\frac{1}{4}$ mile along the tunnel. How many lights does the tunnel have?

Set 9-6 (pages 516–519)

Write an equivalent fraction for $\frac{1}{3}$.

One Way:
Use Fraction Strips

$\frac{1}{3} = \frac{2}{6}$

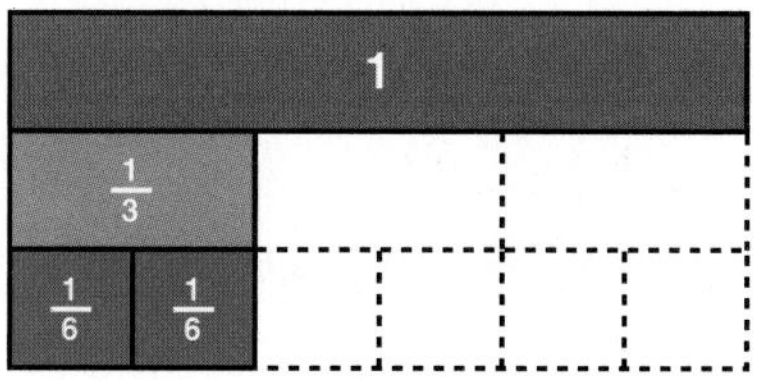

Another Way:
Multiply.

$\times 2$

$\frac{1}{3} = \frac{2}{6}$

$\times 2$

Remember that you can divide the numerator and denominator by the same number to write an equivalent fraction.

Find an equivalent fraction.

1. $\div 2$ $\frac{6}{10} = \frac{\square}{\square}$ $\div 2$

2. $\times 2$ $\frac{3}{7} = \frac{\square}{\square}$ $\times 2$

Set 9-7 (pages 520–521)

Write $\frac{4}{10}$ in simplest form.

2 is a common factor of 4 and 10.

$$\frac{4}{10} \overset{\div 2}{=} \frac{2}{5}$$

The only factor of both 2 and 5 is 1.

So, $\frac{2}{5}$ is in simplest form.

$\frac{4}{10}$ in simplest form is $\frac{2}{5}$.

Remember that a fraction is in simplest form if the numerator and denominator have no common factor other than 1.

Write each fraction in simplest form. If it is in simplest form, write simplest form.

1. $\frac{3}{9}$
2. $\frac{2}{14}$
3. $\frac{5}{8}$
4. $\frac{10}{15}$
5. $\frac{11}{13}$
6. $\frac{4}{20}$

Set 9-8 (pages 522–523)

Which fraction is greater, $\frac{2}{5}$ or $\frac{1}{2}$?

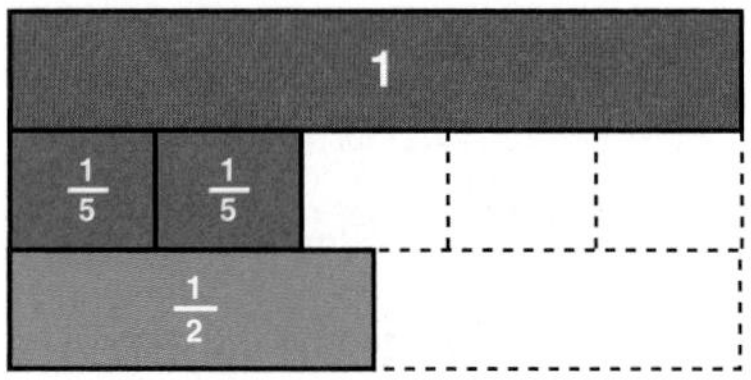

$\frac{1}{2}$ is greater than $\frac{2}{5}$.

$\frac{1}{2} > \frac{2}{5}$.

Remember that > means greater than, and < means less than.

Write >, <, or = for each ○. You may use fraction strips to help.

1. $\frac{1}{8}$ ○ $\frac{1}{4}$
2. $\frac{3}{9}$ ○ $\frac{1}{3}$
3. $\frac{3}{10}$ ○ $\frac{1}{5}$
4. $\frac{6}{7}$ ○ $\frac{4}{7}$
5. $\frac{5}{8}$ ○ $\frac{3}{8}$
6. $\frac{3}{4}$ ○ $\frac{6}{12}$

Set 9-9 (pages 524–527)

Order $\frac{5}{6}$, $\frac{7}{12}$, and $\frac{3}{4}$ from least to greatest.

Use equivalent fractions.

$$\frac{5}{6} \overset{\times 2}{=} \frac{10}{12} \qquad \frac{3}{4} \overset{\times 3}{=} \frac{9}{12}$$

$\frac{7}{12}$, $\frac{9}{12}$, $\frac{10}{12}$

The fractions in order are $\frac{7}{12}$, $\frac{3}{4}$, $\frac{5}{6}$.

Remember that you can draw pictures or compare each fraction to $\frac{1}{2}$ when you compare fractions.

Write > or < for each ○.

1. $\frac{3}{5}$ ○ $\frac{5}{6}$
2. $\frac{2}{3}$ ○ $\frac{5}{12}$

Order the numbers from least to greatest.

3. $\frac{7}{9}$, $\frac{2}{3}$, $\frac{5}{9}$
4. $\frac{1}{2}$, $\frac{7}{20}$, $\frac{3}{10}$
5. $\frac{3}{5}$, $\frac{3}{10}$, $\frac{3}{8}$
6. $\frac{2}{3}$, $\frac{1}{4}$, $\frac{5}{8}$

Set 9-10 (pages 530–533)

Write $2\frac{4}{5}$ as an improper fraction.

1 Multiply the whole number by the denominator. $2 \times 5 = 10$

2 Add the numerator. $10 + 4 = 14$

3 Write the sum as the numerator. The denominator stays the same.

$2\frac{4}{5} = \frac{14}{5}$

Remember when you change an improper fraction to a mixed number, you divide the numerator by the denominator.

Write each as an improper fraction.

1. $2\frac{1}{2}$ **2.** $1\frac{3}{4}$ **3.** $4\frac{2}{3}$

Write each as a mixed number.

4. $\frac{10}{3}$ **5.** $\frac{37}{5}$ **6.** $\frac{23}{4}$

Set 9-11 (pages 534–535)

Compare $2\frac{1}{2}$ and $2\frac{3}{8}$.

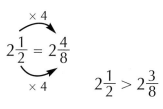

$2\frac{1}{2} = 2\frac{4}{8}$ (× 4 numerator and denominator)

$2\frac{1}{2} > 2\frac{3}{8}$

Remember, you can use a number line to compare mixed numbers.

Write > or < for each ●.

1. $2\frac{1}{3}$ ● $2\frac{2}{5}$ **2.** $3\frac{7}{8}$ ● $3\frac{3}{4}$

3. $5\frac{5}{6}$ ● $5\frac{11}{12}$ **4.** $3\frac{2}{3}$ ● $4\frac{9}{18}$

Set 9-12 (pages 536–537)

What activity does Ken spend about $\frac{1}{4}$ of his day doing?

Ken spends about $\frac{1}{4}$ of his day at school.

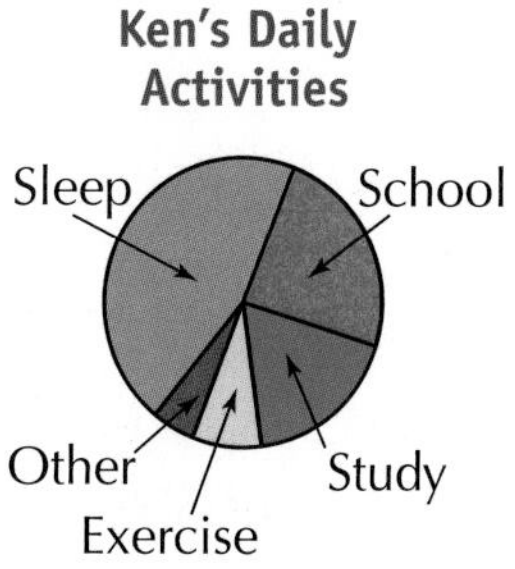

Remember that a circle graph shows data as parts of a whole.

1. About what fraction of Ken's day is spent studying?
2. Which activity takes up about $\frac{1}{2}$ of Ken's day?

Set 9-13 (pages 538–539)

Estimate what fraction of the banner is blue. Explain.

The banner is about $\frac{1}{4}$ blue. Four of the 16 triangles are blue. $\frac{4}{16} = \frac{1}{4}$

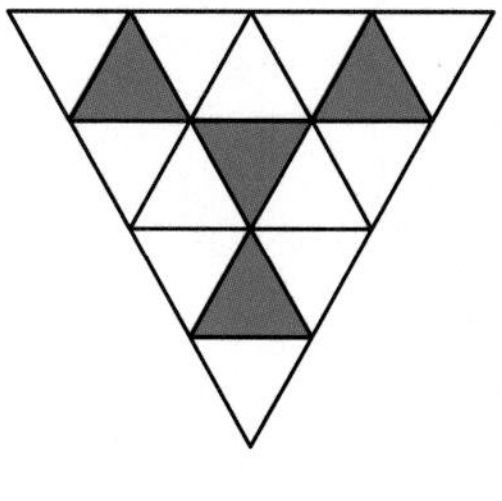

Remember to explain the order of steps you followed when asked to explain your estimate.

1. Tina is $4\frac{3}{4}$ feet tall. Mary is $4\frac{1}{6}$ feet tall. Estimate to decide who is taller. Explain your estimate.

More Practice

Set 9-1 (pages 500–501)

Write a fraction for the part of each region that is blue.

1. 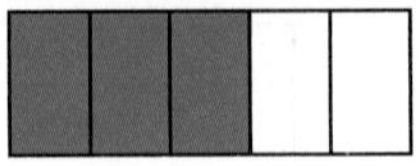
2. 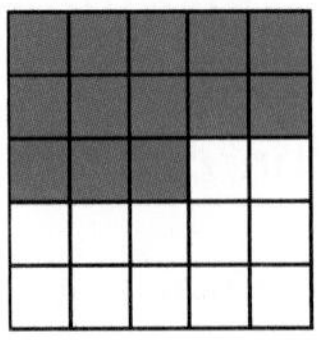
3. 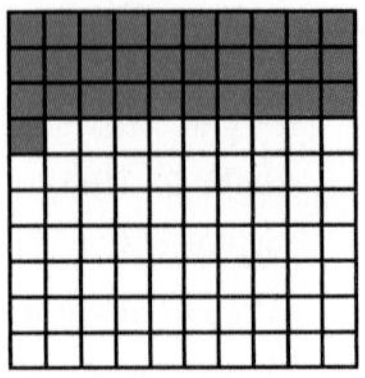
4. 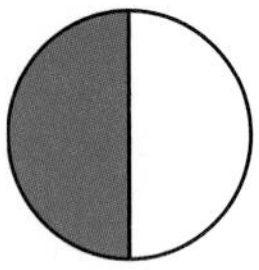

5. Tony cut a piece of wood into 10 equal pieces. He used 7 pieces for a birdhouse. Draw a model to show what fraction of the pieces of wood Tony used for the birdhouse.

Set 9-2 (pages 502–503)

What fraction of each set is red?

1. 
2. 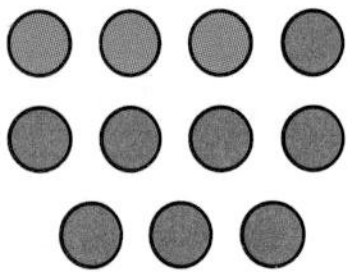
3. 
4. 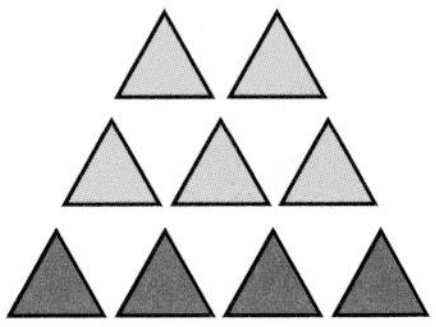

Draw a picture to show each fraction as part of a set.

5. $\frac{2}{5}$ 6. $\frac{7}{9}$ 7. $\frac{3}{14}$ 8. $\frac{6}{6}$

9. What fraction of the marbles is blue?

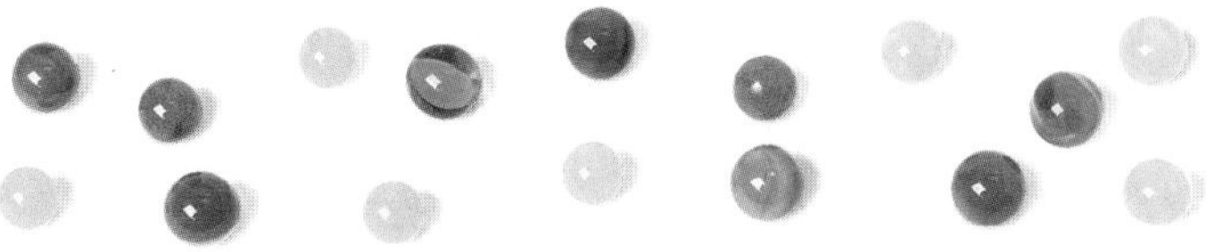

Set 9-3 (pages 504–507)

Write a fraction for the part of each length that is green.

1. 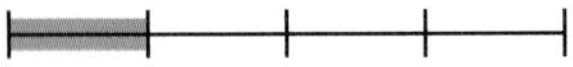
2. 
3. 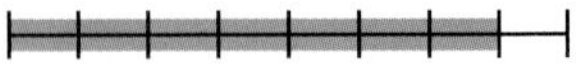

What fraction should be written at each point?

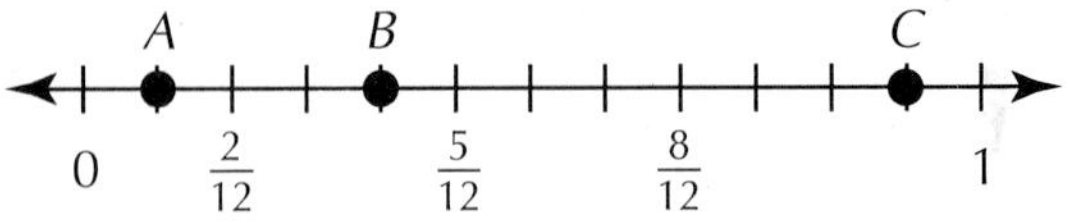

4. *A* 5. *B* 6. *C*

Write the missing fractions.

7. 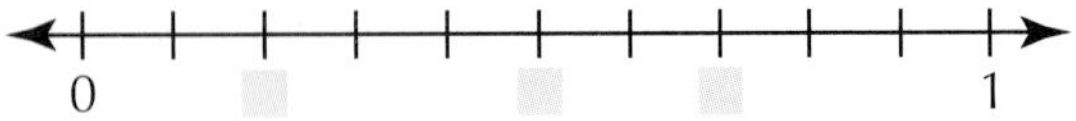

8. 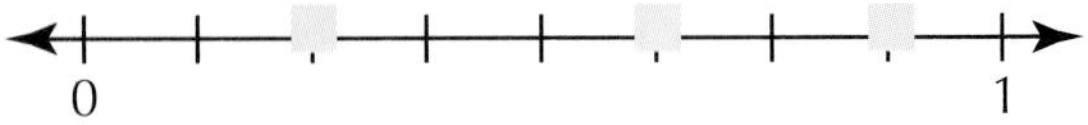

Take It to the NET
More Practice
www.scottforesman.com

Set 9-4 (pages 508–509)

Estimate the part of the figure that is yellow.

1. 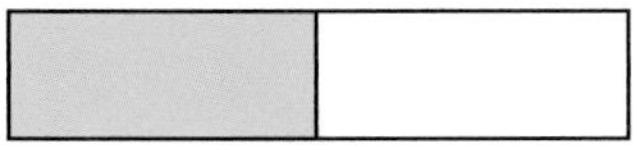

2. 

3. 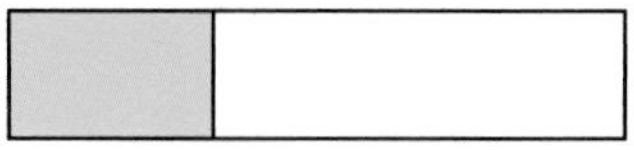

Set 9-5 (pages 512–513)

Draw a picture to solve each problem. Write the answer in a complete sentence.

1. A 3-mile nature trail has a marker at its beginning and a marker at its end. A group of hikers pass a marker every $\frac{1}{2}$ mile. How many markers are used on the trail?

2. Jack used 25 tiles to cover his square floor. He laid the tiles in a checkerboard pattern alternating between white tiles and black tiles. The corner tiles were white. What fraction of the tiles on Jack's floor is white? What fraction is black?

Set 9-6 (pages 516–519)

Multiply or divide to find equivalent fractions.

1. $\frac{1}{3} \overset{\times 5}{=}$ (× 5 on numerator and denominator)

2. $\frac{8}{10} \overset{\div 2}{=}$ (÷ 2 on numerator and denominator)

3. $\frac{5}{7} \overset{\times 3}{=}$ (× 3 on numerator and denominator)

4. $\frac{3}{12} \overset{\div 3}{=}$ (÷ 3 on numerator and denominator)

5. $\frac{1}{6}$　6. $\frac{2}{3}$　7. $\frac{10}{20}$　8. $\frac{6}{18}$　9. $\frac{9}{27}$

10. Draw a picture to show a fraction equivalent to $\frac{6}{8}$.

Set 9-7 (pages 520–521)

Write each fraction in simplest form. If it is in simplest form, Write simplest form.

1. $\frac{3}{15}$　2. $\frac{6}{7}$　3. $\frac{20}{30}$　4. $\frac{4}{16}$　5. $\frac{2}{3}$

6. $\frac{7}{42}$　7. $\frac{6}{8}$　8. $\frac{9}{18}$　9. $\frac{5}{20}$　10. $\frac{3}{12}$

11. Explain how you can tell if $\frac{3}{14}$ is in simplest form.

More Practice

Set 9-8 (pages 522–523)

Write >, <, or = for each ○. You may use fraction strips to help.

1. $\frac{3}{4}$ ○ $\frac{5}{8}$　**2.** $\frac{7}{10}$ ○ $\frac{4}{10}$　**3.** $\frac{2}{5}$ ○ $\frac{4}{10}$　**4.** $\frac{1}{2}$ ○ $\frac{1}{4}$

5. $\frac{3}{6}$ ○ $\frac{1}{4}$　**6.** $\frac{5}{12}$ ○ $\frac{1}{2}$　**7.** $\frac{3}{4}$ ○ $\frac{4}{5}$　**8.** $\frac{6}{10}$ ○ $\frac{4}{10}$

9. $\frac{2}{8}$ ○ $\frac{1}{4}$　**10.** $\frac{6}{8}$ ○ $\frac{3}{8}$　**11.** $\frac{5}{6}$ ○ $\frac{4}{5}$　**12.** $\frac{2}{3}$ ○ $\frac{6}{10}$

13. Dorothy finished $\frac{3}{5}$ of her homework. Amanda finished $\frac{1}{2}$ of her homework. Which girl finished more of her homework?

Set 9-9 (pages 524–527)

Write >, <, or = for each ○.

1. $\frac{5}{6}$ ○ $\frac{1}{4}$　**2.** $\frac{2}{5}$ ○ $\frac{7}{10}$　**3.** $\frac{3}{8}$ ○ $\frac{4}{8}$　**4.** $\frac{4}{5}$ ○ $\frac{1}{10}$

5. $\frac{4}{5}$ ○ $\frac{7}{10}$　**6.** $\frac{4}{7}$ ○ $\frac{8}{14}$　**7.** $\frac{3}{100}$ ○ $\frac{3}{10}$　**8.** $\frac{6}{25}$ ○ $\frac{2}{100}$

Order the numbers from least to greatest.

9. $\frac{1}{2}, \frac{3}{4}, \frac{3}{8}$　**10.** $\frac{3}{4}, \frac{7}{12}, \frac{2}{3}$　**11.** $\frac{2}{5}, \frac{3}{5}, \frac{7}{10}$　**12.** $\frac{5}{6}, \frac{1}{3}, \frac{1}{6}$

13. For a science project, Maria measured how much a plant grew over several weeks. By the end of Week 1, the plant had grown $\frac{5}{8}$ of an inch. It grew another $\frac{1}{2}$ of an inch during Week 2. In Week 3, the plant grew $\frac{7}{16}$ of an inch. During which week did Maria's plant grow the most?

Set 9-10 (pages 530–533)

Write each mixed number as an improper fraction.

1. $1\frac{5}{7}$　**2.** $3\frac{1}{4}$　**3.** $5\frac{1}{2}$　**4.** $2\frac{4}{5}$　**5.** $4\frac{2}{3}$

Write each improper fraction as a mixed number.

6. $\frac{9}{4}$　**7.** $\frac{16}{7}$　**8.** $\frac{22}{3}$　**9.** $\frac{22}{4}$　**10.** $\frac{17}{5}$

11. $\frac{11}{10}$　**12.** $\frac{30}{6}$　**13.** $\frac{15}{2}$　**14.** $\frac{16}{8}$　**15.** $\frac{29}{9}$

16. Amy wrote three different improper fractions that each equal the whole number 3. What could those three fractions be?

Set 9-11 (pages 534–535)

Compare. Write >, <, or = for each ○.

1. $2\frac{3}{5}$ ○ $2\frac{7}{10}$
2. $4\frac{2}{9}$ ○ $4\frac{4}{18}$
3. $7\frac{1}{2}$ ○ $7\frac{6}{20}$
4. $6\frac{1}{3}$ ○ $5\frac{1}{3}$
5. $1\frac{2}{8}$ ○ $1\frac{1}{4}$
6. $7\frac{3}{10}$ ○ $9\frac{4}{5}$
7. $10\frac{7}{9}$ ○ $10\frac{2}{3}$
8. $5\frac{6}{10}$ ○ $5\frac{3}{5}$
9. $6\frac{4}{5}$ ○ $9\frac{2}{5}$
10. $2\frac{2}{3}$ ○ $2\frac{4}{6}$
11. $3\frac{1}{8}$ ○ $3\frac{3}{4}$
12. $5\frac{3}{5}$ ○ $5\frac{9}{10}$
13. In the long jump competition, Bill jumped $8\frac{3}{4}$ feet. Carlos jumped $8\frac{4}{7}$ feet. Who jumped further?

Set 9-12 (pages 536–537)

Use the circle graph at the right.

1. About what fraction of all the votes were for baseball?
2. Which sport got almost $\frac{1}{2}$ of all the votes?
3. Did football receive more or less than $\frac{1}{4}$ of all the votes?
4. Which two sports together had about $\frac{1}{4}$ of all the votes?

Class Favorite Sport

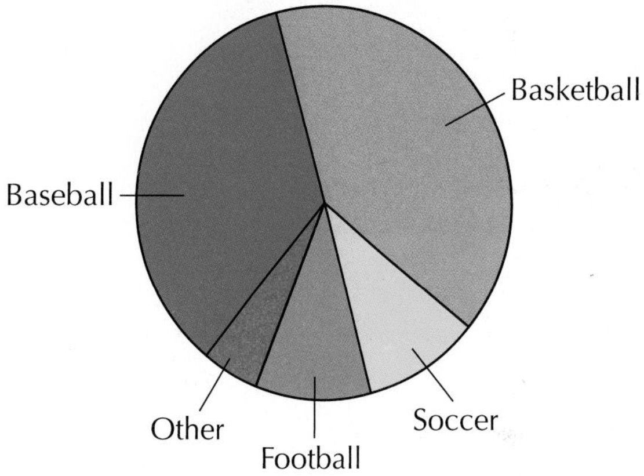

Set 9-13 (pages 538–539)

1. Amber's goal is to save \$100 from her part-time job to buy a new CD player. She saved \$20 the first week and \$25 the second week. Estimate what fraction of her goal Amber has saved. Explain how you estimated.
2. Fifty people were surveyed about their favorite type of music. Of these, 10 said that rock music was their favorite. If you make a circle graph to show the results of the survey, what fraction of the graph will be for rock music? Explain how you decided.
3. Explain how you can estimate if an improper fraction equals a whole number.

CHAPTER 10

Fraction Operations and Customary Measurement

DIAGNOSING READINESS

A Vocabulary

(pages 500, 520, Gr. 3)

Choose the best term from the box.

1. A unit used to measure the weight of an object is a(n) _?_.
2. _?_ is a measure of the amount a container will hold when filled.
3. A standard unit used to measure length is the _?_.
4. A fraction is in _?_ if the _?_ and denominator have no common factors other than 1.

Vocabulary

- **capacity** *(Gr. 3)*
- **inch** *(Gr. 3)*
- **pound** *(Gr. 3)*
- **denominator** *(p. 500)*
- **numerator** *(p. 500)*
- **simplest form** *(p. 520)*

B Add and Subtract Fractions *(Gr. 3)*

Add or subtract. You may use fraction strips or draw a picture to help.

5. $\frac{2}{5} + \frac{1}{5}$

6. $\frac{2}{10} + \frac{3}{10}$

7. $\frac{1}{4} + \frac{2}{4}$

8. $\frac{5}{6} - \frac{1}{6}$

9. Karen ate $\frac{3}{8}$ of a pizza, and Darin ate $\frac{4}{8}$ of the same pizza. Write an addition sentence that shows what fraction of the pizza they ate in all.

Do You Know...

How much does the Empire State Building sway in high winds?

You will find out in Lesson 10-13.

C Length, Weight, and Capacity *(Gr. 3)*

Choose the best unit to measure each length. Write *inch, foot, yard,* or *mile.*

10. shoelace

11. marathon race

12. football field

13. classroom

Choose the best unit to measure each weight. Write *ounce* or *pound.*

14. slice of bread

15. bowling ball

16. bicycle

17. pencil

Choose the best unit to measure the capacity of each. Write *cup* or *gallon.*

18. fish tank

19. soup bowl

20. mug

21. bathtub

D Change Units of Measure *(Gr. 3)*

Complete each table.

22. How many inches are in 4 feet?

Feet	1	2	3	4
Inches	12	24	36	

23. How many gallons are in 16 quarts?

Gallons	1	2	3	
Quarts	4	8	12	16

24. How many ounces are in 1 pound?

Pounds	1	2	3	4
Ounces		32	48	64

Key Idea
To estimate when adding fractions, compare the numbers you are adding to $\frac{1}{2}$.

Materials
- fraction strips or eTools

TEST TALK

Think It Through
I can **use a model** and **look for a pattern** to find a rule.

Estimating Fraction Sums

WARM UP

Draw a picture to show each fraction.

1. $\frac{1}{2}$ 2. $\frac{1}{4}$
3. $\frac{2}{5}$ 4. $\frac{7}{8}$

LEARN

Activity

How do you estimate fraction sums?

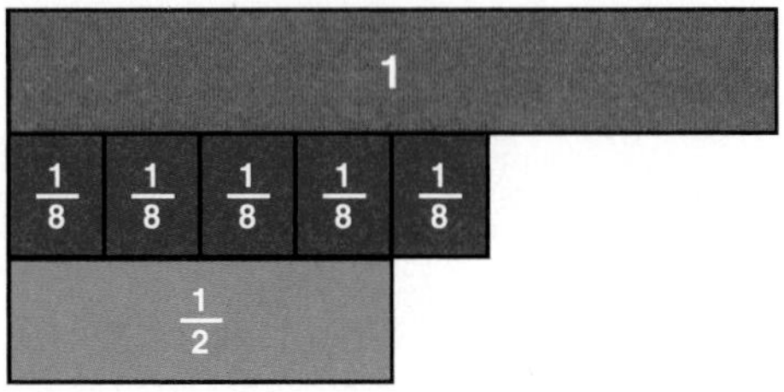

a. Show $\frac{3}{8} + \frac{2}{8}$ with fraction strips. Then, show $\frac{1}{2}$. Write < or > for each ●.

$\frac{3}{8}$ ● $\frac{1}{2}$ $\quad$ $\frac{2}{8}$ ● $\frac{1}{2}$ $\quad$ $\frac{3}{8} + \frac{2}{8}$ ● 1

b. Use fraction strips to show each fraction and sum. Write > or < for each ●.

$\frac{2}{6}$ ● $\frac{1}{2}$, $\frac{1}{6}$ ● $\frac{1}{2}$, $\frac{2}{6} + \frac{1}{6}$ ● 1 $\quad$ $\frac{1}{4}$ ● $\frac{1}{2}$, $\frac{1}{3}$ ● $\frac{1}{2}$, $\frac{1}{4} + \frac{1}{3}$ ● 1

c. When you add two fractions that are each less than $\frac{1}{2}$, is the sum less than or greater than 1? State a rule.

d. Use fraction strips to show each fraction and sum. Write >, < or = for each ●.

$\frac{3}{5}$ ● $\frac{1}{2}$, $\frac{4}{5}$ ● $\frac{1}{2}$, $\frac{3}{5} + \frac{4}{5}$ ● 1 $\quad$ $\frac{2}{3}$ ● $\frac{1}{2}$, $\frac{5}{6}$ ● $\frac{1}{2}$, $\frac{2}{3} + \frac{5}{6}$ ● 1

e. When you add two fractions that are each greater than $\frac{1}{2}$, is the sum less than or greater than 1? State a rule.

f. Use fraction strips to show each fraction and sum. Write >, < or = for each ●.

$\frac{3}{4}$ ● $\frac{1}{2}$, $\frac{3}{8}$ ● $\frac{1}{2}$, $\frac{3}{4} + \frac{3}{8}$ ● 1 $\quad$ $\frac{2}{3}$ ● $\frac{1}{2}$, $\frac{2}{6}$ ● $\frac{1}{2}$, $\frac{2}{3} + \frac{2}{6}$ ● 1

$\frac{1}{4}$ ● $\frac{1}{2}$, $\frac{6}{10}$ ● $\frac{1}{2}$, $\frac{1}{4} + \frac{6}{10}$ ● 1

When one fraction is greater than $\frac{1}{2}$, and one fraction is less than $\frac{1}{2}$, you can't tell if the sum is greater than 1, less than 1, or equal to 1.

g. Predict whether each sum is greater than 1 or less than 1. If you can't tell, write *can't tell*. Then, use fraction strips to check your predictions.

$\frac{5}{12} + \frac{4}{12}$ $\quad$ $\frac{2}{3} + \frac{3}{4}$ $\quad$ $\frac{7}{8} + \frac{1}{12}$ $\quad$ $\frac{1}{3} + \frac{5}{6}$

CHECK

For another example, see Set 10-1 on p. 614.

Write > or < or for each ● .

1. $\frac{1}{8} + \frac{2}{6}$ ● 1 **2.** $\frac{8}{12} + \frac{5}{6}$ ● 1 **3.** $\frac{7}{8} + \frac{5}{6}$ ● 1 **4.** $\frac{1}{4} + \frac{1}{3}$ ● 1

5. Estimate to decide whether $\frac{3}{4} + \frac{1}{3}$ is greater than 1 or less than 1. If you cannot tell, explain why.

6. Number Sense Martie said that $\frac{7}{12} + \frac{1}{9}$ is greater than $\frac{1}{2}$ because $\frac{7}{12} > \frac{1}{2}$. Is Martie right? Explain.

PRACTICE

For more practice, see Set 10-1 on p. 618.

A Skills and Understanding

Write > or < or for each ● .

7. $\frac{3}{10} + \frac{1}{6}$ ● 1 **8.** $\frac{5}{8} + \frac{3}{4}$ ● 1 **9.** $\frac{4}{5} + \frac{4}{5}$ ● 1 **10.** $\frac{1}{3} + \frac{2}{5}$ ● 1 **11.** $\frac{1}{4} + \frac{1}{6}$ ● 1

12. $\frac{2}{12} + \frac{3}{8}$ ● 1 **13.** $\frac{9}{10} + \frac{5}{6}$ ● 1 **14.** $\frac{3}{4} + \frac{3}{5}$ ● 1 **15.** $\frac{7}{8} + \frac{4}{5}$ ● 1 **16.** $\frac{7}{10} + \frac{5}{6}$ ● 1

Estimate to decide whether each sum is greater than 1 or less than 1. If you cannot tell, explain why.

17. $\frac{1}{4} + \frac{7}{8}$ **18.** $\frac{9}{12} + \frac{2}{3}$ **19.** $\frac{1}{6} + \frac{1}{8}$ **20.** $\frac{7}{10} + \frac{2}{3}$ **21.** $\frac{5}{6} + \frac{3}{8}$

22. Number Sense Since $\frac{7}{8}$ and $\frac{11}{12}$ are both close to 1, is the sum $\frac{7}{8} + \frac{11}{12}$ close to 2? Explain.

B Reasoning and Problem Solving

23. Is one-half hour plus three quarters hour more or less than 1 hour?

24. Is one-half hour plus one quarter hour more or less than 1 hour?

25. Writing in Math Kristen said $\frac{7}{8} + \frac{1}{4} > 1$ because $\frac{7}{8} + \frac{1}{8} = 1$ and $\frac{1}{4} > \frac{1}{8}$. Explain how to use Kristen's method to decide whether $\frac{5}{6} + \frac{1}{12}$ is greater than or less than 1.

Mixed Review and Test Prep

Take It to the NET
Test Prep
www.scottforesman.com

26. Can four friends equally share 10 books? Explain how you decided.

27. $7.24 ÷ 4

A. $1.01 **B.** $1.56 **C.** $1.81 **D.** $1.90

Key Idea
When two fractions have the same denominator, their sum has the same denominator.

Vocabulary
- simplest form (p. 520)

Materials
- fraction strips or e tools

Adding Fractions with Like Denominators

WARM UP

Draw a picture to show each fraction.

1. $\frac{3}{4}$
2. $\frac{5}{6}$
3. $\frac{2}{3}$
4. $\frac{3}{10}$

LEARN

Activity

How do you add fractions with fraction strips?

Here's how to find $\frac{5}{8} + \frac{7}{8}$ in **simplest form,** with fraction strips.

Step 1: Use fraction strips to combine $\frac{5}{8}$ and $\frac{7}{8}$.

$$\frac{5}{8} + \frac{7}{8} = \frac{12}{8}$$

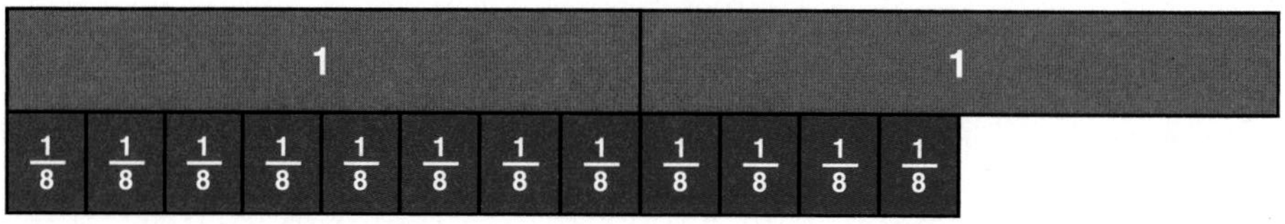

Step 2: Rewrite the sum as a mixed number, if necessary.

$$\frac{12}{8} = 1\frac{4}{8}$$

Step 3: Simplify the fraction if necessary.

$$1\frac{4}{8} = 1\frac{1}{2}$$

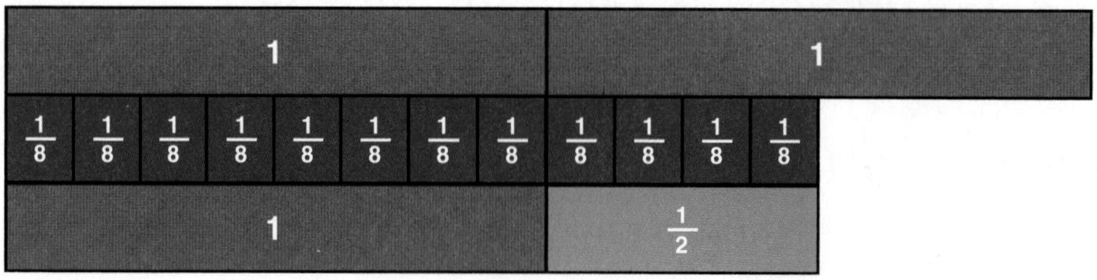

a. Use fraction strips to add. Write the sum in simplest form.

$\frac{5}{12} + \frac{6}{12}$ $\frac{2}{5} + \frac{1}{5}$ $\frac{3}{6} + \frac{2}{6}$

$\frac{3}{5} + \frac{4}{5}$ $\frac{3}{4} + \frac{2}{4}$ $\frac{1}{8} + \frac{5}{8}$

$\frac{3}{10} + \frac{2}{10}$ $\frac{5}{12} + \frac{3}{12}$ $\frac{9}{10} + \frac{5}{10}$

b. Write a rule for adding two fractions with like denominators.

TEST TALK

Think It Through
I can **use objects** or **draw a picture** to add fractions.

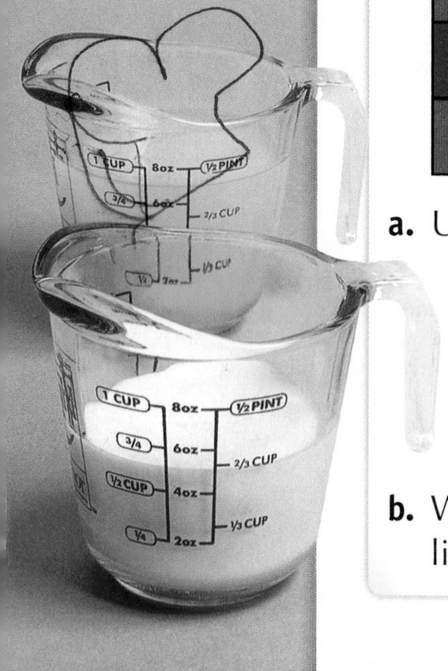

How do you add fractions with paper and pencil?

	Example A	Example B	Example C
	$\frac{7}{10} + \frac{6}{10}$	$\frac{5}{12} + \frac{4}{12}$	$\frac{5}{6} + \frac{5}{6}$
Estimate.	$\frac{7}{10} > \frac{1}{2}$ and $\frac{6}{10} > \frac{1}{2}$, so $\frac{7}{10} + \frac{6}{10} > 1$	$\frac{5}{12} < \frac{1}{2}$ and $\frac{4}{12} < \frac{1}{2}$, so $\frac{5}{12} + \frac{4}{12} < 1$	$\frac{5}{6} > \frac{1}{2}$, so $\frac{5}{6} + \frac{5}{6} > 1$
STEP 1 Add the **numerators.** Write the sum over the like **denominator.**	$\frac{7}{10} + \frac{6}{10} = \frac{13}{10}$	$\frac{5}{12} + \frac{4}{12} = \frac{9}{12}$	$\frac{5}{6} + \frac{5}{6} = \frac{10}{6}$
STEP 2 Simplify, if necessary.	$\frac{13}{10} = 1\frac{3}{10}$ $\frac{3}{10}$ is in simplest form. So $\frac{7}{10} + \frac{6}{10} = 1\frac{3}{10}$. The answer is reasonable since $1\frac{3}{10} > 1$.	$\frac{9}{12} = \frac{3}{4}$ ÷ 3 $\frac{9}{12} = \frac{3}{4}$ ÷ 3 So $\frac{5}{12} + \frac{4}{12} = \frac{3}{4}$. The answer is reasonable since $\frac{3}{4} < 1$.	$\frac{10}{6} = 1\frac{4}{6} = 1\frac{2}{3}$ ÷ 2 $\frac{4}{6} = \frac{2}{3}$ ÷ 2 So $\frac{5}{6} + \frac{5}{6} = 1\frac{2}{3}$. The answer is reasonable since $1\frac{2}{3} > 1$.

Talk About It

1. In Example C, why isn't $1\frac{4}{6}$ in simplest form?
2. In Example A, how does the estimate tell you the sum is a mixed number?

Take It to the NET
More Examples
www.scottforesman.com

CHECK

For another example, see Set 10-2 on p. 614.

Find each sum.

1. $\frac{1}{5} + \frac{1}{5}$ **2.** $\frac{5}{9} + \frac{1}{9}$ **3.** $\frac{7}{8} + \frac{2}{8}$ **4.** $\frac{5}{6} + \frac{2}{6}$ **5.** $\frac{7}{10} + \frac{5}{10}$

6. Number Sense Explain how to add and simplify $\frac{3}{4} + \frac{1}{4}$.

PRACTICE

For more practice, see Set 10-2 on p. 618.

A Skills and Understanding

Find each sum.

7. $\frac{3}{8} + \frac{4}{8}$ **8.** $\frac{1}{4} + \frac{1}{4}$ **9.** $\frac{7}{8} + \frac{7}{8}$ **10.** $\frac{3}{20} + \frac{6}{20}$ **11.** $\frac{4}{25} + \frac{7}{25}$

12. $\frac{2}{9} + \frac{7}{9}$ **13.** $\frac{1}{6} + \frac{3}{6}$ **14.** $\frac{3}{5} + \frac{1}{5}$ **15.** $\frac{7}{12} + \frac{10}{12}$ **16.** $\frac{1}{3} + \frac{2}{3}$

17. $\frac{3}{6} + \frac{5}{6}$ **18.** $\frac{3}{12} + \frac{6}{12}$ **19.** $\frac{7}{15} + \frac{11}{15}$ **20.** $\frac{5}{7} + \frac{5}{7}$ **21.** $\frac{9}{10} + \frac{7}{10}$

22. Number Sense Is $1\frac{1}{8}$ a reasonable answer for $\frac{3}{8} + \frac{2}{8}$? Explain.

B Reasoning and Problem Solving

Math and Art

People use art to communicate their thoughts, feelings, and views of the world.

What fraction of the artists listed at the right

23. were born in the 1800s?

24. were born in the 1400s?

25. lived more than 90 years?

26. lived less than 40 years?

Ten Famous Artists

Michelangelo Buonarroti	1475–1564
Mary Cassatt	1844–1926
Leonardo da Vinci	1452–1519
Vincent van Gogh	1853–1890
Alexander Calder	1898–1976
M.C. Escher	1898–1972
Georgia O'Keeffe	1887–1986
Rembrandt van Rijn	1606–1669
Henri de Toulouse-Lautrec	1864–1901
Pablo Picasso	1881–1973

27. Writing in Math Is the explanation below correct? If not, tell why and write a correct response. If so, draw a picture to show the sum.

> Add $\frac{1}{4} + \frac{1}{4}$.
>
> $\frac{1}{4} + \frac{1}{4} = \frac{1+1}{4+4} = \frac{2}{8} = \frac{1}{4}$

Think It Through
I should always **check that my answer is reasonable.**

C Extensions

Algebra Evaluate each expression for $k = \frac{1}{10}$.

28. $k + \frac{4}{10}$ **29.** $k + \frac{1}{10}$ **30.** $k + \frac{7}{10}$ **31.** $k + \frac{9}{10}$

Algebra Use try, check, and revise to solve each equation.

32. $y + \frac{1}{5} = 1$ **33.** $y + \frac{1}{8} = 1$ **34.** $y + \frac{1}{3} = 1$ **35.** $y + \frac{1}{6} = 1$

Mixed Review and Test Prep

Take It to the NET
Test Prep
www.scottforesman.com

Write > or < for each ●.

36. $\frac{3}{4} + \frac{5}{6}$ ● 1 **37.** $\frac{7}{10} + \frac{7}{8}$ ● 1 **38.** $\frac{1}{6} + \frac{3}{8}$ ● 1 **39.** $\frac{1}{12} + \frac{2}{5}$ ● 1

Write the word form and the decimal for each shaded part.

40.
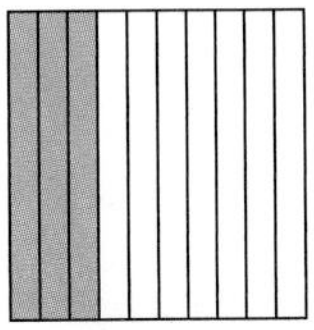

41.
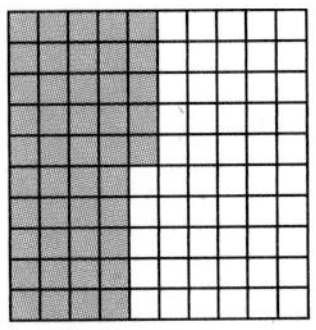

42.
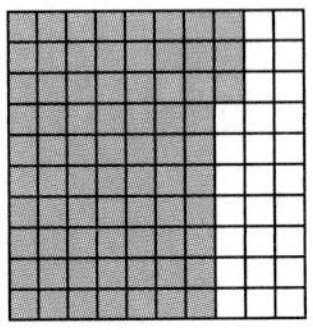

43. **Writing in Math** Explain why the 8 in \$1.89 represents eight tenths of a dollar.

44. $\begin{array}{r} 1{,}284 \\ +\ 3{,}576 \\ \hline \end{array}$ **45.** $\begin{array}{r} \$9.58 \\ +\ \ 6.25 \\ \hline \end{array}$ **46.** $\begin{array}{r} 275 \\ \times\ \ \ 6 \\ \hline \end{array}$ **47.** $\begin{array}{r} 59 \\ \times\ 27 \\ \hline \end{array}$

48. 67 + 489 + 34

A. 470 **C.** 556

B. 523 **D.** 590

49. Which shape is a quadrilateral?

A. square **C.** circle

B. triangle **D.** pentagon

Enrichment

Adding Mixed Numbers with Like Denominators

To add mixed numbers, add the fractions, and then add the whole numbers. Then simplify the answer, if necessary.

$$\begin{array}{r} 1\frac{3}{8} \\ +\ 2\frac{2}{8} \\ \hline 3\frac{5}{8} \end{array}$$

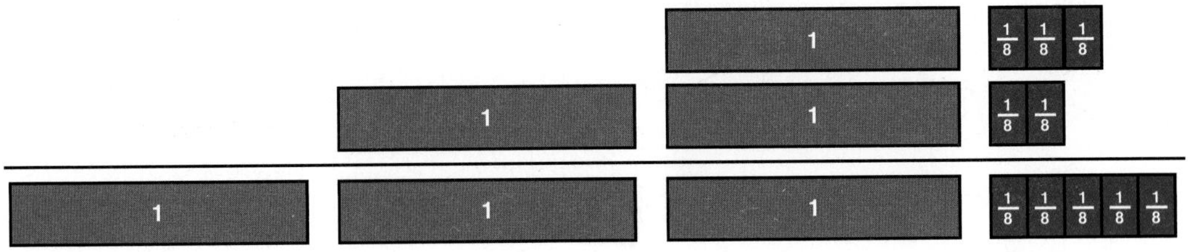

Find each sum.

1. $\begin{array}{r} 1\frac{1}{9} \\ +\ 2\frac{3}{9} \\ \hline \end{array}$ **2.** $\begin{array}{r} 3\frac{1}{5} \\ +\ 4\frac{2}{5} \\ \hline \end{array}$ **3.** $\begin{array}{r} 4\frac{5}{10} \\ +\ 1\frac{3}{10} \\ \hline \end{array}$ **4.** $\begin{array}{r} 2\frac{1}{6} \\ +\ 3\frac{1}{6} \\ \hline \end{array}$

Key Idea
To add fractions with unlike denominators, it is necessary to change to like denominators.

Materials
- fraction strips or e tools

Vocabulary
- factor (p. 124)

Think It Through
I can **use objects** to add fractions.

Adding Fractions with Unlike Denominators

WARM UP

1. $\frac{1}{8} + \frac{2}{8}$
2. $\frac{5}{7} + \frac{1}{7}$
3. $\frac{2}{5} + \frac{2}{5}$
4. $\frac{3}{10} + \frac{3}{10}$
5. $\frac{1}{6} + \frac{5}{6}$
6. $\frac{5}{12} + \frac{1}{12}$

LEARN

Activity

How do you add fractions when the denominators are different?

Here is how to find $\frac{2}{3} + \frac{1}{6}$.

Step 1: Use fraction strips to combine the fractions.

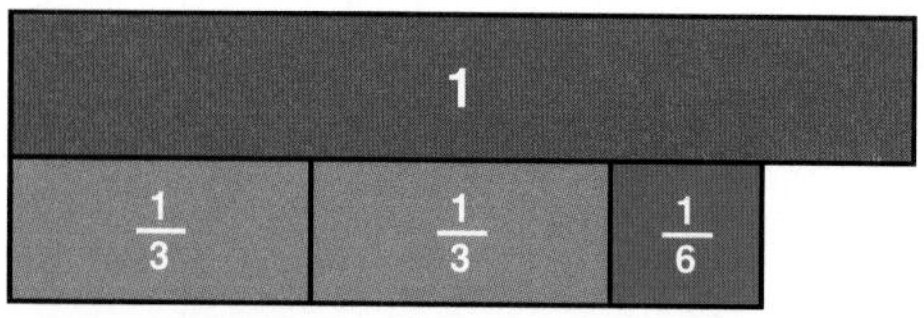

Step 2: Find equivalent fractions with like denominators.

$\frac{2}{3} = \frac{4}{6}$

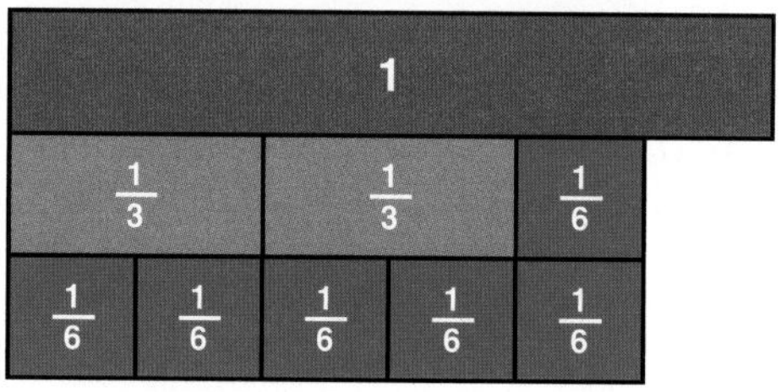

Step 3: Add.

$\frac{2}{3} + \frac{1}{6} = \frac{4}{6} + \frac{1}{6} = \frac{5}{6}$

Find $\frac{1}{4} + \frac{2}{3}$.

Find equivalent fractions with like denominators.

$\frac{1}{4} + \frac{2}{3} = \frac{3}{12} + \frac{8}{12} = \frac{11}{12}$

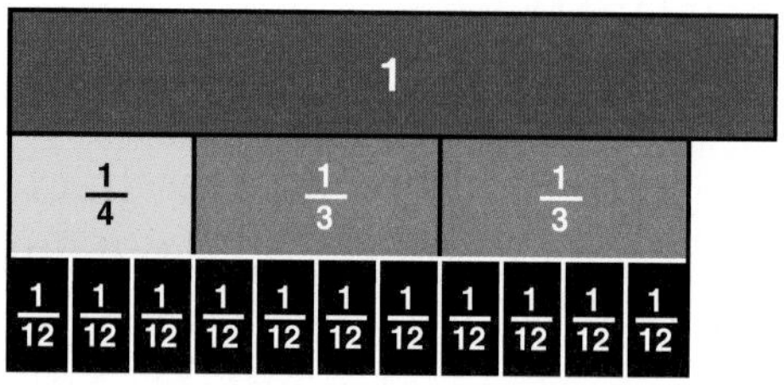

a. Use fraction strips to add. Write the answer in the simplest form.

$\frac{1}{4} + \frac{3}{8}$ $\quad$ $\frac{2}{5} + \frac{3}{10}$ $\quad$ $\frac{3}{4} + \frac{1}{2}$

$\frac{1}{3} + \frac{1}{4}$ $\quad$ $\frac{1}{2} + \frac{2}{3}$ $\quad$ $\frac{2}{5} + \frac{1}{2}$

b. Write a rule for adding fractions with unlike denominators.

c. To add $\frac{1}{4} + \frac{2}{3}$, you can use a denominator of 12. Is 4 a **factor** of 12? Is 3 a factor of 12?

How do you add fractions with paper and pencil?

	Example A	Example B
	Kevin and and his grandfather walked the Robin Trail and the Bluebird Trail. The Robin Trail is $\frac{7}{10}$ mile and the Bluebird Trail is $\frac{3}{5}$ mile. How far did they walk in all?	Lisa and and her grandmother walked the Bluebird Trail and the Hummingbird Trail. The Bluebird Trail is $\frac{3}{5}$ mile and the Hummingbird Trail is $\frac{1}{3}$ mile. How far did they walk in all?
Estimate.	$\frac{7}{10} > \frac{1}{2}$ and $\frac{3}{5} > \frac{1}{2}$, so $\frac{7}{10} + \frac{3}{5} > 1$.	$\frac{3}{5} > \frac{1}{2}$ and $\frac{1}{3} < \frac{1}{2}$, so I can't tell if the sum is less than or greater than 1.
STEP 1 Find equivalent fractions with like denominators.	$\frac{7}{10} = \frac{7}{10}$ $+\ \frac{3}{5} = \frac{6}{10}$	$\frac{3}{5} = \frac{9}{15}$ $+\ \frac{1}{3} = \frac{5}{15}$
STEP 2 Add the numerators. Write the sum over the like denominator. Simplify, if necessary.	$\frac{7}{10} + \frac{6}{10} = \frac{13}{10} = 1\frac{3}{10}$ $\frac{7}{10} + \frac{3}{5} = 1\frac{3}{10}$	$\frac{9}{15} + \frac{5}{15} = \frac{14}{15}$ $\frac{3}{5} + \frac{1}{3} = \frac{14}{15}$
	The sum $1\frac{3}{10}$ is reasonable because $1\frac{3}{10} > 1$. Kevin and his grandfather walked $1\frac{3}{10}$ miles in all.	The sum $\frac{14}{15}$ is reasonable because $\frac{14}{15}$ is about 1. Lisa and her grandmother walked $\frac{14}{15}$ mile in all.

Talk About It

1. In Example A, Step 1, why does $\frac{3}{5} = \frac{6}{10}$?

2. What denominator could you use to find the length of the Robin Trail and the Hummingbird Trail?

Take It to the NET
More Examples
www.scottforesman.com

CHECK

For another example, see Set 10-3 on p. 614.

1. $\frac{3}{8} + \frac{1}{2}$ **2.** $\frac{5}{6} + \frac{1}{3}$ **3.** $\frac{1}{10} + \frac{3}{20}$ **4.** $\frac{3}{25} + \frac{1}{50}$ **5.** $\frac{3}{4} + \frac{1}{3}$

6. Number Sense Could you use 6 as a denominator to add $\frac{1}{3}$ and $\frac{1}{4}$? Explain.

PRACTICE

For more practice, see Set 10-3 on p. 618.

A Skills and Understanding

7. $\frac{1}{2} + \frac{1}{4}$ **8.** $\frac{2}{3} + \frac{1}{4}$ **9.** $\frac{3}{4} + \frac{2}{3}$ **10.** $\frac{4}{5} + \frac{1}{2}$ **11.** $\frac{3}{4} + \frac{5}{8}$

12. $\frac{2}{3} + \frac{5}{6}$ **13.** $\frac{3}{5} + \frac{1}{3}$ **14.** $\frac{1}{3} + \frac{2}{5}$ **15.** $\frac{1}{2} + \frac{5}{8}$ **16.** $\frac{2}{3} + \frac{4}{5}$ **17.** $\frac{7}{20} + \frac{7}{10}$

18. $\frac{1}{3} + \frac{1}{9}$ **19.** $\frac{7}{8} + \frac{1}{4}$ **20.** $\frac{6}{7} + \frac{1}{2}$ **21.** $\frac{1}{6} + \frac{5}{12}$ **22.** $\frac{3}{4} + \frac{4}{5}$ **23.** $\frac{2}{5} + \frac{7}{15}$

24. Number Sense Could you use 12 as a denominator to add $\frac{1}{3}$ and $\frac{1}{2}$? Explain.

B Reasoning and Problem Solving

25. Reasoning Use the information in Examples A and B on page 569. If you hiked the Robin Trail, the Bluebird Trail, and the Hummingbird Trail, how far would you hike in all?

Opera attendance across America has been increasing for the past 20 years.

Math and Music

The table below shows what fraction of the 50 states has one or more opera companies.

Opera Companies

Number of companies	1	2	3 or 4	5 or more
Fraction of states	$\frac{2}{5}$	$\frac{1}{10}$	$\frac{7}{50}$	$\frac{1}{25}$

What fraction of the states has

26. 1 or 2 opera companies?

27. more than 2 opera companies?

28. Are there more states with 1 opera company than states with 3 or more opera companies? Explain.

29. **Writing in Math** Is the explanation below correct? If not, tell why and write a correct response. If so, draw a picture to show the sum.

$$\frac{2}{8} + \frac{1}{2} = \frac{1}{4} + \frac{2}{4} = \frac{3}{4}$$

TEST TALK

Think It Through
I can add fractions in **more than one way.**

C Extensions

Algebra Evaluate each expression for $n = \frac{3}{8}$.

30. $\frac{1}{6} + n$ **31.** $n + \frac{2}{3}$ **32.** $\frac{1}{2} + n$ **33.** $n + n$

Mixed Review and Test Prep

Take It to the NET
Test Prep
www.scottforesman.com

34. $\frac{2}{4} + \frac{1}{4}$ **35.** $\frac{1}{6} + \frac{4}{6}$ **36.** $\frac{7}{20} + \frac{11}{20}$ **37.** $\frac{4}{5} + \frac{4}{5}$ **38.** $\frac{3}{10} + \frac{9}{10}$

39. Maggie's dance recital began at 5:15 P.M. The recital ended at 6:45 P.M. How long did the recital last?

A. 30 minutes **B.** 45 minutes **C.** 1 hour, 15 minutes **D.** 1 hour, 30 minutes

DISCOVERY CHANNEL SCHOOL™

Discover Math in Your World

Ocean Deep

We know less about the ocean floor than we know about the surface of the Moon. One reason is that the water above the ocean floor exerts almost 3 tons of pressure per square inch. This tremendous pressure limits the depths that divers can reach.

1. The deepest recorded dive by a skin diver is about $\frac{4}{50}$ mile. The deepest recorded dive by a scuba diver is about $\frac{19}{100}$ mile. Which diving depth is greater?

2. A special suit called a *jimsuit* enables divers to reach depths up to $\frac{19}{50}$ mile. Is this more or less than $\frac{1}{2}$ mile? Explain.

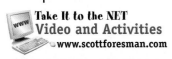

Take It to the NET
Video and Activities
www.scottforesman.com

Section A: Lessons 10-1 through 10-3

Review

Do You Know How?

Estimating Fraction Sums (10-1)

Write $>$ or $<$ for each ○.

1. $\frac{1}{2} + \frac{5}{6}$ ○ 1
2. $\frac{1}{5} + \frac{1}{5}$ ○ 1
3. $\frac{4}{5} + \frac{6}{10}$ ○ 1
4. $\frac{9}{10} + \frac{7}{8}$ ○ 1
5. $\frac{1}{6} + \frac{2}{5}$ ○ 1
6. $\frac{2}{3} + \frac{9}{12}$ ○ 1
7. $\frac{3}{4} + \frac{5}{8}$ ○ 1
8. $\frac{1}{3} + \frac{1}{6}$ ○ 1
9. $\frac{7}{10} + \frac{7}{10}$ ○ 1
10. $\frac{5}{8} + \frac{3}{5}$ ○ 1

Do You Understand?

A Tell how you estimated the sum in Exercise 2.

B Without adding, write two fractions with a sum less than one and two fractions with a sum greater than one.

Adding Fractions with Like Denominators (10-2)

11. $\frac{7}{9} + \frac{7}{9}$
12. $\frac{1}{8} + \frac{3}{8}$
13. $\frac{1}{6} + \frac{1}{6}$
14. $\frac{3}{10} + \frac{8}{10}$
15. $\frac{3}{8} + \frac{7}{8}$
16. $\frac{4}{5} + \frac{2}{5}$
17. $\frac{5}{6} + \frac{4}{6}$
18. $\frac{6}{7} + \frac{6}{7}$
19. $\frac{4}{5} + \frac{1}{5}$
20. $\frac{4}{12} + \frac{11}{12}$
21. $\frac{7}{8} + \frac{5}{8}$
22. $\frac{1}{3} + \frac{2}{3}$
23. $\frac{1}{4} + \frac{2}{4}$
24. $\frac{9}{10} + \frac{3}{10}$

C Tell how you found the sum, in simplest form, in Exercise 12.

D Explain how you know your answer to Exercise 11 is reasonable.

Adding Fractions with Unlike Denominators (10-3)

25. $\frac{4}{5} + \frac{9}{10}$
26. $\frac{5}{6} + \frac{5}{12}$
27. $\frac{5}{8} + \frac{1}{4}$
28. $\frac{9}{20} + \frac{3}{10}$
29. $\frac{1}{3} + \frac{1}{6}$
30. $\frac{9}{10} + \frac{1}{2}$
31. $\frac{3}{4} + \frac{2}{5}$
32. $\frac{4}{5} + \frac{1}{3}$
33. $\frac{4}{15} + \frac{3}{5}$
34. $\frac{2}{3} + \frac{7}{9}$

E Tell how you found the sum in Exercise 27.

F Explain how you know without adding that the sum of $\frac{2}{5} + \frac{4}{15}$ is less than one.

Diagnostic Checkpoint

TEST TALK

Think It Through
I can **use objects** to add fractions.

MULTIPLE CHOICE

1. Mr. Nelson bought $\frac{1}{4}$ pound of turtle food and $\frac{1}{4}$ pound of goldfish food. How many pounds of pet food did he buy? (10-2)

A. $\frac{1}{16}$ **B.** $\frac{1}{8}$ **C.** $\frac{1}{4}$ **D.** $\frac{1}{2}$

2. Mrs. Murphy bought $\frac{2}{3}$ yards of green material and $\frac{5}{6}$ yards of yellow material. How many yards of material did she buy? (10-3)

A. $\frac{7}{9}$ **B.** $1\frac{1}{6}$ **C.** $1\frac{1}{2}$ **D.** $2\frac{1}{3}$

FREE RESPONSE

Write > or < for each ●. (10-1)

3. $\frac{1}{3} + \frac{3}{8}$ ● 1 **4.** $\frac{7}{12} + \frac{3}{4}$ ● 1 **5.** $\frac{1}{10} + \frac{1}{6}$ ● 1 **6.** $\frac{4}{5} + \frac{9}{10}$ ● 1 **7.** $\frac{11}{12} + \frac{5}{8}$ ● 1

Add. (10-2 and 10-3)

8. $\frac{1}{8} + \frac{1}{8}$ **9.** $\frac{5}{6} + \frac{1}{6}$ **10.** $\frac{1}{2} + \frac{1}{5}$ **11.** $\frac{4}{5} + \frac{7}{10}$ **12.** $\frac{9}{12} + \frac{5}{12}$

13. $\frac{7}{10} + \frac{4}{10}$ **14.** $\frac{2}{9} + \frac{1}{3}$ **15.** $\frac{11}{12} + \frac{1}{6}$ **16.** $\frac{2}{3} + \frac{3}{4}$ **17.** $\frac{3}{4} + \frac{1}{5}$

Use the information at the right for 18–25. (10-2 and 10-3)

What is the weight of

18. 2 packages of peas? **19.** 2 packages of carrots?

20. peas and green beans? **21.** peas and carrots?

22. corn and peas? **23.** green beans and carrots?

24. green beans and corn? **25.** carrots and corn?

Vegetables for Camp Stew

Package	Pounds
Carrots	$\frac{3}{4}$
Corn	$\frac{1}{2}$
Green Beans	$\frac{1}{4}$
Peas	$\frac{3}{4}$

Writing in Math

26. Explain how to tell that $\frac{1}{4} + \frac{5}{12}$ is less than 1. (10-1 and 10-3)

27. Write a question that could be answered by adding $\frac{3}{10}$ and $\frac{4}{5}$. (10-3)

Key Idea
When two fractions have the same denominator, their difference has the same denominator.

Materials
- fraction strips or eTools

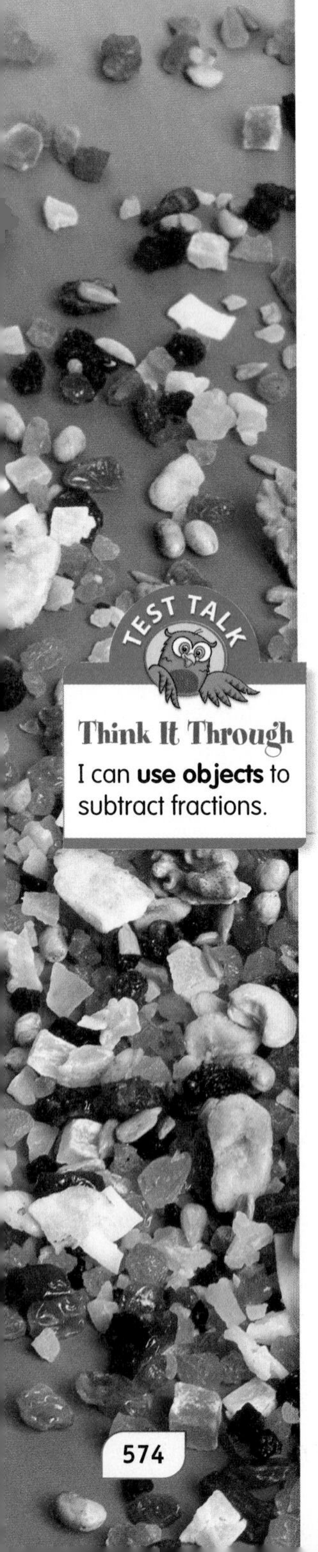

TEST TALK

Think It Through
I can **use objects** to subtract fractions.

Subtracting Fractions with Like Denominators

WARM UP

1. $\frac{1}{5} + \frac{3}{5}$
2. $\frac{3}{8} + \frac{2}{8}$
3. $\frac{4}{9} + \frac{2}{9}$
4. $\frac{5}{12} + \frac{1}{12}$
5. $\frac{1}{5} + \frac{7}{10}$
6. $\frac{1}{2} + \frac{2}{3}$

LEARN

Activity

How do you subtract fractions with fraction strips?

Here is how to find $\frac{11}{12} - \frac{3}{12}$ using fraction strips.

Step 1: Use fraction strips to show $\frac{11}{12}$.

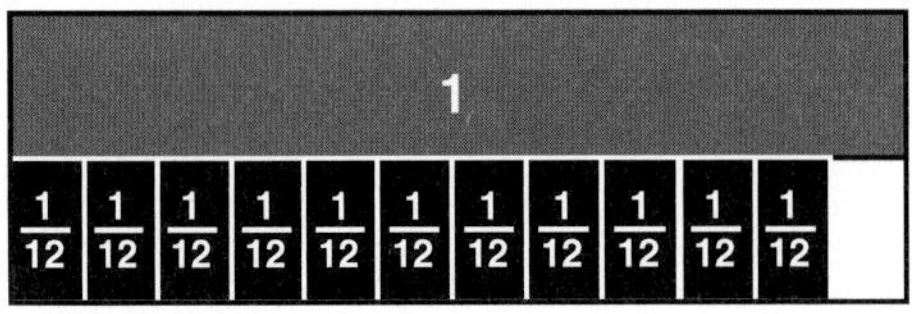

Step 2: Take away $\frac{3}{12}$.

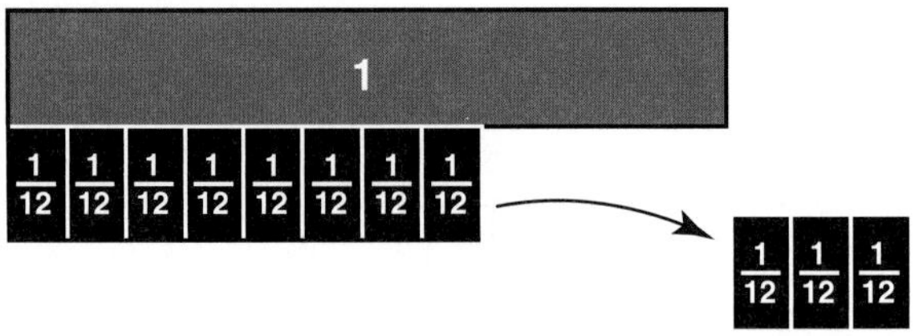

Step 3: Simplify the difference if necessary.

$\frac{11}{12} - \frac{3}{12} = \frac{8}{12} = \frac{2}{3}$

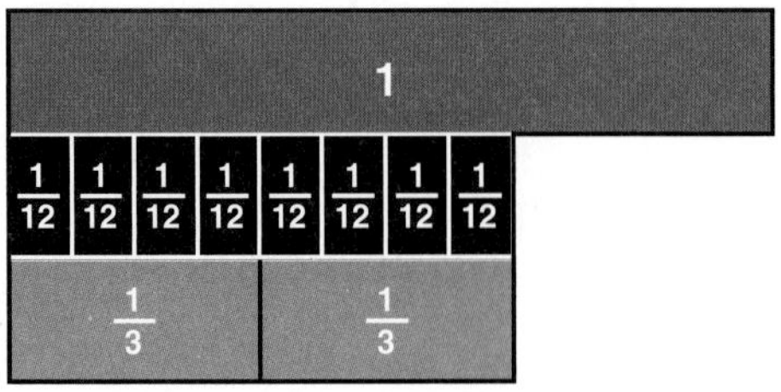

a. Use fraction strips to subtract. Write each difference in simplest form.

$\frac{3}{4} - \frac{2}{4}$ $\frac{7}{12} - \frac{2}{12}$ $\frac{4}{5} - \frac{2}{5}$

$\frac{5}{8} - \frac{3}{8}$ $\frac{5}{6} - \frac{1}{6}$ $\frac{7}{10} - \frac{3}{10}$

b. Write a rule for subtracting two fractions with like denominators.

How do you subtract fractions with paper and pencil?

Rodney bought $\frac{7}{8}$ pound of trail mix and $\frac{2}{6}$ pound of dried fruit.

Hannah bought $\frac{2}{8}$ pound of trail mix and $\frac{5}{6}$ pound of dried fruit.

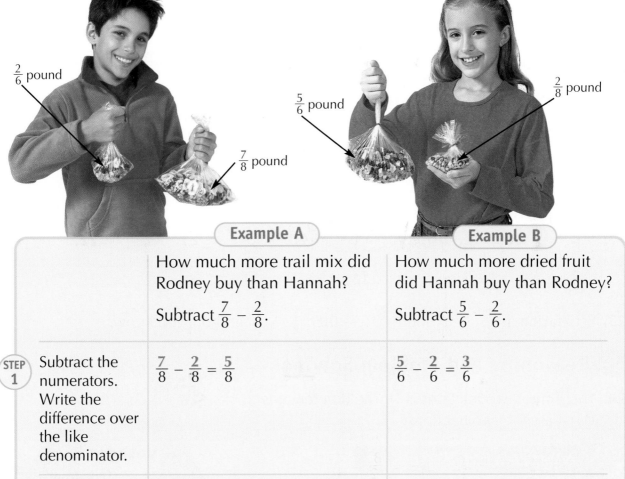

	Example A	Example B
	How much more trail mix did Rodney buy than Hannah? Subtract $\frac{7}{8} - \frac{2}{8}$.	How much more dried fruit did Hannah buy than Rodney? Subtract $\frac{5}{6} - \frac{2}{6}$.
STEP 1 Subtract the numerators. Write the difference over the like denominator.	$\frac{7}{8} - \frac{2}{8} = \frac{5}{8}$	$\frac{5}{6} - \frac{2}{6} = \frac{3}{6}$
STEP 2 Simplify, if necessary.	The only common factor of 5 and 8 is 1. So, $\frac{5}{8}$ is in simplest form. $\frac{7}{8} - \frac{2}{8} = \frac{5}{8}$ Rodney bought $\frac{5}{8}$ of a pound more trail mix than Hannah.	Simplify $\frac{3}{6}$. $\frac{3 \div 3}{6 \div 3} = \frac{1}{2}$ Hannah bought $\frac{1}{2}$ of a pound more dried fruit than Rodney.

Talk About It

1. Why is it necessary to simplify in Example B, but not in Example A?
2. **Reasoning** Explain how to subtract $\frac{12}{25} - \frac{2}{25}$.

Take It to the NET
More Examples
www.scottforesman.com

CHECK ✓

For another example, see Set 10-4 on p. 615.

Find the difference.

1. $\frac{2}{3} - \frac{1}{3}$ **2.** $\frac{5}{7} - \frac{2}{7}$ **3.** $\frac{8}{20} - \frac{1}{20}$ **4.** $\frac{7}{10} - \frac{3}{10}$ **5.** $\frac{9}{12} - \frac{5}{12}$

6. Number Sense Is $1\frac{1}{9}$ a reasonable answer for $\frac{8}{9} - \frac{2}{9}$? Explain.

PRACTICE

For more practice, see Set 10-4 on p. 619.

A Skills and Understanding

Find the difference.

7. $\frac{7}{8} - \frac{3}{8}$ **8.** $\frac{3}{4} - \frac{1}{4}$ **9.** $\frac{4}{7} - \frac{2}{7}$ **10.** $\frac{7}{10} - \frac{1}{10}$ **11.** $\frac{4}{5} - \frac{3}{5}$

12. $\frac{5}{9} - \frac{2}{9}$ **13.** $\frac{11}{20} - \frac{7}{20}$ **14.** $\frac{4}{6} - \frac{1}{6}$ **15.** $\frac{7}{9} - \frac{4}{9}$ **16.** $\frac{6}{50} - \frac{3}{50}$

17. $\frac{3}{5} - \frac{1}{5}$ **18.** $\frac{9}{10} - \frac{7}{10}$ **19.** $\frac{8}{12} - \frac{3}{12}$ **20.** $\frac{17}{25} - \frac{8}{25}$ **21.** $\frac{1}{2} - \frac{1}{2}$ **22.** $\frac{13}{15} - \frac{7}{15}$

23. Estimation Is $\frac{19}{20} - \frac{2}{20}$ more or less than $\frac{1}{2}$? Explain how you know.

B Reasoning and Problem Solving

24. The sum of two fractions is $\frac{7}{8}$. The difference is $\frac{3}{8}$. What are the two fractions?

Math and Science

Voyager 2 was launched from Earth on August 20, 1977. It took *Voyager 2* twelve years to reach Neptune. What fraction of its time to reach Neptune did it spend between

Voyager 2

Planet	Time from Launch
Jupiter	2 years
Saturn	4 years
Neptune	12 years

25. Earth and Jupiter? **26.** Saturn and Neptune?

27. Reasoning In *Miss Opal's Auction,* Miss Opal had written "Use $\frac{1}{2}$ cup less sugar next time" next to her mother's favorite recipe. If the recipe called for 3 cups of sugar, how much should Miss Opal use next time?

28. Writing in Math Jake said that he knew that $\frac{4}{5} - \frac{1}{5} = \frac{3}{5}$ because $\frac{3}{5} + \frac{1}{5} = \frac{4}{5}$. Explain his reasoning.

C Extensions

Evaluate each expression for $s = \frac{5}{12}$.

29. $\frac{6}{12} - s$ **30.** $s - \frac{3}{12}$ **31.** $s - \frac{5}{12}$ **32.** $1 - s$

Mixed Review and Test Prep

Take It to the NET
Test Prep
www.scottforesman.com

33. $\frac{4}{9} + \frac{2}{9}$ **34.** $\frac{7}{12} + \frac{9}{12}$ **35.** $\frac{2}{3} + \frac{5}{9}$ **36.** $\frac{5}{6} + \frac{7}{12}$

37. $\begin{array}{r} 5,682 \\ +\ 6,829 \\ \hline \end{array}$ **38.** $\begin{array}{r} \$5.73 \\ -\ 2.82 \\ \hline \end{array}$ **39.** $\begin{array}{r} 8,004 \\ -\ 835 \\ \hline \end{array}$ **40.** $\begin{array}{r} 45 \\ \times\ 37 \\ \hline \end{array}$ **41.** $\begin{array}{r} \$3.87 \\ \times\ 48 \\ \hline \end{array}$

42. Which is the best estimate for 7,792 + 3,288?

A. 11,000 **C.** 12,000

B. 5,000 **D.** 10,000

43. Which is the best estimate for 9,287 − 4,109?

A. 13,000 **C.** 4,000

B. 5,000 **D.** 2,000

Enrichment

Subtracting Mixed Numbers

To subtract mixed numbers, subtract the fractions, subtract the whole numbers, and then simplify if necessary.

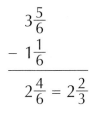

$$\begin{array}{r} 3\frac{5}{6} \\ -\ 1\frac{1}{6} \\ \hline 2\frac{4}{6} = 2\frac{2}{3} \end{array}$$

Start with $3\frac{5}{6}$. **Subtract $1\frac{1}{6}$.** **$2\frac{4}{6} = 2\frac{2}{3}$**

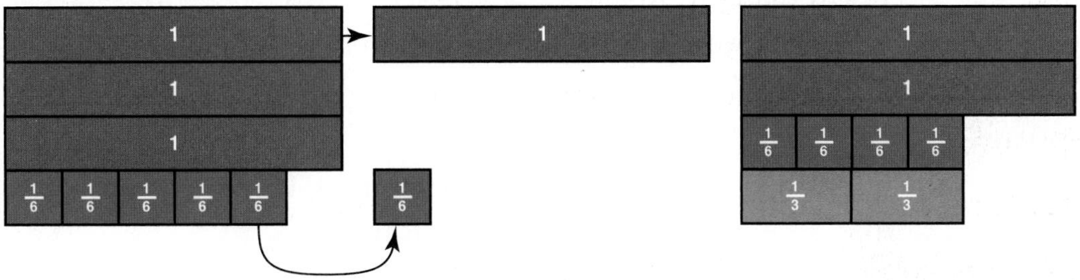

Subtract.

1. $\begin{array}{r} 4\frac{6}{8} \\ -\ 1\frac{5}{8} \\ \hline \end{array}$ **2.** $\begin{array}{r} 7\frac{2}{3} \\ -\ 2\frac{1}{3} \\ \hline \end{array}$ **3.** $\begin{array}{r} 6\frac{8}{12} \\ -\ 4\frac{5}{12} \\ \hline \end{array}$ **4.** $\begin{array}{r} 2\frac{7}{10} \\ -\ 1\frac{1}{10} \\ \hline \end{array}$

5. Reasoning Find $2\frac{1}{4} - 1\frac{3}{4}$. You may use fraction strips to help Write your answer in simplest form.

Key Idea
To subtract fractions with unlike denominators, it is necessary to change to like denominators.

Materials
- fraction strips or e tools

Subtracting Fractions with Unlike Denominators

WARM UP

1. $\frac{7}{8} - \frac{4}{8}$
2. $\frac{7}{9} - \frac{5}{9}$
3. $\frac{2}{3} + \frac{1}{6}$
4. $\frac{4}{8} + \frac{1}{4}$

LEARN

Activity

How do you subtract fractions when the denominators are different?

Here is how to find $\frac{2}{3} - \frac{1}{2}$.

Step 1: Use fraction strips to find a like denominator.

$\frac{2}{3} = \frac{4}{6}$ $\frac{1}{2} = \frac{3}{6}$

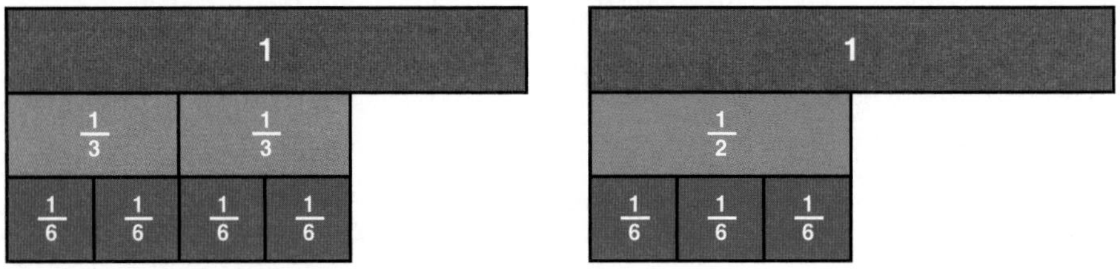

Step 2: Take $\frac{3}{6}$ away from $\frac{4}{6}$.

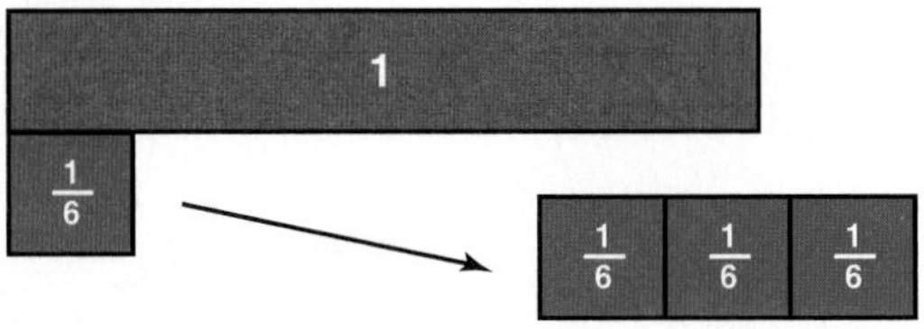

Step 3: Simplify the difference, if necessary.

$$\frac{4}{6} - \frac{3}{6} = \frac{1}{6}$$

$\frac{1}{6}$ is in simplest form.

a. Use fraction strips to subtract. Write each difference in simplest form.

$\frac{3}{4} - \frac{1}{2}$	$\frac{7}{8} - \frac{1}{4}$	$\frac{2}{3} - \frac{1}{6}$
$\frac{2}{3} - \frac{1}{2}$	$\frac{1}{2} - \frac{2}{5}$	$\frac{3}{4} - \frac{1}{3}$
$\frac{5}{6} - \frac{1}{3}$	$\frac{2}{3} - \frac{7}{12}$	$\frac{9}{10} - \frac{3}{5}$

b. Write a rule for subtracting fractions with unlike denominators.

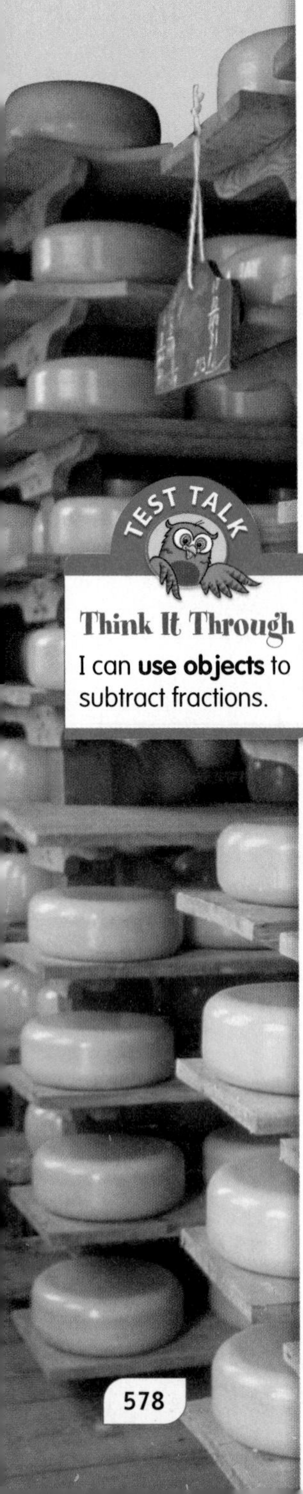

TEST TALK

Think It Through
I can **use objects** to subtract fractions.

How do you subtract fractions with paper and pencil?

Isabella and Danny are making macaroni and cheese. They bought $\frac{3}{4}$ pound of cheese.

	Example A	Example B
	How much cheese will Isabella and Danny have left if they use $\frac{1}{2}$ pound of cheese?	How much cheese will Isabella and Danny have left if they use $\frac{1}{3}$ pound of cheese?
STEP 1 Find equivalent fractions with like denominators.	Subtract $\frac{3}{4} - \frac{1}{2}$. $\frac{3}{4} = \frac{3}{4}$ $-\frac{1}{2} = -\frac{2}{4}$	Subtract $\frac{3}{4} - \frac{1}{3}$. $\frac{3}{4} = \frac{9}{12}$ $-\frac{1}{3} = -\frac{4}{12}$
STEP 2 Subtract the numerators. Write the difference over the like denominator. Simplify, if necessary.	$\frac{3}{4} = \frac{3}{4}$ $-\frac{1}{2} = -\frac{2}{4}$ $\frac{1}{4}$	$\frac{3}{4} = \frac{9}{12}$ $-\frac{1}{3} = -\frac{4}{12}$ $\frac{5}{12}$
	So, $\frac{3}{4} - \frac{1}{2} = \frac{1}{4}$. Isabella and Danny would have $\frac{1}{4}$ pound of cheese left.	So, $\frac{3}{4} - \frac{1}{3} = \frac{5}{12}$. Isabella and Danny would have $\frac{5}{12}$ pound of cheese left.

Talk About It

1. In Example B, why does $\frac{3}{4} = \frac{9}{12}$?

2. What like denominator could you use to subtract $\frac{5}{6} - \frac{2}{3}$?

Take It to the NET
More Examples
www.scottforesman.com

CHECK

For another example, see Set 10-5 on p. 615.

1. $\frac{3}{4} - \frac{3}{8}$ **2.** $\frac{5}{12} - \frac{1}{6}$ **3.** $\frac{4}{5} - \frac{3}{10}$ **4.** $\frac{1}{2} - \frac{1}{3}$ **5.** $\frac{3}{4} - \frac{2}{3}$

6. Number Sense Could you use 20 as a like denominator to subtract $\frac{1}{2} - \frac{1}{5}$? Explain.

PRACTICE

For more practice, see Set 10-5 on p. 619.

A Skills and Understanding

Find each difference. Simplify if necessary.

7. $\frac{1}{3} - \frac{1}{6}$ **8.** $\frac{2}{3} - \frac{1}{4}$ **9.** $\frac{1}{2} - \frac{3}{8}$ **10.** $\frac{2}{3} - \frac{5}{12}$ **11.** $\frac{7}{10} - \frac{1}{2}$

12. $\frac{5}{6} - \frac{5}{12}$ **13.** $\frac{4}{5} - \frac{1}{2}$ **14.** $\frac{11}{12} - \frac{3}{4}$ **15.** $\frac{3}{5} - \frac{1}{2}$ **16.** $\frac{5}{6} - \frac{2}{3}$

17. $\frac{3}{5} - \frac{3}{10}$ **18.** $\frac{1}{3} - \frac{1}{4}$ **19.** $\frac{1}{4} - \frac{1}{8}$ **20.** $\frac{7}{8} - \frac{3}{4}$ **21.** $\frac{3}{5} - \frac{2}{25}$ **22.** $\frac{4}{5} - \frac{2}{3}$

23. Estimation Is the difference of $\frac{24}{25} - \frac{4}{5}$ more or less than $\frac{1}{2}$? Explain.

B Reasoning and Problem Solving

24. Find $\left(\frac{11}{12} - \frac{1}{2}\right) - \frac{1}{3}$.

25. Find $\frac{11}{12} - \left(\frac{1}{2} - \frac{1}{3}\right)$.

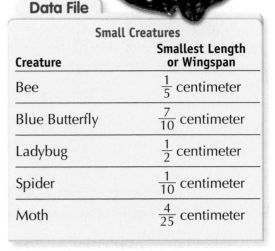

Math and Science

How much longer is

26. a blue butterfly than a spider?

27. a bee than a spider?

28. a ladybug than a bee?

29. a moth than a spider?

30. Reasoning Is a ladybug more or less than twice as long as a bee? Explain.

31. Writing in Math Is the explanation below correct? If not, tell why and write a correct response. If so, draw a picture to show the difference.

> Subtract $\frac{4}{5} - \frac{1}{10}$.
>
> $\frac{4}{5} - \frac{1}{10} = \frac{3}{10}$
>
> I subtracted 4 − 1 = 3 and put it over 10.

Data File

Small Creatures

Creature	Smallest Length or Wingspan
Bee	$\frac{1}{5}$ centimeter
Blue Butterfly	$\frac{7}{10}$ centimeter
Ladybug	$\frac{1}{2}$ centimeter
Spider	$\frac{1}{10}$ centimeter
Moth	$\frac{4}{25}$ centimeter

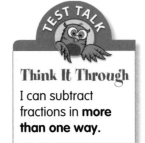

TEST TALK

Think It Through

I can subtract fractions in **more than one way.**

C Extensions

Algebra Evaluate each expression for $n = \frac{1}{4}$.

32. $n - \frac{1}{12}$ **33.** $\frac{3}{4} - n$ **34.** $\frac{1}{2} - n$ **35.** $n - \frac{1}{8}$ **36.** $\frac{7}{8} - n$

Mixed Review and Test Prep

Take It to the NET
Test Prep
www.scottforesman.com

37. $\frac{14}{15} - \frac{4}{15}$ **38.** $\frac{9}{25} - \frac{6}{25}$ **39.** $\frac{8}{9} - \frac{2}{9}$ **40.** $\frac{5}{7} + \frac{6}{7}$ **41.** $\frac{1}{3} + \frac{1}{6}$

42. Use the information at the right. What is the median?

A. 204 **B.** 54

C. 199 **D.** 200

Riverside School District

Grade	K	1	2	3	4	5	6
Number of Students	232	207	194	207	199	182	179

Learning with Technology

Using the Fraction eTool to Add and Subtract Fractions

Select the Strips workspace.

Show the sum of $\frac{1}{4} + \frac{1}{3}$.

a. What is the common denominator?

b. Is the answer in simplest form?

Use the Fraction eTool to find each sum or difference. Write your answer in simplest form.

1. $\frac{3}{8} + \frac{1}{2}$ **2.** $\frac{3}{8} + \frac{1}{4}$

3. $\frac{3}{8} + \frac{5}{8}$ **4.** $\frac{5}{8} - \frac{3}{8}$

5. $\frac{7}{10} + \frac{1}{5}$ **6.** $\frac{7}{10} - \frac{1}{5}$

7. $\frac{5}{6} + \frac{1}{6}$ **8.** $\frac{5}{6} - \frac{1}{6}$

9. $\frac{5}{12} + \frac{1}{6}$ **10.** $\frac{5}{12} - \frac{1}{6}$

11. $\frac{5}{8} + \frac{7}{8}$ **12.** $\frac{7}{12} + \frac{5}{6}$

Reading For Math Success

Draw Conclusions

Drawing conclusions when you read in math can help you use the **problem-solving strategy, *Use Logical Reasoning,*** in the next lesson.

In reading, drawing conclusions can help you make sense of things as you think through a story. In math, drawing conclusions can help you use logical reasoning as you think through a problem.

First I'll make a chart to record the given information.

Our nation's four largest states in terms of area are Montana, Alaska, California, and Texas. Texas is not the largest. California is third largest. Montana is smaller than California. List these states in order, starting with the largest.

To fill in the rest of the chart, I need to look at each column and row and ***draw conclusions.***

Our Nation's Largest States

	First	Second	Third	Fourth
Montana				Yes
Alaska				
California			Yes	
Texas	No			

If there is a *Yes*, then you can conclude that the other cells in that row and column have to be *No*.

After you fill in more cells, continue to ***use logical reasoning*** *to complete all the cells and solve the problem.*

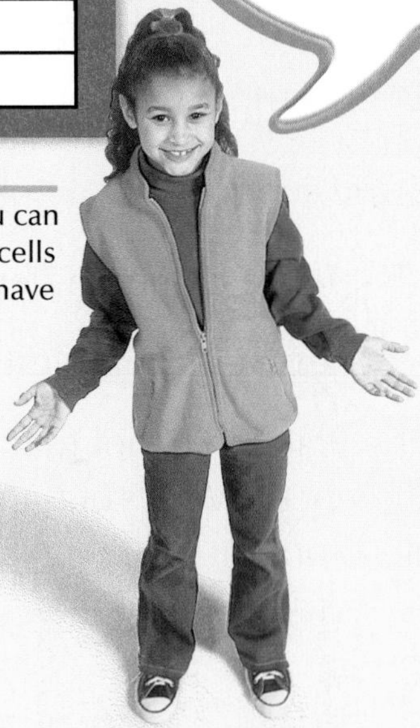

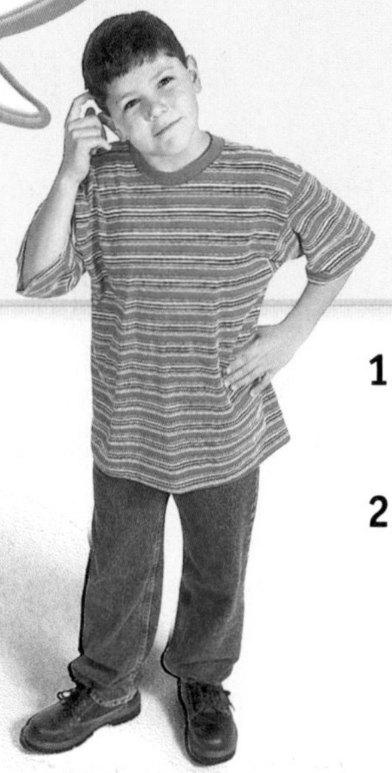

1. How can you draw the conclusion that Alaska is largest?

2. In each row and column of the completed chart, how many cells should say *Yes*?

For 3–5, use the problem below.

Four children have their birthdays in different seasons. Cecelia was born in January. Nola was not born in the fall. Matt was born in the spring.

	Winter	Spring	Summer	Fall
Nola				No
Berto				
Cecelia	Yes			
Matt		Yes		

3. Why can you draw the conclusion that Cecelia was not born in the fall?

4. Why can you draw the conclusion that Berto was not born in February?

5. **Writing in Math** Could Nola have a summer birthday? Why or why not?

For 6–8, use the problem below.

Anita, Tyler, Pete, and Alex won the first four prizes in the school art contest. Pete won 4th prize. Tyler did not win 2nd prize. Alex won 3rd prize. Who won 1st prize?

	First	Second	Third	Fourth
Anita				
Tyler		No		
Pete				Yes
Alex			Yes	

6. **Writing in Math** As you complete table, how do you know what to fill in for the row labeled "third"?

7. Why can you draw the conclusion that Tyler did not win third prize?

8. Why can you draw the conclusion that Anita won second prize?

Problem-Solving Strategy

Reading Helps!
Drawing conclusions
can help you with...
the problem-solving strategy, *Use Logical Reasoning.*

Key Idea
Learning how and when to use logical reasoning can help you solve problems.

Use Logical Reasoning

LEARN

How do you use logical reasoning to solve a problem?

New Friends Annie, Nancy, Linda, and Maria met on vacation. They are from New York, Florida, Texas, and Maine. Maria is from New York and Nancy is not from Florida. If Linda is from Texas, where is Annie from?

TEST TALK
Think It Through
I can **use information** from the problem to help draw conclusions.

Read and Understand

What do you know? Maria is from New York and Linda is from Texas. Nancy is not from Florida.

What are you trying to find? Find what state Annie lives in.

Plan and Solve

What strategy will you use? **Strategy: Use Logical Reasoning.**

Step 1 Make a table.
Step 2 Fill in the table. Each row and each column can have only 1 **Yes** because each girl lives in only 1 state and not more than 1 girl can live in the same state. Fill in the table with No's.
Step 3 Use reasoning to draw conclusions. There are 3 No's in Nancy's row. She must live in Maine. Put a **Yes** in the Maine cell. Complete the chart.

	NY	FL	TX	ME
Annie				
Nancy		**No**		
Linda			**Yes**	
Maria	**Yes**			

	NY	FL	TX	ME
Annie	No	**Yes**	No	No
Nancy	No	**No**	No	**Yes**
Linda	No	No	**Yes**	No
Maria	**Yes**	No	No	No

Answer: Annie is from Florida.

Look Back and Check

Is your work correct? Yes, I filled in the information I was given. I made the right conclusions.

✓ Talk About It

1. When a **Yes** is placed in a cell, what gets placed in the other cells in the same row and column? Why?

CHECK ✓

For another example, see Set 10-6 on p. 615.

Make a chart and use logical reasoning to solve. Write the answer in a complete sentence.

1. **Exploring Antarctica** Five of the early explorers of Antarctica are listed at the right. Two were British and one Russian. The other two were from the United States. Palmer and Wilkes were from the same country. Cook was British. Weddell was from the same country as Cook. Where was von Bellingshausen from?

Early Antarctic Explorers

James Cook

Fabian von Bellingshausen

Nathaniel Palmer

Charles Wilkes

James Weddell

PRACTICE

For more practice, see Set 10-6 on p. 619.

Solve each problem. Write the answer in a complete sentence.

STRATEGIES

- **Show What You Know**
  - Draw a Picture
  - Make an Organized List
  - Make a Table
  - Make a Graph
  - Act It Out or Use Objects
- **Look for a Pattern**
- **Try, Check, and Revise**
- **Write a Number Sentence**
- **Use Logical Reasoning**
- **Solve a Simpler Problem**
- **Work Backward**

Choose a tool

Mental Math

2. **Thompsons** There are 5 people in the Thompson family, Mary, Karl, Todd, Lindsey, and Ari. Their ages are 36, 35, 12, 9, and 4. Karl is the oldest, and Ari is the youngest. Lindsey is 12. Mary is not 9. She is older than Todd. How old is Todd?

3. **Dancers** Twelve dancers want to form a triangle so the same number of dancers is on each side. How should they stand?

4. What shape comes next?

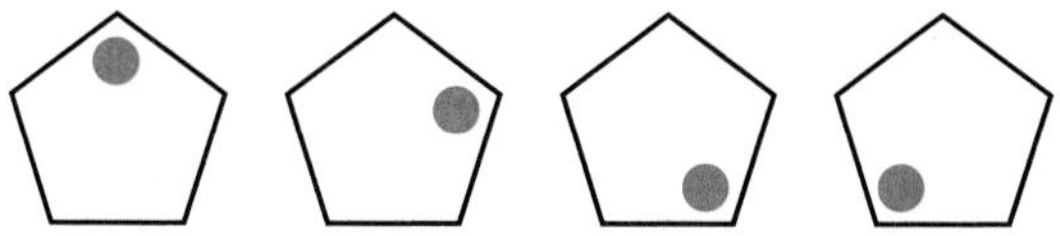

5. Ali and Tim have 12 sheets of paper that are each 9 inches by 12 inches. They want to use all 12 sheets to make a sign for a basketball game. They plan to put a strip of cardboard around the outside edge of the sign. How should they arrange the 12 sheets of paper to use the least cardboard?

6. **Writing in Math** **Rabbits** Marcie has 4 rabbits named Rosie, Clark, Peep, and Lewis. One is orange, one gray, one black, and one spotted. Rosie is orange. Lewis is not gray. Peep is black. What color is Clark? Explain how you found your answer.

Review

Do You Know How?

Do You Understand?

Subtracting Fractions with Like Denominators (10-4)

1. $\frac{5}{6} - \frac{3}{6}$
2. $\frac{5}{12} - \frac{1}{12}$
3. $\frac{7}{8} - \frac{5}{8}$
4. $\frac{3}{5} - \frac{2}{5}$
5. $\frac{6}{7} - \frac{2}{7}$
6. $\frac{9}{10} - \frac{3}{10}$
7. $\frac{8}{9} - \frac{5}{9}$
8. $\frac{17}{20} - \frac{7}{20}$
9. $\frac{2}{3} - \frac{2}{3}$
10. $\frac{5}{8} - \frac{1}{8}$

A Tell how you found the difference Exercise 2.

B How can you tell when an answer is in simplest form?

Subtracting Fractions with Unlike Denominators (10-5)

11. $\frac{5}{8} - \frac{1}{4}$
12. $\frac{5}{6} - \frac{3}{4}$
13. $\frac{7}{9} - \frac{1}{3}$
14. $\frac{1}{2} - \frac{2}{7}$
15. $\frac{5}{6} - \frac{1}{3}$
16. $\frac{4}{5} - \frac{1}{10}$
17. $\frac{3}{4} - \frac{2}{5}$
18. $\frac{1}{4} - \frac{1}{12}$
19. $\frac{1}{2} - \frac{3}{10}$
20. $\frac{7}{12} - \frac{1}{6}$
21. $\frac{7}{10} - \frac{2}{5}$
22. $\frac{3}{8} - \frac{1}{4}$

C Tell how you found the difference in Exercise 16.

D Explain why you could use 15 for a like denominator to add the fractions $\frac{2}{3}$ and $\frac{2}{5}$.

Problem-Solving Strategy: Use Logical Reasoning (10-6)

23. **Book Covers** Mandy put blue, green, yellow, and orange book covers on her math, science, spelling, and history books. She did not put green on her math book. She put blue on her science book and yellow on her history book. What color cover did she put on her spelling book?

E Explain how you could use logical reasoning to solve the Book Covers problem.

F Why does making a chart make it easier to use logical reasoning?

Diagnostic Checkpoint

TEST TALK

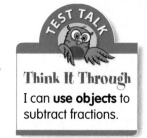

Think It Through
I can **use objects** to subtract fractions.

MULTIPLE CHOICE

1. Jenny used $\frac{3}{4}$ cup of orange juice and $\frac{2}{3}$ cup of pineapple juice in a fruit punch. How much more orange juice did Jenny use than pineapple juice? (10-5)

A. $\frac{1}{12}$ cup **B.** $\frac{1}{4}$ cup **C.** $\frac{1}{3}$ cup **D.** $1\frac{5}{12}$ cups

2. How much more is $\frac{11}{12}$ than $\frac{7}{12}$? (10-4)

A. $\frac{1}{2}$ **B.** $\frac{1}{3}$ **C.** $\frac{1}{4}$ **D.** $\frac{1}{12}$

FREE RESPONSE

Subtract. Simplify if necessary. (10-4 and 10-5)

3. $\frac{4}{5} - \frac{1}{5}$ **4.** $\frac{5}{8} - \frac{2}{8}$ **5.** $\frac{5}{6} - \frac{7}{12}$ **6.** $\frac{3}{10} - \frac{1}{5}$ **7.** $\frac{3}{8} - \frac{1}{4}$

8. $\frac{4}{6} - \frac{2}{6}$ **9.** $\frac{11}{12} - \frac{5}{12}$ **10.** $\frac{2}{3} - \frac{4}{15}$ **11.** $\frac{3}{5} - \frac{1}{6}$ **12.** $\frac{5}{6} - \frac{1}{4}$

13. $\frac{5}{7} - \frac{3}{7}$ **14.** $\frac{9}{10} - \frac{1}{10}$ **15.** $\frac{7}{12} - \frac{1}{4}$ **16.** $\frac{13}{25} - \frac{2}{5}$ **17.** $\frac{8}{9} - \frac{2}{3}$ **18.** $\frac{5}{8} - \frac{1}{2}$

Use the information at the right for 19–20. (10-5)

How much more is needed of

19. the blue material than the green material?

20. the blue material than the white material?

Object	
Length of this book	
Length of the room	

Writing in Math

21. Explain why Tom's answer is not reasonable. Then, tell what he did incorrectly. (10-5)

Tom

$\frac{11}{12} - \frac{2}{3} = \frac{9}{9} = 1$

22. The four teams in the fourth-grade basketball league are the Giants, the Stars, the Tigers, and the Panthers. Each team wears a different color T-shirt. The colors are red, blue, green, and yellow. The Giants wear green. The Panthers do not wear red. If the Stars wear yellow, what color do the Tigers wear? Explain how you solved the problem. (10-6)

Key Idea
Customary units are used to estimate and measure length.

Vocabulary
- customary units of measure
- inch (in.)
- foot (ft)
- yard (yd)
- mile (mi)

Materials
- inch ruler
- yardstick

Length and Customary Units

WARM UP

1. 12 × 3
2. 48 ÷ 12
3. 12 × 5
4. 36 ÷ 3
5. 12 × 6
6. 24 ÷ 12

LEARN

What are units of length?

In the United States, **customary units of measure** are used. Here are some customary units for measuring length.

About 1 **inch (in.)**

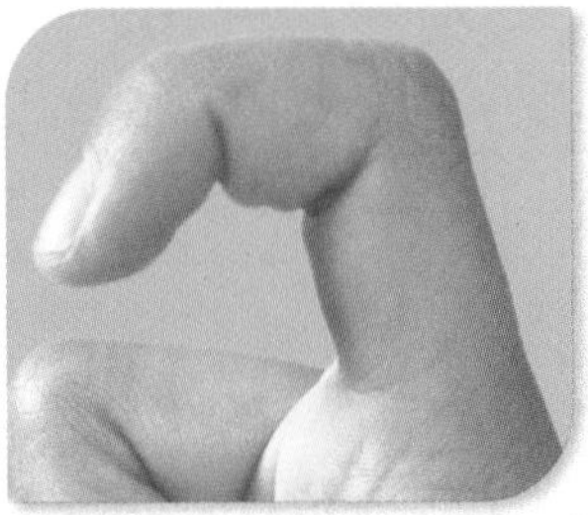

Almost 1 **foot (ft)**

1 ft = 12 in.

About 1 **yard (yd)**

1 yd = 36 in.
1 yd = 3 ft

Talk About It

1. Which is greater, an inch or a yard?
2. What customary unit would you use to find the distance between two cities?

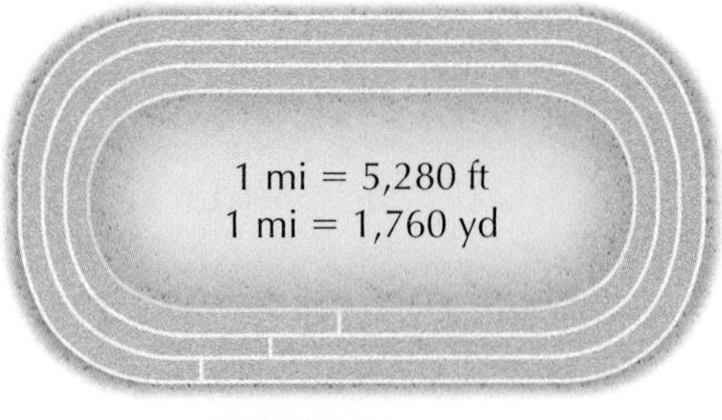

*One **mile (mi)** is the distance around the track twice.*

Activity

How do you measure length?

a. Make a table like the one shown below. Select 10 objects of various lengths. Estimate the length of each object.

b. Measure each object to the nearest inch. If the length is more than a foot, give the measure in feet and inches.

Object	Estimated Length	Length to the Nearest Inch
Length of this book		
Length of the room		

c. Which of the objects that you measured is the longest? Which is the shortest?

TEST TALK

Think It Through
I can **use objects,** like a ruler or yardstick, to measure length.

CHECK

For another example, see Set 10-7 on p. 616.

Estimate first. Then, measure each length to the nearest inch.

1.

2.

3. Reasoning To measure the width of your desk, which would be the better unit to use, your hand span or your height? Explain.

PRACTICE

For more practice, see Set 10-7 on p. 620.

A Skills and Understanding

Estimate first. Then, measure each length to the nearest inch.

4.

5.

Choose the most appropriate unit to measure the length of each. Write in., ft, yd, or mi.

6. pencil **7.** tree **8.** football field **9.** stapler

10. flower garden **11.** shoe **12.** room **13.** mountain

14. Number Sense Would a yardstick be the best tool to use to measure the length of a fly? Explain why or why not.

B Reasoning and Problem Solving

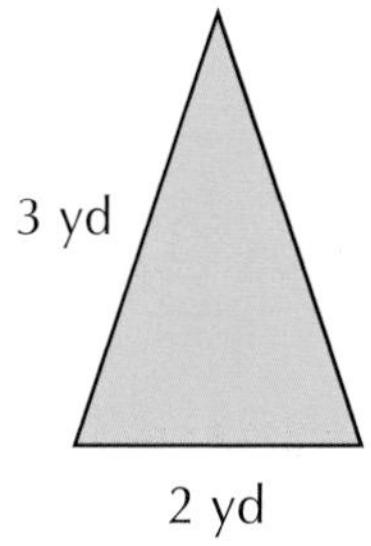

15. If the perimeter of the triangle at the right is 8 yards, what is the length of the third side?

16. Use a ruler to find the perimeter of the rectangle at the right.

17. Writing in Math Explain how you can use a string to compare the distance around a can to its height.

Mixed Review and Test Prep

Take It to the NET
Test Prep
www.scottforesman.com

18. Carlos has a turtle, a shark, a lizard, and a dog. Their names are Biter, Snapper, Koko, and Charlie. Snapper is the turtle. Biter is not the dog or the lizard. Koko is the dog. What is the lizard's name?

19. Write sixty-four million, one thousand, thirty-two in standard form.

A. 64,132 **B.** 64,001,032 **C.** 64,001,320 **D.** 64,010,032

Key Idea
You can get closer measurements if you use fractions of an inch.

Materials
- inch rulers

Fractions of an Inch

LEARN

How can you make measurements more accurate?

Suppose you are building a model airplane and need to cut a 2-inch piece. When you measure to the nearest inch, you could get a piece that is a little more than 2 inches long or a little less than 2 inches long.

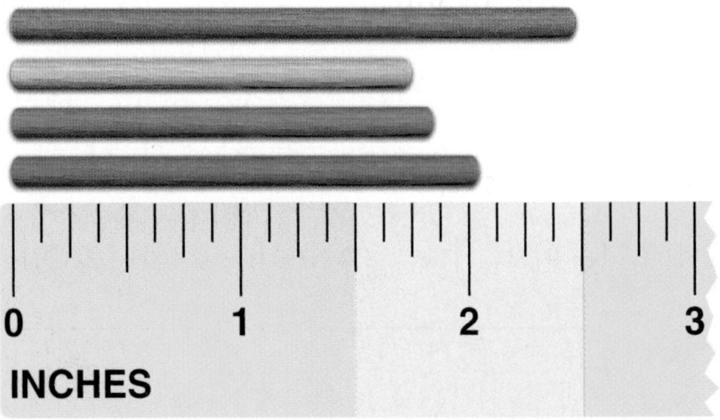

All four pieces above are 2 inches long to the nearest inch.

WARM UP

Draw a picture to show each fraction as part of a length.

1. $\frac{1}{2}$
2. $\frac{1}{6}$
3. $\frac{2}{3}$
4. $\frac{3}{4}$

Example

Measure the blue piece to the nearest $\frac{1}{2}$ inch, the nearest $\frac{1}{4}$ inch, and the nearest $\frac{1}{8}$ inch.

To the nearest $\frac{1}{2}$ inch, the blue piece is 2 inches long.

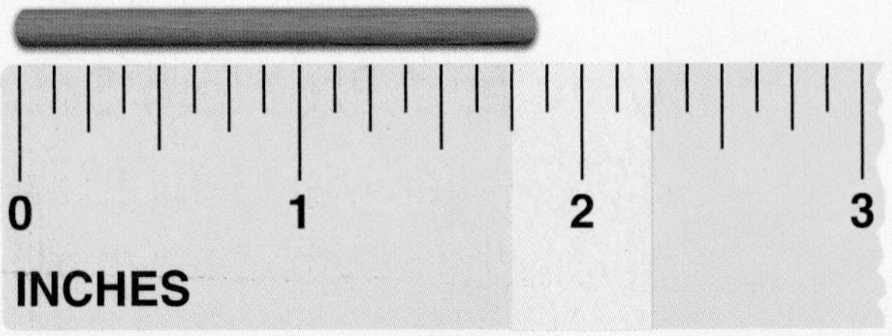

To the nearest $\frac{1}{4}$ inch, the blue piece is $1\frac{3}{4}$ inches long.

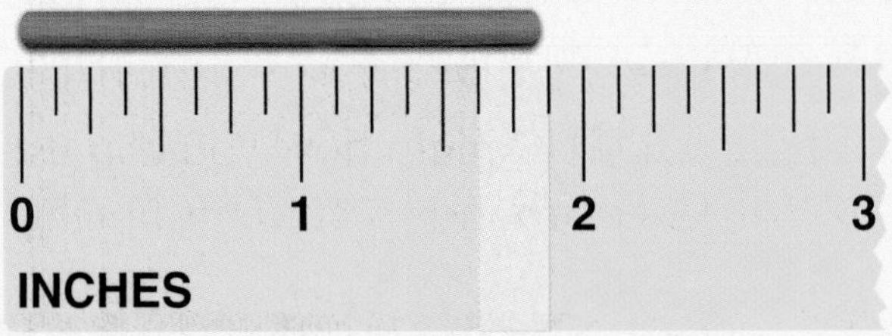

To the nearest $\frac{1}{8}$ inch the blue piece is $1\frac{7}{8}$ inches long.

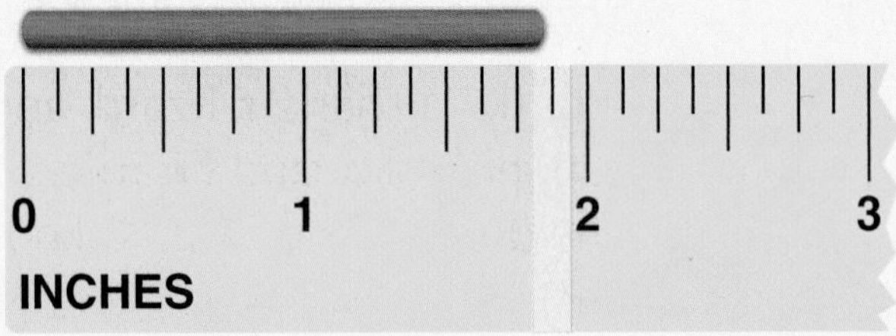

TEST TALK

Think It Through
I can **draw a conclusion.** The smaller the measurement unit I use, the closer I will get to the actual measurement.

Talk About It

1. Draw a line segment that to the nearest $\frac{1}{4}$ inch is $1\frac{1}{2}$ inches long.

CHECK

For another example, see Set 10-8 on p. 618.

Measure each piece on page 590 to the nearest inch, $\frac{1}{2}$ inch, $\frac{1}{4}$ inch, and $\frac{1}{8}$ inch.

1. red dowel **2.** yellow dowel **3.** green dowel

4. Number Sense Draw a picture to explain how an object can be 1 inch long to the nearest $\frac{1}{8}$ inch.

PRACTICE

For more practice, see Set 10-8 on p. 620.

A Skills and Understanding

Measure each piece below to the nearest $\frac{1}{2}$ inch, $\frac{1}{4}$ inch, and $\frac{1}{8}$ inch.

5. 

6.  **7.** 

8. Draw a segment that is $5\frac{1}{8}$ inch long to the nearest $\frac{1}{8}$ inch.

9. Number Sense Draw one segment that is both $1\frac{1}{4}$ inches long to the nearest $\frac{1}{4}$ inch and $1\frac{1}{8}$ inches long to the nearest $\frac{1}{8}$ inch. Explain.

B Reasoning and Problem Solving

Trace each object. Then measure to the nearest $\frac{1}{8}$ inch.

10. Length of your shoe **11.** Width of your hand

12. The perimeter of a triangle is $\frac{5}{8}$ inches. Two sides are $\frac{1}{4}$ inch each. What is the length of the third side?

13. Writing in Math Explain how you could compare the distance around your head at your forehead to the distance around your wrist.

TEST TALK

Think It Through

Sometimes I can explain how to do something by **drawing a picture.**

Mixed Review and Test Prep

Take It to the NET
Test Prep
www.scottforesman.com

Estimate first. Then, find each length to the nearest inch.

14. **15.**

16. Whitney has one \$5 bill, 3 quarters, 4 dimes, and 2 pennies. How much money does Whitney have?

A. \$5.97 **B.** \$6.12 **C.** \$6.17 **D.** \$6.19

Key Idea
Customary units are used to estimate and measure capacity.

Vocabulary
- capacity
- teaspoon (tsp)
- tablespoon (tbsp)
- fluid ounce (fl oz)
- cup (c)
- pint (pt)
- quart (qt)
- gallon (gal)

Materials
- measuring cup
- quart container
- gallon container
- measuring spoons
- containers of different sizes
- water, sand, or rice.

TEST TALK

Think It Through
- I can **use objects,** like measuring cups or spoons, to measure capacity.
- I need to **decide what units to use.**

Capacity and Customary Units

WARM UP

Choose the most appropriate unit to measure the length of each. Write in., ft, yd, or mi.

1. road
2. board
3. finger
4. field

LEARN

What are units of capacity?

Capacity is the amount a container can hold. Here are some customary units for measuring capacity.

1 **cup (c)**
8 **fluid ounces (fl oz)**
1 fl oz = 2 tbsp
1 c = 8 fl oz

1 **teaspoon (tsp)**

1 **tablespoon (tbsp)**
1 tbsp = 3 tsp

1 **pint (pt)**
1 pt = 2 c

1 **quart (qt)**
1 qt = 2 pt

1 **gallon (gal)**
1 gal = 4 qt

Talk About It

1. Which is greater, a pint or a gallon?

Take It to the NET
More Examples
www.scottforesman.com

Activity

How do you measure capacity?

a. Make a table like the one shown below. Select six containers with various capacities. Decide what unit to use to measure each container. Estimate the capacity of each.

b. Use a measuring spoon, measuring cup, or a quart or gallon container to measure the capacity of each container to the nearest unit. Use water, sand, or rice to measure.

Container	Estimated Capacity	Capacity to the Nearest Unit
Bowl		
Vase		

c. Which of the containers you measured had the greatest capacity? What unit did you use to measure it?

CHECK

For another example, see Set 10-9 on p. 616.

Choose the most appropriate unit or units to measure the capacity of each. Write tsp, tbsp, fl oz, c, pt, qt, or gal.

1. soup bowl **2.** salt in a recipe **3.** pond **4.** sugar in a recipe

5. Reasoning Which would be the better unit to measure the water in a swimming pool, the number of juice glasses or the number of bathtubs?

PRACTICE

For more practice, see Set 10-9 on p. 620.

A Skills and Understanding

Choose the most appropriate unit or units to measure the capacity of each. Write tsp, tbsp, fl oz, c, pt, qt, or gal.

6. sink **7.** juice carton **8.** bucket **9.** gasoline tank

10. paper cup **11.** yogurt container **12.** mug **13.** spice in a recipe

14. Number Sense Would a gallon container be the best tool to use to measure the water in an ice cube tray? Explain.

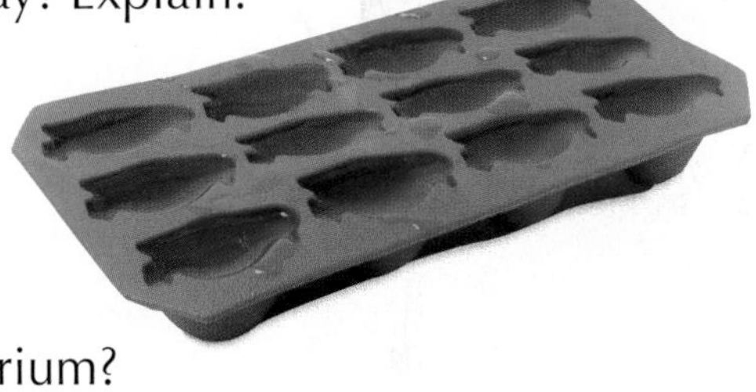

B Reasoning and Problem Solving

You need to add 2 teaspoons of water conditioner for every 20 gallons of water in an aquarium. How much of the water conditioner should you add to each aquarium?

15. 10 gallon **16.** 80 gallon

17. Reasoning Leah said, "The aquarium holds 30 bowls of water." Why isn't this a good description of the capacity?

18. Writing in Math A recipe uses 2 cups of flour. If you measure this flour in tablespoons, would the number of tablespoons be greater than or less than 2? Explain.

Mixed Review and Test Prep

Take It to the NET
Test Prep
www.scottforesman.com

19. Find the length to the nearest $\frac{1}{8}$ inch.

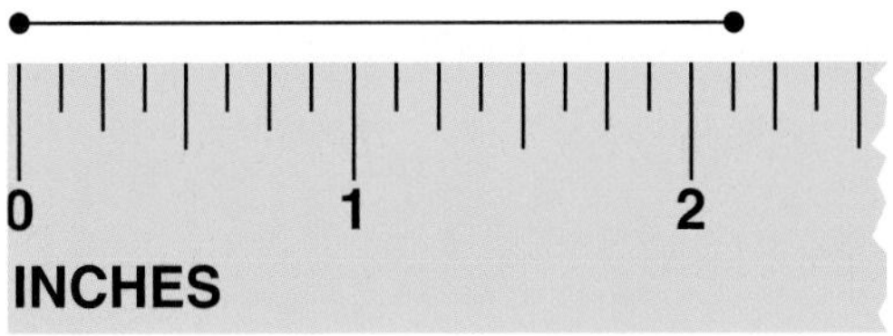

20. Find the elapsed time from 8:15 A.M. and 12:30 P.M.

A. 4 hr 15 min **C.** 3 hr 45 min

B. 4 hr **D.** 3 hr 15 min

Key Idea
Customary units are used to estimate and measure weight.

Vocabulary
- ounce (oz)
- pound (lb)
- ton (T)

Materials
- pan balance
- ounce and pound weights
- objects to weigh

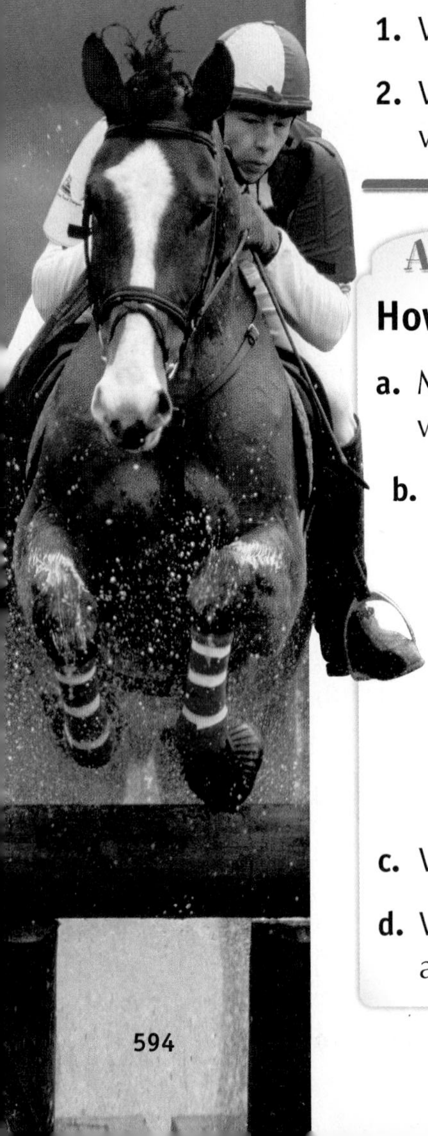

Weight and Customary Units

WARM UP

Choose the most appropriate unit to measure the capacity of each. Write tsp, tbsp, fl oz, c, pt, qt, or gal.

1. fountain **2.** thimble

3. pitcher **4.** vase

LEARN

What are units of weight?

Here are some customary units for measuring weight.

A hummingbird might weigh 1 ***ounce (oz).***

A kitten might weigh 1 ***pound (lb).***
1 lb = 16 oz

A horse might weigh 1 ***ton (T).***
1 T = 2,000 lb

Talk About It

1. Which is greater, an ounce or a pound?

2. What customary unit would you use to find the weight of a large bag of flour?

Activity

How do you measure weight?

a. Make a table like the one shown below. Select six objects with different weights. Estimate the weight of each.

b. Use the pan balance to measure each object to the nearest ounce. Start by using ounce weights. If the object weighs more than a pound, use pounds and ounces.

Object	Estimated Weight	Weight to the Nearest Ounce
Weight of this book		
Weight of notebook		

c. Which of the objects you measured weighs the least?

d. Which of the objects you measured weighs more than a pound?

CHECK

For another example, see Set 10-10 on p. 617.

Choose the most appropriate unit to measure the weight of each. Write oz, lb, or T.

1. loaf of bread **2.** bowl of cereal **3.** truck

4. Reasoning Would a scale used to weigh trucks be the best tool to use to weigh a puppy? Explain why or why not.

PRACTICE

For more practice, see Set 10-10 on p. 621.

A Skills and Understanding

Choose the most appropriate unit to measure the weight of each. Write oz, lb, or T.

5. whale **6.** apple **7.** box of books **8.** letter

9. bag of potatoes **10.** basketball **11.** puppy **12.** house

13. Number Sense Which number would be greater, the number of pounds a box weighs or the number of ounces the same box weighs?

B Reasoning and Problem Solving

14. Reasoning Some dog biscuits comes in boxes like the one shown. Name 3 different things about the box that you can measure. Give a reasonable estimate of each measure.

15. One of the first computers, the Eniac, was completed in 1946. It weighed 30 tons. What unit would you use to measure the weight of a modern personal computer?

16. Writing in Math Explain why using pounds to measure weight is better than using something like rocks.

Mixed Review and Test Prep

Take It to the NET
Test Prep
www.scottforesman.com

Choose the most appropriate unit or units to measure the capacity of each. Write tsp, tbsp, fl oz, c, pt, qt, or gal.

17. fish bowl **18.** can of vegetables **19.** eyedropper

20. $\frac{5}{8} + \frac{1}{4}$

A. $\frac{6}{12}$ **B.** $\frac{7}{4}$ **C.** $\frac{7}{8}$ **D.** $\frac{6}{8}$

21. $\frac{11}{12} - \frac{2}{3}$

A. $\frac{13}{12}$ **B.** $\frac{9}{9}$ **C.** $\frac{3}{4}$ **D.** $\frac{1}{4}$

Key Idea
To compare measures, you may need to change units.

TEST TALK

Think It Through
I can **draw a picture** to help me decide how to change units.

Changing Units and Comparing Measures

WARM UP

1. 24 ÷ 2
2. 36 ÷ 4
3. 9 × 8
4. 15 × 4
5. 3 × 16
6. 32 ÷ 16

LEARN

How do you change customary units?

Customary Units

Length	Capacity	Weight
1 ft = 12 in.	1 tbsp = 3 tsp	1 lb = 16 oz
1 yd = 36 in.	1 fl oz = 2 tbsp	1 T = 2,000 lb
1 yd = 3 ft	1 c = 8 fl oz	
1 mi = 5,280 ft	1 pt = 2 c	
1 mi = 1,760 yd	1 qt = 2 pt	
	1 gal = 4 qt	

To change larger units to smaller units, *multiply*.

Example A

3 gal = ■ qt

Think: 1 gal = 4 qt

3 × 4 = 12

3 gal = 12 qt

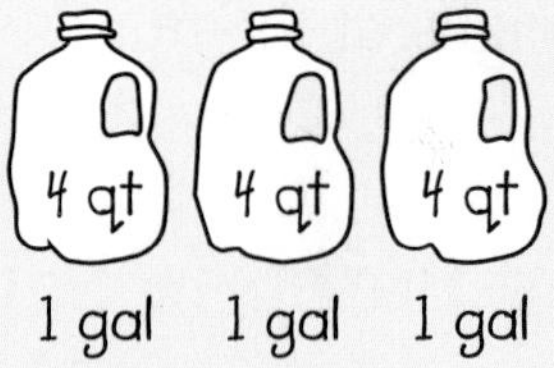

Example B

5 lb 12 oz = ■ oz

Think: 1 lb = 16 oz

$$\begin{array}{r} \overset{3}{16} \\ \times\ 5 \\ \hline 80 \end{array} \qquad \begin{array}{r} 80 \\ +\ 12 \\ \hline 92 \end{array}$$

5 lb 12 oz = 92 oz

To change smaller units to larger units, *divide*.

Example C

15 ft = ■ yd

Think: 3 ft = 1 yd

15 ÷ 3 = 5

15 ft = 5 yd

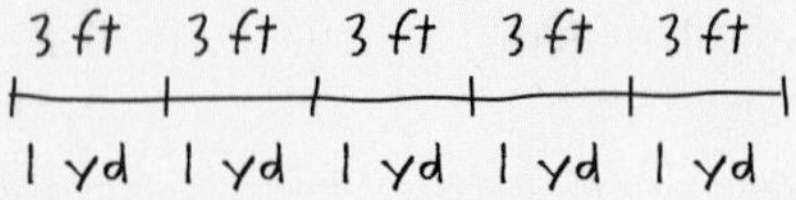

Talk About It

1. Do you multiply or divide to change feet to inches?
2. Do you multiply or divide to change quarts to gallons?
3. In Example B, why do you add 80 + 12?

How do you compare measures?

You can use customary units to compare measures.

	Example D	Example E
	Devon brought 2 gallons of lemonade to the school picnic. If each person gets 1 cup of lemonade, did Devon bring enough lemonade for 36 people? Compare. 2 gal ● 36 c	On track and field day, Emily jumped 2 yards 6 inches in the long jump and Tracy jumped 75 inches. Who jumped farther? Compare. 2 yd 6 in. ● 75 in.
STEP 1 Change to the same units.	2 gal = 8 qt — Think: 1 gal = 4 qt, $2 \times 4 = 8$ 8 qt = 16 pt — Think: 1 qt = 2 pt, $8 \times 2 = 16$ 16 pt = 32 c — Think: 1 pt = 2 c, $16 \times 2 = 32$	Think: 1 yd = 36 in. $36 \times 2 = 72$ $72 + 6 = 78$ 2 yd = 72 in. 2 yd 6 in. = 78 in.
STEP 2 Compare.	32 c < 36 c So, 2 gal < 36 c Devon did not bring enough lemonade for 36 people.	78 in. > 75 in. So, 2 yd 6 in. > 75 in. Emily jumped farther.

Talk About It

4. Do you multiply or divide to change yards to inches?

5. Do you multiply or divide to change gallons to cups?

Take It to the NET
More Examples
www.scottforesman.com

CHECK

For another example, see Set 10-11 on p. 617.

Find each missing number.

1. 4 T = ■ lb

2. 2 yd 1 ft = ■ ft

3. 8 qt = ■ gal

Compare. Write > or < for each ●.

4. 2 ft ● 18 in.

5. 18 fl oz ● 2 cup

6. 2 lb ● 38 oz

7. Number Sense Pierre said that 4 feet is more than 32 inches because 4 feet is more than a yard and 32 inches is less. Is Pierre correct? Explain.

For more practice, see Set 10-11 on p. 621.

A Skills and Understanding

Find each missing number.

8. 5 pt = ■ c
9. 9 lb = ■ oz
10. 6 ft 2 in. = ■ in.
11. 4 qt 1 pt = ■ pt
12. 15 ft = ■ yd
13. 12 qt = ■ gal

Compare. Write > or < for each ●.

14. 2 gal ● 7 qt
15. 4,000 yd ● 2 mi
16. 4,012 lb ● 2 T
17. 8 tsp ● 3 tbsp
18. 24 oz ● 1 lb 10 oz
19. 74 in. ● 2 yd

20. Number Sense Explain how to use quarts to compare 1 gallon and 10 pints.

B Reasoning and Problem Solving

21. Which of the boxes of cereal shown at the right weighs more?

Math and Science

Have you ever noticed how much more a bucket weighs when it is full of water than when it is empty? Use the data file at the right. What is the weight in ounces of

22. 1 quart of water?
23. 1 gallon of water?
24. 1 cubic foot of water?

25. What is the weight in pounds of 500 gallons of water?

Data File

Water Is Heavy

Amount of Water	Weight at 68°F
1 quart	2 lb 1 oz
1 gallon	8 lb 4 oz
1 cubic foot (about $7\frac{1}{2}$ gal)	62 lb 6 oz
500 gallons	2 T 125 lb

26. Writing in Math Is the explanation below correct? If not, tell why and write a correct response. If so, explain how to solve the problem another way.

How many tablespoons are in a cup? Explain.

1 fl oz = 2 tbsp and 1 c = 8 fl oz

fl oz	1	2	3	4	5	6	7	8
tbsp	2	4	6	8	10	12	14	16

There are 16 tablespoons in a cup.

TEST TALK

Think It Through

- I can **make a table** to solve the problem.
- I can solve the problem in **more than one way**.

PRACTICE

C Extensions

You can add or subtract measures.

$$\begin{array}{r} 4 \text{ yd } 2 \text{ ft} \\ + 1 \text{ yd } 2 \text{ ft} \\ \hline 5 \text{ yd } 4 \text{ ft} = 6 \text{ yd } 1 \text{ ft} \end{array}$$

Think: 3 ft = 1 yd,
so 4 ft = 1 yd 1 ft

$$\begin{array}{r} \overset{4}{\cancel{5}} \text{ gal } \overset{5}{\cancel{1}} \text{ qt} \\ - 3 \text{ gal } 2 \text{ qt} \\ \hline 1 \text{ gal } 3 \text{ qt} \end{array}$$

Think: 1 gal = 4 qt
Rename 5 gal as 4 gal + 4 qt.
5 gal 1 qt = 4 gal 5 qt

27. 2 lb 7 oz + 1 lb 3 oz **28.** 2 ft 7 in. + 3 ft 11 in. **29.** 1 qt 1 pt + 2 qt 1 pt

30. 4 gal 3 qt − 2 gal 1 qt **31.** 2 T 500 lb − 1 T 800 lb **32.** 5 yd − 2 ft

Mixed Review and Test Prep

Take It to the NET
Test Prep
www.scottforesman.com

Choose the most appropriate unit to measure the weight of each. Write oz, lb, or T.

33. cherry **34.** truck **35.** apple **36.** watermelon

37. Writing in Math Would a measuring cup be the best tool to use to measure the water in a bathtub? Explain why or why not.

38. $\frac{1}{5} + \frac{7}{10}$

A. $\frac{8}{15}$ **B.** $\frac{9}{10}$ **C.** $\frac{4}{5}$ **D.** $1\frac{3}{5}$

Practice Game

Match Them

Number of Players: 2 or 3
Materials: Customary Measurement Cards

Mix the cards and place them face down in four rows of six each. The first player turns over two cards. If the cards show equivalent measures, the player keeps both cards and takes another turn. If the cards do not match, the cards are returned face down to their original place in the array, and the next player takes a turn. The game ends when all the cards have been correctly matched. The winner is the player with the most cards at the end of the game.

Problem-Solving Skill

Reading Helps!

Making judgments

can help you with...

identifying whether you need an exact answer or an estimate.

Key Idea
Sometimes you need an exact answer to solve a problem, and sometimes an estimate is enough.

TEST TALK

Think It Through
In Example B, the problem is not asking for the exact amount of string, so I can **make the judgment** that all I need is an estimate.

Exact Answer or Estimate

LEARN

When do you need to measure and when is an estimate enough?

The real-world situation indicates whether you need to measure or if you can estimate to tell how much.

Example A

A window shade needs to be ordered for the window shown. What are the inside dimensions of the window?

What are you trying to find? Do you need to measure or estimate?

You want to know the inside dimensions of the window. The shade needs to fit well, so the window needs to be measured.

Example B

A recycling center requires that string be tied around stacks of cardboard boxes. How much string do you need to tie this pile of boxes?

What are you trying to find? Do you need to measure or estimate?

You want to know the amount of string needed to tie the boxes together. You just need to have enough string, so an estimate is OK.

Talk About It

1. Suppose the outside dimensions of the window in Example A are 36 inches by 28 inches and the frame is 3 inches wide. What are the inside dimensions of the window?

2. Suppose the pile of boxes in Example B is about 2 feet long, 2 feet wide, and 2 feet high. About how much string is needed to tie the boxes together?

CHECK

For another example, see Set 10-12 on p. 617.

Tell whether an exact answer is needed or if an estimate is enough. Then solve.

1. You want to put the juice shown below into a gallon jug. Will the juice fit?

2. You put $\frac{1}{2}$ cup of flour in a mixing bowl with other ingredients. Then, you realize the recipe takes $\frac{3}{4}$ cup. How much more flour should you put in the bowl?

PRACTICE

For more practice, see Set 10-12 on p. 621.

For 3–5, use the Running for Charity problem.

Running for Charity Carly runs for a charity. She earns $25 for each total mile she runs in two tries, but nothing for parts of a mile. She runs $\frac{3}{4}$ mile on her first try and $\frac{2}{3}$ mile her second try.

3. Are the $\frac{3}{4}$ mile and $\frac{2}{3}$ mile distances estimates or measures?

4. To find how much money Carly earned, do you need to add $\frac{3}{4} + \frac{2}{3}$ and get an exact answer, or is an estimate enough?

5. Find how much money Carly earned and explain how you found the answer.

For 6–9, tell whether an exact answer is needed or if an estimate is enough. Then solve.

6. Marcel has $20. Can he buy 2 books and a poster?

7. How much change should Mary Ann get from a $10 bill, if she buys one book?

8. How much should the clerk charge Anthony for one book and two posters?

9. Madison has $10. Can she buy one book, one poster, and one bookmark?

Writing in Math For 10–12, tell the appropriate unit of measure for each. Write and tell how you decided.

10. The school bus was about 48 __?__ long.

11. The top of the table was 36 __?__ from the ground.

12. You held your breath for about 48 __?__.

Problem-Solving Applications

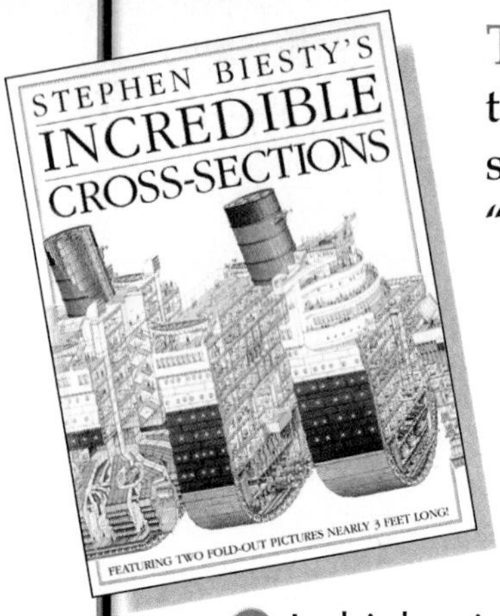

The Empire State Building This skyscraper is more than a tall stack of offices. Since its construction, it has been a symbol of New York City. When it was built, it was called the "Eighth Wonder of the World."

Trivia People on the observation deck of the Empire State Building often see raindrops going up instead of down. This is because the drops are being blown upward by winds passing the building.

1 In high winds, the building may lean $\frac{1}{4}$ inch to one side, then lean $\frac{1}{4}$ inch to the other side. How much does the building move when there are high winds?

2 There are 70 miles of water pipes in the building. How many feet is this?

Using Key Facts

3 How many pounds of steel were used in the building's frame? Write the word name for this amount.

Key Facts
The Empire State Building

- Built in 410 days
- 1,454 feet high
- 102 floors
- 73 elevators
- 1,860 steps to the top
- 6,500 windows
- 60,000 ton steel frame

4 Some steel beams weigh 50 pounds per foot of length. How many pounds would such a beam that is 4 yards long weigh?

5 **Writing in Math** At one time, there were 384 brick laborers and 105 electricians working at the building. Malinda said that there were about 4 times as many brick laborers as electricians. Max said that there were only about twice as many brick laborers as electricians. Who is right and why?

6 **Decision Making** Suppose you could design a 10-story building. Make a chart to show which floors would have stores, restaurants, offices, or apartments. Floors may have more than one use. What fraction of the floors would have stores? Restaurants? Offices? Apartments?

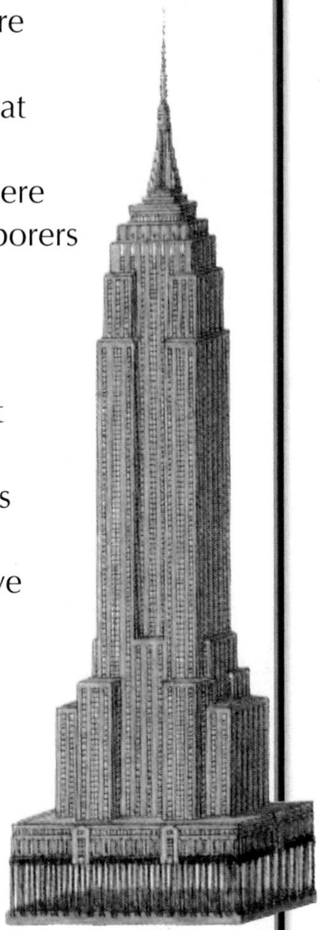

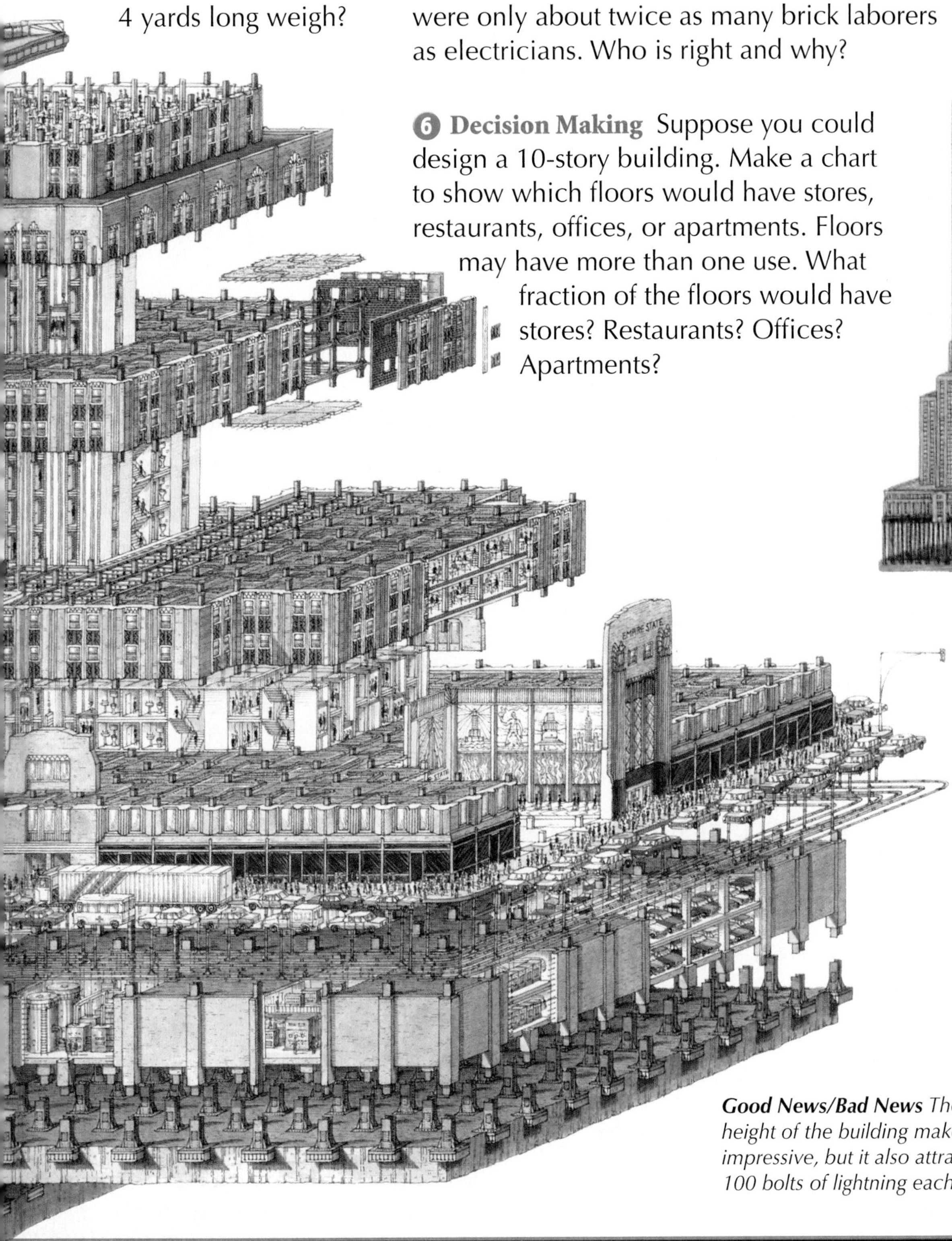

Good News/Bad News *The soaring height of the building makes it very impressive, but it also attracts about 100 bolts of lightning each year.*

Review

Do You Know How? / Do You Understand?

Length and Customary Units (10-7); Capacity and Customary Units (10-9); Weight and Customary Units (10-10)

A box holds 24 cans of tomatoes for shipping. Choose the most appropriate unit to measure

1. the length of the box.
2. the weight of the box.
3. the capacity of one can.
4. the capacity of all the cans.

A Explain why you have a different answer in Exercise 4 than Exercise 3.

B What is the best tool to use to measure the length of a tissue box? Explain.

Fractions of an Inch (10-8)

Give each length to the nearest $\frac{1}{2}$ inch, $\frac{1}{4}$ inch, and $\frac{1}{8}$ inch.

5. 
6. 
7. 

C Is a measurement to the nearest $\frac{1}{4}$ inch or to the nearest $\frac{1}{8}$ inch a closer measurement?

D Are all line segments that measure 3 inches long to the nearest $\frac{1}{2}$ inch the same length? Explain.

Changing Units and Comparing Measures (10-11)

Compare. Write > or < for each ○.

8. 1,670 yd ○ 1 mi
9. 3 gal ○ 20 pt
10. 4 lb ○ 50 oz
11. 5,000 lb ○ 3 T

E Explain how you compared the measures in Exercise 9.

F Do you multiply or divide to change pounds to tons?

Problem-Solving Skill: Exact Answer or Estimate (10-12)

12. Solve the Juice problem.

    Juice If an orange contains about 2 fluid ounces of juice, about how many oranges should you use to make a pint of juice?

G Is 2 fluid ounces in the Juice problem an exact measure or an estimate?

H Do you need to find the exact number of oranges, or an estimate?

Chapter 10 Section C

Diagnostic Checkpoint

Test Talk

Think It Through

I can **draw a picture** to explain my thinking.

MULTIPLE CHOICE

1. Kari made 1 quart of lemonade. How many cups of lemonade did she make? (10-11)

A. 2 cups **B.** 4 cups **C.** 6 cups **D.** 8 cups

2. Which of the following is the most appropriate unit to use to measure the height of a one-story house? (10-7)

A. inch **B.** foot **C.** mile **D.** pound

FREE RESPONSE

Measure each line segment to the nearest $\frac{1}{2}$ inch, $\frac{1}{4}$ inch, and $\frac{1}{8}$ inch. (10-8)

3. 

4. 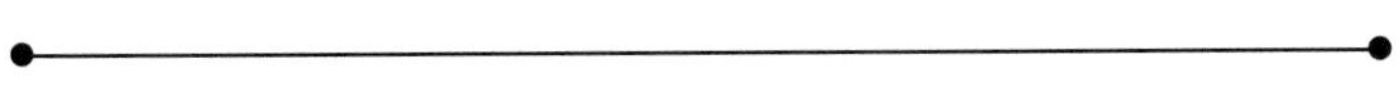

What is the most appropriate unit to use to measure a water bottle's (10-7, 10-9, 10-10)

5. length? **6.** capacity? **7.** weight?

Find each missing number. (10-11)

8. 6 lb 4 oz = ___ oz **9.** 64 oz = ___ lb **10.** 4,000 lb = ___ T

11. 9 yd 2 ft = ___ ft **12.** 72 in = ___ ft **13.** 12 ft = ___ yd

For 14–15, use the data file at the right.

14. Which has a longer wingspan, an eagle or a crane? (10-11)

15. Can two condors fly side-by-side through a 20-foot wide canyon? Tell whether you need an exact answer or an estimate. Then, solve. (10-12)

Data File

Wingspans of Birds

Bird	Wingspan
Eagle	2 yd 1 ft
Condor	8 ft 6 in.
Crane	72 in.
Pelican	2 yd 2 ft

Writing in Math

16. List three things you might measure about the juice box at the right. Then, give an estimate of each measure. (10-7, 10-9, 10-10)

17. Explain how you would compare the distance around your math book to the distance around your desk. (10-7)

Test-Taking Strategies

- Understand the question.
- Get information for the answer.
- → Plan how to find the answer.
- Make smart choices.
- Use writing in math.
- Improve written answers.

Plan How to Find the Answer

After you understand a test question and get needed information, you need to plan how to find the answer. Think about problem-solving skills and strategies and computation methods.

1. The basketball coach recorded the heights of the team's starting players.

How many inches tall is the tallest starting player on the team?

1 foot = 12 inches

A. 18 inches

B. 63 inches

C. 72 inches

D. 75 inches

Basketball Team Heights

Player	Height
Alex	5 feet 7 inches
Bryant	6 feet 3 inches
Frank	5 feet 9 inches
Juan	6 feet 1 inch
Peter	5 feet 11 inches

Understand the question.

*I need to find out the **tallest** player's height in **inches.***

Get information for the answer.

The table shows the heights of each of the players in feet and inches. The text tells me that 1 foot = 12 inches.

Plan how to find the answer.

- Think about problem-solving skills and strategies.

First I need to find the tallest player listed in the table. So I need to compare measurements. Then I need to find this player's height in inches. To change from larger units to smaller units, I multiply. So, I can use multiplication.

- **Choose computation methods.**

I can use mental math to estimate first. But then I'll use paper and pencil to find an exact answer. I need to remember to add the inches in the player's height after I multiply the number of feet by 12.

$6 \times 12 = 72$, $72 + 3 = 75$.

The correct answer is D, 75 inches.

2. All of the students at Washington Elementary School voted for their school mascot. The circle graph shows what part of the total votes each mascot got.

School Mascot Vote

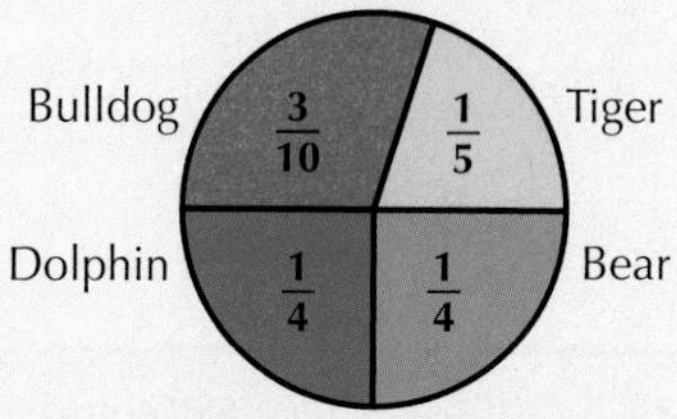

According to the information in the graph, what fraction of all the votes did the tiger and bear mascots get altogether?

A. $\frac{2}{9}$ **C.** $\frac{9}{20}$

B. $\frac{1}{20}$ **D.** $\frac{2}{5}$

Think It Through

I need to find out what fraction of the votes the tiger and bear got in all. The graph shows what fraction of the total votes each mascot got. First, I need to read the graph to find what fraction of the total votes the tiger and bear each got. Then I need to add those two fractions to find how much they got in all. Since the fractions have unlike denominators, I will use paper and pencil to find the sum.

Now it's your turn.

For each problem, describe a plan for finding the answer.

3. The eraser is $1\frac{1}{2}$ inches long. About how long is the crayon?

A. 1 inch **C.** 3 inches

B. $1\frac{1}{2}$ inches **D.** 4 inches

4. Toby bought $\frac{7}{8}$ of a yard of denim cloth. He used $\frac{1}{5}$ yard to patch his jeans.

Which computation could be used to calculate the amount of cloth Toby had left over?

A. $\frac{7}{8} + \frac{1}{5}$ **C.** $\frac{1}{5} + \frac{7}{8}$

B. $\frac{7}{8} - \frac{1}{5}$ **D.** $\frac{1}{5} - \frac{7}{8}$

Chapter 10

Key Vocabulary and Concept Review

Small numbers are simpler to work with than large numbers.
Remember, when the numerator and denominator of a fraction have no common factors other than 1, the fraction is in ***simplest form****. (p. 520)*

Self Check

Estimate fraction sums and add or subtract fractions with like denominators. (Lessons 10-1, 10-2, 10-4)

Sometimes you can estimate by comparing each fraction to $\frac{1}{2}$.

Is $\frac{5}{12} + \frac{1}{4}$ greater than 1 or less than 1?

$\frac{5}{12} + \frac{1}{4} < 1$ because $\frac{5}{12} < \frac{1}{2}$ and $\frac{1}{4} < \frac{1}{2}$.

When the denominators are like, add or subtract the numerators. Write the sum or difference over the common denominator. Write each answer in **simplest form.**

$\frac{4}{9} + \frac{2}{9} = \frac{6}{9} = \frac{2}{3}$

$\frac{5}{9} - \frac{2}{9} = \frac{3}{9} = \frac{1}{3}$

1. Use estimation to tell if $\frac{7}{10} + \frac{3}{4}$ is greater than or less than 1.

2. Find $\frac{1}{5} + \frac{4}{5}$ and $\frac{7}{8} - \frac{3}{8}$.

The factors of 10 are 1, 2, 5, and 10.
Remember, a ***factor*** *of a number is a whole number that divides into the number without a remainder. (p. 402)*

Self Check

Add or subtract fractions with unlike denominators. (Lessons 10-3, 10-5)

Find equivalent fractions with like denominators.

$$\begin{array}{rcr} \frac{3}{5} & = & \frac{6}{10} \\ +\frac{1}{2} & = & +\frac{5}{10} \\ \hline & & \frac{11}{10} = 1\frac{1}{10} \end{array}$$

5 and 2 are both **factors** of 10, so use 10 as the like denominator.

$$\begin{array}{rcr} \frac{7}{12} & = & \frac{7}{12} \\ -\frac{1}{6} & = & -\frac{2}{12} \\ \hline & & \frac{5}{12} \end{array}$$

12 and 6 are both factors of 12, so use 12 as the like denominator.

3. Find $\frac{1}{4} + \frac{7}{8}$ and $\frac{5}{6} - \frac{1}{2}$.

"Custom" is part of customary units.
It has been the custom in the United States to use **customary units of measure** such as **inch, gallon,** and **pound.** (p. 588)

Self Check

Use customary measures. (Lessons 10-7, 10-8, 10-9, 10-10, 10-11)

Measure to the nearest $\frac{1}{8}$ inch.

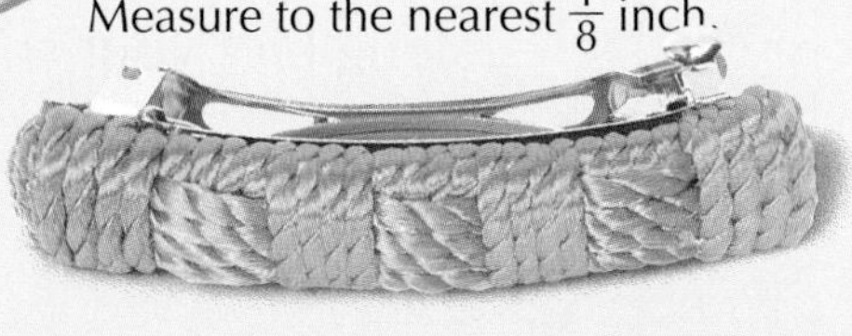

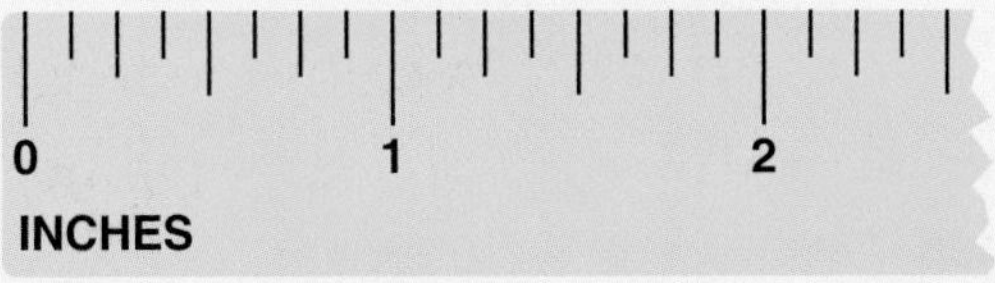

8 lb = ▢ oz	24 qt = ▢ gal
To change to a smaller unit, multiply.	To change to a larger unit, divide.
$8 \times 16 = 128$	$24 \div 4 = 6$
8 lb = 128 oz	24 qt = 6 gal

Customary Units of Length
1 foot (ft) = 12 inches (in.)
1 yard (yd) = 3 ft = 36 in.
1 mile (mi) = 1,760 yd = 5,280 ft

Customary Units of Capacity
1 tablespoon (tbsp) = 3 teaspoons (tsp)
1 fluid ounce (fl oz) = 2 tbsp
1 cup (c) = 8 fl oz
1 pint (pt) = 2 c
1 quart (qt) = 2 pt
1 gal (gal) = 4 qt

Customary Units of Weight
1 pound (lb) = 16 ounces (oz)
1 ton (T) = 2,000 lb

4. Find each missing number: 7 pt = ▢ c and 11 ft = ▢ yd ▢ ft.

Self Check

My desk is filled to capacity.
Capacity is the amount a container can hold. (p. 592)

Use logical reasoning or decide whether an estimate is enough. (Lessons 10-6, 10-12)

Sometimes you only need to find an estimate.

Will needs 7 feet of wire. He has 68 inches. Does he have enough?

Estimate. 7 ft = 7×12 in. So, 7 ft is more than 7×10 in. = 70 in.

No, Will does not have enough wire.

Make a chart with given information and use logical reasoning to make conclusions.

Myrna, Jan, and Zach are a dancer, a painter, and a banker. Myrna is the painter, and Zach is not the banker. Who is the dancer?

	dancer	painter	banker
Myrna	No	Yes	No
Jan	No	No	Yes
Zach	Yes	No	No

Zach is the dancer.

5. Trish has 16 quart bottles of juice. She needs 44 pints. Does she have enough?

Answers: **1.** Greater than 1 **2.** 1; $\frac{1}{2}$ **3.** $1\frac{1}{8}$; $\frac{1}{3}$ **4.** 14; 3; 2 **5.** No

CHAPTER
10 Chapter Test

MULTIPLE CHOICE

Choose the correct letter for each answer.

1. Which sum is less than 1?

A. $\frac{3}{4} + \frac{5}{6}$ **C.** $\frac{3}{7} + \frac{4}{9}$

B. $\frac{1}{2} + \frac{2}{3}$ **D.** $\frac{3}{5} + \frac{6}{7}$

2. Brenda used $\frac{4}{9}$ pound of clay to make a vase and $\frac{2}{9}$ pound of clay to make refrigerator magnets. How much clay did she use in all?

A. $\frac{2}{9}$ pound **C.** $\frac{2}{3}$ pound

B. $\frac{6}{18}$ pound **D.** $\frac{8}{9}$ pound

3. What is the sum of $\frac{1}{3}$ and $\frac{5}{6}$?

A. $\frac{4}{3}$ **C.** $\frac{6}{9}$

B. $1\frac{1}{6}$ **D.** $\frac{4}{9}$

4. Subtract $\frac{7}{10} - \frac{3}{10}$.

A. $\frac{1}{5}$

B. $\frac{1}{2}$

C. $\frac{2}{5}$

D. $\frac{4}{5}$

Think It Through
I can **try working backward from the answer choices.**

5. Pounds would be the most appropriate unit for measuring the weight of which object?

A. paper clip **C.** cargo ship

B. desk **D.** envelope

6. Which would be the most appropriate unit to measure the length of your shoe?

A. inch **C.** yard

B. foot **D.** mile

7. What is the length of this crayon to the nearest $\frac{1}{8}$ inch?

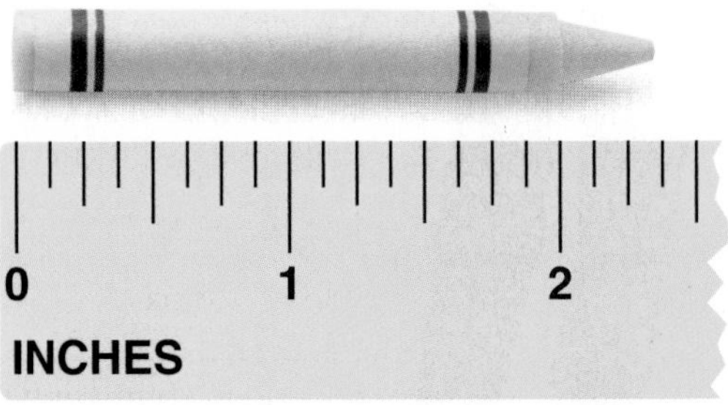

A. 2 inches **C.** $2\frac{1}{2}$ inches

B. $2\frac{3}{8}$ inches **D.** $2\frac{7}{8}$ inches

8. Which would be the most appropriate unit to measure the capacity of a fish pond?

A. cup **C.** quart

B. pint **D.** gallon

9. Calvin bought $\frac{5}{8}$ pound of sliced turkey. He used $\frac{1}{2}$ pound to make sandwiches. How much turkey did he have left over?

A. $\frac{4}{6}$ pound **C.** $\frac{1}{2}$ pound

B. $\frac{2}{3}$ pound **D.** $\frac{1}{8}$ pound

10. Find the missing number.

24 ft = ■ yd

A. 2 **B.** 3 **C.** 6 **D.** 8

11. Which of the following is less than 4 cups?

A. 1 gallon **C.** 2 quarts

B. 4 pints **D.** 10 fluid ounces

12. John's cat weighs 12 pounds. How many ounces does it weigh?

A. 48 ounces

B. 120 ounces

C. 192 ounces

D. 256 ounces

FREE RESPONSE

Find each sum or difference. Simplify if possible.

13. $\frac{3}{5} + \frac{7}{10}$ **14.** $\frac{1}{2} - \frac{4}{9}$

15. $\frac{1}{6} + \frac{1}{5}$ **16.** $\frac{7}{8} + \frac{3}{8}$

17. $\frac{4}{10} - \frac{3}{10}$ **18.** $\frac{1}{3} + \frac{3}{6}$

Find each missing number.

19. 2 T = ■ lb

20. 2 ft 5 in. = ■ in.

21. 18 yd = ■ ft

22. 8 qt = ■ pt

Compare. Write >, or <, or = for each ●.

23. 18 in. ● 2 ft

24. 14 qt ● 3 gal

25. 7 pt ● 10 c

26. 3 T ● 3,000 lb

27. Use logical reasoning to solve this problem.

> **TEST TALK**
> **Think It Through**
> I can **make a chart** to organize the facts.

Carol, Tina, and Annie take music lessons. They take piano, violin, and flute. Tina carries her instrument to her lesson. Annie's instrument does not have strings. What instrument does each girl play?

Writing in Math

28. Tell whether an exact answer or an estimate is needed to solve this problem. Then solve and explain your answer.

Michael's truck can safely carry 1 ton. He has 15 televisions that he needs to deliver. Each television weighs 95 pounds. Can Michael safely carry all the televisions in his truck?

29. What is the first step needed to add or subtract fractions with unlike denominators? Explain.

30. What do a teaspoon, a fluid ounce, and a pint have in common? How are they different? Explain.

Cumulative Review and Test Prep

Number and Operation

MULTIPLE CHOICE

1. At Maria's school, $\frac{3}{8}$ of the students are in sixth grade, $\frac{1}{4}$ are in seventh grade, and $\frac{3}{8}$ are in eighth grade. What fraction of all the students are in either seventh or eighth grade?

A. $\frac{5}{8}$ **B.** $\frac{4}{12}$ **C.** $\frac{6}{8}$ **D.** $\frac{3}{4}$

2. What is 117 divided by 8?

A. 13 R6 **C.** 14 R5

B. 14 **D.** 109

3. Which number below is thirty and eight tenths in standard form?

A. 3.008 **C.** 30.8

B. 3.08 **D.** 30.08

FREE RESPONSE

4. A 10-mile racecourse has markers posted at the beginning, at the end, and every 2 miles. How many markers are posted altogether?

5. What is the product of 75 and 12?

Writing in Math

6. Estimate to decide whether $\frac{3}{5} + \frac{6}{9}$ is greater or less than 1. Explain how you estimated.

TEST TALK

Think It Through
I will make my explanation brief, but complete.

Geometry and Measurement

MULTIPLE CHOICE

7. What is the length of this ribbon to the nearest $\frac{1}{8}$ inch?

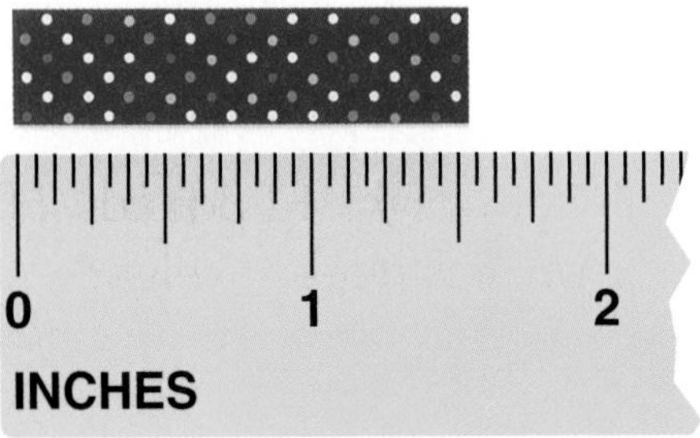

A. $1\frac{3}{8}$ inches **C.** $1\frac{5}{8}$ inches

B. $1\frac{1}{2}$ inches **D.** $1\frac{7}{8}$ inches

8. The concert started at 7:45 P.M. It lasted 1 hour and 45 minutes. At what time did the concert end?

A. 6:00 P.M. **C.** 9:15 P.M.

B. 8:45 P.M. **D.** 9:30 P.M.

FREE RESPONSE

9. A small box of crackers weighs 20 oz. A large box weighs 2 lb. What is the difference in their weights?

10. The perimeter of an equilateral triangle is 27 yards. What is the length of each side of the triangle?

Writing in Math

11. Put the words below into three groups. Explain why you grouped them as you did.

yard	fluid ounce	ton
foot	ounce	mile
teaspoon	quart	inch

Data Analysis and Probability

MULTIPLE CHOICE

12. You spin the spinner below once. Describe the likelihood of landing on a 6.

A. certain

B. likely

C. unlikely

D. impossible

13. To find the score you earned most often on your math tests, you should find the

A. range. **C.** average.

B. mode. **D.** median.

FREE RESPONSE

Use the pictograph for 14–16.

State Populations, 2000

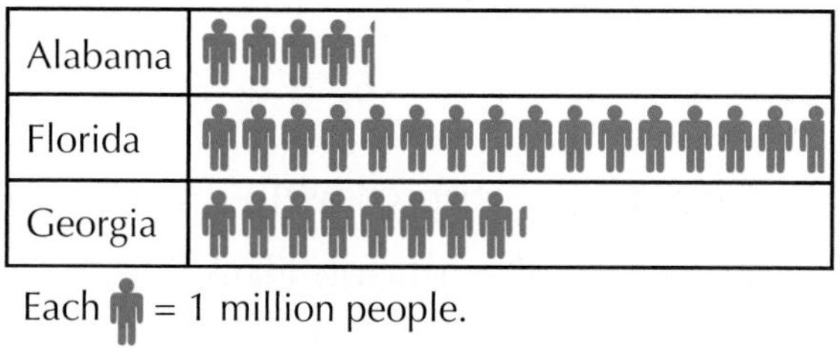

14. Which state shown on the graph has the largest population?

15. About how many times greater is the population of Georgia than the population of Alabama?

Writing in Math

16. About how many people live in Florida? Explain how you used the graph to find your answer.

Algebra

MULTIPLE CHOICE

17. Which number goes in the ▢ to complete the pattern?

81, 64, 49, ▢, 25, 16, ...

A. 36 **B.** 34 **C.** 31 **D.** 29

18. The sum of 2 and n is 45. Which equation models this sentence?

A. $2 + 2 = n$ **C.** $45 + n = 2$

B. $n + 45 = 2$ **D.** $2 + n = 45$

FREE RESPONSE

19. Complete the table and write the rule.

In	17	25	33	41
Out	8	16	24	

20. Bill used 4 toothpicks to make a square. He used 7 toothpicks to make 2 squares side-by-side, and 10 toothpicks to make 3 squares side-by-side. How many toothpicks will Bill use to make 4 squares side-by-side?

Think It Through

I can draw pictures to show the problem.

Writing in Math

21. Susan made 3 gallons of fruit punch. How many cups of fruit punch did she make? Explain how you found your answer.

Reteaching

Set 10-1 (pages 562–563)

Is the sum $\frac{3}{5} + \frac{3}{4}$ greater than or less than 1?

Compare each fraction to $\frac{1}{2}$.

$\frac{3}{5} > \frac{1}{2}$

$\frac{3}{4} > \frac{1}{2}$

$\frac{3}{5} + \frac{3}{4} > 1$

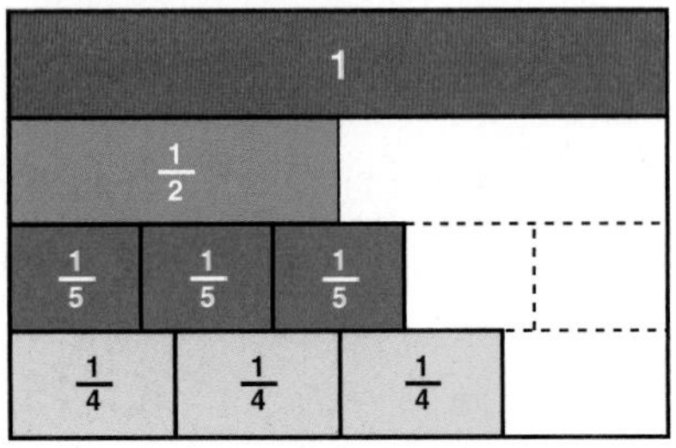

Because both fractions are greater than $\frac{1}{2}$, their sum is greater than 1.

Remember that when two fractions are both less than $\frac{1}{2}$, their sum is less than 1.

Write > or < for each ○.

1. $\frac{1}{8} + \frac{1}{4}$ ○ 1
2. $\frac{2}{9} + \frac{1}{3}$ ○ 1
3. $\frac{7}{10} + \frac{4}{5}$ ○ 1
4. $\frac{6}{7} + \frac{4}{7}$ ○ 1
5. $\frac{1}{8} + \frac{3}{11}$ ○ 1
6. $\frac{3}{4} + \frac{8}{12}$ ○ 1
7. Can you estimate to decide whether the sum $\frac{5}{7} + \frac{1}{3}$ is greater than or less than 1? Explain why or why not.

Set 10-2 (pages 564–567)

Find $\frac{5}{12} + \frac{3}{12}$.

1 Estimate.

$\frac{5}{12} < \frac{1}{2}$

$\frac{3}{12} < \frac{1}{2}$

$\frac{5}{12} + \frac{3}{12} < 1$

2 Add the numerators. Write the sum over the like denominator

$\frac{5}{12} + \frac{3}{12}$

$= \frac{8}{12}$

3 Simplify, if necessary.

$\frac{8}{12} = \frac{2}{3}$

Remember to write your answer in simplest form.

1. $\frac{1}{4} + \frac{2}{4}$
2. $\frac{1}{2} + \frac{1}{2}$
3. $\frac{5}{6} + \frac{3}{6}$
4. $\frac{7}{10} + \frac{1}{10}$
5. $\frac{3}{5} + \frac{1}{5}$
6. $\frac{2}{9} + \frac{4}{9}$
7. Sam used $\frac{3}{8}$ cup of white flour and $\frac{5}{8}$ cup of wheat flour. How much flour did he use in all?

Set 10-3 (pages 568–571)

Find $\frac{1}{3} + \frac{5}{6}$.

1 Find equivalent fractions with like denominators.

$\frac{1}{3} = \frac{2}{6}$

$\frac{5}{6} = \frac{5}{6}$

2 Add the numerators. Write the sum over the like denominator.

$\frac{2}{6} + \frac{5}{6} = \frac{7}{6}$

3 Simplify, if necessary.

$\frac{7}{6} = 1\frac{1}{6}$

Remember that you can estimate to check that your answer is reasonable.

1. $\frac{2}{7} + \frac{1}{2}$
2. $\frac{4}{5} + \frac{7}{10}$
3. $\frac{3}{4} + \frac{3}{8}$
4. $\frac{1}{6} + \frac{5}{12}$
5. Anita bought $\frac{5}{9}$ yard of black ribbon and $\frac{1}{3}$ yard of white ribbon. How much ribbon did she buy in all?

Set 10-4 (pages 576–577)

Find $\frac{7}{9} - \frac{4}{9}$.

1 Subtract the numerators. Write the difference over the like denominator.

$\frac{7}{9} - \frac{4}{9} = \frac{3}{9}$

2 Simplify, if necessary.

$\frac{3}{9} = \frac{1}{3}$

Remember that simplifying a fraction requires division.

1. $\frac{7}{8} - \frac{5}{8}$
2. $\frac{5}{6} - \frac{1}{6}$
3. $\frac{9}{10} - \frac{4}{10}$
4. $\frac{8}{9} - \frac{2}{9}$
5. Angela practiced piano for $\frac{3}{4}$ of an hour. Matthew practiced for $\frac{1}{4}$ of an hour. How much longer did Angela practice than Matthew?

Set 10-5 (pages 578–581)

Find $\frac{6}{8} - \frac{1}{2}$.

1 Find equivalent fractions with like denominators.

$\frac{6}{8} = \frac{6}{8}$

$\frac{1}{2} = \frac{4}{8}$

2 Subtract the equivalent fractions.

$\frac{6}{8} - \frac{4}{8} = \frac{2}{8}$

3 Simplify, if necessary.

$\frac{2}{8} = \frac{1}{4}$

Remember that you can also use fraction strips or draw pictures to subtract.

1. $\frac{7}{9} - \frac{2}{3}$
2. $\frac{3}{4} - \frac{1}{8}$
3. $\frac{4}{5} - \frac{3}{10}$
4. $\frac{1}{2} - \frac{1}{3}$
5. A beetle is $\frac{7}{12}$ inch wide. A ladybug is $\frac{1}{4}$ inch wide. What is the difference in the two insects' widths?

Set 10-6 (pages 584–585)

When you use logical reasoning to solve a problem, follow these steps.

Step 1: Make a chart with the needed labels.

Step 2: Fill in the chart with the information you are given.

Step 3: Use what you are given and reasoning to make conclusions.

Remember that there can only be one YES in each row and column of a logic chart.

1. Andrea, Bill, and Andy bought $\frac{3}{4}$ pound, $\frac{1}{3}$ pound, and $\frac{5}{6}$ pound of nuts. Andrea bought less than $\frac{1}{2}$ pound. Andy bought more than Bill. How much did each person buy?

Reteaching

Set 10-7 (pages 588–589)

What customary unit would you use to measure the length of a kitchen?

An inch is too small, and a yard and mile are too large. The length of a kitchen would be measured in feet.

Remember that you can visualize the length of an inch, a foot, and a yard to help solve a problem.

Choose the most appropriate unit to measure the length of each.

1. swimming pool **2.** scissors

3. mountain tunnel **4.** telephone pole

Set 10-8 (pages 590–591)

Measure this line segment to the nearest $\frac{1}{2}$ inch, $\frac{1}{4}$ inch, and $\frac{1}{8}$ inch.

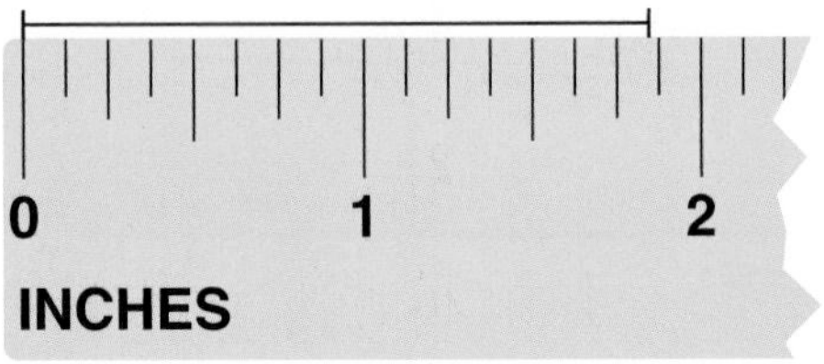

To the nearest $\frac{1}{2}$ inch = 2 inches long.

To the nearest $\frac{1}{4}$ inch = $1\frac{3}{4}$ inches long.

To the nearest $\frac{1}{8}$ inch = $1\frac{7}{8}$ inches long.

Remember that measuring to different fractions of an inch will not always give you different measurements.

Measure each line segment to the nearest $\frac{1}{2}$ inch, $\frac{1}{4}$ inch, and $\frac{1}{8}$ inch.

1.

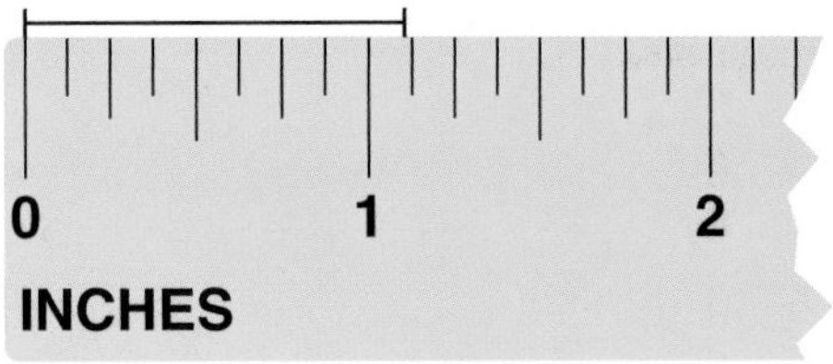

2.

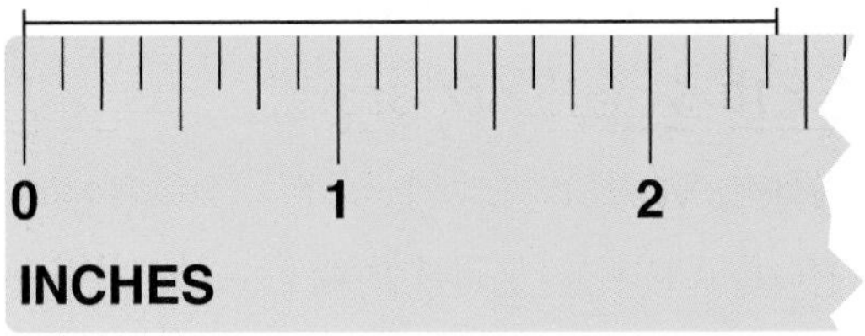

Set 10-9 (pages 592–593)

What is the most appropriate unit to measure the capacity of a sink—teaspoon, tablespoon, fluid ounce, cup, pint, quart, or gallon?

It would take more than 1 gallon to fill a sink, so a gallon is the best unit to use.

Remember capacity is the amount a container can hold.

Choose the most appropriate unit to measure the capacity of each. Write tsp, tbsp, fl oz, c, pt, qt, or gal.

1. swimming pool **2.** soup pot

3. juice box **4.** thimble

Set 10-10 (pages 594–595)

What customary unit would you use to find the weight of a dog—ounce, pound, or ton?

Think about an object that weighs each unit. Then compare to decide if that unit would be best to measure the weight of a dog.

You should use pounds to measure the weight of a dog.

Remember that a ton is equal to 2,000 pounds.

Choose the most appropriate unit to measure the weight of each. Write oz, lb, or T.

1. bowling ball

2. piece of chalk

3. mouse

4. elephant

Set 10-11 (pages 596–599)

How many inches are in 3 feet?

1 ft = 12 inches

3 feet = 3 × 12 inches

3 feet = 36 inches

How many pints are in 14 cups?

2 cups = 1 pint

14 cups = 7 pints

Remember to multiply to change larger units to smaller units.

Find each missing number.

1. 5 lb = ▢ oz

2. 12 ft = ▢ yd

3. 3 c = ▢ fl oz

4. 4 gal = ▢ pt

5. 3 T = ▢ lb

6. 2 yd = ▢ in.

7. 20 qt = ▢ gal

8. 6 tsp = ▢ tbsp

Set 10-12 (pages 600–601)

Paula has $60 to buy art supplies. She wants to buy colored pencils for $6.95, a pad of drawing paper for $12.50, and an easel for $47.25. Does she have enough money to buy all of the items?

Think: I only need to know if Paula has enough money to buy the items. So I only need an estimate of their total cost.

Estimate: $7 + $13 + $50 = $70.

$70 > $60. No, Paula does not have enough money to buy all of the items.

Remember that sometimes an estimate is all you need to solve a problem.

Tell whether an exact answer is needed or if an estimate is enough. Then solve.

1. Carl bought 5 pounds of ground beef. He will use 4 ounces to make each hamburger. Does he have enough beef to make 15 hamburgers?

2. Rosi bought 3 plants for $2.75 each. How much did she spend?

More Practice

Set 10-1 (pages 562–563)

Write > or < for each ●.

1. $\frac{1}{7} + \frac{2}{9}$ ● 1
2. $\frac{3}{4} + \frac{2}{3}$ ● 1
3. $\frac{7}{8} + \frac{6}{10}$ ● 1
4. $\frac{1}{4} + \frac{1}{5}$ ● 1
5. $\frac{10}{11} + \frac{9}{11}$ ● 1
6. $\frac{1}{3} + \frac{1}{6}$ ● 1
7. $\frac{5}{6} + \frac{4}{5}$ ● 1
8. $\frac{1}{8} + \frac{3}{7}$ ● 1
9. At the gym, Lisa stretched for a $\frac{1}{4}$ hour. Then she ran on the treadmill for $\frac{1}{2}$ hour. Did Lisa spend more or less than an hour stretching and running? Explain how you know.

Set 10-2 (pages 564–567)

Find each sum. Simplify, if necessary.

1. $\frac{2}{5} + \frac{1}{5}$
2. $\frac{4}{9} + \frac{1}{9}$
3. $\frac{3}{10} + \frac{4}{10}$
4. $\frac{7}{8} + \frac{5}{8}$
5. $\frac{1}{2} + \frac{1}{2}$
6. $\frac{1}{4} + \frac{3}{4}$
7. $\frac{6}{7} + \frac{5}{7}$
8. $\frac{2}{5} + \frac{4}{5}$
9. $\frac{11}{12} + \frac{9}{12}$
10. $\frac{3}{8} + \frac{3}{8}$
11. $\frac{3}{8} + \frac{5}{8}$
12. $\frac{25}{100} + \frac{50}{100}$
13. $\frac{5}{6} + \frac{5}{6}$
14. $\frac{2}{3} + \frac{1}{3}$
15. $\frac{9}{10} + \frac{7}{10}$
16. Bill bought $\frac{5}{8}$ of a yard of denim cloth. He already had $\frac{1}{8}$ of a yard of the same cloth. How much denim cloth does Bill now have altogether?

Set 10-3 (pages 568–571)

Find each sum. Simplify, if necessary.

1. $\frac{1}{8} + \frac{1}{4}$
2. $\frac{10}{12} + \frac{1}{6}$
3. $\frac{3}{5} + \frac{7}{10}$
4. $\frac{2}{3} + \frac{5}{9}$
5. $\frac{1}{2} + \frac{5}{6}$
6. $\frac{1}{10} + \frac{2}{5}$
7. $\frac{5}{12} + \frac{1}{6}$
8. $\frac{1}{2} + \frac{1}{5}$
9. $\frac{2}{3} + \frac{5}{12}$
10. $\frac{3}{4} + \frac{2}{6}$
11. $\frac{1}{3} + \frac{4}{9}$
12. $\frac{1}{2} + \frac{7}{8}$
13. $\frac{4}{5} + \frac{9}{10}$
14. $\frac{6}{7} + \frac{5}{14}$
15. $\frac{3}{16} + \frac{5}{8}$
16. Denise ate $\frac{1}{6}$ of a pizza. Sharon ate $\frac{1}{4}$ of the same pizza. How much of the whole pizza did they eat together?
17. Patrick added $\frac{3}{4}$ cup brown sugar and $\frac{7}{8}$ cup white sugar to his apple pie recipe. How much total sugar did he add to the recipe?

Set 10-4 (pages 574–577)

Find each difference. Simplify, if necessary.

1. $\frac{4}{7} - \frac{1}{7}$ **2.** $\frac{8}{11} - \frac{5}{11}$ **3.** $\frac{13}{20} - \frac{9}{20}$ **4.** $\frac{5}{6} - \frac{2}{6}$ **5.** $\frac{7}{9} - \frac{4}{9}$

6. $\frac{9}{12} - \frac{7}{12}$ **7.** $\frac{5}{8} - \frac{3}{8}$ **8.** $\frac{4}{5} - \frac{1}{5}$ **9.** $\frac{9}{10} - \frac{7}{10}$ **10.** $\frac{2}{3} - \frac{1}{3}$

11. Rachel added $\frac{1}{4}$ cup of butter to a mixing bowl. Then she realized that the recipe calls for $\frac{3}{4}$ cup of butter. How much more butter should Rachel add to the bowl?

Set 10-5 (pages 578–581)

Find each difference. Simplify, if necessary.

1. $\frac{7}{8} - \frac{1}{4}$ **2.** $\frac{6}{10} - \frac{1}{5}$ **3.** $\frac{8}{9} - \frac{1}{3}$ **4.** $\frac{5}{6} - \frac{1}{2}$ **5.** $\frac{1}{2} - \frac{1}{8}$

6. $\frac{7}{12} - \frac{1}{6}$ **7.** $\frac{3}{4} - \frac{1}{8}$ **8.** $\frac{9}{10} - \frac{15}{100}$ **9.** $\frac{5}{6} - \frac{2}{3}$ **10.** $\frac{11}{12} - \frac{2}{3}$

11. $\begin{array}{r} \frac{1}{3} \\ -\frac{1}{6} \\ \hline \end{array}$ **12.** $\begin{array}{r} \frac{3}{8} \\ -\frac{1}{4} \\ \hline \end{array}$ **13.** $\begin{array}{r} \frac{11}{12} \\ -\frac{5}{6} \\ \hline \end{array}$ **14.** $\begin{array}{r} \frac{3}{4} \\ -\frac{3}{8} \\ \hline \end{array}$ **15.** $\begin{array}{r} \frac{7}{10} \\ -\frac{1}{2} \\ \hline \end{array}$

16. Jennifer bought $\frac{4}{5}$ pound of cashews. She gave $\frac{1}{2}$ pound to her sister. How much did Jennifer have left?

Set 10-6 (pages 584–585)

Make a chart and use logical reasoning to solve. Write the answer in a complete sentence.

1. Last year, all teams in a baseball league played the same number of games. The Tigers, Lions, and Bears had the best records. They won $\frac{7}{10}$, $\frac{5}{9}$, and $\frac{1}{2}$ of their games. The Tigers had the best record. The Lions won fewer games than the Bears. What fraction of their games did each team win?

2. A pet store has four snakes named Victor, Annie, Bob, and Carl. They are a python, cobra, anaconda, and boa constrictor. Carl is a boa constrictor, and Annie is not a cobra. If Victor is an anaconda, what is Bob?

More Practice

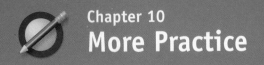

Set 10-7 (pages 588–589)

Estimate first. Then, find each length to the nearest inch.

1. 

2.

Choose the most appropriate unit to measure the length of each. Write in., ft, yd, or mi.

3. soccer field
4. automobile
5. toothbrush
6. river
7. Tim has a ruler and a yardstick. Which would be the best tool to measure the length of a school bus? Explain your answer.

Set 10-8 (pages 590–591)

Measure each ribbon to the nearest $\frac{1}{2}$ inch, $\frac{1}{4}$ inch, and $\frac{1}{8}$ inch.

1. 

2. 

3. 

4. 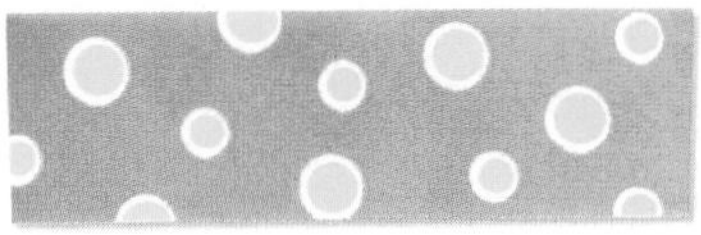

5. Jack says that the line segment at the right is 2 inches long. Did he measure it to the nearest $\frac{1}{2}$ inch or nearest inch? Explain.

Set 10-9 (pages 592–593)

Choose the most appropriate unit or units to measure the capacity of each. Write tsp, tbsp, fl oz, c, pt, qt, or gal.

1. aquarium
2. eye dropper
3. small milk container
4. flour in a recipe
5. bathtub
6. ice cube tray
7. Which is larger, a teaspoon or a tablespoon?
8. The yellow thermos at right holds 16 fluid ounces of water. About how much water can the green thermos hold? Explain how you estimated.

Take It to the NET
More Practice
www.scottforesman.com

Set 10-10 (pages 594–595)

Choose the most appropriate unit or units to measure the weight of each. Write oz, lb, or T.

1. granola bar **2.** canary **3.** bag of flour

4. delivery truck **5.** television **6.** eraser

7. Name three different animals for which an ounce, a pound, and a ton would be the most appropriate units to measure their weights. Tell which animal goes with each unit of weight.

Set 10-11 (pages 596–599)

Find each missing number.

1. 7 ft = ■ in. **2.** 5 c = ■ fl oz **3.** 15 lb = ■ oz

4. 24 pt = ■ gal **5.** 6,000 lb = ■ T **6.** 5 mi = ■ yd

Compare. Write > or < for each ●.

7. 4 ft 3 in. ● 48 in. **8.** 50 lb ● 1,000 oz **9.** 12 tsp ● 6 tbsp

10. 30 pt ● 10 qt **11.** 4,000 yd ● 1 mi **12.** 2 T ● 2,100 lb

13. Shawn is 68 inches tall. Brent is 5 feet 9 inches tall. Who is taller?

Set 10-12 (pages 600–601)

Tell whether an exact answer is needed or if an estimate is enough. Then solve. Write your answer in a complete sentence.

1. Carla brought 2 gallons of juice to the soccer game. Each player will drink 2 cups of juice. Did Carla bring enough juice for the 15 players?

2. Anita bought 2 pounds of sliced turkey for $6.75 a pound and 3 pounds of sliced ham for $5.99 a pound. She also bought a loaf of bread for $1.57. If Anita paid with two $20 bills, how much change did she get back?

3. William has $100.00 to buy tennis equipment. He wants to buy a racket for $75.99, a sun visor for $8.99, and two cans of tennis balls for $3.50 each. Does he have enough money to buy all the equipment?

CHAPTER 11

Decimals and Metric Measurement

DIAGNOSING READINESS

A Vocabulary
(page 28, Gr. 3)

Choose the best term from the box.

1. A metric unit used to measure the length of small objects is a __?__.

2. The decimal 1.38 has a three in the __?__ place and an eight in the __?__ place.

3. The basic metric unit of capacity is the __?__.

Vocabulary

- **centimeter** *(Gr. 3)*
- **hundredths** *(p. 28)*
- **meter** *(Gr. 3)*
- **gram** *(Gr. 3)*
- **liter** *(Gr. 3)*
- **tenths** *(p. 28)*

B Decimals *(Gr. 3)*

Write a decimal for each shaded part.

4.

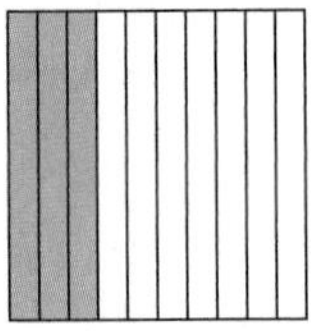

5.

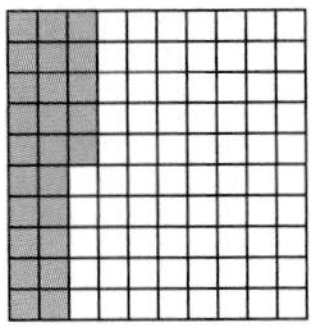

Write each as a decimal.

6. sixteen hundredths

7. three and four tenths

Compare. Use <, >, or =.

8.

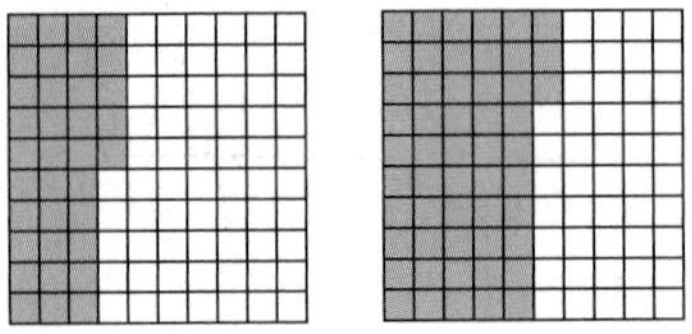

0.35 ● 0.53

Do You Know...

What fraction of Earth's land is covered by woodlands?

You will find out in Lesson 11-15.

C Add and Subtract Decimals

(Gr. 3)

Add or subtract.

9. $\begin{array}{r} 2.4 \\ +\ 3.1 \\ \hline \end{array}$

10. $\begin{array}{r} 5.8 \\ -\ 1.7 \\ \hline \end{array}$

11. $\begin{array}{r} 0.82 \\ +\ 0.16 \\ \hline \end{array}$

12. $\begin{array}{r} 0.45 \\ -\ 0.24 \\ \hline \end{array}$

13. $\begin{array}{r} 1.39 \\ +\ 1.52 \\ \hline \end{array}$

14. $\begin{array}{r} 2.70 \\ -\ 1.38 \\ \hline \end{array}$

15. Karen bought 3.8 pounds of peanuts and 2.4 pounds of cashews. How many pounds of nuts did she buy in all? How much more peanuts did she buy than cashews?

D Metric Units of Measure *(Gr. 3)*

Choose the best estimate for each measurement.

16. length of a bike trail — **A.** 3 m
17. length of a worm — **B.** 3 km
18. length of a bench — **C.** 3 cm

19. capacity of a spoon — **A.** 5 L
20. capacity of a bathtub — **B.** 5 mL
21. capacity of a soup pot — **C.** 500 L

22. mass of a dime — **A.** 2 kg
23. mass of a dog — **B.** 20 kg
24. mass of a bag of flour — **C.** 2 g

Key Idea
Decimals and fractions can be used to name the same amounts.

Vocabulary
- hundredths (p. 28)
- tenths (p. 28)
- equivalent

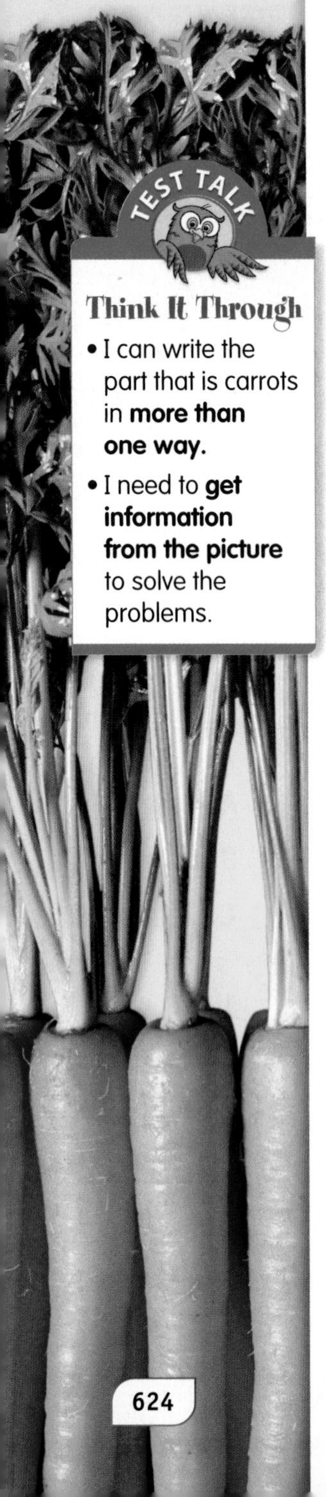

TEST TALK

Think It Through
- I can write the part that is carrots in **more than one way.**
- I need to **get information from the picture** to solve the problems.

Decimals and Fractions

WARM UP

Multiply or divide to find an equivalent fraction.

1. $\frac{4}{5}$
2. $\frac{25}{100}$
3. $\frac{5}{10}$
4. $\frac{3}{20}$

LEARN

How are decimals and fractions related?

Dawn has divided her vegetable garden into 5 equal parts. The grid below shows how she planted her garden.

Example A

Write a fraction for the part of the garden that is carrots.

$\frac{20}{100}$ ← Parts that are orange for carrots / ← Parts in all

$$\frac{20}{100} \overset{\div 20}{=} \frac{1}{5}$$ Write the fraction in simplest form.

$\frac{20}{100}$ or $\frac{1}{5}$ of the garden is carrots.

Example B

Write a decimal for the part of the garden that is carrots.

20 out of 100 parts are orange for carrots.

Twenty **hundredths** or 0.20 is orange.

Also, 2 out of 10 parts are orange. Two **tenths** or 0.2 is orange.

0.20 or 0.2 of the garden is carrots.

The numbers $\frac{20}{100}$, $\frac{1}{5}$, 0.20, and 0.2 are **equivalent.** Numbers that are equivalent name the same amount.

$$\frac{20}{100} = \frac{1}{5} = 0.20 = 0.2$$

Talk About It

1. Are the word names for $\frac{20}{100}$ and 0.20 the same?

How do you change between fractions and decimals?

Example C

Write 0.4 as a fraction in simplest form.

0.4 is four tenths or $\frac{4}{10}$.

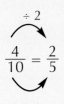

$$\frac{4}{10} \overset{\div 2}{=} \frac{2}{5}$$

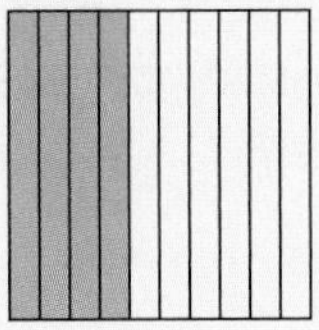

$0.4 = \frac{2}{5}$

Example D

Write $\frac{3}{4}$ as a decimal.

First, write $\frac{3}{4}$ as an equivalent fraction with a denominator of 100.

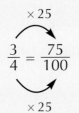

$$\frac{3}{4} \overset{\times 25}{=} \frac{75}{100}$$

Some fractions can be written with a denominator of 100.

75 out of 100 is 0.75.

So, $\frac{3}{4} = 0.75$.

I can think about money to remember decimal equivalents for the benchmark fractions $\frac{1}{2}$, $\frac{1}{4}$, and $\frac{3}{4}$.

$\frac{1}{2}$ of \$1 = \$0.50 or 0.5

$\frac{1}{4}$ of \$1 = \$0.25

$\frac{3}{4}$ of \$1 = \$0.75

You can write mixed numbers as decimals and decimals as mixed numbers.

Since $\frac{3}{4} = 0.75$, $2\frac{3}{4} = 2.75$.

Since $0.4 = \frac{2}{5}$, $7.4 = 7\frac{2}{5}$.

Talk About It

2. In Example C, why does $0.4 = \frac{4}{10}$?

3. In Example D, why is $\frac{3}{4}$ written as a fraction with a denominator of 100 and not a denominator of 10?

CHECK

For another example, see Set 11-1 on p. 678.

Write a fraction and a decimal for the part of each grid that is blue.

1. 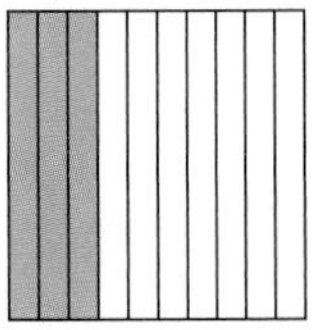

2. 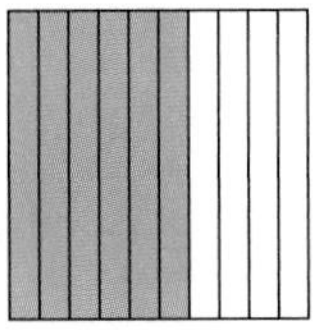

3. 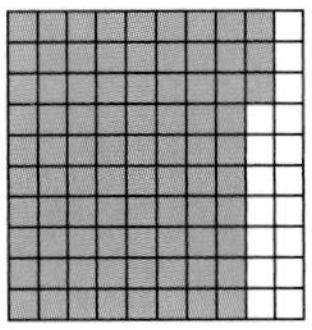

4. 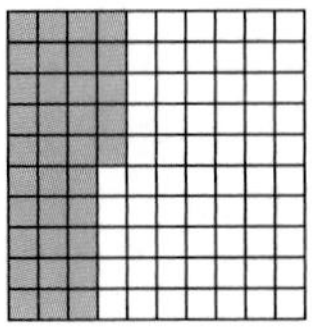

Write each number as a decimal.

5. $\frac{7}{10}$

6. $3\frac{19}{100}$

Write each decimal as a fraction or mixed number, in simplest form.

7. 0.56

8. 2.7

9. Reasoning How can you write $\frac{6}{5}$ as a decimal?

PRACTICE

For more practice, see Set 11-1 on p. 682.

A Skills and Understanding

Write a fraction and a decimal for the part of each grid that is blue.

10. 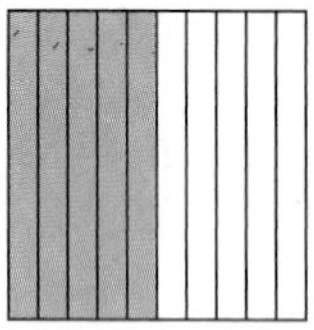

11. 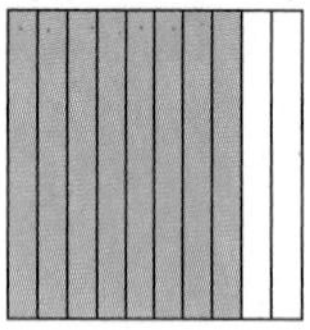

12. 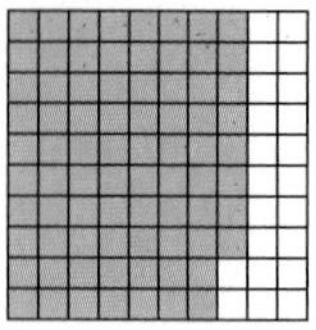

13. 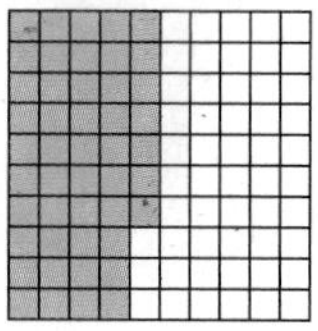

Write each number as a decimal.

14. $\frac{30}{100}$ **15.** $\frac{3}{100}$ **16.** $\frac{7}{20}$ **17.** $\frac{4}{5}$

18. $\frac{1}{2}$ **19.** $\frac{1}{4}$ **20.** $7\frac{4}{100}$ **21.** $6\frac{2}{100}$

Write each decimal as a fraction or mixed number, in simplest form.

22. 0.73 **23.** 0.27 **24.** 0.6 **25.** 0.2

26. 0.15 **27.** 0.16 **28.** 3.25 **29.** 6.5

30. Number Sense Name six numbers that are equivalent to 0.5. Include at least one fraction and one other decimal.

B Reasoning and Problem Solving

Math and Social Studies

Use the data file at the right for 31–34.

A person who can read and write is literate. Write a decimal for the fraction of the population that is literate in

31. Russia. **32.** Argentina.

33. Central African Republic.

34. Which fraction in the data file is not in simplest form? Write it in simplest form.

Data File

Literacy Rates

Country	Fraction of Population That Is Literate
Argentina	$\frac{24}{25}$
Central African Republic	$\frac{3}{5}$
Russia	$\frac{99}{100}$
United States	$\frac{97}{100}$
Brazil	$\frac{90}{100}$

35. Writing in Math Is the answer below correct? If not, tell why and write a correct response. If so, draw a picture to show why the numbers are equal and explain your picture.

Does $\frac{7}{10}$ = 0.70?

Yes, 0.70 = 0.7. Both are seven tenths.

Think It Through
I should make sure my **explanation is clear and complete.**

C Extensions

Percent means *per one hundred* or *out of one hundred.* In the grid at the right, 25 out of 100 squares are shaded, or 25 percent is shaded. You can write 25 percent as 25%.

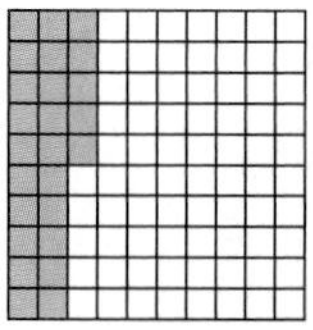

$25\% = 0.25 = \frac{25}{100} = \frac{1}{4}$

Write a fraction, a decimal, and a percent for the part of each grid that is blue.

36. 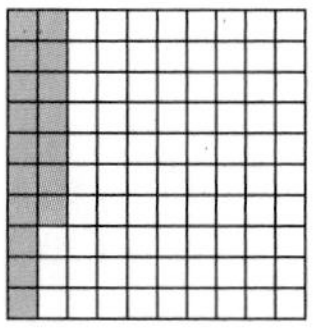

37. 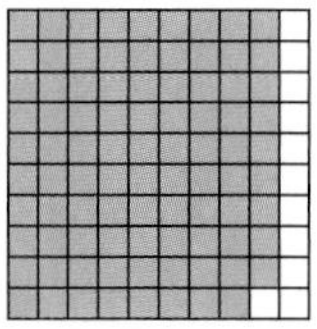

38. 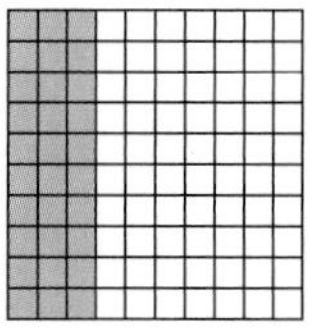

39. 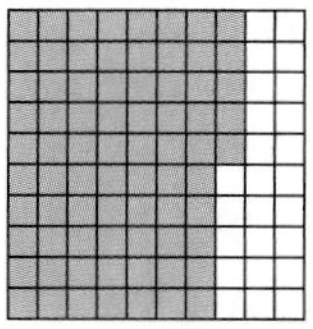

Mixed Review and Test Prep

Take It to the NET
Test Prep
www.scottforesman.com

40. Chris ran $\frac{1}{3}$ mile one day and $\frac{2}{5}$ mile the next. Did he run one mile in all? Tell whether an exact answer is needed or if an estimate is enough. Then, solve.

41. What is the perimeter of a rectangle 4 inches long and 2 inches wide?

A. 6 inches **B.** 8 inches **C.** 10 inches **D.** 12 inches

Discovery CHANNEL SCHOOL™

Discover Math in Your World

Branch Out

The world's largest living thing, the General Sherman Giant Sequoia is in Sequoia National Park in California. In 1978, a 140-foot branch fell off this tree. The branch had a radius of 3.25 feet, a diameter of $6\frac{1}{2}$ feet, and a length of 140 feet. This branch would be a large tree in some parts of the United States.

1. Write $6\frac{1}{2}$ as a decimal.

2. Write 3.25 as a fraction.

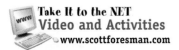

Take It to the NET
Video and Activities
www.scottforesman.com

Key Idea
There are many ways to represent decimal numbers.

TEST TALK

Think It Through
I can **use objects, draw pictures,** or **make a chart** to represent 1.48.

Decimal Place Value

WARM UP

Tell the value of the red digit for each number.

1. 8,264
2. 17,932
3. 2,925
4. 5,924

LEARN

What are some ways to represent decimals?

Here are different ways to represent 1.48.

Number line:

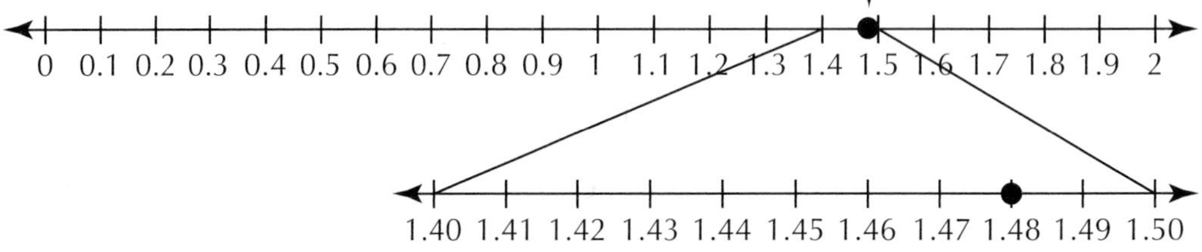

Grids:

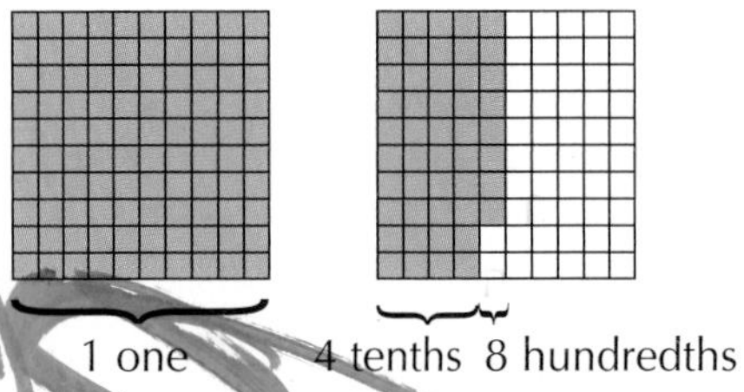

Place-value chart:

tens	ones	.	tenths	hundredths
	1	.	4	8

Expanded form: 1 + 0.4 + 0.08

Standard form: 1.48

Word form: One and forty-eight hundredths

Example

Write the word form and the expanded form for 5.02. Then, tell the value of the red digit.

Word form: five and two hundredths

Expanded form: 5 + 0.02

The red digit is in the hundredths place, so its value is 2 hundredths, 0.02.

I write the word ***and*** *for the decimal point.*

Talk About It

1. Which digit is in the tenths place in 1.48?
2. Explain how to locate 1.48 on a number line.

Take It to the NET
More Examples
www.scottforesman.com

CHECK

For another example, see Set 11-2 on p. 678.

1. Write eight and seven hundredths in standard form.
2. Write the word form and tell the value of the red digit for 25.82.
3. **Reasoning** Write a number that has a 3 in the tens place and a 4 in the tenths place.

PRACTICE

For more practice, see Set 11-2 on p. 682.

A Skills and Understanding

Write each number in standard form.

4. Twelve and fifty-three hundredths **5.** 30 + 6 + 0.8 + 0.09

Write the word form and tell the value of the red digit for each number.

6. 4.27 **7.** 5.56 **8.** 46.91 **9.** 19.03

10. Number Sense Kevin said a number was six tenths, four hundredths. What is the word form for Kevin's number?

B Reasoning and Problem Solving

Write the word form for each decimal measure.

11.

0.86 lb

12.

3.78 L

13.

2.25 yd

14. Writing in Math Kayla found a pattern in decimal and whole number place values. Using Kayla's pattern, what place do you think is right of hundredths? Explain.

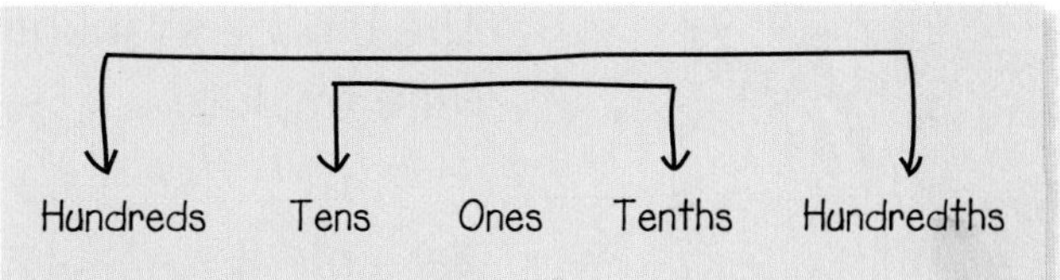

Mixed Review and Test Prep

Take It to the NET
Test Prep
www.scottforesman.com

Write each number as a decimal.

15. $\frac{9}{10}$ **16.** $3\frac{7}{100}$ **17.** $\frac{65}{100}$ **18.** $2\frac{75}{100}$

19. Kay bought 24 jump ropes. Each jump rope cost $1.27. How much did she spend?

A. $7.62 **B.** $19.28 **C.** $30.48 **D.** $30.98

Key Idea
Place value can help you compare and order decimals.

Comparing and Ordering Decimals

WARM UP

Tell the value of the red digit for each number.

1. 0.46
2. 0.79
3. 6.08
4. 3.84

LEARN

How do you compare and order decimals?

Fishing lures are sold by their weight.

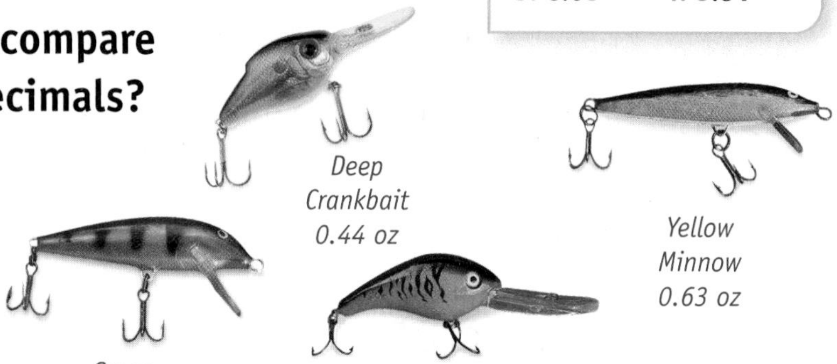

TEST TALK

Think It Through
I can compare decimals in **more than one way.**

Example A

Which lure is heavier, Yellow Minnow or Diving Crankbait?

Compare 0.63 ounce and 0.69 ounce.

One Way: Use grids.

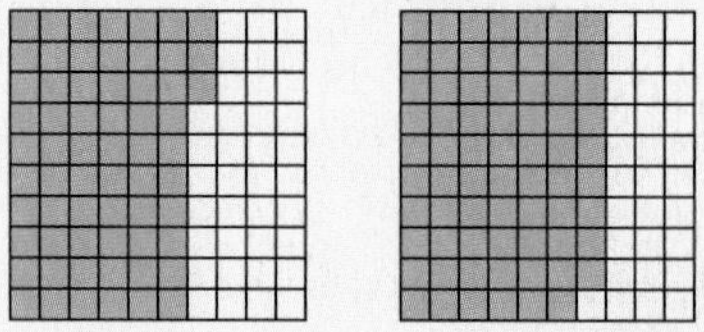

63 hundredths < 69 hundredths

0.63 < 0.69

Another Way: Use place value.

Begin at the left and find the first place where the digits are different. Compare.

0.63 0.69

3 hundredths < 9 hundredths

0.63 < 0.69

The Diving Crankbait lure is heavier than the Yellow Minnow lure.

Example B

I know 0.5 = 0.50

Put the weights of the fishing lures in order from least to greatest.

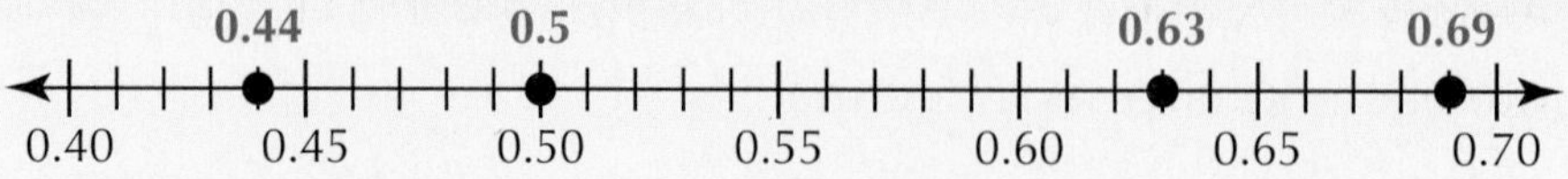

From least to greatest, the weights are 0.44, 0.5, 0.63, 0.69.

Talk About It

1. Which lure weighs the least?

Take It to the NET
More Examples
www.scottforesman.com

CHECK

For another example, see Set 11-3 on p. 678.

Compare. Write >, <, or = for each ●.

1. 0.56 ● 0.71 **2.** 1.48 ● 0.49 **3.** 3.76 ● 3.67 **4.** 0.30 ● 0.3

Order the numbers from least to greatest.

5. 0.85, 0.89, 0.9, 0.8 **6.** 0.25, 0.4, 0.04, 0.35 **7.** 1.7, 1.07, 1.75

8. Number Sense Which is greater, 0.9 or 0.09? Explain.

PRACTICE

For more practice, see Set 11-3 on p. 682.

A Skills and Understanding

Compare. Write >, <, or = for each ●.

9. 0.81 ● 0.76 **10.** 0.36 ● 0.39 **11.** 2.98 ● 3.79 **12.** 3.24 ● 3.42

13. 8.32 ● 7.46 **14.** 4.01 ● 4.1 **15.** 6.19 ● 5.19 **16.** 7.6 ● 7.60

Order the numbers from least to greatest.

17. 3.5, 2.2, 1.9 **18.** 4.7, 5.6, 3.8 **19.** 1.54, 1.45, 1.58

20. 2.24, 2.28, 2.21 **21.** 0.7, 0.9, 0.75, 0.78 **22.** 0.62, 0.6, 0.5, 0.67

23. Number Sense Which is greater, 15.99 or 16?

B Reasoning and Problem Solving

Lengths of Fish Caught

Fish A	11.75 inches
Fish B	12.5 inches
Fish C	11.5 inches
Fish D	11.25 inches

Which fish is longer?

24. Fish A or B **25.** Fish B or C **26.** Fish C or D

27. Show all the fish sizes on a number line.

28. **Writing in Math** What place would you use to compare 2.77 and 2.57? What about 2.77 and 2.75? Explain.

Mixed Review and Test Prep

Take It to the NET
Test Prep
www.scottforesman.com

Write the word form and tell the value of the red digit for each number.

29. 8,273,521 **30.** 0.19 **31.** 2.64 **32.** 35.4

33. Round 765,293 to the nearest ten thousand.

A. 765,290 **B.** 760,000 **C.** 770,000 **D.** 800,000

Key Idea
Place value can help you round decimals

Rounding Decimals

LEARN

How do you round decimals?

Sally's class uses the carpet below in their reading area.

3.43 meters wide

4.68 meters long

	Example A	Example B
	Round the width of the carpet to the nearest whole meter.	Round the length of the carpet to the nearest tenth of a meter.
STEP 1 Find the rounding place.	<u>3</u>.43 ↑ 3 is in the ones place.	4.<u>6</u>8 ↑ 6 is in the tenths place.
STEP 2 Look at the digit to the right. If it is 5 or more, change to the next greatest digit. If it is less than 5, leave the number as is.	<u>3</u>.43 ↑ Leave the number as is, since 4 < 5. 3.43 rounds to 3. The carpet is about 3 meters wide.	4.<u>6</u>8 ↑ Change 6 to 7, since 8 > 5. 4.68 rounds to 4.7. The carpet is about 4.7 meters long.

The number line shows that 4.68 is closer to 4.7 than 4.6.

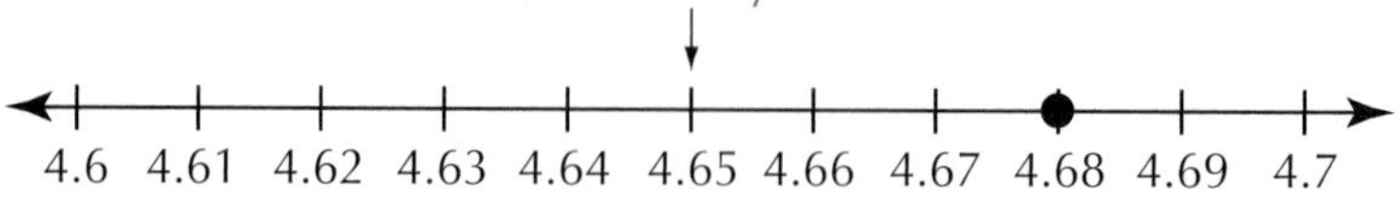

Think It Through
I can **draw** a number line to find the closest number.

WARM UP

Round each number to the nearest thousand.

1. 5,422 **2.** 8,567

3. 19,026 **4.** 47,912

Talk About It

1. Explain why 3.43 rounds to 3 and not 4.

2. What is the halfway number between 4.6 and 4.7?

CHECK

For another example, see Set 11-4 on p. 679.

Round each number to the nearest whole number and to the nearest tenth.

1. 0.83 **2.** 0.76 **3.** 34.33 **4.** 72.56 **5.** 87.12

6. Number Sense Is 55.5 closer to 55 or 56? What about 55.51? Explain.

PRACTICE

For more practice, see Set 11-4 on p. 683.

A Skills and Understanding

Round each number to the nearest whole number.

7. 67.8 **8.** 23.4 **9.** 0.8 **10.** 0.9 **11.** 51.70

12. 21.7 **13.** 35.56 **14.** 7.58 **15.** 10.75 **16.** 20.92

Round each number to the nearest tenth.

17. 0.94 **18.** 4.71 **19.** 8.65 **20.** 0.85 **21.** 14.06

22. Number Sense Write five numbers that round to 2, when rounded to the nearest whole number.

B Reasoning and Problem Solving

For each city in the data file at the right, round the inches of precipitation to the nearest

23. whole inch. **24.** tenth of an inch.

25. Which of the cities has the least precipitation in a year? Which has the most?

26. Writing in Math Use a number line to explain why 0.35 rounded to the nearest whole number is 0.

Data File

Average Yearly Precipitation

City	Inches
Houston, TX	46.07
Los Angeles, CA	14.77
Miami, FL	55.91
Reno, NV	7.53
Richmond, VA	43.16
Washington, D.C.	38.63

Mixed Review and Test Prep

Take It to the NET
Test Prep
www.scottforesman.com

Compare. Write >, <, or = for each ●.

27. 31,462 ● 32,540 **28.** $\frac{3}{4}$ ● $\frac{3}{8}$ **29.** $2\frac{2}{3}$ ● $2\frac{4}{9}$

30. 4.62 ● 6.24 **31.** 0.5 ● 0.53 **32.** 8.29 ● 8.37

33. After Jeb ate 6 grapes he had 24 left. How many grapes did Jeb have to start?

A. 4 grapes **B.** 18 grapes **C.** 30 grapes **D.** 32 grapes

Review

Do You Know How?

Decimals and Fractions (11-1)

Write each number as a decimal.

1. $\frac{3}{5}$ **2.** $2\frac{17}{100}$ **3.** $1\frac{7}{10}$

Write each decimal as a fraction or mixed number, in simplest form.

4. 0.85 **5.** 3.08 **6.** 2.6

Decimal Place Value (11-2)

Write each number in standard form.

7. four and thirteen hundredths

8. 10 + 8 + 0.3 + 0.07

Write the word form and tell the value of the red digit for each number.

9. 27.49 **10.** 3.18 **11.** 15.93

Comparing and Ordering Decimals (11-3)

Compare. Write >, <, or = for each ●.

12. 0.42 ● 0.47 **13.** 0.9 ● 0.90

14. 4.18 ● 4.2 **15.** 3.45 ● 3.43

16. Order 0.66, 0.63, 0.56, 0.65 from least to greatest.

Rounding Decimals (11-4)

Round each number to the nearest whole number and the nearest tenth.

17. 15.34 **18.** 3.55 **19.** 6.03

Do You Understand?

A Tell how you found the decimal in Exercise 1.

B Tell how you found the mixed number in Exercise 5.

C Name the place value position to the right of the ones place.

D How would you write 4 + 0.08 in standard form?

E Explain how you compared the decimals in Exercise 15.

F How did you use place value to find the least number in Exercise 16?

G What is the halfway number between 3.6 and 3.7?

H Explain why 3.66 rounds to 3.7 and not 3.6.

Diagnostic Checkpoint

TEST TALK

Think It Through

I can **use objects, draw pictures,** or **make a chart** to represent decimals.

MULTIPLE CHOICE

1. Which decimal is equivalent to $1\frac{5}{100}$? (11-1)

A. 0.05 **B.** 1.05 **C.** 1.15 **D.** 1.5

2. Which decimal has a 2 in the tenths place? (11-2)

A. 34.52 **B.** 62.87 **C.** 23.01 **D.** 15.29

FREE RESPONSE

Write each decimal as a fraction or mixed number, in simplest form. (11-1)

3. 0.28 **4.** 2.16 **5.** 0.1 **6.** 3.55

Write each number in standard form. (11-2)

7. 20 + 7 + 0.4 + 0.01 **8.** one and thirty-two hundredths

Write the word form and tell the value of the red digit for each number. (11-2)

9. 0.25 **10.** 22.8 **11.** 1.94 **12.** 42.36

Write >, <, or = for each ●. (11-3)

13. 1.26 ● 1.51 **14.** 6.92 ● 6.91

Order the numbers from least to greatest. (11-3)

15. 0.76, 0.67, 0.75 **16.** 2.37, 2.41, 1.23, 2.33

Round each number to the nearest whole number and nearest tenth. (11-4)

17. 20.6 **18.** 9.73 **19.** 6.07 **20.** 12.11

Use the information at the right for 21–23. (11-3 and 11-4)

Which student ran the race in the least amount of time?

21. Paul or Michael? **22.** Paul or Elliot?

23. Order the students from 1st to 4th place.

Results of Fun Day Race

Runner	Seconds
Paul	58.61
Andrew	59.02
Elliot	58.15
Michael	57.85

Writing in Math

24. Explain why $\frac{9}{20}$ and 0.45 are equivalent. (11-1)

25. Explain why 7.06 and 7.6 are not equivalent. (11-2)

Key Idea
To estimate, you change numbers to the ones that are easy to add and subtract.

TEST TALK

Think It Through

- I can **use what I know** about estimating whole number sums and differences to estimate decimal sums and differences.
- I need to **use information from the picture** to solve the problems.

Estimating Decimal Sums and Differences

WARM UP

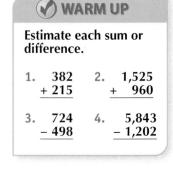

Estimate each sum or difference.

1. 382 + 215
2. 1,525 + 960
3. 724 − 498
4. 5,843 − 1,202

LEARN

How do you estimate when you add and subtract decimals?

Sara lives close to school and the park.

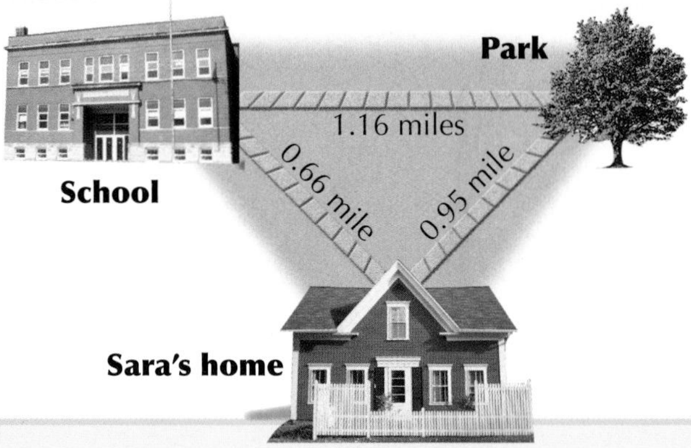

Example A

About how far does Sara walk if she walks to the park after school and then home?

Estimate by rounding to the nearest whole number.

1.16 + 0.95
↓ ↓
1 + 1 = 2 Sara walks about 2 miles.

Example B

About how much farther does Sara walk when she walks to the park and then home for 5 days, a total of 10.55 miles, than when she walks directly home for 5 days, a total of 3.3 miles?

Estimate by rounding to the nearest whole number.

10.55 − 3.3
↓ ↓
11 − 3 = 8 Sara walks about 8 miles farther.

✓ Talk About It

1. Explain why 1.2 and 0.85 both round to 1.
2. **Reasoning** How would you estimate 3.1 − 0.2?

Take It to the NET
More Examples
www.scottforesman.com

CHECK ✓

For another example, see Set 11-5 on p. 679.

Estimate each sum or difference.

1. 3.4 + 5.6 **2.** 7.21 + 8.9 **3.** 2.45 − 1.36 **4.** 7.85 − 3.28

5. Number Sense Tina estimated 2.15 + 1.38 by adding 2 + 1. Did she find an overestimate or an underestimate? Explain.

PRACTICE

For more practice, see Set 11-5 on p. 683.

A Skills and Understanding

Estimate each sum or difference.

6. 0.51 + 0.76 **7.** 4.8 + 0.9 **8.** 15.84 − 8.34 **9.** 4.1 − 1.63

10. 15.3 + 4.74 **11.** 11.92 + 13.4 **12.** 8.94 − 2.33 **13.** 3.37 − 0.8

14. $\begin{array}{r} 3.1 \\ +\ 6.8 \\ \hline \end{array}$ **15.** $\begin{array}{r} 8.08 \\ +\ 4.25 \\ \hline \end{array}$ **16.** $\begin{array}{r} 12.5 \\ -\ 11.4 \\ \hline \end{array}$ **17.** $\begin{array}{r} 4.38 \\ -\ 1.87 \\ \hline \end{array}$ **18.** $\begin{array}{r} 12.01 \\ +\ \ 0.99 \\ \hline \end{array}$

19. Number Sense Brett estimated 8.8 − 6.2 by subtracting 9 − 6 = 3. Did he find an overestimate or an underestimate? Explain.

B Reasoning and Problem Solving

To the nearest mile per hour, how much faster was the record set on October 15, 1997 than the record set on

20. September 25, 1997?

21. October 4, 1983?

22. October 23, 1970?

23. Writing in Math Explain how to estimate 5.68 + 3.4 + 12.97.

Data File

One-Mile Land Speed Records

Date	Speed in Miles per Hour
Oct. 23, 1970	622.41
Oct. 4, 1983	633.47
Sept. 25, 1997	714.14
Oct. 15, 1997	763.04

Mixed Review and Test Prep

Take It to the NET
Test Prep
www.scottforesman.com

Round each number to the nearest tenth.

24. 0.87 **25.** 15.24 **26.** 47.31 **27.** 63.09

28. Algebra Evaluate $a + 17$ for $a = 25$.

A. 8 **B.** 32 **C.** 42 **D.** 425

Key Idea
Adding and subtracting decimals is similar to adding and subtracting whole numbers and money.

Materials
- grid paper
- crayons or markers

Think It Through
I can **use objects** or **draw pictures** to add and subtract decimals.

Using Grids to Add and Subtract Decimals

WARM UP

Tell the value of the red digit for each number.

1. 4.32 2. 8.4
3. 17.6 4. 9.18

LEARN

How do you add decimals with grids?

Activity

Here's how to use a hundredths grid to add 0.4 + 0.32.

Step 1: Shade 4 columns of 10 squares to show 0.4.

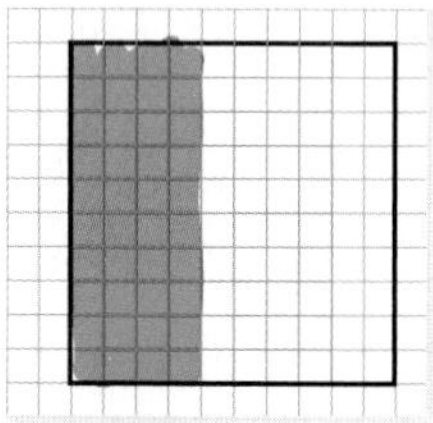

Step 2: Using a different color, shade 32 squares to show 0.32.

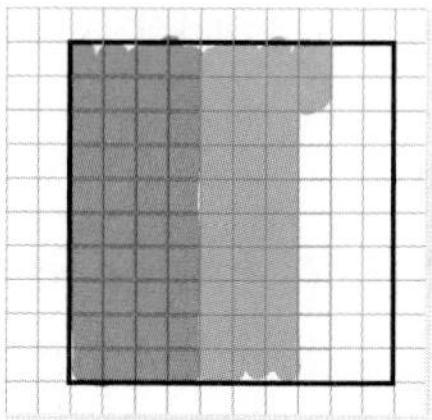

0.4 + 0.32 = 0.72

Step 3: Count all the shaded squares. How many hundredths are shaded in all? Write the decimal for the total number of shaded squares.

Here's how to use hundredths grids to add 0.68 + 0.67.

Shade 68 squares to show 0.68. Use a different color. Shade 67 more squares to show 0.67. Count the shaded squares.

0.68 + 0.67 = 1.35

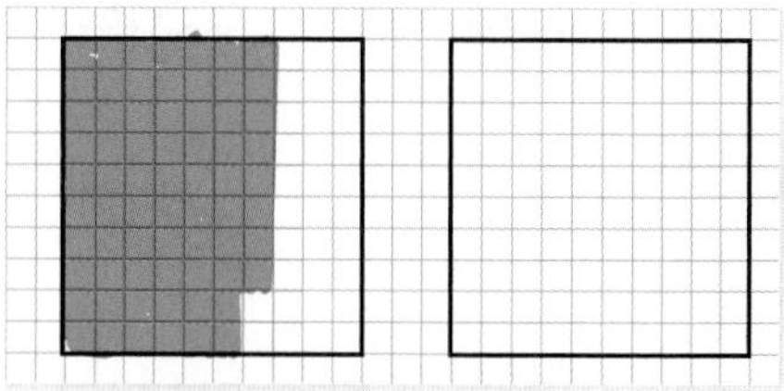

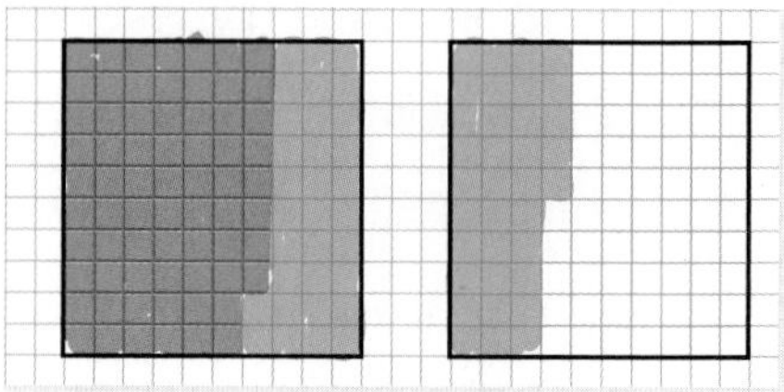

a. Use grids to add.

1.16 + 0.59	0.84 + 0.47	1.62 + 1.78
0.48 + 0.25	1.5 + 0.34	2.32 + 0.9

How do you subtract decimals with grids?

Use the data file at the right. How much longer is the Akashi Kaikyo Bridge than the Golden Gate Bridge?

Data File

Suspension Bridges

Bridge	Country	Length in Miles
Akashi Kaikyo	Japan	2.4
Golden Gate	U.S.A.	1.7
Bosphorus II	Turkey	0.68
Bosphorus I	Turkey	0.67

Activity

Here's how to subtract 2.4 − 1.7 with hundred grids.

Step 1: Shade two grids and 40 squares on another grid to show 2.4.

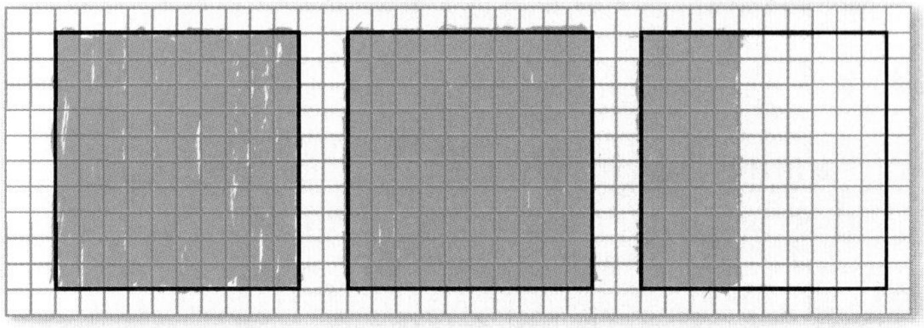

Step 2: Cross out 17 columns of shaded grids to show 1.7.

Step 3: Count the squares that are shaded but not crossed out. Write the decimal.

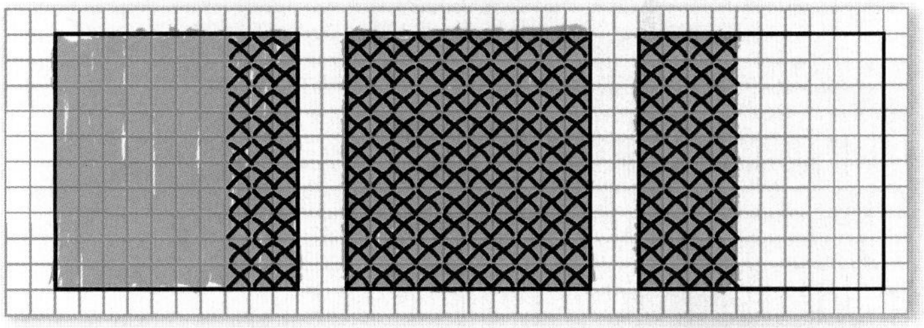

2.4 − 1.7 = 0.7

The Akashi Kaikyo Bridge is 0.7 miles longer than the Golden Gate Bridge.

a. Use grids to subtract.

1.79 − 0.36   1.56 − 1.28   2.34 − 0.75

2.4 − 0.25   1.8 − 0.64   1.03 − 0.4

CHECK

For another example, see Set 11-6 on p. 679.

Add or subtract. Use the grids to help.

1. 0.2 + 0.63

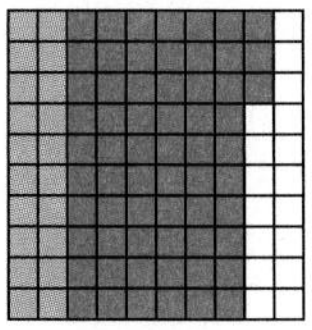

2. 0.9 + 0.25

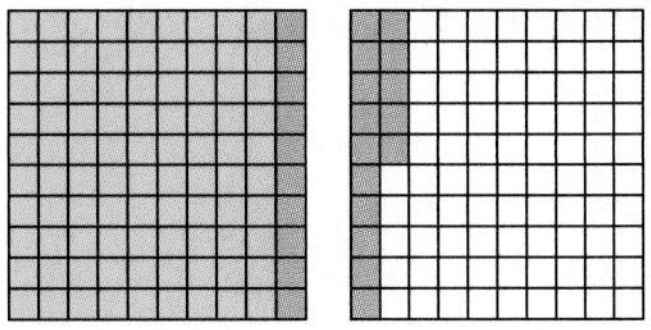

3. 1.45 − 0.29

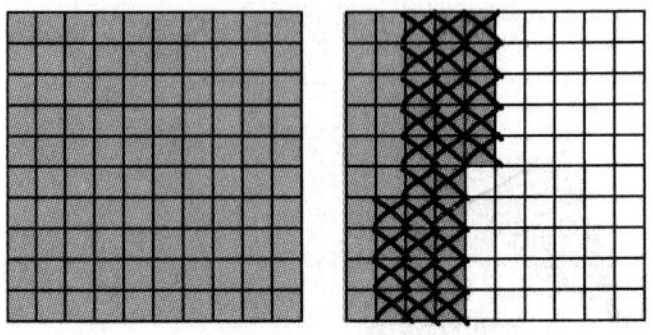

4. Number Sense Do you think the difference 1.2 − 0.85 is less than one or greater than one? Explain.

For more practice, see Set 11-6 on p. 683.

A Skills and Understanding

Add or subtract. Use the grids to help.

5. 0.35 + 0.42

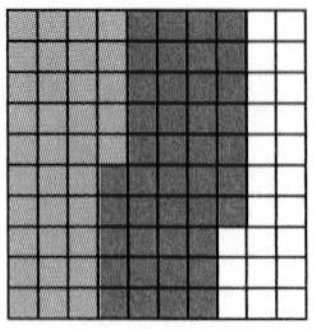

6. 0.57 − 0.28

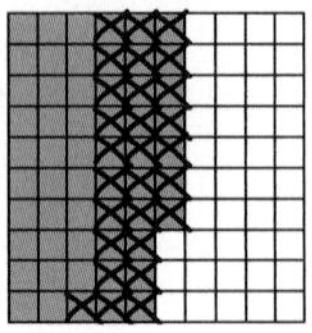

7. 2.19 − 1.4

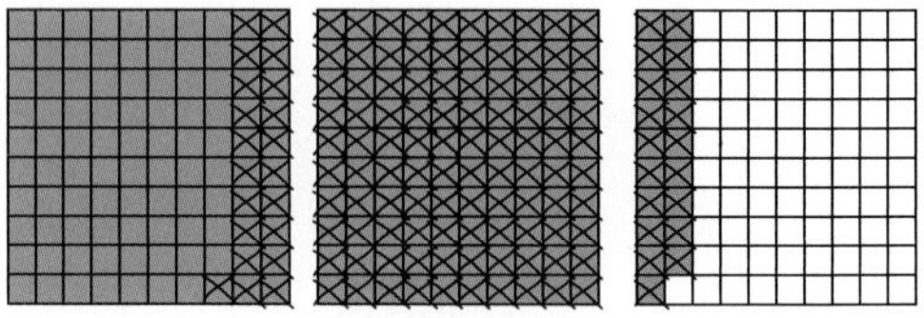

8. 0.3 + 0.58 **9.** 1.06 + 0.37 **10.** 1.7 − 0.64 **11.** 0.9 − 0.15

12. Number Sense Do you think the sum 0.24 + 0.45 is less than one or greater than one? Explain.

B Reasoning and Problem Solving

Math and Everyday Life

Use the data file at the right. How much higher did the gold medal winner jump

13. in 1964 than in 1928?

14. in 2000 than in 1964?

15. in 2000 than in 1928?

16. The women's high jump winner in 1932 jumped 0.06 meters higher than the 1928 winner. How high did the 1932 winner jump?

Data File

Olympic High Jump Women's Gold Medal Winning Heights for Selected Years

Year	Country	Height
1928	Canada	1.59 m
1964	Romania	1.90 m
2000	Russia	2.01 m

17. Writing in Math How is adding 2.35 + 1.92 like adding \$2.35 + \$1.92?

C Extensions

18. Find five examples of decimals in your daily life. You might start by looking at signs and in the newspaper.

Mixed Review and Test Prep

Take It to the NET
Test Prep
www.scottforesman.com

Estimate each sum or difference.

19. 0.85 + 2.33 **20.** 4.47 + 3.82 **21.** 9.71 − 3.61 **22.** 5.72 − 2.18

23. Find the average, or mean, of 20, 38, 22, and 20.

A. 20 **B.** 25 **C.** 26 **D.** 100

Learning with Technology

Using a Calculator to Find Decimal Patterns

1. Use a calculator to find each product.

4.2 × 10	0.56 × 10	0.08 × 10
4.2 × 100	0.56 × 100	0.08 × 100
4.2 × 1,000	0.56 × 1,000	0.08 × 1,000

2. Find each product without a calculator.
Then check your answer with a calculator.

7.84 × 10	0.03 × 10	24.5 × 10
7.84 × 100	0.03 × 100	24.5 × 100
7.84 × 1,000	0.03 × 1,000	24.5 × 1,000

3. Describe a rule that tells how to find each product.

4. Use a calculator to find each quotient.

9,470 ÷ 10	860 ÷ 10	28,520 ÷ 10
9,470 ÷ 100	860 ÷ 100	28,520 ÷ 100
9,470 ÷ 1,000	860 ÷ 1,000	28,520 ÷ 1,000

5. Find each quotient without a calculator.
Then check your answer with a calculator.

3,080 ÷ 10	50 ÷ 10	75,100 ÷ 10
3,080 ÷ 100	50 ÷ 100	75,100 ÷ 100
3,080 ÷ 1,000	50 ÷ 1,000	75,100 ÷ 1,000

6. Describe a rule that tells how to find each quotient.

Find each product or quotient.

7. 0.93 × 100	**8.** 0.3 × 10	**9.** 324 ÷ 100
10. 2.45 × 10	**11.** 0.62 × 10	**12.** 36.4 × 100
13. 810 ÷ 1,000	**14.** 519 ÷ 100	**15.** 72.3 × 10
16. 40 ÷ 10	**17.** 23.5 × 100	**18.** 6,040 ÷ 100
19. 7.6 × 100	**20.** 1,200 ÷ 10	**21.** 6,820 ÷ 1,000

Key Idea
You can add decimals by adding one place at a time, starting from the right.

TEST TALK

Think It Through
- I can **draw a picture** to help solve the problem.
- I can **use what I know** about adding whole numbers and money to add decimals

Adding and Subtracting Decimals

WARM UP

1. 861 + 409
2. 7,040 + 984
3. 3,841 + 2,268
4. 6,096 + 2,085

LEARN

How is adding decimals like adding whole numbers?

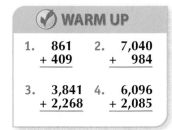

Tuesdays and Fridays are trash collection days on Craig's block.

How much trash was collected from Craig's block for the week?

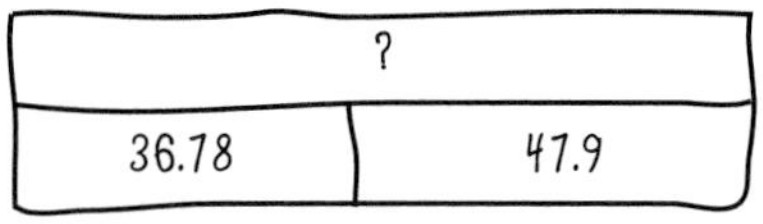

Trash Collected from Craig's Block
Collection Day
Kilograms of Trash
Tuesday
36.78
Friday
47.9

Example A

Estimate: 40 + 50 = 90

STEP 1
Line up the decimal points. Write zeros as place holders, if necessary.

$$\begin{array}{r} 36.78 \\ +\ 47.90 \\ \hline \end{array}$$

Remember, 47.9 = 47.90.

STEP 2
Add the hundredths. Regroup if necessary.

$$\begin{array}{r} 36.78 \\ +\ 47.90 \\ \hline 8 \end{array}$$

STEP 3
Add the tenths. Regroup if necessary.

$$\begin{array}{r} \scriptstyle 1 \\ 36.78 \\ +\ 47.90 \\ \hline 68 \end{array}$$

STEP 4
Add the ones, then the tens. Place the decimal point.

$$\begin{array}{r} \scriptstyle 11 \\ 36.78 \\ +\ 47.90 \\ \hline 84.68 \end{array}$$

The sum 84.68 is reasonable because it is close to the estimate of 90.

For the week, 84.68 kilograms of trash were collected from Craig's block.

Line up the decimal points to add decimals. Then, adding decimals is like adding whole numbers.

Talk About It

1. Between which two places does the decimal point always go?

2. How would you write 2.3 to add it to 0.45?

How is subtracting decimals like subtracting whole numbers?

How much more trash was collected from Craig's neighborhood on Friday than on Tuesday?

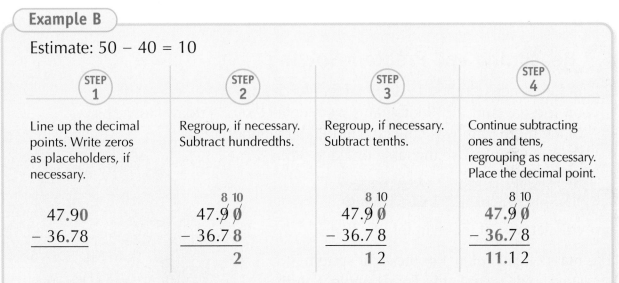

47.9	
36.78	?

Example B

Estimate: 50 − 40 = 10

STEP 1	STEP 2	STEP 3	STEP 4
Line up the decimal points. Write zeros as placeholders, if necessary.	Regroup, if necessary. Subtract hundredths.	Regroup, if necessary. Subtract tenths.	Continue subtracting ones and tens, regrouping as necessary. Place the decimal point.
47.90 − 36.78	8 10 47.9̸0̸ − 36.78 2	8 10 47.9̸0̸ − 36.78 12	8 10 47.9̸0̸ − 36.78 11.12

The difference 11.12 is reasonable because it is close to the estimate of 10.

On Friday, 11.12 more kilograms of trash were collected than on Tuesday.

Line up the decimal points to subtract decimals. Then, subtracting decimals is like subtracting whole numbers.

Talk About It

3. In Step 4, how do you know where to put the decimal point?

Take It to the NET
More Examples
www.scottforesman.com

CHECK

For another example, see Set 11-7 on p. 680.

1. 4.38 + 17.19

2. 54.76 + 89.88

3. 28.56 − 17.79

4. 45.65 − 34.18

5. 84.87 − 35.69

6. 4.3 + 0.85

7. 0.94 + 0.6

8. 0.7 − 0.36

9. 1.4 − 0.92

10. Number Sense Is 9.7 − 0.32 greater or less than 9? Explain how you know without subtracting.

For more practice, see Set 11-7 on p. 684.

A Skills and Understanding

11. $\begin{array}{r} 3.73 \\ +\ 0.68 \\ \hline \end{array}$ **12.** $\begin{array}{r} 14.95 \\ +\ 15.36 \\ \hline \end{array}$ **13.** $\begin{array}{r} 9.13 \\ -\ 0.84 \\ \hline \end{array}$ **14.** $\begin{array}{r} 27.6 \\ -\ 13.72 \\ \hline \end{array}$ **15.** $\begin{array}{r} 56.18 \\ -\ 19.34 \\ \hline \end{array}$

16. 0.86 + 0.4 **17.** 5.13 + 19.9 **18.** 36.1 − 7.55 **19.** 84.23 − 9.9

20. 49.2 + 0.74 **21.** 24.16 + 37.9 **22.** 94.6 − 27.81 **23.** 46.88 − 29.9

24. Number Sense Is 14.8 + 0.76 greater or less than 15? Explain how you know without adding.

B Reasoning and Problem Solving

25. In Julia's neighborhood, 35.94 kilograms of trash were collected on Tuesday and 51.49 kilograms were collected on Friday. How much more trash was collected in Julia's neighborhood than in Craig's? Use the table on page 642.

Math and Science

Use the data file at the right for 26–29.

The mass of each planet in the solar system is measured relative to Earth. For example, Saturn has a mass equal to 95.16 Earths.

Is the mass of Earth less than or greater than the mass of

26. Saturn? **27.** Venus? **28.** Neptune?

29. How much more is the mass of Neptune than Mercury?

30. Algebra Evaluate $n + 3.2$ for $n = 0.35$.

31. Algebra Evaluate $0.84 - t$ for $t = 0.6$.

32. Writing in Math Is the explanation below correct? If not, tell why and write a correct response. If so, explain the problem another way.

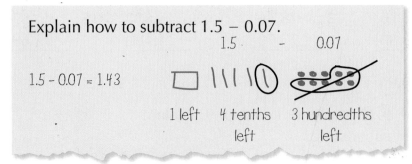

> Explain how to subtract 1.5 − 0.07.
>
> 1.5 - 0.07 = 1.43
>
> 1.5 − 0.07
>
> 
>
> 1 left 4 tenths left 3 hundredths left

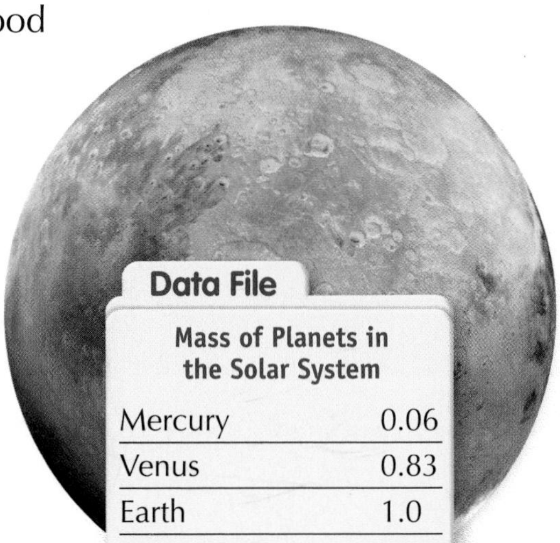

Data File

Mass of Planets in the Solar System

Mercury	0.06
Venus	0.83
Earth	1.0
Mars	0.11
Jupiter	317.8
Saturn	95.16
Uranus	14.54
Neptune	17.15
Pluto	Less than 0.01

TEST TALK

Think It Through

I can **draw pictures to explain my thinking.**

Mixed Review and Test Prep

Take It to the NET
Test Prep
www.scottforesman.com

33. $1.3 + 0.77$ **34.** $0.83 + 1.7$ **35.** $0.8 - 0.12$ **36.** $1.3 - 0.61$

37. $\frac{7}{9} - \frac{1}{3}$

A. $\frac{6}{6}$ **B.** $\frac{5}{9}$ **C.** $\frac{4}{9}$ **D.** $\frac{6}{27}$

Enrichment

Multiplying and Dividing with Decimals

You can find 3×0.24 by adding $0.24 + 0.24 + 0.24$.

Here's how to multiply 3×0.24 with repeated addition and grids.

Step 1: Shade a grid to show 0.24.

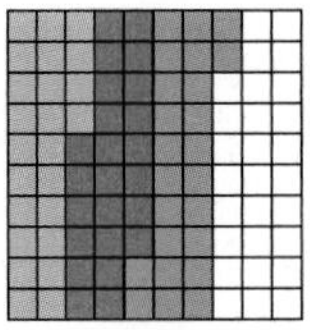

Step 2: Shade 0.24 more in a different color. Then, shade 0.24 more in a third color.

Step 3: Find the number of hundredths shaded in all.

So, $3 \times 0.24 = 0.72$.

Use grids to multiply.

1. 3×0.32 **2.** 2×0.56 **3.** 3×0.46 **4.** 4×0.15

You also can use grids to divide with decimals. Here's how to divide $1.35 \div 3$.

Step 1: Shade a grid to show 1.35.

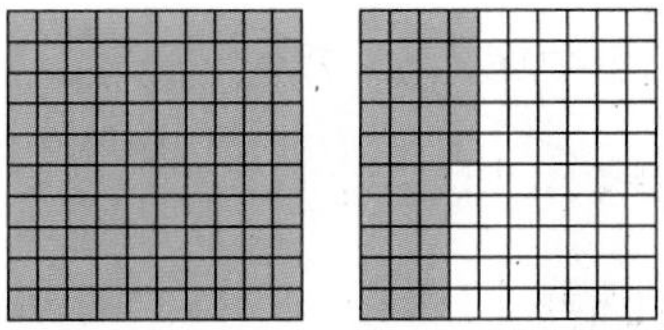

Step 2: Cut out the shaded squares and divide them into 3 equal groups.

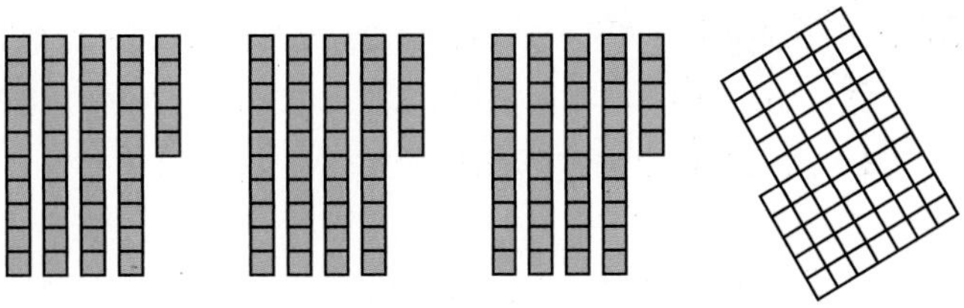

Step 3: Find the number of hundredths in each group. Write the quotient.

$1.35 \div 3 = 0.45$

Use grids to divide.

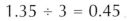

5. $0.32 \div 2$ **6.** $0.42 \div 3$ **7.** $1.12 \div 2$ **8.** $1.14 \div 3$

Reading For Math Success

Activate Prior Knowledge

Activating prior knowledge when you read in math can help you use the **problem-solving strategy, *Solve a Simpler Problem,*** in the next lesson.

In reading, activating prior knowledge can help you connect new ideas to what you know. In math, activating prior knowledge can help you connect a new problem to one you know how to solve.

I already know about perimeter and area of squares.

Mrs. Samuels used 15 carpet squares to cover a portion of her classroom floor. The perimeter of each carpet square was 8 feet. What is the area of the floor Mrs. Samuels covered with all the carpet squares?

Length of each side of 1 square:
$8 \div 4 = 2$ feet
Area of 1 square:
$2 \times 2 = 4$ square feet

*So I'll start with the **simpler problem** of finding the area of just one carpet square.*

Then I'll use the answer to the simpler problem to find the total area covered by 15 carpet squares.

1. Could you have solved this problem without using what you know about squares? Explain.

2. How can you use the answer to the simpler problem to solve the original problem?

For 3–5, use the problem below.

On Saturdays, Claudia earns $15 for mowing the neighbors' lawns and $12 for gardening. On Sundays, she earns twice as much. How much will she earn in 6 weekends?

3. How much does Claudia earn on Saturdays? on Sundays?

4. How much does Claudia earn each weekend?

5. **Writing in Math** How can you use the answers to these simpler problems to solve the original problem?

2-by-2 "L"

3-by-3 "L"

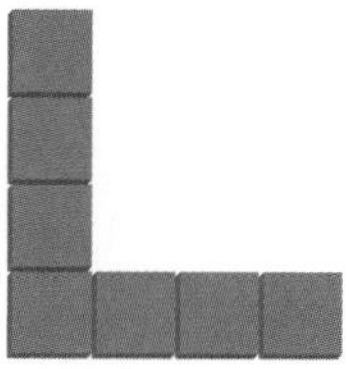

4-by-4 "L"

For 6–7, use the problem below and the picture at the left.

Liam is making his initial, L, out of squares. He wants the same number of squares going across and down. How many squares would he need for a 10-by-10 "L"?

6. How many squares are needed for a 2-by-2 "L"? a 3-by-3 "L"? a 4-by-4 "L"?

7. **Writing in Math** Do you see a pattern in the answers to the simpler problems? If so, describe it.

For 8–9, use the problem below.

Jack has the money shown at the right. If his Dad exchanges it for all quarters, how many quarters would Jack get?

8. How many quarters would Jack get for each dollar? for the 50-cent piece?

9. **Writing in Math** How can you use the answers to these simpler problem to solve the original problem?

Reading Helps!
Activating prior knowledge can help you with...
the problem-solving strategy, ***Solve a Simpler Problem.***

Key Idea
Learning how and when to solve a simpler problem can help you solve problems.

Solve a Simpler Problem

LEARN

How do you solve a simpler problem?

Triangle Trains Each side of each triangle in the figure at the right is one inch. If there are 12 triangles in a row, what is the perimeter of the figure?

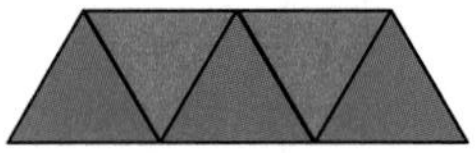

Read and Understand

What do you know? Triangles are being connected. Each side of each triangle is one inch.

What are you trying to find? Find the perimeter of the figure with 12 triangles.

Plan and Solve

What strategy will you use? **Strategy: Solve a Simpler Problem.**

I can look at 1 triangle, then 2 triangles, then 3 triangles.

Step 1 Break apart or change the problem into problems that are simpler to solve.
Step 2 Solve the simpler problems.
Step 3 Use the answers to the simpler problems to solve the original problem.

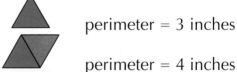

perimeter = 3 inches

perimeter = 4 inches

perimeter = 5 inches

Answer: The perimeter is 2 more than the number of triangles. For 12 triangles, the perimeter is 14 inches.

Look Back and Check

Is your work correct? Yes, I saw a correct pattern.

Talk About It

1. How was the problem broken apart into simpler problems?

2. Describe the pattern in the simpler problems.

CHECK

For another example, see Set 11-8 on p. 680.

Solve the Fences problem. Use the solutions from the simpler problem to help you. Write the answer in a complete sentence.

1. **Fences** Each fence section has a post at each end. How many posts are needed to build a fence with 10 sections?

    Simpler problem: How many posts are needed to build a fence with 1 section? 2 sections? 3 sections? Look for a pattern.

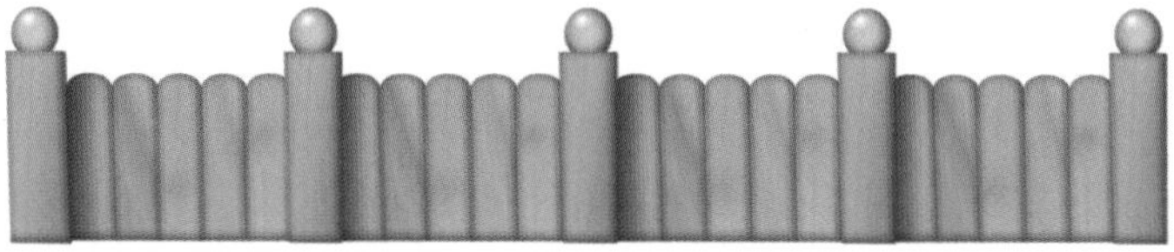

PRACTICE

For more practice, see Set 11-8 on p. 684.

Solve each problem. Write the answer in a complete sentence.

2. **Bracelets** Karina has a 30-inch necklace she wants to have cut into 5 bracelets for her friends. A jeweler charges $2 for each cut. How much does Karina need to pay for the cuts?
3. Troy is entering a 32-player chess tournament. Players are out of the tournament as soon as they lose one match. The winners of each round play again until there is just one champion. How many chess matches are there in all in Troy's tournament?
4. Stacey is entering a different type of chess tournament. Each of the eight players in the tournament plays all the other players. How many chess matches are there in all in Stacey's tournament?
5. **Schedule** The missing classes in the schedule at the right are Math, Reading, Spelling, Social Studies, and Science. Math is at 9:40. Social Studies and Science are after lunch. Reading is before morning recess. At what time is Spelling?

STRATEGIES

- **Show What You Know**
  - Draw a Picture
  - Make an Organized List
  - Make a Table
  - Make a Graph
  - Act It Out or Use Objects
- **Look for a Pattern**
- **Try, Check, and Revise**
- **Write a Number Sentence**
- **Use Logical Reasoning**
- **Solve a Simpler Problem**
- **Work Backward**

Choose a tool

our schedule

8:30	opening
8:45	
9:30	break
9:40	
10:25	recess
10:55	
11:30	lunch
12:15	
1:00	break
1:10	
1:55	recess
2:05	art, music, or P.E.
2:40	school's out

Review

Do You Know How?

Do You Understand?

Estimating Decimal Sums and Differences (11-5)

Estimate each sum or difference.

1. 0.98 + 4.36
2. 3.7 + 3.4
3. 4.3 + 5.17
4. 15.8 + 8.1
5. 6.6 − 2.92
6. 8.78 − 3.25
7. 5.81 − 1.77
8. 36.7 − 25.02

A Explain how you estimated the difference in Exercise 5.

B In Exercise 3, did you get an overestimate or an underestimate? Explain.

Using Grids to Add and Subtract Decimals (11-6)
Adding and Subtracting Decimals (11-7)

9. 0.64 + 0.36
10. 1.25 + 0.8
11. 1.17 + 1.8
12. 1.4 − 0.6
13. 1.63 − 0.92
14. 2.8 − 1.82
15. 8.77 + 5.25
16. 17.21 + 47.9
17. 78.2 + 56.32
18. 37.46 − 18.4
19. 22.4 − 19.6
20. 63.8 − 29.98

C Draw grids to show the difference in Exercise 13.

D Explain how to add 6.2 + 0.59.

Problem-Solving Strategy: Solve a Simpler Problem (11-8)

21. **Tables** You are arranging tables for a pizza party. Each table seats four people, as shown below. However, you want to place the tables end-to-end to form one long table. How many tables are needed for 24 people?

E Describe how solving a simpler problem could help you solve the Tables problem.

F Name two strategies you used to solve the Tables problem.

Chapter 11 Section B
Diagnostic Checkpoint

MULTIPLE CHOICE

1. Mr. Kelly drove 147.6 miles on Saturday and 99.6 miles on Sunday. About how far did he drive over the weekend? (11-5)

A. 50 miles **B.** 100 miles **C.** 250 miles **D.** 300 miles

2. A quarter-pound hamburger weighed 0.25 pound before it was cooked and 0.16 pound after. How much weight was lost during cooking? (11-7)

A. 0.09 lb **B.** 0.11 lb **C.** 0.9 lb **D.** 1.1 lbs

TEST TALK

Think It Through

I need to decide whether I need an **exact answer** or an **estimate** before I solve a problem.

FREE RESPONSE

Add or subtract. For 3–6, you may use grids to help. (11-6 and 11-7)

3. 0.4 + 1.73 **4.** 0.35 + 1.6 **5.** 0.68 − 0.39 **6.** 1.4 − 1.33

7. 46.8 + 4.75 **8.** 87.8 − 12.93 **9.** 75.53 − 29.6 **10.** 26.17 + 54.9

Estimate each sum or difference. (11-6)

11. 3.96 − 1.45 **12.** 2.12 + 8.76 **13.** 6.4 + 3.25 **14.** 5.81 − 2.28

Use the information at the right for 15–17. (11-7)

How much more average annual precipitation does

15. Atlanta receive than Reno?

16. Memphis receive than Houston?

17. Memphis receive than Reno?

Data File

Average Annual Precipitation

Location	Inches
Atlanta, Georgia	50.77
Houston, Texas	46.07
Memphis, Tennessee	52.1
Reno, Nevada	7.53

18. It takes a plumber 5 minutes to cut a pipe. How long does it take the plumber to cut a long pipe into 6 pieces? (11-8)

Writing in Math

19. Use the data file above. Estimate how many more inches of average annual precipitation fall in Memphis than in Atlanta. Is your estimate an overestimate or an underestimate? Explain how you know. (11-5)

20. Explain how you can use estimation to decide which has the greater sum, 5.68 + 2.75 or 3.01 + 4.32. (11-5)

Key Idea
Metric units are used to estimate and measure length.

Vocabulary
- millimeter (mm)
- centimeter (cm)
- decimeter (dm)
- meter (m)
- kilometer (km)

Materials
- metric ruler
- meter stick
- objects to measure

Length and Metric Units

WARM UP

Choose the most appropriate unit to use to measure each. Write in., ft, yd, or mi.

1. width of a large city
2. width of a juice glass

LEARN

What are metric units of length?

Most countries in the world use metric units of measure. The metric units of length used most often are the **millimeter (mm), centimeter (cm), decimeter (dm), meter (m),** and **kilometer (km).**

Metric Units of Length
1 cm = 10 mm
1 dm = 10 cm
1 m = 100 cm
1 km = 1,000 m

A worm is about 1 dm.

A snake is about 1 m.

A ladybug is about 1 cm. A spot is about 1 mm.

A kilometer is the length of about 40 blue whales placed end to end.

Activity

How do you measure length with metric units?

a. Make a table like the one shown below. Select ten objects of various lengths. Estimate the length of each object. Then use a metric ruler or meter stick to measure to the nearest centimeter. If an object is more than a meter long, write the measure in meters and centimeters.

Object	Estimated Length	Length to the Nearest Centimeter
Length of this book		
Length of the room		

b. Which of the objects you measured is the shortest?

Talk About It

1. Which is greater, 1 centimeter or 1 meter?
2. Which is greater, 1 meter or 1 kilometer?

CHECK ✓

For another example, see Set 11-9 on p. 680.

1. Estimate first. Then find the length to the nearest centimeter.

2. Number Sense Choose the most appropriate unit to measure the length of a fire truck. Write mm, cm, dm, m, or km.

PRACTICE

For more practice, see Set 11-9 on p. 684.

A Skills and Understanding

Estimate first. Then find each length to the nearest centimeter.

3.

4.

Choose the most appropriate unit to measure each. Write mm, cm, dm, m, or km.

5. length of an airplane ride

6. width of a kernel of corn

7. length of a shoe

8. height of a tree

Find each missing number.

9. 1 m = ☐ cm

10. 1 km = ☐ m

11. 1 cm = ☐ mm

12. Number Sense Name 3 things you might measure in centimeters.

B Reasoning and Problem Solving

13. Reasoning Use a metric ruler to find the perimeter of the rectangle at the right.

14. Writing in Math Would a 30-centimeter ruler be the best tool to use to measure the distance you live from school? Explain why or why not.

Mixed Review and Test Prep

Take It to the NET
Test Prep
www.scottforesman.com

15. 11.37 − 5.64

16. 42.51 + 6.5

17. 38.5 − 17.4

18. A tunnel is 200 feet long. How many lights are needed if there is one light at the beginning of the tunnel, one at the end, and one every 20 feet?

19. 533 ÷ 6

A. 90 R3 **B.** 89 R1 **C.** 88 R1 **D.** 88 R5

Key Idea
Metric units are used to estimate and measure capacity.

Vocabulary
- liter (L)
- milliliter (mL)

Materials
- a 1-liter measuring cup marked in milliliters
- containers of different sizes
- water or sand

Capacity and Metric Units

WARM UP

Choose the most appropriate unit to use to measure the capacity of each. Write tsp or qt.

1. pitcher of lemonade
2. salt in a recipe

LEARN

What are metric units of capacity?

The two metric units of capacity used most often are the **liter (L)** and the **milliliter (mL).** One liter = 1,000 milliliters.

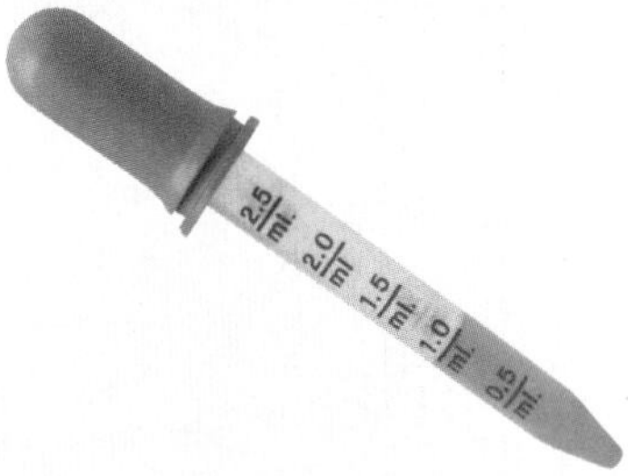

An eye dropper can be used to measure 1 milliliter.

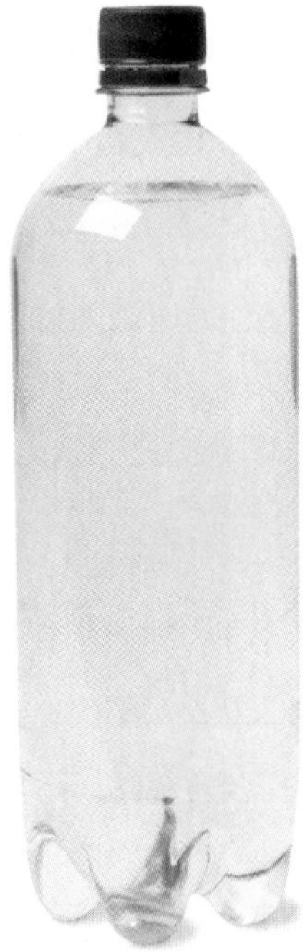

Some water bottles hold one liter.

Talk About It

1. Which is greater, a liter or a milliliter?
2. What metric unit would you use to find the capacity of a car's gas tank?

Activity

How do you measure capacity with metric units?

a. Make a table like the one shown below. Select six containers with various capacities. Estimate the capacity of each. Then use the metric measuring cup and water or sand to measure to the nearest milliliter. If the capacity is more than a liter, give the measure in liters and milliliters.

Object	Estimated Capacity	Capacity to the Nearest Milliliter

b. Which of the containers you measured had the least capacity?

CHECK

For another example, see Set 11-10 on p. 680.

1. Choose the most appropriate unit to use to measure the perfume in a bottle. Write L or mL.

2. **Number Sense** Would a liter bottle or a medicine dropper be a better tool to use to measure the water in a bathtub? Explain.

PRACTICE

For more practice, see Set 11-10 on p. 684.

A Skills and Understanding

Choose the most appropriate unit to measure the capacity of each. Write L or mL.

3. water in a washing machine
4. juice in a glass
5. bleach in a bottle
6. ink in a pen

7. **Number Sense** Which number would be greater, the number of milliliters of milk in a pitcher or the number of liters of milk in the same pitcher?

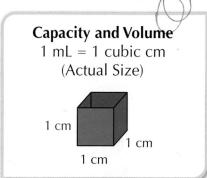

Capacity and Volume
1 mL = 1 cubic cm
(Actual Size)

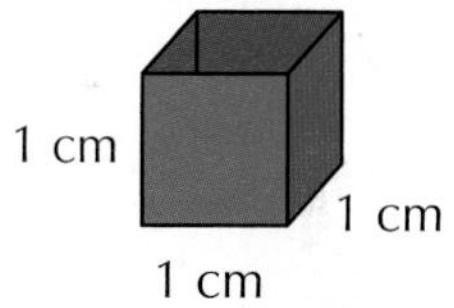

B Reasoning and Problem Solving

A milliliter is the amount of liquid that fits in a container with a volume of 1 cubic cm.

Find the capacity in milliliters of each container.

8. 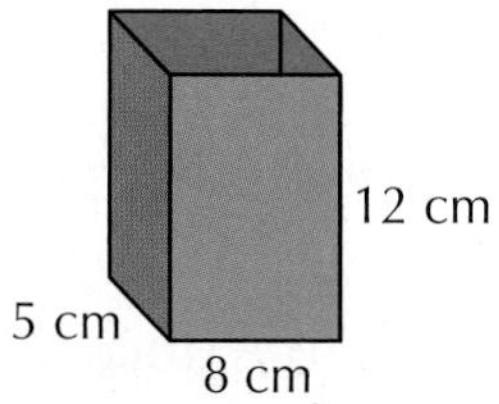

9. 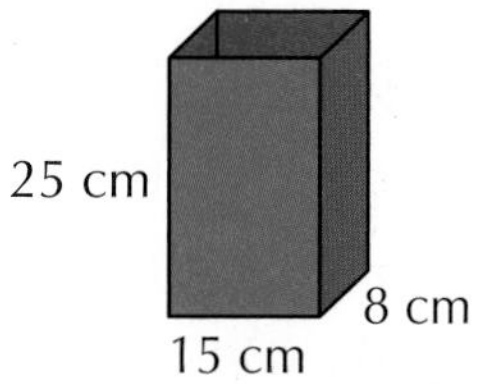

10. 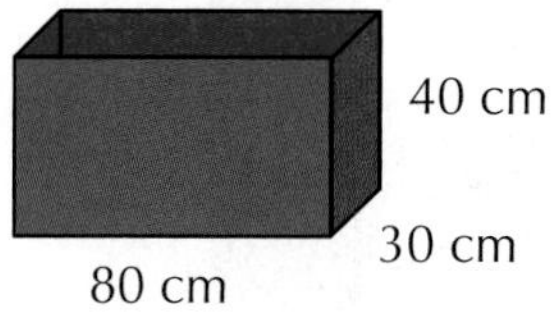

11. **Writing in Math** Alex said he poured lemonade from a 300-liter pitcher into a 20-milliliter glass. Do you think he is right? Explain why or why not.

Mixed Review and Test Prep

Take It to the NET
Test Prep
www.scottforesman.com

12. Choose the most appropriate unit to measure the length of a river. Write mm, cm, dm, m, or km.

13. 19×309

A. 3,090 **B.** 3,440 **C.** 5,771 **D.** 5,871

Key Idea
Metric units are used to estimate and measure mass.

Vocabulary
- mass
- gram (g)
- kilogram (kg)

Materials
- pan balance
- grams and kilograms
- objects to measure mass

TEST TALK

Think It Through
I can **use objects** like a pan balance and weights to measure mass.

Mass and Metric Units

WARM UP

Choose the most appropriate unit to use to measure the weight of each. Write oz, lb, or T.

1. a gallon of milk
2. a bumble bee

LEARN

What are metric units of mass?

Mass is the amount of matter that something contains. The two metric units of mass used most often are the **gram (g)** and the **kilogram (kg).** One kilogram = 1,000 grams.

A grape has a mass of about 1 gram (g).

A cantaloupe has a mass of about 1 kilogram (kg).

Talk About It

1. Which is greater, one gram or one kilogram?
2. **Reasoning** Which number would be less, the number of grams in a watermelon or the number of kilograms in the same watermelon?

Activity

How do you measure mass?

a. Make a table like the one shown below. Select six objects with different masses. Estimate the mass of each. Then use a pan balance to measure each object to the nearest gram. Start by using grams. If the object has a mass greater than a kilogram, use kilograms and grams.

Object	Estimated Mass	Mass to the Nearest Gram

b. Which of the objects you measured had the least mass?

c. Which of the objects you measured has a mass greater than a kilogram?

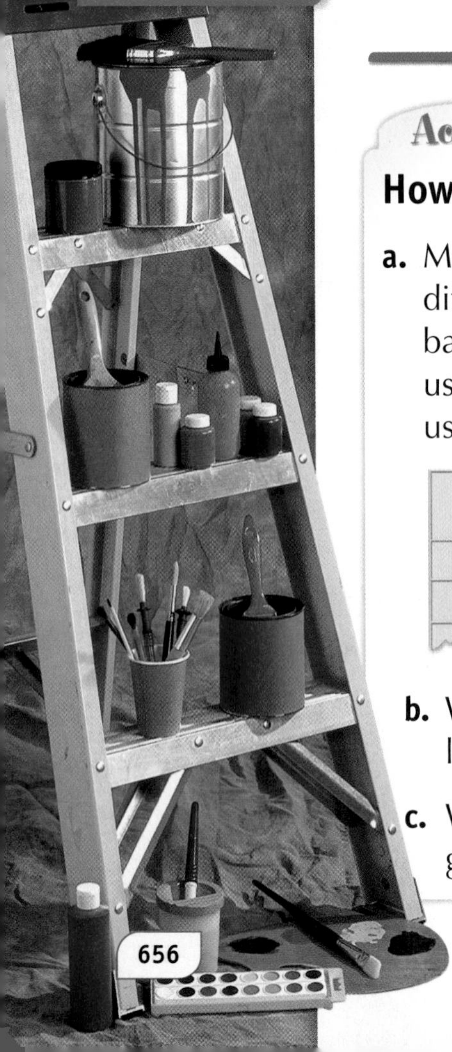

CHECK ✓

For another example, see Set 11-11 on p. 681.

Choose the most appropriate unit to measure the mass of each. Write g or kg.

1. Baseball **2.** Sofa **3.** Horse **4.** Wallet

5. Reasoning A milligram is related to a gram the same way a millimeter is related to a meter. How many milligrams equal a gram?

PRACTICE

For more practice, see Set 11-11 on p. 685.

A Skills and Understanding

Choose the most appropriate unit to measure the mass of each. Write g or kg.

6. Dog **7.** Pencil **8.** Potato **9.** Car

10. Magazine **11.** Television **12.** Bar of soap **13.** Calculator

14. Number Sense Which number would be greater, the mass of a carrot in grams or the mass of the same carrot in kilograms?

B Reasoning and Problem Solving

Use the information at the right for 15–18.

What is the total mass of

15. 2 apples? **16.** 2 slices of watermelon?

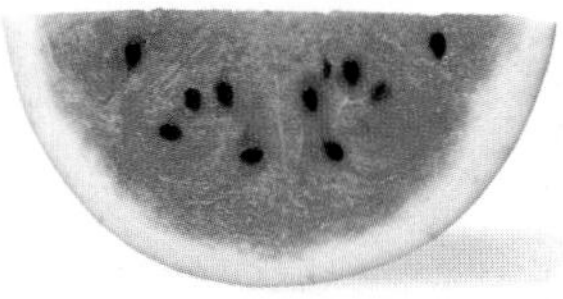

0.5 kg

0.16 kg

How much more is the mass of

17. the slice of watermelon than the apple?

18. the slice of watermelon than 3 apples?

19. **Writing in Math** Would a bathroom scale be the best tool to use to weigh an elephant? Why or why not?

Mixed Review and Test Prep

Take It to the NET
Test Prep
www.scottforesman.com

Choose the most appropriate unit to measure the capacity of each. Write L or mL.

20. Bucket **21.** Mug **22.** Drink box **23.** Bathtub

24. 12 ft 5 in. =

A. 125 in. **B.** 144 in. **C.** 149 in. **D.** 155 in.

Key Idea
To compare measures, you may need to change metric units.

TEST TALK

Think It Through
I can **use what I know.**
1 cm = 10 mm
1 dm = 10 cm
1 m = 100 cm
1 m = 1,000 mm
1 km = 1,000 m
1 L = 1,000 mL
1 kg = 1,000 g

Changing Units and Comparing Measures

WARM UP

Find each missing number.

1. 5 cm = ▢ mm
2. 8 m = ▢ cm
3. 21 km = ▢ m

LEARN

How do you change metric units?

Like metric units of length, metric units of capacity and mass are based on multiples of ten.

To change larger units to smaller units, *multiply.*

Example A

3 m = ▢ cm

Think: 1 m = 100 cm

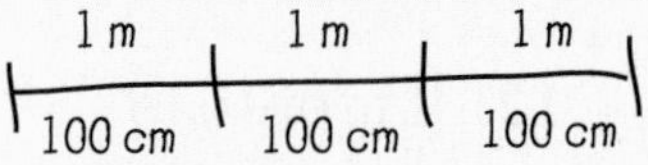

3 × 100 = 300

3 m = 300 cm

Example B

2 L = ▢ mL

Think: 1 L = 1,000 mL

2 × 1,000 = 2,000

2 L = 2,000 mL

To change smaller units to larger units, *divide.*

Example C

50 mm = ▢ cm

Think: 1 cm = 10 mm

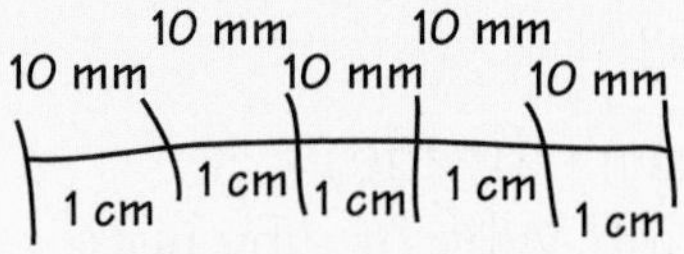

50 ÷ 10 = 5

50 mm = 5 cm

Example D

4,000 g = ▢ kg

Think: 1 kg = 1,000 g

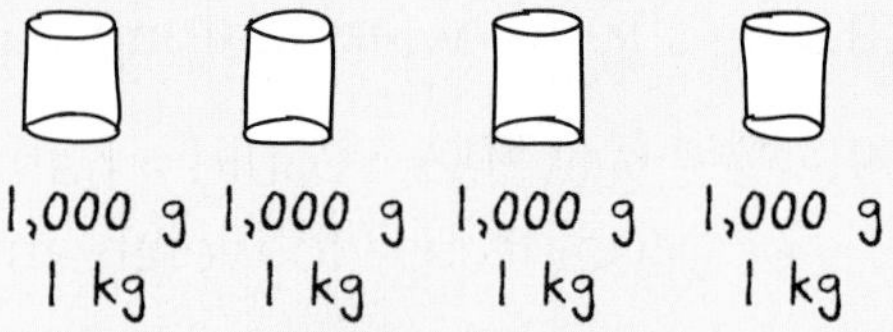

4,000 ÷ 1,000 = 4

4,000 g = 4 kg

Talk About It

1. Do you multiply or divide to change from centimeters to meters?
2. Why do you divide to change grams to kilograms?

How do you compare measures?

You can use metric units to compare measures. When the units are the same, compare the numbers.

Example E

Which watering can is larger?

Compare. 0.75 L ○ 0.85 L

The units are the same. Compare the numbers.

$$\begin{array}{r} 0.75 \\ 0.85 \\ 0.75 < 0.85 \end{array}$$

0.75 L $<$ 0.85 L

0.85 L   0.75 L

When the units are not the same, change units so they are the same.

Example F

Brock is 1 meter 48 centimeters tall and Brandon is 157 centimeters tall. Who is taller, Brock or Brandon?

STEP 1	STEP 2
Change to the same units.	
Think: 1 m = 100 cm	Compare.
100 + 48 = 148	148 cm $<$ 157 cm
1 m 48 cm = 148 cm	1 m 48 cm $<$ 157 cm

Brandon is taller than Brock.

Talk About It

3. Reasoning Explain how to compare 3,200 g and 2 kg 500 g.

Take It to the NET
More Examples
www.scottforesman.com

CHECK

For another example, see Set 11-12 on p. 681.

Find each missing number.

1. 37 cm = □ mm **2.** 4 cm 6 mm = □ mm **3.** 11,000 g = □ kg

Compare. Write > or < for each ○.

4. 0.75 kg ○ 0.85 kg **5.** 6 m ○ 750 cm **6.** 8 L 400 mL ○ 7,540 mL

7. Number Sense Trina said 5,600 mL is greater than 4.8 L because 5,600 mL is more than 5 L and 4.8 L is less. Is Trina correct?

PRACTICE

For more practice, see Set 11-12 on p. 685.

A Skills and Understanding

Find each missing number.

8. 9 km = ■ m **9.** 30 kg = ■ g **10.** 4,000 m = ■ km

11. 80 mm = ■ cm **12.** 1 km 500 m = ■ m **13.** 2 m 70 cm = ■ cm

Compare. Write > or < for each ●.

14. 2.4 km ● 2.5 km **15.** 1.25 L ● 1.5 L **16.** 45 mm ● 4 cm 2 mm

17. 180 g ● 18 kg **18.** 6 m 5 cm ● 639 cm **19.** 8 km 400 m ● 8,200 m

20. Number Sense If 1 g = 1,000 mg, would you multiply or divide to change 5 g to milligrams? Explain why.

B Reasoning and Problem Solving

Math and Science

Use the data file at the right for 21–24.

21. How much farther can a cheetah travel in one minute than a wolf?

Find the distance, in meters, each animal can travel in one minute.

22. Cheetah **23.** Land snail

24. List the animals in order from the animal that travels the least distance in one minute to the animal that travels the greatest distance in one minute.

25. Writing in Math Explain how to change 80 mm to centimeters.

Data File

Distances Animals Can Travel in One Minute

Animal	Distance
Cheetah	1 km 800 m
Land snail	83 cm
Sloth	33 m
Wolf	750 m

Mixed Review and Test Prep

Take It to the NET
Test Prep
www.scottforesman.com

Choose the most appropriate unit to measure the mass of each. Write g or kg.

26. stocking cap **27.** refrigerator **28.** pencil sharpener **29.** file cabinet

30. What digit is in the hundredths place in 516.78?

A. 1 **B.** 5 **C.** 7 **D.** 8

Enrichment

Comparing Metric and Customary Measures

The symbol ≈ is read "is approximately equal to." The table lists some comparable measures.

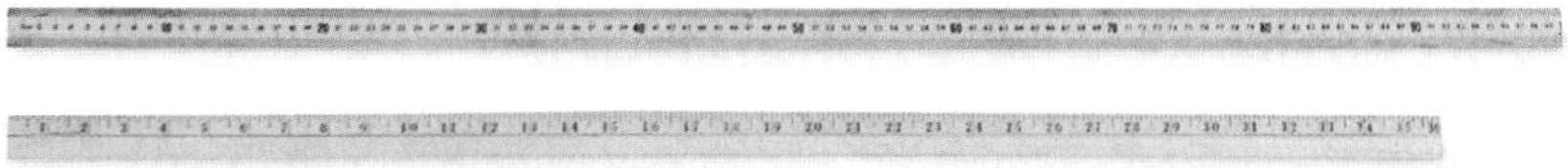

A meter is a little more than a yard.

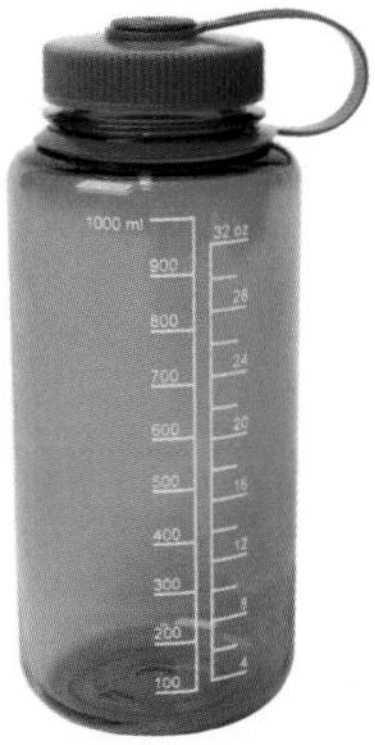

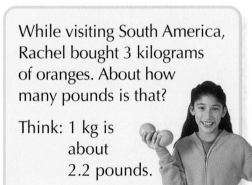

A liter is a little more than a quart.

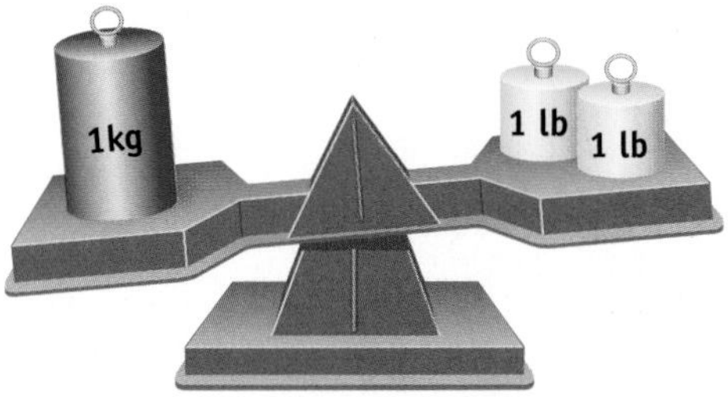

A kilogram is a little more than 2 pounds.

Customary and Metric Unit Equivalents

Length
1 in. = 2.54 cm
1 m ≈ 39.37 in.
1 m ≈ 1.09 yd
1 km ≈ 0.6 mi
1 mi ≈ 1.6 km

Capacity
1 L ≈ 1.06 qt
1 gal ≈ 3.8 L

Weight and Mass
1 oz ≈ 28 g
1 kg ≈ 2.2 lb

While visiting South America, Rachel bought 3 kilograms of oranges. About how many pounds is that?

Think: 1 kg is about 2.2 pounds.

2.2 + 2.2 + 2.2 = 6.6

3 kg ≈ 6.6 lb

While visiting from France, Cecelia ran 4 miles a day. About how many kilometers is that?

Think: A mile is about 1.6 km or 1,600 m.

$$\begin{array}{r} 1{,}600 \\ \times \quad 4 \\ \hline 6{,}400 \end{array}$$

6,400 m = 6.4 km

Estimate each measure in the units given.

1. 5 L ≈ ___ qt **2.** 3 in. = ___ cm **3.** 8 kg ≈ ___ lb **4.** 2 gal ≈ ___ L

5. In France, Steven saw a sign that said 20 km to Paris. About how many miles is that?

6. Number Sense Carl said 30 cm is about 1 foot. Explain why he is correct.

Problem-Solving Skill

Reading Helps!
Identifying steps in a process
can help you with...
writing to explain.

Key Idea
There are specific things you can do to write a good explanation in math.

Writing to Explain

LEARN

How do you write a good explanation?

When you write to explain a prediction you need to tell why something will happen.

And the Winner Is The 611 residents of Alpine Valley are going to vote on a snowboarding location. Four people each surveyed 25 residents about their choice. Here are the results.

Results of the Survey for Snowboarding Location

	Windy Gap	Pine Ridge
Vince's Survey	10	15
Maria's Survey	12	13
Kyle's Survey	6	19
Quentin's Survey	7	18

Predict which location will win. Then predict about how many votes out of 611 each location will get. Explain your prediction.

Writing a Math Explanation

- Make sure your prediction is clearly stated.
- Use steps to make your explanation clear.
- Show and explain carefully how you used the numbers to make your prediction.

I think Pine Ridge will win. Here is why.
1. I added the votes. Pine Ridge got 65 and Windy Gap got 35. That is 100 in all.
2. Windy Gap got 35 out of 100 or about $\frac{1}{3}$ of the votes. There are a little more than 600 residents, so Windy Gap would get about $\frac{1}{3}$ of 600, or about 200 votes.
3. This means that Pine Ridge would get about 400 votes. (600 − 200 = 400)

TEST TALK

Think It Through
I should make sure my explanations are clear so that others can understand them.

Talk About It

1. Why can you estimate when making a prediction?

CHECK

For another example, see Set 11-13 on p. 681.

1. Sally surveyed 25 fourth-grade students and asked them how many hours of sleep they got each night. The results are shown in the table. Use these results to predict about how many fourth-graders out of 102 sleep more than 9 hours. Explain how you made your prediction.

Hours of Sleep Each Night

Fewer than 7 hours	6 students
7 to 9 hours	14 students
More than 9 hours	5 students

PRACTICE

For more practice, see Set 11-13 on p. 685.

Write to explain. Use the bar graph at the right for 2 and 3.

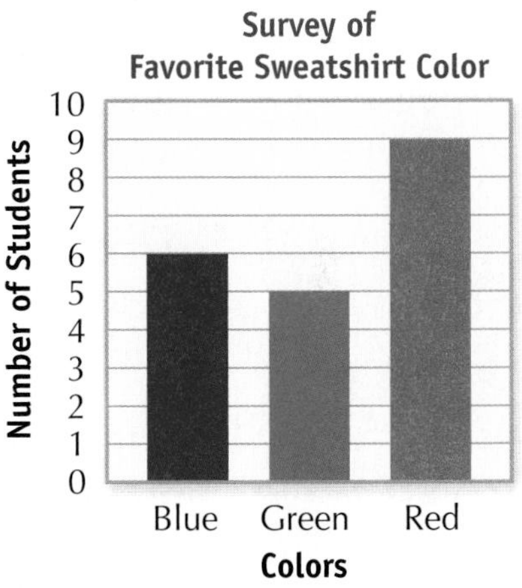

2. The bar graph shows the result of a survey asking 20 students what color sweatshirt they would buy. Based on the survey, predict how many red sweatshirts out of 400 the Pep Club will sell. Explain how you made your prediction.

3. Based on the survey predict about how many green and blue sweatshirts out of 400 the Pep Club will sell.

4. The last digit of the serial number on a one-dollar bill can be any number from 0 through 9. Mrs. Greene is a bank teller. She has 310 one-dollar bills in her drawer. Predict about how many of the dollar bills have a serial number that ends in 4. Explain how you made your prediction.

5. Jake folded a piece of paper in half as shown below. Then he cut out the part shown in orange. Show how the paper will look when it is opened.

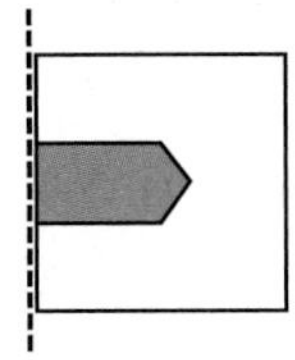

6. The figure below is made using craft sticks. Explain how the number of craft sticks needed changes as the number of squares increases.

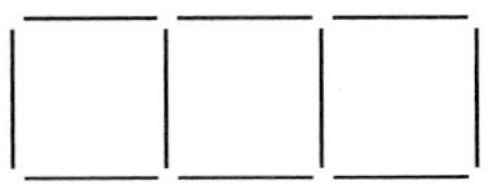

Key Idea
Temperatures can be read in degrees Fahrenheit or degrees Celsius.

Vocabulary
- degrees Fahrenheit (°F)
- degrees Celsius (°C)

Temperature

WARM UP

Show the following numbers on a number line.

1. 8
2. 15
3. 3.5
4. $6\frac{1}{4}$

LEARN

How do you measure how hot or cold it is?

On February 13, 1899, the temperature in Tallahassee, Florida, dropped to −2°F. It was the coldest day ever recorded in Florida.

Degrees Fahrenheit (°F) are standard units of temperature. Water boils at 212°F and freezes at 32°F.

Degrees Celsius (°C) are metric units of temperature. Water boils at 100°C and freezes at 0°C.

A temperature that is below 0° is read as a **negative.** This thermometer shows negative 2 degrees Fahrenheit, written −2°F.

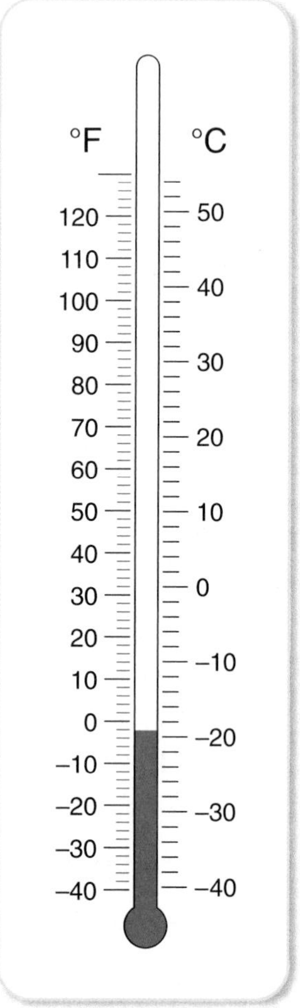

Example A

Read the thermometer at the right. Write the temperature in °C.

Use the °C scale.

The temperature is about −19°C.

Example B

Could you go swimming when it is 30°C? 30°F?

When it is 30°C, it is very warm. You could go swimming. However, when it is 30°F, it is below freezing. It is too cold to swim.

Talk About It

1. How can you tell −2°F from 2°F on a thermometer?

2. Reasoning Which is warmer, −12°C or −20°C?

CHECK ✓

For another example, see Set 11-14 on p. 681.

Read each thermometer. Write the temperature in °F and in °C.

1. 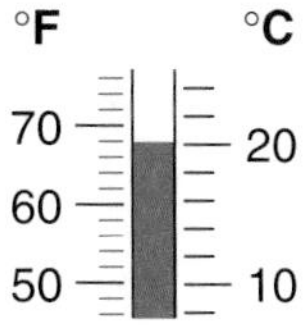

2. 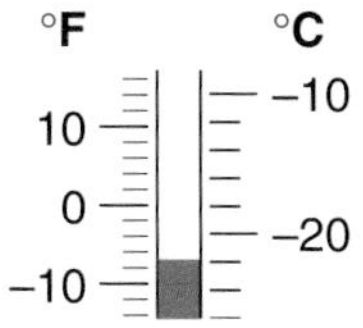

3. 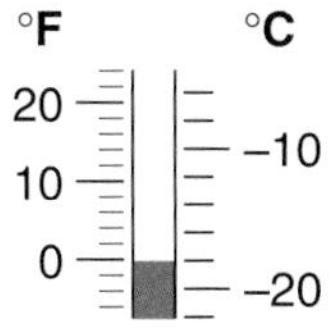

4. 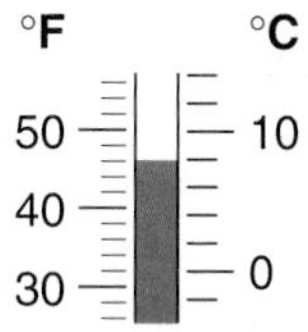

5. **Number Sense** Which is colder, −6°F or −8°F?

PRACTICE

For more practice, see Set 11-14 on p. 685.

A Skills and Understanding

Read each thermometer. Write the temperature in °F and in °C.

6. 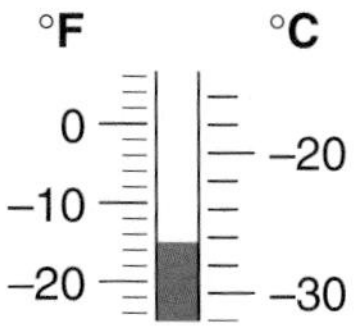

7. 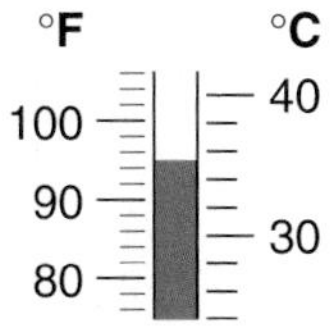

8. 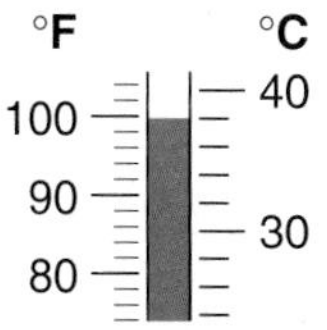

9. 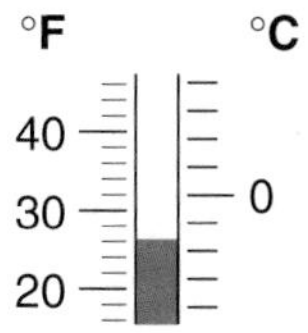

10. **Number Sense** Could you build a snow fort when it is 10°C? Explain why or why not.

B Reasoning and Problem Solving

11. The Canadian weather report said it was 32°C. Would you need to wear a jacket? Explain why or why not.

12. **Estimation** Would the temperature in your classroom be about 25°C or 45°C? Explain.

13. **Reasoning** In the morning the temperature was −5°C. Three hours later, it was 10°C. How many degrees did the temperature rise?

14. **Writing in Math** Normal human body temperature is 98.6°F. About what is this in degrees Celsius? Explain how you decided.

Mixed Review and Test Prep

Take It to the NET
Test Prep
www.scottforesman.com

15. Explain how to compare 0.8 L and 0.75 L.

16. $\frac{2}{3} + \frac{1}{6}$

A. $\frac{3}{9}$ B. $\frac{1}{2}$ C. $\frac{5}{6}$ D. $1\frac{1}{3}$

Problem-Solving Applications

Woodland Wildlife Woodlands are home for many living things, from small insects and tiny sprouting seeds to large bears and redwood trees. Researchers spend their careers studying these living things and how they affect each other.

Trivia When a woodpecker taps a hole in a tree, its head moves at about 13 miles per hour. To catch bugs in the tree, the bird uses its sticky tongue that extends from inside its nostrils, around its skull, and up to 4 inches out its beak.

1 About $\frac{7}{10}$ of the animals in woodlands are insects. What fraction of woodland animals are NOT insects?

Using Key Facts

2 List the animals in the Key Facts chart in order of size, from largest to smallest.

Key Facts

Animal	Body Size
• Badger	0.8 m
• Boar	1.30 m
• Brown bear	2.5 m
• Brown hare	0.76 m
• Red fox	0.86 m

3 About 26 out of every 100 acres of Earth's land are covered by woodlands. What fraction of Earth's lands are woodlands?

Dorling Kindersley

❹ Bristlecone pines are among the oldest and slowest growing trees in the world. One tree is believed to be 4,600 years old. These trees may grow only 0.01 inch each year. How long would it take this tree to grow 1 inch?

❺ **Writing in Math** Write your own word problem about woodland wildlife. Write the answer to your question in a complete sentence.

❻ **Decision Making** Name 6 different animals shown in this lesson that you would like to see on a walk through a forest. What fraction of these 6 animals are mammals?

❼ A Pacific mole has a 55 millimeter tail, a European mole has a 3.75 centimeter tail, a hairy-tailed mole has a 35 millimeter tail, and a star-nosed mole has a $7\frac{1}{4}$ centimeter tail. Order these moles from the one with the shortest tail to the one with the longest tail.

Good News/Bad News *Fire departments have protected many woodlands from fires caused by lightning. Unfortunately, this has allowed dead leaves, grass, and wood to accumulate which may make future fires more difficult to extinguish.*

Review

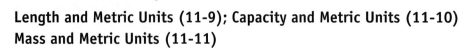

Do You Know How? | Do You Understand?

Length and Metric Units (11-9); Capacity and Metric Units (11-10) Mass and Metric Units (11-11)

Write the most appropriate metric unit to use to measure each.

1. Mass of a tomato

2. Length of a mosquito

3. Capacity of the kitchen sink

A Explain how you decided which unit to use in Exercise 2.

B Tell how you would decide how many centimeters are equal to 4 m 50 cm.

Changing Units and Comparing Measures (11-12)

Find each missing number.

4. 5 km = ___ m **5.** 2 L = ___ mL

6. 60 cm = ___ mm **7.** 3 m = ___ dm

C Explain how you decided whether to multiply or divide in Exercise 5.

D Tell how you would decide which is larger, 9 m 80 cm or 950 cm.

Problem-Solving Skill: Writing to Explain (11-13)

8. Survey of Favorite Kind of Pizza

	Cheese	Veggie	Sausage
3rd grade	6	3	11
4th grade	6	5	9
5th grade	7	2	11

Based on the survey, predict how many out of 298 students will order cheese pizza. Explain.

E How many students were surveyed in each grade?

F Tell what numbers you used in your explanation.

Temperature (11-14)

Write the temperature in °F or °C.

9.
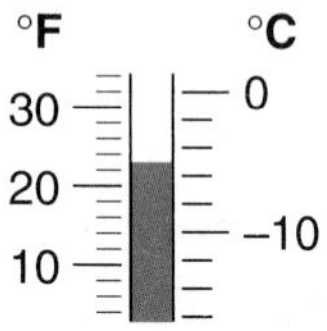

10.
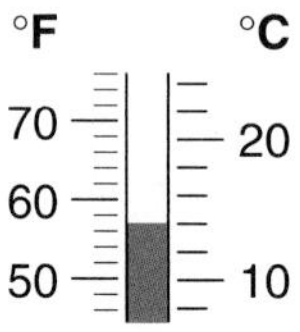

G Is 30°C or 30°F colder?

H Explain how to name a temperature that is 8° below 0°C.

Chapter 11 Section C
Diagnostic Checkpoint

TEST TALK

Think It Through
I can **use what I know** to change units.
1 L = 1,000 mL
1 kg = 1,000 g
1 m = 100 cm

MULTIPLE CHOICE

1. Which is the best estimate for the length of a canoe? (11-9)

A. 4 mm **B.** 4 cm **C.** 4 m **D.** 4 km

2. Which is equal to 2 L 500 mL? (11-12)

A. 25 mL **B.** 2500 mL **C.** 25 L **D.** 2500 L

FREE RESPONSE

3. Estimate first. Then, find the length to the nearest centimeter. (11-9)

Find each missing number. (11-12)

4. 5 kg = ■ g **5.** 100 cm = ■ m **6.** 2 L = ■ mL

Compare. Write > or <, for each ●. (11-12)

7. 3 L ● 3,200 mL **8.** 7,500 g ● 7 kg **9.** 9 m 60 cm ● 950 cm

Read each thermometer. Write the temperature in °F and °C. (11-14)

10. 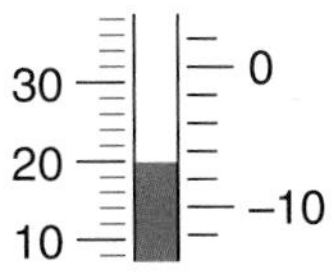

11. 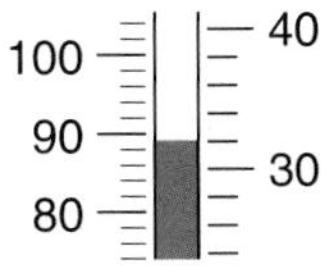

12. 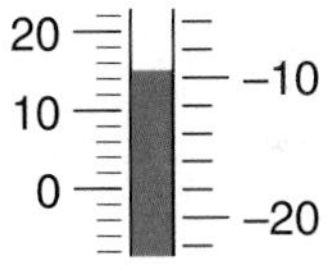

What is the best tool to use to find each measure of a bag of flour like the one shown at the right? (11-9, 11-10, 11-11)

13. Height **14.** Capacity **15.** Mass

Use metric units to give a reasonable estimate of each measure of the bag of flour at the right. (11-9, 11-10, 11-11)

16. Height **17.** Capacity **18.** Mass

Writing in Math

19. Explain how to choose which units to use to measure the mass of a table, grams or kilograms. (11-11)

20. A number cube shows 1, 2, 3, 4, 5, and 6. If you tossed the number cube 30 times, predict about how many 6s you would toss. Explain how you made your prediction. (11-13)

Test-Taking Strategies

- Understand the question.
- Get information for the answer.
- Plan how to find the answer.
- **Make smart choices.**
- Use writing in math.
- Improve written answers.

Make Smart Choices

To answer a multiple-choice test question, you need to choose an answer from answer choices. The steps below will help you make a smart choice.

1. Mr. Halpern's 4th-grade class collected newspapers for recycling. Last week the class collected 16.4 kilograms of newspapers. The girls collected 9.7 kilograms of newspapers. How much did the boys collect?

A. 6.7 kilograms of newspapers

B. 7.7 kilograms of newspapers

C. 26.1 kilograms of newspapers

D. 77 kilograms of newspapers

Understand the question.

__I need to find__ the amount of newspapers the boys collected.

Get information for the answer.

The __text__ gives me the numbers I need to solve the problem.

Plan how to find the answer.

I can __draw a picture__ to show the main idea and then select the right answer from the answer choices.

Make Smart Choices.

- Eliminate wrong answers.

The amount the boys collected cannot be more than the total. So answer choices C and D are wrong.

- Check answers for reasonableness; estimate.

I can __estimate__ the difference. 16 − 10 = 6. So both answer choices A and B are reasonable.

- Try working backward from answer.

I can __use addition to work backward.__ Start with answer choice A.

6.7 + 9.7 = 16.4. That works.

The correct answer is A, 6.7.

2. What unit of measure would be the most appropriate for measuring the actual distance from Iowa City to Des Moines?

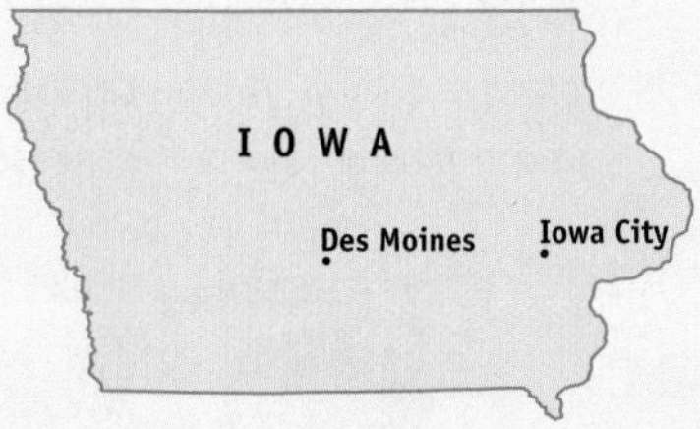

A. centimeters

B. millimeters

C. kilometers

D. decimeters

Think It Through

I need to choose the best units for measuring the distance between two cities. A stick of chalk is about a centimeter thick and a decimeter long. So, answer choices A and D are too small, and I should eliminate them. Millimeters are even smaller, like the thickness of pencil lead. So, I'll eliminate answer choice B. That leaves answer choice C, which is reasonable because kilometers are used to measure long distances. Answer choice C, kilometers, is the best choice.

Now it's your turn.

For each problem, give the answer and explain how you made your choice.

3. The capacity of which item is most appropriately measured in milliliters?

A. paint bucket

B. dosage of cough syrup

C. garbage can

D. water tank

4. Ben follows an 8.3-kilometer route from home to his grandfather's house. He rides a bus for 5.5 kilometers and walks the rest of the distance. How far does Ben walk?

A. 28 kilometers

B. 13.8 kilometers

C. 3.8 kilometers

D. 2.8 kilometers

Key Vocabulary and Concept Review

The "th" in tenths and hundredths tell you they represent fractional parts.

*Remember, a dime is one **tenth** of a dollar, and a penny is one **hundredth** of a dollar. (p. 625)*

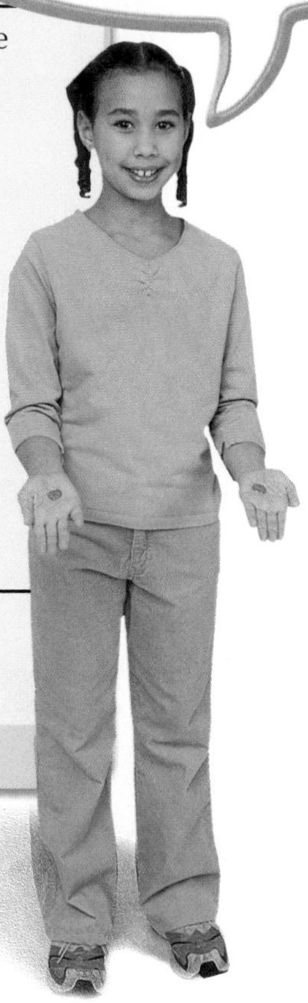

Self Check

Write, compare, and round decimals. (Lessons 11-1, 11-2, 11-3, 11-4)

Show ways to write decimals.

Place-value chart:

ones	tenths	hundredths
2 .	1	5

Standard form: 2.15

Expanded form: 2 + 0.1 + 0.05

Word form: Two and fifteen hundredths

Fraction form: $2\frac{15}{100} = 2\frac{3}{20}$

Compare.

3.76 ○ 3.67.

Line up the places. Begin at the left. Find the first place where the digits are different and compare.

3.**7**6

3.**6**7 — 7 tenths > 6 tenths

So, 3.76 > 3.67.

Round 0.37 to the nearest tenth.

rounding place ↓

0.37

↑ 7 ≥ 5, so change 3 to 4.

So, 0.37 rounds to 0.4.

1. Write 0.75 as a fraction in simplest form.

2. Compare 0.59 to 0.53, and round 3.54 to the nearest tenth.

*Remember, to **estimate**, you use numbers that are easy to work with to find an amount close to the actual answer. (p. 636)*

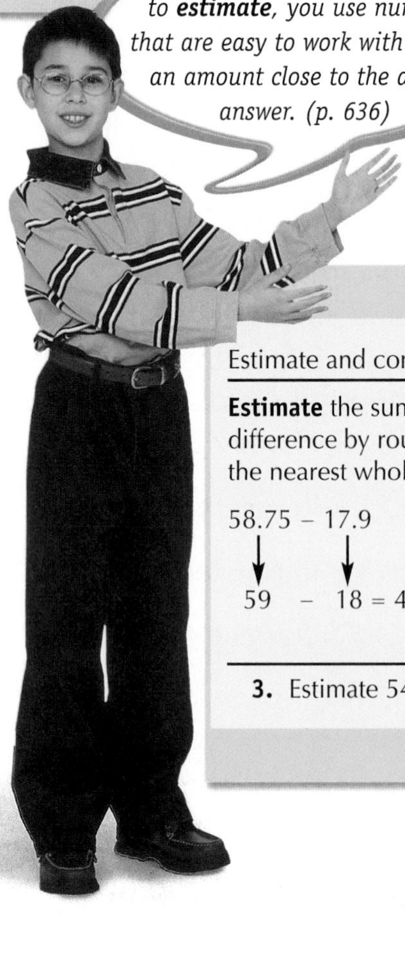

Self Check

Estimate and compute sums and differences of decimals. (Lessons 11-5, 11-6, 11-7)

Estimate the sum or difference by rounding to the nearest whole number.

58.75 − 17.9

↓ ↓

59 − 18 = 41

Add or subtract by lining up the decimal points. Write zeros as placeholders, if needed. Regroup as necessary. Place the decimal point in the answer.

$$\begin{array}{r} {}^{1\,1}\\ 19.40 \\ +\ \ 6.83 \\ \hline 26.23 \end{array} \qquad \begin{array}{r} {}^{7\ 17}\\ 5\,\not{8}.\not{7}\,5 \\ -\,1\,7.9\,0 \\ \hline 4\,0.8\,5 \end{array}$$

3. Estimate 54.3 + 41.25 and find 87.28 − 61.9 and 1.04 + 1.65.

Metric sounds similar to "meter."

*For measuring length, the **meter** is the basic **metric unit of measure.** (p. 652)*

Self Check

Use metric units of measurement. (Lessons 11-9, 11-10, 11-11, 11-12, 11-14)

Measure the worm to the nearest millimeter.

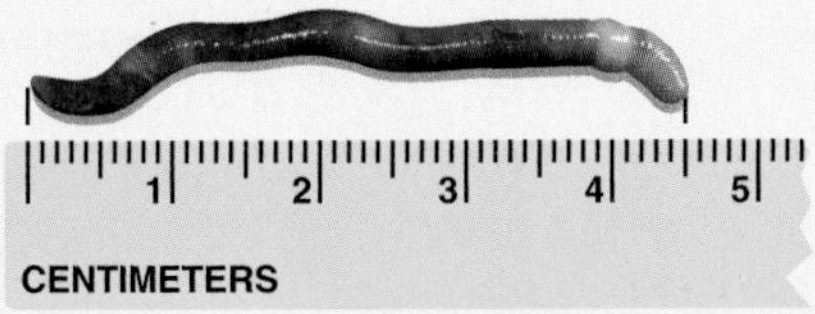

Tell an appropriate unit to measure each.

Capacity of a water bottle

Liter Some water bottles hold 1 L.

Mass of a raisin

Gram The mass of a raisin is about 1 g.

Metric Units of Length
1 centimeter (cm) = 10 millimeters (mm)
1 decimeter (dm) = 10 cm
1 meter (m) = 100 cm
1 kilometer (km) = 1,000 m

Metric Units of Capacity
1 liter (L) = 1,000 milliliters (mL)

Metric Units of Mass
1 kilogram (kg) = 1,000 grams (g)

4. Tell an appropriate unit to measure the length of a belt.

5° and −5° are on opposite sides of 0°.

*5° is above 0°, and **negative** 5 degrees is below 0°. (p. 664)*

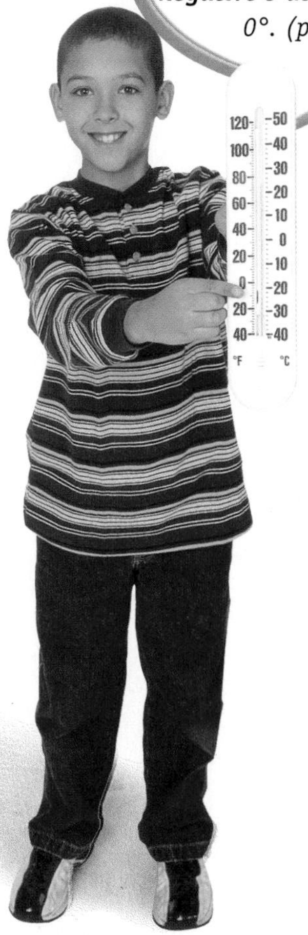

Self Check

Solve simpler problems, use thermometers, and write to explain. (Lessons 11-8, 11-13, 11-14)

How many towels can you hang on a line if you have 14 clothespins?

Simpler problems:
2 clothespins: 1 towel
3 clothespins: 2 towels
4 clothespins: 3 towels

You can hang 13 towels.

Use mathematical terms to explain the temperature shown on the thermometer.

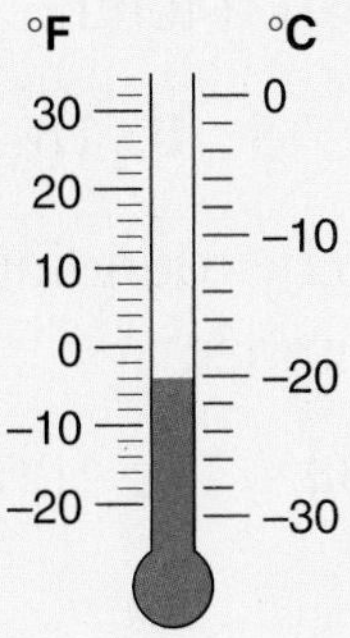

The temperature is −4 **degrees Fahrenheit** (°F). This is the same as −20 **degrees Celsius** (°C). Both temperatures are **negative**, which means they are below 0°.

5. How many knots would you have to tie to make one long rope out of 10 pieces?

Answers: 1. $\frac{3}{4}$ 2. 0.59 > 0.53; 3.5 3. Sample estimate: 95; 25.38; 2.69 4. Sample answer: centimeters 5. 9 knots

CHAPTER 11
Chapter Test

MULTIPLE CHOICE

Choose the correct letter for each answer.

1. What is $\frac{2}{5}$ written as a decimal?

A. 0.10 **C.** 0.25

B. 0.4 **D.** 2.5

2. Which of the following is NOT a way to write 3.54?

A. 3 + 0.5 + 0.04

B. $3\frac{54}{100}$

C. Three and fifty-four hundredths

D. 3 + 0.5 + 0.4

3. Which of the following numbers are written in order from least to greatest?

A. 2.11, 2.09, 2.5, 2.24

B. 2.5, 2.09, 2.11, 2.24

C. 2.09, 2.11, 2.24, 2.5

D. 2.24, 2.11, 2.5, 2.09

4. Round 17.45 to the nearest tenth.

A. 17 **B.** 17.4 **C.** 17.5 **D.** 18

5. Estimate 34.08 + 58.16 by rounding to the nearest whole number.

A. 80 **B.** 92 **C.** 94 **D.** 100

6. Ellen bought 3.75 yards of rope. She used 1.8 yards. How much rope did she have left over?

A. 1.95 yd **C.** 2.67 yd

B. 2.05 yd **D.** 5.55 yd

7. 19.5 + 16.21

A. 3.29

B. 13.71

C. 18.16

D. 35.71

TEST TALK

Think It Through
I can use **estimation to eliminate wrong answers.**

8. Which is the most reasonable estimate for the length of this ribbon?

A. 7 mm **C.** 7 dm

B. 7 cm **D.** 7 m

9. Which would be the most appropriate unit to measure the height of an apartment building?

A. millimeter **C.** meter

B. centimeter **D.** kilometer

10. Which object's capacity would best be measured in milliliters?

A. test tube **C.** fish tank

B. can of paint **D.** washing machine

11. What temperature is shown on this thermometer?

A. 13°F

B. 13°C

C. –13°F

D. –13°C

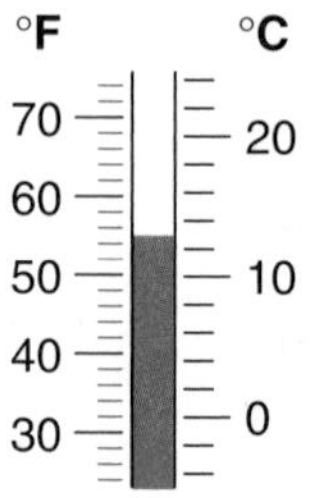

12. How many millimeters equal 7 centimeters?

A. 0.7 **C.** 700

B. 70 **D.** 7,000

13. Which is the best estimate for the mass of a bowling ball?

A. 6 g **C.** 60 g

B. 6 kg **D.** 60 kg

14. Which of the following is greater than 40 meters?

A. 40 mm **C.** 4 km

B. 400 cm **D.** 4 dm

15. One lap around a field is 500 m. If you ran 4 laps around the field, how many kilometers did you run?

A. 1 km **C.** 3 km

B. 2 km **D.** 4 km

FREE RESPONSE

Find each sum or difference.

16. 3.8 + 1.5

17. 12.8 − 7.04

18. 1.16 − 0.6

19. 37.2 + 14.18

20. 58.3 + 19.2

21. 10 − 4.19

Find each missing number.

22. 2 L = ■ mL

23. 2 m 5 cm = ■ cm

24. 18 km = ■ m

25. 9 kg = ■ g

26. 3 cm = ■ mm

Compare. Write >, <, or = for each ●.

27. 18 m ● 200 cm

28. 5,400 mL ● 6 L

29. 25 kg ● 2,500 g

30. Solve the problem. Write the answer in a complete sentence.

Squares Each side of a square is 2 cm long. Eight of these squares are placed end to end to form a rectangle. What is the perimeter of that rectangle?

Writing in Math

31. Sam asked 30 students to name their favorite season.

These are the results:

Favorite Season

Winter	Spring	Summer	Fall
4	6	15	5

Use these results to predict how many out of 516 students in his school would name summer as their favorite season. Explain how you made your prediction.

32. Explain the steps you would follow to find 4.17 − 2.9. Find the difference.

33. How are a meter, a gram, and a liter the same? How are they different? Explain.

Cumulative Review and Test Prep

Number and Operation

MULTIPLE CHOICE

1. Anthony has one quarter, one dime, one nickel, and one penny. How much money does he have in all?

A. \$4.10 **C.** \$0.50

B. \$0.95 **D.** \$0.41

2. Wendy had 50 fruit bars to put in bags for a bake sale. She put 4 bars in each bag. She ate the remaining bars. How many bars did Wendy eat?

A. 2 **C.** 46

B. 12 **D.** 54

3. Write seventy and five hundredths as a decimal.

A. 7.05 **C.** 70.5

B. 7.5 **D.** 70.05

FREE RESPONSE

4. Sam bought 3 books for \$7.00 each, and 2 CDs for \$12.00 each. He paid a total of \$2.25 in sales tax. How much did Sam spend in all?

5. Write the numbers in order from least to greatest.

2.65 2.56 2.26 2.52

Writing in Math

6. Explain how to write $\frac{4}{5}$ as a decimal.

Geometry and Measurement

MULTIPLE CHOICE

7. Which is the most reasonable estimate for the length of this screw?

A. 6 mm **C.** 6 m

B. 6 cm **D.** 6 km

8. What transformation was applied to triangle A to get triangle B?

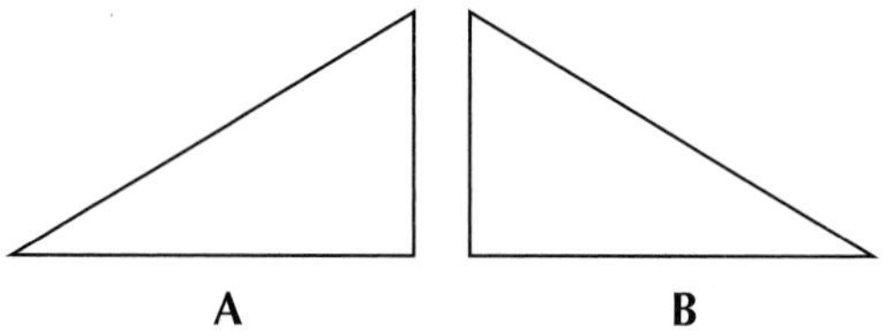

A. Translation **C.** Reflection

B. Rotation **D.** Slide

FREE RESPONSE

9. What time will it be 1 hour and 25 minutes after 11:30 A.M.?

10. A penguin has a mass of 20 kilograms. What is the bird's mass in grams?

11. Each side of a square is 4.5 m long. What is the perimeter of the square?

Writing in Math

12. Describe the figure at the right using geometry words and ideas.

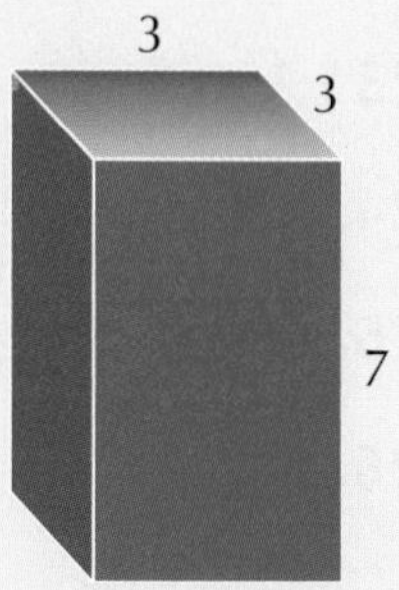

Data Analysis and Probability

MULTIPLE CHOICE

13. Which color marble are you least likely to pick from this bag?

A. green

B. yellow

C. black

D. red

14. What is the median of this data set?

15, 19, 11, 16, 16, 14, 13

A. 9 **C.** 15

B. 11 **D.** 16

FREE RESPONSE

Use the line graph for Items 15–17.

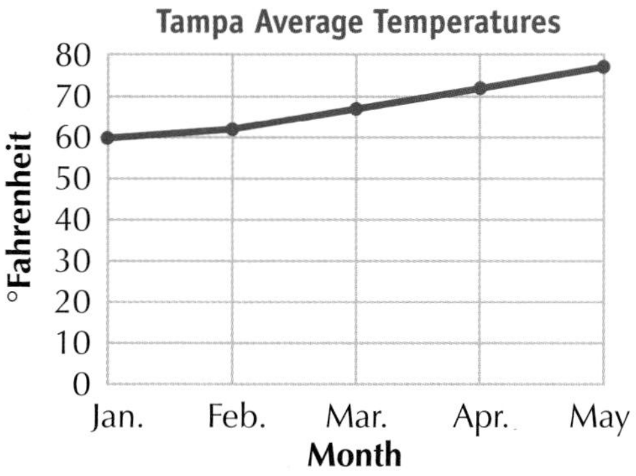

15. What is the average temperature in Tampa in January?

16. Describe the trend in the data in the graph.

Writing in Math

17. Do you think Tampa's average temperature will continue to increase through December? Explain.

Algebra

MULTIPLE CHOICE

18. What is the missing number in the pattern?

100, 10, 1, ___, 0.01, 0.001, ...

A. 1.1 **C.** 0.1

B. 1.0 **D.** 0

19. Evaluate the expression $1.18 + m$, for $m = 0.9$.

A. 0.28 **C.** 2.08

B. 1.27 **D.** 10.18

20. What property of multiplication states that $a \times (b \times c) = (a \times b) \times c$?

A. Commutative **C.** Identity

B. Associative **D.** Distributive

FREE RESPONSE

21. Complete the table and describe the rule you used.

In	0.8	1.6	2.4	3.2
Out	1.7	2.5	3.3	

22. For every kilometer that Sandy walks, she raises $20 for charity. How many kilometers will she have to walk to raise $100?

TEST TALK

Think It Through

I can **solve simpler problems** and **look for a pattern.**

Writing in Math

23. Describe how to evaluate $46 + (18 \div 3)$.

Chapter 11

Reteaching

Set 11-1 (pages 624–627)

Write $\frac{2}{5}$ as a decimal.

1	2	3
Write as an equivalent fraction with 10 or 100 as the denominator.	Read the fraction in word form.	Write what you read as a decimal.
$\frac{2}{5} = \frac{4}{10}$	four tenths	0.4

Remember, to write a decimal as a fraction, read the decimal in word form, and then write what you say as a fraction. Write the fraction in simplest form.

Write each fraction as a decimal and each decimal as a fraction.

1. $\frac{1}{4}$ **2.** 0.13 **3.** $\frac{7}{10}$ **4.** 0.5

Set 11-2 (pages 628–629)

Write the decimal shown in expanded, standard, and word form.

ones	.	tenths	hundredths
2	.	3	7

Expanded form: 2 + 0.3 + 0.07

Standard form: 2.37

Word form: Two and thirty-seven hundredths

Remember to use *and* for the decimal point when you write a decimal in word form.

1. Write twelve and sixteen hundredths in standard and expanded form.

2. Write 20 + 4 + 0.05 in standard and word form.

3. Write the word form for 37.29, and tell the value of the blue digit.

Set 11-3 (pages 630–631)

Compare 0.37 and 0.31.

One Way: Use grids.

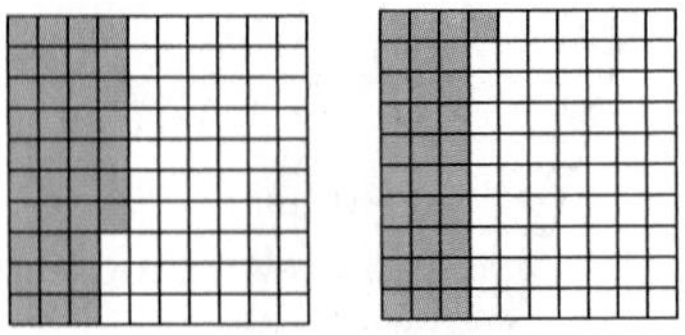

0.37 > 0.31

Another Way: Use place value.

Write the numbers, lining up the decimal points. Then compare digits by place value.

0.37 **7** hundredths > **1** hundredth

0.31 So, 0.37 > 0.31

Remember that zeros at the end of a decimal do not change its value.

Compare. Write >, <, or = for each ○.

1. 0.81 ○ 0.18 **2.** 1.07 ○ 1.7

3. 6.4 ○ 6.40 **4.** 0.52 ○ 0.25

Order from least to greatest.

5. 3.75, 3.57, 5.37

6. 0.69, 0.96, 0.6, 0.9

7. What place value would you use to compare 19.48 and 19.39? Explain.

Set 11-4 (pages 632–633)

Round 4.27 to the nearest whole number and to the nearest tenth.

1	2	3
Find the rounding place.	Compare the digit to its right to 5.	Change the rounding digit to the next greater digit or leave as is.
4.27 (4 underlined)	2 < 5	4.27 rounds to 4.
4.27 (2 underlined)	7 ≥ 5	4.27 rounds to 4.3.

Remember that if the digit to the right of the rounding digit is 5 or more, change the rounding digit to the next greatest digit. If it less than 5, leave the rounding digit as it is.

Round each number to the nearest whole number and to the nearest tenth.

1. 0.71 **2.** 5.26 **3.** 65.43

4. 4.85 **5.** 12.09 **6.** 30.68

Set 11-5 (pages 636–637)

Estimate 12.64 + 7.29.

Round each number to the nearest whole number. Then add or subtract.

12.64 + 7.29
↓ ↓
13 + 7 = 20

Remember to compare the digit in the tenths place to 5 when you round to the nearest whole number.

1. 1.8 + 0.75 **2.** 36.89 − 14.5

3. 52.3 − 11.9 **4.** 6.27 + 6.72

Set 11-6 (pages 638–641)

Find 0.75 + 0.34.

Shade 75 squares to show 0.75.

Shade 34 more squares a different color to show 0.34.

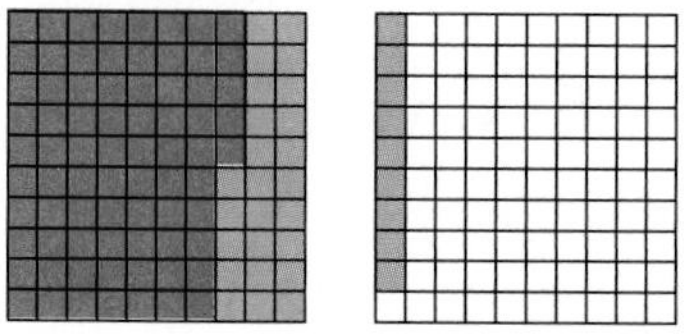

Find how much is colored in all.

0.75 + 0.34 = 1.09

Remember to subtract decimals, shade a grid or grids to show the greater number. Then cross out the lesser number of grid squares. The amount left is the difference.

1. 0.3 + 0.49

2. 0.68 − 0.17

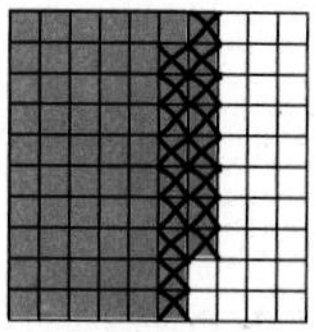

3. 0.92 − 0.55

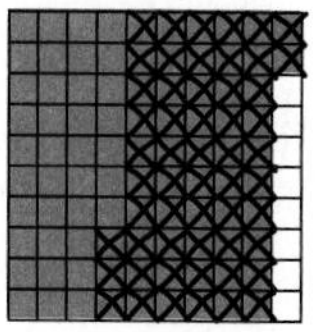

4. 0.61 + 0.25

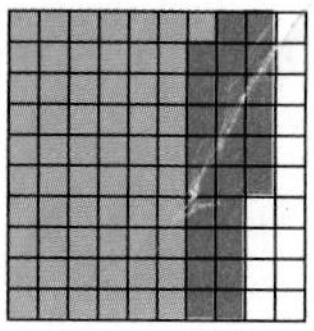

Reteaching

Set 11-7 (pages 642–645)

Find 34.27 + 16.5.

Estimate: 30 + 20 = 50

$$\begin{array}{r} 34.27 \\ +\ 16.5\mathbf{0} \\ \hline \end{array} \qquad \begin{array}{r} {}^{1} \\ 34.27 \\ +\ 16.50 \\ \hline \mathbf{50.77} \end{array}$$

Remember to line up decimal points and write zeros as placeholders if needed.

1. $\begin{array}{r} 3.28 \\ +\ 41.92 \\ \hline \end{array}$

2. $\begin{array}{r} 29.15 \\ -\ 12.07 \\ \hline \end{array}$

3. 31 − 10.5

4. 6.9 + 0.27

5. 5.64 + 3.8

6. 75.04 − 21.5

Set 11-8 (pages 648–649)

When you use simpler problems to solve a problem, follow these steps.

Step 1: Break apart or change the problem into problems that are simpler to solve.

Step 2: Solve the simpler problems.

Step 3: Use the answers to the simpler problems to solve the original problem.

Remember to look for a pattern to help solve problems.

1. Each box of nails has a label on its top and a label on each of its 4 side faces. There are 12 boxes stacked on top of each other. How many labels are visible? (Hint: Find how many labels are visible with 1 box, 2 boxes, and so on)

Set 11-9 (pages 652–653)

Which would be the most appropriate unit to measure the length of a train ride—mm, cm, dm, m, or km?

A train ride usually covers a long distance.

So mm, cm, dm, and m are too small. So, a kilometer is the best unit to use.

Remember that 1,000 meters = 1 kilometer.

Choose the most appropriate unit to measure the length of each. Write mm, cm, dm, m, or km.

1. your arm

2. your finger

3. your toenail

4. your height

Set 11-10 (pages 654–655)

Which would be the most appropriate unit to measure the capacity of a sink—mL or L?

A sink usually can hold a lot of water. So, a milliliter is too small. A liter is the best unit to use.

Remember that capacity is the amount a container can hold.

Choose the most appropriate unit to measure the capacity of each. Write mL or L.

1. an eyedropper

2. a bathtub

3. a gas tank

4. spoon

Set 11-11 (pages 656–657)

What is the most appropriate unit to measure the mass of a spider—g or kg?

A spider is very light, so it has a small mass. A kilogram is too large.

A gram is the best unit to use.

Remember that *kilo* means 1,000. So a kilogram is 1,000 grams.

Choose the most appropriate unit to measure the mass of each. Write g or kg.

1. peanut **2.** bowling ball

3. bicycle **4.** pair of socks

Set 11-12 (pages 658–661)

Find the missing number: 8 cm = ☐ mm.

Think: 1 cm = 10 mm

8 × 10 = 80

8 cm = 80 mm

Multiply to change larger units to smaller units.

Remember to change smaller units to larger units, divide.

1. 5 km = ☐ m **2.** 12 kg = ☐ g

3. 2L = ☐ mL **4.** 300 cm = ☐ m

Set 11-13 (pages 662–663)

When you write to explain a prediction, follow these steps.

Step 1: If the problem has choices, explain why some of the choices do not make sense.

Step 2: If possible, make connections between tables and graphs to help you explain your prediction.

Step 3: Use specific numbers in your explanation.

Remember to make your explanations clear so others will understand them.

1.

Survey of Students' Favorite Pet

Pet	Bird	Dog	Cat	Fish	Other
Number	4	6	5	3	2

Tammy asked 20 students to name their favorite pet. Use these results to predict about how many out of 824 students in the school would name a cat as their favorite pet. Explain your prediction.

Set 11-14 (pages 664–665)

Read the thermometer below. Write the temperature in °F and °C.

The temperature is about 50°F and about 10°C.

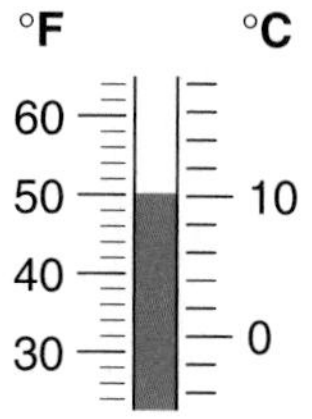

Remember that any temperature below zero is read as a negative.

Write the temperature in °C or °F.

1.

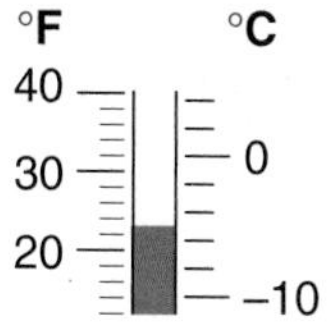

2.

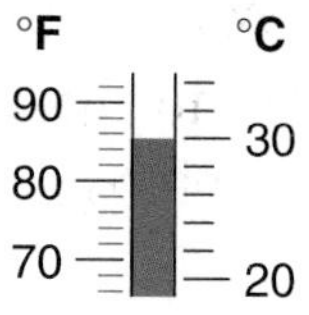

Chapter 11
More Practice

Set 11-1 (pages 624–627)

Write each number as a decimal.

1. $\frac{3}{4}$ **2.** $\frac{1}{5}$ **3.** $3\frac{9}{10}$ **4.** $1\frac{4}{5}$ **5.** $2\frac{17}{100}$

Write each decimal as a fraction or mixed number in simplest form.

6. 0.28 **7.** 1.8 **8.** 0.04 **9.** 2.5 **10.** 0.40

11. Write a decimal and a fraction for the part of the grid at the right that is blue.

12. Write a decimal and a fraction for the part of the grid at the right that is not shaded.

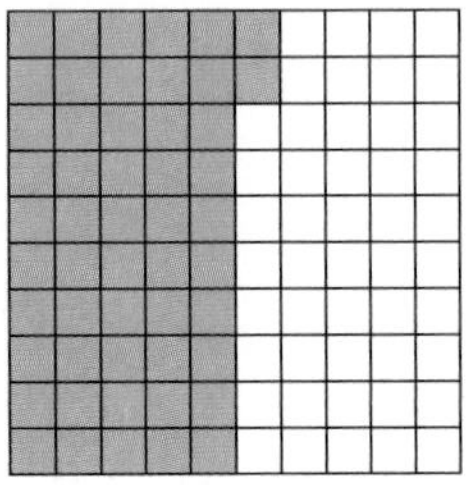

Set 11-2 (pages 628–629)

Write each number in standard form.

1. 40 + 1 + 0.5 + 0.09 **2.** Twelve and seven hundredths

3. Six and forty-nine hundredths **4.** 10 + 8 + 0.03

Write the word form for each number, and tell the value of the red digit.

5. 3.58 **6.** 12.7 **7.** 37.51 **8.** 10.69 **9.** 63.42

10. Caroline wrote a number greater than 50 and less than 100. The number had one tenth and three hundredths. Two of the digits in the number were 0 and 6. What number did Caroline write?

Set 11-3 (pages 630–631)

Compare. Write >, <, or = for each ●.

1. 0.15 ● 0.51 **2.** 3.16 ● 3.19 **3.** 0.8 ● 0.80 **4.** 1.72 ● 1.56

5. 7.08 ● 7.80 **6.** 12.4 ● 1.24 **7.** 0.29 ● 0.19 **8.** 0.34 ● 0.43

Order the numbers from least to greatest.

9. 1.65, 1.56, 1.5 **10.** 0.38, 0.8, 0.3, 0.83 **11.** 2.47, 2.54, 2.45

12. Tony caught three fish on Saturday. The cod weighed 2.35 pounds, the haddock weighed 2.5 pounds, and the shad weighed 2.55 pounds. Which fish weighed the most? Which weighed the least?

Set 11-4 (pages 632–633)

Round each number to the nearest whole number and to the nearest tenth.

1. 0.96 **2.** 5.16 **3.** 12.75 **4.** 41.23 **5.** 0.18

6. 33.07 **7.** 5.24 **8.** 0.49 **9.** 10.62 **10.** 1.99

11. Use the number line at the right. Round 4.42 to the nearest tenth. Explain how the number line helped you round.

Set 11-5 (pages 636–637)

Estimate each sum or difference to the nearest whole number.

1. 4.9 + 3.8 **2.** 9.14 − 7.2 **3.** 8.51 − 1.54 **4.** 6.7 + 2.1

5. 2.5 + 6.1 **6.** 5.09 − 4.35 **7.** 11.03 + 0.84 **8.** 8.16 − 3.45

9. The Johnsons have two dogs named Ginger and Ralph. Ginger weighs 68.16 pounds. Ralph weighs 42.75 pounds. About how much do the two dogs weigh together? About how much more does Ginger weigh than Ralph?

Set 11-6 (pages 638–641)

Add or subtract. You may use grids to help.

1. 0.3 + 0.54

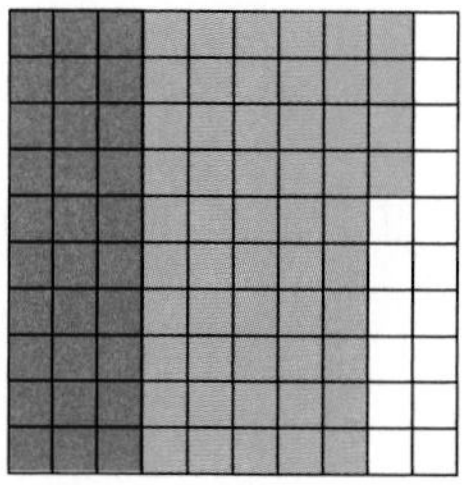

2. 0.81 − 0.17

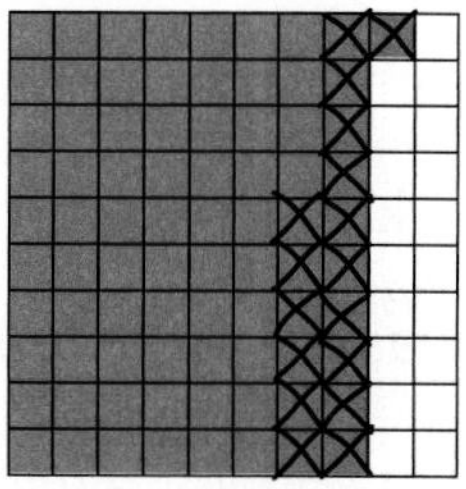

3. 0.56 − 0.28

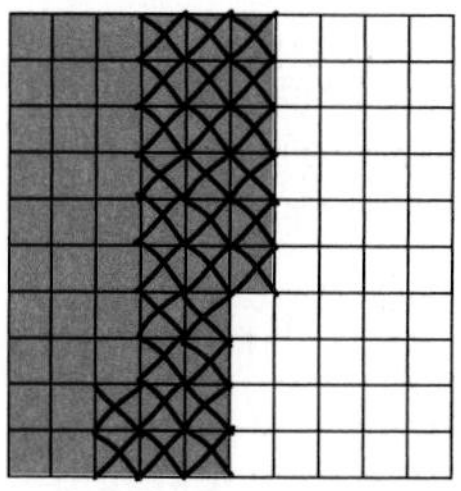

4. 0.6 + 0.83 **5.** 1.4 − 0.6 **6.** 0.47 − 0.09 **7.** 1.5 + 1.5

8. Sharon mixed 0.38 ounce musk oil with 0.5 ounce of sandalwood oil to make perfume. Did she make more or less than one ounce of perfume? Explain.

More Practice

Set 11-7 (pages 642–645)

Find each sum or difference.

1. $7.9 + 0.8$
2. $3.55 - 1.6$
3. $27.04 - 11.25$
4. $34.8 + 0.17$
5. $60.92 + 11.29$
6. $0.43 - 0.05$
7. $64.13 + 9.87$
8. $74.13 - 26.40$
9. In May, Elm Grove received 4.07 inches of rain. In June, the city received 3.5 inches of rain. How much rain did Elm Grove get during the two months in all? What was the difference in the two rainfall amounts?

Set 11-8 (pages 648–649)

Solve the simpler problems. Use the solutions to help you solve the original problem. Write the answer in a complete sentence.

1. Dylan made a 50-page book for his social studies project. How many digits will he write to number all the pages in his book?

   Simpler problem: How many digits are needed for pages 1 to 9? for pages 10 to 19? for pages 20 to 29? Look for a pattern.

2. Each pipe section needs a fitting placed at each end. One fitting is used to connect 2 pipe sections. How many fittings are needed to install plumbing with 12 pipe sections?

Set 11-9 (pages 652–653)

Choose the most appropriate unit to measure each. Write mm, cm, dm, m, or km.

1. length of a notebook
2. height of a Ferris wheel
3. width of a fingernail
4. distance across Iowa
5. thickness of a dime
6. length of tennis racket
7. Name three things you might measure in meters.

Set 11-10 (pages 654–655)

Choose the most appropriate unit to measure the capacity of each. Write mL or L.

1. juice glass
2. can of soup
3. bucket
4. washing machine
5. milk carton
6. spoon
7. How many milliliters equal one liter?

Take It to the NET
More Practice
www.scottforesman.com

Set 11-11 (pages 656–657)

Choose the most appropriate unit to measure the mass of each. Write g or kg.

1. party balloon **2.** baseball bat **3.** limousine

4. slice of bread **5.** encyclopedia **6.** vitamin pill

7. Which number would be greater, the mass of a CD in grams or the mass of the same CD in kilograms? Explain.

Set 11-12 (pages 658–661)

Find each missing number.

1. 2,000 mL = ■ L **2.** 5 m = ■ cm **3.** 70 g = ■ kg

4. 50 cm = ■ mm **5.** 6,000 m = ■ km **6.** 120 cm = ■ dm

Compare. Write > or < for each ●.

7. 100 g ● 1 kg **8.** 400 cm ● 40 m **9.** 28,000 g ● 2.8 kg

10. 5,680 m ● 5 km **11.** 17 L ● 7,000 mL **12.** 25 kg ● 250,000 g

13. In the long-jump competition, Lewis jumped 6 meters. Mike jumped 700 cm, and Will jumped 85 dm. Who jumped the farthest?

Set 11-13 (pages 662–663)

Write to explain.

1. At five times during the day, students checked 20 cars that passed the school and noted whether the driver was wearing a seat belt. The results are shown in the table. Use these results to predict about how many drivers out of 1,000 were not wearing a seat belt. Explain how you made your prediction.

Seat Belt Survey

Time	Wearing Seat Belt	Not Wearing Seat Belt
8 A.M.	18	2
10 A.M.	17	3
Noon	19	1
2 P.M.	19	1
4 P.M.	16	4

Set 11-14 (pages 664–665)

Read each thermometer. Write the temperature in °F and °C.

1.
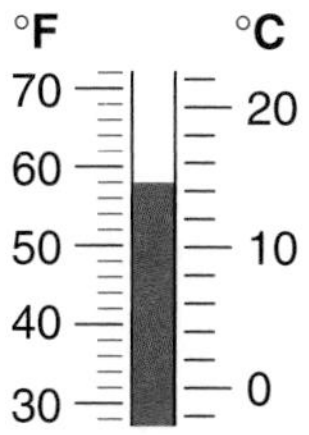

2.
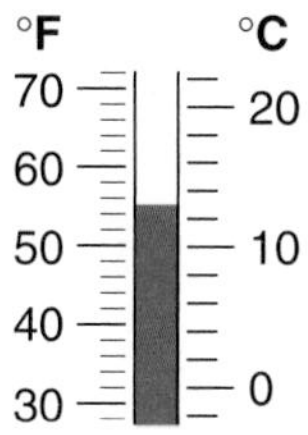

3.
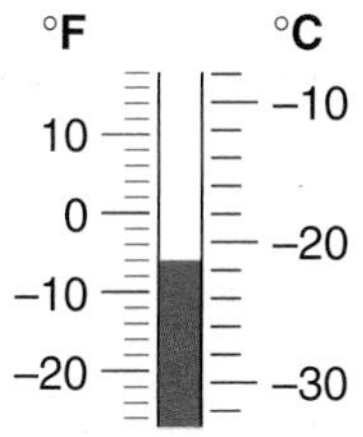

4. There was a snowstorm in Chicago today. Was the temperature outside 25°F or 25°C? Explain.

CHAPTER 12

Graphing and Probability

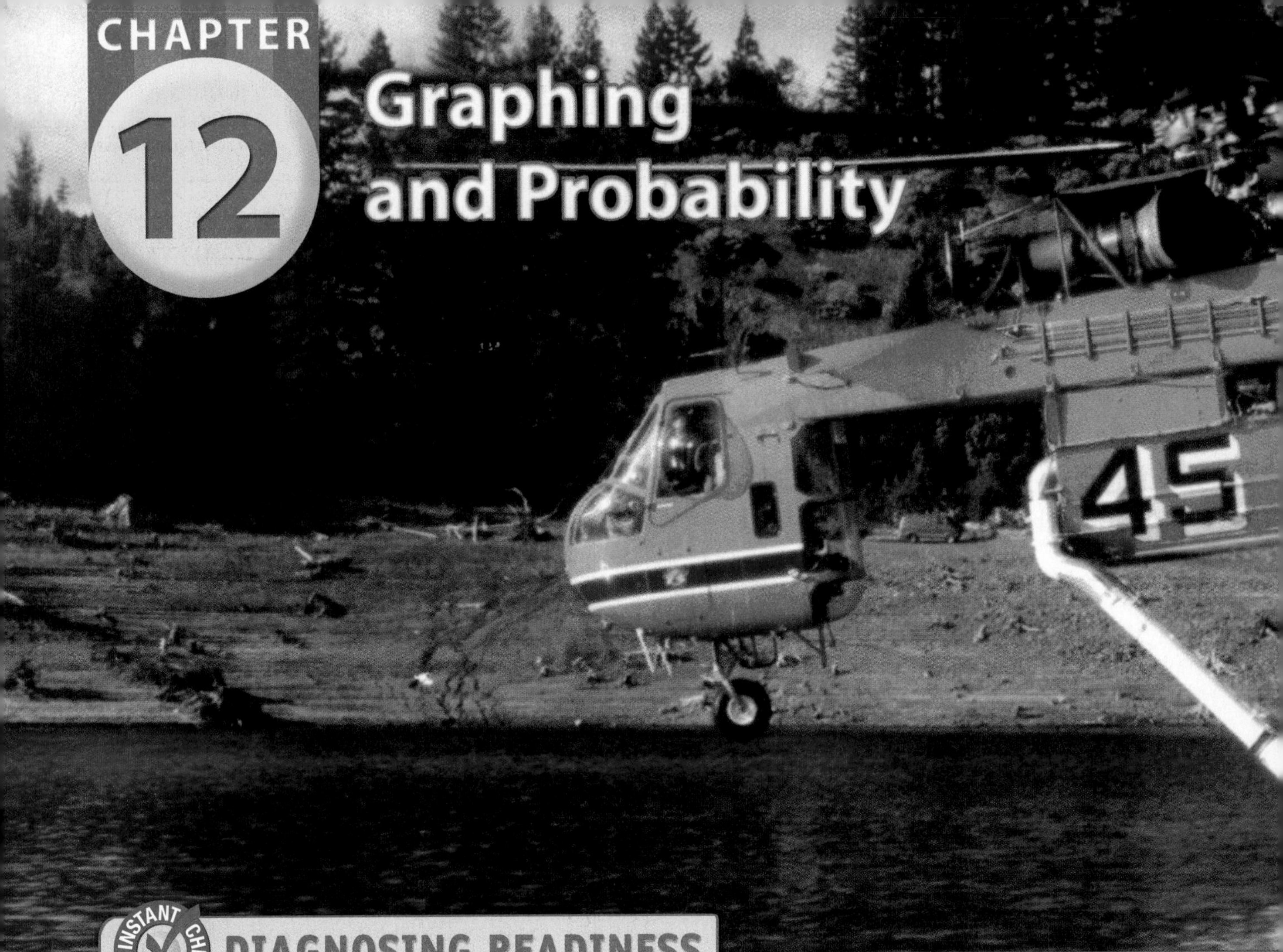

DIAGNOSING READINESS

A Vocabulary

(pages 100, 212, 516, 520)

Choose the best term from the box.

1. A pair of numbers that names a point on a coordinate grid is an __?__.

2. Fractions that name the same amount are __?__.

3. A fraction is written in __?__ if the numerator and denominator have no common factors other than 1.

Vocabulary

- **equation** *(p. 100)*
- **solution** *(p. 100)*
- **ordered pair** *(p. 212)*
- **equivalent fractions** *(p. 516)*
- **simplest form** *(p. 520)*

B Graphing Ordered Pairs

(pages 212–215)

Name the ordered pair for each point.

4. *A* **5.** *B*

6. *C* **7.** *D*

8. *E* **9.** *F*

10. *G* **11.** *H*

12. *K*

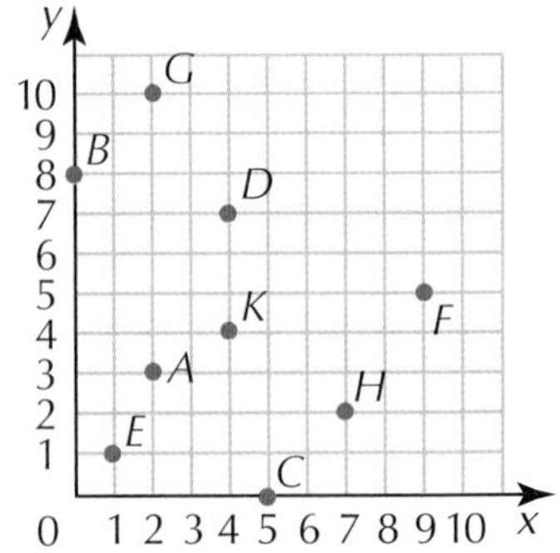

13. On a coordinate grid, start at 0 and move right 3 units. Name the coordinates of the point where you end.

Do You Know...

How many gallons of water can a helicopter drop in one hour?

You'll find out in Lesson 12-10.

C Fractions

(pages 516–521)

Multiply or divide to find an equivalent fraction.

14. $\frac{2}{3} = \frac{\square}{\square}$ (× 4 numerator, × 4 denominator)

15. $\frac{25}{35} = \frac{\square}{\square}$ (÷ 5 numerator, ÷ 5 denominator)

16. $\frac{1}{8}$ **17.** $\frac{3}{18}$ **18.** $\frac{8}{12}$ **19.** $\frac{5}{9}$

Write each fraction in simplest form.

20. $\frac{4}{8}$ **21.** $\frac{5}{15}$ **22.** $\frac{10}{12}$ **23.** $\frac{18}{24}$

24. Explain how you can tell that $\frac{7}{8}$ is in simplest form.

D Algebra

(pages 94–99)

Write an expression for each phrase.

25. 3 more than *t*

26. the total of 30 mm and *k* mm

27. *a* apples, but 7 fewer oranges

28. 8 times a number *n*

29. the cost of 7 books if each one costs *d* dollars

30. the cost of each book if 4 cost *d* dollars

31. Evaluate $2k - 1$ for $k = 3$.

Algebra

Key Idea
To solve an inequality, find values of the variable that make the inequality true.

Vocabulary
- inequality
- solution

Materials
- number lines
- crayons or markers

TEST TALK

Think It Through
- I can **try, check, and revise** to solve an inequality.
- I can **draw a number line** to show the solutions of an inequality.

Inequalities on a Number Line

WARM UP

Evaluate each expression for $x = 16$.

1. $x + 5$
2. $x - 10$
3. $2x$
4. $x \div 4$

LEARN

Activity

How do you solve an inequality?

A number sentence that uses > and < to show that two expressions do not have the same value is an **inequality.** For example, $x > 3$ is an inequality.

The number 4 is one **solution** of $x > 3$, because $4 > 3$ is true. The number 3 is not a solution, because $3 > 3$ is not true.

$x > 3$	$x > 3$
↓	↓
$4 > 3$ True	$3 > 3$ False

Inequalities have more than one solution. Some other solutions to $x > 3$ are $x = 4$, 5, 7, and 9.

Here's how to graph all the solutions of $x > 3$.

Step 1: Draw an open circle at 3 on a number line. This shows that 3 is not a solution, but numbers greater than 3 are.

Step 2: Find several solutions and color those on a number line.

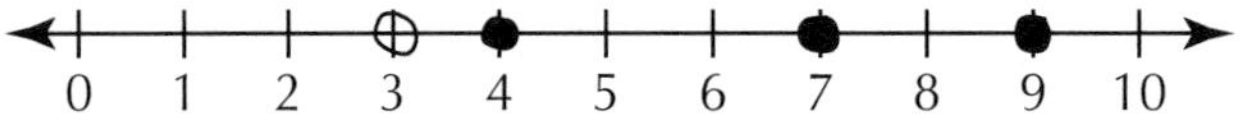

Step 3: Start at the open circle and color over the solutions you found. Draw an arrow, to show the solutions go on forever.

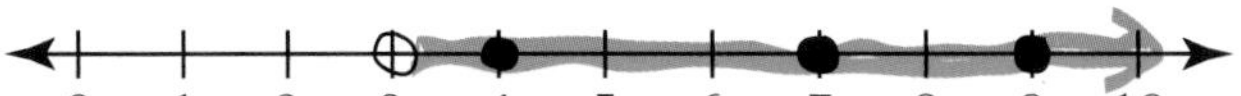

a. The number 8 is colored on the number line above. Explain why 8 is a solution of $x > 3$.

b. The number line above also implies that numbers like 100 and 3.2 are solutions. Explain why 100 and 3.2 are solutions.

c. Name three solutions to each inequality and graph all the solutions on a number line.

$x < 4$ $n > 1$ $m < 6$

CHECK

For another example, see Set 12-1 on p. 728.

Name three solutions to each inequality and graph all the solutions on a number line.

1. $m > 16$ **2.** $z < 5$ **3.** $k < 15$ **4.** $p > 7$

5. Number Sense The number line at the right shows the solutions to an inequality. Is 2 a solution? Is 6.25? Is $7\frac{1}{2}$? Explain how you can tell.

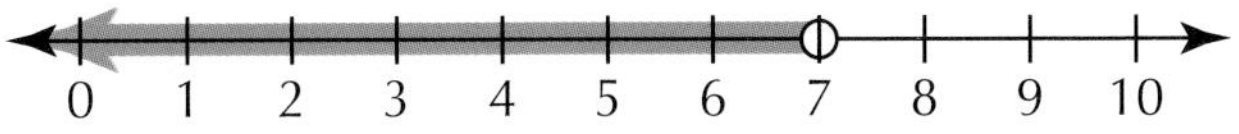

PRACTICE

For more practice, see Set 12-1 on p. 731.

A Skills and Understanding

Name three solutions to each inequality and graph all the solutions on a number line.

6. $a < 3$ **7.** $t > 12$ **8.** $r > 2$ **9.** $k > 4$

10. $b > 9$ **11.** $n < 7$ **12.** $c < 2$ **13.** $h > 6$

14. $p < 20$ **15.** $m < 9$ **16.** $f > 10$ **17.** $u < 21$

18. Number Sense Could 18 + 4 be a solution to the inequality $x < 18$? Explain.

B Reasoning and Problem Solving

In 1952, Japanese inventor, Yoshiro NakaMats, obtained a patent for the 'floppy' disk technology. Dr. NakaMats also claims the invention of CDs among his accomplishments.

19. Katie had \$19 when she went shopping. She had enough money to buy a CD holder. Use the inequality $d < 19$ to find three possible prices of the CD holder.

20. Writing in Math Explain how the number line at the right shows all the solutions of $x > 6$.

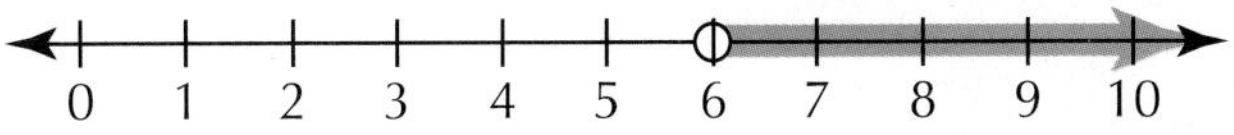

Mixed Review and Test Prep

Take It to the NET
Test Prep
www.scottforesman.com

Write the temperature in °F and °C.

21.

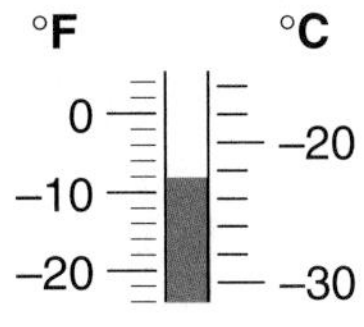

22.

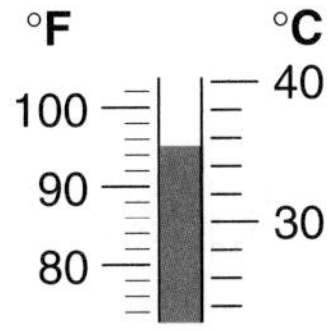

23. 6 lb 1 oz =

A. 72 oz
B. 73 oz
C. 96 oz
D. 97 oz

Algebra

Key Idea
Equations can help you solve problems.

Vocabulary
- equation (p. 100)

TEST TALK

Think It Through
- I can **draw a picture** and **write an equation** to represent the situation.
- I can **try, check, and revise** to solve an equation.

Translating Words to Equations

WARM UP

Evaluate each expression.

1. $n + 7$ for $n = 14$
2. $n - 8$ for $n = 28$
3. $5n$ for $n = 7$

LEARN

How do you write an equation?

A Great Dane puppy weighed 4 pounds when it was born. After 3 weeks, it weighed 6 pounds.

Example

Write an equation to show how much weight the puppy gained in 3 weeks.

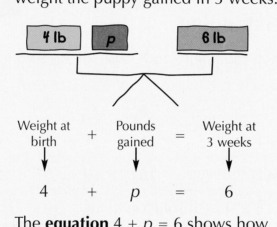

Weight at birth	+	Pounds gained	=	Weight at 3 weeks
↓		↓		↓
4	+	p	=	6

The **equation** $4 + p = 6$ shows how much weight the puppy gained in 3 weeks.

Talk About It

1. What does p stand for in the Example?
2. After 5 weeks, the puppy weighed 8 pounds. Write an equation to show how much weight the puppy gained in 5 weeks.

CHECK

For another example, see Set 12-2 on p. 728.

Write an equation for each sentence.

1. p pages plus 7 pages equals 17 pages.
2. 8 less than k is 15.
3. 9 times n is 27.
4. 36 divided by y is 12.
5. **Reasoning** Kate wanted to find how many centimeters equal 80 millimeters. She used the equation $10x = 80$. Is Kate's equation correct? Explain.

PRACTICE

For more practice, see Set 12-2 on p. 731.

A Skills and Understanding

Write an equation for each sentence.

6. 8 eggs plus r eggs equal 12 eggs.

7. k less than 14 apples is 2 apples.

8. 7 multiplied by a is 21.

9. n divided by 7 is 3.

10. h times 4 is 20.

11. 9 more than t is 15.

12. Number Sense Which equation has a greater solution, $5n = 30$ or $6n = 30$? Explain how you can tell without solving.

B Reasoning and Problem Solving

Write an equation for 13–14.

13. Terri spent \$60 to feed her full-grown Great Dane for 4 weeks. How much did Terri spend each week?

14. Troy delivered 46 newspapers on Tuesday. He delivered 62 papers on Thursday. How many fewer papers did he deliver on Tuesday?

Use the graph at the right for 15–16.

15. The students in grades 3 and 4 made \$200 washing cars. How much did they charge to wash each car?

16. Writing in Math The 7th and 8th graders needed to wash 8 more cars to equal the cars washed by the 5th and 6th graders. Explain how to find how many cars the 7th and 8th graders washed.

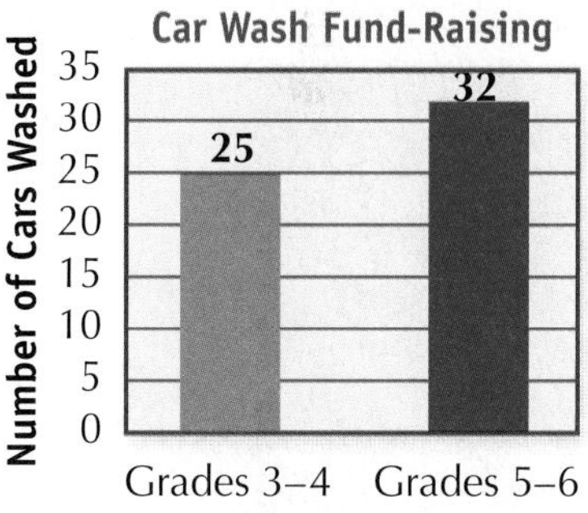

Mixed Review and Test Prep

Take It to the NET
Test Prep
www.scottforesman.com

Name three solutions to each inequality and graph all the solutions on a number line.

17. $n > 5$

18. $z > 20$

19. $k < 12$

20. $x < 2$

21. Jay started reading at 4:20 P.M. He read for 35 minutes. At what time did he finish reading?

A. 4:35 P.M. **B.** 4:50 P.M. **C.** 4:55 P.M. **D.** 4:55 A.M.

Algebra

Key Idea
Equations and their graphs can represent situations.

Vocabulary
- ordered pair (p. 212)

Materials
- grid paper or e tools

TEST TALK

Think It Through
I can write $2 \times x$ as $2x$.

Equations and Graphs

WARM UP

Evaluate each expression for $x = 5$.

1. $x + 10$
2. $x - 1$
3. $7x$
4. $2x - 3$

LEARN

How do you graph an equation?

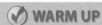

Jacob earns $2 each time he washes the dishes. The table shows the total money, y, Jacob earns when he washes the dishes x times.

Dishes, x	Money, y
0	0
1	2
2	4
3	6

The rule for the table is multiply by 2. Use the rule to write an equation.

Total earned = 2 × Number of times he washes dishes

$y = 2 \times x$

Example A

Graph the equation $y = 2x$.

Use the numbers in the table above to write ordered pairs. Plot the ordered pairs on a coordinate grid. The dashed line shows that all the points lie on a straight line.

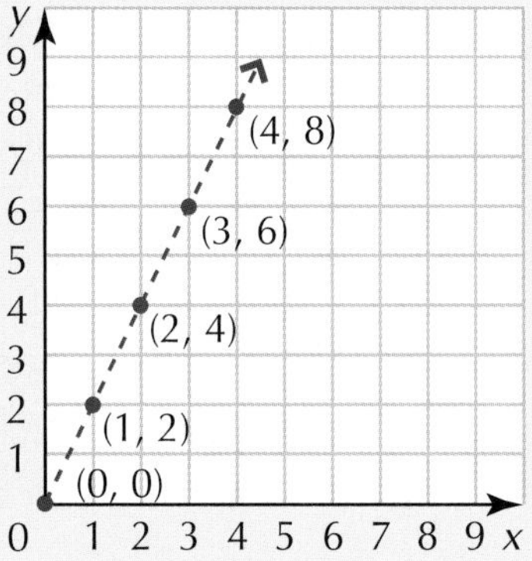

The graph of the equation $y = 2x$ is a straight line.

Example B

Graph $y = x - 2$. Use $x = 2, 3, 4, 5,$ and 6.

x	$y = x - 2$	(x, y)
2	$y = 2 - 2 = 0$	(2, 0)
3	$y = 3 - 2 = 1$	(3, 1)
4	$y = 4 - 2 = 2$	(4, 2)
5	$y = 5 - 2 = 3$	(5, 3)
6	$y = 6 - 2 = 4$	(6, 4)

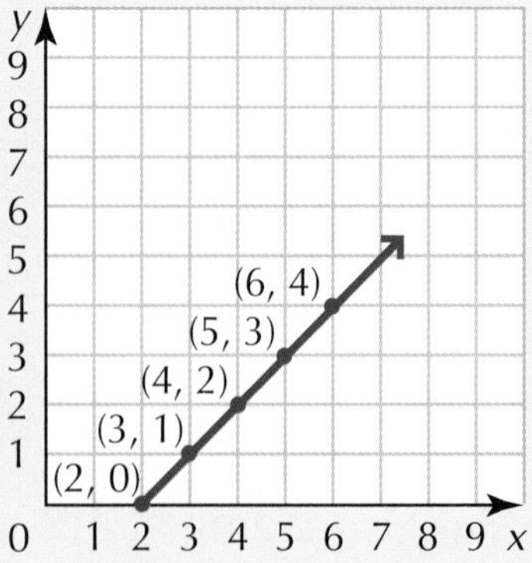

Talk About It

1. What do you notice about the graphs in Examples A and B?

2. Reasoning The graph in Example A shows a trend in the data. Describe the trend.

How do you find ordered pairs on the graph of an equation?

Example C

Find 5 ordered pairs on the graph of $y = 2x + 1$.

Make a table. Choose 5 values for x. Then, evaluate $2x + 1$ for each value of x.

x	$y = 2x + 1$	(x, y)
0	$y = (2 \times 0) + 1 = 0 + 1 = 1$	(0, 1)
1	$y = (2 \times 1) + 1 = 2 + 1 = 3$	(1, 3)
2	$y = (2 \times 2) + 1 = 4 + 1 = 5$	(2, 5)
3	$y = (2 \times 3) + 1 = 6 + 1 = 7$	(3, 7)
4	$y = (2 \times 4) + 1 = 8 + 1 = 9$	(4, 9)

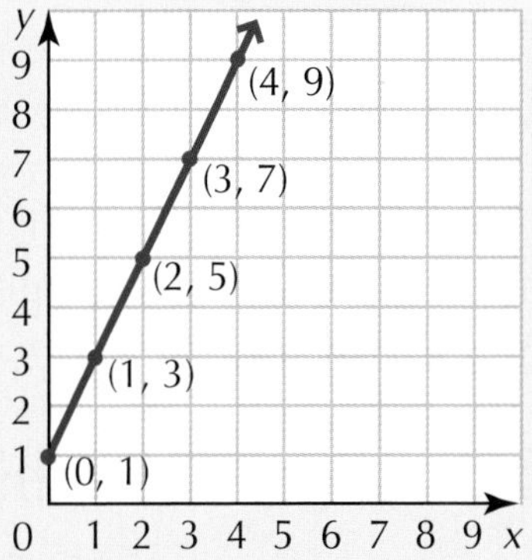

Five ordered pairs on the graph of $y = 2x + 1$ are (0, 1), (1, 3), (2, 5), (3, 7), and (4, 9).

Talk About It

3. In Example C, why do you multiply before you add?

4. Name two more ordered pairs on the graph of the equation $y = 2x + 1$.

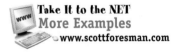

Take It to the NET
More Examples
www.scottforesman.com

For another example, see Set 12-3 on p. 728.

CHECK

For 1–4, use the equation $y = 3x + 1$. Find the value of y for each value of x.

1. $x = 2$ **2.** $x = 5$ **3.** $x = 10$ **4.** $x = 0$

5. Graph $y = x + 2$ on a coordinate grid.

6. Reasoning Roger says (3, 8) is a solution of the equation $y = 4x$. Is he correct? Explain how you can tell.

PRACTICE

For more practice, see Set 12-3 on p. 731.

A Skills and Understanding

For 7–12, use the equation $y = 5x - 2$. Find the value of y for each value of x.

7. $x = 4$ **8.** $x = 3$ **9.** $x = 10$ **10.** $x = 0$ **11.** $x = 20$ **12.** $x = 8$

For 13–15, graph each equation on a separate coordinate grid.

13. $y = 3x$ **14.** $y = x - 1$ **15.** $y = 2x - 1$

For 16–18, find five ordered pairs on the graph of each equation.

16. $y = x - 4$ **17.** $y = x + 7$ **18.** $y = 3x - 3$

19. Number Sense The graph of an equation is shown at the right. Name three solutions to the equation.

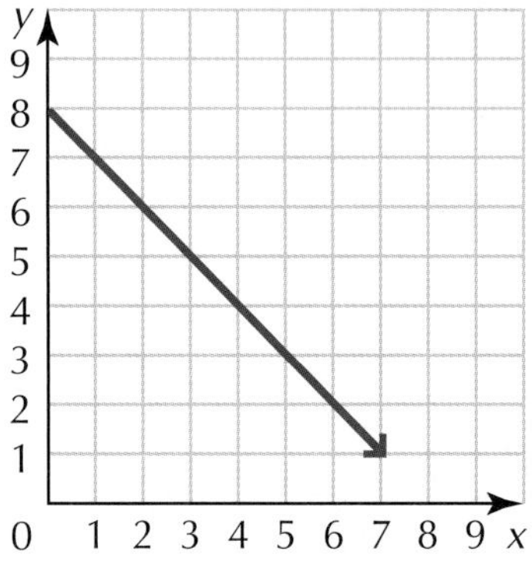

B Reasoning and Problem Solving

20. Use the data on page 692. Suppose Jacob owes his little sister \$5. How much money does Jacob have if he washes the dishes 4 times, and then pays his sister?

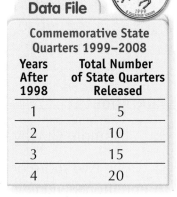

Math and Social Studies

21. The data file at the right shows the total number of different state quarters in circulation each year after 1998. Find a rule for the table. Then, write an equation.

22. The year 2004 is 6 years after 1998. How many different commemorative state quarters were in circulation by 2004?

Data File

Commemorative State Quarters 1999–2008

Years After 1998	Total Number of State Quarters Released
1	5
2	10
3	15
4	20

The new quarters are being issued in the order in which the states signed the Constitution or joined the Union.

23. **Writing in Math** Is the explanation below correct? If not, explain why.

> Is (7, 6) a solution of $y = x - 1$?
>
> $y = x - 1$
>
> ↓ ↓
>
> $7 = 6 - 1$
>
> $7 = 5$
>
> No, (7, 6) is not a solution.

TEST TALK

Think It Through

I can show that an ordered pair is a solution to an equation in **more than one way.**

PRACTICE

Mixed Review and Test Prep

Take It to the NET
Test Prep
www.scottforesman.com

Write an equation for each sentence.

24. 6 less than t is 1.

25. n divided by 8 is 8.

Find each missing number.

26. 2 mi = ___ ft

27. 4 L 500 mL = ___ mL

28. 32 oz = ___ lb

29. Heather's cat eats 3 cans of food in 2 days. How many cans will the cat eat in 2 weeks?

A. 6 cans **B.** 21 cans **C.** 28 cans **D.** 42 cans

TEST TALK

Think It Through

I can **use what I know.**

1 mi = 5,280 ft

1 L = 1,000 mL

1 lb = 16 oz

Enrichment

Distances on Coordinate Grids

Find the length of the horizontal line segment joining (5, 3) and (9, 3).

You can count units on the coordinate grid from one point to the other. The length is 4 units.

You can also use the ordered pairs.

Notice the second number in each ordered pair is the same. Subtract the first numbers.

(5, 3) to (9, 3) 9 − 5 = 4

The length is 4 units.

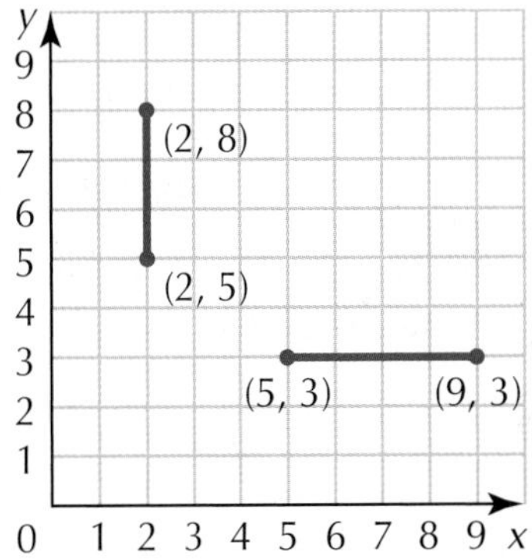

The graph above is part of a Cartesian plane. It is named for the French philosopher and mathematican Rene Descartes (1596-1650).

Find the length of the vertical line segment joining (2, 8) and (2, 5). You can count units on the coordinate grid. The length is 3 units.

You can also use the ordered pairs. Notice, the first number in each ordered pair is the same. Subtract the second numbers.

(2, 8) and (2, 5) 8 − 5 = 3

The length is 3 units.

Find the length of the line segment joining each set of points.

1. (0, 4) and (0, 9) **2.** (3, 1) and (3, 7) **3.** (1, 8) and (4, 8)

4. (6, 0) and (4, 0) **5.** (5, 2) and (1, 2) **6.** (5, 9) and (5, 2)

Lesson 12-4

Problem-Solving Skill

Key Idea
Some problems have extra information and some do not have enough information to solve them.

Reading Helps!

Identifying supporting details

can help you with...

identifying extra or missing information.

Extra or Missing Information

LEARN

Do word problems contain only the information needed to solve them?

Sports Shoes Twice as many running shoes were sold as tennis shoes. How many fewer golf shoes were sold than running shoes?

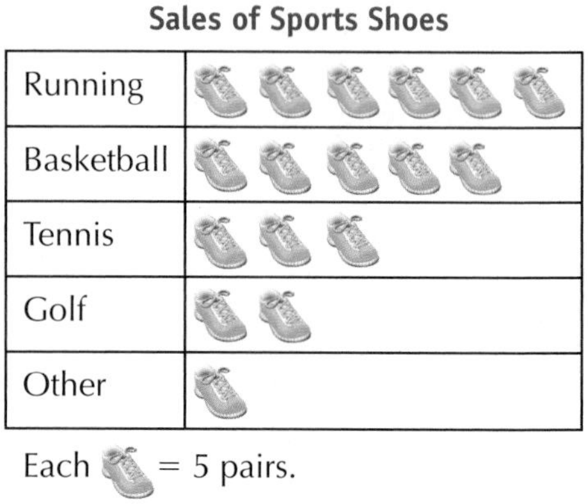

TEST TALK

Think It Through
- I need to **use details** about the number of golf and running shoes sold to help me solve the problem.

Read and Understand

Step 1: What do you know?

- Tell the problem in your own words. — A pictograph shows the number of shoes sold.
- Identify key details and facts. — Six shoes are shown for running shoes, and two shoes are shown for golf shoes.

Step 2: What are you trying to find?

- Tell what the question is asking. — How many fewer golf shoes than running shoes were sold?
- Show the main idea.

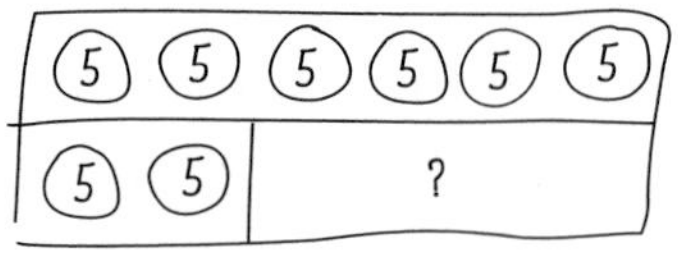

Plan and Solve

- Find and use the needed information. — 30 pairs of running shoes and 10 pairs of golf shoes were sold. So, 30 − 10 = 20 fewer pairs of golf shoes were sold.

Talk About It

1. What was the extra information in the Sports Shoes problem?

CHECK

For another example, see Set 12-4 on p. 729.

Decide if each problem has extra information or not enough information. Tell any information that is not needed or that is missing. Solve if you have enough information.

1. A notebook costs $2.48 and a pen costs $1.49. Does Sarah have enough money to buy a notebook and two pens?

2. A box holds 200 ski caps. Each cap sells for $6. The first day 28 caps were sold. How many caps were left in the box?

PRACTICE

For more practice, see Set 12-4 on p. 732.

For 3–8, decide if each problem has extra information or not enough information. Tell any information that is not needed or that is missing. Solve the problem if you have enough information.

3. Maggie has 2 turtles and 3 cats. She gave her turtles 100 feeder fish. After 3 days, she counted 34 feeder fish left. How many feeder fish did the turtles eat in 3 days?

The circle graph at the right shows the results of a survey of fourth graders. Use the graph for 4–6.

Favorite Computers

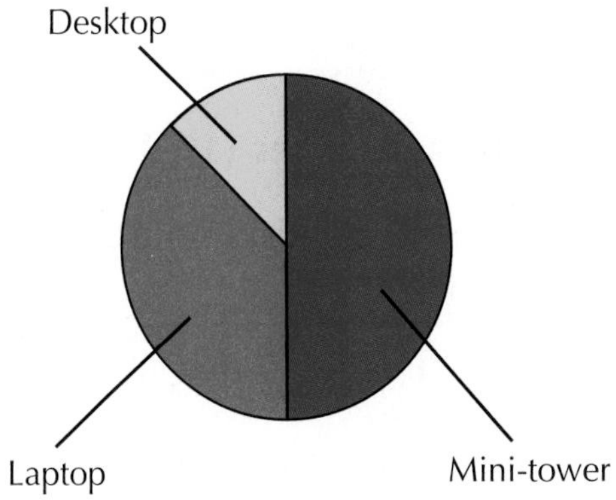

4. What fraction of the fourth graders said a mini-tower is their favorite type of computer?

5. How many of the fourth graders said a laptop is their favorite type of computer?

6. How many more fourth graders said a laptop is their favorite type of computer than said a desktop computer is?

For 7–8, use the graph on page 696.

7. How many pairs of shoes were sold in all?

8. How much more money was made on basketball shoes than on tennis shoes?

9. **Writing in Math** Make up the missing information needed to solve one of the problems above. Then find the answer.

Review

Do You Know How?

Do You Understand?

Inequalities on a Number Line (12-1)

Name three solutions to each inequality and graph all the solutions on a number line.

1. $m < 10$
2. $z > 4$
3. $k > 14$
4. $p < 5$

A Tell how you know a number is a solution to an inequality.

B Explain how your number line in Exercise 2 shows that 7 is a solution of $z > 4$.

Translating Words to Equations (12-2)

Write an equation for each sentence.

5. 5 more than s is equal to 14.
6. t less than 16 is 13.
7. k times 8 is 24.

C Tell how you wrote the equation in Exercise 7.

D Explain how you know which operation to use in Exercise 6.

Equations and Graphs (12-3)

Graph each equation on a separate coordinate grid.

8. $y = x + 3$
9. $y = 3x$

Use the equation $y = 5x + 3$. Find the value of y for each value of x.

10. $x = 2$
11. $x = 9$

E Tell how you graphed the equation in Exercise 8.

F Name 5 ordered pairs on the graph of the equation in Exercise 9.

Problem-Solving Skill: Extra or Missing Information (12-4)

Decide if the problem has extra information or not enough information. Solve if you have enough information.

12. **Doll Dresses** Madison has 6 dolls. Each doll has 2 dresses and 1 pair of shoes. How many doll dresses does Madison have?

G Tell the key details and facts of the Doll Dresses problem.

H Tell what information was not needed to solve the Doll Dresses problem.

Diagnostic Checkpoint

MULTIPLE CHOICE

1. Which ordered pair is a solution for the equation $y = x + 7$? (12-3)

   A. (2, 8) **B.** (8, 2) **C.** (1, 8) **D.** (3, 8)

2. 5 is NOT a solution for which inequality? (12-1)

   A. $x > 1$ **B.** $x < 3$ **C.** $x > 4$ **D.** $x < 7$

TEST TALK

Think It Through
I can **draw a picture** to find the solution to an inequality, to represent a situation, and to graph an equation.

FREE RESPONSE

Name three solutions to each inequality and graph all the solutions on a number line. (12-1)

3. $a < 3$ **4.** $r < 8$ **5.** $k > 11$ **6.** $n > 0$

Write an equation for each sentence. (12-2)

7. 2 bees plus *d* bees equal 11 bees. **8.** *n* divided by 6 is 7.

For 9–12, use the equation $y = 4x - 3$. Find the value of y for each value of x. (12-3)

9. $x = 3$ **10.** $x = 6$ **11.** $x = 1$ **12.** $x = 10$

Graph each equation on a separate coordinate grid. (12-3)

13. $y = x + 4$ **14.** $y = x - 6$ **15.** $y = x$ **16.** $y = 2x + 3$

Use the information at the right for 17–18. Decide if each problem has extra information or not enough information. Tell any information that is not needed or that is missing. Solve if you have enough information. (12-4)

Minutes Dana Walked First Week of June

Day	Minutes
Monday	28
Tuesday	35
Wednesday	40
Thursday	33
Saturday	25

17. Dana walked twice as many minutes the second week of June as Pam walked the first week. How many minutes did Dana walk the first week of June?

18. How many minutes did Dana and Sally walk together?

Writing in Math

19. Explain why 9 cannot be a solution for $s < 9$. (12-1)

20. Explain why (3, 6) would be a point on the graph of the equation $y = 2x$. (12-3)

Key Idea
Words like likely, impossible, and fair describe probability.

Vocabulary
- probability
- likely
- unlikely
- impossible
- certain
- equally likely
- fair
- unfair

Materials
- number cubes labeled 1 to 6 or e tools

TEST TALK

Think It Through
I can **use logical reasoning** to decide whether an event is likely, unlikely, impossible, or certain.

Understanding Probability

WARM UP

Draw a set to show each fraction.

1. $\frac{2}{3}$ 2. $\frac{5}{5}$

3. $\frac{0}{6}$ 4. $\frac{1}{2}$

LEARN

How do you describe probability?

Jake is playing a game at the summer picnic in which he catches a fish. The fish have the numbers shown below.

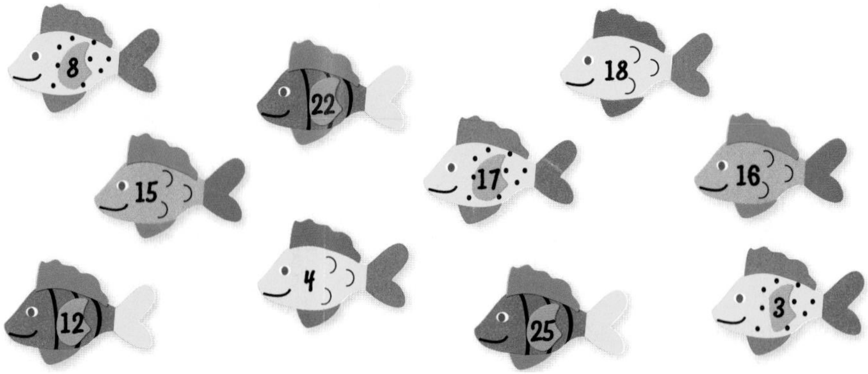

Probability is the likelihood that an event will happen. You can describe the probability that Jake will win with the words **likely, unlikely, impossible,** and **certain.** An event that is impossible can not happen. An event that is certain will happen. Most events are between impossible and certain.

Example

Is it likely, unlikely, impossible, or certain that Jake will win for each of the following winning rules?

Winning Rules

A fish with a number less than 10 wins!	Fewer than $\frac{1}{2}$ of the fish have numbers less than 10, so it is unlikely Jake will win.
A fish with a number greater than 30 wins!	None of the fish have numbers greater than 30, so it is impossible for Jake to win.
A fish with a number between 10 and 20 wins!	The same number of fish are winners as losers, so it is **equally likely** that Jake will win as lose.

Talk About It

1. How can you tell that fewer than $\frac{1}{2}$ of the fish have a number less than 10?

Activity

Is it fair?

A game is **fair** if each player is equally likely to win. If not, the game is **unfair.**

Play each game with a partner. As you play, think about whether or not the game is fair.

a. Play **Matching Numbers.**

Player A tosses two number cubes each numbered 1–6 and Player B keeps score. Player A gets a point when the numbers on the two cubes are the same. Player B gets a point when the numbers are different. The first player with 20 points wins.

b. Is Matching Numbers a fair game? Explain why or why not.

c. Play **Lesser-Greater.**

Player A keeps score and Player B tosses one number cube. Player A gets a point if the number on the cube is 3 or less. Player B gets a point if the number is greater than 3. The first player with 10 points wins.

d. Is Lesser-Greater a fair game? Explain why or why not.

Take It to the NET
More Examples
www.scottforesman.com

CHECK

For another example, see Set 12-5 on p. 729.

Tell whether it is likely, unlikely, impossible, or certain to land on red when each spinner is spun once.

1. 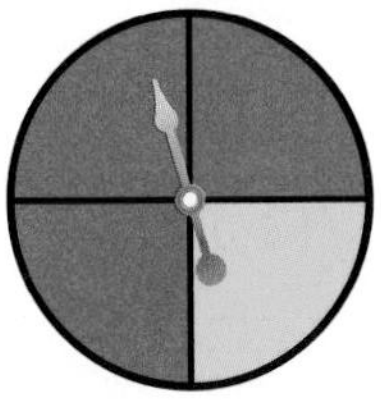

2. 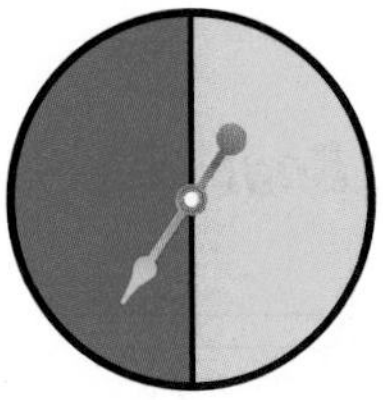

3. 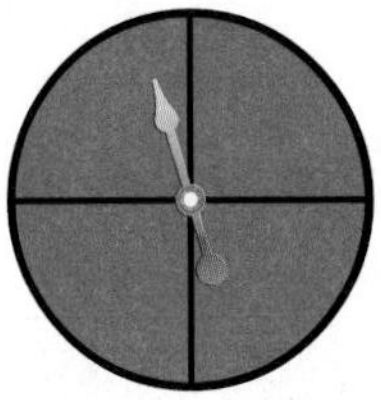

4. 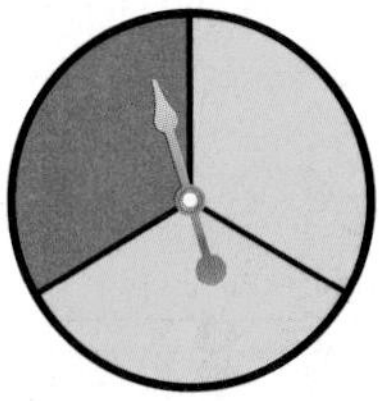

5. **Number Sense** A bag has 8 blocks that are green and orange. You are equally likely to draw a green block or an orange block from the bag. How many of each color block are in the bag?

For more practice, see Set 12-5 on p. 732.

A Skills and Understanding

Tell whether it is likely, unlikely, impossible, or certain to get each color when a marble is taken out of a bag like the one at the right.

6. red **7.** not red **8.** green

9. red or blue **10.** dark blue **11.** not orange

Number Sense In a game, Player A gets a point when a spinner lands on red and Player B gets a point when it lands on blue. Neither player gets a point for another color. Is the game fair or unfair for each spinner at the right? Explain.

12.

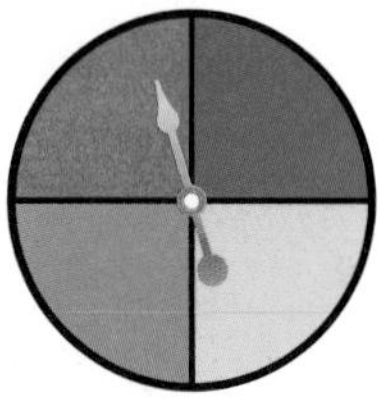

13.

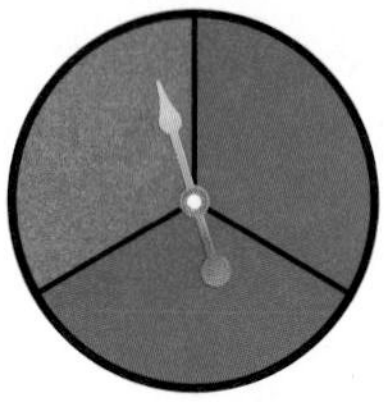

B Reasoning and Problem Solving

Math and Music

Musical notes are named after fractions that indicate the amount of time a note lasts.

Note Values

Name	Whole Note	Half Note	Quarter Note	Eighth Note	Sixteenth Note
Note	𝅝	𝅗𝅥	♩	♪	𝅘𝅥𝅯

You write the notes in the song below on cards, put them in a bag, and pick one, without looking. Is it likely, unlikely, impossible, or certain that you pick

14. a quarter note? **15.** a half note? **16.** a whole note?

17. a quarter note or sixteenth note? **18.** a note that is not a whole note? **19.** a note that is not a half note?

Row, Row, Row, Your Boat

E. O. Lyte

Row, row, row, your boat Gent - ly down the stream;

20. Writing in Math Describe an unfair game.

PRACTICE

C Extensions

Draw and color a picture of a spinner for each.

21. It is certain to spin blue.

22. It is equally likely to spin blue, red, or yellow.

23. It is likely to spin red and unlikely to spin yellow.

Mixed Review and Test Prep

Take It to the NET
Test Prep
www.scottforesman.com

24. Decide if the following problem has extra information or not enough information. Tell any information that is not needed or that is missing. Solve if you have enough information.

Kristie and Nathan are framing pictures to sell at the carnival. Kristie has framed 3 more pictures than Nathan. How many has Nathan framed?

25. 0.75 + 1.2

A. 0.87 **B.** 0.97 **C.** 1.77 **D.** 1.95

Discovery CHANNEL SCHOOL

Discover Math in Your World

Do You Have Enough Energy?

In the United States our energy today comes from petroleum, natural gas, coal, nuclear power, and water power.

1. Use the graph at the right. Petroleum, coal, and natural gas account for what fraction of the energy produced in the United States?

2. In 1950, the United States used 6.84 million barrels of petroleum each day. By 2000, this number was 12.86 million barrels greater. How many million barrels of petroleum were used each day in 2000?

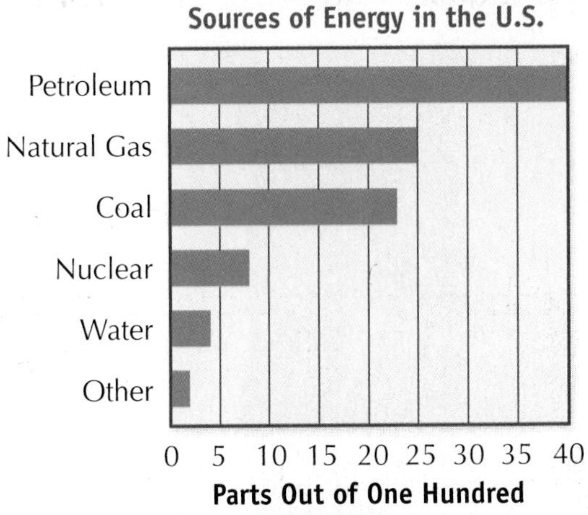

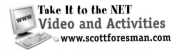

Take It to the NET
Video and Activities
www.scottforesman.com

Key Idea
You can list all the possible outcomes for probability.

Vocabulary
- outcome
- tree diagram

TEST TALK

Think It Through
I can **draw a picture** of a tree diagram to list all possible outcomes.

Listing Outcomes

WARM UP

1. Frank, Kitty, and Joanne are lining up for the spelling bee. List all the ways they could line up.

LEARN

What are the possible results?

Tamika and Janette are selecting tiles from the bag shown at the right. The possible colors they can select are *red, blue, green,* and *yellow.* Each possible result is an **outcome.**

Example

List all the possible outcomes for spinning the spinner shown and tossing a number cube with numbers 1 to 6.

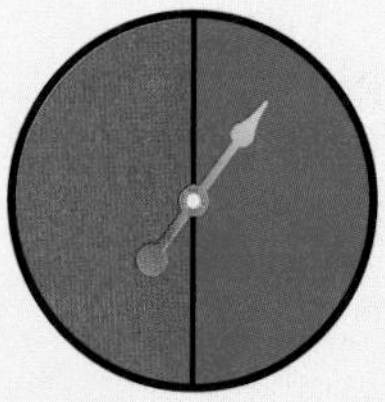

You can use a **tree diagram** to find the possible outcomes.

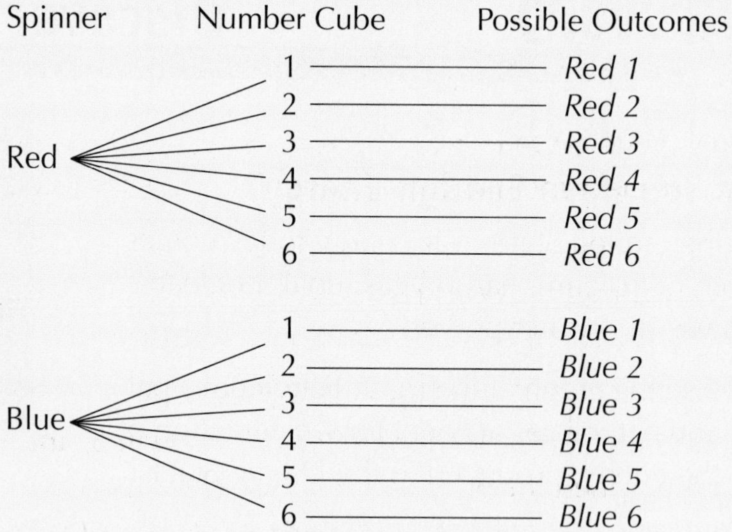

There are 12 possible outcomes.

Talk About It

1. Can Tamika and Janette select an orange tile?
2. In the Example, is Red 8 a possible outcome?

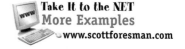

Take It to the NET
More Examples
www.scottforesman.com

CHECK

For another example, see Set 12-6 on p. 729.

List all the possible outcomes for each situation.

1. Spinning Spinner 1
2. Spinning Spinner 2
3. Spinning Spinners 1 and 2

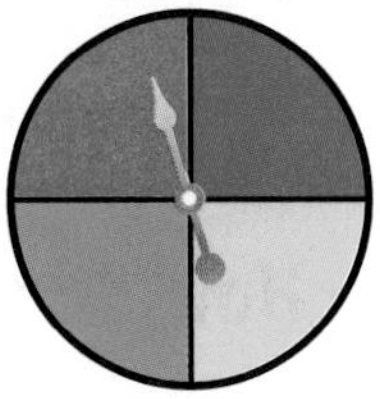
Spinner 1

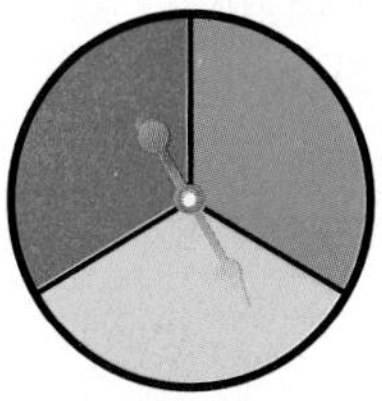
Spinner 2

4. **Reasoning** Make a tree diagram to show all the possible outcomes for spinning Spinner 2 and then tossing a number cube with numbers 0, 2, 4, 6, 8, and 10.

PRACTICE

For more practice, see Set 12-6 on p. 732.

A Skills and Understanding

List all the possible outcomes for selecting a card from each bag, without looking.

Bag 1

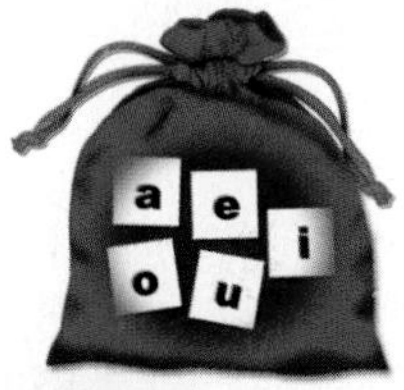

Bag 2

Bag 3

5. Bag 1
6. Bags 1 and 2
7. Bags 1 and 3
8. John is tossing two number cubes each numbered 1–6. If he adds the two numbers, what are all the possible sums?

B Reasoning and Problem Solving

You want to go to one of the restaurants listed in the table at the right and then to one of the movies listed.

Restaurants
Movies
Great Subs
Adventure
Burgers n' more
Comedy
HA HA
Wok World
Best Bar-B-Q
FANTASY

9. Make a tree diagram to show all the possible outcomes of selecting a restaurant and a movie. How many possible outcomes are there?
10. Writing in Math Andrea said that she tossed two number cubes, each numbered 1 through 6, and multiplied the two numbers. Are there more even or odd products? Explain how you know.

Mixed Review and Test Prep

Take It to the NET
Test Prep
www.scottforesman.com

11. 405 ÷ 5
12. 4.5 − 2.78
13. 373 × 45
14. Which best describes the likelihood of getting a vowel when you select a card from the bag at the right?

A. Likely **B.** Unlikely **C.** Impossible **D.** Certain

Key Idea
You can use fractions to describe probabilities.

Finding Probability

WARM UP

What part of each is green?

1. 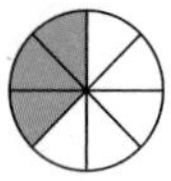
2. 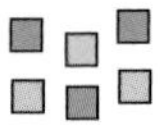

LEARN

How do you find a probability?

You can use fractions to describe the probability of an event.

$$\text{Probability} = \frac{\text{number of favorable outcomes}}{\text{number of possible outcomes}}$$

Example A

Tiffany tosses a number cube with numbers 1 to 6. Find the probability she tosses an even number.

There are 6 possible outcomes: 1, 2, 3, 4, 5, and 6.

There are 3 favorable outcomes: 2, 4, and 6.

$$\text{Probability} = \frac{\text{number of favorable outcomes}}{\text{number of possible outcomes}} = \frac{3}{6} = \frac{1}{2}$$

The probability Tiffany tosses an even number is $\frac{1}{2}$.

Example B

Miguel spins the spinner shown at the right. Find the probability he does not spin yellow.

There are 4 possible outcomes: Red, Blue, Yellow, and Green.

There are 3 favorable outcomes: Red, Blue, and Green.

$$\text{Probability} = \frac{\text{number of favorable outcomes}}{\text{number of possible outcomes}} = \frac{3}{4}$$

The probability Miguel does not spin yellow is $\frac{3}{4}$.

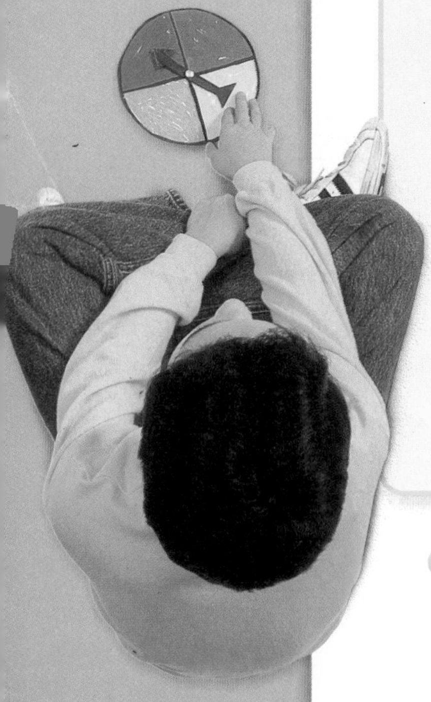

Talk About It

1. Why are there 3 favorable outcomes in Example B?
2. **Reasoning** Can there ever be more favorable outcomes than possible outcomes?

What is the probability of an impossible or certain event?

Example C

You toss a number cube with numbers 1 to 6. Find the probability you toss a number less than 7. Then find the probability you toss a 7.

There are 6 possible outcomes. All the possible outcomes are less than 7. It is certain you will toss a number less than 7.

$$\text{Probability} = \frac{\text{number of favorable outcomes}}{\text{number of possible outcomes}} = \frac{6}{6} = 1$$

None of the possible outcomes is 7. It is impossible to toss a 7.

$$\text{Probability} = \frac{\text{number of favorable outcomes}}{\text{number of possible outcomes}} = \frac{0}{6} = 0$$

The probability that you toss a number less than 7 is 1 and the probability that you toss a 7 is 0.

An impossible event has a probability of 0. A certain event has a probability of 1. Any other event has a probability between 0 and 1.

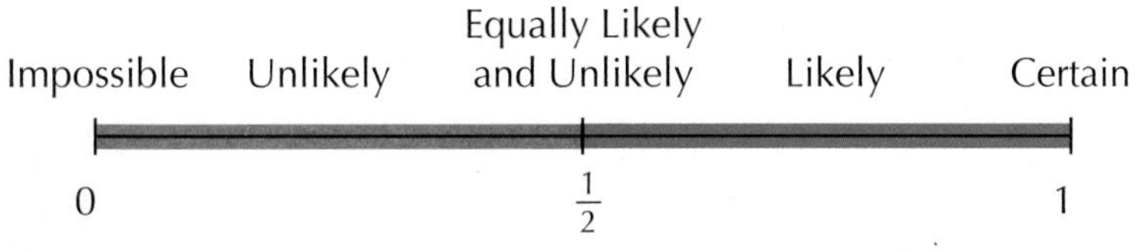

Talk About It

3. The probability an event occurs is $\frac{2}{3}$. Is the event likely, unlikely, impossible, or certain?

4. Reasoning Can an event have a probability of $\frac{9}{8}$? Explain why or why not.

Take It to the NET
More Examples
www.scottforesman.com

CHECK

For another example, see Set 12-7 on p. 730.

When the spinner at the right is spun once write the probability of landing on

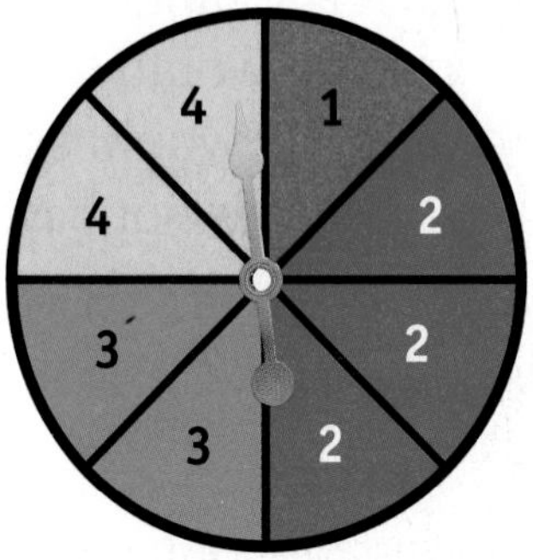

1. 2. **2.** 3. **3.** 5. **4.** a number less than 5.

5. Reasoning Is the spinner more likely to land on a 2 or a 4? Explain.

For more practice, see Set 12-7 on p. 733.

A Skills and Understanding

Write the probability of selecting each shape when you select a tile from those at the right, without looking.

6. diamond **7.** moon **8.** heart

9. heart or moon **10.** not a circle

11. Number Sense The probability an event occurs is $\frac{1}{5}$. Is the event likely, unlikely, impossible, or certain?

B Reasoning and Problem Solving

Math and Science

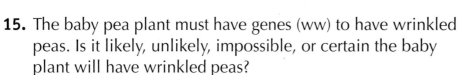

Gregor Mendel was a scientist during the 1800s. He studied thousands of pea plants.

When a pea plant that has two genes for round peas (RR) is crossed with a plant that has two genes for wrinkled peas (ww) you get plants with one gene for round peas and one gene for wrinkled peas (Rw).

The spinner at the right shows the results when two plants with (Rw) genes are crossed. Find the probability of the baby pea plants having the following genes.

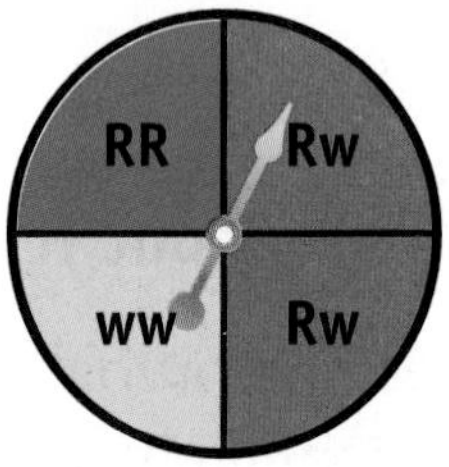

12. RR **13.** Rw **14.** ww

15. The baby pea plant must have genes (ww) to have wrinkled peas. Is it likely, unlikely, impossible, or certain the baby plant will have wrinkled peas?

16. Writing in Math Mr. Martinez said that each Thursday he would spin a spinner like the one at the right. If the spinner lands on red, he would not assign homework. If the spinner lands on blue, he would assign homework. Estimate the probability the class does not have homework this Thursday. Explain.

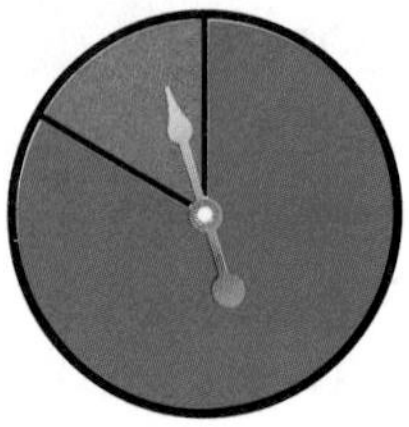

C Extensions

17. You toss a number cube with numbers 1 to 6, twice. List all possible outcomes. Use your list to find the probability that the sum of the numbers on two tosses is 7.

PRACTICE

Mixed Review and Test Prep

Take It to the NET
Test Prep
www.scottforesman.com

18. List all possible outcomes for choosing a letter from the word MATH and then a letter from the word FUN.

Use the graph at the right for 19–21.

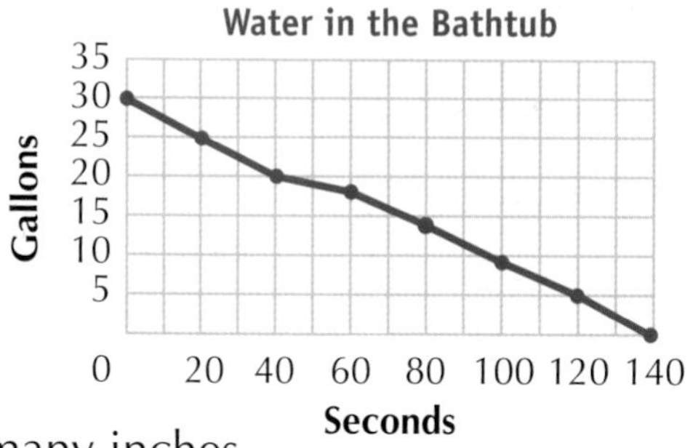

How many gallons of water were in the bathtub after

19. 20 seconds?

20. 120 seconds?

21. Reasoning What is the trend in the data? Is the bathtub filling up or draining?

22. Maureen bought 3 yards of yellow ribbon. How many inches of ribbon did she buy?

A. 42 inches **B.** 105 inches **C.** 108 inches **D.** 126 inches

Learning with Technology

Spinning Spinners and Flipping Coins

Using the **Probability eTool,** you can simulate spinning a spinner or flipping coins.

Select the spinner tool and the number of equal sections you want the spinner to have. Then use the palette to give each section a different color. Assume that the computer will spin the spinner 120 times. Write down what you predict the results should be. Now input 120 for the number of spins and watch what happens. How do the computer's results compare to your prediction?

Now select the coin tool and input 120 as the number of times that you want the coin flipped. Write down what you expect the number of heads and number of tails to be. Have the computer do 120 coin flips and record the number of heads and the number of tails that appeared. How do your predictions compare to the computer's results?

Key Idea
You can use probability to make predictions.

Vocabulary
- prediction

Materials
- spinner divided into fourths
- number cubes with numbers 1 to 6

or e tools

TEST TALK

Think It Through
I can **use objects** and **act it out** to make predictions.

Making Predictions

WARM UP

Find equivalent fractions.

1. $\frac{1}{2} = \frac{\square}{10}$ 2. $\frac{3}{4} = \frac{\square}{12}$
3. $\frac{2}{3} = \frac{\square}{24}$ 4. $\frac{1}{5} = \frac{\square}{100}$

LEARN

Activity

How do you make predictions?

A **prediction** is a guess about what will happen.

At the school carnival, a player can win a prize by spinning blue on a spinner like the one at the right. Twelve people play the game. How many people can you expect to win prizes?

a. What is the probability the spinner lands on blue?

The spinner is $\frac{1}{4}$ blue. Since $\frac{1}{4} = \frac{3}{12}$, you can expect 3 people to win prizes when 12 people play the game.

b. Use a spinner divided into fourths, with $\frac{1}{4}$ blue. Spin 12 times. Use tally marks to record your results. How many times did the spinner land on blue?

Blue	
Not blue	

c. Try the experiment 2 more times. Out of each 12 spins, did exactly 3 spins land on blue? Did close to 3 spins land on blue?

d. How many people would you expect to win prizes in 32 games? 100 games?

e. Spin the spinner to test each prediction. Are your results close to your predictions?

CHECK

For another example, see Set 12-8 on p. 730.

How many times would you expect each outcome?

1. Heads when a coin is flipped 30 times

2. Tails when a coin is flipped 24 times

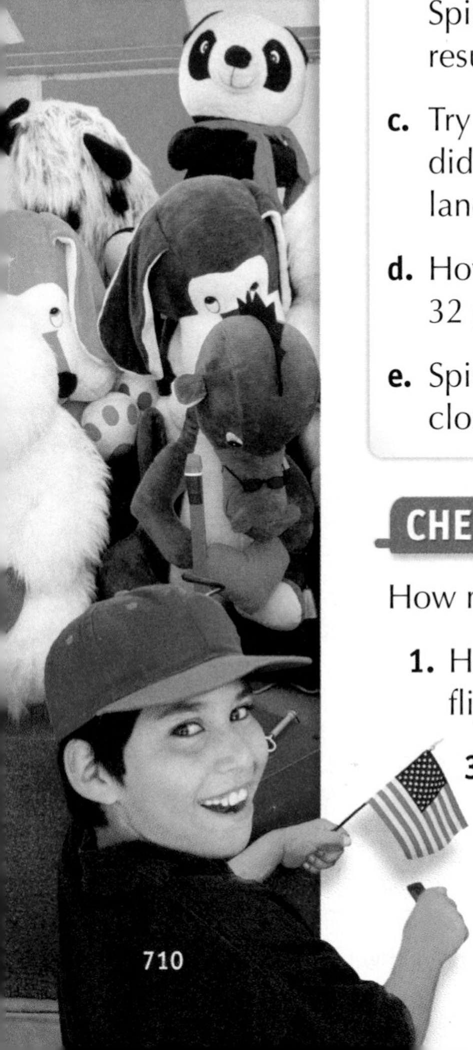

3. Number Sense Suppose a number cube numbered 1 to 6 is tossed 24 times. Would you expect a 6 to be tossed 12 times? Explain.

For more practice, see Set 12-8 on p. 733.

A Skills and Understanding

Use the letters at the right for 4–8. Predict how many times you would pick each letter. You put the letter back after each pick.

4. S when you pick a letter 30 times
5. T when you pick a letter 25 times
6. K when you pick a letter 10 times
7. O when you choose a letter 40 times
8. A letter in the name Scott when you choose a letter 25 times
9. **Number Sense** Suppose a number cube numbered 0, 2, 4, 6, 8, and 10 is tossed 48 times. How many times would you expect an odd number to be tossed?

B Reasoning and Problem Solving

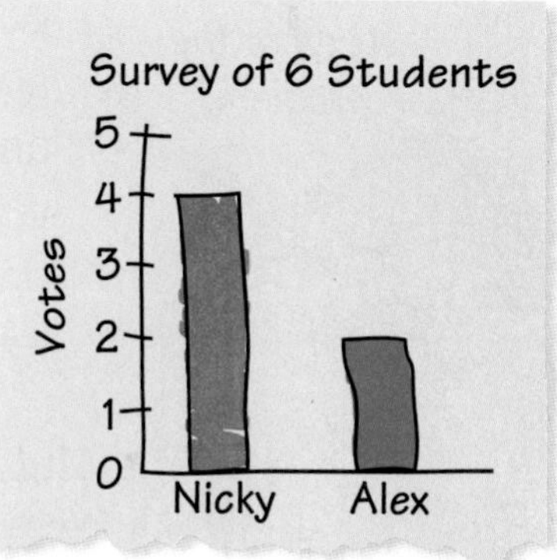

Nicky is running for fourth-grade class president and Alex is running for vice-president. They surveyed 6 students and got the results in the graph at the right. There are 60 fourth-grade students in their school. Based on the survey results, what is the probability

10. Nicky is elected?
11. Alex is elected?

Based on the survey results, predict the number of votes

12. Nicky can expect in the election.
13. Alex can expect in the election.
14. **Writing in Math** Jill and Hank played a game using one of the spinners shown. Here are the results of 21 spins. Which spinner do you think they used? Why?

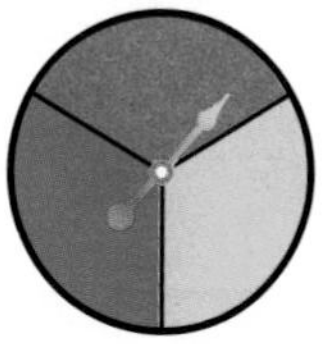
Spinner 1

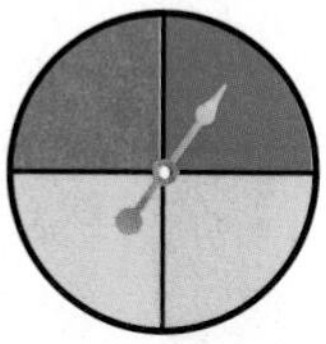
Spinner 2

Color	Blue	Yellow	Red
Number of spins	7	8	6

Mixed Review and Test Prep

Take It to the NET
Test Prep
www.scottforesman.com

Write the probability of each outcome when a number cube numbered 1 to 6 is tossed once.

15. 5
16. an even number
17. a number less than 5
18. Round 23.67 to the nearest tenth.

A. 20 **B.** 23.6 **C.** 23.7 **D.** 24

Reading For Math Success

Identify Steps in a Process

Identifying steps in a process when you read in math can help you use the **problem-solving strategy, *Work Backward,*** in the next lesson.

In reading, identifying steps in a process can help you organize what you read. In math, it can help you work backward to solve problems in which you know the result of a series of steps.

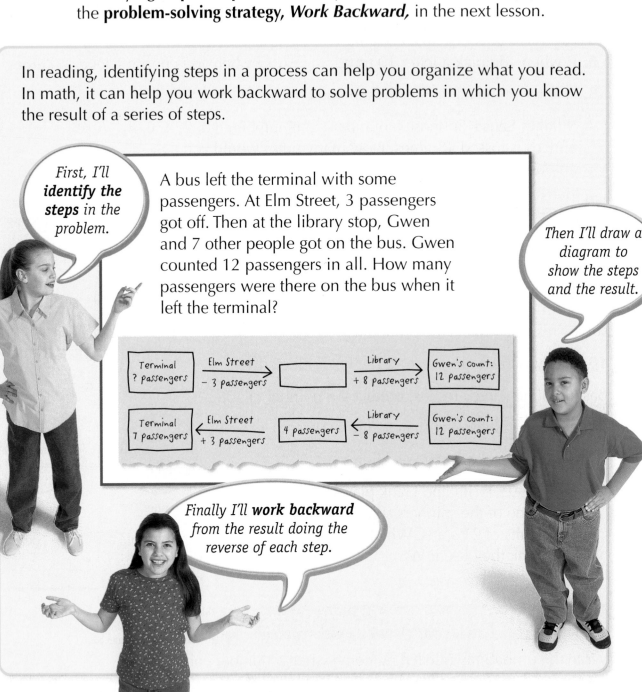

*First, I'll **identify the steps** in the problem.*

A bus left the terminal with some passengers. At Elm Street, 3 passengers got off. Then at the library stop, Gwen and 7 other people got on the bus. Gwen counted 12 passengers in all. How many passengers were there on the bus when it left the terminal?

Then I'll draw a diagram to show the steps and the result.

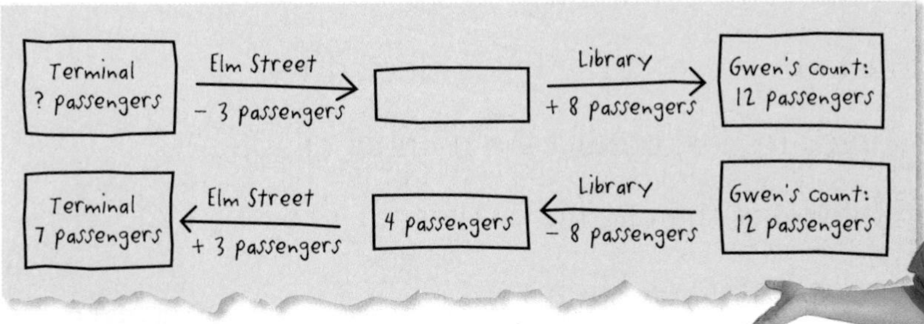

*Finally I'll **work backward** from the result doing the reverse of each step.*

1. How many steps were taken from the starting number to get the result 12?
2. As you work backward, how do you reverse the step where 3 passengers got off at Elm Street?

For 3–5, use the problem below.

Daniel planted rose bushes in his new garden at the beginning of the month. Four plants died. Then, he planted 6 more. Yesterday he transplanted 3 of the plants into his cousin's garden. The picture at the right shows his garden today. How many rose bushes did Daniel plant at the beginning of the month?

3. Draw a diagram to show the steps in the problem.

4. Now work backward. How can you reverse the step where Daniel planted another 6 rose bushes?

5. **Writing in Math** Explain the steps you would use to find how many rose bushes Daniel planted at the beginning of the month.

For 6–8, use the problem below.

Kansas became a state in the 1800s. Nebraska became a state 6 years after Kansas, and 23 years later Idaho became a state. In 1959, 69 years after Idaho, Hawaii became a state. In what year did Kansas become a state?

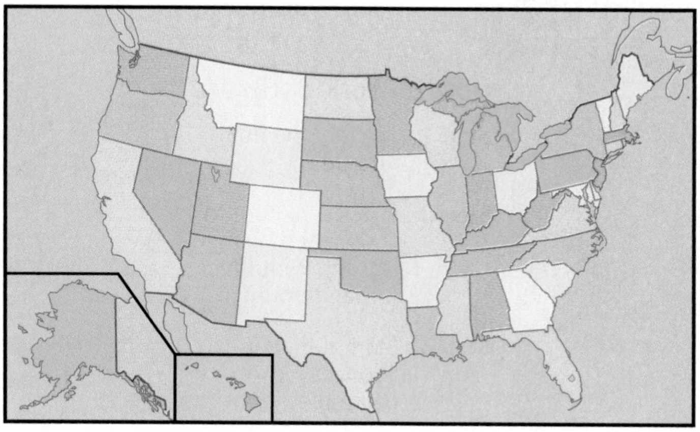

6. Draw a diagram to show the steps in the problem.

7. Now work backward. How can you reverse the step where Hawaii became a state?

8. **Writing in Math** Loren thinks that Kansas became a state in 1851. What steps would you take to check her answer?

Reading Helps!

Identifying steps in a process

can help you with...

the problem-solving strategy, *Work Backward*.

Key Idea
Learning how and when to work backward can help you solve problems.

Work Backward

LEARN

TEST TALK

Think It Through
I need to **reverse the steps** that end with 2 white marbles and 5 black marbles to find the number of each at the start.

How do you work backward to solve a problem?

Marble Exchange A bag contains some white marbles and some black marbles. You put in 3 more black marbles and then take out 1 white marble. You then have 7 marbles and the probability of choosing a white marble is $\frac{2}{7}$. How many marbles of each color were there to start?

Read and Understand

Step 1: What do you know? There were 7 marbles at the end and the probability of selecting white was $\frac{2}{7}$.

Step 2: What are you trying to find? The number of black marbles and white marbles in the bag at the start.

Plan and Solve

What strategy will you use? **Work backward**

How to Work Backward

Step 1 Identify the final amount.

Step 2 Draw a picture to show each change starting with the initial amount.

Step 3 Start at the end. Work backward using the opposite of each change.

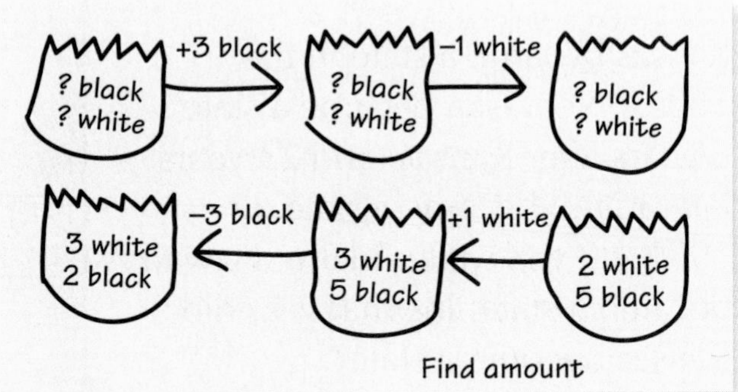

Answer: There were 3 white marbles and 2 black marbles at the start.

Look Back and Check

Is your answer reasonable? Yes, if I start with 3 white and 2 black marbles, I end up with 2 white and 5 black marbles.

✓ Talk About It

1. How do you know there were 2 white marbles and 5 black marbles at the end?

CHECK

For another example, see Set 12-9 on p. 730.

Solve by working backward. Give the answer in a complete sentence.

1. Tracy has band practice at 10:15 A.M. It takes her 20 minutes to get from home to practice and 5 minutes to warm up. What time should she leave home to get to practice on time?

2. A van had 4 fourth-grade students. Two girls got in and 1 boy got out. Then there were 5 students and $\frac{3}{5}$ were girls. How many girls were in the van to start?

PRACTICE

For more practice, see Set 12-9 on p. 733.

Solve. Write the answer in a complete sentence.

3. In the school play Vince, Stan, and Pete are going to be George Washington, Thomas Jefferson, and Patrick Henry. How many different ways can the 3 boys be assigned to the 3 parts?

4. Roberto, Melissa, and Rene are taking turns working in the concession stand at the basketball game. They need to share 2 hours equally. How long should each work?

5. A diagonal connects two vertices of a polygon, but is not a side. How many diagonals does an octagon have?

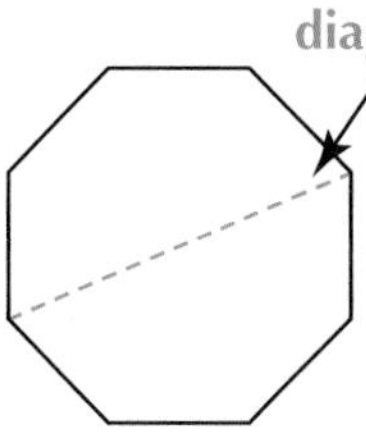

6. The Declaration of Independence was signed in 1776. Three years earlier, the Boston Tea Party took place. Boston was settled 143 years before the Boston Tea Party. What year was Boston settled?

7. **Writing in Math** Solve the following problem. Then, explain how you solved it.

   It takes one-and-one-half hours to get from school to the Revolutionary War museum. The class needs an hour and 45 minutes to tour one part of the museum. They want to finish touring that part before lunch at 11:45. What time should the class leave school?

STRATEGIES

- **Show What You Know**
  - Draw a Picture
  - Make an Organized List
  - Make a Table
  - Make a Graph
  - Act It Out or Use Objects
- **Look for a Pattern**
- **Try, Check, and Revise**
- **Write a Number Sentence**
- **Use Logical Reasoning**
- **Solve a Simpler Problem**
- **Work Backward**

Choose a tool

The amount of tea thrown into the Boston Harbor during the Boston Tea Party was enough to make 24 million cups of tea.

Problem-Solving Applications

Fire-Fighting Helicopters

Fire-fighting helicopters can go where fire trucks cannot. They can drop water on a target more accurately and quickly than an airplane. Their water tanks can be refilled from ponds only 18 inches deep. Helicopters are amazing fire-fighting machines.

Trivia Salt spray can cause problems with a helicopter's engine. To prevent these problems, helicopters that fly over salt water have their engine parts sprayed with a mixture of chemicals and ground apricot stones.

1. The helicopter pictured below looks like a dragonfly. A dragonfly has been observed to fly as fast as 61 miles per hour. The helicopter can fly about twice as fast as this dragonfly. About how fast can this helicopter fly?

2. A small helicopter may drop 75 gallons of water at a time. The large helicopter shown below holds about 35 times as much water. How much water can this helicopter hold?

3. One fire-fighting helicopter may drop 30,000 gallons of water in one hour. At this rate, how many gallons of water could it drop between noon and midnight?

4 Water cannons can be fitted to the helicopter to spray water to a distance of 160 feet at a rate of 300 gallons per minute. How long could the helicopter spray water if it had 2,100 gallons of water in its tank?

Good News/Bad News *Helicopters can fight fires more effectively than trucks or airplanes. However, they can cost $4,000 per hour to operate.*

Key Facts
Aircrane Helitanker

- Height: 25.3 feet
- Length: 70.2 feet
- Rotor diameter: 71.9 feet
- Maximum total weight: 42,000 pounds

Using Key Facts

5 The weight of an empty helicopter is about 19,300 pounds. How much additional weight can it carry?

6 **Writing in Math** Write your own word problem about helicopters. Write the answer to your problem in a complete sentence.

7 **Decision Making** Suppose you wanted to paint a model helicopter in 2 colors. Paints come in sets of 3, 4, or 5 colors shown below. Which set of paints would you buy? How many different 2-color combinations would be possible with that set?

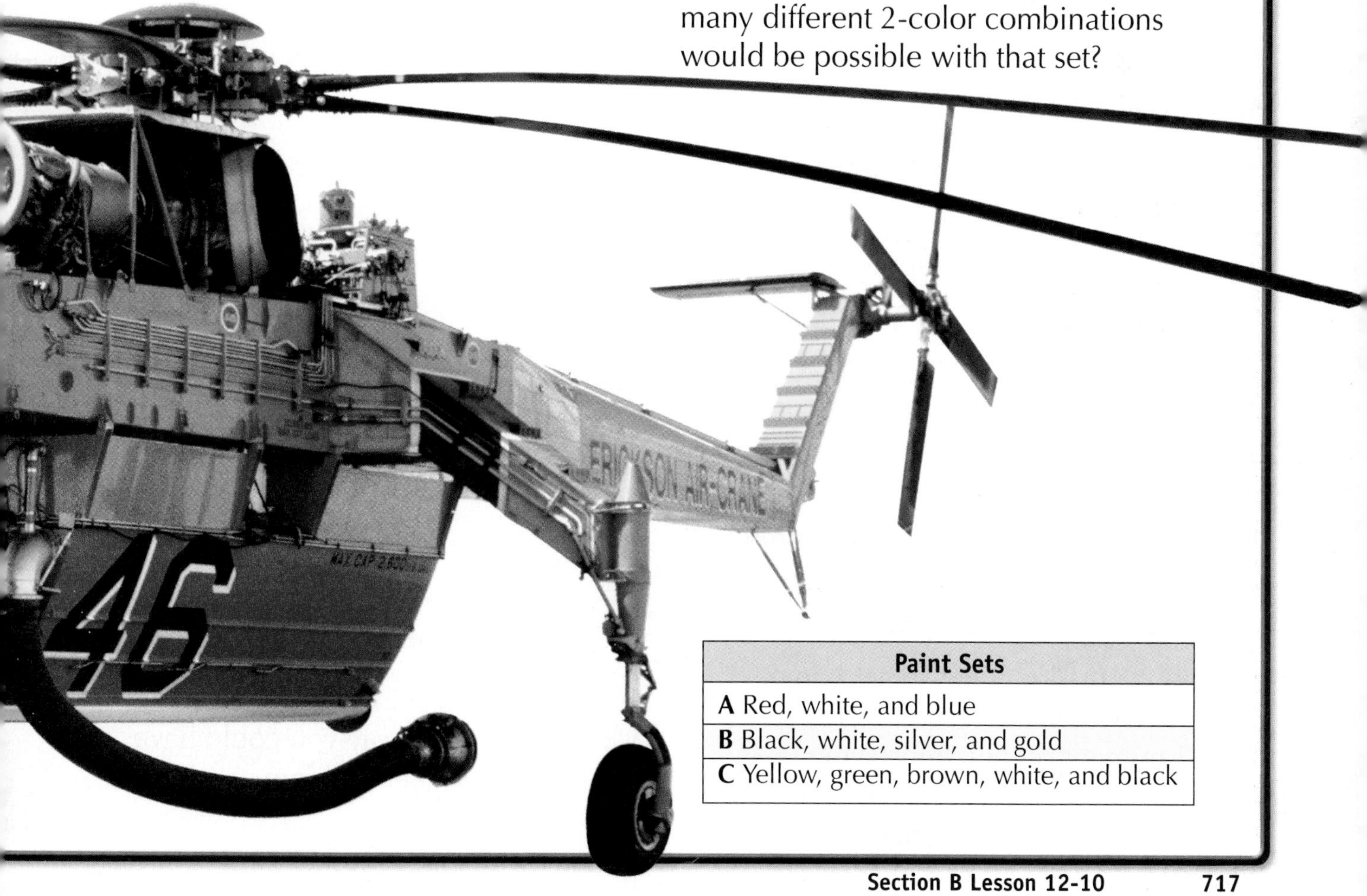

Paint Sets
A Red, white, and blue
B Black, white, silver, and gold
C Yellow, green, brown, white, and black

Review

Do You Know How?

Do You Understand?

Understanding Probability (12-5); Finding Probability (12-7)

1. You spin the spinner at the right. Is it likely, unlikely, impossible, or certain that you spin blue? green?

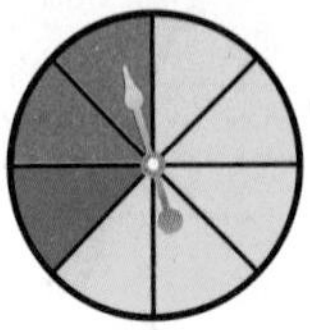

What is the probability of spinning

2. red?
3. yellow?

A Tell how you decided how to describe the probabilities in Exercise 1.

B Explain how you found the probability in Exercise 2.

Listing Outcomes (12-6)

List all the possible outcomes for each situation. You choose a letter from

4. the word Hi.
5. the word Bye.
6. the word Hi and then Bye.

C What is an outcome?

D Explain how you found the outcomes for Exercise 6.

Making Predictions (12-8)

How many times would you expect each outcome?

7. Tails when a coin is flipped 80 times.
8. An odd number when a number cube numbered 1–6 is tossed 60 times.

E Tell how you made your prediction in Exercise 7.

F If you actually toss a number cube 60 times, explain why you would expect to get a 6 *about* 10 times instead of *exactly* 10 times.

Problem-Solving Strategy: Work Backward (12-9)

9. **Soccer** Jackson got home from soccer practice at 6:30 P.M. It took him 15 minutes to get home. His practice was 1 hour and 15 minutes. It took him 10 minutes to get to practice. What time did Jackson leave for practice?

G Explain how you could solve the Soccer problem by working backward.

H Explain another way you could have solved the Soccer problem.

Chapter 12 Section B

Diagnostic Checkpoint

TEST TALK

Think It Through

I can **use logical reasoning** to find outcomes and probability, and to make predictions.

MULTIPLE CHOICE

1. Which best describes the likelihood of spinning red when you spin the spinner at the right? (12-5)

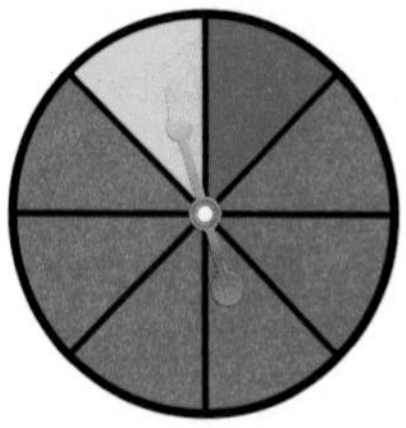

A. Likely **C.** Impossible

B. Unlikely **D.** Certain

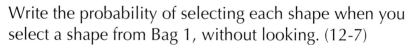

2. Which is NOT a possible outcome when you spin the spinner at the right? (12-6)

A. blue **B.** green **C.** red **D.** yellow

FREE RESPONSE

Tell whether it is likely, unlikely, impossible, or certain to get each shape when a shape is taken out of Bag 1 at the right. (12-5)

Bag 1

3. star **4.** triangle **5.** not a hexagon

6. List all the possible outcomes for pulling a shape from Bag 2 at the right. (12-6)

Write the probability of selecting each shape when you select a shape from Bag 1, without looking. (12-7)

Bag 2

7. a star **8.** a square **9.** not a circle

10. Use Bag 2 at the right. Predict how many times you would pick a triangle if you picked a shape 20 times. You would put the shape back after each pick. (12-8)

Writing in Math

11. Explain whether the following situation is fair or not. If it is not, what could you do to make it fair? (12-5)

The girls line up first for lunch on the weekdays that begin with T. The boys line up first for lunch on the weekdays that do not begin with the letter T.

12. Solve the following problem. Then, explain how you solved it. (12-9)

Linda's father sliced a cantaloupe into equal size pieces. Linda ate 3 pieces. Then, Nora ate 2 pieces, which was $\frac{2}{5}$ of what Linda left for her. How many slices were in the cantaloupe all together?

CHAPTER 12 Test Talk

Test-Taking Strategies

- Understand the question.
- Get information for the answer.
- Plan how to find the answer.
- Make smart choices.
- Use writing in math.
- → Improve written answers.

Improve Written Answers

You can follow the tips below to learn how to improve written answers on a test. It is important to write a clear answer and include only information needed to answer the question.

The rubric below is a scoring guide for Test Questions 1 and 2.

Scoring Rubric

4 points — **Full credit: 4 points**
The prediction is reasonable and the explanation is correct.

3 points — **Partial credit: 3 points**
The prediction is reasonable, but a detail is missing from the explanation.

2 points — **Partial credit: 2 points**
The prediction is reasonable or the explanation is correct, but not both.

1 point — **Partial credit: 1 point**
The prediction is unreasonable. The explanation shows partial understanding.

0 points — **No credit: 0 points**
The prediction and explanation are both incorrect or missing.

1. A spinner is labeled with letters. Ed recorded the results of 12 spins.

Spinner Results

Letter	Number of Spins
Vowel	3
Consonant	9

Suppose Ed spins the spinner 100 times. Based on his data, predict the number of times out of 100 spins the spinner will land on a vowel. Explain how you made your prediction.

Improve Written Answers

- Check if your answer is complete.

  *To **get as many points as possible,** I must predict the number of times the spinner will land on a vowel* and *explain how I made my prediction.*

- Check if your answer makes sense.

  *In Ed's data, a vowel came up on less than half the spins. I should **check my prediction** to see if it is less than half of 100 spins.*

- Check if your explanation is clear and easy to follow.

  *Have I **accurately and clearly** explained my work? Did I **describe the steps in order?** Have I included only the information called for?*

David used the scoring rubric on page 720 to score a student's answer to Test Question 1. The student's paper is shown below.

About 50 times

On the lines below, explain how you made your prediction.

Since there are 2 possible outcomes, each one has a probability of $\frac{1}{2}$. So I found half of 100, and that's 50.

Think It Through

The prediction is unreasonable. It should be less than 50. The explanation is wrong. The student should have figured out the probability from the data. $\frac{3}{12} = \frac{1}{4}$. Then write equivalent fractions: $\frac{1}{4} = \frac{25}{100}$. So 25 is a reasonable prediction. Since the student showed a little knowledge about how to use probability to make predictions, the score is 1 point.

Now it's your turn.

Score the student's paper. If it does not get 4 points, rewrite it so that it does.

2. A spinner has 3 colors. Yolanda recorded the results of 12 spins.

Spinner Results

Color	Number of Spins
Red	2
Green	6
Yellow	4

Suppose Yolanda spins the spinner 60 times. Based on her data, predict the number of times out of 60 spins the spinner will land on red.

Explain how you made your prediction.

I think Yolanda will get red 10 times. First I used the data to find the probability that the spinner will land on red. It's $\frac{2}{12} = \frac{1}{6}$. Then I wrote an equivalent fraction for $\frac{1}{6}$.

Chapter 12

Key Vocabulary and Concept Review

"In-" means not, as in invisible.

*An **inequality** states that quantities are not equal.* *(p. 688)*

Self Check

Graph inequalities on a number line. (Lesson 12-1)

Graph the **inequality** $m < 6$.

Draw an open circle at 6 on a number line. Find several solutions and plot those on the number line. Remember, $m < 6$ means "m is less than 6."

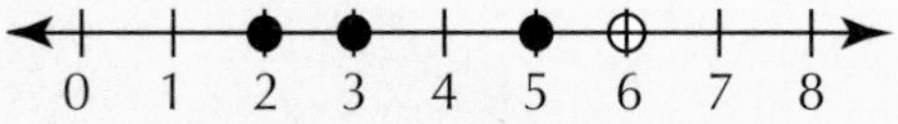

Starting at the open circle, color over the solutions. Put an arrow at the end to show the solutions go on forever.

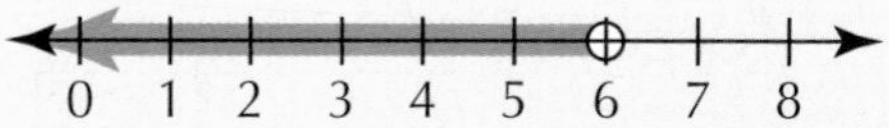

1. Graph $p > 4$ on a number line.

"Order" is part of ordered pair.

*Remember, pay attention to the order of the numbers in an **ordered pair.** (6, 2) and (2, 6) represent different locations.* *(p. 692)*

Self Check

Graph equations. (Lesson 12-3)

Graph $y = x + 3$ on a coordinate grid.

Make a table. Choose 5 values of x and evaluate $x + 3$ for those values.

x	$y = x + 3$	(x, y)
0	$y = 0 + 3$	(0, 3)
1	$y = 1 + 3$	(1, 4)
2	$y = 2 + 3$	(2, 5)
3	$y = 3 + 3$	(3, 6)
4	$y = 4 + 3$	(4, 7)

Plot the **ordered pairs** on a coordinate grid. Connect the points with a line.

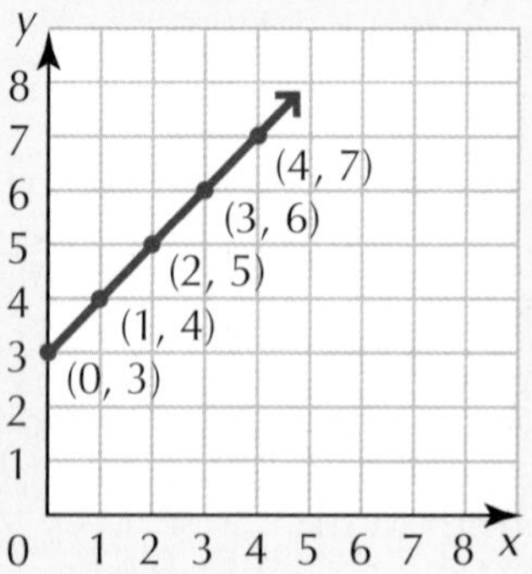

2. Graph $y = x - 2$.

I'm certain I can fit a carton of milk in my lunchbox.

But it's impossible to fit a gallon of milk.

Self Check

Find probability and make predictions. (Lessons 12-5, 12-6, 12-7, 12-8)

Make a **tree diagram** to show the possible **outcomes** if 2 coins are tossed.

Coin 1	Coin 2	Possible Outcomes
H	H	H,H
	T	H,T
T	H	T,H
	T	T,T

H = heads; T = tails

Make a **prediction** about how many times a number cube numbered 1–6 will land on 2 if you toss it 30 times.

Find the **probability:** $\frac{1}{6}$.

Then write it with 30 in the denominator: $\frac{1}{6} = \frac{5}{30}$.

The number cube might land on 2 about 5 times.

The **probability** of an event ranges from 0 to 1.

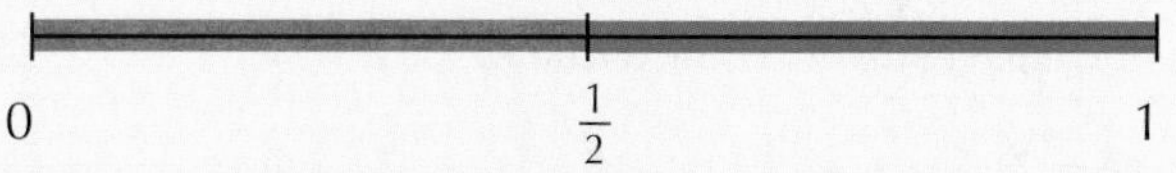

3. If you toss a number cube, what is the probability of getting a number less than 5?

*A **certain** event must happen. It has a probability of 1.*

*An **impossible** event cannot happen. It has a probability of 0.* *(p. 700)*

Self Check

Identify necessary information or work backward. (Lessons 12-4, 12-9)

Find the extra or missing information. Solve the problem, if possible.

A bakery baked 196 donuts. Each one sells for 65¢. The bakery sold 143 donuts. How many were left?

196 − 143 = 53 The information about the price is not needed.

There were 53 donuts left.

Work backward from the end result, using the opposite operation of each change.

Sue's father gave her a piggy bank with money in it. Sue added $7.00 to it and then shook out $4.45. She then had $14.15 in the bank. How much was there to start?

$14.15 + $4.45 − $7.00 = $11.60

There was $11.60 to start.

4. Roy spent $48.16 for 4 CDs and $8.35 for a book. How much did each CD cost?

Answers: 1.

2. Sample graph: See right. 3. $\frac{2}{3}$ 4. $12.04

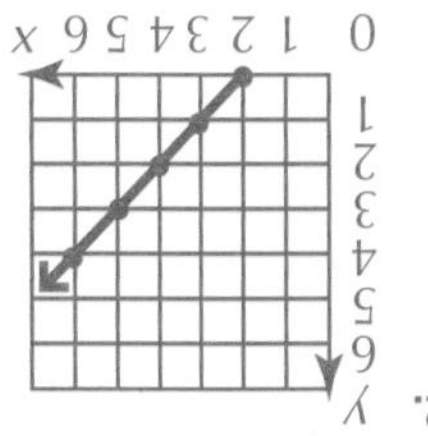

CHAPTER 12

Chapter Test

MULTIPLE CHOICE

Choose the correct letter for each answer.

1. Which inequality is graphed on the number line below?

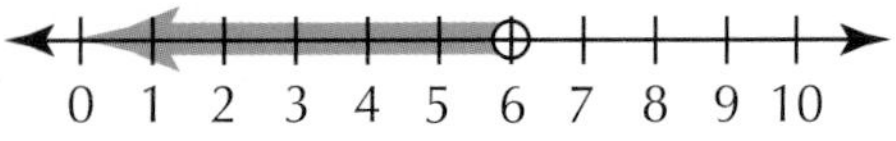

A. $m > 6$ **C.** $m < 6$

B. $m < 4$ **D.** $m > 5$

2. Which equation models the sentence "7 less than q is 21"?

A. $7 - q = 21$ **C.** $q \div 7 = 21$

B. $q < 7$ **D.** $q - 7 = 21$

3. Which ordered pair is a solution for the equation $y = 3x$?

A. (3, 2) **C.** (2, 6)

B. (9, 3) **D.** (2, 3)

4. The graph of an equation is shown below. Which of the following is NOT a solution to that equation?

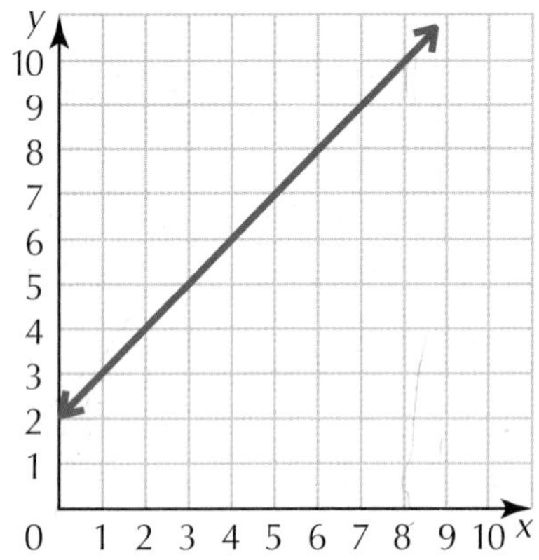

A. (0, 1) **C.** (1, 3)

B. (2, 4) **D.** (5, 7)

5. Which of the following best describes the probability of picking a red marble from this bag?

A. likely

C. unlikely

B. impossible

D. certain

6. How many possible outcomes are there for spinning each of the spinners below at the same time?

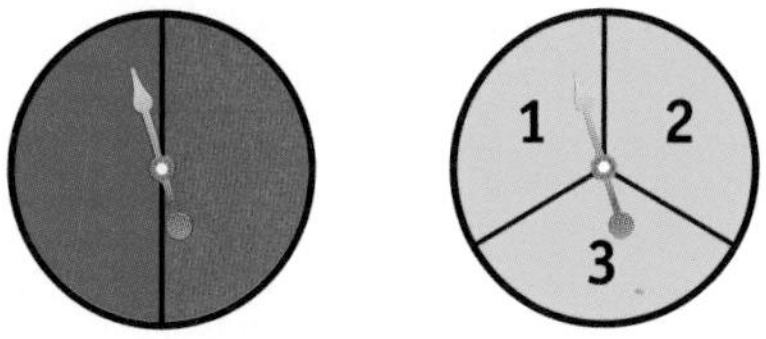

A. 2 **B.** 3 **C.** 5 **D.** 6

7. You toss a number cube numbered 1 to 6. Find the probability of tossing a number less than 3.

A. $\frac{2}{3}$ **C.** $\frac{1}{3}$

B. $\frac{1}{2}$ **D.** $\frac{1}{6}$

TEST TALK

Think It Through

I need to **read each part of the question carefully.**

8. Predict how many times you would pick a **P** from these letters when you pick a letter 30 times. (You put the letter back after each pick.)

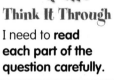

A. 2 **B.** 6 **C.** 10 **D.** 12

9. The number line below shows the solutions to an inequality. Which of the following is NOT a solution?

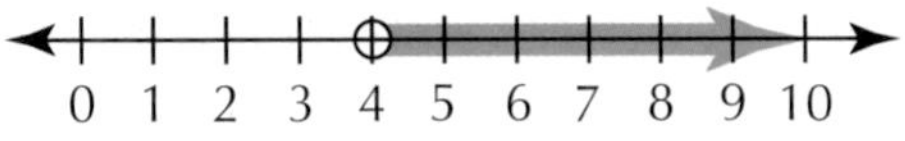

A. $m = 3$

B. $m = 5$

C. $m = 6.75$

D. $m = 7\frac{1}{2}$

10. Tom spins the spinner below. What is the probability that he does NOT land on red?

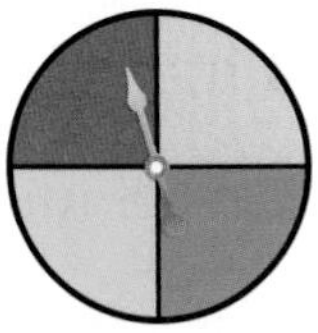

A. $\frac{1}{4}$

B. $\frac{1}{2}$

C. $\frac{3}{4}$

D. 1

FREE RESPONSE

In a game, Player A gets a point when a spinner lands on green and Player B gets a point when it lands on blue. Tell if the game is fair or unfair for each spinner.

11.

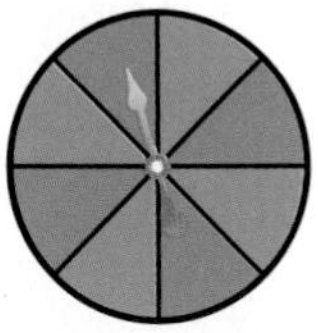

12.

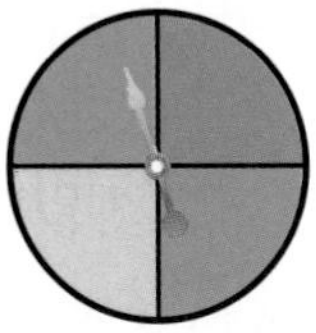

Find the value of y for each value of x using the equation $y = 3x + 4$.

13. $x = 1$

14. $x = 4$

15. $x = 3$

16. $x = 8$

Name 3 solutions to each inequality and graph all the solutions on a number line.

17. $q > 9$

18. $k < 4$

Write an equation for each sentence.

19. 8 cups of flour mixed with p cups of flour make 15 cups of flour.

20. 7 groups of q apples make 14 apples.

21. 24 divided by n is 8.

TEST TALK

Think It Through

I need to **choose operations** to match the words.

22. Solve this problem by working backward.

A bag has some red tiles and some blue tiles. You put in 4 more red tiles and take out 2 blue. The bag then has 6 tiles, and the probability of choosing a red tile is $\frac{5}{6}$. How many tiles of each color were in the bag to start?

Writing in Math

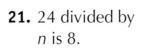

23. Explain if this problem has extra information or not enough information. Tell any information that is not needed or that is missing. Solve if you have enough information.

Alex has 30 rectangular tiles to cover his kitchen floor. The kitchen is 10 feet wide. Does Alex have enough tiles to cover the kitchen floor?

24. Explain the difference between an inequality and an equation.

25. Describe an event for tomorrow whose probability of occurring is impossible.

Cumulative Review and Test Prep

Number and Operation

MULTIPLE CHOICE

1. Which of the following sets of numbers is in order from greatest to least?

A. 6,396 6,936 6,639 6,369

B. 6,369 6,639 6,396 6,936

C. 6,369 6,396 6,639 6,936

D. 6,936 6,639 6,396 6,369

2. A pencil is 17.34 cm long, and a pen is 14.4 cm long. How much longer is the pencil?

A. 3.30 cm **C.** 2.06 cm

B. 2.94 cm **D.** 1.51 cm

3. Find the product of 17 and 28.

A. 45 **C.** 426

B. 224 **D.** 476

FREE RESPONSE

4. Linda walked $\frac{2}{3}$ mile to school, $\frac{1}{2}$ mile to soccer practice after school, and then $\frac{3}{4}$ mile home from practice. How many miles did she walk altogether?

5. If 56 students are divided into 8 teams, how many students will be on each team?

Writing in Math

6. Explain how to round 27,846 to the nearest thousand. Give the answer.

Geometry and Measurement

MULTIPLE CHOICE

7. Use the times shown on the clocks below to find the elapsed time. (Both times are P.M.)

A. 3 h 25 min **C.** 3 h 45 min

B. 2 h 35 min **D.** 2 h 25 min

8. Which pair of lines always forms right angles?

A. parallel **C.** perpendicular

B. intersecting **D.** similar

FREE RESPONSE

9. What is the volume of the cube shown at the right?

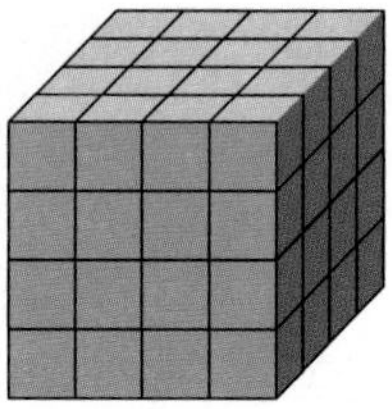

10. When Allen was born, he weighed 7 pounds, 13 ounces. A year later, he weighed 23 pounds, 11 ounces. How much weight did he gain in one year?

Writing in Math

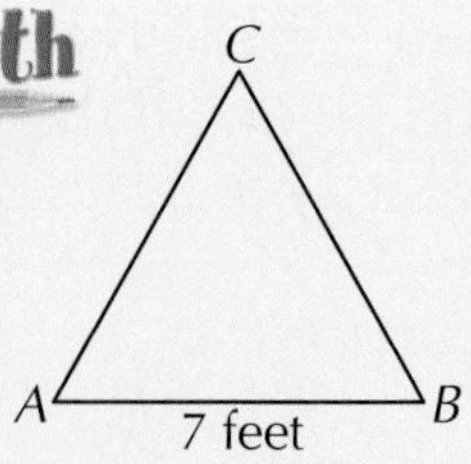

11. All of the sides of triangle *ABC* are congruent. What is the perimeter of the triangle? What kind of triangle is it? Explain your answers.

Data Analysis and Probability

MULTIPLE CHOICE

12. What does the scale of a bar graph tell you?

A. What the graph is about in general

B. The units used on the graph

C. What data is shown on the graph

D. What data set each bar represents

13. What is the mean of this data set?

6, 8, 7, 6, 9, 5, 4, 11

A. 6 **B.** 6.5 **C.** 7 **D.** 8

FREE RESPONSE

Use the spinners for Items 14–16.

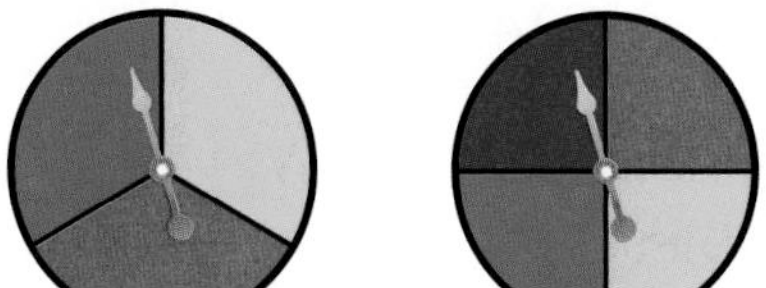

A B

14. Find the probability of the spinner landing on red for each spinner.

15. Describe the probability of Spinner A landing on blue as likely, unlikely, impossible, or certain.

Writing in Math

16. Predict how many times Spinner B would land on blue when you spin it 20 times. Explain how you made your prediction.

Algebra

MULTIPLE CHOICE

17. The graph of an equation is shown below. Which ordered pair is a solution to the equation graphed?

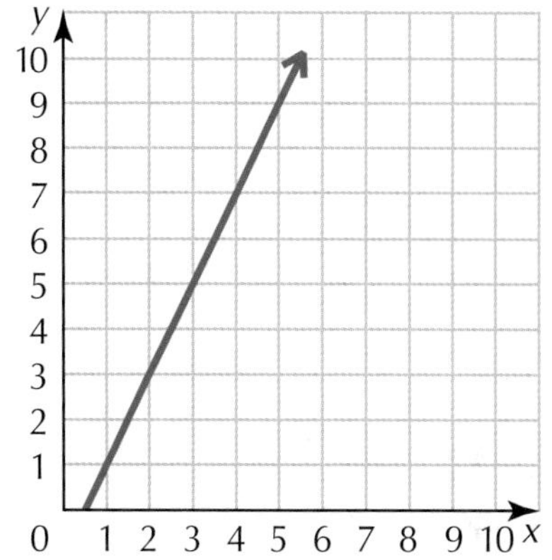

A. (1, 3) **C.** (1, 2)

B. (2, 1) **D.** (3, 5)

18. Which ordered pair is NOT a solution for the equation $y = x + 10$?

A. (0, 10) **C.** (10, 20)

B. (2, 12) **D.** (5, 25)

FREE RESPONSE

19. Use the equation $y = 3x + 2$ to complete this solution table.

x	1	2	3	4
y				

20. Write an equation for the sentence "k less than 13 books is 9 books."

Writing in Math

21. Explain how to graph the inequality $m < 3$ on a number line.

Think It Through

I need to **explain my steps in order.**

Reteaching

Set 12-1 (pages 688–689)

Name three solutions for $a < 4$ and graph all the solutions on a number line.

Three solutions are 0, 2, and 3.

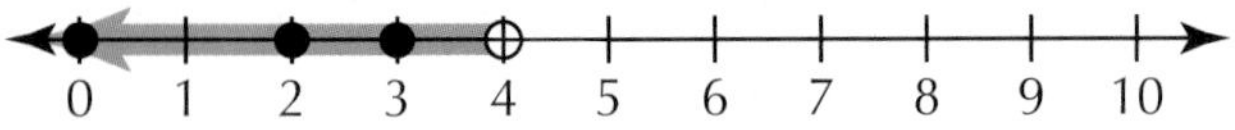

Remember that you use an open circle to show that the number the circle is on is not a solution.

Name three solutions and graph each inequality.

1. $m > 5$
2. $z < 13$
3. $a < 10$
4. $d > 7$
5. $n < 3$
6. $p > 16$

Set 12-2 (pages 690–691)

Write an equation for the problem.

Jason had some pencils. He bought 7 more. Now he has 12 pencils.

Pencils he already had		Pencils he bought		Total number of pencils
p	$+$	7	$=$	12

The equation is $p + 7 = 12$.

Remember that $3 \times p$ is written $3p$.

Write an equation for each problem.

1. 4 balls plus g balls equals 12 balls.
2. s less than 18 is 4.
3. 6 times c is 24.
4. 48 marbles divided by n is 6 marbles.

Set 12-3 (pages 692–695)

Graph $y = x + 3$ on a coordinate grid.

Make a table of ordered pairs.

x	$y = x + 3$	(x, y)
0	$y = 0 + 3 = 3$	(0, 3)
1	$y = 1 + 3 = 4$	(1, 4)
2	$y = 2 + 3 = 5$	(2, 5)
3	$y = 3 + 3 = 6$	(3, 6)

Plot the ordered pairs and connect the points.

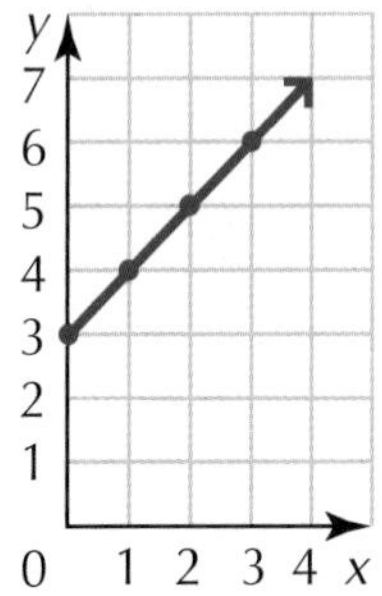

Remember that the first number in an ordered pair tells you how many units to move to the right and the second tells you how many to move up.

Graph each equation.

1. $y = x + 1$
2. $y = x + 4$
3. $y = x - 5$
4. $y = x - 7$
5. $y = x$
6. $y = 5x$

Set 12-4 (pages 696–697)

Decide if the problem has extra information or not enough information. Tell any information that is not needed or that is missing. Solve if you have enough information.

Milk costs $2.79 a gallon. How much did Tami spend on milk?

There is not enough information. You cannot solve this problem because you do not know how many gallons of milk Tami bought.

Remember some problems have information you do not need.

1. Virginia bought 3 packages of invitations and one book of stamps. Each package of invitations cost $2.35. How much did Virginia spend on invitations?
2. Preston reads every night before he goes to bed. Tuesday he read for 25 minutes. How many minutes did Preston read during the week?

Set 12-5 (pages 700–703)

Tell whether it is likely, unlikely, impossible, or certain to pick a yellow tile out of a bag like the one at the right.

Since there is only one yellow tile, it is unlikely you would draw a yellow tile.

Remember that outcomes are *equally likely* if each has the same possibility of occurring.

Tell whether it is likely, unlikely, impossible, or certain to pick each tile from the bag at the left.

1. a blue tile
2. a purple tile
3. a red or blue tile
4. not a brown tile

Set 12-6 (pages 704–705)

List all the possible outcomes for selecting a shape from Bag 1 and Bag 2.

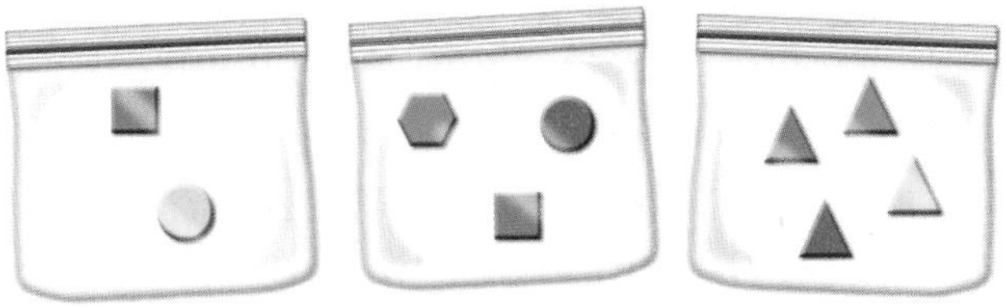

Bag 1 Bag 2 Bag 3

The possible outcomes for selecting a shape from Bag 1 and Bag 2 are square, hexagon; square, circle; square, square; circle, hexagon; circle, circle, circle, square.

Remember that you can list outcomes of more than one event by making a tree diagram or an organized list.

List all the possible outcomes for selecting a shape from

1. Bag 1.
2. Bag 2.
3. Bag 1 and Bag 3.

Set 12-7 (pages 706–709)

Find the probability of selecting a T when you select a letter from the name ROBERT, without looking.

There are 6 possible outcomes: R, R, O, B, E, and T. There is 1 favorable outcome: T

$$\text{Probability} = \frac{\text{number of favorable outcomes}}{\text{number of possible outcomes}} = \frac{1}{6}$$

The probability you will select a T is $\frac{1}{6}$.

Remember that an event can have a probability of 0 or 1.

Find the probability of selecting each letter, from the word MULTIPLY.

1. M
2. L
3. Y
4. U
5. not L
6. S
7. T or L
8. not P
9. a vowel
10. a consonant

Set 12-8 (pages 710–711)

How many times would you expect to select a D when you choose a card from those below 8 times? You put the cards back after each choice.

D A T A

The probability that you pick a D is $\frac{1}{4}$.

Since $\frac{1}{4} = \frac{2}{8}$, you can expect to select a D card 2 times in 8 picks.

Remember that what you expect to happen may be different than what actually happens.

Use the cards at the left. How many times would you expect to select a

1. T when you pick a card 12 times?
2. A when you pick a card 20 times?
3. C when you pick a card 40 times?

Set 12-9 (pages 714–715)

Solve by working backward. Give the answer in a complete sentence.

It takes Marcus 15 minutes to walk to school. He needs 20 minutes to eat breakfast at school. School starts at 8:15 A.M. What is the latest Marcus can leave home and have time for breakfast at school?

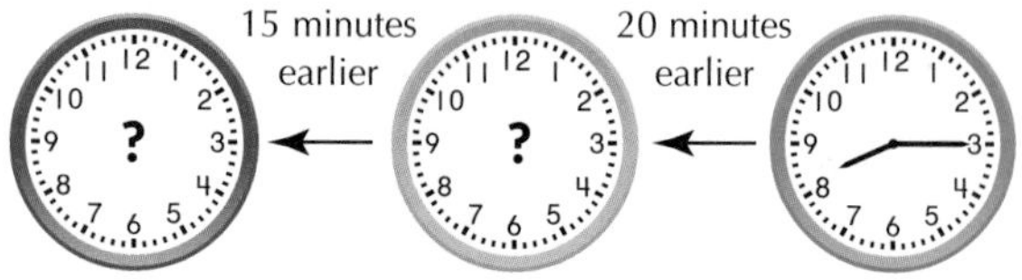

Marcus needs to leave at 7:40 A.M.

Remember that a picture can help you work backward.

1. Mrs. Sandoval likes to get to school a half hour before school starts. It takes her 45 minutes to get to school. School starts at 8:15 A.M. What time should Mrs. Sandoval leave home?

2. Thomas spent \$8.25 bowling and then \$3.60 on a snack. He had \$11.85 left. How much did he have to start?

More Practice

Take It to the NET
More Practice
www.scottforesman.com

Set 12-1 (pages 688–689)

Name three solutions to each inequality and graph all the solutions on a number line.

1. $m > 2$ **2.** $z < 7$ **3.** $f < 17$ **4.** $p > 6$

5. $a < 6$ **6.** $t > 0$ **7.** $r > 11$ **8.** $k < 12$

9. $b > 3$ **10.** $n < 21$ **11.** $c > 2$ **12.** $j > 15$

13. Martha said that 5 is a solution to $d > 5$. Explain why this is not correct.

Set 12-2 (pages 690–691)

Write an equation for each sentence.

1. 8 oranges in addition to *v* oranges equal 17 oranges.

2. *k* less than 9 trucks is 4 trucks.

3. *x* minus 3 is 15.

4. 7 plus an additional *d* is 9.

5. 4 multiplied by *n* is 36.

6. *s* times 7 is 42.

7. *k* divided by 3 is 9.

8. 6 divided by *w* is 2.

9. 56 divided by *t* is 7.

10. 7 less than *x* is 14.

11. Josh scored 18 points in the second half, and a total of 27 points for the entire game. Write and solve an equation to show how many points Josh scored in the first half.

Set 12-3 (pages 692–695)

Use the equation $y = 4x + 2$. Find the value of *y* for each value of *x*.

1. $x = 1$ **2.** $x = 0$ **3.** $x = 5$ **4.** $x = 7$

5. $x = 2$ **6.** $x = 4$ **7.** $x = 3$ **8.** $x = 8$

Graph each equation on a separate coordinate grid.

9. $y = x + 6$ **10.** $y = 4x$ **11.** $y = 3x - 2$ **12.** $y = x - 2$

13. The equation $y = 3x + 2$ represents the total number of books *y* that Erin has read after *x* weeks. How many books has Erin read after 2 weeks?

14. Is the point (2, 8) on the graph $y = 4x + 1$? Explain.

More Practice

Set 12-4 (pages 696–697)

Decide if each problem has extra information or not enough information. Tell any information that is not needed or that is missing. Solve if you have enough information.

1. Malinda had 200 sheets of notebook paper. She put 25 sheets in her science folder, 35 sheets in her social studies folder, 50 sheets in her reading folder, and even more in her math folder. How many sheets did Malinda have left?

2. It costs $4.75 for adults and $2.25 for children for admission to the aquarium. How much will it cost for a group of 16 teachers to get into the aquarium?

Set 12-5 (pages 700–703)

For 1–4, use the picture of the bag at the right. Is it likely, unlikely, impossible, or certain that you pick

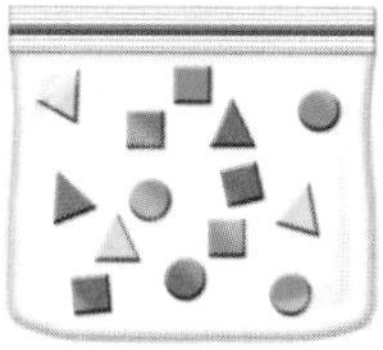

1. a circle? **2.** a green or yellow shape?

3. a blue circle? **4.** a triangle, square, or circle?

For 5–8, use the picture of the cards at the right. Is it likely, unlikely, impossible, or certain that you draw

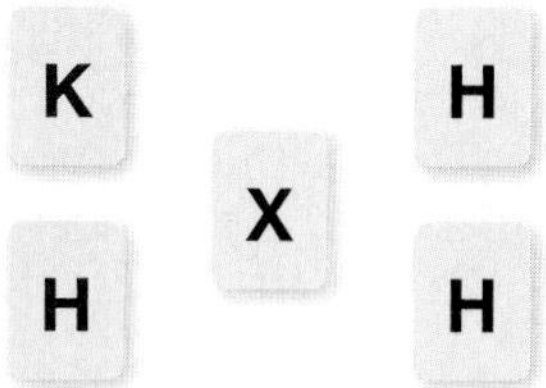

5. a vowel? **6.** an H?

7. a K? **8.** not X?

Set 12-6 (pages 704–705)

List all the possible outcomes for each situation.

Spinner 1

Spinner 2

Spinner 3

1. Spinning Spinner 1 **2.** Spinning Spinner 2

3. Spinning Spinners 1 and 3 **4.** Spinning Spinners 2 and 3

5. Jose says there are 4 possible outcomes of being born in a month that has 30 days. Is he correct? List the possible outcomes.

Set 12-7 (pages 706–709)

Write the probability of the spinner at the right landing on each color when you spin it once.

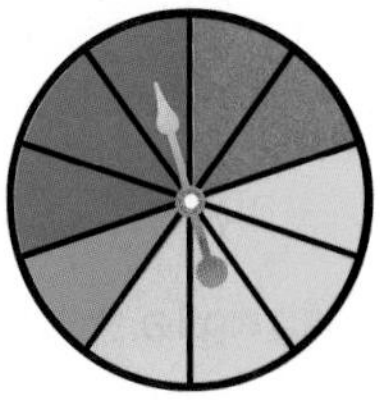

1. yellow
2. blue
3. green
4. not red
5. yellow or green
6. purple
7. Kenny says if the probability of an event is $\frac{4}{5}$, then the event is unlikely. Explain why this is not correct.

Set 12-8 (pages 710–711)

Use the spinner at the right for 1–5. How many times would you expect each outcome?

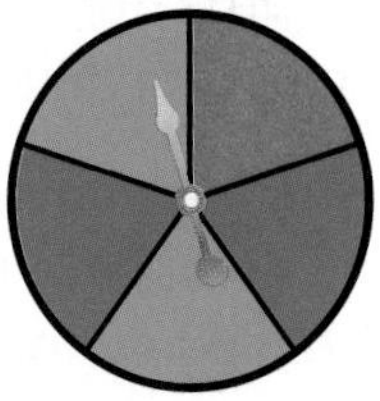

1. landing on red in 10 spins
2. landing on blue in 15 spins
3. landing on yellow in 20 spins
4. landing on a color on the wheel in 35 spins
5. landing on blue or green in 25 spins

Set 12-9 (pages 714–715)

Solve by working backward. Give the answer in a complete sentence.

1. A farmer has chickens and cows. He bought 5 chickens and sold 2 cows. Then, there were 25 animals on the farm and $\frac{17}{25}$ were chickens. How many animals did the farmer have to start?
2. Mr. Richards cut an apple pie into equal size pieces. He served 3 pieces for supper. The next day, he and his daughter ate 2 pieces, which was $\frac{2}{5}$ of the leftovers. Into how many pieces had the pie been cut?
3. Carlos borrowed money from his mother. He spent \$2.86 on snacks and then \$3.50 to get into the skating rink. He had \$3.64 left from the money he borrowed. How much money did he borrow?

A

A.M. Time between midnight and noon. (p. 190)

acute angle An angle that is less than a right angle. (p. 440)

acute triangle A triangle with three acute angles. (p. 444)

addends The numbers that are added together to find a sum. (p. 62)
Example: 2 + 7 = 9
addend

algebraic expression An expression with variables. (p. 98)

analog clock Shows time by pointing to numbers on a face. (p. 190)

angle A figure formed by two rays that have the same endpoint. (p. 440)

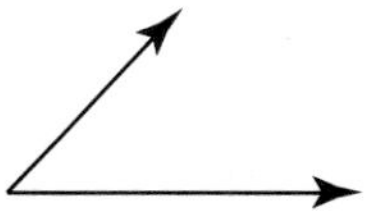

area The number of square units needed to cover the region. (p. 468)

array A way of displaying objects in rows and columns. (p. 124)

Associative Property of Addition Addends can be regrouped and the sum remains the same. (p. 62)

Associative Property of Multiplication Factors can be regrouped and the product remains the same. (p. 288)

average The mean, found by adding all numbers in a set and dividing by the number of values. (p. 404)

B

bar graph A graph using bars to show data. (p. 208)

benchmark fractions Fractions that are commonly used for estimation: $\frac{1}{4}$, $\frac{1}{3}$, $\frac{1}{2}$, $\frac{2}{3}$, and $\frac{3}{4}$. (p. 508)

breaking apart Mental math method used to rewrite a number as the sum of numbers to form an easier problem. (p. 62)

C

capacity The amount a container can hold. (p. 592)

center A point within a circle that is the same distance from all points on a circle. (p. 448)

centimeter (cm) A metric unit of length. 100 centimeters equal 1 meter. (p. 652)

century Unit of time equal to 100 years. (p. 192)

certain (event) An event that is sure to occur. (p. 700)

chord Any line segment that connects any two points on the circle. (p. 448)

circle A closed plane figure in which all the points are the same distance from a point called the center. (p. 448)

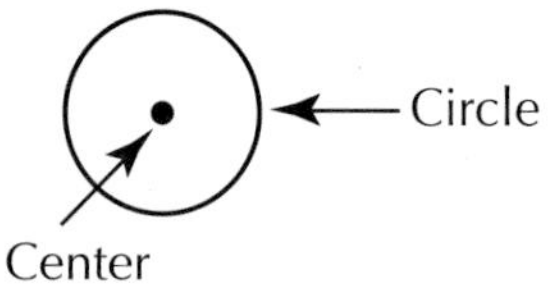

circle graph A graph in the shape of a circle that shows how the whole is broken into parts. (p. 536)

common factor A factor that two or more numbers have in common. (p. 520)

Commutative Property of Addition Numbers can be added in any order and the sum remains the same. (p. 62)

Commutative Property of Multiplication Factors can be multiplied in any order and the product remains the same. (p. 128)

compatible numbers Numbers that are easy to compute mentally. (p. 258)

compensation Adding and subtracting the same number to make the sum or difference easier to find. (pp. 62)

cone A solid figure with a base that is a circle and a curved surface that meets at a point. (p. 434)

congruent figures Figures that have the same shape and size. (p. 452)

coordinate grid A grid used to show ordered pairs. (p. 212)

cube A solid figure with six congruent squares as its faces. (p. 434)

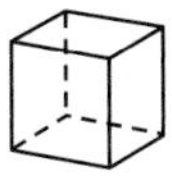

cup (c) A customary unit of capacity. (p. 592)

customary units of measure Units of measure that are used in the United States. (p. 588)

cylinder A solid figure with two congruent circular bases. (p. 434)

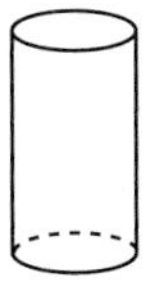

D

data Pieces of collected information. (p. 204)

day A unit of time equal to 24 hours. (p. 192)

decade A unit of time equal to 10 years. (p. 192)

decimal point A dot used to separate dollars from cents or ones from tenths in a number. (p. 28)

decimeter (dm) Metric unit of length equal to 10 centimeters. (p. 652)

degrees Celsius (°C) Metric unit of temperature. (p. 664)

degrees Fahrenheit (°F) Standard unit of temperature. (p. 664)

denominator The number below the fraction bar in a fraction; The total number of equal parts in all. (p. 500)

diameter A line segment that connects two points on a circle and passes through the center. (p. 448)

difference The answer when subtracting two numbers. (p. 64)

digital clock Shows time with numbers. Hours are separated from minutes with a colon. (p. 190)

digits The symbols used to write a number: 0, 1, 2, 3, 4, 5, 6, 7, 8, and 9 (p. 4)

Distributive Property Breaking apart problems into two simpler problems.
Example: $(3 \times 21) = (3 \times 20) + (3 \times 1)$ (p. 132)

divide An operation to find the number in each group or the number of equal groups. (p. 146)

dividend The number to be divided. (p. 146)

divisibility rules The rules that state when a number is divisible by another number. (p. 402)

divisible Can be divided by another number without leaving a remainder.
Example: 10 is divisible by 2. (p. 402)

divisor The number by which another number is divided.
Example: $32 \div 4 = 8$ (p. 146)
↑ Divisor (points to 4)

E

edge A line segment where two faces of a solid figure meet. (p. 434)

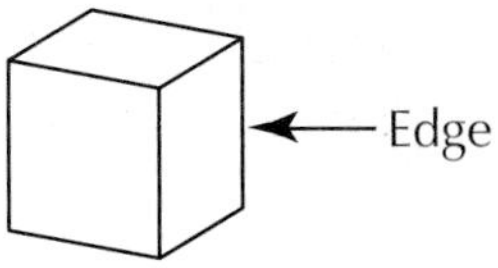

elapsed time The amount of time between the beginning of an event and the end of the event. (p. 196)

equally likely (event) Just as likely to happen as not to happen. (p. 700)

equation A number sentence that uses the equal sign (=) to show that two expressions have the same value. (p. 100)

equilateral triangle A triangle in which all sides are the same length. (p. 444)

equivalent Numbers that name the same amount. (p. 624)

equivalent fractions Fractions that name the same region, part of a set, or part of a segment. (p. 624)

expanded form A number written as the sum of the values of its digits. (p. 4)
Example: 2,000 + 400 + 70 + 6

F

face A flat surface of a solid that does not roll. (p. 434)

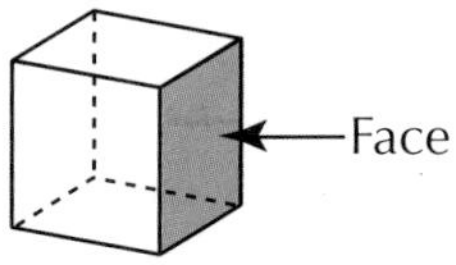

fact family A group of related facts using the same set of numbers. (p. 148)

factors The numbers multiplied together to find a product. (p. 124)
Example: $3 \times 6 = 18$
Factor

fair game A game in which each player is equally likely to win. (p. 700)

flip (reflection) To turn a plane figure over. (p. 452)

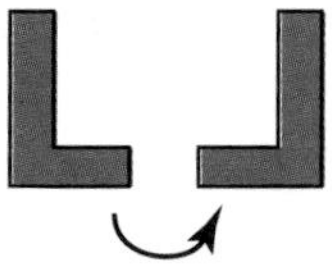

fluid ounce (fl oz) A customary unit of capacity. 1 fluid ounce is equal to 2 tablespoons. (p. 592)

foot (ft) A customary unit of length. 1 foot is equal to 12 inches. (p. 588)

fraction A fraction is a symbol, such as $\frac{2}{3}$, $\frac{5}{1}$, or $\frac{8}{5}$, used to name a part of a whole, a part of a set, a location on a number line, or a division of whole numbers. (p. 500)

front-end estimation A way to estimate a sum by adding the first digit of each addend and adjusting the result based on the remaining digits. (p. 68)

G

gallon (gal) A customary unit of capacity. 1 gallon is equal to 4 quarts. (p. 592)

gram (g) A metric unit of mass. (p. 656)

H

hexagon A polygon with 6 sides. (p. 438)

hour Unit of time equal to 60 minutes (p. 192)

hundredth One part of 100 equal parts of a whole. (p. 28)

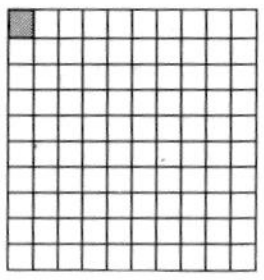

I

Identity Property of Addition The sum of any number and zero is that number. (p. 62)

Identity Property of Multiplication The product of any number and one is that number. (p. 128)

impossible (event) An event that cannot occur. (p. 700)

improper fractions A fraction in which the numerator is greater than or equal to the denominator. (p. 530)

inch (in.) Customary unit of length. (p. 588)

inequality A number sentence that uses the greater than sign (>) or the less than sign (<) to show that two expressions do not have the same value. (p. 688)

intersecting lines Lines that cross at one point. (p. 440)

interval A number which is the difference between two consecutive numbers on the scale of a graph. (p. 208)

inverse operations Two operations that undo each other. Addition and subtraction are inverse operations. Multiplication and division are inverse operations. (pp. 82, 148)
Example: $7 + 10 = 17$; $17 - 10 = 7$
$6 \times 5 = 30$; $30 \div 5 = 6$

isosceles triangle A triangle that has at least two equal sides. (p. 444)

K

key Part of a pictograph that tells what each symbol stands for. (p. 204)

kilogram (kg) A metric unit of mass. 1 kilogram = 1,000 grams. (p. 656)

kilometer (km) A metric unit of length. 1 kilometer = 1,000 meters. (p. 652)

L

leap year Unit of time equal to 366 days. (p. 192)

likely (event) An event that probably will happen. (p. 700)

line A straight path of points that goes on and on in two directions. (p. 440)

line graph A graph that connects points to show how data changes over time. (p. 216)

line of symmetry A line on which a figure can be folded so that both halves are congruent. (p. 456)

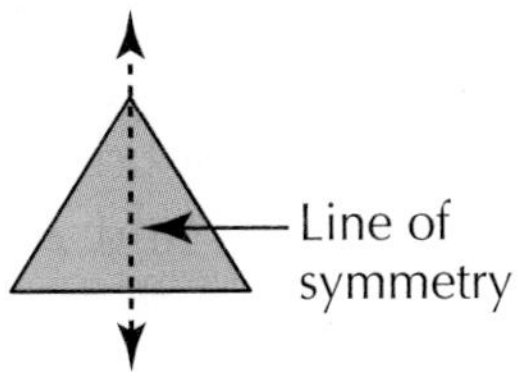

line plot A display of data along a number line. (p. 206)

line segment A part of a line that has two endpoints. (p. 440)

liter (L) A metric unit of capacity. (p. 654)

M

mass The amount of matter that something contains. (p. 656)

mean An average, found by adding all numbers in a set and dividing by the number of values. (p. 404)

median The middle number in an ordered data set. (p. 226)

meter (m) A metric unit of length. (p. 652)

mile (mi) A customary unit of length. 1 mile is equal to 5,280 feet. (p. 588)

millennium A unit for measuring time equal to 1,000 years. (p. 192)

milliliter (mL) A metric unit of capacity. (p. 654)

millimeter (mm) A metric unit of length. (p. 652)

minute A unit of time equal to 60 seconds. (p. 192)

mixed number A number that has a whole number and a fraction. (p. 530)

mode The number or numbers that occur most often in a data set. (p. 226)

month One of the 12 parts into which a year is divided. (p. 192)

multiple The product of any two whole numbers. (p. 128)

N

net A pattern used to make a solid. (p. 434)
Example:

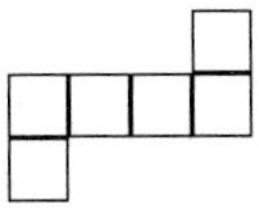

number expression An expression that contains numbers and at least one operation. A number expression is also called a numerical expression. (p. 94)

numerator The number above the fraction bar in a fraction. (p. 500)

O

obtuse angle An angle that is greater than a right angle. (p. 440)

obtuse triangle A triangle in which there is one obtuse angle. (p. 444)

octagon A polygon with 8 sides. (p. 438)

ordered pair A pair of numbers that names a point on a coordinate grid. (p. 212)

ordinal numbers Numbers used to tell order. (p. 200)

ounce (oz) A customary unit of weight. (p. 594)

outcome A possible result of a game or experiment. (p. 704)

outlier A number in a data set that is very different from the rest of the numbers. (p. 206)

overestimate An estimate that is greater than the exact answer. (p. 72)

P

P.M. Time between noon and midnight. (p. 190)

parallel lines In a plane, lines that never intersect. (p. 440)
Example:

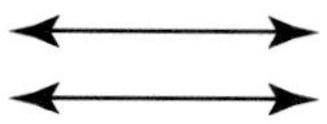

parallelogram A quadrilateral in which opposite sides are parallel. (p. 444)

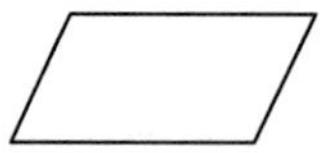

partial products Products found by breaking one factor in a multiplication problem into ones, tens, hundreds, and so on and then multiplying each of these by the other factor. (p. 264)

pentagon A plane figure with 5 sides. (p. 438)

perimeter The distance around a figure. (p. 464)

period In a number, a group of three digits, separated by commas, starting from the right. (p. 5)

perpendicular lines Two intersecting lines that form right angles. (p. 440)
Example:

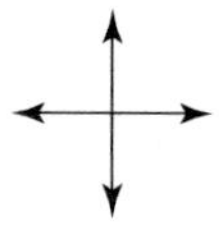

pictograph A graph using pictures or symbols to show data. (p. 206)

pint (pt) A customary unit of capacity. 1 pint is equal to 2 cups. (p. 592)

plane figure A figure with only two dimensions. (p. 434)

plot To locate and mark a point named by an ordered pair on a grid. (p. 212)

point An exact location in space. (p. 440)

polygon A closed plane figure made up of line segments. (p. 438)

pound (lb) A customary unit of weight. 1 pound is equal to 16 ounces. (p. 594)

prediction An informed guess about what will happen. (p. 710)

probability A number telling the likelihood an event will happen. (p. 700)

product The answer to a multiplication problem. (p. 124)

pyramid A solid figure whose base is a polygon and whose faces are triangles with a common vertex. (p. 434)

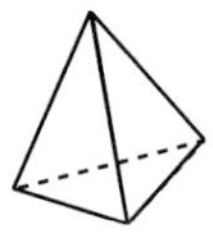

Q

quadrilateral A polygon with 4 sides. (p. 438)

quart (qt) A customary unit of capacity. 1 quart is equal to 2 pints. (p. 592)

quotient The answer to a division problem. (p. 146)

R

radius Any line segment that connects the center to a point on the circle (p. 448)

range The difference between the greatest value and the least value in a data set. (p. 226)

ray A part of a line that has one endpoint and continues endlessly in one direction. (p. 440)

rectangle A quadrilateral with 4 right angles. (p. 444)

rectangular prism A solid figure whose faces are all rectangles. (p. 434)

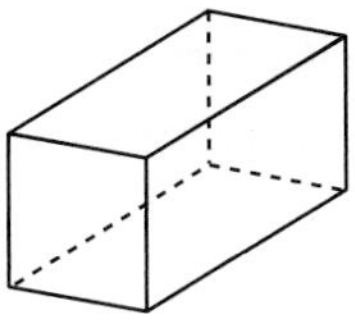

rectangular pyramid A solid figure with a rectangle for its base and triangles for all other faces. (p. 434)

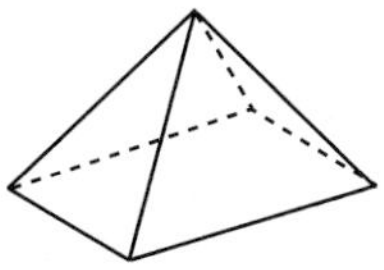

remainder The number that remains after the division is complete. (p. 372)

rhombus A quadrilateral in which opposite sides are parallel and all sides are the same length. (p. 444)

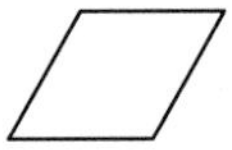

right angle An angle that forms a square corner. (p. 440)

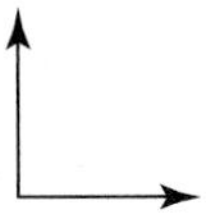

right triangle A triangle in which there is one right angle. (p. 444)

rounding Replacing a number with a number that tells about how many or how much. (p. 20)

S

scale Numbers that show the units used on a graph. (p. 208)

scalene triangle A triangle in which no sides are the same length. (p. 444)

second A unit of time, 60 seconds equal 1 minute. (p. 193)

side Each of the line segments of a polygon. (p. 438)

similar figures Figures that have the same shape and may or may not have the same size. (p. 458)

simplest form A fraction in which the numerator and denominator have no common factors other than 1. (p. 520)

slide (translation) A change in the position of a figure that moves it up, down, or sideways. (p. 452)

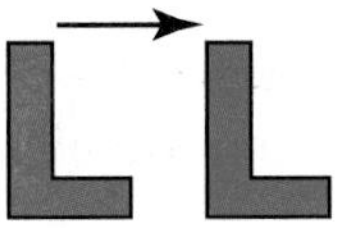

solid figure A figure that has length, width, and height. (p. 434)

solution The value of the variable that makes an equation true. (p. 100)

solve Find a solution to an equation. (p. 100)

sphere A solid figure which include all points the same distance from a point. (p. 434)

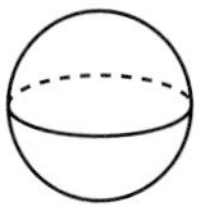

square A quadrilateral with 4 right angles and all sides the same length. (p. 444)

square pyramid A solid figure with a square base and four faces that are triangles. (p. 434)

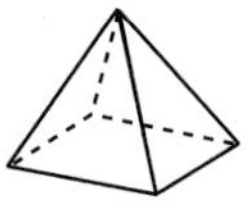

standard form A way to write a number showing only its digits. (p. 4)
Example: 2,613

straight angle An angle that forms a straight line. (p. 440)

sum The result of adding numbers together. (p. 62)

survey Collecting information by asking a number of people the same question and recording their answers. (p. 230)

symmetric A figure is symmetric if it can be folded into two congruent halves that fit on top of each other. (p. 456)

T

tablespoon (tbsp) A customary unit of capacity. 1 tablespoon is equal to 3 teaspoons. (p. 592)

teaspoon (tsp) A customary unit of capacity. 3 teaspoons equal 1 tablespoon. (p. 592)

tenth One of ten equal parts of a whole. (p. 28)

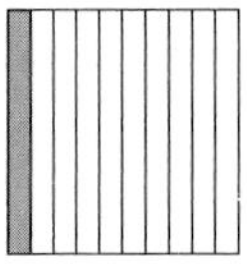

ton (T) A customary unit of weight. 1 ton is equal to 2,000 pounds. (p. 594)

trapezoid A quadrilateral with only one pair of parallel sides. (p. 444)

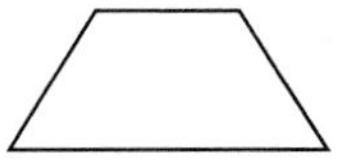

tree diagram A display to show all possible outcomes. (p. 704)

trend A pattern in the data on a line graph, shown by an increase or decrease. (p. 216)

triangle A polygon with 3 sides. (p. 438)

triangular prism A solid figure with two bases that are triangles and the other three faces are rectangles. (p. 434)

turn (rotation) Moves a figure about a point. (p. 452)

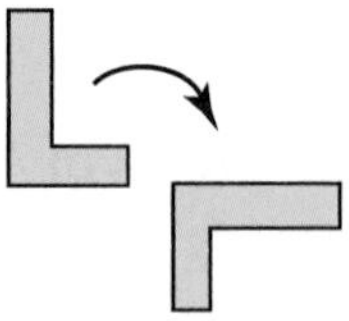

U

underestimate An estimate that is less than the exact answer. (p. 72)

unfair game A game in which each player doesn't have the same chance of winning. (p. 700)

unlikely (event) An event that probably will not happen. (p. 700)

V

variable A symbol or letter that stands for a number. (p. 98)

vertex (plural, vertices) The point where two rays meet. The point where the sides of a polygon meet. The point where three or more edges of a solid figure meet. (pp. 434, 438, 440)

volume The number of cubic units needed to fill a solid figure. (p. 476)

W

week A unit of time equal to 7 days. (p. 192)

word form A number written in words. *Example:* Four thousand, six hundred, thirty-two (p. 4)

Y

yard (yd) A customary unit of length. 1 yard is equal to 3 feet. (p. 588)

year A unit of time equal to 365 days or 52 weeks or 12 months. (p. 192)

Z

Zero Property of Multiplication The product of any number and zero is zero. (p. 128)

Measures–Customary

Length
1 foot (ft) = 12 inches (in)
1 yard (yd) = 3 feet, or 36 inches
1 mile = 5,280 feet, or
1,760 yards

Weight
1 pound (lb) = 16 ounces (oz)
1 ton (T) = 2,000 pounds

Capacity
1 cup (c) = 8 fluid ounces (fl oz), or
16 tablespoons (tbsp)
1 tablespoon (tbsp) = 3 teaspoons (tsp)
1 pint (pt) = 2 cups
1 quart (qt) = 2 pints
1 half-gallon = 2 quarts
1 gallon (gal) = 4 quarts

Time
1 minute (min) = 60 seconds (s)
1 hour (h) = 60 minutes
1 day (d) = 24 hours
1 week (wk) = 7 days
1 year (yr) = 12 months (mo), or
52 weeks, or
365 days
1 leap year = 366 days
(adds one day to
February)
1 decade = 10 years
1 century (c) = 100 years
1 millennium = 1,000 years

Measures–Metric

Length
1 centimeter (cm) = 10 millimeters (mm)
1 decimeter (dm) = 10 centimeters
1 meter (m) = 100 centimeters
1 kilometer (km) = 1,000 meters

Mass/Weight
1 kilogram (kg) = 1,000 grams (g)

Capacity
1 liter (L) = 1,000 milliliters (mL)

Symbols

=	is equal to	$\perp$	is perpendicular
>	is greater than	$\overleftrightarrow{AB}$	line *AB*
<	is less than	$\overline{AB}$	line segment *AB*
°	degree	$\overrightarrow{AB}$	ray *AB*
°C	degree Celsius	$\angle ABC$	angle *ABC*
°F	degree Fahrenheit	(3, 4)	ordered pair 3, 4

Formulas

$P = 2\ell + 2w$	Perimeter of a rectangle
$P = 4s$	Perimeter of a square
$A = \ell \times w$	Area of a rectangle
$A = s \times s$	Area of a square
$V = \ell \times w \times h$	Volume of a rectangular prism

Cover:
Illustration: Jon Goodell
Photograph: Getty Images

Text:
Dorling Kindersley (DK) is an international publishing company specializing in the creation of high-quality reference content for books, CD-ROMs, online materials, and video. The hallmark of DK content is its unique combination of educational value and strong visual style. This combination allows DK to deliver appealing, accessible, and engaging educational content that delights children, parents, and teachers around the world. Scott Foresman is delighted to have been able to use selected extracts of DK content within this Scott Foresman Math program.

40–41: "One Day's Food" from *The World in One Day* by Russell Ash. Text copyright ©1997 by Russell Ash. Compilation and illustration copyright ©1997 by Dorling Kindersley Limited; 102–103: "Mountains" from *Incredible Comparisons* by Russell Ash. Copyright ©1996 by Dorling Kindersley Limited; 168–169: "Animals" from *The World in One Day* by Russell Ash. Text copyright ©1997 by Russell Ash. Compilation and illustration copyright ©1997 by Dorling Kindersley Limited; 234–235: "Tsunami" from *Disaster!* by Richard Platt. Copyright ©1997 by Dorling Kindersley Limited. Text copyright ©1997 by Richard Platt; 292–293: "Jumbo Jet" from *Stephen Biesty's Incredible Cross-Sections* by Richard Platt, illustrated by Stephen Biesty. Copyright ©1992 by Dorling Kindersley Limited; 344–345: "Happy Families" from *Reptile* by Colin McCarthy. Copyright ©2000 by Dorling Kindersley Limited; 412–413: "Sporting Horses" from *Horse* by Juliet Clutton-Brock. Copyright ©2000 by Dorling Kindersley Limited; 478–479: "Big Buildings" from *Incredible Comparisons* by Russell Ash. Copyright ©1996 by Dorling Kindersley Limited; 540–541: "Life on a Coral Reef" from *Coral Reef* by Barbara Taylor. Copyright ©1992 by Dorling Kindersley Limited; 602–603: "Empire State Building" from *Stephen Biesty's Incredible Cross-Sections* by Richard Platt, illustrated by Stephen Biesty. Copyright ©1992 by Dorling Kindersley Limited; 666–667: "Woodland" from *Richard Orr's Nature Cross-Sections* by Moira Butterfield, illustrated by Richard Orr. Copyright ©1995 by Dorling Kindersley Limited; 716–717: "Fire-fighting Helicopter" from *Big Book of Rescue Vehicles* by Caroline Bingham. Copyright ©2000 by Dorling Kindersley Limited.

Illustrations
216, 518, 713 Susan J. Carlson
257 Catherine Twomey
263 Paula Wendland
343 Barbara Cousins

Photographs
Every effort has been made to secure permission and provide appropriate credit for photographic material. The publisher deeply regrets any omission and pledges to correct errors called to its attention in subsequent editions.

Unless otherwise acknowledged, all photographs are the property of Scott Foresman, a division of Pearson Education.

Photo locators denoted as follows: Top (T), Center (C), Bottom (B), Left (L), Right (R), Background (Bkgd)

Front Matter: viii Brand X Pictures **Chapter 1:** 2 ©Izzy Schwartz/Getty Images; 4 ©Ron Chapple/Getty Images; 5 ©Joe Polimeni/Corbis; 8 ©Jake Rajs/Getty Images; 9 Stephen Oliver/©Dorling Kindersley; 10 David Mendelsohn/Masterfile Corporation; 12 ©Ken Tannenbaum/Getty Images; 16 ©Stuart Westmorland/Getty Images; 19 ©Guido Alberto Rossi/Getty Images; 20 ©Joseph Pobereskin/Getty Images; 23 ©Dorling Kindersley; 28 ©Emma Lee/Life File/Getty Images; 29 Getty Images; 30 ©Simon Battensby/Getty Images; 32 Adam Jones/Visuals Unlimited; 34 ©Nick Daly/Getty Images; 36 Corbis; 40 ©Dorling Kindersley; 50 Getty Images **Chapter 2:** 60 R. E. Wilcox/U.S. Geological Survey; 62 ©James Gritz/Getty Images; 63 Hemera Technologies; 64 ©Jon Feingersh/Corbis; 67 ©G. Brad Lewis/Getty Images; 68 Spencer Swanger/Tom Stack & Associates, Inc.; 70 Magrath Photography/Science Photo Library/Photo Researchers, Inc.; 72 ©David Madison/Getty Images; 76 ©Mark E. Gibson Stock Photography; 78 Hemera Technologies; 80 ©Andy Eaves/Getty Images; 82 ©Richard Cummins/Corbis; 84 ©George Hall/Corbis; 86 ©David Madison/Getty Images; 87 (BR) Getty Images, (CR) ©Ryan McVay/Getty Images; 89 (CR) Daryl Benson/Masterfile Corporation, (BR) Hot Ideas/Index Stock Imagery; 90 ©Rex Ziak/Getty Images; 94 ©David Nardini/Getty Images; 96 The Burns Archive, Ltd.; 97 AP/Wide World Photos; 98 Corbis; 102 ©Dorling Kindersley; 107 (TC) Getty Images, (TL) ©Bettmann/Corbis **Chapter 3:** 122 Getty Images; 126 (CR) ©Bettmann/Corbis, (C) Getty Images; 130 ©G. K. and Vikki Hart/Getty Images; 132 Bill Aron/PhotoEdit; 140 ©David H. Wells/Corbis; 141 Leslie Garland Picture Library; 148 ©H. D. Thoreau/Corbis; 150 ©O'Brien Productions/Corbis; 152 ©Kevin Fleming/Corbis; 154 John Warden/SuperStock; 160 ©Kevin Schafer/Corbis; 162 (C, CR) Getty Images, (BR) ©Dorling Kindersley; 163 ©Gunter Marx Photography/Corbis; 164 ©Lawrence Lawry/Getty Images; 166 Clayton-Thompson/Zephyr Images; 168 ©Dorling Kindersley **Chapter 4:** 188 digitalvisiononline.com; 190 ©Michael Yamashita/Corbis; 192 ©Paul Webster/Getty Images; 193 (TL) Getty Images, (TR) Scala/Art Resource, NY; 194 (CR) ©Bettmann/Corbis, (CL) ©C Squared Studios/Getty Images; 195 ©Lawrence Manning/Corbis; 196 ©G. Brad Lewis/Getty Images; 200 ©Dugald Bremmer/Getty Images; 204 ©Ryan McVay/Getty Images; 206 Getty Images; 208 ©David W. Hamilton/Getty Images; 209 Michael K. Nichols/NGS Image Collection; 212 Ron Johnson/Index Stock Imagery; 215 ©Darryl Torckler/Getty Images; 216 ©Bettmann/Corbis; 218 ©Dorling Kindersley; 221 (CR) SuperStock, (BR) ©Rob Lang/Getty Images; 228 ©Galen Rowell/Corbis; 230 ©Comstock Inc.; 231 Getty Images; 232 François Gohier/Photo Researchers, Inc.; 234 Richard Bonson/©Dorling Kindersley; 239 Getty Images **Chapter 5:** 254 (T) Corbis, (C) ©Pictures Colour Library; 257 ©Comstock Inc.; 258 (L, TC) ©Walter Bibikow/Getty Images, (CR) ©James Balog/Getty Images; 259 (TL) ©G. K. and Vikki Hart/Getty Images, (TR) Getty Images; 260 (BRCL) ©Comstock Inc., (BRR) ©Dorling Kindersley; 262 ©Pat O'Hara/Getty Images; 264 ©Steve Cole/Getty Images; 266 (BR) ©Steve Cole/Getty Images, (BC) Christie's Images/SuperStock, (CL) Getty Images; 270 Martin Cameron/©Dorling Kindersley; 272 (B) ©Bruce Clarke/Index Stock Imagery/PictureQuest, (BR) Martin Cameron/©Dorling Kindersley; 273 ©Randy Wells/Getty Images; 275 Rosemary Calvert/Image State/Alamy.com; 277 (B, T) ©Paul Poplis/FoodPix; 279 Alamy.com; 282 ©Richard Nowitz/Phototake/PictureQuest; 283 ©Photolink/Getty Images; 286 ©Erik Dreyer/Getty Images; 290 ©Steve Taylor/Getty Images; 292 ©Stephen Biesty/©Dorling Kindersley; 295 Getty Images; 303 Getty Images **Chapter 6:** 312 Corbis; 316 NASA; 317 NASA/SuperStock; 318 NASA; 320 ©Jake Rajs/Getty Images; 322 Bruce Coleman Inc.; 325 (TR) ©Barney Taxel/Mira.com, (C) Brand X Pictures; 328 ©Museum of the City of New York/Corbis; 332 ©Charlie Borland/Getty Images; 333 ©Alan Carey/Corbis; 336 Michael Abbey/Photo Researchers, Inc.; 338 ©C/B Productions/Corbis; 340 Kindra Clineff/Index Stock Imagery; 342 Brian Hagiwara/FoodPix; 344 ©Dorling Kindersley; 345 ©Dorling Kindersley; 364 ©Kit Houghton/Corbis **Chapter 7:** 368 ©Mark E. Gibson Stock Photography; 373 Corbis; 376 Getty Images; 383 ©Art Wolfe/Getty Images; 384 Getty Images; 386 ©Ryan McVay/Getty Images; 388 ©Dorling Kindersley; 392 Mick Roessler/SuperStock; 397 ©Dagmar/Animals Animals/Earth Scenes; 406 ©D. Falconer/PhotoLink/Getty Images; 407 ©Layne Kennedy/Corbis; 410 Pamela Cemen; 412 (TL, B, C) ©Dorling Kindersley, (TC) Private Collection/Bridgeman Art Library International Ltd.; 413 (TR) British Museum/©Dorling Kindersley, (B) ©Dorling Kindersley; 415 Getty Images; 417 Courtesy of Monroe County, Florida **Chapter 8:** 432 (C) ©Mark Segal/Getty Images, (BR/TRB, R/BL) Getty Images, (BR/BR) ©John Beatty/Getty Images; 436 (CR) Carolyn Ross/Index Stock Imagery, (BC) Corbis, (BRL, BRR) Getty Images, (CL) ©John Beatty/Getty Images, (C) Tony Freeman/PhotoEdit; 438 ©Christine Osbourne/Corbis; 440 digitalvisiononline.com; 442 Alex Maclean/Photonica; 444 Getty Images; 447 James Lemass/Index Stock Imagery; 448 ©Roman Soumar/Corbis; 451 Getty Images; 452 ©Jayne Thornton/Getty Images; 456 ©Charles Lenars/Corbis; 464 Adam Jones/Photo Researchers, Inc.; 466 Kevin Dodge/Masterfile Corporation; 468 ©Dorling Kindersley; 474 Tim Davis/Photo Researchers, Inc.; 476 ©Ron Watts/Corbis; 478 ©Dorling Kindersley; 479 ©Dorling Kindersley **Chapter 9:** 498 digitalvisiononline.com; 500 Getty Images; 507 Hemera Technologies; 508 Getty Images; 509 Hemera Technologies; 511 Getty Images; 512 Aneal N. Vohra/Unicorn Stock Photos; 522 ©Robert Glusic/Getty Images; 523 Getty Images; 524 ©Kevin R. Morris/Corbis; 525 (TC) ©Robert Frerck/Odyssey/Chicago, (TR) ©Geoffrey Clements/Corbis, (TL) ©Cheryl Hatch; 535 Hot Stock/Alamy.com; 536 (TR) Getty Images, (L) ©Myrleen Ferguson Cate/PhotoEdit; 538 (L) ©Philip James Corwin/Corbis, (TC) Mark E. Gibson/©Mark E. Gibson Stock Photography; 540 ©Dorling Kindersley; 541 ©Dorling Kindersley, (BR) Linda Pitkin **Chapter 10:** 560 Corbis; 568 ©Joe McDonald/Corbis; 569 Alan G. Nelson/Animals Animals/Earth Scenes; 570 AP/Wide World Photos; 571 JDC/Visuals Unlimited; 574 ©Kim Zumwalt/Getty Images; 578 ©Dave Bartruff/Corbis; 580 Luiz C. Marigo/Peter Arnold, Inc.; 584 ©Ann Menke/Getty Images; 585 Tom Rosenthal/SuperStock; 592 Getty Images; 594 9L) ©Kit Houghton/Corbis, (TL) Corbis, (CL) Getty Images, (TR) ©William Hamilton/SuperStock; 595 ©Jerry Cooke/Corbis 600 Getty Images; 602 ©Stephen Biesty/©Dorling Kindersley; 603 ©Stephen Biesty/©Dorling Kindersley; 610 Getty Images **Chapter 11:** 622 ©Jeremy Walker/Getty Images; 624 (L) ©Jack Star/PhotoLink/Getty Images, (TL) ©Dorling Kindersley, (TC, TR) Getty Images; 626 ©Stephanie Maze/Corbis; 627 ©Galen Rowell/Corbis; 630 (L) Getty Images, (BL, BR, TR) ©David R. Frazier Photolibrary, (TL) Wally Eberhart/Visuals Unlimited; 631 ©Dale C. Spartas/Corbis; 633 Corbis; 636 (L) ©John Connell/Index Stock Imagery, (TR) Jim Whitmer, (TC) Getty Images; 637 AP/Wide World Photos; 638 ©AFP; 640 ©Karl Weatherly/Corbis; 644 Getty Images; 647 ©Aaron Haupt/Photo Researchers, Inc.; 652 (TL) Visuals Unlimited, (C) ©Jonathan Blair/Corbis, (CL) Getty Images, (CR) ©Mike Johnson Marine Natural History Photography; 656 Getty Images; 657 (CL) ©Siede Preis/Getty Images, (CR) Getty Images; 660 ©Fritz Polking/Visuals Unlimited; 662 (L) ©John Kelly/Getty Images, (C) Getty Images; 664 ©Chris Cole/Getty Images; 666 (TL, C) Richard Orr/©Dorling Kindersley; 673 Visuals Unlimited; 676 Getty Images **Chapter 12:** 686 ©2002 Tom Story; 689 Getty Images; 690 ©Patricia Doyle/Getty Images; 692 ©Francisco Cruz/SuperStock; 694 United States Mint; 696 Bill Bachmann/Index Stock Imagery; 697 ©David Young-Wolff/Getty Images; 700 ©Joyce Choo/Corbis; 703 ©Lester Lefkowitz/Corbis; 708 ©Martin B. Withers; Frank Lane Picture Agency/Corbis; 710 ©Robert Harding Picture Library/Alamy.com; 715 (BR) The Granger Collection, (Frame) Getty Images; 716 (B, CR) ©2002 Tom Story; 717 ©2002 Tom Story

INDEX